HUGMAN'S SWIMMING YEARBOOK 1990

in association with the

Amateur Swimming Association

Adrian Moorhouse: Hugman's Swimming Yearbook *"Swimmer of the Year."*

Allsport Photographic — Simon Bruty

Edited by

BARRY J. HUGMAN

Consultant: Leslie Cranfield (ASA Statistician)

HUGMAN'S
S P O R T I N G
PUBLICATIONS
L I M I T E D

First published in Great Britain in 1989 by
Hugman's Sporting Publications Ltd
24 Notting Hill Gate
London W11 3JQ

ISBN 1 872290 035

Typeset by Area Graphics Ltd, Arden Press Way,
Letchworth, Hertfordshire, SG6 1LH
Printed in Great Britain by LR Printing Services Ltd
Edward Way, Burgess Hill, West Sussex RH15 9UA, England

Front jacket photograph: Adrian Moorhouse (Allsport Photographic)

Contents

Acknowledgements

I am indebted to David Reeves, the Secretary and General Executive of the ASA, for allowing me both the opportunity to produce the first ASA Swimming Yearbook and to be involved in this great sport of his. His encouragement, enthusiasm and support has been first class and much appreciated by me, and I must thank him for putting all the requisite facilities at our disposal. Also, a thank you is in order to Josie Grange, the ASA Registration Officer, for all of her great efforts.

But, if it hadn't been for an introductory meeting with Les Moulsen, a coach at Norwich Penguins, the Yearbook almost certainly would not have come to fruition. It was he who convinced me that swimming deserved the type of Yearbook that I have produced for other sports. Yes, Les Moulsen has a lot to answer for!

I would like to voice my appreciation to the many people, who also gave much valuable help, and if I have missed anyone out, please accept my sincere apologies. They are: E.D. Bowditch, Mrs D. Short, Miss J. Wilding, Col. E.J. Ransley, N. Loasby, Mrs S. Kerswell, Mrs D. Isaac, D. Wear, D. Ashworth, Mrs Neate, Mrs E.J. Gale, I. Martin, F. Lattimer, T. Cooper, I. Watson, J.R. Carrie, R. Proctor, Mrs M. Dodson, F.D.B. Benny, D.S. Harding, Rev. L.S. Pullan, Mrs D. Lowe, L.G. Howe and Mrs M. Tuppen (ASA District and County Honorary Secretaries, who helped co-ordinate the ASA Questionnaire); Margaret Coombes, Trevor Thomas, Harry Booth, Terry Denison, Peter Wilson-Chalon, Joyce Clarke, Peter Hassall, Judy Mott, Aline Williams, Jeff Cook, Wally Clark, Steve Still, Mike Rider, and Anita Lonsbrough (for the supply of up-to-date results); Paul Bush and Viv Firmin (data on the BSCA); Sandra Caldwell, Peter Owen, Brian Relf, Audrey Scott, Trevor Symmons, Irene Williams, Ricky Wood, Tony Warn, Jane Asher, Marie Bracey, Anne Eakin, Kevin Redsull, Steven Downes and Jacquie Cranfield, who produced ASA Milestones (Articles); the legendary Austin Rawlinson (Historical information); Margaret Smith (Registration data on long distance swimming).

I am most grateful to former great stars, Judy Grinham (Roe), Diana Wilkinson (Bishop) and Brian Phelps, for supplying much needed background for the "Where are they now?" articles.

Regarding photographs used in the Yearbook, I must thank A.H. Turner (Chairman) and Karren Glendenning (Editor) of the Swimming Times for allowing us to dip into their magnificent collection. Janie Allbeury and Helen Richards of Alan Pascoe Associates, also supplied many complimentary photographs.

We are very happy to have as our consultant, Leslie Cranfield, the ASA Statistician, who has been involved in the sport for over 20 years. He has compiled the British Rankings since 1966 and has helped with the Press Service at most major events in England since 1979. A member of the International Association of Swimming Statisticians, Leslie has also worked for BBC television and been a regular contributor to *Swimming Times*. He also helped the late Pat Besford with the *IAPS Swimming Bulletin* for many years, and it was her influence that persuaded him to emerge from the spectator's gallery. She would surely have approved of his latest venture!

Finally, much credit must be given to Michael Featherstone and Steve Langbridge for their unstinting efforts in helping to make Hugman's Swimming Yearbook well worth reading.

Misc Abbreviations

B — Borough	R — Region
C — City	S — South
D — District	T — Town
E — East	U — United
N — North	W — West
o — of	
P — Port	PB — Personal Best

Preface

Prior to this publication, sports fans, both on the inside and outside of swimming, must have thought it rather strange that a sport with such a large participation level, whether it be recreational or competitive, did not have its own reference book.

However, Hugman's Swimming Yearbook aims to fill the void, by documenting the history of the sport, as well as current trends in aquatics.

The ASA goes back well over 100 years and researching the past has been fascinating. The archives at Loughborough have revealed a wealth of material and the main problem has been just what to include in the first edition.

To make the Yearbook easy to follow, each discipline of aquatic sport has been sectioned off into Swimming, Diving, Water Polo, Synchronised Swimming, Long Distance, Channel Swimming and the English Schools Swimming Association, categories.

A selection of great moments in British swimming have been recalled, as well as articles on some of the many famous names who have graced the sport. Hopefully, those who remember the events and personalities described, will enjoy reminiscing. But, for the younger reader, maybe it will offer some inspiration; success at the highest level is possible, but it does not come easy!

Rounding off the historical sections is a complete list of champions for all events, including those which have since been discontinued, from junior ASA, right through to Olympic winners.

Also, record progression has been projected on a European and World basis, since the standardisation of 50 metre pool conditions, late in 1956, and for Britain, on going metric in the late '60s.

The 1988–89 season has been documented to show the complete results of the ASA Winter, the ASA National and the National Age Group events, while the international scene for the same period has not been overlooked, and results of the Olympic Games, the European Cup, both the senior and junior European Championships, are fully covered. All other internationals involving Great Britain, or England, along with all major Home competitions, have been included to give a full picture.

A highlight, from my point of view, is the inclusion of Masters Swimming. All of last season's National results are shown, and one has only to pore over the names to evoke memories of a seemingly dim and distant past. Still swimming, and still breaking records, are great names such as Jack Hale, John Mills, John Martin-Dye, Graham Sykes, Peter Jervis, Neil Jackson and Di Harris. More recent stars such as David Wilkie and Maggie Kelly (Hohmann), also get in on the act.

The purpose of the Yearbook is not only to serve swimmers, coaches, clubs, enthusiasts and the ASA, whose structure and its role are fully described herein, but to help promote the sport, giving it a much higher profile than it has enjoyed previously. Everyone with a fascination for any form of swimming should, hopefully, find something of interest within these covers.

In researching out the information already mentioned, the importance of the club and coaching system under the auspices of the ASA, has not been overlooked either. All of the 1,700 clubs affiliated to the ASA are listed, many with key information, including, secretaries' addresses, coaching staff, and the names of many club swimmers.

It can be seen quite clearly from the club section, that although the response in the main was good, there were many affiliated clubs who just did not bother to participate in this, their very own Yearbook, especially as it was backed by the ASA and will serve as a major marketing tool to put swimming well and truly on the map, as well as raising much needed sponsorship funds.

Let us hope that the second edition gets the support we think it deserves, which I am sure it will, probably in the form of the Mums and Dads, whose children should have got a mention first time round.

Finally, to help you find your way around the statistical sections of the book, apart from Progressive/Current Records, which are in reverse order, the style is:

Date/Placing — Competitor's name (Club/Country) — Time
Minutes are suffixed by :
Seconds are suffixed by .

Swimming in Sheffield
Something to look forward to!

Sheffield, in 1990, may well become the Swimming city of the UK. By the end of the year, two exciting new facilities will be opened in the run up to the World Student Games, to compliment the 14 pools already available to the public.

Ponds Forge in the city centre, a truly international facility, has unique features from a number of different countries. The main competition pool will be 50m x 25m, but with a floating floor from Holland, and moving booms from New Zealand, the pool can literally change its shape. There will be spectator seating for 2,900. Also on site will be a leisure pool with state of the art features, including a lazy river, an international diving pool, fitness areas and medical centres.

The Hillsborough pool has been purpose built for water polo competitions, with room for over 800 spectators. Equipped with a floating floor and boom, this pool can be converted to form a leisure pool/competition pool combination. The moving floor will tilt to form a beach area, and can even be raised to allow unique access for disabled users from deck level. The leisure pool side will contain a wave machine, a depth charge, porpoises, and a flume ride.

Existing provision will also be enhanced, and the well established Sheffield training scheme will also benefit. By 1990, it will be possible to swim in pools that span over 100 years of Swimming provision in Sheffield.

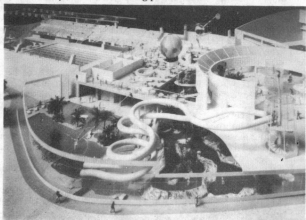

Ponds Forge International Sports Centre

Foreword

**by David Reeves
(Secretary/Chief Executive,
Amateur Swimming
Association)**

Welcome to the first-ever *Swimming Yearbook*, which is published at a time when the profile of swimming, both as a competitive sport and healthy activity, has never been higher.

The first objective of the Amateur Swimming Association is to promote the teaching and practice of swimming, diving, synchronised swimming, and water polo, and stimulate public opinion in favour of providing proper accommodation and facilities for them. Of course, good facilities are of paramount importance, but should we not also be "stimulating public opinion" towards the advantages of swimming, and, indeed, informing the public of just how big and successful the sport is in this country?

The ASA currently has just under 1,700 affiliated clubs, with an estimated total membership of around 300,000, the vast majority of these members being under 16 years of age. The most important work of our clubs is the promotion of "learn to swim" classes and lessons. In 1988, more than 570 people drowned in the United Kingdom, mainly in open water. As an island nation, swimming is more than a sport to us: it can be a life-saver, and everything possible must be done to teach everyone to swim — ideally before they leave school. The re-launch and upgrading of the ASA Proficiency Award Scheme, with the help of sponsorship from TSB England and Wales, has been a tremendous success. In the twelve months since the re-launch, about 1.4 million badges have been issued, with — significantly — Personal Survival Awards topping 100,000 for the first time.

Now that swimming, according to the Sports Council's figures, is the country's most popular participant sporting activity, the ASA are to launch a major campaign to bring the sport to the attention of the public. "Swim-Fit 90" will give everyone the opportunity to join in, from babes in arms to grandparents, the able-bodied and the handicapped. Through swimming, the aim is to improve the health and fitness of the nation.

As a competitive sport, there are exciting times ahead: the Commonwealth Games in New Zealand in January, 1990, with the World Championships in Perth, Australia, a year later. In the longer term, the prospect of the 1991 World Student Games in Sheffield, with possibly the finest swimming facility the world has ever seen.

The sport has a strong base, with 48,000 competitors and officials now registered with the ASA. What better time could there be to launch this excellent publication?

I would like to thank Barry Hugman for his initiative, and the publishers, advertisers, and contributors for making the whole thing possible. I hope the book will do much to "stimulate public opinion" in favour of swimming, and I also hope that every reader will enjoy the wealth of information contained therein.

FINA
FEDERATION INTERNATIONALE DE NATATION AMATEUR

```
ASIA        OCEANIA        EUROPE        AFRICA        AMERICA
                              |
                             LEN
                   LIGUE EUROPÉENNE DE NATATION
                            ASFGB
              AMATEUR SWIMMING FEDERATION OF GREAT BRITAIN
                              |
        ┌─────────────────────┼─────────────────────┐
   SCOTTISH ASA              ASA                 WELSH ASA
                AMATEUR SWIMMING ASSOCIATION
```

MIDLAND DISTRICT ASA	NORTHERN DISTRICT ASA	NORTH EASTERN DISTRICT ASA	SOUTHERN DISTRICT ASA	WESTERN DISTRICT ASA
Bedfordshire	Cheshire	Northumberland	Berkshire	Cornwall
Buckinghamshire	Cumbria	Durham	Buckinghamshire (Part)	Devon
Cambridgeshire	Lancashire	Yorkshire	Channel Islands	Dorset
Derbyshire	Isle of Man		Essex	Gloucestershire
Hereford & Worcester	Staffordshire (Part)		Hampshire	Somerset
Humberside (Part)			Hertfordshire	Wiltshire
Leicestershire			Kent	
Lincolnshire			Middlesex	
Norfolk			Oxfordshire (Part)	
Northamptonshire			Surrey	
Nottinghamshire			Sussex	
Oxfordshire (Part)				
Shropshire				
Staffordshire (Part)				
Suffolk				
Warwickshire				

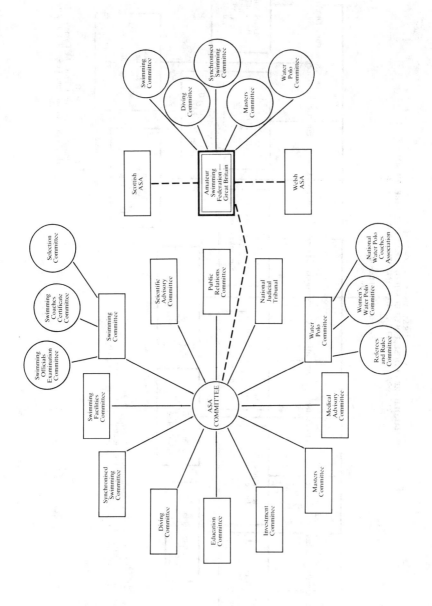

Swimming Committee

Diving Committee

Synchronised Swimming Committee

Masters Committee

Water Polo Committee

Scottish ASA

Amateur Swimming Federation — Great Britain

Welsh ASA

Selection Committee

Swimming Coaches Certificate Committee

Swimming Officials Examination Committee

Swimming Committee

Scientific Advisory Committee

Public Relations Committee

National Judicial Tribunal

National Water Polo Coaches Association

Women's Water Polo Committee

Water Polo Committee

Referees and Rules Committee

Swimming Facilities Committee

ASA COMMITTEE

Medical Advisory Committee

Synchronised Swimming Committee

Diving Committee

Education Committee

Investment Committee

Masters Committee

9

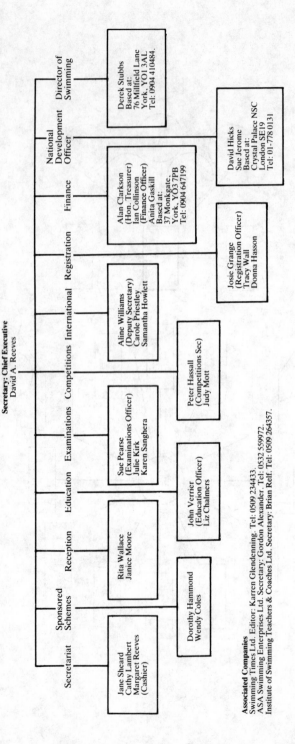

AMATEUR SWIMMING ASSOCIATION
HAROLD FERN HOUSE, LOUGHBOROUGH, LEICESTERSHIRE LE11 0AL.
TEL: 0509 230431. TELEX: 347072 AMSWIMG, FAX: 0509 610720

Secretary: Chief Executive
David A. Reeves

Secretariat
Jane Sheard
Cathy Lambert
Margaret Reeves (Cashier)

Sponsored Schemes
Dorothy Hammond
Wendy Coles

Reception
Rita Wallace
Janice Moore

Education
John Verrier
(Education Officer)
Liz Chalmers

Examinations
Sue Pearse
(Examinations Officer)
Julie Kirk
Karen Sanghera

Competitions
Peter Hassall
(Competitions Sec)
Judy Mott

International

Registration
Josie Grange
(Registration Officer)
Tracy Wall
Donna Hasson

Aline Williams
(Deputy Secretary)
Carole Priestley
Samantha Howlett

Finance
Alan Clarkson
(Hon. Treasurer)
Ian Collinson
(Finance Officer)
Anita Gaskill
Based at:
37 Monkgate,
York, YO3 7PB
Tel: 0904 647199

National Development Officer
David Hicks
Sue Jerome
Based at:
Crystal Palace NSC
London SE19
Tel: 01-778 0131

Director of Swimming
Derek Stubbs
Based at:
76 Millfield Lane
York, YO1 3AL
Tel: 0904 410484.

Associated Companies
Swimming Times Ltd. Editor: Karren Glendenning. Tel: 0509 234433.
ASA Swimming Enterprises Ltd. Secretary: Gordon Alexander. Tel: 0532 559972.
Institute of Swimming Teachers & Coaches Ltd. Secretary: Brian Relf. Tel: 0509 264357.

Hon Medical Adviser: Prof J.M. Cameron. Tel: 01-377 7622
Hon Legal Adviser: John Leach. Tel: 01-680 4387

ASA Milestones

1869 First recorded meeting of representatives of London swimming clubs held in the German Gymnasium, London, on 7 January.
Later that year the title of "Metropolitan Swimming Association" was assumed.
The only National Championship in 1869 was the mile.

1873 The title was changed to "The Swimming Association of Great Britain", though in fact it did not at that time include Scotland.

1878 The 100 yards was instituted, along with the 500 yards freestyle.

1880 Horace Davenport becomes President of the Association, which at that time consisted of 9 London and 11 provincial clubs.

1886 After long disputes over amateurism (during which Horace Davenport resigned), the title of "Amateur Swimming Association" was agreed upon. A new definition of "amateur" was made, and the Association's objectives were revised to include control of race meetings, uniformity of rules, and enforcements of the law.

1887 Royal Patronage granted to the ASA by HRH Queen Victoria.

1890 The first AGM was held, consisting of 135 clubs — first President was Horace Davenport.

1900 John Jarvis claimed Britain's first ever Olympic Gold Medal, when he won the 1000 metres freestyle event.

1901 First Women's Championship (100 yards freestyle).
The Association divided into the five districts we know today.

1903 Sir George Pragnell became President. On accepting office he made a list of reforms which he intended to put forward — a programme which took ten years to implement.

1908 The ASA took a leading part in the organisation of the Olympic Games at the White City, London.

1934 Harold Fern became President of the Association, after serving as Honorary Secretary of the Southern Counties from 1905–21, and then as Honorary Secretary of the ASA.
British Empire Games: swimming events were held at the Empire Pool Wembley (4-11 August).

1935 Diving first came under the control of the ASA when the Amateur Diving Association was wound up.
First centralised Swimming Championship held in Blackpool.

1938 European Championships held at Empire Pool, Wembley (30 July-7 August).

1947 Junior Championships instituted at Hastings.

1948 The ASA again took a leading role in the organisation of the Olympic Games held at Wembley.

1952 Alice M. Austin, of Beckenham Ladies Swimming Club, became the first woman President of the ASA

1956 Judy Grinham became Britain's first Olympic swimming Gold Medallist for 32 years when she won the 100 metres backstroke in Melbourne.

1960 First National Technical Officer appointed. Anita Lonsbrough wins the Olympic 200 metres breaststroke Gold Medal at Rome in world record time.

1962 Institution of Survival Awards.

1969 100th Anniversary of the first reported meeting at the German Gymnasium. Celebrations included a special gala at The Crystal Palace Sports Centre, at which the principal guests were The Association's Royal Patron, Her Majesty Queen Elizabeth II, and The Princess Anne. Later that year a banquet was held at Grosvenor House which was attended by 800 guests, including representatives of FINA. This was followed by a thanksgiving service at Westminster Abbey.

1970 The Martin Report outlining the future development of swimming was published, and accepted by the ASA.
Harold Fern, Honorary Secretary, then President of the ASA for a total of 49 years, retired from office.
Norman Sarsfield appointed first professional Secretary of the ASA.
First Open Age-Group Championships held.

1971 The Association took over publication of "The Swimming Times" from Captain B. W. Cummins, the founder editor.

1973 The ASA's present headquarters in Loughborough were officially opened on 23rd March.

European Junior Championships held in Leeds, in August.

Harold Fern died on 22 August, aged 94. He was Honorary Life President of FINA, as well as Life President of the ASA. For his outstanding life-long contribution to swimming he was inducted as an Honoree of The Hall of Fame in Fort Lauderdale, USA.

1976 David Wilkie becomes Olympic Champion for the 200 metres breaststroke in Montreal.

1977 In celebration of Queen Elizabeth's Silver Jubilee, an International Youth Meeting was held at Crystal Palace in the presence of HRH Princess Margaret. A substantial donation was made to The Appeal Fund of our Patron.

1978 Generous sponsorship from Cadbury's Dairy Milk enabled the setting up of teaching centres for swimmers and the training of teachers under a "Support Swimming" scheme.

1979 There was an increase of over 200% in the number of swimmers, divers, water polo players and synchro swimmers, who benefited from Sports Council Grants, and from The Sports Aid Foundation.

Alf Turner, Honorary Treasurer of the ASA, was honoured with an OBE.

1980 Masters swimming was introduced at National level, initially held in York, for amateurs only.

Duncan Goodhew wins the 100 metres breaststroke Gold Medal in the Moscow Olympics.

1981 Norman Sarsfield retired after 11 years as the first professional Secretary of the ASA, and was awarded the OBE in The New Year's Honours List. Mr Sarsfield was succeeded by Harold W. Hassall, who was in turn succeeded by David Reeves, the current holder.

1984 This year saw the introduction of drug testing in The National Championships.

1987 First European Masters Championships held at Blackpool during September, which was the last major event to be held at the Derby Baths.

1988 The continued growth of masters swimming was shown at The National Masters Championships held in Oxford. Over 500 swimmers competed and some 40 new GB records and 16 world records were set.

The Olympic Games were held in Seoul, South Korea and Adrian Moorhouse won Britain's only swimming Gold Medal in the 100 metres breaststroke.

Ken Martin, MBE, an Honorary Life President, died in September, aged 86. His contribution to swimming was considerable — the "Martin Report" shaped the future development of swimming in the early 1970's and beyond.

Great Britain Swimming Grand Prix launched.

1989 Midland, Northern and Southern Counties Districts, all celebrate their centenaries.

European Junior Swimming and Diving Championships held in Leeds, 27-30 July, 1989.

The ASA Awards Scheme

by Anne Eakin (Awards Convener)

The Awards were first introduced in 1952, with L. Pickering administering two schemes: Proficiency in Diving and Proficiency in Swimming. This grew to four schemes under E.J. Tackley in 1954, with Speed and Diving Awards being introduced. Lily Cook took over as administrator in 1958, and is still there 31 years later! The growth in the number and type of awards during this period has been huge.

In 1958, 8,260 awards were issued, and Lily Cook was able to do the job herself. By 1987, this number had risen to over one million, and involved six to 18 staff.

The very popular Personal Survival Awards were introduced in 1962, followed by The Rainbow series, the Water Skills Awards, and schemes for water-polo and synchronised swimming.

In 1983, fundamental changes were made to the Personal Survival Awards reflecting the latest research in cold water survival, and, at the same time, the Challenge Awards were introduced.

March, 1987 saw the start of a year-long review of the entire scheme, both tests and badges, culminating with the re-launch in March, 1988, sponsored by the TSB. The launch was extensive, involving roadshows, articles, and advertisements in educational journals and the *Swimming Times*.

The process of modernising the Awards Scheme, concentrated on ensuring that any Award would promote good teaching and that, as a result of this, pupils would succeed and be motivated to improve their skills and performance at a higher level. Instant reward for their success was foremost in the thinking of the revision, and therefore the system was changed to permit badges to be ordered prior to the test. The quality of the badges was also improved. So successful was the re-launch, that in March, 1989, the total number of Awards issued during the previous 12-month period was 1.5 million. Awards are invaluable if used correctly. A young girl recently asked an Olympic swimmer:

"When did you know you were going to be famous?"

"When I was ten, and passed the test where you swim in pyjamas — I think it's called the Challenge Two now. I certainly remember feeling very important when my headmaster presented it to me in front of the school. Everybody clapped."

If used correctly, Awards motivate swimmers, and should form a framework for the swimming curriculum.

Teachers should ensure a progressive swimming programme and aim, to provide a constant individual challenge, rather than repetition, which may lack any incentive to achieve better standards.

Concerns over standards of assessment are commonplace. This must remain the major responsibility of teachers and assessors. Poor teaching and low standards achieve nothing, and may, ultimately, give pupils a false sense of security. Those entering for an Award should be 99% certain of attaining it, using the appropriate level of skill.

The new Awards Log Book enables people to see at a glance those to aim for next, and the full range of skills on offer.

THE PUFFIN Award is designed with special needs and pre-school children in mind.

THE RAINBOW scheme is an objective test, asking pupils to swim between two points, without pausing and without stress. Pupils may touch in order to turn, as per the ASA freestyle turn.

PERSONAL SURVIVAL. This scheme is purely educative, and teaches basic principles for procedure, should pupils suddenly find themselves in a cold water emergency situation. The skills must be taught with imagination, and as realistically as possible.

SPEED SWIMMING. With good teaching, efficient strokes develop, which in turn enable pupils to swim further and faster. The scheme is designed to introduce pupils to competitive swimming.

DIVING. The "Preliminary Diving Skills" are designed to develop body awareness, prior to taking up diving seriously. The "Novice Diver" introduces pupils to the spring-board and more advanced techniques.

WATER-POLO. This scheme is designed for school pupils, endeavouring to cultivate an interest in the game.

SYNCHRONISED SWIMMING. The "Preliminary Award" introduces pupils to the basic skills, hopefully whetting their appetites to go on to the more difficult "Proficiency Scheme."

ULTIMATE SWIMMER. This is given freely to those who achieve awards in various schemes. It is designed to encourage pupils to experiment with a range of disciplines.

SWIM FIT. These awards encourage cardio-respiratory fitness, using speed and/or distance. When used regularly and progressively, the scheme can contribute to a health and fitness programme. Suitable for older pupils and adults.

SPECIAL NEEDS. In line with the modern educational trends, the ASA has made several of its Mainstream Awards available to special needs pupils. In particular, the Puffin, Waterskills One and Two, and the Rainbow series, offer those with disability the opportunity to gain the same Awards as their peers.

A sense of achievement is a valuable part of education. The ASA Awards are designed to recognise this achievement. If a child has been properly prepared, there should rarely be a failure. A teacher's duty is to teach success.

Harold Fern, President of the ASA from 1934–1970, shown in his first year of office, presenting the British Empire (Commonwealth) Games 1,500 yards men's freestyle gold medal to N.P. Ryan of Australia.

SWIMMING
SECTION

A Review of the 1988–89 Swimming Season

by Leslie Cranfield

This review covers the period from September 1988 to August 1989. The Seoul Olympics were already the high point of the year, but our swimmers have been in action almost non-stop ever since.

Major honours were achieved at both the European and World Cup competitions during the short-course season of 1988-89. More recently, Adrian Moorhouse and Nick Gillingham each set world records and won gold medals at the 1989 European Championships.

Two new concepts in competitive swimming were launched at the end of 1988 — the British Grand Prix and the FINA World Cup. The overall awards for both competitions were based on stroke categories.

The competitions centred around established meetings on the domestic and international circuits. The British Grand Prix proved very successful during the winter months and attracted the top British swimmers. However, the final, which took place some three months after the preliminary meets, lacked impetus and turned out to be a dull affair.

The World Cup, which was inaugurated with meets in Canada and the USA in November and December, had its problems too. Olympic competitors were not ready to tackle major internationals so soon after the Games. Some meets were cancelled and the rules were changed during the course of the circuit.

The last meet of the World Cup was held at Barnet in late February, and also incorporated a round of the British Grand Prix. Unfortunately, after nearly a month's solid competition on the continent, the top swimmers were weary and the meet somewhat disappointing.

There was delight for Britain at the end of the day, as Suki Brownsdon won both breaststroke and individual medley categories, and Grant Robins surprisingly took the backstroke award.

City of Leeds (men) and Wigan Wasps (women) again won the GB Club Team Championships, held in Leeds in March. These two teams then represented Great Britain at the E.E.C. Club Championships in Hamburg at the end of April.

Wigan, the defending ladies champions, were in contention until the final event, the 4×50 metric freestyle relay, but could only finish fourth. They ended the competition in second spot, five points adrift of the host club, Hamburg.

City of Leeds also finished second, an improvement on last year, but A.S. Roma ran out easy winners of the men's competition.

1988 Olympic Games

The outstanding competitor in the pool proved to be Kristin Otto of East Germany, with her six gold medal haul. Janet Evans (USA), with her predicted three victories, and Krisztina Egerszegi (Hungary), with a surprise win in the 200 backstroke, halted the East German gold rush in the women's events.

Evans' new world record in the 400 freestyle, was a stunning achievement, as she cast aside the East German duo of Frederich and Moehring. Silke Hoerner (GDR) was the only other female world record breaker, with a new mark in the 200 breaststroke.

The men's events were a different story, nine countries claimed gold and nine new world records were set. Matt Biondi (USA), with five gold, one silver and one bronze, did not quite reach the Otto standard, but saved the USA's face. Tamas Darnyi (Hungary) was brilliant with two golden world records in the individual medley. Other world records fell in the 50 freestyle, 200 freestyle, 400 freestyle, 100 backstroke and all three relays. Anthony Nesty (Surinam), in the 100 butterfly, and Daichi Suzuki (Japan), in the 100 backstroke, caused major upsets to win. The most popular winner was Vladimir Salnikov (USSR), who regained the 1500 freestyle title that he won in Moscow, eight years previously.

On paper, Great Britain had possible medals in three events, and these hopes were fulfilled with a gold by Adrian Moorhouse (100 breaststroke), silver by Nick Gillingham (200 breaststroke), and bronze by Andy Jameson (100 butterfly).

These three men did Great Britain proud, and their success is further underlined by the sheer quality of the competition. It was the first Games unaffected by boycott since Montreal, and competition was so intense that making a final was a major achievement.

Adrian Moorhouse suffered much criticism after finishing fourth in Los Angeles, but made his critics eat their words with victories in both the 1985 and 1987 European Championships. However, the turning point for Adrian may have been at the 1986 Commonwealth Games in Edinburgh. Having lost his 100 breaststroke title to arch-rival Victor Davis (Canada), he was determined to make amends, and he did so in style over 200, defeating the Canadian Olympic Champion and World record holder. Disqualification after winning the 1986 World Championships 100 breaststroke title in Madrid, acted as a further spur, and completed his swimming education. The 1988 Moorhouse was altogether a more mature and better prepared competitor.

His new record, set in March, made him the fastest entry in Seoul, and he lived up to expectations by winning his heat, to lead the qualifiers. The final was a race of high drama, as Dmitriy Volkov (USSR) scorched to the halfway turn. This fast start cost Volkov dear, and Moorhouse, who had been well down at 50 metres, made a charge for the wall. As Volkov's stroke shortened, Moorhouse kept his head and reached out to touch the pad, a mere 1/100th of a second ahead of Hungary's unsung Karoly Guttler, with Volkov desperately clinging to the bronze.

Moorhouse's achievement was the start that the British team had dreamed of. On the fourth day of competition, Andy Jameson was the great British hope, and like Moorhouse, he had qualified fastest, setting a new Commonwealth record in the process. However, the final provided a shock winner in Anthony Nesty of Surinam. True, Nesty was the 1987 Pan American Games Champion, but few had expected him to beat Matt Biondi, who blazed up the first length in 24.53 seconds. Biondi seemed to have the gold within his grasp until the final stroke, when he fluffed his finish to allow the fast closing Nesty, past. Meanwhile Jameson, who had been slow into his stroke at the start, caught Australia's Jon Sieben for the bronze. Andy, always the sportsman, said that the final was much harder than the heat. In fact, he had swum the two fastest races of his career — a considerable achievement for this most modest of champions.

Kevin Boyd and friends.   Alan Pascoe Ass.

In the heats of the men's 200 breaststroke, Nick Gillingham broke David Wilkie's British record, set in Montreal 12 years earlier. Gillingham had predicted that he would break the record, but was aware that he would have to go faster still to defeat Hungary's World and European Champion, Joszef Szabo. Two Soviet swimmers tore through the first 100 metres, but trod water when Szabo made his move at the final turn. Gillingham tried all he could to hang on to the Hungarian down that last length, but Szabo would not yield. The English boy swam a brave race, and was rewarded with the silver medal.

Elsewhere, Kevin Boyd broke the national records for both the 400 and 1500 freestyle, and was the only Briton to make two individual finals. Gary Binfield and Paul Howe were other British record breakers, but found their final challenge reduced to the consolations. The last event proved a bitter disappointment. Since the 1987 European Championships in Strasbourg, we had had cause for optimism in the men's medley relay and after qualifying for the final in pole position, our hopes were higher still. However, a disastrous opening backstroke leg blew away our chances and, on the anchor, a desperate Mark Foster earned a disqualification for diving in before Andy Jameson had touched — a sad finale.

Our women's team had their most disappointing Olympics ever, and for the first time failed to produce a single finalist. They found the combination of the occasion and calibre of their oponents overwhelming.

Ruth Gilfillan and Kathy Read were the only record breakers. Ruth twice broke the Scottish 200 freestyle record, and Kathy improved her English record for the 100 backstroke. For the rest, only Helen Bewley, Suki Brownsdon, Jean Hill and Lynne Wilson qualified for the consolations.

The competition in the Chamshil Pool proved electricfying, and although East Germany and the USA took 46 of the medals, 20 other countries also claimed a share of the bounty.

1988 Winter Nationals

These championships, formerly known as the short course Nationals, were bound to be seen by some as an anti-climax, coming so soon after the Olympic Games. However, it did give the opportunity for newcomers to show their hand.

Generally speaking, it was those who missed out on Olympic selection who stole the glory, but Nick Gillingham, Mike Fibbens and Kathy Read maintained their established places on the podium.

Grant Robins and Duncan Rolley, with three titles apiece, dominated the men's division, while Madeleine Scarborough matched them with a hat-trick in the women's events.

Day one brought Grant his first title in the 200 backstroke, and he did it in style, breaking Kevin Boyd's new British record in the process. Ian Wilson completed a tough double with clear victories in the 200 butterfly and 1500 freestyle.

Debbie Tubby looked a class apart when she took her first senior title in the 200 breaststroke. Madeleine Scarborough made it a Pompey double when she successfully defended her 100 butterfly crown.

Day two proved rather more exciting as the meet gained momentum. Duncan Rolley stormed to victory in the 200 freestyle, while younger brother Andy nearly made it a family double in the 400 individual medley. However, the in-form Grant Robins had the last word and snatched the title close to home. In the men's 100 breaststroke, Olympic hero Nick Gillingham, had to battle to shut out the defending champion, Iain Campbell.

For the girls, Rebecca Barden took her first senior title by a mere 3/100th of a second from Helen Walsh in the 200 individual medley. Kathy Read held off a spirited challenge from Gloucester's Joanne Deakins in the 100 backstroke, while Karen Mellor completed a freestyle double with a clear win in the 800, to add to her 400 victory of the previous day.

Day three saw the Portsmouth duo of Robins and Scarborough continuing to dominate, when Robins took a third title in the 100 backstroke, just ahead of Carl Cockcroft. Madeleine made it a butterfly double in the 200, finishing ahead of Olympic representative Caroline Foot for the second time in three days. Later she was back to challenge for the 100 freestyle title, but found a revitalised Karen Pickering just too speedy.

Elsewhere, Duncan Rolley continued to demonstrate new-found freestyle form, this

In typically happy mood, Madeleine Scarborough is seen receiving her World Cup Stroke Award for the butterfly, from Alistair Boyd, Executive Director, TSB. Alan Pascoe Ass.

time over 400, and stopped Ian Wilson from taking a third title. Mike Fibbens had high hopes of a double in the 50 freestyle and 100 butterfly. Sure enough, he took the sprint title, although arch-rival Mark Foster was faster in the consolation. The surprise came in the butterfly, when local hero Rick Leishman caught the early leader David Parker, and a tired Fibbens trailed home last. Lorraine Coombes, who narrowly missed Olympic selection, was a clear winner in the 100 backstroke, recapturing a title that she last won in 1983.

The final day saw Duncan and Madeleine complete their hat-tricks, but it was Caroline Woodcock who made the headlines. Her swift 50 freestyle gave her the overall best performance by a woman.

Duncan had a narrow victory over defending champion Paul Brew in the 200 individual medley. However, moments earlier, Grant Robins had won the consolation final in a new English record time. Mike Fibbens lead all the way to successfully defend his 100 freestyle crown, and Nick Gillingham deposed Iain Campbell in the 200 backstroke.

Madeleine's third Championship win came in the 200 freestyle, and Kathy Read just recaptured the 100 backstroke title that she lost to Helen Slatter. This time it was rising star Joanne Deakins who pushed Read to the limit, while Helen Walsh, who just missed out in the 200 individual medley, made amends in the longer race to claim her first senior title.

1988 European Cup

This annual competition was held in the Royal Commonwealth Pool, Edinburgh, which was converted to 25 metres with the installation of a boom. The meet was most successfully organised by the Scottish A.S.A as a part of their Centenary celebrations.

Mens events: After our prominent showing in Seoul, it was hoped that our boys would offer a challenge to the favourites, the Soviet Union.

However, without Olympic medal winners, Adrian Moorhouse and Andy Jameson, the task proved formidable, even though all our swimmers did qualify for finals.

Kevin Boyd proved to be the outstanding British man with clear victories in the 400

19

and 1500 freestyle. His time for the latter was a new British record of 14:57.36 — a mere 5/100ths of a second short of the Commonwealth best, and his first time under the 15 minute barrier. Nick Gillingham, the Olympic silver medallist, was the only other British man to win a medal. He finished runner-up to Valeriy Lozik (USSR) in the 200 breaststroke, but found the going tougher in the 100, and could only place fourth behind old rival, Dmitriy Volkov (USSR), the bronze medallist in Seoul. The Soviet Union, with eight victories, were always in control and turned out easy winners of the meet. Solid performances by Mike Fibbens, Rick Leishman, Tim Jones and Duncan Rolley put us ahead of the pack, but the all-round power of the two German teams kept us out of the first three places.

Women's events: Three months after their worst ever showing in an Olympic Games, the British girls fought back with some gritty performances. The key to success in a team competition is solid all-round effort, and our girls achieved this by only finishing out of the first four in two events.

Outstanding performances came from Suki Brownsdon, who finished second and third with new British records, in the 100 and 200 breaststroke. In the shorter race, Suki really pushed the Olympic Champion, Tania Bogomilova (Bulgaria), all the way. Kathy Read was also in great form, setting new figures for the 200 backstroke, when finishing second behind Anja Eichhorst (GDR). On the first day she had broken 64 seconds for the first time, to claim an important third place. Madeleine Scarborough was the other Briton to snatch a medal, when she took second place behind Susanne Schuster (W Germany) in the 200 butterfly.

The best performance of all came when Read, Brownsdon, Caroline Foot and Karen Pickering combined to win the final event — the medley relay. Drawn alongside the favourites, GDR, each girl gave their all to secure a famous victory. Read had almost matched Eichhorst on the opening backstroke leg, and then Brownsdon headed Rex on breaststroke. The lead was increased by Foot on fly, who was up against the world champion, Kormelia Gresler. And it was left to Karen Pickering, who had almost quit after a bitter disapointment at the Olympic trials, to finish the job. Sabina Schulze started to close the gap, but Pickering would not yield.

The GDR, with eight wins were clear winners of the Cup, but the British girls were magnificent runners-up.

1989 TSB Nationals

The championships featured a revised programme, and a return to morning heats and late afternoon finals. This format proved more popular with swimmers and coaches, and was reflected in the overall results.

The first day proved successful for Suki Brownsdon and the City of Leeds club. Suki, who has recently shown the best form of her long career, totally dominated the 400 individual medley from the gun, and finished over ten seconds ahead of her nearest rival, Helen Walsh. Inside an hour she was back on the blocks for the 200 breaststroke, and duly collected a fourth successive title.

Jonathan Broughton claimed the first event when he zipped past Paul Brew and Sean McQuaid in the closing stages of the 200 freestyle. The battle for the 100 breaststroke looked intriguing, with Olympic Champion Adrian Moorhouse, defending National champion James Parrack, and Olympic silver medallist Nick Gillingham — the man in form. However, Moorhouse proved that he was hungry for even more success when he kept Gillingham at bay. The surprise of the opening day came in the 100 butterfly, when local hero David Parker (Coventry) flew off the blocks and was never headed. His reward was a first National senior title, a personal best time and automatic selection for the European Championships in Bonn. As hard as they tried, Mike Fibbens and Steven Dronsfield could not close the gap and Parker had put his Coventry club back on the swimming map.

Day two saw backstroke champions Gary Binfield and Kathy Read retain their titles. Read with consumate ease over 100, recording her sixth straight victory in the event that she first won in 1984, while Binfield had a harder task to dislodge the early leader Patrick Blake in the men's 200.

Paul Brew won a thrilling battle with Peter O'Sullivan in the 400 individual medley. O'Sullivan held a 1½ second advantage going into the final freestyle leg, but Brew judged the race perfectly and took control in the final 15 metres.

Mike Fibbens, the runner-up in 1988, showed that he is the fastest British sprinter, when winning the blue riband — the 100 freestyle. Fibbens blazed up the first 50 and held a clear advantage — the second half looked much harder but, nevertheless, he kept cool and proved too good for Steven Dronsfield.

Madeleine Scarborough, who returned to top class swimming in 1987, clinched selection for the European Championships with a clear-cut victory in the 100 butterfly. Former champions, Samantha Purvis and Caroline Foot, were in close attendance at the turn, but suddenly Madeleine found an extra gear, just as the others began to fade. Her final time of 1:02.05 was outstanding and unexpected, since she had missed six weeks training because of a knee injury that required surgery in the spring.

The third day saw the struggle for places on the plane to Bonn intensify, but three National Champions defended their titles successfully — Nick Gillingham (200 breaststroke), Karen Mellor (800 freestyle), and Suki Brownsdon (100 breaststroke). Sharron Davies took her first National title since 1980, with a well-judged victory in the 200 invididual medley.

Davies had been a major talking point of the Championships, and had set her sights on competing at next year's Commonwealth Games in Auckland. She had already revealed how sharp she was with two fourth places in the 100 freestyle and 100 butterfly earlier in the meet. Now, in the short medley, her strongest event, she took on the British record holder, Jean Hill, and World Cup winner, Suki Brownsdon. Davies, despite being behind early leader Samantha Purvis at halfway, had already secured a distinct advantage over Brownsdon and Hill, who had their strongest hand, the breaststroke to follow. So it proved, with Davies holding off the two British breaststroke record holders, and the turn on to freestyle brought a welcome relief as she sailed away to win by almost a second.

Nick Gillingham, the Olympic silver medallist and GB record holder, confirmed his class in the 200 breaststroke, while Neil Hudghton wore down Adrian Moorhouse in the final 50 metres to finish second.

Suki Brownsdon won her third title in a very competitive 100 breaststroke, however, behind her, battle was on for the second spot. Fast-starting Lorraine Coombes and

Nick Gillingham (centre) after winning the TSB National 200 metres breaststroke, with Neil Hudghton (left) in second place and Adrian Moorhouse, third.   Alan Pascoe Ass.

Margaret Hohmann were locked in battle as Brownsdon asserted herself in the second half of the race. Last year Hohmann finished second and went to Seoul. This time Coombes took her revenge and snatched second place.

The men's 400 freestyle brought a second Scottish victory when Campbell McNeil surprisingly swept past long-time leader, Kevin Boyd. The GB record holder and Olympic finalist was lacking condition, because of his final medical school examination, and could not even hold on to second place.

The final day brought more joy for Portsmouth, the club that had been so successful at last November's Winter Championships in Plymouth.

Grant Robins, who had been so disappointing in both the 200 backstroke and 400 individual medley, suddenly found his touch in the shorter medley and headed the field at halfway. Then Peter O'Sullivan made a breaststroke charge to close down on the tiring Robins. But the Portsmouth lad simply refused to give in over the final freestyle leg and took his only title of the meet. This success came with selection for Bonn, Grant's first major senior Games.

Madeleine Scarborough, a club mate of Robins, completed a butterfly double, but only just! Samantha Purvis led for 199 of the 200 metres, but at the end the scoreboard revealed that the pair had touched simultaneously. Both girls had shown tremendous character after suffering misery a year ago at the Olympic trials.

Elsewhere, Kathy Read and Gary Binfield duly collected their second backstroke titles. Caroline Woodcock, the GB record holder, outsprinted Olympic representative Alison Sheppard in the 50 freestyle. Strength of character is also essential in the 1500 freestyle, and Kevin Boyd showed just that in the final individual event. Boyd, who had been pipped at the post over 400 the previous day, made a decisive move at 1200 metres and shook off his only remaining challenger, the defending champion, Tony Day, to grab a place in the team for Bonn.

During the final days prior to the Championships, the country was affected by a series of national strikes and these did disturb the last minute preparations in Coventry. Trains were at a standstill, and the pool closed by the NALGO dispute until the first day of competition. Once underway, some television coverage was lost by the BBC technicians strike, Despite all of these factors, the momentum soon picked up, and there appeared to be no feeling of let down sometimes associated with past Olympic seasons.

1989 European Junior Swimming Championships

Some 30 countries had entered the European Junior Championships, and top quality aquatics were assured. However the atmosphere during the four days at the International Pool, Leeds, was a new experience for British swim fans.

With the call for the competitors in heat 1 of the first event, came the blast of horns, the sound of cowbells, and crowd participation to rival that in Edinburgh for the 1986 Commonwealth Games. It was a meet to remember, and how the British team rose to the occasion, winning eight medals.

The first day saw defending 100 metres breaststroke champion Ian McKenzie, make a brave attempt to get Great Britain off to a golden start. However, Italy's Francesco Postiglione, runner-up in 1988, proved just too powerful, and took his revenge. Ian's early season preparation had been interrupted by illness, and subsequent loss of training cost him dearly. The final event of the session produced another silver medal for the boys 4×100 freestyle team behind hot favourites, the Soviet Union. Michael Hanby set the ball rolling, Sam Ferguson and Mark Jones kept us in touch and Austyn Shortman was outstanding on the anchor leg. Earlier, Christian Robinson and Kevin Crosby set lifetime bests to finish fourth and fifth in the 200 butterfly. Kevin's time of 2:05.81 broke Christian's GB junior record.

The second day saw the East German boys win all three events, but Hungary's Krisztina Egerszegi stopped the East German girls with a double in the 100 backstroke and 400 individual medley. Two personal best swims by Steven Mellor were not rewarded with a medal. He did, however, break the four minute barrier with an improvement of over five seconds. Ian Clayton, in the 100 backstroke, and Lucy Findlay, in the 400 individual medley, were the other British finalists, but found the going tough and finished down the field.

The third day was more successful, and Richard Maden appeared to win the gold medal in the 200 breaststroke after a desperate struggle with Francesco Postiglione.

Sadly, the scoreboard revealed that the Italian had won, but the margin of victory was a cruel 6/100ths of a second. Mark Jones set a Welsh senior record, but even this left him 8/100ths short of a bronze medal. In the boy's 200 backstroke, Ian Clayton's charge over the final 25 metres proved good enough for the bronze. The final day brought Austyn Shortman the bronze in the 100 freestyle, behind the outstanding Soviet sprinter, Raimundas Majolis. This proved to be the limit of our medal winning, despite high hopes in the 1500 freestyle and medley relay. Ross Noble and Steven Mellor had turned in excellent performances in the heats of the 1500 the previous day, but the final produced an outstanding swim by Sebastian Wiese of East Germany, who stormed away from the rest of the field. The British boys found the pace just too hot and had a private battle for fourth spot, which Ross just claimed. Any hope of a medal in the boy's medley relay were dashed by a poor opening backstroke leg. After that we were always fighting a rearguard action, and finished in fourth place.

The Hungarian Olympic backstroke Champion, Krisztina Egerszegi, proved the outstanding swimmer of the meet with four individual golds and a silver — each won with performances of the highest class. Christian Keller (W Germany) proved to be the character of the championships, with victories in the 200 freestyle and 200 individual medley. He also took a silver and bronze in the butterfly events, and further added to his bounty with three relay medals. The young West German relished his success and was warmly greeted by the crowd on his frequent trips to the victory dais. For Great Britain, the boys justified our optimism, with 12 of the team setting personal bests. On the other hand, the girls continue to give cause for concern, producing only two individual finalists, who both finished last.

1989 National Age Group

These Championships followed immediately after the European Juniors, and so many of the British team were putting their reputations on the line by rushing down to Crystal Palace to compete.

Upsets in the current form book were only to be expected, as the veterans of Leeds faced their better prepared rivals.

Christian Robinson (Killerwhales) was one who shook off fatigue, and he did so emphatically. Robinson, who narrowly missed a medal in Leeds, made amends with a remarkable six titles and dominated the 15-16 group. Steven Mellor (Satellite), Robinson's GB team-mate, maintained his new-found form to take three titles in the same section.

Nick Polkinghorne (Truro) scored an unexpected breaststroke double in the 17-18 category. On Tuesday he surprised Richard Maden, a medal-winning hero in Leeds, over the 100 metre sprint. The next day, it was an action replay over 200 metres, and the Cornishman maintained his early lead to set a new Championship best performance. Douglas Gatland (Beckenham) was the most successful competitor in this group with three titles.

Lower down the ranks, Jason Lancaster (Wycombe), and Dominic Sheils (Warrender) scored hat-tricks in the 13-14, but the youngest groups proved more open with a different winner in each of the six events.

Zoe Harrison (Norwich) asserted herself with five victories in the girls 15-16 competition. Previously, in Leeds, she had been unable to make an impression on her European rivals, but a week later she proved more than a match for her British opponents. Dawn Palmer (Killerwhales), the outstanding girl in 1988, was drawn in the same group as Harrison, and found a year's difference in age too big a handicap. Nevertheless she added four more titles to her impressive tally.

In the senior age group, Judy Lancaster (Warriors of Warrington) grabbed three titles, while Jayne Dowling (Bobcats), in the 15-16s, made the dash from Leeds worthwhile with a similar haul. Lee Dalzell (Derwentside) was the most successful in the youngest section.

At the end of a hectic weeks competition, Zoe Harrison and Christian Robinson, with 11 titles between them, were named as the outstanding competitors, while Killerwhales (boys) and City of Chester (girls) took the club honours.

1989 European Championships

The 19th European Championships, held in Bonn, West Germany, were remarkable for the openness of the men's competition, and the continuing reign of the East German women.

Two new world records were set on the first day; one by Adrian Moorhouse in the 100 breaststroke, and the other by Giorgio Lamberti (Italy) in the 200 freestyle. Nick Gillingham equalled Mike Barrowman's new world figures of 2:12.90 for the 200 breaststroke, only to learn that Barrowman had regained the mark within 24 hours. The American, competing in the Pan-Pacific Championship in Tokyo, had shaved 1/100th of a second from his previous record.

Eight countries took a share of gold in the men's events, while only Catherine Plewinski (France), with two titles, prevented a clean sweep by a powerful East German squad. Giorgio Lamberti led the Italian men's team to the top of the medals table with four golds. Apart from his world record, he also set a new European mark in winning the 100 freestyle, and was instrumental in the Italian victory in the long relay.

For Great Britain, it was the breaststroke duo of Adrian Moorhouse and Nick Gillingham, who again proved to be our trump cards. On the first day, Moorhouse, who had broken the world record in the morning heats, successfully defended his 100 metre title ahead of long-time rival Dmitriy Volkov (USSR). This was a third straight victory for Moorhouse, who had previously taken the title in 1985 and 1987, as well as coming second in 1983. Behind the top two, Gillingham finished fastest of all to claim the bronze.

After his fine performance in the sprint, Gillingham had to wait three days to take on the Olympic Champion, Joszef Szabo (Hungry), for the 200 title. The morning heat revealed that Nick was in top form, when breaking the British record, to qualify fastest, but the final turned out to be a solitary affair, as he carved out a furious pace, increasing his lead at every turn. With the crowd behind him from the start, he responded to their frantic cheering to leave the rest nearly three seconds adrift. At the final touch the scoreboard revealed that he had equalled the world record of 2:12.90, and also set a new European mark. Behind Gillingham, the unsung Irishman, Gary O'Toole, swimming in lane eight, overhauled Szabo to claim the silver — a first medal for Ireland in the history of these Championships.

Elsewhere, Kevin Boyd (1500 freestyle), and Tim Jones (200 butterfly) made finals, and both ensured automatic selection for the Commonwealth Games by finishing in the top six. Jones was prominent in the butterfly until the last 50 metres, when Tamas Darnyi (Hungary) applied the pressure to take the crown vacated by Michael Gross. This win, alongside his customary medley double, made the Hungarian the only individual to achieve three golds.

Gary Binfield again broke the British record when taking the consolation final of the 200 metre backstroke. Steven Dronsfield, Campbell McNeil and Peter O'Sullivan all responded well to the challenge of their first European Championships.

After their poor showing in Seoul, the British women's team were determined to improve their international standing. This proved a tough proposition with the almost total East German dominance, leaving the rest fighting for minor places. As in 1987, the British girls failed to take a medal, but gave cause for optimism in some quarters.

Caroline Woodcock, with a new British record in the 50 freestyle, and Karen Pickering, in the 100, revealed a new sprinting prowess. Both girls finished sixth and gained selection for Auckland. Joining them down under will be veterans Lorraine Coombes (100 breaststroke) and Sharron Davies (200 individual medley), who also made the top six.

Kathy Read (backstroke), Suki Brownsdon (breaststroke), and Madeleine Scarborough (100 metres butterfly), ensured a British presence in seven finals, but it was the relay performances that showed true British grit. The medley team finished a highly creditable fifth, and the freestyle quartette, although only sixth, broke the British record.

In the year following an Olympic Games, the sport tends to enter a transitional phase and these Championships showed evidence of this. Only five of the 26 titles were successfully defended in Bonn.

Despite the absence of Michael Gross, and the restricted programme of Kristin Otto, there were memorable moments, especially for Adrian and Nick.

The Evergreen Maggie Hohmann

by Steven Downes (The Times)

At 33 years old, most people are beginning to take their sport a little easier — men who used to be wingers in Sunday morning football might convert to full-backs to prolong their playing careers by a couple of seasons, while women who have run middle distance on the track might think about running a marathon. Maggie Hohmann, though, is different: in the pool, she just keeps going quicker, and come January, she will be aiming at a Commonwealth Games medal, 12 years after winning silvers in Edmonton.

The paradoxes of Hohmann's second swimming career leaves the former Miss Kelly as confused as anyone else: "Now, I'm up half the night with my son, am given the run-around all day, and get into the pool in the evening for training, completely shattered. Yet I improve. The older I get, the more confused I get." Delighted, as well: few of the world record-breakers and winners on last winter's inaugural World Cup circuit could have reacted with such joy as Hohmann after the 100 metres breaststroke in Paris last February. There, she cracked the 70-second barrier for the first time, with 1:09.68 seconds, and nearly leapt from the water like a salmon when she saw the time on the scoreboard. Before the end of the month, Hohmann continued her run of form, improving her own British best for two lengths of a short-course pool to 32.30 seconds.

It is now 23 years since little Maggie Kelly, one of eight children, first joined Bootle Swimming Club. Her swimming career followed conventional lines as she progressed through her teens, with bleary-eyed, sometimes reluctant morning sessions and hard work after school, leading to age group, district and senior honours. Aged 17, she grabbed her first British senior record, although not at breaststroke, for which she is best known, but at 100 metres backstroke.

For three years, she had been training under the guidance of Keith Bewley, now the coach at Wigan Wasps, who has the reputation as one of the best coaches of women in Britain. It was Bewley's style of training which was the key to keeping young Maggie in

An early shot of Maggie Kelly (Hohmann).

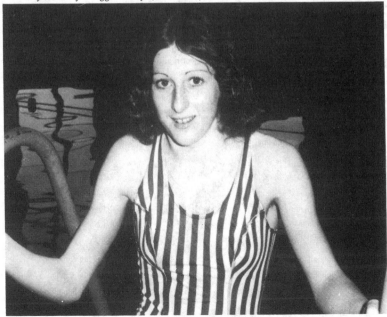

the swim: "I would never have stuck to the sort of regime some of the kids these days are on. Hours and hours of mindless training would just have been too much."

Instead, she thrived on short, sharp, intensive sessions that led her to a World Championship final at 200 metres breaststroke in 1978. The two Commonwealth silvers came the same year, and in 1979, Kelly won a gold in the World Cup, in Tokyo.

But undoubtedly, Maggie's finest moment came as part of the medley relay quartet at the Moscow Olympics when, somehow, and against all odds, the Brits raised and rallied themselves to beat the Soviets to the silver medal.

She retired afterwards, married David Hohmann, an executive with Speedo, moved to Nottingham, and, in June 1986, gave birth to a son, Robert. Her comeback to the competitive pool was partly as a result of becoming a mother: "You've got to have a break from being with the baby all the time and it makes a change doing some training in the evenings."

Within six months of Robert's birth, Hohmann was racing again, swimming a medley relay leg for Wigan after just one training session, although she felt that motherhood had kept her in trim — "Giving birth to a 10lb 10oz baby felt a bit like a competition".

The 18-month term goal was to make the team for the Seoul Olympics, which she did by "just hanging on", as she said on the poolside afterwards, to second place at the Nationals. There, on an emotional Saturday afternoon in Leeds, she gained selection for Korea, where she competed in her third Olympics, the day after her 32nd birthday.

But, while swimming can be a useful escape route from the day-to-day hassle as a wife and mother, the responsibilities cannot be discarded all the time. When Maggie and David are away at a championship, someone has to be found to literally hold the baby, and, with a three-week training camp preceding the European Championships in Bonn in 1989, Maggie knew she could not afford the time off. While she had a claim to a place on the team — second at 200 metres breaststroke and third at 100 metres at the Nationals in Coventry — it was not pressed too hard. Like her Wigan clubmate, June Croft, Hohmann's attention has been fixed firmly on New Zealand, where medals are a much more realistic possibility.

Notably, two other women in Britain's swimming team at the Moscow Games of nearly a decade ago, are still in strong contention for places in England's team for Auckland — Suki Brownsdon and Sharron Davies — and both have conformed to the principles of a lighter, less demanding work load to maintain their enthusiasm for racing, into adulthood. Hohmann has the added difficulty of being coached "by post", with Bewley providing schedules through the mail for her to follow, but it is not a handicap that has stopped her getting faster.

As one of my colleagues in the press box has found to his cost, asking Maggie Hohmann when she intends to retire is a question guaranteed to raise her ire. She cannot foresee a time when she will give up swimming, and as long as she keeps improving, there is no reason why she should opt for an easy life.

Maggie in action during 1978.   Swimming Times

ASA Championships, 1988–89

ASA Winter (Short Course)
Central Park Pool, Plymouth — 16/20 November, 1988

Men

50 Metres Freestyle
Final

1	M. Fibbens (Barnet Copthall)	23.31
2	N. Metcalfe (Co Leeds)	23.43
3	D. Dyke (Walsall)	23.90
4	D. Parker (Co Coventry)	23.91
5	A. Shortman (Bristol Central)	23.95
6	S. Wellington (Portsmouth Northsea)	24.04

Consolation Final

1	M. Foster (Bo Southend)	23.26
2	S. Dronsfield (Co Leeds)	23.92
3	L. Holgate (Oundle & D)	24.20
4	S. Foggo (Co Newcastle)	24.47
5	G. Bulpitt (Co Birmingham)	24.50
6	G. Minns (Co Birmingham)	24.62

Heat Times

1	M. Fibbens (Barnet Copthall)	23.83
2	A. Shortman (Bristol Central)	23.99
3	N. Metcalfe (Co Leeds)	24.00
4	D. Parker (Co Coventry)	24.03
5	D. Dyke (Walsall)	24.04
6	S. Wellington (Portsmouth Northsea)	24.08
7	S. Dronsfield (Co Leeds)	24.11
8	M. Foster (Bo Southend)	24.13
9	G. Bulpitt (Co Birmingham)	24.20
10	G. Minns (Co Birmingham)	24.33
11	L. Holgate (Oundle & D)	24.38
12	S. Foggo (Co Newcastle)	24.39
13	A. Rapley (Buxton & D)	24.42
14	S. Hirst (Barnet Copthall)	24.46
15	T. Hart (Thurrock)	24.55
16	R. Thorp (Millfield)	
	M. Levine (Co Sheffield)	24.67
18	A. Exton (Redditch)	24.68
19	M. Hanby (Nova Centurion)	24.73
20	P. Fakley (Dover Lifeguard)	24.83
21	G. Smith (White Oak)	24.88
22	L. Walker (Kelly College)	24.92
23	A. Moore (Amersham)	
	S. Glover (Salford Triple 'S')	25.07
25	S. Haywood (Co Derby)	25.13
26	C. Strong (Thamesdown)	25.22
27	M. Jones (Co Southampton)	25.27
28	J. Ley (Millfield)	25.35
29	D. Hedley (Chester le Street)	25.37
30	A. Irwin (Kelly College)	25.51
31	S. Morris (Gloucester C)	25.54
32	J. Wallis (Co Peterborough)	25.60
33	J. Hunter (Derwentside)	25.70
34	D. Wright (Co Leicester)	25.82
35	M. Weighton (Wulfrunians)	26.16
36	L. Downham (Bo Burnley CATS)	26.24
	L. Leveridge (Bo Kirklees)	
38	S. Wheeler (Co Sheffield)	26.39
39	N. Williams (Hounslow B)	26.90

Junior Placings: (1) A. Shortman;
(2) T. Hart; (3) M. Hanby.

100 Metres Freestyle
Final

1	M. Fibbens (Barnet Copthall)	50.64
2	S. Dronsfield (Co Leeds)	50.89
3	G. Bulpitt (Co Birmingham)	50.97
4	N. Metcalfe (Co Leeds)	51.24
5	J. Broughton (Co Leeds)	51.40
6	D. Dyke (Walsall)	51.79

Consolation Final

1	R. Greenwood (Co Leeds)	52.21
2	S. Foggo (Co Newcastle)	52.52
3	D. Gatland (Beckenham)	52.70
4	M. Hanby (Nova Centurion)	53.28
5	R. Tozer (Millfield)	53.55
6	L. Bennett (Co Newcastle)	53.66

Heat Times

1	M. Fibbens (Barnet Copthall)	51.04
2	S. Dronsfield (Co Leeds)	51.20
3	G. Bulpitt (Co Birmingham)	51.28
4	N. Metcalfe (Co Leeds)	51.39
5	J. Broughton (Co Leeds)	51.49
6	D. Dyke (Walsall)	51.76
7	M. Foster (Bo Southend)	52.07
8	R. Greenwood (Co Leeds)	52.13
9	L. Bennett (Co Newcastle)	
	S. Foggo (Co Newcastle)	52.45
11	M. Hanby (Nova Centurion)	52.55
12	D. Gatland (Beckenham)	52.61
13	R. Tozer (Millfield)	52.70
14	A. Shortman (Bristol Central)	52.79
15	M. Levine (Co Sheffield)	53.20
16	A. Rapley (Buxton & D)	53.25
17	S. Glover (Salford Triple 'S')	53.32
18	G. Minns (Co Birmingham)	53.33
19	M. Weighton (Wulfrunians)	53.58
20	G. Smith (White Oak)	53.61
21	S. Morris (Gloucester C)	53.71
22	M. Jones (Co Southampton)	53.82
23	J. Thomlinson (Millfield)	
	P. McQuaid (Co Manchester)	53.88
25	L. Walker (Kelly College)	54.00
26	C. Robinson (Killerwhales)	54.02
27	L. Holgate (Oundle & D)	54.27
28	T. Hart (Thurrock)	54.64
29	C. Jones (Co Swansea)	55.20
30	D. Parker (Co Coventry)	55.72

Junior Placings: (1) M. Hanby; (2) A. Shortman;
(3) M. Weighton.

200 Metres Freestyle
Final

1	D. Rolley (Swansea University)	1:50.07
2	P. Brew (Kelly College)	1:51.50
3	J. Broughton (Co Leeds)	1:51.98
4	D. Dyke (Walsall)	1:52.13
5	S. Dronsfield (Co Leeds)	1:52.28
6	L. Bennett (Co Newcastle)	1:52.71

Consolation Final

1	G. Bulpitt (Co Birmingham)	1:50.92
2	D. Gatland (Beckenham)	1:51.43

3	J. Bradley (Bath University)	1:52.77
4	K. Joy (Portsmouth Northsea)	1:53.24
5	R. Tozer (Millfield)	1:55.57
6	K. Renshaw (Chester le Street)	1:56.97

Heat Times

1	D. Rolley (Swansea University)	1:50.89
2	P. Brew (Kelly College)	1:50.98
3	J. Broughton (Co Leeds)	1:51.27
4	S. Dronsfield (Co Leeds)	1:52.36
5	D. Dyke (Walsall)	1:52.42
6	L. Bennett (Co Newcastle)	1:52.68
7	M. Fibbens (Barnet Copthall)	1:53.03
8	G. Bulpitt (Co Birmingham)	1:53.14
9	D. Gatland (Beckenham)	1:53.20
10	J. Bradley (Bath University)	1:53.24
11	K. Joy (Portsmouth Northsea)	1:53.39
12	R. Tozer (Millfield)	1:53.63
13	A. Johnson (Co Newcastle)	1:54.59
14	K. Renshaw (Chester le Street)	1:55.23
15	N. Metcalfe (Co Leeds)	1:55.48
16	C. Robinson (Killerwhales)	1:55.98
17	J. Ley (Millfield)	1:56.35
18	M. Duffy (Co Newcastle)	1:57.32
19	S. Foggo (Co Newcastle)	1:57.37
20	S. Moore (Oundle & D)	1:57.41
21	M. Hanby (Nova Centurion)	1:57.48
22	G. Smith (White Oak)	1:57.52
23	S. Morris (Gloucester C)	1:57.96
24	S. Mellor (Satellite)	1:58.07
25	D. Claridge (Co Birmingham)	1:58.15
26	J. Leveridge (Bo Kirklees)	1:59.16
27	A. Irwin (Kelly College)	1:59.18
28	T. Morgan (Aquabears)	1:59.19
29	C. Jones (Co Swansea)	1:59.21
30	L. Walker (Kelly College)	1:59.83
31	A. Clarke (COSACSS)	1:59.86
32	G. Woolger (Hounslow B)	2:00.73
33	S. Akers (Shiverers)	2:02.33

Junior Placings: (1) C. Robinson; (2) J. Ley; (3) M. Hanby.

400 Metres Freestyle
Final

1	D. Rolley (Swansea University)	3:53.24
2	I. Wilson (Bo Sunderland)	3:53.82
3	J. Broughton (Co Leeds)	3:55.73
4	J. Ong (Kelly College)	3:58.13
5	S. Akers (Shiverers)	3:58.43
6	A. Rolley (Gloucester C)	3:58.73

Consolation Final

1	G. Bulpitt (Co Birmingham)	3:59.90
2	S. Mellor (Satellite)	4:01.64
3	A. Johnson (Co Newcastle)	4:03.83
4	C. Robinson (Killerwhales)	4:04.19
5	G. Donovan (Barking)	4:04.60
6	A. Pearce (Co Leeds)	4:05.12

Heat Times

1	D. Rolley (Swansea University)	3:53.05
2	I. Wilson (Bo Sunderland)	3:54.59
3	J. Broughton (Co Leeds)	3:56.10
4	J. Ong (Kelly College)	3:56.62
5	S. Akers (Shiverers)	3:58.63
6	A. Rolley (Gloucester C)	3:58.69
7	G. Bulpitt (Co Birmingham)	3:59.06
8	G. Robins (Portsmouth Northsea)	3:59.23
9	C. Robinson (Killerwhales)	4:00.29
10	A. Pearce (Co Leeds)	4:00.34
11	A. Johnson (Co Newcastle)	4:02.40
12	S. Mellor (Satellite)	4:05.23

13	G. Donovan (Barking)	4:05.33
14	P. McGillion (Co Coventry)	4:06.22
15	G. Woolger (Hounslow B)	4:06.83
16	P. Stackhouse (Stockport Metro)	4:07.55
17	J. Randell (Co Birmingham)	4:08.33
18	D. Claridge (Co Birmingham)	4:08.83
19	J. Leveridge (Bo Kirklees)	4:12.63
20	S. Clamp (Co Coventry)	4:13.04
21	T. Morgan (Aquabears)	4:13.16

Junior Placings: (1) J. Ong; (2) C. Robinson; (3) S. Mellor.

1500 Metres Freestyle
Heat Times (no final)

1	I. Wilson (Bo Sunderland)	15:27.23
2	S. Akers (Shiverers)	15:36.69
3	J. Ong (Kelly College)	15:37.31
4	S. Mellor (Satellite)	16:05.81
5	S. Clamp (Co Coventry)	16:11.19
6	A. Pearce (Co Leeds)	16:12.79
7	A. Johnson (Co Newcastle)	16:13.95
8	C. Robinson (Killerwhales)	16:20.35
9	T. Lewis (Wycombe & D)	16:20.95
10	G. Woolger (Hounslow B)	16:21.77
11	P. Stackhouse (Stockport Metro)	16:26.90
12	D. Claridge (Co Birmingham)	16:31.07
13	P. Kappes (Killerwhales)	16:37.16
14	T. Morgan (Aquabears)	16:45.50
15	S. Wyer (Co Leeds)	16:55.20
16	I. Lundie (Kelly College)	17:01.61

Junior Placings: (1) J. Ong; (2) S. Mellor; (3) S. Clamp.

100 Metres Backstroke
Final

1	G. Robins (Portsmouth Northsea)	58.04
2	C. Cockcroft (Co Leeds)	58.18
3	M. O'Connor (Co Manchester)	58.40
4	I. Panting (Kelly College)	58.79
5	M. Harris (Barnet Copthall)	59.04
6	P. Blake (Torquay Leander)	59.21

Consolation Final

1	A. Shortman (Bristol Central)	59.60
2	J. Kearney (Nova Centurion)	59.63
3	M. Nolan (Ashton Central)	59.71
4	I. Stewart (York C)	59.77
5	N. Sherringham (Co Sheffield)	1:00.90
6	I. Brown (Ferndown Otters)	1:01.05

Heat Times

1	G. Robins (Portsmouth Northsea)	58.42
2	C. Cockcroft (Co Leeds)	58.56
3	M. O'Connor (Co Manchester)	58.80
4	I. Panting (Kelly College)	59.28
5	M. Harris (Barnet Copthall)	59.42
6	P. Blake (Torquay Leander)	59.50
7	M. Nolan (Ashton Central)	59.83
8	A. Shortman (Bristol Central)	59.84
9	J. Kearney (Nova Centurion)	1:00.06
10	I. Stewart (York C)	1:00.25
11	N. Sherringham (Co Sheffield)	1:00.35
12	I. Brown (Ferndown Otters)	1:00.71
13	C. Biss (Barnet Copthall)	1:00.79
14	M. Templeton (Co Newcastle)	1:00.97
15	D. McNulty (Chester le Street)	1:01.13
16	D. Francis (Colchester)	1:01.35
17	C. Jones (Co Swansea)	1:01.46
18	J. Fleet (Bo Waltham Forest)	1:01.48
19	M. Hooper (Portsmouth Northsea)	1:01.63
20	G. Williams (Rushmoor Royals)	1:01.77

16	C. Cockcroft (Co Leeds)	2:13.30
17	C. Jones (Co Swansea)	2:13.84
18	G. Williams (Rushmoor Royals)	2:13.99
19	I. Hardern (Salford Triple 'S')	2:14.69
20	M. Templeton (Co Newcastle)	2:15.02
21	J. Austin (Co Sheffield)	2:15.39
22	J. Hunter (Derwentside)	2:15.62
23	C. Sharpe (York C)	2:15.83
24	P. Speller (Barking)	2:17.43
25	R. Birch (Millfield)	2:17.64
26	J. Eldridge (Hounslow B)	2:20.65
	J. Kerr (Warrender)	DIS

Junior placings: (1) J. Kearney; (2) P. Pederzolli; (3) S. Mellor.

100 Metres Breaststroke
Final

1	N. Gillingham (Co Birmingham)	1:02.73
2	I. Campbell (Beckenham)	1:03.15
3	P. Shackley (York C)	1:03.99
4	D. Mason (Co Newcastle)	1:04.46
5	P. Blake (Torquay Leander)	1:04.78
6	I. McKenzie (Braintree & Bocking)	1:05.37

Consolation Final

1	J. Hender (Co Chester)	1:04.66
2	D. Gatland (Beckenham)	1:05.02
3	R. Maden (Aquabears)	1:05.49
4	J. Cole (Co Leicester)	1:06.24
5	I. Cotton (Nova Centurion)	1:06.48
6	T. Ashwell (Ipswich)	1:06.54

Heat Times

1	I. Campbell (Beckenham)	1:03.61
2	P. Shackley (York C)	1:03.63
3	N. Gillingham (Co Birmingham)	1:03.87
4	I. McKenzie (Braintree & Bocking) P. Blake (Torquay Leander)	1:04.80
6	D. Mason (Co Newcastle)	1:04.88
7	J. Hender (Co Chester)	1:05.19
8	R. Maden (Aquabears) J. Cole (Co Leicester)	1:05.37
10	D. Gatland (Beckenham)	1:05.59
11	I. Cotton (Nova Centurion)	1:05.96
12	T. Ashwell (Ipswich)	1:06.26
13	R. Wilkes (Portsmouth Northsea)	1:06.29
14	T. Evans (Oundle & D)	1:06.71
15	K. Joy (Portsmouth Northsea)	1:06.83
16	A. Murdock (Nova Centurion)	1:06.89
17	P. Hennys (Soundwell)	1:06.98
18	N. Polkinghorne (Truro C)	1:07.13
19	T. Redfearn (Kelly College)	1:08.04
20	G. Bennett (Bracknell)	1:08.09
21	D. Carr (Co Newcastle)	1:08.17
22	M. Whittaker (Co Southampton)	1:08.21
23	M. Wynn (Kelly College)	1:08.31
24	P. McQuaid (Co Manchester)	1:08.33
25	D. Warren (Tynemouth)	1:08.43
26	A. Smith (Eastbourne)	1:08.45
27	D. Entwistle (Royton)	1:08.67
28	J. Curry (Co Bristol)	1:08.76
29	P. Clark (Braintree & Bocking)	1:09.12
30	J. Snape (Ledbury & D)	1:09.14
31	W. O'Gorman (Millfield)	1:09.22
32	J. Randell (Co Birmingham)	1:09.35
33	R. Thorp (Millfield)	1:09.86
34	N. Poole (Eastbourne)	1:09.90
35	B. Rees (Wycombe & D)	1:09.92
36	R. Laidlow (Cockermouth)	1:09.35

Junior Placings: (1) I. McKenzie; (2) R. Maden; (3) T. Ashwell.

Grant Robins

21	I. Hardern (Salford Triple 'S')	1:02.25
22	J. Kerr (Warrender)	1:02.43
23	S. Mellor (Satellite)	1:02.51
24	J. Hunter (Derwentside)	1:02.66
25	R. Birch (Millfield) P. Gore (Exeter C)	1:02.79
27	S. Wainwright (Millfield)	1:02.89
28	P. Speller (Barking)	1:02.90
29	S. Handley (RTW Monson)	1:03.19
30	M. Salway (Ferndown Otters)	1:03.62

Junior Placings: (1) A. Shortman; (2) J. Kearney; (3) S. Mellor.

200 Metres Backstroke
Final

1	G. Robins (Portsmouth Northsea)	2:02.04
2	P. Blake (Torquay Leander)	2:04.27
3	I. Stewart (York C)	2:07.43
4	A. Rolley (Gloucester C)	2:08.09
5	M. Harris (Barnet Copthall)	2:10.43
6	I. Panting (Kelly College)	2:13.38

Consolation Final

1	M. O'Connor (Co Manchester)	2:06.45
2	J. Kearney (Nova Centurion)	2:07.09
3	M. Nolan (Ashton Central)	2:08.82
4	J. Fleet (Bo Waltham Forest)	2:08.96
5	N. Sherringham (Co Sheffield)	2:08.97
6	P. Pederzolli (Gloucester C)	2:10.70

Heat Times

1	P. Blake (Torquay Leander)	2:06.70
2	G. Robins (Portsmouth Northsea)	2:06.83
3	I. Stewart (York C)	2:07.55
4	M. Harris (Barnet Copthall)	2:07.84
5	A. Rolley (Gloucester C)	2:08.56
6	I. Panting (Kelly College)	2:08.62
7	J. Kearney (Nova Centurion)	2:08.63
8	N. Sherringham (Co Sheffield)	2:09.64
9	P. Pederzolli (Gloucester C)	2:09.68
10	J. Fleet (Bo Waltham Forest)	2:10.05
11	M. Nolan (Ashton Central)	2:10.11
12	M. O'Connor (Co Manchester)	2:10.50
13	M. Hooper (Portsmouth Northsea)	2:11.68
14	S. Mellor (Satellite)	2:12.09
15	C. Biss (Barnet Copthall)	2:12.55

200 Metres Breaststroke
Final

1	N. Gillingham (Co Birmingham)	2:16.30
2	I. Campbell (Beckenham)	2:17.57
3	P. Shackley (York C)	2:19.64
4	D. Mason (Co Newcastle)	2:21.44
5	I. McKenzie (Braintree & Bocking)	2:21.63
6	R. Maden (Aquabears)	2:23.89

Consolation Final

1	J. Hender (Co Chester)	2:21.83
2	R. Wilkes (Portsmouth Northsea)	2:22.80
3	K. Joy (Portsmouth Northsea)	2:23.54
4	J. Randell (Co Birmingham)	2:24.42
5	I. Cotton (Nova Centurion)	2:25.02
6	D. Entwistle (Royton)	2:28.42

Heat Times

1	I. Campbell (Beckenham)	2:17.10
2	N. Gillingham (Co Birmingham)	2:18.58
3	P. Shackley (York C)	2:19.67
4	D. Mason (Co Newcastle)	2:20.27
5	R. Maden (Aquabears)	2:21.11
6	I. McKenzie (Braintree & Bocking)	2:21.92
7	R. Wilkes (Portsmouth Northsea)	2:22.84
8	I. Cotton (Nova Centurion)	2:23.50
9	K. Joy (Portsmouth Northsea)	2:23.52
10	J. Hender (Co Chester)	2:23.75
11	D. Entwistle (Royton)	2:24.15
12	J. Randell (Co Birmingham)	2:24.51
13	A. Murdock (Nova Centurion)	2:24.83
14	T. Ashwell (Ipswich)	2:24.90
15	N. Polkinghorne (Truro C)	2:26.39
16	D. Warren (Tynemouth)	2:26.59
17	D. Carr (Co Newcastle)	2:27.67
18	P. Hennys (Soundwell)	2:28.49
19	P. McQuaid (Co Manchester)	2:28.69
20	P. Clark (Braintree & Bocking)	2:29.37
21	T. Evans (Oundle & D)	2:29.46
22	J. Curry (Co Bristol)	2:32.77
23	W. O'Gorman (Millfield)	2:32.89
24	J. Gregory (Co Leeds)	2:38.40

Junior Placings: (1) I. McKenzie; (2) R. Maden; (3) D. Entwistle.

100 Metres Butterfly
Final

1	R. Leishman (Kelly College)	55.38
2	D. Parker (Co Coventry)	55.58
3	S. Dronsfield (Co Leeds)	55.65
4	R. Greenwood (Co Leeds)	56.39
5	N. Metcalfe (Co Leeds)	56.79
6	M. Fibbens (Barnet Copthall)	57.82

Consolation Final

1	D. Gatland (Beckenham)	57.72
2	P. Pederzolli (Gloucester C)	57.88
3	C. Wilson (Co Southampton)	57.92
4	T. Hart (Co Southampton)	58.10
5	D. McNulty (Chester le Street)	58.23
6	N. Bridge (Millfield)	58.59

Heat Times

1	R. Leishman (Kelly College)	55.59
2	R. Greenwood (Co Leeds)	56.00
3	S. Dronsfield (Co Leeds)	56.02
4	D. Parker (Co Coventry)	56.53
5	N. Metcalfe (Co Leeds)	57.04
6	M. Fibbens (Barnet Copthall)	57.19
7	P. Shackley (York C)	57.42
8	D. McNulty (Chester le Street)	57.54
9	T. Hart (Thurrock)	57.67
10	C. Wilson (Co Southampton)	57.79

11	M. Foster (Bo Southend)	57.90
12	D. Gatland (Beckenham)	57.93
13	N. Bridge (Millfield)	58.04
	P. Pederzolli (Gloucester C)	
15	L. Bennett (Co Newcastle)	58.06
	M. Weighton (Wulfrunians)	
	N. Parish (Oundle & D)	
18	J. Thomlinson (Millfield)	58.20
19	A. Quinn (Co Manchester)	58.21
20	A. Clarke (COSACCS)	58.34
21	K. Renshaw (Chester le Street)	58.41
22	C. Bird (Kelly College)	58.61
23	B. Rees (Wycombe & D)	58.97
24	J. Gray (RTW Monson)	58.98
25	M. Jones (Co Southampton)	59.01
26	R. Tozer (Millfield)	59.02
27	C. Moulson (Forward Hill)	59.05
28	C. Robinson (Killerwhales)	59.16
29	R. Crabtree (Stockport Metro)	59.36
30	S. Hanton (Co Leeds)	59.39
31	M. Smallbone (Millfield)	59.46
32	D. Hedley (Chester le Street)	59.49
33	M. Jenkins (Ferndown Otters)	59.50
34	A. Johnson (Co Newcastle)	59.60
35	J. Wallis (Co Peterborough)	59.67
36	A. Exton (Redditch)	59.69
37	I. Hardern (Salford Triple 'S')	59.81
38	M. Fellows (Co Birmingham)	59.94
39	M. Duffy (Co Newcastle)	1:00.05
40	S. Wyer (Co Leeds)	1:00.13
41	R. Birch (Millfield)	1:00.25
42	H. Sheraton (Millfield)	1:00.43
43	M. Cantrill (Tupton Hall)	1:00.71
	D. Warren (Tynemouth)	
45	J. Eldridge (Hounslow B)	1:00.75
46	T. Evans (Oundle & D)	1:00.76
47	A. Quinn (Salford Triple 'S')	1:01.10
48	M. Hanby (Nova Centurion)	1:01.21
49	G. Williams (Rushmoor Royals)	1:01.35
50	J. Groom (Co Peterborough)	1:01.55

Junior Placings: (1) T. Hart; (2) P. Pederzolli; (3) M. Weighton.

200 Metres Butterfly
Final

1	I. Wilson (Bo Sunderland)	2:02.81
2	D. McNulty (Chester le Street)	2:04.58

Steven Dronsfield Swimming Times

3 A. Quinn (Co Manchester) 2:04.59
4 K. Renshaw (Chester le Street) 2:04.92
5 C. Bird (Kelly College) 2:05.52
6 C. Robinson (Killerwhales) 2:05.70
Consolation Final
1 R. Leishman (Kelly College) 2:03.39
2 N. Parish (Oundle & D) 2:06.22
3 S. Wainwright (Millfield) 2:06.83
4 C. Wilson (Co Southampton) 2:06.99
5 J. Gray (RTW Monson) 2:08.32
6 G. Donovan (Barking) 2:09.68
Heat times
1 I. Wilson (Bo Sunderland) 2:02.09
2 D. McNulty (Chester le Street) 2:03.60
3 C. Robinson (Killerwhales) 2:04.19
4 A. Quinn (Co Manchester) 2:04.50
5 C. Bird (Kelly College) 2:04.71
6 K. Renshaw (Chester le Street) 2:05.03
7 R. Leishman (Kelly College) 2:05.19
8 P. Shackley (York C) 2:05.27
9 N. Parish (Oundle & D) 2:06.65
10 G. Donovan (Barking) 2:06.70
11 D. Rolley (Swansea University) 2:07.02
12 S. Wainwright (Millfield) 2:07.19
13 C. Wilson (Co Southampton) 2:07.30
14 J. Gray (RTW Monson) 2:07.33
15 M. Hooper (Portsmouth Northsea) 2:08.57
16 A. Johnson (Co Newcastle) 2:08.80
17 R. Tozer (Millfield) 2:08.85
18 S. Hanton (Co Leeds) 2:09.18
19 B. Rees (Wycombe & D) 2:10.06
20 N. Beacham (Co Coventry) 2:10.24
21 D. Claridge (Co Birmingham) 2:10.50
22 J. Groom (Co Peterborough) 2:10.74
23 A. Clarke (COSACSS) 2:11.59
24 M. Smallbone (Millfield) 2:12.21
25 D. Bullock (Millfield) 2:13.40
26 P. Kappes (Killerwhales) 2:13.94
27 G. Hall (Nova Centurion) 2:13.95
28 A. Quinn (Salford Triple 'S') 2:14.27
29 D. Hedley (Chester le Street) 2:16.12
Junior Placings: (1) C. Robinson; (2) B. Rees; (3) D. Claridge.

200 Metres Individual Medley
Final
1 D. Rolley (Swansea University) 2:04.37
2 P. Brew (Kelly College) 2:04.44
3 P. Blake (Torquay Leander) 2:05.78
4 P. Pederzolli (Gloucester C) 2:06.87
5 A. Rolley (Gloucester C) 2:07.92
6 I. Stewart (York C) 2:08.81
Consolation Final
1 G. Robins (Portsmouth Northsea) 2:03.51
2 A. Greig (Barnet Copthall) 2:07.55
3 L. Bennett (Co Newcastle) 2:08.20
4 J. Kearney (Nova Centurion) 2:08.92
5 B. Rees (Wycombe & D) 2:11.44
Heat Times
1 D. Rolley (Swansea University) 2:04.69
2 P. Blake (Torquay Leander) 2:05.92
3 P. Brew (Kelly College) 2:06.10
4 P. Pederzolli (Gloucester C) 2:06.41
5 A. Rolley (Gloucester C) 2:06.75
6 I. Stewart (York C) 2:07.59
7 G. Robins (Portsmouth Northsea) 2:07.70
8 L. Bennett (Co Newcastle) 2:07.76
9 A. Greig (Barnet Copthall) 2:07.93
10 J. Kearney (Nova Centurion) 2:09.18

11 D. Gatland (Beckenham) 2:09.46
12 B. Rees (Wycombe & D) 2:09.84
13 K. Joy (Portsmouth Northsea) 2:10.09
14 D. McNulty (Chester le Street) 2:10.22
15 I. Wilson (Bo Sunderland) 2:10.48
16 M. Weighton (Wulfrunians) 2:10.62
17 M. Hooper (Portsmouth Northsea) 2:11.26
18 S. Harding (Sale) 2:11.27
19 S. Hanton (Co Leeds) 2:11.71
20 T. Evans (Oundle & D) 2:11.88
21 R. Crabtree (Stockport Metro) 2:12.17
22 J. Randell (Co Birmingham) 2:12.58
23 N. Parish (Oundle & D) 2:12.85
24 D. Warren (Tynemouth) 2:13.48
25 C. Jones (Co Swansea) 2:13.58
26 S. Wainwright (Millfield) 2:13.95
27 J. Eldridge (Hounslow B) 2:14.13
28 G. Donovan (Barking) 2:14.47
29 P. McGillion (Co Coventry) 2:14.67
30 R. Thorp (Millfield) 2:14.77
31 J. Kerr (Warrender) 2:15.90
32 M. O'Connor (Co Manchester) 2:17.48
Junior Placings: (1) P. Pederzolli; (2) J. Kearney; (3) B. Rees.

400 Metres Individual Medley
Final
1 G. Robins (Portsmouth Northsea) 4:22.15
2 A. Rolley (Gloucester C) 4:22.99
3 P. Brew (Kelly College) 4:30.69
4 A. Greig (Barnet Copthall) 4:30.78
5 I. Stewart (York C) 4:31.70
6 D. McNulty (Chester le Street) 4:34.29
Consolation Final
1 K. Joy (Portsmouth Northsea) 4:32.43
2 M. Hooper (Portsmouth Northsea) 4:32.66
3 G. Donovan (Barking) 4:38.34
4 S. Harding (Sale) 4:39.28
5 S. Hanton (Co Leeds) 4:40.89
6 D. Warren (Tynemouth) 4:41.31
Heat Times
1 G. Robins (Portsmouth Northsea) 4:28.78
2 P. Brew (Kelly College) 4:29.19
3 A. Rolley (Gloucester C) 4:29.52
4 A. Greig (Barnet Copthall) 4:29.80
5 D. Rolley (Swansea University) 4:30.60
6 I. Stewart (York C) 4:31.81
7 D. McNulty (Chester le Street) 4:33.84
8 M. Hooper (Portsmouth Northsea) 4:35.36
9 S. Harding (Sale) 4:35.41
10 K. Joy (Portsmouth Northsea) 4:36.50
11 D. Warren (Tynemouth) 4:39.09
12 G. Donovan (Barking) 4:39.54
13 C. Robinson (Killerwhales) 4:39.92
14 S. Hanton (Co Leeds) 4:39.99
15 P. McGillion (Co Coventry) 4:40.11
16 M. O'Connor (Co Manchester) 4:40.75
17 S. Wainwright (Millfield) 4:41.62
18 N. Sherringham (Co Sheffield) 4:41.91
19 R. Crabtree (Stockport Metro) 4:42.47
20 M. Nolan (Ashton Central) 4:42.75
21 B. Rees (Wycombe & D) 4:42.83
22 C. Biss (Barnet Copthall) 4:43.25
23 P. Kappes (Killerwhales) 4:43.43
24 N. Parish (Oundle & D) 4:43.54
25 T. Evans (Oundle & D) 4:44.73
26 S. Wyer (Co Leeds) 4:44.79
27 A. Quinn (Co Manchester) 4:44.86
28 S. Clamp (Co Coventry) 4:45.71

29 J. Kerr (Warrender)   4:50.52
Junior Placings: (1) C. Robinson; (2) B. Rees; (3)
P. Kappes.

4×100 Metres Freestyle Club Relay
Final

1	Co Leeds	3:25.46
2	Co Birmingham	3:25.68
3	Co Newcastle	3:29.56
4	Portsmouth Northsea	3:31.68
5	Millfield	3:33.83
6	Co Southampton	3:37.10

Heat Times

1	Co Leeds	3:31.99
2	Co Birmingham	3:32.17
3	Co Newcastle	3:32.21
4	Millfield	3:33.32
5	Portsmouth Northsea	3:34.40
6	Kelly College	3:35.86
7	Co Southampton	3:36.29
8	Oundle & D	3:36.55

4×100 Metres Medley Club Relay
Final

1	Co Birmingham	3:50.10
2	Co Leeds	3:51.87
3	Kelly College	3:52.17
4	Portsmouth Northsea	3:52.89
5	Nova Centurion	4:00.08
6	Co Newcastle	4:00.28

Heat Times

1	Co Leeds	3:57.29
2	Portsmouth Northsea	3:57.46
3	Kelly College	3:57.87
4	Co Birmingham	3:57.95
5	Nova Centurion	3:58.32
6	Co Newcastle	4:00.34
7	Oundle & D	4:00.67
8	Millfield	4:02.76
9	Co Southampton	4:05.37
10	Braintree & Bocking	4:11.48

Women

50 Metres Freestyle
Final

1	C. Woodcock (Haywards Heath)	26.18
2	K. Pickering (Ipswich)	26.61
3	J. Gorst (Co Leeds)	26.84
4	A. Kindon (Co Birmingham)	27.10
5	N. Kennedy (Nova Centurion)	27.13
6	J. Wilkinson (St Helens)	27.44

Consolation Final

1	N. Williams (Stockport Metro)	27.35
2	J. Waite (Co Southampton)	27.42
3	L. Graham (Barnet Copthall)	27.71
4	G. Atkins (Portsmouth Northsea)	27.80
5	J. Coull (Co Birmingham)	27.93
6	H. Sanderson (Nova Centurion)	27.95

Heat Times

1	C. Woodcock (Haywards Heath)	26.20
2	J. Gorst (Co Leeds)	26.92
3	K. Pickering (Ipswich)	26.93
4	N. Kennedy (Nova Centurion)	27.03
5	J. Wilkinson (St Helens)	27.04
6	A. Kindon (Co Birmingham)	27.32
7	L. Graham (Barnet Copthall)	27.40
8	N. Williams (Stockport Metro)	27.44
9	J. Waite (Co Southampton)	27.62

10	G. Atkins (Portsmouth Northsea)	27.64
11	H. Sanderson (Nova Centurion)	27.73
12	J. Coull (Co Birmingham)	27.74
13	L. Arrowsmith (Deane Dolphins)	27.83
14	C. Horton (Norwich Penguins)	27.84
	A. Clarke (Tiverton)	
16	H. Tooke (Chatteris Kingfisher)	27.85
17	E. Archer (Haverhill)	27.86
18	E. Brooks (Redbridge B)	27.87
	G. Brooks (Greenwich B Mariners)	
	G. Lavin (Derwentside)	
21	P. Rickard (Co Newcastle)	27.94
22	R. Bowden (Co Southampton)	27.95
23	J. McHarg (Portsmouth Northsea)	27.97
24	J. Constable (Thornbury)	28.13
25	S. Vick (Co Sheffield)	28.28
26	A. Dronsfield (Co Manchester)	28.43
27	R. Brinn (Kelly College)	28.55
28	N. Cumbers (Kelly College)	28.58
29	A. Derby (Harrow & Wealdstone)	28.70
30	C. Foot (Millfield)	29.07
31	J. Punter (Hounslow B)	29.11
32	V. Bagot (Amersham)	29.25

Junior Placings: (1) C. Woodcock; (2) A. Kindon;
(3) J. Waite.

100 Metres Freestyle
Final

1	K. Pickering (Ipswich)	57.20
2	M. Scarborough (Portsmouth Northsea)	57.82
3	J. Wilmot (Loughborough University)	58.28
4	C. Horton (Norwich Penguins)	58.31
5	N. Bates (Norwich Penguins)	58.62
6	N. Williams (Stockport Metro)	59.68

Consolation Final

1	J. Gorst (Co Leeds)	58.95
2	J. Coull (Co Birmingham)	58.96
3	C. Woodcock (Haywards Heath)	59.08
4	G. Atkins (Portsmouth Northsea)	59.16
5	J. Wilkinson (St Helens)	59.24
6	L. Graham (Barnet Copthall)	1:00.02

Heat Times

1	K. Pickering (Ipswich)	57.22
2	C. Horton (Norwich Penguins)	58.13
3	J. Wilmot (Loughborough University)	58.45
4	M. Scarborough (Portsmouth Northsea)	58.52
5	N. Bates (Norwich Penguins)	58.56
6	N. Williams (Stockport Metro)	58.93
7	J. Coull (Co Birmingham)	58.96
8	J. Wilkinson (St Helens)	59.06
9	J. Gorst (Co Leeds)	59.12
10	G. Atkins (Portsmouth Northsea)	59.20
11	C. Woodcock (Haywards Heath)	59.25
12	L. Graham (Barnet Copthall)	59.34
13	A. Kindon (Co Birmingham)	59.63
14	C. Huddart (Salford Triple 'S')	59.70
15	E. Brooks (Redbridge B)	59.95
16	H. Sanderson (Nova Centurion)	59.99
17	E. Archer (Haverhill)	1:00.02
18	N. Sommers (Beckenham)	1:00.21
19	H. Tooke (Chatteris Kingfisher)	1:00.29
20	S. Vick (Co Sheffield)	1:00.34
21	C. Mayor (Bodmin & D)	1:00.40
22	D. Palmer (Killerwhales)	1:00.49
23	P. Rickard (Co Newcastle)	1:00.51
24	M. George (Bo Waltham Forest)	1:00.52
25	D. Salmon (Kelly College)	1:00.63
26	N. Cumbers (Kelly College)	1:00.65
27	A. Baker (Norwich Penguins)	1:00.74

28 A. Dronsfield (Co Manchester)	1:00.80	
29 G. Brooks (Greenwich B Mariners)	1:01.19	
30 J. McHarg (Portsmouth Northsea)	1:01.26	
31 A. Clarke (Tiverton)	1:01.33	
32 L. Smart (Co Chester)	1:01.42	
33 K. Johnson (Colchester)	1:01.80	
34 J. Punter (Hounslow B)	1:02.74	
35 V. Bagot (Amersham)	1:05.50	

Junior Placings: (1) N. Bates; (2) J. Coull; (3) C. Woodcock.

200 Metres Freestyle
Final

1 M. Scarborough (Portsmouth Northsea)	2:03.78
2 M. George (Bo Waltham Forest)	2:05.37
3 J. Wilmot (Loughborough University)	2:05.38
4 N. Bates (Norwich Penguins)	2:06.87
5 H. Jepson (Bo Kirklees)	2:08.12
6 N. Sommers (Beckenham)	2:08.29

Consolation Final

1 C. Horton (Norwich Penguins)	2:06.47
2 D. Salmon (Kelly College)	2:08.11
3 E. Brooks (Redbridge B)	2:08.19
4 L. Smart (Co Chester)	2:08.62
5 N. Cumbers (Kelly College)	2:08.83
6 G. Cook (Bo Kirklees)	2:09.27

Heat Times

1 J. Wilmot (Loughborough University)	2:04.43
2 M. Scarborough (Portsmouth Northsea)	2:05.30
3 M. George (Bo Waltham Forest)	2:05.46
4 N. Sommers (Beckenham)	2:06.47
5 N. Bates (Norwich Penguins)	2:06.57
6 H. Jepson (Bo Kirklees)	2:07.57
7 L. Smart (Co Chester)	2:07.64
8 C. Horton (Norwich Penguins)	2:07.74
9 G. Cook (Bo Kirklees)	2:08.07
10 E. Brooks (Redbridge B)	2:08.33
11 M. Walsh (Millfield)	2:08.42
12 N. Cumbers (Kelly College)	2:08.84
13 D. Salmon (Kelly College)	2:08.94
14 G. Atkins (Portsmouth Northsea)	2:09.35

Karen Pickering   Jack Hickes

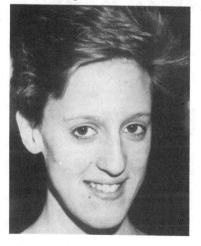

15 H. Sanderson (Nova Centurion)	2:10.10	
16 N. Williams (Stockport Metro)	2:10.34	
17 L. Matthews (Redbridge B)	2:10.90	
18 R. Bennett (Nova Centurion)	2:11.33	
19 L. Sonn (Co Southampton)	2:11.84	
20 J. Gorst (Co Leeds)	2:11.93	
21 P. Herron (Co Newcastle)	2:13.46	

Junior Placings: (1) M. George; (2) N. Bates; (3) H. Jepson.

400 Metres Freestyle
Final

1 K. Mellor (Co Sheffield)	4:18.22
2 J. Wilmot (Loughborough University)	4:20.11
3 N. Sommers (Beckenham)	4:21.54
4 M. George (Bo Waltham Forest)	4:22.40
5 C. Horton (Norwich Penguins)	4:23.37
6 G. Cook (Bo Kirklees)	4:23.76

Consolation Final

1 L. Matthews (Redbridge B)	4:22.88
2 D. Salmon (Kelly College)	4:23.11
3 N. Bates (Norwich Penguins)	4:27.15
4 L. Kilgour (Co Birmingham)	4:27.66
5 L. Sonn (Co Southampton)	4:31.96
6 P. Herron (Co Newcastle)	4:34.13

Heat Times

1 K. Mellor (Co Sheffield)	4:17.76
2 J. Wilmot (Loughborough University)	4:18.67
3 M. George (Bo Waltham Forest)	4:21.19
4 N. Sommers (Beckenham)	4:22.57
5 C. Horton (Norwich Penguins)	4:22.75
6 G. Cook (Bo Kirklees)	4:23.09
7 D. Salmon (Kelly College)	4:24.02
8 L. Sonn (Co Southampton)	4:24.54
9 N. Bates (Norwich Penguins)	4:24.78
10 L. Matthews (Redbridge B)	4:24.89
11 P. Herron (Co Newcastle)	4:25.52
12 J. Deakins (Gloucester C)	4:26.27
13 L. Kilgour (Co Birmingham)	4:26.93
14 D. Churchman (Co Leeds)	4:28.53
15 S. Foggo (Co Newcastle)	4:28.96
16 C. Piggott (Orion)	4:32.35
17 E. Brooks (Redbridge B)	4:32.54
18 E. Archer (Haverhill)	4:32.56
19 K. Boucher (Norwich Penguins)	4:32.96

Junior Placings: (1) M. George; (2) G. Cook; (3) P. Salmon.

800 Metres Freestyle
Heat Times (No Final)

1 K. Mellor (Co Sheffield)	8:42.73
2 M. Scarborough (Portsmouth Northsea)	8:49.72
3 L. Matthews (Redbridge B)	8:55.69
4 G. Cook (Bo Kirklees)	8:55.85
5 N. Sommers (Beckenham)	8:57.54
6 L. Smart (Co Chester)	9:01.21
7 M. George (Bo Waltham Forest)	9:01.62
8 D. Churchman (Co Leeds)	9:05.94
9 L. Sonn (Co Southampton)	9:07.19
10 L. Kilgour (Co Birmingham)	9:10.98
11 D. Palmer (Killerwhales)	9:14.87
12 R. Brinn (Kelly College)	9:15.29
13 A. Sanderson (Rushmoor Royals)	9:15.93
14 S. Foggo (Co Newcastle)	9:19.07
15 K. Boucher (Norwich Penguins)	9:22.20
16 J. Wilcock (St Helens)	9:32.65

Junior Placings: (1) G. Cook; (2) L. Smart; (3) M. George.

100 Metres Backstroke
Final

1	K. Read (Norwich Penguins)	1:04.65
2	J. Deakins (Gloucester C)	1:04.78
3	C. Huddart (Salford Triple 'S')	1:05.47
4	M. Scarborough (Portsmouth Northsea)	1:06.39
5	J. Kelly (Co Southampton)	1:07.05
6	J. Riegal (Harrow & Wealdstone)	1:07.68

Consolation Final

1	K. Britton (Bristol Central)	1:06.84
2	L. Racster (Portsmouth Northsea)	1:07.15
3	L. Gahan (Kelly College)	1:07.75
4	J. Wright (Co Chester)	1:07.94
5	E. Hall (Portsmouth Northsea)	1:08.23
6	P. Rickard (Co Newcastle)	1:09.59

Heat Times

1	K. Read (Norwich Penguins)	1:04.14
2	J. Deakins (Gloucester C)	1:05.32
3	C. Huddart (Salford Triple 'S')	1:06.12
4	M. Scarborough (Portsmouth Northsea)	1:06.43
5	J. Kelly (Co Southampton)	1:07.36
6	J. Riegal (Harrow & Wealdstone)	1:07.65
7	L. Racster (Portsmouth Northsea)	1:07.66
8	L. Gahan (Kelly College)	1:07.70
9	J. Wright (Co Chester)	1:07.90
	K. Britton (Bristol Central)	1:07.90
11	E. Hall (Portsmouth Northsea)	1:07.93
12	R. Bowden (Co Southampton)	1:07.96
13	P. Rickard (Co Newcastle)	1:08.18
14	R. Hamilton (Ipswich)	1:08.41
15	L. Jackson (Everton)	1:08.51
16	T. Loveman (Co Southampton)	1:08.57
17	J. Corbett (Co Birmingham)	1:08.64
18	P. Rickard (Co Newcastle)	1:08.80
19	P. Herron (Co Newcastle)	1:08.94
20	L. Lennon (Nova Centurion)	1:09.02
21	H. Williamson (Harrow & Wealdstone)	1:09.06
22	G. Harvey (Thornbury)	1:09.39
23	A. Sedgebeer (Epping Forest)	1:09.59
24	J. Austin (Wycombe & D)	1:09.65
25	K. Johnson (Colchester)	1:09.76
26	H. Osborne (Co Birmingham)	1:09.93
27	Z. Blake (Torquay Leander)	1:10.12

Junior Placings: (1) J. Deakins; (2) L. Racster; (3) L. Gahan.

200 Metres Backstroke
Final

1	K. Read (Norwich Penguins)	2:17.60
2	J. Deakins (Gloucester C)	2:18.28
3	C. Huddart (Salford Triple 'S')	2:19.74
4	J. Riegal (Harrow & Wealdstone)	2:21.60
5	J. Wright (Co Chester)	2:24.16
6	A. Sedgebeer (Epping Forest)	2:26.54

Consolation Final

1	P. Rickard (Co Newcastle)	2:21.05
2	J. Kelly (Co Southampton)	2:21.25
3	D. Salmon (Kelly College)	2:22.25
4	L. Gahan (Kelly College)	2:25.44
5	J. Corbett (Co Birmingham)	2:25.89
6	S. Bowman (Co Newcastle)	2:27.90

Heat Times

1	K. Read (Norwich Penguins)	2:18.82
2	J. Deakins (Gloucester C)	2:19.66
3	J. Riegal (Harrow & Wealdstone)	2:21.96
4	C. Huddart (Salford Triple 'S')	2:22.01
5	A. Sedgebeer (Epping Forest)	2:22.02
6	J. Wright (Co Chester)	2:22.11
7	P. Rickard (Co Newcastle)	2:22.97
8	J. Kelly (Co Southampton)	2:24.45
9	L. Gahan (Kelly College)	2:24.83
10	D. Salmon (Kelly College)	2:25.27
11	J. Corbett (Co Birmingham)	2:25.72
12	S. Bowman (Co Newcastle)	2:25.75
13	K. Johnson (Colchester)	2:25.78
14	L. Jackson (Everton)	2:26.12
15	E. Hall (Portsmouth Northsea)	2:26.50
16	P. Herron (Co Newcastle)	2:27.11
17	K. Britton (Bristol Central)	2:27.25
18	N. Thompson (Torquay Leander)	2:27.73
19	H. Williamson (Harrow & Wealdstone)	2:27.85
20	R. Britton (Bristol Central)	2:28.21
21	R. Hamilton (Ipswich)	2:29.10
22	K. Pickering (Ipswich)	2:30.20
23	J. Austin (Wycombe & D)	2:30.63
24	Z. Blake (Torquay Leander)	2:31.04

Junior Placings: (1) J. Deakins; (2) J. Wright; (3) L. Gahan.

100 Metres Breaststroke
Final

1	L. Coombes (Co Southampton)	1:12.05
2	D. Tubby (Norwich Penguins)	1:12.87
3	A. Baker (Norwich Penguins)	1:12.96
4	H. Alder (Harrow & Wealdstone)	1:13.11
5	H. Walsh (Millfield)	1:15.36
6	N. James (Nova Centurion)	1:15.96

Consolation Final

1	R. Gillatt (Co Sheffield)	1:13.36
2	J. Henwood (Swansea Valley)	1:14.71
3	L. Findlay (Northampton)	1:14.94
4	R. Swain (Co Derby)	1:15.36
5	M. Young (Colchester)	1:15.72
6	J. Martin (Hounslow B)	1:17.36

Heat Times

1	L. Coombes (Co Southampton)	1:13.27
2	D. Tubby (Norwich Penguins)	1:13.56
3	H. Alder (Harrow & Wealdstone)	1:13.91
4	A. Baker (Norwich Penguins)	1:14.40
5	H. Walsh (Millfield)	1:14.89
6	N. James (Nova Centurion)	1:14.93
7	J. Henwood (Swansea Valley)	1:15.07
8	L. Findlay (Northampton)	1:15.62
9	R. Gillatt (Co Sheffield)	1:15.66
10	R. Swain (Co Derby)	1:15.76
11	J. Martin (Hounslow B)	1:15.88
12	M. Young (Colchester)	1:16.00
13	H. Gorman (Nova Centurion)	1:16.10
	J. Kearley (Co Derby)	1:16.10
15	A. Lynch (Co Sheffield)	1:16.14
16	J. Hocking (Truro C)	1:16.15
17	S. Jefford (Exeter C)	1:16.18
18	J. Terry (Nova Centurion)	1:16.47
19	A. Bird (Bristol Central)	1:16.48
20	A. Murphy (Salford Triple 'S')	1:16.60
21	J. Farnsworth (Co Leeds)	1:16.81
22	R. Newey (Ledbury & D)	1:16.92
23	G. Brooks (Greenwich B Mariners)	1:17.00
24	H. Goddard (Gloucester C)	1:17.02
25	A. Whittle (Hindley)	1:17.14
	K. Seaborn (Co Manchester)	1:17.14
27	E. Wilkinson (Millfield)	1:17.72
28	C. Piggott (Orion)	1:17.87
29	J. Harrison (Bo Kirklees)	1:18.09
30	A. Warner (Co Birmingham)	1:18.17
31	M. Hynes (Co Manchester)	1:18.38

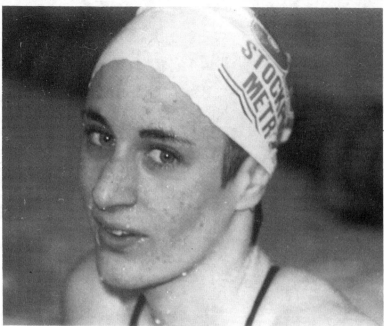

Kathy Read

32 D. Atkins (Mendip)	1:18.57
33 T. Sullivan (Piranha)	1:19.07

Junior Placings: (1) H. Alder; (2) N. James; (3) L. Findlay.

200 Metres Breaststroke
Final

1	D. Tubby (Norwich Penguins)	2:36.22
2	H. Walsh (Millfield)	2:38.43
3	J. Henwood (Swansea Valley)	2:39.74
4	J. Farnsworth (Co Leeds)	2:40.24
5	J. Harrison (Bo Kirklees)	2:42.87
6	J. Martin (Hounslow B)	2:45.05

Consolation Final

1	N. James (Nova Centurion)	2:41.60
2	L. Findlay (Northampton)	2:41.69
3	A. Murphy (Salford Triple 'S')	2:42.07
4	K. Seaborn (Co Manchester)	2:42.20
5	H. Goddard (Gloucester C)	2:42.57
6	H. Alder (Harrow & Wealdstone)	2:43.38

Heat Times

1	D. Tubby (Norwich Penguins)	2:36.80
2	J. Farnsworth (Co Leeds)	2:38.45
3	J. Henwood (Swansea Valley)	2:38.70
4	J. Harrison (Bo Kirklees)	2:39.09
5	H. Walsh (Millfield)	2:39.97
6	L. Coombes (Co Southampton)	2:40.89
7	J. Martin (Hounslow B)	2:42.51
8	K. Seaborn (Co Manchester)	2:42.62
9	A. Murphy (Salford Triple 'S')	2:42.80
10	N. James (Nova Centurion)	2:42.97
11	L. Findlay (Northampton)	2:43.41
12	H. Alder (Harrow & Wealdstone)	2:43.60
13	H. Goddard (Gloucester C)	2:43.61

14	E. Wilkinson (Millfield)	2:43.75
15	H. Gorman (Nova Centurion)	2:43.77
16	S. Solly (Nova Centurion)	2:45.21
17	C. Piggott (Orion)	2:45.58
18	M. Hynes (Co Manchester)	2:46.53
19	R. Gillatt (Co Sheffield)	2:46.83

Junior Placings: (1) J. Farnsworth; (2) J. Harrison; (3) K. Seaborn.

100 Metres Butterfly
Final

1	M. Scarborough (Portsmouth Northsea)	1:02.07
2	C. Foot (Millfield)	1:03.04
3	A. Baker (Norwich Penguins)	1:03.39
4	G. Atkins (Portsmouth Northsea)	1:03.43
5	L. Wilson (Bo Sunderland)	1:04.13
6	N. Bates (Norwich Penguins)	1:04.84

Consolation Final

1	M. O'Fee (Co Newcastle)	1:04.51
2	S. Buxton (Nova Centurion)	1:04.64
3	H. Jepson (Bo Kirklees)	1:05.10
4	S. McGill (Ferndown Otters)	1:05.69
5	J. Taylor (Portsmouth Northsea)	1:05.70
6	M. Hadden (Beckenham)	1:06.41

Heat Times

1	M. Scarborough (Portsmouth Northsea)	1:02.49
2	C. Foot (Millfield)	1:02.92
3	A. Baker (Norwich Penguins)	1:03.64
4	G. Atkins (Portsmouth Northsea)	1:03.94
5	N. Bates (Norwich Penguins)	1:04.26
6	L. Wilson (Bo Sunderland)	1:04.40
7	M. O'Fee (Co Newcastle)	1:04.44

8 S. Buxton (Nova Centurion)   1:04.97
9 R. Bowden (Co Southampton)   1:05.00
10 H. Jepson (Bo Kirklees)   1:05.06
11 M. Hadden (Beckenham)   1:05.32
12 S. McGill (Ferndown Otters)
    J. Taylor (Portsmouth Northsea)   } 1:05.45
14 H. Osborne (Co Birmingham)   1:05.72
15 J. Dowling (Bo Burnley CATS)   1:05.83
16 M. George (Bo Waltham Forest)   1:05.84
17 T. Day (Beckenham)   1:05.95
18 A. Duffy (Derwentside)   1:06.02
19 N. Sommers (Beckenham)   1:06.16
20 L. Graham (Barnet Copthall)   1:07.16
21 A. Clarke (Tiverton)   1:07.34
22 E. Brooks (Redbridge B)   1:07.59
23 T. Sullivan (Piranha)   1:07.62
24 M. Kowalski (Beckenham)   1:07.71
25 J. Corbett (Co Birmingham)   1:09.09
26 A. Murphy (Salford Triple 'S')   1:09.47

Junior Placings: (1) N. Bates; (2) S. Buxton; (3) H.
Jepson.

200 Metres Butterfly
Final
1 M. Scarborough
   (Portsmouth Northsea)   2:15.08
2 C. Foot (Millfield)   2:15.96
3 H. Jepson (Bo Kirklees)   2:16.18
4 L. Wilson (Bo Sunderland)   2:17.42
5 M. Bradley (Oundle & D)   2:20.25
6 M. O'Fee (Co Newcastle)   2:20.43
Consolation Final
1 A. Baker (Norwich Penguins)   2:18.39
2 J. Taylor (Portsmouth Northsea)   2:18.51
3 N. Ballard (Beckenham)   2:20.70
4 A. Duffy (Derwentside)   2:21.81
5 J. Stark (Nova Centurion)   2:23.18
6 S. McGill (Ferndown Otters)   2:24.15
Heat Times
1 L. Wilson (Bo Sunderland)   2:15.31
2 H. Jepson (Bo Kirklees)   2:15.93
3 C. Foot (Millfield)   2:16.63
4 M. Scarborough
   (Portsmouth Northsea)   2:18.51
5 M. O'Fee (Co Newcastle)   2:18.71
6 M. Bradley (Oundle & D)   2:19.76
7 J. Taylor (Portsmouth Northsea)   2:19.89
8 A. Baker (Norwich Penguins)   2:20.34
9 A. Duffy (Derwentside)   2:20.83
10 N. Ballard (Beckenham)   2:21.18
11 M. George (Bo Waltham Forest)   2:21.28
12 J. Stark (Nova Centurion)   2:22.52
13 S. McGill (Ferndown Otters)   2:23.21
14 R. Bennett (Nova Centurion)   2:23.26
15 J. Dowling (Bo Burnley CATS)   2:24.46
16 A. Cashmore (Co Birmingham)   2:26.79
Junior Placings: (1) H. Jepson; (2) N. Ballard; (3)
M. George.

200 Metres Indvidual Medley
Final
1 R. Bowden (Co Southampton)   2:22.69
2 H. Walsh (Millfield)   2:22.72
3 H. Osborne (Co Birmingham)   2:23.33
4 J. Dowling (Bo Burnley CATS)   2:23.59
5 L. Findlay (Northampton)   2:24.09
6 S. Vick (Co Sheffield)   2:26.07
Consolation Final
1 A. Baker (Norwich Penguins)   2:22.64

2 K. Read (Norwich Penguins)   2:25.94
3 N. Ballard (Beckenham)   2:26.47
4 D. Palmer (Killerwhales)   2:27.28
5 J. Stark (Nova Centurion)   2:27.99
6 J. Harrison (Bo Kirklees)   2:29.97
Heat Times
1 R. Bowden (Co Southampton)   2:22.07
2 H. Osborne (Co Birmingham)   2:22.72
3 J. Dowling (Bo Burnley CATS)   2:23.13
4 H. Walsh (Millfield)   2:23.54
5 S. Vick (Co Sheffield)   2:24.15
6 L. Findlay (Northampton)   2:24.39
7 A. Baker (Norwich Penguins)   2:24.51
8 K. Read (Norwich Penguins)   2:25.26
9 J. Stark (Nova Centurion)   2:25.93
10 N. Ballard (Beckenham)   2:26.04
11 D. Palmer (Killerwhales)   2:26.12
12 J. Harrison (Bo Kirklees)   2:26.42
13 R. Brinn (Kelly College)   2:26.75
14 M. Hynes (Co Manchester)   2:27.65
15 H. Sanderson (Nova Centurion)   2:27.97
16 E. Wilkinson (Millfield)   2:28.19
17 S. McGill (Ferndown Otters)   2:28.66
18 J. Manning (Beaufort)   2:29.49
19 S. Buxton (Nova Centurion)   2:29.56
20 G. Brooks (Greenwich B Mariners)   2:30.27
21 Z. Blake (Torquay Leander)   2:30.78
22 E. Archer (Haverhill)   2:31.17
Junior Placings: (1) H. Osborne; (2) J. Dowling; (3)
L. Findlay.

400 Metres Individual Medley
Final
1 H. Walsh (Millfield)   4:57.58
2 K. Mellor (Co Sheffield)   4:59.45
3 R. Bowden (Co Southampton)   5:00.13
4 A. Baker (Norwich Penguins)   5:05.97
5 H. Osborne (Co Birmingham)   5:06.81
6 R. Brinn (Kelly College)   5:13.65
Consolation Final
1 D. Tubby (Norwich Penguins)   5:03.61
2 M. Hollingsworth (Chase)   5:05.44
3 S. Southern (Redditch)   5:09.69
4 J. Stark (Nova Centurion)   5:10.28
5 J. Harrison (Bo Kirklees)   5:10.64

Caroline Foot

6 S. Vick (Co Sheffield) — 5:10.93

Heat Times

1	R. Bowden (Co Southampton)	4:59.01
2	H. Walsh (Millfield)	5:00.55
3	H. Osborne (Co Birmingham)	5:03.17
4	K. Mellor (Co Sheffield)	5:03.95
5	R. Brinn (Kelly College)	5:04.99
6	L. Wilson (Bo Sunderland)	5:05.06
7	J. Dowling (Bo Burnley CATS)	5:05.15
8	A. Baker (Norwich Penguins)	5:06.69
9	M. Hollingsworth (Chase)	5:07.11
10	D. Tubby (Norwich Penguins)	5:07.17
11	J. Harrison (Bo Kirklees)	5:07.58
12	S. Vick (Co Sheffield)	5:09.29
13	S. Southern (Redditch)	5:09.89
14	J. Stark (Nova Centurion)	5:10.95
15	S. Foggo (Co Newcastle)	5:12.83
16	S. Solly (Nova Centurion)	5:14.29
17	K. Boucher (Norwich Penguins)	5:14.33

Junior Placings: (1) H. Osborne; (2) J. Dowling; (3) J. Harrison.

4×100 Metres Freestyle Club Relay
Final

1	Portsmouth Northsea	3:56.33
2	Co Birmingham	3:59.39
3	Kelly College	3:59.70
4	Nova Centurion	4:00.19
5	Millfield	4:00.95

6 Norwich Penguins — 4:01.06

Heat Times

1	Portsmouth Northsea	4:00.76
2	Kelly College	4:00.98
3	Co Birmingham	4:02.48
4	Millfield	4:03.01
5	Nova Centurion	4:03.61
6	Norwich Penguins	4:03.76
7	Co Southampton	4:05.54
8	Haverhill	4:09.71
9	Bodmin & D	4:12.90

4×100 Metres Medley Club Relay
Final

1	Norwich Penguins	4:22.00
2	Portsmouth Northsea	4:24.01
3	Nova Centurion	4:26.50
4	Millfield	4:28.23
5	Co Southampton	4:28.59
6	Co Leeds	4:36.72

Heat Times

1	Norwich Penguins	4:23.76
2	Portsmouth Northsea	4:26.56
3	Nova Centurion	4:27.02
4	Millfield	4:28.00
5	Co Southampton	4:29.24
6	Co Leeds	4:33.43
7	Kelly College	4:37.38
8	Co Birmingham	4:38.91

ASA National (Long Course)

The Sports Centre, Coventry — 13/16 July, 1989

Men

50 Metres Freestyle
Final

1	M. Fibbens (Barnet Copthall)	23.87
2	M. Foster (Bo Southend)	24.02
3	N. Metcalfe (Co Leeds)	24.22
4	S. Dronsfield (Co Leeds)	24.30
5	J. Bradley (Bo S Tyneside)	24.47
6	A. Rapley (Buxton & D)	24.48
7	D. Parker (Co Coventry)	24.54
8	G. Watson (Carnegie)	24.71

Consolation Final

1	G. Bulpitt (Co Birmingham)	24.59
2	P. Pederzolli (Hounslow B)	24.75
3	M. Levine (Co Sheffield)	24.76
4	S. Wellington (Portsmouth Northsea)	24.79
5	M. Arnold (Co Swansea)	24.80
6	I. Teaz (Glasgow Nomads)	24.91
7	S. Foggo (Co Newcastle)	24.97
8	S. Hirst (Barnet Copthall)	25.18

Heat Times

1	M. Fibbens (Barnet Copthall)	23.73
2	M. Foster (Bo Southend)	24.06
3	S. Dronsfield (Co Leeds)	24.22
4	N. Metcalfe (Co Leeds)	24.33
5	D. Parker (Co Coventry)	24.41
6	A. Rapley (Buxton & D)	24.49
7	J. Bradley (Bo S Tyneside)	24.62
8	G. Watson (Carnegie)	24.63
9	G. Bulpitt (Co Birmingham)	24.66
10	S. Wellington (Portsmouth Northsea)	24.68
11	S. Foggo (Co Newcastle)	24.77
12	M. Arnold (Co Swansea)	24.79
13	M. Levine (Co Sheffield)	24.80
14	P. Pederzolli (Hounslow B)	24.91
15	I. Teaz (Glasgow Nomads)	24.97
16	S. Hirst (Barnet Copthall)	25.03
17	D. Dyke (Walsall)	25.13
18	R. Cole (Co Manchester)	25.14
19	P. McQuaid (Co Manchester)	25.16
20	R. Greenwood (Co Leeds)	25.26
21	L. Holgate (Oundle & D)	25.31
22	W. Howarth (Witney & D)	25.41
23	G. Goudie (Warrender)	25.43
24	M. Flowers (Northampton)	25.60
25	A. Nannini (Eton College)	25.63
26	S. Handley (RTW Monson)	25.65
27	I. Stewart (York C)	25.69
28	A. Irwin (Kelly College)	25.71
29	C. Hale (Hull Olympic)	25.75
30	C. Moxham (Barnet Copthall)	25.84
31	S. Glover (Manchester U Salford)	25.88
32	J. Cunningham (Co Leeds)	25.98
33	S. Haywood (Co Derby)	26.00
34	K. Westwood (Co Derby)	26.02
35	L. Piggott (Beckenham)	26.08
36	D. Wright (Co Leicester)	26.21
37	J. Thubron (Chester le Street)	26.29
38	D. Beswick (Co Manchester)	26.34
39	S. Adamson (Co Southampton)	26.40

100 Metres Freestyle
Final

1	M. Fibbens (Barnet Copthall)	51.68
2	S. Dronsfield (Co Leeds)	51.92

3 G. Bulpitt (Co Birmingham)	51.98
4 T. Hodges (Hounslow B)	52.38
5 M. Foster (Bo Southend)	52.53
6 J. Broughton (Co Leeds)	52.57
7 N. Metcalfe (Co Leeds)	53.17
8 S. Foggo (Co Newcastle)	53.44

Consolation Final

1 D. Parker (Co Coventry)	52.82
2 S. McQuaid (Co Manchester)	53.60
3 J. Bradley (Bo S Tyneside)	53.87
4 C. McNeil (Paisley)	53.89
5 D. Dyke (Walsall)	54.00
6 L. Bennett (Co Newcastle)	54.35
7 M. Arnold (Co Swansea)	55.19
8 M. Hanby (Nova Centurion)	56.08

Heat Times

1 M. Fibbens (Barnet Copthall)	
S. Dronsfield (Co Leeds)	51.94
3 G. Bulpitt (Co Birmingham)	52.71
4 T. Hodges (Hounslow B)	52.84
5 N. Metcalfe (Co Leeds)	52.99
6 J. Broughton (Co Leeds)	53.03
7 S. Foggo (Co Newcastle)	53.07
8 M. Foster (Bo Southend)	53.20
9 J. Bradley (Bo S Tyneside)	53.27
10 S. McQuaid (Co Manchester)	53.43
11 D. Dyke (Walsall)	53.54
12 D. Parker (Co Coventry)	54.12
13 C. McNeil (Paisley)	54.20
14 M. Hanby (Nova Centurion)	54.47
15 L. Bennett (Co Newcastle)	54.84
16 M. Arnold (Co Swansea)	54.99
17 M. Jones (Co Southampton)	55.03
18 P. McQuaid (Co Manchester)	55.19
19 C. Moxham (Barnet Copthall)	55.29
20 C. Jones (Co Swansea)	55.41
21 S. Glover (Manchester U Salford)	55.43
22 W. Howarth (Witney & D)	55.60
23 I. Teaz (Glasgow Nomads)	
A. Irwin (Kelly College)	55.84
25 C. James (Darran Park)	55.87
26 R. Greenwood (Co Leeds)	55.89
27 S. Patch (Lincoln)	56.11
28 A. Nannini (Eton Manor)	56.18
29 P. Chick (Beckenham)	56.25
30 C. Robinson (Killerwhales)	56.29
31 G. Thomas (Rochford & D)	
J. Leveridge (Bo Kirklees)	56.47
33 P. Henry (Edinburgh)	57.21
34 S. Haywood (Co Derby)	57.95

200 Metres Freestyle
Final

1 J. Broughton (Co Leeds)	1:53.34
2 P. Brew (Kelly College)	1:53.85
3 S. McQuaid (Co Manchester)	1:54.15
4 T. Hodges (Hounslow B)	
J. Davey (Co Leeds)	1:54.87
6 G. Bulpitt (Co Birmingham)	1:55.22
7 C. McNeil (Paisley)	1:55.70
8 L. Bennett (Co Newcastle)	1:56.59

Consolation Final

1 D. Rolley (Co Southampton)	1:58.12
2 D. Dyke (Walsall)	1:58.51
3 A. Irwin (Kelly College)	1:58.89
4 K. Joy (Portsmouth Northsea)	1:59.52
5 P. Henry (Edinburgh)	1:59.94
6 C. Robinson (Killerwhales)	2:00.03
7 A. Clayton (Co Leeds)	2:00.46

8 S. Carroll (Windsor)	2:00.48

Heat Times

1 P. Brew (Kelly College)	1:53.75
2 M. Fibbens (Barnet Copthall)	1:54.46
3 S. McQuaid (Co Manchester)	1:54.63
4 J. Davey (Co Leeds)	1:54.80
5 J. Broughton (Co Leeds)	1:54.99
6 T. Hodges (Hounslow B)	1:55.95
7 C. McNeil (Paisley)	1:56.05
8 L. Bennett (Co Newcastle)	1:56.89
9 G. Bulpitt (Co Birmingham)	1:56.92
10 D. Dyke (Walsall)	1:58.00
11 D. Rolley (Co Southampton)	1:58.57
12 A. Irwin (Kelly College)	1:59.88
13 K. Joy (Portsmouth Northsea)	1:59.95
14 A. Clayton (Co Leeds)	2:00.42
15 S. Carroll (Windsor)	2:00.56
16 P. Henry (Edinburgh)	2:00.63
17 C. Robinson (Killerwhales)	2:00.77
18 A. Rolley (Portsmouth Northsea)	2:00.86
19 S. Patch (Lincoln)	2:02.44
20 J. Leveridge (Bo Kirklees)	2:02.96
21 C. Edwards (Killerwhales)	2:03.59
22 S. Wells (Norwich Penguins)	2:03.94
23 S. Lille (Co Swansea)	2:04.45

400 Metres Freestyle
Final

1 C. McNeil (Paisley)	3:58.84
2 J. Broughton (Co Leeds)	3:58.98
3 K. Boyd (Bo S Tyneside)	3:59.20
4 P. Brew (Kelly College)	4:00.17
5 T. Day (Co Leeds)	4:03.99
6 S. Moore (Oundle & D)	4:06.22
7 J. Ong (Kelly College)	4:10.25
8 S. Akers (Shiverers)	4:11.13

Consolation Final

1 A. Clayton (Co Leeds)	4:10.35
2 M. Hooper (Portsmouth Northsea)	4:11.38
3 S. Hanton (Co Leeds)	4:11.44
4 D. Rolley (Co Southampton)	4:11.47
5 A. Rolley (Portsmouth Northsea)	4:13.30
6 A. Stevens (Co Birmingham)	4:15.19
7 S. Carroll (Windsor)	4:16.82
8 S. Patch (Lincoln)	4:20.93

Heat Times

1 K. Boyd (Bo S Tyneside)	4:00.01
2 C. McNeil (Paisley)	4:01.09
3 T. Day (Co Leeds)	4:01.97
4 P. Brew (Kelly College)	4:03.45
5 J. Broughton (Co Leeds)	4:03.54
6 S. Akers (Shiverers)	4:04.05
7 I. Wilson (Bo Sunderland)	4:04.24
8 J. Ong (Kelly College)	4:09.14
9 S. Moore (Oundle & D)	4:09.36
10 T. Hodges (Hounslow B)	4:09.97
11 A. Rolley (Portsmouth Northsea)	4:11.60
12 A. Clayton (Co Leeds)	4:12.63
13 S. Hanton (Co Leeds)	4:12.85
14 M. Hooper (Portsmouth Northsea)	4:13.28
15 D. Rolley (Co Southampton)	4:13.82
16 S. Carroll (Windsor)	4:15.30
17 G. Woolger (Hounslow B)	4:15.37
18 S. Patch (Lincoln)	4:15.95
19 A. Stevens (Co Birmingham)	4:16.04
20 S. Clamp (Co Coventry)	4:17.11
21 C. Dunmore (Oundle & D)	4:18.91
22 G. Pearson (Derwentside)	4:19.52
23 A. Myers (Fleetwood & D)	4:21.13

24	A. Rosser (Torfaen)	4:24.23
25	C. Edwards (Killerwhales)	4:26.74

1500 Metres Freestyle
Heat Times (no final)

1	K. Boyd (Bo S Tyneside)	15:44.19
2	T. Day (Co Leeds)	15:48.12
3	I. Wilson (Bo Sunderland)	15:57.47
4	C. McNeil (Paisley)	16:02.82
5	J. Ong (Kelly College)	16:02.89
6	S. Akers (Shiverers)	16:12.97
7	A. Clayton (Co Leeds)	16:30.11
8	S. Moore (Oundle & D)	16:33.34
9	M. Hooper (Portsmouth Northsea)	16:38.92
10	S. Clamp (Co Coventry)	16:49.80
11	J. McHale (Co Sheffield)	16:51.22
12	S. Hanton (Co Leeds)	16:58.24
13	A. Woods (Norwich Penguins)	16:58.45
14	N. Robinson (Portsmouth Northsea)	17:02.19
15	T. Hobbs (Co Newcastle)	17:05.47
16	S. Smith (Wigan Wasps)	17:06.31
17	P. Kappes (Killerwhales)	17:10.63
18	B. Lafferty (Co Sheffield)	17:10.77
19	S. Lane (Stockton Aquatics)	17:15.55
20	A. Robinson (Stockton Aquatics)	17:15.67
21	M. Hall (Co Bradford)	17:21.33
22	A. Aitken (Stockton Aquatics)	17:50.13
23	G. Brown (Bo Southend)	18:03.55

100 Metres Backstroke
Final

1	G. Binfield (Maxwell)	58.52
2	G. Robins (Portsmouth Northsea)	58.81
3	M. O'Connor (Co Manchester)	59.00
4	M. Harris (Co Birmingham)	59.31
5	M. Peyrebrune (Warrender)	59.79
6	M. Matthews (Barnet Copthall)	1:00.13
7	I. Panting (Kelly College)	1:00.20
8	I. Rosser (Torfaen)	1:00.23

Consolation Final

1	P. Blake (Wigan Wasps)	1:00.68
2	N. Sherringham (Co Sheffield)	1:01.00
3	J. Kearney (Nova Centurion)	1:01.39
4	I. Stewart (York C)	1:01.42
5	I. Clayton (Wigan Wasps)	1:01.44
6	B. Winter (Swansea University)	1:01.81
7	C. Cockcroft (Co Leeds)	1:02.39
8	M. Nolan (Ashton Central)	1:02.65

Heat Times

1	G. Binfield (Maxwell)	58.87
2	G. Robins (Portsmouth Northsea)	59.30
3	M. Harris (Co Birmingham)	59.41
4	M. O'Connor (Co Manchester)	59.82
5	M. Peyrebrune (Warrender)	1:00.30
6	I. Panting (Kelly College)	1:00.35
7	I. Rosser (Torfaen)	
	M. Matthews (Barnet Copthall)	1:00.41
9	P. Blake (Wigan Wasps)	1:00.97
10	J. Kearney (Nova Centurion)	1:01.26
11	N. Sherringham (Co Sheffield)	1:01.33
12	I. Clayton (Wigan Wasps)	1:01.42
13	C. Cockcroft (Co Leeds)	1:01.61
14	I. Stewart (York C)	1:01.72
15	B. Winter (Swansea University)	1:01.97
16	M. Nolan (Ashton Central)	1:02.14
17	S. Handley (RTW Monson)	1:02.45
18	S. Bisley (Milngarvie)	1:02.66
19	S. Foggo (Co Newcastle)	1:02.75
20	C. Biss (Barnet Copthall)	1:02.82

21	J. Kerr (Kelly College)	1:02.92
22	C. Edwards (Killerwhales)	1:03.18
23	C. Hale (Hull Olympic)	1:03.31
24	G. Goudie (Warrender)	1:03.46
25	T. Hobbs (Co Newcastle)	1:03.59
26	C. Jones (Co Swansea)	1:03.63
27	J. McNeil (Milngarvie)	1:03.82
28	A. Ruckwood (Haden Hill)	1:04.22
29	P. Jones (Bo Burnley CATS)	1:04.25
30	G. Williams (Portsmouth Northsea)	1:04.47
31	M. Hampton (Basildon)	1:04.78
32	I. Hardern (Manchester U Salford)	1:05.07
33	A. Aitken (Stockton Aquatics)	1:05.16
34	S. Adamson (Co Southampton)	1:05.25
35	A. Fry (Manchester U Salford)	1:05.31
36	G. Pearson (Derwentside)	1:05.64
37	K. Westwood (Co Derby)	1:05.74
38	A. Jones (York C)	
	R. Batterby (York C)	1:05.92
40	M. Billam (Hull Olympic)	1:05.93
41	N. Poole (Portsmouth Northsea)	1:05.97
42	S. Parker (Co Coventry)	1:06.75

200 Metres Backstroke
Final

1	G. Binfield (Maxwell)	2:05.26
2	P. Blake (Wigan Wasps)	2:05.56
3	G. Robins (Portsmouth Northsea)	2:06.45
4	I. Clayton (Wigan Wasps)	2:06.80
5	M. O'Connor (Co Manchester)	2:07.12
6	J. Davey (Co Leeds)	2:07.81
7	I. Panting (Kelly College)	2:09.06
8	M. Matthews (Barnet Copthall)	2:11.56

Consolation Final

1	I. Rosser (Torfaen)	2:08.20
2	I. Stewart (York C)	2:09.55
3	D. McNulty (Chester le Street)	2:10.40
4	C. Biss (Barnet Copthall)	2:14.03
5	N. Sherringham (Co Sheffield)	2:14.17
6	B. Winter (Swansea University)	2:15.58
7	A. Rolley (Portsmouth Northsea)	2:16.63
8	J. Austin (Co Sheffield)	2:17.16

Heat Times

1	P. Blake (Wigan Wasps)	
	G. Binfield (Maxwell)	2:07.07
3	I. Clayton (Wigan Wasps)	2:07.75

Jeff Ong

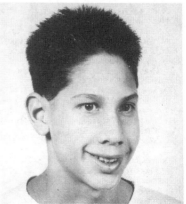

4 G. Robins (Portsmouth Northsea)	2:07.84	
5 M. O'Connor (Co Manchester)	2:07.92	
6 I. Panting (Kelly College)	2:08.42	
7 M. Matthews (Barnet Copthall)	2:09.41	
8 J. Davey (Co Leeds)	2:09.80	
9 I. Stewart (York C)	2:09.83	
10 D. McNulty (Chester le Street)	2:11.51	
11 K. Boyd (Bo S Tyneside)	2:11.63	
12 I. Rosser (Torfaen)	2:11.66	
13 M. Harris (Co Birmingham)	2:12.92	
14 J. Kearney (Nova Centurion)	2:13.13	
15 C. Biss (Barnet Copthall)	2:13.47	
16 N. Sherringham (Co Sheffield)	2:13.79	
17 M. Peyrebrune (Warrender)	2:14.50	
18 J. Austin (Co Sheffield)	2:15.35	
19 B. Winter (Swansea University)	2:15.60	
20 A. Rolley (Portsmouth Northsea)	2:15.69	
21 M. Hooper (Portsmouth Northsea)	2:15.90	
22 J. Kerr (Kelly College)	2:16.39	
23 M. Nolan (Ashton Central)	2:16.76	
24 C. Edwards (Killerwhales)	2:17.01	
25 P. Griffiths (Stroud)	2:17.34	
26 T. Hobbs (Co Newcastle)	2:17.41	
27 A. Ruckwood (Haden Hill)	2:17.43	
28 C. Hale (Hull Olympic	2:17.65	
29 G. Pearson (Derwentside)	2:18.41	
30 A. Aitken (Stockton Aquatics)	2:19.36	
31 S. Lack (Barnet Copthall)	2:19.78	
32 S. Clamp (Co Coventry)	2:19.96	
33 S. Bisley (Milngarvie)	2:20.52	
34 I. Hardern (Manchester U Salford)	2:21.54	
35 A. Fry (Manchester U Salford)	2:21.72	
36 A. Jones (York C)	2:21.77	
37 M. Billam (Hull Olympic)	2:22.11	
38 D. Bradford (Fleetwood & D)	2:23.09	
39 J. McNeil (Milngarvie)	2:28.37	

100 Metres Breaststroke
Final

1 A. Moorhouse (Co Leeds)	1:03.31
2 N. Gillingham (Co Birmingham)	1:03.61
3 J. Parrack (Co Leeds)	1:04.24
4 J. Hender (Co Chester)	1:05.49
5 A. Fitzgerald (Bo Southend)	1:05.60
6 G. Watson (Carnegie)	1:05.66
7 N. Hudghton (Co Dundee)	1:05.74
8 P. O'Sullivan (Hounslow B)	1:07.30

Consolation Final

1 D. Mason (Co Newcastle)	1:07.56
2 R. Brown (Torfaen)	1:07.98
3 I. Cotton (Co Leeds)	1:08.02
4 J. Cole (Co Leicester)	1:09.24
5 M. Whittaker (Co Southampton)	1:09.31
6 G. Bennett (Bracknell)	1:09.90
7 A. Boyd (Co Newcastle)	1:10.02
8 P. Hennys (Soundwell)	1:10.29

Heat Times

1 A. Moorhouse (Co Leeds)	1:04.29
2 N. Gillingham (Co Birmingham)	1:04.34
3 J. Parrack (Co Leeds)	1:04.96
4 J. Hender (Co Chester)	1:05.70
5 A. Fitzgerald (Bo Southend)	1:06.16
6 G. Watson (Carnegie)	1:06.18
7 P. O'Sullivan (Hounslow B)	1:06.65
8 N. Hudghton (Co Dundee)	1:07.17
9 D. Mason (Co Newcastle)	1:07.22
10 I. Cotton (Co Leeds)	1:08.11
11 J. Cole (Co Leicester)	1:08.29
12 R. Brown (Torfaen)	1:08.34

13 G. Bennett (Bracknell)	1:09.45
14 M. Whittaker (Co Southampton)	1:09.65
15 P. Blake (Wigan Wasps)	1:09.80
16 A. Boyd (Co Newcastle)	1:09.95
17 P. Hennys (Soundwell)	1:10.01
18 A. Clapper (Barking)	1:10.02
19 D. Carr (Co Newcastle)	1:10.08
20 T. Ashwell (Ipswich)	1:10.52
21 N. Poole (Portsmouth Northsea)	1:10.59
22 I. Jackson (Paisley)	1:10.78
23 T. Evans (Oundle & D)	1:10.95
24 C. Corbett (Maxwell)	1:10.99
25 J. Spriggs (Basildon)	1:11.10
26 K. Joy (Portsmouth Northsea)	1:11.21
27 P. Melhuish (Co Cardiff)	1:11.24
28 T. Maddocks (Rochford & D)	1:11.40
29 M. Wynn (Kelly College)	1:11.66
30 L. Peterson (Braintree & Bocking)	1:11.90
31 J. Moorfoot (Stockton Aquatics)	1:12.12
32 W. O'Gorman (Millfield)	1:13.05
33 P. Wilkinson (Co Leeds)	1:13.25
34 S. Wells (Norwich Penguins)	1:13.35
S. Handley (RTW Monson)	
36 A. Cooper (Royton)	1:14.27
37 S. Haywood (Co Derby)	1:16.87

200 Metres Breaststroke
Final

1 N. Gillingham (Co Birmingham)	2:18.45
2 N. Hudghton (Co Dundee)	2:19.34
3 A. Moorhouse (Co Leeds)	2:19.55
4 P. O'Sullivan (Hounslow B)	2:22.75
5 A. Fitzgerald (Bo Southend)	2:24.21
6 J. Hender (Co Chester)	2:25.50
7 J. Parrack (Co Leeds)	2:26.93
8 D. Mason (Co Newcastle)	2:27.48

Consolation Final

1 R. Brown (Torfaen)	2:26.12
2 I. Cotton (Co Leeds)	2:27.63
3 I. Swift (Rotherham Metro)	2:28.05
4 D. Entwistle (Royton)	2:28.31
5 G. Bennett (Bracknell)	2:30.40
6 A. Clapper (Barking)	2:31.19
7 P. McGillion (Co Coventry)	2:32.28
8 M. Whittaker (Co Southampton)	2:34.90

Heat Times

1 N. Hudghton (Co Dundee)	2:21.13
2 N. Gillingham (Co Birmingham)	2:21.33
3 A. Moorhouse (Co Leeds)	2:22.68
4 P. O'Sullivan (Hounslow B)	2:24.46
5 J. Hender (Co Chester)	2:25.17
6 A. Fitzgerald (Bo Southend)	2:25.62
7 D. Mason (Co Newcastle)	2:26.54
8 J. Parrack (Co Leeds)	2:26.72
9 R. Brown (Torfaen)	2:27.23
10 I. Cotton (Co Leeds)	2:28.26
11 D. Entwistle (Royton)	2:28.68
12 I. Swift (Rotherham Metro)	2:30.05
13 P. McGillion (Co Coventry)	2:32.02
14 G. Bennett (Bracknell)	2:32.18
15 A. Clapper (Barking)	2:32.69
16 M. Whittaker (Co Southampton)	2:33.65
17 A. Boyd (Co Newcastle)	2:33.79
18 D. Shearsby (Harrow & Wealdstone)	2:33.86
19 T. Ashwell (Ipswich)	2:33.87
20 K. Joy (Portsmouth Northsea)	2:33.97
21 T. Evans (Oundle & D)	2:34.03
22 I. Jackson (Paisley)	2:34.04

David Parker   Alan Pascoe Ass.

9 M. Matthews (Barnet Copthall)	58.22
10 D. McNulty (Chester le Street)	58.34
11 R. Greenwood (Co Leeds)	58.55
12 I. Panting (Kelly College)	58.69
13 C. Wilson (Co Southampton)	58.78
14 M. Smith (Co Swansea)	59.29
15 K. Reynard (Warrender)	59.32
16 A. Quinn (Sale)	59.40
17 M. Foster (Bo Southend)	59.59
18 D. Lo Cascio (Barnet Copthall)	59.90
19 C. Moxham (Barnet Copthall)	1:00.21
20 I. Hardern (Manchester U Salford)	1:00.28
21 C. Bird (Kelly College)	1:00.32
22 C. Robinson (Killerwhales)	1:00.93
23 M. Jones (Co Southampton)	1:01.16
24 P. Edwards (Norwich Penguins)	1:01.77
25 P. Chick (Beckenham)	1:01.92
26 H. Sheraton (Millfield)	1:02.01
27 T. Cook (Barking)	1:03.69
28 S. Wells (Norwich Penguins)	1:03.73
29 S. Haywood (Co Derby)	1:04.12
30 D. Wright (Co Leicester)	1:04.52
31 G. Hall (Nova Centurion)	1:04.74

200 Metres Butterfly
Final

1 A. Quinn (Sale)	2:05.08
2 M. Watkins (Torfaen)	2:05.88
3 C. Robinson (Killerwhales)	2:06.06
4 C. Bird (Kelly College)	2:07.42
5 D. McNulty (Chester le Street)	2:07.57
6 P. Henry (Edinburgh)	2:08.76
7 E. Stewart (Co Leeds)	2:09.89
8 R. Beacham (Co Coventry)	2:10.11

Consolation Final

1 N. Parish (Oundle & D)	2:08.90
2 M. Hooper (Portsmouth Northsea)	2:09.95
3 R. Leishman (Kelly College)	2:09.99
4 K. Renshaw (Chester le Street)	2:10.03
5 C. Wilson (Co Southampton)	2:12.06
6 S. Wainwright (Millfield)	2:13.12
7 C. Dunmore (Oundle & D)	2:15.45
8 S. Smith (Wigan Wasps)	2:17.24

Heat Times

1 T. Jones (Co Birmingham)	2:02.87
2 M. Watkins (Torfaen)	2:06.02
3 A. Quinn (Sale)	2:06.32
4 C. Bird (Kelly College)	2:08.27
5 D. McNulty (Chester le Street)	2:08.31
6 C. Robinson (Killerwhales)	2:08.95
7 R. Beacham (Co Coventry)	2:09.37
8 E. Stewart (Co Leeds)	2:10.20
9 P. Henry (Edinburgh)	2:10.60
10 C. Wilson (Co Southampton)	2:10.77
11 M. Hooper (Portsmouth Northsea)	2:10.97
12 N. Parish (Oundle & D)	2:11.25
13 R. Leishman (Kelly College)	2:11.33
14 K. Renshaw (Chester le Street)	2:11.58
15 S. Wainwright (Millfield)	2:12.68
16 P. Chick (Beckenham)	2:14.78
17 P. Edwards (Norwich Penguins)	2:14.92
18 C. Dunmore (Oundle & D)	2:15.37
19 S. Smith (Wigan Wasps)	2:15.94
20 M. Fellows (Co Birmingham)	2:15.96
21 N. Grundy (Fleetwood & D)	2:20.26
22 M. Simpkins (Co Oxford)	2:20.53
23 D. Bullock (Bo Waltham Forest)	2:20.72
24 R. Copping (Portsmouth Northsea)	2:21.41
25 T. Cook (Barking)	2:23.68

23 P. Hennys (Soundwell)	2:34.11
24 M. Wynn (Kelly College)	2:34.16
25 J. Spriggs (Basildon)	2:34.89
26 J. Brownhill (Beckenham)	
L. Peterson	2:34.97
(Braintree & Bocking)	
28 T. Maddocks (Rochford & D)	2:35.24
29 S. Wells (Norwich Penguins)	2:35.43
30 R. Laidlow (Kelly College)	2:35.87
31 J. Gregory (Co Leeds)	2:36.38
32 P. Kappes (Killerwhales)	2:36.54
33 L. Radwell (Oundle & D)	2:37.31
34 P. Wilkinson (Co Leeds)	2:39.07
35 L. Hammond (Co Leicester)	2:39.38
36 P. Cropper (Manchester U Salford)	2:39.42
37 P. Clark (Bo Southend)	2:39.44
38 D. Carr (Co Newcastle)	2:39.63

100 Metres Butterfly
Final

1 D. Parker (Co Coventry)	55.33
2 M. Fibbens (Barnet Copthall)	55.70
3 S. Dronsfield (Co Leeds)	55.90
4 G. Binfield (Maxwell)	56.24
5 T. Jones (Co Birmingham)	57.09
6 E. Stewart (Co Leeds)	57.10
7 M. Watkins (Torfaen)	57.44
8 R. Leishman (Kelly College)	57.61

Consolation Final

1 D. McNulty (Chester le Street)	58.36
2 I. Panting (Kelly College)	58.51
3 R. Greenwood (Co Leeds)	58.64
4 M. Matthews (Barnet Copthall)	58.95
5 M. Smith (Co Swansea)	59.12
6 C. Wilson (Co Southampton)	59.14
7 A. Quinn (Sale)	59.69
8 K. Reynard (Warrender)	59.92

Heat Times

1 S. Dronsfield (Co Leeds)	56.10
2 G. Binfield (Maxwell)	56.57
3 E. Stewart (Co Leeds)	56.81
4 D. Parker (Co Coventry)	57.10
5 T. Jones (Co Birmingham)	57.42
6 M. Fibbens (Barnet Copthall)	57.72
7 R. Leishman (Kelly College)	57.95
8 M. Watkins (Torfaen)	58.02

200 Metres Individual Medley
Final

1	G. Robins (Portsmouth Northsea)	2:06.05
2	P. O'Sullivan (Hounslow B)	2:06.14
3	J. Davey (Co Leeds)	2:07.34
4	P. Brew (Kelly College)	2:08.48
5	P. Blake (Wigan Wasps)	2:09.65
6	N. Gillingham (Co Birmingham)	2:10.62
7	I. Stewart (York C)	2:10.76
8	P. McGillion (Co Coventry)	2:12.28

Consolation Final

1	D. McNulty (Chester le Street)	2:11.52
2	T. Evans (Oundle & D)	2:12.39
3	L. Bennett (Co Newcastle)	2:12.47
4	J. Kerr (Kelly College)	2:13.28
5	A. Greig (Barnet Copthall)	2:13.71
6	R. Beacham (Co Coventry)	2:14.12
7	J. Brownhill (Beckenham)	2:15.98
8	A. Rolley (Portsmouth Northsea)	2:17.28

Heat Times

1	G. Binfield (Maxwell)	2:07.27
2	P. O'Sullivan (Hounslow B)	2:08.61
3	J. Davey (Co Leeds)	2:08.79
4	G. Robins (Portsmouth Northsea)	2:08.99
5	P. Brew (Kelly College)	2:09.44
6	P. Blake (Wigan Wasps)	2:10.22
7	N. Gillingham (Co Birmingham)	2:10.58
8	P. McGillion (Co Coventry)	2:11.68
9	I. Stewart (York C)	2:11.77
10	M. Hooper (Portsmouth Northsea)	2:12.28
11	A. Greig (Barnet Copthall)	2:12.34
12	L. Bennett (Co Newcastle)	2:12.44
13	J. Kerr (Kelly College)	2:12.57
14	T. Evans (Oundle & D)	2:12.68
15	D. McNulty (Chester le Street)	2:14.72
16	R. Beacham (Co Coventry)	2:15.03
17	A. Rolley (Portsmouth Northsea)	2:16.00
18	J. Brownhill (Beckenham)	2:16.11
19	K. Joy (Portsmouth Northsea)	2:16.20
20	C. Moxham (Barnet Copthall)	2:17.08
21	S. Wells (Norwich Penguins)	2:17.36
22	C. Jones (Co Swansea)	2:17.76
23	I. Hardern (Manchester U Salford)	2:17.78
24	S. Patch (Lincoln)	2:18.46
25	M. Billam (Hull Olympic)	2:18.58
26	N. Poole (Portsmouth Northsea)	2:20.53
27	S. Clamp (Co Coventry)	2:20.67
28	M. Simpkins (Co Oxford)	2:20.69
29	S. Abels (Jersey)	2:21.53
30	L. Radwell (Oundle & D)	2:22.20
31	P. Wilkinson (Co Leeds)	2:22.48
32	G. Pearson (Derwentside)	2:23.34
33	S. Haywood (Co Derby)	2:25.79

400 Metres Individual Medley
Final

1	P. Brew (Kelly College)	4:26.45
2	P. O'Sullivan (Hounslow B)	4:27.16
3	T. Day (Co Leeds)	4:32.31
4	M. Hooper (Portsmouth Northsea)	4:35.32
5	P. McGillion (Co Coventry)	4:37.76
6	I. Stewart (York C)	4:39.90
7	A. Greig (Barnet Copthall)	4:43.57
8	J. Kerr (Kelly College)	4:43.72

Consolation Final

1	A. Rolley (Portsmouth Northsea)	4:42.46
2	S. Hanton (Co Leeds)	4:44.33
3	T. Evans (Oundle & D)	4:46.29
4	P. Kappes (Killerwhales)	4:47.34
5	N. Parrish (Oundle & D)	4:48.67
6	S. Clamp (Co Coventry)	4:49.63
7	S. Wells (Norwich Penguins)	4:51.34
8	J. Ong (Kelly College)	4:51.37

Heat Times

1	P. O'Sullivan (Hounslow B)	4:31.19
2	P. Brew (Kelly College)	4:33.43
3	T. Day (Co Leeds)	4:35.06
4	M. Hooper (Portsmouth Northsea)	4:36.38
5	I. Rosser (Torfaen)	4:38.87
6	P. McGillion (Co Coventry)	4:38.94
7	A. Greig (Barnet Copthall)	4:41.15
8	I. Stewart (York C)	4:41.85
9	J. Kerr (Kelly College)	4:47.50
10	J. Ong (Kelly College)	4:48.06
11	T. Evans (Oundle & D)	4:48.15
12	P. Kappes (Killerwhales)	4:49.30
13	A. Rolley (Portsmouth Northsea)	4:50.00
14	S. Hanton (Co Leeds)	4:50.15
15	N. Parish (Oundle & D)	4:50.48
16	S. Wainwright (Millfield)	4:50.74
17	S. Clamp (Co Coventry)	4:50.93
18	S. Wells (Norwich Penguins)	4:51.25
19	C. Thompson (Co Bradford)	4:53.10
20	I. Hardern (Manchester U Salford)	4:53.96
21	M. Simpkins (Co Oxford)	4:56.82
22	M. Billam (Hull Olympic)	4:57.44
23	P. Wilkinson (Co Leeds)	4:59.00
24	D. Bradford (Fleetwood & D)	4:59.45
25	N. Carr (Barking)	5:03.01
26	R. Copping (Portsmouth Northsea)	5:03.57
	K. Renshaw (Chester le Street)	DIS

4×100 Metres Freestyle Club Relay
Final

1	Co Leeds	3:30.14
2	Co Birmingham	3:34.40
3	Barnet Copthall	3:34.79
4	Hounslow B	3:35.53
5	Co Newcastle	3:35.75
6	Portsmouth Northsea	3:39.23
7	Co Coventry	3:39.74
8	Co Manchester	3:39.85

Paul Brew

Heat Times

1	Barnet Copthall	3:35.65
2	Co Leeds	3:36.70
3	Co Newcastle	3:36.80
4	Co Coventry	3:36.83
5	Co Birmingham	3:37.29
6	Hounslow B	3:37.65
7	Portsmouth Northsea	3:39.47
8	Co Manchester	3:39.86
9	Co Southampton	3:42.38
10	Kelly College	3:44.76
11	Oundle & D	3:44.79
12	Co Derby	3:51.68

4×100 Metres Medley Club Relay

Final

1	Co Leeds	3:49.27
2	Co Birmingham	3:51.33
3	Barnet Copthall	4:01.76
4	Co Manchester	4:04.35
5	Co Newcastle	4:04.43
6	Portsmouth Northsea	4:05.96
7	Co Southampton	4:06.91
8	Co Coventry	4:09.83

Heat Times

1	Co Birmingham	3:50.65
2	Co Leeds	3:58.88
3	Barnet Copthall	4:02.97
4	Co Newcastle	4:03.73
5	Portsmouth Northsea	4:03.93
6	Co Manchester	4:06.70
7	Co Coventry	4:07.75
8	Co Southampton	4:08.79
9	Hounslow B	4:09.53
10	Nova Centurion	4:10.16
11	Oundle & D	4:11.53
12	Killerwhales	4:13.32
13	Co Derby	4:20.10
	Kelly College	DIS

Women

50 Metres Freestyle

Final

1	C. Woodcock (Haywards Heath)	26.49
2	A. Sheppard (Milngarvie)	26.81
3	K. Pickering (Ipswich)	26.92
4	J. Gorst (Co Leeds)	27.07
5	S. Davies (Bracknell)	27.13
	S. Watson (Paisley)	
7	L. Donnelly (Hamilton)	27.42
8	J. Coull (Co Birmingham)	27.43

Consolation Final

1	J. Gunston (Bracknell)	27.50
2	M. Buckley (Co Birmingham)	27.70
3	G. Brooks (Greenwich B Mariners)	27.81
4	J. Waite (Co Southampton)	27.84
5	J. McHarg (Portsmouth Northsea)	27.90
6	J. Scott-Robertson (Halstead)	27.93
7	G. Lavin (Derwentside)	27.97
8	A. Kindon (Co Birmingham)	28.10

Heat Times

1	C. Woodcock (Haywards Heath)	26.88
	A. Sheppard (Milngarvie)	
3	J. Gorst (Co Leeds)	27.19
4	K. Pickering (Ipswich)	27.22
5	J. Coull (Co Birmingham)	27.28
6	S. Watson (Paisley)	27.30
7	S. Davies (Bracknell)	27.60

8	A. Kindon (Co Birmingham)	27.67
	L. Donnelly (Hamilton)	
10	G. Brooks (Greenwich B Mariners)	27.73
	M. Buckley (Co Birmingham)	
12	J. Gunston (Bracknell)	27.75
13	G. Lavin (Derwentside)	27.85
14	J. McHarg (Portsmouth Northsea)	28.00
	J. Scott-Robertson (Halstead)	
16	J. Waite (Co Southampton)	28.08
17	G. Atkins (Portsmouth Northsea)	28.16
18	H. Sanderson (Nova Centurion)	28.23
19	E. Archer (Kelly College)	28.32
20	E. Brooks (Redbridge B)	28.34
21	S. Garrett (Barnet Copthall)	28.37
22	J. Lancaster (Warrington Warriors)	28.40
23	S. Vick (Co Sheffield)	28.45
24	C. Foot (Millfield)	28.52
25	N. Cumbers (Kelly College)	28.54
26	E. McLeod (Lichfield)	28.60
27	E. Gilfillan (Co Dundee)	28.62
28	C. Horton (Norwich Penguins)	28.63
29	K. Cheney (Spondon)	28.70
30	H. Mansfield (Co Chester)	28.72
31	A. Clarke (Kelly College)	28.78
32	H. Johnston (Sale)	28.91
33	L. Clark (Haverhill)	28.94
34	K. Harrison (Rotherham Metro)	29.05
35	M. Berry (Haverhill)	29.28
36	A. Garratt (Co Peterborough)	29.31
37	E. Nathan (Millfield)	29.32
38	A. Christie (Jersey)	29.40
39	C. Harris (Northampton)	29.47
40	J. Punter (Hounslow B)	29.67
41	A. Derby (Harrow & Wealdstone)	29.88

100 Metres Freestyle

Final

1	K. Pickering (Ipswich)	58.21
2	L. Donnelly (Hamilton)	58.57
3	J. Coull (Co Birmingham)	58.83
4	S. Davies (Bracknell)	58.87
5	Z. Long (Beckenham)	58.96
6	S. Watson (Paisley)	59.17
7	J. Gorst (Co Leeds)	59.22
8	J. Gunston (Bracknell)	59.52

Consolation Final

1	A. Sheppard (Milngarvie)	59.36
2	C. Woodcock (Haywards Heath)	59.38
3	H. Mansfield (Co Chester)	59.67
4	E. Gilfillan (Co Dundee)	1:00.30
5	G. Atkins (Portsmouth Northsea)	1:00.33
6	A. Kindon (Co Birmingham)	1:00.49
7	J. Lancaster (Warrington Warriors)	1:00.56
8	G. Brooks (Greenwich B Mariners)	1:01.13

Heat Times

1	J. Coull (Co Birmingham)	58.65
2	L. Donnelly (Hamilton)	59.11
3	K. Pickering (Ipswich)	59.25
4	S. Watson (Paisley)	59.31
5	J. Gunston (Bracknell)	59.43
6	Z. Long (Beckenham)	59.46
7	S. Davies (Bracknell)	59.51
8	J. Gorst (Co Leeds)	59.82
9	G. Atkins (Portsmouth Northsea)	1:00.22
10	E. Gilfillan (Co Dundee)	1:00.25
11	A. Kindon (Co Birmingham)	1:00.30
12	A. Sheppard (Milngarvie)	1:00.31
13	H. Mansfield (Co Chester)	1:00.39
14	J. Lancaster (Warrington Warriors)	1:00.43

15	G. Brooks (Greenwich B Mariners)	1:00.45
16	C. Woodcock (Haywards Heath)	1:00.64
17	M. Scarborough	
	(Portsmouth Northsea)	1:00.79
18	N. Bates (Norwich Penguins)	1:00.80
19	G. Lavin (Derwentside)	1:00.95
20	N. Cumbers (Kelly College)	1:00.97
21	C. Huddart (Manchester U Salford)	1:01.04
22	C. Foot (Millfield)	1:01.05
23	P. Rickard (Tynemouth)	1:01.16
24	M. Riegal (Harrow & Wealdstone)	1:01.22
25	A. Dronsfield (Co Manchester)	1:01.23
26	S. Vick (Co Sheffield)	1:01.27
27	M. Buckley (Co Birmingham)	1:01.30
28	H. Sanderson (Nova Centurion)	1:01.38
29	J. Waite (Co Southampton)	1:01.42
30	C. Horton (Norwich Penguins)	1:01.44
31	D. Salmon (Kelly College)	1:01.54
32	L. Marchant (Nova Centurion)	1:01.87
33	J. McHarg (Portsmouth Northsea)	1:01.88
34	C. Banks (York C)	1:01.93
35	E. Brooks (Redbridge B)	1:02.00
36	A. Clarke (Kelly College)	1:02.04
37	S. Littlewood (Manchester U Salford)	1:02.06
38	D. Palmer (Killerwhales)	1:02.18
39	K. Harrison (Rotherham Metro)	1:02.21
40	C. Shiell (Edinburgh)	1:02.24
41	J. Ewing (Paisley)	1:02.57
42	K. Cheney (Spondon)	1:02.74
43	R. Shurey (Hounslow B)	1:03.13
44	A. Gilmore (Portsmouth Northsea)	1:03.31
45	E. Rumbold (Norwich Penguins)	1:03.36
46	E. Archer (Kelly College)	1:03.68
47	K. Edbrooke (Guildford C)	1:04.21

200 Metres Freestyle

Final

1	J. Coull (Co Birmingham)	2:05.23
2	H. Mansfield (Co Chester)	2:06.15
3	L. Donnelly (Hamilton)	2:06.32
4	J. Lancaster (Warrington Warriors)	2:07.79
5	Z. Long (Beckenham)	2:08.49
6	E. Gilfillan (Co Dundee)	2:08.92
7	K. Mellor (Co Sheffield)	2:08.93
8	D. Churchman (Co Leeds)	2:10.29

Consolation Final

1	N. Cumbers (Kelly College)	2:08.63
2	S. Watson (Paisley)	2:09.79
3	J. Gorst (Co Leeds)	2:10.31
4	C. Banks (York C)	2:10.84
5	C. Piggott (Co Birmingham)	2:11.05
6	D. Salmon (Kelly College)	
	Z. Harrison (Norwich Penguins)	2:11.49
8	M. Ivison (Bo S Tyneside)	2:13.16

Heat Times

1	J. Coull (Co Birmingham)	2:07.48
2	H. Mansfield (Co Chester)	2:08.26
3	L. Donnelly (Hamilton)	2:09.07
4	E. Gilfillan (Co Dundee)	2:09.58
5	J. Lancaster (Warrington Warriors)	2:10.02
6	K. Mellor (Co Sheffield)	2:10.03
7	Z. Long (Beckenham)	2:10.42
8	D. Churchman (Co Leeds)	2:10.85
9	H. Walsh (Swansea University)	2:11.00
10	J. Gorst (Co Leeds)	2:11.02
11	S. Watson (Paisley)	2:11.17
12	N. Cumbers (Kelly College)	2:11.22
13	M. Ivison (Bo S Tyneside)	2:11.37
14	D. Salmon (Kelly College)	2:11.63

15	C. Banks (York C)	2:11.77
16	J. Riegal (Harrow & Wealdstone)	2:11.81
17	C. Piggott (Co Birmingham)	2:11.92
18	Z. Harrison (Norwich Penguins)	2:12.06
19	H. Sanderson (Nova Centurion)	2:12.26
20	A. Kay (Co Bradford)	2:12.28
21	E. Brooks (Redbridge B)	2:12.48
22	G. Brooks (Greenwich B Mariners)	2:12.56
23	C. Shiell (Edinburgh)	2:12.62
24	S. Vick (Co Sheffield)	2:12.68
25	D. Palmer (Killerwhales)	2:12.87
26	N. Sommers (Beckenham)	2:12.89
27	N. Bates (Norwich Penguins)	2:12.92
28	L. Sonn (Co Southampton)	2:13.49
29	C. Horton (Norwich Penguins)	2:14.13
30	K. Harrison (Rotherham Metro)	2:14.96
31	R. Bridger (Nova Centurion)	2:15.86
32	E. Archer (Kelly College)	2:17.52
33	P. Herron (Co Newcastle)	2:19.67

400 Metres Freestyle

Final

1	K. Mellor (Co Sheffield)	4:22.37
2	N. Atkinson (Stockport Metro)	4:24.13
3	H. Walsh (Swansea University)	4:26.05
4	E. Arnold (Nottingham Northern)	4:27.58
5	L. Sonn (Co Southampton)	4:32.39
6	L. Matthews (Redbridge B)	4:32.44
7	C. Piggott (Co Birmingham)	4:32.49
8	D. Evans (Wigan Wasps)	4:33.35

Consolation Final

1	D. Jones (Co Chester)	4:29.69
2	M. Ivison (Bo S Tyneside)	4:30.28
3	D. Churchman (Co Leeds)	4:33.34
4	S. Foggo (Co Newcastle)	4:33.37
5	C. Smith (Wigan Wasps)	4:35.13
6	Z. Harrison (Norwich Penguins)	4:35.72
7	R. Shurey (Hounslow B)	4:36.92
8	J. Davey (Co Newcastle)	4:37.08

Heat Times

1	E. Arnold (Nottingham Northern)	4:27.40
2	K. Mellor (Co Sheffield)	4:27.57
3	N. Atkinson (Stockport Metro)	4:29.22
4	H. Walsh (Swansea University)	4:29.54
5	C. Piggott (Co Birmingham)	4:32.15
6	L. Sonn (Co Southampton)	4:32.57
7	L. Matthews (Redbridge B)	4:32.87
8	D. Evans (Wigan Wasps)	4:33.31
9	M. Ivison (Bo S Tyneside)	4:33.42
10	S. Foggo (Co Newcastle)	4:34.43
11	C. Smith (Wigan Wasps)	4:34.57
12	D. Churchman (Co Leeds)	4:34.90
13	D. Jones (Co Chester)	4:35.75
14	J. Davey (Co Newcastle)	4:36.87
15	N. Sommers (Beckenham)	4:38.10
16	Z. Harrison (Norwich Penguins)	4:38.72
17	R. Shurey (Hounslow B)	4:39.46
18	M. Berry (Haverhill)	4:40.05
19	L. Kilgour (Co Birmingham)	4:40.77
20	S. Brown (Edinburgh)	4:43.18
21	N. Gwynne (Wigan Wasps)	4:44.45
22	D. Palmer (Killerwhales)	4:45.94
23	P. Herron (Co Newcastle)	4:49.75

800 Metres Freestyle

Heat Times (no final)

1	K. Mellor (Co Sheffield)	8:53.39
2	N. Atkinson (Stockport Metro)	8:56.38
3	E. Arnold (Nottingham Northern)	8:59.74

4 P. Hutchinson (Wigan Wasps)	9:09.59
5 D. Evans (Wigan Wasps)	9:12.34
6 L. Matthews (Redbridge B)	9:12.58
7 S. Foggo (Co Newcastle)	9:12.78
8 L. Sonn (Co Southampton)	9:14.13
9 M. Ivison (Bo S Tyneside)	9:16.73
10 C. Smith (Wigan Wasps)	9:16.78
11 J. Davey (Co Newcastle)	9:21.56
12 B. Collier (Wigan Wasps)	9:21.81
13 D. Churchman (Co Leeds)	9:23.74
14 L. Kilgour (Co Birmingham)	9:24.25
15 V. Barnes (Co Manchester)	9:27.01
16 C. Shiell (Edinburgh)	9:30.53
17 S. Brown (Edinburgh)	9:32.31
18 V. Crane (Greenwich B Mariners)	9:32.58
19 K. Dawson (Bracknell)	9:32.96
20 D. Palmer (Killerwhales)	9:37.60
21 J. Owen (Chester le Street)	9:40.37

100 Metres Backstroke
Final

1 K. Read (Barnet Copthall)	1:04.70
2 H. Slater (Kelly College)	1:05.75
3 J. Deakins (Gloucester C)	1:06.18
4 S. Page (Co Birmingham)	1:06.74
5 A. Sheppard (Milngarvie)	1:07.06
6 J. Ewing (Paisley)	1:08.10
7 J. Corbett (Co Birmingham)	1:08.70
8 L. Phimister (Moray & D)	1:08.82

Consolation Final

1 J. Riegal (Harrow & Wealdstone)	1:08.53
2 L. Racster (Portsmouth Northsea)	1:09.09
3 A. Sedgebeer (Epping Forest)	1:09.11
4 J. Evans (Co Swansea)	1:09.12
5 J. Wright (Co Chester)	1:09.23
6 C. Huddart (Manchester U Salford)	1:09.73
7 K. Edbrooke (Guildford C)	1:09.81
8 P. Rickard (Tynemouth)	1:09.91

Heat Times

1 K. Read (Barnet Copthall)	1:04.75
2 H. Slater (Kelly College)	1:05.74
3 S. Page (Co Birmingham)	1:06.74
4 J. Deakins (Gloucester C)	1:07.27
5 A. Sheppard (Milngarvie)	1:07.45
6 L. Phimister (Moray & D)	1:08.06
7 J. Ewing (Paisley)	1:08.34
8 J. Corbett (Co Birmingham)	1:08.40
9 C. Huddart (Manchester U Salford)	1:08.96
10 L. Racster (Portsmouth Northsea)	1:09.00
11 J. Riegal (Harrow & Wealdstone)	1:09.02
12 A. Sedgebeer (Epping Forest)	1:09.07
13 J. Evans (Co Swansea)	1:09.35
14 J. Wright (Co Chester)	1:09.47
15 K. Edbrooke (Guildford C) P. Rickard (Tynemouth)	1:09.56
17 F. Cover (Rotherham Metro)	1:09.70
18 J. Gibson (Nova Centurion)	1:09.75
19 E. Hall (Portsmouth Northsea)	1:09.89
20 J. Kelly (Co Southampton)	1:10.07
21 S. Rosser (Torfaen)	1:10.09
22 L. Gahan (Kelly College)	1:10.28
23 E. Tattam (Bracknell)	1:10.60
24 C. Bailey (Co Birmingham)	1:10.68
25 S. Swettenham (Fleetwood & D)	1:10.69
26 B. Jones (Co Chester)	1:10.74
27 J. Austin (Kelly College)	1:10.81
28 T. Sullivan (Piranha)	1:11.01
29 H. Osborne (Co Birmingham)	1:11.03
30 L. Jackson (Everton)	1:11.34

Sharron Page

31 L. Cunningham (Edinburgh)	1:11.38
32 A. Kay (Co Bradford)	1:11.50
33 P. Herron (Co Newcastle)	1:11.94
34 V. Hale (Co Swansea)	1:11.99
35 A. Clarke (Kelly College)	1:12.22
36 N. Thompson (Exeter C)	1:12.46
37 B. Turner (Manchester U Salford)	1:12.58
38 Y. Lester (Braintree & Bocking)	1:12.61
39 B. Scott (Ferndown Otters)	1:12.95
40 C. Banks (York C)	1:13.45
41 G. Harvey (Millfield)	1:13.51
42 T. Cornish (Frome)	1:14.32

200 Metres Backstroke
Final

1 K. Read (Barnet Copthall)	2:16.11
2 H. Slater (Kelly College)	2:18.12
3 J. Deakins (Gloucester C)	2:19.09
4 J. Riegal (Harrow & Wealdstone)	2:20.96
5 A. Sedgebeer (Epping Forest)	2:25.10
6 J. Wright (Co Chester)	2:25.88
7 P. Rickard (Tynemouth)	2:28.65
8 C. Huddart (Manchester U Salford)	2:29.18

Consolation Final

1 S. Page (Co Birmingham)	2:25.57
2 J. Kelly (Co Southampton)	2:25.97
3 J. Corbett (Co Birmingham)	2:26.38
4 L. Gahan (Kelly College)	2:29.27
5 B. Jones (Co Chester)	2:29.34
6 L. Racster (Portsmouth Northsea)	2:29.74
7 J. Gibson (Nova Centurion)	2:30.87
8 J. Ewing (Paisley)	2:31.15

Heat Times

1 K. Read (Barnet Copthall)	2:17.91
2 J. Deakins (Gloucester C)	2:22.35
3 H. Slater (Kelly College)	2:22.59
4 J. Riegal (Harrow & Wealdstone)	2:23.89
5 A. Sedgebeer (Epping Forest)	2:24.24
6 J. Wright (Co Chester)	2:25.83
7 P. Rickard (Tynemouth)	2:25.97
8 C. Huddart (Manchester U Salford)	2:26.14
9 J. Kelly (Co Southampton)	2:26.50
10 J. Corbett (Co Birmingham)	2:26.93
11 L. Phimister (Moray & D)	2:27.35
12 J. Ewing (Paisley)	2:27.45

45

13 S. Page (Co Birmingham)	2:28.15
14 B. Jones (Co Chester)	2:28.52
15 L. Racster (Portsmouth Northsea)	2:28.75
16 L. Gahan (Kelly College)	2:28.94
17 J. Gibson (Nova Centurion)	2:29.88
18 E. Hall (Portsmouth Northsea)	2:30.16
19 L. Jackson (Everton)	2:30.95
20 H. Osborne (Co Birmingham)	2:30.97
21 C. Bailey (Co Birmingham)	2:31.15
22 L. Heath (Co Birmingham)	2:31.87
23 F. Cover (Rotherham Metro)	2:31.92
24 N. Thompson (Exeter C)	2:32.36
25 S. Swettenham (Fleetwood & D)	2:32.40
26 L. Cunningham (Edinburgh)	2:32.46
27 E. Firbank (Stockton Aquatics)	2:33.03
28 R. Britton (Bristol Central)	2:33.61
29 C. Banks (York C)	2:34.31
30 G. Harvey (Millfield)	2:35.22
31 E. Archer (Kelly College)	2:35.61
32 J. Austin (Kelly College)	2:36.52
33 P. Herron (Co Newcastle)	2:42.30

100 Metres Breaststroke
Final

1 S. Brownsdon (Wigan Wasps)	1:11.55
2 L. Coombes (Co Southampton)	1:12.03
3 M. Hohmann (Wigan Wasps)	1:12.16
4 J. Hill (Cumbernauld)	1:12.97
5 J. Henwood (Torfaen)	1:14.51
6 R. Gillatt (Co Sheffield)	1:15.72
7 H. Alder (Harrow & Wealdstone)	1:15.76
8 D. Tubby (Co Birmingham)	1:16.82

Consolation Final

1 S. MacDonald (Paisley)	1:17.14
2 H. Gorman (Nova Centurion)	1:17.22
3 N. James (Nova Centurion)	1:17.59
4 S. Green (Piranha)	1:17.74
5 S. Smart (Co Chester)	1:18.30
6 R. Swain (Co Derby)	1:18.50
7 C. Piggott (Co Birmingham)	1:19.06
8 A. Lynch (Co Sheffield)	1:19.12

Heat Times

1 S. Brownsdon (Wigan Wasps)	1:12.14
2 L. Coombes (Co Southampton)	1:12.28
3 M. Hohmann (Wigan Wasps)	1:13.02
4 J. Hill (Cumbernauld)	1:13.89
5 J. Henwood (Torfaen)	1:15.17
6 R. Gillatt (Co Sheffield)	1:15.21
7 H. Alder (Harrow & Wealdstone)	1:16.28
8 D. Tubby (Co Birmingham)	1:17.07
9 H. Gorman (Nova Centurion)	1:17.20
10 A. Sheppard (Milngarvie)	1:17.25
11 S. MacDonald (Paisley)	1:17.38
12 A. Baker (Norwich Penguins)	1:17.64
13 R. Swain (Co Derby)	1:17.75
14 C. Piggott (Co Birmingham) N. James (Nova Centurion)	1:17.83
16 S. Smart (Co Chester)	1:17.88
17 A. Lynch (Co Sheffield)	1:17.99
18 S. Green (Piranha)	1:18.45
19 A. McKellican (Co Leeds)	1:19.10
20 K. Pountney (Co Coventry)	1:19.12
21 L. Clarke (Co Newcastle)	1:19.44
22 J. Terry (Nova Centurion)	1:19.49
23 J. Swindlehurst (Sale)	1:19.96
24 J. Kearley (Co Derby)	1:20.38
25 N. Wood (Killerwhales)	1:20.57
26 T. Sullivan (Piranha)	1:20.60
27 R. Newey (Ledbury & D)	1:20.65

28 E. Rumbold (Norwich Penguins)	1:20.75
29 J. Williamson (Co Southampton)	1:20.99
30 K. Grange (Nova Centurion)	1:21.15
31 L. Harding (Saxon Crown)	1:21.21
32 J. Matheron (Bo Southend)	1:22.01
33 L. James (Witney & D)	1:22.39
34 D. Atkins (Mendip)	1:22.59
35 A. Christie (Jersey)	1:22.97

200 Metres Breaststroke
Final

1 S. Brownsdon (Wigan Wasps)	2:35.01
2 M. Hohmann (Wigan Wasps)	2:38.12
3 J. Hill (Cumbernauld)	2:38.36
4 J. Henwood (Torfaen)	2:40.46
5 R. Gillatt (Co Sheffield)	2:43.23
6 H. Gorman (Nova Centurion)	2:43.52
7 L. Coombes (Co Southampton)	2:44.12
8 D. Tubby (Co Birmingham)	2:47.33

Consolation Final

1 N. James (Nova Centurion)	2:46.30
2 C. Piggott (Co Birmingham)	2:46.45
3 A. McKellican (Co Leeds)	2:47.60
4 J. Harrison (Bo Kirklees)	2:48.73
5 J. Swindlehurst (Sale)	2:48.74
6 L. Clarke (Co Newcastle)	2:48.90
7 A. Warner (Co Birmingham)	2:49.20
8 A. Lynch (Co Sheffield)	2:50.91

Heat Times

1 S. Brownsdon (Wigan Wasps)	2:39.07
2 M. Hohmann (Wigan Wasps)	2:40.59
3 J. Hill (Cumbernauld)	2:40.78
4 J. Henwood (Torfaen)	2:41.45
5 H. Gorman (Nova Centurion)	2:42.27
6 L. Coombes (Co Southampton)	2:44.16
7 R. Gillatt (Co Sheffield)	2:44.36
8 H. Walsh (Swansea University)	2:44.38
9 D. Tubby (Co Birmingham)	2:44.64
10 C. Piggott (Co Birmingham)	2:45.91
11 J. Harrison (Bo Kirklees)	2:46.49
12 A. McKellican (Co Leeds)	2:46.86
13 N. James (Nova Centurion)	2:47.34
14 J. Swindlehurst (Sale)	2:48.24
15 L. Clarke (Co Newcastle)	2:49.28
16 A. Warner (Co Birmingham)	2:49.94
17 A. Lynch (Co Sheffield)	2:50.36
18 S. Green (Piranha)	2:50.68
19 P. Mitchell (Epping Forest)	2:51.16
20 R. Swain (Co Derby)	2:52.00
21 J. Williamson (Co Southampton)	2:52.77
22 L. Hall (Co Bradford)	2:54.33
23 A. Howse (Taunton)	2:54.38
24 C. Powell (Torfaen)	2:54.74
25 Z. Harrison (Norwich Penguins)	2:55.45
26 J. Matheron (Bo Southend)	2:58.93

100 Metres Butterfly
Final

1 M. Scarborough (Portsmouth Northsea)	1:02.05
2 S. Purvis (Wigan Wasps)	1:03.32
3 C. Foot (Millfield)	1:03.33
4 S. Davies (Bracknell)	1:03.52
5 S. Brownsdon (Wigan Wasps)	1:03.64
6 J. Lancaster (Warrington Warriors)	1:04.19
7 S. Brooksbank (Co Leeds)	1:04.36
8 L. Wilson (Bo Sunderland)	1:05.06

Consolation Final

1 J. Hill (Cumbernauld)	1:04.84

2	A. Baker (Norwich Penguins)	1:04.88
3	M. McKinnell (Co Cardiff)	1:04.91
4	H. Bewley (Swansea University)	1:05.25
5	A. Duffy (Derwentside)	1:05.68
6	S. Lewis (Swansea University)	1:05.76
7	J. Taylor (Portsmouth Northsea)	1:05.95
8	H. Jepson (Bo Kirklees)	1:06.54

Heat Times

1	M. Scarborough (Portsmouth Northsea)	1:03.64
2	S. Purvis (Wigan Wasps)	1:03.97
3	C. Foot (Millfield)	1:04.35
4	S. Brooksbank (Co Leeds)	1:04.37
5	S. Davies (Bracknell) S. Brownsdon (Wigan Wasps)	1:04.65
7	L. Wilson (Bo Sunderland)	1:05.18
8	J. Lancaster (Warrington Warriors)	1:05.34
9	A. Baker (Norwich Penguins)	1:05.36
10	H. Bewley (Swansea University)	1:05.39
11	J. Hill (Cumbernauld)	1:05.52
12	S. Lewis (Swansea University)	1:05.70
13	A. Duffy (Derwentside)	1:05.79
14	M. McKinnell (Co Cardiff)	1:05.85
15	H. Jepson (Bo Kirklees)	1:05.88
16	J. Taylor (Portsmouth Northsea)	1:06.10
17	G. Atkins (Portsmouth Northsea)	1:06.22
18	P. Trickett (DARTES)	1:06.61
19	D. Evans (Wigan Wasps)	1:07.05
20	S. McGill (Ferndown Otters)	1:07.21
21	H. Welford (Neston)	1:07.24
22	L. Kilgour (Co Birmingham)	1:07.59
23	S. MacDonald (Paisley)	1:07.74
24	E. Strange (Co Oxford)	1:07.88
25	C. Coward (Wigan Wasps)	1:08.24

26	J. Gunston (Bracknell)	1:08.41
27	E. Rumbold (Norwich Penguins)	1:08.45
28	J. Owen (Chester le Street)	1:08.60
29	Z. Long (Beckenham)	1:08.65
30	H. Paull (Kelly College)	1:08.75
31	N. Bates (Norwich Penguins)	1:08.88
32	E. Brooks (Redbridge B)	1:09.16
33	S. Buxton (Nova Centurion)	1:09.29
34	G. Brooks (Greenwich B Mariners)	1:12.09

200 Metres Butterfly
Final

1	S. Purvis (Wigan Wasps) M. Scarborough (Portsmouth Northsea)	2:15.24
3	H. Bewley (Swansea University)	2:17.91
4	L. Wilson (Bo Sunderland)	2:18.57
5	H. Jepson (Bo Kirklees)	2:19.78
6	N. Atkinson (Stockport Metro)	2:19.89
7	D. Evans (Wigan Wasps)	2:19.91
8	A. Duffy (Derwentside)	2:21.52

Consolation Final

1	H. Welford (Neston)	2:20.54
2	C. Foot (Millfield)	2:20.62
3	A. Baker (Norwich Penguins)	2:22.49
4	S. Lewis (Swansea University)	2:22.63
5	J. Taylor (Portsmouth Northsea)	2:22.67
6	A. Kay (Co Bradford)	2:22.96
7	L. Kilgour (Co Birmingham)	2:25.73
8	C. Coward (Wigan Wasps)	DNF

Heat Times

1	S. Purvis (Wigan Wasps)	2:16.94
2	L. Wilson (Bo Sunderland)	2:18.86
3	H. Jepson (Bo Kirklees)	2:19.00

Sharron Davies Swimming Times

4 H. Bewley (Swansea University)	2:19.42
5 M. Scarborough (Portsmouth Northsea)	2:19.55
6 D. Evans (Wigan Wasps)	2:20.23
7 N. Atkinson (Stockport Metro)	2:20.49
8 A. Duffy (Derwentside)	2:20.87
9 H. Welford (Neston)	2:21.15
10 C. Foot (Millfield)	2:21.20
11 S. Lewis (Swansea University)	2:21.93
12 A. Kay (Co Bradford)	2:22.26
13 J. Taylor (Portsmouth Northsea)	2:22.77
14 A. Baker (Norwich Penguins)	2:24.04
15 L. Kilgour (Co Birmingham)	2:26.01
16 C. Coward (Wigan Wasps)	2:26.68
17 S. Smart (Co Chester)	2:27.57
18 P. Trickett (DARTES)	2:28.16
19 S. Jamison (York C)	2:28.28
20 G. Holland (Oldham)	2:28.30
21 Z. Harrison (Norwich Penguins)	2:28.35
22 J. Owen (Chester le Street)	2:28.52
23 N. Gwynne (Wigan Wasps)	2:29.08
24 E. Brooks (Redbridge B)	2:29.54
25 E. Strange (Co Oxford)	2:29.65
26 J. Stark (Co Sheffield)	2:30.25
27 K. Dawson (Bracknell)	2:30.55
28 H. Koban (Nova Centurion)	2:31.68
29 D. Palmer (Killerwhales)	2:34.14
30 P. Adams (Co Leeds)	2:34.52
31 R. Shurey (Hounslow B)	2:34.93

200 Metres Individual Medley
Final

1 S. Davies (Bracknell)	2:19.29
2 J. Hill (Cumbernauld)	2:20.18
3 S. Brownsdon (Wigan Wasps)	2:20.51
4 S. Purvis (Wigan Wasps)	2:20.98
5 K. Read (Barnet Copthall)	2:22.83
6 J. Lancaster (Warrington Warriors)	2:25.12
7 H. Slatter (Kelly College)	2:26.31
8 S. Smart (Co Chester)	2:26.96

Consolation Final

1 K. Pickering (Ipswich)	2:23.29
2 H. Walsh (Swansea University)	2:24.55
3 H. Mansfield (Co Chester)	2:26.34
4 A. Baker (Norwich Penguins)	2:26.89
5 J. Riegal (Harrow & Wealdstone)	2:26.96
6 C. Piggott (Co Birmingham)	2:27.40
7 S. Garrett (Barnet Copthall)	2:27.57
8 R. Bowden (Co Southampton)	2:29.17

Heat Times

1 S. Davies (Bracknell)	2:20.68
2 S. Purvis (Wigan Wasps)	2:20.84
3 J. Hill (Cumbernauld)	2:21.14
4 S. Brownsdon (Wigan Wasps)	2:22.29
5 K. Read (Barnet Copthall)	2:24.99
6 H. Slatter (Kelly College)	2:25.00
7 S. Smart (Co Chester)	2:25.25
8 J. Lancaster (Warrington Warriors)	2:25.35
9 H. Walsh (Swansea University)	2:25.70
10 R. Bowden (Co Southampton)	2:25.92
11 A. Baker (Norwich Penguins)	2:26.53
12 K. Pickering (Ipswich)	2:26.59
13 C. Piggott (Co Birmingham)	2:26.73
14 J. Riegal (Harrow & Wealdstone)	2:26.81
15 Z. Long (Beckenham)	2:27.15
16 S. Garrett (Barnet Copthall)	2:27.19
17 H. Mansfield (Co Chester)	2:27.26
18 B. Jones (Co Chester)	2:27.81
19 L. Phimister (Moray & D)	2:28.66

20 T. Atkin (Lincoln)	2:28.98
21 D. Palmer (Killerwhales)	2:29.45
22 H. Osborne (Co Birmingham)	2:29.79
23 Z. Harrison (Norwich Penguins)	2:29.83
24 T. Sullivan (Piranha)	2:29.90
25 C. Upton (Beckenham)	2:29.91
26 E. Rumbold (Norwich Penguins)	2:30.35
27 M. Berry (Haverhill)	2:31.34
28 L. Wall (Co Bradford)	2:31.99
29 P. Rickard (Tynemouth)	2:32.08
30 C. Brookes (Co Coventry)	2:32.16
31 S. Jamison (York C)	2:32.62
32 L. Marchant (Nova Centurion)	2:32.68
33 C. Coward (Wigan Wasps)	2:32.86
34 S. Solly (Nova Centurion)	2:32.90
35 Z. Platt (Portsmouth Northsea)	2:33.18
36 A. Lynch (Co Sheffield)	2:33.30
37 V. Hale (Co Swansea)	2:35.08
38 G. Brooks (Greenwich B Mariners)	2:35.09
39 L. Cunningham (Edinburgh)	2:35.71
40 A. Sedgebeer (Epping Forest)	2:36.02
41 G. Harvey (Millfield)	2:36.77
S. Vick (Co Sheffield)	DIS

400 Metres Individual Medley
Final

1 S. Brownsdon (Wigan Wasps)	4:51.91
2 H. Walsh (Swansea University)	5:02.00
3 S. Smart (Co Chester)	5:05.35
4 K. Read (Barnet Copthall)	5:05.83
5 T. Atkin (Lincoln)	5:06.99
6 D. Evans (Wigan Wasps)	5:09.74
7 J. Harrison (Bo Kirklees)	5:12.42
H. Slatter (Kelly College)	DIS

Consolation Final

1 R. Bowden (Co Southampton)	5:07.40
2 D. Palmer (Killerwhales)	5:09.68
3 C. Piggott (Co Birmingham)	5:10.90
4 L. Phimister (Moray & D)	5:11.73
5 J. Riegal (Harrow & Wealdstone)	5:12.90
6 L. Wall (Co Bradford)	5:13.47
7 S. Foggo (Co Newcastle)	5:13.48
8 S. Garrett (Barnet Copthall)	5:14.18

Heat Times

1 S. Brownsdon (Wigan Wasps)	4:58.54
2 H. Slatter (Kelly College)	5:04.17
3 H. Walsh (Swansea University)	5:04.18
4 K. Read (Barnet Copthall)	5:05.91
5 S. Smart (Co Chester)	5:06.80
6 T. Atkin (Lincoln)	5:07.09
7 J. Harrison (Bo Kirklees)	5:07.36
8 D. Evans (Wigan Wasps)	5:08.21
9 L. Phimister (Moray & D)	5:09.96
10 C. Piggott (Co Birmingham)	5:10.41
11 J. Deakins (Gloucester C)	5:11.78
12 J. Riegal (Harrow & Wealdstone)	5:12.84
13 D. Palmer (Killerwhales)	5:14.21
14 L. Wall (Co Bradford)	5:14.85
15 R. Bowden (Co Southampton)	5:14.90
16 S. Foggo (Co Newcastle)	5:15.97
17 S. Garrett (Barnet Copthall)	5:16.29
18 A. Baker (Norwich Penguins)	5:16.35
19 H. Osborne (Co Birmingham)	5:16.77
20 Z. Harrison (Norwich Penguins)	5:17.37
21 J. Smith (Oundle & D)	5:19.92
22 E. Rumbold (Norwich Penguins)	5:20.55
23 Z. Platt (Portsmouth Northsea)	5:20.70
24 J. Davey (Co Newcastle)	5:21.43
25 J. Wright (Co Chester)	5:21.83

26 S. Solly (Nova Centurion)	5:22.56	
27 V. Crane (Greenwich B Mariners)	5:23.59	
28 P. Adams (Co Leeds)	5:23.92	
29 J. Owen (Chester le Street)	5:25.73	
30 R. Loveman(Co Southampton)	5:26.24	
31 T. Sullivan (Piranha)	5:26.38	
32 C. Coward (Wigan Wasps)	5:29.18	
33 A. Howse (Taunton)	5:32.38	
34 G. Harvey (Millfield)	5:32.80	
35 J. Matheron (Bo Southend)	5:33.58	
C. Upton (Beckenham)	DIS	

4×100 Metres Freestyle Club Relay
Final

1 Co Birmingham	3:58.54
2 Portsmouth Northsea	4:00.66
3 Bracknell	4:01.25
4 Norwich Penguins	4:03.09
5 Kelly College	4:03.84
6 Wigan Wasps	4:03.90
7 Nova Centurion	4:07.25
8 Co Southampton	4:12.90

Heat Times

1 Co Birmingham	4:02.47
2 Portsmouth Northsea	4:02.74
3 Bracknell	4:04.18

4 Norwich Penguins	4:04.57
5 Kelly College	4:05.68
6 Nova Centurion	4:07.45
7 Wigan Wasps	4:08.54
8 Co Coventry	4:12.16

4×100 Metres Medley Club Relay
Final

1 Wigan Wasps	4:27.29
2 Co Birmingham	4:29.86
3 Co Southampton	4:30.02
4 Portsmouth Northsea	4:30.30
5 Norwich Penguins	4:31.96
6 Kelly College	4:31.98
7 Nova Centurion	4:36.95
8 Co Derby	4:44.18

Heat Times

1 Wigan Wasps	4:32.95
2 Norwich Penguins	4:34.23
3 Portsmouth Northsea	4:34.45
4 Co Birmingham	4:35.26
5 Co Southampton	4:35.52
6 Kelly College	4:36.87
7 Nova Centurion	4:37.87
8 Co Derby	4:43.77
9 Co Newcastle	4:45.69

ASA National Age Group

National Sports Centre, Crystal Palace — 31 July/5 August, 1989

12 Years Age Group

Boys

100 Metres Freestyle
Final

1 D. Ingram (Calne Alpha)	1:02.18
2 D. Ellis (COSACSS)	1:02.72
3 R. Arnott (Co Leicester)	1:03.04
4 W. Simmons (Millfield)	1:04.49
5 S. Mount (Tynemouth)	1:04.52
6 S. Pickup (Co Bristol)	1:04.71
7 M. Cooper (Co Hull)	1:04.80
8 M. Page (Co Coventry)	1:05.55

Heat Times

1 D. Ellis (COSACSS)	1:02.83
2 D. Ingram (Calne Alpha)	1:03.25
3 R. Arnott (Co Leicester)	1:03.77
4 S. Pickup (Co Bristol)	1:07.78
5 M. Page (Co Coventry)	1:04.19
6 M. Cooper (Co Hull)	1:04.32
7 W. Simmons (Millfield),	1:04.42
8 S. Mount (Tynemouth)	1:04.48
9 N. Tyas (Co Leeds)	1:04.50
10 T. Hadley (Dudley Metro)	1:04.59
11 J. Bayles (Runnymede)	1:04.63
12 M. Brehaut (Regent Tigers)	1:04.85
13 K. James (Co Newcastle)	1:05.22
14 J. Harris (Leander)	1:05.48
15 R. Allcote (Swadlincote)	1:05.61
16 J. Collins (Shiverers)	1:05.67
17 R. Gudgin (Walsall)	1:05.68
18 D. Pipes (Co Hull)	1:05.89
19 N. Rhodes (Newton Hall)	1:05.94
20 P. Potter (York C)	1:06.18
21 D. Gurney (Reading)	1:06.28
22 R. Underwood (Killerwhales)	1:06.40

23 J. Openshaw (Co Leeds)	1:06.52
24 S. Mosley (Co Birmingham)	1:06.64
25 J. Peet (Southgate)	1:06.89
26 S. Prichard (Luton)	1:07.11
27 M. Gordon (Runnymede)	1:07.33
28 L. Carnwell (Cheadle & D)	1:07.37
29 M. Cooke (Killerwhales)	1:07.55
30 R. Manby (Barking)	1:07.73
31 R. Stevens (Maxwell)	1:07.98
32 R. Barr (Broadway)	1:08.22
33 A. Turner (Manchester U Salford)	1:08.27
34 R. Wardle (Co Birmingham)	1:08.44
35 K. Palmer (Co Lincoln Pentaqua)	1:08.47

400 Metres Freestyle
Heat Times (no final)

1 N. Tyas (Co Leeds)	4:40.13
2 T. Hadley (Dudley Metro)	4:40.77
3 D. Ellis (COSACSS)	4:43.18
4 M. Cooper (Co Hull)	4:48.09
5 D. Pipes (Co Hull)	4:48.84
6 R. Paterson (Killerwhales)	4:50.31
7 P. Potter (York C)	4:50.42
8 S. Mount (Tynemouth)	4:50.45
9 R. Underwood (Killerwhales)	4:50.53
10 J. Openshaw (Co Leeds)	4:52.28
11 M. Brehaut (Regent Tigers)	4:52.51
12 K. Seidl (Australia)	4:53.72
13 B. Gemmill (Killerwhales)	4:54.97
14 G. Vowles (Killerwhales)	4:55.43
15 N. Rhodes (Newton Hall)	4:56.36
16 M. Page (Co Coventry)	4:57.80
17 S. Pickup (Co Bristol)	4:58.91
18 O. Webb (Co Sheffield)	5:00.12
19 M. Cooke (Killerwhales)	5:00.87
20 J. Bayles (Runnymede)	5:02.51
21 L. Carnwell (Cheadle & D)	5:02.93

49

22	R. Stevens (Maxwell)	5:03.07
23	C. Myers (Co Leeds)	5:03.63
24	J. Blood (Cheadle & D)	5:04.07
25	I. Fowler (Warrington Warriors)	5:04.34
26	M. Gordon (Runnymede)	5:06.14

100 Metres Backstroke
Final

1	J. Bayles (Runnymede)	1:14.37
2	R. Arnott (Co Leicester)	1:15.33
3	R. Paterson (Killerwhales)	1:15.34
4	S. Parry (Co Liverpool)	1:15.47
5	D. Ingram (Calne Alpha)	1:15.76
6	S. Prichard (Luton)	1:16.00
7	L. Jamieson (Bo Kirklees)	1:16.09
8	G. Vowles (Killerwhales)	1:16.49

Heat Times

1	R. Paterson (Killerwhales)	1:14.88
2	S. Parry (Co Liverpool)	1:15.13
3	R. Arnott (Co Leicester)	1:15.42
4	J. Bayles (Runnymede)	1:15.75
5	S. Prichard (Luton)	1:15.84
6	G. Vowles (Killerwhales)	1:16.03
7	D. Ingram (Calne Alpha)	1:16.28
8	L. Jamieson (Bo Kirklees)	1:16.31
9	M. Cooper (Co Hull)	1:16.64
10	T. Hadley (Dudley Metro)	1:16.65
11	J. Harris (Leander)	1:16.67
12	K. James (Co Newcastle)	1:16.75
13	W. Simmons (Millfield)	1:16.76
14	R. Gudgin (Walsall)	1:16.79
15	L. Whitehead (Radford)	1:16.80
16	M. Snape (Aberdeen)	1:17.25
17	P. Anderson (Carlisle C)	1:17.42
18	M. Gordon (Runnymede)	1:17.43
19	P. Farrall (Orion)	1:17.50
20	S. Mount (Tynemouth)	1:17.61
21	A. Turner (Manchester U Salford)	1:17.87
22	J. Blood (Cheadle & D)	1:18.01
23	N. Tyas (Co Leeds)	1:18.11
24	L. Taylor (Cheltenham)	1:18.48
25	N. Manson (Ringwood)	1:18.56
26	G. Meadows (Co Leeds)	1:18.58
27	J. Collins (Shiverers)	1:18.60
28	D. Ellis (COSACSS)	1:18.64
29	P. Potter (York C)	1:18.96
30	S. Pickup (Co Bristol)	1:18.99
31	A. Gray (Hartlepool)	1:19.06
32	R. McQuillan (Co Bristol)	1:19.46
33	C. Colley (Co Sheffield)	1:20.29
34	R. Stevens (Maxwell)	1:20.52
35	K. Palmer (Co Lincoln Pentaqua)	1:20.59
36	D. Grassby (Co Coventry)	1:20.73
37	M. Swarbrick (Bournemouth Dolphins)	1:23.45

100 Metres Breaststroke
Final

1	D. Gurney (Reading)	1:18.39
2	R. Goodchild (Co Leeds)	1:18.62
3	J. Collins (Shiverers)	1:19.52
4	M. Brehaut (Regent Tigers)	1:19.90
5	J. Harris (Leander)	1:22.14
6	M. Gartside (Warrington Warriors)	1:22.33
7	J. Marshall (Bath Dolphins)	1:22.61
8	J. Sherriff-Geary (Redbridge B)	1:23.37

Heat Times

1	R. Goodchild (Co Leeds)	1:18.56
2	D. Gurney (Reading)	1:18.93
3	J. Collins (Shiverers)	1:19.12

4	M. Brehaut (Regent Tigers)	1:20.20
5	M. Gartside (Warrington Warriors)	1:21.32
6	J. Harris (Leander)	1:21.48
7	J. Marshall (Bath Dolphins)	1:22.09
8	J. Sherriff-Geary (Redbridge B)	1:22.78
9	N. Greenland (Banbury)	1:23.53
10	P. Buck (Ruislip)	1:23.84
11	R. McGuire (Thurrock)	1:24.15
12	D. Brewis (Washington)	1:24.25
13	R. Arnott (Co Leicester)	1:24.52
14	P. Wordsworth (Rotherham Metro)	1:24.63
15	R. Johnson (Colchester)	1:24.64
16	M. Snape (Aberdeen)	1:24.69
17	D. Whinham (Tynemouth)	1:24.87
18	D. Freeman (Nuneaton)	1:24.90
19	M. Cooke (Killerwhales)	1:25.01
20	A. Wilde (Fleetwood & D)	1:25.18
21	S. Mosley (Co Birmingham)	1:25.25
22	K. James (Co Newcastle)	1:25.45
23	D. Pipes (Co Hull)	1:25.56
24	T. Tryhorn (Bognor Regis)	1:25.77
25	B. Rowbery (Pontypool)	1:25.82
26	A. Turner (Manchester U Salford)	1:26.38
27	G. Morgan (Maxwell)	1:26.50
28	N. Manson (Ringwood)	1:26.51
29	M. Whorwood (Harrow & Wealdstone)	1:26.64
30	S. Roberts (Clacton)	1:26.68
31	D. Gregory (York C)	1:26.79
32	J. Howell (Co Liverpool)	1:27.02
33	D. Cottrell (Everton)	1:27.20
34	D. Ingram (Calne Alpha)	1:27.29
35	M. Woolridge (Ferndown Otters)	1:27.30
36	S. Isherwood (Co Derby)	1:27.37
37	D. Grosvenor (Bo Kirklees)	1:27.75
38	S. Carr (Leicester Penguins)	1:27.96
39	A. Warren (Brentwood)	1:28.26
40	A. Dawson (Nuneaton)	1:28.28
41	D. Ellis (COSACSS)	1:28.29
42	S. Hoare (Teddington)	1:28.36
43	K. Seidl (Australia)	1:29.09

100 Metres Butterfly
Final

1	S. Mount (Tynemouth)	1:10.15
2	M. Brehaut (Regent Tigers)	1:10.65
3	M. Snape (Aberdeen)	1:11.29
4	N. Rhodes (Newton Hall)	1:11.62
5	M. Gartside (Warrington Warriors)	1:11.71
6	T. Hadley (Dudley Metro)	1:12.13
7	D. Grassby (Co Coventry)	1:12.37
8	J. Harris (Leander)	1:13.05

Heat Times

1	S. Mount (Tynemouth)	1:11.34
2	M. Snape (Aberdeen)	1:12.01
3	N. Rhodes (Newton Hall)	1:12.32
4	J. Harris (Leander)	1:12.78
5	T. Hadley (Dudley Metro)	1:13.06
6	M. Brehaut (Regent Tigers)	1:13.10
7	M. Gartside (Warrington Warriors)	1:13.14
8	D. Grassby (Co Coventry)	1:13.27
9	D. Ingram (Calne Alpha)	1:13.62
10	J. Openshaw (Co Leeds)	1:13.69
11	D. Gurney (Reading)	1:14.38
12	R. Paterson (Killerwhales)	1:14.66
13	S. Parry (Co Liverpool)	1:14.79
14	L. Jamieson (Bo Kirklees)	1:15.26
15	J. Collins (Shiverers)	1:15.66
16	A. Turner (Manchester U Salford)	1:15.80
17	R. Arnott (Co Leicester)	1:16.08

18 O. Webb (Co Sheffield)	1:16.14	
19 M. Cooke (Killerwhales)	1:16.44	
20 K. James (Co Newcastle)	1:16.98	
21 S. Prichard (Luton)	1:17.27	
22 G. Beadle (Southgate)	1:17.40	
23 D. Penfold (Reading)	1:20.32	
24 M. Gordon (Runnymede)	1:22.97	

200 Metres Individual Medley
Final

1 R. Arnott (Co Leicester)	2:36.57
2 N. Tyas (Co Leeds)	2:37.54
3 M. Brehaut (Regent Tigers)	2:37.82
4 T. Hadley (Dudley Metro)	2:38.10
5 O. Webb (Co Sheffield)	2:40.21
6 J. Bayles (Runnymede)	2:41.22
7 M. Gartside (Warrington Warriors)	2:41.32
8 A. Turner (Manchester U Salford)	2:41.84

Heat Times

1 N. Tyas (Co Leeds)	2:37.69
2 R. Arnott (Co Leicester)	2:37.89
3 T. Hadley (Dudley Metro)	2:38.68
4 M. Brehaut (Regent Tigers)	2:39.77
5 A. Turner (Manchester U Salford)	2:40.37
6 M. Gartside (Warrington Warriors)	2:40.39
7 O. Webb (Co Sheffield)	2:41.23
8 J. Bayles (Runnymede)	2:41.26
9 J. Openshaw (Co Leeds)	2:41.28
10 J. Harris (Leander)	2:41.94
11 M. Cooke (Killerwhales)	2:42.05
12 D. Ellis (COSACSS)	2:42.64
13 B. Gemmill (Killerwhales)	2:42.92
14 S. Pritchard (Luton)	2:43.34
15 M. Snape (Aberdeen)	2:43.61
16 D. Gurney (Reading)	2:44.03
D. Pipes (Co Hull)	
18 R. Paterson (Killerwhales)	2:44.18
19 K. James (Co Newcastle)	2:44.19
20 S. Pickup (Co Bristol)	2:44.52
21 S. Parry (Co Liverpool)	2:45.50
22 S. Mount (Tynemouth)	2:45.51
23 K. Seidl (Australia)	2:45.54
24 D. Grassby (Co Coventry)	2:47.97
25 D. Ingram (Calne Alpha)	2:48.87
26 G. Meadows (Co Leeds)	2:49.05
27 M. Swarbrick (Bournemouth Dolphins)	2:51.17
28 K. Palmer (Co Lincoln Pentaqua)	2:52.53
J. Collins (Shiverers)	DIS
P. Anderson (Carlisle C)	DIS

4×50 Metres Freestyle Club Relay
Final

1 Co Leeds	2:00.88
2 Co Hull	2:01.19
3 Co Coventry	2:01.94
4 Killerwhales	2:03.68
5 Maxwell	2:04.27
6 Reading	2:05.22
7 Millfield	2:05.48
8 Cheadle & D	2:06.89

Heat Times

1 Co Leeds	2:03.15
2 Co Coventry	2:03.39
3 Co Hull	2:04.03
4 Killerwhales	2:04.24
5 Reading	2:04.94
6 Maxwell	2:04.96
7 Millfield	2:06.32
8 Cheadle & D	2:06.96

9 York C	2:07.31
10 Beckenham	2:07.48
11 Co Sheffield	2:07.58
12 Boldon	2:07.89
13 Cheltenham	2:07.91
14 Manchester U Salford	2:07.97
15 Cranleigh	2:08.02
16 Southgate Leatherhead	2:08.08
18 Runnymede	2:08.13
19 Co Chester	2:10.09
20 Co Liverpool	2:10.26
21 Shiverers	2:10.42
22 Stockport Metro	2:12.93
23 Redbridge B	2:15.78

4×50 Metres Medley Club Relay
Final

1 Co Leeds	2:15.23
2 Co Sheffield	2:18.59
3 Reading	2:18.66
4 Killerwhales	2:20.28
5 Maxwell	2:21.65
6 Dudley Metro	2:21.90
7 Co Coventry	2:22.16
8 Manchester U Salford	2:22.19

Heat Times

1 Co Leeds	2:17.61
2 Reading	2:20.72
3 Maxwell	2:21.08
4 Co Sheffield	2:21.09
5 Co Coventry	2:22.77
6 Killerwhales	2:22.82
7 Dudley Metro	2:23.80
8 Manchester U Salford	2:24.19
9 Beckenham	2:24.38
10 Leicester Penguins	2:24.49
11 Millfield	2:25.54
12 York C	2:25.74
13 Co Chester	2:25.76
14 Runnymede	2:25.78
15 Redbridge B	2:26.24
16 Co Hull	2:26.33
17 Southgate	2:27.57
18 Cheltenham	2:27.60
19 Co Liverpool	2:27.85
20 Shiverers	2:28.08
21 Leatherhead	2:28.35
22 Cranleigh	2:32.15
Stockport Metro	DIS

Girls

100 Metres Freestyle
Final

1 L. Dalzell (Derwentside)	1:03.11
2 C. Batty (Trenton Dolphins)	1:03.76
3 E. Komlosy (Teddington)	1:03.99
4 K. Walton (Oundle & D)	1:04.02
5 J. Scott (Bexley)	1:04.25
6 R. Holland (Millfield)	1:04.63
7 J. Kent-Brown (Oldham)	1:05.60
8 B. Stevenson (DARTES)	1:06.28

Heat Times

1 L. Dalzell (Derwentside)	1:03.63
2 C. Batty (Trenton Dolphins)	1:04.54
3 K. Walton (Oundle & D)	1:04.76
4 E. Komlosy (Teddington)	1:05.37
5 R. Holland (Millfield)	1:05.40

51

6 J. Scott (Bexley)	1:05.75
7 B. Stevenson (DARTES)	1:05.82
8 J. Kent-Brown (Oldham)	1:05.94
9 L. Rogers (Co Bristol)	1:06.31
10 S. Henderson (Nova Centurion)	1:06.63
11 A. Bennett (Satellite)	1:06.73
12 T. Honstein (Canada)	1:06.75
13 C. McInnes (White Oak)	1:06.83
14 K. Goddard (Gloucester C)	1:07.13
15 K. Bennett (Harrow & Wealdstone)	1:07.32
16 E. Lang (Bo Burnley CATS)	1:07.45
17 K. Milnes (Co Bradford)	1:07.61
18 L. Bulbeck (Portsmouth Northsea)	1:07.67
19 N. Steel (Livingston)	1:07.85
20 E. James (Chester le Street)	1:07.93
21 N. Tindall (Co Hull)	1:08.08
22 T. Fullbrandt (Canada)	1:08.09
23 K. Herbert (Redbridge B)	1:08.11
24 K. Burnage (Weyport Olympians)	1:08.35
25 J. Wilcock (St Helens)	1:08.63
26 S. Chew (Luton) K. Russen (Kidlington & Gosford)	1:09.56

400 Metres Freestyle
Heat Times (no final)

1 L. Dalzell (Derwentside)	4:47.17
2 K. Milnes (Co Bradford)	4:48.92
3 E. Weatherhead (USA)	4:52.93
4 J. Wilcock (St Helens)	4:54.93
5 K. Walton (Oundle & D)	4:55.76
6 C. Batty (Trenton Dolphins)	4:56.06
7 J. Brignall (Bo Southend)	4:56.17
8 R. Taylor (Co Birmingham)	4:57.73
9 J. Cowan (Portsmouth Northsea)	4:57.82
10 T. Fullbrandt (Canada)	4:58.72
11 A. Bennett (Satellite)	4:59.30
12 J. Kent-Brown (Oldham)	5:00.39
13 A. Rowley (Dudley Metro)	5:00.96
14 L. Stroud (Co Southampton)	5:01.75
15 L. Rogers (Co Bristol)	5:01.89
16 E. Lewis (Co Leeds)	5:02.80
17 N. Tindall (Co Hull)	5:02.84
18 S. Herridge (Guernsey)	5:02.88
19 L. Godber (Nova Centurion)	5:03.22
20 K. Burnage (Weyport Olympians)	5:03.32
21 L. Bulbeck (Portsmouth Northsea)	5:09.33
22 C. Swatman (Co Bradford)	5:12.18
23 K. Herbert (Redbridge B)	5:12.68

100 Metres Backstroke
Final

1 T. Fullbrandt (Canada)	1:11.65
2 A. Bennett (Satellite)	1:13.20
3 D. Watson (Teddington)	1:13.73
4 K. Bennett (Harrow & Wealdstone)	1:14.13
5 N. Steel (Livingston)	1:14.70
6 E. Komlosy (Teddington)	1:15.40
7 R. Brewer (Jersey)	1:16.12
8 S. Harrison (Barrow Beavers)	1:16.37

Heat Times

1 T. Fullbrandt (Canada)	1:14.10
2 D. Watson (Teddington)	1:14.80
3 A. Bennett (Satellite)	1:14.91
4 N. Steel (Livingston)	1:15.09
5 E. Komlosy (Teddington)	1:15.44
6 S. Harrison (Barrow Beavers)	1:15.56
7 K. Bennett (Harrow & Wealdstone)	1:15.72
8 R. Brewer (Jersey)	1:16.10
9 K. Walton (Oundle & D)	1:16.42

10 C. Swatman (Co Bradford)	1:16.56
11 R. Rayworth (Co Liverpool)	1:16.92
12 K. Price (Leicester Penguins)	1:17.52
13 J. Scott (Bexley)	1:17.55
14 K. Leibe (Walsall)	1:17.57
15 J. Jones (Co Chester)	1:17.81
16 A. Bland (Hartlepool)	1:17.94
17 L. Dalzell (Derwentside)	1:18.25
18 E. Jack (Co Coventry)	1:18.30
19 H. Cox (Maxwell)	1:18.31
20 J. Evans (Nova Centurion)	1:18.41
21 H. Cantwell (Rhymney Valley)	1:18.60
22 R. Taylor (Co Birmingham)	1:18.95
23 L. Johnstone (Derwentside)	1:19.08
24 W. Greaves (Nova Centurion)	1:19.16
25 A. Minter (Ipswich)	1:19.18
26 E. Lang (Bo Burnley CATS)	1:19.50
27 A. Rowley (Dudley Metro)	1:19.66
28 R. Perry (Cranleigh)	1:19.70
29 L. Brialey (Maxwell)	1:19.78
30 S. Brown (Beckenham)	1:19.96
31 N. Read (Killerwhales)	1:20.00
32 S. Ringwood (Co Manchester)	1:20.07
33 N. Jeffries (Co Lincoln Pentaqua)	1:20.08
34 S. McGowan (Black Lion)	1:20.10
35 T. Honstein (Canada)	1:20.98
36 L. Bulbeck (Portsmouth Northsea)	1:22.24
37 B. Stevenson (DARTES)	1:22.48

100 Metres Breaststroke
Final

1 L. Rogers (Co Bristol)	1:18.86
2 L. Dalzell (Derwentside)	1:19.06
3 C. Baddley (Atherton)	1:22.21
4 T. Honstein (Canada)	1:23.68
5 B. Stevenson (DARTES)	1:24.01
6 D. Watson (Teddington)	1:24.33
7 K. Goom (Bournemouth Dolphins)	1:24.41
8 J. Cotton (Maxwell)	1:26.30

Heat Times

1 L. Rogers (Co Bristol)	1:20.36
2 L. Dalzell (Derwentside)	1:20.58
3 C. Baddley (Atherton)	1:22.51
4 K. Goom (Bournemouth Dolphins)	1:23.05
5 T. Honstein (Canada)	1:23.44
6 B. Stevenson (DARTES)	1:23.70
7 D. Watson (Teddington)	1:23.99
8 J. Cotton (Maxwell)	1:24.46
9 H. Wilby (Co Birmingham)	1:24.68
10 E. Lang (Bo Burnley CATS)	1:24.74
11 H. Bain (Oswestry Otters)	1:24.76
12 N. O'Hara (Saxon Crown)	1:25.14
13 C. Niblett (Dover Lifeguard)	1:25.35
14 M. Wong (Gloucester C)	1:25.39
15 N. Steel (Livingston)	1:25.54
16 L. Keen (Norwich Penguins)	1:25.63
17 C. Batty (Trenton Dolphins)	1:25.81
18 L. Cousins (RTW Monson)	1:25.84
19 H. Hughes (Slough Dolphins)	1:26.29
20 M. Brennan (Shiverers)	1:26.37
21 K. Leibe (Walsall)	1:26.57
22 E. Komlosy (Teddington)	1:26.76
23 J. Turner (Walsall)	1:26.80
24 J. Sullivan (Bo Kirklees)	1:27.01
25 E. Weatherhead (USA)	1:27.12
26 S. Moore (Runnymede)	1:27.52
27 J. Waterworth (Wulfrunians)	1:27.53
28 E. James (Chester le Street)	1:27.68
29 N. Tindall (Co Hull)	1:28.01

30	N. Williams (Killerwhales)	1:28.18
31	K. Walton (Oundle & D)	1:28.63
32	E. Weedon (Stockport Metro)	1:28.76
33	K. Horgan (Co Leeds)	1:28.93
34	A. Rowley (Dudley Metro)	1:29.10
35	R. Rajput (Co Birmingham)	1:29.60
36	L. Walden (Rugby)	1:29.76
37	S. Chew (Luton)	1:29.83
38	S. Jenkins (Pontypool)	1:30.60
39	K. Mullins (Eckington)	1:30.67

100 Metres Butterfly
Final

1	K. Milnes (Co Bradford)	1:10.18
2	E. Lang (Bo Burnley CATS)	1:10.25
3	J. Kent-Brown (Oldham)	1:11.87
4	A. Bennett (Satellite)	1:12.39
5	K. Bennett (Harrow & Wealdstone)	1:12.42
6	K. Walton (Oundle & D)	1:12.88
7	L. Dalzell (Derwentside)	1:13.08
8	J. Wilcock (St Helens)	1:13.40

Heat Times

1	E. Lang (Bo Burnley CATS)	1:12.15
2	K. Milnes (Co Bradford)	1:12.52
3	K. Bennett (Harrow & Wealdstone)	1:13.23
4	L. Dalzell (Derwentside)	1:13.31
5	J. Wilcock (St Helens)	1:13.46
6	A. Bennett (Satellite)	1:13.67
7	K. Walton (Oundle & D)	1:13.75
8	J. Kent-Brown (Oldham)	1:13.84
9	L. Rogers (Co Bristol)	1:14.07
10	J. Cowan (Portsmouth Northsea)	1:14.11
11	T. Honstein (Canada)	1:14.17
12	A. Rowley (Dudley Metro)	1:14.31
13	J. Jones (Co Chester)	1:15.69
14	B. Stevenson (DARTES)	1:16.07
15	P. Overy (Shiverers)	1:16.08
16	V. Jamieson-Pate (Barnet Copthall)	1:16.18
17	P. Henry (North Devon)	1:16.42
18	K. Goddard (Gloucester C)	1:16.72
19	J. Brignall (Bo Southend)	1:16.77
20	R. Taylor (Co Birmingham)	1:16.81
21	E. Komlosy (Teddington)	1:16.91
22	L. Gibbons (Co Newcastle)	1:17.04
	L. Bulbeck (Portsmouth Northsea)	
24	S. Dawson (Co Leeds)	1:17.31
25	S. Greenep (Ferndown Otters)	1:17.43
26	E. Weatherhead (USA)	1:17.45
27	T. Fullbrandt (Canada)	1:17.89
28	R. Harvey (Walsall)	1:18.07
29	L. Hatty (Co Leeds)	1:18.27
30	J. Laundon (Northampton)	1:18.42
31	N. Steel (Livingston)	1:18.50
32	K. Burnage (Weyport Olympians)	1:18.52
33	M. Swift (Bo Southend)	1:18.85
34	R. Holland (Millfield)	1:19.69
35	S. Henderson (Nova Centurion)	1:20.05
36	E. Goldsmith (Shiverers)	1:21.24
37	E. James (Chester le Street)	1:24.69

200 Metres Individual Medley
Final

1	L. Dalzell (Derwentside)	2:32.93
2	L. Rogers (Co Bristol)	2:37.29
3	E. Lang (Bo Burnley CATS)	2:37.91
4	K. Bennett (Harrow & Wealdstone)	2:38.53
5	K. Walton (Oundle & D)	2:38.84
6	E. Komlosy (Teddington)	2:41.46
7	E. Weatherhead (USA)	2:41.96

8	K. Milnes (Co Bradford)	2:42.34

Heat Times

1	L. Dalzell (Derwentside)	2:34.97
2	L. Rogers (Co Bristol)	2:39.90
3	K. Bennett (Harrow & Wealdstone)	2:39.94
4	K. Walton (Oundle & D)	2:40.30
5	E. Komlosy (Teddington)	2:40.53
6	E. Weatherhead (USA)	2:41.09
7	E. Lang (Bo Burnley CATS)	2:41.29
8	K. Milnes (Co Bradford)	2:41.43
9	A. Rowley (Dudley Metro)	2:41.70
10	B. Stevenson (DARTES)	2:41.95
11	A. Bennett (Satellite)	2:41.98
12	T. Fullbrandt (Canada)	2:42.07
13	C. Batty (Trenton Dolphins)	2:43.37
14	D. Watson (Teddington)	2:43.44
15	J. Cowan (Portsmouth Northsea)	2:43.55
16	S. Mostyn (Oswestry Otters)	2:44.17
17	T. Honstein (Canada)	2:44.53
18	K. Goddard (Gloucester C)	2:44.62
19	L. Bulbeck (Portsmouth Northsea)	2:45.05
20	J. Jones (Co Chester)	2:45.30
21	N. Steel (Livingston)	2:45.57
22	C. Baddley (Atherton)	2:46.21
23	R. Taylor (Co Birmingham)	2:47.24
24	K. Burke (Cockermouth)	2:48.41
25	L. Keen (Norwich Penguins)	2:48.80
26	S. Chew (Luton)	2:50.14
27	L. Hatty (Co Leeds)	2:50.51
28	K. Burnage (Weyport Olympians)	2:51.17
29	K. Russen (Kidlington & Gosford)	2:51.47
30	E. James (Chester le Street)	2:51.51
31	K. Howes (Kidlington & Gosford)	2:51.67
32	R. Armel (Hounslow B)	2:52.13

4×50 Metres Freestyle Club Relay
Final

1	Nova Centurion	2:03.16
2	DARTES	2:04.19
3	Co Birmingham	2:04.42
4	Stockport Metro	2:04.54
	Teddington	
6	Gloucester C	2:04.87
7	Maxwell	2:04.97
8	Kidlington & Gosford	2:06.62

Heat Times

1	Nova Centurion	2:04.72
2	Teddington	2:04.88
3	Co Birmingham	2:05.26
4	Gloucester C	2:05.31
5	Maxwell	2:05.32
6	DARTES	2:06.15
7	Stockport Metro	2:06.46
8	Kidlington & Gosford	2:06.67
9	Hounslow B	2:07.39
10	Millfield	2:07.89
11	Co Liverpool	2:07.90
12	Co Bradford	2:08.25
13	Derwentside	2:08.34
14	Co Leeds	2:09.08
15	Reading	2:10.17
16	Hull Olympic	2:10.30
17	Bracknell	2:11.31
18	Bodmin & D	2:11.47
19	Forward Hillingdon	2:11.60
20	Co Manchester	2:12.12
21	Killerwhales	2:12.45
22	Cranleigh	2:14.07

23	Runnymede	2:14.68
24	Manchester U Salford	2:17.84

4×50 Metres Medley Club Relay
Final

1	Co Bradford	2:18.84
2	DARTES	2:19.87
3	Stockport Metro	2:20.12
4	Gloucester C	2:20.67
5	Maxwell	2:20.68
6	Nova Centurion	2:20.96
7	Co Liverpool	2:21.91
8	Millfield	2:22.67

Heat Times

1	Co Bradford	2:20.23
2	Gloucester C	2:20.72
3	Maxwell	2:21.55
4	Co Liverpool	2:22.27
5	DARTES	2:23.40
6	Millfield	2:23.69
7	Nova Centurion	2:23.78
8	Stockport Metro	2:23.93
9	Co Leeds	2:24.10
10	Shiverers	2:24.85
11	Derwentside	2:25.46
12	Co Birmingham	2:25.78
13	Teddington	2:26.52
14	Hounslow B	2:26.88
15	Kidlington & Gosford	2:27.78
16	Bracknell	2:28.04
17	Bo Waltham Forest	2:28.13
18	Reading	2:28.32
19	Killerwhales	2:29.42
20	Co Manchester	2:29.43
21	Cranleigh	2:29.55
22	Hull Olympic	2:30.23
23	Wycombe & D	2:30.46
24	Witham Dolphins	2:30.55
25	Cheadle & D	2:30.66
26	Bodmin & D	2:30.72
27	Forward Hillingdon	2:31.33
28	Manchester U Salford	2:32.59
29	Southgate	2:35.71
30	Runnymede	2:36.97

13/14 Years Age Group
Boys

100 Metres Freestyle
Final

1	J. Lancaster (Wycombe & D)	57.06
2	D. Forster (Atherton)	57.40
3	M. Wilson (Co Leeds)	57.51
4	D. Sheils (Warrender)	57.62
5	S. Mavin (Co Peterborough)	57.66
6	R. Calvo (Spain)	57.76
7	M. Carl (Redbridge B)	58.82
8	T. Quilt (Co Cardiff)	59.28

Heat Times

1	J. Lancaster (Wycombe & D)	56.66
2	D. Forster (Atherton)	57.73
3	R. Calvo (Spain)	57.78
4	S. Mavin (Co Peterborough)	57.85
5	D. Sheils (Warrender)	57.92
6	M. Carl (Redbridge B)	58.30
7	T. Quilt (Co Cardiff)	58.39
8	M. Wilson (Co Leeds)	58.44
9	C. Eldred (Co Newcastle)	58.47

10	G. Prentice (Co Southampton)	58.79
11	R. Kirk (Llanelli)	58.80
12	N. Skinner (Portsmouth Northsea)	59.02
13	D. Shaw (Wycombe & D)	59.10
14	D. Lodge (Nova Centurion)	59.22
15	M. Whitton (Co Hull)	59.36
16	A. Roberts (COSACSS)	59.49
17	M. Robilliard (Leicester Penguins)	59.54
18	J. Runnacles (Co Peterborough)	59.55
19	B. Stericker (Royton)	59.67
	M. Eastment (Millfield)	
21	P. Baxter (Oundle & D)	59.82
22	S. Darling (Millfield)	59.86
23	S. Smalley (Hull Olympic)	59.88
24	L. Coton (Co Birmingham)	59.92
25	M. Colclough (Hindley)	59.94
26	S. Crozier (Bo Burnley CATS)	59.97
27	P. Roberts (COSACSS)	1:00.05
28	M. Vu-Hong (Chelsea & Kensington)	1:00.09
29	S. Guigarro (Spain)	1:00.10
30	S. Powell (Beckenham)	1:00.14
31	G. Connor (Runnymede)	1:00.30
32	A. Godwin (Portsmouth Northsea)	1:00.31
33	B. Shaw (Harrogate & D)	1:00.41
34	K. Mutton (Thamesdown)	1:00.66
35	A. Ward (Chippenham)	1:00.71
	M. Heil (Barking)	
37	S. Watkin (Co Newcastle)	1:00.92
38	D. Brace (Barnet Copthall)	1:01.30
39	S. Flin (Beckenham)	1:01.33
40	M. Vallis (Canada)	1:03.86
41	B. Armitstead (Canada)	1:04.56
42	B. MacCallum (Canada)	1:05.18

200 Metres Freestyle
Final

1	J. Lancaster (Wycombe & D)	2:01.44
2	D. Forster (Atherton)	2:02.13
3	D. Sanz (Spain)	2:03.80
4	R. Calvo (Spain)	2:05.80
5	M. Colclough (Hindley)	2:06.22
6	N. Skinner (Portsmouth Northsea)	2:07.26
7	D. Paxton (Bishop Stortford)	2:07.52
8	C. Eldred (Co Newcastle)	2:07.66

Heat Times

1	J. Lancaster (Wycombe & D)	2:03.13
2	D. Forster (Atherton)	2:05.82
3	M. Colclough (Hindley)	2:06.42
4	N. Skinner (Portsmouth Northsea)	2:06.84
5	D. Sanz (Spain)	2:06.86
6	C. Eldred (Co Newcastle)	2:06.87
7	R. Calvo (Spain)	2:07.02
8	D. Paxton (Bishop Stortford)	2:07.26
9	S. Mavin (Co Peterborough)	2:07.71
10	S. Smalley (Hull Olympic)	2:08.20
11	M. Wilson (Co Leeds)	2:08.42
12	M. Carl (Redbridge B)	2:08.45
13	M. Whitton (Co Hull)	2:08.67
14	B. Shaw (Harrogate & D)	2:09.82
15	S. Hamer (Bo Burnley CATS)	2:10.14
16	S. Guigarro (Spain)	2:10.41
17	M. Heil (Barking)	2:10.50
18	G. Brown (Bo Southend)	2:11.46
19	S. Crozier (Bo Burnley CATS)	2:14.26

400 Metres Freestyle
Heat Times (no final)

1	D. Sanz (Spain)	4:18.41
2	D. Forster (Atherton)	4:19.22

3	C. Eldred (Co Newcastle)	4:23.03	29	P. Howard (Co Leeds)	1:10.35
4	M. Colclough (Hindley)	4:23.82	30	M. Vallis (Canada)	1:10.45
5	G. Brown (Bo Southend)	4:26.54	31	J. Salter (Redditch)	1:10.56
6	D. Paxton (Bishop Stortford)	4:28.28	32	B. Hughes (Co Coventry)	1:10.63
7	D. Smith (Bo Waltham Forest)	4:30.82	33	T. Eland (DARTES)	1:10.79
8	S. Smalley (Hull Olympic)	4:33.41	34	C. Jones (Bo Southend)	1:11.18
9	L. Windle (Killerwhales)	4:33.49	35	S. Pearson (Co Milton Keynes)	1:11.48
10	G. Ale (Luton)	4:33.59	36	A. Carnegie (Darlington)	1:11.88
11	B. Gray (Co Newcastle)	4:33.81	37	C. Robinson (Manchester U Salford)	1:11.97
12	N. Skinner (Portsmouth Northsea)	4:34.05	38	D. Mack (Co Newcastle)	1:12.07
13	M. Heil (Barking)	4:35.90			

200 Metres Backstroke

14	M. Clements (Portsmouth Northsea)	4:36.17	**Final**		
15	M. Carl (Redbridge B)	4:36.29	1	N. Skinner (Portsmouth Northsea)	2:17.38
16	L. Sutherland (Stockport Metro)	4:36.30	2	M. Wilson (Co Leeds)	2:19.52
17	J. Ellis (Bracknell)	4:37.72	3	L. Windle (Killerwhales)	2:21.81
18	D. Gates (Satellite)	4:39.15	4	J. Lancaster (Wycombe & D)	2:21.92
19	B. Shaw (Harrogate & D)	4:41.34	5	M. Carl (Redbridge B)	2:22.23
20	L. Portingale (Co Bristol)	4:43.00	6	R. Searle (Beckenham)	2:22.76

1500 Metres Freestyle

Heat Times (no final)

			7	S. Caballero (Spain)	2:22.79
1	D. Sanz (Spain)	17:09.11	8	D. Paxton (Bishop Stortford)	2:23.61
2	G. Brown (Bo Southend)	17:29.26	**Heat Times**		
3	D. Paxton (Bishop Stortford)	17:31.65	1	N. Skinner (Portsmouth Northsea)	2:18.88
4	C. Eldred (Co Newcastle)	17:46.87	2	M. Wilson (Co Leeds)	2:20.82
5	M. Clements (Portsmouth Northsea)	17:48.72	3	S. Caballero (Spain)	2:21.93
6	D. Gates (Satellite)	17:54.27	4	M. Carl (Redbridge B)	2:22.31
7	D. Forster (Atherton)	18:00.04	5	D. Paxton (Bishop Stortford)	2:22.89
8	M. Heil (Barking)	18:06.38	6	L. Windle (Killerwhales)	2:23.13
			7	R. Searle (Beckenham)	2:23.34

100 Metres Backstroke

Final			8	J. Lancaster (Wycombe & D)	2:23.61
1	M. Wilson (Co Leeds)	1:04.22	9	B. Stericker (Royton)	2:23.62
2	N. Skinner (Portsmouth Northsea)	1:04.28	10	D. Forster (Atherton)	2:24.79
3	J. Lancaster (Wycombe & D)	1:04.73	11	P. Baxter (Oundle & D)	2:26.81
4	D. Forster (Atherton)	1:05.74	12	A. Weltch (Portsmouth Northsea)	2:27.22
5	M. Carl (Redbridge B)	1:05.93	13	B. Armitstead (Canada)	2:27.31
6	S. Caballero (Spain)	1:06.04	14	L. Portingale (Co Bristol)	2:27.81
7	S. Mavin (Co Peterborough)	1:06.09	15	M. Holroyd (Co Bradford)	2:28.69
8	D. Paxton (Bishop Stortford)	1:06.26	16	M. Haynes (Gloucester C)	2:28.75
Heat Times			17	F. Birch (Co Sheffield)	2:28.81
1	J. Lancaster (Wycombe & D)	1:04.37	18	J. Salter (Redditch)	2:29.06
2	M. Wilson (Co Leeds)	1:04.80	19	T. Eland (DARTES)	2:29.42
3	N. Skinner (Portsmouth Northsea)	1:04.96	20	J. Sutcliffe (Co Leeds)	2:29.43
4	M. Carl (Redbridge B)	1:06.09	21	M. Clements (Portsmouth Northsea)	2:29.44
5	S. Mavin (Co Peterborough)	1:06.23	22	S. Binks (DARTES)	2:30.02
6	D. Paxton (Bishop Stortford)	1:06.61	23	S. Barry (Romford T)	2:30.29
7	D. Forster (Atherton)	1:06.62	24	W. Reece (Aquabears)	2:30.42
8	S. Caballero (Spain)	1:06.70	25	C. Williams (Nova Centurion)	2:30.51
9	B. Stericker (Royton)	1:06.99	26	S. Crozier (Bo Burnley CATS)	2:30.55
10	B. Armitstead (Canada)	1:07.67	27	R. Kirk (Llanelli)	2:30.56
11	R. Searle (Beckenham)	1:07.96	28	A. Roberts (COSACSS)	2:31.05
12	C. Williams (Nova Centurion)	1:08.05	29	N. Hambleton (DARTES)	2:31.49
13	S. Binks (DARTES)	1:08.07	30	B. Gray (Co Newcastle)	2:31.63
14	L. Portingale (Co Bristol)	1:08.12	31	R. Hinton (Barnstaple)	2:33.02
15	P. Baxter (Oundle & D)	1:08.25	32	R. Murray (Gloucester C)	2:33.51
16	J. Sutcliffe (Co Leeds)	1:08.38	33	S. Pearson (Co Milton Keynes)	2:36.14
17	L. Windle (Killerwhales)	1:08.49	34	M. Vallis (Canada)	2:37.22
18	M. Murray (Gloucester C)	1:08.75			

100 Metres Breaststroke

19	S. Crozier (Bo Burnley CATS)	1:08.86	**Final**		
20	D. Sheils (Warrender)	1:09.22	1	D. Sheils (Warrender)	1:09.79
21	T. Quilt (Co Cardiff)	1:09.29	2	S. Hamer (Bo Burnley CATS)	1:11.15
22	B. Gray (Co Newcastle)	1:09.41	3	J. Moreno (Co Southampton)	1:11.51
23	A. Roberts (COSACSS)	1:09.43	4	F. Aymerich (Spain)	1:12.18
	D. Brace (Barnet Copthall)		5	C. Mee (Barnstaple)	1:14.21
25	A. Rowlands (Sandbach Sharks)	1:09.70	6	P. Guy (Leander)	1:14.59
26	W. Reece (Aquabears)	1:09.87	7	P. Baxter (Oundle & D)	1:14.69
27	A. Weltch (Portsmouth Northsea)	1:09.94	8	G. Roberts (Clacton)	1:14.77
28	M. Haynes (Gloucester C)	1:10.09	**Heat Times**		
			1	D. Sheils (Warrender)	1:11.81

2	J. Moreno (Co Southampton)	1:12.01
3	S. Hamer (Bo Burnley CATS)	1:12.94
4	F. Aymerich (Spain)	1:13.20
5	P. Guy (Leander)	1:14.18
6	C. Mee (Barnstaple)	1:14.31
7	G. Roberts (Clacton)	1:14.99
8	P. Baxter (Oundle & D)	1:15.02
9	B. Pitts (Croydon Amphibians)	1:15.03
10	S. Mavin (Co Peterborough)	1:15.25
11	I. Croft (Bexley)	1:15.50
12	C. Nicholas (Thamesdown)	1:15.57
13	C. Rippon (Nova Centurion)	1:15.85
14	J. Leech (Derwentside)	1:15.99
15	R. Graham (Blackpool)	1:16.09
16	D. Mack (Co Newcastle)	1:16.14
17	P. French (Thamesdown)	1:16.26
18	G. Evans (Haden Hill)	1:16.65
19	L. Windle (Killerwhales)	1:16.77
20	D. Paxton (Bishop Stortford)	1:16.85
21	A. Day (Co Newcastle)	1:17.06
	R. Walker (S Hunsley)	
23	M. Colclough (Hindley)	1:17.13
24	R. Gordon (Co Southampton)	1:17.16
25	R. Pedrick (Brixham)	1:17.24
26	B. Hughes (Co Coventry)	1:17.56
27	T. Attfield (Rushmoor Royals)	1:17.73
28	P. Burch (Beckenham)	1:17.83
29	S. Powell (Beckenham)	1:17.84
	S. Jones (Co Bristol)	
31	S. Tilley (Killerwhales)	1:18.08
	R. Ronca (Millfield)	
33	M. Sharples (Atherton)	1:18.46
34	S. Moss (Derby Phoenix)	1:18.54
35	S. Darling (Millfield)	1:18.61
36	S. Watkin (Co Newcastle)	1:18.62
37	G. Davies (Reading)	1:18.99
38	S. Griffin (Oundle & D)	1:19.00
39	B. MacCallum (Canada)	1:19.36
40	S. Rose (Bracknell)	1:19.68
41	N. Sultman (Co Newcastle)	1:20.16

200 Metres Breaststroke
Final

1	D. Sheils (Warrender)	2:32.93
2	F. Aymerich (Spain)	2:35.83
3	J. Moreno (Co Southampton)	2:37.39
4	S. Hamer (Bo Burnley CATS)	2:38.11
5	G. Roberts (Clacton)	2:39.93
6	P. Guy (Leander)	2:40.40
7	P. Baxter (Oundle & D)	2:42.31
8	I. Croft (Bexley)	2:43.44

Heat Times

1	F. Aymerich (Spain)	2:37.32
2	D. Sheils (Warrender)	2:37.39
3	J. Moreno (Co Southampton)	2:38.51
4	S. Hamer (Bo Burnley CATS)	2:39.33
5	P. Baxter (Oundle & D)	2:40.39
6	P. Guy (Leander)	2:40.78
7	I. Croft (Bexley)	2:42.34
8	G. Roberts (Clacton)	2:42.40
9	C. Mee (Barnstaple)	2:42.57
10	L. Windle (Killerwhales)	2:42.96
11	D. Paxton (Bishop Stortford)	2:43.41
12	J. Leech (Derwentside)	2:44.52
13	G. Evans (Haden Hill)	2:44.77
14	B. Hughes (Co Coventry)	2:45.20
15	D. Mack (Co Newcastle)	2:45.46
16	M. Colclough (Hindley)	2:45.76
17	C. Rippon (Nova Centurion)	2:46.09
18	S. Notman (Braintree & Bocking)	2:46.35

19	R. Gordon (Co Southampton)	2:46.56
20	T. Attfield (Rushmoor Royals)	2:47.32
21	D. Smallbone (Millfield)	2:47.50
22	M. James (Co Southampton)	2:48.56
23	B. Pitts (Croydon Amphibians)	2:48.91
24	P. Grainger (Warrington Warriors)	2:49.08
25	P. French (Thamesdown)	2:49.19
26	I. Chandler (Runnymede)	2:49.22
27	P. Burch (Beckenham)	2:49.37
28	S. Watkin (Co Newcastle)	2:50.05
29	M. Sharples (Atherton)	2:50.25
30	P. Melhuish (Eastleigh)	2:50.48
31	N. Sultman (Co Newcastle)	2:50.56
32	A. Day (Co Newcastle)	2:50.62
33	M. Higginbotham (Stockport Metro)	2:50.73
34	S. Jones (Co Bristol)	2:52.00
35	K. Etheridge (Walsall)	2:52.12
36	D. Gates (Satellite)	2:52.99
37	T. Read (Hounslow B)	2:53.27
38	S. McGaw (Manchester U Salford)	2:54.13
39	N. Caverly (Manchester U Salford)	2:54.54
40	M. Hanham (Luton)	2:55.83
41	A. Wilmott (Soundwell)	2:56.28
42	S. Moss (Derby Phoenix)	2:57.18
43	G. Davies (Reading)	2:57.57
44	B. MacCallum (Canada)	3:00.75

100 Metres Butterfly
Final

1	J. Lancaster (Wycombe & D)	1:00.94
2	A. Lopez (Spain)	1:02.05
3	S. Mavin (Co Peterborough)	1:02.96
4	X. Fortuno (Spain)	1:03.17
5	B. Vickery (Isle of Thanet)	1:04.29
6	P. Roberts (COSACSS)	1:04.42
7	M. Heil (Barking)	1:04.86
8	D. Paxton (Bishop Stortford)	1:05.07

Heat Times

1	J. Lancaster (Wycombe & D)	59.29
2	A. Lopez (Spain)	1:02.98
3	S. Mavin (Co Peterborough)	1:03.42
4	X. Fortuno (Spain)	1:03.90
5	P. Roberts (COSACSS)	1:04.40
6	D. Paxton (Bishop Stortford)	1:04.50
7	M. Heil (Barking)	1:04.52
8	B. Vickery (Isle of Thanet)	1:04.81
9	N. Skinner (Portsmouth Northsea)	1:04.84
10	D. Brace (Barnet Copthall)	1:05.04
11	D. Forster (Atherton)	1:05.14
12	S. Crozier (Bo Burnley CATS)	1:05.34
13	S. Darling (Millfield)	1:05.70
14	R. Calvo (Spain)	1:05.78
15	M. Eastment (Millfield)	1:05.99
16	A. Carnegie (Darlington)	1:06.17
	B. Armitstead (Canada)	
18	R. Kirk (Llanelli)	1:06.23
19	D. Gates (Satellite)	1:06.36
	R. Searle (Beckenham)	
21	J. Ellis (Bracknell)	1:06.53
22	L. Coton (Co Birmingham)	1:06.80
23	S. Hamer (Bo Burnley CATS)	1:06.90
24	P. Howard (Co Leeds)	1:07.04
25	C. Eldred (Co Newcastle)	1:07.07
	C. Robinson (Manchester U Salford)	
27	S. Powell (Beckenham)	1:07.12
28	B. Stericker (Royton)	1:07.16
29	L. Windle (Killerwhales)	1:07.24
30	D. Sheils (Warrender)	1:07.26
31	M. Colclough (Hindley)	1:07.34
32	B. Hughes (Co Coventry)	1:07.52
33	P. Baxter (Oundle & D)	1:07.53

34	O. Sherlock (Southgate)	1:07.57
35	A. Coll (Co Chester)	1:07.89
36	R. Satchwell (Basingstoke)	1:08.32
37	S. Firbank (DARTES)	1:08.39
38	G. Connor (Runnymede)	1:08.56
39	M. Vallis (Canada)	1:11.25
40	B. MacCallum (Canada)	1:12.41

200 Metres Butterfly

Final

1	A. Lopez (Spain)	2:16.13
2	J. Lancaster (Wycombe & D)	2:16.42
3	D. Paxton (Bishop Stortford)	2:19.04
4	M. Heil (Barking)	2:19.21
5	D. Forster (Atherton)	2:20.53
6	D. Gates (Satellite)	2:24.64
7	J. Ellis (Bracknell)	2:25.69
8	A. Coll (Co Chester)	2:28.63

Heat Times

1	A. Lopez (Spain)	2:16.92
2	J. Lancaster (Wycombe & D)	2:17.64
3	M. Heil (Barking)	2:19.93
4	D. Paxton (Bishop Stortford)	2:21.60
5	D. Forster (Atherton)	2:22.82
6	J. Ellis (Bracknell)	2:23.73
7	A. Coll (Co Chester)	2:25.57
8	D. Gates (Satellite)	2:25.96
9	S. Crozier (Bo Burnley CATS)	2:26.29
10	M. Colclough (Hindley)	2:26.83
11	C. Eldred (Co Newcastle)	2:27.21
12	G. Ale (Luton)	2:27.63
13	M. Clements (Portsmouth Northsea)	2:27.83
14	R. Pearson (Co Sheffield)	2:27.90
15	S. Hamer (Bo Burnley CATS)	2:28.10
16	S. Firbank (DARTES)	2:28.31
17	J. Gibson (Killerwhales)	2:28.77
18	B. Vickery (Isle of Thanet)	2:29.10
19	R. Newbould (Stockport Metro)	2:29.49
20	B. Armitstead (Canada)	2:31.02
21	R. Murray (Isle of Thanet)	2:31.54
22	P. Lawson (Norton)	2:32.01
23	M. Eastment (Millfield)	2:32.61
24	B. Hughes (Co Coventry)	2:32.90
25	R. Satchwell (Basingstoke)	2:38.43
26	K. Wilkin (Bo Kirklees)	2:41.25
27	A. Godwin (Portsmouth Northsea)	2:41.85

200 Metres Individual Medley

Final

1	D. Sheils (Warrender)	2:17.60
2	J. Lancaster (Wycombe & D)	2:18.59
3	D. Paxton (Bishop Stortford)	2:20.22
4	X. Fortuno (Spain)	2:21.00
5	L. Windle (Killerwhales)	2:22.07
6	N. Skinner (Portsmouth Northsea)	2:22.65
7	F. Aymerich (Spain)	2:23.32
8	P. Baxter (Oundle & D)	2:24.23

Heat Times

1	J. Lancaster (Wycombe & D)	2:19.61
2	D. Sheils (Warrender)	2:21.51
3	X. Fortuno (Spain)	2:21.64
4	F. Aymerich (Spain)	2:22.05
	L. Windle (Killerwhales)	
6	P. Baxter (Oundle & D)	2:22.49
7	N. Skinner (Portsmouth Northsea)	2:22.60
8	D. Paxton (Bishop Stortford)	2:23.05
9	S. Mavin (Co Peterborough)	2:23.18
10	D. Forster (Atherton)	2:23.92
11	S. Hamer (Bo Burnley CATS)	2:25.70
12	D. Gates (Satellite)	2:26.77
13	B. Stericker (Royton)	2:27.32

14	S. Crozier (Bo Burnley CATS)	2:27.68
15	N. Sultman (Co Newcastle)	2:27.93
16	M. Colclough (Hindley)	2:27.94
17	B. Hughes (Co Coventry)	2:28.07
18	R. Murray (Gloucester C)	2:28.10
19	S. Darling (Millfield)	2:28.25
20	A. Godwin (Portsmouth Northsea)	2:28.95
21	S. Watson (Cranleigh)	2:29.94
22	R. Kirk (Llanelli)	2:30.04
23	P. Roberts (COSACSS)	2:30.08
24	J. Gibson (Killerwhales)	2:30.30
25	M. Heil (Barking)	2:30.38
26	P. Lawson (Norton)	2:30.58
27	K. Wilkin (Bo Kirklees)	2:31.29
28	M. Parkinson (DARTES)	2:31.59
29	L. Coton (Co Birmingham)	2:31.60
30	G. Ale (Luton)	2:31.74
31	B. Shaw (Harrogate & D)	2:32.14
32	A. Coll (Co Chester)	2:32.72
33	D. Brace (Barnet Copthall)	2:32.76
34	J. Passmore (Brixham)	2:33.86
35	D. Smith (Bo Waltham Forest)	2:34.22
36	D. Mack (Co Newcastle)	2:34.88
	S. Powell (Beckenham)	DIS

400 Metres Individual Medley

Heat Times (no final)

1	D. Paxton (Bishop Stortford)	4:55.54
2	L. Windle (Killerwhales)	4:56.44
3	X. Fortuno (Spain)	4:57.59
4	J. Lancaster (Wycombe & D)	5:00.06
5	D. Forster (Atherton)	5:01.76
6	D. Sheils (Warrender)	5:02.12
7	D. Gates (Satellite)	5:03.10
8	N. Skinner (Portsmouth Northsea)	5:05.64
9	P. Baxter (Oundle & D)	5:08.23
10	S. Hamer (Bo Burnley CATS)	5:10.52
11	M. Colclough (Hindley)	5:11.05
12	G. Ale (Luton)	5:12.89
13	S. Mavin (Co Peterborough)	5:13.23
14	P. Roberts (COSACSS)	5:13.41
15	B. Gray (Co Newcastle)	5:13.56
16	A. Coll (Co Chester)	5:14.29
17	M. Heil (Barking)	5:14.30
	P. Lawson (Norton)	
19	M. Clements (Portsmouth Northsea)	5:14.48
20	P. Howard (Co Leeds)	5:14.80
21	S. Crozier (Bo Burnley CATS)	5:15.15
22	A. Godwin (Portsmouth Northsea)	5:15.37
23	D. Smith (Bo Waltham Forest)	5:16.51
24	N. Sultman (Co Newcastle)	5:16.69
25	R. Murray (Gloucester C)	5:17.02
26	R. Pearson (Co Sheffield)	5:20.14
27	C. Mee (Barnstable)	5:20.28

4×50 Metres Freestyle Club Relay

Final

1	Co Newcastle	1:48.25
2	COSACSS	1:48.85
3	Co Leeds	1:49.64
4	Portsmouth Northsea	1:50.11
5	Beckenham	1:50.42
6	Barnet Copthall	1:50.47
7	Millfield	1:50.87
8	Thamesdown Tigersharks	1:51.49

Heat Times

1	COSACSS	1:49.08
2	Co Newcastle	1:49.60
3	Co Leeds	1:50.57
4	Portsmouth Northsea	1:50.67
5	Beckenham	1:51.05

6 Barnet Copthall	1:51.20
7 Millfield	1:51.37
8 Thamesdown Tigersharks	1:51.59
9 DARTES	1:51.68
10 Nova Centurion	1:51.85
11 Isle of Thanet	1:52.43
12 Wycombe & D	1:52.51
13 Co Southampton	1:52.81
14 Bo Burnley CATS	1:53.02
15 Croydon Amphibians	1:54.51
16 Co Birmingham	1:54.66
17 Co Milton Keynes	1:54.95
18 Manchester U Salford	1:55.10
19 Killerwhales	1:55.14
20 Reading	1:56.08
21 Stockport Metro	1:56.10
22 Cranleigh	1:56.21
23 Runnymede	1:56.67
24 Co Coventry	1:56.87
25 Hull Olympic	1:56.96
26 Hounslow B	1:57.75
27 Leatherhead	1:58.26
28 Brixham	1:58.60
29 Bodmin & D	1:59.19
30 Everton	2:00.11

4×50 Metres Medley Club Relay
Final

1 DARTES	2:02.06
2 Bo Burnley CATS	2:02.73
3 Beckenham	2:03.07
4 Nova Centurion	2:04.01
Co Leeds	
6 COSACSS	2:04.39
7 Co Newcastle	2:04.87
8 Millfield	2:05.61

Heat times

1 DARTES	2:04.43
2 Bo Burnley CATS	2:04.50
3 COSACSS	2:04.87
4 Beckenham	2:04.96
5 Co Leeds	2:05.30
6 Millfield	2:05.45
7 Co Newcastle	2:05.64
8 Nova Centurion	2:06.34
9 Co Southampton	2:06.66
10 Thamesdown Tigersharks	2:06.85
11 Isle of Thanet	2:07.03
12 Co Peterborough	2:07.44
13 Barnet Copthall	2:07.45
14 Killerwhales	2:07.47
15 Portsmouth Northsea	2:07.98
16 Croydon Amphibians	2:08.82
17 Stockport Metro	2:08.83
18 Manchester U Salford	2:08.96
19 Brixham	2:09.39
20 Gloucester C	2:09.45
21 Co Birmingham	2:10.42
22 Reading	2:10.79
23 Hounslow B	2:11.13
24 Co Coventry	2:11.86
25 Leatherhead	2:12.49
26 Everton	2:12.86
27 Runnymede	2:14.27

Girls

100 Metres Freestyle
Final

1 A. Dronsfield (Co Manchester)	59.76

2 G. Lavin (Derwentside)	1:00.15
3 A. Gilmore (Portsmouth Northsea)	1:01.38
4 Z. Harrison (Norwich Penguins)	1:01.56
5 D. Herrero (Spain)	1:01.58
6 J. Mallison (Co Coventry)	1:01.65
7 K. Cheney (Spondon)	1:02.01
8 G. Holland (Oldham)	1:02.02

Heat Times

1 A. Dronsfield (Co Manchester)	1:00.23
2 G. Lavin (Derwentside)	1:00.84
3 A. Gilmore (Portsmouth Northsea)	1:01.33
4 J. Mallison (Co Coventry)	1:01.74
5 D. Herrero (Spain)	1:01.79
6 K. Cheney (Spondon)	1:01.82
7 Z. Harrison (Norwich Penguins)	1:02.18
8 G. Holland (Oldham)	1:02.21
9 N. Elliott (Co Bristol)	1:02.30
10 N. Vafiadis (Hounslow B)	1:02.69
11 J. Phillips (Bo Kirklees)	1:02.72
12 V. Horner (Gateshead)	1:02.73
13 K. Harrison (Rotherham Metro)	1:02.75
14 M. Bates (Dudley Metro)	1:02.77
15 D. Palmer (Killerwhales)	1:03.12
16 E. Cook (Stockton Aquatics)	1:03.21
17 L. Jackson (Derwentside)	1:03.34
18 L. Wyatt (Beckenham)	1:03.51
19 P. Trickett (DARTES)	1:03.53
20 S. Smith (Bo Kirklees)	1:03.59
21 T. Jameson (Aquabears)	1:03.72
22 J. Lee (Luton)	1:03.77
23 N. Hawkes (Dudley Metro)	1:03.81
24 E. Gibbons (St Helens)	1:03.90
25 R. Jack (Maxwell)	1:04.03
M. Rustellet (Spain)	
27 P. Alcock (Warrington Warriors)	1:04.08
28 E. Watson (Nova Centurion)	1:04.12
29 T. Billanie (Newburn)	1:04.22
30 D. Rimmer (Co Liverpool)	1:04.54
31 M. Harley (Barnet Copthall)	1:04.56
32 A. Farrants (Canada)	1:04.59
33 H. Kemball-Cook (Lowestoft)	1:04.69
34 S. Brown (Co Bradford)	1:04.71
35 J. Park (Co Newcastle)	1:04.83
36 V. Hale (Co Swansea)	1:04.90
37 C. Grayson (York C)	1:04.94
38 T. Hill (Greenwich B Mariners)	1:05.18
39 S. O'Flanagan (Rochford & D)	1:05.35
40 N. Eldridge (Hounslow B)	1:05.49
41 K. Axford (Beckenham)	1:05.57
42 E. Hazelwood (Co Leeds)	1:05.85
43 K. Orrey (Lincoln)	1:06.34

200 Metres Freestyle
Final

1 Z. Harrison (Norwich Penguins)	2:09.19
2 N. Elliott (Co Bristol)	2:10.97
3 V. Horner (Gateshead & Whickham)	2:11.11
4 D. Palmer (Killerwhales)	2:11.46
5 A. Dronsfield (Co Manchester)	2:13.32
6 G. Holland (Oldham)	2:14.65
7 K. Harrison (Rotherham Metro)	2:15.34
8 G. Lavin (Derwentside)	2:15.62

Heat Times

1 A. Dronsfield (Co Manchester)	2:10.95
2 Z. Harrison (Norwich Penguins)	2:11.91
3 V. Horner (Gateshead & Whickham)	2:13.04
4 G. Holland (Oldham)	2:13.07
5 N. Elliott (Co Bristol)	2:13.25
6 G. Lavin (Derwentside)	2:13.49

3	G. Holland (Oldham)	4:35.16
4	P. Alcock (Warrington Warriors)	4:35.24
5	V. Horner (Gateshead & Whickham)	4:36.81
6	K. Blackshaw (Bo Southend)	4:36.87
7	E. Cook (Stockton Aquatics)	4:39.72
8	J. Phillips (Co Bradford)	4:40.43
9	S. Brown (Co Bradford)	4:41.92
10	E. Gibbons (St Helens)	4:43.29
11	L. Wyatt (Beckenham)	4:44.44
12	T. Billanie (Newburn)	4:44.59
13	S. Green (Piranha)	4:45.34
14	J. Hayter (Aquabears)	4:45.43
15	K. Orrey (Lincoln)	4:46.21
16	H. Leek (Chase)	4:46.31
17	S. Colling (Derwentside)	4:47.00
18	E. Montes (Spain)	4:47.75
19	C. Fawkes (Manchester U Salford)	4:48.31
20	C. Meredith (Aquabears)	4:49.79
21	N. Hawkes (Dudley Metro)	4:49.95
22	C. Cowburn (Fleetwood & D)	4:51.93
23	S. O'Flanagan (Rochford & D)	4:56.36
24	N. Solsona (Spain)	5:05.72

800 Metres Freestyle
Heat Times (no final)

1	D. Palmer (Killerwhales)	9:23.48
2	Z. Harrison (Norwich Penguins)	9:27.03
3	P. Alcock (Warrington Warriors)	9:31.73
4	S. Colling (Derwentside)	9:33.22
5	L. Wyatt (Beckenham)	9:34.93
6	K. Blackshaw (Bo Southend)	9:35.06
7	E. Gibbons (St Helens)	9:36.85
8	G. Holland (Oldham)	9:37.87
9	S. Green (Piranha)	9:40.01
10	J. Hayter (Aquabears)	9:40.85
11	T. Billanie (Newburn)	9:42.40
12	L. Jackson (Derwentside)	9:42.80
13	S. Brown (Co Bradford)	9:43.38
14	E. Montes (Spain)	9:44.17
15	C. Meredith (Aquabears)	9:44.93
16	H. Leek (Chase)	9:45.76
17	S. Strahan (Co Lincoln Pentaqua)	9:45.96
18	E. Cook (Stockton Aquatics)	9:47.55
19	E. Arter (Co Leeds)	9:49.20
20	C. Cowburn (Fleetwood & D)	9:49.43
21	N. Elliott (Co Bristol)	9:51.68
22	H. Downes (Derwentside)	9:55.31
23	E. Smith (Co Leeds)	10:00.78
24	C. Waterfield (Co Leeds)	10:04.66

100 Metres Backstroke
Final

1	K. Harrison (Rotherham Metro)	1:09.03
2	D. Palmer (Killerwhales)	1:09.65
3	A. Gray (Fleetwood & D)	1:10.26
4	V. Horner (Gateshead & Whickham)	1:10.38
5	K. Axford (Beckenham)	1:10.65
6	H. Kemball-Cook (Lowestoft)	1:10.77
7	V. Hale (Co Swansea)	1:10.78
8	M. Soler (Spain)	1:12.58

Heat Times

1	K. Harrison (Rotherham Metro)	1:09.74
2	M. Soler (Spain)	1:10.85
3	A. Gray (Fleetwood & D)	1:10.86
4	K. Axford (Beckenham)	1:10.92
5	V. Hale (Co Swansea)	1:11.26
6	H. Kemball-Cook (Lowestoft)	1:11.31
7	V. Horner (Gateshead & Whickham)	1:11.39
8	D. Palmer (Killerwhales)	1:11.46

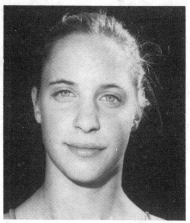

Zoe Harrison

7	K. Harrison (Rotherham Metro)	2:13.70
8	D. Palmer (Killerwhales)	2:14.35
9	P. Alcock (Warrington Warriors)	2:14.52
10	L. Wyatt (Beckenham)	2:14.73
11	K. Orrey (Lincoln)	2:14.90
12	S. Colling (Derwentside)	2:15.39
13	L. Jackson (Derwentside)	
	E. Cook (Stockton Aquatics)	2:15.81
15	J. Phillips (Bo Kirklees)	2:15.83
16	K. Blackshaw (Bo Southend)	2:16.13
17	S. Brown (Co Bradford)	2:16.40
18	A. Gilmore (Portsmouth Northsea)	2:16.48
19	T. Billanie (Newburn)	2:16.52
20	V. Hale (Co Swansea)	2:16.53
21	C. Fawkes (Manchester U Salford)	2:16.66
22	S. Green (Piranha)	2:17.13
23	T. Hill (Greenwich B Mariners)	2:17.16
24	D. Herrero (Spain)	2:17.19
25	T. Jameson (Aquabears)	2:17.20
26	E. Gibbons (St Helens)	2:17.39
27	N. Wood (Killerwhales)	2:17.52
28	N. Vafiadis (Hounslow B)	2:17.58
29	M. Thorn (North Devon)	2:18.12
30	H. Leek (Chase)	2:18.53
31	N. Hawkes (Dudley Metro)	
	G. Spier (Beckenham)	2:18.63
33	G. Palmer (Satellite)	2:18.75
34	S. Strahan (Co Lincoln Pentaqua)	2:18.86
35	J. Lee (Luton)	2:18.97
36	M. Harley (Barnet Copthall)	2:19.24
37	C. Cowburn (Fleetwood & D)	2:19.92
38	S. O'Flanagan (Rochford & D)	2:19.98
39	M. Hardiman (Co Birmingham)	2:19.99
40	M. Rustullet (Spain)	2:21.51
41	H. Downes (Derwentside)	2:22.00
42	A. Farrants (Canada)	2:22.47
43	T. Charles (Pontypool)	2:22.82
44	C. Grayson (York C)	2:23.58
45	E. Hazelwood (Co Leeds)	2:24.21
46	N. Solsona (Spain)	2:36.86

400 Metres Freestyle
Heat Times (no finals)

| 1 | Z. Harrison (Norwich Penguins) | 4:32.85 |
| 2 | D. Palmer (Killerwhales) | 4:35.00 |

9 L. Stent (Chalfont Otters)	1:11.53
10 N. Vafiadis (Hounslow B)	1:11.61
11 A. Foggo (Aquabears)	1:11.75
12 C. Halsall (Co Liverpool)	1:11.79
13 T. Billanie (Newburn)	1:11.80
14 A. Dronsfield (Co Manchester)	1:12.11
15 T. Hill (Greenwich B Mariners)	1:12.12
16 L. Hurst (Smiths)	1:12.17
17 C. Knight (Fleetwood & D)	1:12.34
18 M. Harley (Barnet Copthall)	1:12.44
19 P. Trickett (DARTES)	1:12.53
20 M. Bates (Dudley Metro)	1:12.59
21 C. Fawkes (Manchester U Salford)	1:12.66
22 J. Ricketts (Millfield)	1:12.81
23 H. Oates (Fleetwood & D)	1:12.98
24 P. Alcock (Warrington Warriors)	1:13.01
25 E. Watson (Nova Centurion)	1:13.05
26 S. Hartshorn (Haverhill)	1:13.08
27 L. Carroll (Runnymede)	1:13.60
28 S. Darcy (Cranleigh)	1:13.62
29 A. Gilmore (Portsmouth Northsea)	1:13.71
30 K. Herranz (Spain)	1:13.89
31 C. Hughes (DARTES)	1:13.97
32 J. Lee (Luton)	1:14.14
33 T. Cooper (Deane Dolphins)	1:14.23
34 J. Slater (Royton)	1:14.33
35 G. Palmer (Satellite)	1:14.52
36 S. Ward (Co Sheffield)	1:14.61
37 V. Griffin (Reading)	1:15.07
38 K. Gray (Co Newcastle)	1:15.18
39 S. Thomas (Tenby & D)	1:15.59
40 A. Farrants (Canada)	1:15.91

200 Metres Backstroke
Final

1 D. Palmer (Killerwhales)	2:30.21
2 K. Axford (Beckenham)	2:31.09
3 K. Harrison (Rotherham Metro)	2:31.54
4 V. Horner (Gateshead & Whickham)	2:32.16
5 E. Watson (Nova Centurion)	2:33.25
6 T. Billanie (Newburn)	2:34.20
7 C. Fawkes (Manchester U Salford)	2:35.83
8 A. Foggo (Aquabears)	2:36.40

Heat Times

1 A. Foggo (Aquabears)	2:31.90
2 K. Harrison (Rotherham Metro)	2:32.54
3 D. Palmer (Killerwhales)	2:32.89
4 E. Watson (Nova Centurion)	2:33.11
5 T. Billanie (Newburn)	2:33.59
6 K. Axford (Beckenham)	2:33.77
7 V. Horner (Gateshead & Whickham)	2:33.78
8 C. Fawkes (Manchester U Salford)	2:33.93
9 J. Slater (Royton)	2:34.60
10 L. Wyatt (Beckenham)	2:34.64
11 P. Alcock (Warrington Warriors)	2:34.76
12 G. Hughes (DARTES)	2:35.25
13 V. Hale (Co Swansea)	2:35.74
14 N. Ryder (Thurrock)	2:35.84
15 J. Ricketts (Millfield)	2:35.86
16 M. Quinn (Gloucester C)	2:35.99
17 C. Knight (Fleetwood & D)	2:36.15
18 H. Oates (Fleetwood & D)	2:36.24
19 N. Vafiadis (Hounslow B)	2:36.27
20 T. Hill (Greenwich B Mariners)	2:36.55
21 T. Cooper (Deane Dolphins)	2:37.14
22 A. Gilmore (Portsmouth Northsea)	2:37.62
23 S. Lightfoot (Co Leeds)	2:38.27
24 A. Farrants (Canada)	2:38.36
25 G. Palmer (Satellite)	2:38.46

26 A. Gray (Fleetwood & D)	2:38.90
27 M. Soler (Spain)	2:39.97
28 S. Bass (Co Bradford)	2:41.46
29 K. Herranz (Spain)	2:42.01
30 K. Gray (Co Newcastle)	2:42.42

100 Metres Breaststroke
Final

1 S. Masquera (Spain)	1:17.44
2 N. Cohen (Co Oxford)	1:18.15
3 S. Green (Piranha)	1:18.19
4 E. Firth (Bo Kirklees)	1:18.45
5 A. Creasey (Beckenham)	1:19.31
6 J. Marsh (Hindley)	1:19.58
7 K. Grange (Nova Centurion)	1:20.08
8 L. Benson (Crawley)	1:20.20

Heat Times

1 S. Masquera (Spain)	1:18.34
2 S. Green (Piranha)	1:18.73
3 L. Benson (Crawley)	1:19.17
4 N. Cohen (Co Oxford)	1:19.36
5 A. Creasey (Beckenham)	1:19.47
6 K. Grange (Nova Centurion)	1:19.75
7 J. Marsh (Hindley)	1:19.80
8 E. Firth (Bo Kirklees)	1:20.10
9 L. Saunders (Ferndown Otters)	1:20.12
10 C. Campbell (Co Newcastle)	1:20.23
11 M. Hardiman (Co Birmingham)	1:20.25
12 N. Wood (Killerwhales)	1:20.32
K. Cheney (Spondon)	
14 M. Smith (Harrogate & D)	1:20.38
15 D. Palmer (Killerwhales)	1:20.40
16 J. Peace (Rotherham Metro)	1:20.67
17 S. Strahan (Co Lincoln Pentaqua)	1:20.69
18 C. Hughes (DARTES)	1:20.77
J. Robinson (Middlesbrough)	
20 K. McNeil (Milngarvie)	1:20.86
N. Fox (Chelmsford)	
22 K. Merritt (Chalfont Otters)	1:21.25
23 A. Richardson (Sale)	1:21.28
24 J. Lee (Luton)	1:21.42
25 E. Crapper (Co Sheffield)	1:21.44
26 M. Thorn (North Devon)	1:21.45
27 A. Lovell (Epping Forest)	1:21.83
28 J. Hayter (Aquabears)	1:21.90
29 H. Pickersgill (Stockport Metro)	1:21.99
30 S. Travers (Portsmouth Northsea)	1:22.00
31 F. Heppell (York C)	1:22.54
32 A. Freeman (Oundle & D)	1:22.57
33 C. Grayson (York C)	1:22.77
K. Ferrill (Co Sheffield)	
35 E. Cook (Stockton Aquatics)	1:22.87
36 J. Marvin (Co Derby)	1:22.88
37 H. Watts (Beau Sejour)	1:23.23
38 E. Watson (Nova Centurion)	1:23.33
39 S. Hanscombe (Co Cardiff)	1:23.36
40 H. Eyles (Reading)	1:23.47
41 J. Marsh (Chatteris Kingfisher)	1:23.50
42 D. Craven (Darlington)	1:23.59
43 B. Marshall (Norwich Penguins)	1:23.60
44 N. Bott (Redditch)	1:23.64
45 F. Skipworth (Oundle & D)	1:23.95
46 N. Robinson (Chester le Street)	1:24.20
47 D. Perriam (Weyport Olympians)	1:24.27
48 H. Kemball-Cook (Lowestoft)	1:24.31
49 K. Orrey (Co Lincoln Pentaqua)	1:24.67
50 E. Clapper (Barking)	1:25.26
51 V. Hale (Co Swansea)	1:25.63
52 S. Hunter (Derwentside)	1:26.43

53 K. Crowther (Warrington Warriors)   1:26.71

200 Metres Breaststroke
Final

1	D. Palmer (Killerwhales)	2:47.24
2	S. Masquera (Spain)	2:47.59
3	J. Marsh (Hindley)	2:48.17
4	N. Wood (Killerwhales)	2:50.35
5	S. Green (Piranha)	2:51.00
6	Z. Harrison (Norwich Penguins)	2:51.38
7	M. Hardiman (Co Birmingham)	2:51.68
8	C. Hughes (DARTES)	2:52.82

Heat Times

1	M. Hardiman (Co Birmingham)	2:48.87
2	S. Masquera (Spain)	2:49.48
3	D. Palmer (Killerwhales)	2:49.75
4	Z. Harrison (Norwich Penguins)	2:50.83
5	J. Marsh (Hindley)	2:50.97
6	S. Green (Piranha)	2:51.17
7	C. Hughes (DARTES)	2:51.49
8	N. Wood (Killerwhales)	2:51.74
9	L. Benson (Crawley)	2:51.78
10	A. Creasey (Beckenham)	2:51.81
11	J. Peace (Rotherham Metro)	2:51.89
12	J. Lee (Luton)	2:52.45
13	K. McNeil (Milngarvie)	2:52.47
14	M. Fairhurst (Tyldesley)	2:52.72
15	K. Merritt (Chalfont Otters)	2:52.90
16	L. Saunders (Ferndown Otters)	2:53.03
17	E. Firth (Bo Kirklees)	2:53.38
18	K. Grange (Nova Centurion)	2:53.51
19	N. Cohen (Co Oxford)	2:54.41
20	D. Craven (Darlington)	2:54.93
21	A. Freeman (Oundle & D)	2:55.53
22	F. Heppell (York C)	2:55.58
23	N. Fox (Chelmsford)	2:55.81
24	D. Murphy (Norwich Penguins)	2:56.06
25	M. Thorn (North Devon)	2:56.25
26	S. Strahan (Co Lincoln Pentaqua)	2:56.59
27	A. Richardson (Sale)	2:56.67
28	J. Marsh (Chatteris Kingfisher)	2:57.32
29	G. Benson (Co Bradford)	2:57.61
30	H. Watts (Beau Sejour)	2:57.65
31	C. Campbell (Co Newcastle)	2:57.85
32	K. Ferrill (Co Sheffield)	2:58.10
33	N. Robinson (Chester le Street)	2:58.37
34	E. Crapper (Co Sheffield)	2:58.40
35	C. Stubley (Co Leicester)	2:58.47
36	K. Orrey (Co Lincoln Pentaqua)	2:58.70
37	S. Hunter (Derwentside)	2:59.76
38	B. Marshall (Norwich Penguins)	3:00.19
39	J. Helliar (Killerwhales)	3:00.21
40	J. Hayter (Aquabears)	3:00.96
41	L. Earl (Beckenham)	3:01.29
42	N. Bott (Redditch)	3:01.45
43	R. Blair (Aquabears)	3:01.78
44	B. Golland (Wulfrunians)	3:04.57
45	H. Bowler (Manchester U Salford)	3:06.35

100 Metres Butterfly
Final

1	Z. Harrison (Norwich Penguins)	1:05.31
2	P. Trickett (DARTES)	1:06.08
3	A. Gray (Fleetwood & D)	1:06.53
4	G. Holland (Oldham)	1:07.62
5	S. Smith (Bo Kirklees)	1:07.64
6	E. Strange (Co Oxford)	1:08.18
7	P. Alcock Warrington Warriors)	1:08.27
8	S. Ward (Co Sheffield)	1:08.48

Heat Times

1	A. Gray (Fleetwood & D)	1:07.13
2	Z. Harrison (Norwich Penguins)	1:07.61
3	P. Trickett (DARTES)	1:07.67
4	S. Ward (Co Sheffield)	1:08.21
5	E. Strange (Co Oxford)	1:08.26
6	S. Smith (Bo Kirklees)	1:08.59
7	G. Holland (Oldham)	1:08.82
8	P. Alcock (Warrington Warriors)	1:08.95
9	L. Wyatt (Beckenham)	1:09.61
10	D. Palmer (Killerwhales)	1:10.03
11	E. Skews (Co Sheffield)	1:10.30
12	T. Hill (Greenwich B Mariners)	1:10.35
13	V. Horner (Gateshead & Whickham) S. Green (Piranha)	1:10.56
15	J. Slater (Royton)	1:10.65
16	C. Fawkes (Manchester U Salford)	1:10.69
17	J. Hayter (Aquabears)	1:10.79
18	A. Dronsfield (Co Manchester)	1:10.87
19	C. Battye (Bo Kirklees)	1:10.94
20	P. Barron (Pioneer '79)	1:11.05
21	K. Orrey (Co Lincoln Pentaqua)	1:11.23
22	S. O'Flanagan (Rochford & D)	1:11.25
23	R. Jack (Maxwell)	1:11.51
24	M. Hinton (Barnstable)	1:11.58
25	C. Cowburn (Fleetwood & D) M. Sanchez (Spain)	1:11.85
27	S. Romano (Co Swansea)	1:11.89
28	V. Hale (Co Swansea)	1:12.03
29	H. Gill (Norwich Penguins)	1:12.28
30	N. Elliott (Co Bristol)	1:12.30
31	D. Craven (Darlington) L. Waller (Southgate)	1:12.37
33	C. Shephard (Grimsby Santa Marina)	1:12.62
34	L. Wigham (Gateshead & Whickham)	1:12.82
35	E. Gibbons (St Helens)	1:12.86
36	D. Murphy (Norwich Penguins)	1:13.29
37	C. Diggle (Nova Centurion)	1:13.36
38	N. Cohen (Co Oxford)	1:13.74
39	K. Reed (York C)	1:13.96
40	R. Dewhurst (Lancaster C)	1:16.02

200 Metres Butterfly
Final

1	Z. Harrison (Norwich Penguins)	2:22.62
2	P. Trickett (DARTES)	2:24.93
3	G. Holland (Oldham)	2:25.19
4	D. Palmer (Killerwhales)	2:27.43
5	E. Strange (Co Oxford)	2:29.75
6	P. Alcock (Warrington Warriors)	2:30.34
7	J. Slater (Royton)	2:30.62
8	K. Orrey (Co Lincoln Pentaqua)	2:32.77

Heat Times

1	G. Holland (Oldham)	2:27.93
2	P. Trickett (DARTES)	2:28.83
3	Z. Harrison (Norwich Penguins)	2:28.93
4	D. Palmer (Killerwhales)	2:29.19
5	J. Slater (Royton)	2:29.61
6	P. Alcock (Warrington Warriors)	2:30.38
7	E. Strange (Co Oxford)	2:30.65
8	K. Orrey (Co Lincoln Pentaqua)	2:31.53
9	J. Hayter (Aquabears)	2:31.66
10	C. Cowburn (Fleetwood & D)	2:31.90
11	M. Sanchez (Spain)	2:32.43
12	S. O'Flanagan (Rochford & D)	2:32.69
13	S. Smith (Bo Kirklees)	2:32.95
14	S. Ward (Co Sheffield)	2:33.27
15	E. Montes (Spain)	2:33.74
16	M. Fairhurst (Tyldesley)	2:34.03

17	C. Fawkes (Manchester U Salford)	2:34.04
18	P. Baron (Pioneer '79)	2:34.10
19	S. Green (Piranha)	2:34.24
20	H. Gill (Norwich Penguins)	2:34.53
21	E. Skews (Co Sheffield)	2:34.80
22	C. Battye (Bo Kirklees)	2:34.96
23	J. Adkins (Co Coventry)	2:35.49
24	V. Horner (Gateshead & Whickham)	2:35.57
25	L. Wyatt (Beckenham)	2:36.09
26	E. Arter (Co Leeds)	2:36.97
27	D. Craven (Darlington)	2:36.99
28	M. Hinton (Barnstable)	2:37.10
29	D. Murphy (Norwich Penguins)	2:37.16
30	S. Read (Hatfield)	2:37.82
31	C. Shephard (Grimsby Santa Marina)	2:38.15
32	A. Martin (Norwich Penguins)	2:38.92
33	N. Ryder (Thurrock)	2:39.91
34	T. Billanie (Newburn)	2:40.47
35	K. Wrigley (Warrington Warriors)	2:40.58
36	J. Turnbull (Aquabears)	2:40.84
37	E. Gibbons (St Helens)	2:41.65
38	S. Romano (Co Swansea)	2:42.87
39	H. Downes (Derwentside)	2:43.44
40	S. Camy (Beckenham)	2:43.96
41	K. Reed (York C)	2:48.21

200 Metres Individual Medley
Final

1	Z. Harrison (Norwich Penguins)	2:26.85
2	D. Palmer (Killerwhales)	2:27.16
3	P. Alcock (Warrington Warriors)	2:32.33
4	N. Wood (Killerwhales)	2:32.81
5	J. Lee (Luton)	2:33.24
6	E. Cook (Stockton Aquatics)	2:33.95
7	V. Hale (Co Swansea)	2:34.38
8	T. Billanie (Newburn)	2:34.75

Heat Times

1	D. Palmer (Killerwhales)	2:29.88
2	Z. Harrison (Norwich Penguins)	2:31.51
3	P. Alcock (Warrington Warriors)	2:33.18
4	E. Cook (Stockton Aquatics)	2:33.22
	T. Billanie (Newburn)	
6	N. Wood (Killerwhales)	2:33.51
7	V. Hale (Co Swansea)	2:33.70
8	J. Lee (Luton)	2:33.84
9	C. Fawkes (Manchester U Salford)	2:34.07
10	J. Jackson (Derwentside)	2:34.15
11	P. Trickett (DARTES)	2:34.31
12	M. Palau (Spain)	2:34.60
13	J. Hayter (Aquabears)	2:34.96
14	S. Brown (Co Bradford)	2:35.04
15	S. Green (Piranha)	2:35.15
16	A. Dronsfield (Co Manchester)	2:35.23
17	K. Orrey (Co Lincoln Pentaqua)	2:35.32
18	K. Harrison (Rotherham Metro)	2:35.39
19	V. Horner (Gateshead & Whickham)	2:35.44
20	J. Helliar (Killerwhales)	2:35.48
21	C. Hughes (DARTES)	2:35.60
22	S. Strahan (Co Lincoln Pentaqua)	2:35.70
23	J. Park (Co Newcastle)	2:35.77
24	E. Pengelly (Satellite)	2:35.88
25	A. Gray (Fleetwood & D)	2:36.27
26	J. Peace (Rotherham Metro)	2:36.33
27	S. O'Flanagan (Rochford & D)	2:36.56
28	S. Ward (Co Sheffield)	2:37.20
29	R. Avalos (Spain)	2:37.25
30	G. Palmer (Satellite)	2:38.52
31	H. Kemball-Cook (Lowestoft)	2:38.56
32	A. Gilmore (Portsmouth Northsea)	2:38.77

33	M. Thorn (North Devon)	2:39.15
34	Y. Roberts (Hounslow B)	2:39.42
35	N. Cohen (Co Oxford)	2:39.78
36	N. Elliott (Co Bristol)	2:40.19
37	M. Hinton (Barnstable)	2:40.50
38	M. Harley (Barnet Copthall)	2:40.74
39	R. Blair (Aquabears)	2:41.06
40	C. Cowburn (Fleetwood & D)	2:41.53
41	A. Farrants (Canada)	2:43.71

400 Metres Individual Medley
Heat Times (no finals)

1	D. Palmer (Killerwhales)	5:12.47
2	Z. Harrison (Norwich Penguins)	5:19.32
3	J. Hayter (Aquabears)	5:21.48
4	V. Horner (Gateshead & Whickham)	5:21.63
5	S. Green (Piranha)	5:21.99
6	P. Alcock (Warrington Warriors)	5:23.30
7	K. Orrey (Co Lincoln Pentaqua)	5:23.32
8	E. Cook (Stockton Aquatics)	5:24.09
9	R. Avalos (Spain)	5:25.18
10	C. Fawkes (Manchester U Salford)	5:25.52
11	N. Ryder (Thurrock)	5:26.17
12	S. Brown (Co Bradford)	5:27.18
13	J. Peace (Rotherham Metro)	5:27.83
14	T. Billanie (Newburn)	5:27.48
15	E. Arter (Co Leeds)	5:28.88
16	J. Helliar (Killerwhales)	5:28.94
17	H. Gill (Norwich Penguins)	5:29.04
18	J. Slater (Royton)	5:29.32
19	N. Wood (Killerwhales)	5:29.87
20	E. Montes (Spain)	5:30.11
21	P. Trickett (DARTES)	5:31.14
22	M. Palau (Spain)	5:31.56
23	V. Hale (Co Swansea)	5:32.75
24	D. Murphy (Norwich Penguins)	5:33.03
25	E. Gibbons (St Helens)	5:33.23
26	S. Ward (Co Sheffield)	5:33.66
27	L. Jackson (Derwentside)	5:33.83
28	G. Palmer (Satellite)	5:33.92
29	J. Woodward (Thamesdown)	5:35.86
30	S. Strahan (Co Lincoln Pentaqua)	5:36.73
31	E. Skews (Co Sheffield)	5:37.27
32	E. Pengelly (Satellite)	5:38.96
33	N. Cohen (Co Oxford)	5:41.37
34	C. Diggle (Nova Centurion)	5:43.65
35	C. Cowburn (Fleetwood & D)	5:44.04
36	M. Hinton (Barnstable)	5:44.97
37	S. Gray (Co Leeds)	5:46.84

4×50 Metres Freestyle Club Relay
Final

1	Derwentside	1:54.42
2	Killerwhales	1:57.22
3	Nova Centurion	1:57.34
4	Beckenham	1:57.57
5	Norwich Penguins	1:57.81
6	Dudley Metropolitan	1:57.93
7	Co Birmingham	1:58.97
8	Portsmouth Northsea	1:59.14

Heat Times

1	Derwentside	1:56.45
2	Killerwhales	1:58.72
3	Nova Centurion	1:58.75
4	Dudley Metropolitan	1:59.06
5	Beckenham	1:59.31
6	Norwich Penguins	1:59.40
7	Co Birmingham	1:59.83
8	Portsmouth Northsea	1:59.96

9	Aquabears	2:00.09
10	Hounslow B	2:00.18
11	Maxwell	2:00.25
12	Pioneer '79	2:00.50
13	Co Liverpool	2:00.73
14	Co Coventry	2:00.75
15	Holylake	2:01.21
16	Co Leeds	2:01.31
17	Gateshead & Whickham	2:01.63
18	Co Sheffield	2:01.67
19	Co Newcastle	2:01.69
20	Fleetwood & D	2:01.70
21	Regent Tigers	2:01.98
22	Sale	2:02.03
23	Reading	2:02.46
24	Southgate	2:03.29
25	Beau Sejour	2:03.50
26	Harrow & Wealdstone	2:03.71
27	York C	2:03.75
28	Haverhill	2:04.72
29	Guildford C	2:04.90
30	Forward Hillingdon	2:05.21
31	Warrington Warriors	2:05.25
32	Manchester U Salford	2:06.38
	Stockport Metro	DIS

4×50 Metres Medley Club Relay
Final

1	Beckenham	2:10.53
2	Norwich Penguins	2:11.21
3	DARTES	2:11.70
4	Nova Centurion	2:11.89
5	Co Sheffield	2:12.31
6	Co Oxford	2:13.97
7	Co Newcastle	2:14.75
8	Co Liverpool	2:15.27

Heat Times

1	Norwich Penguins	2:12.20
2	DARTES	2:12.84
3	Beckenham	2:13.14
4	Co Sheffield	2:13.16
5	Co Oxford	2:13.35
6	Co Newcastle	2:13.92
7	Co Liverpool	2:14.02
8	Nova Centurion	2:14.07
9	Killerwhales	2:14.53
10	Portsmouth Northsea	2:14.57
11	Co Birmingham	2:14.68
12	Gateshead & Whickham	2:15.30
13	Southgate	2:15.37
14	Aquabears	2:15.58
15	Derwentside	2:16.08
16	Sale	2:16.12
17	Stockport Metro	2:16.40
18	Reading	2:16.52
19	Co Coventry	2:16.57
20	Hounslow B	2:16.74
21	Chalfont Otters	2:17.01
22	Beau Sejour	2:17.21
23	Fleetwood & D	2:17.28
24	Haverhill	2:17.41
25	Co Leeds	2:18.03
26	Guildford C	2:18.11
27	York C	2:18.22
28	Forward Hillingdon	2:18.52
29	Manchester U Salford	2:19.82
30	Warrington Warriors	2:20.01
31	Pioneer '79	2:21.29
32	Harrow & Wealdstone	2:22.19

15/16 Years Age Group
Boys

100 Metres Freestyle
Final

1	C. Robinson (Killerwhales)	53.43
2	S. Mellor (Satellite)	54.04
3	P. Chick (Beckenham)	54.27
4	C. Moxham (Barnet Copthall)	54.51
5	S. Patch (Co Lincoln Pentaqua)	54.53
6	J. Leveridge (Bo Kirklees)	54.73
7	O. Gallienne (Gloucester C)	55.22
8	M. Watt (Portsmouth Northsea)	55.86

Heat Times

1	C. Moxham (Barnet Copthall)	54.56
2	S. Patch (Co Lincoln Pentaqua)	54.80
3	S. Mellor (Satellite)	55.01
4	C. Robinson (Killerwhales)	55.04
5	J. Leveridge (Bo Kirklees)	55.11
6	P. Chick (Beckenham)	55.17
7	O. Galliene (Gloucester C)	55.25
8	M. Watt (Portsmouth Northsea)	55.44
9	A. Nannini (Eton College)	55.71
10	P. Hutchings (Torfaen)	55.78
11	C. Edwards (Killerwhales)	55.82
12	S. Haywood (Co Derby)	56.01
13	K. Westwood (Co Derby)	56.08
14	D. Claridge (Co Birmingham)	56.10
15	S. Handley (RTW Monson)	56.17
16	I. Swift (Rotherham Metro)	56.20
17	G. Thomas (Rochford & D)	56.41
18	M. Cary (Wycombe &D)	56.42
19	I. Trinder (Co Newcastle)	56.43
20	J. Sanders (Ferndown Otters)	56.52
21	P. Regan (Sale)	56.59
	N. King (Wandsworth)	
23	D. Hill (Luton)	56.67
24	L. Grenyer (Beckenham)	56.68
25	D. Smith (Dudley Metro)	56.82
26	S. Adamson (Co Southampton)	56.84
27	N. Collins (Kelly College)	56.91
28	T. Stephenson (Co Newcastle)	56.98
29	P. Edwards (Norwich Penguins)	57.01
30	P. Ouldcott (Sale)	57.08
31	H. Sheraton (Millfield)	57.11
32	P. Palmer (Co Lincoln Pentaqua)	57.13
33	D. Wright (Co Leicester)	57.16
34	S. McGreevy (Eastbourne)	57.25
35	K. Gammon (North Devon)	57.64
36	S. Aucott (Co Leicester)	57.68
	D. Major (Co Southampton)	
38	M. Wolfendon (Co Chester)	57.76
39	L. Tyson (Co Birmngham)	57.89
40	N. Randle (Co Coventry)	57.90
41	M. Browne (Canada)	58.32
42	A. Chamberlain (Yeovil & D)	58.34
43	A. Fletcher (Bo Burnley CATS)	58.44
44	J. Kirkin (Warrington Warriors)	58.64
45	L. Radwell (Oundle & D)	58.69
46	A. Smith (Co Chester)	59.11
47	D. Braiden (Canada)	59.26

200 Metres Freestyle
Final

1	C. Robinson (Killerwhales)	1:56.11
2	S. Mellor (Satellite)	1:56.26
3	J. Leveridge (Bo Kirklees)	1:58.27
4	S. Patch (Co Lincoln Pentaqua)	1:58.57
5	P. Chick (Beckenham)	1:59.02

6 A. Clayton (Co Leeds)		1:59.07
7 C. Edwards (Killerwhales)		1:59.88
8 P. Palmer (Co Lincoln Pentaqua)		2:00.63

Heat Times

1 J. Leveridge (Bo Kirklees)		1:58.81
2 S. Patch (Co Lincoln Pentaqua)		1:59.50
A. Clayton (Co Leeds)		
4 C. Robinson (Killerwhales)		1:59.80
5 S. Mellor (Satellite)		1:59.92
6 P. Chick (Beckenham)		2:00.07
7 P. Palmer (Co Lincoln Pentaqua)		2:00.28
C. Edwards (Killerwhales)		
9 S. Haywood (Co Derby)		2:00.79
10 D. Claridge (Co Birmingham)		2:01.04
11 M. Watt (Portsmouth Northsea)		2:01.68
12 J. Gonzalez (Spain)		2:01.99
13 K. Crosby (Warrington Warriors)		2:02.03
14 N. King (Wandsworth)		2:02.06
15 G. Morgan (Co Birmingham)		2:02.29
16 P. Hutchings (Torfaen)		2:02.37
17 O. Gallienne (Gloucester C)		2:02.57
18 P. Edwards (Norwich Penguins)		2:02.63
19 S. Houlton (Luton)		2:02.83
20 D. Hill (Luton)		2:03.20
S. Wells (Norwich Penguins)		
22 C. Moxham (Barnet Copthall)		2:03.38
23 A. Aitken (Stockton Aquatics)		2:03.99
24 L. Radwell (Oundle & D)		2:04.15
25 M. Hickey (Warrington Warriors)		2:04.30
26 K. Westwood (Co Derby)		2:04.49
27 G. Thomas (Rochford & D)		2:04.58
28 D. Bradford (Fleetwood & D)		2:04.66
29 S. Clamp (Co Coventry)		2:04.81
30 A. Chamberlain (Yeovil & D)		2:04.85
31 I. Diez (Spain)		2:04.95
32 A. Smith (Co Chester)		2:05.08
33 D. Smith (Dudley Metro)		2:05.18
34 L. Grenyer (Beckenham)		2:05.56
35 S. Aucott (Co Leicester)		2:05.78
36 G. Pearson (Derwentside)		2:05.83
37 M. Lundie (Swansea Valley)		2:06.28
38 K. Gammon (North Devon)		2:06.40
39 T. Stephenson (Co Newcastle)		2:06.51
40 J. Kirkin (Warrington Warriors)		2:06.74
41 D. Newton (Stockton Aquatics)		2:07.21
42 N. Collins (Kelly College)		2:07.29
43 A. Wooldridge (Co Birmingham)		2:07.72
44 D. Braiden (Canada)		2:09.66
45 M. Browne (Canada)		2:12.26

400 Metres Freestyle

Heat Times (no final)

1 S.Mellor (Satellite)		4:01.27
2 C. Robinson (Killerwhales)		4:08.40
3 A. Clayton (Co Leeds)		4:12.40
4 P. Palmer (Co Lincoln Pentaqua)		4:12.84
5 P. Edwards (Norwich Penguins)		4:13.46
6 J. Leveridge (Bo Kirklees)		4:14.89
7 S. Patch (Co Lincoln Pentaqua)		4:15.76
8 P. Chick (Beckenham)		4:16.39
9 D. Pye (St Helens)		4:16.46
10 I. Diez (Spain)		4:16.50
11 A. Aitken (Stockton Aquatics)		4:16.63
12 G. Pearson (Derwentside)		4:17.39
13 M. Hickey (Warrington Warriors)		4:17.71
14 D. Claridge (Co Birmingham)		4:17.82
15 C. Edwards (Killerwhales)		4:17.96
16 D. Bradford (Fleetwood & D)		4:18.67
17 S. Houlton (Luton)		4:19.03
18 A. Rosser (Torfaen)		4:19.27
19 S. Clamp (Co Coventry)		4:19.34
20 N. King (Wandsworth)		4:20.21
21 N. Carr (Barking)		4:20.87
22 G. Rosser (Torfaen)		4:22.16
23 J. Kirkin (Warrington Warriors)		4:23.20
24 A. Smith (Co Chester)		4:24.55
25 S. Smith (Wigan Wasps)		4:25.25
26 A. Wooldridge (Co Birmingham)		4:25.43
27 N. Collins (Kelly College)		4:25.39
28 D. Newton (Stockton Aquatics)		4:27.67
29 I. Shearer (Reading)		4:30.18

1500 Metres Freestyle

Heat Times (no final)

1 A. Clayton (Co Leeds)		16:29.41
2 I. Diez (Spain)		16:47.62
3 S. Clamp (Co Coventry)		16:51.14
4 R. Copping (Portsmouth Northsea)		16:53.29
5 G. Pearson (Derwentside)		16:56.08
6 D. Pye (St Helens)		17:00.63
7 S. Smith (Wigan Wasps)		17:08.79
8 S. Lane (Stockton Aquatics)		17:10.13
9 P. Edwards (Norwich Penguins)		17:15.08
10 N. Carr (Barking)		17:20.00
11 D. Belcourt (Harrow & Wealdstone)		17:21.85
12 J. Kirkin (Warrington Warriors)		17:22.85
13 G. Rosser (Torfaen)		17:23.92
14 A. Rosser (Torfaen)		17:24.94
15 N. Speed (Co Leeds)		17:32.23
16 J. Ratcliffe (Co Bristol)		17:33.03
17 A. Wooldridge (Co Birmingham)		17:34.52
18 S. Houlton (Luton)		17:34.78
19 A. Smith (Co Chester)		17:36.82
20 P. Daintith (Warrington Warriors)		17:38.60
21 S. Hall (DARTES)		17:49.92
22 I. Shearer (Reading)		17:56.72

100 Metres Backstroke

Final

1 S. Mellor (Satellite)		1:01.16
2 S. Handley (BTW Monson)		1:01.67
3 C. Edwards (Killerwhales)		1:02.15
4 K. Westwood (Co Derby)		1:03.06
5 J. McNeil (Milngavie)		1:03.08
6 A. Ruckwood (Haden Hill)		1:03.21
7 K. Crosby (Warrington Warriors)		1:03.44
8 S. Parker (Co Coventry)		1:03.52

Heat Times

1 S. Mellor (Satellite)		1:02.67
2 S. Handley (BTW Monson)		1:02.82
3 C. Edwards (Killerwhales)		1:03.08
4 J. McNeil (Milngavie)		1:03.22
K. Westwood (Co Derby)		
6 S. Parker (Co Coventry)		1:03.48
7 A. Ruckwood (Haden Hill)		1:03.67
8 K. Crosby (Warrington Warriors)		1:03.76
9 P. Hutchings (Torfaen)		1:03.93
10 S. Summers (Bo Kirklees)		1:04.27
11 A. Jones (York C)		1:04.39
12 S. Adamson (Co Southampton)		1:04.56
M. Hampton (Basildon)		
N. King (Wandsworth)		
15 J. Manzio (Spain)		1:04.57
16 A. Aitken (Stockton Aquatics)		1:04.64
17 D. Hill (Luton)		1:04.79
18 D. Hudson (Norwich Swan)		1:05.05
19 H. Sheraton (Millfield)		1:05.15
20 M. Billam (Hull Olympic)		1:05.16

21	R. Batterby (York C)	1:05.22
22	J. Fitzgerald (Chelsea & Kensington)	1:05.36
23	G. Pearson (Derwentside)	1:05.37
24	M. Browne (Canada)	1:05.51
25	J. Holmes (Hatfield)	1:05.52
26	N. English (Southgate)	1:05.56
	N. Poole (Portsmouth Northsea)	
28	K. Fleet (Bo Waltham Forest)	1:05.59
29	K. Gammon (North Devon)	1:05.91
30	A. Chamberlain (Yeovil & D)	1:05.96
31	M. Rolfe (Oundle & D)	1:06.03
32	A. Fry (Manchester U Salford)	1:06.06
33	D. Bradford (Fleetwood & D)	1:06.45
34	S. Bradley (Barking)	1:06.68
35	S. Lack (Barnet Copthall)	1:06.70
	R. Toolen (Wroughton)	
37	P. Ouldcott (Sale)	1:07.16
38	M. Watt (Portsmouth Northsea)	1:07.24
39	S. Kelly (Co Newcastle)	1:07.33
40	A. Lysak (Stockton Aquatics)	1:07.78
41	P. Hinxman (Canterbury)	1:08.03
42	P. Barnett (Holywell)	1:08.44

200 Metres Backstroke
Final

1	S. Mellor (Satellite)	2:09.79
2	C. Edwards (Killerwhales)	2:14.13
3	K. Crosby (Warrington Warriors)	2:15.49
4	J. Manzano (Spain)	2:17.17
5	G. Pearson (Derwentside)	2:17.82
6	P. Hutchings (Torfaen)	2:18.01
7	A. Ruckwood (Haden Hill)	2:18.66
8	S. Handley (RTW Monson)	2:22.36

Heat Times

1	C. Edwards (Killerwhales)	2:15.56
2	S. Mellor (Satellite)	2:15.61
3	K. Crosby (Warrington Warriors)	2:16.41
4	P. Hutchings (Torfaen)	2:17.28
5	J. Manzano (Spain)	2:17.30
6	S. Handley (RTW Monson)	2:17.63
7	A. Ruckwood (Haden Hill)	2:18.00
8	G. Pearson (Derwentside)	2:18.18
9	S. Summers (Bo Kirklees)	2:18.79
10	K. Fleet (Bo Waltham Forest)	2:19.59
11	K. Westwood (Co Derby)	2:19.89
12	D. Hill (Luton)	2:19.91
13	R. Batterby (York C)	2:20.04
14	D. Belcourt (Harrow & Wealdstone)	2:20.22
15	A. Aitken (Stockton Aquatics)	2:20.34
16	L. Williams (Wigan Wasps)	2:20.36
17	A. Jones (York C)	2:20.37
18	C. Alderson (Norwich Penguins)	2:20.51
19	J. Holmes (Hatfield)	2:20.61
20	S. Adamson (Co Southampton)	2:20.64
21	S. Lack (Barnet Copthall)	2:20.76
22	S. Wells (Norwich Penguins)	2:21.02
23	D. Bradford (Fleetwood & D)	2:21.21
24	M. Hampton (Basildon)	2:21.83
25	S. Clamp (Co Coventry)	2:22.27
26	J. McNeil (Milngarvie)	2:22.28
27	P. Chick (Beckenham)	2:22.44
28	K. Gammon (North Devon)	2:22.70
29	S. Barnes (Fareham Nomads)	2:22.95
30	M. Watt (Portsmouth Northsea)	2:23.40
31	N. Wilkin (Bo Kirklees)	2:23.64
32	P. Simpson (Stockton Aquatics)	2:23.68
33	N. King (Wandsworth)	2:23.74
34	J. Fitzgerald (Chelsea & Kensington)	2:23.76
35	A. Fry (Manchester U Salford)	2:23.77

Steven Mellor Artwood Photography

36	A. Lysak (Stockton Aquatics)	2:24.62
37	N. English (Southgate)	2:24.63
38	M. Williams (Maxwell)	2:24.76
39	M. Wolfenden (Co Chester)	2:24.83
40	S. Kelly (Co Newcastle)	2:25.08
41	P. Ouldcott (Sale)	2:25.27
42	A. Chamberlain (Yeovil & D)	2:25.48
43	H. Sheraton (Millfield)	2:25.64
44	A. Wooldridge (Co Birmingham)	2:25.89
45	L. Dormer (Bournemouth Dolphins)	2:26.49
46	J. Ralph (Portsmouth Northsea)	2:26.55
47	G. Newton (Oundle & D)	2:26.75
48	S. Bradley (Barking)	2:26.94
49	P. Daintith (Warrington Warriors)	2:27.34
50	R. Stannard (Leatherhead)	2:27.65
51	M. Browne (Canada)	2:28.62
52	D. Hidle (Bo Sunderland)	2:28.70

100 Metres Breaststroke
Final

1	I. Swift (Rotherham Metro)	1:08.08
2	N. Pope (Portsmouth Northsea)	1:08.50
3	A. Clapper (Barking)	1:08.88
4	T. Maddocks (Rochford & D)	1:09.36
5	A. Aguilar (Spain)	1:09.95
6	A. Cooper (Royton)	1:10.27
7	P. Simpson (Stockton Aquatics)	1:10.75
8	J. Moorfoot (Stockton Aquatics)	1:10.77

Heat Times

1	I. Swift (Rotherham Metro)	1:08.51
2	N. Pope (Portsmouth Northsea)	1:09.20
3	A. Aguilar (Spain)	1:09.87
4	T. Maddocks (Rochford & D)	1:10.05
5	A. Cooper (Royton)	1:10.14
6	A. Clapper (Barking)	1:10.24
7	J. Moorfoot (Stockton Aquatics)	1:10.62
8	P. Simpson (Stockton Aquatics)	1:10.94
9	S. Davison (Middlesbrough)	1:11.06
10	K. Lancaster (Warrington Warriors)	1:11.10
11	M. Douglas (Co Newcastle)	1:11.30
12	P. Wilkinson (Co Leeds)	1:11.34
	S. Handley (RTW Monson)	
14	J. Leveridge (Bo Kirklees)	1:11.47
15	D. Shearsby (Harrow & Wealdstone)	1:11.75

16	B. Barraclough (Bo Kirklees)	1:11.85
17	I. Seidl (Australia)	1:11.98
18	S. Wells (Norwich Penguins)	1:12.00
19	L. Peterson (Braintree & Bocking)	1:12.03
20	S. Hutchinson (Nova Centurion)	1:12.11
21	C. Andrews (Bournemouth Dolphins)	1:12.55
22	P. Bimrose (Kippax)	1:12.56
23	D. Beswick (Co Manchester)	1:12.94
24	M. Dunstone (Co Bristol)	1:12.96
25	M. Baker (Barnet Copthall)	1:13.04
26	R. Milloy (Co Coventry)	1:13.22
27	R. Laidlow (Kelly College)	1:13.23
28	S. Haywood (Co Derby)	1:13.24
29	A. McPeake (Washington)	1:13.25
30	K. Dougan (Oundle & D)	1:13.26
31	M. Roe (Nova Centurion)	1:13.28
32	D. Smith (Dudley Metro)	1:13.39
33	W. O'Gorman (Millfield)	1:13.41
34	S. Lodge (Bo Kirklees)	1:13.48
35	D. Murdock (Nova Centurion)	1:13.53
36	A. Brown (Torfaen)	1:13.69
37	L. Radwell (Oundle & D)	1:13.84
38	C. Robinson (Killerwhales)	1:14.00
39	T. McKenny (Haverhill)	1:14.11
40	I. Wright (Co Bradford)	1:14.32
41	S. Collett (Bracknell)	1:14.42
42	A. Medlycott (Co Newcastle)	1:14.56
43	S. Abels (Jersey)	1:14.76
44	P. Fitzpatrick (Redditch)	1:14.81
45	S. Patch (Co Lincoln Pentaqua)	1:15.11
46	R. Howe (Bo Sunderland)	1:15.15
47	A. Fletcher (Bo Burnley CATS)	1:15.20
48	D. Tobin (RTW Monson)	1:16.65
49	D. Braiden (Canada)	1:18.77
50	S. Aucott (Co Leicester)	1:18.80
51	N. Fairbrother (Braunstone)	1:20.30

200 Metres Breaststroke
Final

1	I. Swift (Rotherham Metro)	2:26.49
2	J. Leveridge (Bo Kirklees)	2:30.64
3	L. Peterson (Braintree & Bocking)	2:31.37
4	A. Clapper (Barking)	2:31.73
5	D. Shearsby (Harrow & Wealdstone)	2:32.36
6	T. Maddocks (Rochford & D)	2:32.75
7	A. Aguilar (Spain)	2:32.80
8	M. Douglas (Co Newcastle)	2:33.81

Heat Times

1	I. Swift (Rotherham Metro)	2:29.80
2	L. Peterson (Braintree & Bocking)	2:33.41
3	J. Leveridge (Bo Kirklees)	2:33.63
4	T. Maddocks (Rochford & D)	2:33.73
5	M. Douglas (Co Newcastle)	2:33.75
6	A. Clapper (Barking)	2:33.89
7	D. Shearsby (Harrow & Wealdstone)	2:33.97
8	A. Aguilar (Spain)	2:34.00
9	A. Cooper (Royton) P. Wilkinson (Co Leeds)	2:34.08
11	K. Lancaster (Warrington Warriors)	2:34.38
12	S. Wells (Norwich Penguins)	2:34.71
13	N. Poole (Portsmouth Northsea)	2:35.02
14	I. Seidl (Australia)	2:35.03
15	P. Beacham (Co Coventry)	2:35.28
16	D. Beswick (Co Manchester)	2:35.42
17	T. McKenny (Haverhill)	2:35.54
18	R. Laidlow (Kelly College)	2:35.72
19	S. Davison (Middlesbrough)	2:35.86
20	B. Barraclough (Bo Kirklees)	2:36.54
21	D. Murdock (Nova Centurion)	2:37.10

22	S. Hutchinson (Nova Centurion)	2:37.39
23	P. Simpson (Stockton Aquatics)	2:38.66
24	J. Moorfoot (Stockton Aquatics)	2:38.82
25	P. Bimrose (Kippax)	2:38.85
26	S. Lodge (Bo Kirklees)	2:39.17
27	M. Dunstone (Co Bristol)	2:39.22
28	R. Fish (Co Coventry)	2:39.28
29	M. Simpkins (Co Oxford)	2:40.00
30	M. Roe (Nova Centurion)	2:40.10
31	G. Johnson (Co Leeds)	2:41.22
32	L. Radwell (Oundle & D)	2:42.68
33	S. Abels (Jersey)	2:43.08
34	M. Baker (Barnet Copthall)	2:43.51
35	S. Patch (Co Lincoln Pentaqua)	2:43.55
36	L. Williams (Wigan Wasps)	2:43.68
37	D. Collins (Maxwell)	2:44.17
38	A. McPeake (Washington)	2:44.69
39	W. O'Gorman (Millfield)	2:44.77
40	S. Hill (Co Peterborough)	2:45.49
41	P. Fitzpatrick (Redditch)	2:45.79
42	A. Firbank (DARTES)	2:46.02
43	I. Winmill (Runnymede)	2:46.76
44	P. McCloud (Co Leicester)	2:46.95

100 Metres Butterfly
Final

1	C. Robinson (Killerwhales)	59.10
2	C. Moxham (Barnet Copthall)	59.16
3	S. Haywood (Co Derby)	59.55
4	K. Crosby (Warrington Warriors)	59.67
5	M. Mellor (Satellite)	59.92
6	M. Browne (Canada)	1:00.25
7	P. Chick (Beckenham)	1:00.31
8	H. Sheraton (Millfield)	1:00.54

Heat Times

1	S. Haywood (Co Derby)	59.58
2	K. Crosby (Warrington Warriors)	59.93
3	C. Robinson (Killerwhales)	1:00.15
4	C. Moxham (Barnet Copthall) S. Mellor (Satellite)	1:00.19
6	P. Chick (Beckenham)	1:00.39
7	M. Browne (Canada)	1:00.72
8	H. Sheraton (Millfield)	1:00.73
9	T. Cook (Barking)	1:00.76
10	P. Edwards (Norwich Penguins)	1:00.99

Ian Swift　　　　　　　　　　　Artwood Photography

11	N. Grundy (Fleetwood & D)	1:01.50
12	C. Edwards (Killerwhales)	1:01.64
13	D. Wright (Co Leicester)	1:01.72
14	G. Hall (Nova Centurion)	1:01.87
15	P. Hutchings (Torfaen)	1:02.05
16	D. Hill (Luton)	1:02.18
17	N. King (Wandsworth)	1:02.23
18	D. Claridge (Co Birmingham)	1:02.25
19	M. Wolfenden (Co Chester)	1:02.32
20	M. Cary (Wycombe & D)	1:02.38
21	A. Romero (Spain)	1:02.40
22	D. Allen (Shiverers)	1:02.51
23	A. Nannini (Eton College)	1:02.64
24	G. Morgan (Co Birmingham)	1:02.72
25	A. Chamberlain (Yeovil & D)	1:02.73
26	R. Ashcroft (Hindley)	1:02.89
27	P. Lowe (Co Manchester)	1:02.90
28	S. Wells (Norwich Penguins)	1:02.91
29	D. Case (Barking)	1:03.35
30	P. Simpson (Stockton Aquatics)	1:03.39
31	C. Baker (Cheadle & D)	1:03.43
32	N. Randle (Co Coventry)	1:03.72
33	D. Braiden (Canada)	1:08.67

200 Metres Butterfly
Final

1	C. Robinson (Killerwhales)	2:07.92
2	K. Crosby (Warrington Warriors)	2:09.04
3	P. Edwards (Norwich Penguins)	2:10.90
4	P. Chick (Beckenham)	2:11.19
5	S. Smith (Wigan Wasps)	2:15.34
6	D. Claridge (Co Birmingham)	2:15.60
7	P. Hutchings (Torfaen)	2:15.74
8	G. Hall (Nova Centurion)	2:16.13

Heat Times

1	P. Edwards (Norwich Penguins)	2:11.09
2	C. Robinson (Killerwhales)	2:12.71
3	K. Crosby (Warrington Warriors)	2:12.89
4	G. Hall (Nova Centurion)	2:13.43
5	P. Chick (Beckenham)	2:13.55
6	S. Smith (Wigan Wasps)	2:15.32
7	D. Claridge (Co Birmingham)	2:15.43
8	P. Hutchings (Torfaen)	2:15.45
9	R. Copping (Portsmouth Northsea)	2:15.54
10	D. Allen (Shiverers)	2:15.59
11	H. Sheraton (Millfield)	2:15.63
12	D. Pye (St Helens)	2:15.77
13	R. Ashcroft (Hindley)	2:15.96
14	D. Hill (Luton)	2:17.47
15	L. Tyson (Co Birmingham)	2:17.57
16	M. Herbert (Runnymede)	2:17.98
17	M. Simpkins (Co Oxford)	2:18.04
18	M. Hickey (Warrington Warriors)	2:18.37
19	T. Cook (Barking)	2:18.66
20	A. Romero (Spain)	2:18.67
21	C. Baker (Cheadle & D)	2:18.72
22	C. Edwards (Killerwhales)	2:18.77
23	P. Lowe (Co Manchester)	2:20.06
24	A. Jones (York C)	2:20.40
25	S. Houlton (Luton)	2:20.84
26	N. Grundy (Fleetwood & D)	2:21.14
27	A. Moss (Chelmsford)	2:21.72
28	S. Bradley (Barking)	2:22.00
29	A. McLeish (Co Lincoln Pentaqua)	2:22.03
30	G. Axford (Beckenham)	2:23.10
31	A. Flint (Nova Centurion)	2:23.80
32	N. Speed (Co Leeds)	2:23.88
33	J. Thubron (Chester le Street)	2:64.64
	M. Cary (Wycombe & D)	DIS

200 Metres Individual Medley
Final

1	C. Robinson (Killerwhales)	2:13.79
2	C. Moxham (Barnet Copthall)	2:15.36
3	C. Patch (Co Lincoln Pentaqua)	2:16.75
4	K. Crosby (Warrington Warriors)	2:16.95
5	C. Edwards (Killerwhales)	2:17.11
6	S. Haywood (Co Derby)	2:17.43
7	M. Billam (Hull Olympic)	2:17.67
8	S. Wells (Norwich Penguins)	2:17.68

Heat Times

1	C. Moxham (Barnet Copthall)	2:16.21
2	C. Patch (Co Lincoln Pentaqua)	2:17.16
3	C. Edwards (Killerwhales)	2:17.63
4	K. Crosby (Warrington Warriors)	2:17.66
5	C. Robinson (Killerwhales)	2:18.39
6	S. Wells (Norwich Penguins)	2:18.44
7	S. Haywood (Co Derby)	2:18.91
8	M. Billam (Hull Olympic)	2:19.14
9	I. Swift (Rotherham Metro)	2:19.22
10	P. Simpson (Stockton Aquatics)	2:19.23
11	J. Leveridge (Bo Kirklees)	2:19.31
12	D. Smith (Dudley Metro)	2:19.42
13	P. Wilkinson (Co Leeds)	2:19.83
14	S. Summers (Bo Kirklees)	2:19.87
15	N. Poole (Portsmouth Northsea)	2:20.19
16	D. Bradford (Fleetwood & D)	2:20.33
17	A. Aitken (Stockton Aquatics)	2:20.50
18	D. Beswick (Co Manchester)	2:20.68
19	P. Chick (Beckenham)	
	A. Chamberlain (Yeovil & D)	2:20.79
21	A. Cooper (Royton)	2:20.97
22	B. Barraclough (Bo Kirklees)	2:21.21
23	J. Holmes (Hatfield)	2:21.37
24	M. Simpkins (Co Oxford)	2:21.50
25	N. Carr (Barking)	2:21.58
26	A. Clapper (Barking)	2:21.66
27	H. Sheraton (Millfield)	2:21.82
28	R. Copping (Portsmouth Northsea)	2:21.88
29	P. Barnett (Holywell)	2:21.91
30	R. Laidlow (Kelly College)	2:21.97
31	S. Abels (Jersey)	2:22.05
32	D. Murdock (Nova Centurion)	
	G. Morgan (Co Birmingham)	2:22.08
34	M. Cary (Wycombe & D)	2:22.18
35	N. King (Wandsworth)	2:22.49
36	L. Radwell (Oundle & D)	2:22.52
37	D. Hill (Luton)	2:22.55
38	J. Ralph (Portsmouth Northsea)	2:22.56
39	S. Adamson (Co Southampton)	2:23.01
40	G. Pearson (Derwentside)	2:23.19
41	D. Belcourt (Harrow & Wealdstone)	2:23.28
42	S. Clamp (Co Coventry)	2:23.58
43	K. Gammon (North Devon)	2:25.10
44	S. Lane (Stockton Aquatics)	2:26.11
45	K. Lancaster (Warrington Warriors)	2:26.21
46	T. Cook (Barking)	2:29.11

400 Metres Individual Medley
Heat Times (no final)

1	C. Robinson (Killerwhales)	4:40.20
2	K. Crosby (Warrington Warriors)	4:48.02
3	R. Copping (Portsmouth Northsea)	4:51.84
4	C. Edwards (Killerwhales)	4:51.94
5	D. Bradford (Fleetwood & D)	4:53.49
6	S. Summers (Bo Kirklees)	4:54.48
7	S. Patch (Co Lincoln Pentaqua)	4:54.65
8	M. Simpkins (Co Oxford)	4:54.73
9	S. Lane (Stockton Aquatics)	4:54.94

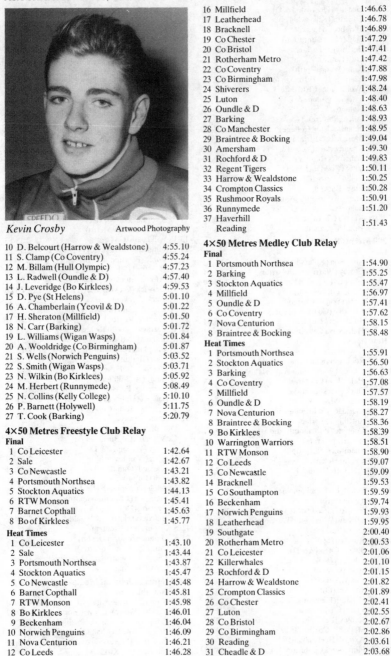

Kevin Crosby   Artwood Photography

10 D. Belcourt (Harrow & Wealdstone)	4:55.10
11 S. Clamp (Co Coventry)	4:55.24
12 M. Billam (Hull Olympic)	4:57.23
13 L. Radwell (Oundle & D)	4:57.40
14 J. Leveridge (Bo Kirklees)	4:59.53
15 D. Pye (St Helens)	5:01.10
16 A. Chamberlain (Yeovil & D)	5:01.22
17 H. Sheraton (Millfield)	5:01.50
18 N. Carr (Barking)	5:01.72
19 L. Williams (Wigan Wasps)	5:01.84
20 A. Wooldridge (Co Birmingham)	5:01.87
21 S. Wells (Norwich Penguins)	5:03.52
22 S. Smith (Wigan Wasps)	5:03.71
23 N. Wilkin (Bo Kirklees)	5:05.92
24 M. Herbert (Runnymede)	5:08.49
25 N. Collins (Kelly College)	5:10.10
26 P. Barnett (Holywell)	5:11.75
27 T. Cook (Barking)	5:20.79

4×50 Metres Freestyle Club Relay

Final

1 Co Leicester	1:42.64
2 Sale	1:42.67
3 Co Newcastle	1:43.21
4 Portsmouth Northsea	1:43.82
5 Stockton Aquatics	1:44.13
6 RTW Monson	1:45.41
7 Barnet Copthall	1:45.63
8 Bo of Kirklees	1:45.77

Heat Times

1 Co Leicester	1:43.10
2 Sale	1:43.44
3 Portsmouth Northsea	1:43.87
4 Stockton Aquatics	1:45.47
5 Co Newcastle	1:45.48
6 Barnet Copthall	1:45.81
7 RTW Monson	1:45.98
8 Bo Kirklees	1:46.01
9 Beckenham	1:46.04
10 Norwich Penguins	1:46.09
11 Nova Centurion	1:46.21
12 Co Leeds	1:46.28
13 Loughborough T	1:46.30
14 Co Southampton	1:46.39
15 Killerwhales	1:46.60

16 Millfield	1:46.63
17 Leatherhead	1:46.78
18 Bracknell	1:46.89
19 Co Chester	1:47.29
20 Co Bristol	1:47.41
21 Rotherham Metro	1:47.42
22 Co Coventry	1:47.88
23 Co Birmingham	1:47.98
24 Shiverers	1:48.24
25 Luton	1:48.40
26 Oundle & D	1:48.63
27 Barking	1:48.93
28 Co Manchester	1:48.95
29 Braintree & Bocking	1:49.04
30 Amersham	1:49.30
31 Rochford & D	1:49.83
32 Regent Tigers	1:50.11
33 Harrow & Wealdstone	1:50.25
34 Crompton Classics	1:50.28
35 Rushmoor Royals	1:50.91
36 Runnymede	1:51.20
37 Haverhill	1:51.43
Reading	

4×50 Metres Medley Club Relay

Final

1 Portsmouth Northsea	1:54.90
2 Barking	1:55.25
3 Stockton Aquatics	1:55.47
4 Millfield	1:56.97
5 Oundle & D	1:57.41
6 Co Coventry	1:57.62
7 Nova Centurion	1:58.15
8 Braintree & Bocking	1:58.48

Heat Times

1 Portsmouth Northsea	1:55.91
2 Stockton Aquatics	1:56.50
3 Barking	1:56.63
4 Co Coventry	1:57.08
5 Millfield	1:57.57
6 Oundle & D	1:58.19
7 Nova Centurion	1:58.27
8 Braintree & Bocking	1:58.36
9 Bo Kirklees	1:58.39
10 Warrington Warriors	1:58.51
11 RTW Monson	1:58.90
12 Co Leeds	1:59.07
13 Co Newcastle	1:59.09
14 Bracknell	1:59.53
15 Co Southampton	1:59.59
16 Beckenham	1:59.74
17 Norwich Penguins	1:59.93
18 Leatherhead	1:59.95
19 Southgate	2:00.40
20 Rotherham Metro	2:00.53
21 Co Leicester	2:01.06
22 Killerwhales	2:01.10
23 Rochford & D	2:01.15
24 Harrow & Wealdstone	2:01.82
25 Crompton Classics	2:01.89
26 Co Chester	2:02.41
27 Luton	2:02.55
28 Co Bristol	2:02.67
29 Co Birmingham	2:02.86
30 Reading	2:03.61
31 Cheadle & D	2:03.68
32 Co Manchester	2:03.83
33 Loughborough T	2:04.67
34 Shiverers	2:05.22

35	Runnymede	2:05.98
36	Haverhill	2:06.33
37	Rushmoor Royals	2:07.12
	Sale	DIS
	Barnet Copthall	DIS

Girls

100 Metres Freestyle
Final

1	D. Morgan (Derwentside)	59.27
2	J. McHarg (Portsmouth Northsea)	59.39
3	D. Jones (Co Chester)	59.50
4	G. Brooks (Greenwich B Mariners)	59.65
5	L. Smart (Co Chester)	1:00.60
6	R. Shurey (Hounslow B)	1:00.69
7	J. Waite (Co Southampton)	1:01.11
8	J. Constable (Thornbury)	1:01.20

Heat Times

1	G. Brooks (Greenwich B Mariners)	1:00.09
2	D. Morgan (Derwentside)	1:00.12
3	J. McHarg (Portsmouth Northsea)	1:00.34
4	D. Jones (Co Chester)	1:00.48
5	L. Smart (Co Chester)	1:00.63
6	J. Waite (Co Southampton)	1:00.73
7	J. Constable (Thornbury)	1:00.78
8	R. Shurey (Hounslow B)	1:01.00
9	C. Mayor (Bodmin & D)	1:01.01
10	D. Salmon (Kelly College)	1:01.08
11	E. Brooks (Redbridge B)	1:01.10
12	C. Piggott (Co Birmingham)	1:01.54
13	N. Matthews (Shiverers)	1:01.56
14	J. Ratcliffe (Co Manchester)	1:01.59
15	K. Johnson (Colchester)	1:01.60
16	J. Dowling (Bo Burnley CATS)	1:01.61
17	S. Ridler (Rochford & D)	1:01.66
18	S. Vick (Co Sheffield)	1:01.84
19	M. George (Bo Waltham Forest)	1:01.90
20	L. Marchant (Nova Centurion)	1:01.96
21	L. Findlay (Kelly College)	1:02.05
22	J. Evans (Co Swansea)	1:02.17
23	C. Banks (York C)	1:02.18
24	L. Kilgour (Co Birmingham)	1:02.33

Debbie Morgan   Artwood Photography

25	E. Rumbold (Norwich Penguins)	1:02.40
26	S. Littlewood (Manchester U Salford)	1:02.44
27	C. Harris (Northampton)	1:02.73
28	J. Marshall (Norwich Penguins)	1:02.79
29	R. Garry (Warrington Warriors)	1:02.81
30	R. Swain (Co Derby)	1:02.85
31	S. Eade (Ipswich)	1:03.17
32	H. Corlett (Satellite)	1:03.18
33	R. Brown (Bo Burnley CATS)	1:03.19
34	C. Hall (Thurrock)	1:03.29
	M. Hynes (Co Manchester)	1:03.29
36	L. Appleton (Warrington Warriors)	1:03.32
37	S. Kench (Co Chester)	1:03.57
38	M. Read (Guildford C)	1:03.67
39	G. Cook (Bo Kirklees)	1:03.74
40	D. Powell (Maxwell)	1:04.22
41	G. Harvey (Millfield)	1:04.27
42	B. Turner (Manchester U Salford)	1:04.31
43	J. Punter (Hounslow B)	1:04.71
44	R. Bridger (Nova Centurion)	1:04.85
45	P. Hudson (Ferndown Otters)	1:05.01

200 Metres Freestyle
Final

1	D. Morgan (Derwentside)	2:06.37
2	D. Jones (Co Chester)	2:07.35
3	L. Smart (Co Chester)	2:08.82
4	L. Sonn (Co Southampton)	2:09.93
5	M. George (Bo Waltham Forest)	2:10.03
6	C. Banks (York C)	2:10.53
7	S. Foggo (Co Newcastle)	2:10.62
8	L. Kilgour (Co Birmingham)	2:12.00

Heat Times

1	D. Morgan (Derwentside)	2:09.07
2	D. Jones (Co Chester)	2:09.26
3	L. Smart (Co Chester)	2:09.54
4	C. Banks (York C)	2:10.70
5	L. Sonn (Co Southampton)	2:11.28
	M. George (Bo Waltham Forest)	2:11.28
7	S. Foggo (Co Newcastle)	2:11.31
8	L. Kilgour (Co Birmingham)	2:11.47
9	C. Piggott (Co Birmingham)	2:11.83
10	E. Brooks (Redbridge B)	2:11.91
11	K. Johnson (Colchester)	2:12.33
12	J. Waite (Co Southampton)	2:12.55
13	S. Vick (Co Sheffield)	2:12.79
14	R. Shurey (Hounslow B)	2:12.85
15	E. Rumbold (Norwich Penguins)	2:12.89
16	A. Thorpe (Co Leeds)	2:12.92
17	J. McHarg (Portsmouth Northsea)	2:13.03
18	H. Osborne (Co Birmingham)	2:13.12
19	L. Marchant (Nova Centurion)	2:13.33
20	J. Marshall (Norwich Penguins)	2:13.42
21	R. Garry (Warrington Warriors)	2:13.74
22	J. Evans (Co Swansea)	2:13.94
23	G. Brooks (Greenwich B Mariners)	2:13.97
24	J. Ratcliffe (Co Manchester)	2:14.02
25	C. Harris (Northampton)	2:14.03
26	C. Mayor (Bodmin & D)	2:14.11
27	P. Richardson (Eastbourne)	2:14.57
28	H. Goddard (Gloucester C)	2:14.66
29	V. Crane (Greenwich B Mariners)	2:14.84
30	L. Appleton (Warrington Warriors)	2:15.12
31	A. Dean (Warrington Warriors)	2:15.34
32	P. Adams (Co Leeds)	2:15.93
33	S. Kench (Co Chester)	2:15.96
34	H. Corlett (Satellite)	2:16.24
35	N. Matthews (Shiverers)	2:16.36
36	E. Jones (Co Chester)	2:16.43

37	S. Littlewood (Manchester U Salford)	2:16.88
38	C. Stirrup (Hindley)	2:17.29
39	L. Kettle (Stockton Aquatics)	2:17.37
40	R. Brown (Bo Burnley CATS)	2:17.42
41	S. Akers (Co Cardiff)	2:17.58
42	J. Pitt (Beckenham)	2:18.21
43	S. Ridler (Rochford & D)	2:18.45
44	J. Corbett (Co Birmingham)	2:18.76
45	L. Gahan (Kelly College)	2:19.29
46	J. Birkett (Co Lincoln Pentaqua)	2:23.00

400 Metres Freestyle
Heat Times (no final)

1	D. Jones (Co Chester)	4:26.33
2	D. Morgan (Derwentside)	4:26.59
3	L. Sonn (Co Southampton)	4:27.98
4	L. Smart (Co Chester)	4:28.48
5	R. Shurey (Hounslow B)	4:31.32
6	L. Kilgour (Co Birmingham)	4:31.36
7	D. Salmon (Kelly College)	4:31.62
8	M. George (Bo Waltham Forest)	4:31.71
9	S. Foggo (Co Newcastle)	4:32.31
10	C. Piggott (Co Birmingham)	4:32.38
11	A. Thorpe (Co Leeds)	4:36.82
12	K. Johnson (Colchester)	4:37.81
13	L. Wall (Co Bradford)	4:38.58
	P. Richardson (Eastbourne)	
15	J. Ratcliffe (Co Manchester)	4:38.75
16	C. Mayor (Bodmin & D)	4:38.84
17	S. Kench (Co Chester)	4:39.12
18	E. Brooks (Redbridge B)	4:39.21
19	V. Barnes (Co Manchester)	4:39.76
20	L. Appleton (Warrington Warriors)	4:40.14
21	V. Crane (Greenwich B Mariners)	4:40.31
22	K. Jones (Co Chester)	4:41.24
23	P. Adams (Co Leeds)	4:41.30
24	L. Kettle (Stockton Metro)	4:41.70
25	E. Jones (Co Chester)	4:41.84
26	H. Paull (Kelly College)	4:43.57
27	S. Akers (Co Cardiff)	4:46.14
28	C. Wanbon (Warrington Warriors)	4:46.83
29	J. Marshall (Norwich Penguins)	4:48.23

800 Metres Freestyle
Heat Times (no final)

1	E. Arnold (Nottingham Northern)	8:58.15
2	L. Smart (Co Chester)	9:01.69
3	S. Foggo (Co Newcastle)	9:05.58
4	L. Sonn (Co Southampton)	9:09.54
5	D. Morgan (Derwentside)	9:10.47
6	C. Piggott (Co Birmingham)	9:12.59
7	R. Shurey (Hounslow B)	9:15.43
8	L. Kilgour (Co Birmingham)	9:15.95
9	D. Jones (Co Chester)	9:17.29
10	A. Thorpe (Co Leeds)	9:20.12
11	G. Cook (Bo Kirklees)	9:25.69
	K. Johnson (Colchester)	
13	V. Barnes (Co Manchester)	9:26.13
14	V. Crane (Greenwich B Mariners)	9:26.59
15	L. Appleton (Warrington Warriors)	9:27.25
16	J. Farnsworth (Co Leeds)	9:28.90
17	S. Kench (Co Chester)	9:30.24
18	C. Mayor (Bodmin & D)	9:32.79
19	K. Jones (Co Chester)	9:33.85
20	M. George (Bo Waltham Forest)	9:34.96
21	R. Loveman (Co Southampton)	9:36.52
22	H. Speed (Co Leeds)	9:40.00
23	S. Akers (Co Cardiff)	9:43.03
24	J. Owen (Chester le Street)	9:44.17

25	P. Richardson (Eastbourne)	9:44.64
26	C. Wanbon (Warrington Warriors)	9:45.10
27	E. Jones (Co Chester)	9:47.08
28	H. Thistlewaite (Piranha)	9:50.12
29	J. Wilcock (St Helens)	9:59.68

100 Metres Backstroke
Final

1	L. Racster (Portsmouth Northsea)	1:07.13
2	J. Corbett (Co Birmingham)	1:07.82
3	J. Evans (Co Swansea)	1:08.27
4	E. Tattum (Bracknell)	1:08.60
5	H. Osborne (Co Birmingham)	1:09.09
6	M. Read (Guildford C)	1:09.76
7	S. Swettenham (Fleetwood & D)	1:10.29
8	L. Gahan (Kelly College)	1:10.65

Heat Times

1	L. Racster (Portsmouth Northsea)	1:07.63
2	E. Tattum (Bracknell)	1:08.63
3	J. Corbett (Co Birmingham)	1:08.76
4	M. Read (Guildford C)	1:09.44
5	H. Osborne (Co Birmingham)	1:09.68
6	S. Swettenham (Fleetwood & D)	1:09.72
7	L. Gahan (Kelly College)	1:09.86
8	J. Evans (Co Swansea)	1:09.96
9	E. Firbank (Stockton Aquatics)	1:10.61
10	T. Sullivan (Piranha)	1:10.83
11	Z. Cray (Clacton)	1:10.88
12	K. Johnson (Colchester)	1:11.09
13	C. Maggs (Co Bristol)	1:11.28
14	R. Brown (Bo Burnley CATS)	1:11.33
15	G. Harvey (Millfield)	1:11.52
16	R. Jenkins (Torfaen)	1:11.68
17	Y. Lester (Braintree & Bocking)	1:11.69
18	B. Turner (Manchester U Salford)	1:11.71
19	A. Mackay (Warrington Warriors)	1:11.80
20	R. Britton (Bristol Central)	1:11.83
	E. Rumbold (Norwich Penguins)	
22	J. Pitt (Beckenham)	1:12.07
23	L. Figes (Bristol Central)	1:12.27
24	L. Evans (Thurrock)	1:12.41
25	L. Neale (Chase)	1:12.63
26	A. Wood (Haden Hill)	1:12.72
27	H. Koban (Nova Centurion)	1:12.73
28	S. Littlewood (Manchester U Salford)	1:12.90

Linda Racster   Artwood Photography

29 K. Jones (Co Milton Keynes) 1:12.99
30 H. Storey (Co Newcastle) 1:13.11
31 C. Nash (Co Oxford)
    M. Hynes (Co Manchester) 1:13.20
33 C. Banks (York C) 1:13.30
34 K. Colby (Bracknell) 1:13.78
35 J. Sheppard (Nova Centurion) 1:14.06
36 L. Mee (Smiths) 1:14.11
37 S. Mackley (Rochford & D) 1:14.14
38 S. Higgins (Hounslow B) 1:14.46
39 M. Vanderstelt (Canada) 1:14.77
40 V. Keat (Bodmin & D) 1:16.48

200 Metres Backstroke
Final

1 L. Racster (Portsmouth Northsea) 2:23.71
2 D. Salmon (Kelly College) 2:27.00
3 J. Corbett (Co Birmingham) 2:27.21
4 E. Tattum (Bracknell) 2:28.89
5 J. Evans (Co Swansea) 2:29.12
6 R. Britton (Bristol Central) 2:29.53
7 M. Read (Guildford C) 2:30.02
8 L. Gahan (Kelly College) 2:30.43

Heat Times

1 L. Racster (Portsmouth Northsea) 2:25.37
2 D. Salmon (Kelly College) 2:26.63
3 L. Gahan (Kelly College) 2:28.12
4 J. Corbett (Co Birmingham) 2:28.90
5 E. Tattum (Bracknell) 2:29.27
6 M. Read (Guildford C) 2:29.75
7 J. Evans (Co Swansea) 2:30.29
8 R. Britton (Bristol Central) 2:30.65
9 H. Osborne (Co Birmingham) 2:31.48
10 S. Swettenham (Fleetwood & D) 2:31.50
11 A. Mackay (Warrington Warriors) 2:31.58
12 R. Loveman (Co Southampton) 2:32.20
13 D. Jones (Co Chester) 2:32.44
14 K. Johnson (Colchester) 2:32.81
15 H. Koban (Nova Centurion) 2:33.63
16 E. Firbank (Stockton Aquatics) 2:33.72
17 C. Maggs (Co Bristol) 2:34.22
18 L. Wall (Co Bradford) 2:34.35
19 L. Evans (Thurrock) 2:34.78
20 M. Hynes (Co Manchester) 2:35.39
21 Y. Lester (Braintree & Bocking) 2:35.56
22 B. Turner (Manchester U Salford) ... 2:36.15
23 S. Higgins (Hounslow B) 2:36.63
24 M. Vanderstelt (Canada) 2:36.96
25 C. Nash (Co Oxford) 2:37.47
26 J. Whiting (Croydon Amphibians) 2:37.81
27 P. Richardson (Eastbourne) 2:37.95
28 V. Goodwin (Millfield) 2:37.98
29 P. Adams (Co Leeds) 2:38.05
30 G. Harvey (Millfield) 2:38.06
31 C. Banks (York C) 2:38.60
32 G. Thompson
    (Gateshead & Whickham) 2:39.32
33 H. Storey (Co Newcastle) 2:40.80
34 S. Littlewood (Manchester U Salford) . 2:41.00
35 C. Harris (Northampton) 2:41.23
36 J. Sheppard (Nova Centurion) 2:41.73
37 R. Rowlands (Prescot) 2:41.93
38 C. Russ (Harrow & Wealdstone) 2:42.24
39 S. Mackley (Rochford & D) .... DNF

100 Metres Breaststroke
Final

1 H. Alder (Harrow & Wealdstone) 1:15.25
2 R. Swain (Co Derby) 1:15.93

Hazel Alder   Artwood Photography

3 C. Gable (Stockport Metro) 1:16.27
4 J. Swindlehurst (Sale) 1:16.88
5 C. Piggott (Co Birmingham) 1:17.16
6 G. Brooks (Greenwich B Mariners) 1:18.18
7 N. James (Nova Centurion) 1:18.32
8 J. Williamson (Co Southampton) 1:18.52

Heat Times

1 H. Alder (Harrow & Wealdstone) 1:16.96
2 R. Swain (Co Derby) 1:17.90
3 J. Swindlehurst (Sale)
   C. Piggott (Co Birmingham) 1:17.94
5 C. Gable (Stockport Metro) 1:18.08
6 N. James (Nova Centurion) 1:18.28
7 G. Brooks (Greenwich B Mariners) 1:18.47
8 J. Williamson (Co Southampton) 1:18.55
9 S. Brown (Douglas) 1:18.92
10 L. Findlay (Kelly College) 1:19.26
11 J. Terry (Nova Centurion) 1:19.44
12 L. Clarke (Co Newcastle) 1:19.69
13 Z. Platt (Portsmouth Northsea) 1:19.77
14 J. Kearley (Co Derby) 1:19.91
15 C. Wilson (Hindley) 1:20.06
16 G. Price (Satellite)
    A. Pickersgill (Stockport Metro) . 1:20.18
18 T. Sullivan (Piranha) 1:20.30
19 E. Rumbold (Norwich Penguins) 1:20.34
20 J. Waite (Co Southampton) 1:20.35
21 P. Richardson (Eastbourne) 1:20.38
22 J. Constable (Thornbury) 1:20.57
23 A. Dean (Warrington Warriors)
    H. Corlett (Satellite) 1:20.60
25 M. Young (Colchester)
    K. Poutney (Co Coventry) 1:20.64
27 H. Douthwaite (York C) 1:20.98
28 L. Harding (Saxon Crown) 1:21.09
29 J. Morton (Jersey) 1:21.19
30 S. Collins (Colchester) 1:21.47
31 T. Gee (Bo Burnley CATS) 1:21.61
32 J. Coventry (Keynsham) 1:21.68
33 L. Miller (Beckenham) 1:21.91
34 L. James (Witney & D) 1:22.07
35 C. Soper (Ferndown Otters) 1:22.31
36 K. Jones (Co Chester) 1:22.40
37 J. Farnsworth (Co Leeds) 1:22.41

71

38	S. Swettenham (Fleetwood & D)	1:22.43
39	K. Jackson (Greenwich B Mariners)	1:22.65
40	T. Sim (Chester le Street)	1:22.72
41	L. Wall (Co Bradford)	1:22.76
42	G. Bennett (Gosport Dolphins)	1:22.78
43	S. Vick (Co Sheffield)	1:23.07
44	A. Cawdery (Newport & Maindee)	1:23.10
45	J. Buddle (Maxwell)	1:23.35
46	D. Garrod (Hatfield)	1:23.74
47	S. Ridler (Rochford & D)	1:23.85
48	C. Walbyoff (Pontypool)	1:24.44
49	J. Matheron (Bo Southend)	1:24.52
50	A. Clinkard (Middlesbrough)	1:24.64
51	C. Harris (Northampton)	1:25.24
52	M. Lister (Co Leicester)	1:26.37

200 Metres Breaststroke
Final

1	C. Piggott (Co Birmingham)	2:41.60
2	H. Alder (Harrow & Wealdstone)	2:42.71
3	N. James (Nova Centurion)	2:45.77
4	C. Gable (Stockport Metro)	2:47.36
5	R. Swain (Co Derby)	2:49.92
6	J. Swindlehurst (Sale)	2:50.20
7	S. Brown (Douglas)	2:50.26
8	L. Clarke (Co Newcastle)	2:51.34

Heat Times

1	C. Piggott (Co Birmingham)	2:42.70
2	H. Alder (Harrow & Wealdstone)	2:44.66
3	C. Gable (Stockport Metro)	2:46.89
4	N. James (Nova Centurion)	2:47.09
5	L. Clarke (Co Newcastle)	2:48.45
6	J. Swindlehurst (Sale)	2:48.88
7	S. Brown (Douglas)	2:48.91
8	R. Swain (Co Derby)	2:49.60
9	Z. Platt (Portsmouth Northsea)	2:49.62
10	J. Williamson (Co Southampton)	2:49.99
11	G. Price (Satellite)	2:50.16
12	K. Poutney (Co Coventry)	2:50.22
13	A. Dean (Warrington Warriors)	2:50.30
14	P. Richardson (Eastbourne)	2:50.41
15	H. Corlett (Satellite)	2:51.17
16	E. Rumbold (Norwich Penguins)	2:51.24
17	I. Farnsworth (Co Leeds)	2:51.45
18	S. Collins (Colchester)	2:51.48
19	T. Sullivan (Piranha)	2:51.57
20	J. Terry (Nova Centurion)	2:51.67
21	K. Jones (Co Chester)	2:51.84
22	H. Goddard (Gloucester C)	2:51.95
23	C. Powell (Torfaen)	2:52.66
24	J. Matheron (Bo Southend)	2:53.14
25	T. Sim (Chester le Street)	2:53.16
26	J. Kearley (Co Derby)	2:54.54
27	T. Gee (Bo Burnley CATS)	2:54.56
28	C. Wilson (Hindley)	2:54.85
29	E. Spokes (Co Coventry)	2:55.02
30	L. Harding (Saxon Crown)	2:55.05
31	F. O'Reilly (Co Coventry)	2:55.61
32	J. Morton (Jersey)	2:56.15
33	A. Pickersgill (Stockport Metro)	2:56.30
34	L. Marchant (Nova Centurion)	2:56.82
35	D. Lancaster (Warrington Warriors)	2:57.31
36	M. Young (Colchester)	2:57.34
37	V. Crane (Greenwich B Mariners)	2:57.48
38	K. Fellows (Soundwell)	2:57.50
39	C. Walbyoff (Pontypool)	2:57.68
40	J. Austin (Ruislip & Northwood)	2:58.47
41	J. Clowes (COSACSS)	2:58.89
42	A. Diskin (Co Manchester)	2:58.96

43	J. Smith (Oundle & D)	2:58.98
44	S. Swettenham (Fleetwood & D)	2:59.26
45	A. Clinkard (Middlesbrough)	2:59.96
46	S. Davies (Fareham Nomads)	3:02.13
47	H. Worth (Darlington)	3:02.28
48	K. Owen (Killerwhales)	3:02.44
49	M. Lister (Co Leicester)	3:03.40

100 Metres Butterfly
Final

1	J. Dowling (Bo Burnley CATS)	1:04.13
2	C. Coward (Wigan Wasps)	1:06.16
3	A. Mackay (Warrington Warriors)	1:06.54
4	R. Shurey (Hounslow B)	1:06.62
5	L. Kilgour (Co Birmingham)	1:07.74
6	S. McGill (Ferndown Otters)	1:07.83
7	Z. Platt (Portsmouth Northsea)	1:08.46
8	H. Paull (Kelly College)	1:09.33

Heat Times

1	J. Dowling (Bo Burnley CATS)	1:06.35
2	C. Coward (Wigan Wasps)	1:07.16
3	A. Mackay (Warrington Warriors)	1:07.20
4	L. Kilgour (Co Birmingham)	1:07.46
5	S. McGill (Ferndown Otters)	1:07.58
6	R. Shurey (Hounslow B)	1:07.65
7	Z. Platt (Portsmouth Northsea)	1:08.26
8	H. Paull (Kelly College)	1:08.29
9	M. Lang (Warrington Warriors)	1:08.43
10	M. Hynes (Co Manchester)	1:08.66
11	G. Bennett (Gosport Dolphins)	1:08.72
12	E. Rumbold (Norwich Penguins)	1:08.88
13	E. Brooks (Redbridge B)	1:08.94
14	G. Berger (Ferndown Otters)	1:09.07
15	L. Smart (Co Chester)	1:09.13
16	J. Constable (Thornbury)	1:09.19
17	L. Richards (Stockton Aquatics)	1:09.29
18	H. Osborne (Co Birmingham)	1:09.42
19	R. Cooper (Warrington Warriors)	1:09.46
20	J. Crewdson (Co Manchester)	1:09.52
21	T. Sullivan (Piranha)	1:09.57
22	K. Jones (Co Chester)	1:09.63
23	D. Morgan (Derwentside)	1:09.67
24	M. George (Bo Waltham Forest)	1:09.72
25	L. Appleton (Warrington Warriors)	1:09.75

Caroline Gable   Artwood Photography

26 J. Owen (Chester le Street)	1:09.78
27 J. Corbett (Co Birmingham)	1:09.88
28 K. Seymour (Southwold)	1:09.91
29 R. Brown (Bo Burnley CATS)	1:10.06
30 J. Evans (Co Swansea)	1:10.18
31 J. Smith (Oundle & D)	1:10.30
32 S. Duggan (Hounslow B)	1:10.53
33 P. Richardson (Eastbourne)	1:10.68
34 J. Birkett (Co Lincoln Pentaqua)	1:10.82
35 P. Adams (Co Leeds)	1:10.86
36 S. Foggo (Co Newcastle)	1:10.88
37 H. Koban (Nova Centurion)	1:10.92
38 J. Waite (Co Southampton)	1:10.96
39 C. Mabb (Beckenham)	1:11.02
40 C. Dancer (Dover Lifeguard)	1:11.11
41 R. Kench (Co Chester)	1:11.23
42 H. Corlett (Satellite)	1:11.42
43 P. Hudson (Ferndown Otters)	1:12.76
44 D. Garrod (Hatfield)	1:12.95
45 G. Harvey (Millfield)	1:13.64
46 M. Vanderstelt (Canada)	1:13.92
47 J. Broome (Co Milton Keynes)	1:15.01

200 Metres Butterfly
Final

1 J. Dowling (Bo Burnley CATS)	2:21.35
2 L. Kilgour (Co Birmingham)	2:22.51
3 C. Coward (Wigan Wasps)	2:22.77
4 S. McGill (Ferndown Otters)	2:25.59
5 R. Shurey (Hounslow B)	2:26.02
6 L. Smart (Co Chester)	2:26.19
7 L. Appleton (Warrington Warriors)	2:26.22
8 A. Mackay (Warrington Warriors)	2:28.21

Heat Times

1 J. Dowling (Bo Burnley CATS)	2:23.75
2 L. Kilgour (Co Birmingham)	2:24.30
3 C. Coward (Wigan Wasps)	2:25.38
4 S. McGill (Ferndown Otters)	2:26.42
5 R. Shurey (Hounslow B)	2:27.26
6 L. Appleton (Warrington Warriors)	2:27.40
7 A. Mackay (Warrington Warriors)	2:27.98
8 L. Smart (Co Chester)	2:28.20
9 R. Cooper (Warrington Warriors)	2:28.55
10 J. Owen (Chester le Street)	2:28.96
11 H. Osborne (Co Birmingham)	2:30.02
12 P. Richardson (Eastbourne)	2:30.06
13 E. Brooks (Redbridge B)	2:30.30
14 G. Bennett (Gosport Dolphins)	2:30.33
15 P. Adams (Co Leeds)	2:30.57
16 J. Crewdson (Co Manchester)	2:30.74
17 H. Koban (Nova Centurion)	2:30.75
18 J. Ratcliffe (Co Manchester)	2:31.32
19 J. Evans (Co Swansea)	2:31.42
20 K. Jones (Co Chester)	2:31.43
21 J. Wilcock (St Helens)	2:32.05
22 Z. Platt (Portsmouth Northsea)	2:32.29
23 K. Dawson (Bracknell)	2:32.60
24 E. Jones (Co Chester)	2:32.79
25 J. Smith (Oundle & D)	2:32.98
26 M. Lang (Warrington Warriors)	2:33.05
27 S. Preece (Warrington Warriors)	2:34.09
28 V. Crane (Greenwich B Mariners)	2:34.41
29 K. Seymour (Southwold)	2:34.56
30 K. Berry (Norwich Penguins)	2:34.76
31 M. Vanderstelt (Canada)	2:35.27
32 A. Griffin (Co Bradford)	2:35.64
33 J. Corbett (Co Birmingham)	2:35.95
34 R. Brown (Bo Burnley CATS)	2:37.36
35 S. Miller (Killerwhales)	2:37.56

36 D. Murray (Isle of Thanet)	2:38.46
37 C. Dancer (Dover Lifeguard)	2:41.15
38 J. Cooke (Poole)	2:41.92
39 H. Thistlewaite (Piranha)	2:42.55
40 J. Matheron (Bo Southend)	2:43.92

200 Metres Individual Medley
Final

1 J. Dowling (Bo Burnley CATS)	2:22.74
2 C. Piggott (Co Birmingham)	2:24.47
3 S. Vick (Co Sheffield)	2:27.79
4 Z. Platt (Portsmouth Northsea)	2:28.94
5 E. Rumbold (Norwich Penguins)	2:29.44
6 H. Osborne (Co Birmingham)	2:29.67
7 L. Wall (Co Bradford)	2:30.61
8 K. Jones (Co Chester)	2:31.27

Heat Times

1 C. Piggott (Co Birmingham)	2:26.59
2 J. Dowling (Bo Burnley CATS)	2:27.34
3 Z. Platt (Portsmouth Northsea)	2:28.90
4 H. Osborne (Co Birmingham)	2:28.95
5 S. Vick (Co Sheffield)	2:29.19
6 E. Rumbold (Norwich Penguins)	2:29.44
7 L. Wall (Co Bradford)	2:29.62
8 K. Jones (Co Chester)	2:29.95
9 K. Johnson (Colchester)	2:30.08
10 P. Richardson (Eastbourne)	2:30.37
11 T. Sullivan (Piranha)	2:30.54
12 J. Smith (Oundle & D)	2:30.56
13 A. Dean (Warrington Warriors)	2:30.61
14 A. Mackay (Warrington Warriors)	2:31.14
15 H. Goddard (Gloucester C)	2:31.60
16 S. McGill (Ferndown Otters)	2:31.85
17 L. Marchant (Nova Centurion)	2:31.88
18 L. Richards (Stockton Aquatics)	2:32.54
19 D. Morgan (Derwentside)	2:32.59
20 L. Appleton (Warrington Warriors)	2:32.63
21 H. Corlett (Satellite)	2:32.72
22 C. Banks (York C)	2:32.82
23 R. Shurey (Hounslow B)	2:32.84
24 D. Salmon (Kelly College)	2:32.90
25 S. Foggo (Co Newcastle)	2:33.06
26 S. Swettenham (Fleetwood & D)	2:33.13
27 J. Swindlehurst (Sale)	2:33.59
28 M. Read (Guildford C)	2:33.78
29 M. Hynes (Co Manchester)	2:34.28
30 G. Brooks (Greenwich B Mariners)	2:34.47
31 G. Harvey (Millfield)	2:35.94
32 D. Garrod (Hatfield)	2:36.68
33 E. Firbank (Stockton Aquatics)	2:36.93
34 M. Vanderstelt (Canada)	2:37.81

400 Metres Individual Medley
Heat Times (no final)

1 L. Findlay (Kelly College)	5:01.59
2 J. Dowling (Bo Burnley CATS)	5:03.62
3 C. Piggott (Co Birmingham)	5:04.10
4 S. Foggo (Co Newcastle)	5:11.99
5 L. Smart (Co Chester)	5:12.23
6 K. Jones (Co Chester)	5:13.49
7 S. Vick (Co Sheffield)	5:15.24
8 L. Kilgour (Co Birmingham)	5:16.00
9 L. Wall (Co Bradford)	5:16.10
10 H. Osborne (Co Birmingham)	5:16.52
11 Z. Platt (Portsmouth Northsea)	5:17.32
12 R. Shurey (Hounslow B)	5:18.17
13 P. Richardson (Eastbourne)	5:20.05
14 A. Mackay (Warrington Warriors)	5:20.11
15 T. Sullivan (Piranha)	5:20.38

Lucy Findlay

16	J. Smith (Oundle & D)	5:20.97
17	E. Rumbold (Norwich Penguins)	5:21.54
18	V. Crane (Greenwich B Mariners)	5:23.06
19	L. Appleton (Warrington Warriors)	5:24.38
20	L. Marchant (Nova Centurion)	5:24.74
21	R. Cooper (Warrington Warriors)	5:24.95
22	H. Koban (Nova Centurion)	5:25.29
23	R. Loveman (Co Southampton)	5:26.44
24	P. Adams (Co Leeds)	5:26.67
25	A. Thorpe (Co Leeds)	5:26.72
26	J. Owen (Chester le Street)	5:27.10
27	M. Vanderstelt (Canada)	5:28.60
28	J. Matheron (Bo Southend)	5:33.45
29	H. Thistlethwaite (Piranha)	5:35.02
	C. Harris (Northampton)	DIS
	C. Banks (York C)	DIS

4×50 Metres Freestyle Club Relay
Final

1	Kelly College	1:55.22
2	Portsmouth Northsea	1:55.27
	Co Chester	
4	Co Birmingham	1:55.65
5	Co Manchester	1:55.70
6	Rochford & D	1:56.10
7	Warrington Warriors	1:56.18
8	Beckenham	1:57.07

Heat Times

1	Co Chester	1:55.75
2	Portsmouth Northsea	1:56.02
3	Co Manchester	1:56.53
4	Kelly College	1:56.58
5	Co Birmingham	1:56.64
6	Beckenham	1:56.71
7	Rochford & D	1:56.89
8	Warrington Warriors	1:57.24
9	Hounslow B	1:57.61
10	Nova Centurion	1:58.04
11	Ferndown Otters	1:58.25
12	York C	1:58.40
13	Co Southampton	1:58.58
14	Co Leeds	1:58.78
15	Thornbury	1:58.87
16	Norwich Penguins	1:59.36

17	Fareham Nomads	1:59.45
18	Bracknell	1:59.56
19	Harrow & Wealdstone	1:59.85
20	Co Newcastle	1:59.98
21	Greenwich B Mariners	2:00.23
22	Colchester	2:00.24
23	Orpington	2:00.29
24	Co Leicester	2:00.83
25	Thurrock	2:01.13
26	Woodside & Thornton Heath	2:01.49
27	Manchester U Salford	2:01.76
28	Reading	2:01.91
	Co Coventry	
30	Rushmoor Royals	2:01.97
31	Barking	2:02.67
32	Millfield	2:04.01
	Sale	DIS

4×50 Metres Medley Club Relay
Final

1	Kelly College	2:04.56
2	Portsmouth Northsea	2:05.39
3	Co Birmingham	2:07.13
4	Co Southampton	2:08.82
5	Warrington Warriors	2:09.08
6	Beckenham	2:09.12
7	Nova Centurion	2:09.54
8	Ferndown Otters	2:10.03

Heat Times

1	Kelly College	2:07.36
2	Portsmouth Northsea	2:07.41
3	Co Birmingham	2:08.50
4	Co Southampton	2:10.52
5	Warrington Warriors	2:10.61
6	Nova Centurion	2:10.94
7	Beckenham	2:11.05
8	Ferndown Otters	2:11.60
9	Harrow & Wealdstone	2:11.83
10	Colchester	2:12.42
11	Co Newcastle	2:12.62
12	Co Manchester	2:13.35
13	Co Leeds	2:13.45
	Co Chester	
15	York C	2:13.50
16	Norwich Penguins	2:13.74
17	Hounslow B	2:14.02
18	Greenwich B Mariners	2:14.36
19	Fareham Nomads	2:14.50
20	Rochford & D	2:15.21
21	Manchester U Salford	2:15.77
22	Rushmoor Royals	2:15.90
23	Bracknell	2:15.92
24	Sale	2:15.94
25	Thurrock	2:16.16
26	Millfield	2:16.60
27	Co Leicester	2:17.09
28	Reading	2:17.25
29	Co Coventry	2:18.47
30	Barking	2:19.37

17/18 Years Age Group Boys

100 Metres Freestyle
Final

1	A. Shortman (Bristol Central)	52.73
2	D. Gatland (Beckenham)	52.83
3	M. Hanby (Nova Centurion)	53.12

4	M. Levine (Co Sheffield)	53.63
5	J. Kearney (Nova Centurion)	54.83
6	C. Jones (Co Swansea)	54.98
7	T. Hart (Thurrock)	55.18
8	M. Poole (Co Coventry)	55.57

Heat Times

1	D. Gatland (Beckenham)	
	M. Levine (Co Sheffield)	53.75
3	A. Shortman (Bristol Central)	54.10
4	M. Hanby (Nova Centurion)	54.27
5	M. Poole (Co Coventry)	54.66
6	J. Kearney (Nova Centurion)	54.75
7	C. Jones (Co Swansea)	54.77
8	T. Hart (Thurrock)	54.94
9	M. O'Connor (Co Manchester)	55.26
10	J. Brownhill (Beckenham)	55.54
11	S. Moore (Oundle & D)	55.56
12	J. Sadler (Witney & D)	55.81
13	M. Austin (Newport & Maindee)	55.97
14	C. Smith (Co Chester)	56.02
15	L. Piggott (Beckenham)	56.04
16	M. Smith (Co Swansea)	56.09
17	S. Lee (Haverhill)	56.15
18	H. Wakeling (Broadway)	56.29
19	M. Wells (Manchester U Salford)	
	S. Taylor (Trenton Dolphins)	56.33
21	S. Akers (Shiverers)	58.54

200 Metres Freestyle
Final

1	D. Gatland (Beckenham)	1:54.68
2	M. Hanby (Nova Centurion)	1:56.12
3	S. Akers (Shiverers)	1:56.72
4	S. Moore (Oundle & D)	1:57.00
5	C. Jones (Co Swansea)	1:57.38
6	M. Poole (Co Coventry)	1:59.65
7	S. Lee (Haverhill)	1:59.70
8	M. O'Connor (Co Manchester)	2:02.93

Heat Times

1	C. Jones (Co Swansea)	1:58.13
2	S. Moore (Oundle & D)	1:58.67
3	S. Akers (Shiverers)	1:58.72
4	M. O'Connor (Co Manchester)	1:59.04
5	M. Poole (Co Coventry)	1:59.13

Austyn Shortman   Artwood Photography

6	D. Gatland (Beckenham)	1:59.37
7	S. Lee (Haverhill)	1:59.61
8	M. Hanby (Nova Centurion)	1:59.72
9	J. Gray (RTW Monson)	2:00.22
10	J. Brownhill (Beckenham)	2:00.26
11	M. Levine (Co Sheffield)	2:00.47
12	G. Hall (Reading)	2:00.73
13	D. Warren (Tynemouth)	2:01.26
14	M. Jones (Co Southampton)	2:01.39
15	T. Evans (Oundle & D)	2:01.58
16	R. Garbutt (Hull Olympic)	2:01.78
17	A. Palmer (Chester le Street)	2:01.97
18	A. McCarney (Enniskillen)	2:02.14
19	T. Lewis (Wycombe & D)	2:02.31
20	M. Wells (Manchester U Salford)	2:02.40
21	T. Morgan (Aquabears)	
	C. Heathcote (Nova Centurion)	2:02.78
23	J. McHale (Co Sheffield)	2:03.10
24	C. Smith (Co Chester)	2:03.34
25	M. Austin (Newport & Maindee)	2:03.40
26	T. Hart (Thurrock)	2:03.75
27	E. Goodson-Piper	
	(Camden Swiss Cottage)	2:03.76
28	J. Groom (Co Peterborough)	2:04.04
29	J. Hunter (Derwentside)	2:07.38

400 Metres Freestyle
Heat Times (no final)

1	S. Akers (Shiverers)	4:01.98
2	S. Moore (Oundle & D)	4:09.65
3	G. Hall (Reading)	4:12.24
4	C. Heathcote (Nova Centurion)	4:12.78
5	D. Warren (Tynemouth)	4:13.62
6	T. Lewis (Wycombe & D)	4:14.80
7	J. Gray (RTW Monson)	4:15.58
8	T. Morgan (Aquabears)	4:16.76
9	J. McHale (Co Sheffield)	4:17.54
10	S. Lee (Haverhill)	4:17.69
11	A. Palmer (Chester le Street)	4:18.99
12	C. Smith (Co Chester)	4:19.72
13	M. Poole (Co Coventry)	4:19.90
14	M. Hall (Co Bradford)	4:21.06
15	R. Garbutt (Hull Olympic)	4:21.81
16	D. Akers (Co Leeds)	4:22.27
17	E. Goodson-Piper	
	(Camden Swiss Cottage)	4:27.65
18	M. West (Co Milton Keynes)	4:35.92

1500 Metres Freestyle
Heat Times (no final)

1	S. Akers (Shiverers)	15:59.20
2	S. Moore (Oundle & D)	16:25.67
3	A. Robinson (Stockton Aquatics)	16:35.16
4	T. Lewis (Wycombe & D)	16:43.30
5	P. Kappes (Killerwhales)	16:48.90
6	G. Hall (Reading)	16:50.78
7	S. McQuaid (Co Manchester)	16:55.90
8	J. McHale (Co Sheffield)	16:59.26
9	B. Nowell (Torfaen)	16:59.38
10	B. Lafferty (Co Sheffield)	17:05.60
11	M. Hall (Co Bradford)	17:07.94
12	T. Morgan (Aquabears)	17:09.14
13	J. Hague (York C)	17:47.45
14	M. Bell (Canada)	18:53.15

100 Metres Backstroke
Final

1	M. O'Connor (Co Manchester)	59.82
2	A. Shortman (Bristol Central)	59.97

75

3 J. Kearney (Nova Centurion) — 1:00.53
4 J. Fleet (Bo Waltham Forest) — 1:01.03
5 N. Sherringham (Co Sheffield) — 1:01.29
6 G. Williams (Portsmouth Northsea) — 1:01.95
7 C. Jones (Co Swansea) — 1:02.10
8 J. Hunter (Derwentside) — 1:03.26

Heat Times

1 M. O'Connor (Co Manchester) — 1:01.38
2 J. Fleet (Bo Waltham Forest) — 1:01.44
3 A. Shortman (Bristol Central) — 1:01.65
4 J. Kearney (Nova Centurion) — 1:01.76
5 N. Sherringham (Co Sheffield) — 1:01.86
6 G. Williams (Portsmouth Northsea) — 1:02.15
7 J. Hunter (Derwentside) — 1:02.46
8 C. Jones (Co Swansea) — 1:02.57
9 C. Biss (Barnet Copthall) — 1:03.01
10 C. Hale (Hull Olympic) — 1:03.68
11 B. Rees (Wycombe & D) — 1:03.85
12 J. Brownhill (Beckenham) — 1:03.92
13 P. Barlow (Bracknell) — 1:04.06
14 A. Clarke (COSACSS) — 1:04.13
15 H. Wakeling (Broadway) — 1:04.30
16 R. Birch (Millfield) — 1:04.38
17 R. Pilling (Bo Kirklees) — 1:04.43
18 J. Wallis (Co Peterborough) — 1:04.51
19 A. Jefferson (Nova Centurion) — 1:04.65
20 B. Lafferty (Co Sheffield) — 1:04.68
21 S. Lee (Haverhill) — 1:05.04
22 S. Taylor (Co Peterborough) — 1:05.16
23 H. Lewisman (Co Oxford) — 1:05.30
24 L. Delaney (Manchester U Salford) — 1:05.46
25 P. Speller (Barking) — 1:05.73
26 J. Hague (York C) — 1:05.97
27 C. Sharpe (York C) — 1:06.07
28 M. Osteritter (Haverhill) — 1:07.03
29 H. Gell (Norwich Penguins) — 1:07.17

200 Metres Backstroke
Final

1 M. O'Connor (Co Manchester) — 2:09.04
2 J. Fleet (Bo Waltham Forest) — 2:09.60
3 J. Kearney (Nova Centurion) — 2:10.93
4 G. Williams (Portsmouth Northsea) — 2:13.24
5 C. Biss (Barnet Copthall) — 2:15.27
6 R. Pilling (Bo Kirklees) — 2:16.82
7 J. Hunter (Derwentside) — 2:17.40
8 B. Lafferty (Co Sheffield) — 2:18.36

Heat Times

1 J. Fleet (Bo Waltham Forest) — 2:12.31
2 G. Williams (Portsmouth Northsea) — 2:12.81
3 M. O'Connor (Co Manchester) — 2:14.53
4 J. Kearney (Nova Centurion) — 2:14.82
5 C. Biss (Barnet Copthall) — 2:16.20
6 R. Pilling (Bo Kirklees) — 2:17.21
7 J. Hunter (Derwentside) — 2:18.06
8 B. Lafferty (Co Sheffield) — 2:18.90
9 P. Kappes (Killerwhales) — 2:19.03
10 C. Hale (Hull Olympic) — 2:19.19
11 A. Roberts (Co Leeds) — 2:19.55
12 C. Sharpe (York C) — 2:19.61
13 J. McHale (Co Sheffield) — 2:20.10
14 G. Hall (Reading)
   A. Jefferson (Nova Centurion) — 2:20.23
16 D. Warren (Tynemouth) — 2:20.25
17 J. Hague (York C) — 2:20.91
18 C. Smith (Co Chester) — 2:21.02
19 M. Ellett (Killerwhales) — 2:21.40
20 H. Lewisman (Co Oxford) — 2:21.55
21 P. Barlow (Bracknell) — 2:22.48

22 P. Falle (Regent Tigers) — 2:22.72
23 G. Cowburn (Fleetwood & D) — 2:22.90
24 S. Taylor (Co Peterborough) — 2:22.98
25 R. Birch (Millfield) — 2:23.40
26 P. Martin (Co Sheffield) — 2:23.54
27 R. Morris (Norwich Penguins) — 2:23.61
28 J. Beale (Millfield) — 2:24.11
29 M. Flint (Co Southampton) — 2:25.20
30 M. Hall (Co Bradford) — 2:25.78
31 M. Osteritter (Haverhill) — 2:27.83
32 P. Speller (Barking) — 2:28.37
33 M. Bell (Canada) — 2:30.89

100 Metres Breaststroke
Final

1 N. Polkinghorne (Truro C) — 1:06.69
2 R. Maden (Aquabears) — 1:06.95
3 C. Thompson (Co Bradford) — 1:07.50
4 T. Ashwell (Ipswich) — 1:08.24
5 D. Entwistle (Royton) — 1:08.57
6 M. Whittaker (Co Southampton) — 1:09.43
7 M. Weighton (Wulfrunians) — 1:09.55
8 A. Buller (Stockport Metro) — 1:10.83

Heat Times

1 N. Polkinghorne (Truro C) — 1:07.69
2 R. Maden (Aquabears) — 1:07.71
3 D. Entwistle (Royton) — 1:08.35
4 C. Thompson (Co Bradford) — 1:08.86
5 T. Ashwell (Ipswich) — 1:09.03
6 M. Whittaker (Co Southampton) — 1:09.42
7 A. Buller (Stockport Metro) — 1:09.92
8 M. Weighton (Wulfrunians) — 1:10.25
9 J. Brownhill (Beckenham) — 1:10.37
10 T. Evans (Oundle & D) — 1:10.74
11 J. Clark (Royton) — 1:10.78
12 M. de Ville (Reading) — 1:11.25
13 D. Spence (Co Leeds) — 1:11.50
14 R. Pilling (Bo Kirklees) — 1:11.63
15 N. Millar (Co Cardiff) — 1:11.90
16 P. Kappes (Killerwhales) — 1:12.02
17 D. Knight (Hounslow B) — 1:12.32
18 S. Horsley (Co Lincoln Pentaqua) — 1:12.44
19 S. Taylor (Trenton Dolphins) — 1:12.53
20 M. McCamley (Derwentside) — 1:12.78

Jamie Fleet

21 R. Hocquard (Jersey)	1:12.80
22 D. Akers (Co Leeds)	1:12.89
23 N. Mitchell (Swindon Dolphins)	1:12.95
24 L. Hammond (Co Leicester)	1:12.99
25 D. Goodwin (Co Lincoln Pentaqua)	1:13.06
26 B. Rees (Wycombe & D)	1:13.07
27 A. Clarke (COSACSS)	1:13.12
28 C. Arnold (Co Derby)	
C. Sultman (Co Newcastle)	1:13.17
30 M. Ellett (Killerwhales)	1:13.24
31 I. Jones (Bournemouth Dolphins)	1:13.26
32 D. Anscombe (Nova Centurion)	1:13.33
33 P. Ford (Bath University)	1:13.46
34 N. Masters (Ferndown Otters)	1:13.63
35 J. Curry (Co Bristol)	1:13.80
36 M. Falkous (York C)	1:13.82
37 S. Ankin (St Ives)	1:13.88
38 G. Dyball (Thamesdown)	1:13.89
39 J. Mortimer (Fleetwood & D)	1:14.15
40 J. Whittles (Co Birmingham)	1:14.22
41 S. Lee (Haverhill)	1:14.82
42 M. Smallbone (Millfield)	1:14.83
43 C. Kelly (Shark, Eire)	1:15.23

200 Metres Breaststroke
Final

1 N. Polkinghorne (Truro C)	2:22.73
2 R. Maden (Aquabears)	2:24.10
3 D. Entwistle (Royton)	2:25.60
4 C. Thompson (Co Bradford)	2:26.13
5 P. Pederzolli (Hounslow B)	2:31.15
6 J. Brownhill (Beckenham)	2:33.18
7 M. Whittaker (Co Southampton)	2:33.38
8 T. Ashwell (Ipswich)	2:36.31

Heat Times

1 D. Entwistle (Royton)	2:26.73
2 R. Maden (Aquabears)	2:28.92
3 C. Thompson (Co Bradford)	2:29.52
4 N. Polkinghorne (Truro C)	2:29.74
5 P. Pederzolli (Hounslow B)	2:30.62
6 J. Brownhill (Beckenham)	2:31.72
7 T. Ashwell (Ipswich)	2:32.02
8 M. Whittaker (Co Southampton)	2:32.73
9 A. Buller (Stockport Metro)	2:33.21
10 D. Warren (Tynemouth)	2:33.31
11 P. Kappes (Killerwhales)	2:33.64
12 T. Evans (Oundle & D)	2:33.85
13 D. Goodwin (Co Lincoln Pentaqua)	2:34.39
14 C. Heathcote (Nova Centurion)	2:34.83
15 M. de Ville (Reading)	2:34.93
16 J. Clark (Royton)	2:35.29
17 M. Ellett (Killerwhales)	
M. Pickett (Camden Swiss Cottage)	2:35.96
19 L. Hammond (Co Leicester)	2:36.16
20 M. McCamley (Derwentside)	2:36.17
21 S. Taylor (Trenton Dolphins)	2:36.39
22 D. Knight (Hounslow B)	2:36.84
23 B. Rees (Wycombe & D)	2:37.39
24 D. Akers (Co Leeds)	2:38.07
25 J. Whittles (Co Birmingham)	2:38.67
26 C. Arnold (Co Derby)	2:39.07
27 R. Pilling (Bo Kirklees)	2:39.14
28 J. Mortimer (Fleetwood & D)	2:39.20
29 I. Jones (Bournemouth Dolphins)	2:39.26
30 M. Falkous (York C)	2:39.78
31 R. Hocquard (Jersey)	2:40.48
32 J. Curry (Co Bristol)	2:40.55
33 P. Newsham (Beckenham)	2:40.64
34 E. Ruddick (Sale)	2:41.78

35 C. Sultman (Co Newcastle)	
M. Smallbone (Millfield)	2:41.84
37 N. Masters (Ferndown Otters)	2:43.95
38 M. Hall (Co Bradford)	2:45.12
39 S. Horsley (Co Lincoln Pentaqua)	2:45.60
40 M. Godsave (Runnymede)	2:47.30

100 Metres Butterfly
Final

1 M. Smith (Co Swansea)	57.81
2 T. Hart (Thurrock)	57.86
3 D. Gatland (Beckenham)	58.21
4 M. Weighton (Wulfrunians)	58.52
5 J. Gray (RTW Monson)	59.81
6 M. Hanby (Nova Centurion)	59.88
7 B. Rees (Wycombe & D)	59.89
8 D. Warren (Tynemouth)	59.97

Heat Times

1 D. Gatland (Beckenham)	58.56
2 M. Smith (Co Swansea)	59.24
3 M. Weighton (Wulfrunians)	59.54
4 T. Hart (Thurrock)	59.57
5 M. Hanby (Nova Centurion)	59.72
6 J. Gray (RTW Monson)	59.76
7 D. Warren (Tynemouth)	1:00.07
8 B. Rees (Wycombe & D)	1:00.13
9 A. Clarke (COSACSS)	
J. Wallis (Co Peterborough)	1:00.16
11 J. Lynas (Kelly College)	1:00.34
12 S. Taylor (Trenton Dolphins)	1:00.40
13 M. Smallbone (Millfield)	1:00.47
14 P. Buswell (Beckenham)	1:00.98
15 M. O'Connor (Co Manchester)	
M. Jones (Co Southampton)	1:01.22
17 T. Evans (Oundle & D)	1:01.26
18 R. Garbutt (Hull Olympic)	1:01.86
19 M. Austin (Newport & Maindee)	1:01.89
20 J. Sadler (Witney & D)	1:02.38
21 H. Wakeling (Broadway)	1:02.70
22 R. Birch (Millfield)	1:02.98
23 J. Maher (Northampton)	1:03.07
24 M. Bell (Canada)	1:05.81

Richard Maden

200 Metres Butterfly
Final

1	D. Gatland (Beckenham)	2:06.07
2	T. Hart (Thurrock)	2:11.01
3	J. Gray (RTW Monson)	2:11.12
4	D. Warren (Tynemouth)	2:11.97
5	S. Moore (Oundle & D)	2:12.48
6	C. Heathcote (Nova Centurion)	2:13.13
7	S. McQuaid (Co Manchester)	2:13.25
8	J. Lynas (Kelly College)	2:13.82

Heat Times

1	D. Gatland (Beckenham)	2:10.67
2	J. Gray (RTW Monson)	2:11.40
3	D. Warren (Tynemouth)	2:11.56
4	J. Lynas (Kelly College)	2:11.85
5	S. Moore (Oundle & D)	2:12.30
6	T. Hart (Thurrock)	2:12.45
7	S. McQuaid (Co Manchester)	2:12.91
8	C. Heathcote (Nova Centurion)	2:13.55
9	J. Groom (Co Peterborough)	2:13.80
10	P. Kappes (Killerwhales)	2:14.45
11	D. Anscombe (Nova Centurion)	2:14.89
12	A. Clarke (COSACSS)	2:14.97
13	A. McCarney (Enniskillen)	2:15.27
14	M. Smallbone (Millfield)	2:15.59
15	S. Lee (Haverhill)	2:15.89
16	A. Quinn (Co Manchester)	2:16.37
17	M. O'Connor (Co Manchester)	2:16.43
18	B. Lafferty (Co Sheffield)	2:17.18
19	P. Loring (Braintree & Bocking)	2:18.71
20	R. Garbutt (Hull Olympic)	2:19.01
21	D. Spence (Co Leeds)	2:19.17
22	J. Hague (York C)	2:19.43
23	M. Smith (Co Swansea)	2:19.48
24	T. Morgan (Aquabears)	2:19.55
25	D. Coates (Northampton)	2:19.99
26	A. Singh (Hounslow B)	2:20.53
27	J. Maher (Northampton)	2:20.91
28	G. Collier (Bracknell)	2:21.06
29	P. Newsham (Beckenham)	2:21.33
30	J. Fleet (Bo Waltham Forest)	2:22.20
31	P. Thomas (Reading)	2:22.55
32	A. Storey (Killerwhales)	2:23.41
33	S. Martin (Co Leicester)	2:24.79
34	R. Birch (Millfield)	2:26.30
35	J. Bennett (Co Sheffield)	2:26.99
36	M. Bell (Canada)	2:27.59
	C. Darlaston (Sale)	DIS

200 Metres Individual Medley
Final

1	D. Gatland (Beckenham)	2:08.95
2	M. Hanby (Nova Centurion)	2:11.21
3	J. Kearney (Nova Centurion)	2:12.88
4	T. Evans (Oundle & D)	2:13.27
5	M. O'Connor (Co Manchester)	2:13.31
6	J. Brownhill (Beckenham)	2:13.67
7	D. Warren (Tynemouth)	2:14.37
8	C. Thompson (Co Bradford)	2:16.17

Heat Times

1	M. Hanby (Nova Centurion)	2:12.21
2	J. Kearney (Nova Centurion)	2:12.58
3	M. O'Connor (Co Manchester)	2:12.99
4	T. Evans (Oundle & D)	2:14.09
5	D. Warren (Tynemouth)	2:14.48
6	C. Thompson (Co Bradford)	2:14.96
7	D. Gatland (Beckenham)	2:15.22
8	J. Brownhill (Beckenham)	2:15.33
9	B. Rees (Wycombe & D)	2:15.68

Timothy Hart　　　　Artwood Photography

10	N. Sherringham (Co Sheffield)	2:15.76
11	S. Lee (Haverhill)	2:15.89
12	C. Jones (Co Swansea)	2:16.06
13	R. Pilling (Bo Kirklees)	2:16.17
14	S. Taylor (Trenton Dolphins)	2:16.27
15	P. Kappes (Killerwhales)	2:16.56
16	D. Anscombe (Nova Centurion)	2:16.81
17	T. Lewis (Wycombe & D)	2:17.33
18	A. Clarke (COSACSS)	2:17.34
19	J. Fleet (Bo Waltham Forest)	2:17.44
20	A. McCarney (Enniskillen)	2:17.69
21	B. Lafferty (Co Sheffield)	2:17.79
22	S. Moore (Oundle & D)	2:17.97
23	J. Groom (Co Peterborough)	2:18.31
24	D. Entwistle (Royton)	2:18.46
25	C. Smith (Co Chester)	2:18.70
26	D. Spence (Co Leeds)	2:18.99
27	S. McQuaid (Co Manchester)	2:19.46
28	A. Buller (Stockport Metro)	2:19.60
29	R. Maden (Aquabears)	2:19.90
30	M. Ellett (Killerwhales)	2:20.46
31	A. Jefferson (Nova Centurion)	2:20.68
32	T. Ashwell (Ipswich)	2:21.04
33	T. Hart (Thurrock)	2:21.10
34	D. Akers (Co Leeds)	2:21.19
35	J. Eldridge (Kelly College)	2:21.67
36	J. Curry (Co Bristol)	2:23.99
37	M. Godsave (Runnymede)	2:24.20
38	M. Bell (Canada)	2:27.37

400 Metres Individual Medley
Heat Times (no final)

1	D. Warren (Tynemouth)	4:38.19
2	P. Kappes (Killerwhales)	4:41.25
3	C. Biss (Barnet Copthall)	4:43.29
4	C. Heathcote (Nova Centurion)	4:46.58
5	D. Entwistle (Royton)	4:47.73
6	S. McQuaid (Co Manchester)	4:47.92
7	T. Evans (Oundle & D)	4:49.63
8	D. Anscombe (Nova Centurion)	4:50.22
9	M. O'Connor (Co Manchester)	4:50.41
10	R. Pilling (Bo Kirklees)	4:51.77
11	M. Ellett (Killerwhales)	4:52.32
12	T. Lewis (Wycombe & D)	4:52.87

13 N. Sherringham (Co Sheffield)	4:53.60
14 B. Lafferty (Co Sheffield)	4:54.78
15 D. Spence (Co Leeds)	4:54.97
16 J. Groom (Co Peterborough)	4:55.87
17 J. Fleet (Bo Waltham Forest)	4:56.19
18 D. Akers (Co Leeds)	4:56.86
19 T. Morgan (Aquabears)	4:58.26
20 J. Hague (York C)	4:58.52
21 B. Rees (Wycombe & D)	4:58.71
22 M. Hall (Co Bradford)	4:59.48
23 J. McHale (Co Sheffield)	5:00.76
24 A. McCarney (Enniskillen)	5:01.14
25 M. Bell (Canada)	5:06.03
26 P. Newsham (Beckenham)	5:06.97
27 G. Cowburn (Fleetwood & D)	5:08.95
C. Thompson (Co Bradford)	DIS

4×50 Metres Freestyle Club Relay
Final

1 Co Sheffield	1:39.50
2 Beckenham	1:39.63
3 Bristol Central	1:39.91
4 Co Peterborough	1:40.89
5 Nova Centurion	1:41.64
6 Hounslow B	1:42.44
7 Braintree & Bocking	1:43.89
8 Co Southampton	1:44.53

Heat Times

1 Bristol Central	1:41.01
2 Beckenham	1:41.21
3 Co Sheffield	1:41.53
4 Co Peterborough	1:41.74
5 Hounslow B	1:42.25
6 Nova Centurion	1:42.66
7 Co Southampton	1:43.45
8 Braintree & Bocking	1:43.76
9 Hull Olympic	1:44.31
10 Aquabears	1:44.82
11 Haverhill	1:44.95
12 Forward Hillingdon	1:45.46
13 Orpington	1:45.62
14 Wycombe & D	1:45.91
15 Bracknell	1:45.94
16 Co Coventry	1:46.39
17 Reading	1:48.70

4×50 Metres Medley Club Relay
Final

1 Co Sheffield	1:51.74
2 Co Southampton	1:51.96
3 Beckenham	1:52.49
4 Aquabears	1:54.31
5 Nova Centurion	1:54.39
6 Braintree & Bocking	1:54.87
7 Hounslow B	1:55.82
8 Co Peterborough	1:57.59

Heat Times

1 Co Southampton	1:53.78
2 Beckenham	1:53.92
3 Nova Centurion	1:54.95
4 Aquabears	1:55.05
5 Co Sheffield	1:55.16
6 Braintree & Bocking	1:55.97
7 Hounslow B	1:57.18
8 Co Peterborough	1:57.65
9 Hull Olympic	1:57.91
10 Millfield	1:57.95
11 Reading	1:58.62
12 Orpington	1:58.90

13 Bracknell	1:59.37
14 Haverhill	2:00.79
15 Forward Hillingdon	2:01.16
16 Shiverers	2:08.11

Women

100 Metres Freestyle
Final

1 J. Lancaster (Warrington Warriors)	59.61
2 H. Mansfield (Co Chester)	59.64
3 N. Bates (Norwich Penguins)	1:00.29
4 C. Horton (Norwich Penguins)	1:00.65
5 N. Sommers (Beckenham)	1:00.75
6 B. Jones (Co Chester)	1:00.85
7 J. Wilkinson (St Helens)	1:01.57
8 P. Rickard (Tynemouth)	1:01.66

Heat Times

1 H. Mansfield (Co Chester)	1:00.19
2 J. Lancaster (Warrington Warriors)	1:00.66
3 J. Wilkinson (St Helens)	1:00.78
4 N. Sommers (Beckenham)	1:00.83
5 N. Bates (Norwich Penguins)	1:01.05
6 C. Horton (Norwich Penguins)	1:01.07
7 P. Rickard (Tynemouth)	1:01.30
8 B. Jones (Co Chester)	1:01.34
9 S. Buxton (Nova Centurion)	1:01.53
10 A. Kindon (Co Birmingham)	1:01.56
11 J. Riegal (Harrow & Wealdstone)	1:01.59
12 C. Huddart (Manchester U Salford)	
H. Jepson (Bo Kirklees)	1:01.92
14 A. Spark (Bishop Auckland)	1:01.98
15 A. Clarke (Kelly College)	1:02.16
16 J. Travis (Aquabears)	1:02.17
17 J. Andrews (Amersham)	1:02.32
18 H. Lawrence (Beckenham)	1:02.33
19 A. Sanderson (Rushmoor Royals)	1:02.36
20 H. Tooke (Kelly College)	1:02.55
21 A. Duffy (Derwentside)	
S. Dykes (Co Bristol)	1:02.72
23 C. Upton (Beckenham)	1:02.74
24 D. Harding (Rushmoor Royals)	1:02.81
25 D. Tothill (Co Oxford)	
E. Nathan (Millfield)	1:02.89
27 C. Brookes (Co Coventry)	1:03.00
28 A. Mackintosh (Nova Centurion)	1:03.05
29 E. Archer (Kelly College)	1:03.06
30 L. Hawking (Nova Centurion)	1:03.10
31 R. Thomas (Wycombe & D)	1:03.42
32 J. Davey (Co Newcastle)	1:03.73
33 R. Howell (Weyport Olympians)	1:04.02
34 E. Hansford (Forward Hillingdon)	1:04.54
35 A. Howse (Taunton)	1:04.61
36 S. Crook (Co Southampton)	1:04.87
37 M. Middle (Weyport Olympians)	1:05.03
38 R. Looye (Canada)	1:07.88
39 M. Towers (Canada)	1:08.77

200 Metres Freestyle
Final

1 H. Mansfield (Co Chester)	2:07.22
2 J. Riegal (Harrow & Wealdstone)	2:07.27
3 J. Lancaster (Warrington Warriors)	2:07.39
4 H. Jepson (Bo Kirklees)	2:08.86
5 D. Churchman (Co Leeds)	2:09.84
6 N. Sommers (Beckenham)	2:09.87
7 S. Smart (Co Chester)	2:12.09
8 S. Dykes (Co Bristol)	2:12.60

Claire Huddart

Heat Times

1	H. Jepson (Bo Kirklees)	2:09.48
2	N. Sommers (Beckenham)	2:09.76
3	H. Mansfield (Co Chester)	2:10.09
4	S. Smart (Co Chester)	2:10.46
5	J. Lancaster (Warrington Warriors)	2:10.51
6	S. Dykes (Co Bristol)	2:10.58
7	J. Riegal (Harrow & Wealdstone)	2:10.59
8	D. Churchman (Co Leeds)	2:10.74
9	C. Horton (Norwich Penguins)	2:11.28
10	B. Jones (Co Chester)	2:11.78
11	S. Buxton (Nova Centurion)	2:12.10
12	A. Duffy (Derwentside)	2:12.21
13	N. Bates (Norwich Penguins)	2:12.47
14	J. Taylor (Portsmouth Northsea)	2:13.20
15	L. Hawking (Nova Centurion)	2:13.85
16	A. Sanderson (Rushmoor Royals)	2:13.86
17	A. Spark (Bishop Auckland)	2:14.12
18	S. Jamison (York C)	2:14.27
19	A. Baker (Norwich Penguins)	2:14.36
20	C. Huddart (Manchester U Salford)	2:14.47
21	D. Tothill (Co Oxford)	2:14.84
22	J. Wilkinson (St Helens)	2:14.92
23	J. Andrews (Amersham)	2:15.14
24	E. Nathan (Millfield)	2:15.60
25	P. Rickard (Tynemouth)	2:15.84
26	A. Mackintosh (Nova Centurion)	2:15.95
27	J. Travis (Aquabears)	2:16.25
28	A. Lynch (Co Sheffield)	2:16.47
29	L. Heath (Co Birmingham)	2:16.59
30	H. Brocklehurst (Co Derby)	2:17.27
31	R. Thomas (Wycombe & D)	2:17.33
32	J. Davey (Co Newcastle)	2:17.40
33	A. Howse (Taunton)	2:17.87
34	R. Dickinson (Bodmin & D)	2:18.74
35	T. Watkinson (Rykneld)	2:19.05
36	K. Unsworth (Millfield)	2:20.19
37	H. Tooke (Kelly College)	2:20.46
38	C. Brookes (Kelly College)	2:21.09
39	B. Chalmers (Kelly College)	2:21.37
40	R. Looye (Canada)	2:23.60

400 Metres Freestyle
Heat Times (no final)

1	H. Jepson (Bo Kirklees)	4:27.63
2	A. Kay (Co Bradford)	4:29.96
3	N. Sommers (Beckenham)	4:30.47
4	D. Churchman (Co Leeds)	4:30.48
5	J. Lancaster (Warrington Warriors)	4:31.00
6	H. Mansfield (Co Chester)	4:32.76
7	C. Horton (Norwich Penguins)	4:32.97
8	N. Bates (Norwich Penguins)	4:36.25
9	S. Dykes (Co Bristol)	4:36.41
10	P. Rickard (Tynemouth)	4:37.42
11	S. Buxton (Nova Centurion)	4:38.75
12	C. Huddart (Manchester U Salford)	4:39.05
13	A. Sanderson (Rushmoor Royals)	4:40.00
14	A. Baker (Norwich Penguins)	4:41.34
15	L. Heath (Co Birmingham)	4:41.74
16	J. Davey (Co Newcastle)	4:42.05
17	L. Hawking (Nova Centurion)	4:42.93
18	D. Tothill (Co Oxford)	4:46.87
19	H. Welford (Neston)	4:47.11
20	H. Brocklehurst (Co Derby)	4:48.16
21	R. Dickinson (Bodmin & D)	4:48.77
22	B. Hill (Hatfield)	4:50.80
	A. Spark (Bishop Auckland)	
24	R. Love (Canada)	4:55.21
25	C. Penrose (Barking)	4:55.75
26	B. Chalmers (Kelly College)	4:55.85
27	S. Collins (Harrow & Wealdstone)	4:56.35
28	K. Unsworth (Millfield)	4:57.34
29	E. Nathan (Millfield)	4:58.32

800 Metres Freestyle
Heat Times (no final)

1	N. Sommers (Beckenham)	9:06.32
2	A. Kay (Co Bradford)	9:13.99
3	D. Churchman (Co Leeds)	9:22.69
4	J. Davey (Co Newcastle)	9:23.70
5	J. Taylor (Portsmouth Northsea)	9:29.27
6	R. Dickinson (Bodmin & D)	9:39.03
7	H. Welford (Neston)	9:40.65

100 Metres Backstroke
Final

1	J. Riegal (Harrow & Wealdstone)	1:07.72
2	A. Sedgebeer (Epping Forest)	1:07.81
3	C. Huddart (Manchester U Salford)	1:07.88
	J. Kelly (Co Southampton)	
5	F. Cover (Rotherham Metro)	1:08.29
6	J. Wright (Co Chester)	1:09.36
7	K. Britton (Bristol Central)	1:09.83
8	A. Dullforce (Camden Swiss Cottage)	1:09.93

Heat Times

1	A. Sedgebeer (Epping Forest)	1:09.11
2	J. Kelly (Co Southampton)	1:09.30
3	C. Huddart (Manchester U Salford)	1:09.39
4	F. Cover (Rotherham Metro)	1:09.48
5	J. Wright (Co Chester)	1:09.57
6	J. Riegal (Harrow & Wealdstone)	1:09.73
7	A. Dullforce (Camden Swiss Cottage)	1:09.78
8	K. Britton (Bristol Central)	1:09.91
9	P. Rickard (Tynemouth)	1:10.05
	L. Jackson (Everton)	
11	S. Rosser (Torfaen)	1:10.34
12	J. Gibson (Nova Centurion)	1:10.49
13	C. Bailey (Co Birmingham)	1:10.67
14	S. Smart (Co Chester)	1:11.07
15	B. Jones (Co Chester)	1:11.23
16	E. Archer (Kelly College)	1:11.27
17	M. Tomlin (Guernsey)	1:11.38
18	E. Platt (Portsmouth Northsea)	1:11.43
19	L. Heath (Co Birmingham)	1:12.22

20 J. Harrison (Bo Kirklees)	1:12.27
21 H. Washbourne (Co Birmingham)	1:12.33
22 M. Towers (Canada)	1:12.80
23 R. Thomas (Wycombe & D)	1:12.94
24 A. Clarke (Kelly College)	1:13.00
25 K. Haugh (Black Lion)	1:13.04
26 H. Fouracres (Hatfield)	1:13.20
27 K. Nuttall (Warrington Warriors)	1:13.26
28 S. Buxton (Nova Centurion)	1:13.32
29 C. Upton (Beckenham)	1:13.46
30 S. Embleton (Co Newcastle)	1:13.66
31 T. Cornish (Frome)	1:13.75
32 A. Spark (Bishop Auckland)	1:13.79

200 Metres Backstroke
Final

1 J. Riegal (Harrow & Wealdstone)	2:22.30
2 A. Sedgebeer (Epping Forest)	2:23.41
3 J. Kelly (Co Southampton)	2:25.16
4 P. Rickard (Tynemouth)	2:26.25
5 L. Jackson (Everton)	2:27.57
6 B. Jones (Co Chester)	2:27.81
7 C. Huddart (Manchester U Salford)	2:28.13
8 J. Wright (Co Chester)	2:29.53

Heat times

1 P. Rickard (Tynemouth)	2:25.99
2 J. Riegal (Harrow & Wealdstone)	2:26.46
3 A. Sedgebeer (Epping Forest)	2:27.31
4 J. Kelly (Co Southampton)	2:27.34
5 J. Wright (Co Chester)	2:27.39
6 L. Jackson (Everton)	2:27.81
7 C. Huddart (Manchester U Salford)	2:27.86
8 B. Jones (Co Chester)	2:28.10
9 C. Bailey (Co Birmingham)	2:28.12
10 K. Britton (Bristol Central)	2:29.45
11 A. Kay (Co Bradford)	2:29.49
12 F. Cover (Rotherham Metro)	2:30.07
13 L. Heath (Co Birmingham)	2:31.17
14 J. Harrison (Bo Kirklees)	2:32.25
15 J. Gibson (Nova Centurion)	2:32.73
16 K. Nuttall (Warrington Warriors)	2:32.98
17 R. Thomas (Wycombe & D)	2:33.09
18 H. Washbourne (Co Birmingham)	2:33.13
19 A. Dullforce (Camden Swiss Cottage)	2:33.32

Anna Baker

20 E. Platt (Portsmouth Northsea)	2:34.31
21 A. Sanderson (Rushmoor Royals)	2:34.57
22 J. Austin (Kelly College)	2:35.29
23 E. Archer (Kelly College)	2:35.62
24 S. Dykes (Co Bristol)	2:36.32
25 C. Hawkins (Ruislip & Northwood)	2:36.56
26 S. Solly (Nova Centurion)	2:36.74
27 H. Fouracres (Hatfield)	2:36.95
28 S. Jamison (York C)	2:37.27
29 M. Towers (Canada)	2:37.44
30 D. Tothill (Co Oxford)	2:37.78
31 S. Embleton (Co Newcastle)	2:37.87
32 C. Armstrong (Co Coventry)	2:38.31
33 H. Tooke (Kelly College)	2:38.95
34 L. Goodfellow (Greenwich B Mariners)	2:41.80
35 S. Bourton (Shiverers)	2:42.30
36 M. Proe (Shiverers)	2:43.25

100 Metres Breaststroke
Final

1 A. Baker (Norwich Penguins)	1:14.94
2 R. Gillatt (Co Sheffield)	1:15.16
3 J. Hocking (Truro C)	1:15.89
4 S. Smart (Co Chester)	1:16.47
5 H. Gorman (Nova Centurion)	1:17.29
6 A. Warner (Co Birmingham)	1:18.04
7 A. Lynch (Co Sheffield)	1:18.18
8 S. Brown (Lisburn)	1:18.68

Heat Times

1 R. Gillatt (Co Sheffield)	1:15.35
2 A. Baker (Norwich Penguins)	1:16.52
3 J. Hocking (Truro)	
H. Gorman (Nova Cenurion)	1:17.63
5 S. Smart (Co Chester)	1:18.27
6 A. Lynch (Co Sheffield)	1:18.42
7 S. Brown (Lisburn)	1:18.60
8 A. Warner (Co Birmingham)	1:18.77
9 R. Newey (Ledbury & D)	
J. Harrison (Bo Kirklees)	1:19.44
11 J. Travis (Aquabears)	1:19.80
12 A. Kindon (Co Birmingham)	1:19.81
13 P. Mitchell (Epping Forest)	1:20.30
14 C. Upton (Beckenham)	1:20.33
15 A. Bird (Bristol Central)	1:20.83
16 C. Brookes (Co Coventry)	1:20.96
17 T. Watkinson (Rykneld)	1:21.02
18 D. Atkins (Mendip)	1:21.12
19 K. Senior (Bracknell)	1:21.25
20 R. Morris (Jersey)	1:21.44
21 S. Solly (Nova Centurion)	1:21.78
22 B. Darley (Hull Olympic)	1:21.83
23 A. Howse (Taunton)	1:22.06
24 A. Lucas (Co Coventry)	1:22.27
25 L. Sturgeon (Edinburgh)	1:22.61
26 R. Thomas (Wycombe & D)	1:22.65
27 C. Hurst (Bo Waltham Forest)	1:22.94
28 L. Eyles (Co Coventry)	1:23.27
29 S. Linnell (Stockport Metro)	1:23.37
30 J. Usher (Taunton)	1:26.03
31 Y. Brown (Co Coventry)	1:26.17

200 Metres Breaststroke
Final

1 R. Gillatt (Co Sheffield)	2:42.92
2 S. Smart (Co Chester)	2:43.90
3 H. Gorman (Nova Centurion)	2:44.22
4 J. Harrison (Bo Kirklees)	2:44.53
5 J. Hocking (Truro C)	2:45.03
6 A. Baker (Norwich Penguins)	2:47.39

7 S. Brown (Lisburn)	2:48.30
8 A. Lynch (Co Sheffield)	2:50.76

Heat Times

1 J. Harrison (Bo Kirklees)	2:44.57
2 R. Gillatt (Co Sheffield)	2:45.02
3 J. Hocking (Truro C)	2:45.33
4 H. Gorman (Nova Centurion)	2:45.58
5 S. Smart (Co Chester)	2:46.11
6 S. Brown (Lisburn)	2:46.46
7 A. Baker (Norwich Penguins)	2:46.77
8 A. Lynch (Co Sheffield)	2:47.86
9 A. Warner (Co Birmingham)	2:48.84
10 P. Mitchell (Epping Forest)	2:49.27
11 S. Solly (Nova Centurion)	2:50.02
12 A. Howse (Taunton)	2:51.05
13 C. Upton (Beckenham)	2:51.60
14 N. Sommers (Beckenham)	2:51.87
15 D. Atkins (Mendip)	2:52.35
16 J. Travis (Aquabears)	2:53.21
17 K. Senior (Bracknell)	2:53.76
18 C. Hurst (Bo Waltham Forest)	
B. Darley (Hull Olympic)	2:54.68
20 L. Eyles (Co Coventry)	2:54.74
21 T. Watkinson (Rykneld)	2:55.91
22 C. Brookes (Co Coventry)	2:56.04
23 L. Sturgeon (Edinburgh)	2:56.06
24 R. Thomas (Wycombe & D)	2:56.22
25 S. Linnell (Stockport Metro)	2:57.85
26 C. Green (Bournemouth Dolphins)	2:58.61
27 A. Lucas (Co Coventry)	2:58.76
28 J. Pearson (Kelly College)	3:00.45
29 F. Cover (Rotherham Metro)	3:00.61
30 E. Watson (Basildon)	3:04.12
31 R. Dickinson (Bodmin & D)	3:05.25
32 J. Hansford (Poole)	3:07.56
33 H. Morgan (Wulfrunians)	3:11.45

100 Metres Butterfly
Final

1 J. Lancaster (Warrington Warriors)	1:04.53
2 A. Baker (Norwich Penguins)	1:04.65
3 A. Duffy (Derwentside)	1:04.82
4 H. Jepson (Bo Kirklees)	1:05.20
5 J. Taylor (Portsmouth Northsea)	1:05.70
6 C. Horton (Norwich Penguins)	1:06.56
7 S. Buxton (Nova Centurion)	1:07.04
8 N. Sommers (Beckenham)	1:07.36

Heat Times

1 A. Duffy (Derwentside)	1:04.72
2 A. Baker (Norwich Penguins)	1:05.02
3 J. Lancaster (Warrington Warriors)	1:05.56
4 H. Jepson (Bo Kirklees)	1:05.90
5 J. Taylor (Portsmouth Northsea)	1:06.55
6 S. Buxton (Nova Centurion)	1:06.75
7 C. Horton (Norwich Penguins)	1:06.81
8 N. Sommers (Beckenham)	1:06.89
9 H. Welford (Neston)	1:07.23
10 B. Jones (Co Chester)	1:07.31
11 J. Barker (Co Leicester)	1:07.67
12 A. Kay (Co Bradford)	1:08.05
13 C. Upton (Beckenham)	1:08.18
14 T. Day (Beckenham)	1:08.30
15 J. Hocking (Truro C)	1:08.31
16 N. Bates (Norwich Penguins)	1:08.39
17 S. Jamison (York C)	1:08.41
18 S. Smart (Co Chester)	1:08.69
19 S. Solly (Nova Centurion)	1:08.70
20 R. Thomas (Wycombe & D)	1:08.90

21 D. Harding (Rushmoor Royals)	1:08.97
22 K. Senior (Bracknell)	1:09.17
23 A. Kindon (Co Birmingham)	1:09.24
24 A. Sanderson (Rushmoor Royals)	1:09.35
J. Wright (Co Chester)	
26 S. Dykes (Co Bristol)	1:09.49
27 J. Andrews (Amersham)	1:09.50
28 A. Clarke (Kelly College)	1:09.61
29 R. Goss (Truro C)	1:09.67
30 H. Fouracres (Hatfield)	1:09.76
31 H. Brocklehurst (Co Derby)	1:09.87
32 C. Armstrong (Co Coventry)	1:10.72
33 R. Newey (Ledbury & D)	1:11.03
34 A. Dullforce (Camden Swiss Cottage)	1:11.10
35 L. Collingwood (Co Manchester)	1:11.34
36 L. Balch (Oundle & D)	1:11.55
37 A. Sedgebeer (Epping Forest)	1:12.79
38 R. Looye (Canada)	1:13.46
39 M. Towers (Canada)	1:15.32

200 Metres Butterfly
Final

1 A. Duffy (Derwentside)	2:17.75
2 H. Jepson (Bo Kirklees)	2:18.10
3 J. Taylor (Portsmouth Northsea)	2:18.94
4 H. Welford (Neston)	2:20.56
5 J. Lancaster (Warrington Warriors)	2:20.76
6 A. Baker (Norwich Penguins)	2:21.54
7 A. Kay (Co Bradford)	2:21.66
8 S. Smart (Co Chester)	2:27.26

Heat Times

1 A. Duffy (Derwentside)	2:19.32
2 H. Jepson (Bo Kirklees)	2:20.06
3 H. Welford (Neston)	2:20.94
4 J. Lancaster (Warrington Warriors)	2:22.08
5 J. Taylor (Portsmouth Northsea)	2:22.11
6 A. Kay (Co Bradford)	2:22.23
7 A. Baker (Norwich Penguins)	2:22.41
8 S. Smart (Co Chester)	2:25.82
9 B. Jones (Co Chester)	2:27.67
10 S. Jamison (York C)	2:27.80
11 J. Davey (Co Newcastle)	2:28.76
12 H. Brocklehurst (Co Derby)	2:31.10

Rachel Gillatt

13 M. Tomlin (Guernsey)	2:31.27	
14 C. Horton (Norwich Penguins)	2:31.57	
15 S. Reading (Barking)	2:31.84	
16 A. Cashmore (Kelly College)	2:31.85	
17 K. Senior (Bracknell)	2:31.93	
18 H. Fouracres (Hatfield)	2:33.62	
19 C. Bishop (Avon Neptune)	2:34.74	
20 B. Chalmers (Kelly College)	2:40.02	
21 C. Parker (Ipswich)	2:40.74	
22 C. Armstrong (Co Coventry)	2:45.30	

200 Metres Individual Medley
Final

1 S. Smart (Co Chester)	2:23.58
2 J. Riegal (Harrow & Wealdstone)	2:24.75
3 J. Lancaster (Warrington Warriors)	2:24.92
4 C. Upton (Beckenham)	2:26.10
5 J. Harrison (Bo Kirklees)	2:26.26
6 H. Mansfield (Co Chester)	2:26.73
7 B. Jones (Co Chester)	2:28.56
8 A. Baker (Norwich Penguins)	2:29.56

Heat Times

1 J. Harrison (Bo Kirklees)	2:26.59
2 S. Smart (Co Chester)	2:26.64
3 C. Upton (Beckenham)	2:26.73
4 H. Mansfield (Co Chester)	2:27.66
5 J. Riegal (Harrow & Wealdstone)	2:27.75
6 J. Lancaster (Warrington Warriors)	2:28.00
7 B. Jones (Co Chester)	2:28.34
8 A. Baker (Norwich Penguins)	2:29.29
9 N. Sommers (Beckenham)	2:29.62
10 S. Solly (Nova Centurion)	2:30.16
11 P. Rickard (Tynemouth)	2:30.36
12 S. Buxton (Nova Centurion)	2:30.94
13 R. Thomas (Wycombe & D)	2:31.45
14 A. Lynch (Co Sheffield)	2:31.66
15 A. Kindon (Co Birmingham)	2:31.88
16 J. Davey (Co Newcastle)	2:31.91
17 C. Horton (Norwich Penguins)	2:32.15
18 H. Gorman (Nova Centurion)	2:32.49
19 C. Huddart (Manchester U Salford)	2:32.58
20 J. Travis (Aquabears)	2:33.00
21 S. Dykes (Co Bristol)	2:33.26
22 A. Howse (Taunton)	2:33.45
23 C. Brookes (Co Coventry)	2:33.50
24 J. Wright (Co Chester)	2:33.94
25 R. Dickinson (Bodmin & D)	2:34.11
26 D. Atkins (Mendip)	2:34.35
27 A. Sanderson (Rushmoor Royals)	2:34.48
28 B. Darley (Hull Olympic)	2:34.70
29 K. Senior (Bracknell)	2:35.07
30 F. Cover (Rotherham Metro)	2:35.17
31 L. Heath (Co Birmingham)	2:35.28
32 A. Sedgebeer (Epping Forest)	2:35.29
33 H. Brocklehurst (Co Derby)	2:35.70
34 E. Nathan (Millfield)	2:36.03
35 P. Mitchell (Epping Forest)	2:36.16
36 J. Taylor (Portsmouth Northsea)	2:36.58
37 R. Newey (Ledbury & D)	2:36.68
38 R. Looye (Canada)	2:42.72
39 E. Turner (Bournemouth Dolphins)	2:44.14

400 Metres Individual Medley
Heat Times (no final)

1 J. Lancaster (Warrington Warriors)	5:03.04
2 J. Harrison (Bo Kirklees)	5:05.13
3 S. Smart (Co Chester)	5:05.64
4 H. Mansfield (Co Chester)	5:08.53
5 C. Upton (Beckenham)	5:09.36

6 J. Riegal (Harrow & Wealdstone)	5:10.05
7 H. Jepson (Bo Kirklees)	5:11.43
8 B. Jones (Co Chester)	5:13.23
9 N. Sommers (Beckenham)	5:14.90
10 A. Baker (Norwich Penguins)	5:15.94
11 S. Solly (Nova Centurion)	5:17.26
12 J. Wright (Co Chester)	5:20.09
13 J. Davey (Co Newcastle)	5:20.44
14 C. Brookes (Co Coventry)	5:24.02
15 A. Lynch (Co Sheffield)	5:24.08
16 A. Howse (Taunton)	5:26.75
17 H. Gorman (Nova Centurion)	5:26.83
18 K. Senior (Bracknell)	5:28.83
19 S. Jamison (York C)	5:31.29
20 A. Sanderson (Rushmoor Royals)	5:32.95
21 B. Hill (Hatfield)	5:34.37
22 R. Looye (Canada)	5:35.34
23 S. Reading (Barking)	5:36.37
24 S. Collins (Harrow & Wealdstone)	5:42.14
25 L. Sturgeon (Edinburgh)	5:42.60
P. Howard (Co Manchester)	DIS

4×50 Metres Freestyle Club Relay
Final

1 Beckenham	1:52.81
2 Norwich Penguins	1:52.84
3 Co Chester	1:53.88
4 Kelly College	1:53.93
5 Nova Centurion	1:55.36
6 Co Birmingham	1:58.21
7 Co Coventry	1:59.84
8 Bracknell	2:00.39

Heat Times

1 Beckenham	1:53.86
2 Norwich Penguins	1:54.27
3 Kelly College	1:54.41
4 Co Chester	1:54.57
5 Nova Centurion	1:56.44
6 Co Birmingham	1:58.29
7 Bracknell	2:00.88
8 Co Coventry	2:00.96
9 Hatfield	2:02.41
10 Rushmoor Royals	2:02.67
11 Shiverers	2:03.62
12 Harrow & Wealdstone	2:05.04

4×50 Metres Medley Club Relay
Final

1 Nova Centurion	2:05.88
2 Co Chester	2:06.91
3 Beckenham	2:08.56
4 Norwich Penguins	2:09.31
5 Co Birmingham	2:09.77
6 Kelly College	2:11.55
7 Hatfield	2:15.16
8 Co Coventry	2:15.89

Heat Times

1 Nova Centurion	2:07.86
2 Co Chester	2:09.00
3 Norwich Penguins	2:09.46
4 Beckenham	2:10.61
5 Kelly College Co Birmingham	2:10.79
7 Hatfield	2:14.72
8 Co Coventry	2:15.11
9 Harrow & Wealdstone	2:16.47
10 Bracknell	2:18.98
11 Shiverers	2:20.36
12 Rushmoor Royals	2:20.81

Other Major Competitions, 1988–89

National Speedo Inter-League Cup Final
The National Sports Centre, Crystal Palace — 11 September, 1988

Senior

Men

100 Metres Freestyle
1	N. Metcalfe (Co Leeds)	53.51
2	G. Robins (Portsmouth Northsea)	54.45
3	D. Gatland (Beckenham)	55.13
4	R. Tozer (Millfield)	55.65
5	J. Langdown (Co Southampton)	56.21
6	S. Mansbridge (Stockport Metro)	56.79
7	R. Moulson (Norwich Penguins)	56.94
8	J. Kearney (Radford)	57.90

100 Metres Backstroke
1	C. Cockcroft (Co Leeds)	1:02.07
2	M. Hooper (Portsmouth Northsea)	1:02.75
3	J. Kearney (Radford)	1:02.99
4	S. Wainwright (Millfield)	1:03.81
5	J. Chatten (Norwich Penguins)	1:05.73
6	T. Stone (Co Southampton)	1:08.02
7	A. Lysak (Stockport Metro)	1:09.81
8	R. Stapleton (Beckenham)	1:09.84

100 Metres Breaststroke
1	I. Campbell (Beckenham)	1:08.59
2	R. Wilkes (Portsmouth Northsea)	1:09.19
3	A. Murdock (Radford)	1:09.87
4	A. Butler (Stockport Metro)	1:12.84
5	S. Wells (Norwich Penguins)	1:13.47
6	R. Thorp (Millfield)	1:14.57
7	J. Gregory (Co Leeds)	1:15.21
8	C. Wilson (Co Southampton)	1:15.79

100 Metres Butterfly
1	R. Crabtree (Stockport Metro)	59.46
2	N. Bridge (Millfield)	59.58
3	R. Greenwood (Co Leeds)	1:00.14
4	D. Gatland (Beckenham)	1:00.48
5	M. Jones (Co Southampton)	1:00.57
6	P. Hawkins (Portsmouth Northsea)	1:01.67
7	C. Proctor (Radford)	1:03.41
8	P. Edwards (Norwich Penguins)	1:03.50

200 Metres Individual Medley
1	G. Robins (Portsmouth Northsea)	2:11.84
2	M. Buswell (Beckenham)	2:12.61
3	R. Crabtree (Stockport Metro)	2:16.07
4	S. Wyer (Co Leeds)	2:17.06
5	D. Anscombe (Radford)	2:19.55
6	C. Wilson (Co Southampton)	2:19.80
7	R. Moulson (Norwich Penguins)	2:22.24
8	R. Thorp (Millfield)	2:22.77

6×50 Metres Freestyle Club Relay
1	Millfield	2:29.49
2	Co Leeds	2:30.22
3	Portsmouth Northsea	2:31.28
4	Beckenham	2:35.68
5	Co Southampton	2:35.85
6	Radford	2:36.29
7	Stockport Metro	2:38.46
8	Norwich Penguins	2:41.11

4×50 Metres Medley Club Relay
1	Portsmouth Northsea	1:52.66
2	Co Leeds	1:52.71
3	Radford	1:53.04
4	Millfield	1:53.82
5	Beckenham	1:54.42
6	Co Southampton	1:56.45
7	Stockport Metro	1:57.83
8	Norwich Penguins	2:00.92

Women

100 Metres Freestyle
1	N. Williams (Stockport Metro)	1:00.85
2	G. Atkins (Portsmouth Northsea)	1:00.92
3	N. Bates (Norwich Penguins)	1:01.10
4	D. Churchman (Co Leeds)	1:02.21
	N. Sommers (Beckenham)	
6	S. Crook (Co Southampton)	1:02.93
7	L. Hawking (Radford)	1:03.76
8	C. Roberts (Millfield)	1:07.15

100 Metres Backstroke
1	J. Wood (Radford)	1:08.66
2	J. Kelly (Co Southampton)	1:08.73
3	E. Armstrong (Co Leeds)	1:10.50
4	E. Hall (Portsmouth Northsea)	1:10.59
5	S. Green (Beckenham)	1:12.77
6	K. Boucher (Norwich Penguins)	1:13.34
7	J. Bennett (Stockport Metro)	1:13.68
8	E. Wilkinson (Millfield)	1:15.24

100 Metres Breaststroke
1	D. Tubby (Norwich Penguins)	1:15.67
2	L. Coombes (Co Southampton)	1:16.06
3	A. McKellican (Co Leeds)	1:19.39
4	C. Gable (Stockport Metro)	1:21.06
5	J. Wood (Radford)	1:22.48
6	M. Kowalski (Beckenham)	1:23.27
7	E. Wilkinson (Millfield)	1:24.52
8	E. Grygoruk (Portsmouth Northsea)	1:26.14

100 Metres Butterfly
1	M. Scarborough (Portsmouth Northsea)	1:04.30
2	A. Baker (Norwich Penguins)	1:05.61
3	M. Hadden (Beckenham)	1:06.33
4	S. Buxton (Radford)	1:08.14
5	B. Bowden (Co Southampton)	1:08.15
6	N. Atkinson (Stockport Metro)	1:08.38
7	H. Walsh (Millfield)	1:09.48
8	D. Churchman (Co Leeds)	1:10.19

200 Metres Individual Medley
1	B. Bowden (Co Southampton)	2:27.33
2	M. Scarborough (Portsmouth Northsea)	2:27.70
3	A. Baker (Norwich Penguins)	2:28.12
4	N. Sommers (Beckenham)	2:31.41

5	A. McKellican (Co Leeds)	2:32.17
6	S. Buxton (Radford)	2:33.05
7	H. Walsh (Millfield)	2:35.40
8	N. Atkinson (Stockport Metro)	2:35.80

6×50 Metres Freestyle Club Relay

1	Portsmouth Northsea	2:53.38
2	Beckenham	2:53.87
3	Co Southampton	2:55.68
4	Stockport Metro	2:56.86
5	Co Leeds	2:57.33
6	Norwich Penguins	2:57.57
7	Radford	2:58.84
8	Millfield	2:59.10

4×50 Metres Medley Club Relay

1	Co Southampton	2:06.92
2	Portsmouth Northsea	2:08.46
3	Stockport Metro	2:09.72
4	Norwich Penguins	2:09.91
5	Co Leeds	2:11.62
6	Beckenham	2:11.67
7	Millfield	2:11.94
8	Radford	2:12.06

10-11 Years Age Group

Boys

50 Metres Freestyle

1	A. Godwin (Portsmouth Northsea)	29.77
2	L. Sutton (Millfield)	31.70
3	N. Tyas (Co Leeds)	32.16
4	R. Marley (Beckenham)	32.39
5	D. Blanchard (Norwich Penguins)	33.40
6	B. Oliver (Radford)	33.72
7	A. Jones (Co Southampton)	34.99
8	J. Hutchinson (Stockport Metro)	35.68

50 Metres Backstroke

1	A. Prendergast (Co Leeds)	32.32
2	A. Witt (Portsmouth Northsea)	36.75
3	L. Whitehead (Radford)	37.26
4	P. Gillings (Beckenham)	37.49
5	M. Finn (Co Southampton)	39.05
6	D. Staines (Stockport Metro)	41.38
7	J. Snelling (Norwich Penguins)	42.31
8	J. Goddard (Millfield)	44.63

50 Metres Breaststroke

1	A. Prendergast (Co Leeds)	40.59
2	S. Stimpson (Beckenham)	41.50
3	A. Simmonds (Norwich Penguins)	42.45
4	P. Glass (Co Southampton)	43.06
5	A. Witt (Portsmouth Northsea)	43.57
6	G. Jukes (Radford)	44.74
7	J. Newcombe (Stockport Metro)	45.70
8	C. Simmons (Millfield)	45.74

50 Metres Butterfly

1	A. Godwin (Portsmouth Northsea)	32.75
2	L. Whitehead (Radford)	36.13
3	J. Openshaw (Co Leeds)	36.35
4	T. Ward (Beckenham)	37.56
5	P. Houghton (Stockport Metro)	37.60
6	M. Finn (Co Southampton)	37.99
7	J. Snelling (Norwich Penguins)	38.64
8	L. Sutton (Millfield)	38.73

4×50 Metres Freestyle Club Relay

1	Portsmouth Northsea	2:08.23

2	Co Leeds	2:11.11
3	Beckenham	2:12.73
4	Radford	2:15.11
5	Norwich Penguins	2:17.00
6	Stockport Metro	2:17.27
7	Co Southampton	2:19.93
8	Millfield	2:20.57

4×50 Metres Medley Club Relay

1	Co Leeds	2:27.35
2	Beckenham	2:33.88
3	Norwich Penguins	2:38.66
4	Radford	2:40.16
5	Stockport Metro	2:44.53
6	Millfield	2:51.66
	Portsmouth Northsea	DIS

Girls

50 Metres Freestyle

1	E. Watson (Radford)	31.27
2	A. Rigby (Norwich Penguins)	31.40
3	L. Bulbeck (Portsmouth Northsea)	31.85
4	L. Hatty (Co Leeds)	32.97
5	C. Bates (Stockport Metro)	33.82
6	L. Stroud (Co Southampton)	33.91
7	M. Atkinson (Beckenham)	35.19
8	V. Cooke (Millfield)	35.43

50 Metres Backstroke

1	E. Watson (Radford)	35.70
2	A. Rigby (Norwich Penguins)	37.34
3	E. Hazelwood (Co Leeds)	38.90
4	S. Brown (Beckenham)	39.15
5	J. Cowan (Portsmouth Northsea)	39.54
6	M. Owen (Millfield)	40.19
7	G. Ross (Stockport Metro)	40.68
8	S. Mayes (Co Southampton)	43.44

50 Metres Breaststroke

1	L. Keen (Norwich Penguins)	40.58
2	C. Waterfield (Co Leeds)	41.36
3	E. Weedon (Stockport Metro)	41.93
4	J. Darby (Radford)	42.89
5	G. Chillingworth (Co Southampton)	43.37
6	M. Owen (Millfield)	43.55
7	J. Cowan (Portsmouth Northsea)	44.98
8	J. Hanley (Beckenham)	48.60

50 Metres Butterfly

1	E. Hazelwood (Co Leeds)	34.41
2	L. Bulbeck (Portsmouth Northsea)	35.03
3	L. Keen (Norwich Penguins)	35.94
4	A. Riley (Radford)	37.78
5	V. Cooke (Millfield)	38.06
6	L. Stroud (Co Southampton)	38.63
7	E. Weedon (Stockport Metro)	38.80
8	S. Brown (Beckenham)	45.37

4×50 Metres Freestyle Club Relay

1	Co Leeds	2:11.05
2	Norwich Penguins	2:11.54
3	Radford	2:13.03
4	Portsmouth Northsea	2:14.12
5	Stockport Metro	2:16.29
6	Co Southampton	2:22.38
7	Beckenham	2:25.98
8	Millfield	2:27.92

4×50 Metres Medley Club Relay

1	Co Leeds	2:27.66

2 Norwich Penguins	2:30.52
3 Radford	2:32.59
4 Stockport Metro	2:39.57
5 Millfield	2:40.41
6 Co Southampton	2:45.30
7 Beckenham	2:55.79
Portsmouth Northsea	DIS

13/U Years Age Group
Boys

100 Metres Freestyle

1 N. Collins (Millfield)	59.22
2 N. Skinner (Portsmouth Northsea)	1:00.91
3 M. Wilson (Co Leeds)	1:02.26
4 D. Lodge (Radford)	1:02.54
5 G. Smith (Stockport Metro)	1:05.14
6 J. Moreno (Co Southampton)	1:05.17
7 S. Feek (Norwich Penguins)	1:06.62
8 S. Flin (Beckenham)	1:07.48

100 Metres Backstroke

1 A. Weltch (Portsmouth Northsea)	1:10.99
2 D. Fletcher (Radford)	1:11.08
3 R. Searle (Beckenham)	1:12.82
4 J. Sutcliffe (Co Leeds)	1:13.66
5 F. Anderson (Co Southampton)	1:14.14
6 I. Palmer-Barnes (Millfield)	1:15.93
7 N. Rounce (Norwich Penguins)	1:16.23
8 R. Newbold (Stockport Metro)	1:17.39

100 Metres Breaststroke

1 J. Moreno (Co Southampton)	1:16.39
2 R. Ronca (Millfield)	1:20.15
3 P. Gouruish (Norwich Penguins)	1:20.59
4 D. Rawlinson (Stockport Metro)	1:21.17
5 A. Burrett (Co Leeds)	1:22.79
6 P. Burch (Beckenham)	1:23.03
7 I. Palmer (Radford)	1:25.89
8 A. Nancarrow (Portsmouth Northsea)	1:27.42

100 Metres Butterfly

1 N. Skinner (Portsmouth Northsea)	1:08.91
2 N. Collins (Millfield)	1:09.25
3 R. Searle (Beckenham)	1:11.00
4 C. Scotney (Co Leeds)	1:11.07
5 D. Rawlinson (Stockport Metro)	1:15.35
6 S. Feek (Norwich Penguins)	1:15.86
7 D. Fletcher (Radford)	1:16.12
8 G. Prentice (Co Southampton)	1:19.61

4×50 Metres Freestyle Club Relay

1 Co Leeds	1:55.14
2 Millfield	1:55.47
3 Portsmouth Northsea	1:55.98
4 Co Southampton	1:58.34
5 Radford	2:00.05
6 Stockport Metro	2:01.32
7 Beckenham	2:01.33
8 Norwich Penguins	2:03.51

4×50 Metres Medley Club Relay

1 Co Southampton	2:08.64
2 Co Leeds	2:10.56
3 Millfield	2:10.61
4 Portsmouth Northsea	2:11.77
5 Radford	2:13.77
6 Beckenham	2:13.96
7 Stockport Metro	2:15.13
8 Norwich Penguins	2:17.02

Girls

100 Metres Freestyle

1 A. Gilmore (Portsmouth Northsea)	1:04.61
2 A. Runnicles (Millfield)	1:04.94
3 A. Harriott (Beckenham)	1:06.20
4 H. Gill (Norwich Penguins)	1:06.90
5 S. Gray (Co Leeds)	1:07.92
6 S. Lockyer (Co Southampton)	1:08.04
7 E. Watson (Radford)	1:09.09
8 L. Henderson (Stockport Metro)	1:09.78

100 Metres Backstroke

1 K. Axford (Beckenham)	1:12.44
2 H. Kemball-Cook (Norwich Penguins)	1:14.13
3 E. Keates (Portsmouth Northsea)	1:17.16
4 J. Ricketts (Millfield)	1:17.19
5 S. Lightfoot (Co Leeds)	1:17.92
6 E. Watson (Radford)	1:19.65
7 G. Beaton (Co Southampton)	1:20.07
8 H. Jepson (Stockport Metro)	1:20.10

100 Metres Breaststroke

1 Z. Harrison (Norwich Penguins)	1:21.19
2 A. Creasey (Beckenham)	1:24.86
3 S. Travers (Portsmouth Northsea)	1:25.16
4 R. Boultby (Radford)	1:25.74
5 S. Lockyer (Co Southampton)	1:25.89
6 C. Espley (Millfield)	1:27.93
7 S. Bishop (Stockport Metro)	1:28.08
8 V. Lee (Co Leeds)	1:28.70

100 Metres Butterfly

1 Z. Harrison (Norwich Penguins)	1:08.71
2 E. Arter (Co Leeds)	1:14.62
3 H. Paddock (Co Southampton)	1:15.98
4 A. Gilmore (Portsmouth Northsea)	1:16.00
5 H. Kenworthy (Stockport Metro)	1:16.01
6 C. O'Leary (Beckenham)	1:16.60
7 J. Reed (Millfield)	1:19.85
8 R. Boultby (Radford)	1:20.21

4×50 Metres Freestyle Club Relay

1 Beckenham	2:00.59
2 Norwich Penguins	2:01.25
3 Millfield	2:03.61
4 Portsmouth Northsea	2:04.04
5 Co Leeds	2:04.53
6 Stockport Metro	2:08.35
7 Co Southampton	2:09.13
8 Radford	2:10.48

4×50 Metres Medley Club Relay

1 Norwich Penguins	2:13.33
2 Beckenham	2:16.94
3 Millfield	2:17.75
4 Portsmouth Northsea	2:18.00
5 Co Southampton	2:19.74
6 Co Leeds	2:20.31
7 Stockport Metro	2:23.05
8 Radford	2:23.30

15/U Years Age Group
Boys

100 Metres Freestyle

1 P. Edwards (Norwich Penguins)	57.69
2 L. Grenyer (Beckenham)	58.34
3 J. Miller (Co Leeds)	58.49
4 D. Griffin (Stockport Metro)	58.97

5 M. Watt (Portsmouth Northsea)	59.06
6 S. Adamson (Co Southampton)	59.89
7 W. O'Gorman (Millfield)	1:00.13
8 G. Hall (Radford)	1:00.37

100 Metres Backstroke

1 J. Boags (Norwich Penguins)	1:06.44
2 P. Chick (Beckenham)	1:06.74
3 D. Blakeley (Co Leeds)	1:07.64
4 J. Ralph (Portsmouth Northsea)	1:07.83
5 A. Lysak (Stockport Metro)	1:09.22
6 H. Sheraton (Millfield)	1:09.64
7 C. Alderson (Radford)	1:10.85
8 H. Osborn (Co Southampton)	1:13.32

100 Metres Breaststroke

1 S. Wells (Norwich Penguins)	1:13.68
2 P. McGinty (Beckenham)	1:14.47
3 P. Wilkinson (Co Leeds)	1:14.59
4 W. O' Gorman (Millfield)	1:15.34
5 M. Whittaker (Co Southampton)	1:16.09
6 D. Griffin (Stockport Metro)	1:17.79
7 J. Ralph (Portsmouth Northsea)	1:20.55
8 M. Stott (Radford)	1:21.92

100 Metres Butterfly

1 P. Edwards (Norwich Penguins)	1:02.68
2 P. Chick (Beckenham)	1:04.30
3 G. Hall (Radford)	1:05.15
4 D. Blakeley (Co Leeds)	1:05.76
5 P. Butt (Co Southampton)	1:06.61
6 H. Sheraton (Millfield)	1:08.03
7 P. Woodrow (Stockport Metro)	1:08.15
8 R. Copping (Portsmouth Northsea)	1:09.21

4×50 Metres Freestyle Club Relay

1 Co Leeds	1:46.82
2 Stockport Metro	1:47.53
3 Beckenham	1:47.72
4 Norwich Penguins	1:48.08
5 Portsmouth Northsea	1:48.25
6 Millfield	1:49.64
7 Radford	1:50.39
8 Co Southampton	1:50.50

Stuart Wells

4×50 Metres Medley Club Relay

1 Co Leeds	1:59.42
2 Beckenham	2:02.25
3 Millfield	2:03.02
4 Norwich Penguins	2:03.41
5 Portsmouth Northsea	2:04.66
6 Stockport Metro	2:04.92
7 Co Southampton	2:05.94
8 Radford	2:07.82

Girls

100 Metres Freestyle

1 J. Pitt (Beckenham)	1:03.43
2 L. Sonn (Co Southampton)	1:04.10
3 J. Marshall (Norwich Penguins)	1:04.15
4 L. Racster (Portsmouth Northsea)	1:04.45
5 H. Cross (Co Leeds)	1:04.79
6 L. Merchant (Radford)	1:05.27
7 T. Gorham (Millfield)	1:06.92
8 L. Kettle (Stockport Metro)	1:07.05

100 Metres Backstroke

1 L. Racster (Portsmouth Northsea)	1:10.79
2 S. Green (Beckenham)	1:12.55
3 V. Goodwin (Millfield)	1:13.03
4 R. Loveman (Co Southampton)	1:15.55
5 B. Simmonds (Co Leeds)	1:16.15
6 K. Mellors (Radford)	1:16.28
7 A. Law (Norwich Penguins)	1:16.47
8 Y. Frayne (Stockport Metro)	1:18.89

100 Metres Breaststroke

1 C. Gable (Stockport Metro)	1:20.41
2 Z. Platt (Portsmouth Northsea)	1:21.66
3 J. Williamson (Co Southampton)	1:21.71
4 J. Farnsworth (Co Leeds)	1:22.21
5 M. Donaughy (Radford)	1:24.72
6 K. Marley (Beckenham)	1:25.42
7 M. Willsea (Norwich Penguins)	1:25.97
8 K. Wilson (Millfield)	1:31.22

100 Metres Butterfly

1 Z. Harrison (Norwich Penguins)	1:08.87
2 Z. Platt (Portsmouth Northsea)	1:09.31
3 P. Adams (Co Leeds)	1:10.94
4 C. Gable (Stockport Metro)	1:14.47
5 L. Sonn (Co Southampton)	1:15.04
6 V. Goodwin (Millfield)	1:15.20
7 C. Mabb (Beckenham)	1:15.55
8 K. Mellors (Radford)	1:16.12

4×50 Metres Freestyle Club Relay

1 Beckenham	1:57.64
2 Portsmouth Northsea	1:58.04
3 Stockport Metro	2:00.50
4 Norwich Penguins	2:00.51
5 Co Southampton	2:01.88
6 Co Leeds	2:02.09
7 Radford	2:02.58
8 Millfield	2:03.18

4×50 Metres Medley Club Relay

1 Beckenham	2:15.26
2 Portsmouth Northsea	2:15.74
3 Co Leeds	2:17.08
4 Norwich Penguins	2:17.91
5 Millfield	2:18.51
6 Radford	2:18.62
7 Co Southampton	2:18.67

8	Stockport Metro	2:19.18

Final Points Tables

1	Co Leeds	282.5
2	Portsmouth Northsea	279.0
3	Beckenham	253.5
4	Norwich Penguins	247.0
5	Co Southampton	194.0
6	Radford	186.0
7	Millfield	180.0
8	Stockport Metro	176.0

SPEEDO Swimmer of the Meet Awards:
Womens: Debbie Tubby (Norwich Penguins)
Mens: Neil Metcalfe (City of Leeds)
SPEEDO Prizes to Junior Age-Groupers:
15/u girls: Lynda Racster (Portsmouth Northsea)
15/u boys: Paul Edwards (Norwich Penguins)
13/u girls: Zoe Harrison (Norwich Penguins)
13/u boys: Neil Collins (Millfield)
11/u girls: Esther Watson (Radford)
11/u boys: Adrian Godwin (Portsmouth Northsea)

Debbie Tubby

British Club Team Championships
International Pool, Leeds – 10/11 March, 1989
Men

50 Metres Freestyle
Final

1	R. Cole (Co Manchester)	24.12
2	M. Fibbens (Barnet Copthall)	24.28
3	N. Metcalfe (Co Leeds)	24.55
4	G. Bulpitt (Co Birmingham)	24.73
5	D. Dyke (Co Coventry)	25.03
6	L. Holgate (Oundle & D)	25.04
7	S. Leith (Co Dundee)	25.26
8	J. Thomlinson (Millfield)	25.38

Heat Times

1	M. Fibbens (Barnet Copthall)	24.05
2	N. Metcalfe (Co Leeds)	24.76
3	G. Bulpitt (Co Birmingham)	24.95
4	R. Cole (Co Manchester)	25.06
5	L. Holgate (Oundle & D)	25.16
6	D. Dyke (Co Coventry)	25.38
7	J. Thomlinson (Millfield)	25.48
8	S. Leith (Co Dundee)	25.56
9	S. Foggo (Co Newcastle)	25.64
10	D. Robinson (Portsmouth Northsea)	25.73
11	R. Jennings (Nova Centurion)	25.89
12	A. Irwin (Kelly College)	25.90
13	I. McCallum (Paisley)	25.94
14	L. Piggott (Beckenham)	26.21
15	P. Faulkener (Wigan Wasps)	26.54
16	A. Jones (Torfaen)	26.61

100 Metres Freestyle
Final

1	M. Fibbens (Barnet Copthall)	51.86
2	N. Metcalfe (Co Leeds)	53.04
3	G. Bulpitt (Co Birmingham)	53.27
4	P. Brew (Kelly College)	53.93
5	S. Foggo (Co Newcastle)	54.84
6	D. Dyke (Co Coventry)	55.08
7	I. McCallum (Paisley)	55.34
8	L. Holgate (Oundle & D)	57.12

Heat Times

1	M. Fibbens (Barnet Copthall)	51.38
2	G. Bulpitt (Co Birmingham)	53.81
3	N. Metcalfe (Co Leeds)	53.91
4	P. Brew (Kelly College)	53.93
5	D. Dyke (Co Coventry)	55.15
6	S. Foggo (Co Newcastle)	55.20
7	I. McCallum (Paisley)	55.70
8	L. Holgate (Oundle & D)	55.85
9	P. Chick (Beckenham)	56.19
10	R. Tozer (Millfield)	56.27
11	R. Jennings (Nova Centurion)	56.42
12	D. Robinson (Portsmouth Northsea)	56.46
13	P. McQuaid (Co Manchester)	56.60
14	S. Leith (Co Dundee)	57.01
15	A. Jones (Torfaen)	57.41
16	P. Firth (Wigan Wasps)	57.87

400 Metres Freestyle
Final

1	J. Ong (Kelly College)	4:02.43
2	C. McNeil (Paisley)	4:02.86
3	J. Broughton (Co Leeds)	4:08.44
4	G. Robins (Portsmouth Northsea)	4:11.33
5	S. Moore (Oundle & D)	4:11.62
6	T. Jones (Co Birmingham)	4:12.68
7	A. May (Co Dundee)	4:14.86
8	S. McQuaid (Co Manchester)	4:18.64

Heat Times

1	J. Ong (Kelly College)	4:07.66
2	C. McNeil (Paisley)	4:07.69
3	J. Broughton (Co Leeds)	4:07.96
4	G. Robins (Portsmouth Northsea)	4:11.24
5	S. Moore (Oundle & D)	4:11.38
6	S. McQuaid (Co Manchester)	4:11.41
7	T. Jones (Co Birmingham)	4:12.40
8	A. May (Co Dundee)	4:13.55
9	I. Rosser (Torfaen)	4:13.88
10	A. Johnson (Co Newcastle)	4:17.30
11	S. Smith (Wigan Wasps)	4:22.30
12	R. Stapleton (Beckenham)	4:22.61
13	P. McGillion (Co Coventry)	4:22.67
14	C. Heathcote (Nova Centurion)	4:23.21

15	C. Biss (Barnet Copthall)	4:26.13
16	J. Ley (Millfield)	4:27.23

1500 Metres Freestyle
Heat Times (No Final)

1	J. Ong (Kelly College)	15:50.66
2	C. McNeil (Paisley)	16:15.20
3	T. Day (Co Leeds)	16:17.76
4	S. Moore (Oundle & D)	16:40.15
5	G. Bulpitt (Co Birmingham)	16:49.70
6	R. Stapleton (Beckenham)	16:50.01
7	A. Johnson (Co Newcastle)	16:57.41
8	N. Robinson (Portsmouth Northsea)	17:01.24
9	S. Smith (Wigan Wasps)	17:01.27
10	C. Heathcote (Nova Centurion)	17:01.51
11	S. McQuaid (Co Manchester)	17:12.23
12	B. Nowell (Torfaen)	17:12.55
13	H. Sheraton (Millfield)	17:34.73
14	C. Biss (Barnet Copthall)	17:45.83
15	J. Thompson (Co Coventry)	17:48.98
16	F. Thirde (Co Dundee)	18:20.94

50 Metres Backstroke
Final

1	M. Harris (Co Birmingham)	27.69
2	C. Cockcroft (Co Leeds)	27.95
3	M. O'Connor (Co Manchester)	28.85
4	I. Panting (Kelly College)	29.47
5	S. Foggo (Co Newcastle)	29.79
6	M. Hooper (Portsmouth Northsea)	30.06
7	N. Bridge (Millfield)	30.32
8	N. Michael (Beckenham)	30.47

Heat Times

1	M. Harris (Co Birmingham)	27.58
2	C. Cockcroft (Co Leeds)	27.97
3	M. O'Connor (Co Manchester)	29.17
4	S. Foggo (Co Newcastle)	29.59
5	I. Panting (Kelly College)	29.63
6	N. Bridge (Millfield)	30.12
7	M. Hooper (Portsmouth Northsea)	30.17
8	N. Michael (Beckenham)	30.18
9	D. Lo Cascio (Barnet Copthall)	30.20
10	S. Parker (Co Coventry)	30.43
11	P. Blake (Wigan Wasps)	30.49
12	A. May (Co Dundee)	30.51
13	C. Dunmore (Oundle & D)	30.52
14	S. Ferguson (Paisley)	31.04
15	M. Watkins (Torfaen)	31.31
16	C. Proctor (Nova Centurion)	31.64

100 Metres Backstroke
Final

1	C. Cockcroft (Co Leeds)	59.73
2	M. Harris (Co Birmingham)	59.82
3	G. Robins (Portsmouth Northsea)	59.83
4	M. O'Connor (Co Manchester)	1:00.61
5	I. Panting (Kelly College)	1:01.25
6	I. Rosser (Torfaen)	1:02.09
7	P. Blake (Wigan Wasps)	1:03.36
8	S. Wainwright (Millfield)	1:03.49

Heat Times

1	G. Robins (Portsmouth Northsea)	59.72
2	C. Cockcroft (Co Leeds)	1:00.02
3	M. Harris (Co Birmingham)	1:00.04
4	M. O'Connor (Co Manchester)	1:01.31
5	I. Panting (Kelly College)	1:01.62
6	I. Rosser (Torfaen)	1:01.76
7	S. Wainwright (Millfield)	1:03.20
8	P. Blake (Wigan Wasps)	1:03.22

9	T. Hobbs (Co Newcastle)	1:03.88
10	D. Lo Cascio (Barnet Copthall)	1:04.46
11	A. May (Co Dundee)	1:04.58
12	S. Parker (Co Coventry)	1:04.98
13	C. Dunmore (Oundle & D)	1:05.31
14	J. Brownhill (Beckenham)	1:05.84
15	S. Hooper (Nova Centurion)	1:07.95
16	S. Ferguson (Paisley)	1:08.05

50 Metres Breaststroke
Final

1	A. Moorhouse (Co Leeds)	29.93
2	N. Gillingham (Co Birmingham)	30.36
3	I. Campbell (Beckenham)	30.79
4	N. Hudghton (Co Dundee)	31.01
5	R. Wilkes (Portsmouth Northsea)	31.76
6	M. Wynn (Kelly College)	31.89
7	D. Mason (Co Newcastle)	32.05
8	A. Murdock (Nova Centurion)	32.36

Heat Times

1	A. Moorhouse (Co Leeds)	30.44
2	I. Campbell (Beckenham)	31.09
3	N. Hudghton (Co Dundee)	
	N. Gillingham (Co Birmingham)	31.28
5	R. Wilkes (Portsmouth Northsea)	31.41
6	D. Mason (Co Newcastle)	31.78
7	M. Wynn (Kelly College)	32.05
8	A. Murdock (Nova Centurion)	32.06
9	N. Gaggini (Oundle & D)	32.31
10	N. Curran (Paisley)	32.44
11	R. Norgrove (Torfaen)	32.46
12	M. Hodgson (Wigan Wasps)	32.81
13	A. Greig (Barnet Copthall)	32.92
14	P. McQuaid (Co Manchester)	33.02
15	W. O'Gorman (Millfield)	33.72
16	S. Penny (Co Coventry)	33.78

100 Metres Breaststroke
Final

1	N. Gillingham (Co Birmingham)	1:04.94
2	A. Moorhouse (Co Leeds)	1:05.13
3	N. Hudghton (Co Dundee)	1:06.80
4	I. Campbell (Beckenham)	1:07.15
5	M. Wynn (Kelly College)	1:09.29
6	A. Murdock (Nova Centurion)	1:09.43
7	R. Wilkes (Portsmouth Northsea)	1:10.10
8	N. Curran (Paisley)	1:12.14

Heat Times

1	A. Moorhouse (Co Leeds)	1:05.47
2	N. Gillingham (Co Birmingham)	1:07.26
3	N. Hudghton (Co Dundee)	1:07.97
4	I. Campbell (Beckenham)	1:08.63
5	R. Wilkes (Portsmouth Northsea)	1:09.37
6	M. Wynn (Kelly College)	1:09.62
7	N. Curran (Paisley)	1:10.34
8	A. Murdock (Nova Centurion)	1:10.52
9	R. Brown (Torfaen)	1:11.32
10	T. Evans (Oundle & D)	1:11.42
11	D. Mason (Co Newcastle)	1:11.55
12	A. Greig (Barnet Copthall)	1:11.64
13	M. Hodgson (Wigan Wasps)	1:11.93
14	P. Crewdson (Co Manchester)	1:12.04
15	S. Penny (Co Coventry)	1:12.95
16	W. O'Gorman (Millfield)	1:14.26

50 Metres Butterfly
Final

1	D. Parker (Co Coventry)	25.94
2	M. Fibbens (Barnet Copthall)	26.28

OTHER MAJOR COMPETITIONS, 1988-89

3 S. Dronsfield (Co Leeds) 26.36
4 R. Leishman (Kelly College) 26.45
5 R. Lee (Co Birmingham) 26.76
6 N. Parish (Oundle & D) 27.18
7 N. Bridge (Millfield) 27.20
8 M. Watkins (Torfaen) 27.49

Heat Times
1 M. Fibbens (Barnet Copthall) 25.85
2 S. Dronsfield (Co Leeds) 26.03
3 D. Parker (Co Coventry) 26.19
4 R. Leishman (Kelly College) 26.69
5 R. Lee (Co Birmingham) 27.22
6 N. Bridge (Millfield) 27.34
7 N. Parish (Oundle & D) 27.37
8 M. Watkins (Torfaen) 27.43
9 M. Hodgson (Wigan Wasps) 27.48
10 A. Quinn (Co Manchester) 27.59
11 C. Proctor (Nova Centurion) 27.81
12 J. Corless (Portsmouth Northsea) 27.82
13 S. Albin (Co Dundee) 27.86
14 D. Mason (Co Newcastle) 27.87
15 I. McCallum (Paisley) 28.25
16 N. Grenyer (Beckenham) 28.61

100 Metres Butterfly
Final
1 S. Dronsfield (Co Leeds) 57.22
2 T. Jones (Co Birmingham) 57.47
3 D. Parker (Co Coventry) 57.99
4 R. Leishman (Kelly College) 58.22
5 N. Parish (Oundle & D) 59.38
6 A. Quinn (Co Manchester) 59.48
7 M. Watkins (Torfaen) 1:00.10
8 N. Bridge (Millfield) 1:00.74

Heat Times
1 S. Dronsfield (Co Leeds) 57.36
2 T. Jones (Co Birmingham) 57.41
3 D. Parker (Co Coventry) 57.98
4 R. Leishman (Kelly College) 58.07
5 A. Quinn (Co Manchester) 59.63
6 N. Bridge (Millfield) 59.67
7 N. Parish (Oundle & D) 59.78
8 M. Watkins (Torfaen) 1:00.06
9 D. Lo Cascio (Barnet Copthall) 1:00.29
10 M. Hooper (Portsmouth Northsea) 1:00.86
11 L. Bennett (Co Newcastle) 1:01.09
12 S. Ferguson (Paisley) 1:03.08
13 G. Hall (Nova Centurion) 1:03.59
14 N. Grenyer (Beckenham) 1:03.73
15 S. Smith (Wigan Wasps) 1:04.01
16 N. Glave (Co Dundee) 1:04.14

200 Metres Individual Medley
Final
1 P. Brew (Kelly College) 2:08.43
2 T. Day (Co Leeds) 2:12.08
3 C. McNeil (Paisley) 2:13.56
4 I. Rosser (Torfaen) 2:13.72
5 A. Greig (Barnet Copthall) 2:14.37
6 N. Gillingham (Co Birmingham) 2:14.98
7 L. Bennett (Co Newcastle) 2:17.29
8 G. Robins (Portsmouth Northsea) 2:22.30

Heat Times
1 P. Brew (Kelly College) 2:12.48
2 G. Robins (Portsmouth Northsea) 2:13.24
3 N. Gillingham (Co Birmingham) 2:13.35
4 T. Day (Co Leeds) 2:13.71
5 I. Rosser (Torfaen) 2:13.94
6 C. McNeil (Paisley) 2:14.92

Tim Jones

7 A. Greig (Barnet Copthall) 2:15.24
8 L. Bennett (Co Newcastle) 2:16.16
9 T. Evans (Oundle & D) 2:16.52
10 R. Beacham (Co Coventry) 2:17.00
11 N. Hudghton (Co Dundee) 2:17.17
12 P. Blake (Wigan Wasps) 2:17.40
13 S. Wainwright (Millfield) 2:17.63
14 J. Brownhill (Beckenham) 2:18.63
15 S. McQuaid (Co Manchester) 2:23.80
    D. Anscombe (Nova Centurion) DIS

4×50 Metres Freestyle Club Relay
Final
1 Co Manchester 1:37.96
2 Co Birmingham 1:38.62
3 Co Leeds 1:39.01
4 Barnet Copthall 1:40.54
5 Co Newcastle 1:40.67
6 Millfield 1:41.87
7 Oundle & D 1:44.25
8 Co Coventry 1:45.43

Heat Times
1 Co Leeds 1:38.22
2 Co Manchester 1:39.49
3 Co Birmingham 1:39.84
4 Barnet Copthall 1:39.85
5 Millfield 1:40.67
6 Co Newcastle 1:41.20
7 Co Coventry 1:41.58
8 Oundle & D 1:41.70
9 Portsmouth Northsea 1:41.74
10 Kelly College 1:42.09
11 Paisley 1:42.10
12 Nova Centurion 1:42.40
13 Beckenham 1:42.56
14 Co Dundee 1:43.00
15 Torfaen 1:44.29
16 Wigan Wasps 1:44.39

4×50 Metres Medley Club Relay
Final
1 Co Leeds 1:48.78
2 Co Birmingham 1:48.93
3 Kelly College 1:51.29
4 Portsmouth Northsea 1:52.67

5	Co Dundee	1:52.71
6	Co Manchester	1:52.84
7	Oundle & D	1:54.77
8	Co Newcastle	1:56.17

Heat Times

1	Co Leeds	1:49.59
2	Co Birmingham	1:51.60
3	Portsmouth Northsea	1:52.06
4	Kelly College	1:53.02
5	Oundle & D	1:53.46
6	Co Dundee	1:53.69
7	Co Manchester	1:53.72
8	Co Newcastle	1:53.86
9	Barnet Copthall	1:53.90
10	Co Coventry	1:54.06
11	Torfaen	1:54.45
12	Beckenham	1:54.68
13	Millfield	1:55.03
14	Nova Centurion	1:55.64
15	Paisley	1:58.49
16	Wigan Wasps	1:59.17

Women

50 Metres Freestyle
Final

1	J. Waite (Co Southampton)	27.75
2	J. Gorst (Co Leeds)	27.90
3	J. McHarg (Portsmouth Northsea)	27.95
4	J. Coull (Co Birmingham)	28.09
5	J. Croft (Wigan Wasps)	28.13
6	N. Kennedy (Nova Centurion)	28.26
7	H. Mansfield (Co Chester)	28.51
8	H. Turk (Gloucester C)	28.75

Heat Times

1	J. McHarg (Portsmouth Northsea)	27.63
2	J. Gorst (Co Leeds)	27.72
3	J. Waite (Co Southampton)	27.75
4	J. Coull (Co Birmingham)	27.81
5	J. Croft (Wigan Wasps)	27.88
6	H. Mansfield (Co Chester)	27.97
7	N. Kennedy (Nova Centurion)	28.31
8	H. Turk (Gloucester C)	28.37
9	C. Horton (Norwich Penguins)	28.39
10	E. Archer (Kelly College)	28.53
11	L. Graham (Barnet Copthall)	28.62
12	S. Vick (Co Sheffield)	28.64
13	N. Pinch (Torfaen)	28.85
14	E. Gilfillan (Co Dundee)	29.03
15	J. Bryce (Warrender)	29.21
16	H. Lawrence (Beckenham)	29.25

100 Metres Freestyle
Final

1	R. Gilfillan (Co Dundee)	59.29
2	J. Croft (Wigan Wasps)	59.32
3	J. Coull (Co Birmingham)	59.47
4	G. Atkins (Portsmouth Northsea)	59.74
5	H. Mansfield (Co Chester)	1:00.10
6	J. Gorst (Co Leeds)	1:01.21
7	H. Sanderson (Nova Centurion)	1:01.85
8	J. Waite (Co Southampton)	1:02.39

Heat Times

1	J. Coull (Co Birmingham)	59.18
2	J. Croft (Wigan Wasps)	1:00.11
3	R. Gilfillan (Co Dundee)	1:00.31
4	H. Mansfield (Co Chester)	1:00.59
5	G. Atkins (Portsmouth Northsea)	1:00.62
6	J. Gorst (Co Leeds)	1:00.89
7	J. Waite (Co Southampton)	1:01.14
8	H. Sanderson (Nova Centurion)	1:01.52
9	S. Vick (Co Sheffield)	1:01.91
10	N. Bates (Norwich Penguins)	1:01.95
11	H. Tooke (Kelly College)	1:02.09
12	L. Graham (Barnet Copthall)	1:02.29
13	R. Smart (Gloucester C)	1:02.43
14	N. Pinch (Torfaen)	1:03.44
15	H. Lawrence (Beckenham)	1:03.85
16	K. Robson (Warrender)	1:04.56

400 Metres Freestyle
Final

1	K. Mellor (Co Sheffield)	4:20.77
2	J. Croft (Wigan Wasps)	4:20.94
3	R. Gilfillan (Co Dundee)	4:25.37
4	M. Scarborough (Portsmouth Northsea)	4:31.30
5	L. Smart (Co Chester)	4:31.74
6	D. Churchman (Co Leeds)	4:34.80
7	J. Coull (Co Birmingham)	4:35.96
8	J. Marshall (Norwich Penguins)	4:42.42

Heat Times

1	K. Mellor (Co Sheffield)	4:25.67
2	R. Gilfillan (Co Dundee)	4:29.15
3	L. Smart (Co Chester)	4:29.33
4	J. Coull (Co Birmingham)	4:31.04
5	J. Croft (Wigan Wasps)	4:32.39
6	M. Scarborough (Portsmouth Northsea)	4:32.99
7	D. Churchman (Co Leeds)	4:33.71
8	J. Marshall (Norwich Penguins)	4:41.31
9	N. Cumbers (Kelly College)	4:41.48
10	L. Hawking (Nova Centurion)	4:41.79
11	N. Sommers (Beckenham)	4:42.43
12	N. Pinch (Torfaen)	4:43.49
13	M. Harley (Barnet Copthall)	4:46.99
14	R. Loveman (Co Southampton)	4:47.25
15	A. Elder (Warrender)	4:47.42
16	E. O'Sullivan (Gloucester C)	4:57.29

800 Metres Freestyle
Heat Times (No Final)

1	K. Mellor (Co Sheffield)	8:53.00
2	P. Hutchinson (Wigan Wasps)	9:05.89
3	R. Gilfillan (Co Dundee)	9:07.73
4	M. Scarborough (Portsmouth Northsea)	9:09.91
5	L. Smart (Co Chester)	9:12.00
6	K. Read (Norwich Penguins)	9:15.01
7	J. Deakins (Gloucester C)	9:15.09
8	D. Churchman (Co Leeds)	9:24.38
9	C. Piggott (Co Birmingham)	9:26.93
10	N. Sommers (Beckenham)	9:28.33
11	L. Hawking (Nova Centurion)	9:34.31
12	A. Elder (Warrender)	9:39.99
13	R. Loveman (Co Southampton)	9:42.46
14	N. Cumbers (Kelly College)	9:42.59
15	C. Bowen (Torfaen)	9:54.23
16	M. Harley (Barnet Copthall)	10:00.21

50 Metres Backstroke
Final

1	S. Page (Co Birmingham)	31.18
2	K. Read (Norwich Penguins)	31.92
3	J. Deakins (Gloucester C)	32.19
4	L. Racster (Portsmouth Northsea)	32.37
5	H. Slatter (Kelly College)	32.58
6	J. Kelly (Co Southampton)	32.66
7	S. Rosser (Torfaen)	33.12
8	S. Garrett (Barnet Copthall)	33.70

Heat Times

1 S. Page (Co Birmingham) — 31.49
2 K. Read (Norwich Penguins) — 31.76
3 J. Deakins (Gloucester C) — 32.19
4 H. Slatter (Kelly College) — 32.99
5 J. Kelly (Co Southampton) — 32.53
6 S. Rosser (Torfaen) — 32.88
7 S. Garrett (Barnet Copthall) — 32.96
8 L. Racster (Portsmouth Northsea) — 33.21
9 E. Armstrong (Co Leeds) — 33.47
10 J. Wright (Co Chester) — 33.50
11 L. Lennon (Nova Centurion) — 33.53
12 S. Green (Beckenham) — 33.59
13 S. Hindmarch (Wigan Wasps) — 33.81
    K. Mellor (Co Sheffield)
15 J. Latimer (Warrender) — 34.22
16 S. Gilfillan (Co Dundee) — 34.70

100 Metres Backstroke
Final

1 S. Page (Co Birmingham) — 1:06.11
2 K. Read (Norwich Penguins) — 1:06.92
3 J. Deakins (Gloucester C) — 1:06.97
4 H. Slatter (Kelly College) — 1:07.73
5 J. Kelly (Co Southampton) — 1:09.58
6 L. Racster (Portsmouth Northsea) — 1:09.66
7 J. Wood (Nova Centurion) — 1:09.72
8 J. Wright (Co Chester) — 1:10.22

Heat Times

1 K. Read (Norwich Penguins) — 1:06.61
2 J. Deakins (Gloucester C) — 1:07.07
3 H. Slatter (Kelly College) — 1:07.69
4 S. Page (Co Birmingham) — 1:08.26
5 J. Kelly (Co Southampton) — 1:08.95
6 J. Wood (Nova Centurion) — 1:08.97
7 J. Wright (Co Chester) — 1:09.15
8 L. Racster (Portsmouth Northsea) — 1:09.69
9 S. Green (Beckenham) — 1:11.03
10 J. Latimer (Warrender) — 1:11.33
11 R. Jenkins (Torfaen) — 1:11.93
12 E. Armstrong (Co Leeds) — 1:12.29
13 D. Evans (Wigan Wasps) — 1:12.44
14 S. Garrett (Barnet Copthall) — 1:13.22
15 S. Tanner (Co Sheffield) — 1:13.48
16 F. Morrison (Co Dundee) — 1:15.55

50 Metres Breaststroke
Final

1 M. Hohmann (Wigan Wasps) — 33.47
2 L. Coombes (Co Southampton) — 33.76
3 R. Gillatt (Co Sheffield) — 34.70
4 A. Baker (Norwich Penguins) — 35.51
5 J. Henwood (Torfaen) — 35.55
6 H. Frank (Co Leeds) — 36.22
7 S. Smart (Co Chester) — 36.52
8 L. Spiller (Barnet Copthall) — 36.72

Heat Times

1 M. Hohmann (Wigan Wasps) — 33.59
2 L. Coombes (Co Southampton) — 34.33
3 R. Gillatt (Co Sheffield) — 34.91
4 J. Henwood (Torfaen) — 35.21
5 A. Baker (Norwich Penguins) — 35.49
6 H. Frank (Co Leeds) — 35.69
7 S. Smart (Co Chester) — 36.04
8 L. Spiller (Barnet Copthall) — 36.39
9 N. James (Nova Centurion) — 36.53
    E. Alexander (Co Dundee)
11 A. Kindon (Co Birmingham) — 36.70

12 H. Goddard (Gloucester C) — 37.06
13 Z. Platt (Portsmouth Northsea) — 37.37
14 R. Brinn (Kelly College) — 37.42
15 L. McLaren (Warrender) — 37.49
16 E. Burns (Beckenham) — 37.82

100 Metres Breaststroke
Final

1 M. Hohmann (Wigan Wasps) — 1:13.13
2 R. Gillatt (Co Sheffield) — 1:16.52
3 J. Henwood (Torfaen) — 1:16.57
4 L. Coombes (Co Southampton) — 1:16.81
5 H. Frank (Co Leeds) — 1:16.92
6 S. Smart (Co Chester) — 1:17.06
7 A. Baker (Norwich Penguins) — 1:18.49
8 L. McLaren (Warrender) — 1:19.40

Heat Times

1 M. Hohmann (Wigan Wasps) — 1:15.84
2 R. Gillatt (Co Sheffield) — 1:16.39
3 L. Coombes (Co Southampton) — 1:16.75
4 J. Henwood (Torfaen) — 1:17.00
5 J. Frank (Co Leeds) — 1:17.46
6 A. Baker (Norwich Penguins) — 1:18.56
7 S. Smart (Co Chester) — 1:18.81
8 L. McLaren (Warrender) — 1:19.50
9 N. James (Nova Centurion) — 1:19.20
10 E. Burns (Beckenham) — 1:20.32
11 C. Piggott (Co Birmingham) — 1:20.51
12 E. Alexander (Co Dundee) — 1:21.10
13 H. Goddard (Gloucester C) — 1:21.11
14 Z. Platt (Portsmouth Northsea) — 1:22.33
15 L. Spiller (Barnet Copthall) — 1:23.61
16 R. Brinn (Kelly College) — 1:23.83

50 Metres Butterfly
Final

1 M. Scarborough (Portsmouth Northsea) — 29.57
2 N. Kennedy (Nova Centurion) — 29.70
3 S. Brooksbank (Co Leeds) — 30.31
4 H. Turk (Gloucester C) — 30.46
5 S. Brownsdon (Wigan Wasps) — 30.57
6 M. Hadden (Beckenham) — 30.86
7 N. Bates (Norwich Penguins) — 30.92
8 H. Paull (Kelly College) — 31.25

Heat Times

1 M. Scarborough (Portsmouth Northsea) — 29.72
2 N. Kennedy (Nova Centurion) — 29.81
3 S. Brooksbank (Co Leeds) — 30.10
4 N. Bates (Norwich Penguins) — 30.38
5 M. Hadden (Beckenham) — 30.40
6 H. Turk (Gloucester C) — 30.59
7 S. Brownsdon (Wigan Wasps) — 30.60
8 H. Paull (Kelly College) — 31.04
9 S. Page (Co Birmingham) — 31.05
10 B. Bowden (Co Southampton) — 31.20
11 B. Jones (Co Chester) — 31.28
12 S. Rosser (Torfaen) — 31.60
13 J. Stark (Co Sheffield) — 31.80
14 E. Gilfillan (Co Dundee) — 31.85
15 K. Robson (Warrender) — 32.09
16 D. Nissim (Barnet Copthall) — 32.34

100 Metres Butterfly
Final

1 S. Brooksbank (Co Leeds) — 1:06.02
2 N. Kennedy (Nova Centurion) — 1:06.17
3 G. Atkins (Portsmouth Northsea) — 1:06.40
4 S. Brownsdon (Wigan Wasps) — 1:06.53
5 M. Hadden (Beckenham) — 1:08.73

6	B. Jones (Co Chester)	1:09.03
7	G. Kerr (Warrender)	1:10.70
8	H. Osborne (Co Birmingham)	1:12.52

Heat Times

1	G. Atkins (Portsmouth Northsea)	1:05.34
2	S. Brooksbank (Co Leeds)	1:06.66
3	N. Kennedy (Nova Centurion)	1:07.29
4	M. Hadden (Beckenham)	1:07.60
5	H. Osborne (Co Birmingham)	1:08.14
6	S. Brownsdon (Wigan Wasps)	1:08.33
7	B. Jones (Co Chester)	1:08.68
8	R. Smart (Gloucester C)	1:08.95
	G. Kerr (Warrender)	
10	J. Stark (Co Sheffield)	1:08.98
11	N. Bates (Norwich Penguins)	1:09.02
12	H. Paull (Kelly College)	1:09.70
13	S. Rosser (Torfaen)	1:10.29
14	E. Gilfillan (Co Dundee)	1:10.50
15	D. Nissim (Barnet Copthall)	1:11.63
16	B. Bowden (Co Southampton)	1:12.60

200 Metres Individual Medley
Final

1	S. Brownsdon (Wigan Wasps)	2:22.83
2	S. Slatter (Kelly College)	2:23.57
3	S. Smart (Co Chester)	2:25.77
4	G. Atkins (Portsmouth Northsea)	2:29.46
5	C. Upton (Beckenham)	2:30.68
6	S. Vick (Co Sheffield)	2:30.79
7	H. Osborne (Co Birmingham)	2:31.82
8	G. Kerr (Warrender)	2:32.47

Heat Times

1	S. Smart (Co Chester)	2:24.34
2	H. Slatter (Kelly College)	2:25.48
3	S. Brownsdon (Wigan Wasps)	2:26.59
4	G. Atkins (Portsmouth Northsea)	2:28.68
5	S. Vick (Co Sheffield)	2:29.57
6	G. Kerr (Warrender)	2:29.73
7	C. Upton (Beckenham)	2:29.74
	H. Osborne (Co Birmingham)	
9	A. Baker (Norwich Penguins)	2:29.85
	S. Garrett (Barnet Copthall)	
11	S. Gilfillan (Co Dundee)	2:30.53
12	A. McKellican (Co Leeds)	2:30.56
13	R. Smart (Gloucester C)	2:31.08

Susan Vick

14	H. Sanderson (Nova Centurion)	2:33.19
15	B. Bowden (Co Southampton)	2:33.66
16	R. Jenkins (Torfaen)	2:40.75

4×50 Metres Freestyle Club Relay
Final

1	Co Birmingham	1:50.82
2	Portsmouth Northsea	1:52.73
3	Wigan Wasps	1:53.87
4	Co Leeds	1:54.05
5	Kelly College	1:54.57
6	Norwich Penguins	1:55.21
7	Nova Centurion	1:55.39
8	Co Chester	1:56.64

Heat Times

1	Co Birmingham	1:51.69
2	Norwich Penguins	1:54.37
3	Portsmouth Northsea	1:54.41
4	Co Leeds	1:54.51
5	Nova Centurion	1:54.86
6	Wigan Wasps	1:54.91
7	Kelly College	1:55.35
8	Co Chester	1:55.41
9	Co Southampton	1:55.57
10	Barnet Copthall	1:56.08
11	Co Dundee	1:56.72
12	Gloucester C	1:56.84
13	Co Sheffield	1:57.48
14	Beckenham	1:57.62
15	Warrender	1:57.88
16	Torfaen	1:58.09

4×50 Metres Medley Club Relay
Final

1	Wigan Wasps	2:03.16
2	Co Southampton	2:04.54
3	Norwich Penguins	2:06.28
4	Co Leeds	2:07.60
5	Portsmouth Northsea	2:07.89
6	Nova Centurion	2:08.16
7	Co Chester	2:11.37
8	Barnet Copthall	2:12.69

Heat Times

1	Wigan Wasps	2:04.53
2	Co Southampton	2:05.36
3	Norwich Penguins	2:05.88
4	Nova Centurion	2:06.50
5	Portsmouth Northsea	2:07.40
6	Co Leeds	2:08.06
7	Barnet Copthall	2:08.71
8	Co Chester	2:08.74
9	Kelly College	2:09.02
10	Co Birmingham	2:09.19
11	Beckenham	2:09.91
12	Co Sheffield	2:10.59
13	Warrender	2:10.94
14	Gloucester C	2:11.04
15	Co Dundee	2:11.05
16	Torfaen	2:11.59

Final Points Tables
Men

1	Co Leeds	237
2	Co Birmingham	221
3	Kelly College	199
4	Portsmouth Northsea	152
5	Oundle & D	148

6	Co Manchester	144
7	Co Newcastle	140
	Barnet Copthall	
9	Co Coventry	121
10	Paisley	116
11	Co Dundee	111
12	Millfield	106
13	Torfaen	104
14	Beckenham	103
15	Nova Centurion	79
16	Wigan Wasps	74

Women

1	Wigan Wasps	207

2	Portsmouth Northsea	190
3	Co Leeds	177
4	Co Birmingham	171
5	Norwich Penguins	168
	Co Chester	
7	Nova Centurion	147
8	Co Southampton	144
9	Co Sheffield	136
10	Kelly College	125
11	Gloucester C	117
12	Co Dundee	102
13	Beckenham	100
14	Torfaen	87
15	Barnet Copthall	85
16	Warrender	76

Edinburgh Open Meet (Finals)

Royal Commonwealth Pool, Edinburgh – 23/25 March, 1989

NOTE: Owing to lack of space, senior heats, consolation finals, and junior events held at the meet, are not recorded.

Men

50 Metres Freestyle

1	W. Johnston (Ulster)	24.19
2	D. Miller (Stockport Metro)	24.63
3	G. Watson (Carnegie)	24.64
4	B. Bell (Ulster)	24.73
5	S. Ferguson (Paisley)	24.76
6	J. Bradley (Bath University)	24.83
7	O. Andreson (Norway)	25.37
8	J. Nygard (Norway)	25.43

100 Metres Freestyle

1	J. Bradley (Bath University)	53.16
2	W. Johnston (Ulster)	53.48
3	P. Easter (Norwich Penguins)	54.11
4	P. Henry (Edinburgh)	54.13
5	D. Miller (Stockport Metro)	54.36
6	P. McQuaid (Co Manchester)	54.49
7	C. McNeil (Paisley)	54.66
8	K. Boyd (Bo S Tyneside)	55.30

200 Metres Freestyle

1	C. McNeil (Paisley)	1:55.17
2	P. Henry (Edinburgh)	1:55.64
3	K. Boyd (Bo S Tyneside)	1:56.54
4	P. Easter (Norwich Penguins)	1:57.56
5	A. Dahl (Norway)	1:58.53
6	J. Bradley (Bath University)	1:59.82
7	D. Miller (Stockport Metro)	2:01.49
8	P. McGillion (Ulster)	2:03.57

400 Metres Freestyle

1	K. Boyd (Bo S Tyneside)	3:59.69
2	C. McNeil (Paisley)	4:00.58
3	P. Henry (Edinburgh)	4:04.68
4	A. Dahl (Norway)	4:14.09
5	A. Brown (Edinburgh)	4:14.89
6	R. Noble (Stirling)	4:16.13
7	I. McIntyre (Edinburgh)	4:16.36
8	S. McKinlay (Cumbernauld)	4:16.85

1500 Metres Freestyle

1	K. Boyd (Bo S Tyneside)	16:01.57
2	C. McNeil (Paisley)	16:16.06
3	R. Noble (Stirling)	16:33.09
4	A. Brown (Edinburgh)	16:39.25
5	I. McIntyre (Edinburgh)	16:51.31
6	J. McHale (Co Sheffield)	17:01.42
7	G. Hall (Reading)	17:06.82
8	B. Lafferty (Co Sheffield)	17:14.61
	S. Leitch (Warrender)	

100 Metres Backstroke

1	K. Boyd (Bo S Tyneside)	59.97
2	J. Fleet (Essex County)	1:01.87
3	P. Blake (Wigan Wasps)	1:02.42
4	U. Weuder (Denmark)	1:02.71
5	J. Kerr (Warrender)	1:02.77
6	E. Stewart (Co Dundee)	1:03.30
7	T. Hobbs (Co Newcastle)	1:03.83
8	M. Kofoed (Denmark)	1:04.76

200 Metres Backstroke

1	K. Boyd (Bo S Tyneside)	2:08.49
2	P. Blake (Wigan Wasps)	2:10.02
3	U. Weuder (Denmark)	2:13.30
4	D. McNulty (Chester le Street)	2:13.61
5	J. Fleet (Essex County)	2:16.36
6	T. Hobbs (Co Newcastle)	2:17.33
7	M. Kofoed (Denmark)	2:18.88
8	J. Austin (Co Sheffield)	2:19.34

100 Metres Breaststroke

1	A. Marcek (Czechoslovakia)	1:04.45
2	R. Beinhaver (Czechoslovakia)	1:05.45
3	G. Watson (Carnegie)	1:05.54
4	N. Hughton (Co Dundee)	1:06.64
5	A. Murdock (Nova Centurion)	1:09.41
6	O. Andreson (Norway)	1:10.13
7	J. Lant (Co Sheffield)	1:10.68
8	P. McGillion (Ulster)	1:13.34

200 Metres Breaststroke

1	A. Marcek (Czechoslovakia)	2:18.61
2	R. Beinhaver (Czechoslovakia)	2:19.17
3	N. Hughton (Co Dundee)	2:21.79
4	S. Stigant (Douglas)	2:33.48
5	A. Murdock (Nova Centurion)	2:34.54
6	P. McGillion (Ulster)	2:34.81
7	P. Crewsdon (Co Manchester)	2:37.60
8	C. With (Norway)	2:38.49

100 Metres Butterfly

1	E. Stewart (Co Dundee)	58.85
2	A. Quinn (Co Manchester)	58.99
3	D. McNulty (Chester le Street)	59.39
4	W. Johnston (Ulster)	59.57
5	N. Waterson (Cumbernauld)	59.59
6	E. Clasen (Norway)	1:00.00
7	S. Milne (Peterhead)	1:00.40
8	J. Thomlinson (Millfield)	1:01.05

200 Metres Butterfly

1	A. Quinn (Co Manchester)	2:08.22
2	D. McNulty (Chester le Street)	2:08.36
3	S. Milne (Peterhead)	2:09.30
4	P. Henry (Edinburgh)	2:12.57
5	K. Renshaw (Chester le Street)	2:13.96
6	A. Buchanan (Stirling)	2:15.19
7	S. McQuaid (Co Manchester)	2:16.14
8	N. Waterson (Cumbernauld)	2:17.30

200 Metres Individual Medley

1	P. McGillion (Ulster)	2:12.68
2	P. Henry (Edinburgh)	2:12.81
3	P. Blake (Wigan Wasps)	2:13.44
4	J. Kerr (Warrender)	2:14.89
5	D. Anscombe (Nova Centurion)	2:17.37
6	A. Quinn (Co Manchester)	2:18.24
7	K. Dick (Chester le Street)	2:20.33
8	C. With (Norway)	2:20.43

400 Metres Individual Medley

1	P. Blake (Wigan Wasps)	4:41.57
2	P. Henry (Edinburgh)	4:42.14
3	D. McNulty (Chester le Street)	4:44.08
4	P. Kappes (Essex County)	4:45.12
5	J. Kerr (Warrender)	4:46.51
6	S. McKinlay (Cumbernauld)	4:46.63
7	P. McGillion (Ulster)	4:49.18
8	C. Thompson (Co Bradford)	4:49.32

Women

50 Metres Freestyle

1	A. Sheppard (Milngarvie)	26.79
2	K. Nygard (Norway)	27.32
3	N. Williams (Stockport Metro)	27.69
4	F. Phimister (Moray & D)	27.80
5	B. Greenwood (Aberdeen)	28.23
6	A. Askland (Norway)	28.27
7	G. Lavin (Derwentside)	28.40
8	H. Mansfield (Co Chester)	28.43

100 Metres Freestyle

1	L. Donnelly (Hamilton Baths)	58.54
2	A. Sheppard (Milngarvie)	59.14
3	N. Williams (Stockport Metro)	59.90
4	H. Mansfield (Co Chester)	59.91
5	B. Greenwood (Aberdeen)	1:00.38
6	T. Aasbo (Norway)	1:00.64
7	E. Gilfillan (Co Dundee)	1:00.98
8	A. Ewing (Paisley)	1:01.55

200 Metres Freestyle

1	L. Donnelly (Hamilton Baths)	2:05.03
2	H. Mansfield (Co Chester)	2:08.04
3	C. Shiell (Edinburgh)	2:08.13
4	L. Smart (Co Chester)	2:09.77
5	B. Greenwood (Aberdeen)	2:11.48
6	T. Aasbo (Norway)	2:12.10
7	J. Thurgoland (Sale)	2:13.42
8	P. Herron (Co Newcastle)	2:14.69

400 Metres Freestyle

1	N. Atkinson (Stockport Metro)	4:24.05
2	C. Shiell (Edinburgh)	4:24.40
3	M. Ivison (Bo S Tyneside)	4:32.14
4	J. Thurgoland (Sale)	4:34.13
5	L. Smart (Co Chester)	4:36.21
6	L. Matthews (Essex County)	4:41.10

800 Metres Freestyle

1	N. Atkinson (Stockport Metro)	9:01.33
2	C. Shiell (Edinburgh)	9:06.37
3	L. Matthews (Essex County)	9:14.05
4	L. Smart (Co Chester)	9:15.66
5	M. Ivison (Bo S Tyneside)	9:19.32
6	M. Madine (Ulster)	9:21.55
7	V. Barnes (Co Manchester)	9:32.54
8	J. Davey (Co Newcastle)	9:33.46

100 Metres Backstroke

1	J. Ewing (Paisley)	1:05.83
2	L. Phimister (Moray & D)	1:07.19
3	S. Belaire (Denmark)	1:08.43
4	B. Greenwood (Aberdeen)	1:09.11
5	A. Sedgebeer (Essex County)	1:10.49
6	L. Cunningham (Edinburgh)	1:11.66

200 Metres Backstroke

1	J. Ewing (Paisley)	2:23.27
2	L. Cunningham (Edinburgh)	2:25.04
3	L. Phimister (Moray & D)	2:25.87
4	A. Sedgebeer (Essex County)	2:25.98
5	J. Bennett (Stockport Metro)	2:27.40
6	P. Herron (Co Newcastle)	2:29.91
7	B. Greenwood (Aberdeen)	2:31.73
8	A. Granli (Norway)	2:32.62

100 Metres Breaststroke

1	J. Hill (Cumbernauld)	1:15.32
2	C. Gable (Stockport Metro)	1:15.60
3	L. Aanesen (Norway)	1:16.45
4	H. Gorman (Nova Centurion)	1:16.46
5	B. Shimmons (Stirling)	1:16.92
6	S. Brown (Douglas)	1:16.99
7	D. Campbell (Cumbernauld)	1:18.10
8	S. Smart (Co Chester)	1:22.15

Pippa Herron

200 Metres Breaststroke

1 J. Hill (Cumbernauld)	2:39.04
2 H. Gorman (Nova Centurion)	2:46.66
3 S. Smart (Co Chester)	2:46.94
C. Gable (Stockport)	
5 S. Brown (Ulster)	2:47.21
6 J. Wood (Radford)	2:48.94
7 B. Shimmons (Stirling)	2:50.58

100 Metres Butterfly

1 C. Foot (Millfield)	1:04.41
2 N. Kennedy (Nova Centurion)	1:04.57
3 A. Baker (Norwich Penguins)	1:04.83
4 A. Duffy (Derwentside)	1:05.25
5 M. Madine (Ulster)	1:05.29
6 S. Buxton (Nova Centurion)	1:05.68
7 L. Appleton (Warrington Warriors)	1:08.20
8 N. Appleton (Stockport Metro)	1:11.51

200 Metres Butterfly

1 N. Atkinson (Stockport Metro)	2:21.31
A. Baker (Norwich Penguins)	
3 C. Foot (Millfield)	2:22.14
4 M. Madine (Ulster)	2:22.72

5 S. Smart (Co Chester)	2:24.41
6 L. Appleton (Warrington Warriors)	2:27.20
7 G. Kerr (Warrender)	2:28.87
8 J. Stark (Co Sheffield)	2:35.10

200 Metres Individual Medley

1 J. Hill (Cumbernauld)	2:21.76
2 S. Smart (Co Chester)	2:24.73
3 L. Phimister (Moray & D)	2:27.32
4 H. Mansfield (Co Chester)	2:27.36
5 S. Vick (Co Sheffield)	2:29.26
6 T. Aasbo (Norway)	2:30.63
7 S. Gilfillan (Co Dundee)	2:31.32
8 J. Wood (Radford)	2:31.38

400 Metres Individual Medley

1 S. Smart (Co Chester)	5:03.24
2 L. Phimister (Moray & D)	5:07.94
3 H. Mansfield (Co Chester)	5:08.78
4 A. Baker (Norwich Penguins)	5:11.07
5 D. Palmer (Essex County)	5:14.12
6 S. Gilfillan (Co Dundee)	5:16.24
7 G. Kerr (Warrender)	5:16.71
8 S. Vick (Co Sheffield)	5:17.99

Cardiff Speedo Meet (Finals)

Empire Pool, Cardiff – 29 April/1 May, 1989

NOTE: Owing to lack of space, heats and consolation finals held at the meet, are not recorded.

Men

50 Metres Freestyle

1 M. Foster (Bo Southend)	23.90
2 M. Fibbens (Barnet Copthall)	23.97
3 W. Johnston (Ulster)	24.36
4 A. Shortman (Bristol Central)	24.47
5 A. Rapley (Buxton & D)	24.52
6 S. Foggo (Co Newcastle)	24.84
7 R. Clarke (Canada)	24.96
8 P. Brew (Kelly College)	25.42

100 Metres Freestyle

1 M. Fibbens (Barnet Copthall)	52.44
2 M. Foster (Bo Southend)	52.96
3 S. McQuaid (Loughborough University)	53.11
4 G. Bulpitt (Co Birmingham)	53.36
W. Johnston (Ulster)	
6 R. Clarke (Canada)	54.14
7 M. Hanby (Nova Centurion)	54.63
8 J. Cunningham (Munster)	54.88

200 Metres Freestyle

1 S. McQuaid (Loughborough University)	1:54.03
2 P. Brew (Kelly College)	1:54.86
3 G. Bulpitt (Co Birmingham)	1:55.05
4 M. Weighton (Wulfrunians)	1:57.44
5 R. Clarke (Canada)	1:57.55
6 C. Jones (Co Swansea)	1:57.58
7 J. Ong (Kelly College)	1:58.60
8 I. Stewart (York C)	1:59.58

400 Metres Freestyle

1 I. Wilson (Bo Sunderland)	3:59.54
2 P. Brew (Kelly College)	4:02.62
3 J. Ong (Kelly College)	4:07.22
4 R. Clarke (Canada)	4:08.23
5 G. Hall (Reading)	4:13.21
6 A. Johnson (Co Newcastle)	4:14.30
7 V. Leon (Barnet Copthall)	4:19.33
8 T. Hobbs (Co Newcastle)	4:19.47

1500 Metres Freestyle

1 I. Wilson (Bo Sunderland)	15:51.33
2 J. Ong (Kelly College)	16:18.98
3 S. Clamp (Co Coventry)	16:37.89
4 S. Smith (Wigan Wasps)	16:46.24
5 B. Woolhouse (Canada)	16:53.66
6 T. Hobbs (Co Newcastle)	16:53.84
7 D. Pye (St Helens)	17:04.45
8 S. S. Houlton (Luton)	17:13.16

50 Metres Backstroke

1 M. Peyrebrune (Loughborough University)	28.18
2 A. Rapley (Buxton & D)	28.29
3 I. Panting (Kelly College)	28.72
4 M. Matthews (Barnet Copthall)	28.74
5 M. O'Conner (Co Manchester)	28.76
6 A. Pfeiffer (Switzerland)	28.79
7 C. Jones (Co Swansea)	29.09
8 R. Gheel (Ulster)	29.10

100 Metres Backstroke

1 M. O'Connor (Co Manchester)	1:00.33
I. Rosser (Torfaen)	
3 M. Peyrebrune (Loughborough University)	1:00.78
4 I. Panting (Kelly College)	1:00.94
5 R. Gheel (Ulster)	1:01.12
6 M. Matthews (Barnet Copthall)	1:01.16
7 J. Kearney (Nova Centurion)	1:01.30
8 B. Winter (Swansea University)	1:01.69

200 Metres Backstroke

1	I. Rosser (Torfaen)	2:07.94
2	M. O'Connor (Co Manchester)	2:08.73
3	R. Gheel (Ulster)	2:10.71
4	M. Matthews (Barnet Copthall)	2:11.30
5	I. Stewart (York C)	2:11.54
6	J. Kearney (Nova Centurion)	2:11.65
7	B. Winter (Swansea University)	2:14.33
8	J. Kerr (Kelly College)	2:15.55

50 Metres Breaststroke

1	I. Campbell (Beckenham)	30.67
2	M. Weighton (Wulfrunians)	31.37
3	P. Hennys (Soundwell)	31.48
4	D. Mason (Co Newcastle)	31.63
5	M. Wynn (Kelly College)	31.68
6	P. Ford (Bath University)	31.88
7	D. Carr (Co Newcastle)	32.21
8	R. Brown (Torfaen)	32.22

100 Metres Breaststroke

1	I. Campbell (Beckenham)	1:05.86
2	D. Mason (Co Newcastle)	1:07.24
3	R. Brown (Torfaen)	1:07.99
4	C. Thompson (Co Bradford)	1:08.85
5	P. Hennys (Soundwell)	1:08.96
6	M. Wynn (Kelly College)	1:09.08
7	P. Melhuish (Co Cardiff)	1:10.54
8	D. Bearman (Holywell)	1:11.73

200 Metres Breaststroke

1	N. Gillingham (Co Birmingham)	2:22.36
2	I. Campbell (Beckenham)	2:24.63
3	R. Brown (Torfaen)	2:27.68
4	D. Entwistle (Royton)	2:28.31
5	C. Thompson (Co Bradford)	2:28.85
6	P. Hennys (Soundwell)	2:32.23
7	R. Laidlow (Kelly College)	2:32.58
8	P. Melhuish (Co Cardiff)	2:33.69

50 Metres Butterfly

1	M. Foster (Bo Southend)	25.73
2	W. Johnston (Ulster)	25.96
3	M. Fibbens (Barnet Copthall)	26.10
4	M. Smith (Co Swansea)	26.28
5	G. Bulpitt (Co Birmingham)	26.80
6	M. Watkins (Torfaen)	26.93

Guy Bulpitt

98

7	J. Cunningham (Munster)	27.02
8	N. Bridge (Millfield)	27.18

100 Metres Butterfly

1	M. Watkins (Torfaen)	57.70
2	M. Smith (Co Swansea)	58.14
3	W. Johnston (Ulster)	58.31
4	G. Bulpitt (Co Birmingham)	58.37
5	M. Weighton (Wulfrunians)	58.40
6	I. Panting (Kelly College)	58.54
7	M. Matthews (Barnet Copthall)	58.93
8	T. Hart (Thurrock)	58.97

200 Metres Butterfly

1	I. Wilson (Bo Sunderland)	2:04.95
2	M. Watkins (Torfaen)	2:05.30
3	C. Bird (Kelly College)	2:09.94
4	T. Hart (Thurrock)	2:10.28
5	D. Pye (St Helens)	2:12.55
6	S. Smith (Wigan Wasps)	2:12.82
7	M. Smith (Co Swansea)	2:13.81
8	K. Crosby (Warrington Warriors)	2:14.64

200 Metres Individual Medley

1	P. Brew (Kelly College)	2:09.02
2	I. Rosser (Torfaen)	2:10.98
3	I. Stewart (York C)	2:12.51
4	M. Weighton (Wulfrunians)	2:13.52
5	C. Jones (Co Swansea)	2:13.98
6	J. Kerr (Kelly College)	2:15.38
7	M. Hanby (Nova Centurion)	2:18.19
8	J. Kearney (Nova Centurion)	2:20.31

400 Metres Individual Medley

1	P. Brew (Kelly College)	4:33.02
2	I. Wilson (Bo Sunderland)	4:36.00
3	I. Rosser (Torfaen)	4:38.05
4	I. Stewart (York C)	4:43.89
5	P. McGillion (Ulster)	4:46.65
6	C. Heathcote (Nova Centurion)	4:47.52
7	J. Kerr (Kelly College)	4:48.02
8	J. Ong (Kelly College)	4:52.74

Women

50 Metres Freestyle

1	J. Coull (Co Birmingham)	27.42
2	R. Vogelaar (Canada)	27.57
3	M. McKinnell (Co Cardiff)	27.76
4	A. Kindon (Co Birmingham)	27.79
5	C. Foot (Millfield)	28.02
6	J. Wilkinson (St Helens)	28.09
7	J. Lancaster (Warrington Warriors)	28.24
8	H. Mansfield (Co Chester)	28.27

100 Metres Freestyle

1	J. Coull (Co Birmingham)	58.80
2	H. Mansfield (Co Chester)	1:00.05
3	R. Vogelaar (Canada)	1:00.16
4	E. Archer (Kelly College)	1:00.31
5	A. Kindon (Co Birmingham)	1:00.49
6	S. Page (Co Birmingham)	1:00.53
7	J. Lancaster (Warrington Warriors)	1:00.68
8	D. Jones (Co Chester)	1:00.84

200 Metres Freestyle

1	J. Coull (Co Birmingham)	2:06.42
2	H. Mansfield (Co Chester)	2:06.55
3	D. Jones (Co Chester)	2:08.81
4	N. Cumbers (Kelly College)	2:08.83
5	J. Henwood (Torfaen)	2:09.84

6 H. Walsh (Swansea University)	2:10.38
7 E. Archer (Kelly College)	2:11.93
8 J. Lancaster (Warrington Warriors)	2:12.49

400 Metres Freestyle

1 T. Atkin (Co Lincoln Pentaqua)	4:27.21
2 L. Matthews (Redbridge B)	4:28.50
3 G. Cook (Bo Kirklees)	4:28.56
4 C. Smith (Wigan Wasps)	4:28.69
5 L. Smart (Co Chester)	4:30.77
6 S. Foggo (Co Newcastle)	4:31.09
7 D. Jones (Co Chester)	4:34.28
8 L. Kilgour (Co Birmingham)	4:35.58

800 Metres Freestyle

1 S. Foggo (Co Newcastle)	9:08.81
2 L. Matthews (Redbridge B)	9:09.10
3 C. Smith (Wigan Wasps)	9:11.08
4 G. Cook (Bo Kirklees)	9:12.50
5 J. Deakins (Gloucester C)	9:12.86
6 L. Smart (Co Chester)	9:16.50
7 J. Davey (Co Newcastle)	9:21.16
8 L. Pagnucco (Canada)	9:22.32

50 Metres Backstroke

1 S. Page (Co Birmingham)	30.40
2 K. Read (Barnet Copthall)	30.86
3 H. Slatter (Kelly College)	31.46
4 T. Atkin (Co Lincoln Pentaqua)	31.81
5 L. Gahan (Kelly College)	32.18
6 C. Buhl (Switzerland)	
C. Huddart (Manchester U Salford)	32.19
8 J. Corbett (Co Birmingham)	32.67

100 Metres Backstroke

1 S. Page (Co Birmingham)	1:04.92
2 K. Read (Barnet Copthall)	1:05.00
3 H. Slatter (Kelly College)	1:05.23
4 J. Deakins (Gloucester C)	1:06.61
5 C. Huddart (Manchester U Salford)	1:08.95
6 J. Corbett (Co Birmingham)	1:09.14
7 J. Wright (Co Chester)	1:09.51
8 L. Gahan (Kelly College)	1:09.74

200 Metres Backstroke

1 H. Slatter (Kelly College)	2:17.74
2 J. Deakins (Gloucester C)	2:19.14
3 K. Read (Barnet Copthall)	2:19.70
4 J. Wright (Co Chester)	2:25.07
5 C. Huddart (Manchester U Salford)	2:26.10
6 D. Salmon (Kelly College)	2:27.03
7 B. Jones (Co Chester)	2:27.55
8 L. Gahan (Kelly College)	2:28.00

50 Metres Breaststroke

1 J. Henwood (Torfaen)	34.71
2 S. Jefford (Co Exeter)	35.09
3 D. Tubby (Co Birmingham)	35.40
4 A. Schweizer (Switzerland)	35.60
5 R. Vogelaar (Canada)	35.69
6 A. Kindon (Co Birmingham)	36.26
7 R. Newey (Ledbury & D)	36.27
8 S. Brown (Ulster)	36.64

100 Metres Breaststroke

1 J. Henwood (Torfaen)	1:14.75
2 D. Tubby (Co Birmingham)	1:15.51
3 C. Piggott (Co Birmingham)	1:17.31
4 S. Jefford (Co Exeter)	1:18.03
5 S. Brown (Ulster)	1:18.22
6 H. Walsh (Swansea University)	1:18.24

7 R. Vogelaar (Canada)	1:19.02
8 A. Schweizer (Switzerland)	1:19.60

200 Metres Breaststroke

1 J. Henwood (Torfaen)	2:39.85
2 D. Tubby (Co Birmingham)	2:41.08
3 C. Piggott (Co Birmingham)	2:44.80
4 H. Walsh (Swansea University)	2:45.78
5 A. Schweizer (Switzerland)	2:45.92
6 T. Gouthuey (Switzerland)	2:47.95
7 L. Findlay (Kelly College)	2:48.55

50 Metres Butterfly

1 C. Foot (Millfield)	29.16
2 R. Vogelaar (Canada)	29.44
3 M. McKinnell (Co Cardiff)	29.50
4 J. Lancaster (Warrington Warriors)	29.92
5 M. Hadden (Beckenham)	30.24
6 S. Dougherty (Ulster)	30.38
7 A. Mackay (Warrington Warriors)	30.43
8 S. Lewis (Swansea University)	30.58

100 Metres Butterfly

1 M. McKinnell (Co Cardiff)	1:04.48
2 C. Foot (Millfield)	1:04.79
3 L. Wilson (Bo Sunderland)	1:04.95
4 A. Mackay (Warrington Warriors)	1:05.80
5 Z. Harrison (Norwich Penguins)	1:05.90
6 H. Bewley (Swansea University)	1:06.15
7 S. Lewis (Swansea University)	1:06.17
8 T. Atkin (Co Lincoln Pentaqua)	1:06.81

200 Metres Butterfly

1 L. Wilson (Bo Sunderland)	2:16.48
2 T. Atkin (Co Lincoln Pentaqua)	2:17.46
3 H. Slatter (Kelly College)	2:20.84
4 H. Welford (Neston)	2:21.23
5 H. Bewley (Swansea University)	2:21.46
6 S. Lewis (Swansea University)	2:22.04
7 A. Kay (Co Bradford)	2:23.47
8 L. Appleton (Warrington Warriors)	2:25.11

200 Metres Individual Medley

1 H. Slatter (Kelly College)	2:21.01
2 T. Atkin (Co Lincoln Pentaqua)	2:22.15
3 K. Read (Barnet Copthall)	2:23.89

Lynne Wilson   Jack Hickes

4	H. Walsh (Swansea University)	2:25.52	2	H. Slatter (Kelly College)	5:00.78
5	H. Mansfield (Co Chester)	2:27.26	3	H. Mansfield (Co Chester)	5:06.47
6	S. Garrett (Barnet Copthall)	2:27.79	4	J. Deakins (Gloucester C)	5:08.36
7	L. Findlay (Kelly College)	2:28.61	5	K. Jones (Co Chester)	5:09.87
8	K. Jones (Co Chester)	2:29.78	6	S. Foggo (Co Newcastle)	5:10.58
			7	L. Findlay (Kelly College)	5:10.78

400 Metres Individual Medley

1 T. Atkin (Co Lincoln Pentaqua)   5.00.37

8 C. Buhl (Switzerland)   5:12.05

European Community Club Finals

Hamburg, W Germany – 29/30 April, 1989

NOTE: City of Leeds (men) and Wigan Wasps (women), as the British club team champions for 1989, were automatically selected to represent Britain in these championships.

Men

50 Metres Freestyle

1	Y. Clausse (Luxemburg)	24.32
2	S. Fraschi (Rome)	24.38
3	B. Zikarsky (Hamburg)	24.43
4	S. Lopez (Barcelona)	
	N. Metcalfe (Leeds)	24.80
6	S. Cullen (Dublin)	24.89
7	P. Rollin (Canet & Roussillon)	25.08
8	H. Villaret (Lisboa)	25.46

100 Metres Freestyle

1	B. Zikarsky (Hamburg)	
	S. Fraschi (Rome)	52.30
3	H. Olbrecht (Dilbeek)	53.36
4	R. Sloeserwij (Amsterdam)	53.38
5	Y. Clausse (Luxemburg)	53.44
6	N. Metcalf (Leeds)	53.60
7	F. Schott (Canet & Roussillon)	53.61
8	A. Jonama (Barcelona)	54.13

400 Metres Freestyle

1	S. Pfeiffer (Hamburg)	4:00.50
2	J. Broughton (Leeds)	4:02.24
3	J. Faure (Canet & Roussillon)	4:04.14
4	G. Braglia (Rome)	4:08.74
5	R. Sloeserwij (Amsterdam)	4:09.70
6	J. Marti (Barcelona)	4:10.76
7	J. Santos (Lisboa)	4:15.33
8	B. Segers (Dilbeek)	4:18.10

1500 Metres Freestyle

1	S. Pfeiffer (Hamburg)	15:50.41
2	T. Day (Leeds)	15:59.70
3	Y. Cardineau (Canet & Roussillon)	16:10.94
4	D. Jordana (Barcelona)	16:18.21
5	M. Bertinetti (Rome)	16:42.12
6	M. Madeira (Lisboa)	16:54.16
7	D. Alfagis (Piraeus)	16:58.12
8	D. Ravijts (Dilbeek)	17:06.92

50 Metres Backstroke

1	L. Sorensen (Holstebro)	27.60
2	F. Schoot (Canet & Roussillon)	27.83
3	C. Cockcroft (Leeds)	28.08
4	S. Cullen (Dublin)	28.12
5	F. Imperadore (Rome)	28.58
6	S. Hackmann (Hamburg)	28.72
7	P. de Rover (Amsterdam)	28.74
8	E. Slachmuylders (Dilbeek)	29.13

100 Metres Backstroke

1	L. Sorensen (Holstebro)	58.94
2	B. Dumas (Canet & Roussillon)	59.78
3	S. Hackmann (Hamburg)	59.99
4	O. Barrufet (Barcelona)	1:00.56
5	R. Cassio (Rome)	1:00.89
6	C. Cockcroft (Leeds)	1:01.24
7	E. Slachmuylders (Dilbeek)	1:02.20
8	C. Stivenson (Piraeus)	1:02.91

50 Metres Breaststroke

1	L. Carbonari (Rome)	29.40
2	A. Moorhouse (Leeds)	29.66
3	T. Pata (Canet & Roussillon)	
	A. Sorensen (Holstebro)	31.10
5	S. Steegeling (Amsterdam)	31.15
6	A. Yokochi (Lisboa)	31.18
7	J. McGrath (Dublin)	31.62
8	G. Masden (Barcelona)	32.04

100 Metres Breaststroke

1	A. Moorhouse (Leeds)	1:03.67
2	S. Lopez (Barcelona)	1:05.99
3	L. Carbonari (Rome)	1:06.03
4	G. O'Toole (Dublin)	1:07.04
5	A. Yokochi (Lisboa)	1:07.21
6	A. Sorensen (Holstebro)	1:07.35
7	S. Steegeling (Amsterdam)	1:07.85
8	T. Pata (Canet & Roussillon)	1:08.17

50 Metres Butterfly

1	F. Schott (Canet & Roussillon)	25.88
2	S. Dronsfield (Leeds)	25.95
3	C. Stivenson (Piraeus)	26.25
4	C. Hoffmann (Hamburg)	26.44
5	M. Braida (Rome)	26.52
6	A. Jonama (Spain)	26.82
7	M. Seimetz (Luxemburg)	26.84
8	D. Madeira (Lisboa)	27.12

100 Metres Butterfly

1	M. Braida (Rome)	56.74
2	S. Dronsfield (Leeds)	57.46
3	C. Hoffmann (Hamburg)	57.51
4	C. Stivenson (Piraeus)	57.54
5	D. Madeira (Lisboa)	57.64
6	P. Rollin (Canet & Roussillon)	59.15
7	M. Seimetz (Luxemburg)	59.33
8	J. Rodriguez (Barcelona)	59.63

200 Metres Individual Medley

1	P. Bermel (Hamburg)	
	R. Cassio (Rome)	2:07.37
3	L. Sorensen (Holstebro)	2:08.09
4	S. Lopez (Barcelona)	2:08.16
5	L. Journet (Canet & Roussillon)	2:09.15
6	D. Madeira (Lisboa)	2:10.70
7	S. Steegeling (Amsterdam)	2:11.44
8	G. O'Toole (Dublin)	2:11.47

4×50 Metres Freestyle Relay

1	Rome	1:36.94
2	Hamburg	1:37.04
3	Leeds	1:37.07
4	Amsterdam	1:38.31
5	Canet & Roussillon	1:38.52
6	Holstebro	1:39.20
7	Dublin	1:39.25
8	Barcelona	1:39.60

4×50 Metres Medley Relay

1	Rome	1:46.04
2	Leeds	1:46.34
3	Canet & Roussillon	1:48.14
4	Hamburg	1:48.20
5	Barcelona	1:48.92
6	Holstebro	1:49.80
7	Lisboa	1:50.57
8	Dublin	1:50.58

Final Points Table

1	Rome	138.0
2	Leeds	125.5
3	Hamburg	124.0
4	Canet	114.5
5	Barcelona	92.5
6	Holstebro	81.5
7	Amsterdam	73.0
8	Lisboa	71.0
9	Dublin	61.0
10	Dilbeek	50.0
11	Piracus	49.0
12	Luxemburg	48.0

Women

50 Metres Freestyle

1	K. Seick (Hamburg)	27.03
2	K. Sciorelli (Torino)	27.09
3	J. Reggiany (Clichy)	27.47
4	J. Croft (Wigan)	27.81
5	E. Martinez (Sabadell)	28.24
6	E. Paraskevopoulou (Thessaloniki)	28.46
7	R. Wyerink (Denekamp)	28.51
8	S. Lytje (Kastrup)	28.76

100 Metres Freestyle

1	K. Seick (Hamburg)	58.19
2	J. Croft (Wigan)	58.71
3	K. Sciorelli (Torino)	58.95
4	S. Kamoun (Clichy)	58.99
5	E. Martinez (Sabadell)	1:00.50
6	R. Wyering (Denekamp)	1:01.93
7	C. Ortiga (Porto)	1:02.81
8	S. Lytje (Kastrup)	1:03.02

400 Metres Freestyle

1	L. Bensimon (Clichy)	4:17.98
2	J. Croft (Wigan)	4:21.23
3	S. Nimtz (Hamburg)	4:22.75
4	M. Hansen (Kastrup)	4:29.30
5	N. Claes (Seraing)	4:30.59
6	N. Pantasso (Torino)	4:30.79
7	N. Campbell (Dublin)	4:31.84
8	M. Costa (Porto)	4:42.76

800 Metres Freestyle
(Results not available)

50 Metres Backstroke

1	S. Schlicht (Hamburg)	30.81
2	L. Savarino (Torino)	31.92
3	A. Mathieu (Clichy)	31.93
4	N. Sousa (Porto)	32.30
5	K. Klepkou (Thessaloniki)	32.90
6	S. Hindmarch (Wigan)	33.02
7	D. Bonnes (Denekamp)	33.89
8	M. Collette (Luxemburg)	33.96

100 Metres Backstroke

1	S. Schlicht (Hamburg)	1:05.70
2	L. Savarino (Torino)	1:06.80
3	I. Westerin (Denekamp)	1:08.77
4	A. Mathieu (Clichy)	1:09.29
5	K. Klepkou (Thessaloniki)	1:09.35
6	N. Sousa (Porto)	1:09.74
7	D. Evans (Wigan)	1:11.01
8	L. Bernabeu (Sabadell)	1:11.34

50 Metres Breaststroke

1	M. Hohmann (Wigan)	32.95
2	P. Peracini (Clichy)	34.39
3	J. Beilfub (Hamburg)	34.64
4	C. Giordano (Torino)	35.13
5	W. Ligtenberg (Denekamp)	35.16
6	B. Lourdes (Sabadell)	35.20
7	M. Osweiler (Luxemburg)	36.20
8	D. Sorensen (Kastrup)	37.39

100 Metres Breaststroke

1	M. Hohmann (Wigan)	1:12.02
2	C. Giordano (Torino)	1:14.34
3	N. Arendt (Luxemburg)	1:14.57
4	B. Lourdes (Sabadell)	1:15.77
5	J. Belfub (Hamburg)	1:15.94
6	W. Ligtenberg (Denekamp)	1:17.76
7	V. Andre (Clichy)	1:19.39
8	N. Byrne (Dublin)	1:19.54

50 Metres Butterfly

1	S. Brownsdon (Wigan)	29.02
2	S. Kamoun (Clichy)	29.12
3	N. Tabe (Hamburg)	29.40
4	E. Viola (Torino)	29.48
5	M. Cuervo (Sabadell)	30.52
6	N. Campbell (Dublin)	30.65
7	B. Meyners (Denekamp)	31.51
8	M. Lenoir (Seraing)	31.74

100 Metres Butterfly

1	S. Brownsdon (Wigan)	1:03.68
2	I. Beyermann (Hamburg)	1:04.34
3	E. Viola (Torino)	1:05.11
4	B. Poggaard (Kastrup)	1:05.36
5	S. Pinault (Clichy)	1:05.66
6	R. Wigger (Denekamp)	1:06.28
7	M. Cuervo (Sabadell)	1:08.03
8	M. Lenoir (Seraing)	1:08.95

200 Metres Individual Medley

1	L. Bensimon (Clichy)	2:18.48

2 S. Brownsdon (Wigan)	2:22.70	
3 S. Schlicht (Hamburg)	2:23.96	
4 C. Giordano (Torino)	2:24.69	
5 R. Wigger (Denekamp)	2:25.99	
6 N. Arendt (Luxemburg)	2:26.42	
7 N. Claes (Seraing)	2:28.01	
8 B. Lourdes (Sabadell)	2:32.96	

3 Torino	2:02.62
4 Clichy	2:02.77
5 Denekamp	2:06.10
6 Sabadell	2:06.96
7 Dublin	2:09.47
8 Luxemburg	2:11.20

4×50 Metres Freestyle Relay

1 Clichy	1:48.49
2 Hamburg	1:48.65
3 Torino	1:49.96
4 Wigan	1:50.44
5 Denekamp	1:51.76
6 Sabadell	1:53.53
7 Porto	1:54.71
8 Kastrup	1:55.04

Final Points Table

1 Hamburg	143.0
2 Wigan	138.0
3 Clichy	135.0
4 Torino	126.0
5 Denekamp	88.0
6 Sabadell	83.5
7 Kastrup	69.0
8 Dublin	57.5
9 Porto	54.0
10 Thessaloniki	46.0
11 Luxemburg	46.0
12 Seraing	41.0

4×50 Metres Medley Relay

1 Wigan	2:01.36
2 Hamburg	2:01.57

Grand Prix

NOTE: Only the first three in each event are recorded.

Tryst Sports Centre, Cumbernauld — 11/13 November, 1988

Men

50 Metres Freestyle

1 S. Gusgen (W Germany)	22.77
2 M. Fibbens (Barnet Copthall)	23.17
3 S. Caron (France)	23.34

100 Metres Freestyle

1 S. Caron (France)	50.25
2 M. Fibbens (Barnet Copthall)	50.35
3 S. McQuaid (Co Manchester)	51.51

200 Metres Freestyle

1 S. McQuaid (Co Manchester)	1:51.31
2 K. Turner (Aer Lingus)	1:51.99
3 K. Boyd (Bo S Tyneside)	1:52.10

400 Metres Freestyle

1 K. Boyd (Bo S Tyneside)	3:52.64
2 S. McQuaid (Co Manchester)	3:55.77
3 P. Henry (Edinburgh)	3:57.86

1500 Metres Freestyle

1 C. McNeil (Paisley)	15:47.67
2 J. Barth (W Germany)	15:50.94
3 R. Noble (Stirling)	15:51.37

100 Metres Backstroke

1 M. Peyrebrune (Warrender)	1:00.61
2 I. Clayton (Wigan Wasps)	1:00.63
3 A. May (Co Dundee)	1:01.26

200 Metres Backstroke

1 K. Boyd (Bo S Tyneside)	2:02.68
2 I. Clayton (Wigan Wasps)	2:07.20
3 A. May (Co Dundee)	2:09.31

100 Metres Breaststroke

1 N. Hudghton (Aberdeen)	1:04.38
2 G. Watson (Carnegie)	1:04.43
3 R. Beab (W Germany)	1:04.57

200 Metres Breaststroke

1 N. Gillingham (Co Birmingham)	2:15.52
2 N. Hudghton (Aberdeen)	2:17.57
3 P. Kaschub (W Germany)	2:24.23

100 Metres Butterfly

1 T. Buchholz (W Germany)	56.06
2 M. Fibbens (Barnet Copthall)	56.35
3 S. Gusgen (W Germany)	56.49

200 Metres Butterfly

1 M. Fibbens (Barnet Copthall)	2:05.93
2 N. Waterson (Co Dundee)	2:06.78
3 P. Henry (Edinburgh)	2:07.13

200 Metres Individual Medley

1 R. Diegel (W Germany)	2:08.82
2 A. May (Co Dundee)	2:10.70
3 S. McKinlay (Co Dundee)	2:13.55

400 Metres Individual Medley

1 R. Diegel (W Germany)	4:35.15
2 S. McKinlay (Co Dundee)	4:39.29
3 A. May (Co Dundee)	4:41.07

Women

50 Metres Freestyle

1 A. Sheppard (Milngarvie)	26.19
2 J. Croft (Wigan Wasps)	27.33
3 R. Gilfillan (Co Dundee)	27.52

100 Metres Freestyle

1 J. Croft (Wigan Wasps)	58.01
2 R. Gilfillan (Co Dundee)	58.12
3 A. Sheppard (Milngarvie)	58.59

200 Metres Freestyle

1 J. Croft (Wigan Wasps)	2:02.50
2 R. Gilfillan (Co Dundee)	2:04.93
3 P. Hutchinson (Wigan Wasps)	2:07.33

400 Metres Freestyle

1 J. Croft (Wigan Wasps)	4:20.99

2	P. Hutchinson (Wigan Wasps)	4:22.40
3	R. Gilfillan (Co Dundee)	4:24.68

800 Metres Freestyle

1	P. Hutchinson (Wigan Wasps)	8:51.01
2	J. Croft (Wigan Wasps)	8:55.62
3	R. Gilfillan (Co Dundee)	9:04.88

100 Metres Backstroke

1	K. Read (Norwich Penguins)	1:05.43
2	L. Phimister (Moray & D)	1:05.88
3	A. Sheppard (Milngarvie)	1:06.13

200 Metres Backstroke

1	K. Read (Norwich Penguins)	2:18.41
2	L. Cunningham (Edinburgh)	2:21.92
3	L. Phimister (Moray & D)	2:23.86

100 Metres Breaststroke

1	S. Brownsdon (Wigan Wasps)	1:10.85
2	M. Hohmann (Wigan Wasps)	1:11.65
3	A. McKellican (Co Dundee)	1:15.49

200 Metres Breaststroke

1	M. Hohmann (Wigan Wasps)	2:33.55
2	S. Brownsdon (Wigan Wasps)	2:34.37
3	A. McKellican (Co Dundee)	2:39.16

100 Metres Butterfly

1	S. Brownsdon (Wigan Wasps)	1:03.22
2	D. Evans (Wigan Wasps)	1:05.14
3	C. Coward (Wigan Wasps)	1:05.71

200 Metres Butterfly

1	D. Evans (Wigan Wasps)	2:16.94
2	S. Brownsdon (Wigan Wasps)	2:19.36
3	A. Duffy (Derwentside)	2:21.39

200 Metres Individual Medley

1	S. Brownsdon (Wigan Wasps)	2:20.51
2	L. Phimister (Moray & D)	2:22.00
3	K. Read (Norwich Penguins)	2:24.81

400 Metres Individual Medley

1	S. Brownsdon (Wigan Wasps)	4:58.86
2	L. Phimister (Moray & D)	5:01.12
3	D. Evans (Wigan Wasps)	5:01.84

Leisure Centre, Dundee — 2/4 December, 1988

Men

50 Metres Freestyle

1	R. Dekker (Holland)	23.07
2	P. Brew (Kelly College)	23.76
3	L. Holgate (Oundle & D)	24.22

100 Metres Freestyle

1	R. Dekker (Holland)	51.14
2	P. Brew (Kelly College)	51.33
3	S. McQuaid (Loughborough University)	51.34

200 Metres Freestyle

1	P. Brew (Kelly College)	1:51.62
2	S. McQuaid (Loughborough University)	1:51.89
3	J. Broughton (Co Leeds)	1:52.05

400 Metres Freestyle

1	K. Boyd (Bo S Tyneside)	3:46.06
2	I. Wilson (Bo Sunderland)	3:53.99
3	C. McNeil (Paisley)	3:57.59

1500 Metres Freestyle

1	I. Wilson (Bo Sunderland)	15:21.17
2	C. McNeil (Paisley)	15:50.63
3	R. Noble (Stirling)	15:57.27

50 Metres Backstroke

1	G. Binfield (Milton Keynes)	27.32
2	G. Robins (Portsmouth Northsea)	27.55
3	I. Panting (Kelly College)	27.68

100 Metres Backstroke

1	G. Robins (Portsmouth Northsea)	57.29
2	M. O'Connor (Co Manchester)	58.27
3	G. Binfield (Milton Keynes)	58.40

200 Metres Backstroke

1	K. Boyd (Bo S Tyneside)	2:00.07
2	G. Robins (Portsmouth Northsea)	2:03.41
3	G. Binfield (Milton Keynes)	2:05.25

50 Metres Breaststroke

1	R. Dekker (Holland)	28.53
2	G. Watson (Edinburgh)	28.98
3	J. Parrack (Co Leeds)	29.30

100 Metres Breaststroke

1	R. Dekker (Holland)	1:02.75
2	J. Parrack (Co Leeds)	1:03.89
3	N. Hudghton (Aberdeen)	1:04.42

200 Metres Breaststroke

1	N. Hudghton (Aberdeen)	2:18.54
2	R. Dekker (Holland)	2:20.41
3	D. Mason (Co Newcastle)	2:21.13

50 Metres Butterfly

1	R. Leishman (Kelly College)	25.23
2	R. Dekker (Holland)	25.91
3	E. Stewart (Co Dundee)	26.27

100 Metres Butterfly

1	R. Leishman (Kelly College)	55.65
2	G. Binfield (Milton Keynes)	57.24
3	A. Quinn (Co Manchester)	57.73

200 Metres Butterfly

1	I. Wilson (Bo Sunderland)	2:02.97
2	P. Brew (Kelly College)	2:03.43
3	R. Leishman (Kelly College)	2:03.82

200 Metres Individual Medley

1	P. Brew (Kelly College)	2:03.72
2	G. Robins (Portsmouth Northsea)	2:03.92
3	G. Binfield (Milton Keynes)	2:06.46

400 Metres Individual Medley

1	G. Robins (Portsmouth Northsea)	4:28.88
2	I. Wilson (Bo Sunderland)	4:29.30
3	G. Donovan (Barking)	4:40.01

Women

50 Metres Freestyle

1	A. Sheppard (Milngarvie)	26.09
2	M. A. Muis (Holland)	26.37
3	K. Brienesse (Holland)	26.69

100 Metres Freestyle

1	M. A. Muis (Holland)	56.69
2	M. I. Muis (Holland)	56.86
3	K. Brienesse (Holland)	56.96

200 Metres Freestyle

1	M. A. Muis (Holland)	2:01.55

2	M. I. Muis (Holland)	2:01.93
3	J. Croft (Wigan Wasps)	2:01.97

400 Metres Freestyle

1	J. Croft (Wigan Wasps)	4:17.05
2	P. Hutchinson (Wigan Wasps)	4:19.14
3	M. George (Bo Waltham Forest)	4:23.56

800 Metres Freestyle

1	J. Croft (Wigan Wasps)	8:43.71
2	P. Hutchinson (Wigan Wasps)	8:55.54
3	H. Slatter (Kelly College)	8:55.74

50 Metres Backstroke

1	S. Page (Stockport Metro)	30.30
2	K. Read (Norwich Penguins)	30.50
3	J. Ewing (Paisley)	31.14

100 Metres Backstroke

1	K. Read (Norwich Penguins)	1:05.06
2	S. Page (Stockport Metro)	1:05.24
3	H. Slatter (Kelly College)	1:06.01

200 Metres Backstroke

1	K. Read (Norwich Penguins)	2:17.39
2	H. Slatter (Kelly College)	2:20.83
3	J. Ewing (Paisley)	2:22.47

50 Metres Breaststroke

1	S. Brownsdon (Wigan Wasps)	32.58
2	M. Hohmann (Wigan Wasps)	32.63
3	L. Coombes (Co Southampton)	33.48

100 Metres Breaststroke

1	S. Brownsdon (Wigan Wasps)	1:09.98
2	M. Hohmann (Wigan Wasps)	1:10.34
3	L. Coombes (Co Southampton)	1:12.39

200 Metres Breaststroke

1	S. Brownsdon (Wigan Wasps)	2:31.09
2	L. Coombes (Co Southampton)	2:37.33
3	A. McKellican (Co Dundee)	2:38.83

50 Metres Butterfly

1	K. Brienesse (Holland)	28.37
2	S. Brownsdon (Wigan Wasps)	28.93
3	S. Buxton (Nova Centurion)	29.16

Suki Brownsdon

100 Metres Butterfly

1	K. Brienesse (Holland)	1:01.79
2	S. Brownsdon (Wigan Wasps)	1:04.04
3	H. Bewley (Swansea University)	1:04.28

200 Metres Butterfly

1	H. Bewley (Swansea University)	2:16.26
2	D. Evans (Wigan Wasps)	2:17.06
3	L. Wilson (Bo Sunderland)	2:18.33

200 Metres Individual Medley

1	M. A. Muis (Holland)	2:17.87
2	M. I. Muis (Holland)	2:18.82
3	S. Brownsdon (Wigan Wasps)	2:18.94

400 Metres Individual Medley

1	S. Brownsdon (Wigan Wasps)	4:53.61
2	H. Slatter (Kelly College)	4:58.48
3	D. Evans (Wigan Wasps)	5:00.95

Barton Pool, Gloucester — 16/19 December, 1988
Men

50 Metres Freestyle

1	M. Fibbens (Barnet Copthall)	23.32
2	S. Wellington (Portsmouth Northsea)	24.00
3	R. Lee (Co Birmingham)	24.20

100 Metres Freestyle

1	M. Fibbens (Barnet Copthall)	49.78
2	G. Bulpitt (Co Birmingham)	51.23
3	D. Dyke (Walsall)	51.99

200 Metres Freestyle

1	D. Rolley (Swansea University)	1:51.80
2	G. Bulpitt (Co Birmingham)	1:52.25
3	P. Pederzolli (Gloucester C)	1:52.85

400 Metres Freestyle

1	D. Rolley (Swansea University)	3:57.10
2	G. Bulpitt (Co Birmingham)	3:58.42
3	P. Pederzolli (Gloucester C)	4:00.85

100 Metres Backstroke

1	J. Davey (Co Leeds)	58.80
2	C. Cockcroft (Co Leeds)	59.35
3	P. Blake (Wigan Wasps)	59.86

200 Metres Backstroke

1	P. Blake (Wigan Wasps)	2:07.95
2	C. Cockcroft (Co Leeds)	2:09.64
3	C. Jones (Swansea University)	2:10.79

100 Metres Breaststroke

1	I. Campbell (Beckenham)	1:04.21
2	I. McKenzie (Braintree & Bocking)	1:05.09
3	M. Buswell (Beckenham)	1:05.19

200 Metres Breaststroke

1	I. McKenzie (Braintree & Bocking)	2:21.86
2	D. Mason (Co Newcastle)	2:22.97
3	M. Arzoz (Barnet Copthall)	2:23.81

50 Metres Butterfly

1	M. Fibbens (Barnet Copthall)	25.58
2	R. Greenwood (Co Leeds)	26.05
3	M. Jones (Co Southampton)	26.24

100 Metres Butterfly

1	M. Fibbens (Barnet Copthall)	55.32
2	R. Greenwood (Co Leeds)	57.47
3	C. Wilson (Bo Sunderland)	57.91

200 Metres Individual Medley
1 D. Rolley (Swansea University)	2:03.99
2 J. Davey (Co Leeds)	2:04.81
3 A. Rolley (Gloucester C)	2:07.19

400 Metres Individual Medley
1 A. Rolley (Gloucester C)	4:26.71
2 A. Greig (Barnet Copthall)	4:32.26
3 M. Hooper (Portsmouth Northsea)	4:37.51

Women

50 Metres Freestyle
1 C. Woodcock (Haywards Heath)	26.73
2 J. Gorst (Co Leeds)	26.77
3 C. Foot (Millfield)	26.84

100 Metres Freestyle
1 J. Croft (Wigan Wasps)	57.63
2 J. Gorst (Co Leeds)	57.94
3 C. Foot (Millfield)	58.45

200 Metres Freestyle
1 J. Croft (Wigan Wasps)	2:02.33
2 N. Sommers (Beckenham)	2:06.30
3 H. Sanderson (Nova Centurion)	2:08.67

400 Metres Freestyle
1 J. Croft (Wigan Wasps)	4:15.97
2 N. Sommers (Beckenham)	4:24.19
3 L. Matthews (Redbridge B)	4:25.99

100 Metres Backstroke
1 K. Read (Norwich Penguins)	1:03.60
2 C. Huddart (Salford Triple 'S')	1:06.10
3 J. Riegal (Harrow & Wealdstone)	1:08.20

200 Metres Backstroke
1 K. Read (Norwich Penguins)	2:18.55
2 C. Huddart (Salford Triple 'S')	2:21.75
3 J. Riegal (Harrow & Wealdstone)	2;22.36

100 Metres Breaststroke
1 M. Hohmann (Wigan Wasps)	1:10.19
2 L. Coombes (Co Southampton)	1:13.62
3 H. Frank (Co Leeds)	1:14.89

Helen Frank

200 Metres Breaststroke
1 M. Hohmann (Wigan Wasps)	2:32.82
2 H. Frank (Co Leeds)	2:38.43
3 L. Coombes (Co Southampton)	2:38.64

50 Metres Butterfly
1 C. Foot (Millfield)	28.86
2 M. McKinnell (Co Cardiff)	29.25
3 M. Hadden (Beckenham)	29.71

100 Metres Butterfly
1 C. Foot (Millfield)	1:02.68
2 M. McKinnell (Co Cardiff)	1:03.52
3 D. Newell (Redbridge B)	1:05.03

200 Metres Individual Medley
1 K. Read (Norwich Penguins)	2:20.70
2 R. Smart (Gloucester C)	2:24.56
3 J. Riegal (Harrow & Wealdstone)	2:24.90

400 Metres Individual Medley
1 K. Read (Norwich Penguins)	4:55.69
2 H. Slatter (Kelly College)	5:02.19
3 H. Osborne (Co Birmingham)	5:04.11

Centre 2000, Southampton — 20/22 January, 1989

Men

50 Metres Freestyle
1 M. Fibbens (Barnet Copthall)	22.83
2 S. Wellington (Portsmouth Northsea)	23.70
3 D. Parker (Co Cardiff)	24.07

100 Metres Freestyle
1 M. Fibbens (Barnet Copthall)	49.42
2 D. Dyke (Walsall)	51.98
3 P. Easter (Norwich Penguins)	52.10

200 Metres Freestyle
1 P. Brew (Kelly College)	1:50.39
2 P. Easter (Norwich Penguins)	1:52.61
3 G. Robins (Portsmouth Northsea)	1:52.76

400 Metres Freestyle
1 P. Brew (Kelly College)	3:54.24
2 I. Wilson (Bo Sunderland)	3:54.82
3 G. Robins (Portsmouth Northsea)	3:56.97

1500 Metres Freestyle
1 I. Wilson (Bo Sunderland)	15:15.70
2 J. Ong (Kelly College)	15:33.94
3 S. Akers (Shiverers)	16:10.25

50 Metres Backstroke
1 G. Robins (Portsmouth Northsea)	27.45
2 I. Clayton (Wigan Wasps)	27.60
3 I. Panting (Kelly College)	27.74

100 Metres Backstroke
1 G. Robins (Portsmouth Northsea)	57.17
2 M. O'Connor (Co Manchester)	58.56
3 I. Clayton (Wigan Wasps)	58.66

200 Metres Backstroke
1 G. Robins (Portsmouth Northsea)	2:04.25
2 I. Clayton (Wigan Wasps)	2:04.28
3 P. Blake (Wigan Wasps)	2:06.62

50 Metres Breaststroke
1 I. Campbell (Beckenham)	29.67
2 N. Hudghton (Aberdeen)	29.93
3 R. Wilkes (Portsmouth Northsea)	30.00

105

100 Metres Breaststroke
1 N. Gillingham (Co Birmingham)	1:02.73
2 M. Buswell (Beckenham)	1:03.97
3 N. Hudghton (Aberdeen)	1:04.34

200 Metres Breaststroke
1 N. Hudghton (Aberdeen)	2:16.54
2 M. Buswell (Beckenham)	2:19.28
3 I. Campbell (Beckenham)	2:19.89

50 Metres Butterfly
1 D. Parker (Co Cardiff)	25.23
2 M. Fibbens (Barnet Copthall)	
R. Leishman (Kelly College)	25.33

100 Metres Butterfly
1 M. Fibbens (Barnet Copthall)	55.08
2 R. Leishman (Kelly College)	55.75
3 D. Parker (Co Cardiff)	55.98

200 Metres Butterfly
1 R. Leishman (Kelly College)	2:02.74
2 I. Wilson (Bo Sunderland)	2:03.74
3 A. Quinn (Co Manchester)	2:04.49

200 Metres Individual Medley
1 P. Brew (Kelly College)	2:05.25
2 G. Robins (Portsmouth Northsea)	2:05.44
3 A. Rolley (Gloucester C)	2:07.14

400 Metres Individual Medley
1 P. Brew (Kelly College)	4:21.35
2 G. Robins (Portsmouth Northsea)	4:21.47
3 A. Rolley (Gloucester C)	4:32.86

Women

50 Metres Freestyle
1 C. Woodcock (Haywards Heath)	26.14
2 A. Sheppard (Milngarvie)	26.35
3 C. Foot (Millfield)	26.76

100 Metres Freestyle
1 J. Croft (Wigan Wasps)	57.35
2 L. Donnelly (Hamilton)	57.54
3 R. Gilfillan (Co Dundee)	57.56

200 Metres Freestyle
1 J. Croft (Wigan Wasps)	2:01.21
2 R. Gilfillan (Co Dundee)	2:01.24
3 L. Donnelly (Hamilton)	2:03.73

400 Metres Freestyle
1 K. Mellor (Co Sheffield)	4:12.45
2 R. Gilfillan (Co Dundee)	4:14.11
3 J. Croft (Wigan Wasps)	4:14.82

800 Metres Freestyle
1 K. Mellor (Co Sheffield)	8:44.42
2 R. Gilfillan (Co Dundee)	8:47.60
3 J. Croft (Wigan Wasps)	8:51.80

50 Metres Backstroke
1 J. Ewing (Paisley)	30.49
2 K. Edbrooke (Guildford C)	30.61
3 C. Huddart (Salford Triple 'S')	30.75

100 Metres Backstroke
1 C. Huddart (Salford Triple 'S')	1:04.61
2 J. Ewing (Paisley)	1:05.58
3 H. Slatter (Kelly College)	1:05.83

200 Metres Backstroke
1 C. Huddart (Salford Triple 'S')	2:19.22

2 H. Slatter (Kelly College)	2:20.74
3 A. Sedgebeer (Epping Forest)	2:22.07

50 Metres Breaststroke
1 S. Brownsdon (Wigan Wasps)	32.39
2 M. Hohmann (Wigan Wasps)	32.63
3 L. Coombes (Co Southampton)	32.64

100 Metres Breaststroke
1 S. Brownsdon (Wigan Wasps)	1:10.26
2 M. Hohmann (Wigan Wasps)	1:10.92
3 L. Coombes (Co Southampton)	1:11.52

200 Metres Breaststroke
1 S. Brownsdon (Wigan Wasps)	2:29.25
2 M. Hohmann (Wigan Wasps)	2:32.10
3 H. Alder (Harrow & Wealdstone)	2:39.52

50 Metres Freestyle
1 C. Foot (Millfield)	28.58
2 M. Scarborough (Portsmouth Northsea)	28.61
3 S. Brownsdon (Wigan Wasps)	28.72

100 Metres Butterfly
1 M. Scarborough (Portsmouth Northsea)	1:02.00
2 C. Foot (Millfield)	1:02.14
3 S. Brownsdon (Wigan Wasps)	1:02.47

200 Metres Butterfly
1 C. Foot (Millfield)	2:16.05
2 M. Scarborough (Portsmouth Northsea)	2:16.13
3 L. Wilson (Bo Sunderland)	2:16.91

200 Metres Individual Medley
1 S. Brownsdon (Wigan Wasps)	2:16.61
2 H. Slatter (Kelly College)	2:22.14
3 T. Atkin (Co Lincoln Pentaqua)	2:22.99

400 Metres Individual Medley
1 S. Brownsdon (Wigan Wasps)	4:49.04
2 H. Slatter (Kelly College)	4:56.02
3 T. Atkin (Co Lincoln Pentaqua)	4:58.14

Copthall Stadium, Hendon — 2/23 February, 1989
Men

25 Metres Freestyle
1 D. Halsall (Switzerland)	10.17
2 S. Volery (Switzerland)	10.60
3 B. Hoffmeister (W Germany)	10.91

50 Metres Freestyle
1 D. Halsall (Switzerland)	22.66
2 B. Gutzeit (France)	22.89
3 S. Volery (Switzerland)	22.94

100 Metres Freestyle
1 M. Fibbens (Barnet Copthall)	49.85
2 A. Holmertz (Sweden)	50.64
3 T. Werner (Sweden)	50.73

200 Metres Freestyle
1 A. Holmertz (Sweden)	1:48.29
2 T. O'Hare (Canada)	1:49.56
3 M. Phillips (Canada)	1:50.59

400 Metres Freestyle
1 K. Boyd (Bo S Tyneside)	3:50.50
2 T. O'Hare (Canada)	3:54.25
3 J. Broughton (Co Leeds)	3:56.30

1500 Metres Freestyle
1 T. O'Hare (Canada)	15:26.63
2 J. Ong (Kelly College)	15:27.05
3 C. Marchand (France)	15:38.10

50 Metres Backstroke
1 C. Cockcroft (Co Leeds)	27.07
2 M. Harris (Co Birmingham)	27.25
3 G. Robins (Portsmouth Northsea)	27.60

100 Metres Backstroke
1 C. Cockroft (Co Leeds)	57.71
2 R. Boucher (France)	57.79
3 G. Robins (Portsmouth Northsea)	57.85

200 Metres Backstroke
1 G. Robins (Portsmouth Northsea)	2:02.66
2 M. Woolhouse (Canada)	2:06.95
3 I. Rosser (Torfaen)	2:06.96

50 Metres Breaststroke
1 G. Watson (Edinburgh)	28.79
2 J. Stensson (Sweden)	29.25
3 P. Suominen (Finland)	29.33

100 Metres Breaststroke
1 N. Gillingham (Co Birmingham)	1:03.10
2 J. Cleveland (Canada)	1:03.33
3 I. Campbell (Beckenham)	1:03.99

200 Metres Breaststroke
1 N. Gillingham (Co Birmingham)	2:13.29
2 J. Cleveland (Canada)	2:17.30
3 N. Hudghton (Aberdeen)	2:19.48

100 Metres Butterfly
1 M. Fibbens (Barnet Copthall)	54.99
2 B. Gutzeit (France)	55.58
3 S. Dronsfield (Co Leeds)	56.10

200 Metres Butterfly
1 T. Jones (Co Birmingham)	2:01.03
2 C. Hoffman (W Germany)	2:01.94
3 I. Wilson (Bo Sunderland)	2:04.50

100 Metres Individual Medley
1 B. Gutzeit (France)	57.54
2 J. Sheehan (Canada)	57.59
3 A. Peterson (Sweden)	57.91

400 Metres Individual Medley
1 P. Brew (Kelly College)	4:19.84
2 A. Peterson (Sweden)	4:27.42
3 G. Robins (Portsmouth Northsea)	4:30.19

Women

25 Metres Freestyle
1 D. Hunger (GDR)	12.25
2 C. Woodcock (Haywards Heath)	12.28
3 A. Sheppard (Milngarvie)	12.30

100 Metres Freestyle
1 M. Stellmach (GDR)	57.36
2 R. Gilfillan (Co Dundee)	57.44
3 L. Donnelly (Hamilton)	57.52

200 Metres Freestyle
1 H. Friedrich (GDR)	2:02.13
2 M. Stallmach (GDR)	2:02.41
3 R. Gilfillan (Co Dundee)	2:02.43

400 Metres Freestyle
| 1 D. Wurzburger (Canada) | 4:13.46 |

Linda Donnelly

| 2 J. Croft (Wigan Wasps) | 4:13.77 |
| 3 L. Bensimon (France) | 4:15.54 |

800 Metres Freestyle
1 D. Wurzburger (Canada)	8:35.34
2 F. Cambrini (Italy)	8:45.44
3 E. Holland (Canada)	8:47.04

50 Metres Backstroke
1 B. Weigang (GDR)	29.69
2 S. Page (Stockport Metro)	30.08
3 A. Anderson (Canada)	30.13

100 Metres Backstroke
1 A. Anderson (Canada)	1:03.36
2 T. Szabo (Hungary)	1:04.03
3 N. Cribben (Canada)	1:04.71

200 Metres Backstroke
1 A. Anderson (Canada)	2:15.60
2 T. Szabo (Hungary)	2:16.93
3 C. Olsson (Sweden)	2:17.31

50 Metres Breaststroke
1 M. Hohmann (Wigan Wasps)	32.30
2 S. Brownsdon (Wigan Wasps)	32.43
3 A. Higson (Canada)	32.68

100 Metres Breaststroke
1 S. Boernike (GDR)	1:09.66
2 S. Brownsdon (Wigan Wasps)	1:09.75
3 A. Higson (Canada)	1:09.77

200 Metres Breaststroke
1 S. Boernike (GDR)	2:27.03
2 S. Brownsdon (Wigan Wasps)	2:31.52
3 A. Nisiro (Italy)	2:31.75

50 Metres Butterfly
1 B. Weigang (GDR)	28.35
2 C. Foot (Millfield)	28.66
3 M. Scarborough (Millfield)	29.01

100 Metres Butterfly
1 B. Weigang (GDR)	1:00.82
2 M. Scarborough (Portsmouth Northsea)	1:02.16
3 M. Cater (Canada)	1:02.62

200 Metres Butterfly
1	B. Weigang (GDR)	2:10.86
2	M. Cater (Canada)	2:14.12
3	M. Scarborough (Portsmouth Northsea)	2:14.94

100 Metres Individual Medley
1	D. Hunger (GDR)	1:03.17
2	S. Brownsdon (Wigan Wasps)	1:04.06
3	A. Higson (Canada)	1:04.11

200 Metres Individual Medley
1	A. Higson (Canada)	2:15.46
2	S. Boernike (GDR)	2:15.78
3	S. Brownsdon (Wigan Wasps)	2:16.88

400 Metres Individual Medley
1	S. Brownsdon (Wigan Wasps)	4:50.89
2	S. Smart (Co Chester)	4:58.88
3	H. Slatter (Kelly College)	4:59.10

International Pool, Leeds — 11/13 May, 1989
Mens

50 Metres Freestyle
1	M. Fibbens (Barnet Copthall)	24.12
2	S. Dronsfield (Co Leeds)	24.51
3	N. Metcalfe (Co Leeds)	24.92

100 Metres Freestyle
1	M. Fibbens (Barnet Copthall)	52.11
2	S. Dronsfield (Co Leeds)	53.08
3	S. McQuaid (Co Manchester)	53.56

200 Metres Freestyle
1	P. Brew (Kelly College)	1:56.14
2	J. Broughton (Co Leeds)	1:56.17
3	C. McNeil (Paisley)	1:56.22

400 Metres Freestyle
1	P. Brew (Kelly College)	4:04.63
2	C. McNeil (Paisley)	4:04.87
3	N. Waterson (Cumbernauld)	4:10.18

1500 Metres Freestyle
1	C. McNeil (Paisley)	16:11.20
2	R. Noble (Stirling)	16:15.73
3	P. Henry (Edinburgh)	16:55.43

50 Metres Backstroke
1	M. Peyrebrune (Warrender)	28.52
2	M. Matthews (Barnet Copthall)	28.82
3	I. Panting (Kelly College)	28.87

100 Metres Backstroke
1	G. Robins (Portsmouth Northsea)	1:00.81
2	M. O'Connor (Co Manchester)	1:00.92
3	M. Peyrebrune (Warrender)	1:00.97

200 Metres Backstroke
1	G. Robins (Portsmouth Northsea)	2:09.20
2	I. Clayton (Wigan Wasps)	2:11.40
3	J. Perez (Spain)	2:11.72

50 Metres Breaststroke
1	G. Watson (Carnegie)	29.57
2	N. Hudghton (Co Dundee)	30.57
3	D. Mason (Co Newcastle)	31.52

100 Metres Breaststroke
1	G. Watson (Carnegie)	1:06.00
2	I. McKenzie (Braintree & Bocking)	1:06.93
3	N. Hudghton (Co Dundee)	1:07.07

200 Metres Breaststroke
1	N. Hudghton (Co Dundee)	2:22.93
2	I. McKenzie (Braintree & Bocking)	2:27.14
3	M. Arzoz (Spain)	2:29.75

50 Metres Butterfly
1	M. Fibbens (Barnet Copthall)	25.69
2	A. Jameson (Co Liverpool)	25.72
3	S. Dronsfield (Co Leeds)	25.85

100 Metres Butterfly
1	M. Fibbens (Barnet Copthall)	57.61
2	S. Dronsfield (Co Leeds)	58.22
3	R. Leishman (Kelly College)	58.23

200 Metres Butterfly
1	A. Quinn (Co Manchester)	2:08.43
2	R. Leishman (Kelly College)	2:09.46
3	R. Font (Spain)	2:09.97

200 Metres Individual Medley
1	G. Robins (Portsmouth Northsea)	2:07.89
2	P. Brew (Kelly College)	2:08.84
3	J. Kerr (Kelly College)	2:14.94

400 Metres Individual Medley
1	P. Brew (Kelly College)	4:35.83
2	G. Robins (Portsmouth Northsea)	4:38.04
3	P. Pederzolli (Hounslow B)	4:43.49

Women

50 Metres Freestyle
1	A. Sheppard (Milngarvie)	26.82
2	C. Woodcock (Haywards Heath)	26.91
3	J. Gorst (Co Leeds)	27.28

100 Metres Freestyle
1	R. Gilfillan (Co Dundee)	58.81
2	L. Donnelly (Hamilton)	58.84
3	J. Croft (Wigan Wasps)	58.97

200 Metres Freestyle
1	R. Gilfillan (Co Dundee)	2:04.16
2	L. Donnelly (Hamilton)	2:06.47
3	J. Croft (Wigan Wasps)	2:07.63

400 Metres Freestyle
1	K. Mellor (Co Sheffield)	4:20.71
2	J. Croft (Wigan Wasps)	4:22.88
3	R. Gilfillan (Co Dundee)	4:26.28

800 Metres Freestyle
1	K. Mellor (Co Sheffield)	8:49.29
2	C. Smith (Wigan Wasps)	9:06.65
3	L. Matthews (Redbridge B)	9:09.37

50 Metres Backstroke
1	K. Read (Barnet Copthall)	30.98
2	H. Slatter (Kelly College)	31.25
3	J. Ewing (Paisley)	31.41

100 Metres Backstroke
1	H. Slatter (Kelly College)	1:05.75
2	K. Read (Barnet Copthall)	1:05.88
3	J. Ewing (Paisley)	1:07.80

200 Metres Backstroke
1	K. Read (Barnet Copthall)	2:18.63
2	H. Slatter (Kelly College)	2:19.93
3	J. Riegal (Harrow & Wealdstone)	2:23.12

50 Metres Breaststroke
1 S. Brownsdon (Wigan Wasps)   33.44
2 L. Coombes (Co Southampton)   33.54
3 M. Prat (Spain)   35.09

100 Metres Breaststroke
1 L. Coombes (Co Southampton)   1:13.20
2 S. Brownsdon (Wigan Wasps)   1:13.24
3 M. Prat (Spain)   1:15.34

200 Metres Breaststroke
1 S. Brownsdon (Wigan Wasps)   2:34.38
2 L. Coombes (Co Southampton)   2:43.25
3 H. Alder (Harrow & Wealdstone)   2:44.23

50 Metres Butterfly
1 S. Brownsdon (Wigan Wasps)   29.21
2 C. Foot (Millfield)   29.40
3 J. Gunston (Bracknell)   29.61

100 Metres Butterfly
1 S. Brownsdon (Wigan Wasps)   1:03.44
2 C. Foot (Millfield)   1:04.11
3 S. Brooksbank (Co Leeds)   1:04.32

200 Metres Butterfly
1 L. Wilson (Bo Sunderland)   2:17.42
2 T. Atkin (Co Lincoln Pentaqua)   2:19.44
3 A. Duffy (Derwentside)   2:20.09

200 Metres Individual Medley
1 H. Slatter (Kelly College)   2:21.80
2 K. Bald (Canada)   2:22.62
3 S. Brownsdon (Wigan Wasps)   2:23.10

400 Metres Individual Medley
1 T. Atkin (Co Lincoln Pentaqua)   4:55.76
2 S. Brownsdon (Wigan Wasps)   4:59.40
3 K. Read (Barnet Copthall)   5:02.04

Final Points Tables
Men

Sprint Freestyle
1 M. Fibbens (Barnet Copthall)   138
2 S. McQuaid (Co Manchester)   106
3 P. McQuaid (Co Manchester)   73

Distance Freestyle
1 C. McNeil (Paisley)   121
2 S. McQuaid (Co Manchester)   98
3 N. Waterson (Cumbernauld)   78

Backstroke
1 G. Robins (Portsmouth Northsea)   132
2 I. Clayton (Wigan Wasps)   111
3 M. O'Connor (Co Manchester)   106

Breaststroke
1 N. Hudghton (Aberdeen)   127
2 G. Watson (Carnegie)   118
3 D. Mason (Co Newcastle)   92

Butterfly
1 M. Fibbens (Barnet Copthall)   138
2 R. Leishman (Kelly College)   119
3 A. Quinn (Co Manchester)   102

Individual Medley
1 G. Robins (Portsmouth Northsea)   123
2 P. Brew (Kelly College)   117
3 A. Greig (Barnet Copthall)   100

Women

Sprint Freestyle
1 A. Sheppard (Milngarvie)   119
2 C. Woodcock (Haywards Heath)   118
3 J. Croft (Wigan Wasps)   117

Distance Freestyle
1 J. Croft (Wigan Wasps)   131
2 R. Gilfillan (Co Dundee)   122
3 P. Hutchinson (Wigan Wasps)   107

Backstroke
1 K. Read (Barnet Copthall)   136
2 J. Ewing (Paisley)   117
3 H. Slatter (Kelly College)   116

Breaststroke
1 S. Brownsden (Wigan Wasps)   136
2 L. Coombes (Co Southampton)   118
3 M. Hohmann (Wigan Wasps)   100

Butterfly
1 C. Foot (Millfield)   130
2 S. Brownsdon (Wigan Wasps)   128
3 L. Wilson (Bo Sunderland)   105

Individual Medley
1 S. Brownsdon (Wigan Wasps)   132
2 H. Slatter (Kelly College)   116
3 K. Read (Barnet Copthall)   109

Tracey Atkin

109

Adrian Moorhouse Scales the Olympic Peaks

by Kevin Redsull (The Press Association)

When Adrian Moorhouse triumphantly punched the air after his 100 metres breaststroke victory at the Seoul Olympics, it represented the natural response of a competitor who had finally erased the memory of a failure, which had threatened to cast a permanent shadow over his career.

The Yorkshireman's inability to live up to the expectations of both himself and, just as critically, of the British media at the Los Angeles Games four years earlier, led to a temporary rift with his coach and mentor at the City of Leeds Club, Terry Denison. And it almost persuaded Moorhouse to turn his back on a sport in which he clearly possessed the talent to be a world beater.

Now, with an Olympic gold medal proudly adorning an impressive collection of swimming hardware at the family home in Bingley, near Bradford, Moorhouse is able to reflect frankly and thoughtfully on the painful aftermath of his LA experience.

Yet, as he recalled, 1984 could hardly have started more encouragingly. "I swam a very fast time in the January and from that moment the press started saying I could win the gold medal, and that built my confidence up.

"I was feeling good and Terry set me a lot of work, but then about April, I started feeling down and I didn't know why. I tried to get through it by working even harder in training, but that didn't work, and then I had a blood test which revealed I had suffered from German measles for a couple of months."

That meant an unwanted break in his Olympic build-up, and when Moorhouse got back into the water he was determined to make up for lost time. He admitted: "I was so intense about doing well that I overworked, and when I got to the Games I hadn't rested enough."

And with it had disappeared the spark in his performance, with the consequence that Moorhouse finished fourth in the 100 metres after starting as one of the favourites for the gold. Worse then followed in the 200 metres where, despite being the reigning European champion, he failed to even make the final.

Then the media backlash started, fuelled partly by the refusal of both swimmer and coach to publicly discuss afterwards what had gone wrong. The late Pat Besford, writing in the *Daily Telegraph*, accused Moorhouse of swimming "a foolish race" in his 200 metres heat and of being over-confident, while Athol Still in *The Times* claimed that Moorhouse's performances " . . . fell so far short of expectation that it is clear his preparation for the Games have been little short of disastrous." The damage had been done, both in and out of the water, as far as Moorhouse was concerned. He returned home with his self-confidence, in his own words, "shot to pieces".

"It wasn't just because of how I'd swum, but because of the media thing as well. Basically my reaction stemmed from being a fairly private sort of person, and I didn't want to share the worst moment of my life with anybody else. But the media interpreted that as a bit of a prima-donna response because I had got beat, so when I returned home I said 'right, I'm not going to say anything to the press', and that caused more bad feeling."

There were suggestions from some quarters that Moorhouse should retire, while the swimmer himself did not venture back into the water for several weeks after returning from America. And when he made his return to competition the following December, the result was almost as disastrous.

Moorhouse finished 13th in both the 100 and 200 breaststroke events at the European Cup in Norway, and he admitted: "That was the real low point, because I had won a European Cup title the year before. But when I got back into training I didn't want to know — I suppose I was burned out.

"When I got back from Norway, Terry suggested that I should go and see a hypnotist. But I said 'No, I will sort my own head out'. But Terry's suggestion made me sit down and re-evaluate what I wanted from swimming. So, on New Year's Eve, while everybody was out at parties, I sat down and wrote a list of targets which I knew I would have to

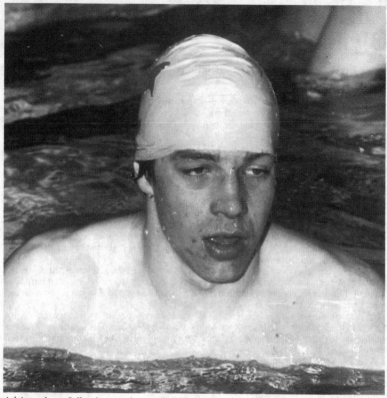

Adrian relaxes following another great swim.

Swimming Times

achieve at the national short course championships the following April if I was going to carry on. I thought that four more months out of life wasn't that long, and that I would give it a go."

He certainly did. Moorhouse achieved his target time for the 100 metres by the emphatic method of setting a new world best time of 1 minute 00.58 seconds at Sharston, and in the 200 meres he set a new British record of 2 minutes 14.30 seconds. Moorhouse recalled: "I knew then that my confidence was back and that I was a world class performer. But if I hadn't swum those times I would have retired."

From the point of view of neat packaging, it would be tempting to say at this juncture that the rest is now history. But that would be much too simplistic in assessing a career which has been characterised by a series of dramatic "highs" and "lows", apart from what happened in Los Angeles.

For a start, there was his relationship with Denison, which Moorhouse admits ran into "a rough patch" after the '84 Games. "It took a long time for the relationship to settle down again. Before LA, it was a 'teacher-pupil' situation, Terry was lecturing me and I found I couldn't handle it."

So after Sharston, Moorhouse decided to go to Hong Kong to train under another acknowledged breaststroke expert, former GB Olympic coach, Dave Haller, as part of his preparation for the 1985 European Championships in Sofia.

"Dave worked my nuts off for a couple of months, and then I came back and worked with Terry for a couple of weeks before going off to Sofia, where Paul Hickson took charge of my training. So I had three different coaches in the space of a few weeks, which didn't help my taper at all, and I felt lousy."

Even so, Moorhouse still landed the 100 metres title which had eluded him at two previous European Championships, only to tarnish that success by failing to qualify for the final of the 200 metres, where he was the defending champion, after swimming a poor tactical heat. To rub salt into the wound, Moorhouse then won the 'B' final in a time faster than that achieved by the winner of the gold medal, and once again the media knives were out. "A tactical blunder of colossal magnitude" claimed Athol Still, while Moorhouse conceded ruefully at the time: "I blew it, what more can I say?"

Apart from the obvious disappointment felt in British quarters, it also increased the suspicion that perhaps there was something in his make-up, or maybe it was just fate, that was always going to prevent Moorhouse from doing his talent full justice.

The next "chapter" came at the 1986 Commonwealth Games, where the men's breaststroke events developed into a straight head-to-head confrontation between Moorhouse and the Canadian, Victor Davis. The media latched onto it and built up the rivalry between the two men, and neither they nor the spectators were left disappointed by what followed.

The African boycott inevitably devalued the athletics events in Edinburgh, but the swimming events were unaffected. And the fierce battle for supremacy between the three leading swimming countries, Australia, Canada and England, produced genuine atmosphere in the Royal Commonwealth Pool, with the duel between Moorhouse and Davis being one of the focal points.

Davis drew first blood, depriving Moorhouse of the 100 metres title which he had won in Brisbane four years earlier. The Englishman finished second and commented: "The times were poor, we both should have gone faster, but the pressure got to us a bit. I was choked off afterwards with losing to him, and he started slagging me off in the press for the slow time, and so you had a real pot-boiler situation for the 200 metres final."

That was three days later, and it produced one of the highlights of the Games. Davis was supremely confident, and with good reason. He was the existing world record holder and Olympic champion, and hadn't been beaten over the distance for three years. But Moorhouse destroyed that record. Davis turned slightly ahead going into the final length, but the Englishman produced a powerful late surge to gain thrilling revenge for his 100 metres defeat.

"I love watching that race on video, it's got to be one of the highspots of my career," said Moorhouse. "I honestly felt pleased just to be swimming that night because of the atmosphere in the pool, and to beat Davis was very satisfying."

But his elation evaporated in the most cruel way possible at the world championships, in Madrid, a fortnight later.

Moorhouse swam superbly in his heat of the 100 metres, setting the fastest qualifying time in a new European record of 1 minute 2.01 seconds, and then went faster by 0.27 seconds when touching for the final. But he was subsequently disqualified for an alleged "dolphin kick" at the halfway turn.

It remains the only occasion in his career that Moorhouse has been disqualified in such a manner, and the reaction of many of those present was summed up by an official of the United States team who said, bluntly: "Adrian was robbed."

Whatever the merits of the decision, it seemed that his major championship "bogey" had struck again, but Moorhouse adopted a much more positive approach.

"I couldn't believe it at first, but when I went away and thought about what had happened, I didn't find it that depressing, because I had touched the wall first nearly a second ahead of Davis (who was awarded the gold medal).

"Until Madrid, I hadn't swum with any real authority in a major championship, but my time in the heats put me on top of the world rankings for that year, and so I was able to sit back and say to myself I am now the 'best in the world' at the end of 1986, which was really the turning point in relation to my success in Seoul."

And, at that point, the rest virtually is history. In pre-Olympic year, Moorhouse provided a clear warning of what was to come in Seoul by becoming the first man to beat the one minute barrier for the 100 metres breaststroke, when he won the prestigious Arena short course title, in Bonn, in 59.75 seconds. "That was the best short course swim I have ever produced. Everything went right," he recalled fondly.

Moorhouse then confirmed his increased authority in the water by impressively retaining the European 100 metres title in Strasbourg, while finishing third in the 200 for good measure.

James Parrack (facing camera) caused a major upset when he defeated the future Olympic Champion, Moorhouse, to win the 1988 National 100 metres breaststroke title.

Jack Hickes

And so to Seoul. Once again, in a repeat of what happened before the Los Angeles Games, Moorhouse threw down the gauntlet early in the year by setting a fast time. He won a major American meet in March with a new European record of 1 minute 01.78 seconds, only .13 seconds outside the world record, which Steve Lundquist set in winning the '84 Olympic title.

But this time Moorhouse ensured there was no other repeat of his ill-fated LA build-up. He kept a low profile and did not overwork in training, and when he again posted the fastest time in the heats in Seoul, it looked as though his moment had finally arrived. Yet, in keeping with what had gone before, there was still one more twist in the script.

It was provided by the talented Russian competitor, Dmitriy Volkov, who covered the first 50 metres of the final as if life depended on it, and who still had a clear advantage over Moorhouse with 25 metres still to go. Moorhouse said: "I remember thinking, I hope he dies soon, or else I won't catch him, but whatever happens I'm going to race him to the wall, because that's what I came here for."

The television cameras graphically captured the fluctuating reactions of his watching parents as Moorhouse thrillingly overhauled Volkov over the closing few metres, while remaining oblivious to the late challenge of the Hungarian, Karoly Gutter, who eventually finished second just one hundredth of a second behind the Briton.

But this was one occasion where the time really didn't matter, for Moorhouse had finally erased that LA nightmare. "When I got back into the water after LA, I knew that I had to win the gold in Seoul, there was nothing else I could do which would rectify what had happened there. I knew that otherwise I would always be remembered as a nearly man." Suffice to say, that description no longer applies.

British Stars: Pen Portraits

Men

GARY BINFIELD
Born: 13.3.66. *Club:* Maxwell. *Coaches:* Mike Wakeley/Clive Rushton. PB: 100 metres backstroke 57.73 (1989), 200 metres backstroke 2:03.56 (1989), 200 metres individual medley 2:05.41 (1987). ASA National Champion 100 and 200 metres backstroke (1989). GB record holder (long course) 200 metres backstroke. Has won seven National titles since 1984. GB international since 1985. Student University of South Carolina. Competed in Commonwealth Games 1986, World Championships 1986, European Championships 1987 and 1989, and Olympic Games 1988.

Kevin Boyd

KEVIN BOYD
Born: 23.6.66. *Club:* Borough of South Tyneside. *Coach:* Paddy Hayes. PB: 200 metres freestyle 1:51.71 (1986), 400 metres freestyle 3:50.01 (1988), 800 metres freestyle 8:01.87 (1988), 1500 metres freestyle 15:17.56 (1988). ASA National Champion 1500 metres freestyle (1989). GB record holder (long course), 400, 800 and 1500 metres freestyle. GB record holder (short course), 200 metres backstroke, 200, 400, 800 and 1500 metres freestyle. Has won five National titles and seven short course titles since 1984. Completed final medical school examinations, Newcastle University, June 1988. GB in-

ternational since 1984. Silver medallist Commonwealth Games 1986 (400 metres freestyle). Also competed in the World Championships 1986, Olympic Games 1988, and European Championships 1987 and 1989.

PAUL BREW
Born: 20.11.65. *Club:* Kelly College. *Coach:* Archie Brew (father). PB: 200 metres freestyle 1:51.96 (1989), 200 metres individual medley 2:05.72 (1987), 400 metres individual medley 4:25.25 (1988). ASA National Champion 400 metres individual medley (1989). GB record holder (short course), 200 and 400 metres individual medley. Has won three National titles and three short course titles since 1984. GB international since 1984. Scottish international. Competed in Commonwealth Games 1986, Olympic Games 1988, and European Championships 1989.

JONATHAN BROUGHTON
Born: 1.7.67. *Club:* City of Leeds. *Coach:* Terry Denison. PB: 200 metres freestyle 1:51.84 (1987), 400 metres freestyle 3:58.98 (1989). ASA National Champion 200 metres freestyle (1989). Previously won this title in 1987. GB international since 1986. Competed in Commonwealth Games 1986 (relay bronze medallist), European Championships 1987 and 1989. Olympic Games 1988.

Tony Day

115

TONY DAY

Born: 14.4.65. *Club:* City of Leeds.. *Coach:* Terry Denison. PB: 400 metres freestyle 3:57.18 (1988), 1500 metres freestyle 15:21.25 (1988), 400 metres individual medley 4:30.02 (1986). Has won the National 1500 metres title twice and short course 1500 metres title four times. Competed in Commonwealth Games 1982 and 1986, European Championships 1985 and 1987, Olympic Games 1988. Bronze medallist 1500 metres freestyle World Student Games (1985). GB international since 1982. Just completed Ph D studies at University of Leeds. Welsh record holder 400 and 1500 metres freestyle, 200 and 400 metres individual medley.

STEVEN DRONSFIELD

Born: 21.7.71. *Club:* City of Leeds. *Coach:* Terry Denison. PB: 50 metres freestyle 23.71 (1989), 100 metres freestyle 51.47 (1989), 100 metres butterfly 55.90 (1989). Yet to win a senior title at the Nationals. Won one silver and three bronze medals European Championships 1987. Competed in European Championships 1989 — his first major senior games and set lifetime bests in 50 and 100 metres freestyle.

MICHAEL FIBBENS

Born: 31.5.68. *Club:* Barnet Copthall. *Coach:* Doug Campbell (brother-in-law). PB: 50 metres freestyle 23.33 (1989), 100 metres freestyle 50.91 (1989), 100 metres butterfly 55.46 (1989). ASA National Champion 50 and 100 metres freestyle (1989). ASA Winter Champion 50 and 100 metres freestyle (1988). Has won two National titles and four short course titles, GB record holder (short course) 50 metres freestyle 22.52 (1989), 100 metres freestyle 48.95 (1989) and 100 metres butterfly 54.00 (1989). GB international since 1986. Competed in European Championships 1987 and 1989 and Olympic Games 1988. Sister Nicola was a GB international and still holds GB record for 100 metres butterfly set at Los Angeles Olympics.

MARK FOSTER

Born: 12.5.70. *Club:* Borough of Southend. *Coach:* Mike Higgs. PB: 50 metres freestyle 23.13 (1987), 100 metres freestyle 51.15 (1987). Previously won 50 metres freestyle sprint National title three times (1986-1988) and took four short course titles in 1986/1987. GB record

Mark Foster

holder (long course) 50 metres freestyle. GB international since 1985. Competed in Commonwealth Games 1986 (relay bronze medallist), World Championships 1986, European Championships 1987 and Commonwealth Games 1988. Former GB short course record holder for 50 and 100 metres freestyle.

NICK GILLINGHAM

Born: 21.1.67. *Club:* City of Birmingham. *Coach:* Barry Prime. PB: 100 metres breaststroke 1:02.12 (1989), 200 metres breaststroke 2:12.90 (1989). ASA National Champion 200 metres breaststroke for past three years. ASA Winter Champion 100 and 200 metres breaststroke (1988). European 200 metres breaststroke Champion (1989). European, Commonwealth and GB record holder (long course) 200 metres breaststroke. European and GB record holder (short course) 200 metres breaststroke. GB international since 1985. Gold medallist 200 metres breaststroke, bronze 100 metres breaststroke, European Championships 1989. Silver medallist Olympic Games 1988 (200 metres breaststroke), bronze medallist Commonwealth Games 1986 (200 metres breaststroke). Also competed in European Championships 1987 and World Championships 1986.

PAUL HOWE

Born: 8.1.68. *Club:* City of Birmingham. *Coach:* Barry Prime. PB: 200 metres freestyle 1:51.22 (1988), 400 metres freestyle 3:57.90 (1988). Former ASA National 400 metres freestyle Champion

(1988). Won two short course National titles (1985). GB record holder (long course) 200 metres freestyle. Relay bronze medallist Olympic Games 1984, aged 16 years. Another relay bronze Commonwealth Games 1986. GB international since 1984. Also competed in Olympic Games 1988. Student Arizona State University.

NEIL HUDGHTON
Born: 13.7.69. *Club:* City of Dundee. *Coach:* Jim Gilfillan. PB: 200 metres breaststroke 2:19.34 (1989). GB international since 1989 but long time Scottish international. Competed in Commonwealth Games 1986 and European Championships 1989. Scottish 200 metres breaststroke short course record holder. GB Grand Prix category winner breaststroke.

TIM JONES
Born: 16.1.67. *Club:* City of Birmingham. *Coach:* Barry Prime. PB: 100 metres butterfly 56.03 (1989), 200 metres butterfly 2:00.32 (1988). Former ASA National 200 metres butterfly Champion (1988). Also won two ASA short course titles. GB record holder (short course) 200 metres butterfly 1:58.81. GB international since 1986. Competed in Commonwealth Games 1986 and European Championships 1989.

CAMPBELL McNEIL
Born: 2.3.69. *Club:* Paisley. *Coach:* Jim Park. PB: 400 metres freestyle 3:56.29 (1989), 1500 metres freestyle 15:46.89 (1989). GB Grand Prix category winner distance freestyle. ASA National 400 metres freestyle Champion (1989). Won three freestyle titles at Scottish long course Championships (1989). GB international since 1989, but had previously represented Scotland on many occasions. Scottish record holder 400 metres freestyle. Competed in Commonwealth Games 1986 and European Championships 1989.

ADRIAN MOORHOUSE
Born: 24.5.64. *Club:* City of Leeds. *Coach:* Terry Denison. PB: 100 metres breaststroke 1:01.49 (1989), 200 metres breaststroke 2:15.78 (1987). Olympic Champion, European Champion, World, European and Commonwealth record holder 100 metres breaststroke. ASA National 100 metres breaststroke Champion

seven times (1981-1983, 1985-1987 and 1989), 200 metres breaststroke Champion five times (1981-1983, 1985-1986). Also won ten breaststroke short course titles. GB international since 1980. European 100 metres breaststroke Champion 1985, 1987 and 1989, 200 metres breaststroke Champion 1983. Commonwealth Games 100 metres breaststroke Champion 1982, 200 metres breaststroke Champion 1986. First man to break the minute over 100 metres breaststroke in 25 metre pool with 59.75 in 1987 — the world's fastest time.

PETER O'SULLIVAN
Born: 23.12.67. *Club:* Hounslow Borough. *Coach:* Malcolm Staight. PB: 200 metres individual medley 2:06.14 (1989), 400 metres individual medley 4:26.38 (1989). Student University of Georgia. GB international since 1986. Competed in European Championships 1989 — his first major games.

DAVID PARKER
Born: 31.3.71. *Club:* City of Coventry. *Coach:* Nick Selwood. PB: 100 metres butterfly 55.33 (1989). ASA National 100 metres butterfly Champion (1989). Competed in European Championships 1989 — his first major games. GB international since 1989 after graduating from the English intermediate squad. Improved his personal best by over two seconds in 1989.

James Parrack

JAMES PARRACK
Born: 10.3.67. *Club:* City of Leeds. *Coach:* Terry Denison. PB: 100 metres breaststroke 1:03.71 (1988). Surprise winner of 100 metres breaststroke National

title in 1988 beating illustrious club mate, Adrian Moorhouse. Competed in Olympic Games 1988 — his first GB international.

Alastair Quinn

ALASTAIR QUINN
Born: 13.6.67. *Club:* Sale. *Coach:* Paddy Griffin. PB: 200 metres butterfly 2:05.08 (1989). National 200 metres butterfly Champion (1989). Competed in European Championships 1989 — his GB senior international debut.

GRANT ROBINS
Born: 21.5.69. *Club:* Portsmouth Northsea. *Coach:* Chris Nesbit. PB: 100 metres backstroke 58.53 (1988), 200 metres backstroke 2:04.10 (1989), 200 metres individual medley 2:06.05 (1989). ASA National 200 metres individual medley Champion (1989) and previously won the 400 metres individual medley in 1985. Named the outstanding male competitor at the 1988 Winter Championships where he won three titles. GB record holder (short course) 100 metres backstroke. GB international since 1985, but had to wait four more years to gain selection for a major Games — the European Championships 1989. World Cup category winner, backstroke. GB Grand Prix category winner, individual medley and backstroke.

IAN WILSON
Born: 19.12.70. *Club:* Borough of Sunderland. *Coach:* Steven Poulter. PB: 400 metres freestyle 3:59.54 (1989), 1500 metres freestyle 15:43.15 (1988), 200

metres butterfly 2:04.95 (1989). ASA Winter Champion for 1500 metres freestyle and 200 metres butterfly in 1988. GB international since 1989 but illness has hampered his progress. Sister Lynne competed in Olympic Games 1988 in 200 metres butterfly.

Women

TRACEY ATKIN
Born: 14.8.71. *Club:* City of Lincoln Pentaqua. *Coach:* Ian Turner. PB: 200 metres butterfly 2:15.21 (1989), 400 metres individual medley 4:51.85 (1988). Former ASA National 400 metres individual medley Champion (1988). GB international since 1987. Competed in Olympic Games 1988.

Helen Bewley   Jack Hickes

HELEN BEWLEY
Born: 14.5.68. *Club:* University of Swansea. *Coach:* Paul Hickson. PB: 200 metres butterfly 2:15.28 (1987). Former ASA National 200 metres butterfly Champion in 1986 and 1987. She also captured the short course 200 metres butterfly title in 1986 and 1987. GB international since 1985. Competed in Commonwealth Games 1986 and European Championships 1987, reaching the final of 200 metres butterfly. Also competed in the 1988 Olympic Games.

SUKI BROWNSDON
Born: 14.10.65. *Club:* Wigan Wasps. *Coach:* Keith Bewley. PB: 100 metres breaststroke 1:10.39 (1987), 200 metres

breaststroke 2:33.16 (1985), 200 metres individual medley 2:20.29 (1988), 400 metres individual medley 4:51.45 (1988). ASA National Champion 100, 200 metres breaststroke and 400 metres individual medley 1989. Also won the breaststroke titles on four other occasions, 1981 and 1986-1988. Collected four ASA short course titles (1981-1982). GB international since Moscow Olympics 1980. Competed in three Olympic Games, five European Championships, two World Championships and two Commonwealth Games. Silver medallist 100 metres breaststroke, European Championships 1981. Bronze medallist 100 metres breaststroke, Commonwealth Games 1982. Gold medallist 4×100 metres relay Commonwealth Games 1986. 1989 World Cup category winner in breaststroke and individual medley. GB record holder 100 metres breaststroke (long course) and 100 and 200 metres breaststroke (short course).

LORRAINE COOMBES
Born: 28.10.60. *Club:* City of Southampton. *Coach:* Dave Heathcock. PB: 100 metres breaststroke 1:11.24 (1989), 200 metres breaststroke 2:38.46 (1984). 1988 ASA Winter Champion 100 metres breaststroke. She also previously won both short course breaststroke titles in 1983. Former ASA National 100 metres breaststroke Champion (1983). GB record holder (long course) 50 metres breaststroke 32.94 (1989). GB international since 1982. Competed in European Championships 1983 and 1989, and Commonwealth Games 1986.

Joanna Coull   Eric Palmer

JOANNA COULL
Born: 4.12.73. *Club:* City of Birmingham. *Coach:* Barry Prime. PB: 100 metres freestyle 57.95 (1989), 200 metres freestyle 2:04.27 (1984). ASA National 200 metres freestyle Champion 1989. Surprisingly has never won a National Age Group Title. GB international since 1988. Competed in Olympic Games 1988 and European Championships 1989.

JUNE CROFT
Born: 17.6.63. *Club:* Wigan Wasps. *Coach:* Keith Bewley. PB: 50 metres freestyle 26.48 (1981), 100 metres freestyle 56.60 (1982), 200 metres freestyle 1:59.74 (1982), 400 metres freestyle 4:11.49 (1984). Has won eight ASA National titles and 16 ASA short course titles since 1979. GB international since 1979. Commonwealth record holder 200 metres freestyle. GB record holder (long course) 100 and 200 metres freestyle and GB record holder (short course) for 100, 200 and 400 metres freestyle. Former Commonwealth Games Champion for 100 and 200 metres freestyle, Brisbane 1982. Bronze medallist 400 metres freestyle Olympic Games 1984. Silver medallist 4×100 metres medley relay Olympic Games 1980.

SHARRON DAVIES
Born: 1.11.62. *Club:* Bracknell. *Coach:* Rosa Gallop. PB: 200 metres individual medley 2:17.31 (1980), 400 metres individual medley 4:46.83 (1980). 1989 ASA National Champion 200 metres individual medley, a title that she had previously won on five other occasions (1976-1980). Has also won 16 other senior national titles and 15 senior short course titles. GB international 1976-1980 and returned to the team for the 1989 European Championships. Olympic Silver medallist 400 metres individual medley in 1980 in a GB record time that still stands. Double Commonwealth Games Champion (200 and 400 metres individual medley) in 1978. Also competed in World Championships 1978, and was bronze medallist in 400 metres individual medley at the European Championships 1977. GB short course record holder for 200 and 400 metres individual medley, both set in 1980.

CAROLINE FOOT
Born: 14.3.65. *Club:* Millfield. *Coach:* Paddy Garratt. PB: 100 metres butterfly 1:02.18 (1988). GB Grand Prix category

winner butterfly. Former ASA National 100 metres butterfly Champion (1986). Silver medallist 100 metres butterfly Commonwealth Games 1986. GB team member since 1982. Competed in World Championships 1982 and 1986, European Championships 1983 and 1987, and Olympic Games 1988.

Ruth Gilfillan

RUTH GILFILLAN

Born: 6.3.67. *Club:* City of Dundee. *Coach:* James Gilfillan (father). PB: 100 metres freestyle 58.00 (1988), 200 metres freestyle 2:01.66 (1988), 400 metres freestyle 4:14.89 (1987). Former ASA National 200 metres freestyle Champion (1987 and 1988) and 400 metres freestyle Champion (1988). GB international since 1984. Bronze medallist Commonwealth Games 1986, 200 metres freestyle. Also competed in World Championships 1986, Olympic Games 1988 and European Championships 1987. Scottish long course record holder 100, 200, 400 and 800 metres freestyle. Ruth missed most of the 1989 summer season because of injury.

JEAN HILL

Born: 15.7.64. *Club:* Cumbernauld. *Coach:* Danny McGowan. PB: 100 metres breaststroke 1:11.26 (1984), 200 metres breaststroke 2:31.57 (1987), 200 metres individual medley 2:17.21 (1986). GB record holder (long course) for 200 metres breaststroke and 200 metres individual medley, but has never won an ASA National title. GB international since 1984. Scottish international since 1978. Gave up competition in 1979, but returned in 1982. Double silver medallist Commonwealth Games 1986 (100 metres breaststroke and 200 metres individual medley). Finalist

100 metres breaststroke at Los Angeles Olympic Games. Also competed in Commonwealth Games 1978, three European Championships (1986, 1987 and 1989) and the Olympic Games 1988. Scottish long course record holder for 100 and 200 metres breaststroke, 100 metres butterfly, 200 and 400 metres individual medley.

MARGARET HOHMANN

Born: 22.9.56. *Club:* Wigan Wasps. *Coach:* Keith Bewley. PB: 100 metres breaststroke 1:11.48 (1980), 200 metres breaststroke 2:36.46 (1980). Former GB record holder for 100 and 200 metres breaststroke who retired after the 1980 Olympics, later returning to competition in 1987. Winner of 11 ASA National titles between 1973-1980 and 11 short course titles during the same period. She crowned her comeback in 1987 by taking the 100 metres breaststroke short course title that she had last won in 1980. Within 12 months she competed in her third Olympic Games and celebrated her 32nd birthday in Seoul. Dissatisfied with her performance at the 1988 Olympics, she determined to carry on and set new GB records for both 50 metres breaststroke short and long course in 1989. GB international 1973-1980 and 1988, relay silver medallist Olympic Games 1980, bronze medallist 100 metres breaststroke World Championships 1978. Silver and bronze medallist Commonwealth Games 1978 (100 and 200 metres breaststroke).

KAREN MELLOR

Born: 6.5.69. *Club:* City of Sheffield. *Coach:* Fred Furniss. PB: 200 metres freestyle 2:05.41 (1986), 400 metres freestyle 4:16.16 (1988), 800 metres freestyle 8:40.41 (1988). 1989 ASA National Champion and 1988 ASA Winter Champion 400 metres and 800 metres freestyle. Has won seven ASA National titles and four ASA short course titles. GB team member since 1985. Fourth in 800 metres freestyle, Commonwealth Games 1986. Also competed in the World Championships 1986, European Championships 1987 and Olympic Games 1988. Selected for the 1989 European Championships, but illness forced her to withdraw.

KAREN PICKERING

Born: 19.12.71. *Club:* Ipswich. *Coach:* Dave Champion. PB: 50 metres freestyle 26.92 (1989), 100 metres freestyle 56.82 (1989). 1989 ASA National Champion and ASA Winter Champion 1988 100 metres freestyle. GB international since 1987. Competed in the European Championships 1987 and 1989. In Bonn she became the first girl to threaten June Croft's National record for 100 metres freestyle which has stood since 1982. She later turned in outstanding times in both relays.

SAMANTHA PURVIS
Born: 24.6.67. *Club:* Wigan Wasps. *Coach:* Keith Bewley. PB: 100 metres butterfly 1:02.17 (1984), 200 metres butterfly 2:11.97 (1984), 200 metres individual medley 2:20.84 (1989). 1989 joint ASA National Champion for 200 metres butterfly. Has won six National butterfly titles since 1984 and one short course title. GB record holder (long/short course) for 200 metres butterfly. GB international since 1983. Bronze medallist 100 metres butterfly Commonwealth Games 1986. Competed in four European Championships (1983-1989), the Olympic Games 1988, and World Championships 1986.

KATHERINE READ
Born: 30.6.69. *Club:* Barnet Copthall. *Coach:* Doug Campbell. PB: 100 metres backstroke 1:04.27 (1988), 200 metres backstroke 2:14.87 (1986). 1989 ASA National Champion and 1988 ASA Winter Champion 100 and 200 metres backstroke. Kathy has run up a remarkable sequence of victories at the Nationals. She has won the title six consecutive times (1984-1989) and only Holland's Jolanda de Rover in 1988 prevented a similar run over 200 metres. GB record holder for 200 metres backstroke long and short course pools. GB international since 1984 and has competed in all major championships since the Los Angeles Olympics. Silver medallist at 200 metres backstroke in the 1986 Commonwealth Games.

MADELEINE SCARBOROUGH
Born: 18.8.64. *Club:* Portsmouth Northsea. *Coach:* Chris Nesbit. PB: 100 metres butterfly 1:01.94 (1989), 200 metres butterfly 2:15.24 (1989). 1989 ASA National Champion 100 metres butterfly and Joint Champion 200 metres butterfly. 1988 ASA Winter Champion 100 and 200 metres butterfly. Former junior international who gave up top class competition after the 1983 World Student Games. She returned in 1987 and won the ASA short course 100 metres butterfly title at

Ipswich. GB international since 1987. Competed in the European Championships 1989.

Helen Slatter Tavistock Times

HELEN SLATTER
Born: 7.6.70. *Club:* Kelly College. *Coach:* Archie Brew. PB: 100 metres backstroke 1:05.23 (1989), 200 metres backstroke 2:17.59 (1989). Former ASA short course champion 100 and 200 metres backstroke (1987). GB international since 1987.

ALISON SHEPPARD
Born: 5.11.72. *Club:* Milngarvie. *Coach:* Alec McNeil. PB: 50 metres freestyle 26.43 (1988). GB Grand Prix winner sprint freestyle category 1989. Scottish Champion 50 metres freestyle and 100 metres backstroke. GB international since 1988. Competed in the Olympic Games 1988.

CAROLINE WOODCOCK
Born: 23.8.72. *Club:* Haywards Heath. *Coach:* Kevin Banfield. PB: 50 metres freestyle 26.01 (1989), 100 metres freestyle 58.82 (1989). 1989 ASA National Champion 50 metres freestyle and 1988 ASA Winter Champion 50 metres freestyle. Won the "outstanding female competitor award" at the 1988 ASA Winter Championships in Plymouth. GB record holder (long course) 50 metres freestyle, a record she has broken twice in 1989. Has improved her personal best by an amazing 1.40 seconds over the one length this year. GB international in 1989. Competed in the European Championships 1989, her first major competition, finishing fifth in the 50 metres freestyle. And was a member of the GB team that came sixth in a new GB record time.

SPLASH OUT IN STYLE
at
BARNET COPTHALL POOLS

GREAT NORTH WAY, HENDON, LONDON NW4

SWIMMING
DIVING
SYNCHRO
FITNESS CENTRE

BEGINNER, COUNTY, NATIONAL AND INTERNATIONAL LEVELS

*9 Training Squads *Weight Training Facilities *Dry Land Exercises*
*Video Work *Electronic Timing in Training *Underwater Speakers*
*Underwater Viewing Facilities *Full Underwater Markings for
Synchronised Swimming *8-Lane 25m Pool *6-Lane 25yd Pool *Anti-wave
Lane Ropes *Fully Qualified Coaches and Teachers *Nearby College of
Further Education *Diving Pool 4m deep *2 x 1m Springboards*
*1m Springboard *3m Springboard *5m Platform*

WE TAKE OUR SWIMMING SERIOUSLY
WE TAKE <u>YOUR</u> SWIMMING SERIOUSLY

FOR FURTHER DETAILS CONTACT:-
DOUG CAMBELL TELEPHONE: 01-203 4187

LONDON BOROUGH
barnet
Directorate of Technical Services

International Results, 1988–89

Olympic Games
Seoul, S Korea — 18/25 September, 1988

Men

50 Metres Freestyle
Final
1	M. Biondi (USA)	22.14
2	T. Jager (USA)	22.38
3	G. Prigoda (USSR)	22.71
4	D. Halsall (Switzerland)	22.83
5	S. Volery (Switzerland)	22.84
6	V. Tkashenko (USSR)	22.88
7	F. Henter (W Germany)	23.03
8	A. Baildon (Australia)	23.15

Consolation Final
1	G. Titus (Sweden)	23.28
2	P. Johansson (Sweden)	23.37
3	P-S. Ang (Singapore)	23.39
4	J. Shen (China)	23.40
5	C. Kalfayan (France)	23.45
6	S. Guesgen (W Germany)	23.55
7	M. Andrews (Canada)	23.64
8	H. Woods (Netherlands Antilles)	23.65

British Competitors
22	M. Foster (GBR)	23.51
25	M. Fibbens (GBR)	23.67

100 Metres Freestyle
Final
1	M. Biondi (USA)	48.63
2	C. Jacobs (USA)	49.06
3	S. Caron (France)	49.62
4	G. Prigoda (USSR)	49.75
5	I. Bachkatov (USSR)	50.08
6	A. Baildon (Australia)	50.23
7	P. Johansson (Sweden)	50.35
8	T. Werner (Sweden)	50.54

Consolation Final
1	T. Stachewicz (Australia)	50.71
2	D. Goss (Canada)	50.73
3	S. Volery (Switzerland)	50.74
4	S. Lodziewski (GDR)	51.00
5	F. Mortensen (Denmark)	51.05
6	T. Fahrner (W Germany)	51.12
7	T. Golomeev (Bulgaria)	51.16
8	H. Woods (Netherlands Antilles)	51.25

British Competitors
21	A. Jameson (GBR)	51.18
22	R. Lee (GBR)	51.20

200 Metres Freestyle
Final
1	D. Armstrong (Australia)	1:47.25
2	A. Holmertz (Sweden)	1:47.89
3	M. Biondi (USA)	1:47.99
4	A. Wojdat (Poland)	1:48.40
5	M. Gross (W Germany)	1:48.59
6	S. Zesner (GDR)	1:48.77
7	T. Dalbey (USA)	1:48.86
8	T. Fahrner (W Germany)	1:49.19

Consolation Final
1	R. Gleria (Italy)	1:49.28
2	T. Flemming (GDR)	1:50.18
3	T. Stachewicz (Australia)	1:50.83
4	A. Kouznetsov (USSR)	1:51.03
5	F. Mortensen (Denmark)	1:51.44
6	M. Podkoscielny (Poland)	1:51.63
7	S. Ogata (Japan)	1:51.89
8	P. Howe (GBR)	1:51.99

Other British Competitors
27	M. Green (GBR)	1:53.03

400 Metres Freestyle
Final
1	U. Dassler (GDR)	3:46.95
2	D. Armstrong (Australia)	3:47.15
3	A. Wojdat (Poland)	3:47.34
4	M. Cetlinski (USA)	3:48.09
5	M. Podkoscielny (Poland)	3:48.59
6	S. Pfeiffer (W Germany)	3:49.96
7	K. Boyd (GBR)	3:50.16
8	A. Holmertz (Sweden)	3:51.04

Consolation Final
1	J. Hoffmann (GDR)	3:52.13
2	V. Kalaus (Hungary)	3:53.24
3	T. O'Hare (Canada)	3:54.33
4	C. Scanavino (Uruguay)	3:54.36
5	I. Brown (Australia)	3:54.63
6	D. Jorgensen (USA)	3:55.34
7	S. Vassallo (Puerto Rico)	3:55.39
8	Z. Szilagyi (Hungary)	3:56.00

Other British Competitors
24	T. Day (GBR)	3:57.91

1500 Metres Freestyle
Final
1	V. Salnikov (USSR)	15:00.40
2	S. Pfeiffer (W Germany)	15:02.69
3	U. Dassler (GDR)	15:06.15
4	M. Cetlinski (USA)	15:06.42
5	M. Podkoscielny (Poland)	15:14.76
6	R. Henkel (W Germany)	15:18.19
7	K. Boyd (GBR)	15:21.16
8	D. Petric (Yugoslavia)	15:37.12

Other British Competitors
22	T. Day (GBR)	15:38.75

100 Metres Backstroke
Final
1	D. Suzuki (Japan)	55.05
2	D. Berkoff (USA)	55.18
3	I. Polianski (USSR)	55.20
4	S. Zabolotnov (USSR)	55.37
5	M. Tewksbury (Canada)	56.09
6	F. Baltrusch (GDR)	56.10
7	F. Hoffmeister (W Germany)	56.19
8	S. Murphy (Canada)	56.32

Consolation Final
1	D. Richter (GDR)	56.66
2	F. Schott (France)	56.98
3	J. Mortensen (USA)	57.06
4	S. Maruyana (Japan)	57.13

5	G. Mikhalev (Bulgaria)	57.17
6	D. Lim (Singapore)	57.72
7	M. Guzman (Puerto Rico)	57.95
8	E. Edvardsson (Iceland)	58.20

British Competitors

22	N. Harper (GBR)	58.02
25	N. Cochran (GBR)	58.25

200 Metres Backstroke
Final

1	I. Polianski (USSR)	1:59.37
2	F. Baltrusch (GDR)	1:59.60
3	P. Kingsman (New Zealand)	2:00.48
4	S. Zabolotnov (USSR)	2:00.52
5	D. Richter (GDR)	2:01.67
6	J. Berndt (W Germany)	2:01.84
7	D. Veatch (USA)	2:02.26
8	R. Romero (Brazil)	2:02.28

Consolation Final

1	F. Hoffmeister (W Germany)	2:01.65
2	S. Bigelov (USA)	2:02.95
3	M. Lopez-Zubero (Spain)	2:03.70
4	M. Tewksbury (Canada)	2:03.79
5	G. Mikhalev (Bulgaria)	2:04.24
6	T. Deutsch (Hungary)	2:04.42
7	D. Suzuki (Japan)	2:04.67
8	G. Binfield (GBR)	2:04.90

100 Metres Breaststroke
Final

1	A. Moorhouse (GBR)	1:02.04
2	K. Guttler (Hungary)	1:02.05
3	D. Volkov (USSR)	1:02.20
4	V. Davis (Canada)	1:02.38
5	T. Debnar (Hungary)	1:02.50
6	R. Schroeder (USA)	1:02.55
7	G. Minervini (Italy)	1:02.93
8	C. Poswiat (GDR)	1:03.43

Consolation Final

1	A. Matveev (USSR)	1:03.01
2	R. Dekker (Holland)	1:03.22
3	M. Marnecke (W Germany)	1:03.40
4	A. Mayer (W Germany)	1:03.85
5	H. Nagahata (Japan)	1:03.89
6	P. Suominen (Finland)	1:04.04
7	D. Watters (USA)	1:04.17
8	J. Chen (China)	1:04.72

Other British Competitors

17	J. Parrack (GBR)	1:04.23

200 Metres Breaststroke
Final

1	J. Szabo (Hungary)	2:13.52
2	N. Gillingham (GBR)	2:14.12
3	S. Lopez (Spain)	2:15.21
4	M. Barrowman (USA)	2:15.45
5	V. Lozik (USSR)	2:16.16
6	V. Alexeev (USSR)	2:16.70
7	J. Cleveland (Canada)	2:17.10
8	P. Szabo (Hungary)	2:17.12

Consolation Final

1	A. Yokochi (Puerto Rico)	2:18.01
2	S. Takahashi (Japan)	2:18.03
3	S. Appleboom (Belgium)	2:18.08
4	R. Beinhauer (Czechoslovakia)	2:18.13
5	E. Dagon (Switzerland)	2:18.17
6	C. Grant (Canada)	2:18.36
7	A. Marcek (Czechoslovakia)	2:18.51
8	C. Penicaud (France)	2:18.95

Neil Cochran   Swimming Times

Other British Competitors

15	A. Moorhouse (GBR)	2:18.51

100 Metres Butterfly
Final

1	A. Nesty (Surinam)	53.00
2	M. Biondi (USA)	53.01
3	A. Jameson (GBR)	53.30
4	J. Sieben (Australia)	53.33
5	M. Gross (W Germany)	53.44
6	J. Mortensen (USA)	54.07
7	T. Ponting (Canada)	54.09
8	V. Iaroschuk (USSR)	54.60

Consolation Final

1	J. Shen (China)	54.52
2	A. Mosse (New Zealand)	54.63
3	B. Nielsen (Denmark)	54.77
4	V. Cerny (Canada)	54.79
5	R. Szukala (Poland)	54.80
6	H. Miura (Japan)	54.98
7	J. Zheng (China)	55.05
8	N. Cochran (GBR)	55.22

200 Metres Butterfly
Final

1	M. Gross (W Germany)	1:56.94
2	B. Nielsen (Denmark)	1:58.24
3	A. Mosse (New Zealand	1:58.28
4	T. Ponting (Canada)	1:58.91
5	M. Stewart (USA)	1:59.19
6	D. Wilson (Australia)	1:59.20
7	J. Kelly (Canada)	1:59.48
8	A. Nesty (Surinam)	2:00.80

Consolation Final

1	M. Dean (USA)	2:00.26
2	T. Jones (GBR)	2:00.32
3	V. Iaroschuk (USSR)	2:00.34
4	N. Hodgson (GBR)	2:01.09
5	C. Bordeau (France)	2:01.46
6	F. Drost (Holland)	2:01.59
7	S. Takeda (Japan)	2:02.18
8	M. Roberts (Australia)	2:04.28

200 Metres Individual Medley
Final

1	T. Darnyi (Hungary)	2:00.17

2 P. Kuehl (GDR)	2:01.61
3 V. Iaroschuk (USSR)	2:02.40
4 M. Zoubkov (USSR)	2:02.92
5 P. Bermel (W Germany)	2:03.81
6 R. Bruce (Australia)	2:04.34
7 R. Hannemann (GDR)	2:04.82
8 G. Anderson (Canada)	2:06.35

Consolation Final

1 D. Wharton (USA)	2:03.05
2 J. Davey (GBR)	2:04.17
3 N. Cochran (GBR)	2:05.44
4 C. Bordeau (France)	2:05.51
5 L. Sacchi (Italy)	2:05.68
6 C. Papanikolaou (Greece)	2:06.61
7 J. Berndt (W Germany)	2:06.76
8 B. Stapleton (USA)	2:06.82

400 Metres Individual Medley
Final

1 T. Darnyi (Hungary)	4:14.75
2 D. Wharton (USA)	4:17.36
3 S. Battistelli (Italy)	4:18.01
4 J. Szabo (Hungary)	4:18.15
5 P. Kuehl (GDR)	4:18.44
6 J. Berndt (W Germany)	4:21.71
7 L. Sacchi (Italy)	4:23.23
8 P. Bermel (W Germany)	4:24.02

Consolation Final

1 J. Kostoff (USA)	4:22.95
2 C. Bordeau (France)	4:23.39
3 R. Bruce (Australia)	4:24.33
4 J. Kelly (Canada)	4:25.02
5 M. Zoubkov (USSR)	4:25.44
6 R. Woodhouse (Australia)	4:26.14
7 P. Brew (GBR)	4:26.77
8 C. Papanikolaou (Greece)	4:27.95

Other British Competitors

J. Davey (GBR)	DIS

4×100 Metres Freestyle Relay
Final

1 USA	3:16.53
2 USSR	3:18.33
3 GDR	3:19.82
4 France	3:20.02
5 Sweden	3:21.07
6 W Germany	3:21.65
7 GBR	3:21.71
8 Italy	3:22.93

4×200 Metres Freestyle Relay
Final

1 USA	7:12.51
2 GDR	7:13.68
3 W Germany	7:14.35
4 Australia	7:15.23
5 Italy	7:16.00
6 Sweden	7:19.10
7 France	7:24.69
8 Canada	7:24.91

British Team

9 GBR	7:29.77

4×100 Metres Medley Relay
Final

1 USA	3:36.93
2 Canada	3:39.28
3 USSR	3:39.96
4 W Germany	3:42.98
5 Japan	3:44.36

6 Australia	3:45.85
7 Holland	3:46.55
GBR	DIS

Women

50 Metres Freestyle
Final

1 K. Otto (GDR)	25.49
2 W. Yang (China)	25.64
3 K. Meissner (GDR)	25.71
J. Sterkel (USA)	
5 L. Fetter (USA)	25.78
6 T. Costache (Rumania)	25.80
7 C. Plewinski (France)	25.90
8 K. van Wirdum (Australia)	26.01

Consolation Final

1 M. Aizpors (W Germany)	26.17
2 C. Pielke (W Germany)	26.22
3 M. Armentero (Switzerland)	26.34
4 K. Tophan (Canada)	26.45
A. Nakano (Japan)	
6 I. Abranova (USSR)	26.48
7 K. Brienesse (Holland)	26.66
8 D. van der Plaats (Holland)	26.80

British Competitors

25 A. Sheppard (GBR)	27.14
27 A. Cripps (GBR)	27.17

100 Metres Freestyle
Final

1 K. Otto (GDR)	54.93
2 Y. Zhuang (China)	55.47
3 C. Plewinski (France)	55.49
4 M. Stellmach (GDR)	55.52
5 S. Poll (Costa Rica)	55.90
6 K. Brienesse (Holland)	56.15
7 D. Torres (USA)	56.25
8 C. van Bentum (Holland)	56.54

Consolation Final

1 N. Trefilova (USSR)	56.48
2 A. Nakano (Japan)	56.72
3 L. Dobrescu (Rumania)	56.79
4 M. Kremer (USA)	56.83
5 G. Jensen (Denmark)	57.02
6 K. van Wirdum (Australia)	57.04
7 S. Issakova (USSR)	57.07
8 T. Costache (Rumania)	57.11

British Competitors

25 A. Cripps (GBR)	57.81
28 J. Croft (GBR)	58.19

200 Metres Freestyle
Final

1 H. Friedrich (GDR)	1:57.65
2 S. Poll (Costa Rica)	1:58.67
3 M. Stellmach (GDR)	1:59.01
4 M. Wayte (USA)	1:59.04
5 N. Trefilova (USSR)	1:59.24
6 M. Kremer (USA)	2:00.23
7 S. Ortwig (W Germany)	2:00.73
8 C. Prunier (France)	2:02.88

Consolation Final

1 P. Noall (Canada)	2:00.77
2 R. Gilfillan (GBR)	2:01.66
3 M. Jacobsen (Denmark)	2:01.84
4 L. Dobrescu (Rumania)	2:01.98
5 M. Pura (Rumania)	2:02.30
6 C. Nakamori (Japan)	2:02.31

125

7 B. Schulz-Lohberg (W Germany)	2:02.32
8 Y. Zhuang (China)	2:14.23

Other British Competitors

21 J. Croft (GBR)	2:03.63

400 Metres Freestyle
Final

1 J. Evans (USA)	4:03.85
2 H. Friedrich (GDR)	4:05.94
3 A. Moehring (USA)	4:06.62
4 T. Bruce (USA)	4:08.16
5 J. Elford (Australia)	4:10.64
6 I. Arnould (Belgium)	4:11.73
7 S. Ortwig (W Germany)	4:13.05
8 N. Trefilova (USSR)	4:13.92

Consolation Final

1 S. Burge-Lopez (Australia)	4:10.21
2 N. Lung (Rumania)	4:11.68
3 M. Pura (Rumania)	4:12.14
4 A. Strumenlieva (Bulgaria)	4:13.43
5 P. Noall (Canada)	4:14.70
6 M. Melchiorri (Italy)	4:14.90
7 C. Nakamori (Japan)	4:15.59
8 C. Prunier (France)	4:21.03

British Competitors

18 R. Gilfillan (GBR)	4:16.66
27 J. Croft (GBR)	4:21.98

800 Metres Freestyle
Final

1 J. Evans (USA)	8:20.20
2 A. Strauss (GDR)	8:22.09
3 J. McDonald (Australia)	8:22.93
4 A. Moehring (GDR)	8:23.09
5 B. Tami (USA)	8:30.86
6 J. Elford (Australia)	8:30.94
7 I. Arnould (Belgium)	8:37.47
8 A. Strumenlieva (Bulgaria)	8:41.05

British Competitors

16 K. Mellor (GBR)	8:44.64
25 T. Atkin (GBR)	9:00.04

100 Metres Backstroke
Final

1 K. Otto (GDR)	1:00.89
2 K. Egerszegi (Hungary)	1:01.56
3 C. Sirch (GDR)	1:01.57
4 B. Mitchell (USA)	1:02.71
5 B. Barr (USA)	1:02.78
6 S. Poll (Costa Rica)	1:03.34
7 N. Livingstone (Australia)	1:04.15
8 M. Aizpors (W Germany)	1:04.19

Consolation Final

1 A. Patrascoiu (Rumania)	1:03.33
2 S. Schlicht (W Germany)	1:03.68
3 M. Carosi (Italy)	1:03.80
4 L. Melien (Canada)	1:03.87
5 L. Vigarani (Italy)	1:03.88
6 J. de Rover (Holland)	1:04.11
7 S. Musson (New Zealand)	1:04.17
8 K. Read (GBR)	1:04.27

Other British Competitors

18 S. Page (GBR)	1:04.75

200 Metres Backstroke
Final

1 K. Egerszegi (Hungary)	2:09.29
2 K. Zimmermann (GDR)	2:10.61
3 C. Sirch (GDR)	2:11.45
4 B. Barr (USA)	2:12.39

5 N. Livingstone (Australia)	2:13.43
6 A. Hayes (USA)	2:15.02
7 J. de Rover (Holland)	2:15.17
8 S. Schlicht (W Germany)	2:15.94

Consolation Final

1 A. Patrascoiu (Rumania)	2:15.75
2 S. Musson (New Zealand)	2:16.06
3 L. Lin (China)	2:16.68
4 K. Read (GBR)	2:18.20
5 L. Vigarani (Italy)	2:18.69
6 K. Lord (Australia)	
S. Morishita (Japan)	2:18.78
J. Larsson (Sweden)	DIS

Other British Competitors

22 H. Slatter (GBR)	2:21.66

100 Metres Breaststroke
Final

1 T. Dangalakova (Bulgaria)	1:07.95
2 A. Frenkeva (Bulgaria)	1:08.74
3 S. Hoerner (GDR)	1:08.83
4 A. Higson (Canada)	1:08.86
5 E. Volkova (USSR)	1:09.24
6 T. McFarlane (USA)	1:09.60
7 X. Huang (China)	1:10.53
8 A. Rex (GDR)	1:10.67

Consolation Final

1 S. Kouzmina (USSR)	1:10.42
2 K. Duggan (Canada)	1:10.58
3 I. Lempereur (Belgium)	1:10.86
4 M. Dalla-Valle (Italy)	1:10.95
5 S. Johnson (USA)	1:11.08
6 G. Csepe (Hungary)	1:11.24
7 L. Hooiveld (Australia)	1:11.26
8 S. Brownsdon (GBR)	1:11.95

Other British Competitors

20 M. Hohmann (GBR)	1:12.67

200 Metres Breaststroke
Final

1 S. Hoerner (GDR)	2:26.71
2 X. Huang (China)	2:27.49
3 A. Frenkeva (Bulgaria)	2:28.34
4 T. Dangalokova (Bulgaria)	2:28.43
5 I. Bogatcheva (USSR)	2:28.54
6 I. Lempereur (Belgium)	2:29.42
7 A. Higson (Canada)	2:29.60
8 M. Dalla-Valle (Italy)	2:29.86

Consolation Final

1 S. Boernike (GDR)	2:28.55
2 S. Kouzmina (USSR)	2:30.03
3 L. Moes (Holland)	2:30.83
4 A. Nisiro (Italy)	2:31.19
5 S. Rapp (USA)	2:32.90
6 T. McFarlane (USA)	2:33.46
7 G. Clouthier (Canada)	2:33.55
8 B. Becue (Belgium)	2:34.10

British Competitors

20 S. Brownsdon (GBR)	2:36.14
33 H. Frank (GBR)	2:41.12

100 Metres Butterfly
Final

1 K. Otto (GDR)	59.00
2 B. Weigang (GDR)	59.45
3 W. Qian (China)	59.52
4 C. Plewinski (France)	59.58
5 J. Jorgensen (USA)	1:00.48
6 C. van Bentum (Holland)	1:00.62

7 M. Meagher (USA)	1:00.97	
8 X. Wang (China)	1:01.15	

Consolation Final

1 S. Koptchikova (USSR)	1:01.48
2 K. Takahashi (Japan)	1:01.80
3 J. Delord (France)	1:02.45
4 N. Miteva (Bulgaria)	1:02.47
5 F. Alessandri (Australia)	1:02.51
6 T. Kitano (Japan)	1:02.53
7 G. Rehaa (W Germany)	1:02.63
8 I. Tocchini (Italy)	1:02.78

British Competitors

21 A. Cripps (GBR)	1:03.34

200 Metres Butterfly
Final

1 K. Nord (GDR)	2:09.51
2 B. Weigang (GDR)	2:09.91
3 M. Meagher (USA)	2:10.80
4 S. Pura (Rumania)	2:11.28
5 T. Radke (USA)	2:11.55
6 K. Takahashi (Japan)	2:11.62
7 X. Wang (China)	2:12.34
8 C. van Bentum (Holland)	2:13.17

Consolation Final

1 M. Cater (Canada)	2:12.66
2 I. Beyermann (W Germany)	2:13.74
3 G. Rehaa (W Germany)	2:14.20
4 S. Koptchikova (USSR)	2:14.43
5 N. Jacobsen (Denmark)	2:15.60
6 T. Kitano (Japan)	2:15.61
7 H. Bewley (GBR)	2:17.11
8 L. Wilson (GBR)	2:18.66

200 Metres Individual Medley
Final

1 D. Hunger (GDR)	2:12.59
2 E. Dendeberova (USSR)	2:13.31
3 N. Lung (Rumania)	2:14.85
4 J. Clatworthy (Australia)	2:16.31
5 M. A. Muis (Holland)	2:16.40
6 A. Patrascoiu (Rumania)	2:16.70
7 L. Lin (China)	2:17.42
8 W. Hedgepeth (USA)	2:17.99

Consolation Final

1 M. I. Muis (Holland)	2:17.73
2 B. Lohberg-Schulz (W Germany)	2:17.85
3 J. Hill (GBR)	2:19.20
4 A. Philipsson (Sweden)	2:19.35
5 R. Pelotti (Italy) A. Petricevic (Yugoslavia)	2:19.63
7 I. Bogatcheva (USSR)	2:19.91

8 Y. Mishioka (Japan)	2:20.43	

Other British Competitors

23 Z. Long (GBR)	2:22.64

400 Metres Individual Medley
Final

1 J. Evans (USA)	4:37.76
2 N. Lung (Rumania)	4:39.46
3 D. Hunger (GDR)	4:39.76
4 E. Dendeberova (USSR)	4:40.44
5 K. Nord (GDR)	4:41.64
6 J. Clatworthy (Australia)	4:45.86
7 L. Lin (China)	4:47.05
8 D. Procter (Australia)	4:47.51

Consolation Final

1 R. Felotti (Italy)	4:49.53
2 B. Lohberg-Schulz (W Germany)	4:50.54
3 E. Hansen (USA)	4:51.93
4 A. Strumenlieva (Bulgaria)	4:52.33
5 A. Philipsson (Sweden)	4:52.77
6 C. Magnier (France)	4:53.29
7 A. Poulsen (Denmark)	4:54.40
8 M. Yan (China)	4:55.92

British Competitors

18 S. Brownsdon (GBR)	4:54.66
24 T. Atkin (GBR)	5:01.34

4×100 Metres Freestyle Relay
Final

1 GDR	3:40.63
2 Holland	3:43.39
3 USA	3:44.25
4 China	3:44.69
5 USSR	3:44.99
6 Canada	3:46.75
7 W Germany	3:46.90
8 Denmark	3:49.25

British Team

10 GBR	3:50.84

4×100 Medley Relay
Final

1 GDR	4:03.74
2 USA	4:07.90
3 Canada	4:10.49
4 Australia	4:11.57
5 Holland	4:12.19
6 Bulgaria	4:12.36
7 W Germany	4:12.89
8 Italy	4:13.85

British Team

9 GBR	4:16.18

Europa Cup
Royal Commonwealth Pool, Edinburgh — 10/11 December, 1988

Men

100 Metres Freestyle
Final

1 V. Tkashenko (USSR)	49.55
2 S. Volery (Switzerland)	49.59
3 J. Bruha (W Germany)	49.95
4 J. Holmqvist (Sweden)	50.12
5 T. Golomeev (Bulgaria)	50.22
6 T. Flemming (GDR)	50.23

7 M. Fibbens (GBR)	50.31
8 J. Melberg (Norway)	50.56

Heat Times

1 S. Volery (Switzerland)	49.63
2 J. Bruha (W Germany)	49.64
3 T. Flemming (GDR)	50.15
4 V. Tkashenko (USSR)	50.25
5 J. Holmqvist (Sweden)	50.28
6 J. Melberg (Norway)	50.36
7 T. Golomeev (Bulgaria)	50.66

8	M. Fibbens (GBR)	50.67
9	R. Gleria (Italy)	50.97
10	J. Hernando (Spain)	51.22
11	H. Kroes (Holland)	51.86
12	J. Vermasheina (Finland)	52.43

200 Metres Freestyle
Final

1	A. Matzk (GDR)	1:47.48
2	J. Bruha (W Germany)	1:48.64
3	N. Evseev (USSR)	1:48.70
4	D. Serra (Spain)	1:49.27
5	C. Wallin (Sweden)	1:49.69
6	J. Melberg (Norway)	1:49.71
7	A. Bottini (Switzerland)	1:51.29
8	P. Howe (GBR)	1:51.90

Heat Times

1	J. Melberg (Norway)	1:50.14
2	D. Serra (Spain)	1:50.36
3	A. Matzk (GDR)	1:50.71
4	P. Howe (GBR)	1:51.05
5	N. Evseev (USSR)	1:51.17
6	J. Bruha (W Germany)	1:51.93
7	A. Bottini (Switzerland)	1:52.22
8	C. Wallin (Sweden)	1:52.58
9	R. Sloeserwij (Holland)	1:52.91
10	V. Koshanov (Bulgaria)	1:52.98
11	M. Trevisan (Italy)	1:53.11
12	D. Alfatzis (Greece)	1:56.79

400 Metres Freestyle
Final

1	K. Boyd (GBR)	3:45.18
2	A. Matzk (GDR)	3:47.54
3	R. Dauranov (USSR)	3:49.83
4	M. Goetze (W Germany)	3:50.80
5	M. Trevisan (Italy)	3:52.60
6	J. Vallejo (Spain)	3:52.87
7	V. Koshanov (Bulgaria)	3:55.88
8	A. Bottini (Switzerland)	3:56.98

Heat Times

1	R. Dauranov (USSR)	3:50.27
2	K. Boyd (GBR)	3:50.46
3	A. Matzk (GDR)	3:52.06
4	M. Goetze (W Germany)	3:53.46
5	V. Koshanov (USSR)	3:54.52
6	J. Vallejo (Spain)	3:54.83
7	M. Trevisan (Italy)	3:55.16
8	A. Bottini (Switzerland)	3:57.48
9	J. Melberg (Norway)	4:00.50
10	R. Sloeserwij (Holland)	4:05.11
11	R. Gudmundsson (Iceland)	4:08.71

1500 Metres Freestyle
Final

1	K. Boyd (GBR)	14:57.36
2	M. Goetze (W Germany)	15:10.71
3	R. Dauranov (USSR)	15:15.54
4	F. Calmasini (Italy)	15:18.15
5	C. Kuehlmoergen (GDR)	15:22.78
6	R. Bustelli (Switzerland)	16:00.85
7	M. van de Spoel (Holland)	16:00.88
8	R. Gudmundsson (Iceland)	16:21.01

100 Metres Backstroke
Final

1	S. Zabolotnov (USSR)	56.03
2	G. Mikhalev (Bulgaria)	56.29
3	T. Kaiser (GDR)	56.60
4	P. Ferland (Switzerland)	57.22

5	C. Beimel (W Germany)	57.30
6	M. Ranis (Czechoslovakia)	57.75
7	G. Binfield (GBR)	57.88
	C. Ventosa (Spain)	DIS

Heat Times

1	G. Mikhalev (Bulgaria)	56.79
2	S. Zabolotnov (USSR)	57.29
3	T. Kaiser (GDR)	57.65
4	P. Ferland (Switzerland)	57.75
5	C. Beimel (W Germany)	57.94
6	G. Binfield (GBR)	57.98
7	M. Ranis (Czechoslovakia)	58.12
8	C. Ventosa (Spain)	58.34
9	M. Kandris (Greece)	58.62
10	R. Riem (Italy)	58.70
11	R. Kristensen (Norway)	58.73
12	H. Kroes (Holland)	58.81

200 Metres Backstroke
Final

1	S. Zabolotnov (USSR)	1:59.76
2	T. Weber (GDR)	2:00.52
3	M. Ranis (Czechoslovakia)	2:00.96
4	S. Battistelli (Italy)	2:01.39
5	G. Mikhalev (Bulgaria)	2:01.53
6	S. Hackman (W Germany)	2:02.42
7	M. Lopez-Zubero (Spain)	2:02.51
8	G. Binfield (GBR)	2:05.52

Heat Times

1	M. Lopez-Zubero (Spain)	2:01.94
2	S. Battistelli (Italy)	2:02.93
3	M. Ranis (Czechoslovakia)	2:03.09
4	T. Weber (GDR)	2:03.13
5	S. Hackman (W Germany)	2:03.15
6	S. Zabolotnov (USSR)	2:03.28
7	G. Mikhalev (Bulgaria)	2:03.42
8	G. Binfield (GBR)	2:05.13
9	C. Papanikolaou (Greece)	2:05.15
10	G. Horsthuis (Holland)	2:07.01
11	P. Ferland (Switzerland)	2:07.70
12	R. Kristensen (Norway)	2:10.25

100 Metres Breaststroke
Final

1	D. Volkov (USSR)	1:00.36
2	B. Goebel (W Germany)	1:01.23
3	C. Poswiat (GDR)	1:01.53
4	N. Gillingham (GBR)	1:02.38
5	R. Dekker (Holland)	1:03.17
6	P. Eberle (Switzerland)	1:03.35
7	M. Saporiti (Italy)	1:04.45
8	I. Drambas (Greece)	1:04.76

Heat Times

1	D. Volkov (USSR)	1:00.90
2	B. Goebel (W Germany)	1:01.31
3	N. Gillingham (GBR)	1:03.17
4	R. Dekker (Holland)	1:03.26
5	P. Eberle (Switzerland)	1:03.40
6	C. Poswiat (GDR)	1:03.51
7	M. Saporiti (Italy)	1:04.06
8	I. Drambas (Greece)	1:04.37
9	R. Camallonga (Spain)	1:04.72
10	M. Lohi (Finland)	1:06.28

200 Metres Breaststroke
Final

1	V. Lozik (USSR)	2:12.55
2	N. Gillingham (GBR)	2:13.49
3	S. Lopez (Spain)	2:14.25

4 B. Goebel (W Germany)	2:16.85
5 P. Eberle (Switzerland)	2:17.96
6 R. Dekker (Holland)	2:18.07
7 F. Fusi (Italy)	2:19.66
8 I. Drambas (Greece)	2:20.58

Heat Times

1 V. Lozik (USSR)	2:16.96
2 N. Gillingham (GBR)	2:17.99
3 B. Goebel (W Germany)	2:18.29
4 S. Lopez (Spain)	2:18.41
5 R. Dekker (Holland)	2:19.11
6 P. Eberle (Switzerland)	2:19.25
7 F. Fusi (Italy)	2:20.34
8 I. Drambas (Greece)	2:20.51
9 R. Faerber (GDR)	2:20.54
10 M. Lohi (Finland)	2:28.10

100 Metres Butterfly
Final

1 V. Iaroschuk (USSR)	53.97
2 N. Rudolph (GDR)	55.31
3 J. Ballester (Spain)	55.35
4 R. Leishman (GBR)	55.55
5 C. Kjolholdt (Norway)	55.76
6 A. Ioannidis (Greece)	56.26
7 J. Nyholm (Sweden)	56.38
8 M. Braida (Italy)	56.98

Heat Times

1 V. Iaroschuk (USSR)	55.56
2 C. Kjolholdt (Norway)	55.93
3 J. Ballester (Spain)	56.00
4 N. Rudolph (GDR)	56.05
5 R. Leishman (GBR)	56.08
6 M. Braida (Italy)	56.15
7 A. Ioannidis (Greece)	56.29
8 J. Nyholm (Sweden)	56.49
9 K. van Dam (Holland)	56.50
10 F. Henter (W Germany)	56.59
11 R. Birrer (Switzerland)	56.63
12 J. Vermasheina (Finland)	58.01

200 Metres Butterfly
Final

1 K. Hoffmann (W Germany)	2:00.20
2 A. Savchenko (USSR)	2:00.41
3 J. Ballester (Spain)	2:00.91
4 C. Gessner (GDR)	2:01.57
5 T. Jones (GBR)	2:02.37
6 M. Braida (Italy)	2:02.56
7 D. Alfatzis (Greece)	2:02.86
8 C. Kjolholdt (Norway)	2:05.69

Heat Times

1 A. Savchenko (USSR)	2:00.69
2 K. Hoffmann (W Germany)	2:02.06
3 J. Ballester (Spain)	2:02.15
4 M. Braida (Italy) C. Gessner (GDR)	2:02.86
6 T. Jones (GBR)	2:02.98
7 D. Alfatzis (Greece)	2:03.84
8 C. Kjolholdt (Norway)	2:04.63
9 K. van Dam (Holland)	2:05.88
10 J. Nyholm (Sweden)	2:05.91
11 D. Jordi (Switzerland)	2:07.90

200 Metres Individual Medley
Final

1 J. Hladky (W Germany)	2:00.37
2 C. Gessner (GDR)	2:01.09
3 V. Iaroschuk (USSR)	2:01.35
4 L. Sacchi (Italy)	2:02.28

5 D. Rolley (GBR)	2:04.79
6 O. Barrufet (Spain)	2:06.62
7 M. Kandris (Greece)	2:07.27
8 P. Ferland (Switzerland)	2:12.55

Heat Times

1 J. Hladky (W Germany)	2:02.74
2 C. Gessner (GDR)	2:04.26
3 V. Iaroschuk (USSR)	2:04.30
4 D. Rolley (GBR)	2:04.57
5 L. Sacchi (Italy)	2:06.27
6 M. Kandris (Greece)	2:07.03
7 O. Barrufet (Spain)	2:08.82
8 P. Ferland (Switzerland)	2:09.20
9 O. Joustra (Holland)	2:09.27

400 Metres Individual Medley
Final

1 C. Gessner (GDR)	4:15.72
2 L. Sacchi (Italy)	4:18.85
3 C. Papanikolaou (Greece)	4:22.58
4 M. Zubkov (USSR)	4:24.27
5 P. Hermanspann (W Germany)	4:25.05
6 O. Barrufet (Spain)	4:29.18
7 A. Rolley (GBR)	4:32.03
8 A. Andermatt (Switzerland)	4:33.25

Heat Times

1 C. Gessner (GDR)	4:25.00
2 C. Papanikolaou (Greece)	4:26.53
3 L. Sacchi (Italy)	4:27.41
4 A. Rolley (GBR)	4:29.55
5 M. Zubkov (USSR)	4:29.82
6 P. Hermanspann (W Germany)	4:31.41
7 O. Barrufet (Spain)	4:33.58
8 A. Andermatt (Switzerland)	4:34.76
9 S. Steegeling (Holland)	4:34.89

4×100 Metres Freestyle Relay
Final

1 USSR	3:17.01
2 W Germany	3:17.16
3 GDR	3:18.70
4 Switzerland	3:21.46
5 GBR	3:21.52
6 Italy	3:21.63

Gary Binfield

7 Holland	3:28.13
Spain	DIS

4×100 Metres Medley Relay
Final

1	USSR	3:40.66
2	GDR	3:41.20
3	W Germany	3:42.59
4	Switzerland	3:46.33
5	GBR	3:46.36
6	Spain	3:49.04
7	Holland	3:49.49
	Italy	DIS

Heat Times

1	W Germany	3:44.15
2	USSR	3:46.15
3	GDR	3:46.55
4	GBR	3:47.19
5	Switzerland	3:48.59
6	Holland	3:49.81
7	Spain	3:49.93
8	Italy	3:50.31
9	Greece	3:52.80

Women

100 Metres Freestyle
Final

1	S. Schulze (GDR)	55.93
2	M. Mastebroek (Holland)	56.32
3	K. Zilliox (W Germany)	56.36
4	K. Pickering (GBR)	57.13
5	A. Garbayo (Spain)	57.36
6	E. Dendeberova (USSR)	57.67
7	P. Soerensen (Denmark)	57.81
8	L. Karlsson (Sweden)	57.87

Heat Times

1	S. Schulze (GDR)	56.11
2	K. Zilliox (W Germany)	56.79
3	M. Mastebroek (Holland)	56.97
4	K. Pickering (GBR)	57.40
5	E. Dendeberova (USSR)	57.87
6	P. Soerensen (Denmark)	57.91
7	L. Karlsson (Sweden)	58.10
8	N. Hristova (Bulgaria)	
	A. Garbayo (Spain)	58.23
10	L. Spinadin (Italy)	58.60
11	V. Jaskova (Czechoslovakia)	58.61
12	S. Spaeti (Switzerland)	58.97
13	M. Salmela (Finland)	59.01
14	M. Fuglem (Norway)	59.56

200 Metres Freestyle
Final

1	S. Ortwig (W Germany)	1:59.78
2	D. Hase (GDR)	2:00.44
3	I. Dalby (Norway)	2:01.44
4	J. Croft (GBR)	2:01.59
5	N. Trefilova (USSR)	2:01.65
6	M. Jacobsen (Denmark)	2:02.20
7	M. Masseurs (Holland)	2:05.23
8	A. Garbayo (Spain)	2:05.81

Heat Times

1	J. Croft (GBR)	2:01.25
2	S. Ortwig (W Germany)	2:02.37
3	I. Dalby (Norway)	2:02.77
4	D. Hase (GDR)	2:03.22
5	M. Jacobsen (Denmark)	2:04.37
6	N. Trefilova (USSR)	2:05.03
7	M. Masseurs (Holland)	2:05.52

8	A. Garbayo (Spain)	2:05.77
9	S. Rusinova (Czechoslovakia)	2:05.78
10	S. Spaeti (Switzerland)	2:06.27
11	A. Borisova (Bulgaria)	2:06.55
12	N. Pautasso (Italy)	2:06.67

400 Metres Freestyle
Final

1	G. Mueller (GDR)	4:09.55
2	I. Dalby (Norway)	4:10.51
3	S. Ortwig (W Germany)	4:10.83
4	J. Croft (GBR)	4:15.46
5	F. Cambrini (Italy)	4:16.01
6	M. Jacobsen (Denmark)	4:16.04
7	N. Trefilova (USSR)	4:18.06
8	N. Krueger (Switzerland)	4:27.71

Heat Times

1	I. Dalby (Norway)	4:13.56
2	G. Mueller (GDR)	4:16.36
3	S. Ortwig (W Germany)	4:16.80
4	F. Cambrini (Italy)	4:17.20
5	N. Trefilova (USSR)	4:17.60
6	M. Jacobsen (Denmark)	4:19.26
7	J. Croft (GBR)	4:19.27
8	N. Krueger (Switzerland)	4:21.54
9	S. Rusinova (Czechoslovakia)	4:21.98
10	A. Strumenlieva (Bulgaria)	4:23.64
11	T. Kourti (Greece)	4:28.26
12	M. Masseurs (Holland)	4:28.37

800 Metres Freestyle
Final

1	H. Grein (GDR)	8:26.59
2	M. Melchiorri (Italy)	8:43.16
3	N. Trefilova (USSR)	8:47.13
4	P. Hutchinson (GBR)	8:48.91
5	A. Strumenlieva (Bulgaria)	8:51.55
6	O. Splichalova (Czechoslovakia)	8:52.28
7	S. Nimtz (W Germany)	8:53.08
8	N. Krueger (Switzerland)	8:56.17
9	L. Madsen (Norway)	9:01.46
10	B. Puggard (Denmark)	9:07.46
11	T. Kourti (Greece)	9:07.57
12	J. Westheim (Holland)	9:19.52

100 Metres Backstroke
Final

1	A. Eichhorst (GDR)	1:02.90
2	F. Elzerman (Holland)	1:03.43
3	K. Read (GBR)	1:03.86
4	L. Vigarani (Italy)	1:03.90
5	K. Zilliox (W Germany)	1:04.06
6	N. Krupskaia (USSR)	1:04.96
7	E. Gysling (Switzerland)	1:05.04
8	J. Korbasova (Czechoslovakia)	1:06.62

Heat Times

1	A. Eichhorst (GDR)	1:03.43
2	F. Elzerman (Holland)	1:03.61
3	K. Read (GBR)	1:04.60
4	L. Vigarani (Italy)	1:04.91
5	K. Zilliox (W Germany)	1:05.09
6	N. Krupskaia (USSR)	1:05.57
7	E. Gysling (Switzerland)	1:06.08
8	J. Korbasova (Czechoslovakia)	1:06.17
9	M. Marchena (Spain)	1:06.25
10	K. Klepkou (Greece)	1:06.69
11	V. Svensson (Sweden)	1:06.70
12	S. Bellaire (Denmark)	1:07.25
13	N. Hristova (Bulgaria)	1:08.26

200 Metres Backstroke
Final

1	A. Eichhorst (GDR)	2:14.10
2	K. Read (GBR)	2:14.27
3	F. Elzerman (Holland)	2:15.01
4	N. Krupskaia (USSR)	2:16.35
5	L. Vigarani (Italy)	2:17.21
6	M. Marchena (Spain)	2:17.69
7	C. Thielemann (W Germany)	2:18.82
8	M. Jacobsen (Denmark)	2:19.57

Heat Times

1	F. Elzerman (Holland)	2:15.96
2	A. Eichhorst (GDR)	2:16.49
3	K. Read (GBR)	2:17.25
4	N. Krupskaia (USSR)	2:18.20
5	L. Vigarani (Italy)	2:18.41
6	M. Marchena (Spain)	2:18.63
7	C. Thielemann (W Germany)	2:19.29
8	M. Jacobsen (Denmark)	2:19.87
9	J. Korbasova (Czechoslovakia)	2:21.13
10	L. Madsen (Norway)	2:22.17
11	K. Klepkou (Greece)	2:23.97
12	E. Gysling (Switzerland)	2:26.01
13	V. Svensson (Sweden)	2:26.23

100 Metres Breaststroke
Final

1	T. Bogomilova (Bulgaria)	1:08.20
2	S. Brownsdon (GBR)	1:08.96
3	A. Rex (GDR)	1:09.21
4	E. Volkova (USSR)	1:09.86
5	M. Dalla-Valle (Italy)	1:09.87
6	A. Haenel (W Germany)	1:10.79
7	K. Bulten (Holland)	1:11.64
8	R. Runolfsdottir (Iceland)	1:11.81

Heat Times

1	S. Brownsdon (GBR)	1:09.96
2	E. Volkova (USSR)	1:10.03
3	M. Dalla-Valle (Italy)	1:10.11
4	A. Rex (GDR)	1:10.28
5	T. Bogomilova (Bulgaria)	1:10.37
6	K. Bulten (Holland)	1:11.64
7	R. Runolfsdottir (Iceland)	1:11.99
8	A. Haenel (W Germany)	1:12.04
9	M. Splichalova (Czechoslovakia)	1:13.11
10	M. Mantzius (Denmark)	1:13.90
11	A. Schweizer (Switzerland)	1:14.32
12	S. Parera (Spain)	1:15.01
13	Y. Poulopoulou (Greece)	1:16.47

200 Metres Breaststroke
Final

1	D. Brendel (GDR)	2:26.54
2	T. Bogacheva (USSR)	2:28.51
3	S. Brownsdon (GBR)	2:28.53
4	M. Dalla-Valle (Italy)	2:29.80
5	A. Frenkeva (Bulgaria)	2:32.12
6	A. Haenel (W Germany)	2:32.74
7	R. Runolfsdottir (Iceland)	2:32.99
8	L. Karlsson (Sweden)	2:34.88

Heat Times

1	D. Brendel (GDR)	2:29.19
2	S. Brownsdon (GBR)	2:31.79
3	A. Haenel (W Germany)	2:32.32
4	M. Dalla-Valle (Italy)	2:32.42
5	T. Bogacheva (USSR)	2:33.22
6	R. Runolfsdottir (Iceland)	2:33.25
7	L. Karlsson (Sweden)	2:33.41
8	A. Frenkeva (Bulgaria)	2:34.39

9	M. Splichalova (Czechoslovakia)	2:37.07
10	S. Parera (Spain)	2:37.22
11	M. van Breen (Holland)	2:40.70
12	A. Schweizer (Switzerland)	2:41.77
13	M. Mantzius (Denmark)	2:44.62
	Y. Poulopoulou (Greece)	DIS

100 Metres Butterfly
Final

1	N. Koekkoek (Holland)	1:01.75
2	K. Gressler (GDR)	1:02.08
3	S. Schuster (W Germany)	1:02.40
4	M. Scarborough (GBR)	1:02.57
5	M. Fernandez (Spain)	1:02.84
6	S. Kopshikova (USSR)	1:02.98
7	N. Miteva (Bulgaria)	1:03.10
8	M. Jacobsen (Denmark)	1:03.61

Heat Times

1	N. Koekkoek (Holland)	1:01.86
2	M. Scarborough (GBR)	1:02.53
3	S. Schuster (W Germany)	1:02.67
4	K. Gressler (GDR)	1:02.78
5	M. Jacobsen (Denmark)	1:03.20
6	M. Fernandez (Spain)	1:03.24
	N. Miteva (Bulgaria)	
8	S. Kopshikova (USSR)	1:03.42
9	C. Brook (Switzerland)	1:04.28
10	E. Viola (Italy)	1:04.44
11	M. Johannessen (Norway)	1:04.49
12	E. Nikolaidou (Greece)	1:04.78
13	M. Salmela (Finland)	1:05.48
14	E. Klatova (Czechoslovakia)	1:05.62

200 Metres Butterfly
Final

1	S. Schuster (W Germany)	2:13.68
2	M. Scarborough (GBR)	2:14.80
3	G. Heide (GDR)	2:15.05
4	B. Puggard (Denmark)	2:15.17
5	E. Roussaki (Greece)	2:15.64
6	N. Miteva (Bulgaria)	2:16.36
7	S. Kopshikova (USSR)	2:16.64
8	O. Splichalova (Czechoslovakia)	2:22.21

Heat Times

1	S. Schuster (W Germany)	2:17.13
2	H. Grein (GDR)	2:17.19
3	B. Puggard (Denmark)	2:17.26
4	M. Scarborough (GBR)	2:17.41
5	S. Kopshikova (USSR)	2:17.96
6	E. Roussaki (Greece)	2:18.12
7	N. Miteva (Bulgaria)	2:19.31
8	O. Splichalova (Czechoslovakia)	2:19.85
9	E. Fiano (Italy)	2:20.12
10	M. Cuervo (Spain)	2:20.59
11	M. Johannessen (Norway)	2:21.72
12	I. Bernardi (Switzerland)	2:23.72
13	N. Koekkoek (Holland)	2:25.03

200 Metres Individual Medley
Final

1	E. Dendeberova (USSR)	2:13.62
2	C. Meier (GDR)	2:16.31
3	R. Felotti (Italy)	2:16.52
4	S. Brownsdon (GBR)	2:17.45
5	T. Bogomilova (Bulgaria)	2:19.24
6	P. Hausmann (W Germany)	2:19.98
7	A. Poulsen (Denmark)	2:20.90
8	N. Koekkoek (Holland)	2:21.79

Heat Times

1	C. Meier (GDR)	2:19.35

2	S. Brownsdon (GBR)	2:19.63
3	R. Felotti (Italy)	2:19.72
4	E. Dendeberova (USSR)	2:20.36
5	P. Hausmann (W Germany)	2:21.00
6	T. Bogomilova (Bulgaria)	2:21.68
7	N. Kockkoek (Holland)	2:21.79
8	A. Poulsen (Denmark)	2:22.53
9	R. Runolfsdottir (Iceland)	2:22.86
10	K. Myras (Norway)	2:22.99
11	M. Safont (Spain)	2:24.19
12	K. Remaeus (Sweden)	2:24.28
13	M. Santalo (Finland)	2:24.88
14	F. Egli (Switzerland)	2:28.23
15	O. Splichalova (Czechoslovakia)	2:29.56

400 Metres Individual Medley
Final

1	G. Mueller (GDR)	4:41.53
2	E. Dendeberova (USSR)	4:43.98
3	R. Felotti (Italy)	4:50.06
4	P. Hausmann (W Germany)	4:51.89
5	B. Wiersma (Holland)	4:55.85
6	H. Walsh (GBR)	4:56.95
7	A. Poulsen (Denmark)	4:58.42
8	M. Safont (Spain)	4:59.74

Heat Times

1	E. Dendeberova (USSR)	4:49.86
2	G. Mueller (GDR)	4:54.00
3	B. Wiersma (Holland)	4:55.58
4	P. Hausmann (W Germany)	4:55.60
5	R. Felotti (Italy)	4:55.69
6	H. Walsh (GBR)	4:56.22
7	A. Poulsen (Denmark)	4:59.24
8	M. Safont (Spain)	5:00.38
9	K. Myras (Norway)	5:00.68
10	V. Svensson (Sweden)	5:01.16
11	M. Santalo (Finland)	5:02.82
12	A. Strumenlieva (Bulgaria)	5:04.57
13	I. Bernardi (Switzerland)	5:13.44
	S. Rusinova (Czechoslovakia)	DIS

4×100 Metres Freestyle Relay
Final

1	GDR	3:43.20
2	W Germany	3:44.58
3	Holland	3:48.99
4	USSR	3:50.31
5	GBR	3:50.78
6	Denmark	3:51.74
7	Norway	3:53.24
8	Bulgaria	3:54.94

Heat Times

1	W Germany	3:47.25
2	GDR	3:47.47
3	Holland	3:49.29
4	GBR	3:49.56
5	USSR	3:50.19
6	Denmark	3:53.31
7	Bulgaria	3:53.52
8	Norway	3:53.82
9	Italy	3:54.51
10	Switzerland	3:57.70
11	Czechoslovakia	4:03.23

4×100 Metres Medley Relay
Final

1	GBR	4:11.80
2	GDR	4:12.28
3	W Germany	4:14.09
4	USSR	4:14.56
5	Italy	4:15.80
6	Bulgaria	4:19.86
7	Czechoslovakia	4:21.49
8	Switzerland	4:22.08

Heat Times

1	GDR	4:14.87
2	GBR	4:17.26
3	USSR	4:17.45
4	Italy	4:17.47
5	W Germany	4:20.96
6	Switzerland	4:21.19
7	Bulgaria	4:22.13
8	Czechoslovakia	4:23.61
9	Denmark	4:24.43
10	Spain	4:26.69
11	Greece	4:33.50
	Holland	DIS
	Norway	DIS

Final Points Table (Top 4)
Men

1	USSR	238
2	GDR	208
3	W Germany	203
4	GBR	179

Women

1	GDR	256
2	GBR	220
3	W Germany	212
4	USSR	204

Three Nations Junior Meet – Holland

Maastricht, Holland — 11/12 March, 1989

Note: Junior men born in 1972/3 and junior women in 1974/5.

Junior Men

100 Metres Freestyle

1	E. Buchholz (GDR)	53.57
2	A. Heidrich (GDR)	53.76
3	A. Shortman (England)	53.77
4	W. van de Akker (Holland)	54.55
5	M. Hanby (England)	54.58
6	R. Blank (Holland)	55.27

200 Metres Freestyle

1	A. Heidrich (GDR)	1:57.16
2	W. Torsten (GDR)	1:57.72
3	P. Pederzolli (England)	1:57.84
4	R. Blank (Holland)	1:58.64
5	V. Elgersma (Holland)	2:00.90
6	M. Hanby (England)	2:00.92

400 Metres Freestyle

1	T. Wilhelm (GDR)	4:01.05
2	H. Drabo (GDR)	4:06.20
3	C. Robinson (England)	4:07.69
4	S. Mellor (England)	4:08.02
5	A. van der Meer (Holland)	4:09.19
6	V. Elgersma (Holland)	4:12.80

1500 Metres Freestyle

1	T. Wilhelm (GDR)	15:52.35
2	H. Drabo (GDR)	16:01.74
3	S. Mellor (England)	16:12.97
4	S. Clamp (England)	16:59.64
5	P. Jordan (Holland)	17:21.99
6	V. Elgersma (Holland)	17:22.05

100 Metres Backstroke

1	R. Braun (GDR)	1:00.16
2	A. Shortman (England)	1:00.42
3	I. Clayton (England)	1:00.91
4	M. Hogerbrug (Holland)	1:01.07
5	R. Blank (Holland)	1:02.91
6	E. Buchholz (GDR)	1:03.24

200 Metres Backstroke

1	I. Clayton (England)	2:07.85
2	R. Braun (GDR)	2:08.53
3	E. Buchholz (GDR)	2:12.34
4	M. Hogerbrug (Holland)	2:12.92
5	J. Kearney (England)	2:13.91
6	J. Sonneveld (Holland)	2:15.86

100 Metres Breaststroke

1	M. van Brummelen (Holland)	1:05.49
2	R. Maden (England)	1:07.01
3	C. Eger (GDR)	1:07.42
4	J. Fiechter (Holland)	1:09.52
5	H. Schmidt (GDR)	1:09.56
6	T. Ashwell (England)	1:10.22

200 Metres Breaststroke

1	G. Donkers (Holland)	2:27.36
2	R. Maden (England)	2:27.51
3	I. Swift (England)	2:30.17
4	C. Eger (GDR)	2:30.19
5	H. Schmidt (GDR)	2:31.58
6	M. Wouda (Holland)	2:34.92

Ian Clayton   Artwood Photography

100 Metres Butterfly

1	T. Hart (England)	58.79
2	B. Friedrich (GDR)	59.51
3	S. Sturm (GDR)	1:00.01
4	D. Parlevliet (Holland)	1:00.17
	A. Clarke (England)	
6	R. Boon (Holland)	1:00.71

200 Metres Butterfly

1	C. Robinson (England)	2:08.00
2	S. Sturm (GDR)	2:08.57
3	K. Crosby (England)	2:11.10
4	B. Friedrich (GDR)	2:11.50
5	R. Boon (Holland)	2:13.35
6	D. Parlevliet (Holland)	2:15.13

200 Metres Individual Medley

1	R. Domschke (GDR)	2:09.32
2	M. Weighton (England)	2:09.54
3	P. Pederzolli (England)	2:10.57
4	C. Dahle (GDR)	2:12.42
5	M. Wouda (Holland)	2:13.91
6	M. Hogerbrug (Holland)	2:14.73

400 Metres Individual Medley

1	R. Domschke (GDR)	4:39.81
2	C. Dahle (GDR)	4:40.98
3	B. Rees (England)	4:47.56
4	C. Robinson (England)	4:48.39
5	M. Wouda (Holland)	4:51.25
6	V. Elgersma (Holland)	5:13.00

4×100 Metres Freestyle Relay

1	GDR	3:35.98
2	England	3:36.14
3	Holland	3:37.85
4	England 2	3:42.63

4×200 Metres Freestyle Relay

1	GDR	7:49.40
2	England	7:51.47
3	Holland	7:55.90
4	England 2	8:13.02

4×100 Metres Medley Relay

1	England	3:59.37
2	GDR	3:59.77
3	Holland	3:59.89
4	England 2	4:02.34

Junior Women

100 Metres Freestyle

1	S. Hellmer (GDR)	57.92
2	M. Masseurs (Holland)	59.12
3	J. Rotermund (GDR)	59.64
4	B. Starink (Holland)	1:00.23
5	D. Salmon (England)	1:00.92
6	D. Morgan (England)	1:01.14

200 Metres Freestyle

1	S. Gutsche (GDR)	2:04.11
2	J. Rotermund (GDR)	2:06.37
3	M. Masseurs (Holland)	2:08.90
4	D. Salmon (England)	2:10.75
5	B. Starink (Holland)	2:12.30
6	E. Brooks (England)	2:12.67

400 Metres Freestyle

1	S. Gutsche (GDR)	4:19.50
2	J. Rotermund (GDR)	4:23.61
3	M. Masseurs (Holland)	4:25.00

4 G. Cook (England)	4:28.53
5 L. Sonn (England)	4:36.11
6 B. Starink (Holland)	4:36.56

800 Metres Freestyle

1 C. Kynast (GDR)	8:57.96
2 M. Bude (GDR)	8:58.03
3 G. Cook (England)	9:10.82
4 S. Foggo (England)	9:20.43
5 M. Smit (Holland)	9:37.92
6 L. van de Bosch (Holland)	9:46.54

100 Metres Backstroke

1 S. Henke (GDR)	1:04.53
2 S. Krause (GDR)	1:05.16
3 H. Mullins (England)	1:07.87
4 S. van de Hanenberg (Holland)	1:08.31
5 I. Westrik (Holland)	1:08.94
6 J. Corbett (England)	1:09.08

200 Metres Backstroke

1 M. Bude (GDR)	2:17.00
2 S. Krause (GDR)	2:18.76
3 H. Mullins (England)	2:25.25
4 I. Westrik (Holland)	2:27.16
5 L. Gahan (England)	2:28.81
6 S. van de Hanenberg (Holland)	2:33.37

100 Metres Breaststroke

1 J. Rodchau (GDR)	1:13.94
2 P. Neumerkel (GDR)	1:14.53
3 H. Alder (England)	1:16.33
4 K. Tellegen (Holland)	1:16.35
5 R. Swain (England)	1:16.71
6 H. Koopmans (Holland)	1:17.40

200 Metres Breaststroke

1 J. Rodchau (GDR)	2:37.38
2 K. Tellegen (Holland)	2:44.72
3 P. Neumerkel (GDR)	2:44.90
4 H. Alder (England)	2:45.88
5 H. Koopmans (Holland)	2:47.33
6 K. Seaborn (England)	2:50.63

100 Metres Butterfly

1 P. Conrad (GDR)	1:03.91
2 S. Herbst (GDR)	1:05.12
3 Z. Harrison (England)	1:05.86
4 J. Dowling (England)	1:05.92
5 L. van Duijnhoven (Holland)	1:07.54
6 M. Vos (Holland)	1:08.67

200 Metres Butterfly

1 P. Conrad (GDR)	2:18.75
2 S. Herbst (GDR)	2:18.90
3 J. Dowling (England)	2:25.53
4 E. Brooks (England)	2:33.42
5 C. Alberts (Holland)	2:35.14
6 M. Vos (Holland)	2:39.38

200 Metres Individual Medley

1 S. Herbst (GDR)	2:21.95
2 M. Bude (GDR)	2:22.47
3 L. Findlay (England)	2:23.60
4 K. Tellegen (Holland)	2:28.48
5 D. Morgan (England)	2:30.92
6 I. Westrik (Holland)	2:33.67

400 Metres Individual Medley

1 S. Herbst (GDR)	4:56.20
2 J. Rodchau (GDR)	4:56.88
3 L. Findlay (England)	5:06.72
4 J. Dowling (England)	5:15.80
5 M. Masseurs (Holland)	5:23.32
B. Starink (Holland)	DIS

4×100 Metres Freestyle Relay

1 GDR	3:57.56
2 Holland	4:02.32
3 England 2	4:02.84
4 England	4:04.00

4×200 Metres Freestyle Relay

1 GDR	8:36.38
2 Holland	8:49.31
3 England	8:52.03
4 England 2	8:59.91

4×100 Metres Medley Relay

1 GDR	4:20.89
2 GDR 2	4:27.90
3 England	4:31.73
4 Holland	4:31.97
5 England 2	4:36.30

Final Points Table

1 GDR	337.0
2 GBR	221.5
3 Holland	160.5

Eight Nations Junior Meet – Holland

Amersfoort, Holland — 25/26 March, 1989

Note: Junior men born in 1972/3 and junior women in 1974/5.

Junior Men

100 Metres Freestyle

1 F. Letzler (Sweden)	52.89
2 A. Shortman (England)	53.05
3 C. Thumser (W Germany)	53.11
4 J. Lukeman (Canada)	53.26
5 P. Helgesson (Sweden)	53.39
6 J. Langfeldt (W Germany)	53.43
7 M. Munoz (Spain)	53.52
8 D. Kondziolka (Canada)	53.54
9 E. Merisi (Italy)	53.81
10 P. Pederzolli (England)	54.03
11 D. del Campo (Spain)	54.17
12 A. Tessier (France)	54.47
13 J-P. Leclanche (France)	54.53
14 W. van der Akker (Holland)	54.60
15 V. Elgersma (Holland)	54.72
16 R. Lo Cocciolo (Italy)	54.89

200 Metres Freestyle

1 C. Keller (W Germany)	1:54.40

2	C. Thumser (W Germany)	1:56.13
3	E. Merisi (Italy)	1:56.20
4	P. Helgeson (Sweden)	1:56.78
5	J. Baeza (Spain)	1:56.96
6	G. Ciutto (Italy)	1:56.98
7	F. Letzler (Sweden)	1:57.08
8	C. Robinson (England)	1:57.15
9	P. Pederzolli (England)	1:57.31
10	R. Blank (Holland)	1:57.69
11	J. Lukeman (Canada)	1:57.98
12	D. Francis (Canada)	1:58.83
13	B. Gourves (France)	1:59.19
14	I. Garcia (Spain)	2:01.20
15	B. Rosique (France)	2:01.24
16	V. Elgersma (Holland)	2:03.02

400 Metres Freestyle

1	C. Robinson (England)	4:04.11
2	B. Gourves (France)	4:04.27
3	S. Mellor (England)	4:05.14
4	D. Chisholm (Canada)	4:05.22
5	S. Bahr (W Germany)	4:05.72
6	F. Fabron (France)	4:06.23
7	A. van der Meer (Holland)	4:06.88
8	J. Baeza (Spain)	4:06.95
9	M. Tolosa (Spain)	4:07.26
10	G. Ciutto (Italy)	4:07.35
11	R. Blank (Holland)	4:07.82
12	D. Francis (Canada)	4:09.16
13	P. Helgesson (Sweden)	4:10.33
14	B. Moller (Sweden)	4:10.65
15	T. Rexhausen (W Germany)	4:13.16
16	E. Bellardi (Italy)	4:17.23

1500 Metres Freestyle

1	B. Gourves (France)	15:56.94
2	B. Lomax (Canada)	15:59.26
3	L. Kalenka (W Germany)	15:59.95
4	S. Mellor (England)	16:05.60
5	S. Bahr (W Germany)	16:06.14
6	F. Fabron (France)	16:15.45
7	P. Stackhouse (England)	16:15.55
8	S. Roure (Spain)	16:21.14
9	B. Moller (Sweden)	16:24.76
10	D. Royo (Spain)	16:26.39
11	S. Baird (Canada)	16:26.62
12	A. van der Meer (Holland)	16:38.15
13	E. Bellardi (Italy)	16:44.57
14	J. Adolfsson (Sweden)	16:48.64
15	M. Salvagni (Italy)	16:59.42
16	P. Jordan (Holland)	17:04.93

100 Metres Backstroke

1	E. Merisi (Italy)	58.90
2	R. Daigneault (Canada)	59.71
3	D. Lonnberg (Sweden)	59.90
4	F. Wenck (W Germany)	1:00.39
5	E. Rebourg (France)	1:00.50
6	L. Kalenka (W Germany)	1:00.51
7	J. Perez (Spain)	1:00.54
8	A. Shortman (England)	1:00.79
9	M. Hogerbrug (Holland)	1:00.98
10	I. Clayton (England)	1:01.37
11	A. Lucia (Italy)	1:01.79
12	W. van der Akker (Holland)	1:01.90
13	M. Adams (Canada)	1:02.04
14	T. le Leuch (France)	1:02.09
15	D. Dolz (Spain)	1:02.55
16	K. Asp (Sweden)	1:03.50

200 Metres Backstroke

1	L. Kalenka (W Germany)	2:06.27
2	E. Merisi (Italy)	2:06.46
3	E. Rebourg (France)	2:08.55
4	J. Perez (Spain)	2:08.91
5	F. Wenck (W Germany)	2:09.15
6	I. Clayton (England)	2:09.36
7	M. Adams (Canada)	2:11.84
8	D. Lonnberg (Sweden)	2:12.18
9	R. Daigneault (Canada)	2:12.35
10	J. Aparicio (Spain)	2:12.82
11	M. Hogerbrug (Holland)	2:12.83
12	J. Kearney (England)	2:14.18
13	L. Spelers (France)	2:15.42
14	K. Asp (Sweden)	2:17.07
15	R. de Lucia (Italy)	2:17.71
16	J. Sonneveld (Holland)	2:18.09

100 Metres Breaststroke

1	F. Postiglione (Italy)	1:04.98
2	M. van Brummelen (Holland)	1:05.87
3	V. Latocha (France)	1:06.40
4	T. Gluck (W Germany)	1:07.13
5	A. Trussler (Canada)	1:07.48
6	R. Maden (England)	1:07.58
7	M. Lamothe (Canada)	1:08.37
8	I. Swift (England)	1:08.65
9	N. Milhau (France)	1:08.68
10	A. Hellgren (Sweden)	1:08.76
11	F. Pighetti (Italy)	1:09.11
12	F. Tebar (Spain)	1:09.31
13	F. Viciano (Spain)	1:09.43
14	J. Fiechter (Holland)	1:09.64
15	M. Alpfors (Sweden)	1:09.97
16	R. Sutschek (W Germany)	1:10.40

200 Metres Breaststroke

1	F. Postiglione (Italy)	2:20.32
2	A. Trussler (Canada)	2:22.00
3	G. Donkers (Holland)	2:25.35
4	M. Lamothe (Canada)	2:26.41
5	T. Gluck (W Germany)	2:27.24
6	M. van Brummelen (Holland)	2:27.51
7	V. Latocha (France)	2:27.61
8	O. Gelies (France)	2:27.74
9	R. Maden (England)	2:27.81
10	I. Swift (England)	2:28.24
11	F. Viciano (Spain)	2:29.45
12	F. Tebar (Spain)	2:29.68
13	B-O. Eriksson (Sweden)	2:30.43
14	A. Tonci (Italy)	2:31.61
15	N. Boman (Sweden)	2:33.54
16	R. Sutschek (W Germany)	2:34.99

100 Metres Butterfly

1	R. Font (Spain)	57.97
2	O. Corpel (France)	58.06
3	T. Johnsen (Canada)	58.29
4	J. Langfeldt (W Germany)	58.34
5	D. Block (Canada)	58.45
6	N. Pau (Italy)	58.92
7	O. Soderholm (Sweden)	59.12
8	J. Alvarez (Spain)	59.22
9	T. Sohlke (W Germany)	59.24
10	D. Parlevliet (Holland)	59.42
11	B. Rees (England)	59.53
12	M. Alpfors (Sweden)	59.59
13	L. Belfiore (Italy)	59.67
14	T. Hart (England)	59.69

15 V. Elgersma (Holland)	1:00.20
16 L. Bordeau (France)	1:01.00

200 Metres Butterfly

1 X. Aguilar (Spain)	2:05.61
2 C. Robinson (England)	2:05.92
3 C. Keller (W Germany)	2:06.13
4 O. Corpel (France)	2:06.54
5 D. Block (Canada)	2:06.68
6 R. Font (Spain)	2:08.05
7 R. McFarlane (Canada)	2:08.74
8 M. Ciafrei (Italy)	2:09.12
9 A. Forvass (Sweden)	2:09.78
10 K. Crosby (England)	2:10.08
11 O. Soderholm (Sweden)	2:11.34
12 T. Sohlke (W Germany)	2:11.46
13 L. Bordeau (France)	2:12.97
14 R. Boon (Holland)	2:15.16
15 D. Parlevliet (Holland)	2:15.24
16 G. Leone (Italy)	2:22.00

200 Metres Individual Medley

1 C. Keller (W Germany)	2:08.75
2 E. Merisi (Italy)	2:08.92
3 C. Myden (Canada)	2:09.35
4 M. Weighton (England)	2:10.38
5 J. Pratt (Canada)	2:10.51
6 D. Lonnberg (Sweden)	2:12.19
7 P. Pederzolli (England)	2:12.29
8 B-O. Eriksson (Sweden)	2:12.47
9 C. Tardito (France)	2:12.54
10 P. Maigret (France)	2:13.15
11 J. Perez (Spain)	2:13.74
12 I. Fulquet (Spain)	2:14.30
13 M. Hogerbrug (Holland)	2:15.10
14 M. Ciafrei (Italy)	2:15.23
15 J. Fiechter (Holland)	2:16.61
16 M. Gehring (W Germany)	2:19.25

400 Metres Individual Medley

1 S. Baird (Canada)	4:37.43
2 C. Keller (W Germany)	4:39.17
3 J. Perez (Spain)	4:41.66
4 C. Tardoti (France)	4:42.75
5 P. Maigret (France)	4:43.81
6 M. Ciafrei (Italy)	4:44.76
7 B. Moller (Sweden)	4:45.42
8 B. Rees (England)	4:45.53
9 P. Pederzolli (England)	4:45.89
10 M. Hiller (W Germany)	4:48.99
11 A. van der Meer (Holland)	4:49.38
12 M. Claudio (Italy)	4:52.01
13 V. Elgersma (Holland)	4:57.58
B-O. Eriksson (Sweden)	DIS
J. Pratt (Canada)	DIS
I. Fulquet (Spain)	DIS

4×100 Metres Freestyle Relay

1 W Germany	3:32.60
2 Canada	3:32.76
3 Sweden	3:33.06
4 England	3:34.79
5 Spain	3:36.24
6 France	3:37.06
7 Italy	3:37.39
8 Holland	3:37.46

4×200 Metres Freestyle Relay

1 W Germany	7:47.06
2 Canada	7:51.54

Magnus Weighton

3 England	7:51.92
4 Italy	7:51.96
5 France	7:53.67
6 Sweden	7:54.49
7 Holland	7:56.40
8 Spain	7:58.94

4×100 Metres Medley Relay

1 Italy	3:57.04
2 W Germany	3:58.17
3 France	3:58.25
4 Canada	3:59.03
5 Sweden	3:59.53
6 Holland	4:00.83
7 Spain	4:01.96
England	DIS

Junior Women

100 Metres Freestyle

1 P. Lessard (Canada)	57.62
2 M. Masseurs (Holland)	58.43
3 E. Cernigio (Italy)	58.59
4 I. Sciorelli (Italy)	59.01
5 B. Starink (Holland)	59.78
6 M. Sarrailh (France)	1:00.04
7 J. Lakusiak (Canada)	1:00.47
8 C. Clapies (France)	1:00.53
9 E. Brooks (England)	1:00.60
10 B. Grosse (W Germany)	1:00.66
11 M. Ulveklint (Sweden)	1:00.75
12 H. Mullins (England)	1:00.93
13 A. Soderstrom (Sweden)	1:00.99
14 R. Pascual (Spain)	1:01.06
15 T. PhanTan (W Germany)	1:01.15
16 N. Barberi (Spain)	1:02.82

200 Metres Freestyle

1 P. Lessard (Canada)	2:04.88
2 M. Masseurs (Holland)	2:06.77
3 U. Lunenschloss (W Germany)	2:08.14
4 E. Cernigoi (Italy)	2:08.46
5 D. Salmon (England)	2:08.81
6 C. Clapies (France)	2:08.89

7	M. Krauze (W Germany)	2:08.93
8	M. Data (Italy)	2:09.16
9	D. Morgan (England)	2:09.71
10	B. Starink (Holland)	2:09.98
11	J. Savege (Canada)	2:10.54
12	C. Ohlund (Sweden)	2:11.27
13	R. Pascual (Spain)	2:11.59
14	A. Soderstrom (Sweden)	2:12.18
15	E. Martin (France)	2:14.55
16	A. Vinals (Spain)	2:20.57

400 Metres Freestyle

1	M. Masseurs (Holland)	4:21.55
2	M. Krause (W Germany)	4:21.62
3	M. Data (Italy)	4:24.92
4	G. Cook (England)	4:24.96
5	G. Fiscon (Italy)	4:25.10
6	U. Lunenschloss (W Germany)	4:28.37
7	D. Salmon (England)	4:28.53
8	C. Clapies (France)	4:30.86
9	S. Shewchuk (Canada)	4:31.12
10	A-S. Jonsson (Sweden)	4:31.24
11	S. Merritt (Canada)	4:32.66
12	B. Starink (Holland)	4:33.73
13	C. Faudel (France)	4:33.75
14	A. Soderstrom (Sweden)	4:33.99
15	A. Vinals (Spain)	4:34.78
16	M. Gaztanaga (Spain)	4:36.76

800 Metres Freestyle

1	M. Krause (W Germany)	9:01.73
2	G. Fiscon (Italy)	9:03.99
3	M. Data (Italy)	9:06.41
4	G. Cook (England)	9:06.81
5	U. Lunenschloss (W Germany)	9:12.80
6	S. Foggo (England)	9:14.10
7	A-S. Jonsson (Sweden)	9:15.37
8	S. Merritt (Canada)	9:18.52
9	S. Shewchuk (Canada)	9:22.21
10	A. Lindbom (Sweden)	9:26.58
11	G. Fernandez (Spain)	9:27.05
12	C. Faudel (France)	9:28.30
13	A. Vinals (Spain)	9:33.22
14	L. van der Bosch (Holland)	9:33.99
15	M. Smit (Holland)	9:36.66
16	A. Bollonjeon (France)	9:38.15

100 Metres Backstroke

1	S. Volker (W Germany)	1:04.41
2	P. Lessard (Canada)	1:06.05
3	S. Revelant (Italy)	1:06.07
4	M. Lischinsky (Canada)	1:07.10
5	L. Bianconi (Italy)	1:07.35
6	V. Svensson (Sweden)	1:07.66
7	C. Heinrichs (W Germany)	1:07.77
8	H. Mullins (England)	1:08.09
9	I. Westrik (Holland)	1:08.52
10	J. Corbett (England)	1:08.59
11	T. Trueba (Spain)	1:08.82
12	M. Sarrailh (France)	1:09.00
13	W. Leemker (Holland)	1:09.52
14	H. Ricardo (France)	1:10.09
15	S. Carlos (Spain)	1:10.26
16	C. Johansson (Sweden)	1:10.67

200 Metres Backstroke

1	S. Volker (W Germany)	2:18.39
2	L. Bianconi (Italy)	2:22.83
3	M. von Moller (W Germany)	2:23.48
4	J. Malar (Canada)	2:24.89

Samantha Foggo Artwood Photography

5	M. Lischinsky (Canada)	2:24.93
6	I. Westrik (Holland)	2:24.97
7	H. Mullins (England)	2:25.24
8	T. Trueba (Spain)	2:26.40
9	H. Ricardo (France)	2:27.07
10	V. Svensson (Sweden)	2:27.26
11	M. Olive (Spain)	2:27.55
12	C. Cron (France)	2:28.31
13	D. Curradi (Italy)	2:28.94
14	L. Gahan (England)	2:29.71
15	C. Johansson (Sweden)	2:31.38
16	W. Leemker (Holland)	2:32.10

100 Metres Breaststroke

1	A. Hanel (W Germany)	1:11.93
2	C. Giordano (Italy)	1:14.33
3	H. Alder (England)	1:14.68
4	K. Tellegen (Holland)	1:14.82
5	M. Prat (Spain)	1:15.19
6	L. Karlsson (Sweden)	1:15.37
7	A. Guery (France)	1:16.18
8	J. Karlsson (Sweden)	1:16.24
9	R. Vacchetta (Italy)	1:16.27
10	A. Kube (W Germany)	1:16.47
11	E. Garcia (Spain)	1:16.50
12	R. Swain (England)	1:16.64
13	I. Groulx (Canada)	1:16.66
14	K. Kaye (Canada)	1:17.14
15	I. Jeannot (France)	1:17.56
16	H. Koopmans (Holland)	1:17.72

200 Metres Breaststroke

1	A. Hanel (W Germany)	2:34.71
2	C. Giordano (Italy)	2:38.38
3	K. Tellegen (Holland)	2:41.84
4	R. Vacchetta (Italy)	2:42.33
5	H. Alder (England)	2:43.14
6	L. Karlsson (Sweden)	2:43.57
7	M. Prat (Spain)	2:44.65
8	K. Kaye (Canada)	2:44.67
9	S. Jeannot (France)	2:45.53
10	L. Findlay (England)	2:45.75
11	J. Karlsson (Sweden)	2:46.49
12	I. Groulx (Canada)	2:47.66
13	H. Koopmans (Holland)	2:47.88

137

14	N. Eliorreta (France)	2:49.22
15	E. Tejero (Spain)	2:49.71
	S. Schober (W Germany)	DIS

100 Metres Butterfly

1	A. de Hoop (Holland)	1:04.40
2	J. Dowling (England)	1:05.02
3	Z. Harrison (England)	1:05.03
4	J. Pineau (Canada)	1:05.61
5	C. Ohlund (Sweden)	1:05.96
6	E. Natali (Italy)	1:06.09
7	E. Cernigoi (Italy)	1:06.26
8	E. Martin (France)	1:06.30
9	S. Volker (W Germany)	1:06.33
10	D. Siskovic (W Germany)	1:06.39
11	C. Harrison (Canada)	1:06.85
12	F. Feret (France)	1:07.04
13	K. Kjaerulff (Spain)	1:07.26
14	M. Mar Serra (Spain)	1:07.43
15	V. Svensson (Sweden)	1:08.20
16	L. van Duijnhoven (Holland)	1:08.44

200 Metres Butterfly

1	A. de Hoop (Holland)	2:18.55
2	M. Amadori (Italy)	2:19.93
3	K. Kimber (Canada)	2:20.69
4	M. Krause (W Germany)	2:22.01
5	E. Martin (France)	2:23.30
6	A. Zizzamia (Italy)	
	K. Kjaerulff (Spain)	2:23.59
8	C. Harrison (Canada)	2:23.70
9	C. Ohlund (Sweden)	2:24.96
10	V. Svensson (Sweden)	2:25.07
11	J. Dowling (England)	2:25.12
12	Z. Harrison (England)	2:27.77
13	K. Riand (France)	2:28.14
14	D. Siskovic (W Germany)	2:28.92
15	M. Mar Serra (Spain)	2:29.76
16	C. Alberts (Holland)	2:33.27

200 Metres Individual Medley

1	A. Hanel (W Germany)	2:22.42
2	J. Dowling (England)	2:23.16
3	J. Malar (Canada)	2:23.34
4	L. Bianconi (Italy)	2:23.92
5	U. Jardfeldt (Sweden)	2:24.17
6	C. Giordano (Italy)	2:24.25
7	L. Findlay (England)	2:24.91
8	T. PhanTan (W Germany)	2:26.73
9	A. Bollenjeon (France)	2:27.35
10	K. Tellegen (Holland)	2:28.03
11	T. Trueba (Spain)	2:28.73
12	V. Svensson (Sweden)	2:28.80
13	E. Perez (Spain)	2:28.89
14	L. Wilkinson (Canada)	2:29.15
15	N. Florrieta (France)	2:32.86
16	I. Westrik (Holland)	2:33.40

400 Metres Individual Medley

1	J. Malar (Canada)	5:01.62
2	L. Findlay (England)	5:04.72
3	A. Bollejeon (France)	5:05.60
4	U. Jardfeldt (Sweden)	5:06.11
5	C. Giordano (Italy)	5:06.17
6	A. Zizzamia (Italy)	5:06.56
7	L. Wilkinson (Canada)	5:07.45
8	J. Dowling (England)	5:08.06
9	T. Phan Tan (W Germany)	5:09.96
10	E. Perez (Spain)	5:10.32
11	M. Gaztanaga (Spain)	5:13.99

Laura Gahan Artwood Photography

12	A. Jonsson (Sweden)	5:14.48
13	N. Buhring (W Germany)	5:14.90
14	A. de Hoop (Holland)	5:16.17
15	N. Eliobreta (France)	5:17.44
16	L. van der Bosch (Holland)	5:17.92

4×100 Metres Freestyle Relay

1	Sweden	3:58.04
2	Canada	3:59.21
3	Holland	3:59.57
4	Italy	4:00.06
5	W Germany	4:00.13
6	England	4:00.15
7	France	4:02.38
8	Spain	4:09.84

4×200 Metres Freestyle Relay

1	Italy	8:36.79
2	Holland	8:38.74
3	England	8:39.27
4	W Germany	8:41.48
5	Canada	8:42.78
6	Sweden	8:50.32
7	Spain	8:53.46
8	France	8:57.98

4×100 Metres Medley Relay

1	W Germany	4:24.33
2	Italy	4:25.54
3	Canada	4:26.82
4	England	4:28.00
5	Holland	4:28.74
6	Spain	4:33.36
7	France	4:34.86
	Sweden	DIS

Final Points Table

1	W Germany	599
2	Canada	562
3	Italy	558
4	GBR	517
5	France	405
6	Sweden	388
7	Holland	354
8	Spain	339

Seven Nations Intermediate Meet – Sweden

Molndal, Sweden — 25/26 March, 1989
Note: Men born in 1970/1 and women in 1972/3

Men

50 Metres Freestyle
1	H. Karlsson (Sweden)	23.31
2	R. Gusperti (Italy)	23.66
3	A. Coll (Spain)	23.73
4	V. Drews (W Germany)	23.74
5	P. Lindstrom (Sweden)	23.93
6	A. Hickman (W Germany)	24.02
7	M. Tilro (Holland)	24.14
8	D. Parker (England)	24.20
9	I. Garcia (Spain)	24.22
10	S. Barbetti (France)	24.26
11	L. Journet (France)	24.32
12	M. van de Spoel (Holland)	24.67
13	S. Foggo (England)	24.90
14	A. Gallo (Italy)	24.92

100 Metres Freestyle
1	H. Karlsson (Sweden)	51.53
2	M. Herrmann (W Germany)	51.62
3	C. Ventosa (Spain)	52.03
4	A. Hickmann (W Germany)	52.51
5	A. Coll (Spain)	52.72
6	S. Baudoux (France)	52.87
7	E. Idini (Italy)	53.16
8	S. Barbetti (France)	53.17
9	R. Gusperti (Italy)	53.40
10	S. Foggo (England)	53.46
11	M. Tilro (Holland)	53.85
12	P. Lindstrom (Sweden)	54.29
13	D. Bouwens (Holland)	54.32
14	D. Parker (England)	55.16

200 Metres Freestyle
1	M. Herrmann (W Germany)	1:53.21
2	E. Idini (Italy)	1:53.32
3	M. Annad (France)	1:54.13
4	D. Gatland (England)	1:55.17
5	A. Hickmann (W Germany)	1:55.28
6	P. Miomandre (France)	1:55.75
7	D. Bertolani (Italy)	1:56.28
8	A. Coll (Spain)	1:56.81
9	H. Karlsson (Sweden)	1:56.91
10	M. Jimenez (Spain)	1:56.96
11	M. Hall (Sweden)	1:57.02
12	D. Bouwens (Holland)	1:58.10
13	L. Bennett (England)	1:58.33
14	M. van de Spoel (Holland)	1:58.58

400 Metres Freestyle
1	L. Journet (France)	3:59.21
2	E. Idini (Italy)	4:00.56
3	C. Marchand (France)	4:00.63
4	P. Mnich (W Germany)	4:01.47
5	S. Akers (England)	4:01.55
6	C. Bremer (W Germany)	4:02.55
7	B. Zorzan (Italy)	4:06.58
8	R. Vinasco (Sweden)	4:07.54
9	M. Jimenez (Spain)	4:07.65
10	X. Lastra (Spain)	4:08.98
11	M. Ronnevall (Sweden)	4:09.13
12	M. van de Spoel (Holland)	4:09.39
13	G. Woolgar (England)	4:12.92
14	J. Geutjes (Holland)	4:14.84

1500 Metres Freestyle
1	C. Marchand (France)	15:43.20
2	B. Sanson (France)	15:44.63
3	P. Mnich (W Germany)	15:49.99
4	C. Bremer (W Germany)	15:55.81
5	S. Akers (England)	15:55.98
6	M. Longo (Italy)	16:02.04
7	H. Rosmark (Sweden)	16:11.17
8	M. van de Spoel (Holland)	16:23.04
9	X. Lastra (Spain)	16:27.61
10	C. Cattaneo (Italy)	16:30.90
11	O. Stromberg (Sweden)	16:39.01
12	G. Woolger (England)	16:41.39
13	J. Geutjes (Holland)	16:48.73
14	R. Trani (Spain)	16:52.04

100 Metres Backstroke
1	S. Battistelli (Italy)	57.02
2	C. Ventosa (Spain)	58.26
3	M. Masanelli (France)	58.44
4	N. Dubreuil (France)	58.87
5	S. Hackmann (W Germany)	59.21
6	C. Jonsson (Sweden)	59.47
7	P. Parlklo (Sweden)	59.64
8	F. Ter Brugge (Holland)	59.82
9	P. Hermanspann (W Germany)	59.92
10	M. O'Connor (England)	1:00.41
11	F. Iannarelli (Italy)	1:00.44
12	N. Sherringham (England)	1:00.81
13	J. Dijkstra (Holland)	1:00.88
14	T. Sopp (Spain)	1:02.06

200 Metres Backstroke
1	S. Battistelli (Italy)	2:01.66
2	D. Holderbach (France)	2:03.75
3	B. Dumas (France)	2:06.03
4	C. Ventosa (Spain)	2:06.44
5	L. Bianchin (Italy)	2:06.83
6	S. Hackmann (W Germany)	2:07.55

Steven Foggo

7	P. Hermanspann (W Germany)	2:08.91
8	N. Hakansson (Sweden)	2:09.64
9	C. Jonsson (Sweden)	2:10.32
10	I. Stewart (England)	2:10.52
11	D. Zafra (Spain)	2:11.16
12	F. Ter Brugge (Holland)	2:11.64
13	M. O'Connor (England)	2:12.91
14	D. Nelson (Holland)	2:16.22

100 Metres Breaststroke

1	C. Bourdon (France)	1:05.42
2	J. Balle (W Germany)	1:05.68
3	F. de Cristofaro (Italy)	1:06.22
4	J. Hender (England)	1:06.52
5	J. Fernandez (Spain)	1:06.59
6	F. Civallero (Italy)	1:06.61
7	J. Rey (France)	1:06.71
8	E. de Vadder (W Germany)	1:07.33
9	C. van Dam (Holland)	1:07.45
10	P. Karlsson (Sweden)	1:07.54
11	M. van Rijn (Holland)	1:07.87
12	L. Tasias (Spain)	1:08.35
13	P. Strom (Sweden)	1:08.87
14	D. Mason (England)	1:08.90

200 Metres Breaststroke

1	J. Rey (France)	2:19.62
2	C. Bourdon (France)	2:20.47
3	J. Fernandez (Sweden)	2:22.48
4	F. de Cristofaro (Italy)	2:24.23
5	T. Brinkhaus (W Germany)	2:26.09
6	J. Hender (England)	2:26.47
7	F. Civallero (Italy)	2:26.64
8	S. Steegeling (Holland)	2:28.14
9	L. Tasias (Spain)	2:28.20
10	T. Andersson (Sweden)	2:28.37
11	J. Palle (W Germany)	2:28.92
12	P. Karlsson (Sweden)	2:29.90
13	M. van de Maagdenberg (Holland)	2:31.70
14	D. Mason (England)	2:32.35

100 Metres Butterfly

1	M. Herrmann (W Germany)	56.20
2	C. van Dam (Holland)	56.44
3	C. Sanmartino (Spain)	56.51
4	J. Nyholm (Sweden)	56.80
5	F. Scaramelli (Italy)	56.90
6	F. Eposito (France)	56.97
7	M. Rasmusson (Sweden)	57.22
8	D. Parker (England)	57.29
9	S. Baudoux (France)	57.75
10	G. Lapucci (Italy)	58.24
11	F. der Brugge (Holland)	58.39
12	E. Lopez (Spain)	58.40
13	T. Osterkamp (W Germany)	58.97
14	N. Bridge (England)	1:00.86

200 Metres Butterfly

1	M. Maltagliati (Italy)	2:04.47
2	M. Herrmann (W Germany)	2:05.10
3	F. Esposito (France)	2:05.20
4	P. Mnich (W Germany)	2:06.25
5	S. Andersson (Sweden)	2:06.79
6	A. Palloni (Italy)	2:07.25
7	S. Wainwright (England)	2:07.30
8	M. Rasmusson (Sweden)	2:08.05
9	C. Cuscusa (France)	2:08.45
10	D. Granados (Spain)	2:08.54
11	N. Parish (England)	2:08.88
12	C. van Dam (Holland)	2:10.64

13	C. Sanmartino (Spain)	2:10.98
14	R. Beelaerts (Holland)	2:24.29

200 Metres Individual Medley

1	S. Battistelli (Italy)	2:04.13
2	B. Sanson (France)	2:05.02
3	P. Hermanspann (W Germany)	2:08.97
4	B. Dumas (France)	2:09.89
5	J. Fernandez (Spain)	2:10.47
6	S. Hackmann (W Germany)	2:11.08
7	A. Coll (Spain)	2:11.73
8	D. Galeone (Italy)	2:11.74
9	S. Steegeling (Holland)	2:11.85
10	J. Prelner (Sweden)	2:11.98
11	H. Jonsson (Sweden)	2:12.93
12	I. Stewart (England)	2:14.32
13	L. Bennett (England)	2:14.40
14	J. Dijkstra (Holland)	2:16.19

400 Metres Individual Medley

1	B. Sanson (France)	4:29.95
2	L. Journet (France)	4:31.21
3	F. de Cristofaro (Italy)	4:37.86
4	A. Palloni (Italy)	4:39.40
5	P. Hermanspann (W Germany)	4:39.55
6	J. Fernandez (Spain)	4:39.89
7	M. Hooper (England)	4:40.89
8	C. Bremer (W Germany)	4:40.97
9	T. Arman (Sweden)	4:42.29
10	M. van de Spoel (Holland)	4:42.70
11	H. Jonsson (Sweden)	4:42.77
12	M. Claramunt (Spain)	4:44.02
13	S. Steegeling (Holland)	4:46.90
14	L. Bennett (England)	4:50.08

4×100 Metres Freestyle Relay

1	Sweden	3:28.83
2	W Germany	3:29.18
3	France	3:30.73
4	Spain	3:32.20
5	Holland	3:35.80
6	Italy	3:35.83
7	England	3:36.34

4×200 Metres Freestyle Relay

1	France	7:38.25
2	W Germany	7:41.65
3	Italy	7:41.95
4	Sweden	7:42.69
5	Spain	7:47.17
6	England	7:53.42
7	Holland	8:07.45

4×100 Metres Medley Relay

1	Italy	3:51.27
2	Spain	3:52.82
3	W Germany	3:53.80
4	France	3:54.37
5	Sweden	3:57.62
6	Holland	3:58.75
7	England	4:00.37

Women

50 Metres Freestyle

1	C. Woodcock (England)	26.19
2	I. de Bruijn (Holland)	26.76
3	L. Olofsson (Spain)	26.83
4	L. Trionfetti-Nisini (Italy)	27.04
5	C. Landin (Sweden)	27.06
6	N. Pautasso (Italy)	27.15

7	N. Robert (Holland)	27.17
8	N. Gil (Spain)	27.24
9	J. Lancaster (England)	27.25
10	E. Boronat (Spain)	27.27
11	K. Borys (France)	27.41
12	B. Emig (W Germany)	27.44
13	M. Giraudon (France)	27.58
14	H. Korner (W Germany)	28.00

100 Metres Freestyle

1	N. Robert (Holland)	58.83
2	L. Trionfetti-Nisini (Italy)	59.11
3	M. Giraudon (France)	59.13
4	C. Woodcock (England)	59.19
5	N. Pautasso (Italy)	59.23
6	N. Bates (England)	59.58
7	C. Landin (Sweden)	59.64
	E. Boronat (Spain)	
9	N. Gil (Spain)	1:00.12
10	L. Olofsson (Sweden)	1:00.14
11	B. Emig (W Germany)	1:00.32
12	H. Korner (W Germany)	1:00.46
13	K. Borys (France)	1:00.60
14	C. Martens (Holland)	1:00.84

200 Metres Freestyle

1	H. Lunenschloss (W Germany)	2:03.68
2	O. Patron (Italy)	2:04.93
3	L. Pettersson (Sweden)	2:06.44
4	M. Giraudon (France)	2:07.11
5	J. Lancaster (England)	2:07.12
6	N. Pautasso (Italy)	2:07.78
7	C. Jeanson (France)	2:08.23
8	B. Emig (W Germany)	2:08.31
9	M. George (England)	2:08.97
10	N. Robert (Holland)	2:09.35
11	C. Holm (Sweden)	2:11.31
12	E. Boronat (Spain)	2:11.32
13	J. Westheim (Holland)	2:12.18
14	N. Gil (Spain)	2:12.82

400 Metres Freestyle

1	O. Patron (Italy)	4:16.83
2	H. Lunenschloss (W Germany)	4:18.01
3	E. Arnold (England)	4:23.60
4	S. Garrel (France)	4:25.03
5	S. Nimtz (W Germany)	4:25.86
6	I. Bertrand (France)	4:26.27
7	M. George (England)	4:30.14
8	M. Pasquali (Italy)	4:30.77
9	M. Sastre (Spain)	4:31.40
10	N. Hansen (Sweden)	4:31.61
11	C. Holm (Sweden)	4:31.92
12	R. Mulder (Holland)	4:33.44
13	J. Westheim (Holland)	4:35.89
14	M. Vila (Spain)	4:41.80

800 Metres Freestyle

1	H. Lunenschloss (W Germany)	8:52.89
2	O. Patron (Italy)	8:53.90
3	E. Arnold (England)	8:55.60
4	P. Haussmann (W Germany)	9:12.10
5	S. Garrel (France)	9:12.35
6	M. Pasquali (Italy)	9:16.60
7	I. Bertrand (France)	9:19.09
8	M. George (England)	9:20.46
9	A. Blom (Sweden)	9:21.42
10	R. Mulder (Holland)	9:22.08
11	C. Holm (Sweden)	9:27.16
12	M. Sastre (Sweden)	9:27.93

13	J. Westheim (Holland)	9:29.61
14	C. Gil (Spain)	9:46.50

100 Metres Backstroke

1	C. Melwani (Spain)	1:05.30
2	J. Larsson (Sweden)	1:05.91
3	J. Wildeman (Holland)	1:05.94
4	A. Kempf (France)	1:06.12
5	F. Salvalaio (Italy)	1:06.43
6	B. de Wit (Holland)	1:06.93
7	R. Aehle (W Germany)	1:07.41
8	L. Racster (England)	1:07.76
9	I. Wirth (France)	1:07.78
10	T. Papandrea (Italy)	1:07.83
11	E. Firbank (England)	1:07.95
12	E. Anderweit (W Germany)	1:08.01
13	M. Hakansson (Sweden)	1:08.25
14	V. Torres (Spain)	1:08.96

200 Metres Backstroke

1	J. Larsson (Sweden)	2:18.17
2	F. Salvalaio (Italy)	2:21.81
3	J. Wildeman (Holland)	2:21.85
4	G. Ceccarelli (Italy)	2:21.99
5	I. Wirth (France)	2:22.06
6	M. Olsson (Sweden)	2:22.78
7	R. Aehle (W Germany)	2:23.17
8	E. Anderweit (W Germany)	2:23.96
9	A. Kempf (France)	2:24.06
10	C. Melwani (Spain)	2:25.33
11	E. Firbank (England)	2:25.69
12	B. de Wit (Holland)	2:26.07
13	J. Wright (England)	2:26.22
14	V. Torres (Spain)	2:27.68

100 Metres Breaststroke

1	M. Naeckel (W Germany)	1:12.50
2	K. Bulten (Holland)	1:13.13
3	N. Saint Cyr (France)	1:14.46
4	R. Gillatt (England)	1:15.46
5	E. Lesinigo (Italy)	1:15.51
6	H. Aude (France)	1:15.72
7	K. Remeus (Sweden)	1:15.75
8	S. Hjort (Sweden)	1:16.44
9	Y. Gandia (Spain)	1:16.60
10	M. Riecken (W Germany)	1:16.92

Nicole Bates

11	R. Gagliardo (Italy)	1:17.21
12	N. James (England)	1:17.54
13	M. Vazquez (Spain)	1:20.03
14	I. de Bruijn (Holland)	1:20.28

200 Metres Breaststroke

1	M. Naeckel (W Germany)	2:40.18
2	N. Saint Cyr (France)	2:40.90
3	E. Lesinigo (Italy)	2:42.82
4	K. Remaeus (Sweden)	2:43.30
5	Y. Gandia (Spain)	2:43.36
6	M. Riecken (W Germany)	2:44.46
7	J. Harrison (England)	2:45.99
8	S. Raedts (Holland)	2:46.57
9	K. Bulten (Holland)	2:47.01
10	R. Gagliardo (Italy)	2:47.12
11	H. Aude (France)	2:47.25
12	S. Hjort (Sweden)	2:48.54
13	J. Farnsworth (England)	2:49.85
14	M. Vazquez (Spain)	2:49.96

100 Metres Butterfly

1	A. Lindberg (Sweden)	1:02.25
2	C. Jeanson (France)	1:02.94
3	J. Lancaster (England)	1:03.73
4	E. Viola (Italy)	1:03.78
5	M. Persson (Sweden)	1:03.96
6	S. Schueren (W Germany)	1:04.65
7	P. Bartolini (Italy)	1:05.11
8	J. Timmermans (Holland)	1:05.28
9	G. Navarro (France)	1:05.49
10	C. Stephan (W Germany)	1:05.84
11	N. Bates (England)	1:06.05
12	R. Salguero (Spain)	1:06.41
13	R. Tomas (Spain)	1:06.89
14	I. de Bruijn (Holland)	1:07.39

200 Metres Butterfly

1	C. Jeanson (France)	2:16.04
2	S. Schueren (W Germany)	2:19.54
3	P. Bartolini (Italy)	2:20.81
4	M. Persson (Sweden)	2:20.82
5	H. Jepson (England)	2:21.41
6	H. Welford (England)	2:21.70
7	A. Angelot (France)	2:22.21
8	T. Papandrea (Italy)	2:23.48
9	C. Magnusson (Sweden)	2:24.08
10	D. Veenhuizen (Holland)	2:24.48
11	R. Salguero (Spain)	2:27.18
12	C. Stephan (W Germany)	2:27.34

Heather Osborne

13	E. Vega (Spain)	2:28.08
14	I. de Bruijn (Holland)	2:29.24

200 Metres Individual Medley

1	P. Haussmann (W Germany)	2:21.92
2	C. Mattsson (Sweden)	2:23.72
3	N. Saint Cyr (France)	2:23.87
4	A. Angelot (France)	2:24.75
5	D. Veenhuizen (Holland)	2:25.26
6	L. Trionfetti-Nisini (Italy)	2:25.89
7	P. Bartolini (Italy)	2:26.10
8	S. Hjort (Sweden)	2:27.01
9	M. Vela (Spain)	2:27.02
10	M. Riecken (W Germany)	2:27.94
11	G. van der Meer (Holland)	2:29.16
12	H. Osborne (England)	2:31.00
13	J. Drewitt (England)	2:31.04
14	E. Vega (Spain)	2:31.11

400 Metres Individual Medley

1	P. Haussmann (W Germany)	4:56.90
2	S. Garrel (France)	5:03.81
3	A. Angelot (France)	5:05.16
4	M. Persson (Sweden)	5:07.64
5	J. Harrison (England)	5:07.90
6	C. Mattsson (Sweden)	5:09.39
7	R. Mulder (Holland)	5:10.12
8	M. Vela (Spain)	5:10.31
9	M. Menegon (Italy)	5:11.06
10	D. Veenhuizen (Holland)	5:11.14
11	M. Riecken (W Germany)	5:12.45
12	M. Passarello (Italy)	5:14.27
13	J. Drewitt (England)	5:14.41
14	M. Vila (Spain)	5:21.24

4×100 Metres Freestyle Relay

1	Sweden	3:56.12
2	France	3:57.40
3	Italy	3:59.14
4	W Germany	3:59.16
5	England	4:00.57
6	Spain	4:00.69
	Holland	DIS

4×200 Metres Freestyle Relay

1	Italy	8:32.38
2	W Germany	8:32.66
3	Sweden	8:38.08
4	France	8:38.39
5	England	8:38.75
6	Holland	8:47.73
7	Spain	8:52.96

4×100 Metres Medley Relay

1	W Germany	4:22.94
2	Sweden	4:23.33
3	France	4:23.62
4	Holland	4:23.92
5	England	4:24.65
6	Spain	4:28.46
7	Italy	4:29.18

Final Points Table

1	France	587.0
2	Italy	553.0
3	W Germany	549.0
4	Sweden	463.5
5	GBR	339.0
6	Spain	325.5
7	Holland	285.0

Three Nations Spring Trophy – Sweden
Orebro, Sweden — 1/2 April, 1989

Men

50 Metres Freestyle
1 J. Holmqvist (Sweden)	22.90
2 R. Dekker (Holland)	23.34
3 P. Johansson (Sweden)	23.43
4 M. Fibbens (GBR)	23.47
5 M. Kroes (Holland)	23.86
6 N. Metcalfe (GBR)	24.12

100 Metres Freestyle
1 T. Werner (Sweden)	50.23
2 J. Holmqvist (Sweden)	50.89
3 M. Fibbens (GBR)	51.15
4 N. Metcalfe (GBR)	52.63
P. Dybiona (Holland)	
6 H. Kooes (Holland)	52.66

200 Metres Freestyle
1 A. Holmertz (Sweden)	1:51.35
2 M. Soderlund (Sweden)	1:52.83
3 J. Broughton (GBR)	1:53.83
4 F. Drost (Holland)	1:53.90
5 K. Boyd (GBR)	1:55.04
6 P. Dybiona (Holland)	1:55.63

400 Metres Freestyle
1 K. Boyd (GBR)	3:58.19
2 H. Jangwall (Sweden)	3:58.83
3 I. Wilson (GBR)	3:59.94
4 U. Eriksson (Sweden)	4:06.90
5 R. Blank (Holland)	4:09.44
6 M. van der Spoel (Holland)	4:09.90

1500 Metres Freestyle
1 K. Boyd (GBR)	15:47.09
2 H. Jangwall (Sweden)	15:49.29
3 I. Wilson (GBR)	15:50.59
4 H. Nilsson (Sweden)	16:03.44
5 M. van der Spoel (Holland)	16:17.98
6 A. de Kort (Holland)	16:40.91

100 Metres Backstroke
1 G. Robins (GBR)	59.28
2 H. Fredin (Sweden)	59.33
3 G. Skold (Sweden)	59.88
4 G. Horsthuis (Holland)	59.90
5 C. Cockcroft (GBR)	59.91
6 G. Keutgen (Holland)	1:00.07

200 Metres Backstroke
1 G. Robins (GBR)	2:05.83
2 K. Boyd (GBR)	2:09.16
3 H. Fredin (Sweden)	2:09.26
4 G. Horsthuis (Holland)	2:11.76
5 N. Hakansson (Sweden)	2:11.86
6 P. Horsthuis (Holland)	2:12.19

100 Metres Breaststroke
1 A. Moorhouse (GBR)	1:04.46
2 N. Gillingham (GBR)	1:04.47
3 R. Dekker (Holland)	1:04.48
4 P. Berggren (Sweden)	1:05.80
5 J. Stensson (Sweden)	1:05.84
6 A. Weerden (Holland)	1:06.47

200 Metres Breaststroke
1 N. Gillingham (GBR)	2:19.87

2 J. Bidrman (Sweden)	2:20.51
3 N. Hudghton (GBR)	2:22.90
4 P. Guldbrand (Sweden)	2:25.01
5 R. Dekker (Holland)	2:26.60
6 A. van Waerden (Holland)	2:27.06

100 Metres Butterfly
1 A. Rasmusson (Sweden)	56.09
2 C. van Dam (Holland)	56.24
3 M. Fibbens (GBR)	56.72
4 T. Jones (GBR)	56.87
5 C. Wallin (Sweden)	56.96
6 F. Drost (Holland)	57.14

200 Metres Butterfly
1 C. Wallin (Sweden)	2:02.75
2 T. Jones (GBR)	2:02.89
3 F. Drost (Holland)	2:07.30
4 S. Gullberg (Sweden)	2:07.42
5 C. van Dam (Holland)	2:08.24
6 R. Leishman (GBR)	2:09.84

200 Metres Individual Medley
1 J. Bidrman (Sweden)	2:04.14
2 A. Petersson (Sweden)	2:06.12
3 P. Brew (GBR)	2:06.41
4 G. Robins (GBR)	2:07.85
5 R. Dekker (Holland)	2:07.96
6 M. Hogerbrug (Holland)	2:14.26

400 Metres Individual Medley
1 J. Bidrman (Sweden)	4:29.18
2 P. Brew (GBR)	4:31.56
3 R. Wiiand (Sweden)	4:37.69
4 M. van der Spoel (Holland)	4:41.24
5 A. Rolley (GBR)	4:45.26
6 M. Hogerbrug (Holland)	4:48.31

4×100 Metres Freestyle Relay
1 Sweden	3:23.15
2 Holland	3:28.64
3 GBR	3:29.12

4×200 Metres Freestyle Relay
1 Sweden	7:27.92
2 GBR	7:39.50
3 Holland	7:51.76

4×100 Metres Medley Relay
1 Sweden	3:50.58
2 GBR	3:51.12
3 Holland	3:52.24

Women

50 Metres Freestyle
1 M. Mastebroek (Holland)	26.69
2 H. Aberg (Sweden)	26.87
3 M.A. Muis (Holland)	26.96
4 L. Olofsson (Sweden)	27.13
5 C. Woodcock (GBR)	27.20
6 A. Sheppard (GBR)	27.41

100 Metres Freestyle
1 D. van der Plaats (Holland)	56.96
2 M.A. Muis (Holland)	57.53
3 K. Pickering (GBR)	58.07

4 E. Nyberg (Sweden)		58.09
5 H. Kalvehed (Sweden)		58.38
6 R. Gilfillan (GBR)		59.29

200 Metres Freestyle

1 J. Croft (GBR)	2:04.66
2 M.A. Muis (Holland)	2:05.22
3 R. Gilfillan (GBR)	2:05.38
4 K. Brienesse (Holland)	2:05.50
5 M. Gustavsson (Sweden)	2:06.85
6 A. Hansen (Sweden)	2:07.14

400 Metres Freestyle

1 R. Gilfillan (GBR)	4:20.86
2 K. Mellor (GBR)	4:23.48
3 D. van der Plaats (Holland)	4:23.50
4 L. Ronnback (Sweden)	4:25.07
5 B. Wiersma (Holland)	4:25.73
6 M. Nilsson (Sweden)	4:32.27

800 Metres Freestyle

1 K. Mellor (GBR)	8:59.50
2 P. Hutchinson (GBR)	9:05.40
3 K. Silvester (Holland)	9:11.46
4 L. Ronnback (Sweden)	9:13.30
5 A. Rosengren (Sweden)	9:25.60
6 N. Rubert (Holland)	9:32.20

100 Metres Backstroke

1 E. Elzerman (Holland)	1:04.42
2 J. Deakins (GBR)	1:05.59
3 J. Larsson (Sweden)	1:06.07
4 A. Eriksson (Sweden)	1:06.35
5 J. Wildeman (Holland)	1:06.42
6 C. Huddart (GBR)	1:07.21

200 Metres Backstroke

1 J. Deakins (GBR)	2:18.05
2 E. Elzerman (Holland)	2:19.39
3 J. Larsson (Sweden)	2:21.29
4 J. Wildeman (Holland)	2:22.00
5 A. Eriksson (Sweden)	2:23.83
6 C. Huddart (GBR)	2:25.64

100 Metres Breaststroke

1 S. Brownsdon (GBR)	1:12.71
2 A. Persson (Sweden)	1:12.82
3 L. Karlsson (Sweden)	1:14.96
4 M.I. Muis (Holland)	1:15.06
5 D. Tubby (GBR)	1:16.53
6 L. Moes (Holland)	1:17.36

200 Metres Breaststroke

1 S. Brownsdon (GBR)	2:36.43
2 A. Persson (Sweden)	2:38.87
3 A. Rosengren (Sweden)	2:40.21

4 Y. Smit (Holland)	2:41.02
5 L. Moes (Holland)	2:41.31
6 D. Tubby (GBR)	2:41.40

100 Metres Butterfly

1 K. Brienesse (Holland)	1:01.78
2 J. Anema (Holland)	1:02.36
3 A. Lindberg (Sweden)	1:04.08
4 M. Persson (Sweden)	1:04.23
5 C. Foot (GBR)	1:04.39
6 G. Atkins (GBR)	1:05.15

200 Metres Butterfly

1 T. Atkin (GBR)	2:15.21
2 K. Brienesse (Holland)	2:16.62
3 C. van Bentum (Holland)	2:18.02
4 H. Bewley (GBR)	2:19.44
5 C. Johansson (Sweden)	2:22.55
6 A. Nilsson (Sweden)	2:23.70

200 Metres Individual Medley

1 M.I. Muis (Holland)	2:19.59
2 M.A. Muis (Holland)	2:19.81
3 H. Kalvehed (Sweden)	2:20.68
4 S. Brownsdon (GBR)	2:21.67
5 H. Slatter (GBR)	2:23.16
6 M. Gustavsson (Sweden)	2:23.19

400 Metres Individual Medley

1 T. Atkin (GBR)	4:54.31
2 S. Brownsdon (GBR)	4:56.42
3 M.A. Muis (Holland)	5:01.54
4 M.I. Muis (Holland)	5:02.27
5 A. Nilsson (Sweden)	5:09.40
6 U. Jardfelt (Sweden)	5:12.73

4×100 Metres Freestyle Relay

1 Holland	3:50.16
2 GBR	3:52.09
3 Sweden	3:52.69

4×200 Metres Freestyle Relay

1 Holland	8:20.20
2 GBR	8:25.19
3 Sweden	8:26.21

4×100 Metres Medley Relay

1 Holland	4:18.01
2 GBR	4:18.22
3 Sweden	4:21.30

Final Points Table

1 GBR	271.5
2 Sweden	261.0
3 Holland	231.5

Four Nations Fast Water Meet – Holland
Amersfoort, Holland — 22/23 April, 1989

Men

50 Metres Freestyle

1 R. Dekker (Holland)	23.84
2 Y. Bachkatov (USSR)	24.09
3 B. Hoffmeister (W Germany)	24.59
4 D. Hogerbrug (Holland)	24.69
5 G. Bulpitt (GBR)	24.74
6 M. Mueller (W Germany)	24.75

7 S. Dronsfield (GBR)	24.99
8 A. Kuznetsov (USSR)	25.04

100 Metres Freestyle

1 Y. Bachkatov (USSR)	52.04
2 R. Dekker (Holland)	52.97
3 G. Bulpitt (GBR)	53.11
4 S. Lasz (W Germany)	53.19
5 M. Mueller (W Germany)	53.59

6 A. Kuznetsov (USSR)	53.83
7 R. Sloeserwij (Holland)	53.89
8 S. Dronsfield (GBR)	53.90

50 Metres Backstroke

1 S. Zabolotnov (USSR)	27.10
2 F. Hoffmeister (W Germany)	27.62
3 M. Harris (GBR)	27.68
I. Polianski (USSR)	
5 G. Keutgen (Holland)	27.98
6 R. Sloeserwij (Holland)	28.64
7 H. Botz (W Germany)	29.03
8 M. O'Connor (GBR)	29.16

100 Metres Backstroke

1 S. Zabolotnov (USSR)	57.51
2 F. Hoffmeister (W Germany)	58.31
3 M. Harris (GBR)	58.61
4 I. Polianski (USSR)	1:00.03
5 R. Sloeserwij (Holland)	1:00.27
6 P. Hermanspann (W Germany)	1:00.34
7 M. O'Connor (GBR)	1:00.73
8 G. Keutgen (Holland)	1:01.04

50 Metres Breaststroke

1 R. Dekker (Holland)	29.18
2 G. Watson (GBR)	29.41
3 D. Volkov (USSR)	29.49
4 V. Lozik (USSR)	30.14
5 H. Wedekind (W Germany)	30.47
6 N. Hudghton (GBR)	30.80
7 S. Steegeling (Holland)	31.05
8 H. Botz (W Germany)	35.20

100 Metres Breaststroke

1 R. Dekker (Holland)	1:05.18
2 D. Volkov (USSR)	1:05.20
3 N. Hudghton (GBR)	1:06.37
4 H. Wedekind (W Germany)	1:06.39
5 G. Watson (GBR)	1:06.45
6 V. Lozik (USSR)	1:07.03
7 S. Steegeling (Holland)	1:08.39

50 Metres Butterfly

1 C. van Dam (Holland)	25.74
2 D. Volkov (USSR)	25.76
3 D. Parker (GBR)	25.77
4 V. Iaroschuk (USSR)	26.04
5 S. Dronsfield (GBR)	26.18
6 S. Lasz (W Germany)	26.19
7 D. Vandenhirtz (GDR)	26.28
8 D. Hogerbrug (Holland)	26.49

100 Metres Butterfly

1 V. Iaroschuk (USSR)	55.79
2 C. van Dam (Holland)	56.21
3 D. Vandenhirtz (W Germany)	58.39
4 D. Parker (GBR)	58.43
5 D. Hogerbrug (Holland)	58.61
6 S. Dronsfield (GBR)	58.87
7 S. Lasz (W Germany)	59.02

200 Metres Individual Medley

1 V. Iaroschuk (USSR)	2:07.60
2 S. Zabolotnov (USSR)	2:09.64
3 A. Rolley (GBR)	2:11.49
4 S. Steegeling (Holland)	2:11.73
5 R. Dekker (Holland)	2:12.72
6 G. Bulpitt (GBR)	2:13.59
7 F. Hoffmeister (W Germany)	2:14.10
8 H. Botz (W Germany)	2:15.71

4×50 Metres Freestyle Relay

1 Holland	1:36.80
2 USSR	1:37.27
3 GBR	1:37.57
4 W Germany	1:37.72

4×100 Metres Freestyle Relay

1 Holland	3:32.49
2 USSR	3:33.10
3 W Germany	3:33.15
4 GBR	3:34.37

4×50 Metres Medley Relay

1 USSR	1:45.54
2 W Germany	1:46.14
3 GBR	1:47.24
4 Holland	1:47.95

4×100 Metres Medley Relay

1 USSR	3:51.80
2 W Germany	3:54.88
3 Holland	3:55.48
4 GBR	3:55.51

Women

50 Metres Freestyle

1 D. van de Plaats (Holland)	26.46
2 M. A. Muis (Holland)	26.54
3 M. Aizpors (W Germany)	26.61
4 K. Zilliox (W Germany)	26.96
5 N. Trefilova (USSR)	27.03
6 C. Woodcock (GBR)	27.20
7 J. Gorst (GBR)	27.40
8 Y. Shamarova (USSR)	27.93

100 Metres Freestyle

1 M. A. Muis (Holland)	56.84
2 D. van de Plaats (Holland)	57.47
3 M. Aizpors (W Germany)	58.18
4 N. Trefilova (USSR)	58.20
5 Y. Shamarova (USSR)	59.07
6 K. Zilliox (W Germany)	59.14
7 C. Woodcock (GBR)	59.58
8 J. Gorst (GBR)	59.73

50 Metres Backstroke

1 E. Elzerman (Holland)	30.41
2 M. Zoller (W Germany)	31.19
3 J. Wildeman (Holland)	31.48
4 C. Huddart (GBR)	32.21
5 J. Deakin (GBR)	32.22
6 N. Trefilova (USSR)	32.53
7 C. Thielemann (W Germany)	33.13

100 Metres Backstroke

1 E. Elzerman (Holland)	1:04.19
2 M. Aizpors (W Germany)	1:04.43
3 M. Zoller (W Germany)	1:05.46
4 J. Deakins (GBR)	1:05.94
5 J. Wildeman (Holland)	1:06.17
6 C. Huddart (GBR)	1:08.42
7 N. Trefilova (USSR)	1:10.17

50 Metres Breaststroke

1 L. Coombs (GBR)	33.52
2 M. A. Muis (Holland)	34.45
3 A. Baker (GBR)	34.46
4 L. Moes (Holland)	34.82
5 S. Koptchikova (USSR)	34.99

145

6	M. Gelhar (W Germany)	35.01
7	B. Dahm (W Germany)	35.07

100 Metres Breaststroke

1	L. Coombs (GBR)	1:12.87
2	M. A. Muis (Holland)	1:14.25
3	L. Moes (Holland)	1:14.50
4	B. Dahm (W Germany)	1:14.57
5	A. Baker (GBR)	1:15.44
6	M. Gelhar (W Germany)	1:15.77
7	S. Koptchikova (USSR)	1:18.14

50 Metres Butterfly

1	K. Brienesse (Holland)	28.08
2	J. Anema (Holland)	28.68
3	N. Kennedy (GBR)	28.87
4	S. Koptchikova (USSR)	29.90
5	M. Pieroth (W Germany)	30.02
6	S. Purvis (GBR)	30.08
7	K. Eschmann (W Germany)	30.15
8	Y. Shamarova (USSR)	30.77

100 Metres Butterfly

1	K. Brienesse (Holland)	1:01.06
2	J. Anema (Holland)	1:03.62
3	S. Koptchikova (USSR)	1:03.74
4	N. Kennedy (GBR)	1:04.97
5	S. Purvis (GBR)	1:05.51
6	Y. Shamarova (USSR)	1:05.85
7	M. Pieroth (W Germany)	1:06.11
8	K. Eschmann (W Germany)	1:06.15

200 Metres Individual Medley

1	M. A. Muis (Holland)	2:18.25

2	M.I. Muis (Holland)	2:20.67
3	Y. Shamarova (USSR)	2:21.28
4	S. Koptchikova (USSR)	2:23.07
5	M. Zoller (W Germany)	2:24.06
6	C. Thielemann (W Germany)	2:25.62
7	S. Purvis (GBR)	2:25.86
8	A. Baker (GBR)	2:26.45

4×50 Metres Freestyle Relay

1	Holland	1:45.67
2	W Germany	1:49.19
3	GBR	1:49.34

4×100 Metres Freestyle Relay

1	Holland	3:49.90
2	W Germany	3:58.41
3	GBR	4:02.73

4×50 Metres Medley Relay

1	Holland	1:58.36
2	GBR	2:01.06
3	W Germany	2:02.46

4×100 Metres Medley Relay

1	Holland	4:17.88
2	W Germany	4:23.47
3	GBR	4:24.19

Final Points Table

1	USSR	3,456.64
2	W Germany	3,428.61
3	GBR	3,423.02
4	Holland	3,361.09

European Junior Championships
The International Pool, Leeds — 27/30 July, 1989

Junior Men
100 Metres Freestyle
Final

1	R. Mazhuolis (USSR)	50.41
2	I. Sey (USSR)	52.29
3	A. Shortman (GBR)	52.43
4	E. Bucholz (GDR)	52.60
5	R. Jensen (Denmark)	53.09
6	F. Letzler (Sweden)	53.20
7	C. Thumser (W Germany)	53.56
8	M. Hanby (GBR)	53.60

Consolation Final

1	C. Koprowicz (Poland)	53.61
2	M. Munoz (Spain)	53.82
3	F. Reimann (GDR)	53.83
4	M. Bralski (Poland)	54.03
5	J. Blomqvist (Finland)	54.36
6	J. Nygard (Norway)	54.60
7	R. Lo Cocciolo (Italy)	54.80
8	A. O'Connor (Ireland)	55.03

200 Metres Freestyle
Final

1	C. Keller (W Germany)	1:51.48
2	S. Wiese (GDR)	1:52.67
3	A. Romanov (USSR)	1:52.74
4	D. Lepikov (USSR)	1:53.05
5	A. Kasvio (Finland)	1:54.02

6	E. Merisi (Italy)	1:54.29
7	M. Hanby (GBR)	1:54.59
8	E. Buchholz (GDR)	1:55.06

Consolation Final

1	C. Thumser (W Germany)	1:54.79
2	V. Elgersma (Holland)	1:55.37
3	R. Jensen (Denmark)	1:55.96
4	M. Kanellopoulos (Greece)	1:56.73
5	J. Baeza (Spain)	1:56.76
6	G. Jurak (Yugoslavia)	1:57.39
7	C. Koprowicz (Poland)	1:57.42
8	T. le Leuch (France)	2:01.76

Other British Competitors

18	P. Pederzolli (GBR)	1:57.22

400 Metres Freestyle
Final

1	S. Wiese (GDR)	3:56.78
2	T. Wilhelm (GDR)	3:56.82
3	A. Kudriavtsev (USSR)	3:57.90
4	A. Kasvio (Finland)	3:59.47
5	S. Mellor (GBR)	3:59.72
6	G. Kovacs (Hungary)	4:03.34
7	G. Jurak (Yugoslavia)	4:03.90
8	M. Kanellopoulos (Greece)	4:05.67

Consolation Final

1	B. Gourves (France)	4:03.16
2	D. Alexandrov (USSR)	4:03.68

3 R. Rychlowski (Poland)	4:04.37
4 S. Bahr (W Germany)	4:06.47
5 Z. Kade (Hungary)	4:07.77
6 C. Thumser (W Germany)	4:09.00
7 A. van der Meer (Holland)	4:09.77
8 P. Rothbauer (Austria)	4:13.50

Other British Competitors

15 C. Robinson (GBR)	4:09.72

1500 Metres Freestyle
Final

1 S. Wiese (GDR)	15:29.13
2 T. Wilhelm (GDR)	15:37.28
3 A. Kudriavtsev (USSR)	15:38.61
4 R. Noble (GBR)	15:45.98
5 S. Mellor (GBR)	15:46.01
6 S. Bahr (W Germany)	16:03.02
7 F. Sawalla (W Germany)	16:08.57
8 B. Gourves (France)	16:11.27

100 Metres Backstroke
Final

1 R. Braun (GDR)	59.05
2 S. Grishaev (USSR)	59.36
3 D. Kharitonov (USSR)	59.41
4 E. Merisi (Italy)	59.73
5 S. Maene (Belgium)	59.80
6 L. Kalenka (W Germany)	59.88
7 I. Clayton (GBR)	59.94
8 M. Crisan (Rumania)	1:00.23

Consolation Final

1 R. Bizub (Czechoslovakia)	1:00.10
2 D. Lonnberg (Sweden)	1:00.38
3 P. Nagy (Hungary)	1:00.45
4 F. Wenck (W Germany)	1:00.61
5 E. Rebourg (France)	1:00.78
6 V. Kozobolis (Greece)	1:00.83
7 M. Sedrowski (Poland)	1:00.88
8 T. Jorgensen (Denmark)	1:01.13

200 Metres Backstroke
Final

1 R. Braun (GDR)	2:04.78
2 E. Merisi (Italy)	2:04.93
3 I. Clayton (GBR)	2:06.18
4 R. Bizub (Czechoslovakia)	2:06.93
5 D. Kharitonov (USSR)	2:07.17
6 L. Kalenka (W Germany)	2:07.56
7 F. Wenck (W Germany)	2:08.25
8 M. Sedrowski (Poland)	2:10.27

Consolation Final

1 S. Maene (Belgium)	2:08.91
2 J. Kearney (GBR)	2:09.00
3 A. O'Connor (Ireland)	2:09.01
4 H. Cleverdal (Sweden)	2:09.35
5 E. Rebourg (France)	2:09.43
6 J. Perez (Spain)	2:09.75
7 T. Jorgensen (Denmark)	2:12.04
8 M. Hogerbrug (Holland)	2:12.26

100 Metres Breaststroke
Final

1 F. Postiglione (Italy)	1:05.03
2 I. McKenzie (GBR)	1:05.47
3 N. Rozsa (Hungary)	1:05.61
4 A. Dzhaburia (USSR)	1:05.68
5 T. Gluck (W Germany)	1:05.87
6 V. Latocha (France)	1:06.19
7 R. Maden (GBR)	1:06.47
8 F. de Burchgraeve (Belgium)	1:07.13

Consolation Final

1 C. Eger (GDR)	1:07.29
2 F. Pighetti (Italy)	1:07.52
3 L. Bang (Denmark)	1:07.68
4 E. Pahoulakis (Greece)	1:07.69
5 J. Vracun (Yugoslavia)	1:07.83
6 C. Braunsteiner (Hungary)	1:07.84
7 F. Viciano (Spain)	1:08.03
8 A. Hellgren (Sweden)	1:08.55

200 Metres Breaststroke
Final

1 F. Postiglione (Italy)	2:21.97
2 R. Maden (GBR)	2:22.03
3 T. Gluck (W Germany)	2:23.05
4 S. Remy (France)	2:23.68
5 C. Braunsteiner (Hungary)	2:24.86
6 P. Kisielewski (Poland)	2:25.01
7 F. Viciano (Spain)	2:26.55
8 G. Donkers (Holland)	2:27.39

Consolation Final

1 A. Dzhaburia (USSR)	2:23.36
2 C. Thompson (GBR)	2:23.67
3 A. Kachel (Poland)	2:25.27
4 M. Wouda (Holland)	2:25.65
5 G. Almassy (Austria)	2:26.27
6 M. Arzoz (Spain)	2:27.22
7 F. de Burchbraeve (Belgium)	2:28.17
8 C. Eger (GDR)	2:31.47

100 Metres Butterfly
Final

1 D. Kudinov (USSR)	56.08
2 C. Keller (W Germany)	56.57
3 M. Milosevic (Yugoslavia)	56.63
4 M. Jones (GBR)	56.71
5 M. Gromov (USSR)	56.72
6 R. Font (Spain)	57.52
7 F. Nitu (Rumania)	57.78
8 S. Wandl (Austria)	58.02

Consolation Final

1 G. Leone (Italy)	57.74
2 M. Weighton (GBR)	58.08
3 J. Mikula (Czechoslovakia)	58.35
4 O. Corpel (France)	58.49

Craig Thompson   Artwood Photography

5 M. Pietraszewski (Poland)	58.58	
6 D. Larsson (Sweden)	58.67	
7 G. Giziotis (Greece)	59.03	
8 L. Belfiore (Italy)	1:00.25	

200 Metres Butterfly
Final

1 D. Kudinov (USSR)	2:03.19
2 J. Aguilar (Spain)	2:04.11
3 C. Keller (W Germany)	2:04.55
4 C. Robinson (GBR)	2:04.93
5 K. Crosby (GBR)	2:05.81
6 J. Mikula (Czechoslovakia)	2:06.41
7 O. Corpel (USSR)	2:07.15
8 M. Gromov (USSR)	2:07.79

Consolation Final

1 M. Milosevic (Yugoslavia)	2:05.39
2 M. Klechammer (Poland)	2:07.22
3 A. Piukovich (Hungary)	2:08.40
4 R. Font (Spain)	2:08.54
5 P. Slawek (Poland)	2:09.25
6 F. Sawalla (W Germany)	2:09.39
7 M. Ciafrei (Italy)	2:09.45
8 G. Leone (Italy)	2:11.27

200 Metres Individual Medley
Final

1 C. Keller (W Germany)	2:07.05
2 R. Domschke (GDR)	2:08.38
3 I. Fedoseev (USSR)	2:09.13
4 P. Kovacs (Hungary)	2:10.50
5 B. Eriksson (Sweden)	2:10.74
6 C. Dahle (GDR)	2:10.92
7 D. Kalchev (Belgium)	2:11.03
8 M. Wouda (Holland)	2:11.43

Consolation Final

1 M. Malinski (Poland)	2:09.82
2 P. Pederzolli (GBR)	2:10.37
3 S. Maene (Belgium)	2:11.63
4 J. Langfeldt (W Germany)	2:11.82
5 D. Byrne (Ireland)	2:13.09
6 P. Maigret (France)	2:14.70
7 S. Wandl (Austria)	2:14.79
8 I. Luczak (Poland)	2:15.81

Other British Competitors

18 M. Weighton (GBR)	2:13.74

400 Metres Individual Medley
Final

1 R. Domschke (GDR)	4:33.02
2 M. Malinski (Poland)	4:33.36
3 H. Cleverdal (Sweden)	4:33.47
4 P. Kovacs (Hungary)	4:35.68
5 I. Fedoseev (USSR)	4:36.26
6 D. Kalchev (Bulgaria)	4:36.90
7 M. Wouda (Holland)	4:37.95
8 B. Eriksson (Sweden)	4:41.91

Consolation Final

1 M. Ciafrei (Italy)	4:37.45
2 S. McKinlay (GBR)	4:40.28
3 C. Tardito (France)	4:40.59
4 D. Christensen (Denmark)	4:40.72
5 I. Fulquet (Spain)	4:41.12
6 J. Aguilar (Spain)	4:43.61
7 J. Langfeldt (W Germany)	4:48.05
8 R. Stapleton (GBR)	4:49.79

4×100 Metres Freestyle Relay
Final

1 USSR	3:25.42

2 GBR	3:29.12
3 W Germany	3:29.34
4 Sweden	3:30.12
5 GDR	3:31.87
6 Finland	3:34.96
7 Holland	3:36.87
8 Italy	3:38.25

4×200 Metres Freestyle Relay
Final

1 USSR	7:33.91
2 W Germany	7:38.26
3 GDR	7:39.82
4 GBR	7:42.05
5 Sweden	7:50.15
6 France	7:51.65
7 Holland	7:55.77
8 Poland	7:56.22

4×100 Metres Medley Relay
Final

1 USSR	3:50.21
2 W Germany	3:54.01
3 Italy	3:55.04
4 GBR	3:55.40
5 Hungary	3:55.74
6 Sweden	3:58.08
7 France	3:58.46
8 GDR	3:59.93

Junior Women

100 Metres Freestyle
Final

1 S. Henke (GDR)	57.65
2 S. Hellmer (GDR)	57.84
3 A. Hadding (W Germany)	58.46
4 I. Sciorelli (Italy)	58.67
5 M. Masseurs (Holland)	58.79
6 S. Volker (W Germany)	59.51
7 G. Balyi (Hungary)	59.67
8 B. Starink (Holland)	59.80

Consolation Final

1 D. Morgan (GBR)	59.51
2 L. Sarrailh (France)	59.55
3 K. Nygard (Norway)	59.75
4 M. Ulveklint (Sweden)	59.84
5 E. Cernigoi (Italy)	59.96
6 L. Karlsson (Sweden)	1:00.02
7 R. Lahtinen (Finland)	1:01.21
8 C. Clapies (France)	1:01.30

Other British Competitors

19 D. Jones (GBR)	1:01.30

200 Metres Freestyle
Final

1 S. Gutsche (GDR)	2:02.65
2 S. Hellmer (GDR)	2:02.98
3 B. Coada (Rumania)	2:04.55
4 H. Cerna (Czechoslovakia)	2:06.08
5 M. Masseurs (Holland)	2:06.27
6 C. Negrea (Rumania)	2:06.50
7 E. Berzlanovits (Hungary)	2:07.51
8 U. Lunenschloss (W Germany)	2:08.84

Consolation Final

1 G. Balyi (Hungary)	2:06.47
2 A. Zizzamia (Italy)	2:06.92
3 B. Starink (Holland)	2:07.18
4 D. Jones (GBR)	2:07.48

Gillian Cook Artwood Photography

5	O. Sozdateleva (USSR)	2:08.23
6	A. Smith (Denmark)	2:10.27
7	A. Lindbom (Sweden)	2:10.30
8	M. Data (Italy)	2:10.64

400 Metres Freestyle
Final

1	S. Gutsche (GDR)	4:15.52
2	C. Kynast (GDR)	4:17.74
3	O. Splichalova (Czechoslovakia)	4:18.13
4	Z. Buth (Hungary)	4:19.78
5	E. Berzlanovits (Hungary)	4:22.17
6	A. Zizzamia (Italy)	4:24.33
7	O. Sozdateleva (USSR)	4:25.15
8	M. Krause (W Germany)	4:25.75

Consolation Final

1	U. Lunenschloss (W Germany)	4:22.16
2	M. Masseurs (Holland)	4:26.73
3	A. Smith (Denmark)	4:28.35
4	A. Lindbom (Sweden)	4:28.87
5	C. Shiell (GBR)	4:30.45
6	R. Engen (Norway)	4:30.92
7	M. Hansen (Denmark)	4:31.17
8	G. Cook (GBR)	4:33.25

800 Metres Freestyle
Final

1	C. Kynast (GDR)	8:46.63
2	O. Splichalova (Czechoslovakia)	8:48.51
3	E. Berzlanovits (Hungary)	8:49.47
4	V. Funk (GDR)	8:50.93
5	G. Fiscon (Italy)	8:51.31
6	A. Zizzamia (Italy)	8:51.68
7	Z. Buth (Hungary)	8:57.93
8	O. Kuznetsova (USSR)	9:01.98

British Competitors

18	C. Shiell (GBR)	9:29.45

100 Metres Backstroke
Final

1	K. Egerszegi (Hungary)	1:02.24
2	T. Szabo (Hungary)	1:02.81
3	S. Henke (GDR)	1:03.18
4	S. Volker (W Germany)	1:03.46
5	S. Krause (GDR)	1:04.18
6	M. Kocheva (Bulgaria)	1:05.39
7	M. von Moller (W Germany)	1:05.60
8	W. Leemker (Holland)	1:07.23

Consolation Final

1	J. Korbasova (Czechoslovakia)	1:06.34
2	L. Bianconi (Italy)	1:06.57
3	S. Revelant (Italy)	1:07.62
4	I. Westrik (Holland)	1:08.01
5	H. Mullins (GBR)	1:08.07
6	T. Kolianova (USSR)	1:08.27
7	L. Sarrailh (France)	1:08.34
8	C. Negrea (Rumania)	1:08.80

Other British Competitors

16	D. Salmon (GBR)	2:26.67

200 Metres Backstroke
Final

1	K. Egerszegi (Hungary)	2:10.69
2	T. Szabo (Hungary)	2:14.99
3	S. Krause (GDR)	2:15.87
4	S. Volker (W Germany)	2:18.30
5	M. Bude (GDR)	2:19.33
6	J. Korbasova (Czechoslovakia)	2:21.39
7	M. Kocheva (Bulgaria)	2:23.26
8	M. von Moller (W Germany)	2:23.30

Consolation Final

1	L. Bianconi (Italy)	2:21.49
2	T. Kolianova (USSR)	2:22.87
3	I. Westrik (Holland)	2:23.19
4	A. Oberwaldner (Austria)	2:25.91
5	S. Revelant (Italy)	2:26.42
6	H. Mullins (GBR)	2:26.97
7	M. Trueba (Spain)	2:27.10
8	C. Negrea (Rumania)	2:31.87

Other British Competitors

16	D. Salmon (GBR)	2:26.67

100 Metres Breaststroke
Final

1	I. Landik (USSR)	1:10.88
2	J. Dorries (GDR)	1:11.38
3	A. Hanel (W Germany)	1:11.52
4	N. Goossens (Belgium)	1:11.99
5	L. Manhalova (Czechoslovakia)	1:12.37
6	M. Tarasova (USSR)	1:13.42
7	C. Giordano (Italy)	1:13.68
8	J. Rodehau (GDR)	1:14.51

Consolation Final

1	K. Tellegen (Holland)	1:14.08
2	K. Eleki (Hungary)	1:14.64
3	K. de Witte (Belgium)	1:14.71
4	D. Salzani (Italy)	1:14.81
5	L. Poulsen (Denmark)	1:14.93
6	A. Kube (W Germany)	1:15.09
7	H. Alder (GBR)	1:15.55
8	M. Prat (Spain)	1:16.46

200 Metres Breaststroke
Final

1	M. Tarasova (USSR)	2:32.69
2	N. Goossens (Belgium)	2:33.20
3	A. Hanel (W Germany)	2:34.19
4	I. Landik (USSR)	2:34.97
5	J. Dorries (GDR)	2:36.23
6	C. Giordano (Italy)	2:36.91
7	L. Poulsen (Denmark)	2:38.95
8	S. Schober (W Germany)	2:41.74

Consolation Final

1	K. Tellegen (Holland)	2:39.69
	L. Manhalova (Czechoslovakia)	
3	R. Vacchetta (Italy)	2:40.21
4	J. Rodehau (GDR)	2:41.97

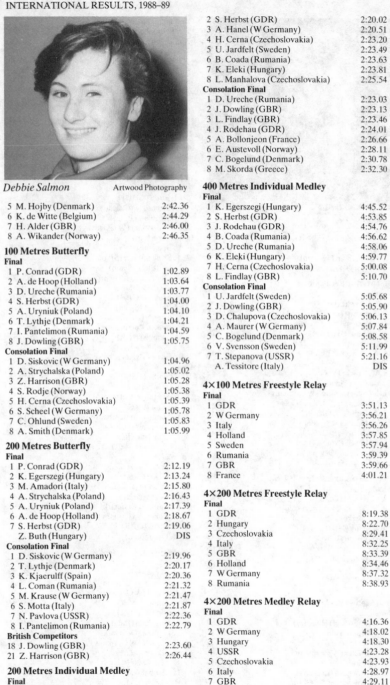

Debbie Salmon   Artwood Photography

5 M. Hojby (Denmark)	2:42.36
6 K. de Witte (Belgium)	2:44.29
7 H. Alder (GBR)	2:46.00
8 A. Wikander (Norway)	2:46.35

100 Metres Butterfly
Final

1 P. Conrad (GDR)	1:02.89
2 A. de Hoop (Holland)	1:03.64
3 D. Ureche (Rumania)	1:03.77
4 S. Herbst (GDR)	1:04.00
5 A. Uryniuk (Poland)	1:04.10
6 T. Lythje (Denmark)	1:04.21
7 I. Pantelimon (Rumania)	1:04.59
8 J. Dowling (GBR)	1:05.75

Consolation Final

1 D. Siskovic (W Germany)	1:04.96
2 A. Strychalska (Poland)	1:05.02
3 Z. Harrison (GBR)	1:05.28
4 S. Rodje (Norway)	1:05.38
5 H. Cerna (Czechoslovakia)	1:05.39
6 S. Scheel (W Germany)	1:05.78
7 C. Ohlund (Sweden)	1:05.83
8 A. Smith (Denmark)	1:05.99

200 Metres Butterfly
Final

1 P. Conrad (GDR)	2:12.19
2 K. Egerszegi (Hungary)	2:13.24
3 M. Amadori (Italy)	2:15.80
4 A. Strychalska (Poland)	2:16.43
5 A. Uryniuk (Poland)	2:17.39
6 A. de Hoop (Holland)	2:18.67
7 S. Herbst (GDR)	2:19.06
Z. Buth (Hungary)	DIS

Consolation Final

1 D. Siskovic (W Germany)	2:19.96
2 T. Lythje (Denmark)	2:20.17
3 K. Kjaerulff (Spain)	2:20.36
4 L. Coman (Rumania)	2:21.32
5 M. Krause (W Germany)	2:21.47
6 S. Motta (Italy)	2:21.87
7 N. Pavlova (USSR)	2:22.36
8 I. Pantelimon (Rumania)	2:22.79

British Competitors

18 J. Dowling (GBR)	2:23.60
21 Z. Harrison (GBR)	2:26.44

200 Metres Individual Medley
Final

1 K. Egerszegi (Hungary)	2:16.03

2 S. Herbst (GDR)	2:20.02
3 A. Hanel (W Germany)	2:20.51
4 H. Cerna (Czechoslovakia)	2:23.20
5 U. Jardfelt (Sweden)	2:23.49
6 B. Coada (Rumania)	2:23.63
7 K. Eleki (Hungary)	2:23.81
8 L. Manhalova (Czechoslovakia)	2:25.54

Consolation Final

1 D. Ureche (Rumania)	2:23.03
2 J. Dowling (GBR)	2:23.13
3 L. Findlay (GBR)	2:23.46
4 J. Rodehau (GDR)	2:24.01
5 A. Bollonjeon (France)	2:26.66
6 E. Austevoll (Norway)	2:28.11
7 C. Bogelund (Denmark)	2:30.78
8 M. Skorda (Greece)	2:32.30

400 Metres Individual Medley
Final

1 K. Egerszegi (Hungary)	4:45.52
2 S. Herbst (GDR)	4:53.85
3 J. Rodehau (GDR)	4:54.76
4 B. Coada (Rumania)	4:56.62
5 D. Ureche (Rumania)	4:58.06
6 K. Eleki (Hungary)	4:59.77
7 H. Cerna (Czechoslovakia)	5:00.08
8 L. Findlay (GBR)	5:10.70

Consolation Final

1 U. Jardfelt (Sweden)	5:05.68
2 J. Dowling (GBR)	5:05.90
3 D. Chalupova (Czechoslovakia)	5:06.13
4 A. Maurer (W Germany)	5:07.84
5 C. Bogelund (Denmark)	5:08.58
6 V. Svensson (Sweden)	5:11.99
7 T. Stepanova (USSR)	5:21.16
A. Tessitore (Italy)	DIS

4×100 Metres Freestyle Relay
Final

1 GDR	3:51.13
2 W Germany	3:56.21
3 Italy	3:56.26
4 Holland	3:57.85
5 Sweden	3:57.94
6 Rumania	3:59.39
7 GBR	3:59.66
8 France	4:01.21

4×200 Metres Freestyle Relay
Final

1 GDR	8:19.38
2 Hungary	8:22.70
3 Czechoslovakia	8:29.41
4 Italy	8:32.25
5 GBR	8:33.39
6 Holland	8:34.46
7 W Germany	8:37.32
8 Rumania	8:38.93

4×200 Metres Medley Relay
Final

1 GDR	4:16.36
2 W Germany	4:18.02
3 Hungary	4:18.30
4 USSR	4:23.28
5 Czechoslovakia	4:23.93
6 Italy	4:28.97
7 GBR	4:29.11
8 Bulgaria	4:30.53

European Championships
Bonn, W Germany — 12/20 August, 1989

Men

50 Metres Freestyle
Final
1	V. Tkashenko (USSR)	22.64
2	E. Kotriaga (USSR)	22.67
3	N. Rudolph (GDR)	22.76
4	D. Halsall (Switzerland)	22.89
5	R. Dekker (Holland)	23.06
6	S. Volery (Switzerland)	23.13
7	C. Kalfayan (France)	23.22
8	B. Hoffmeister (W Germany)	23.36

Consolation Final
1	G. Titus (Sweden)	23.26
2	F. Mortensen (Denmark)	23.41
3	E. Ran (Holland)	23.46
4	M. Fibbens (GBR)	23.47
5	B. Zikarsky (W Germany)	23.54
6	J. Holmqvist (Sweden)	23.56
7	P. Rohde (Denmark)	23.59
8	P. Kladiva (Czechoslovakia)	23.64

Other British Competitors
21	S. Dronsfield (GBR)	23.71

100 Metres Freestyle
Final
1	G. Lamberti (Italy)	49.24
2	I. Bachkatov (USSR)	50.13
3	R. Mazhoulis (USSR)	50.15
4	S. Caron (France)	50.16
5	T. Werner (Sweden)	50.44
6	R. Gleria (Italy)	50.46
7	P. Sitt (W Germany)	50.61
8	F. Mortensen (Denmark)	51.32

Consolation Final
1	E. Ran (Holland)	50.91
2	M. Fibbens (GBR)	50.95
3	J. Melberg (Norway)	50.97
	A. Schadt (W Germany)	
5	S. Volery (Switzerland)	51.06
6	C. Kalfayan (France)	51.18
	D. Richter (GDR)	
8	P. Kladiva (Czechoslovakia)	52.09

Other British Competitors
20	S. Dronsfield (GBR)	51.66

200 Metres Freestyle
Final
1	G. Lamberti (Italy)	1:46.69
2	A. Wojdat (Poland)	1:47.96
3	A. Holmertz (Sweden)	1:48.06
4	R. Gleria (Italy)	1:48.37
5	P. Sitt (W Germany)	1:49.06
6	S. Zesner (GDR)	1:49.31
7	U. Dassler (GDR)	1:49.62
8	V. Taianovich (USSR)	1:50.27

Consolation Final
1	M. Herrmann (W Germany)	1:50.48
2	M. Podkoscielny (Poland)	1:50.53
3	N. Agh (Hungary)	1:50.73
4	J. Melberg (Norway)	1:50.75
5	R. Granneman (Holland)	1:51.65
6	F. Mortensen (Denmark)	1:51.88
7	P. Brew (GBR)	1:51.96
8	I. Bachkatov (USSR)	1:52.95

Other British Competitors
23	J. Broughton (GBR)	1:52.89

400 Metres Freestyle
Final
1	A. Wojdat (Poland)	3:47.78
2	S. Pfeiffer (W Germany)	3:48.68
3	M. Podkoscielny (Poland)	3:49.29
4	A. Holmertz (Sweden)	3:49.58
5	U. Dassler (GDR)	3:49.78
6	J. Hoffmann (GDR)	3:50.52
7	Z. Szilagyi (Hungary)	3:52.68
8	J. Bucar (Yugoslavia)	3:55.36

Consolation Final
1	E. Logvinov (USSR)	3:54.79
2	M. Trevisan (Italy)	3:55.57
3	H. Jangwall (Sweden)	3:55.72
4	A. Gaidukevich (USSR)	3:55.73
5	D. Serra (Spain)	3:55.95
6	C. McNeil (GBR)	3:56.29
7	N. Agh (Hungary)	3:59.29

Other British Competitors
24	J. Broughton (GBR)	4:03.78

1500 Metres Freestyle
Final
1	J. Hoffmann (GDR)	15:01.52
2	S. Pfeiffer (W Germany)	15:01.93
3	M. Podkoscielny (Poland)	15:19.29
4	S. Persson (Sweden)	15:23.73
5	K. Boyd (GBR)	15:25.15
6	A. Gaidukevich (USSR)	15:25.28
7	E. Logvinov (USSR)	15:28.50
8	M. Bensi (Italy)	15:43.84

Other British Competitors
11	C. McNeil (GBR)	15:46.89

100 Metres Backstroke
Final
1	M. Lopez-Zubero (Spain)	56.44
2	S. Zabolotnov (USSR)	56.45

Jonathan Broughton

3 D. Richter (GDR)	56.52	
4 F. Hoffmeister (W Germany)	56.66	
5 I. Polianski (USSR)	56.97	
6 T. Weber (GDR)	57.04	
7 T. Duetsch (Hungary)	57.56	
8 L. Soerensen (Denmark)	57.69	

Consolation Final

1 F. Schott (France)	57.23
2 C. Ventosa (Spain)	58.08
3 G. Binfield (GBR)	58.10
4 G. Mikhalev (Bulgaria)	58.28
5 S. Cullen (Ireland)	58.64
6 P. Oberglock (W Germany)	58.65
7 G. Robins (GBR)	58.66
8 M. Ranis (Czechoslovakia)	58.89

200 Metres Backstroke
Final

1 S. Battistelli (Italy)	1:59.96
2 V. Selkov (USSR)	2:00.02
3 T. Weber (GDR)	2:00.54
4 F. Hoffmeister (W Germany)	2:01.44
5 M. Lopez-Zubero (Spain)	2:02.31
6 D. Holderbach (France)	2:02.93
7 M. Ranis (Czechoslovakia)	2:04.29
8 T. Deutsch (Hungary)	2:08.72

Consolation Final

1 G. Binfield (GBR)	2:03.56
2 P. Kuehl (GDR)	2:04.02
3 G. Robins (GBR)	2:04.10
4 L. Soersensen (Denmark)	2:04.48
5 E. Merisi (Italy)	2:04.77
6 S. Zabolotnov (USSR)	2:05.13
7 S. Hackmann (W Germany)	2:05.68
8 G. Mikhalev (Bulgaria)	2:06.69

100 Metres Breaststroke
Final

1 A. Moorhouse (GBR)	1:01.71
2 D. Volkov (USSR)	1:01.94
3 N. Gillingham (GBR)	1:02.12
4 G. Minervini (Italy)	1:02.33
5 R. Dekker (Holland)	1:02.56
6 T. Debnar (Hungary)	1:03.05
7 V. Alexeev (USSR)	1:03.31
8 M. Warnecke (W Germany)	1:03.57

Consolation Final

1 C. Penicaud (France)	1:03.69
2 R. Faerber (GDR)	1:03.75
3 T. Boehm (Austria)	
M. Cagelli (Italy)	1:03.76
5 K. Guettler (Hungary)	1:03.84
6 P. Suominen (Finland)	1:03.89
7 R. Camallonga (Spain)	1:04.02
8 B. Goebel (W Germany)	1:04.69

200 Metres Breaststroke
Final

1 N. Gillingham (GBR)	2:12.90
2 G. O'Toole (Ireland)	2:15.73
3 J. Szabo (Hungary)	2:16.05
4 R. Beinhauer (Czechoslovakia)	2:16.37
5 S. Lopez (Spain)	2:16.66
6 T. Debnar (Hungary)	2:16.90
7 V. Lozik (USSR)	2:17.74
8 J. Fernandez (Spain)	2:19.24

Consolation Final

1 C. Penicaud (France)	2:16.60
2 A. Marcek (Czechoslovakia)	2:17.72
3 T. Mueller (GDR)	2:17.81

4 A. Yokochi (Portugal)	2:17.96
5 J. Beck (W Germany)	2:19.17
6 R. Faerber (GDR)	2:19.78
7 S. Appleboom (Belgium)	2:20.04
8 D. Leblanc (France)	2:21.38

Other British Competitors

19 N. Hudghton (GBR)	2:20.39

100 Metres Butterfly
Final

1 R. Szukala (Poland)	54.47
2 B. Gutzeit (France)	54.50
3 M. Herrmann (W Germany)	54.54
4 N. Rudolph (GDR)	54.55
5 V. Iaroschuk (USSR)	54.59
6 H. Baric (Yugoslavia)	54.65
7 V. Kovalski (USSR)	54.85
8 J. Ballester (Spain)	55.34

Consolation Final

1 E. Ran (Holland)	55.24
2 M. Fibbens (GBR)	55.46
3 C. Wallin (Sweden)	55.75
4 U. Schnabel (GDR)	55.84
5 L. Depickere (France)	55.98
6 M. Lopez-Zubero (Spain)	56.02
7 D. Parker (GBR)	56.22
8 C. Kjolholdt (Norway)	56.41

200 Metres Butterfly
Final

1 T. Darnyi (Hungary)	1:58.87
2 R. Szukala (Poland)	2:00.62
3 K. Matijaz (Yugoslavia)	2:00.73
4 W. Wyzga (Poland)	2:00.87
5 C. Bordeau (France)	2:01.05
6 T. Jones (GBR)	2:01.12
7 M. Braida (Italy)	2:01.36
8 M. Herrmann (W Germany)	2:02.22

Consolation Final

1 C. Wallin (Sweden)	2:01.08
2 C. Gessner (GDR)	2:01.89
3 A. Savchenko (USSR)	2:02.19
4 J. Ballester (Spain)	2:02.25
5 T. Kiss (Hungary)	2:03.18
6 R. Leitner (Austria)	2:03.35
7 V. Iaroschuk (USSR)	2:03.40
8 C. Hoffmann (W Germany)	2:03.75

Other British Competitors

25 A. Quinn (GBR)	2:05.55

200 Metres Individual Medley
Final

1 T. Darnyi (Hungary)	2:01.03
2 R. Hannemann (GDR)	2:03.07
3 J. Hladky (W Germany)	2:03.21
4 V. Iaroschuk (USSR)	2:03.23
5 P. Kuehl (GDR)	2:03.84
6 F. Lefevre (France)	2:04.14
7 J. Bidrman (Sweden)	2:04.81
8 P. Bermel (W Germany)	2:04.83

Consolation Final

1 G. O'Toole (Ireland)	2:05.46
2 L. Sacchi (Italy)	2:05.52
3 L. Soerensen (Denmark)	2:05.74
4 B. Sanson (France)	2:06.11
5 M. Zubkov (USSR)	2:06.29
6 G. Robins (GBR)	2:06.68
7 C. Papanikolaou (Greece)	2:07.48
8 P. O'Sullivan (GBR)	2:07.52

400 Metres Individual Medley
Final

1 T. Darnyi (Hungary)	4:15.25
2 P. Kuehl (GDR)	4:16.08
3 S. Battistelli (Italy)	4:19.13
4 C. Gessner (GDR)	4:19.71
5 J. Szabo (Hungary)	4:21.69
6 L. Sacchi (Italy)	4:22.96
7 S. Marniuk (USSR)	4:25.10
8 C. Papanikolaou (Greece)	4:33.79

Consolation Final

1 F. Lefevre (France)	4:23.96
2 J. Bidrman (Sweden)	4:25.78
3 P. O'Sullivan (GBR)	4:26.38
4 M. Zubkov (USSR)	4:28.14
5 P. Brew (GBR)	4:31.08
6 M. Konecki (Poland)	4:31.93
7 A. Kudritzki (W Germany)	4:33.60
8 O. Bures (Czechoslovakia)	4:41.40

4×100 Metres Freestyle Relay
Final

1 W Germany	3:19.68
2 France	3:19.73
3 Sweden	3:19.76
4 USSR	3:19.77
5 GDR	3:21.36
6 Italy	3:21.37
7 Holland	3:23.98
GBR	DIS

4×200 Metres Freestyle Relay
Final

1 Italy	7:15.39
2 W Germany	7:17.38
3 GDR	7:17.79
4 Sweden	7:20.76
5 USSR	7:22.14
6 Poland	7:25.19
7 Hungary	7:26.95
8 Spain	7:37.24

British Team

9 GBR	7:29.86

4×100 Metres Medley Relay
Final

1 USSR	3:41.44
2 France	3:43.09
3 Italy	3:43.14
4 W Germany	3:43.58
5 GBR	3:44.11
6 GDR	3:44.14
7 Spain	3:47.29
8 Holland	3:47.73

Women

50 Metres Freestyle
Final

1 C. Plewinski (France)	25.63
2 D. Hunger (GDR)	25.64
3 K. Meissner (GDR)	25.87
4 G. Jensen (Denmark)	25.94
5 M. Aizpors (W Germany)	26.11
6 C. Woodcock (GBR)	26.12
7 M. A. Muis (Holland)	26.13
8 T. Costache (Rumania)	26.21

Consolation Final

1 K. Zilliox (W Germany)	26.53
2 S. Persi (Italy)	26.56
3 J. Draxler (Austria)	26.62
4 B. Jus (Austria)	26.65
5 M. I. Muis (Holland)	26.75
6 H. Aberg (Sweden)	26.80
7 E. Kurchina (USSR) P. Verbauwen (Belgium)	26.92

Other British Competitors

18 K. Pickering (GBR)	27.16

100 Metres Freestyle
Final

1 K. Meissner (GDR)	55.38
2 M. Stellmach (GDR)	55.40
3 M. A. Muis (Holland)	55.61
4 C. Plewinski (France)	55.66
5 M.I. Muis (Holland)	56.24
6 K. Pickering (GBR)	56.87
7 G. Jensen (Denmark)	56.89
8 M. Aizpors (W Germany)	56.97

Consolation Final

1 E. Nyberg (Sweden)	57.51
2 S. Persi (Italy)	57.65
3 V. Jardin (France)	57.85
4 J. Coull (GBR)	57.95
5 N. Pulido (Spain)	58.03
6 J. Draxler (Austria)	58.04
7 T. Costache (Rumania)	58.31
8 P. Verbauwen (Belgium)	58.33

200 Metres Freestyle
Final

1 M. Stellmach (GDR)	1:58.93
2 M. A. Muis (Holland)	1:59.96
3 M. Jacobsen (Denmark)	2:00.35
4 H. Friedrich (GDR)	2:00.48
5 C. Plewinski (France)	2:00.55
6 I. Dalby (Norway)	2:02.35
7 C. Prunier (France)	2:03.08
8 H. Lunenschloss (W Germany)	2:03.69

Consolation Final

1 M. I. Muis (Holland)	2:01.46
2 B. Puggard (Denmark)	2:02.47
3 I. Shamorova (USSR)	2:03.12
4 E. Nyberg (Sweden)	2:03.21
5 O. Patron (Italy)	2:04.21
6 J. Coull (GBR)	2:04.27
7 I. Arnould (Belgium) T. Mahera (Greece)	2:04.40

400 Metres Freestyle
Final

1 A. Moehring (GDR)	4:05.84
2 H. Friedrich (GDR)	4:10.14
3 M. Melchiorri (Italy)	4:10.89
4 I. Dalby (Norway)	4:11.51
5 O. Patron (Italy)	4:13.09
6 I. Arnould (Belgium)	4:14.41
7 S. Cam (Belgium)	4:16.49
8 N. Lung (Rumania)	4:19.44

Consolation Final

1 H. Lunenschloss (W Germany)	4:15.86
2 C. Prunier (France)	4:17.49
3 E. Mortensen (Denmark)	4:19.07
4 S. Nimtz (W Germany)	4:19.80
5 J. Schmich (Austria)	4:22.23
6 N. Pulido (Spain)	4:22.71
7 K. Silvester (Holland)	4:24.28
8 N. Krueger (Switzerland)	4:29.93

153

800 Metres Freestyle
Final

1 A. Moehring (GDR)	8:23.99
2 A. Strauss (GDR)	8:28.24
3 I. Dalby (Norway)	8:28.59
4 C. Sossi (Italy)	8:28.92
5 M. Melchiorri (Italy)	8:36.57
6 H. Lunenschloss (W Germany)	8:45.98
7 I. Arnould (Belgium)	8:47.67
8 K. Faure (France)	8:53.01

100 Metres Backstroke
Final

1 K. Otto (GDR)	1:01.86
2 K. Egerszegi (Hungary)	1:02.44
3 A. Eichhorst (GDR)	1:03.10
4 S. Voelker (W Germany)	1:03.63
5 M. Aizpors (W Germany)	1:03.64
6 E. Elzerman (Holland)	1:03.80
7 K. Read (GBR)	1:04.60
8 N. Shibaeva (USSR)	1:04.80

Consolation Final

1 L. Vigarani (Italy)	1:04.54
2 M. Kocheva (Bulgaria)	1:05.30
3 C. Melwani (Spain)	1:05.63
4 H. Slatter (GBR)	1:05.76
5 D. Alauf (Yugoslavia)	1:06.15
6 N. Krupskaia (USSR)	1:06.31
7 T. Lund (Denmark)	1:06.49
8 P. Dejonckheere (Belgium)	1:06.81

200 Metres Backstroke
Final

1 D. Hase (GDR)	2:12.46
2 K. Egerszegi (Hungary)	2:12.61
3 K. Otto (GDR)	2:14.29
4 E. Elzerman (Holland)	2:14.94
5 L. Vigarani (Italy)	2:15.92
6 N. Shibaeva (USSR)	2:16.50
7 K. Read (GBR)	2:16.85
8 M. Zoller (W Germany)	2:18.73

Consolation Final

1 C. Marchena (Spain)	2:18.90
2 N. Krupskaia (USSR)	2:19.12
3 D. Alauf (Yugoslavia)	2:19.37
4 H. Slatter (GBR)	2:19.50
5 S. Voelker (W Germany)	2:20.07
6 T. Godina (Yugoslavia)	2:21.72
7 A. Barros (Portugal)	2:22.04
8 M. Kotcheva (Bulgaria)	2:23.35

100 Metres Breaststroke
Final

1 S. Boernike (GDR)	1:09.55
2 T. Dangalakova (Bulgaria)	1:09.65
3 M. Dalla-Valle (Italy)	1:10.39
4 E. Volkova (USSR)	1:10.47
5 B. Becue (Belgium)	1:10.60
6 L. Coombes (GBR)	1:11.24
7 S. Kuzmina (USSR)	1:11.32
8 S. Brownsdon (GBR)	1:11.63

Consolation Final

1 A. Haenel (W Germany)	1:11.81
2 K. Bulten (Holland)	1:12.27
3 M. Splichalova (Czechoslovakia)	1:12.34
4 A. Frenkeva (Bulgaria)	1:12.50
5 N. Goossens (Belgium)	1:12.53
6 G. Csepe (Hungary)	1:12.77

7 B. Kaszuba (Poland)	1:12.90
8 L. Moes (Holland)	1:12.93

200 Metres Breaststroke
Final

1 S. Boernike (GDR)	2:27.77
2 B. Becue (Belgium)	2:29.94
3 E. Volkova (USSR)	2:29.95
4 M. Dalla-Valle (Italy)	2:30.11
5 S. Kuzmina (USSR)	2:31.67
6 V. Bojaryn (France)	2:33.37
7 B. Kaszuba (Poland)	2:34.09
8 S. Brownsdon (GBR)	2:35.78

Consolation Final

1 A. Nisiro (Italy)	2:32.88
2 A. Haenel (W Germany)	2:34.75
3 L. Moes (Holland)	2:34.92
4 A. Peczak (Poland)	2:35.17
5 M. Splichalova (Czechoslovakia)	2:36.44
6 R. Runolfsdottir (Iceland)	2:36.76
7 J. Hill (GBR)	2:38.15
8 A. Frenkeva (Bulgaria)	2:40.63

100 Metres Butterfly
Final

1 C. Plewinski (France)	59.08
2 J. Jakob (GDR)	1:00.42
3 K. Nord (GDR)	1:00.81
4 J. Delord (France)	1:01.31
5 J. Anema (Holland)	1:01.48
6 M. Carosi (Italy)	1:01.85
7 M. Scarborough (GBR)	1:01.94
8 M. Jacobsen (Denmark)	1:02.28

Consolation Final

1 S. Bosserhoff (W Germany)	1:02.45
2 A. Lindberg (Sweden)	1:02.51
3 G. Rcha (W Germany)	1:02.53
4 N. Iakovleva (USSR)	1:03.12
5 S. Purvis (GBR)	1:03.40
6 M. Fernandez (Spain)	1:03.56
7 N. Robert (Holland)	1:03.94
8 N. Miteva (Bulgaria)	1:04.28

200 Metres Butterfly
Final

1 K. Nord (GDR)	2:09.33
2 J. Jakob (GDR)	2:10.94
3 M. Jacobsen (Denmark)	2:12.63
4 B. Puggaard (Denmark)	2:14.23
5 G. Rcha (W Germany)	2:14.75
6 C. Jeanson (France)	2:15.53
7 I. Beyermann (W Germany)	2:16.80
8 M. Fernandez (Spain)	2:17.81

Consolation Final

1 M. Scarborough (GBR)	2:15.78
2 F. Cambrini (Italy)	2:15.85
3 S. Purvis (GBR)	2:15.87
4 N. Iakovleva (USSR)	2:17.58
5 S. Gordon (Ireland)	2:17.74
6 N. Meskovska (Yugoslavia)	2:18.17
7 J. Arantes (Portugal)	2:18.93
8 M. Cuervo (Spain)	2:19.73

200 Metres Individual Medley
Final

1 D. Hunger (GDR)	2:13.26
2 M. A. Muis (Holland)	2:15.85
3 M. I. Muis (Holland)	2:17.23
4 I. Bogacheva (USSR)	2:17.87

5	B. Lohberg (W Germany)	2:17.93
6	S. Davies (GBR)	2:18.05
7	I. Shamarova (USSR)	2:18.34
8	N. Lung (Rumania)	2:18.45

Consolation Final

1	B. Becue (Belgium)	2:18.92
2	A. Petricevic (Yugoslavia)	2:19.01
3	S. Parera (Spain)	2:19.59
4	J. Hill (GBR)	2:20.57
5	R. Felotti (Italy)	2:20.75
6	S. Cam (Belgium)	2:20.81
7	L. Bensimon (France)	2:21.92
8	H. Kaelvehed (Sweden)	2:22.14

400 Metres Individual Medley
Final

1	D. Hunger (GDR)	4:41.82
2	K. Egerszegi (Hungary)	4:44.75
3	G. Mueller (GDR)	4:46.06
4	N. Lung (Rumania)	4:46.75
5	A. Petricevic (Yugoslavia)	4:51.34
6	I. Bogacheva (USSR)	4:52.55
7	S. Cam (Belgium)	4:54.03
8	N. Castello (Spain)	4:56.28

Consolation Final

1	S. Brownsdon (GBR)	4:51.45
2	P. Hausmann (W Germany)	4:54.77
3	M. Smith (Ireland)	5:04.55
4	G. Poulopoulou (Greece)	5:04.94
5	A. Peczak (Poland)	5:06.53
6	S. Gordon (Ireland)	5:07.77

4×100 Metres Freestyle Relay
Final

1	GDR	3:42.46
2	Holland	3:43.66
3	W Germany	3:46.15
4	Denmark	3:46.94
5	France	3:47.04
6	GBR	3:48.87
7	Sweden	3:52.20
8	USSR	3:52.21

4×200 Metres Freestyle Relay
Final

1	GDR	7:58.54
2	Holland	8:08.00
3	Italy	8:10.49
4	Denmark	8:11.53
5	USSR	8:15.08
6	W Germany	8:18.10
7	Belgium	8:31.51
8	Ireland	8:41.25

4×100 Metres Medley Relay
Final

1	GDR	4:07.40
2	Italy	4:10.78
3	Holland	4:11.53
4	W Germany	4:12.26
5	GBR	4:13.45
6	USSR	4:15.48
7	Denmark	4:17.11
8	Bulgaria	4:17.27

Caroline Woodcock

155

GO FOR "GOLD" WITH LEEDS BRITAINS TOP SWIM SCHEME

ADRIAN MOORHOUSE
Olympic Champion and World Record Holder

700+
Swimmers in
Training Scheme

Learn to Swim Scheme
19 Pools
Over 1 million lessons per year

Telephone Leeds 443713 or 421959 TODAY!

For your Information Brochure

LEEDS
LEISURE
SERVICES

LEEDS
LEISURE
SERVICES

Great Post-War British Victories
by Leslie Cranfield

Britain's Girls Break the World Record, and Take the Commonwealth Games Medley Relay Title

The final night of the sixth Commonwealth Games held in Cardiff on 25 July, 1958, turned out to be one of the most exciting in the history of the sport.

One event more than any other captured the public's imagination — the women's medley relay. The race was billed as a straight fight between Australia and England, since each country had included two individual gold medal winners in their quartette.

England were to be led off by Olympic Champion, and World record holder, Judy Grinham, while Australia were to be anchored by the incomparable Dawn Fraser, the fastest female swimmer of the era.

For England to have a chance of victory, the first three swimmers needed to hand over a big lead to their freestyler, the young Diana Wilkinson.

Judy Grinham set the ball rolling by equalling her world record on backstroke to leave her Australian rival Anne Nelson, over four seconds in arrears. Anita Lonsbrough, the newly crowned 200 metres breaststroke champion, increased the lead by a further second on the next leg. The English aces had now been played and a powerful Australian response was expected over the latter half of the race.

England's Christine Gosden had been expected to lose ground to Beverley Bainbridge, the individual butterfly winner. Gosden, however, surpassed herself, and yielded only ³⁄₁₀ths of a second and a five second advantage was handed over to Diana Wilkinson on freestyle.

The 14-year-old Wilkinson, competing in her first major Games, showed remarkable calm in the face of the Olympic freestyle champion, Dawn Fraser. Gradually, the huge lead began to dwindle, as Fraser charged off in hot pursuit. With the crowd in the Empire Pool reaching fever ptich, Wilkinson held on to bring the English team home first. Fraser, despite recording the fastest split time ever, had failed by 1.1 seconds to catch England, who had amazingly broken the World record.

This race was the final chapter of a series of triumphs by England's women swimmers at these Games.

Ian Black Wins Three European Gold Medals

It was a warm September evening in Budapest on 2 September, 1958, and the packed crowd in the Margaret Island pool was buzzing with excitement at the prospect of the competition to come. If the weather was warm, the swimming proved to be even hotter, and it turned out to be a night to remember for Britain.

Some of the most famous names in the history of British swimming were in action and how they did our country proud. But the man everyone had come to see, was Ian Black, the 17-year-old schoolboy from Aberdeen.

Black had already had an exhausting, but successful summer, winning a gold and two silver medals at the Commonwealth Games in July. Soon after the Cardiff Games ended, he took the National one mile title in New Brighton, and two weeks later, won four more ASA titles at Blackpool. On this particular Wednesday, he was competing in both the 400 metres freestyle and the 200 metres butterfly finals, hoping to complete a gruelling double.

When Black stepped onto the block for the freestyle he had two problems — to win the title and yet save enough energy for the butterfly race, scheduled some 40 minutes later. Ian was the current European record holder and his main opposition was expected to come from Boris Nikitin (USSR), the previous owner of the record. Nikitin led at the halfway mark, but then Black put on the pressure and took over shortly afterwards. This move proved crucial, and Black led by 1.7 seconds at the 300 metre turn. He had broken his Soviet rival and his decisive lead enabled him to relax a little over the closing stages. At the finish he had almost five seconds to spare over Nikitin.

Ian Black

Gerry Granham

As soon as the race was over, Black paddled back the full length of the pool to relax and prepare for his next final. Meanwhile, thanks to team-mate Graham Sykes, who was involved in a swim-off for a place in the backstroke final, there was a ten minute delay in the programme.

Then, all to soon, Black was lining up alongside his British colleague Graham Symonds, for the 200 metres butterfly final. From the gun it was the Czech, Pavel Pasdirek, who swept into an early lead, ahead of Symonds. At the halfway turn the Czech still dictated the pace and held an advantage of 1.1 seconds over Black, who was still behind Symonds. Somehow, the Scot summoned up the strength to urge himself on, and passed the flagging Symonds in pursuit of Pasdirek. He continued to defy the pain barrier and challenged the leader. Now, with the bit between his teeth, victory was assured and he passed the Czech to bring off a marvellous double triumph. Symonds, meanwhile, had clung desparately to the bronze.

Sandwiched between these two victories, Judy Grinham had taken the 100 metres backstroke title, after a tremendous race with team-mate, Margaret Edwards. The British team were jubilant.

Great Britain, who had not won a gold medal in these Championships since John Besford's backstroke victory in 1934, had just claimed three within the space of 45 minutes!

Later in the week, Black overcame fatigue once more and took the 1500 metres freestyle title, to become the first individual to score a hat-trick of gold medals since the legendary Arne Borg of Sweden, in 1927.

These magnificent achievements earned Black the "Sportsman of the Year" award for 1958 — a fitting tribute to a man, who had pushed his body to the very limit in search of success.

Anita Lonsbrough Captures an Olympic Title

The women's 200 metres breaststroke was the first title to be decided in the Stadio del Nuoto at the Rome Olympics on 27 August, 1960.

Two girls dominated the event; the blonde German World record holder, Urselmann, and Great Britain's former World record holder, Anita Lonsbrough.

Urselmann had qualified fastest when setting a new Olympic record in the third heat. Lonsbrough, meanwhile, had been equally impressive in winning the second heat by over five seconds, and the stage was set for an intriguing final.

Urselmann, the superior sprinter, started fast and held a significant advantage of two seconds on the halfway turn. The German challenge had been laid down, but the Yorkshire girl did not panic. She raised her tempo and stormed down the third length to level at the final turn.

The last 50 metres was a dramatic affair as the two girls, side by side in the centre lanes, fought for the lead. Each time Lonsbrough edged ahead, the German responded, and drew level. The closing 20 metres were agony to watch as the British girl refused to give way again. Her legs had gone, but somehow she willed her powerful arms to keep stroking towards the wall, through sheer determination.

At the end, the scoreboard revealed that the Briton had won by half a second — a surprising margin, which did not seem possible after such a close struggle. Both girls had broken the World record and Lonsbrough had not only taken the gold medal, but had become the first woman to dip under two minutes, 50 seconds.

This victory marked only the second occasion that Britain had won the event, following Lucy Morton, 36 years earlier, in Paris.

Anita Lonsbrough

Bobby McGregor Finally Strikes Gold

The first final to be decided at the 11th European Championships in Utrecht on 22 August, 1966, was the blue riband event — the men's 100 metres freestyle.

British hopes of success in the Den Hommel pool rested on Scotland's super sprinter, Bobby McGregor, from Falkirk. McGregor, a hero for Britain and Scotland on so many occasions, had never won a major title. He had finished second in the 1962 Commonwealth Games, second to the mighty Don Schollander (USA) at the 1964 Olympics and second a few weeks earlier, behind Australia's new star, Mike Wenden, at the 1966 Commonwealth Games.

Now, aged 22, the architectural student had qualified second fastest behind Leonid Ilichev (USSR) for the final, but the doubts remained.

The big three were in the centre lanes, Udo Poser (GDR) in three, Ilichev in four and McGregor in five. At the start the Soviet sprinter appeared to overbalance and McGregor convinced that the starter would recall the swimmers was left stranded on the block. Meanwhile, another East German had streaked ahead. To the suprise of the crowd, the race went on with McGregor hopelessly adrift, after he had literally flopped into the water. Bad luck seemed to have struck the Scot again.

However, this disastrous start must have galvanised McGregor, for he stormed after the others in hot pursuit. Incredibly, by the turn, McGregor had taken the lead after an astonishing first 50 metres. This superhuman effort appeared to demoralise Ilichev and McGregor, once in the lead, never looked back. He claimed the title, with a time of 53.7 seconds, amazingly, only just outside his best ever.

Later, there was much discussion concerning the amount of time that Bobby had lost at the start. Estimates ranged from 0.3 to 0.8 of a second. Certainly, if the latter was correct, then the World record which stood at 52.9 seconds, would have been under threat. Never had a triumph been so richly deserved, for McGregor, who had dominated British sprinting since 1962, had seemed fated to be the permanent runner-up at major events.

Bobby McGregor

Past Championship Winners, 1869–1989

National Age Group Champions, 1968-1989

11 Years Age Group
Boys

110 Yards Freestyle

1968	T. Sims (Chelsea & Kensington)	1:10.00
1969	B. Lonsdale (Hounslow B)	1:09.50
1970	G. Davis (St. James)	1:09.50

100 Metres Freestyle

1972	S. King (Southend & Leigh)	1:08.80
1973	M. Fenner (Wembley)	1:09.97
1974	R. Winter (Elmbridge Phoenix)	1:07.96
1975	K. Walker (Canada)	1:06.66
1976	E. Stirk (Bradford Metro)	1:06.49
1977	J. Matkin (Oak Street)	1:05.60
1978	G. Richardson (Barking)	1:05.90
1979	G. O'Toole (Trojan, Eire)	1:05.12
1980	P. Burgess (Camden Swiss Cottage)	1:04.81
1981	M. Foster (Southend on Sea)	1:03.12
1982	S. Dronsfield (Salford Triple 'S')	1:03.04
1983	A. Shortman (Bristol Central)	1:03.88
1984	P. Edwards (Norwich Penguins)	1:04.85

200 Metres Freestyle

1976	T. Barrett (Motherwell)	2:22.03
1977	J. Matkin (Oak Street)	2:21.20
1978	G. Richardson (Barking)	2:22.28
1979	G. O'Toole (Trojan, Eire)	2:18.69
1980	P. Burgess (Camden Swiss Cottage)	2:21.13
1981	M. Foster (Southend on Sea)	2:18.23
1982	S. Dronsfield (Salford Triple 'S')	2:18.83
1983	J. Ley (Redbridge Metro)	2:15.79
1984	P. Edwards (Norwich Penguins)	2:21.49

110 Yards Backstroke

1968	N. Culverwell (Modernians)	1:19.60
1969	G. Fell	1:21.80
1970	R. Waller (Edmonton Phoenix)	1:18.20

100 Metres Backstroke

1972	K. Mulholland (Walton)	1:19.40
1973	M. Fenner (Wembley)	1:16.26
1974	N. Harrison (Durham C)	1:17.80
1975	M. Rickhuss (Darlaston)	1:17.53
1976	T. Barrett (Motherwell)	1:15.68
1977	S. Cooper (Guisborough)	1:14.40
1978	B. Greensmith (Durham C)	1:16.97
1979	R. Lee (Gosport St Vincent)	1:16.50
1980	R. Nagle (Camden Swiss Cottage)	1:13.47
1981	M. Foster (Southend on Sea)	1:14.16
1982	S. Dronsfield (Salford Triple 'S')	1:14.35
1983	A. Shortman (Bristol Central)	1:13.87
1984	P. Edwards (Norwich Penguins)	1:15.18

110 Yards Breaststroke

1968	P. Ball	1:31.80
1969	J. Dobb (Hucknall & Linby)	1:31.40
1970	J. Bulbeck (Ipswich)	1:32.50

100 Metres Breaststroke

1972	J. Brett (Warrender)	1:30.99
1973	R. Stafford (Sun Phoenix)	1:28.49

1974	G. Cook (Lamorna)	1:26.83
1975	S. Willis (Billingham Forum)	1:27.01
1976	D. Moores (Hatfield)	1:24.87
1977	A. Allchurch (Co Sheffield)	1:25.50
1978	R. MacNamee (Beckenham)	1:25.34
1979	M. Guest (Halesowen)	1:26.62
1980	M. McHaffie (Cranleigh)	1:20.93
1981	M. Maidment (Harrow & Wealdstone)	1:23.42
1982	A. Murdoch (Derby Phoenix)	1:23.90
1983	I. McKenzie (Braintree & Bocking)	1:23.73
1984	W. O'Gorman (Reading)	1:23.00

110 Yards Butterfly

1968	C. Hodgson	1:18.60
1969	B. Lonsdale (Hounslow B)	1:15.00
1970	A. Raspin (Hull Olympic)	1:17.90

100 Metres Butterfly

1972	D. Evitts (Onward Dolphin)	1:16.80
1973	M. Davies (Welsh Cygnets)	1:17.02
1974	M. Rickhuss (Walsall)	1:15.71
1975	M. Rickhuss (Darlaston)	1:13.11
1976	K. Craddock (Junction Ten)	1:12.15
1977	J. Matkin (Oak Street)	1:13.30
1978	A. Pullan (Luton & Vauxhall)	1:14.29
1979	G. O'Toole (Trojan, Eire)	1:12.52
1980	M. McHaffie (Cranleigh)	1:12.26
1981	M. Foster (Southend on Sea)	1:11.09
1982	S. Dronsfield (Salford Triple 'S')	1:10.06
1983	S. McQuaid (Co Manchester)	1:11.23
1984	P. Edwards (Norwich Penguins)	1:11.49

200 Metres Individual Medley

1974	G. Cook (Lamorna)	2:47.04
1975	M. Rickhuss (Darlaston)	2:45.13
1976	T. Barrett (Motherwell)	2:39.89
1977	S. Jackson (SASA)	2:46.60
1978	R. MacNamee (Beckenham)	2:43.88
1979	G. O'Toole (Trojan, Eire)	2:42.91
1980	M. McHaffie (Cranleigh)	2:39.62
1981	M. Foster (Southend on Sea)	2:39.73
1982	S. Dronsfield (Salford Triple 'S')	2:39.75
1983	J. Ley (Redbridge Metro)	2:36.91
1984	W. O'Gorman (Reading)	2:40.02

4×50 Metres Freestyle Club Relay

1972	Southend & Leigh	2:16.90
1973	Leeds Central	2:14.81
1974	Elmbridge Phoenix	2:11.54
1975	Warrington Warriors	2:13.66
1976	Leeds Central	2:11.26
1977	Co Manchester	2:08.70
1978	Fleetwood & D	2:10.05
1979	Camden Swiss Cottage	2:09.61
1980	Southend on Sea	2:06.68
1981	Rotherham Metro	2:07.75
1982	Hounslow B	2:08.38
1983	Co Liverpool	2:07.42
1984	Killerwhales	2:05.26

4×50 Metres Medley Club Relay

1972	Southend & Leigh	2:36.20
1973	Oak Street	2:32.27
1974	Elmbridge Phoenix	2:24.79
1975	COSACSS	2:31.66
1976	Southend & Leigh	2:26.39
1977	Wigan Wasps	2:26.30
1978	Lincoln Vulcan	2:25.55
1979	Co Coventry	2:22.17
1980	Southend on Sea	2:21.76
1981	Harrow & Wealdstone	2:23.00
1982	Salford Triple 'S'	2:26.04
1983	Co Liverpool	2:24.42
1984	Killerwhales	2:24.64

Girls

110 Yards Freestyle

1968	E. Horton	1:13.00
1969	H. Crow	1:11.20
1970	J. Green (Heath T)	1:10.90

100 Metres Freestyle

1972	A. Machin (Gloucester C)	1:11.70
1973	K. Archer (Chelsea & Kensington)	1:08.97
1974	D. Cox (Co Coventry)	1:09.23
1975	J. Archer (St James)	1:07.48
1976	J. Willmott (Southend & Leigh)	1:06.07
1977	G. Stanley (Co Manchester)	1:06.50
1978	D. Gore (Fleetwood & D)	1:06.41
1979	J. Kerr (Canada)	1:05.90
1980	C. Byfield (Harlow)	1:04.03
1981	J. Illingworth (Leeds Central)	1:06.23
1982	S. Brooks (Salford Triple 'S')	1:05.63
1983	H. Long (Beckenham)	1:06.70
1984	J. Drewitt (Luton & Vauxhall)	1:05.94

200 Metres Freestyle

1976	J. Willmott (Southend & Leigh)	2:22.01
1977	G. Stanley (Co Manchester)	2:21.50
1978	D. Gore (Fleetwood & D)	2:24.32
1979	J. Kerr (Canada)	2:19.51
1980	S. Hardcastle (Southend on Sea)	2:15.87
1981	J. Illingworth (Leeds Central)	2:20.36
1982	S. Brooks (Salford Triple 'S')	2:23.55
1983	H. Long (Beckenham)	2:22.73
1984	J. Drewitt (Luton & Vauxhall)	2:21.78

110 Yards Backstroke

1968	A. Wheatley	1:21.30
1969	D. Viccajee	1:19.80
1970	J. Green (Heath T)	1:18.90

100 Metres Backstroke

1972	A. Wilson (Modernians)	1:19.50
1973	A. Wilson (Modernians)	1:15.23
1974	D. Cox (Co Coventry)	1:17.28
1975	M. Charles (Orion)	1:17.52
1976	A. Dix (Co Cardiff))	1:16.08
1977	A. Horsfield (Co Manchester)	1:15.90
1978	T. Tether (Dudley)	1:13.73
1979	D. Sampson (Chelsea & Kensington)	1:16.25
1980	C. Byfield (Harlow)	1:15.69
1981	A. Ratcliffe (Orpington)	1:14.82
1982	J. Bennett (Stockport Metro)	1:18.32
1983	S. Colledge (Orion)	1:16.93
1984	H. Pluck (Middlesbrough)	1:17.00

110 Yards Breaststroke

1968	S. Bailey	1:30.10
1969	F. Bills	1:31.50
1970	E. Riches (Luton & Vauxhall)	1:30.30

100 Metres Breaststroke

1972	L. Rothwell (Atherton)	1:29.10
1973	A. Wright (Junction Ten)	1:29.92
1974	K. Evans (Po Plymouth)	1:29.12
1975	M. Spring (Beckenham)	1:27.01
1976	A. Shepherd (Sutton & Cheam)	1:27.98
1977	G. Stanley (Co Manchester)	1:21.70
1978	M. Los (Canada)	1:26.01
1979	S. Hardcastle (Southend on Sea)	1:25.98
1980	S. Hardcastle (Southend on Sea)	1:22.90
1981	J. Cooke (Co Liverpool)	1:24.25
1982	H. Frank (Leeds Central)	1:24.08
1983	H. Long (Beckenham)	1:24.90
1984	C. Gable (Hyde Seal)	1:26.19

110 Yards Butterfly

1968	L. Allardice (Killerwhales)	1:21.40
1969	D. Binks (Soundwell)	1:19.80
1970	S. Kemp (Feltham)	1:18.30

100 Metres Butterfly

1972	L. Motley (Sheffield C)	1:22.40
1973	F. Coull (Southend & Leigh)	1:13.91
1974	D. Cox (Co Coventry)	1:18.30
1975	M. Charles (Orion)	1:16.92
1976	J. Christian (Bosworthians)	1:15.29
1977	G. Stanley (Co Manchester)	1:12.60
1978	S. Inkson (Moray & D)	1:13.55
1979	T. Zomopoulos (Camden Swiss Cottage)	1:13.95
1980	S. Hardcastle (Southend on Sea)	1:13.16
1981	J. Illingworth (Leeds Central)	1:13.64
1982	J. Buckley (Northampton)	1:15.16
1983	C. Hung (Hong Kong)	1:13.00
1984	J. Drewitt (Luton & Vauxhall)	1:12.49

200 Metres Individual Medley

1974	D. Cox (Co Coventry)	2:47.14
1975	M. Charles (Orion)	2:44.14
1976	J. Willmott (Southend & Leigh)	2:42.98
1977	G. Stanley (Co Manchester)	2:38.50
1978	S. Inkson (Moray & D)	2:41.78
1979	J. Kerr (Canada)	2:39.31
1980	S. Hardcastle (Southend on Sea)	2:35.57
1981	J. Illingworth (Leeds Central)	2:40.84
1982	A. Fieldhouse (Bristol North)	2:44.63
1983	H. Long (Beckenham)	2:41.88
1984	J. Drewitt (Luton & Vauxhall)	2:41.05

4×50 Metres Freestyle Club Relay

1972	Hartlepool	2:23.40
1973	Southend & Leigh	2:16.30
1974	Chelsea & Kensington	2:15.61
1975	St James	2:12.56
1976	Southend & Leigh	2:10.52
1977	Co Manchester	2:10.90
1978	Leeds Central	2:09.71
1979	Southend & Leigh	2:07.35
1980	Leeds Central	2:10.12
1981	Leeds Central	2:07.34
1982	Stockport Metro	2:11.40
1983	Camp Hill Edwardians	2:09.87
1984	Luton & Vauxhall	2:10.72

4×50 Metres Medley Club Relay

1972	Leeds Central	2:39.60
1973	Sheffield C	2:34.61
1974	Camp Hill Edwardians	2:32.65
1975	St James	2:30.68

1976	Leeds Central	2:28.12
1977	COSACSS	2:29.10
1978	Chelsea & Kensington	2:26.78
1979	Southend & Leigh	2:24.90
1980	Stockport Metro	2:27.86
1981	Leeds Central	2:23.28
1982	Leeds Central	2:25.58
1983	Luton & Vauxhall	2:27.66
1984	Runnymede	2:25.46

12 Years Age Group Boys

110 Yards Freestyle
1968	C. King	1:07.20
1969	M. Muhl	1:07.90
1970	B. Lonsdale (Hounslow B)	1:06.30

100 Metres Freestyle
1985	S. Ferguson (Paisley)	1:01.97
1986	J. Bainbridge (Camp Hill Edwardians)	1:02.22
1987	M. Carl (Redbridge B)	1:02.75
1988	B. Shaw (Harrogate & D)	1:01.97
1989	P. Ingram (Calne Alpha)	1:02.18

400 Metres Freestyle
1985	S. Mellor (Co Manchester)	4:38.58
1986	S. Dugmore (Walsall)	4:43.48
1987	M. Carl (Redbridge B)	4:48.05
1988	G. Ale (Luton)	4:40.19
1989	M. Tyas (Co Leeds)	4:40.13

110 Yards Backstroke
1968	M. Simmons	1:15.90
1969	N. Culverwell	1:12.50
1970	P. Middlemiss (Hounslow B)	1:16.10

100 Metres Backstroke
1985	S. Mellor (Co Manchester)	1:10.45
1986	C. Edwards (Killerwhales)	1:11.38
1987	M. Carl (Redbridge B)	1:10.93
1988	T. Eland (DARTES)	1:12.83
1989	J. Bayles (Runnymede)	1:14.37

110 Yards Breaststroke
1968	C. Basse	1:23.60
1969	P. Allison	1:23.00
1970	J. Dobb (Hucknall & Linby)	1:27.00

100 Metres Breaststroke
1985	P. Simpson (Stockton Aquatics)	1:18.37
1986	L. Peterson (Witham Dolphins)	1:19.90
1987	D. Sheils (Midlothian)	1:17.07
1988	R. Ronca (Millfield)	1:18.75
1989	D. Gurney (Reading)	1:18.39

110 Yards Butterfly
1968	S. Johnson	1:14.10
1969	T. Simms	1:14.40
1970	B. Lonsdale (Hounslow B)	1:11.80

100 Metres Butterfly
1985	K. Crosby (Warrington Warriors)	1:08.31
1986	S. Dugmore (Walsall)	1:09.00
1987	D. Molloy (Crawley)	1:09.85
1988	A. Godwin (Portsmouth Northsea)	1:10.04
1989	S. Mount (Tynemouth)	1:10.15

220 Yards Individual Medley
1968	S. Johnson	2:48.50
1969	N. Culverwell	2:44.00

1970	B. Lonsdale (Hounslow B)	2:45.60

200 Metres Individual Medley
1985	S. Mellor (Co Manchester)	2:30.41
1986	C. Edwards (Killerwhales)	2:33.04
1987	D. Paxton (Bishop Stortford)	2:33.40
1988	G. Ale (Luton)	2:33.30
1989	R. Arnott (Co Leicester)	2:36.57

4×50 Metres Freestyle Club Relay
1985	Reading	1:58.86
1986	Killerwhales	1:56.90
1987	Co Newcastle	2:01.07
1988	Salford Triple 'S'	2:00.58
1989	Co Leeds	2:00.88

4×50 Metres Medley Club Relay
1985	Reading	2:13.80
1986	Killerwhales	2:13.78
1987	Co Liverpool	2:13.90
1988	Harrogate & D	2:17.20
1989	Co Leeds	2:15.23

Girls

110 Yards Freestyle
1968	A. Willington	1:08.70
1969	E. Horton	1:09.50
1970	D. Fairman (Sutton & Cheam)	1:11.10

100 Metres Freestyle
1985	J. Drewitt (Luton & Vauxhall)	1:01.72
1986	D. Morgan (Consett)	1:02.89
1987	J. Mallison (Avon Neptune)	1:03.36
1988	D. Palmer (Killerwhales)	1:01.48
1989	L. Dalzell (Derwentside)	1:03.11

400 Metres Freestyle
1985	J. Drewitt (Luton & Vauxhall)	4:37.73
1986	D. Morgan (Consett)	4:42.12
1987	E. Cook (Stockton Aquatics)	4:45.46
1988	V. Horner (Gateshead Metro)	4:42.40
1989	L. Dalzell (Derwentside)	4:47.17

110 Yards Backstroke
1968	L. Dean	1:18.00
1969	J. Thompson	1:17.00
1970	L. Reale (Aldershot)	1:17.60

Joanne Drewitt Artwood Photography

100 Metres Backstroke

1985	M. Dougan (St Ives)	1:11.81
1986	I. Gahan (Po Plymouth)	1:12.71
1987	K. Axeford (Beckenham)	1:12.65
1988	D. Palmer (Killerwhales)	1:11.54
1989	T. Fullbrandt (Canada)	1:11.65

110 Yards Breaststroke

1968	M. Donnelly	1:26.00
1969	D. Johns	1:25.00
1970	J. Dalkin (Henleaze)	1:26.60

100 Metres Breaststroke

1985	C. Powell (Newport & Monmouth)	1:22.26
1986	L. Findlay (Northampton)	1:21.32
1987	J. Campbell (Co Newcastle)	1:22.25
1988	S. Green (Leyland Barracuda)	1:19.74
1989	L. Rogers (Co Bristol)	1:18.86

110 Yards Butterfly

1968	S. Hazelby	1:19.50
1969	E. Horton	1:17.60
1970	D. Binks (Soundwell)	1:15.90

100 Metres Butterfly

1985	J. Drewitt (Luton & Vauxhall)	1:09.48
1986	J. Dowling (Bo Burnley CATS)	1:11.23
1987	P. Trickett (DARTES)	1:10.10
1988	D. Palmer (Killerwhales)	1:09.43
1989	K. Milnes (Co Bradford)	1:10.18

220 Yards Individual Medley

1968	A. Willington	2:50.40
1969	J. Jackson	2:51.00
1970	D. Binks (Soundwell)	2:48.50

200 Metres Individual Medley

1985	J. Drewitt (Luton & Vauxhall)	2:32.20
1986	J. Birkett (Co Lincoln Pentaqua)	2:37.40
1987	E. Cook (Stockton Aquatics)	2:34.90
1988	D. Palmer (Killerwhales)	2:30.45
1989	L. Dalzell (Derwentside)	2:32.93

4×50 Metres Freestyle Club Relay

1985	Luton & Vauxhall	2:05.14
1986	Co Birmingham	2:02.95
1987	Norwich Penguins	2:02.93
1988	Nova Centurion	2:00.52
1989	Nova Centurion	2:03.16

4×50 Metres Medley Club Relay

1985	Colchester	2:18.36
1986	Co Birmingham	2:19.85
1987	Warrender	2:16.58
1988	Beckenham	2:17.66
1989	Co Bradford	2:18.84

12/13 Years Age Group
Boys

100 Metres Freestyle

1971	C. Birbeck (Torquay Leander)	1:01.90
1972	K. Longland (Beckenham)	1:02.60
1973	P. Hare (Addington)	1:01.16
1974	J. Sexton (Marlin)	1:01.34
1975	C. van der Merwe (Canada)	59.65
1976	J. Fraser (NCR Dundee)	59.25
1977	M. Pickering (Hatfield)	59.90
1978	D. Somerton (Sutton & Cheam)	1:00.05
1979	J. Matkin (Oak Street)	58.72
1980	J. Cattle (Slough Dolphins)	59.89
1981	P. Howe (Co Coventry)	59.49

1982	P. Burgess (Camden Swiss Cottage)	59.32
1983	M. Foster (Redbridge B)	58.27
1984	A. Hindson (Stanley)	58.38

400 Metres Freestyle

1976	M. Jones (Warrington)	4:37.74
1977	M. Pickering (Hatfield)	4:34.40
1978	I. Greyson (Broadlands)	4:30.30
1979	J. Matkin (Oak Street)	4:29.63
1980	P. Baldasera (York C)	4:32.03
1981	P. Howe (Co Coventry)	4:25.14
1982	P. Burgess (Camden Swiss Cottage)	4:33.63
1983	M. Foster (Redbridge B)	4:25.77
1984	S. Wainwright (Co Lincoln Pentaqua)	4:28.60

100 Metres Backstroke

1971	P. Middlemiss (Hounslow B)	1:09.30
1972	G. Abraham (Co Southampton)	1:10.30
1973	C. Taylor (Bristol Grammar School)	1:11.44
1974	J. Cotton (COSACSS)	1:09.64
1975	S. Barnicoat (USA)	1:08.45
1976	J. Fraser (NCR Dundee)	1:10.36
1977	C. Spence (NCR Dundee)	1:08.20
1978	I. Grayson (Broadlands)	1:07.17
1979	S. Cooper (Guisborough)	1:08.45
1980	A. Pullan (Luton & Vauxhall)	1:07.44
1981	R. Lee (Gosport)	1:07.14
1982	R. Stirk (Co Bradford)	1:09.01
1983	M. Hillier (Maxwell)	1:08.12
1984	M. Nolan (Ashton Central)	1:06.48

100 Metres Breaststroke

1971	P. Lee (Heston)	1:20.50
1972	I. Corry (Leander)	1:17.10
1973	S. Goldstone (Welsh Cygnets)	1:18.47
1974	A. Cunningham (Wigan Wasps)	1:18.35
1975	M. Porter (Teesside)	1:17.35
1976	D. Fereday (Wolverhampton)	1:16.07
1977	C. Tragant (Barracuda)	1:18.40
1978	G. Hegedus (Harrow & Wealdstone)	1:14.26
1979	A. Carr (Grimsby Santa Marina)	1:14.56
1980	M. Baldwin (Salford Triple 'S')	1:13.11
1981	R. Hodges (Bognor Regis)	1:17.19
1982	R. Stirk (Co Bradford)	1:16.27
1983	M. Maidment (Harrow & Wealdstone)	1:14.00
1984	A. Murdock (Spondon)	1:14.96

100 Metres Butterfly

1971	B. Lonsdale (Hounslow B)	1:07.20
1972	G. Mond (Anaconda)	1:08.00
1973	K. Fox (Junction Ten)	1:07.37
1974	J. Cotton (COSACSS)	1:08.50
1975	P. Morgan (Co Cardiff)	1:06.59
1976	J. Bott (Hatfield)	1:07.51
1977	M. Pickering (Hatfield)	1:04.40
1978	I. Grayson (Broadlands)	1:05.59
1979	D. Shaw (Co Manchester)	1:04.92
1980	A. Price (Shrewsbury)	1:03.92
1981	B. Lang (Guernsey)	1:04.49
1982	A. Stock (Co Leicester)	1:05.06
1983	M. Foster (Redbridge B)	1:04.02
1984	S. Dronsfield (Stockport Metro)	1:03.39

200 Metres Individual Medley

1972	A. Parry (Tyldesley)	2:34.70
1973	P. Sparkes (St James)	2:33.48
1974	J. Cotton (COSACSS)	2:29.31
1975	C. van der Myc (Canada)	2:26.43
1976	G. Cook (Totnes)	2:29.35

1977 M. Pickering (Hatfield)	2:28.60
1978 G. Hegedus (Harrow & Wealdstone)	2:25.14
1979 M. Cavazzoni (Pointe Claire)	2:28.07
1980 A. Price (Shrewsbury)	2:27.55
1981 B. Lang (Guernsey)	2:27.02
1982 P. Burgess (Camden Swiss Cottage)	2:28.38
1983 M. Foster (Redbridge B)	2:24.86
1984 S. Dronsfield (Stockport Metro)	2:24.37

4×50 Metres Freestyle Club Relay

1972 Co Southampton	1:56.70
1973 Junction Ten	2:00.12
1974 Marlin	2:00.78
1975 Leeds Central	2:00.21
1976 Darlington	1:57.50
1977 Newcastle	1:57.20
1978 Broadlands	1:55.35
1979 Co Manchester	1:53.24
1980 Co Cardiff	1:55.54
1981 Camden Swiss Cottage	1:54.63
1982 Co Leicester	1:55.63
1983 Co Milton Keynes	1:54.68
1984 Camp Hill Edwardians	1:56.01

4×50 Metres Medley Club Relay

1972 Co Southampton	2:14.00
1973 Reading	2:12.20
1974 Co Coventry	2:16.22
1975 Teesside	2:14.45
1976 Elmbridge Phoenix	2:13.32
1977 Hatfield	2:10.90
1978 Broadlands	2:10.19
1979 Co Manchester	2:07.73
1980 Salford Triple 'S'	2:07.38
1981 Co Southampton	2:08.88
1982 Co Leicester	2:11.76
1983 Co Milton Keynes	2:10.99
1984 Stockton Aquatics	2:09.95

Girls

100 Metres Freestyle

1971 J. Atkinson (Darlington)	1:07.00
1972 J. Atkinson (Darlington)	1:04.40
1973 F. Fraser (NCR Dundee)	1:05.22
1974 K. Archer (St James)	1:04.92
1975 K. Archer (St James)	1:02.82
1976 C. Brazendale (Norbreck Castle)	1:00.74
1977 J. Willmott (Southend & Leigh)	1:02.00
1978 J. Willmott (Southend & Leigh)	59.98
1979 M. McPherson (Canada)	1:00.73
1980 S. Inkson (Moray & D)	1:01.83
1981 S. Hardcastle (Southend on Sea)	1:02.67
1982 L. Masters (Fleetwood & D)	1:01.18
1983 M. Ticktin (Pointe Claire)	1:00.54
1984 H. Mansfield (Co Chester)	1:01.71

400 Metres Freestyle

1976 C. Brazendale (Norbreck Castle)	4:33.57
1977 M. Charles (Co Coventry)	4:36.40
1978 J. Willmott (Southend & Leigh)	4:34.80
1979 N. Moffat (Killerwhales)	4:33.58
1980 P. Barnes (Newton Hall)	4:42.08
1981 S. Hardcastle (Southend on Sea)	4:30.61
1982 S. Hardcastle (Southend on Sea)	4:23.43
1983 M. Ticktin (Pointe Claire)	4:32.46
1984 M. Ivison (Bo S Tyneside)	4:36.31

100 Metres Backstroke

1971 K. Walker (Welsh Cygnets)	1:15.00

1972 M. Crook (Co Southampton)	1:14.40
1973 L. Taylor (Junction Ten)	1:11.82
1974 K. Wilkinson (Co Coventry)	1:14.04
1975 J. Beasley (Halesowen)	1:10.19
1976 D. Cox (Co Coventry)	1:10.11
1977 I. Beasley (Junction Ten)	1:09.50
1978 S. Hill (Leeds Central)	1:10.30
1979 A. Horsfield (Co Manchester)	1:09.18
1980 S. Inkson (Moray & D)	1:09.01
1981 T. Zomopoulos (Camden Swiss Cottage)	1:09.02
1982 K. Read (Norwich Penguins)	1:08.80
1983 J. Wood (Nova Centurion)	1:09.64
1984 S. Page (Norwich Penguins)	1:10.27

100 Metres Breaststroke

1971 S. Phillips (Sheffield C)	1:24.20
1972 C. Latendresse (Pointe Claire)	1:23.47
1973 F. Coull (Southend & Leigh)	1:12.23
1974 C. Guy (Gloucester C)	1:22.38
1975 C. Mason (Southport)	1:19.33
1976 A. Vasey (Bo Sunderland)	1:20.84
1977 J. Dodds (Co Chester)	1:19.00
1978 J. Seymour (Sutton & Cheam)	1:18.25
1979 G. Stanley (Co Manchester)	1:17.25
1980 D. Bowman (Darlington)	1:18.20
1981 C. Brock (Radford)	1:16.53
1982 S. Hammerton (Bo Sunderland)	1:17.38
1983 J. Wood (Nova Centurion)	1:16.38
1984 H. Frank (Co Leeds)	1:16.42

100 Metres Butterfly

1971 J. Atkinson (Darlington)	1:12.30
1972 J. Atkinson (Darlington)	1:08.70
1973 L. Wittey (Wembley)	1:10.05
1974 F. Coull (Southend & Leigh)	1:12.23
1975 J. Stables (Dewsbury)	1:08.79
1976 T. Probert (Wythenshawe)	1:08.85
1977 A. Horsfield (Co Manchester)	1:08.90
1978 L. Purchon (Leeds Central)	1:08.54
1979 M. McPherson (Canada)	1:05.79
1980 P. Barnes (Newton Hall)	1:08.13
1981 L. Montford (Nova Centurion)	1:07.37
1982 S. Hardcastle (Southend on Sea)	1:06.94
1983 S. Lewis (Orpington)	1:07.45
1984 G. Atkins (Portsmouth Northsea)	1:07.77

200 Metres Individual Medley

1972 J. Atkinson (Hollyburn)	2:36.10
1973 C. Latendresse (Pointe Claire)	2:36.96
1974 A. Wilson (Modernians)	2:39.15
1975 K. Archer (St James)	2:31.64
1976 D. Cox (Co Coventry)	2:32.11
1977 J. Harwood (Warrington Warriors)	2:30.20
1978 L. Purchon (Leeds Central)	2:28.18
1979 A. Horsfield (Co Manchester)	2:27.15
1980 S. Inkson (Moray & D)	2:30.34
1981 S. Hardcastle (Southend on Sea)	2:28.98
1982 S. Hardcastle (Southend on Sea)	2:27.32
1983 Z. Long (Beckenham)	2:27.24
1984 S. Travis (Portsmouth Northsea)	2:28.79

4×50 Metres Freestyle Club Relay

1972 Hollyburn	2:07.50
1973 Beckenham	2:04.30
1974 Co Southampton	2:03.51
1975 Co Southampton	2:02.13
1976 Co Southampton	2:01.94
1977 Southend & Leigh	1:59.50
1978 Leeds Central	1:56.87

1979	Beckenham	1:58.69
1980	Ealing B	1:56.82
1981	Nova Centurion	1:59.89
1982	Nova Centurion	2:01.03
1983	Stockport Metro	1:59.08
1984	Norwich Penguins	1:59.21

4×50 Metres Medley Club Relay

1972	Reading	2:22.00
1973	Pointe Claire	2:18.61
1974	Co Southampton	2:19.06
1975	St James	2:16.62
1976	Reading	2:16.37
1977	Leeds Central	2:13.90
1978	Leeds Central	2:12.61
1979	Canada	2:10.72
1980	Ealing B	2:11.87
1981	Nova Centurion	2:13.43
1982	Orpington	2:11.44
1983	Co Leeds	2:11.43
1984	Co Chester	2:13.44

13 Years Age Group
Boys

110 Yards Freestyle

1968	K. Burns	1:03.90
1969	S. Meredith	1:03.60
1970	J. Thompson (Irlam & Cadishead)	1:04.00

110 Yards Backstroke

1968	J. Clarke	1:12.50
1969	H. Burgess	1:11.00
1970	N. Culverwell (Modernians)	1:09.10

110 Yards Breaststroke

1968	M. O'Connell	1:22.00
1969	D. Leigh	1:20.00
1970	M. Williams (Bristol Central)	1:22.50

110 Yards Butterfly

1968	J. Sheddon	1:10.90
1969	S. Meredith	1:08.10
1970	T. Sims (Chelsea & Kensington)	1:09.60

220 Yards Individual Medley

1968	P. Manning	2:41.10
1969	S. Johnson	2:38.20
1970	N. Culverwell (Modernians)	2:35.30

Girls

110 Yards Freestyle

1968	S. McPherson	1:09.40
1969	S. Edmondson	1:07.60
1970	S. Simpson (Everton)	1:07.20

110 Yards Backstroke

1968	E. Irwin	1:15.90
1969	L. Dean	1:15.50
1970	S. Simpson (Everton)	1:14.60

110 Yards Breaststroke

1968	J. Parry	1:24.60
1969	M. Donnelly	1:24.90
1970	D. Johns (Po Plymouth)	1:23.60

110 Yards Butterfly

1968	J. Collinson	1:15.40
1969	J. Secker	1:14.10
1970	S. Simpson (Everton)	1:13.90

220 Yards Individual Medley

1968	J. Barnes	2:45.60

1969	J. Jeavons	2:44.30
1970	S. Simpson (Everton)	2:42.40

13/14 Years Age Group
Boys

100 Metres Freestyle

1985	S. Dronsfield (Salford Triple 'S')	54.80
1986	M. Hanby (Nova Centurion)	56.33
1987	C. Robinson (Killerwhales)	56.19
1988	C. Edwards (Killerwhales)	57.03
1989	J. Lancaster (Wycombe & D)	57.06

200 Metres Freestyle

1985	S. Dronsfield (Salford Triple 'S')	2:00.23
1986	J. Ley (Millfield)	2:03.29
1987	C. Robinson (Killerwhales)	2:00.38
1988	J. Randall (Co Birmingham)	2:01.03
1989	J. Lancaster (Wycombe & D)	2:01.44

400 Metres Freestyle

1985	S. Wainwright (Co Lincoln Pentaqua)	4:22.50
1986	J. Ley (Millfield)	4:15.63
1987	C. Robinson (Killerwhales)	4:16.79
1988	J. Randall (Co Birmingham)	4:16.46
1989	D. Sanz (Spain)	4:18.41

1500 Metres Freestyle

1985	S. Wainwright (Co Lincoln Pentaqua)	17:16.69
1986	J. Ley (Millfield)	16:59.66
1987	C. Robinson (Killerwhales)	16:48.68
1988	P. Madden (Canada)	17:12.13
1989	D. Sanz (Spain)	17:09.11

100 Metres Backstroke

1985	M. Nolan (Ashton Central)	1:03.00
1986	P. Pederzolli (Kelly College)	1:05.44
1987	S. Mellor (Co Manchester)	1:05.23
1988	C. Edwards (Killerwhales)	1:02.59
1989	M. Wilson (Co Leeds)	1:04.22

200 Metres Backstroke

1985	G. Williams (Rushmoor Royals)	2:16.78
1986	S. Mellor (Co Manchester)	2:20.05
1987	S. Mellor (Co Manchester)	2:18.13

James Ley Artwood Photography

1988 C. Edwards (Killerwhales)	2:17.30	
1989 N. Skinner (Portsmouth Northsea)	2:17.38	

100 Metres Breaststroke

1985 T. Evans (Kettering)	1:10.85
1986 I. McKenzie (Braintree & Bocking)	1:08.86
1987 P. Simpson (Stockton Aquatics)	1:12.95
1988 S. Wells (Norwich Penguins)	1:11.14
1989 D. Sheils (Warrender)	1:09.79

200 Metres Breaststroke

1985 T. Evans (Kettering)	2:37.13
1986 I. McKenzie (Braintree & Bocking)	2:30.78
1987 C. Robinson (Killerwhales)	2:37.60
1988 J. Randall (Co Birmingham)	2:32.56
1989 D. Sheils (Warrender)	2:32.93

100 Metres Butterfly

1985 S. Dronsfield (Salford Triple 'S')	1:00.00
1986 P. Pederzolli (Kelly College)	1:02.13
1987 H. Sheraton (Millfield)	1:01.70
1988 A. Cheung (Hong Kong)	1:00.72
1989 J. Lancaster (Wycombe & D)	1:00.94

200 Metres Butterfly

1985 S. Hurlford (Ro Waterloo)	2:13.94
1986 R. Stapleton (Beckenham)	2:14.82
1987 C. Robinson (Killerwhales)	2:14.32
1988 D. Pye (St Helens)	2:15.40
1989 A. Lopez (Spain)	2:16.13

200 Metres Individual Medley

1985 S. Dronsfield (Salford Triple 'S')	2:18.48
1986 R. Stapleton (Beckenham)	2:15.83
1987 C. Robinson (Killerwhales)	2:20.66
1988 J. Randall (Co Birmingham)	2:16.33
1989 D. Sheils (Warrender)	2:17.60

400 Metres Individual Medley

1985 S. Wainwright (Co Lincoln Pentaqua)	4:55.60
1986 R. Stapleton (Beckenham)	4:47.71
1987 C. Robinson (Killerwhales)	4:55.99
1988 P. Madden (Canada)	4:49.81
1989 D. Paxton (Bishop Stortford)	4:55.54

4×50 Metres Freestyle Club Relay

1985 Salford Triple 'S'	1:50.10
1986 Nova Centurion	1:47.93
1987 Co Birmingham	1:48.71
1988 Hong Kong	1:45.55
1989 Co Newcastle	1:48.25

4×50 Metres Medley Club Relay

1985 Salford Triple 'S'	2:00.59
1986 Nova Centurion	2:02.46
1987 Beckenham	2:03.42
1988 Hong Kong	1:58.14
1989 DARTES	2:02.06

Girls

100 Metres Freestyle

1985 K. Pickering (Shiverers)	1:00.46
1986 N. Bates (Norwich Penguins)	1:00.04
1987 J. Drewitt (Luton)	59.63
1988 G. Brooks (Greenwich B Mariners)	1:00.17
1989 A. Dronsfield (Co Manchester)	59.76

200 Metres Freestyle

1985 M. Ivinson (Bo S Tyneside)	2:10.82
1986 N. Bates (Norwich Penguins)	2:07.49
1987 J. Drewitt (Luton)	2:08.94

1988 D. Salmon (Kelly College)	2:09.52
1989 Z. Harrison (Norwich Penguins)	2:09.19

400 Metres Freestyle

1985 J. Parrott (Norwich Penguins)	4:31.90
1986 N. Bates (Norwich Penguins)	4:28.92
1987 J. Drewitt (Luton)	4:30.97
1988 D. Morgan (Consett)	4:30.30
1989 Z. Harrison (Norwich Penguins)	4:32.85

800 Metres Freestyle

1985 M. Ivinson (Bo Tyneside)	9:19.57
1986 L. Banks (Bo Southend)	9:20.02
1987 L. Banks (Bo Southend)	9:10.89
1988 S. Foggo (Co Newcastle)	9:16.67
1989 D. Palmer (Killerwhales)	9:23.48

100 Metres Backstroke

1985 S. Page (Stockport Metro)	1:08.14
1986 R. Smith (Reading)	1:08.82
1987 L. Raester (Poole)	1:09.25
1988 H. Mullins (Harrogate & D)	1:08.16
1989 K. Harrison (Rotherham Metro)	1:09.03

200 Metres Backstroke

1985 S. Page (Stockport Metro)	2:26.59
1986 R. Smith (Reading)	2:28.81
1987 H. Osborne (Co Birmingham)	2:26.86
1988 D. Salmon (Kelly College)	2:27.19
1989 D. Palmer (Killerwhales)	2:30.21

100 Metres Breaststroke

1985 S. Smart (Co Chester)	1:16.18
1986 C. Gable (Stockport Metro)	1:15.19
1987 L. Findlay (Northampton)	1:14.42
1988 L. Findlay (Northampton)	1:15.99
1989 S. Masquera (Spain)	1:17.44

200 Metres Breaststroke

1985 S. Smart (Co Chester)	2:45.97
1986 H. Watson (Nova Centurion)	2:43.96
1987 C. Gable (Stockport Metro)	2:44.38
1988 K. Seaborn (Co Manchester)	2:44.98
1989 D. Palmer (Killerwhales)	2:47.24

100 Metres Butterfly

1985 G. Atkins (Portsmouth Northsea)	1:05.37
1986 J. Lancaster (Warrington Warriors)	1:06.89
1987 L. Kilgour (Co Birmingham)	1:06.54
1988 J. Dowling (Bo Burnley CATS)	1:06.03
1989 Z. Harrison (Norwich Penguins)	1:05.31

200 Metres Butterfly

1985 T. Atkin (Co Lincoln Pentaqua)	2:23.97
1986 J. Rowland (Wigan Wasps)	2:27.07
1987 L. Appleton (St Helens)	2:23.79
1988 J. Dowling (Bo Burnley CATS)	2:24.54
1989 Z. Harrison (Norwich Penguins)	2:22.62

200 Metres Individual Medley

1985 S. Travis (Portsmouth Northsea)	2:26.76
1986 J. Drewitt (Luton)	2:28.29
1987 J. Drewitt (Luton)	2:27.15
1988 L. Findlay (Northampton)	2:25.88
1989 Z. Harrison (Norwich Penguins)	2:26.85

400 Metres Individual Medley

1985 S. Travis (Portsmouth Northsea)	5:08.59
1986 J. Rowland (Wigan Wasps)	5:15.84
1987 J. Drewitt (Luton)	5:16.06
1988 J. Dowling (Bo Burnley CATS)	5:10.24
1989 D. Palmer (Killerwhales)	5:12.47

4×50 Metres Freestyle Club Relay

1985	Stockport Metro	1:56.20
1986	Nova Centurion	1:56.09
1987	Co Birmingham	1:54.32
1988	Salford Triple 'S'	1:55.74
1989	Derwentside	1:54.42

4×50 Metres Medley Club Relay

1985	Stockport Metro	2:09.85
1986	Nova Centurion	2:09.96
1987	Co Birmingham	2:08.76
1988	Salford Triple 'S'	2:10.38
1989	Beckenham	2:10.53

14 Years Age Group Boys

110 Yards Freestyle

1968	I. Stansfield	1:01.40
1969	K. Burns	59.50
1970	C. Harrison (Wythenshawe)	1:02.60

110 Yards Backstroke

1968	P. Williams	1:09.50
1969	J. Clarke	1:07.20
1970	M. Simmons (Addington)	1:08.20

110 Yards Breaststroke

1968	D. Batten	1:18.50
1969	D. Waller (Edmonton Phoenix)	1:17.60
1970	D. Leigh (Oak Street)	1:16.70

110 Yards Butterfly

1968	F. Edwards	1:08.70
1969	N. Dexter	1:05.70
1970	S. Johnson (Torquay Leander)	1:06.60

220 Yards Individual Medley

1968	V. Hare	2:33.90
1969	N. Dexter	2:30.80
1970	S. Johnson (Torquay Leander)	2:33.30

Girls

110 Yards Freestyle

1968	D. Sutherland	1:05.80
1969	S. Richardson	1:07.00
1970	S. Edmondson (Hull Olympic)	1:06.20

110 Yards Backstroke

1968	P. Bairstrow	1:13.30
1969	G. Palmer	1:14.40
1970	M. McNutt (Aldershot)	1:13.10

110 Yards Breaststroke

1968	A. Radojoic	1:24.30
1969	J. Parry	1:23.00
1970	P. Thornhill (Watford)	1:24.30

110 Yards Butterfly

1968	S. Cronin	1:14.00
1969	L. Walker	1:13.60
1970	J. Machin (Gloucester C)	1:12.00

220 Yards Individual Medley

1968	D. Sutherland	2:43.80
1969	S. Richardson	2:42.00
1970	D. Banks (Chelmsford)	2:38.80

14/15 Years Age Group Boys

100 Metres Freestyle

1971	S. Veale (Torquay Leander)	58.70

1972	A. Devlin (Warrender)	58.30
1973	G. Hewitt (Middlesbrough)	56.74
1974	S. Whiteley (Oak Street)	57.48
1975	P. Hare (Amphibians)	56.46
1976	J. Cotton (COSACSS)	57.62
1977	K. Pacey (Millfield)	55.70
1978	D. Lamontagne (Canada)	55.53
1979	M. Sheldon (Beckenham)	56.38
1980	A. Jameson (Kelly College)	55.05
1981	C. Bole (Warrender)	55.31
1982	P. Howe (Co Coventry)	56.01
1983	P. Howe (Co Coventry)	54.08
1984	M. Foster (Millfield)	55.00

200 Metres Freestyle

1971	S. Veale (Torquay Leander)	2:07.60
1972	A. Devlin (Warrender)	2:06.10
1973	G. Hewitt (Middlesbrough)	2:04.30
1974	D. Parker (Co Coventry)	2:03.86
1975	P. Hare (Amphibians)	2:01.39
1976	J. Cotton (COSACSS)	2:02.36
1977	G. McCaffery (Co Manchester)	2:01.70
1978	D. Lamontagne (Canada)	2:00.96
1979	D. Shemilt (Canada)	2:00.17
1980	D. Stacey (Broadlands)	1:59.13
1981	C. Bole (Warrender)	1:59.88
1982	P. Howe (Co Coventry)	2:00.09
1983	P. Howe (Co Coventry)	1:56.14
1984	G. Robins (Portsmouth Northsea)	2:00.93

400 Metres Freestyle

1976	J. Cotton (COSACSS)	4:20.51
1977	R. Pavitt (Reading)	4:18.14
1978	A. Hughes (Tigersharks)	4:20.15
1979	D. Shemilt (Canada)	4:10.26
1980	D. Stacey (Broadlands)	4:08.53
1981	D. Matkin (Rotherham Metro)	4:16.71
1982	P. Baldasera (York C)	4:16.14
1983	P. Howe (Co Coventry)	4:03.59
1984	G. Robins (Portsmouth Northsea)	4:15.51

1500 Metres Freestyle

1982	T. Hodges (Hounslow B)	16:54.09
1983	B. Volz (N York Aquatic)	16:13.15
1984	G. Robins (Portsmouth Northsea)	16:44.15

100 Metres Backstroke

1971	N. Culverwell (Modernians)	1:05.20
1972	A. Watson (Onward Dolphins)	1:03.90
1973	I. Hughes (Co Southampton)	1:04.28
1974	G. Abraham (Co Southampton)	1:03.64
1975	P. Hubble (W London Dolphins)	1:05.61
1976	J. Cotton (COSACSS)	1:03.74
1977	I. Collins (Millfield)	1:03.10
1978	J. Bott (Millfield)	1:01.86
1979	G. Mason (New Zealand)	1:03.43
1980	A. Jameson (Kelly College)	1:01.62
1981	G. Goudie (Warrender)	1:03.62
1982	R. Lee (Gosport St Vincent)	1:04.26
1983	S. Flowers (Canada)	1:02.07
1984	I. Panting (Brixham)	1:03.74

200 Metres Backstroke

1971	P. Robinson (Darlington)	2:20.60
1972	A. Watson (Onward Dolphins)	2:16.80
1973	G. Abraham (Co Southampton)	2:19.73
1974	R. Waller (Edmonton Phoenix)	2:15.33
1975	P. Hubble (W London Dolphins)	2:21.08
1976	J. Cotton (COSACSS)	2:18.81
1977	I. Collins (Millfield)	2:14.60
1978	J. Bott (Millfield)	2:13.45

1979	R. Morris (Pointe Claire)	2:17.01
1980	A. Jameson (Kelly College)	2:12.54
1981	G. Binfield (Co Milton Keynes)	2:16.92
1982	P. Baldasera (York C) R. Lee (Gosport St Vincent)	2:18.80
1983	S. Flowers (Canada)	2:12.27
1984	I. Panting (Brixham)	2:17.10

100 Metres Breaststroke

1971	D. Leigh (Oak Street)	1:12.30
1972	P. Lee (Heston)	1:15.40
1973	P. Lee (Heston)	1:13.48
1974	D. Hills (Elmbridge Phoenix)	1:12.27
1975	D. Hills (Feltham)	1:13.22
1976	M. Porter (Teesside)	1:14.21
1977	S. Pratt (Saxon Crown)	1:11.30
1978	K. Kiff (Millfield)	1:13.33
1979	M. Brickman (Canada)	1:11.06
1980	I. Campbell (NCR Dundee)	1:09.35
1981	A. Carr (Grimsby)	1:10.35
1982	P. Crook (Co Manchester)	1:11.36
1983	A. Nicoll (Co Dundee)	1:10.70
1984	G. Watson (FINS)	1:08.16

200 Metres Breaststroke

1971	D. Leigh (Oak Street)	2:37.70
1972	P. Lee (Heston)	2:43.10
1973	P. Lee (Heston)	2:38.80
1974	I. Corry (Leander)	2:38.84
1975	A. Rollo (Glasgow)	2:38.34
1976	N. McLeish (Bosworthians)	2:37.96
1977	I. France (Wigan Wasps)	2:35.70
1978	K. Kiff (Millfield)	2:34.49
1979	A. Moorhouse (Co Bradford)	2:35.13
1980	G. Hegedus (Harrow & Wealdstone)	2:31.40
1981	A. Carr (Grimsby)	2:30.51
1982	P. Crook (Co Manchester)	2:34.59
1983	A. Nicoll (Co Dundee)	2:32.32
1984	N. Hudghton (Aberdeen)	2:31.53

100 Metres Butterfly

1971	S. Nash (Lucas)	1:02.40
1972	T. Sims (Chelsea & Kensington)	1:03.40
1973	B. Lonsdale (Hounslow B)	1:01.67
1974	G. Abraham (Co Southampton)	1:02.09
1975	P. Hubble (W London Dolphins)	1:01.69
1976	J. Cotton (COSACSS)	1:01.32
1977	M. Clarke (Norwich Penguins)	1:01.50
1978	J. Walker (Beckenham)	1:02.16
1979	M. Pickering (Hatfield)	1:00.43
1980	A. Jameson (Kelly College)	58.03
1981	L. Badaway (Camp Hill Edwardians)	1:00.85
1982	T. Jones (Walsall)	1:00.92
1983	S. Flowers (Canada)	1:00.52
1984	R. Leishman (Bo Kirklees)	59.49

200 Metres Butterfly

1982	M. Webster (Leeds Central)	2:14.49
1983	S. Flowers (Canada)	2:12.90
1984	S. Ferriday (Co Leeds)	2:11.02

200 Metres Individual Medley

1971	D. Leigh (Oak Street)	2:28.00
1972	A. Devlin (Warrender)	2:21.50
1973	I. MacVay (Canada)	2:22.51
1974	A. Parry (Tyledesley)	2:21.99
1975	P. Sparkes (Merton Swordfish)	2:19.98
1976	J. Cotton (COSACSS)	2:17.80
1977	K. Pacey (Millfield)	2:18.20
1978	B. Dickinson (Marlins)	2:18.78

1979	J. Davey (Co Manchester)	2:16.85
1980	G. Hegedus (Harrow & Wealdstone)	2:12.97
1981	G. Binfield (Co Milton Keynes)	2:16.60
1982	P. Baldasera (York C)	2:19.10
1983	S. Flowers (Canada)	2:16.17
1984	G. Robins (Portsmouth Northsea)	2:17.33

400 Metres Individual Medley

1982	G. Richardson (Barking)	4:56.06
1983	B. Volz (N York Aquatic)	4:45.89
1984	G. Robins (Portsmouth Northsea)	4:53.02

4×50 Metres Freestyle Club Relay

1972	St James	1:50.90
1973	St James	1:51.91
1974	Co Southampton	1:49.22
1975	Hatfield	1:52.21
1976	Co Leicester	1:49.22
1977	Millfield	1:48.70
1978	Darlington	1:46.72
1979	NCR Dundee	1:45.98
1980	Harrow & Wealdstone	1:45.04
1981	Camp Hill Edwardians	1:46.40
1982	Co Manchester	1:45.38
1983	Co Manchester	1:44.19
1984	Millfield	1:45.01

4×50 Metres Medley Club Relay

1972	Nottingham Northern	2:04.90
1973	St James	2:03.92
1974	Co Southampton	2:02.31
1975	Junction Ten	2:03.96
1976	Hatfield	2:02.40
1977	Co Manchester	1:59.90
1978	Millfield	1:57.30
1979	NCR Dundee	1:57.25
1980	Millfield	1:57.05
1981	Co Manchester	1:59.17
1982	York C	2:00.14
1983	Co Manchester	1:58.98
1984	Nova Centurion	1:58.15

Girls

100 Metres Freestyle

1971	C. Thurgar (Worthing)	1:04.00
1972	S. Cooksley (Woolwich)	1:04.00
1973	W. Quirk (Pointe Claire)	1:01.51
1974	D. Hill (Portsmouth Northsea)	1:03.68
1975	S. Barnard (Beckenham)	1:00.77
1976	M. Houston (Leeds Central)	1:00.62
1977	C. Brazendale (Norbreck Castle)	57.50
1978	H. Jameson (Co Liverpool)	1:00.81
1979	K. Lovatt (Leeds Central)	1:00.09
1980	J. Willmott (Southend on Sea)	58.53
1981	S. Inkson (Millfield)	1:00.28
1982	D. Gore (Fleetwood & D)	59.67
1983	J. McEnroy (Ro Waterloo)	1:00.34
1984	C. Frain (Aquabears)	1:00.38

200 Metres Freestyle

1971	S. Edmondson (Hull Olympic)	2:22.00
1972	S. Cooksley (Woolwich)	2:19.10
1973	W. Quirk (Pointe Claire)	2:12.10
1974	C. Trew (Bristol North)	2:17.59
1975	S. Barnard (Beckenham)	2:12.47
1976	M. Houston (Leeds Central)	2:09.94
1977	C. Brazendale (Norbreck Castle)	2:04.40
1978	J. Harwood (St Helens)	2:09.85
1979	J. Archer (Beckenham)	2:08.68

1980	J. Willmott (Southend on Sea)	2:04.87
1981	S. Inkson (Millfield)	2:09.05
1982	D. Gore (Fleetwood & D)	2:07.24
1983	J. McEnroy (Ro Waterloo)	2:07.60
1984	K. Mellor (Co Manchester)	2:07.74

400 Metres Freestyle

1976	A. Kenney (Kingston)	4:30.91
1977	C. Brazendale (Norbreck Castle)	4:23.50
1978	J. Croft (Wigan Wasps)	4:30.80
1979	N. Muir-Cochrane (Leeds Central)	4:25.59
1980	J. Willmott (Southend on Sea)	4:19.95
1981	J. Robertson (Paisley)	4:30.41
1982	R. Gilfillan (Co Dundee)	4:31.02
1983	K. Hodgson (Co Milton Keynes)	4:29.27
1984	K. Mellor (Norwich Penguins)	4:21.12

800 Metres Freestyle

1982	R. Gifillan (Co Dundee)	9:30.21
1983	K. Hodgson (Co Milton Keynes)	9:07.11
1984	K. Mellor (Norwich Penguins)	8:53.57

100 Metres Backstroke

1971	J. Oldham (Wythenshawe)	1:11.40
1972	G. Fordyce (Criterion)	1:12.40
1973	M. Hartnell (CDSC)	1:10.22
1974	B. Roughley (Swinton)	1:09.52
1975	P. Crane (Bradford)	1:09.47
1976	J. Beasley (Junction Ten)	1:07.96
1977	L. Hilder (Worthing)	1:09.40
1978	S. Cooper (Harrow & Wealdstone)	1:07.68
1979	S. Hill (Leeds Central)	1:07.89
1980	K. McDermott (Southend on Sea)	1:09.41
1981	S. Inkson (Millfield)	1:08.44
1982	M. Wheeler (Fleetwood & D)	1:07.27
1983	K. Hodgson (Co Milton Keynes)	1:08.92
1984	K. Hodgson (Co Milton Keynes)	1:07.55

200 Metres Backstroke

1971	J. Oldham (Wythenshawe)	2:32.00
1972	K. Drucker (Enfield)	2:34.30
1973	M. Hartnell (Canada)	2:32.20
1974	B. Roughley (Swinton)	2:28.72
1975	J. Melchoir (Ravensbourne)	2:27.20
1976	S. Davies (Po Plymouth)	2:24.88
1977	S. Davies (Po Plymouth)	2:18.80

Gaynor Stanley

1978	M. Charles (Co Coventry)	2:22.75
1979	M. Charles (Co Coventry)	2:22.45
1980	L. Driver (Dudley Metro)	2:24.71
1981	A. Horsfield (Wigan Wasps)	2:24.29
1982	S. Inkson (Aberdeen)	2:26.48
1983	K. Hodgson (Co Milton Keynes)	2:25.70
1984	J. Wood (Nova Centurion)	2:22.37

100 Metres Breaststroke

1971	P. Wilson (Warrender)	1:21.60
1972	C. Gaskell (Rochdale)	1:19.80
1973	A. Dickie (Paisley)	1:19.22
1974	D. Rudd (Orion)	1:20.81
1975	C. Guy (Gloucester C)	1:19.11
1976	C. Mason (Southport)	1:17.03
1977	C. Mason (Wigan Wasps)	1:17.20
1978	S. Cooper (Harrow & Wealdstone)	1:17.93
1979	M. Hayward (Camp Hill Edwardians)	1:17.92
1980	S. Brownsdon (RTW Monson)	1:13.55
1981	G. Stanley (Wigan Wasps)	1:15.74
1982	C. Brock (Millfield)	1:14.14
1983	C. Brock (Millfield)	1:15.57
1984	S. Parker (Cockermouth)	1:14.07

200 Metres Breaststroke

1971	P. Wilson (Warrender)	2:55.30
1972	C. Gaskell (Rochdale)	2:54.30
1973	A. Dickie (Paisley)	2:52.54
1974	D. Rudd (Orion)	2:53.58
1975	E. Burroughs (Warrington)	2:50.38
1976	C. Mason (Southport)	2:45.92
1977	C. Mason (Wigan Wasps)	2:44.70
1978	S. Cooper (Harrow & Wealdstone)	2:49.85
1979	C. Bohan (Kings Hospital, Eire)	2:43.44
1980	S. Brownsdon (RTW Monson)	2:38.33
1981	G. Stanley (Wigan Wasps)	2:43.01
1982	L. Tate (Leeds Central)	2:44.02
1983	R. Gloor (Harrow & Wealdstone)	2:42.43
1984	S. Parker (Cockermouth)	2:37.91

100 Metres Butterfly

1971	A. Willington (Warley Wasps)	1:09.90
1972	D. Binks (Soundwell)	1:10.50
1973	W. Quirk (Pointe Claire)	1:08.37
1974	J. Atkinson (Millfield)	1:08.36
1975	A. Taylor (Junction Ten)	1:06.78
1976	K. Archer (Chelsea & Kensington)	1:06.30
1977	S. Davies (Po Plymouth)	1:05.50
1978	J. Osgerby (Wigan Wasps)	1:04.52
1979	N. Fibbens (Hatfield)	1:05.22
1980	F. Ross (Bexley)	1:04.74
1981	L. Criddle (Millfield)	1:04.36
1982	S. Purvis (Sedgefield)	1:04.43
1983	L. Montford (Nova Centurion)	1:05.22
1984	N. Kennedy (Avon Neptunes)	1:04.42

200 Metres Butterfly

1982	A. Dadd (Co Manchester)	2:21.11
1983	L. Montford (Nova Centurion)	2:21.53
1984	L. Wilson (Bo S Tyneside)	2:20.85

200 Metres Individual Medley

1971	P. Wilson (Warrender)	2:37.80
1972	D. Johns (Po Plymouth)	2:37.70
1973	D. Simpson (NCR Dundee)	2:32.69
1974	J. Atkinson (Millfield)	2:32.42
1975	S. Barnard (Beckenham)	2:32.48
1976	A. Kenney (Kingston)	2:27.58
1977	S. Davies (Po Plymouth)	2:25.10
1978	S. Cooper (Harrow & Wealdstone)	2:25.10
1979	M. Scott (Fleetwood & D)	2:26.98

1980 G. Stanley (Co Manchester)   2:25.50
1981 G. Stanley (Wigan Wasps)   2:24.84
1982 S. Bowman (Darlington)   2:25.20
1983 J. McElroy (Ro Waterloo)   2:23.03
1984 J. Wood (Nova Centurion)   2:26.62

400 Metres Individual Medley
1982 S. Bowman (Darlington)   5:09.92
1983 J. McElroy (Ro Waterloo)   5:05.07
1984 K. Mellor (Norwich Penguins)   5:03.94

4×50 Metres Freestyle Club Relay
1972 Leeds Central   2:02.09
1973 Pointe Claire   1:59.16
1974 Paisley   1:59.75
1975 Beckenham   1:57.34
1976 York C   1:56.37
1977 Wigan Wasps   1:56.00
1978 Millfield   1:54.14
1979 Leeds Central   1:52.88
1980 Co Manchester   1:54.28
1981 Wigan Wasps   1:54.06
1982 Fleetwood & D   1:53.49
1983 Fleetwood & D   1:55.80
1984 Aquabears   1:54.65

4×50 Metres Medley Club Relay
1972 Killerwhales   2:16.30
1973 Pointe Claire   2:10.62
1974 Orion   2:13.79
1975 Leeds Central   2:13.98
1976 St James   2:10.92
1977 Wigan Wasps   2:08.40
1978 Killerwhales   2:08.30
1979 Leeds Central   2:06.59
1980 Co Manchester   2:06.51
1981 Wigan Wasps   2:07.63
1982 Millfield   2:06.02
1983 Millfield   2:05.15
1984 Orpington   2:08.06

15 Years Age Group
Boys

110 Yards Freestyle
1968 J. Mills   1:00.20
1969 P. Faharty   1:00.50
1970 K. Burns (Sheffield C)   1:57.10

110 Yards Backstroke
1968 M. Every   1:07.50
1969 C. Cunningham   1:07.10
1970 J. Clarke (Starfish)   1:05.00

110 Yards Breaststroke
1968 J. Anderson (St James)   1:17.20
1969 V. Hare   1:17.50
1970 M. O'Connell (Co Southampton)   1:12.80

110 Yards Butterfly
1968 J. Mills (St James)   1:02.80
1969 G. Milne   1:04.70
1970 G. Cashin (New Kingston)   1:05.10

220 Yards Individual Medley
1968 R. Stephenson   2:30.40
1969 C. Cunningham   2:25.20
1970 D. Waller (Edmonton Phoenix)   2:27.80

Girls

110 Yards Freestyle
1968 L. Wedge   1:07.30

1969 D. Sutherland (Sutton & Cheam)   1:04.90
1970 J. Sloane (Warrington)   1:06.00

110 Yards Backstroke
1968 M. Dyason   1:15.30
1969 S. Grant   1:11.30
1970 S. Savage (Co Southampton)   1:14.40

110 Yards Breaststroke
1968 A. Parkinson   1:25.40
1969 M. Borlase   1:23.60
1970 J. Parry (Darlington)   1:21.70

110 Yards Butterfly
1968 M. Weymouth   1:12.20
1969 S. Gorman   1:13.80
1970 L. Walker (Watford)   1:13.30

220 Yards Individual Medley
1968 K. Smith   2:44.80
1969 P. Bairstow (Huddersfield B)   2:39.50
1970 S. Richardson (Co Southampton)   2:39.90

15/16 Years Age Group
Boys

100 Metres Freestyle
1985 M. Foster (Millfield)   54.10
1986 S. Dronsfield (Salford Triple 'S')   53.80
1987 D. Parker (Co Coventry)   53.41
1988 M. Hanby (Nova Centurion)   53.21
1989 C. Robinson (Killerwhales)   53.43

200 Metres Freestyle
1985 G. Robins (Portsmouth Northsea)   1:58.05
1986 S. Dronsfield (Salford Triple 'S')   1:58.05
1987 D. Gatland (Beckenham)   1:55.91
1988 M. Hanby (Nova Centurion)   1:56.17
1989 C. Robinson (Killerwhales)   1:56.11

400 Metres Freestyle
1985 G. Robins (Portsmouth Northsea)   4:08.96
1986 M. Botterill (Bo Kirklees)   4:12.40
1987 D. Weatherford (USA)   4:06.90
1988 J. Ong (Kelly College)   4:03.78
1989 S. Mellor (Satellite)   4:01.27

1500 Metres Freestyle
1985 G. Robins (Portsmouth Northsea)   16:23.64
1986 I. Wilson (Bo Sunderland)   16:13.87
1987 S. Akers (Shiverers)   16:21.37
1988 J. Ong (Kelly College)   16:00.12
1989 A. Clayton (Co Leeds)   16:29.41

100 Metres Backstroke
1985 I. Panting (Brixham)   1:01.70
1986 M. O'Connor (Co Manchester)   1:01.94
1987 D. Weatherford (USA)   59.71
1988 A. Shortman (Bristol Central)   1:01.43
1989 S. Mellor (Satellite)   1:01.16

200 Metres Backstroke
1985 I. Panting (Brixham)   2:13.64
1986 G. Williams (Rushmoor Royals)   2:12.95
1987 D. Weatherford (USA)   2:09.15
1988 J. Kearney (Nova Centurion)   2:12.71
1989 S. Mellor (Satellite)   2:09.79

100 Metres Breaststroke
1985 A. Fitzgerald (Bo Southend)   1:08.31
1986 T. Evans (Kelly College)   1:09.37
1987 I. McKenzie (Braintree & Bocking)   1:06.59

171

1988 R. Maden (Aquabears)	1:08.67
1989 I. Swift (Rotherham Metro)	1:08.08

200 Metres Breaststroke

1985 N. Hudghton (Aberdeen)	2:27.87
1986 T. Evans (Kelly College)	2:32.27
1987 R. Brown (Torfaen)	2:30.72
1988 R. Maden (Aquabears)	2:27.50
1989 I. Swift (Rotherham Metro)	2:26.49

100 Metres Butterfly

1985 R. Leishman (Bo Kirklees)	58.24
1986 S. Dronsfield (Salford Triple 'S')	58.45
1987 D. Parker (Co Coventry)	57.62
1988 M. Jones (Co Southampton)	57.73
1989 C. Robinson (Killerwhales)	59.10

200 Metres Butterfly

1985 R. Leishman (Bo Kirklees)	2:08.15
1986 J. Stout (Wigan Wasps)	2:09.65
1987 D. Weatherford (USA)	2:09.62
1988 C. Robinson (Killerwhales)	2:08.64
1989 C. Robinson (Killerwhales)	2:07.92

200 Metres Individual Medley

1985 G. Robins (Portsmouth Northsea)	2:13.87
1986 L. Bennett (Gateshead Metro)	2:14.39
1987 D. Weatherford (USA)	2:10.65
1988 P. Pederzolli (Gloucester C)	2:11.06
1989 C. Robinson (Killerwhales)	2:13.79

400 Metres Individual Medley

1985 G. Robins (Portsmouth Northsea)	4:45.29
1986 D. Morgan (Co Swansea)	4:41.88
1987 D. Weatherford (USA)	4:36.80
1988 C. Robinson (Killerwhales)	4:45.19
1989 C. Robinson (Killerwhales)	4:40.20

4×50 Metres Freestyle Club Relay

1985 Co Leicester	1:43.10
1986 Nova Centurion	1:43.34
1987 Salford Triple 'S'	1:42.38
1988 Co Newcastle	1:43.93
1989 Co Leicester	1:42.64

4×50 Metres Medley Club Relay

1985 Barking	1:57.24
1986 Co Manchester	1:54.55
1987 Salford Triple 'S'	1:53.83
1988 Nova Centurion	1:54.50
1989 Portsmouth Northsea	1:54.90

Girls

100 Metres Freestyle

1985 C. Frain (Aquabears)	59.93
1986 K. Pickering (Shiverers)	59.14
1987 G. Atkins (Portsmouth Northsea)	59.64
1988 J. Lancaster (Warrington Warriors)	59.67
1989 D. Morgan (Derwentside)	59.27

200 Metres Freestyle

1985 S. Hardcastle (Southend Synchronettes)	2:04.95
1986 N. Cumbers (Pontypool)	2:08.38
1987 R. Knight (Camp Hill Edwardians)	2:07.85
1988 J. Lancaster (Warrington Warriors)	2:07.93
1989 D. Morgan (Derwentside)	2:06.37

400 Metres Freestyle

1985 S. Hardcastle (Southend Synchronettes)	4:17.08

1986 M. Ivison (Bo S Tyneside)	4:26.80
1987 M. Ivison (Bo S Tyneside)	4:26.26
1988 E. Arnold (Nottingham Northern)	4:23.03
1989 D. Jones (Co Chester)	4:26.33

800 Metres Freestyle

1985 S. Hardcastle (Southend Synchronettes)	8:39.68
1986 M. Ivison (Bo S Tyneside)	9:09.46
1987 M. Ivison (Bo S Tyneside)	9:04.98
1988 E. Arnold (Nottingham Northern)	8:52.38
1989 E. Arnold (Nottingham Northern)	8:58.15

100 Metres Backstroke

1985 H. Slatter (Norwich Penguins)	1:07.66
1986 S. Page (Stockport Metro)	1:07.33
1987 T. Atkin (Co Lincoln Pentaqua)	1:06.91
1988 L. Phimister (Moray & D)	1:06.84
1989 L. Racster (Portsmouth Northsea)	1:07.13

200 Metres Backstroke

1985 K. Read (Stockport Metro)	2:20.46
1986 J. Wood (Nova Centurion)	2:22.85
1987 T. Atkin (Co Lincoln Pentaqua)	2:22.35
1988 J. Deakins (Gloucester C)	2:02.61
1989 L. Racster (Portsmouth Northsea)	2:23.71

100 Metres Breaststroke

1985 D. Tubby (Norwich Penguins)	1:16.89
1986 D. Tubby (Norwich Penguins)	1:15.46
1987 H. Frank (Co Leeds)	1:14.35
1988 R. Gillatt (Co Sheffield)	1:16.78
1989 H. Alder (Harrow & Wealdstone)	1:15.25

200 Metres Breaststroke

1985 S. Parker (Cockermouth)	2:39.98
1986 H. Frank (Co Leeds)	2:41.92
1987 H. Frank (Co Leeds)	2:42.28
1988 J. Harrison (Bo Kirklees)	2:46.10
1989 C. Piggott (Co Birmingham)	2:41.60

100 Metres Butterfly

1985 N. Kennedy (Avon Neptunes)	1:05.43
1986 M. O'Fee (Wigan Wasps)	1:05.12
1987 G. Atkins (Portsmouth Northsea)	1:04.11
1988 J. Lancaster (Warrington Warriors)	1:04.63
1989 J. Dowling (Bo Burnley CATS)	1:04.13

200 Metres Butterfly

1985 M. O'Fee (Wigan Wasps)	2:18.66
1986 M. O'Fee (Wigan Wasps)	2:18.23
1987 S. Smart (Co Chester)	2:19.02
1988 H. Welford (Neston)	2:19.13
1989 J. Dowling (Bo Burnley CATS)	2:21.35

200 Metres Individual Medley

1985 Z. Long (Kelly College)	2:22.63
1986 S. Smart (Co Chester)	2:22.93
1987 S. Smart (Co Chester)	2:23.95
1988 J. Drewitt (Luton)	2:24.95
1989 J. Dowling (Bo Burnley CATS)	2:22.74

400 Metres Individual Medley

1985 S. Hardcastle (Southend Synchronettes)	4:56.66
1986 S. Smart (Co Chester)	5:04.66
1987 S. Smart (Co Chester)	5:02.31
1988 J. Drewitt (Luton)	5:06.38
1989 L. Findlay (Kelly College)	5:01.59

4×50 Metres Freestyle Club Relay

1985 Bracknell	1:53.97
1986 Stockport Metro	1:52.99

1987 Norwich Penguins	1:54.01
1988 Co Chester	1:53.32
1989 Kelly College	1:55.22

4×50 Metres Medley Club Relay

1985 Orpington	2:06.09
1986 Stockport Metro	2:05.51
1987 Nova Centurion	2:06.76
1988 Beckenham	2:07.38
1989 Kelly College	2:04.56

16/17 Years Age Group Boys

100 Metres Freestyle

1971 S. Clarke (Nottingham Northern)	57.10
1972 K. Burns (Sheffield C)	57.30
1973 S. Meredith (Crawley)	56.00
1974 G. Hewitt (Middlesbrough)	56.15
1975 R. Burrell (Co Southampton)	56.36
1976 R. Burrell (Co Southampton)	55.15
1977 P. Hare (Amphibians)	54.70
1978 S. North (Oak Street)	55.47
1979 B. Porter (Barnet Copthall)	55.01
1980 M. Reynolds (Barnet Copthall)	54.07
1981 P. Michaelson (Camden Swiss Cottage)	53.53
1982 E. Stirk (Co Bradford)	54.81
1983 D. Dyke (Walsall)	53.45
1984 T. Hodges (Hounslow B)	53.92

200 Metres Freestyle

1976 D. Parker (Co Coventry)	1:59.41
1977 P. Sparkes (Merton Swordfish)	1:57.50
1978 K. Lee (Hatfield)	2:00.00
1979 J. Randall (Co Leicester)	1:58.09
1980 J. Davey (Co Manchester)	1:56.57
1981 J. Davey (Co Manchester)	1:56.42
1982 S. Cooper (Co Coventry)	1:57.48
1983 I. Mulcahy (Stockton Aquatics)	1:56.24
1984 T. Hodges (Hounslow B)	1:58.24

400 Metres Freestyle

1971 N. Dexter (Luton & Vauxhall)	4:28.80
1972 S. Veale (Lamorna)	4:25.00
1973 S. Veale (Lamorna)	4:21.60
1974 D. Smith (Co Coventry)	4:17.00
1975 P. Nash (Co York)	4:10.56
1976 D. Parker (Co Coventry)	4:08.45
1977 P. Sparkes (Merton Swordfish)	4:06.40
1978 R. Pavitt (Reading)	4:13.64
1979 S. Harris (Co Manchester)	4:07.68
1980 J. Davey (Co Manchester)	4:02.68
1981 J. Davey (Co Manchester)	4:00.40
1982 S. Cooper (Co Coventry)	4:07.29
1983 I. Mulcahy (Stockton Aquatics)	4:07.00
1984 T. Hodges (Hounslow B)	4:09.76

800 Metres Freestyle

1971 N. Dexter (Luton & Vauxhall)	9:17.20
1972 S. Veale (Lamorna)	9:15.90
1973 S. Veale (Lamorna)	9:11.49
1974 D. Smith (Co Coventry)	8:55.64

1500 Metres Freestyle

1975 P. Nash (York)	16:29.10
1976 A. Astbury (Leeds Central)	16:32.22
1977 A. Astbury (Leeds Central)	16:46.70
1978 R. Pavitt (Reading)	16:53.60
1979 J. Randall (Co Leicester)	16:30.07
1980 J. Davey (Co Manchester)	16:26.52
1981 R. Williams (Kelly College)	16:30.38

1982 I. Greyson (Norwich Penguins)	16:41.73
1983 T. Jakisch (Canada)	16:29.07
1984 A. Pearce (Co Leeds)	16:31.33

100 Metres Backstroke

1971 B. Prime (Modernians)	1:04.60
1972 G. Johnson (Consett)	1:04.50
1973 S. Bunce (Otters)	1:02.16
1974 I. Hughes (Co Southampton)	1:02.83
1975 G. Abraham (Co Southampton)	1:02.02
1976 G. Abraham (Co Southampton)	1:01.34
1977 D. Campbell (NCR Dundee)	1:02.30
1978 M. Fenner (Kelly College)	1:02.83
1979 M. Fenner (Kelly College)	1:01.52
1980 J. Pearson (Sutton & Cheam)	1:00.98
1981 A. Jameson (Kelly College)	1:00.51
1982 N. Harper (Millfield)	1:00.22
1983 K. Boyd (Hull Olympic)	1:01.42
1984 R. Lee (Gosport St Vincent)	1:02.17

200 Metres Backstroke

1971 J. Scott (Stoke Newington)	2:21.60
1972 P. Robinson (Darlington)	2:18.20
1973 A. Watson (Progress)	2:13.90
1974 I. Hughes (Co Southampton)	2:14.33
1975 R. Waller (Edmonton)	2:15.31
1976 G. Abraham (Co Southampton)	2:13.60
1977 L. Patrickson (Wigan Wasps)	2:14.00
1978 M. Fenner (Kelly College)	2:11.81
1979 M. Fenner (Kelly College)	2:11.63
1980 J. Bott (Millfield)	2:11.49
1981 J. Davey (Co Manchester)	2:08.98
1982 N. Harper (Millfield)	2:13.45
1983 D. Botsford (Canada)	2:10.83
1984 I. Rosser (Torfaen)	2:12.84

100 Metres Breaststroke

1971 D. Waller (Edmonton Phoenix)	1:11.80
1972 D. Leigh (Oak Street)	1:10.30
1973 D. Leigh (Oak Street)	1:08.56
1974 B. O'Brien (Co Coventry)	1:10.68
1975 C. Pryke (Ipswich)	1:10.23
1976 C. Marshall (SASA)	1:12.38
1977 D. Bryant (Gateshead Metro)	1:11.10
1978 D. Bryant (Gateshead Metro)	1:09.83
1979 S. Pratt (Beckenham)	1:08.78
1980 A. Moorhouse (Leeds Central)	1:07.18
1981 S. Driscoll (Beckenham)	1:08.42
1982 M. Warnes (Thamesdown)	1:08.37
1983 G. Binfield (Co Milton Keynes)	1:08.50
1984 R. Wilkes (Portsmouth Northsea)	1:09.03

200 Metres Breaststroke

1971 D. Waller (Edmonton Phoenix)	2:36.30
1972 D. Leigh (Oak Street)	2:31.60
1973 D. Leigh (Oak Street)	2:29.96
1974 B. O'Brien (Co Coventry)	2:31.15
1975 C. Pryke (Ipswich)	2:34.50
1976 C. Marshall (SASA)	2:36.66
1977 N. McLeish (Bosworthians)	2:34.50
1978 N. McLeish (Bosworthians)	2:32.19
1979 S. Pratt (Beckenham)	2:29.81
1980 A. Moorhouse (Leeds Central)	2:25.39
1981 F. August (Beckenham)	2:28.10
1982 A. Carr (Co Lincoln Pentaqua)	2:28.23
1983 G. Binfield (Co Milton Keynes)	2:28.12
1984 R. Wilkes (Portsmouth Northsea)	2:28.39

100 Metres Butterfly

1971 M. Edwards (Camp Hill Edwardians)	1:02.80
1972 S. Nash (Westminster)	1:01.00

1973	S. Nash (Orion)	1:00.24
1974	G. Hewitt (Middlesbrough)	1:00.15
1975	S. Penprase (Totnes)	59.88
1976	P. Hubble (Chelsea & Kensington)	59.44
1977	P. Hubble (Chelsea & Kensington)	58.20
1978	K. Lee (Hatfield)	59.51
1979	P. Ward (Canada)	58.01
1980	J. Walker (Co Manchester)	58.64
1981	N. Hodgson (Wigan Wasps)	58.01
1982	D. Williams (Fleetwood & D)	57.51
1983	G. Binfield (Co Milton Keynes)	58.41
1984	T. Jones (Walsall)	59.08

200 Metres Butterfly

1971	M. Edwards (Camp Hill Edwardians)	2:19.20
1972	M. Benny (Spondon)	2:15.40
1973	S. Nash (Orion)	2:11.57
1974	B. Lonsdale (Hounslow B)	2:11.64
1975	S. Penprase (Totnes)	2:12.12
1976	P. Hubble (Chelsea & Kensington)	2:10.61
1977	P. Hubble (Chelsea & Kensington)	2:06.80
1978	P. Morris (Bracknell)	2:08.69
1979	P. Ward (Canada)	2:06.29
1980	J. Walker (Co Manchester)	2:08.01
1981	N. Hodgson (Wigan Wasps)	2:07.77
1982	I. Ridyard (Co Manchester)	2:09.64
1983	G. Binfield (Co Milton Keynes)	2:08.35
1984	T. Jones (Walsall)	2:07.98

200 Metres Individual Medley

1982	D. Williams (Fleetwood & D)	2:13.88
1983	G. Binfield (Co Milton Keynes)	2:11.05
1984	I. Rosser (Torfaen)	2:13.62

400 Metres Individual Medley

1971	B. Prime (Modernians)	5:07.30
1972	V. Davies (Co Southampton)	4:59.30
1973	J. Cleworth (Tyldesley)	5:00.66
1974	D. Smith (Co Coventry)	4:53.16
1975	M. Thorne (Thornbury)	4:56.24
1976	P. Sparkes (Merton Swordfish)	4:49.00
1977	P. Sparkes (Merton Swordfish)	4:34.80
1978	G. Sykes (Co Coventry)	4:43.77
1979	R. Brew (Kelly College)	4:42.83
1980	J. Davey (Co Manchester)	4:40.95
1981	J. Davey (Co Manchester)	4:36.29
1982	G. Binfield (Co Milton Keynes)	4:44.66
1983	G. Binfield (Co Milton Keynes)	4:37.62
1984	A. Smith (Reading)	4:42.80

4×50 Metres Freestyle Club Relay

1972	Amphibians	1:48.00
1973	Amphibians	1:46.24
1974	Co Cardiff	1:46.12
1975	Co Southampton	1:42.69
1976	Co Southampton	1:43.63
1977	NCR Dundee	1:44.40
1978	Hatfield	1:43.31
1979	Millfield	1:42.42
1980	Kelly College	1:42.14
1981	Kelly College	1:41.75
1982	Millfield	1:41.61
1983	Co Manchester	1:42.98
1984	Co Leeds	1:41.70

4×50 Metres Club Relay

1972	Nottingham Northern	2:01.00
1973	St James	1:58.73
1974	Millfield	1:58.12
1975	Co Southampton	1:57.29

1976	Co Southampton	1:54.45
1977	NCR Dundee	1:57.30
1978	Hatfield	1:56.96
1979	Millfield	1:53.92
1980	Millfield	1:53.52
1981	Beckenham	1:53.82
1982	Millfield	1:52.66
1983	Harrow & Wealdstone	1:55.12
1984	Walsall	1:54.79

Girls

100 Metres Freestyle

1971	J. Turley (Consett)	1:03.80
1972	M. McGlashan (Warrender)	1:03.20
1973	J. Simpson (NCR Dundee)	1:02.93
1974	L. Allardice (Killerwhales)	1:02.88
1975	E. Gray (Glasgow)	1:03.20
1976	D. Hill (Portsmouth Northsea)	1:00.74
1977	M. Houston (Leeds Central)	1:00.10
1978	L. Holland (Warrington Warriors)	1:00.79
1979	S. Davies (Kelly College)	59.60
1980	J. Croft (Wigan Wasps)	57.09
1981	C. Foot (Millfield)	59.57
1982	M. Dixon (Sheffield C)	59.69
1983	A. James (Kelly College)	59.25
1984	E. Williams (Co Manchester)	1:00.29

200 Metres Freestyle

1976	D. Hill (Portsmouth Northsea)	2:11.39
1977	D. Hill (Portsmouth Northsea)	2:09.80
1978	L. Holland (Warrington Warriors)	2:08.52
1979	S. Davies (Kelly College)	2:07.40
1980	J. Croft (Wigan Wasps)	2:05.04
1981	C. Heavy (Trojan, Eire)	2:08.44
1982	S. Kerswell (Camden Swiss Cottage)	2:06.14
1983	A. James (Kelly College)	2:08.06
1984	J. Willmott (Nova Centurion)	2:08.74

400 Metres Freestyle

1971	S. Richardson (Beckenham)	4:52.40
1972	C. Bodle (Gloucester C)	4:45.20
1973	D. Mills (St James)	4:43.80
1974	S. Cooksley (Beckenham)	4:38.73
1975	S. Cooksley (Beckenham)	4:39.05
1976	T. Burke (Tower Hamlets)	4:37.56
1977	D. Hill (Portsmouth Northsea)	4:33.00
1978	L. Heggie (Co Coventry)	4:27.88
1979	S. Davies (Kelly College)	4:26.35
1980	J. Croft (Wigan Wasps)	4:23.47
1981	J. Archer (Beckenham)	4:29.74
1982	S. Kerswell (Camden Swis Cottage)	4:26.01
1983	M. Willey (Co Derby)	4:28.10
1984	J. Willmott (Nova Centurion)	4:28.07

800 Metres Freestyle

1971	J. Hunter (Killerwhales)	10:04.10
1972	C. Bodle (Gloucester C)	9:52.40
1973	D. Mills (St James)	9:43.15
1974	C. Robertson (Paisley)	9:41.99
1975	G. Gibson (Beckenham)	9:36.51
1976	T. Burke (Tower Hamlets)	9:30.93
1977	M. Houston (Leeds Central)	9:24.30
1978	L. Heggie (Co Coventry)	9:11.60
1979	S. Davies (Kelly College)	9:07.61
1980	J. Croft (Wigan Wasps)	9:02.77
1981	J. Archer (Beckenham)	9:15.05
1982	S. Kerswell (Camden Swiss Cottage)	9:00.17
1983	M. Willey (Co Derby)	9:06.37
1984	S. Munro (Stockton Aquatics)	9:11.74

100 Metres Backstroke

1971	P. Bairstow (Huddersfield B)	1:10.80
1972	M. Kelly (Everton)	1:11.70
1973	E. George (St James)	1:11.06
1974	K. Walker (Welsh Cygnets)	1:09.68
1975	B. Roughley (Swinton)	1:07.67
1976	J. Melchoir (St James)	1:09.01
1977	H. Gilyard (Bradford Metro)	1:07.80
1978	K. Wilkinson (USA)	1:07.90
1979	C. Sanders (Orion)	1:08.08
1980	J. Holmes (Co Manchester)	1:08.35
1981	A. Mason (Wigan Wasps)	1:05.97
1982	C. White (Bo S Tyneside)	1:06.49
1983	A. Horsfield (Wigan Wasps)	1:07.77
1984	S. Hindmarsh (Millfield)	1:07.38

200 Metres Backstroke

1971	L. Armour (Warrender)	2:38.50
1972	M. Kelly (Everton)	2:32.70
1973	G. Fordyce (Criterion)	2:33.04
1974	J. Alexander (Everton)	2:34.21
1975	B. Roughley (Swinton)	2:26.64
1976	J. Melchoir (St James)	2:28.46
1977	H. Gilyard (Bradford Metro)	2:26.90
1978	K. Wilkinson (Co Coventry)	2:23.91
1979	S. Davies (Kelly College)	2:22.49
1980	M. Charles (Co Coventry)	2:24.00
1981	C. White (Bo S Tyneside)	2:23.68
1982	K. Connolly (Hounslow B)	2:23.87
1983	J. Woolley (Co Manchester)	2:23.04
1984	J. Woolley (Co Manchester)	2:23.20

100 Metres Breaststroke

1971	J. Parry (Darlington)	1:20.80
1972	P. Wilson (Warrender)	1:19.90
1973	C. Gaskell (Rochdale)	1:18.00
1974	N. Fletcher (Sheffield C)	1:18.78
1975	D. Rudd (Orion)	1:19.81
1976	D. Rudd (Co Coventry)	1:17.10
1977	K. Stanley (Co Manchester)	1:19.10
1978	P. Waters (USA)	1:14.48
1979	J. North (Beckenham)	1:17.60
1980	K. Jones (Pontypool Dolphins)	1:16.76
1981	J. Dodds (Co Manchester)	1:16.19
1982	J. Seymour (Camp Hill Edwardians)	1:14.58
1983	S. Bowman (Darlington)	1:14.64
1984	C. Brock (Millfield)	1:15.23

200 Metres Breaststroke

1971	J. Parry (Darlington)	2:54.50
1972	P. Wilson (Warrender)	2:47.60
1973	C. Gaskell (Rochdale)	2:48.03
1974	N. Fletcher (Co Sheffield)	2:51.52
1975	D. Rudd (Orion)	2:49.52
1976	D. Rudd (Co Coventry)	2:41.80
1977	C. Guy (Weston super Mare)	2:50.50
1978	P. Waters (USA)	2:43.99
1979	C. Mason (Kelly College)	2:45.33
1980	K. Jones (Pontypool Dolphins)	2:45.46
1981	J. Dodds (Co Manchester)	2:46.35
1982	J. Seymour (Camp Hill Edwardians)	2:44.42
1983	S. Bowman (Darlington)	2:41.04
1984	H. Guest (Nova Centurion)	2:43.79

100 Metres Butterfly

1971	S. Richardson (Beckenham)	1:11.30
1972	K. Wickham (Darlington)	1:09.30
1973	K. Wickham (Darlington)	1:07.96
1974	S. Dickie (Paisley)	1:08.24
1975	L. Foyster (Lichfield)	1:08.83

1976	S. Jenner (Mermaid)	1:04.98
1977	M. Hopkins (Kings Hospital, Eire)	1:05.40
1978	K. Archer (Chelsea & Kensington)	1:04.11
1979	S. Davies (Kelly College)	1:04.30
1980	S. Cooper (Harrow & Wealdstone)	1:03.29
1981	L. Purchon (Leeds Central)	1:03.61
1982	L. Purchon (Leeds Central)	1:03.62
1983	L. Criddle (Millfield)	1:03.51
1984	L. Montford (Nova Centurion)	1:04.59

200 Metres Butterfly

1972	J. Barnes (Woolwich)	2:30.50
1973	S. Simpson (Everton)	2:32.28
1974	J. Alexander (Everton)	2:29.15
1975	L. Foyster (Lichfield)	2:27.34
1976	S. Jenner (Mermaid)	2:22.07
1977	L. Taylor (Co Coventry)	2:22.50
1978	K. Archer (Chelsea & Kensington)	2:21.32
1979	J. Osgerby (Wigan Wasps)	2:20.79
1980	A. Osgerby (Wigan Wasps)	2:18.74
1981	F. Ross (Bexley)	2:18.97
1982	F. Ross (Bexley)	2:17.54
1983	L. Criddle (Millfield)	2:19.04
1984	L. Montford (Nova Centurion)	2:19.38

200 Metres Individual Medley

1982	L. Tate (Leeds Central)	2:23.31
1983	A. Horsfield (Wigan Wasps)	2:24.00
1984	H. Guest (Nova Centurion)	2:26.03

400 Metres Individual Medley

1971	D.B. Walker (Thistle)	5:31.50
1972	C. Tamlyn (Beckenham)	5:26.50
1973	A. Willington (Junction Ten)	5:25.13
1974	S. Dickie (Paisley)	5:25.05
1975	C. Griffith (S London)	5:25.31
1976	D. Rudd (Co Coventry)	5:21.57
1977	S. Broadbent (Dewsbury)	5:13.00
1978	K. Wilkinson (Co Coventry)	5:06.80
1979	S. Davies (Kelly College)	4:57.44
1980	M. Scott (Fleetwood & D)	5:06.09
1981	L. Tate (Leeds Central)	5:06.35
1982	L. Tate (Leeds Central)	5:06.07
1983	A. Horsfield (Wigan Wasps)	5:06.56
1984	H. Guest (Nova Centurion)	5:09.70

4×50 Metres Freestyle Club Relay

1972	Warrender	2:03.20
1973	Pointe Claire	2:02.39
1974	Beckenham	2:01.30
1975	Newcastle	1:57.11
1976	Otter	1:59.14
1977	Co Manchester	1:55.60
1978	Co Manchester	1:55.67
1979	Canada	1:54.48
1980	Canada	1:51.76
1981	Co Manchester	1:53.54
1982	Co Manchester	1:55.06
1983	Kelly College	1:53.22
1984	Co Leeds	1:52.67

4×50 Metres Medley Club Relay

1972	Warrender	2:17.40
1973	Pointe Claire	2:15.05
1974	Killerwhales	2:16.82
1975	Millfield	2:12.50
1976	Co Coventry	2:10.18
1977	Co Coventry	2:08.00
1978	Chelsea & Kensington	2:08.49
1979	Beckenham	2:07.56

1980	Harrow & Wealdstone	2:06.86
1981	Co Manchester	2:05.94
1982	Camp Hill Edwardians	2:06.65
1983	Co Southampton	2:06.26
1984	Co Leeds	2:04.92

17/18 Years Age Group

Boys

100 Metres Freestyle
1985	G. Smith (White Oak)	54.07
1986	M. Fibbens (Kelly College)	53.46
1987	N. Metcalfe (Co Leeds)	52.95
1988	S. Foggo (Co Newcastle)	53.49
1989	A. Shortman (Bristol Central)	52.73

200 Metres Freestyle
1985	J. Broughton (Co Leeds)	1:55.83
1986	G. Robins (Portsmouth Northsea)	1:55.97
1987	I. Stewart (Co York)	1:56.73
1988	D. Gatland (Beckenham)	1:56.39
1989	D. Gatland (Beckenham)	1:54.68

400 Metres Freestyle
1985	D. Legge (York C)	4:08.05
1986	S. Willis (Beckenham)	4:03.26
1987	G. Robins (Portsmouth Northsea)	4:05.72
1988	I. Wilson (Bo Sunderland)	4:00.77
1989	S. Akers (Shiverers)	4:01.98

1500 Metres Freestyle
1985	G. Donovan (Barking)	16:26.07
1986	S. Willis (Beckenham)	15:57.30
1987	G. Robins (Portsmouth Northsea)	16:10.75
1988	I. Wilson (Bo Sunderland)	15:43.15
1989	S. Akers (Shiverers)	15:59.20

100 Metres Backstroke
1985	I. Rosser (Torfaen)	1:01.84
1986	G. Robins (Portsmouth Northsea)	1:01.64
1987	M. Harris (Camden Swiss Cottage)	1:00.99
1988	M. O'Connor (Co Manchester)	1:00.41
1989	M. O'Connor (Co Manchester)	59.82

200 Metres Backstroke
1985	I. Rosser (Torfaen)	2:11.30
1986	I. Panting (Kelly College)	2:11.40
1987	I. Panting (Kelly College)	2:10.74
1988	M. O'Connor (Co Manchester)	2:08.78
1989	M. O'Connor (Co Manchester)	2:09.04

100 Metres Breaststroke
1985	N. Gillingham (Perry Beeches)	1:06.44
1986	A. Fitzgerald (Bo Southend)	1:08.28
1987	A. Fitzgerald (Bo Southend)	1:07.21
1988	I. Cotton (Nova Centurion)	1:08.27
1989	N. Polkinghorne (Truro C)	1:06.69

200 Metres Breaststroke
1985	N. Gillingham (Perry Beeches)	2:25.69
1986	A. Fitzgerald (Bo Southend)	2:25.85
1987	A. Fitzgerald (Bo Southend)	2:24.49
1988	A. Murdock (Nova Centurion)	2:27.85
1989	N. Polkinghorne (Truro C)	2:22.73

100 Metres Butterfly
1985	A. Quinn (Co Manchester)	58.74
1986	R. Leishman (Kelly College)	57.48
1987	R. Leishman (Kelly College)	57.80
1988	N. Bridge (Millfield)	57.30
1989	M. Smith (Co Swansea)	57.81

Neil Metcalfe

200 Metres Butterfly
1985	A. Quinn (Co Manchester)	2:06.48
1986	R. Leishman (Kelly College)	2:07.79
1987	I. Panting (Kelly College)	2:08.40
1988	I. Wilson (Bo Sunderland)	2:05.85
1989	D. Gatland (Beckenham)	2:06.07

200 Metres Individual Medley
1985	D. Rolley (Gloucester C)	2:09.56
1986	G. Robins (Portsmouth Northsea)	2:11.72
1987	G. Robins (Portsmouth Northsea)	2:11.57
1988	I. Stewart (York C)	2:11.06
1989	D. Gatland (Beckenham)	2:08.95

400 Metres Individual Medley
1985	D. Rolley (Gloucester C)	4:36.59
1986	G. Robins (Portsmouth Northsea)	4:35.96
1987	G. Robins (Portsmouth Northsea)	4:38.62
1988	I. Wilson (Bo Sunderland)	4:37.42
1989	D. Warren (Tynemouth)	4:38.19

4×50 Metres Freestyle Club Relay
1985	Hounslow B	1:40.92
1986	Nova Centurion	1:39.80
1987	Portsmouth Northsea	1:38.85
1988	Millfield	1:40.06
1989	Co Sheffield	1:39.50

4×50 Metres Medley Club Relay
1985	Newcastle	1:54.00
1986	Kelly College	1:52.33
1987	Co Leeds	1:51.86
1988	Oundle & D	1:52.16
1989	Co Sheffield	1:51.74

Girls

100 Metres Freestyle
1985	E. Williams (Co Manchester)	59.96
1986	C. Frain (Aquabears)	1:00.33
1987	H. Sanderson (Rushmoor Royals)	1:00.12
1988	G. Atkins (Portsmouth Northsea)	59.63
1989	J. Lancaster (Warrington Warriers)	59.61

200 Metres Freestyle
| 1985 | J. Willmott (Nova Centurion) | 2:08.17 |

1986	H. Day (Bracknell)	2:08.20
1987	R. Bennett (Nova Centurion)	2:08.72
1988	C. Horton (Edinburgh)	2:06.12
1989	H. Mansfield (Co Chester)	2:07.22

400 Metres Freestyle

1985	J. Willmott (Nova Centurion)	4:25.65
1986	P. Hutchinson (Wigan Wasps)	4:26.99
1987	R. Bennett (Nova Centurion)	4:28.07
1988	C. Smith (Wigan Wasps)	4:28.92
1989	H. Jepson (Bo Kirklees)	4:27.63

800 Metres Freestyle

1985	A. Cripps (Wigan Wasps)	8:59.59
1986	P. Hutchinson (Wigan Wasps)	9:02.43
1987	L. Matthews (Redbridge B)	9:08.96
1988	C. Horton (Edinburgh)	9:04.98
1989	N. Sommers (Beckenham)	9:06.32

100 Metres Backstroke

1985	E. Armstrong (Co Southampton)	1:08.89
1986	J. Burford (Gloucester C)	1:09.44
1987	J. Wood (Nova Centurion)	1:07.97
1988	J. Wood (Nova Centurion)	1:07.97
1989	J. Riegal (Harrow & Wealdstone)	1:07.72

200 Metres Backstroke

1985	E. Armstrong (Co Southampton)	2:24.91
1986	R. Bowden (Bo Southend)	2:27.36
1987	S. Brinson (USA)	2:24.88
1988	L. Cunningham (Co Manchester)	2:22.86
1989	J. Riegal (Harrow & Wealdstone)	2:22.30

100 Metres Breaststroke

1985	S. Bowman (Darlington)	1:15.47
1986	S. Parker (Wigan Wasps)	1:16.00
1987	D. Tubby (Norwich Penguins)	1:15.28
1988	D. Tubby (Norwich Penguins)	1:15.71
1989	A. Baker (Norwich Penguins)	1:14.94

200 Metres Breaststroke

1985	S. Bowman (Darlington)	2:43.78
1986	S. Parker (Darlington)	2:40.88
1987	D. Tubby (Norwich Penguins)	2:42.81

1988	D. Tubby (Norwich Penguins)	2:40.72
1989	R. Gillett (Co Sheffield)	2:42.92

100 Metres Butterfly

1985	M. Buckley (Perry Beeches)	1:04.57
1986	S. Brooksbank (Co Leeds)	1:04.18
1987	N. Kennedy (Avon Neptune)	1:04.19
1988	G. Atkins (Portsmouth Northsea)	1:03.75
1989	J. Lancaster (Warrington Warriors)	1:04.53

200 Metres Butterfly

1985	H. Bewley (Millfield)	2:19.32
1986	L. Wilson (Bo Sunderland)	2:20 12
1987	L. Wilson (Bo Sunderland)	2:18.62
1988	N. Atkinson (Stockport Metro)	2:18.63
1989	A. Duffy (Derwentside)	2:17.75

200 Metres Individual Medley

1985	S. Bowman (Darlington)	2:24.82
1986	L. Graham (Bo Ealing)	2:26.48
1987	R. Bowden (Co Southampton)	2:26.09
1988	S. Smart (Co Chester)	2:24.32
1989	S. Smart (Co Chester)	2:23.58

400 Metres Individual Medley

1985	S. Bowman (Darlington)	5:06.49
1986	L. Graham (Bo Ealing)	5:07.62
1987	L. Wilson (Bo Sunderland)	5:10.73
1988	S. Smart (Co Chester)	5:04.60
1989	J. Lancaster (Warrington Warriors)	5:03.04

4×50 Metres Freestyle Club Relay

1985	Co Leeds	1:52.89
1986	Co Southampton	1:54.42
1987	Harrow & Wealdstone	1:55.39
1988	Stockport Metro	1:55.71
1989	Beckenham	1:52.81

4×50 Metres Medley Club Relay

1985	Co Southampton	2:07.80
1986	Co Southampton	2:08.03
1987	Bracknell	2:09.37
1988	Nova Centurion	2:09.42
1989	Nova Centurion	2:05.88

Junior ASA (Short Course) Champions, 1971–1988

Note: Competitors must be under 17 on 31 December during the championship year.

Junior Men

50 Metres Freestyle

1985	M. Foster (Millfield)	24.78
1986	M. Foster (Millfield)	24.21
1987	S. Dronsfield (Salford Triple 'S')	24.34
1988	A. Shortman (Bristol Central)	23.95

110 Yards Freestyle

1972	S. Nash (W Handsworth)	57.50
1974	G. Hewit (Middlesbrough)	56.40
1975	S. Whiteley (Oak Street)	57.10
1976	P. Hare (Amphibians)	55.20

100 Metres Freestyle

1971	K. Burns (Sheffield C)	58.00
1973	T. Townend (Hull Olympic)	57.90
1977	P. Marshall (NCR Dundee)	56.50
1978	K. Pacey (Millfield)	56.87
1979	A. Doubleday (Portsmouth Northsea)	54.51

1980	M. Pickering (Tigersharks)	54.09
1981	G. Wilson (Carnegie)	53.14
1982	C. Bole (Warrender)	52.85
1983	P. Howe (Co Coventry)	54.13
1984	P. Howe (Millfield)	52.74
1985	G. Robins (Portsmouth Northsea)	53.52
1986	M. Foster (Millfield)	50.81
1987	S. Dronsfield (Salford Triple 'S')	51.22
1988	M. Hanby (Nova Centurion)	52.55

220 Yards Freestyle

1972	S. Veale (Lamorna)	2:06.70
1974	G. Hewit (Middlesbrough)	2:01.50
1975	D. Parker (Co Coventry)	2:04.50
1976	P. Sparkes (Merton Swordfish)	1:59.10

200 Metres Freestyle

1971	N. Dexter (Luton & Vauxhall)	2:08.60
1973	T. Townend (Hull Olympic)	2:05.10

1977 P. Marshall (NCR Dundee)	2:03.25	
1978 P. Morgan (Co Cardiff)	2:02.23	
1979 A. Doubleday		
(Portsmouth Northsea)	1:58.43	
1980 D. Stacey (Broadland)	1:58.75	
1981 G. Wilson (Carnegie)	1:54.34	
1982 C. Bole (Warrender)	1:55.62	
1983 P. Howe (Co Coventry)	1:54.67	
1984 P. Howe (Millfield)	1:52.28	
1985 G. Robins (Portsmouth Northsea)	1:57.07	
1986 M. Foster (Millfield)	1:55.69	
1987 D. Gatland (Beckenham)	1:52.39	
1988 C. Robinson (Killerwhales)	1:55.98	

440 Yards Freestyle

1972 S. Veale (Lamorna)	4:32.50
1974 D. Smith (Co Coventry)	4:16.60
1975 D. Parker (Co Coventry)	4:16.30
1976 P. Sparkes (Merton Swordfish)	4:08.10

400 Metres Freestyle

1971 N. Dexter (Luton & Vauxhall)	4:27.70
1973 J. Cleworth (Tyldesley)	4:27.90
1977 P. Morgan (Co Cardiff)	4:21.45
1978 R. Pavitt (Reading)	4:17.34
1979 J. Davey (Co Manchester)	4:13.24
1980 D. Stacey (Broadland)	4:02.2‡
1981 D. Stacey (Norwich Penguins)	4:01.69
1982 I. Ridyard (Co Manchester)	4:10.74
1983 P. Howe (Co Coventry)	4:03.42
1984 P. Howe (Millfield)	3:57.19
1985 G. Robins (Portsmouth Northsea)	4:05.17
1986 M. Botterill (Bo Kirklees)	4:11.52
1987 S. Akers (Shiverers)	4:00.98
1988 J. Ong (Kelly College)	3:58.13

1650 Yards Freestyle

1972 S. Veale (Lamorna)	17:54.50
1974 D. Smith (Co Coventry)	16:50.90
1975 D. Parker (Co Coventry)	16:40.50
1976 P. Sparkes (Merton Swordfish)	16:13.90

1500 Metres Freestyle

1971 A. Devlin (Warrender)	17:40.90
1973 D. Smith (Coventry Three Spires)	17:11.10
1977 D. Taylor (Warrender)	16:53.30
1978 R. Pavitt (Reading)	16:31.68
1979 A. Hughes (Tigersharks)	16:25.40
1980 D. Stacey (Broadland)	15:50.76
1981 D. Stacey (Norwich Penguins)	15:44.62
1982 I. Ridyard (Co Manchester)	16:13.46
1983 S. Gwynne (Co Cardiff)	16:25.15
1984 G. Robins (Portsmouth Northsea)	15:53.29
1985 G. Robins (Portsmouth Northsea)	15:46.88
1986 M. Botterill (Bo Kirklees)	16:32.80
1987 S. Akers (Shiverers)	15:46.78
1988 J. Ong (Kelly College)	15:37.31

110 Yards Backstroke

1972 A. Watson (Onward Dolphin)	1:04.80
1974 I. Hughes (Co Southampton)	1:01.60
1975 G. Abraham (Co Southampton)	1:02.50
1976 S. Purchase (Wolverhampton)	1:04.90

100 Metres Backstroke

1971 J. Clarke (Starfish)	1:04.80
1973 S. Bunce (Otter)	1:02.20
1977 I. Collins (Millfield)	1:04.83
1978 M. Fenner (Kingsbury & Wembley)	1:02.91
1979 J. Bott (Millfield)	1:00.72
1980 A. Jameson (Kelly College)	1:01.47

1981 N. Harper (Millfield)	59.77	
1982 K. Boyd (Hull Olympic)	1:01.21	
1983 R. Lee (Gosport St Vincent)	1:02.16	
1984 R. Lee (Gosport St Vincent)	1:01.30	
1985 N. Bridge (Millfield)	1:02.15	
1986 N. Bridge (Millfield)	1:01.70	
1987 M. Nolan (Ashton Central)	1:00.30	
1988 A. Shortman (Bristol Central)	59.84	

220 Yards Backstroke

1972 A. Watson (Onward Dolphin)	2:19.30
1974 I. Hughes (Co Southampton)	2:12.90
1975 G. Abraham (Co Southampton)	2:15.80
1976 C. Tainty (Camp Hill Edwardians)	2:18.60

200 Metres Backstroke

1971 G. Lamping (Hull Olympic)	2:22.10
1973 N. Culverwell (Modernians)	2:18.40
1977 P. Marshall (NCR Dundee)	2:17.58
1978 M. Fenner (Kingsbury & Wembley)	2:16.64
1979 J. Bott (Millfield)	2:07.93
1980 A. Jameson (Kelly College)	2:11.32
1981 N. Harper (Millfield)	2:10.29
1982 K. Boyd (Hull Olympic)	2:12.54
1983 G. Lilley (Hounslow B)	2:13.63
1984 I. Rosser (Torfaen)	2:11.77
1985 G. Robins (Portsmouth Northsea)	2:13.21
1986 A. Whitehead (Co Manchester)	2:14.17
1987 M. O'Connor (Co Manchester)	2:10.55
1988 J. Kearney (Nova Centurion)	2:08.63

110 Yards Breaststroke

1972 D. Leigh (Oak Street)	1:10.90
1974 P. Lee (Hounslow B)	1:12.50
1975 C. Pryke (Ipswich)	1:11.50
1976 N. Jones (Bilston)	1:12.90

100 Metres Breaststroke

1971 M. O'Connell (Co Southampton)	1:10.50
1973 B. O'Brien (Co Coventry)	1:11.50
1977 N. McLeish (Bosworthians)	1:12.60
1978 L. France (Wigan Wasps)	1:11.44
1979 D. Fereday (Wolverhampton)	1:09.62
1980 A. Moorhouse (Leeds Central)	1:07.92
1981 G. Hegedus (Harrow & Wealdstone)	1:06.13
1982 A. Carr (Co Lincoln Pentaqua)	1:07.74
1983 P. Mason (Portsmouth Northsea)	1:07.98
1984 K. Milburn (Stockport Metro)	1:08.18
1985 M. Maidment	
(Harrow & Wealdstone)	1:08.77
1986 M. Maidment	
(Harrow & Wealdstone)	1:07.93
1987 I. McKenzie (Braintree & Bocking)	1:06.57
1988 I. McKenzie (Braintree & Bocking)	1:05.37

220 Yards Breaststroke

1972 D. Leigh (Oak Street)	2:36.20
1974 J. Cullum (Rochdale)	2:35.70
1975 C. Pryke (Ipswich)	2:37.30
1976 J. McKeown (Modernians)	2:35.20

200 Metres Breaststroke

1971 M. O'Connell (Co Southampton)	2:33.80
1973 B. O'Brien (Co Coventry)	2:32.80
1977 N. McLeish (Bosworthians)	2:34.64
1978 L. France (Killerwhales)	2:30.75
1979 M. Clarke (Killerwhales)	2:31.29
1980 A. Moorhouse (Leeds Central)	2:23.18
1981 G. Hegedus	
(Harrow & Wealdstone)	2:26.68
1982 A. Carr (Co Lincoln Pentaqua)	2:28.71

1983	P. Mason (Portsmouth Northsea)	2:25.03
1984	K. Milburn (Stockport Metro)	2:26.49
1985	A. Fitzgerald	
	(Southend Synchronettes)	2:27.25
1986	P. McQuaid (Co Manchester)	2:29.20
1987	I. McKenzie (Braintree & Bocking)	2:24.69
1988	I. McKenzie (Braintree & Bocking)	2:21.63

110 Yards Butterfly

1972	S. Nash (W Handsworth)	1:02.20
1974	B. Lonsdale (Hounslow B)	1:00.20
1975	P. Morris (Clacton)	1:02.60
1976	P. Hubble (Chelsea & Kensington)	1:00.20

100 Metres Butterfly

1971	P. Manning (Woolwich)	1:04.00
1973	B. Lonsdale (Hounslow B)	1:02.60
1977	A. Trower (Gloucester C)	1:01.39
1978	M. Clarke (Norwich Penguins)	1:00.99
1979	J. Walker (Beckenham)	1:00.58
1980	N. Hodgson (Wigan Wasps)	59.85
1981	A. Jameson (Kelly College)	57.60
1982	I. Ridyard (Co Manchester)	58.81
1983	T. Jones (Walsall)	59.65
1984	I. Campbell (Largs)	59.08
1985	R. Leishman (Bo Kirklees)	57.61
1986	M. Foster (Millfield)	58.82
1987	P. Pederzolli (Kelly College)	58.28
1988	T. Hart (Thurrock)	57.67

220 Yards Butterfly

1972	S. Nash (W Handsworth)	2:18.80
1974	B. Lonsdale (Hounslow B)	2:12.70
1975	A. Parry (Tyldesley)	2:18.00
1976	P. Hubble (Chelsea & Kensington)	2:15.00

200 Metres Butterfly

1971	N. Dexter (Luton & Vauxhall)	2:22.80
1973	I. Hicks (St James)	2:18.20
1977	A. Trower (Gloucester C)	2:16.00
1978	M. Clarke (Norwich Penguins)	2:14.40
1979	A. Hughes (Tigersharks)	2:11.85
1980	N. Hodgson (Wigan Wasps)	2:10.63
1981	A. Jameson (Kelly College)	2:05.47
1982	I. Ridyard (Co Manchester)	2:09.55
1983	A. Pullan (York C)	2:12.04
1984	P. Howe (Millfield)	2:07.15
1985	S. Ferriday (Co Leeds)	2:05.69
1986	M. Iball (Co Chester)	2:13.95
1987	S. Wainwright (Millfield)	2:07.91
1988	C. Robinson (Killerwhales)	2:05.70

146⅔ Yards Individual Medley

1972	M. Thomas (Leicester)	1:33.40
1975	A. Parry (Tyldesley)	1:30.10
1976	P. Sparkes (Merton Swordfish)	1:28.60

133⅓ Metres Individual Medley

1971	V. Davis (Co Southampton)	1:31.40
1973	A. Watson (Progress)	1:31.00
1977	J. Cotton (COSACSS)	1:28.45
1978	I. Collins (Millfield)	1:27.94

220 Yards Individual Medley

1974	G. Hewit (Middlesbrough)	2:20.70

200 Metres Individual Medley

1979	M. Frazer (NCR Dundee)	2:14.61
1980	G. Hegedus (Harrow & Wealdstone)	2:13.19
1981	G. Hegedus (Harrow & Wealdstone)	2:07.52
1982	G. Binfield (Co Milton Keynes)	2:12.17
1983	P. Baldesera (Co Leeds)	2:13.74

1984	A. Smith (Reading)	2:13.90
1985	G. Robins (Portsmouth Northsea)	2:09.81
1986	M. Foster (Millfield)	2:11.21
1987	P. Pederzolli (Kelly College)	2:08.04
1988	P. Pederzolli (Gloucester C)	2:06.87

440 Yards Individual Medley

1972	A. Gittings (Bilston)	5:12.70
1974	I. Hicks (St James)	4:58.80
1975	A. Parry (Tyldesley)	4:59.00
1976	P. Sparkes (Merton Swordfish)	4:50.40

400 Metres Individual Medley

1971	V. Davis (Co Southampton)	5:00.60
1973	I. Hicks (St James)	5:03.40
1977	S. Poulter (Blackburn)	4:56.20
1978	I. Hubble (Reading)	4:50.75
1979	A. Hughes (Tigersharks)	4:53.30
1980	J. Davey (Co Manchester)	4:37.12
1981	G. Hegedus (Harrow & Wealdstone)	4:32.43
1982	G. Binfield (Co Milton Keynes)	4:42.35
1983	P. Baldesera (Co Leeds)	4:42.95
1984	P. Howe (Millfield)	4:41.42
1985	G. Robins (Portsmouth Northsea)	4:38.49
1986	M. Iball (Co Chester)	4:50.03
1987	S. Wainwright (Millfield)	4:39.27
1988	C. Robinson (Killerwhales)	4:39.92

Junior Women

50 Metres Freestyle

1985	H. Day (Bracknell)	27.15
1986	K. Edbrooke (Guildford C)	27.50
1987	C. Woodcock (Haywards Heath)	27.30
1988	C. Woodcock (Haywards Heath)	26.18

110 Yards Freestyle

1972	L. Allardice (Killerwhales)	1:02.40
1974	E. Wright (Newcastle)	1:02.10
1975	D. Hill (Portsmouth Northsea)	1:01.60
1976	D. Hill (Portsmouth Northsea)	1:00.30

100 Metres Freestyle

1971	L. Allardice (Killerwhales)	1:02.80
1973	L. Allardice (Killerwhales)	1:01.80
1977	C. Brazendale (Norbeck Castle)	59.97
1978	C. Brazendale (Norbeck Castle)	58.94
1979	J. Croft (Wigan Wasps)	58.89
1980	J. Willmott (Southend on Sea)	58.86
1981	C. Foot (Millfield)	58.65
1982	J. Elliott (Beckenham)	59.02
1983	A. Cripps (Co Coventry)	58.00
1984	A. Cripps (Wigan Wasps)	56.56
1985	S. Hardcastle	
	(Southend Synchronettes)	58.63
1986	Z. Long (Kelly College)	58.59
1987	K. Pickering (Shiverers)	58.32
1988	N. Bates (Norwich Penguins)	58.62

220 Yards Freestyle

1972	L. Allardice (Killerwhales)	2:14.80
1974	J. Green (Walsall)	2:12.50
1975	S. Barnard (Beckenham)	2:13.60
1976	S. Barnard (Co Cardiff)	2:08.70

200 Metres Freestyle

1971	L. Allardice (Killerwhales)	2:17.90
1973	L. Allardice (Killerwhales)	2:11.70
1977	C. Brazendale (Norbreck Castle)	2:06.60
1978	S. Davies (Po Plymouth)	2:06.64
1979	J. Croft (Wigan Wasps)	2:06.26

179

1980	J. Willmott (Southend on Sea)	2:05.79
1981	J. Willmott (Southend on Sea)	2:03.06
1982	A. Cripps (Co Coventry)	2:06.99
1983	A. Cripps (Co Coventry)	2:04.31
1984	A. Cripps (Wigan Wasps)	1:59.93
1985	S. Hardcastle (Southend Synchronettes)	2:03.00
1986	S. Smart (Co Chester)	2:07.56
1987	N. Sommers (Beckenham)	2:05.83
1988	M. George (Bo Waltham Forest)	2:05.37

440 Yards Freestyle

1972	J. Green (Walsall)	4:43.70
1974	D. Simpson (NCR Dundee)	4:34.80
1975	A. James (Co Cardiff)	4:35.80
1976	D. Hill (Portsmouth Northsea)	4:31.20

400 Metres Freestyle

1971	L. Allardice (Killerwhales)	4:47.00
1973	J. Green (Walsall)	4:35.20
1977	S. Davies (Po Plymouth)	4:28.03
1978	S. Davies (Po Plymouth)	4:20.44
1979	J. Croft (Wigan Wasps)	4:19.86
1980	J. Willmott (Southend on Sea)	4:12.96
1981	S. Kerswell (Camden Swiss Cottage)	4:17.87
1982	A. Cripps (Co Coventry)	4:19.48
1983	S. Hardcastle (Redbridge B)	4:15.28
1984	S. Hardcastle (Southend Synchronettes)	4:04.93
1985	S. Hardcastle (Southend Synchronettes)	4:09.25
1986	L. Matthews (Redbridge B)	4:27.49
1987	M. Ivison (Bo S Tyneside)	4:22.74
1988	M. George (Bo Waltham Forest)	4:22.40

880 Yards Freestyle

1972	J. Green (Walsall)	9:40.50
1974	J. Atkinson (Millfield)	9:20.80
1975	J. Atkinson (Millfield)	9:23.30
1976	L. Heggie (Warrington Warriors)	9:17.60

800 Metres Freestyle

1971	J. Green (Walsall)	10:05.10
1973	J. Green (Walsall)	9:22.80
1977	S. Davies (Po Plymouth)	9:08.48
1978	C. Brazendale (Norbreck Castle)	9:04.77
1979	J. Willmott (Southend & Leigh)	8:50.90
1980	J. Willmott (Southend & Leigh)	8:45.54
1981	J. Willmott (Southend on Sea)	8:45.88
1982	A. Cripps (Co Coventry)	8:51.19
1983	S. Hardcastle (Redbridge B)	8:43.96
1984	S. Hardcastle (Southend Synchronettes)	8:29.01
1985	S. Hardcastle (Southend Synchronettes)	8:31.67
1986	L. Matthews (Redbridge B)	9:05.67
1987	P. Howard (Co Manchester)	8:57.90
1988	G. Cook (Bo Kirklees)	8:55.85

110 Yards Backstroke

1972	M. Kelly (Everton)	1:11.70
1974	M. Crook (Co Southampton)	1:09.00
1975	B. Roughley (Swinton)	1:09.00
1976	J. Beasley (Junction Ten)	1:06.80

100 Metres Backstroke

1971	D. Ashton (Wythenshawe)	1:11.50
1973	M. Crook (Co Southampton)	1:10.70
1977	J. Beasley (Junction Ten)	1:06.92
1978	J. Beasley (Junction Ten)	1:06.62
1979	H. Jameson (Kelly College)	1:05.05

1980	A. Mason (Wigan Wasps)	1:06.45
1981	A. Mason (Wigan Wasps)	1:06.19
1982	M. Wheeler (Fleetwood & D)	1:07.46
1983	S. Purvis (Stockton Aquatics)	1:06.03
1984	M. Wheeler (Fleetwood & D)	1:05.05
1985	K. Read (Stockport Metro)	1:05.08
1986	H. Slatter (Kelly College)	1:05.93
1987	T. Atkin (Co Lincoln Pentaqua)	1:05.58
1988	J. Deakins (Gloucester C)	1:04.78

220 Yards Backstroke

1972	K. Drucker (Enfield)	2:33.90
1974	M. Crook (Co Southampton)	2:26.80
1975	B. Roughley (Swinton)	2:29.40
1976	J. Beasley (Junction Ten)	2:26.30

200 Metres Backstroke

1971	G. Palmer (Leeds Central)	2:37.40
1973	M. Crook (Co Southampton)	2:31.80
1977	J. Beasley (Junction Ten)	2:21.54
1978	S. Davies (Po Plymouth)	2:21.84
1979	H. Jameson (Kelly College)	2:20.60
1980	M. Charles (Co Coventry)	2:23.46
1981	A. Horsfield (Wigan Wasps)	2:21.73
1982	K. Wilson (Co Liverpool)	2:26.29
1983	S. Purvis (Stockton Aquatics)	2:21.82
1984	K. Read (Norwich Penguins)	2:16.68
1985	K. Read (Stockport Metro)	2:15.19
1986	J. Wood (Nova Centurion)	2:19.77
1987	T. Atkin (Co Lincoln Pentaqua)	2:20.85
1988	J. Deakins (Gloucester C)	2:18.28

110 Yards Breaststroke

1972	H. Cox (Co Southampton)	1:20.30
1974	N. Fletcher (Sheffield)	1:19.70
1975	A. Adams (Co Cardiff)	1:18.20
1976	C. Guy (Weston super Mare)	1:16.80

100 Metres Breaststroke

1971	D. Walker (Thistle)	1:19.80
1973	S. Dickie (Paisley)	1:18.40
1977	C. Mason (Wigan Wasps)	1:17.89
1978	M. Campbell (Cumbernauld)	1:14.99
1979	M. Campbell (Cumbernauld)	1:14.26
1980	G. Stanley (Co Manchester)	1:12.76
1981	S. Brownsdon (RTW Monson)	1:11.17
1982	G. Stanley (Wigan Wasps)	1:12.35
1983	C. Brock (Millfield)	1:12.66
1984	C. Brock (Millfield)	1:13.61
1985	Z. Long (Kelly College)	1:14.87
1986	J. Wood (Nova Centurion)	1:13.37
1987	H. Frank (Co Leeds)	1:12.47
1988	H. Alder (Harrow & Wealdstone)	1:13.11

220 Yards Breaststroke

1972	C. Gaskell (Rochdale)	2:53.40
1974	A. Dickie (Paisley)	2:46.70
1975	D. Rudd (Orion)	2:52.30
1976	A. Adams (Co Cardiff)	2:47.20

200 Metres Breaststroke

1971	P. Wilson (Warrender)	2:53.40
1973	H. Cox (Co Southampton)	2:48.90
1977	C. Mason (Wigan Wasps)	2:45.60
1978	M. Campbell (Cumbernauld)	2:39.74
1979	G. Stanley (Co Manchester)	2:36.96
1980	G. Stanley (Co Manchester)	2:35.64
1981	S. Brownsdon (RTW Monson)	2:32.68
1982	G. Stanley (Wigan Wasps)	2:32.16
1983	L. Tate (Co Leeds)	2:35.42

1984 Z. Long (Beckenham)	2:39.29
1985 J. Wood (Nova Centurion)	2:34.93
1986 J. Wood (Nova Centurion)	2:36.24
1987 S. Smart (Co Chester)	2:38.37
1988 J. Farnsworth (Co Leeds)	2:40.24

110 Yards Butterfly

1972 J. Jeavons (Melton Mowbray)	1:08.90
1974 J. Atkinson (Millfield)	1:06.70
1975 J. Atkinson (Millfield)	1:06.50
1976 S. Jenner (Mermaid & Marlin)	1:05.40

100 Metres Butterfly

1971 J. Machin (Gloucester C)	1:10.40
1973 J. Atkinson (Darlington)	1:08.00
1977 K. Archer (Chelsea & Kensington)	1:06.34
1978 S. Davies (Po Plymouth)	1:05.31
1979 A. Osgerby (Wigan Wasps)	1:03.29
1980 L. Purchon (Leeds Central)	1:04.76
1981 L. Criddle (Millfield)	1:03.51
1982 L. Criddle (Millfield)	1:01.43
1983 S. Purvis (Stockton Aquatics)	1:02.67
1984 M. Wheeler (Fleetwood & D)	1:03.86
1985 L. Wilson (Bo S Tyneside)	1:04.30
1986 Z. Long (Kelly College)	1:03.65
1987 J. Lancaster (Warrington Warriors)	1:04.08
1988 N. Bates (Norwich Penguins)	1:04.84

220 Yards Butterfly

1972 J. Machin (Gloucester C)	2:29.90
1974 J. Atkinson (Millfield)	2:26.30
1975 J. Atkinson (Millfield)	2:24.10
1976 S. Jenner (Mermaid & Marlin)	2:20.70

200 Metres Butterfly

1971 A. Willington (Warley)	2:39.30
1973 J. Atkinson (Darlington)	2:26.60
1977 K. Archer (Chelsea & Kensington)	2:28.25
1978 H. Boxall (COSACSS)	2:21.18
1979 A. Osgerby (Wigan Wasps)	2:16.63
1980 S. Kerswell (Camden Swiss Cottage)	2:19.06
1981 L. Criddle (Millfield)	2:16.79
1982 L. Criddle (Millfield)	2:15.07
1983 S. Purvis (Stockton Aquatics)	2:15.09
1984 H. Bewley (Millfield)	2:16.18
1985 M. O'Fee (Wigan Wasps)	2:17.33
1986 M. O'Fee (Wigan Wasps)	2:16.18
1987 T. Atkin (Co Lincoln Pentaqua)	2:17.80
1988 H. Jepson (Bo Kirklees)	2:16.18

146⅔ Yards Individual Medley

1972 D. Banks (Chelmsford)	1:38.60
1975 A. Adams (Co Cardiff)	1:34.90
1976 A. Adams (Co Cardiff)	1:31.70

133⅓ Metres Individual Medley

1971 D. Banks (Chelmsford)	1:39.00
1973 H. Andrew (Bristol Central)	1:40.60
1977 S. Davies (Po Plymouth)	1:34.10
1978 S. Davies (Po Plymouth)	1:31.68

220 Yards Individual Medley

1974 D. Simpson (NCR Dundee)	2:31.10

200 Metres Individual Medley

1979 S. Cooper (Harrow & Wealdstone)	2:23.09
1980 S. Kerswell (Camden Swiss Cottage)	2:22.68
1981 S. Brownsdon (RTW Monson)	2:20.17
1982 G. Stanley (Wigan Wasps)	2:24.65
1983 S. Bowman (Darlington Diana)	2:21.36
1984 S. Hardcastle (Southend Synchronettes)	2:20.68
1985 Z. Long (Kelly College)	2:19.54
1986 Z. Long (Kelly College)	2:18.47
1987 S. Smart (Co Chester)	2:20.15
1988 H. Osborne (Co Birmingham)	2:23.33

440 Yards Individual Medley

1972 A. Willington (Warley)	5:28.10
1974 A. Dickie (Paisley)	5:20.70
1975 A. Adams (Co Cardiff)	5:13.10
1976 S. Barnard (Co Cardiff)	5:07.10

400 Metres Individual Medley

1971 D. Walker (Thistle)	5:31.90
1973 D. Johns (Po Plymouth)	5:33.50
1977 S. Davies (Po Plymouth)	5:02.52
1978 S. Davies (Po Plymouth)	5:01.75
1979 M. Charles (Co Coventry)	5:02.84
1980 S. Kerswell (Camden Swiss Cottage)	4:53.36
1981 S. Kerswell (Camden Swiss Cottage)	4:52.31
1982 S. Hardcastle (Southend on Sea)	5:09.54
1983 S. Hardcastle (Redbridge B)	4:53.04
1984 S. Hardcastle (Southend Synchronettes)	4:45.84
1985 S. Hardcastle (Southend Synchronettes)	4:48.35
1986 Z. Long (Kelly College)	4:55.40
1987 S. Smart (Co Chester)	4:55.33
1988 H. Osborne (Co Birmingham)	5:06.81

Junior ASA (Long Course) Champions, 1947–1987

Note: The championships were discontinued after 1987. Competitors were under 17 on 31 December during the championship year.

Junior Men

50 Metres Freestyle

1987 J. Lukeman (Canada)	25.12

100 Yards Freestyle

1947 T. Miller (Plaistow U)	58.60
1948 J. Wardrop (Motherwell)	57.40
1949 T. Welsh (Galashiels)	58.40
1950 R. Drew (Bristol Central)	57.60
1951 J. Whitehead (Leigh)	57.70
1952 B. Lord (Lowermoor)	55.00

110 Yards Freestyle

1953 W. Chapman (Eccles)	1:03.20
1954 G. Baxter (Gloucester C)	1:00.00
1955 K. Wallwork (Swinton & Pendlebury)	1:01.50
1956 P. Kendrew (York C)	1:00.60
1957 I. Black (Gordon's College)	1:00.00
1958 C. Hansard (Swansea)	1:01.40
1959 C. Hansard (Swansea)	1:00.50
1960 P. Hammond (English Steel)	59.00
1961 P. Sillett (Radcliffe)	59.60

1962	D. Watts (Barracuda)	59.00
1963	S. Brambley (Co Southampton)	59.60
1964	M. Turner (Stockport)	59.40
1965	L. Norris (Barracuda)	1:00.80
1966	M. Windeatt (Torquay Leander)	59.00
1967	M. Windeatt (Torquay Leander)	57.90
1968	M. Windeatt (Torquay Leander)	57.10
1969	R. Terrell (Co Southampton)	57.70
1970	M. Shore (Inverness)	57.10

100 Metres Freestyle

| 1987 | M. Levine (Rotherham Metro) | 54.84 |

220 Yards Freestyle

1952	B. Lord (Lowermoor)	2:24.50
1953	B. Jackson (Southport)	2:26.40
1954	N. McKechnie (Wallasey)	2:20.20
1955	K. Wallwork	
	(Swinton & Pendlebury)	2:19.10
1956	I. Black (Gordon's College)	2:19.20
1957	I. Black (Gordon's College)	2:10.00
1958	A. Galbraith (Carlisle Secondary)	2:18.80
1959	P. Hammond (English Steel)	2:16.90
1960	P. Hammond (English Steel)	2:14.90
1961	R. Lord (Co Coventry)	2:14.70
1962	H. Edwards (St James)	2:13.40
1963	K. Bewley (Bootle)	2:15.20
1964	M. Turner (Stockport)	2:11.70
1965	J. Andrews (Chelsea & Kensington)	2:15.80
1966	M. Windeatt (Torquay Leander)	2:10.20
1967	M. Windeatt (Torquay Leander)	2:08.70
1968	R. van Hamburg (Everton)	2:07.30
1969	R. Terrell (Co Southampton)	2:04.80
1970	M. Shore (Inverness)	2:07.10

200 Metres Freestyle

| 1987 | R. Tozer (Millfield) | 1:59.69 |

400 Metres Freestyle

| 1987 | S. Akers (Shiverers) | 4:07.73 |

1500 Metres Freestyle

| 1987 | S. Akers (Shiverers) | 16:04.41 |

100 Yards Backstroke

1947	R. Wardrop (Motherwell)	1:09.00
1948	R. Wardrop (Motherwell)	1:07.20
1949	A. Gurr (E Ham)	1:07.50
1950	J. Luke (Renfrew Aqua)	1:06.10
1951	A. McTreen (Heath Town)	1:06.50
1952	H. Rigby (Southport)	
	D. Andrews (York C)	1:03.80

110 Yards Backstroke

1953	D. Davies (Bristol Central)	1:14.60
1954	M. Peacock (Sutton & Cheam)	1:11.90
1955	B. Bulmer (York C)	1:11.10
1956	P. Kendrew (York C)	1:11.90
1957	A. Turner (Sheffield C)	1:11.60
1958	A. Galletly (Perth Pullars)	1:11.70
1959	R. Thomas (Bristol C)	1:10.60
1960	R. Jones (Newport)	1:09.20
1961	J. Burt (Southall)	1:09.20
1962	G. Smart (Carnegie)	1:06.60
1963	G. Thwaites (Darlington)	1:06.50
1964	N. Downie (Zenith)	1:08.20
1965	A. Davison (Newcastle under Lyme)	1:07.90
1966	A. Davison (Newcastle under Lyme)	1:04.50
1967	R. Terrell (Co Southampton)	1:06.40
1968	R. Terrell (Co Southampton)	1:05.30

Malcolm Windeatt

1969 R. Terrell (Co Southampton)	1:05.30
1970 J. Scott (Stoke Newington)	1:05.80

100 Metres Backstroke
1987 M. O'Connor (Co Manchester)	1:00.97

200 Metres Backstroke
1987 M. O'Connor (Co Manchester)	2:10.34

100 Yards Breaststroke
1947 R. Thomson (Motherwell)	1:13.00
1948 R. Thomson (Motherwell)	1:14.20
1949 J. Bailey (E Ham)	1:10.50
1950 D. Williamson (Sunderland)	1:13.50
1951 P. Alp (Hounslow B)	1:11.80
1952 T. Holborn (Birkenhead)	1:06.60

110 Yards Breaststroke
1953 H. Smith (Paisley)	1:21.00
1954 A. Longega (Sutton & Cheam)	1:18.10
1955 R. Manning (Sunderland)	1:21.30
1956 R. Manning (Sunderland)	1:20.80
1957 H. Bentham (Trafford Park)	1:21.10
1958 G. Hill (Nottingham Portland)	1:19.70
1959 C. Wilkinson (Stockport)	1:18.20
1960 J. Faben (Southall)	1:19.80
1961 A. Abrey (Isleworth Penguins)	1:18.00
1962 M. Tucker (Southall)	1:16.80
1963 R. Roberts (Stoke Newington)	1:16.00
1964 R. Roberts (Stoke Newington)	1:13.90
1965 D. Marshall (Co Southampton)	1:16.40
1966 W. Price (Hornchurch)	1:16.00
1967 I. Gatward (Aldershot Garrison)	1:18.50
1968 D. Batten (Camden Swiss Cottage)	1:16.30
1969 M. Carty (Stoke Newington)	1:13.80
1970 M. O'Connell (Co Southampton)	1:12.60

100 Metres Breaststroke
1987 I. McKenzie (Braintree & Bocking)	1:06.53

200 Metres Breaststroke
1987 C. Thompson (Co Bradford)	2:32.63

110 Yards Butterfly
1955 G. Bowker (Hyde Seal)	1:15.10
1956 I. Black (Gordon's College)	1:10.30
1957 I. Black (Gordon's College)	1:06.00
1958 I. Blyth (Whitehall)	1:08.20
1959 T. Glenville (Hull Olympic)	1:08.30
1960 I. Williams (Dewsbury)	1:07.90
1961 P. Sillett (Radcliffe)	1:07.20
1962 D. Watts (Barracuda)	1:05.00
1963 E. Hodgson (Huddersfield B)	1:05.70
1964 M. Turner (Stockport)	1:04.30
1965 M. Woodroffe (Cardiff)	1:06.60
1966 L. Norris (Barracuda)	1:03.40
1967 R. Terrell (Co Southampton)	1:04.40
1968 J. Mills (St James)	1:03.00
1969 J. Mills (St James)	1:00.80
1970 S. Maher (Newport)	1:02.30

100 Metres Butterfly
1987 S. Dronsfield (Salford Triple 'S')	59.86

200 Metres Butterfly
1987 S. Wainwright (Millfield)	2:13.62

220 Yards Individual Medley
1967 R. Terrell (Co Southampton)	2:23.50
1968 R. Terrell (Co Southampton)	2:21.30
1969 R. Terrell (Co Southampton)	2:23.90
1970 S. Maher (Newport)	2:22.80

200 Metres Individual Medley
1987 T. Evans (Oundle & D)	2:15.26

400 Metres Individual Medley
1987 M. O'Connor (Co Manchester)	4:46.24

Junior Women

50 Metres Freestyle
1987 A. Kindon (Co Birmingham)	27.70

100 Yards Freestyle
1947 M. Girvan (Motherwell)	1:06.50
1948 D. Wilkinson (Sparkhill)	1:10.20
1949 A. Douglas (Knighton Fields)	1:06.20
1950 J. Botham (S Manchester)	1:05.60
1951 A. Barnwell (Worthing)	1:02.80
1952 F. Ewart (Hastings & St Leonards)	1:04.00

110 Yards Freestyle
1953 F. Hogben (St Thomas)	1:12.50
1954 M. Spooner (Holbeck)	1:11.40
1955 C. Barry (Stoke Newington)	1:10.50
1956 S. Grant (Canada)	1:09.40
1957 D. Wilkinson (Stockport)	1:06.60
1958 D. Wilkinson (Stockport)	1:05.60
1959 M. Toms (Beckenham)	1:06.80
1960 P. Best (Mermaid)	1:06.20
1961 E. Long (Ilford)	1:06.50
1962 L. Amos (Northsea)	1:03.60
1963 S. Keen (Heston)	1:05.50
1964 P. Sillett (Radcliffe)	1:04.40
1965 K. Muir (S Africa)	1:05.90
1966 S. Ratcliffe (Everton)	1:05.40
1967 A. Jackson (Peel)	1:03.30
1968 A. Jackson (Peel)	1:01.10
1969 D. Sutherland (Cheam)	1:04.40
1970 C. Whiting (New Zealand)	1:03.80

100 Metres Freestyle
1987 K. Pickering (Shiverers)	58.97

220 Yards Freestyle
1952 V. Nares-Pillow (Surrey Ladies)	2:41.10
1953 F. Hogben (St Thomas)	2:44.00
1954 B. Kingston (Heston)	2:44.40
1955 C. Barry (Stoke Newington)	2:38.20
1956 S. Grant (Canada)	2:37.30
1957 D. Wilkinson (Stockport)	2:28.60
1958 D. Wilkinson (Stockport)	2:26.40
1959 J. Samuel (Surrey Ladies)	2:25.90
1960 E. Long (Ilford)	2:24.50
1961 E. Long (Ilford)	2:24.30
1962 E. Long (Ilford)	2:20.60
1963 P. Sillett (Radcliffe)	2:28.60
1964 J. Bradford (Gateshead)	2:28.10
1965 K. Muir (S Africa)	2:23.80
1966 S. Williams (Co Exeter)	2:21.40
1967 S. Williams (Co Exeter)	2:19.90
S. Ratcliffe (Everton)	
1968 A. Jackson (Peel)	2:17.90
1969 D. Gurr (Canada)	2:18.10
1970 L. Allardice (Hornchurch)	2:18.60

200 Metres Freestyle
1987 M. Ivison (Bo S Tyneside)	2:08.45

400 Metres Freestyle
1987 P. Howard (Co Manchester)	4:22.83

800 Metres Freestyle
1987 P. Howard (Co Manchester)	8:58.77

183

100 Yards Backstroke

1947	M. Girvan (Motherwell)	1:12.60
1948	M. Girvan (Motherwell)	1:14.40
1949	R. Markland (Kingston)	1:10.80
1950	M. McDowall (Kilmarnock)	1:10.50
1951	M. McDowall (Kilmarnock)	1:08.80
1952	P. Musgrove (York C)	1:09.60

110 Yards Backstroke

1953	S. Tolton (Worthing)	1:17.50
1954	J. Tiso (Sparkhill)	1:16.80
1955	J. Tiso (Sparkhill)	1:15.90
1956	V. Christie (Hampstead)	1:19.10
1957	J. Edwards (Bristol Central)	1:19.10
1958	B. Tyrer (Mermaid)	1:17.00
1959	C. Hussey (Nottingham)	1:16.00
1960	S. Probert (Bristol Central)	1:15.50
1961	C. Dunn (York C)	1:14.90
1962	L. Ludgrove (St James)	1:10.90
1963	L. Ludgrove (St James)	1:12.00
1964	J. Franklin (Taunton)	1:11.00
1965	K. Muir (S Africa)	1:08.90
1966	W. Burrell (Carlisle Secondary)	1:14.30
1967	M. Browning (S Manchester)	1:11.20
1968	W. Burrell (Carlisle Secondary)	1:10.80
1969	D. Gurr (Canada)	1:09.80
1970	D. Sutherland (Cheam)	1:11.70

100 Metres Backstroke

1987	S. Page (Stockport Metro)	1:07.35

200 Metres Backstroke

1987	T. Atkin (Co Lincoln Pentaqua)	2:23.26

100 Yards Breaststroke

1947	E. Gordon (Hamilton)	1:21.40
1948	E. Gordon (Hamilton)	1:23.20
1949	E. Gordon (Hamilton)	1:18.00
1950	J. Wrigley (Lowermoor)	1:19.20
1951	J. Wrigley (Lowermoor)	1:19.10
1952	B. Harvey (Leander)	1:18.00

110 Yards Breaststroke

1953	D. Taylor (Ilford)	1:27.80
1954	M. Grundy (Blackpool)	1:26.80
1955	C. Gosden (Croydon)	1:29.40
1956	P. Powley (Bournemouth)	1:28.20
1957	J. Dyson (Kingston)	1:26.10
1958	J. Dyson (Kingston)	1:25.30
1959	C. Barber (Heston)	1:24.80
1960	S. Hills (Sans Egal)	1:24.50

1961	D. Fraser (Gateshead)	1:23.80
1962	D. Fraser (Gateshead)	1:21.50
1963	S. Mitchell (Hampstead)	1:21.00
1964	D. Harris (Beckenham)	1:20.70
1965	S. Churms (Northampton)	1:23.40
1966	A. Radnage (York C)	1:21.60
1967	J. Bevan (Newport)	1:22.00
1968	L. Dunn (Sheffield)	1:22.30
1969	L. Dunn (Sheffield)	1:20.40
1970	P. Wilson (Warrender)	1:21.80

100 Metres Breaststroke

1987	H. Frank (Co Leeds)	1:14.97

200 Metres Breaststroke

1987	H. Frank (Co Leeds)	2:39.75

110 Yards Butterfly

1955	C. Gosden (Croydon)	1:24.60
1956	S. Grant (Canada)	1:23.40
1957	J. Dyson (Kingston)	1:22.40
1958	J. Oldroyd (Dewsbury)	1:16.00
1959	P. Baines (Ilford)	1:17.60
1960	P. Baines (Ilford)	1:14.20
1961	M. Cotterill (Watford)	1:15.70
1962	D. Akers (Holloway)	1:14.60
1963	J. Price (Worsley)	1:14.80
1964	J. Price (Worsley)	1:15.00
1965	M. Fluxman (S Africa)	1:12.80
1966	M. Auton (W Hartlepool)	1:12.20
1967	J. Burke (Stretford)	1:12.80
1968	M. Weymouth (Hampstead)	1:10.50
1969	A. Pepe (Canada)	1:10.30
1970	C. Whiting (New Zealand)	1:09.00

100 Metres Butterfly

1987	T. Atkin (Co Lincoln Pentaqua)	1:05.45

200 Metres Butterfly

1987	N. Atkinson (Stockport Metro)	2:20.05

220 Yards Individual Medley

1967	S. Ratcliffe (Everton)	2:35.50
1968	S. Ratcliffe (Everton)	2:33.70
1969	D. Gurr (Canada)	2:33.80
1970	G. Hunter (New Zealand)	2:35.00

200 Metres Individual Medley

1987	T. Atkin (Co Lincoln Pentaqua)	2:24.77

400 Metres Individual Medley

1987	T. Atkin (Co Lincoln Pentaqua)	4:59.08

ASA Winter (Short Course) Champions, 1971–1988

Men

50 Metres Freestyle

1985	R. Lee (Co Cardiff)	23.37
1986	M. Foster (Millfield)	23.41
1987	M. Foster (Bo Southend)	22.88
1988	M. Fibbens (Barnet Copthall)	23.31

110 Yards Freestyle

1972	M. Windeatt (Torquay Leander)	54.60
1974	B. Brinkley (Modernians)	53.80
1975	B. Brinkley (Modernians)	53.60
1976	R. Iredale (Co Cardiff)	54.40

100 Metres Freestyle

1971	M. Bailey (Hull)	55.50
1973	M. Windeatt (Torquay Leander)	53.90
1977	D. Dunne (Beckenham)	54.39
1978	R. Burrell (Co Southampton)	53.18
1979	D. Dunne (Beckenham)	51.37
1980	S. Volery (Co Cardiff)	52.06
1981	M. Taylor (Co Cardiff)	51.40
1982	N. Goldsworthy (Camden Swiss Cottage)	51.20
1983	D. Lowe (Harrow & Wealdstone)	49.86
1984	D. Lowe (Harrow & Wealdstone)	50.78
1985	R. Lee (Co Cardiff)	51.38
1986	M. Foster (Millfield)	50.81
1987	M. Fibbens (Beckenham)	49.90
1988	M. Fibbens (Barnet Copthall)	50.64

220 Yards Freestyle
1972	B. Brinkley (Modernians)	2:00.10
1974	B. Brinkley (Modernians)	1:54.70
1975	B. Brinkley (Modernians)	1:56.40
1976	B. Brinkley (Modernians)	1:55.60

200 Metres Freestyle
1971	B. Brinkley (Modernians)	2:02.50
1973	B. Brinkley (Modernians)	1:56.90
1977	A. McClatchey (Warrender)	1:56.83
1978	C. Dale (Beckenham)	1:56.88
1979	A. Astbury (Leeds Central)	1:51.20
1980	D. Dunne (Beckenham)	1:53.27
1981	M. Taylor (Co Cardiff)	1:51.71
1982	P. Hubble (Hounslow B)	1:50.95
1983	P. Easter (Co Coventry)	1:50.54
1984	D. Lowe (Harrow & Wealdstone)	1:52.15
1985	P. Howe (Millfield)	1:50.65
1986	P. Easter (Co Swansea)	1:52.23
1987	M. Fibbens (Beckenham)	1:50.41
1988	D. Rolley (Swansea University)	1:50.07

440 Yards Freestyle
1972	B. Brinkley (Modernians)	4:16.20
1974	B. Brinkley (Modernians)	4:02.90
1975	B. Brinkley (Modernians)	4:10.80
1976	B. Brinkley (Modernians)	4:06.00

400 Metres Freestyle
1971	B. Brinkley (Modernians)	4:20.10
1973	B. Brinkley (Modernians)	4:09.20
1977	D. Parker (Co Coventry)	4:05.75
1978	A. Astbury (Leeds Central)	4:06.00
1979	A. Astbury (Leeds Central)	3:53.31
1980	S. Poulter (Wigan Wasps)	3:58.42
1981	J. Davey (Co Manchester)	3:56.16
1982	S. Harris (Co Manchester)	3:54.59
1983	P. Easter (Co Coventry)	3:51.27
1984	S. Willmott (Stockton Aquatics)	3:56.85
1985	P. Howe (Millfield)	3:53.87
1986	K. Boyd (Bo S Tyneside)	3:55.51
1987	K. Boyd (Bo S Tyneside)	3:52.19
1988	D. Rolley (Swansea University)	3:53.24

1650 Yards Freestyle
1972	R. Terrell (Co Southampton)	17:18.40
1974	D. Smith (Co Coventry)	16:50.90
1975	D. Parker (Co Coventry)	16:40.50
1976	D. Parker (Co Coventry)	16:07.70

1500 Metres Freestyle
1971	A. Devlin (Warrender)	17:40.90
1973	B. Brinkley (Modernians)	16:37.30
1977	D. Parker (Co Coventry)	15:51.00
1978	P. Sparkes (Merton Swordfish)	15:58.53
1979	A. Astbury (Leeds Central)	15:30.13
1980	S. Lewington (Co Coventry)	15:29.69
1981	P. Easter (Norwich Penguins)	15:38.25
1982	P. Easter (Co Coventry)	15:32.82
1983	D. Stacey (Co Coventry)	15:35.61
1984	T. Day (Co Leeds)	15:37.87
1985	T. Day (Co Leeds)	15:34.52
1986	T. Day (Co Leeds)	15:33.56
1987	T. Day (Co Leeds)	15:12.98
1988	I. Wilson (Bo Sunderland)	15:27.23

110 Yards Backstroke
1972	M. Richards (Nottingham Northern)	1:01.10
1974	C. Cunningham (Ilford)	1:00.20
1975	S. Bunce (Co Cardiff)	1:01.00
1976	S. Bunce (Co Cardiff)	1:00.80

100 Metres Backstroke
1971	M. Richards (Nottingham Northern)	1:00.70
1973	C. Cunningham (Co Southampton)	1:00.70
1977	S. Harrison (Co Southampton)	1:00.97
1978	S. Harrison (Co Southampton)	59.88
1979	P. Marshall (NCR Dundee)	59.37
1980	P. Marshall (Beckenham)	58.66
1981	G. Abraham (Co Southampton)	58.17
1982	A. Jameson (Kelly College)	57.94
1983	N. Harper (Millfield)	57.80
1984	S. Harrison (Co Southampton)	58.15
1985	K. Boyd (Bo S Tyneside)	58.68
1986	K. Boyd (Bo S Tyneside)	59.54
1987	M. Peyrebrune (Warrender)	58.35
1988	G. Robins (Portsmouth Northsea)	58.04

220 Yards Backstroke
1972	C. Cunningham (Co Southampton)	2:13.50
1974	C. Cunningham (Ilford)	2:10.60
1975	P. Lerpiniere (Millfield)	2:12.60
1976	P. Lerpiniere (Millfield)	2:10.10

200 Metres Backstroke
1971	M. Richards (Nottingham Northern)	2:14.20
1973	C. Cunningham (Co Southampton)	2:11.40
1977	M. Sloper (Reading)	2:11.49
1978	R. Waller (Edmonton)	2:10.85
1979	P. Marshall (NCR Dundee)	2:07.76
1980	D. Cummins (Kelly College)	2:07.22
1981	J. Davey (Co Manchester)	2:09.23
1982	J. Davey (Co Milton Keynes)	2:05.81
1983	N. Cochran (Aberdeen)	2:05.65
1984	K. Boyd (Hull Olympic)	2:03.70
1985	K. Boyd (Bo S Tyneside)	2:04.32
1986	K. Boyd (Bo S Tyneside)	2:06.57
1987	G. Robins (Portsmouth Northsea)	2:04.78
1988	G. Robins (Portsmouth Northsea)	2:02.04

110 Yards Breaststroke
1972	M. O'Connell (Co Southampton)	1:09.10
1974	D. Leigh (Oak Street)	1:07.00
1975	D. Leigh (Oak Street)	1:06.70
1976	D. Leigh (Co Cardiff)	1:06.80

100 Metres Breaststroke
1971	D. Wilkie (Warrender)	1:09.80
1973	M. O'Connell (Co Southampton)	1:08.50
1977	L. Atkinson (Co Cardiff)	1:07.75
1978	L. Atkinson (Co Cardiff)	1:06.75
1979	L. Atkinson (Co Cardiff)	1:06.79
1980	D. Goodhew (Beckenham)	1:02.78
1981	A. Moorhouse (Leeds Central)	1:03.41
1982	A. Moorhouse (Leeds Central)	1:02.77
1983	F. August (Beckenham)	1:05.36
1984	A. Moorhouse (Co Leeds)	1:02.17
1985	A. Moorhouse (Co Leeds)	1:00.58
1986	A. Moorhouse (Co Leeds)	1:01.45
1987	I. Campbell (Beckenham)	1:02.32
1988	N. Gillingham (Co Birmingham)	1:02.73

220 Yards Breaststroke
1972	D. Wilkie (Warrender)	2:31.60
1974	D. Leigh (Oak Street)	2:24.30
1975	D. Leigh (Oak Street)	2:28.60
1976	D. Leigh (Co Cardiff)	2:25.70

200 Metres Breaststroke
1971	D. Wilkie (Warrender)	2:33.50
1973	B. O'Brian (Coventry Three Spires)	2:32.85
1977	L. Atkinson (Co Cardiff)	2:27.11
1978	L. Atkinson (Co Cardiff)	2:21.64

1979	L. Atkinson (Co Cardiff)	2:22.19
1980	D. Goodhew (Beckenham)	2:16.88
1981	A. Moorhouse (Leeds Central)	2:18.59
1982	A. Moorhouse (Leeds Central)	2:18.22
1983	K. Adkins (Co Cardiff)	2:18.56
1984	A. Moorhouse (Co Leeds)	2:17.09
1985	A. Moorhouse (Co Leeds)	2:14.35
1986	A. Moorhouse (Co Leeds)	2:15.13
1987	I. Campbell (Beckenham)	2:15.11
1988	N. Gillingham (Co Birmingham)	2:16.30

110 Yards Butterfly

1972	J. Mills (St James)	1:00.30
1974	C. Cunningham (Ilford)	58.90
1975	B. Brinkley (Modernians)	58.10
1976	S. Nash (Co Cardiff)	57.70

100 Metres Butterfly

1971	M. Bailey (Hull)	1:00.40
1973	M. Edwards (Camp Hill Edwardians)	58.90
1977	M. Thorne (Co Coventry)	58.18
1978	P. Hubble (Reading)	57.69
1979	J. Mills (Beckenham)	57.83
1980	M. Taylor (Co Cardiff)	57.19
1981	G. Abraham (Co Southampton)	56.02
1982	A. Jameson (Kelly College)	56.00
1983	D. Lowe (Harrow & Wealdstone)	55.17
1984	D. Lowe (Harrow & Wealdstone)	56.17
1985	D. Williams (Fleetwood & D)	56.27
1986	T. Jones (Walsall)	57.40
1987	M. Foster (Bo Southend)	56.28
1988	R. Leishman (Kelly College)	55.38

220 Yards Butterfly

1972	J. Mills (St James)	2:09.20
1974	B. Brinkley (Modernians)	2:06.20
1975	B. Brinkley (Modernians)	2:08.00
1976	B. Brinkley (Modernians)	2:05.50

200 Metres Butterfly

1971	J. Mills (St James)	2:12.50
1973	B. Brinkley (Modernians)	2:09.60
1977	M. Thorne (Co Coventry)	2:06.80
1978	P. Hubble (Reading)	2:05.79
1979	P. Morris (Bracknell)	2:04.38
1980	P. Morris (Bracknell)	2:04.12
1981	I. Collins (Millfield)	2:02.35
1982	P. Hubble (Hounslow B)	2:01.24
1983	N. Hodgson (Wigan Wasps)	2:02.95
1984	N. Hodgson (Wigan Wasps)	2:02.39
1985	S. Poulter (Wigan Wasps)	2:01.91
1986	S. Poulter (Wigan Wasps)	2:02.54
1987	T. Jones (Co Birmingham)	2:03.47
1988	I. Wilson (Bo Sunderland)	2:02.81

146⅔ Yards Individual Medley

1972	R. Terrell (Co Southampton)	1:25.80
1975	D. Cleworth (Tyldesley)	1:27.20
1976	D. Cleworth (Tyldesley)	1:26.00

133⅓ Metres Individual Medley

1971	D. Wilkie (Warrender)	1:28.90
1973	R. Terrell (Co Southampton)	1:26.10
1977	M. Thorne (Co Coventry)	1:26.20
1978	D. Cleworth (Co Manchester)	1:24.84

220 Yards Individual Medley

1974	B. Brinkley (Modernians)	2:14.10

200 Metres Individual Medley

1979	D. Dunne (Beckenham)	2:07.31
1980	D. Cummins (Kelly College)	2:07.59

1981	J. Randall (Co Leicester)	2:07.07
1982	S. Forrest (Wigan Wasps)	2:05.97
1983	R. Brew (Wulfrunians)	2:06.67
1984	R. Brew (Kelly College)	2:02.69
1985	P. Brew (Kelly College)	2:04.65
1986	D. Rolley (Swansea University)	2:06.02
1987	P. Brew (Kelly College)	2:03.25
1988	D. Rolley (Swansea University)	2:04.37

440 Yards Individual Medley

1972	R. Terrell (Co Southampton)	4:50.70
1974	B. Prime (Modernians)	4:44.80
1975	A. McClatchey (Warrender)	4:46.40
1976	B. Prime (Modernians)	4:42.00

400 Metres Individual Medley

1971	S. Grossman (St James)	4:58.20
1973	B. Brinkley (Modernians)	4:42.20
1977	M. Thorne (Co Coventry)	4:39.67
1978	D. Cleworth (Co Manchester)	4:36.51
1979	I. Collins (Millfield)	4:33.00
1980	G. Sykes (Co Coventry)	4:31.37
1981	J. Davey (Co Manchester)	4:29.03
1982	S. Poulter (Wigan Wasps)	4:24.69
1983	P. Easter (Co Coventry)	4:25.69
1984	S. Willmott (Stockton Aquatics)	4:24.57
1985	G. Binfield (Salford Triple 'S')	4:25.17
1986	S. Poulter (Wigan Wasps)	4:24.02
1987	P. Brew (Kelly College)	4:19.83

4×100 Metres Freestyle Club Relay

1987	Co Leeds	3:26.57
1988	Co Leeds	3:25.46

4×100 Metres Medley Club Relay

1987	Co Leeds	3:48.56
1988	Co Birmingham	3:50.10

Women

50 Metres Freestyle

1985	C. Cooper (Potters Bar)	25.93
1986	N. Kennedy (Avon Neptunes)	27.05
1987	J. Croft (Wigan Wasps)	26.77
1988	C. Woodcock (Haywards Heath)	26.18

110 Yards Freestyle

1972	L. Allardice (Killerwhales)	1:02.40
1974	J. Simpson (NCR Dundee)	1:01.20
1975	D. Hill (Portsmouth Northsea)	1:01.60
1976	D. Hill (Portsmouth Northsea)	1:00.30

100 Metres Freestyle

1971	D. Sutherland (Cheam)	1:02.50
1973	J. Sirs (Hartlepool)	1:01.10
1977	C. Brazendale (Norbreck Castle)	59.97
1978	C. Brazendale (Norbreck Castle)	58.94
1979	S. Davies (Kelly College)	57.48
1980	J. Croft (Wigan Wasps)	57.70
1981	J. Croft (Wigan Wasps)	56.77
1982	J. Croft (Wigan Wasps)	55.16
1983	C. Foot (Millfield)	57.20
1984	J. Croft (Wigan Wasps)	55.98
1985	C. Cooper (Potters Bar)	55.79
1986	C. Foot (Millfield)	57.76
1987	J. Croft (Wigan Wasps)	56.72
1988	K. Pickering (Ipswich)	57.20

220 Yards Freestyle

1972	M. Brown (Woolwich)	2:14.70
1974	S. Edmondson (Hull Olympic)	2:11.20

1975	D. Walker (Thistle)	2:13.50
1976	S. Barnard (Co Cardiff)	2:08.70

200 Metres Freestyle

1971	D. Sutherland (Cheam)	2:16.30
1973	L. Allardice (Killerwhales)	2:11.70
1977	C. Brazendale (Norbreck Castle)	2:06.60
1978	S. Davies (Po Plymouth)	2:06.64
1979	S. Davies (Kelly College)	2:05.24
1980	J. Croft (Wigan Wasps)	2:03.05
1981	J. Croft (Wigan Wasps)	2:01.61
1982	J. Croft (Wigan Wasps)	1:57.15
1983	J. Willmott (Redbridge B)	2:01.84
1984	J. Croft (Wigan Wasps)	1:58.53
1985	A. Cripps (Wigan Wasps)	2:01.87
1986	S. Garrett (Beckenham)	2:04.64
1987	J. Croft (Wigan Wasps)	2:00.45
1988	M. Scarborough (Portsmouth Northsea)	2:03.78

440 Yards Freestyle

1972	J. Green (Walsall)	4:43.70
1974	S. Edmondson (Hull Olympic)	4:34.70
1975	D. Walker (Thistle)	4:35.60
1976	G. Gibson (Beckenham)	4:29.80

400 Metres Freestyle

1971	D. Sutherland (Cheam)	4:46.30
1973	J. Green (Walsall)	4:35.20
1977	S. Davies (Po Plymouth)	4:28.03
1978	S. Davies (Po Plymouth)	4:20.44
1979	S. Davies (Kelly College)	4:16.38
1980	J. Willmott (Southend on Sea)	4:12.96
1981	J. Croft (Wigan Wasps)	4:13.45
1982	J. Croft (Wigan Wasps)	4:09.02
1983	J. Willmott (Redbridge B)	4:09.24
1984	J. Croft (Wigan Wasps)	4:04.93
1985	S. Hardcastle (Southend Synchronettes)	4:09.25
1986	S. Hardcastle (Bo Southend)	4:11.08
1987	J. Croft (Wigan Wasps)	4:13.09
1988	K. Mellor (Co Sheffield)	4:18.22

880 Yards Freestyle

1972	J. Green (Walsall)	9:40.50
1974	J. Atkinson (Millfield)	9:20.80
1975	J. Atkinson (Millfield)	9:23.30
1976	G. Gibson (Beckenham)	9:14.40

800 Metres Freestyle

1971	A. Mackie (Thistle)	9:55.80
1973	J. Green (Walsall)	9:22.80
1977	S. Davies (Po Plymouth)	9:08.48
1978	C. Brazendale (Norbreck Castle)	9:04.77
1979	J. Willmott (Southend & Leigh)	8:50.90
1980	J. Willmott (Southend on Sea)	8:45.54
1981	J. Croft (Wigan Wasps)	8:44.29
1982	J. Willmott (Southend on Sea)	8:25.00
1983	J. Willmott (Redbridge B)	8:32.98
1984	J. Croft (Wigan Wasps)	8:27.78
1985	S. Hardcastle (Southend Synchronettes)	8:31.67
1986	K. Mellor (Norwich Penguins)	8:46.94
1987	K. Mellor (Norwich Penguins)	8:37.17
1988	K. Mellor (Co Sheffield)	8:42.73

110 Yards Backstroke

1972	P. Bairstow (Huddersfield)	1:10.70
1974	M. Kelly (Everton)	1:08.00
1975	B. Roughley (Swinton)	1:09.00
1976	J. Beasley (Junction Ten)	1:06.80

100 Metres Backstroke

1971	J. Brown (Hull)	1:10.10
1973	M. Kelly (Everton)	1:09.70
1977	J. Beasley (Junction Ten)	1:06.92
1978	J. Beasley (Junction Ten)	1:06.62
1979	H. Jameson (Kelly College)	1:05.05
1980	H. Jameson (Kelly College)	1:05.62
1981	H. Jameson (Kelly College)	1:05.55
1982	H. Jameson (Kelly College)	1:04.24
1983	C. White (Bo S Tyneside)	1:03.68
1984	C. White (Bo S Tyneside)	1:03.58
1985	C. White (Co Leeds)	1:03.37
1986	K. Read (Stockport Metro)	1:04.83
1987	H. Slatter (Kelly College)	1:04.85
1988	K. Read (Norwich Penguins)	1:04.65

220 Yards Backstroke

1972	P. Bairstow (Huddersfield)	2:30.40
1974	M. Kelly (Everton)	2:26.20
1975	B. Roughley (Swinton)	2:29.40
1976	J. Beasley (Junction Ten)	2:26.30

200 Metres Backstroke

1971	W. Burrell (Carlisle)	2:31.20
1973	D. Ashton (Wythenshawe)	2:28.80
1977	J. Beasley (Junction Ten)	2:21.54
1978	S. Davies (Po Plymouth)	2:21.84
1979	J. Admans (Slough Dolphins)	2:18.45
1980	J. Admans (Slough Dolphins)	2:17.56
1981	J. Admans (Slough Dolphins)	2:18.57
1982	H. Jameson (Kelly College)	2:16.31
1983	C. White (Bo S Tyneside)	2:15.16
1984	C. White (Bo S Tyneside)	2:14.98
1985	K. Read (Stockport Metro)	2:15.19
1986	K. Read (Stockport Metro)	2:16.70
1987	H. Slatter (Kelly College)	2:16.37
1988	K. Read (Norwich Penguins)	2:17.60

110 Yards Breaststroke

1972	C. Jarvis (Modernians)	1:17.90
1974	C. Gaskell (Rochdale)	1:15.60
1975	H. Burnham (Beckenham)	1:17.60
1976	M. Kelly (Co Cardiff)	1:14.20

100 Metres Breaststroke

1971	D. Harrison (Hartlepool)	1:16.80
1973	C. Jarvis (Modernians)	1:17.50
1977	M. Kelly (Cumbernauld)	1:14.80
1978	M. Kelly (Beckenham)	1:12.56
1979	M. Kelly (Beckenham)	1:11.24
1980	M. Kelly (Beckenham)	1:10.13
1981	S. Brownsdon (RTW Monson)	1:11.17
1982	S. Brownsdon (RTW Monson)	1:11.14
1983	L. Burt (Reading)	1:12.31
1984	J. Hill (Larkhall & Avondale)	1:11.38
1985	S. Bowman (Darlington)	1:11.77
1986	J. Wood (Nova Centurion)	1:13.37
1987	M. Hohmann (Wigan Wasps)	1:10.69
1988	L. Coombes (Co Southampton)	1:12.05

220 Yards Breaststroke

1972	P. Beavan (Kingsbury)	2:49.10
1974	C. Gaskell (Rochdale)	2:43.30
1975	H. Burnham (Beckenham)	2:47.40
1976	M. Kelly (Co Cardiff)	2:39.50

200 Metres Breaststroke

1971	D. Harrison (Hartlepool)	2:49.00
1973	C. Tamlyn (Beckenham)	2:45.30
1977	D. Rudd (Co Coventry)	2:38.41
1978	M. Campbell (Cumbernauld)	2:39.74

1979	M. Kelly (Beckenham)	2:34.49
1980	M. Kelly (Beckenham)	2:32.92
1981	S. Brownsdon (RTW Monson)	2:32.68
1982	G. Stanley (Wigan Wasps)	2:32.16
1983	L. Burt (Reading)	2:34.55
1984	J. Seymour (Camp Hill Edwardians)	2:33.90
1985	G. Stanley (Wigan Wasps)	2:31.85
1986	G. Stanley (Stockport Metro)	2:30.72
1987	G. Stanley (Stockport Metro)	2:33.88
1988	D. Tubby (Norwich Penguins)	2:36.22

100 Yards Butterfly

1972	J. Jeavons (Melton Mowbray)	1:08.90
1974	J. Atkinson (Millfield)	1:06.70
1975	J. Atkinson (Millfield)	1:06.50
1976	J. Atkinson (Millfield)	1:04.90

100 Metres Butterfly

1971	J. Machin (Gloucester C)	1:10.40
1973	J. Jeavons (Melton Mowbray)	1:07.30
1977	S. Jenner (Mermaid & Marlin)	1:05.05
1978	L. Taylor (Co Coventry)	1:04.56
1979	A. Osgerby (Wigan Wasps)	1:03.29
1980	A. Osgerby (Wigan Wasps)	1:01.87
1981	A. Osgerby (Wigan Wasps)	1:02.19
1982	L. Criddle (Millfield)	1:01.43
1983	L. Criddle (Millfield)	1:01.84
1984	A. Osgerby (Wigan Wasps)	1:02.24
1985	L. Taylor (Co Manchester)	1:03.60
1986	C. Foot (Millfield)	1:03.38
1987	M. Scarborough (Portsmouth Northsea)	1:01.95
1988	M. Scarborough (Portsmouth Northsea)	1:02.07

220 Yards Butterfly

1972	J. Machin (Gloucester C)	2:29.90
1974	J. Atkinson (Millfield)	2:26.30
1975	J. Atkinson (Millfield)	2:24.10
1976	S. Jenner (Mermaid & Marlin)	2:20.70

200 Metres Butterfly

1971	C. Stockley (Watford)	2:36.60
1973	J. Jeavons (Melton Mowbray)	2:26.40
1977	S. Jenner (Mermaid & Marlin)	2:21.37
1978	S. Jenner (Mermaid & Marlin)	2:18.43
1979	A. Osgerby (Wigan Wasps)	2:16.63
1980	A. Osgerby (Wigan Wasps)	2:15.36
1981	A. Osgerby (Wigan Wasps)	2:13.59
1982	A. Osgerby (Wigan Wasps)	2:14.49
1983	F. Ross (Bexley)	2:13.35
1984	F. Ross (Bexley)	2:13.46
1985	S. Purvis (Stockton Aquatics)	2:12.54
1986	H. Bewley (Millfield)	2:15.66
1987	H. Bewley (Millfield)	2:14.41
1988	M. Scarborough (Portsmouth Northsea)	2:15.08

146⅔ Yards Individual Medley

1972	S. Ratcliffe (Everton)	1:38.00
1975	A. Adams (Co Cardiff)	1:34.90
1976	A. Adams (Co Cardiff)	1:31.70

133⅓ Metres Individual Medley

1971	D. Banks (Chelmsford)	1:39.00
1973	D. Banks (Killerwhales)	1:35.90
1977	M. Kelly (Cumbernauld)	1:32.52
1978	S. Davies (Po Plymouth)	1:31.68

Jean Jeavons

220 Yards Individual Medley

1974	D. Banks (Killerwhales)	2:28.60

200 Metres Individual Medley

1979	S. Davies (Kelly College)	2:19.54
1980	S. Davies (Kelly College)	2:19.31
1981	S. Brownsdon (RTW Monson)	2:20.17
1982	J. Croft (Wigan Wasps)	2:19.00
1983	C. Jackson (Guernsey)	2:20.53
1984	J. Seymour (Camp Hill Edwardians)	2:18.38
1985	S. Purvis (Stockton Aquatics)	2:16.66
1986	Z. Long (Kelly College)	2:18.47
1987	Z. Long (Kelly College)	2:18.97
1988	R. Bowden (Co Southampton)	2:22.69

440 Yards Individual Medley

1972	S. Ratcliffe (Everton)	5:21.90
1974	S. Richardson (Beckenham)	5:14.30
1975	A. Adams (Co Cardiff)	5:13.10
1976	S. Barnard (Co Cardiff)	5:07.10

400 Metres Individual Medley

1971	S. Anslow (Southwark)	5:27.20

1973	S. Richardson (Beckenham)	5:14.40
1977	S. Davies (Po Plymouth)	5:02.52
1978	S. Davies (Po Plymouth)	5:01.75
1979	S. Davies (Kelly College)	4:48.49
1980	S. Davies (Kelly College)	4:50.81
1981	S. Kerswell (Camden Swiss Cottage)	4:52.31
1982	M. Scott (Fleetwood & D)	4:51.76
1983	S. Hardcastle (Redbridge B)	4:53.04
1984	S. Hardcastle (Southend Synchronettes)	4:45.84
1985	S. Hardcastle (Southend Synchronettes)	4:48.35
1986	G. Stanley (Stockport Metro)	4:51.71
1987	G. Stanley (Stockport Metro)	4:51.92
1988	H. Walsh (Millfield)	4:57.58

4×100 Metres Freestyle Club Relay

1987	Stockport Metro	3:56.54
1988	Portsmouth Northsea	3:56.33

4×100 Metres Medley Club Relay

1987	Co Southampton	4:24.31
1988	Norwich Penguins	4:22.00

ASA National (Long Course) Champions, 1869–1989

Note: The men's 440 yards freestyle was held as a salt-water championship until 1934. From 1869–1872, the men's mile was contested on the River Thames — Putney Aquaduct to the Hammersmith Bridge, but thereafter in still water. First competed for in 1909 over 1,200 yards, in honour of Captain Webb, the freestyle team swimming event assumed various distances until withdrawn from the championships in 1948. The men's club medley relay, instituted in 1946, originally with a freestyle, backstroke and breaststroke leg, had a further freestyle leg added in 1947, which was eventually replaced by the butterfly in 1955. In the women's club medley relay, the backstroke, breaststroke and two freestyle legs were the order of the day from 1935–1954, until the butterfly replaced one of the freestyle legs in 1955. Prior to 1953, when held for the first time at the Derby Baths, Blackpool, the championships were not always competed for under long course conditions.

Men

50 Metres Freestyle

1985	M. Reynolds (Barnet Copthall)	24.24
1986	M. Foster (Millfield)	24.17
1987	M. Foster (Bo Southend)	23.30
1988	M. Foster (Bo Southend)	23.55
1989	M. Fibbens (Barnet Copthall)	23.87

100 Yards Freestyle

1878	J. Moore	1:16.75
1879	J. Moore	1:13.25
1880	W. Itter	1:16.75
1881	C. Bettinson	1:16.00
1882	C. Depau	1:12.25
1883	W. Blew-Jones	1:11.00
1884	J. Mayger	1:11.20
1885	J. Mayger	1:12.00
1886	J. Nuttall	1:09.50
1887	J. Nuttall	1:07.80
1888	J. Nuttall	1:06.25
1889	C. Lenton	1:07.80
1890	W. Evans	1:08.75
1891	W. Evans	1:08.40
1892	J. Tyers (Farnworth)	1:05.80
1893	J. Tyers (Farnworth)	1:07.60
1894	J. Tyers (Farnworth)	1:05.60
1895	J. Tyers (Farnworth)	1:04.00

1896	J. Tyers (Farnworth)	1:01.40
1897	J. Tyers (Farnworth)	1:03.60
1898	J. Derbyshire (Osborne)	1:00.80
1899	J. Derbyshire (Osborne)	1:00.40
1900	J. Derbyshire (Osborne)	1:01.00
1901	J. Derbyshire (Osborne)	1:01.40
1902	F. Lane (Australia)	1:00.00
1903	J. Derbyshire (Osborne)	1:01.60
1904	J. Derbyshire (Osborne)	1:00.80
1905	Z. de Halmay (Hungary)	59.00
1906	C. Daniels (USA)	58.60
1907	C. Daniels (USA)	55.40
1908	H. Meyboom (Belgium)	1:00.60
1909	P. Radmilovic (Weston super Mare)	1:01.00
1910	F. Beaurepaire (Australia)	59.80
1911	H. Hardwick (Australia)	58.60
1912	P. McGillivray (USA)	57.70
1913	H. Annison (Croydon)	1:00.00
1920	I. Stedman (Australia)	58.00
1921	M. van Schelle (Belgium)	57.60
1922	M. van Schelle (Belgium)	56.60
1923	M. van Schelle (Belgium)	57.00
1924	E. Henry (Australia)	58.00
1925	S. de Barany (Hungary)	55.80
1926	J. House (USA)	57.40
1927	C. Baillie (Oldham Police)	56.80
1928	P. Samson (USA)	54.40

1929	N. Brooks (Oldham Police)	55.40
1930	N. Brooks (Oldham Police)	56.20
1931	R. Sutton (Plaistow U)	56.20
1932	N. Brooks (Oldham Police)	54.60
1933	R. Sutton (Plaistow U)	56.00
1934	G. Larson (Canada)	54.00
1935	R. Gabrielsen (Beckenham)	55.40
1936	F. Dove (Otter)	55.00
1937	F. Dove (Otter)	55.80
1938	F. Dove (Otter)	55.00
1946	A. Jany (France)	52.00
1947	P. Kendall (Sutton & Cheam)	55.20
1948	R. Stedman (Beckenham)	55.00
1949	R. Stedman (Beckenham)	53.70
1950	P. Kendall (Sutton & Cheam)	54.30
1951	G. Larsson (Sweden)	52.10
1952	J. Wardrop (Motherwell)	53.40

110 Yards Freestyle

1953	R. Roberts (Otter)	59.50
1954	G. Baxter (Gloucester C)	1:00.90
1955	R. Roberts (Otter)	58.50
1956	N. McKechnie (Wallasey)	58.90
1957	N. McKechnie (Wallasey)	59.20
1958	I. Black (Gordon's College)	58.30
1959	I. Black (Gordon's College)	58.00
1960	S. Clarke (Plaistow U)	57.80
1961	J. Martin-Dye (Penguin)	57.20
1962	R. McGregor (Falkirk Otters)	55.60
1963	R. McGregor (Falkirk Otters)	54.10
1964	R. McGregor (Falkirk Otters)	53.90
1965	R. Lord (Co Coventry)	55.20
1966	R. McGregor (Falkirk Otters)	53.50
1967	R. McGregor (Falkirk Otters)	54.00
1968	R. McGregor (Falkirk Otters)	53.90
1969	M. Windeatt (Torquay Leander)	56.30
1970	M. Windeatt (Torquay Leander)	55.20

100 Metres Freestyle

1971	M. Windeatt (Torquay Leander)	55.10
1972	M. Windeatt (Torquay Leander)	54.30
1973	C. Cunningham (Co Southampton)	54.62
1974	B. Brinkley (Modernians)	54.20
1975	B. Brinkley (Modernians)	52.30
1976	K. Burns (York C)	54.04
1977	T. Smith (Radcliffe)	53.25
1978	R. Burrell (Co Southampton)	53.18
1979	R. Burrell (Co Southampton)	52.42
1980	M. Smith (Radcliffe)	52.86
1981	M. Taylor (Co Cardiff)	52.58
1982	D. Lowe (Harrow & Wealdstone)	52.25
1983	D. Lowe (Harrow & Wealdstone)	52.22
1984	D. Lowe (Harrow & Wealdstone)	52.22
1985	M. Reynolds (Barnet Copthall)	52.98
1986	R. Lee (Co Cardiff)	51.66
1987	R. Lee (Co Birmingham)	50.91
1988	A. Jameson (Co Liverpool)	51.31
1989	M. Fibbens (Barnet Copthall)	51.68

220 Yards Freestyle

1880	E. Danels	3:09.75
1881	E. Danels	3:14.50
1882	E. Danels	3:13.25
1883	T. Cairns	2:59.25
1884	T. Cairns	3:02.25
1885	T. Cairns	3:08.25
1886	J. Nuttall	3:04.80
1887	J. Nuttall	2:59.80
1888	J. Nuttall	3:15.60

1889	T. Jones	2:57.50
1890	W. Evans	2:51.20
1891	W. Evans	2:52.00
1892	J. Tyers (Farnworth)	2:46.40
1893	J. Tyers (Farnworth)	2:54.80
1894	J. Tyers (Farnworth)	2:49.00
1895	J. Tyers (Farnworth)	2:41.00
1896	J. Tyers (Farnworth)	2:50.20
1897	J. Tyers (Farnworth)	2:38.80
1898	J. Derbyshire (Osborne)	2:42.40
1900	F. Lane (Blackpool) J. Derbyshire (Osborne)	2:34.80
1901	J. Derbyshire (Osborne)	2:42.00
1902	F. Lane (Australia)	2:28.60
1903	J. Derbyshire (Osborne)	2:46.00
1904	C. Forsyth (Hyde Seal)	2:37.80
1905	B. Kieran (Australia)	2:37.20
1906	C. Healy (Australia)	2:37.40
1907	Z. de Halmay (Hungary)	2:34.00
1908	F. Beaurepaire (Australia)	2:37.00
1909	T. Battersby (Southport)	2:32.80
1910	F. Beaurepaire (Australia)	2:30.00
1911	H. Hardwick (Australia)	2:33.60
1912	J. Hatfield (Middlesbrough)	2:30.20
1913	J. Hatfield (Middlesbrough)	2:30.60
1920	F. Beaurepaire (Australia)	2:29.20
1921	A. Borg (Sweden)	2:29.20
1922	J. Hatfield (Middlesbrough)	2:32.20
1923	A. Borg (Sweden)	2:29.60
1924	H. Annison (Croydon)	2:35.00
1925	J. Hatfield (Middlesbrough)	2:34.40
1926	J. Whiteside (Bolton)	2:31.00
1927	A. Dickin (Polytechnic)	2:36.00
1928	J. Whitehurst (S Manchester)	2:27.20
1929	N. Brooks (Oldham Police)	2:28.00
1930	N. Brooks (Oldham Police)	2:26.00
1931	R. Sutton (Plaistow U)	2:22.20
1932	R. Sutton (Plaistow U)	2:31.50
1933	R. Leivers (Longton)	2:23.60
1934	G. Larson (Canada)	2:20.20
1935	N. Wainwright (Hanley)	2:18.60
1936	N. Wainwright (Hanley)	2:17.80

Jack Hatfield

190

Jack Wardrop (left) with brother, Robert.

1937	N. Wainwright (Hanley)	2:18.60
1938	N. Wainwright (Hanley)	2:16.60
1946	A. Jany (France)	2:14.00
1947	J. Hale (Hull Kingston)	2:20.10
1948	J. Hale (Hull Kingston)	2:16.40
1949	P. Osbrand (Sweden)	2:13.60
1950	J. Wardrop (Motherwell)	2:16.60
1951	G. Larsson (Sweden)	2:12.20
1952	J. Wardrop (Motherwell)	2:11.20
1953	P. Roberts (Otter)	2:15.80
1954	J. Wardrop (Motherwell)	2:11.70
1955	N. McKechnie (Wallasey)	2:13.80
1956	N. McKechnie (Wallasey)	2:11.30
1957	N. McKechnie (Wallasey)	2:12.00
1958	I. Black (Gordon's College)	2:07.20
1959	I. Black (Gordon's College)	2:06.00
1960	S. Clarke (Plaistow U)	2:07.60
1961	J. Martin-Dye (Penguin)	2:06.90
1962	M. McLachlan (Otter)	2:05.50
1963	R. McGregor (Falkirk Otters)	2:04.80
1964	G. Grylls (S Africa)	2:03.50
1965	G. Grylls (S Africa)	2:01.60
1966	R. McGregor (Falkirk Otters)	2:02.60
1967	A. Jarvis (Otter)	2:03.40
1968	A. Jarvis (Otter)	2:00.10
1969	M. Woodroffe (Llanstrisant)	2:01.50
1970	M. Borrie (New Zealand)	2:02.40

200 Metres Freestyle

1971	B. Brinkley (Modernians)	2:02.00
1972	B. Brinkley (Modernians)	1:57.90
1973	B. Brinkley (Modernians)	1:56.68
1974	B. Brinkley (Modernians)	1:57.50

1975	B. Brinkley (Modernians)	1:55.39
1976	A. McClatchey (Warrender)	1:55.94
1977	G. Downie (Warrender)	1:55.69
1978	D. Dunne (Beckenham)	1:54.38
1979	G. Downie (Warrender)	1:54.68
1980	P. Hubble (Slough Dolphins)	1:54.19
1981	A. Astbury (Leeds Central)	1:54.94
1982	J. Davey (Co Milton Keynes)	1:53.87
1983	P. Hubble (Hounslow B)	1:54.12
1984	J. Davey (Salford Triple 'S')	1:54.10
1985	M. Reynold (Barnet Copthall)	1:53.89
1986	K. Boyd (Bo S Tyneside)	1:53.25
1987	J. Broughton (Co Leeds)	1:51.84
1988	R. Lee (Co Birmingham)	1:52.72
1989	J. Broughton (Co Leeds)	1:53.34

440 Yards Freestyle

1884	T. Cairns	6:33.00
1885	H. Schlotel	6:48.20
1886	H. Schlotel	6:21.25
1887	H. Schlotel	6:31.40
1888	J. Nuttall	6:16.50
1889	W. Henry	6:04.00
1890	W. Evans	6:19.20
1891	W. Evans	7:15.00
1892	W. Evans	7:03.00
1893	J. Tyers (Farnworth)	6:33.20
1894	J. Tyers (Farnworth)	7:06.40
1895	J. Tyers (Farnworth)	6:08.80
1896	J. Tyers (Farnworth)	6:18.40
1897	P. Cavill (Australia)	4:50.40
1898	J. Jarvis (Leicester)	6:30.00
1899	F. Lane (Blackpool)	6:30.80

191

1900	J. Jarvis (Leicester)	12:55.00
1901	D. Billington (Bacup)	8:23.20
1902	R. Cavill (Australia)	5:04.80
1903	D. Billington (Bacup)	6:34.60
1904	D. Billington (Bacup)	6:19.00
1905	B. Kieran (Australia)	5:22.20
1906	H. Taylor (Chadderton)	5:42.60
1907	H. Taylor (Chadderton)	4:43.00
1908	F. Beaurepaire (Australia)	4:59.40
1909	T. Battersby (Southport)	S/O
1910	F. Beaurepaire (Australia)	5:38.60
1911	H. Hardwick (Australia)	5:40.40
1912	J. Hatfield (Middlesbrough)	4:54.80
1913	J. Hatfield (Middlesbrough)	5:43.00
1920	H. Annison (Croydon)	5:41.00
1921	E. Peter (Penguin)	5:40.00
1922	E. Peter (Penguin)	5:46.80
1923	E. Peter (Penguin)	5:52.60
1924	J. Hatfield (Middlesbrough)	5:52.60
1925	P. Radmilovic (Weston super Mare)	5:41.20
1926	A. Dickin (Hammersmith)	5:44.60
1927	J. Hatfield (Middlesbrough)	5:51.00
1928	P. Samson (USA)	5:30.80
1929	N. Brooks (Oldham Police)	5:39.20
1930	N. Brooks (Oldham Police)	5:41.80
1931	R. Sutton (Plaistow U)	5:27.40
1932	R. Leivers (Longton)	5:30.40
1933	R. Sutton (Plaistow U)	5:28.00
1934	R. Leivers (Longton)	5:37.00
1935	N. Wainwright (Hanley)	5:05.80
1936	N. Wainwright (Hanley)	4:58.40
1937	N. Wainwright (Hanley)	5:03.40
1938	N. Wainwright (Hanley)	4:59.00
1946	J. Hale (Hull Kingston)	4:56.20
1947	J. Hale (Hull Kingston)	5:00.40
1948	J. Hale (Hull Kingston)	5:02.40
1949	P. Ostrand (Sweden)	4:47.50
1950	J. Wardrop (Motherwell)	4:54.80
1951	J. Wardrop (Motherwell)	4:49.50
1952	J. Wardrop (Motherwell)	4:47.20
1953	R. Sreenan (Whitehall)	4:54.40
1954	G. Symonds (Co Coventry)	4:53.80
1955	N. McKechnie (Wallasey)	4:47.00
1956	N. McKechnie (Wallasey)	4:45.80
1957	R. Sreenan (Whitehall)	4:53.60
1958	I. Black (Gordon's College)	4:28.40
1959	I. Black (Gordon's College)	4:32.90
1960	J. Martin-Dye (Penguin)	4:31.70
1961	J. Martin-Dye (Penguin)	4:34.20
1962	R. Campion (Stoke Newington)	4:32.70
1963	J. Martin-Dye (Penguin)	4:31.30
1964	G. Grylls (S Africa)	4:24.90
1965	G. Grylls (S Africa)	4:22.20
1966	A. Kimber (Co Southampton)	4:24.30
1967	A. Kimber (Co Southampton)	4:23.50
1968	A. Jarvis (Otter)	4:22.00
1969	R. Jacks (Canada)	4:17.90
1970	R. Terrell (Co Southampton)	4:21.40

400 Metres Freestyle

1971	B. Brinkley (Modernians)	4:18.50
1972	B. Brinkley (Modernians)	4:10.20
1973	B. Brinkley (Modernians)	4:10.62
1974	B. Brinkley (Modernians)	4:08.40
1975	B. Brinkley (Modernians)	4:04.03
1976	A. McLatchey (Warrender)	4:05.46
1977	D. Downie (Warrender)	4:03.49
1978	S. Gray (Amateur)	4:00.41
1979	P. Sparkes (Beckenham)	4:00.31

Graham Symonds

1980	A. Astbury (Leeds Central)	3:58.42
1981	A. Astbury (Leeds Central)	3:59.38
1982	A. Astbury (Leeds Central)	3:57.06
1983	J. Davey (Co Milton Keynes)	3:58.84
1984	J. Davey (Salford Triple 'S')	4:00.22
1985	P. Easter (Norwich Penguins)	4:02.49
1986	K. Boyd (Bo S Tyneside)	3:56.85
1987	K. Boyd (Bo S Tyneside)	3:57.88
1988	P. Howe (Co Birmingham)	3:57.90
1989	C. McNeil (Paisley)	3:58.84

500 Yards Freestyle

1878	J. Taylor	8:07.25
1879	E. Danels	7:44.25
1880	E. Danels	7:51.25
1881	E. Danels	7:49.75
1882	E. Danels	7:44.00
1883	E. Danels	7:48.25
1884	T. Cairns	7:32.50
1885	T. Cairns	7:51.75
1886	J. Nuttall	7:19.25
1887	J. Nuttall	7:26.80
1888	J. Nuttall	7:25.20
1889	J. Standring	7:35.20
1890	W. Evans	7:23.80
1891	W. Evans	7:14.00
1892	W. Evans	7:24.00
1893	J. Tyers (Farnworth)	7:07.00
1894	J. Tyers (Farnworth)	6:45.00
1895	J. Tyers (Farnworth)	6:47.40
1896	J. Tyers (Farnworth)	6:55.80
1897	J. Derbyshire (Osborne)	7:02.20
1898	J. Jarvis (Leicester)	6:47.60
1899	J. Jarvis (Leicester)	6:51.00
1900	J. Jarvis (Leicester)	6:49.20
1901	J. Jarvis (Leicester)	6:35.00
1902	D. Billington (Bacup)	6:25.40
1903	D. Billington (Bacup)	6:53.20
1904	C. Forsyth (Hyde Seal)	6:33.20
1905	B. Kieran (Australia)	6:07.20
1906	H. Taylor (Chadderton)	6:24.60
1907	H. Taylor (Chadderton)	6:22.00
1908	H. Taylor (Chadderton)	6:14.00
1909	T. Battersby (Southport)	6:26.20
1910	F. Beaurepaire (Australia)	6:21.00

1911	H. Taylor (Hyde Seal)	6:22.00
1912	J. Hatfield (Middlesbrough)	6:18.80
1913	J. Hatfield (Middlesbrough)	6:13.60
1920	H. Annison (Croydon)	6:31.20
1921	J. Hatfield (Middlesbrough)	6:22.60
1922	J. Hatfield (Middlesbrough)	6:11.40
1923	J. Hatfield (Middlesbrough)	6:18.40
1924	J. Hatfield (Middlesbrough)	6:13.80
1925	J. Hatfield (Middlesbrough)	6:22.60
1926	J. Hatfield (Middlesbrough)	6:32.40
1927	J. Hatfield (Middlesbrough)	6:18.20
1928	A. Vandeplancke (France)	6:18.80
1929	J. Taris (France)	5:56.40
1930	F. Milton (Otter)	6:34.00
1931	A. Taylor (Eccles)	6:11.40
1932	R. Leivers (Longton)	6:12.60
1933	R. Leivers (Longton)	6:02.80
1934	N. Wainwright (Hanley)	5:54.00

½ Mile Freestyle

1881	D. Ainsworth	14:31.50
1882	D. Ainsworth	15:16.75
1883	D. Ainsworth	14:23.50
1884	G. Bell	14:35.50
1885	H. Schlotel	13:04.50
1886	H. Schlotel	14:17.50
1887	J. Nuttall	14:44.00
1888	H. Bowden	14:25.40
1889	J. Standring	14:56.80
1890	W. Evans	14:38.00
1891	S. Greasley	13:42.40
1892	S. Greasley	14:00.80
1893	J. Tyers (Farnworth)	13:41.00
1894	J. Tyers (Farnworth)	13:42.40
1895	J. Tyers (Farnworth)	13:56.00
1897	J. Derbyshire (Osborne)	13:38.80
1898	J. Jarvis (Leicester)	12:52.00
1899	J. Jarvis (Leicester)	12:45.60
1900	J. Jarvis (Leicester)	12:35.00
1901	J. Jarvis (Leicester)	12:42.40
1902	R. Cavill (Australia)	11:50.40
1903	D. Billington (Bacup)	13:10.60
1904	C. Forsyth (Hyde Seal)	12:23.00
1905	B. Kieran (Australia)	11:28.00
1906	H. Taylor (Chadderton)	11:25.40
1907	H. Taylor (Chadderton)	12:16.20
1908	F. Beaurepaire (Australia)	12:44.00
1909	T. Battersby (Southport)	11:47.20
1910	F. Beaurepaire (Australia)	11:39.80
1911	H. Taylor (Chadderton)	12:05.60
1912	J. Hatfield (Middlesbrough)	12:21.20
1913	J. Hatfield (Middlesbrough)	11:46.40
1920	H. Annison (Croydon)	12:21.40
1921	J. Hatfield (Middlesbrough)	11:57.80
1922	J. Hatfield (Middlesbrough)	11:59.20
1923	J. Hatfield (Middlesbrough)	12:15.20
1924	J. Hatfield (Middlesbrough)	12:11.40
1925	J. Hatfield (Middlesbrough)	11:51.00
1926	P. Radmilovic (Weston super Mare)	11:57.40
1927	E. Peter (Hammersmith)	12:02.20
1928	S. White (Bristol C)	13:55.00
1929	J. Taris (France)	11:19.80
1930	F. Bramhall (Terres)	12:46.80
1931	A. Taylor (Eccles)	11:33.20
1932	R. Leivers (Longton)	11:27.40
1933	N. Wainwright (Hanley)	11:31.60
1934	N. Wainwright (Hanley)	10:57.40
1935	N. Wainwright (Hanley)	10:51.60
1936	R. Leivers (Longton)	10:30.00

1937	N. Wainwright (Hanley)	10:26.40
1938	K. Deane (Great Yarmouth)	10:47.00
1946	J. Hale (Hull Kingston)	10:27.40
1947	J. Hale (Hull Kingston)	10:49.80
1948	J. Hale (Hull Kingston)	10:58.60
1949	J. Wardrop (Motherwell)	10:30.30
1950	J. Wardrop (Motherwell)	10:29.10
1951	D. Bland (Lambton)	10:33.10
1952	J. Wardrop (Motherwell)	10:03.60
1953	R. Sreenan (Whitehall)	10:24.60
1954	G. Symonds (Coventry)	10:48.40
1955	R. Sreenan (Whitehall)	10:27.70
1956	N. McKechnie (Wallasey)	10:12.90
1957	R. Sreenan (Whitehall)	10:07.80
1958	R. Sreenan (Whitehall)	10:07.80
1959	R. Campion (Stoke Newington)	10:13.10
1960	R. Campion (Stoke Newington)	9:56.70
1961	W. Kennedy (Otter)	9:52.60
1962	R. Campion (Stoke Newington)	9:47.20
1963	W. Kennedy (Otter)	9:57.60
1964	H. Milton (Otter)	10:13.20
1965	G. Grylls (S Africa)	9:15.50
1966	A. Kimber (Co Southampton)	9:09.30
1967	A. Kimber (Co Southampton)	9:13.30
1968	A. Kimber (Co Southampton)	9:12.70
1969	R. Jacks (Canada)	8:58.00
1970	M. Treffers (New Zealand)	9:03.20

1 Mile Freestyle

1869	T. Morris	27:18.00
1870	H. Parker	26:06.40
1871	H. Parker	24:35.00
1872	H. Parker	29:03.00
1873	D. Ainsworth	30:58.50
1874	H. Davenport	31:09.00
1875	H. Davenport	31:30.00
1876	H. Davenport	33:08.00
1877	H. Davenport	29:25.50
1878	H. Davenport	31:15.25
1879	H. Davenport	34:09.00
1880	J. Taylor	30:38.00
1881	J. Taylor	35:20.00
1882	J. Taylor	32:38.00
1883	E. Danels	31:40.60

Neil McKechnie

1884	G. Bell	31:42.75
1885	S. Sargent	32:11.50
1886	H. Schotel	31:32.75
1887	J. Nuttall	30:38.00
1888	J. Standring	34:01.50
1889	H. Bowden	31:00.80
1890	S. Greasley	29:32.40
1891	S. Greasley	30:33.60
1892	S. Greasley	28:18.40
1893	J. Tyers (Farnworth)	27:21.40
1894	J. Tyers (Farnworth)	27:51.40
1895	J. Tyers (Farnworth)	27:33.80
1896	J. Tyers (Farnworth)	26:46.50
1897	J. Jarvis (Leicester)	32:28.60
1898	J. Jarvis (Leicester)	26:37.20
1899	J. Jarvis (Leicester)	25:13.40
1900	J. Jarvis (Leicester)	26:26.00
1901	J. Jarvis (Leicester)	25:13.80
1902	J. Jarvis (Leicester)	25:32.40
1903	D. Billington (Bacup)	24:56.40
1904	D. Billington (Bacup)	27:18.00
1905	D. Billington (Bacup)	24:42.60
1906	H. Taylor (Chadderton)	27:09.00
1907	H. Taylor (Chadderton)	25:04.60
1908	F. Beaurepaire (Australia)	25:15.40
1909	T. Battersby (Southport)	24:01.40
1910	F. Beaurepaire (Australia)	24:39.40
1911	H. Taylor (Hyde Seal)	23:35.50
1912	J. Hatfield (Middlesbrough)	25:02.80
1913	J. Hatfield (Middlesbrough)	24:55.20
1914	J. Hatfield (Middlesbrough)	24:42.40
1920	H. Annison (Croydon)	25:25.00
1921	J. Hatfield (Middlesbrough)	24:48.80
1922	J. Hatfield (Middlesbrough)	26:46.80
1923	J. Hatfield (Middlesbrough)	24:54.00
1924	J. Hatfield (Middlesbrough)	25:22.40
1925	P. Radmilovic (Weston super Mare)	24:27.00
1926	P. Radmilovic (Weston super Mare)	24:27.00
1927	P. Radmilovic (Weston super Mare)	25:39.80
1928	D. Lindsay (New Zealand)	25:10.80
1929	J. Hatfield (Middlesbrough)	25:40.60
1930	J. Hatfield (Middlesbrough)	25:30.60
1931	F. Milton (Otter)	25:28.40
1932	F. Milton (Otter)	25:58.60
1933	N. Wainwright (Hanley)	23:20.60
1934	N. Wainwright (Hanley)	23:47.00
1935	N. Wainwright (Hanley)	23:19.00
1936	R. Leivers (Longton)	21:49.40
1937	N. Wainwright (Hanley)	22:31.80
1938	R. Leivers (Longton)	22:07.20
1946	J. Hale (Hull Kingston)	21:47.20
1947	J. Hale (Hull Kingston)	21:33.20
1948	J. Hale (Hull Kingston)	21:25.20
1949	D. Bland (Lambton)	22:13.20
1950	D. Bland (Lambton)	21:54.90
1951	D. Bland (Lambton)	21:33.80
1952	J. Wardrop (Motherwell)	20:53.20
1953	R. Sreenan (Whitehall)	21:11.40
1954	R. Sreenan (Whitehall)	22:13.20
1955	R. Sreenan (Whitehall)	21:16.40
1956	R. Sreenan (Whitehall)	20:57.40
1957	R. Sreenan (Whitehall)	21:23.20
1958	I. Black (Gordon's College)	19:17.50
1959	R. Campion (Stoke Newington)	20:48.20
1960	R. Campion (Stoke Newington)	21:00.20
1961	R. Campion (Stoke Newington)	19:50.60
1962	R. Campion (Stoke Newington)	19:30.20
1963	J. Martin-Dye (Penguin)	20:07.50

1964	G. Grylls (S Africa)	19:10.10

1500 Metres Freestyle

1971	J. Mills (St James)	17:21.50
1972	B. Brinkley (Modernians)	16:39.60
1973	J. Carter (Paisley)	16:41.03
1974	J. Carter (Paisley)	16:38.60
1975	P. Nash (York C)	16:28.19
1976	D. Parker (Co Coventry)	16:10.70
1977	P. Sparkes (Merton Swordfish)	15:50.91
1978	S. Gray (Amateur)	15:43.08
1979	A. Astbury (Leeds Central)	15:41.77
1980	A. Astbury (Leeds Central)	15:33.77
1981	A. Astbury (Leeds Central)	15:43.62
1982	A. Astbury (Leeds Central)	15:37.89
1983	A. Astbury (Co Leeds)	15:45.57
1984	T. Day (Co Leeds)	16:01.61
1985	D. Stacey (Co Swansea)	15:44.11
1986	D. Stacey (Co Swansea)	15:49.44
1987	K. Boyd (Bo S Tyneside)	15:49.23
1988	T. Day (Co Leeds)	15:43.41
1989	K. Boyd (Bo S Tyneside)	15:44.19

1650 Yards Freestyle

1965	J. Gilchrist (Canada)	17:33.90
1966	A. Kimber (Co Southampton)	17:52.80
1967	A. Kimber (Co Southampton)	17:33.90
1968	A. Kimber (Co Southampton)	17:48.30
1969	R. Jacks (Canada)	17:20.80
1970	M. Treffers (New Zealand)	17:04.40

100 Yards Backstroke

1947	A. Kinnear (Otter)	1:04.00
1948	W. Brockway (Maindee)	1:02.60
1949	W. Brockway (Maindee)	1:00.80
1950	W. Brockway (Maindee)	1:01.20
1951	W. Brockway (Maindee)	59.70
1952	R. Wardrop (Motherwell)	1:04.10

110 Yards Backstroke

1953	W. Brockway (Maindee)	1:08.80
1954	W. Brockway (Maindee)	1:07.20
1955	W. Brockway (Maindee)	1:08.40
1956	G. Sykes (Coventry)	1:08.20
1957	G. Sykes (Coventry)	1:06.70
1958	G. Sykes (Coventry)	1:07.40
1959	G. Sykes (Standard Triumph)	1:05.50
1960	G. Sykes (Standard Triumph)	1:04.80
1964	B. Stewart (S Africa)	1:03.90
1965	B. Stewart (S Africa)	1:03.10
1966	R. Jones (Stoke Newington)	1:02.20
1967	R. Jones (Stoke Newington)	1:03.00
1968	R. Jones (Stoke Newington)	1:02.40
1969	C. Rushton (Rochdale)	1:02.70
1970	M. Richards (Nottingham Northern)	1:01.80

100 Metres Backstroke

1971	M. Richards (Nottingham Northern)	1:02.60
1972	C. Cunningham (Co Southampton)	1:00.30
1973	C. Cunningham (Co Southampton)	1:00.76
1974	S. Pickell (Canada)	1:00.80
1975	J. Carter (Paisley)	1:00.37
1976	G. Abraham (Co Southampton)	1:01.00
1977	G. Abraham (Co Southampton)	59.84
1978	G. Abraham (Co Southampton)	59.43
1979	G. Abraham (Co Southampton)	58.54
1980	D. Campbell (NCR Dundee)	58.68
1981	G. Abraham (Co Southampton)	58.58
1982	S. Harrison (Co Southampton)	58.50
1983	J. Randall (Co Coventry)	59.45

1984	J. Davey (Salford Triple 'S')	59.30
1985	M. Matthews (Barnet Copthall)	1:00.02
1986	N. Harper (Millfield)	58.85
1987	G. Binfield (Salford Triple 'S')	58.35
1988	N. Cochran (Co Swansea)	58.79
1989	G. Binfield (Maxwell)	58.52

150 Yards Backstroke

1903	W. Call (Sheffield Otter)	2:06.60
1904	W. Call (Sheffield Otter)	2:01.40
1905	W. Call (Sheffield Otter)	2:01.60
1906	F. Unwin (Sheffield Otter)	2:04.00
1907	F. Unwin (Sheffield Otter)	1:59.20
1908	F. Unwin (Sheffield Otter)	2:01.00
1909	F. Unwin (Sheffield Otter)	2:02.20
1910	M. Weckesser (Belgium)	1:57.20
1911	M. Weckesser (Belgium)	1:58.40
1912	G. Webster (Sowerby Bridge)	2:00.00
1913	G. Webster (Sowerby Bridge)	1:59.40
1920	G. Blitz (Belgium)	1:59.80
1921	G. Blitz (Belgium)	1:55.80
1922	A. Rawlinson (Garston)	1:56.20
1923	A. Rawlinson (Garston)	1:55.80
1924	A. Rawlinson (Garston)	1:48.20
1925	A. Rawlinson (Garston)	1:52.40
1926	A. Rawlinson (Garston)	1:51.80
1927	J. Besford (S Manchester)	1:50.00
1928	J. Besford (S Manchester)	1:48.20
1929	J. Trippett (Sheffield C Police)	1:52.00
1930	J. Besford (S Manchester)	1:46.20
1931	J. Besford (S Manchester)	1:45.40
1932	J. Besford (S Manchester)	1:45.00
1933	W. Francis (Renfrew Baths)	1:46.00
1934	W. Francis (Renfrew Baths)	1:45.00

1935	J. Besford (Shiverers)	1:46.80
1936	J. Besford (Shiverers)	1:48.40
1937	M. Taylor (Sheffield Baths)	1:46.40
1938	M. Taylor (Sheffield Baths)	1:46.00
1946	G. Vallerey (France)	1:38.60

220 Yards Backstroke

1961	G. Sykes (Coventry Standard Triumph)	2:23.90
1962	G. Sykes (Coventry Standard Triumph)	2:21.60
1963	R. Jones (Newport Olympic)	2:25.00
1964	B. Stewart (S Africa)	2:20.10
1965	R. Hutton (Canada)	2:16.00
1966	N. Jackson (Southport)	2:18.50
1967	P. Reynolds (Australia)	2:17.90
1968	D. Butler (Gloucester C)	2:17.20
1969	C. Rushton (Rochdale)	2:16.80
1970	M. Richards (Nottingham Northern)	2:15.20

200 Metres Backstroke

1971	M. Richards (Nottingham Northern)	2:15.70
1972	C. Cunningham (Co Southampton)	2:09.50
1973	C. Cunningham (Co Southampton)	2:09.45
1974	S. Pickell (Canada)	2:11.90
1975	J. Carter (Paisley)	2:10.81
1976	J. Carter (Paisley)	2:09.80
1977	J. Carter (Paisley)	2:08.83
1978	G. Abraham (Co Southampton)	2:10.32
1979	D. Campbell (NCR Dundee)	2:07.46
1980	D. Campbell (NCR Dundee)	2:05.31
1981	D. Campbell (Taybridge)	2:07.77
1982	A. Jameson (Kelly College)	2:09.55
1983	J. Davey (Co Milton Keynes)	2:06.04

Gary Abraham   Swimming Times

195

1984	J. Davey (Salford Triple 'S')	2:06.15
1985	M. Matthews (Barnet Copthall)	2:08.63
1986	G. Binfield (Salford Triple 'S')	2:06.08
1987	J. Davey (Salford Triple 'S')	2:04.16
1988	G. Binfield (Salford Triple 'S')	2:05.95
1989	G. Binfield (Maxwell)	2:05.26

110 Yards Breaststroke

1964	N. Nicholson (Gateshead)	1:12.60
1965	B. Hotz (S Africa)	1:12.30
1966	R. Roberts (Stoke Newington)	1:11.10
1967	R. Roberts (Stoke Newington)	1:10.30
1968	J. Roberts (Eccles)	1:11.50
1969	B. Mahoney (Canada)	1:10.20
1970	M. Carty (Stoke Newington)	1:12.10

100 Metres Breaststroke

1971	M. O'Connell (Co Southampton)	1:09.80
1972	M. O'Connell (Co Southampton)	1:08.10
1973	D. Wilkie (Warrender)	1:07.88
1974	D. Wilkie (Warrender)	1:06.96
1975	D. Leigh (Oak Street)	1:08.05
1976	L. Atkinson (Co Cardiff)	1:11.70
1977	P. Naisby (S Shields)	1:05.72
1978	D. Goodhew (Beckenham)	1:04.93
1979	D. Goodhew (Beckenham)	1:05.03
1980	D. Goodhew (Beckenham)	1:03.57
1981	A. Moorhouse (Leeds Central)	1:05.10
1982	A. Moorhouse (Leeds Central)	1:03.43
1983	A. Moorhouse (Co Leeds)	1:04.09
1984	N. Ali (Salford Triple 'S')	1:07.04
1985	A. Moorhouse (Co Leeds)	1:03.38
1986	A. Moorhouse (Co Leeds)	1:02.89
1987	A. Moorhouse (Co Leeds)	1:03.29
1988	J. Parrack (Co Leeds)	1:03.71
1989	A. Moorhouse (Co Leeds)	1:03.31

200 Yards Breaststroke

1903	W. Robinson (Liverpool)	2:49.80
1904	W. Robinson (Liverpool)	2:52.20
1905	W. Robinson (Liverpool)	2:49.00
1906	F. Naylor (Hornsey)	2:58.40
1907	P. Courtman (Old Trafford)	2:55.45
1908	P. Courtman (Old Trafford)	2:47.20
1909	P. Courtman (Old Trafford)	2:46.20
1910	H. Julin (Sweden)	2:53.00
1911	E. Toldi (Hungary)	2:42.00
1912	P. Courtman (Old Trafford)	2:47.80
1913	P. Courtman (Old Trafford)	2:43.00
1920	R. Lassam (Ravensbourne)	2:43.20
1921	S. Leon (France)	2:49.80
1922	J. de Combe (Belgium)	2:58.00
1923	W. Stoney (Huddersfield)	2:51.00
1924	R. Flint (Croft House)	2:51.00
1925	R. Flint (Croft House)	2:50.00
1926	H. Bouvier (France)	2:48.20
1927	L. van Parys (Belgium)	2:42.40
1928	R. Flint (Croft House)	2:42.40
1929	R. Flint (Croft House)	2:44.60
1930	S. Bell (Penguin)	2:43.40
1931	J. Cartonnet (France)	2:42.20
1932	J. Cartonnet (France)	2:39.00
1933	A. Schoebel (France)	2:38.00
1934	N. Hamilton (Western Baths)	2:43.20
1935	N. Hamilton (Western Baths)	2:43.60
1936	N. Hamilton (Western Baths)	2:43.60
1937	J. Davies (Otter)	2:41.20
1938	J. Davies (Otter)	2:39.20
1946	J. Davies (Otter)	2:39.60

1947	R. Romain (King's College)	2:30.00
1948	R. Romain (Otter)	2:30.80
1949	R. Romain (Otter)	2:30.70
1950	P. Jervis (Retford)	2:34.70
1951	D. Snelling (Darwen)	2:34.00
1952	P. Jervis (Retford)	2:29.80

220 Yards Breaststroke

1953	P. Jervis (Retford)	2:53.00
1954	P. Jervis (Retford)	2:51.30
1955	C. Walkden (Beckenham)	2:47.30
1956	C. Walkden (Beckenham)	2:46.00
1957	B. Day (Sheffield TS)	2:50.30
1958	C. Walkden (Beckenham)	2:43.90
1959	G. Rowlinson (Bolton)	2:48.50
1960	G. Rowlinson (Bolton)	2:46.00
1961	C. Wilkinson (Stockport)	2:43.90
1962	C. Wilkinson (Stockport)	2:43.80
1963	N. Nicholson (Gateshead)	2:42.20
1964	B. Hotz (S Africa)	2:39.20
1965	B. Hotz (S Africa)	2:40.30
1966	D. Finnigan (Darlington)	2:39.40
1967	R. Roberts (Stoke Newington)	2:36.10
1968	J. Roberts (Eccles)	2:38.50
1969	B. Mahoney (Canada)	2:33.50
1970	N. Johnson (Millfield)	2:36.10

200 Metres Breaststroke

1971	M. O'Connell (Co Southampton)	2:33.70
1972	D. Wilkie (Warrender)	2:28.00
1973	D. Wilkie (Warrender)	2:27.60
1974	D. Wilkie (Warrender)	2:26.30
1975	B. O'Brien (Co Coventry)	2:31.02
1976	D. Goodhew (Millfield)	2:25.98
1977	P. Naisby (S Shields)	2:24.31
1978	D. Goodhew (Beckenham)	2:22.96
1979	D. Goodhew (Beckenham)	2:24.69
1980	D. Goodhew (Beckenham)	2:19.07
1981	A. Moorhouse (Leeds Central)	2:24.96
1982	A. Moorhouse (Leeds Central)	2:19.97
1983	A. Moorhouse (Co Leeds)	2:24.03
1984	M. Buswell (Co Leeds)	2:22.71
1985	A. Moorhouse (Co Leeds)	2:19.73
1986	A. Moorhouse (Co Leeds)	2:20.65

Chris Walkden

1987	N. Gillingham (Co Birmingham)	2:18.18
1988	N. Gillingham (Co Birmingham)	2:16.29
1989	N. Gillingham (Co Birmingham)	2:18.45

110 Yards Butterfly
1964	V. Slovin (S Africa)	1:00.40
1965	D. Sherry (Canada)	58.10
1966	J. Thurley (Sutton & Cheam)	1:01.70
1967	L. Norris (Barracuda)	1:00.30
1968	M. Woodroffe (Cardiff)	59.80
1969	M. Woodroffe (Llanstrisant)	59.20
1970	M. Woodroffe (Madeley College)	1:00.10

100 Metres Butterfly
1971	B. Robertson (Canada)	58.40
1972	J. Mills (St James)	59.20
1973	M. Edwards (Camp Hill Edwardians)	58.90
1974	B. Brinkley (Modernians)	58.50
1975	B. Brinkley (Modernians)	57.03
1976	J. Mills (Sutton & Cheam)	56.68
1977	J. Mills (Sutton & Cheam)	57.80
1978	J. Mills (Sutton & Cheam)	56.35
1979	P. Hubble (Reading)	57.47
1980	P. Hubble (Slough Dolphins)	56.17
1981	D. Lowe (Harrow & Wealdstone)	56.10
1982	P. Hubble (Hounslow B)	55.61
1983	K. Lee (Barnet Copthall)	56.45
1984	D. Williams (Salford Triple 'S')	57.07
1985	P. Easter (Norwich Penguins)	57.62
1986	A. Jameson (Co Liverpool)	55.98
1987	N. Cochran (Co Swansea)	55.49
1988	A. Jameson (Co Liverpool)	53.85
1989	D. Parker (Co Coventry)	55.33

220 Yards Butterfly
1953	B. Barnes (Preston)	2:44.20
1954	J. Hale (Hull C)	2:39.50
1955	G. Symonds (Coventry)	2:36.30
1956	D. Dickson (Stoke Newington)	2:43.80
1957	R. Campion (Stoke Newington)	2:44.20
1958	I. Black (Gordon's College)	2:25.20
1959	I. Black (Gordon's College)	2:22.70
1960	I. Blyth (Whitehall)	2:23.50
1961	B. Jenkins (Swindon Dolphins)	2:19.00
1962	B. Jenkins (Swindon Dolphins)	2:16.70
1963	B. Jenkins (Swindon Dolphins)	2:17.60
1964	V. Slovin (S Africa)	2:13.50
1965	D. Sherry (Canada)	2:13.50
1966	J. Thurley (Sutton & Cheam)	2:15.10
1967	M. Woodroffe (Cardiff)	2:15.30
1968	M. Woodroffe (Cardiff)	2:11.00
1969	M. Woodroffe (Llanstrisant)	2:09.90
1970	M. Woodroffe (Madeley College)	2:10.70

200 Metres Butterfly
1971	J. Mills (St James)	2:10.10
1972	B. Brinkley (Modernians)	2:05.60
1973	B. Brinkley (Modernians)	2:07.55
1974	B. Brinkley (Modernians)	2:07.30
1975	B. Brinkley (Modernians)	2:05.68
1976	P. Hubble (Chelsea & Kensington)	2:07.04
1977	P. Sparkes (Merton Swordfish)	2:05.19
1978	P. Hubble (Reading)	2:03.66
1979	P. Sparkes (Beckenham)	2:04.66
1980	P. Hubble (Slough Dolphins)	2:01.60
1981	S. Poulter (Wigan Wasps)	2:02.76
1982	P. Hubble (Hounslow B)	2:01.16
1983	P. Hubble (Hounslow B)	2:02.94
1984	D. Emerson (Co Leeds)	2:05.52
1985	N. Hodgson (Wigan Wasps)	2:05.76

Martyn Woodroffe

1986	N. Hodgson (Wigan Wasps)	2:02.85
1987	S. Poulter (Wigan Wasps)	2:03.26
1988	T. Jones (Co Birmingham)	2:02.25
1989	A. Quinn (Sale)	2:05.08

220 Yards Individual Medley
1966	A. Kimber (Co Southampton)	2:21.80
1967	P. Reynolds (Australia)	2:19.80
1968	M. Woodroffe (Cardiff)	2:18.90
1969	M. Woodroffe (Llanstrisant)	2:17.60
1970	M. Woodroffe (Madeley College)	2:18.20

200 Metres Individual Medley
1971	B. Brinkley (Modernians)	2:19.50
1972	R. Terrell (Co Southampton)	2:11.90
1973	B. Brinkley (Modernians)	2:10.95
1974	D. Wilkie (Warrender)	2:12.30
1975	B. Brinkley (Modernians)	2:10.89
1976	J. Carter (Paisley)	2:12.60
1977	D. Cleworth (Co Manchester)	2:11.27
1978	D. Cleworth (Co Manchester)	2:09.98
1979	G. Sykes (Co Coventry)	2:11.89
1980	R. Brew (Kelly College)	2:08.86
1981	G. Sykes (Co Coventry)	2:08.72
1982	I. Collins (Wulfrunians)	2:08.53
1983	R. Brew (Wulfrunians)	2:07.01
1984	P. Brew (Kelly College)	2:08.28
1985	S. Willmott (Stockton Aquatics)	2:07.94
1986	P. Brew (Kelly College)	2:06.62
1987	G. Binfield (Salford Triple 'S')	2:05.41
1988	N. Cochran (Co Swansea)	2:05.59
1989	G. Robins (Portsmouth Northsea)	2:06.05

440 Yards Individual Medley
1963	B. Jenkins (Swindon Dolphins)	5:16.90
1964	T. Lacey (USA)	5:06.70
1965	J. Gilchrist (Canada)	4:55.30
1966	A. Kimber (Co Southampton)	5:02.00
1967	A. Kimber (Co Southampton)	4:54.80
1968	M. Woodroffe (Cardiff) A. Kimber (Co Southampton)	4:55.50
1969	M. Woodroffe (Llanstrisant)	4:55.10
1970	M. Woodroffe (Madeley College)	4:52.50

400 Metres Individual Medley
| 1971 | S. Roxborough (Canada) | 4:58.10 |

Ray Terrell

E. Collinson

1972	R. Terrell (Co Southampton)	4:42.70
1973	B. Brinkley (Modernians)	4:36.29
1974	J. Carter (Paisley)	4:42.00
1975	J. Carter Paisley)	4:38.06
1976	A. McClatchey (Warrender)	4:35.25
1977	A. McClatchey (Warrender)	4:36.18
1978	S. Gray (Amateur)	4:34.92
1979	P. Sparkes (Beckenham)	4:34.57
1980	S. Gray (Harrow & Wealdstone)	4:32.00
1981	S. Poulter (Wigan Wasps)	4:31.98
1982	S. Poulter (Wigan Wasps)	4:36.39
1983	J. Davey (Co Milton Keynes)	4:28.05
1984	G. Binfield (Salford Triple 'S')	4:34.81
1985	G. Robins (Portsmouth Northsea)	4:39.42
1986	J. Davey (Salford Triple 'S')	4:24.70
1987	J. Davey (Salford Triple 'S')	4:24.20
1988	J. Davey (Salford Triple 'S')	4:24.97
1989	P. Brew (Kelly College)	4:26.45

Freestyle Team Swimming

1909 Wigan
1910 Wigan
1911 Hyde Seal
1912 Hyde Seal
1913 Hyde Seal
1920 Hammersmith
1921 Middlesbrough
1922 Penguin
1923 Northumberland
1924 Penguin
1925 Penguin
1926 Penguin
1927 Penguin
1928 S Manchester

1929 Oldham Police
1930 Oldham Police
1931 Oldham Police
1932 Oldham Police
1933 Otter
1934 Oldham Police
1935 Otter
1936 Otter
1937 Otter
1938 Otter
1946 Yorkshire
1947 Yorkshire

4×110 Yards Freestyle Club Relay

1955	Otter	4:06.50
1956	Otter	4:09.50
1957	Wallasey	4:06.10
1958	York C	4:01.40
1959	York C	4:02.60
1960	Stoke Newington	3:58.20
1961	York C	3:57.30
1962	York C	3:55.60
1963	York C	3:54.10
1964	York C	3:52.20
1965	York C	3:53.30
1966	York C	3:52.60
1967	Otter	3:49.50
1968	Co Southampton	3:49.90
1969	Co Southampton	3:48.50
1970	Co Southampton	3:49.10

4×100 Metres Freestyle Club Relay

1971	Nottingham Northern	3:49.60
1972	Co Southampton	3:46.50
1973	Co Southampton	3:45.35

1974	Modernians	3:50.40
1975	Modernians	3:46.05
1976	Modernians	3:40.90
1977	Co Southampton	3:42.04
1978	Beckenham	3:36.51
1979	Beckenham	3:34.39
1980	Beckenham	3:31.22
1981	Co Southampton	3:33.04
1982	Barnet Copthall	3:32.94
1983	Barnet Copthall	3:31.46
1984	Barnet Copthall	3:35.75
1985	Barnet Copthall	3:34.98
1986	Millfield	3:31.07
1987	Co Birmingham	3:26.38
1988	Co Birmingham	3:30.21
1989	Co Birmingham	3:30.14

4×220 Yards Freestyle Club Relay

1952	Sparkhill	9:37.00
1953	Sparkhill	9:42.50
1954	Coventry	9:38.40

4×233⅓ Yards Freestyle Club Relay

1948	Otter	10:54.40
1950	Blackpool	10:58.70
1951	Sparkhill	10:33.60

4×240 Yards Freestyle Club Relay

1949	Otter	11:05.40

3×110 Yards Medley Club Relay

1946	Otter	3:46.40

4×110 Yards Medley Club Relay

1955	Otter	4:36.50
1956	Stoke Newington	4:46.80
1957	Otter	4:46.40
1958	Stoke Newington	4:44.90
1959	Stoke Newington	4:38.00
1960	Stoke Newington	4:34.30
1961	Otter	4:34.50
1962	York C	4:29.40
1963	York C	4:28.00
1964	Otter	4:25.30
1965	Barracuda	4:26.40
1966	Stoke Newington	4:19.20
1967	Stoke Newington	4:18.40
1968	Co Southampton	4:19.30
1969	Co Southampton	4:20.40
1970	Co Southampton	4:16.00

4×100 Metres Medley Club Relay

1971	Nottingham Northern	4:13.50
1972	Co Southampton	4:11.70
1973	Co Southampton	4:07.40
1974	Millfield	4:13.00
1975	Co Southampton	4:07.57
1976	Co Southampton	4:03.28
1977	Co Southampton	4:01.79
1978	Beckenham	3:58.91
1979	Co Southampton	3:57.13
1980	Beckenham	3:53.00
1981	Co Southampton	3:58.21
1982	Co Southampton	3:56.54
1983	Co Leeds	3:58.33
1984	Salford Triple 'S'	3:55.73
1985	Co Leeds	3:58.26
1986	Co Leeds	3:55.58
1987	Co Birmingham	3:54.91
1988	Beckenham	3:52.80
1989	Co Leeds	3:49.27

2×100 + 2×200 Yards Medley Club Relay

1949	Otter	6:52.20
1950	Otter	7:02.00
1951	Penguin	6:56.70

2×110 + 2×200 Yards Medley Club Relay

1947	Otter	7:51.20
1948	Otter	7:53.40
1952	Penguin	7:41.60
1953	Otter	7:46.30
1954	Otter	7:32.20

Women

50 Metres Freestyle

1985	A. Jones (Camden Swiss Cottage)	27.68
1986	N. Fibbens (Beckenham)	26.80
1987	N. Kennedy (Avon Neptunes)	27.14
1988	C. van Bentum (Holland)	26.72
1989	C. Woodcock (Haywards Heath)	26.49

100 Yards Freestyle

1901	H. Thorp (Leeds)	1:30.40
1902	M. Scott (Bacup)	1:25.20
1903	H. Thorp (Leeds)	1:27.60
1904	H. Mackay (Farnfield)	1:25.00
1905	M. Scott (Bacup)	1:24.60
1906	J. Fletcher (Leicester)	1:24.00
1907	J. Fletcher (Leicester)	1:18.00
1908	J. Fletcher (Leicester)	1:18.00
1909	J. Fletcher (Leicester)	1:14.00
1910	I. Steer (Cardiff)	1:13.60
1911	J. Fletcher (Leicester)	1:15.60
1912	J. Fletcher (Leicester)	1:15.20
1913	D. Curwen (Westminster)	1:13.60
1920	C. Jeans (Nottingham)	1:14.00
1921	H. James (Garston)	1:11.00
1922	C. Jeans (Nottingham)	1:09.20
1923	C. Jeans (Nottingham)	1:07.40
1924	C. Jeans (Nottingham)	1:07.20
1925	C. Jeans (Nottingham)	1:07.20
1926	M. Laverty (Moss Side)	1:07.40
1927	M. Hamblen (Hammersmith)	1:08.20
1928	V. Tanner (Eastbourne)	1:06.20
1929	M. Cooper (Mermaid)	1:06.00
1930	E. King (Zenith)	1:09.00
1931	M. Cooper (Mermaid)	1:05.60
1932	M. Cooper (Mermaid)	1:02.80
1933	S. Calderhead (Barrow)	1:07.20
1934	E. Hughes (Walsall)	1:06.80
1935	O. Wadham (Bournemouth)	1:03.60
1936	O. Wadham (Bournemouth)	1:02.80
1937	O. Wadham (Bournemouth)	1:03.40
1938	J. Harrowby (United)	1:02.20
1946	N. Riach (Motherwell)	1:03.00
1947	N. Riach (Motherwell)	1:02.40
1948	M. Wellington (Beckenham)	1:02.80
1949	E. Turner (Galashiels)	1:02.40
1950	P. Linton (Maindee)	1:02.90
1951	P. Linton (Maindee)	1:03.50
1952	A. Barnwell (Worthing)	1:02.20

110 Yards Freestyle

1953	J. Botham (S Manchester)	1:09.70
1954	J. Botham (S Manchester)	1:09.40
1955	F. Ewart (Hastings & St Leonards)	1:08.30
1956	V. Grant (Canada)	1:07.00
1957	D. Wilkinson (Stockport)	1:05.70
1958	J. Grinham (Hampstead)	1:06.80

199

1959	N. Steward (Hornchurch)	1:05.20
1960	N. Steward (Hornchurch)	1:04.90
1961	D. Wilkinson (Stockport)	1:04.90
1962	D. Wilkinson (Stockport)	1:03.30
1963	D. Wilkinson (Stockport)	1:03.30
1964	D. Wilkinson (Stockport)	1:04.40
1965	M. Lay (Canada)	1:01.40
1966	P. Sillett (Radcliffe)	1:02.90
1967	A. Jackson (Peel)	1:02.60
1968	A. Jackson (Peel)	1:01.70
1969	A. Jackson (Peel)	1:03.70
1970	A. Jackson (Peel)	1:01.20

100 Metres Freestyle

1971	L. Hill (Co Southampton)	1:02.20
1972	L. Allardice (Killerwhales)	1:01.20
1973	L. Allardice (Killerwhales)	1:00.71
1974	G. Amundred (Canada)	1:01.00
1975	D. Hill (Portsmouth Northsea)	1:01.21
1976	C. Brazendale (Norbreck Castle)	59.58
1977	V. Bullock (Co Cardiff)	59.14
1978	S. Davies (Po Plymouth)	59.23
1979	J. Croft (Wigan Wasps)	59.15
1980	J. Croft (Wigan Wasps)	57.59
1981	J. Croft (Wigan Wasps)	57.89
1982	J. Croft (Wigan Wasps)	56.71
1983	J. Croft (Wigan Wasps)	58.22
1984	D. Gore (Fleetwood & D)	59.12
1985	A. Jones (Camden Swiss Cottage)	59.71
1986	A. Cowley (Wigan Wasps)	57.51
1987	Z. Long (Kelly College)	58.44
1988	C. van Bentum (Holland)	57.03
1989	K. Pickering (Ipswich)	58.21

220 Yards Freestyle

1912	D. Curwen (Westminster)	3:08.80
1913	D. Curwen (Westminster)	3:12.40
1920	C. Jeans (Nottingham)	3:02.60
1921	H. James (Garston)	3:05.20
1922	H. James (Garston)	3:10.00
1923	C. Jeans (Nottingham)	2:54.00
1924	H. James (Cunard)	2:58.60
1925	C. Jeans (Nottingham)	2:52.80
1926	E. Mayne (Torquay Leander)	2:57.80
1927	M. Cooper (Mermaid)	2:49.40
1928	M. Cooper (Mermaid)	2:46.40
1929	M. Cooper (Mermaid)	2:48.00
1930	B. Yarwood (Eccles)	3:09.00
1931	M. Cooper (Mermaid)	2:50.60
1932	M. Cooper (Mermaid)	2:42.20
1933	B. Wolstenholme (Moss Side)	2:43.80
1934	M. Kenyon (Nelson)	2:44.80
1935	O. Bartle (Croydon)	2:45.00
1936	G. Morcom (Tipton)	2:43.00
1937	O. Bartle (Croydon)	2:42.60
1938	M. Jeffrey (Croydon)	2:40.80
1946	N. Riach (Motherwell)	2:36.00
1947	C. Gibson (Motherwell)	2:29.20
1948	C. Gibson (Motherwell)	2:32.60
1949	M. Wellington (Beckenham)	2:34.20
1950	P. Linton (Maindee)	2:33.10
1951	D. Wilkinson (Woolwich T & SC)	2:31.10
1952	L. Preece (Wallasey)	2:32.00
1953	L. Preece (Wallasey)	2:33.70
1954	J. Botham (S Manchester)	2:34.30
1955	V. Grant (Canada)	2:34.70
1956	V. Grant (Canada)	2:30.60
1957	J. Grinham (Hampstead)	2:30.00
1958	E. Ferguson (York C)	2:28.60

1959	N. Steward (Hornchurch)	2:25.60
1960	N. Steward (Hornchurch)	2:22.10
1961	N. Rae (Motherwell)	2:21.60
1962	D. Wilkinson (Stockport)	2:21.90
1963	A. Lonsbrough (Huddersfield B)	2:19.70
1964	E. Long (Ilford)	2:21.90
1965	E. Long (Ilford)	2:16.10
1966	J. Cave (Bristol Central)	2:20.50
1967	S. Williams (Co Exeter)	2:17.20
1968	A. Jackson (Peel)	2:17.60
1969	S. Ratcliffe (Everton)	2:17.10
1970	A. Jackson (Peel)	2:14.30

200 Metres Freestyle

1971	L. Allardice (Killerwhales)	2:13.90
1972	L. Allardice (Killerwhales)	2:12.20
1973	L. Allardice (Killerwhales)	2:11.19
1974	G. Amundred (Canada)	2:10.42
1975	W. Lee (Canada)	2:09.58
1976	M. Houston (Leeds Central)	2:08.00
1977	S. Davies (Po Plymouth)	2:08.15
1978	S. Davies (Po Plymouth)	2:05.39
1979	S. Davies (Kelly College)	2:04.43
1980	J. Willmott (Southend on Sea)	2:03.23
1981	C. van Bentum (Holland)	2:03.82
1982	J. Croft (Wigan Wasps)	2:01.18
1983	J. Croft (Wigan Wasps)	2:02.94
1984	C. Jackson (Guernsey)	2:06.74
1985	K. Mellor (Norwich Penguins)	2:07.24
1986	A. Cowley (Wigan Wasps)	2:03.16
1987	R. Gilfillan (Co Dundee)	2:03.79
1988	C. van Bentum (Holland)	2:02.20
1989	J. Coull (Co Birmingham)	2:05.23

440 Yards Freestyle

1924	H. James (Cunard)	6:27.00
1925	M. Laverty (Moss Side)	6:18.80
1926	M. Laverty (Moss Side)	6:10.60
1927	M. Laverty (Moss Side)	6:11.40
1928	M. Cooper (Mermaid)	6:08.60
1929	M. Cooper (Mermaid)	6:15.40
1930	M. Cooper (Mermaid)	6:02.40
1931	M. Cooper (Mermaid)	5:58.40
1932	M. Cooper (Mermaid)	6:00.60
1933	B. Wolstenholme (Moss Side)	6:03.00

Lesley Allardice　　　　　　Allsport Photographic

1934	B. Wolstenholme (Moss Side)	5:50.60
1935	B. Wolstenholme (Moss Side)	6:00.00
1936	G. Morcom (Tipton)	5:50.40
1937	O. Bartle (Croydon)	5:50.00
1938	M. Jeffrey (Croydon)	5:43.20
1946	N. Riach (Motherwell)	5:50.00
1947	C. Gibson (Motherwell)	5:23.20
1948	C. Gibson (Motherwell)	5:39.80
1949	M. Wellington (Beckenham)	5:36.40
1950	D. Wilkinson (Sparkhill)	5:26.20
1951	D. Wilkinson (Woolwich T & SC)	5:17.60
1952	D. Wilkinson (Woolwich T & SC)	5:20.40
1953	D. Wilkinson (Woolwich T & SC)	5:29.80
1954	C. Brown (Newcastle under Lyme)	5:33.20
1955	J. Clarke (Isleworth Penguins)	5:34.80
1956	M. Girvan (Motherwell)	5:29.50
1957	E. Ferguson (York C)	5:33.00
1958	E. Ferguson (York C)	5:13.10
1959	N. Steward (Hornchurch)	5:12.90
1960	E. Long (Ilford)	5:05.00
1961	N. Rae (Motherwell)	5:02.80
1962	E. Long (Ilford)	4:53.70
1963	E. Long (Ilford)	4:52.40
1964	E. Long (Ilford)	4:58.50
1965	E. Long (Ilford)	4:48.90
1966	J. Cave (Bristol Central)	4:52.60
1967	S. Williams (Co Exeter)	4:48.50
1968	S. Davison (Chelsea & Kensington)	4:55.80
1969	S. Williams (Co Exeter)	4:51.50
1970	J. Wright (New Zealand)	4:42.60

400 Metres Freestyle

1971	L. Allardice (Killerwhales)	4:44.60
1972	J. Green (Walsall)	4:35.40

1973	J. Green (Walsall)	4:37.28
1974	L. Cliff (Canada)	4:28.50
1975	K. Skilling (Canada)	4:29.51
1976	M. Houston (Leeds Central)	4:28.20
1977	S. Davies (Po Plymouth)	4:26.72
1978	S. Davies (Po Plymouth)	4:20.56
1979	S. Davies (Kelly College)	4:18.59
1980	J. Willmott (Southend on Sea)	4:17.49
1981	J. Willmott (Southend on Sea)	4:16.29
1982	J. Croft (Wigan Wasps)	4:12.72
1983	J. Willmott (Redbridge B)	4:14.36
1984	S. Hardcastle (Southend Synchronettes)	4:20.12
1985	K. Mellor (Norwich Penguins)	4:21.83
1986	S. Hardcastle (Bo Southend)	4:15.39
1987	R. Gilfillan (Co Dundee)	4:18.83
1988	R. Gilfillan (Co Dundee)	4:15.66
1989	K. Mellor (Co Sheffield)	4:22.37

880 Yards Freestyle

1966	J. Cave (Bristol Central)	10:23.50
1967	S. Williams (Co Exeter)	9:59.80
1968	S. Davison (Chelsea & Kensington)	10:04.10
1969	S. Williams (Co Exeter)	10:06.10
1970	J. Wright (New Zealand)	9:48.50

800 Metres Freestyle

1971	J. Green (Walsall)	10:00.10
1972	J. Green (Walsall)	9:31.30
1973	J. Green (Walsall)	9:33.87
1974	L. Cliff (Canada)	9:12.90
1975	K. Skilling (Canada)	9:10.86
1976	A. Nelson (Canada)	9:14.19
1977	L. Heggie (Warrington)	9:09.62

Three Scottish girls: Helen Gordon, Margaret Girvan and Cathie Gibson.

Leicester Evening Mail

1978	S. Davies (Po Plymouth)	8:58.87
1979	J. Willmott (Southend & Leigh)	8:55.14
1980	J. Willmott (Southend on Sea)	8:48.60
1981	J. Willmott (Southend on Sea)	8:38.56
1982	J. Willmott (Southend on Sea)	8:46.73
1983	J. Willmott (Redbridge B)	8:43.98
1984	S. Hardcastle (Southend Synchronettes)	8:52.91
1985	K. Mellor (Norwich Penguins)	9:00.41
1986	S. Hardcastle (Bo Southend)	8:41.11
1987	K. Mellor (Norwich Penguins)	8:54.47
1988	K. Mellor (Co Sheffield)	8:40.41
1989	K. Mellor (Co Sheffield)	8:53.39

100 Yards Backstroke

1947	C. Gibson (Motherwell)	1:10.40
1948	N. Lane (New Zealand)	1:11.80
1949	H. Yate (Mermaid)	1:10.20
1950	M. McDowall (Kilmarnock)	1:11.70
1951	M. McDowall (Kilmarnock)	1:09.20
1952	M. McDowall (Kilmarnock)	1:09.80

110 Yards Backstroke

1953	M. McDowall (Kilmarnock)	1:18.60
1954	J. Symons (Northumberland)	1:16.90
1955	J. Grinham (Hampstead)	1:15.30
1956	J. Grinham (Hampstead)	1:14.50
1957	J. Hoyle (Watford)	1:16.00
1958	J. Grinham (Hampstead)	1:12.90
1959	M. Edwards (Heston)	1:12.50
1960	N. Steward (Hornchurch)	1:11.00
1961	M. Edwards (Heston)	1:13.80
1962	L. Ludgrove (St James)	1:10.90
1963	L. Ludgrove (St James)	1:11.70
1964	L. Ludgrove (Beckenham)	1:09.90
1965	A. Fairlie (S Africa)	1:08.90
1966	L. Ludgrove (Beckenham)	1:09.10
1967	L. Ludgrove (Beckenham)	1:09.50
1968	W. Burrell (Carlisle Secondary)	1:11.20
1969	D. Gurr (Canada)	1:09.10
1970	G. Stirling (New Zealand)	1:08.70

100 Metres Backstroke

1971	J. Brown (Hull Olympic)	1:10.70
1972	J. Brown (Hull Olympic)	1:09.70
1973	M. Kelly (Everton)	1:09.98
1974	W. Cook (Canada)	1:06.20
1975	G. Ladouceur (Canada)	1:07.44
1976	A. James (Co Cardiff)	1:08.50
1977	J. Beasley (Junction Ten)	1:06.82
1978	A. James (Beckenham)	1:06.19
1979	J. Admans (Slough Dolphins)	1:06.71
1980	H. Jameson (Kelly College)	1:05.85
1981	H. Jameson (Kelly College)	1:05.94
1982	C. White (Bo S Tyneside)	1:04.85
1983	C. White (Bo S Tyneside)	1:05.24
1984	K. Read (Norwich Penguins)	1:06.47
1985	K. Read (Stockport Metro)	1:05.94
1986	K. Read (Stockport Metro)	1:05.22
1987	K. Read (Stockport Metro)	1:05.43
1988	K. Read (Norwich Penguins)	1:04.69
1989	K. Read (Barnet Copthall)	1:04.70

150 Yards Backstroke

1920	L. Morton (Blackpool)	2:19.00
1921	M. Spencer (Garston)	2:18.60
1922	I. Gilbert (Attercliffe)	2:16.00
1923	M. Spencer (Garston)	2:18.40
1924	W. Shaw (Sheffield Excelsior)	2:18.60
1925	E. King (Warrender Baths)	2:04.00

1926	E. King (Zenith)	2:04.60
1927	M. Barker (St Pancras)	2:03.80
1928	E. King (Zenith)	1:57.20
1929	M. Cooper (Mermaid)	1:59.20
1930	I. Clifford (Hammersmith)	2:05.00
1931	M. Cooper (Mermaid)	1:55.40
1932	M. Welsh (Northumberland)	S/O
1933	M. McNulty (Moss Side)	2:04.80
1934	B. Wolstenholme (Moss Side)	1:58.40
1935	P. Harding (Coventry Three Spires)	1:56.60
1936	P. Harding (Croydon)	1:55.00
1937	L. Frampton (Hounslow B)	1:56.40
1938	H. Yate (Po Plymouth)	1:56.60
1946	M. Berlioux (France)	1:52.60

220 Yards Backstroke

1964	L. Ludgrove (Beckenham)	2:31.30
1965	A. Fairlie (S Africa)	2:30.20
1966	L. Ludgrove (Beckenham)	2:29.00
1967	L. Ludgrove (Beckenham)	2:29.80
1968	W. Burrell (Carlisle Secondary)	2:32.80
1969	D. Gurr (Canada)	2:28.80
1970	W. Burrell (Carlisle Secondary)	2:28.90

200 Metres Backstroke

1971	D. Ashton (Wythenshawe)	2:30.70
1972	D. Ashton (Wythenshawe)	2:29.00
1973	G. Fordyce (Criterion)	2:29.48
1974	W. Cook (Canada)	2:23.10
1975	G. Ladouceur (Canada)	2:26.09
1976	S. Davies (Po Plymouth)	2:23.63
1977	S. Davies (Po Plymouth)	2:21.18
1978	S. Davies (Po Plymouth)	2:20.10
1979	J. Admans (Slough Dolphins)	2:18.94
1980	J. Admans (Slough Dolphins)	2:19.02
1981	J. de Rover (Holland)	2:17.93
1982	C. White (Bo S Tyneside)	2:19.80
1983	C. White (Bo S Tyneside)	2:20.08
1984	K. Read (Norwich Penguins)	2:21.45
1985	K. Read (Stockport Metro)	2:18.32
1986	K. Read (Stockport Metro)	2:14.87
1987	K. Read (Stockport Metro)	2:18.64
1988	J. de Rover (Holland)	2:17.39
1989	K. Read (Barnet Copthall)	2:16.11

Jill Slattery

110 Yards Breaststroke

1964	J. Slattery (Sheffield C)	1:20.60
1965	D. Harris (Beckenham)	1:19.20
1966	D. Harris (Beckenham)	1:19.20
1967	A. Radnage (York C)	1:19.10
1968	D. Harris (Beckenham)	1:18.80
1969	A. O'Connor (Guinness)	1:19.90
1970	A. Radnage (York C)	1:19.50

100 Metres Breaststroke

1971	D. Harrison (Hartlepool)	1:18.80
1972	C. Jarvis (Modernians)	1:17.40
1973	C. Jarvis (Modernians)	1:17.93
1974	S. Dickie (Paisley)	1:16.40
1975	M. Kelly (Co Cardiff)	1:16.18
1976	M. Kelly (Co Cardiff)	1:14.23
1977	M. Kelly (Cumbernauld)	1:15.32
1978	M. Kelly (Beckenham)	1:13.39
1979	M. Kelly (Beckenham)	1:12.80
1980	M. Kelly (Beckenham)	1:12.21
1981	S. Brownsdon (RTW Monson)	1:12.32
1982	J. Seymour (Camp Hill Edwardians)	1:14.28
1983	L. Burt (Reading)	1:13.64
1984	S. Bowman (Darlington Diana)	1:13.89
1985	S. Bowman (Darlington Diana)	1:15.42
1986	S. Brownsdon (Wigan Wasps)	1:13.78
1987	S. Brownsdon (RTW Monson)	1:12.32
1988	S. Brownsdon (RTW Monson)	1:11.89
1989	S. Brownsdon (Wigan Wasps)	1:11.55

200 Yards Breaststroke

1920	L. Morton (Blackpool)	3:10.00
1921	G. Carson (Leicester)	3:12.40
1922	D. Hart (Mermaid)	3:02.80
1923	D. Hart (Mermaid)	3:03.80
1924	M. Harrison (Sheffield Dolphins)	3:07.60
1925	I. Gilbert (Attercliffe)	3:05.00
1926	E. Morris (Birmingham)	3:11.20
1927	E. King (Zenith)	3:06.40
1928	E. King (Zenith)	3:10.00
1929	M. Hinton (S Manchester)	3:08.00
1930	C. Wolstenholme (Moss Side)	2:56.80
1931	M. Hinton (S Manchester)	2:56.60
1932	M. Hinton (S Manchester)	2:56.60
1933	M. Hinton (S Manchester)	2:58.60
1934	M. Hinton (S Manchester)	2:57.40
1935	V. Kingston (United)	2:53.60
1936	D. Storey (E Leeds)	2:53.60
1937	D. Storey (E Leeds)	2:53.80
1938	D. Storey (Montague Burton)	2:49.20
1946	J. Caplin (Brighton)	3:01.20
1947	E. Church (Northampton)	2:52.80
1948	E. Church (Northampton)	2:54.20
1949	J. Caspers (Sweden)	2:47.10
1950	H. Gordon (Hamilton Baths)	2:46.00
1951	H. Gordon (Hamilton Baths)	2:45.50
1952	H. Gordon (Hamilton Baths)	2:43.00

220 Yards Breaststroke

1953	M. Grundy (Blackpool)	3:07.90
1954	M. Grundy (Blackpool)	3:03.80
1955	H. Gordon (Hamilton Baths)	3:01.10
1956	H. Gordon (Hamilton Baths)	2:59.20
1957	C. Gosden (Croydon)	2:56.50
1958	A. Lonsbrough (Huddersfield B)	2:55.80
1959	A. Lonsbrough (Huddersfield B)	2:54.00
1960	A. Lonsbrough (Huddersfield B)	2:56.10
1961	A. Lonsbrough (Huddersfield B)	2:53.70
1962	A. Lonsbrough (Huddersfield B)	2:52.20
1963	S. Mitchell (Hampstead)	2:52.60

Dorothy Harrison

1964	S. Mitchell (Hampstead)	2:50.50
1965	S. Mitchell (Heston)	2:49.20
1966	S. Mitchell (Heston)	2:49.30
1967	J. Slattery (Sheffield C)	2:49.20
1968	J. Slattery (Attercliffe)	2:49.30
1969	D. Harrison (Hartlepool)	2:50.00
1970	D. Harrison (Hartlepool)	2:48.80

200 Metres Breaststroke

1971	D. Harrison (Hartlepool)	2:51.20
1972	P. Beavan (Kingsbury)	2:46.40
1973	C. Tamlyn (Beckenham)	2:47.18
1974	M. Stuart (Canada)	2:45.10
1975	M. Kelly (Co Cardiff)	2:42.13
1976	D. Rudd (Co Coventry)	2:39.15
1977	M. Kelly (Cumbernauld)	2:39.45
1978	M. Kelly (Beckenham)	2:38.17
1979	D. Rudd (Co Coventry)	2:37.97
1980	M. Kelly (Beckenham)	2:37.16
1981	S. Brownsdon (RTW Monson)	2:36.85

Margaret Grundy

1982 G. Stanley (Wigan Wasps)	2:38.95
1983 G. Stanley (Wigan Wasps)	2:38.92
1984 N. Herbert (Reading)	2:39.69
1985 G. Stanley (Wigan Wasps)	2:38.52
1986 S. Brownsdon (Wigan Wasps)	2:34.17
1987 S. Brownsdon (RTW Monson)	2:34.95
1988 S. Brownsdon (RTW Monson)	2:34.71
1989 S. Brownsdon (Wigan Wasps)	2:35.01

110 Yards Butterfly

1953 M. Ivinson (Border C)	1:24.20
1954 F. Webb (Cheam)	1:24.00
1955 C. MacAdam (Heston)	1:17.70
1956 A. Morton (Blackpool)	1:17.40
1957 C. Gosden (Croydon)	1:16.90
1958 S. Watt (Aberdeen Thistle)	1:14.50
1959 S. Watt (Aberdeen Thistle)	1:13.90
1960 S. Watt (Aberdeen Thistle)	1:12.40
1961 L. Green (Hampstead)	1:12.70
1962 P. Baines (Stoke Newington)	1:11.30
1963 M. Stewart (Canada)	1:08.60
1964 M. Cotterill (Watford)	1:10.20
1965 E. Tanner (Canada)	1:08.10
1966 A. Barner (York C)	1:08.80
1967 A. Barner (York C)	1:08.00
1968 M. Auton (Hartlepool)	1:08.10
1969 M. Auton (Hartlepool)	1:08.10
1970 C. Whiting (New Zealand)	1:08.00

100 Metres Butterfly

1971 J. Jeavons (Melton Mowbray)	1:10.00
1972 J. Jeavons (Melton Mowbray)	1:06.60
1973 J. Atkinson (Darlington)	1:06.26
1974 P. Stenhouse (Canada)	1:06.80
1975 H. Boivin (Canada)	1:05.22
1976 L. Taylor (Co Coventry)	1:04.97
1977 J. Hull (Basildon)	1:05.45
1978 S. Jenner (Mermaid & Marlin)	1:04.29
1979 A. Osgerby (Wigan Wasps)	1:03.33
1980 A. Osgerby (Wigan Wasps)	1:02.47
1981 J. Osgerby (Wigan Wasps)	1:03.40
1982 A. Osgerby (Wigan Wasps)	1:02.60
1983 A. Osgerby (Wigan Wasps)	1:01.87
1984 S. Purvis (Stockton Aquatics)	1:02.17
1985 C. Cooper (Potters Bar)	
S. Purvis (Stockton Aquatics)	1:03.38
1986 C. Foot (Millfield)	1:02.21
1987 S. Purvis (Co Birmingham)	1:03.23
1988 C. van Bentum (Holland)	1:02.10
1989 M. Scarborough (Portsmouth Northsea)	1:02.05

220 Yards Butterfly

1966 A. Barner (York C)	2:34.70
1967 A. Barner (York C)	2:36.40
1968 M. Auton (Hartlepool)	2:32.70
1969 V. Smith (Otter, Dublin)	2:33.10
1970 V. Smith (Otter, Dublin)	2:33.70

200 Metres Butterfly

1971 C. Stockley (Watford)	2:37.20
1972 J. Jeavons (Melton Mowbray)	2:23.60
1973 J. Jeavons (Co Coventry)	2:25.17
1974 P. Stenhouse (Canada)	2:23.50
1975 J. Bonner (Canada)	2:22.96
1976 A. Nelson (Canada)	2:23.50
1977 S. Jenner (Mermaid & Marlin)	2:19.50
1978 S. Jenner (Mermaid & Marlin)	2:16.42
1979 A. Osgerby (Wigan Wasps)	2:18.45
1980 A. Osgerby (Wigan Wasps)	2:15.90

1981 A. Osgerby (Wigan Wasps)	2:18.19
1982 F. Ross (Bexley)	2:16.67
1983 A. Osgerby (Wigan Wasps)	2:13.79
1984 S. Purvis (Stockton Aquatics)	2:15.41
1985 S. Purvis (Stockton Aquatics)	2:17.86
1986 H. Bewley (Millfield)	2:15.87
1987 H. Bewley (Millfield)	2:15.28
1988 C. van Bentum (Holland)	2:12.33
1989 S. Purvis (Wigan Wasps)	2:15.24

220 Yards Individual Medley

1966 J. Turnbull (Hartlepool)	2:37.60
1967 S. Ratcliffe (Everton)	2:34.60
1968 S. Ratcliffe (Everton)	2:34.70
1969 S. Ratcliffe (Everton)	2:34.20
1970 S. Ratcliffe (Everton)	2:30.70

200 Metres Individual Medley

1971 D. Banks (Chelmsford)	2:34.90
1972 S. Richardson (Beckenham)	2:31.40
1973 D. Walker (Thistle)	2:31.81
1974 L. Cliff (Canada)	2:27.20
1975 H. Boivin (Canada)	2:25.72
1976 S. Davies (Po Plymouth)	2:26.46
1977 S. Davies (Po Plymouth)	2:22.95
1978 S. Davies (Po Plymouth)	2:19.75
1979 S. Davies (Kelly College)	2:20.40
1980 S. Davies (Kelly College)	2:20.73
1981 A. Verstappen (Holland)	2:21.66
1982 J. Croft (Wigan Wasps)	2:20.65
1983 M. Scott (Fleetwood & D)	2:22.98
1984 C. Jackson (Guernsey)	2:23.52
1985 Z. Long (Kelly College)	2:22.04
1986 Z. Long (Kelly College)	2:19.96
1987 Z. Long (Kelly College)	2:20.55
1988 M. A. Muis (Holland)	2:19.22
1989 S. Davies (Bracknell)	2:19.29

440 Yards Individual Medley

1963 A. Lonsbrough (Huddersfield B)	5:37.00
1964 A. Lonsbrough (Huddersfield B)	5:39.40
1965 B. Hounsell (Canada)	5:35.00
1966 S. Williams (Co Exeter)	5:37.00
1967 S. Ratcliffe (Everton)	5:27.70
1968 S. Ratcliffe (Everton)	5:31.40

Ann Osgerby   Swimming Times

Shelagh Ratcliffe

Drylegs

1969	S. Ratcliffe (Everton)	5:28.00
1970	S. Ratcliffe (Everton)	5:19.10

400 Metres Individual Medley

1971	D. Banks (Chelmsford)	5:26.90
1972	D. Walker (Thistle)	5:17.30
1973	D. Walker (Thistle)	5:16.20
1974	L. Cliff (Canada)	5:06.12
1975	S. Richardson (Beckenham)	5:08.82
1976	S. Davies (Po Plymouth)	5:03.33
1977	S. Davies (Po Plymouth)	4:56.28
1978	S. Davies (Po Plymouth)	4:56.07
1979	S. Davies (Kelly College)	4:55.08
1980	S. Davies (Kelly College)	4:56.90
1981	M. Scott (Fleetwood & D)	4:56.64
1982	L. Tate (Leeds Central)	4:59.43
1983	S. Hardcastle (Redbridge B)	4:55.17
1984	K. Read (Norwich Penguins)	4:58.53
1985	K. Read (Stockport Metro)	4:53.21
1986	S. Hardcastle (Bo Southend)	4:50.94
1987	G. Stanley (Stockport Metro)	4:56.88
1988	T. Atkin (Co Lincoln Pentaqua)	4:51.85
1989	S. Brownsdon (Wigan Wasps)	4:51.91

4×100 Yards Freestyle Club Relay

1948	Beckenham	4:38.00
1949	Weston super Mare	4:36.60
1950	Croydon	4:40.70
1951	Croydon	4:39.50

4×110 Yards Freestyle Club Relay

1952	Mermaid	4:57.00
1953	Mermaid	5:01.80
1954	Mermaid	4:59.40
1955	Leander	5:02.30

1956	Mermaid	4:53.30
1957	Kingston	4:53.00
1958	Kingston	4:49.80
1959	Beckenham	4:45.30
1960	Mermaid	4:40.50
1961	Hampstead	4:40.00
1962	Hampstead	4:34.30
1963	Hampstead	4:30.30
1964	Stoke Newington	4:33.20
1965	Hampstead	4:31.60
1966	Kingston	4:29.10
1967	Beckenham	4:26.20
1968	Beckenham	4:31.80
1969	Beckenham	4:28.80
1970	Hornchurch	4:25.30

4×100 Metres Freestyle Club Relay

1971	Killerwhales	4:21.90
1972	Cheam	4:17.30
1973	Killerwhales	4:19.68
1974	Paisley	4:19.50
1975	Beckenham	4:13.48
1976	Co Cardiff	4:07.09
1977	Millfield	4:06.55
1978	Co Cardiff	4:03.88
1979	Wigan Wasps	4:03.14
1980	Millfield	4:01.09
1981	Wigan Wasps	4:00.25
1982	Wigan Wasps	3:59.35
1983	Millfield	3:58.44
1984	Co Manchester	4:03.75
1985	Stockport Metro	4:04.50
1986	Wigan Wasps	3:56.51
1987	Wigan Wasps	3:56.56

1988 Wigan Wasps	4:00.40
1989 Co Birmingham	3:58.54

4×100 Yards Medley Club Relay
1935 Coventry Three Spires	
1936 Bournemouth	
1937 Bournemouth	
1938 United	
1949 Northampton	4:55.20
1950 Hampstead	4:56.90
1951 Croydon	4:56.60

4×110 Yards Medley Club Relay
1946 Mermaid	5:59.20
1947 Beckenham	5:38.10
1948 Mermaid	5:27.40
1952 Mermaid	5:26.40
1953 Mermaid	5:19.00
1954 Mermaid	5:22.70
1955 Mermaid	5:15.00
1956 Leander	5:24.70
1957 Heston	5:21.70
1958 Heston	5:14.50
1959 Heston	5:12.40
1960 Heston	5:09.20
1961 Heston	5:04.90
1962 Hampstead	5:05.50
1963 Hampstead	4:58.00

1964 Beckenham	4:51.70
1965 Beckenham	4:52.20
1966 Beckenham	4:50.50
1967 Beckenham	4:48.90
1968 York C	4:55.50
1969 Hartlepool	4:50.40
1970 Beckenham	4:53.10

4×100 Metres Medley Club Relay
1971 Co Southampton	4:53.50
1972 Co Southampton	4:44.40
1973 Beckenham	4:46.13
1974 Beckenham	4:43.50
1975 Co Cardiff	4:35.98
1976 Co Coventry	4:31.06
1977 Co Coventry	4:32.00
1978 Beckenham	4:27.66
1979 Beckenham	4:25.43
1980 Wigan Wasps	4:24.58
1981 Wigan Wasps	4:25.60
1982 Wigan Wasps	4:20.06
1983 Wigan Wasps	4:21.90
1984 Millfield	4:27.48
1985 Wigan Wasps	4:30.57
1986 Wigan Wasps	4:22.93
1987 Stockport Metro	4:23.63
1988 Norwich Penguins	4:23.20
1989 Wigan Wasps	4:27.29

Commonwealth Champions, 1930–1986

Men

100 Yards Freestyle
1930 M. Bourne (Canada)	56.00
1934 G. Burleigh (Canada)	55.00

110 Yards Freestyle
1938 B. Pirie (Canada)	59.60
1950 P. Salmon (Canada)	1:00.40
1954 J. Henricks (Australia)	56.50
1958 J. Devitt (Australia)	56.60
1962 D. Pound (Canada)	55.80
1966 M. Wenden (Australia)	54.00

100 Metres Freestyle
1970 M. Wenden (Australia)	53.06
1974 M. Wenden (Australia)	52.73
1978 M. Morgan (Australia)	52.70
1982 N. Brooks (Australia)	51.14
1986 G. Fasala (Australia)	50.95

200 Metres Freestyle
1970 M. Wenden (Australia)	1:56.69
1974 S. Badger (Canada)	1:56.72
1978 R. McKeon (Australia)	1:52.06
1982 A. Astbury (England)	1:51.52
1986 R. Gleria (Australia)	1:50.57

400 Yards Freestyle
1930 N. Ryan (Australia)	4:39.80

440 Yards Freestyle
1934 N. Ryan (Australia)	5:03.00
1938 B. Pirie (Canada)	4:54.60
1950 G. Agnew (Australia)	4:49.40
1954 G. Chapman (Australia)	4:39.80
1958 J. Konrads (Australia)	4:25.90
1962 M. Rose (Australia)	4:20.00
1966 B. Windle (Australia)	4:15.00

400 Metres Freestyle
1970 G. White (Australia)	4:08.48
1974 J. Kulasalu (Australia)	4:01.44
1978 R. McKeon (Australia)	3:54.43
1982 A. Astbury (England)	3:53.29
1986 D. Armstrong (Australia)	3:52.25

1500 Yards Freestyle
1930 N. Ryan (Australia)	18:55.40
1934 N. Ryan (Australia)	18:25.40

Andy Astbury

1650 Yards Freestyle

1938	B. Leivers (England)	19:46.40
1950	G. Johnston (S Africa)	19:55.70
1954	G. Johnston (S Africa)	19:01.40
1958	J. Konrads (Australia)	17:45.40
1962	M. Rose (Australia)	17:18.10
1966	R. Jackson (Australia)	17:25.90

1500 Metres Freestyle

1970	G. Windeatt (Australia)	16:23.82
1974	S. Holland (Australia)	15:34.73
1978	M. Metzker (Australia)	15:31.92
1982	M. Metzker (Australia)	15:23.94
1986	J. Plummer (Australia)	15:12.62

100 Yards Backstroke

1930	J. Trippett (England)	1:05.40
1934	W. Francis (Scotland)	1:05.20

110 Yards Backstroke

1938	P. Oliver (Australia)	1:07.90
1950	J. Wild (S Africa)	1:07.70
1954	J. Brockway (Wales)	1:06.50
1958	J. Monkton (Australia)	1:01.70
1962	G. Sykes (England)	1:04.50
1966	P. Reynolds (Australia)	1:02.40

100 Metres Backstroke

1970	B. Kennedy (Canada)	1:01.65
1974	M. Tonelli (Australia)	59.65
1978	G. Patching (Australia)	57.90
1982	M. West (Canada)	57.12
1986	M. Tewksbury (Canada)	56.45

220 Yards Backstroke

1962	J. Carroll (Australia)	2:20.90
1966	P. Reynolds (Australia)	2:12.00

200 Metres Backstroke

1970	M. Richards (Wales)	2:14.53
1974	B. Cooper (Australia)	2:06.31
1978	G. Hurring (New Zealand)	2:04.37
1982	C. Henning (Canada)	2:02.88
1986	S. Goss (Canada)	2:02.55

110 Yards Breaststroke

1962	I. O'Brien (Australia)	1:11.40
1966	I. O'Brien (Australia)	1:08.20

100 Metres Breaststroke

1970	B. Mahony (Canada)	1:09.00
1974	D. Leigh (England)	1:06.52
1978	G. Smith (Canada)	1:03.81
1982	A. Moorhouse (England)	1:02.93
1986	V. Davis (Canada)	1:03.01

200 Yards Breaststroke

1930	J. Aubin (Canada)	2:38.40
1934	N. Hamilton (Scotland)	2:41.40

220 Yards Breaststroke

1938	J. Davies (England)	2:51.90
1950	D. Hawkins (Australia)	2:54.10
1954	J. Doms (New Zealand)	2:52.60
1958	T. Gathercole (Australia)	2:41.60
1962	I. O'Brien (Australia)	2:38.20
1966	I. O'Brien (Australia)	2:29.30

200 Metres Breaststroke

1970	B. Mahony (Canada)	2:30.29
1974	D. Wilkie (Scotland)	2:24.42
1978	G. Smith (Canada)	2:20.86
1982	V. Davis (Canada)	2:16.25
1986	A. Moorhouse (England)	2:16.35

110 Yards Butterfly

1962	K. Berry (Australia)	59.05
1966	R. Jacks (Canada)	1:00.30

100 Metres Butterfly

1970	B. MacDonald (Canada)	58.44
1974	N. Rogers (Australia)	56.58
1978	D. Thompson (Canada)	55.04
1982	D. Thompson (Canada)	54.71
1986	A. Jameson (England)	54.07

220 Yards Butterfly

1958	I. Black (Scotland)	2:22.60
1962	K. Berry (Australia)	2:10.80
1966	D. Gerrard (New Zealand)	2:12.70

Brian Brinkley   Allsport Photographic

200 Metres Butterfly

1970	T. Arusoo (Canada)	2:08.97
1974	B. Brinkley (England)	2:04.51
1978	G. Nagy (Canada)	2:01.99
1982	P. Hubble (England)	2:00.98
1986	A. Mosse (New Zealand)	1:57.27

200 Metres Individual Medley

1970	G. Smith (Canada)	2:13.72
1974	D. Wilkie (Scotland)	2:10.11
1978	G. Smith (Canada)	2:05.25
1982	A. Baumann (Canada)	2:02.25
1986	A. Baumann (Canada)	2:01.80

400 Yards Individual Medley

1970	G. Smith (Canada)	4:48.87
1974	M. Treffers (New Zealand)	4:35.90
1978	G. Smith (Canada)	4:27.34
1982	A. Baumann (Canada)	4:23.53
1986	A. Baumann (Canada)	4:18.29

440 Yards Individual Medley

1962	A. Alexander (Australia)	5:15.30
1966	P. Reynolds (Australia)	4:50.80

4×110 Yards Freestyle Team Relay

1962	Australia	3:43.90
1966	Australia	3:35.60

4×100 Metres Freestyle Team Relay

1970	Australia	3:36.02
1974	Canada	3:33.79
1978	Canada	3:27.94
1982	Australia	3:24.17
1986	Australia	3:21.58

4×200 Yards Freestyle Team Relay

1930	Canada	8:42.40
1934	Canada	8:40.60

4×220 Yards Freestyle Team Relay

1938	England	9:19.00
1950	New Zealand	9:27.70
1954	Australia	8:47.60
1958	Australia	8:33.40
1962	Australia	8:13.40
1966	Australia	7:59.50

4×200 Metres Freestyle Team Relay

1970	Australia	7:50.77
1974	Australia	7:50.13
1978	Australia	7:34.83
1982	Australia	7:28.81
1986	Australia	7:23.49

3×100 Yards Medley Team Relay

1934	Canada	3:11.40

3×110 Yards Medley Team Relay

1938	England	3:28.20
1950	England	3:26.60
1954	Australia	3:22.00

4×110 Yards Medley Team Relay

1958	Australia	4:14.20
1962	Australia	4:12.40
1966	Canada	4:10.50

4×100 Metres Medley Team Relay

1970	Canada	4:01.10
1974	Canada	3:52.93
1978	Canada	3:49.76
1982	Australia	3:47.34
1986	Canada	3:44.00

Women

100 Yards Freestyle

1930	J. Cooper (England)	1:07.00
1934	P. Dewar (Canada)	1:03.50

110 Yards Freestyle

1938	E. de Lacy (Australia)	1:10.10
1950	M. McQuade (Australia)	1:09.00
1954	L. Crapp (Australia)	1:05.80
1958	D. Fraser (Australia)	1:01.40
1962	D. Fraser (Australia)	59.50
1966	M. Lay (Canada)	1:02.30

100 Metres Freestyle

1970	A. Coughlan (Canada)	1:01.22
1974	S. Gray (Australia)	59.13
1978	C. Klimpel (Canada)	57.78
1982	J. Croft (England)	56.97
1986	J. Kerr (Canada)	57.62

200 Metres Freestyle

1970	K. Moras (Australia)	2:09.78
1974	S. Gray (Australia)	2:04.27
1978	R. Perrott (New Zealand)	2:00.63
1982	J. Croft (England)	1:59.74
1986	S. Baumer (Australia)	2:00.61

400 Yards Freestyle

1930	J. Cooper (England)	5:25.40

440 Yards Freestyle

1934	P. Dewar (Canada)	5:45.60
1938	D. Green (Australia)	5:39.70
1950	J. Harrison (S Africa)	5:26.40
1954	L. Crapp (Australia)	5:11.40
1958	I. Konrads (Australia)	4:49.40
1962	D. Fraser (Australia)	4:51.40
1966	K. Wainwright (Australia)	4:38.80

400 Metres Freestyle

1970	K. Moras (Australia)	4:27.38
1974	J. Turrall (Australia)	4:22.09
1978	T. Wickham (Australia)	4:08.45
1982	T. Wickham (Australia)	4:08.82
1986	S. Hardcastle (England)	4:07.68

Linda Ludgrove

800 Metres Freestyle

1970	K. Moras (Australia)	9:02.45
1974	J. Parkhouse (New Zealand)	8:58.49
1978	T. Wickham (Australia)	8:24.62
1982	T. Wickham (Australia)	8:29.05
1986	S. Hardcastle (England)	8:24.77

100 Yards Backstroke

1930	J. Cooper (England)	1:15.00
1934	P. Harding (England)	1:13.80

110 Yards Backstroke

1938	P. Norton (Australia)	1:19.50
1950	J. Davies (Australia)	1:18.60
1954	J. Harrison (S Africa)	1:15.20
1958	J. Grinham (England)	1:11.90
1962	L. Ludgrove (England)	1:11.10
1966	L. Ludgrove (England)	1:09.20

100 Metres Backstroke

1970	L. Watson (Australia)	1:07.10
1974	W. Cook (Canada)	1:06.37
1978	D. Forster (Australia)	1:03.97
1982	L. Forrest (Australia)	1:03.48
1986	S. Hume (New Zealand)	1:04.00

220 Yards Backstroke

1962	L. Ludgrove (England)	2:35.20
1966	L. Ludgrove (England)	2:28.50

200 Metres Backstroke

1970	L. Watson (Australia)	2:22.86
1974	W. Cook (Canada)	2:20.37
1978	C. Gibson (Canada)	2:16.57
1982	L. Forrest (Australia)	2:13.36
1986	G. Parkes (Australia)	2:14.88

110 Yards Breaststroke

1962	A. Lonsbrough (England)	1:21.30
1966	D. Harris (England)	1:19.70

100 Metres Breaststroke

1970	B. Whitfield (Australia)	1:17.40
1974	C. Gaskell (England)	1:16.42
1978	R. Corsiglia (Canada)	1:13.56
1982	K. Bald (Canada)	1:11.89
1986	A. Higson (Canada)	1:10.84

200 Yards Breaststroke

1930	C. Wolstenholme (England)	2:54.80
1934	C. Dennis (Australia)	2:50.20

220 Yards Breaststroke

1938	D. Storey (England)	3:06.30
1950	E. Gordon (Scotland)	3:01.70
1954	E. Gordon (Scotland)	2:59.20
1958	A. Lonsbrough (England)	2:53.50
1962	A. Lonsbrough (England)	2:51.70
1966	J. Slattery (England)	2:50.30

200 Metres Breaststroke

1970	B. Whitfield (Australia)	2:44.12
1974	P. Beavan (Wales)	2:43.11
1978	L. Borsholt (Canada)	2:37.70
1982	A. Ottenbrite (Canada)	2:32.07
1986	A. Higson (Canada)	2:31.20

110 Yards Butterfly

1958	B. Bainbridge (Australia)	1:13.50
1962	M. Stewart (Canada)	1:10.10
1966	E. Tanner (Canada)	1:06.80

100 Metres Butterfly

1970	D. Lansley (England)	1:07.90
1974	P. Stenhouse (Canada)	1:05.38
1978	W. Quirk (Canada)	1:01.92
1982	L. Curry (Australia)	1:01.22
1986	C. Cooper (England)	1:02.12

220 Yards Butterfly

1966	E. Tanner (Canada)	2:29.90

200 Metres Butterfly

1970	M. Robinson (Australia)	2:24.67
1974	S. Yost (Australia)	2:20.57
1978	M. Ford (Australia)	2:11.29
1982	M. Ford (Australia)	2:11.89
1986	D. McGinnis (Canada)	2:11.97

200 Metres Individual Medley

1970	D. Langford (Australia)	2:28.89
1974	L. Cliff (Canada)	2:24.13
1978	S. Davies (England)	2:18.37
1982	L. Curry (Australia)	2:16.94
1986	S. Landells (Australia)	2:17.02

440 Yards Individual Medley

1962	A. Lonsbrough (England)	5:38.60
1966	E. Tanner (Canada)	5:26.30

400 Metres Individual Medley

1970	D. Langford (Australia)	5:10.74
1974	L. Cliff (Canada)	5:01.35
1978	S. Davies (England)	4:52.44
1982	L. Curry (Australia)	4:51.95
1986	S. Landells (Australia)	4:45.82

4×100 Yards Freestyle Team Relay

1930	England	4:32.80
1934	Canada	4:21.80

4×110 Yards Freestyle Team Relay

1938	Canada	4:48.30
1950	Australia	4:44.90
1954	S Africa	4:33.90
1958	Australia	4:17.40
1962	Australia	4:11.00
1966	Canada	4:10.80

4×100 Metres Freestyle Team Relay

1970	Australia	4:06.41
1974	Canada	3:57.14
1978	Canada	3:50.28
1982	England	3:54.23
1986	Canada	3:48.45

4×200 Metres Freestyle Team Relay

1986	Australia	8:12.09

3×100 Yards Medley Team Relay

1934	Canada	3:42.00

3×110 Yards Medley Team Relay

1938	England	3:57.70
1950	Australia	3:53.80
1954	Scotland	3:51.00

4×110 Yards Medley Team Relay

1958	England	4:54.00
1962	Australia	4:45.90
1966	England	4:40.60

4×100 Metres Medley Team Relay

1970	Australia	4:30.66
1974	Canada	4:24.77
1978	Canada	4:15.26
1982	Canada	4:14.33
1986	England	4:13.48

European Champions, 1926–1989

Men

50 Metres Freestyle

1987	J. Woithe (GDR)	22.66
1989	T. Tkachenko (USSR)	22.64

100 Metres Freestyle

1926	I. Barany (Hungary)	1:01.00
1927	A. Borg (Sweden)	1:00.00
1931	I. Barany (Hungary)	59.80
1934	F. Csik (Hungary)	59.70
1938	K. Hoving (Holland)	59.80
1947	A. Jany (France)	57.70
1950	A. Jany (France)	57.70
1954	I. Nyeki (Hungary)	57.80
1958	P. Pucci (Italy)	56.30
1962	A. Gottvalles (France)	55.00
1966	R. McGregor (GBR)	53.70
1970	M. Rousseau (France)	52.90
1974	P. Nocke (W Germany)	52.18
1977	P. Nocke (W Germany)	51.55
1981	P. Johansson (Sweden)	50.55
1983	P. Johansson (Sweden)	50.20
1985	S. Caron (France)	50.20
1987	S. Lodziewski (GDR)	49.79
1989	G. Lamberti (Italy)	49.24

200 Metres Freestyle

1970	H. Fassnacht (W Germany)	1:55.20
1974	P. Nocke (W Germany)	1:53.10
1977	P. Nocke (W Germany)	1:51.72
1981	S. Kopliakov (USSR)	1:51.23
1983	M. Gross (W Germany)	1:47.87
1985	M. Gross (W Germany)	1:47.95
1987	A. Holmertz (Sweden)	1:48.44
1989	G. Lamberti (Italy)	1:46.69

400 Metres Freestyle

1926	A. Borg (Sweden)	5:14.20
1927	A. Borg (Sweden)	5:08.60
1931	I. Barany (Hungary)	5:04.00
1934	J. Taris (France)	4:55.50
1938	B. Borg (Sweden)	4:51.60
1947	A. Jany (France)	4:35.20
1950	A. Jany (France)	4:48.00
1954	G. Csordas (Hungary)	4:38.80
1958	I. Black (GBR)	4:31.30
1962	J. Bontekoe (Holland)	4:25.60
1966	F. Wiegand (GDR)	4:11.10
1970	G. Larsson (Sweden)	4:02.60
1974	A. Samsonov (USSR)	4:02.11
1977	S. Rusin (USSR)	3:54.83
1981	B. Petric (Yugoslavia)	3:51.63
1983	V. Salnikov (USSR)	3:49.80
1985	U. Dassler (GDR)	3:51.52
1987	U. Dassler (GDR)	3:48.95
1989	A. Wojdat (Poland)	3:47.78

1500 Metres Freestyle

1926	A. Borg (Sweden)	21:29.20
1927	A. Borg (Sweden)	21:07.20
1931	O. Halassy (Hungary)	20:49.00
1934	J. Taris (France)	20:01.50
1938	B. Borg (Sweden)	19:55.60
1947	G. Mitro (Hungary)	19:28.00
1950	H. Lehmann (W Germany)	19:48.20
1954	G. Csordas (Hungary)	18:57.80
1958	I. Black (GBR)	18:05.80
1962	J. Katona (Hungary)	17:49.50
1966	G. Belitz (USSR)	16:58.50
1970	H. Fassnacht (W Germany)	16:19.90
1974	F. Pfutze (GDR)	15:54.57
1977	V. Salnikov (USSR)	15:16.45
1981	V. Salnikov (USSR)	15:09.17
1983	V. Salnikov (USSR)	15:08.84
1985	U. Dassler (GDR)	15:08.56
1987	R. Henkel (W Germany)	15:02.23
1989	J. Hoffmann (GDR)	15:01.52

100 Metres Backstroke

1926	G. Frohlich (Germany)	1:16.00
1927	E. Lundahl (Sweden)	1:17.40
1931	G. Deutsch (Germany)	1:14.80

Hans Fassnacht (W Germany)

1934 J. Besford (GBR)	1:11.70
1938 H. Schlauch (Germany)	1:09.00
1947 G. Vallerey (France)	1:07.60
1950 G. Larsson (Sweden)	1:09.40
1954 G. Bozon (France)	1:05.10
1958 R. Christophe (France)	1:03.10
1970 R. Matthes (GDR)	58.90
1974 R. Matthes (GDR)	58.21
1977 M. Rolko (Czechoslovakia)	58.35
1981 S. Wladar (Hungary)	56.72
1983 D. Richter (GDR)	56.10
1985 I. Polianski (USSR)	55.24
1987 S. Zabolotnov (USSR)	56.06
1989 M. Lopez-Zubero (Spain)	56.44

200 Metres Backstroke

1962 L. Barbier (USSR)	2:16.60
1966 Y. Gromak (USSR)	2:12.90
1970 R. Matthes (GDR)	2:08.80
1974 R. Matthes (GDR)	2:04.64
1977 Z. Verraszto (Hungary)	2:03.88
1981 S. Wladar (Hungary)	2:00.80
1983 S. Zabolotnov (USSR)	2:01.00
1985 I. Polianski (USSR)	1:58.50
1987 S. Zabolotnov (USSR)	1:59.35
1989 S. Battistelli (Italy)	1:59.96

100 Metres Breaststroke

1970 N. Pankin (USSR)	1:06.80
1974 N. Pankin (USSR)	1:05.63
1977 G. Moerken (W Germany)	1:02.86
1981 Y. Kis (USSR)	1:03.44
1983 R. Zhulpa (USSR)	1:03.32
1985 A. Moorhouse (GBR)	1:02.99
1987 A. Moorhouse (GBR)	1:02.13
1989 A. Moorhouse (GBR)	1:01.71

200 Metres Breaststroke

1926 E. Rademacher (Germany)	2:52.60
1927 E. Rademacher (Germany)	2:55.20
1931 I. Reingoldt (Finland)	2:52.20
1934 E. Sietas (Germany)	2:49.00
1983 J. Balke (Germany)	2:45.80
1947 R. Romain (GBR)	2:40.10
1950 H. Klein (W Germany)	2:38.60
1954 K. Bodinger (W Germany)	2:40.90
1958 L. Kolesnikov (USSR)	2:41.10
1962 G. Prokopenko (USSR)	2:32.80
1966 G. Prokopenko (USSR)	2:30.00
1970 K. Katzur (GDR)	2:26.00
1974 D. Wilkie (GBR)	2:20.42
1977 G. Moerken (W Germany)	2:16.78
1981 R. Zhulpa (USSR)	2:16.15
1983 A. Moorhouse (GBR)	2:17.49
1985 D. Volkov (USSR)	2:19.53
1987 J. Szabo (Hungary)	2:13.87
1989 N. Gillingham (GBR)	2:12.90

100 Metres Butterfly

1970 H. Lampe (W Germany)	57.50
1974 R. Pyttel (GDR)	55.90
1977 R. Pyttel (GDR)	55.49
1981 A. Markovskiy (USSR)	54.39
1983 M. Gross (W Germany)	54.00
1985 M. Gross (W Germany)	54.02
1987 A. Jameson (GBR)	53.62
1989 R. Szukala (Poland)	54.47

200 Metres Butterfly

1954 G. Tumpek (Hungary)	2:32.20

1958 I. Black (GBR)	2:21.90
1962 V. Kuzmin (USSR)	2:14.20
1966 V. Kuzmin (USSR)	2:10.20
1970 U. Poser (GDR)	2:08.00
1974 A. Hargitay (Hungary)	2:03.80
1977 M. Kraus (W Germany)	2:00.40
1981 M. Gross (W Germany)	1:59.19
1983 M. Gross (W Germany)	1:57.05
1985 M. Gross (W Germany)	1:56.65
1987 M. Gross (W Germany)	1:57.59
1989 T. Darnyi (Hungary)	1:58.87

200 Metres Individual Medley

1970 G. Larsson (Sweden)	2:09.30
1974 D. Wilkie (GBR)	2:06.32
1977 A. Hargitay (Hungary)	2:06.82
1981 A. Sidorenko (USSR)	2:03.41
1983 G. Franceschi (Italy)	2:02.48
1985 T. Darnyi (Hungary)	2:03.23
1987 T. Darnyi (Hungary)	2:00.56
1989 T. Darnyi (Hungary)	2:01.03

400 Metres Individual Medley

1962 G. Androsov (USSR)	5:01.30
1966 F. Wiegand (GDR)	4:47.90
1970 G. Larsson (Sweden)	4:36.20
1974 A. Hargitay (Hungary)	4:28.89
1977 S. Fesenko (USSR)	4:26.83
1981 S. Fesenko (USSR)	4:22.77
1983 G. Franceschi (Italy)	4:20.41
1985 T. Darnyi (Hungary)	4:20.70
1987 T. Darnyi (Hungary)	4:15.42
1989 T. Darnyi (Hungary)	4:15.25

4×100 Freestyle Relay

1962 France	3:43.70
1966 GDR	3:36.80
1970 USSR	3:32.30
1974 W Germany	3:30.61
1977 W Germany	3:26.57
1981 USSR	3:21.48
1983 USSR	3:20.88
1985 W Germany	3:22.18
1987 GDR	3:19.17
1989 W Germany	3:19.68

4×200 Metres Freestyle Relay

1926 Germany	9:57.20
1927 Germany	9:49.60
1931 Hungary	9:34.00
1934 Hungary	9:30.20
1938 Germany	9:17.60
1947 Sweden	9:00.50
1950 Sweden	9:06.50
1954 Hungary	8:47.80
1958 USSR	8:33.70
1962 Sweden	8:18.40
1966 USSR	8:00.20
1970 W Germany	7:49.50
1974 W Germany	7:39.70
1977 USSR	7:28.21
1981 USSR	7:24.41
1983 W Germany	7:20.40
1985 W Germany	7:19.23
1987 W Germany	7:13.10
1989 Italy	7:15.39

4×100 Metres Medley Relay

1958 USSR	4:16.50
1962 GDR	4:09.00

211

1966	USSR	4:02.40	1981 C. Schmidt (GDR)	8:32.79
1970	GDR	3:54.40	1983 A. Strauss (GDR)	8:32.12
1974	W Germany	3:51.57	1985 A. Strauss (GDR)	8:32.45
1977	W Germany	3:48.73	1987 A. Moehring (GDR)	8:19.53
1981	USSR	3:44.23	1989 A. Moehring (GDR)	8:23.99
1983	USSR	3:43.99		
1985	W Germany	3:43.59	**100 Metres Backstroke**	
1987	USSR	3:41.51	1927 W. den Turk (Holland)	1:24.60
1989	USSR	3:41.44	1931 M. Braun (Holland)	1:22.80

Women

50 Metres Freestyle

1987 T. Costache (Rumania)	25.50
1989 C. Plewinski (France)	25.63

100 Metres Freestyle

1927 M. Vierdag (Holland)	1:15.00
1931 Y. Godard (France)	1:10.00
1934 W. den Ouden (Holland)	1:07.10
1938 R. Hveger (Denmark)	1:06.20
1947 F. Nathansen (Denmark)	1:07.80
1950 I. Schumacher (Holland)	1:06.40
1954 K. Szoke (Hungary)	1:05.80
1958 K. Jobson (Sweden)	1:04.70
1962 H. Pechstein (GDR)	1:03.30
1966 M. Grunert (GDR)	1:01.20
1970 G. Wetzko (GDR)	59.60
1974 K. Ender (GDR)	56.96
1977 B. Krause (GDR)	56.55
1981 C. Metschuck (GDR)	55.74
1983 B. Meineke (GDR)	55.18
1985 H. Friedrich (GDR)	55.71
1987 K. Otto (GDR)	55.38
1989 K. Meissner (GDR)	55.38

200 Metres Freestyle

1970 G. Wetzko (GDR)	2:08.20
1974 K. Ender (GDR)	2:03.22
1977 P. Thuemer (GDR)	2:00.79
1981 C. Schmidt (GDR)	2:00.27
1983 B. Meineke (GDR)	1:59.45
1985 H. Friedrich (GDR)	1:59.55
1987 H. Friedrich (GDR)	1:58.24
1989 M. Stellmach (GDR)	1:58.93

400 Metres Freestyle

1927 M. Braun (Holland)	6:11.80
1931 M. Braun (Holland)	5:42.00
1934 R. Mastenbroek (Holland)	5:27.40
1938 R. Hveger (Denmark)	5:09.00
1947 K. Harup (Denmark)	5:18.20
1950 G. Andersen (Denmark)	5:30.90
1954 A. Sebo (Hungary)	5:14.40
1958 J. Koster (Holland)	5:02.60
1962 A. Lasterie (Holland)	4:52.40
1966 C. Mandonnaud (France)	4:48.20
1970 E. Sehmisch (GDR)	4:32.90
1974 A. Franke (GDR)	4:17.83
1977 P. Thuemer (GDR)	4:08.91
1981 I. Diers (GDR)	4:08.58
1983 A. Strauss (GDR)	4:08.07
1985 A. Strauss (GDR)	4:09.22
1987 H. Friedrich (GDR)	4:06.39
1989 A. Moehring (GDR)	4:05.84

800 Metres Freestyle

1970 K. Neugebauer (GDR)	9:29.10
1974 C. Doerr (GDR)	8:52.45
1977 P. Thuemer (GDR)	8:38.32

100 Metres Backstroke

1934 R. Mastenbroek (Holland)	1:20.30
1938 C. King (Holland)	1:15.00
1947 K. Harup (Denmark)	1:15.90
1950 R. van den Horst (Holland)	1:17.10
1954 G. Wielema (Holland)	1:13.20
1958 J. Grinham (GBR)	1:12.60
1963 R. van Velsen (Holland)	1:10.50
1966 C. Caron (France)	1:08.10
1970 T. Lekveishvili (USSR)	1:07.80
1974 U. Richter (GDR)	1:03.30
1977 B. Treiber (GDR)	1:02.63
1981 I. Kleber (GDR)	1:02.81
1983 I. Kleber (GDR)	1:01.79
1985 B. Weigang (GDR)	1:02.16
1987 K. Otto (GDR)	1:01.86
1989 K. Otto (GDR)	1:01.86

200 Metres Backstroke

1970 A. Gyarmati (Hungary)	2:25.50
1974 U. Richter (GDR)	2:17.35
1977 B. Treiber (GDR)	2:13.10
1981 C. Polit (GDR)	2:12.55
1983 C. Sirch (GDR)	2:12.05
1985 C. Sirch (GDR)	2:10.89
1987 C. Sirch (GDR)	2:10.20
1989 D. Hase (GDR)	2:12.46

100 Metres Breaststroke

1970 G. Prozumenshikova (USSR)	1:15.60
1974 C. Justen (W Germany)	1:12.55
1977 J. Bogdanova (USSR)	1:11.89
1981 U. Geweniger (GDR)	1:08.60
1983 U. Geweniger (GDR)	1:08.51
1985 S. Gerasch (GDR)	1:08.62
1987 S. Hoerner (GDR)	1:07.91
1989 S. Boernike (GDR)	1:09.55

200 Metres Breaststroke

1927 H. Schrader (Germany)	3:20.40
1931 C. Wolstenholme (GBR)	3:16.20
1934 M. Genenger (Germany)	3:09.10
1938 I. Sorensen (Denmark)	3:05.40
1947 N. van Vliet (Holland)	2:56.60
1950 R. Vergauwen (Belgium)	3:00.10
1954 U. Happe (W Germany)	2:54.90
1958 A. den Haan (Holland)	2:52.00
1962 A. Lonsbrough (GBR)	2:50.20
1966 G. Prozumenshikova (USSR)	2:40.80
1970 G. Prozumenshikova (USSR)	2:40.70
1974 K. Linke (GDR)	2:34.99
1977 J. Bogdanova (USSR)	2:35.04
1981 U. Geweniger (GDR)	2:32.41
1983 U. Geweniger (GDR)	2:30.64
1985 T. Bogomilova (Bulgaria)	2:28.57
1987 S. Hoerner (GDR)	2:27.49
1989 S. Boernike (GDR)	2:27.77

100 Metres Butterfly

1954 J. Langenau (W Germany)	1:16.60
1958 T. Lagerberg (Holland)	1:11.90
1962 A. Kok (Holland)	1:09.00

1966	A. Kok (Holland)	1:05.60
1970	A. Gyarmati (Hungary)	1:05.00
1974	R. Kother (GDR)	1:01.99
1977	A. Pollack (GDR)	1:00.61
1981	U. Geweniger (GDR)	1:00.40
1983	I. Geissler (GDR)	1:00.31
1985	K. Gressler (GDR)	59.46
1987	K. Otto (GDR)	59.52
1989	C. Plewinski (France)	59.08

200 Metres Butterfly

1970	H. Lindner (GDR)	2:20.20
1974	R. Kother (GDR)	2:14.45
1977	A. Fiebig (GDR)	2:12.77
1981	I. Geissler (GDR)	2:08.50
1983	C. Polit (GDR)	2:07.82
1985	J. Alex (GDR)	2:11.78
1987	K. Nord (GDR)	2:08.85
1989	K. Nord (GDR)	2:09.33

200 Metres Individual Medley

1970	M. Grunert (GDR)	2:26.60
1974	U. Tauber (GDR)	2:18.97
1977	U. Tauber (GDR)	2:15.95
1981	U. Geweniger (GDR)	2:12.64
1983	U. Geweniger (GDR)	2:13.07
1985	K. Nord (GDR)	2:16.07
1987	C. Sirch (GDR)	2:15.04
1989	D. Hunger (GDR)	2:13.26

400 Metres Individual Medley

1962	A. Lasterie (Holland)	5:27.80
1966	B. Heukels (Holland)	5:25.00
1970	E. Stolze (GDR)	5:07.00
1974	U. Tauber (GDR)	4:52.42
1977	U. Tauber (GDR)	4:45.22
1981	P. Schneider (GDR)	4:39.30
1983	K. Nord (GDR)	4:39.95
1985	K. Nord (GDR)	4:47.08
1987	N. Lung (Rumania)	4:40.21

Evelyn Stolze (GDR)

1989	D. Hunger (GDR)	4:41.82

4×100 Metres Freestyle Relay

1927	GBR	5:11.00
1931	Holland	4:55.00
1934	Holland	4:41.50
1938	Denmark	4:31.60
1947	Denmark	4:32.30
1950	Holland	4:33.90
1954	Hungary	4:30.60
1958	Holland	4:22.90
1962	Holland	4:15.10
1966	USSR	4:11.30
1970	GDR	4:00.80
1974	GDR	3:52.48
1977	GDR	3:49.52
1981	GDR	3:44.37
1983	GDR	3:44.72
1985	GDR	3:44.48
1987	GDR	3:42.58
1989	GDR	3:42.46

4×200 Metres Freestyle Relay

1983	GDR	8:02.27
1985	GDR	8:03.82
1987	GDR	7:55.47
1989	GDR	7:58.54

4×100 Medley Relay

1958	Holland	4:52.90
1962	GDR	4:40.10
1966	Holland	4:36.40
1970	GDR	4:30.10
1974	GDR	4:13.78
1977	GDR	4:14.35
1981	GDR	4:09.72
1983	GDR	4:05.79
1985	GDR	4:06.93
1987	GDR	4:04.05
1989	GDR	4:07.40

World Champions, 1973–1986

Men

50 Metres Freestyle
1986 T. Jager (USA)	22.49

100 Metres Freestyle
1973 J. Montgomery (USA)	51.70
1975 A. Coan (USA)	51.23
1978 D. McCagg (USA)	50.24
1982 J. Woithe (GDR)	50.18
1986 M. Biondi (USA)	48.94

200 Metres Freestyle
1973 J. Montgomery (USA)	1:53.02
1975 T. Shaw (USA)	1:51.04
1978 W. Forrester (USA)	1:51.02
1982 M. Gross (W Germany)	1:49.84
1986 M. Gross (W Germany)	1:47.92

400 Metres Freestyle
1973 R. de Mont (USA)	3:58.18
1975 T. Shaw (USA)	3:54.88
1978 V. Salnikov (USSR)	3:51.94
1982 V. Salnikov (USSR)	3:51.30
1986 R. Henkel (W Germany)	3:50.05

1500 Metres Freestyle
1973 S. Holland (Australia)	15:31.85
1975 T. Shaw (USA)	15:28.92
1978 V. Salnikov (USSR)	15:03.99
1982 V. Salnikov (USSR)	15:01.77
1986 R. Henkel (W Germany)	15:05.31

100 Metres Backstroke
1973 R. Matthes (GDR)	57.47
1975 R. Matthes (GDR)	58.15
1978 R. Jackson (USA)	56.36
1982 D. Richter (GDR)	55.95
1986 I. Polianski (USSR)	55.58

200 Metres Backstroke
1973 R. Matthes (GDR)	2:01.87
1975 Z. Verraszto (Hungary)	2:05.05
1978 J. Vassallo (USA)	2:02.16
1982 R. Carey (USA)	2:00.82
1986 I. Polianski (USSR)	1:58.78

100 Metres Breaststroke
1973 J. Hencken (USA)	1:04.02
1975 D. Wilkie (GBR)	1:04.26
1978 W. Kusch (W Germany)	1:03.58
1982 S. Lundquist (USA)	1:02.75
1986 V. Davis (Canada)	1:02.71

200 Metres Breaststroke
1973 D. Wilkie (GBR)	2:19.28
1975 D. Wilkie (GBR)	2:18.23
1978 N. Nevid (USA)	2:18.37
1982 V. Davis (Canada)	2:14.77
1986 J. Szabo (Hungary)	2:14.27

100 Metres Butterfly
1973 B. Robertson (Canada)	55.69
1975 G. Jagenburg (USA)	55.63
1978 J. Bottom (USA)	54.30
1982 M. Gribble (USA)	53.88
1986 P. Morales (USA)	53.54

200 Metres Butterfly
1973 R. Backhaus (USA)	2:03.32
1975 W. Forrester (USA)	2:01.95
1978 M. Bruner (USA)	1:59.38
1982 M. Gross (W Germany)	1:58.85
1986 M. Gross (W Germany)	1:56.63

200 Metres Individual Medley
1973 G. Larsson (Sweden)	2:08.36
1975 A. Hargitay (Hungary)	2:07.72
1978 G. Smith (Canada)	2:03.65
1982 A. Sidorenko (USSR)	2:03.30
1986 T. Darnyi (Hungary)	2:01.57

400 Metres Individual Medley
1973 A. Hargitay (Hungary)	4:31.11
1975 A. Hargitay (Hungary)	4:32.57
1978 J. Vassallo (USA)	4:20.05
1982 R. Prado (Brazil)	4:19.78
1986 T. Darnyi (Hungary)	4:18.98

4×100 Metres Freestyle Team Relay
1973 USA	3:27.18
1975 USA	3:24.85
1978 USA	3:19.74
1982 USA	3:19.26
1986 USA	3:19.89

4×200 Metres Freestyle Team Relay
1973 USA	7:33.22
1975 W Germany	7:39.44
1978 USA	7:20.82
1982 USA	7:21.09
1986 GDR	7:15.91

4×100 Metres Medley Team Relay
1973 USA	3:49.49
1975 USA	3:49.00
1978 USA	3:44.63
1982 USA	3:40.84
1986 USA	3:41.25

Women

50 Metres Freestyle
1986 T. Costache (Rumania)	25.28

100 Metres Freestyle
1973 K. Ender (GDR)	57.54
1975 K. Ender (GDR)	56.50
1978 B. Krause (GDR)	55.68
1982 B. Meineke (GDR)	55.79
1986 K. Otto (GDR)	55.05

200 Metres Freestyle
1973 K. Rothhammer (USA)	2:04.99
1975 S. Babashoff (USA)	2:02.50
1978 C. Woodhead (USA)	1:58.53
1982 A. Verstappen (Holland)	1:59.53
1986 H. Friedrich (GDR)	1:58.26

400 Metres Freestyle
1973 H. Greenwood (USA)	4:20.28
1975 S. Babashoff (USA)	4:16.87
1978 T. Wickham (Australia)	4:06.28

1982 C. Schmidt (GDR)	4:08.98
1986 H. Friedrich (GDR)	4:07.45

800 Metres Freestyle

1973 N. Calligaris (Italy)	8:52.97
1975 J. Turrall (Australia)	8:44.75
1978 T. Wickham (Australia)	8:24.94
1982 K. Linehan (USA)	8:27.48
1986 A. Strauss (GDR)	8:28.24

100 Metres Backstroke

1973 U. Richter (GDR)	1:05.42
1975 U. Richter (GDR)	1:03.30
1978 L. Jezek (USA)	1:02.55
1982 K. Otto (GDR)	1:01.30
1986 B. Mitchell (USA)	1:01.74

200 Metres Backstroke

1973 M. Belote (USA)	2:20.52
1975 B. Treiber (GDR)	2:15.46
1978 L. Jezek (USA)	2:11.93
1982 K. Sirch (GDR)	2:09.91
1986 K. Sirch (GDR)	2:11.37

100 Metres Breaststroke

1973 R. Vogel (GDR)	1:13.74
1975 H. Anke (GDR)	1:12.72
1978 J. Bogdanova (USSR)	1:10.31
1982 U. Geweniger (GDR)	1:09.14
1986 S. Gerasch (GDR)	1:08.11

200 Metres Breaststroke

1973 R. Vogel (GDR)	2:40.01
1975 H. Anke (GDR)	2:37.25
1978 L. Kachusite (USSR)	2:31.42
1982 S. Varganova (USSR)	2:28.82
1986 S. Hoerner (GDR)	2:27.40

100 Metres Butterfly

1973 K. Ender (GDR)	1:02.53
1975 K. Ender (GDR)	1:01.24
1978 M. Pennington (USA)	1:00.20
1982 M. Meagher (USA)	59.41
1986 K. Gressler (GDR)	59.51

200 Metres Butterfly

1973 R. Kother (GDR)	2:13.76
1975 R. Kother (GDR)	2:13.82
1978 T. Caulkins (USA)	2:09.87
1982 I. Geissler (GDR)	2:08.66
1986 M. Meagher (USA)	2:08.41

200 Metres Individual Medley

1973 A. Huebner (GDR)	2:20.51
1975 K. Heddy (USA)	2:19.80
1978 T. Caulkins (USA)	2:14.07
1982 P. Schneider (GDR)	2:11.79
1986 K. Otto (GDR)	2:15.56

400 Metres Individual Medley

1973 G. Wegner (GDR)	4:57.51
1975 U. Tauber (GDR)	4:52.76
1978 T. Caulkins (USA)	4:40.83
1982 P. Schneider (GDR)	4:36.10
1986 K. Nord (GDR)	4:43.75

4×100 Metres Freestyle Team Relay

1973 GDR	3:52.45
1975 GDR	3:49.37
1978 USA	3:43.43
1982 GDR	3:43.92
1986 GDR	3:40.57

4×200 Metres Freestyle Team Relay

1986 GDR	7:59.33

4×100 Metres Medley Team Relay

1973 GDR	4:16.84
1975 GDR	4:14.74
1978 USA	4:08.21
1982 GDR	4:05.88
1986 GDR	4:04.82

Olympic Champions, 1896–1988

Men

50 Metres Freestyle

1988 M. Biondi (USA)	22.14

100 Yards Freestyle

1904 Z. Halmay (Hungary)	1:02.80

100 Metres Freestyle

1896 A. Hajos (Hungary)	1:22.20
1906 C. Daniels (USA)	1:13.40
1908 C. Daniels (USA)	1:05.60
1912 D. Kahanamoku (USA)	1:03.40
1920 D. Kahanamoku (USA)	1:01.40
1924 J. Weissmuller (USA)	59.00
1928 J. Weissmuller (USA)	58.60
1932 Y. Miyasaki (Japan)	58.20
1936 F. Csik (Hungary)	57.60
1948 W. Ris (USA)	57.30
1952 C. Scholes (USA)	57.40
1956 J. Henricks (Australia)	55.40
1960 J. Devitt (Australia)	55.20
1964 D. Schollander (USA)	53.40
1968 M. Wenden (Australia)	52.20
1972 M. Spitz (USA)	51.22
1976 J. Montgomery (USA)	49.99
1980 J. Woithe (GDR)	50.40
1984 A. Gaines (USA)	49.80
1988 M. Biondi (USA)	48.63

220 Yards Freestyle

1904 C. Daniels (USA)	2:44.20

200 Metres Freestyle

1900 F. Lane (Australia)	2:25.20
1968 M. Wenden (Australia)	1:55.20
1972 M. Spitz (USA)	1:52.78
1976 B. Furniss (USA)	1:50.29
1980 S. Kopliakov (USSR)	1:49.81
1984 M. Gross (W Germany)	1:47.44
1988 D. Armstrong (Australia)	1:47.25

440 Yards Freestyle

1904 C. Daniels (USA)	6:16.20

500 Yards Freestyle

1896 P. Neumann (Austria)	8:12.60

400 Metres Freestyle

1906 O. Schaeff (Austria)	6:22.80
1908 H. Taylor (GBR)	5:36.80

Mark Spitz (USA)

Allsport Photographic

1912	G. Hodgson (Canada)	5:24.40
1920	N. Ross (USA)	5:26.80
1924	J. Weissmuller (USA)	5:04.20
1928	A. Zorrilla (Argentine)	5:01.60
1932	C. Crabbe (USA)	4:48.40
1936	J. Medica (USA)	4:44.50
1948	W. Smith (USA)	4:41.00
1952	J. Boiteux (France)	4:30.70
1956	M. Rose (Australia)	4:27.30
1960	M. Rose (Australia)	4:18.30
1964	D. Schollander (USA)	4:12.20
1968	M. Burton (USA)	4:09.00
1972	B. Cooper (Australia)	4:00.27
1976	B. Goodell (USA)	3:51.93
1980	V. Salnikov (USSR)	3:51.31
1984	G. di Carlo (USA)	3:51.23
1988	U. Dassler (GDR)	3:46.95

1000 Metres Freestyle

1900	J. Jarvis (GBR)	13:40.20

1200 Metres Freestyle

1896	A. Hajos (Hungary)	18:22.20

1 Mile Freestyle

1904	E. Rausch (Germany)	27:18.20
1906	H. Taylor (GBR)	28:28.00

1500 Metres Freestyle

1906	H. Taylor (GBR)	22:48.40
1912	G. Hodgson (Canada)	22:00.00
1920	N. Ross (USA)	22:23.20
1924	A. Charlton (Australia)	20:06.60
1928	A. Borg (Sweden)	19:51.80
1932	K. Kitamura (Japan)	19:12.40
1936	N. Terada (Japan)	19:13.70
1948	J. McLane (USA)	19:18.50
1952	F. Konno (USA)	18:30.30
1956	M. Rose (Australia)	17:58.90
1960	J. Konrads (Australia)	17:19.60
1964	R. Windle (Australia)	17:01.70
1968	M. Burton (USA)	16:38.90
1972	M. Burton (USA)	15:52.58

1976	B. Goodell (USA)	15:02.40
1980	V. Salnikov (USSR)	14:58.27
1984	M. O'Brien (USA)	15:05.20
1988	V. Salnikov (USSR)	15:00.40

100 Yards Backstroke

1904	W. Brack (Germany)	1:16.80

100 Metres Backstroke

1908	A. Bieberstein (Germany)	1:24.60
1912	H. Hebner (USA)	1:21.20
1920	W. Kealoha (USA)	1:15.20
1924	W. Kealoha (USA)	1:13.20
1928	G. Kojac (USA)	1:08.20
1932	M. Kiyokawa (Japan)	1:08.60
1936	A. Kiefer (USA)	1:05.90
1948	A. Stack (USA)	1:06.40
1952	Y. Oyakawa (USA)	1:05.40
1956	D. Theile (Australia)	1:02.20
1960	D. Theile (Australia)	1:01.90
1968	R. Matthes (GDR)	58.70
1972	R. Matthes (GDR)	56.58
1976	J. Naber (USA)	55.49
1980	B. Baron (Sweden)	56.53
1984	R. Carey (USA)	55.79
1988	D. Suzuki (Japan)	55.05

200 Metres Backstroke

1900	E. Hoppenberg (Germany)	2:47.00
1964	J. Graef (USA)	2:10.30
1968	R. Matthes (GDR)	2:09.60
1972	R. Matthes (GDR)	2:02.82
1976	J. Naber (USA)	1:59.19
1980	S. Wladar (Hungary)	2:01.93
1984	R. Carey (USA)	2:00.23
1988	I. Polianski (USSR)	1:59.37

100 Metres Breaststroke

1968	D. McKenzie (USA)	1:07.70
1972	N. Taguchi (Japan)	1:04.94
1976	J. Hencken (USA)	1:03.11
1980	D. Goodhew (GBR)	1:03.34

1984 S. Lundquist (USA)	1:01.65
1988 A. Moorhouse (GBR)	1:02.04

200 Metres Breaststroke

1908 F. Holman (GBR)	3:09.20
1912 W. Bathe (Germany)	3:01.80
1920 H. Malmroth (Sweden)	3:04.40
1924 R. Skelton (USA)	2:56.60
1928 Y. Tsuruta (Japan)	2:48.80
1932 Y. Tsuruta (Japan)	2:45.40
1936 T. Hamuro (Japan)	2:41.50
1948 J. Verdeur (USA)	2:39.30
1952 J. Davies (Australia)	2:34.40
1956 M. Furukawa (Japan)	2:34.70
1960 W. Mulliken (USA)	2:37.40
1964 I. O'Brien (Australia)	2:27.80
1968 F. Munoz (Mexico)	2:28.70
1972 J. Hencken (USA)	2:21.55
1976 D. Wilkie (GBR)	2:15.11
1980 R. Shulpa (USSR)	2:15.85
1984 V. Davis (Canada)	2:13.34
1988 J. Szabo (Hungary)	2:13.52

100 Metres Butterfly

1968 D. Russell (USA)	55.90
1972 M. Spitz (USA)	54.27
1976 M. Vogel (USA)	54.35
1980 P. Arvidsson (Sweden)	54.92
1984 M. Gross (W Germany)	53.08
1988 A. Nesty (Surinam)	53.00

200 Metres Butterfly

1956 W. Yorzyk (USA)	2:19.30
1960 M. Troy (USA)	2:12.80
1964 K. Berry (USA)	2:06.60
1968 C. Robie (USA)	2:08.70
1972 M. Spitz (USA)	2:00.70
1976 M. Bruner (USA)	1:59.23
1980 S. Fesenko (USSR)	1:59.76
1984 J. Sieben (Australia)	1:57.04
1988 M. Gross (W Germany)	1:56.94

200 Metres Individual Medley

1968 C. Hickcox (USA)	2:12.00
1972 G. Larsson (Sweden)	2:07.17

Duncan Goodhew Swimming Times

1984 A. Baumann (Canada)	2:01.42
1988 T. Darnyi (Hungary)	2:00.17

400 Metres Individual Medley

1964 R. Roth (USA)	4:45.40
1968 C. Hickcox (USA)	4:48.40
1972 G. Larsson (Sweden)	4:31.98
1976 R. Strachan (USA)	4:23.68
1980 A. Sidorenko (USSR)	4:22.89
1984 A. Baumann (Canada)	4:17.41
1988 T. Darnyi (Hungary)	4:14.75

4×100 Metres Freestyle Team Relay

1964 USA	3:33.20
1968 USA	3:31.70
1972 USA	3:26.42
1984 USA	3:19.03
1988 USA	3:16.53

4×200 Metres Freestyle Team Relay

1908 GBR	10:55.60
1912 Australasia	10:11.60
1920 USA	10:04.40
1924 USA	9:53.40
1928 USA	9:36.20
1932 Japan	8:58.40
1936 Japan	8:51.50
1948 USA	8:46.00
1952 USA	8:31.10
1956 Australia	8:23.60
1960 USA	8:10.20
1964 USA	7:52.10
1968 USA	7:52.30
1972 USA	7:35.78
1976 USA	7:23.50
1980 USSR	7:23.22
1984 USA	7:15.69
1988 USA	7:12.51

4×250 Metres Freestyle Team Relay

1906 Hungary	16:52.40

4×100 Metres Medley Team Relay

1960 USA	4:05.40
1964 USA	3:58.40
1968 USA	3:54.90
1972 USA	3:48.16
1976 USA	3:42.22
1980 Australia	3:45.70
1984 USA	3:39.30
1988 USA	3:36.93

Women

50 Metres Freestyle

1988 K. Otto (GDR)	25.49

100 Metres Freestyle

1912 F. Durack (Australia)	1:22.20
1920 E. Bleibtrey (USA)	1:13.60
1924 E. Lackie (USA)	1:12.40
1928 A. Osipowich (USA)	1:11.00
1932 H. Madison (USA)	1:06.80
1936 H. Mastenbroek (Holland)	1:05.90
1948 G. Andersen (Denmark)	1:06.30
1952 K. Szoke (Hungary)	1:06.80
1956 D. Fraser (Australia)	1:02.00
1960 D. Fraser (Australia)	1:01.20
1964 D. Fraser (Australia)	59.50
1968 J. Henne (USA)	1:00.00

217

1972 S. Neilson (USA)	58.59	
1976 K. Ender (GDR)	55.65	
1980 B. Krause (GDR)	54.79	
1984 C. Steinseiffer (USA)		
N. Hogshead (USA)	55.92	
1988 K. Otto (GDR)	54.93	

200 Metres Freestyle

1968 D. Meyer (USA)	2:10.50
1972 S. Gould (Australia)	2:03.56
1976 K. Ender (GDR)	1:59.26
1980 B. Krause (GDR)	1:58.33
1984 A. Wayte (USA)	1:59.23
1988 H. Friedrich (GDR)	1:57.65

300 Metres Freestyle

1920 E. Bleibtrey (USA)	4:34.00

400 Metres Freestyle

1924 M. Norelius (USA)	6:02.20
1928 M. Norelius (USA)	5:42.80
1932 H. Madison (USA)	5:28.50
1936 H. Mastenbroek (Holland)	5:26.40
1948 A. Curtis (USA)	5:17.80
1952 V. Gyenge (Hungary)	5:12.10
1956 L. Crapp (Australia)	4:54.60
1960 C. von Saltza (USA)	4:50.60
1964 V. Duenkel (USA)	4:43.30
1968 D. Meyer (USA)	4:31.80
1972 S. Gould (Australia)	4:14.04
1976 P. Thumer (GDR)	4:09.89
1980 I. Diers (GDR)	4:08.76
1984 T. Cohen (USA)	4:07.10
1988 J. Evans (USA)	4:03.85

800 Metres Freestyle

1968 D. Meyer (USA)	9:24.00
1972 K. Rothhammer (USA)	8:53.68
1976 P. Thumer (GDR)	8:37.14

1980 M. Ford (Australia)	8:28.90
1984 T. Cohen (USA)	8:24.95
1988 J. Evans (USA)	8:20.20

100 Metres Backstroke

1924 S. Bauer (USA)	1:23.20
1928 M. Braun (Holland)	1:22.00
1932 E. Holm (USA)	1:19.40
1936 D. Senff (Holland)	1:18.90
1948 K. Harup (Denmark)	1:14.40
1952 J. Harrison (S Africa)	1:14.30
1956 J. Grinham (GBR)	1:12.90
1960 L. Burke (USA)	1:09.30
1964 C. Ferguson (USA)	1:07.70
1968 K. Hall (USA)	1:06.20
1972 M. Belote (USA)	1:05.78
1976 U. Richter (GDR)	1:01.83
1980 R. Reinisch (GDR)	1:00.86
1984 T. Andrews (USA)	1:02.55
1988 K. Otto (GDR)	1:00.89

200 Metres Backstroke

1968 L. Watson (USA)	2:24.80
1972 M. Belote (USA)	2:19.19
1976 U. Richter (GDR)	2:13.43
1980 R. Reinisch (GDR)	2:11.77
1984 J. de Rover (Holland)	2:12.38
1988 K. Egerszegi (Hungary)	2:09.29

100 Metres Breaststroke

1968 D. Bjedov (Yugoslavia)	1:15.80
1972 C. Carr (USA)	1:13.58
1976 H. Anke (GDR)	1:10.86
1980 U. Geweniger (GDR)	1:10.22
1984 P. van Staveren (Holland)	1:09.88
1988 T. Dangalakova (Bulgaria)	1:07.95

200 Metres Breaststroke

1924 L. Morton (GBR)	3:33.20

Debbie Meyer of America (left), and Karen Moras (Australia); first and third respectively in the 1968 Olympic 400 metres freestyle final. Allsport Photographic

Petra Schneider (GDR)

1928	H. Schrader (Germany)	3:12.60
1932	C. Dennis (Australia)	3:06.30
1936	H. Maehata (Japan)	3:03.60
1948	P. van Vliet (Holland)	2:57.20
1952	E. Szekely (Hungary)	2:51.70
1956	U. Happe (W Germany)	2:53.10
1960	A. Lonsbrough (GBR)	2:49.50
1964	G. Prozumenshikova (USSR)	2:48.40
1968	S. Wichman (USA)	2:44.40
1972	B. Whitfield (Australia)	2:41.71
1976	M. Koshevaia (USSR)	2:33.35
1980	L. Kachusite (USSR)	2:29.54
1984	A. Ottenbrite (Canada)	2:30.38
1988	S. Hoerner (GDR)	2:26.71

100 Metres Butterfly

1956	S. Mann (USA)	1:11.00
1960	C. Schuler (USA)	1:09.50
1964	S. Stouder (USA)	1:04.70
1968	L. McClements (Australia)	1:05.50
1972	M. Aoki (Japan)	1:03.34
1976	K. Ender (GDR)	1:00.13
1980	K. Metschuk (GDR)	1:00.42
1984	M. Meagher (USA)	59.26
1988	K. Otto (GDR)	59.00

200 Metres Butterfly

1968	A. Kok (Holland)	2:24.70
1972	K. Moe (USA)	2:15.57
1976	A. Pollack (GDR)	2:11.41
1980	I. Geissler (GDR)	2:10.44
1984	M. Meagher (USA)	2:06.90
1988	K. Nord (GDR)	2:09.51

200 Metres Individual Medley

1968	C. Kolb (USA)	2:24.70
1972	S. Gould (Australia)	2:23.07
1984	T. Caulkins (USA)	2:12.64
1988	D. Hunger (GDR)	2:12.59

400 Metres Individual Medley

1964	D. de Varona (USA)	5:18.70
1968	C. Kolb (USA)	5:08.50
1972	G. Neall (Australia)	5:02.97
1976	U. Tauber (GDR)	4:42.77
1980	P. Schneider (GDR)	4:36.29
1984	T. Caulkins (USA)	4:39.24
1988	J. Evans (USA)	4:37.76

4×100 Metres Freestyle Team Relay

1912	GBR	5:52.80
1920	USA	5:11.60
1924	USA	4:58.80
1928	USA	4:47.60
1932	USA	4:38.00
1936	Holland	4:36.00
1948	USA	4:29.20
1952	Hungary	4:24.40
1956	Australia	4:17.10
1960	USA	4:08.90
1964	USA	4:03.80
1968	USA	4:02.50
1972	USA	3:55.19
1976	USA	3:44.82
1980	GDR	3:42.71
1984	USA	3:43.43
1988	GDR	3:40.63

4×100 Metres Medley Team Relay

1960	USA	4:41.10
1964	USA	4:33.90
1968	USA	4:28.30
1972	USA	4:20.75
1976	GDR	4:07.95
1980	GDR	4:06.67
1984	USA	4:08.34
1988	GDR	4:03.74

Where Are They Now?

Judy Grinham

On 5 December 1956, Judy Grinham became the first Briton to win an Olympic swimming gold medal since Lucy Morton in 1924.

The instant fame that accompanies such sporting achievement did little to alter the 17-year-old girl from Neasden. Even today, more than 30 years later, she still cannot believe that it really happened to her!

Judy, who swam for the Hampstead Ladies Swimming Club and was coached by Reg Laxton, won her first ASA backstroke title in 1955, and made her international debut the same year. She retained the title the following year and qualified for the Melbourne Olympics with high hopes.

In Melbourne, Judy took the first heat with considerable ease and set a new Olympic record. Carin Cone (USA), the Pan-American champion, won heat two and Margaret Edwards, the other British hope, claimed another Olympic record and became the fastest qualifier from heat three.

In the final, all British eyes were focussed on Edwards in lane four and Grinham in five, with the American forming the other part of the spearhead in three. From the start it was Grinham and Edwards who were locked in battle, as on so many previous occasions, with the American playing the waiting game.

With some 20 metres to the wall, Edwards made a last effort, but Grinham dug in to her reserves and responded to the challenge. Cone, meanwhile, had gone into top gear and was closing fast on the British pair. But in the end it was Judy who touched first after a supreme final effort, which kept her just inches ahead of Cone. Both girls clocked 1:12.90, which broke the Olympic record yet again. Edwards finished third for the bronze, a mere ²⁄₁₀th of a second in arrears.

Judy (centre) shows off her Commonwealth Games 110 yards backstroke gold medal.

Later, Judy's time was recognised as the inaugural world record for a long course pool.

So, in not much more than a minute, Judy had ended our gold medal drought in the Olympic pool and helped to establish Great Britain as a force in world swimming. The next major championships were not scheduled until 1958, but in 1957 Judy went on a tour of China with the British team — an experience that still holds many happy memories for her.

A year later, at the 1958 Commonwealth Games, she again played a major part in the success of the English team. When taking the gold medal in the 110 yards backstroke, ahead of arch-rival Margaret Edwards, she regained the world record in the process with a new mark of 1:11.90.

Judy Grinham

Two days later, Judy played a key role in the magnificent English triumph in the medley relay. Swimming the first leg, she equalled her new world record and lay the foundation for a famous victory over the invincible Australians. The others in the quartette did not let her down and this marvellous team effort was rewarded with gold medals and a world record.

Within six weeks, Grinham and her team-mates were in action again at the European Championships in Budapest, where Judy duly took the backstroke gold ahead of Margaret Edwards once more. This victory made her the first athlete to hold all three major titles at one time. She gained further success in Hungary with a bronze in the 100 metres freestyle, which gave her particular pleasure. On top of this she added two more relay medals to her collection in Budapest. These championships marked the end of her short, but amazingly successful international career.

She announced her retirement on her 20th birthday, in March 1959, to become a sportswriter for the "Daily Express", covering the Rome Olympics and other major events.

Judy was married in 1960 and her son was born in 1961, with daughter Alison, following a year later. Maintaining her links with swimming, she coached and gave private lessons in the '60s, but later, in the '70s, helped her first husband set up and run an international hockey magazine.

1977 marked a change of direction when she started to work for Dr Barnardo's, co-ordinating all the fundraising activities, including arranging functions, the running of charity shops, as well as public relations and publicity. She showed remarkable acumen for the task and was the top fundraiser in 1978-79.

Today, Judy is a Fellow of the Institute of Training and Development and is the National Training Officer (appeals) for Barnardo's. Sadly, she now has no connection with the sport that brought her international fame, but has been involved in other sports such as hockey, golf and football. Currently, Judy is into windsurfing, though she maintains that she is only a beginner.

Her greatest disappointment was coping with defeat for the first time after winning the Olympic title. This, she firmly believes, was a good lesson for life. Surprisingly, she says, her most vivid memory is of the medley team victory in Cardiff, rather than that of her Olympic victory.

The name of Judy Grinham is synonymous with success — one immediately thinks of her magnificent achievements in the pool. Her gold medals and world records stand as a testament to a great, but modest competitor.

Diana Wilkinson

Diana Wilkinson became the youngest swimmer ever to represent Great Britain, back in June 1957. Her international debut, in a match against West Germany in Liverpool, marked the beginning of a career that was to span the next ten years. She competed in two Olympics, three European and three Commonwealth Games, and travelled the world from Australia to Jamaica.

During this period, she reached gold medal winning heights and, on occasions, suffered bitter disappointment.

Diana took her first ASA Senior 110 yards freestyle title in 1957, at the famous Derby Baths in Blackpool. Earlier that summer she had become the first Briton to break the one minute barrier for the 100 yards freestyle. These achievements earned her the "Daily Express" Sportswoman of the Year Award for 1957, at the tender age of 13!

If 1957 was remarkable, 1958 was to prove just as memorable, as the Commonwealth Games and European Championships were scheduled for that summer.

During the Cardiff Games, Diana was involved in one of the races of the Championships — the women's medley relay. Swimming the final freestyle leg, she had to hold off the invincible Dawn Fraser, of Australia, if England were to win. Her colleagues on the team had built up the necessary big lead by the time Diana hit the water, five seconds ahead of her famous Australian rival. Diana responded by swimming her fastest ever time to stave off the Australian challenge. The 14-year-old had shown a remarkable temperament to help the English team, not only to the gold medal, but a world record too!

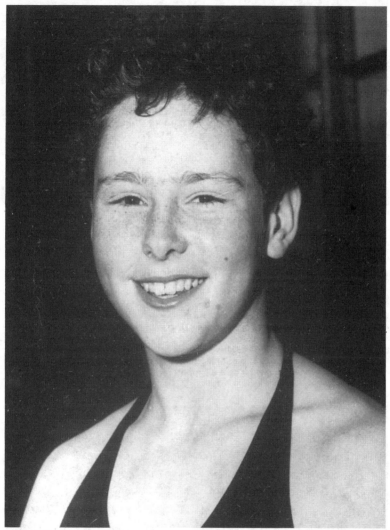

Diana Wilkinson

After the excitement of 1958, the following year was comparatively quiet, and was used as a stepping stone by Diana's coach, Harry Sullivan, with the Rome Olympics in mind. The 1960 Games were not a success and she failed to get through the heats.

In 1961 she reclaimed the National 110 yards freestyle title she had last won in 1957, and this marked a new stage in her career. The following June, at the Derby Baths, Diana broke the European record for the 100 metres freestyle, over the longer linear distance of 110 yards. This made her the favourite for the European title, which would be decided in Leipzig that August.

In Leipzig she was the fastest qualifier for the final, which turned out to be one of the closest ever. Three girls — Diana, Heidi Pechstein (GDR) and Ineke Tigelaar (Holland), seemed to touch simultaneously. Without the benefit of electronic timing, the judges could not agree on the placings, but in the end awarded the gold to Pechstein, with Diana second. This was a bitter blow since the referee, who was not consulted, had placed her first!

She won two more relay medals in Leipzig and added a further couple at the Commonwealth Games in Perth, Australia.

In 1964, Diana collected her last ASA title, and won a place on the Olympic team. However, she suffered another disappointment in Tokyo. A badly administered injection, prior to departure, clearly affected her, and she was unable to recapture her brilliant form of 1962.

Diana qualified as a teacher of physical education in 1966 and taught in Liverpool for two years. After competing in her third Commonwealth Games in Kingston, Jamaica, where she duly won two more relay medals, the 1967 World Student Games brought down the curtain on an international career, which had begun ten years earlier.

In 1968 she married George Bishop and moved South, where she lectured at Chelsea College of Physical Education until 1975. Later that year she gave birth to twins, Susie and Nickie, and within 12 months had returned to Stockport.

By 1979 she had started working for the Local Authority, where she is currently employed as the Leisure Development Officer in charge of a unit responsible for the development of recreational projects throughout Stockport Metropolitan Borough Council. Her brief includes the Stockport Metro Swimming Club where she also has a parental interest.

During her time at the top, Diana was always a key member of the team, but despite her own international success, her most vivid memory is of her brother, Chris, winning the ASA breaststroke Championship in 1961.

These days, Diana's main sporting interest is golf, but she still has strong views on the sport that she excelled at and, in response to being asked to comment on swimming in its current shape, stated: "The present overall National scene seems to lack the thrills and excitement of the 'North v. South' days, and senior National events generate very little atmosphere, which must reflect on performances. Age Group swimming has its advantages, but it is a disadvantage if parents do not understand the philosophy behind the events. Good or average children can blossom into world beaters if handled sensibly and encouraged through their formative years. Too many children disappear from the sport before reaching their full potential, often because parents and coaches are simply too impatient and think that winning is all important."

Chris Wilkinson   Gerry Granham

Progressive/Current Records

Current English Junior (Short Course) Records

Boys

50 Metres Freestyle
23.41 M. Foster (Millfield)   30.03.86

100 Metres Freestyle
50.81 M. Foster (Millfield)   31.03.86

200 Metres Freestyle
1:51.10 P. Howe (Co Coventry)   05.11.83

400 Metres Freestyle
3:55.94 P. Howe (Millfield)   13.11.83

800 Metres Freestyle
8:12.40 D. Stacey (Norwich Penguins) 06.02.81

1500 Metres Freestyle
15:27.87 D. Stacey (Norwich Penguins) 06.02.81

50 Metres Backstroke
27.45 A. Shortman (Bristol Central) 16.10.88

100 Metres Backstroke
59.73 M. Nolan (Ashton Central)   24.01.87

200 Metres Backstroke
2:09.72 P. Pederzolli (Gloucester C) 18.06.88

50 Metres Breaststroke
30.69 N. Poole (Portsmouth Northsea) 03.03.89

100 Metres Breaststroke
1:04.57 I. McKenzie
  (Braintree & Bocking)   30.01.88

200 Metres Breaststroke
2:19.70 I. McKenzie
  (Braintree & Bocking)   27.02.88

50 Metres Butterfly
25.48 M. Foster (Millfield)   07.02.86

100 Metres Butterfly
56.61 S. Dronsfield (Salford Triple 'S') 21.11.86

200 Metres Butterfly
2:04.19 C. Robinson (Killerwhales)   16.11.88

200 Metres Individual Medley
2:07.94 P. Pederzolli (Kelly College) 23.10.87

400 Metres Individual Medley
4:33.61 J. Davey (Co Manchester)   07.12.80

Girls

50 Metres Freestyle
26.75 A. Kindon (Co Birmingham)   25.01.87

100 Metres Freestyle
57.41 K. Pickering (Shiverers)   21.11.86

200 Metres Freestyle
2:01.46 S. Hardcastle
  (Southend Synchronettes)   08.04.84

400 Metres Freestyle
4:08.82 S. Hardcastle
  (Southend Synchronettes)   05.04.84

800 Metres Freestyle
8:27.31 S. Hardcastle
  (Southend Synchronettes)   15.12.84

1500 Metres Freestyle
16:06.68 S. Hardcastle
  (Southend Synchronettes)   10.02.85

50 Metres Backstroke
30.41 S. Page (Stockport Metro)   27.03.87

100 Metres Backstroke
1:04.42 S. Page (Stockport Metro)   25.01.87

200 Metres Backstroke
2:15.19 K. Read (Stockport Metro)   05.04.85

50 Metres Breaststroke
33.01 C. Gable (Stockport Metro)   28.02.87

100 Metres Breaststroke
1:09.85 S. Brownsdon (RTW Monson)   24.01.81

200 Metres Breaststroke
2:32.13 S. Brownsdon (RTW Monson)   21.02.81

50 Metres Butterfly
29.33 J. Lancaster
  (Warrington Warriors)   21.02.88

100 Metres Butterfly
1:02.08 C. Cooper (Barnet Copthall) 01.04.82

200 Metres Butterfly
2:15.09 S. Purvis (Stockton Aquatics) 03.04.83

200 Metres Individual Medley
2:17.77 S. Davies (Po Plymouth)   11.02.78

400 Metres Individual Medley
4:45.84 S. Hardcastle
  (Southend Synchronettes)   08.04.84

Paul Pederzolli   Artwood Photography

225

Current British Junior (Short Course) Records

Boys

50 Metres Freestyle
23.41 M. Foster (England) — 30.03.86

100 Metres Freestyle
50.81 M. Foster (England) — 31.03.86

200 Metres Freestyle
1:51.10 P. Howe (England) — 05.11.83

400 Metres Freestyle
3:55.94 P. Howe (England) — 13.11.83

800 Metres Freestyle
8:12.40 D. Stacey (England) — 06.02.81

1500 Metres Freestyle
15:27.87 D. Stacey (England) — 06.02.81

50 Metres Backstroke
27.45 A. Shortman (England) — 16.10.88

100 Metres Backstroke
59.69 A. May (Scotland) — 02.04.88

200 Metres Backstroke
2:08.07 I. Rosser (Wales) — 02.03.84

50 Metres Breaststroke
30.69 N. Poole (England) — 03.03.89

100 Metres Breaststroke
1:04.57 I. McKenzie (England) — 30.01.88

200 Metres Breaststroke
2:19.70 I. McKenzie (England) — 27.02.88

50 Metres Butterfly
25.48 M. Foster (England) — 07.02.86

100 Metres Butterfly
56.61 S. Dronsfield (England) — 21.11.86

200 Metres Butterfly
2:04.19 C. Robinson (England) — 16.11.88

200 Metres Individual Medley
2:07.94 P. Pederzolli (England) — 23.10.87

400 Metres Individual Medley
4:33.61 J. Davey (England) — 07.12.80

Girls

50 Metres Freestyle
26.32 A. Sheppard (Scotland) — 03.04.88

100 Metres Freestyle
57.41 K. Pickering (England) — 21.11.86

200 Metres Freestyle
2:01.46 S. Hardcastle (England) — 08.04.84

400 Metres Freestyle
4:08.82 S. Hardcastle (England) — 05.04.84

800 Metres Freestyle
8:27.31 S. Hardcastle (England) — 15.12.84

1500 Metres Freestyle
16:06.68 S. Hardcastle (England) — 10.02.85

50 Metres Backstroke
30.41 S. Page (England) — 27.03.87

100 Metres Backstroke
1:04.42 S. Page (England) — 25.01.87

200 Metres Backstroke
2:15.19 K. Read (England) — 05.04.85

50 Metres Breaststroke
33.01 C. Gable (England) — 28.02.87

100 Metres Breaststroke
1:09.85 S. Brownsdon (England) — 24.01.81

200 Metres Breaststroke
2:32.13 S. Brownsdon (England) — 21.02.81

50 Metres Butterfly
29.33 J. Lancaster (England) — 21.02.88

100 Metres Butterfly
1:02.08 C. Cooper (England) — 01.04.82

200 Metres Butterfly
2:15.09 S. Purvis (England) — 03.04.83

200 Metres Individual Medley
2:17.77 S. Davies (England) — 11.02.78

400 Metres Individual Medley
4:45.84 S. Hardcastle (England) — 08.04.84

Paul Howe

Alison Sheppard

Current English Junior (Long Course) Records

Boys

50 Metres Freestyle
24.00 M. Foster (Millfield) 05.05.86

100 Metres Freestyle
52.46 M. Foster (Millfield) 13.04.86

200 Metres Freestyle
1:54.78 P. Howe (Co Coventry) 07.08.83

400 Metres Freestyle
4:02.05 P. Howe (Co Coventry) 06.08.83

800 Metres Freestyle
8:26.64 D. Stacey (Norwich Penguins) 30.01.81

1500 Metres Freestyle
15:59.04 P. Sparkes (Merton Swordfish) 19.07.76

50 Metres Backstroke
28.04 M. Foster (Millfield) 03.05.86

100 Metres Backstroke
1:00.47 A. Shortman (Bristol Central) 31.07.88

200 Metres Backstroke
2:12.17 A. Jameson (Kelly College) 23.05.80

50 Metres Breaststroke
30.54 I. McKenzie
(Braintree & Bocking) 23.07.87

100 Metres Breaststroke
1:05.33 I. McKenzie
(Braintree & Bocking) 23.07.87

200 Metres Breaststroke
2:24.40 I. McKenzie
(Braintree & Bocking) 25.07.87

50 Metres Butterfly
25.96 M. Foster (Millfield) 04.05.86

100 Metres Butterfly
57.65 R. Leishman (Bo Kirklees) 28.07.85

200 Metres Butterfly
2:05.81 K. Crosby
(Warrington Warriors) 27.07.89

200 Metres Individual Medley
2:10.20 P. Pederzolli (Gloucester C) 02.04.88

400 Metres Individual Medley
4:36.60 R. Stapleton (Beckenham) 24.07.87

Girls

50 Metres Freestyle
27.29 A. Kindon (Co Birmingham) 24.07.87

100 Metres Freestyle
57.50 C. Brazendale
(Norbreck Castle) 23.08.77

200 Metres Freestyle
2:03.23 J. Willmott (Southend on Sea) 26.05.80

400 Metres Freestyle
4:10.27 S. Hardcastle
(Southend Synchronettes) 31.07.84

800 Metres Freestyle
8:32.60 S. Hardcastle
(Southend Synchronettes) 03.08.84

1500 Metres Freestyle
16:46.48 J. Willmott (Southend on Sea) 25.04.80

50 Metres Backstroke
31.20 S. Page (Stockport Metro) 11.04.87

100 Metres Backstroke
1:05.69 K. Read (Stockport Metro) 26.05.85

200 Metres Backstroke
2:16.00 K. Read (Stockport Metro) 28.05.84

50 Metres Breaststroke
33.95 C. Gable (Stockport Metro) 05.06.88

100 Metres Breaststroke
1:11.05 S. Brownsdon (RTW Monson) 08.09.81

200 Metres Breaststroke
2:34.43 S. Brownsdon (RTW Monson) 03.07.81

50 Metres Butterfly
29.53 Z. Harrison (Norwich Penguins) 10.06.89

100 Metres Butterfly
1:02.74 A. Osgerby (Wigan Wasps) 23.08.78

200 Metres Butterfly
2:16.01 A. Osgerby (Wigan Wasps) 26.08.78

200 Metres Individual Medley
2:17.82 S. Davies (Po Plymouth) 04.08.78

400 Metres Individual Medley
4:51.05 S. Hardcastle
(Southend Synchronettes) 26.05.84

Current British Junior (Long Course) Records

Boys

50 Metres Freestyle
24.00 M. Foster (England) 05.05.86

100 Metres Freestyle
52.46 M. Foster (England) 13.04.86

200 Metres Freestyle
1:54.78 P. Howe (England) 07.08.83

400 Metres Freestyle
4:02.05 P. Howe (England) 06.08.83

800 Metres Freestyle
8:26.64 D. Stacey (England) 30.01.81

1500 Metres Freestyle
15:59.04 P. Sparkes (England) 19.07.76

50 Metres Backstroke
28.04 M. Foster (England) 03.05.86

100 Metres Backstroke
1:00.47 A. Shortman (England) 31.07.88

200 Metres Backstroke
2:10.47 G. Williams (Wales) 23.05.87

227

50 Metres Breaststroke
30.54 I. McKenzie (England)　　　23.07.87

100 Metres Breaststroke
1:05.33 I. McKenzie (England)　　　23.07.87

200 Metres Breaststroke
2:24.40 I. McKenzie (England)　　　25.07.87

50 Metres Butterfly
25.81 M. Jones (Wales)　　　08.05.88

100 Metres Butterfly
57.65 R. Leishman (England)　　　28.07.85

200 Metres Butterfly
2:05.81 K. Crosby (England)　　　27.07.89

200 Metres Individual Medley
2:10.20 P. Pederzolli (England)　　　02.04.88

400 Metres Individual Medley
4:36.60 R. Stapleton (England)　　　24.07.87

Girls

50 Metres Freestyle
26.43 A. Sheppard (Scotland)　　　24.06.88

100 Metres Freestyle
57.50 C. Brazendale (England)　　　23.08.77

200 Metres Freestyle
2:03.23 J. Willmott (England)　　　26.05.80

400 Metres Freestyle
4:10.27 S. Hardcastle (England)　　　31.07.84

800 Metres Freestyle
8:32.60 S. Hardcastle (England)　　　03.08.84

1500 Metres Freestyle
16:46.48 J. Willmott (England)　　　25.04.80

50 Metres Backstroke
31.20 S. Page (England)　　　11.04.87

100 Metres Backstroke
1:05.69 K. Read (England)　　　26.05.85

200 Metres Backstroke
2:16.00 K. Read (England)　　　28.05.84

50 Metres Breaststroke
33.95 C. Gable (England)　　　05.06.88

100 Metres Breaststroke
1:11.05 S. Brownsdon (England)　　　08.09.81

200 Metres Breaststroke
2:34.43 S. Brownsdon (England)　　　03.07.81

50 Metres Butterfly
29.53 Z. Harrison (England)　　　10.06.89

100 Metres Butterfly
1:02.74 A. Osgerby (England)　　　23.08.78

200 Metres Butterfly
2:16.01 A. Osgerby (England)　　　26.08.78

200 Metres Individual Medley
2:17.82 S. Davies (England)　　　04.08.78

400 Metres Individual Medley
4:51.05 S. Hardcastle (England)　　　26.05.84

Progressive English (Short Course) Records

Men

50 Metres Freestyle
23.33 D. Lowe
　　　　(Harrow & Wealdstone)　　　12.02.83
23.23 D. Lowe
　　　　(Harrow & Wealdstone)　　　12.02.83
23.22 D. Lowe
　　　　(Harrow & Wealdstone)　　　19.02.85
22.88 M. Foster (Bo Southend)　　　22.11.86
22.84 M. Foster (Bo Southend)　　　24.10.87
22.69 M. Foster (Bo Southend)　　　13.02.88
22.57 M. Foster (Bo Southend)　　　14.02.88
22.52 M. Fibbens (Barnet Copthall)　　　12.02.89

100 Metres Freestyle
53.90 M. Windeatt (Torquay Leander)　31.03.73
53.80 B. Brinkley (Modernians)　　　30.03.74
53.60 B. Brinkley (Modernians)　　　15.03.75
52.94 D. Dunne (Beckenham)　　　05.03.77
52.80 M. Smith (Radcliffe)　　　08.05.77
52.00 K. Burns (Co Manchester)　　　05.06.78
51.10 M. Smith (Co Manchester)　　　05.06.78
50.76 M. Smith (Radcliffe)　　　02.01.81
50.59 M. Smith (Radcliffe)　　　02.01.81
50.54 M. Smith (Wigan Wasps)　　　10.01.82
50.50 D. Lowe
　　　　(Harrow & Wealdstone)　　　19.12.82
50.31 D. Lowe
　　　　(Harrow & Wealdstone)　　　04.04.83
49.86 D. Lowe
　　　　(Harrow & Wealdstone)　　　04.04.83

49.26 M. Foster (Bo Southend)　　　23.11.86
48.97 M. Foster (Bo Southend)　　　13.12.87
48.95 M. Fibbens (Barnet Copthall)　　　11.02.89

Mike Fibbens

200 Metres Freestyle

1:58.10	B. Brinkley (Modernians)	04.09.71
1:56.90	B. Brinkley (Modernians)	30.03.73
1:54.55	B. Brinkley (Modernians)	02.03.74
1:52.71	B. Brinkley (Modernians)	22.03.75
1:52.44	B. Brinkley (Modernians)	15.02.76
1:51.20	A. Astbury (Leeds Central)	30.03.79
1:50.95	P. Hubble (Hounslow B)	02.04.82
1:49.59	P. Hubble (Calgary University)	16.03.83
1:48.76	K. Boyd (Bo S Tyneside)	14.12.86
1:48.52	K. Boyd (Bo S Tyneside)	12.02.89

400 Metres Freestyle

4:14.90	B. Brinkley (Modernians)	23.10.71
4:12.10	B. Brinkley (Modernians)	18.06.72
4:09.70	B. Brinkley (Modernians)	24.02.73
4:09.20	B. Brinkley (Modernians)	29.03.73
4:01.54	B. Brinkley (Modernians)	02.03.74
3:58.85	B. Brinkley (Modernians)	23.03.75
3:58.47	B. Brinkley (Modernians)	14.02.76
3:56.43	B. Brinkley (Modernians)	07.03.76
3:53.31	A. Astbury (Leeds Central)	29.03.79
3:50.39	A. Astbury (Leeds Central)	02.12.83
3:46.80	K. Boyd (Bo S Tyneside)	13.12.86
3:45.33	K. Boyd (Bo S Tyneside)	12.12.87
3:44.66	K. Boyd (Bo S Tyneside)	12.12.87

800 Metres Freestyle

8:49.60	B. Brinkley (Modernians)	24.02.73
8:48.50	B. Brinkley (Modernians)	31.03.73
8:42.50	D. Smith (Co Coventry)	15.04.74
8:30.40	B. Brinkley (Modernians)	19.04.75
8:23.10	B. Brinkley (Modernians)	13.02.76
8:18.80	D. Parker (Co Coventry)	23.01.77
8:16.53	S. Lewington (Co Coventry)	28.03.79
8:14.70	S. Lewington (Co Coventry)	22.02.80
8:12.40	D. Stacey (Norwich Penguins)	06.02.81
8:04.12	A. Astbury (Co Leeds)	07.01.83
7:56.42	D. Stacey (Beckenham)	22.11.86
7:54.39	K. Boyd (Bo S Tyneside)	06.02.87
7:52.61	K. Boyd (Bo S Tyneside)	13.11.88
7:48.23	K. Boyd (Bo S Tyneside)	10.02.89

1500 Metres Freestyle

16:47.40	B. Brinkley (Modernians)	24.02.73
16:37.30	B. Brinkley (Modernians)	31.03.73
16:32.70	D. Parker (Co Coventry)	15.02.75
16:04.80	D. Parker (Co Coventry)	30.03.75
15:43.78	B. Brinkley (Modernians)	13.02.76
15:39.40	D. Parker (Co Coventry)	23.01.77
15:30.13	A. Astbury (Leeds Central)	28.03.79
15:27.30	S. Lewington (Co Coventry)	22.02.80
15:23.35	D. Stacey (Co Coventry)	05.02.82
15:22.78	T. Day (Co Leeds)	18.01.85
15:10.12	D. Stacey (Beckenham)	22.11.86
14:57.36	K. Boyd (Bo S Tyneside)	10.12.88

50 Metres Backstroke

26.89	M. Harris (Co Birmingham)	24.02.89

100 Metres Backstroke

1:01.80	A. Davison (Madeley College)	10.04.71
1:01.30	C. Rushton (Madeley College)	01.04.72
1:00.70	C. Cunningham (Co Southampton)	31.03.73
1:00.20	C. Cunningham (Ilford)	30.03.74
1:00.10	S. Harrison (Co Southampton)	12.02.78
59.88	S. Harrison (Co Southampton)	10.03.78
59.39	J. Bott (Millfield)	16.05.79
57.68	G. Abraham (Co Southampton)	04.04.81

57.28	N. Harper (Millfield)	23.06.84
57.25	G. Robins (Portsmouth Northsea)	20.11.88
57.02	G. Robins (Portsmouth Northsea)	16.12.88

200 Metres Backstroke

2:13.50	C. Cunningham (Co Southampton)	30.03.72
2:11.40	C. Cunningham (Co Southampton)	29.03.73
2:10.60	C. Cunningham (Ilford)	28.03.74
2:10.10	P. Lerpiniere (Millfield)	01.04.76
2:09.40	P. Robinson (Darlington)	30.04.78
2:07.93	J. Bott (Millfield)	29.03.79
2:07.47	M. Fenner (Bo S Tyneside)	10.05.81
2:06.95	A. Jameson (Kelly College)	07.02.82
2:05.81	J. Davey (Co Milton Keynes)	01.04.82
2:05.75	K. Boyd (Hull Olympic)	12.02.84
2:05.37	K. Boyd (Hull Olympic)	10.03.84
2:03.70	K. Boyd (Hull Olympic)	05.04.84
2:03.23	K. Boyd (Bo S Tyneside)	08.02.87
2:02.68	K. Boyd (Bo S Tyneside)	13.11.88
2:02.04	G. Robins (Portsmouth Northsea)	17.11.88
2:00.07	K. Boyd (Bo S Tyneside)	04.12.88

50 Metres Breaststroke

28.92	A. Moorhouse (Co Leeds)	25.01.87
28.24	A. Moorhouse (Co Leeds)	06.02.87
28.13	A. Moorhouse (Co Leeds)	13.02.88
27.90	A. Moorhouse (Co Leeds)	14.02.88

100 Metres Breaststroke

1:09.40	M. O'Connell (Co Southampton)	30.10.71
1:09.30	M. O'Connell (Co Southampton)	18.03.72
1:09.10	M. O'Connell (Co Southampton)	31.03.72
1:08.40	D. Leigh (Oak Street)	27.10.72
1:07.00	D. Leigh (Oak Street)	29.03.74
1:06.70	D. Leigh (Oak Street)	13.03.75
1:06.36	D. Leigh (Oak Street)	23.03.75
1:05.75	D. Bryant (Gateshead Metro)	25.02.79
1:01.83	D. Goodhew (Beckenham)	09.02.80
1:01.53	A. Moorhouse (Co Leeds)	05.02.84
1:00.58	A. Moorhouse (Co Leeds)	06.04.85
59.75	A. Moorhouse (Co Leeds)	08.02.87

200 Metres Breaststroke

2:33.80	M. O'Connell (Co Southampton)	09.04.71
2:28.40	D. Leigh (Oak Street)	12.11.73
2:24.30	D. Leigh (Oak Street)	30.03.74
2:23.70	D. Leigh (Oak Street)	01.02.75
2:17.25	D. Goodhew (Beckenham)	10.02.80
2:16.88	D. Goodhew (Beckenham)	06.04.80
2:16.68	A. Moorhouse (Co Leeds)	12.11.83
2:15.49	A. Moorhouse (Co Leeds)	18.12.83
2:15.00	A. Moorhouse (Co Leeds)	09.03.85
2:14.35	A. Moorhouse (Co Leeds)	08.04.85
2:13.14	A. Moorhouse (Co Leeds)	23.01.87
2:12.86	A. Moorhouse (Co Leeds)	01.03.87
2:12.85	A. Moorhouse (Co Leeds)	13.02.88
2:10.79	N. Gillingham (Co Birmingham)	11.02.89
2:09.81	N. Gillingham (Co Birmingham)	11.02.89

50 Metres Butterfly

25.48	M. Foster (Millfield)	07.02.86

25.35	M. Fibbens (Beckenham)	07.02.87
24.97	M. Foster (Kelly College)	27.02.87
24.63	M. Foster (Kelly College)	28.02.87
24.48	M. Foster (Bo Southend)	14.02.88

100 Metres Butterfly

58.90	M. Edwards	
	(Camp Hill Edwardians)	29.03.73
57.40	B. Brinkley (Modernians)	17.02.74
57.26	B. Brinkley (Modernians)	16.02.75
57.14	B. Brinkley (Modernians)	22.03.75
56.64	B. Brinkley (Modernians)	06.03.76
55.83	G. Abraham (Co Southampton)	04.04.81
55.56	P. Hubble (Hounslow B)	08.01.82
55.45	P. Hubble (Hounslow B)	08.01.82
54.94	D. Lowe	
	(Harrow & Wealdstone)	19.12.82
54.82	P. Hubble (Calgary University)	19.03.83
54.77	M. Fibbens (Beckenham)	21.11.86
54.00	M. Fibbens (Barnet Copthall)	04.02.89

200 Metres Butterfly

2:09.20	J. Mills (St James)	31.03.72
2:04.40	B. Brinkley (Modernians)	16.02.74
2:03.86	B. Brinkley (Modernians)	02.03.74
2:03.40	B. Brinkley (Modernians)	16.02.75
2:02.05	B. Brinkley (Modernians)	23.03.75
2:00.36	B. Brinkley (Modernians)	07.03.76
1:59.39	P. Hubble (Calgary University)	16.03.83
1:58.81	T. Jones (Co Birmingham)	11.02.89

200 Metres Individual Medley

2:16.40	R. Terrell (Co Southampton)	19.04.69
2:14.60	B. Brinkley (Modernians)	24.02.73
2:13.50	B. Brinkley (Modernians)	17.02.74
2:07.50	B. Brinkley (Modernians)	21.03.75
2:07.31	D. Dunne (Beckenham)	28.03.79
2:07.07	J. Randall (Co Leicester)	05.04.81
2:07.00	S. Poulter (Wigan Wasps)	08.01.82
2:06.90	S. Poulter (Wigan Wasps)	05.02.82
2:05.97	S. Forrest (Wigan Wasps)	04.04.82
2:05.73	S. Willmott (Stockton Aquatics)	08.04.84
2:05.35	G. Binfield (Salford Triple 'S')	16.06.85
2:05.28	D. Rolley (Swansea University)	09.02.86
2:05.04	J. Davey (Salford Triple 'S')	21.06.86
2:04.38	R. Lee (Co Birmingham)	24.01.87
2:03.51	G. Robins	
	(Portsmouth Northsea)	20.11.88

400 Metres Individual Medley

4:45.60	B. Brinkley (Modernians)	24.02.73
4:42.20	B. Brinkley (Modernians)	31.03.73
4:37.77	B. Brinkley (Modernians)	02.03.74
4:35.04	B. Brinkley (Modernians)	22.03.75
4:32.39	D. Cleworth (Co Manchester)	10.12.78
4:29.24	G. Sykes (Co Coventry)	25.01.80
4:28.56	G. Sykes (Co Coventry)	22.02.80
4:26.20	S. Poulter (Wigan Wasps)	09.01.82
4:24.96	S. Poulter (Wigan Wasps)	06.02.82
4:24.69	S. Poulter (Wigan Wasps)	02.04.82
4:24.02	S. Poulter (Wigan Wasps)	05.02.83
4:23.92	S. Poulter (Wigan Wasps)	07.02.86
4:21.60	G. Robins	
	(Portsmouth Northsea)	22.11.87
4:21.47	G. Robins	
	(Portsmouth Northsea)	22.01.87

4×100 Metres Freestyle Club Relay

3:26.57	Co Leeds	22.11.87
3:25.46	Co Leeds	20.11.88

4×100 Metres Medley Club Relay

3:48.56	Co Leeds	21.11.87

Women

50 Metres Freestyle

29.90	S. Page (Co Birmingham)	03.03.89

100 Metres Freestyle

1:00.20	D. Hill (Portsmouth Northsea)	30.03.75
59.89	D. Hill (Portsmouth Northsea)	06.03.76
59.37	M. Houston (Leeds Central)	05.03.77
58.44	S. Davies (Po Plymouth)	11.12.77
57.48	S. Davies (Kelly College)	30.03.79
57.27	J. Croft (Wigan Wasps)	10.02.80
57.19	J. Croft (Wigan Wasps)	08.02.81
56.69	J. Croft (Wigan Wasps)	08.02.81
56.59	J. Croft (Wigan Wasps)	22.02.81
56.36	J. Croft (Wigan Wasps)	15.11.81
55.47	J. Croft (Wigan Wasps)	10.01.82
55.27	J. Croft (Wigan Wasps)	10.01.82
57.16	J. Croft (Wigan Wasps)	03.04.82

200 Metres Freestyle

2:11.70	L. Allardice (Killerwhales)	29.03.73
2:11.20	S. Edmondson (Hull Olympic)	29.03.74
2:09.90	S. Barnard (Beckenham)	29.03.75
2:09.81	D. Hill (Portsmouth Northsea)	07.03.76
2:09.50	S. Barnard (Beckenham)	24.01.76
2:08.70	S. Barnard (Co Cardiff)	03.04.76
2:08.20	D. Davies (Po Plymouth)	16.01.77
2:05.76	M. Houston (Leeds Central)	12.02.77
2:04.13	S. Davies (Po Plymouth)	10.12.77
2:00.81	S. Davies (Kelly College)	25.02.79
1:59.90	J. Croft (Wigan Wasps)	12.12.81
1:59.40	J. Croft (Wigan Wasps)	08.01.82
1:57.95	J. Croft (Wigan Wasps)	08.01.82
1:57.15	J. Croft (Wigan Wasps)	04.04.82

400 Metres Freestyle

4:42.90	J. Green (Walsall)	26.02.72
4:36.00	J. Green (Walsall)	24.02.73
4:35.20	J. Green (Walsall)	31.03.73
4:34.30	J. Green (Walsall)	22.04.73
4:33.10	J. Green (Walsall)	15.04.74
4:25.10	S. Barnard (Beckenham)	24.01.76
4:20.32	S. Davies (Po Plymouth)	09.12.77
4:15.82	S. Davies (Kelly College)	28.01.79
4:15.02	J. Willmott (Southend & Leigh)	26.01.80
4:12.23	J. Croft (Wigan Wasps)	09.01.82
4:10.29	J. Croft (Wigan Wasps)	09.01.82
4:08.47	J. Croft (Wigan Wasps)	06.02.82
4:04.93	J. Croft (Wigan Wasps)	05.04.84

800 Metres Freestyle

9:57.70	J. Hunter (Killerwhales)	08.04.71
9:36.80	J. Green (Walsall)	26.02.72
9:24.80	J. Green (Walsall)	24.02.73
9:22.80	J. Green (Walsall)	29.03.73
9:20.80	J. Atkinson (Millfield)	28.03.74
9:18.60	J. Green (Bilston)	30.03.75
9:13.00	S. Barnard (Beckenham)	25.01.76
9:09.33	S. Barnard (Beckenham)	13.02.76
9:05.10	S. Davies (Po Plymouth)	15.01.77
9:00.68	M. Houston (Leeds Central)	04.03.77
8:46.06	S. Davies (Po Plymouth)	09.12.77
8:41.50	J. Willmott (Southend & Leigh)	25.01.80
8:35.02	J. Willmott (Southend on Sea)	12.12.81
8:27.08	J. Willmott (Southend on Sea)	05.02.82
8:25.00	J. Willmott (Southend on Sea)	02.04.82

1500 Metres Freestyle

19:23.90	C. Bodle (Gloucester C)	10.06.72
19:00.10	C. Bodle (Gloucester C)	24.03.74
18:36.20	C. Bodle (Gloucester C)	31.03.74
18:06.00	K. Wilkinson (Co Coventry)	11.11.75
17:50.55	T. Burke (Tower Hamlets)	02.12.77
16:56.90	J. Willmott (Southend & Leigh)	16.12.79
16:37.67	J. Willmott (Southend on Sea)	07.12.80
16:19.23	J. Willmott (Southend on Sea)	20.12.81
16:06.68	S. Hardcastle (Southend Synchronettes)	10.02.85
16:00.03	S. Hardcastle (Bo Southend)	23.02.86

100 Metres Backstroke

1:08.40	M. Crook (Co Southampton)	14.04.73
1:08.00	M. Kelly (Everton)	29.03.74
1:06.80	J. Beasley (Junction Ten)	31.03.76
1:06.11	S. Davies (Po Plymouth)	04.12.77
1:05.76	S. Davies (Po Plymouth)	12.02.78
1:05.05	H. Jameson (Kelly College)	28.03.79
1:04.83	L. Hall (Oak Street)	08.03.80
1:04.71	H. Jameson (Kelly College)	07.02.81
1:04.37	C. White (Bo S Tyneside)	06.03.82
1:04.30	H. Jameson (Kelly College)	04.04.82
1:04.24	H. Jameson (Kelly College)	04.04.82
1:03.78	C. White (Bo S Tyneside)	05.02.83
1:03.68	C. White (Bo S Tyneside)	04.04.83
1:03.58	C. White (Bo S Tyneside)	08.04.84
1:03.37	C. White (Co Leeds)	08.04.85

200 Metres Backstroke

2:26.20	M. Kelly (Everton)	30.03.74
2:25.90	M. Kelly (Everton)	26.05.74
2:25.10	K. Wilkinson (Co Coventry)	21.02.76
2:24.34	S. Davies (Po Plymouth)	11.04.76
2:23.50	K. Wilkinson (Co Coventry)	26.04.76
2:19.63	S. Davies (Po Plymouth)	13.02.77
2:17.79	S. Davies (Po Plymouth)	03.12.77
2:16.30	J. Admans (Slough Dolphins)	27.01.80
2:15.16	C. White (Bo S Tyneside)	02.04.83
2:14.98	C. White (Bo S Tyneside)	06.04.84
2:14.27	K. Read (Norwich Penguins)	10.12.88

June Croft

50 Metres Breaststroke

33.30	M. Hohmann (Wigan Wasps)	12.02.88
32.31	M. Hohmann (Wigan Wasps)	13.02.88
32.30	M. Hohmann (Wigan Wasps)	23.02.89

100 Metres Breaststroke

1:15.10	D. Harris (Beckenham)	19.04.69
1:14.20	M. Kelly (Co Cardiff)	03.04.76
1:12.70	D. Rudd (Co Cardiff)	22.01.77
1:12.56	M. Kelly (Beckenham)	11.03.78
1:11.24	M. Kelly (Beckenham)	31.03.79
1:10.75	M. Kelly (Beckenham)	24.02.80
1:10.13	M. Kelly (Beckenham)	06.04.80
1:08.96	S. Brownsdon (Wigan Wasps)	10.12.88

200 Metres Breaststroke

2:42.30	D. Harris (Beckenham)	29.04.69
2:42.20	D. Harrison (Hartlepool)	18.06.72
2:40.40	M. Kelly (Co Cardiff)	17.01.76
2:39.80	M. Kelly (Co Cardiff)	25.01.76
2:39.50	M. Kelly (Co Cardiff)	31.03.76
2:35.40	D. Rudd (Co Coventry)	23.01.77
2:35.21	D. Rudd (Co Coventry)	12.02.77
2:34.49	M. Kelly (Beckenham)	28.03.79
2:33.70	M. Kelly (Beckenham)	10.02.80
2:32.62	M. Kelly (Beckenham)	23.02.80
2:32.13	S. Brownsdon (RTW Monson)	21.02.81
2:30.82	S. Brownsdon (Calgary University)	02.12.84
2:30.72	G. Stanley (Stockport Metro)	28.03.86
2:30.69	G. Stanley (Stockport Metro)	22.11.86
2:30.34	S. Brownsdon (Wigan Wasps)	09.03.87
2:28.53	S. Brownsdon (Wigan Wasps)	09.12.88

100 Metres Butterfly

1:07.00	M. Auton (Hartlepool)	08.03.69
1:06.70	J. Atkinson (Millfield)	30.03.74
1:06.10	J. Atkinson (Millfield)	06.04.74
1:06.00	E. Taylor (Co Coventry)	21.02.76
1:05.90	S. Jenner (Mermaid & Marlin)	28.02.76
1:04.30	S. Jenner (Mermaid & Marlin)	13.03.76
1:04.03	S. Jenner (Mermaid & Marlin)	06.03.77
1:03.33	S. Davies (Po Plymouth)	04.12.77
1:02.36	A. Osgerby (Wigan Wasps)	25.02.79

1:01.94	A. Osgerby (Wigan Wasps)	09.02.80
1:01.43	L. Criddle (Millfield)	01.04.82
1:00.28	C. Cooper (Potters Bar)	05.04.85

200 Metres Butterfly

2:29.90	J. Machin (Gloucester C)	31.03.72
2:27.50	J. Jeavons (Melton Mowbray)	24.02.73
2:26.30	J. Jeavons (Melton Mowbray)	29.03.73
2:24.10	J. Atkinson (Millfield)	14.03.75
2:23.28	J. Atkinson (Millfield)	22.03.75
2:22.80	J. Atkinson (Millfield)	29.03.75
2:21.90	J. Alexander (Co Cardiff)	24.01.76
2:20.70	S. Jenner (Mermaid & Marlin)	02.04.76
2:19.52	S. Jenner (Mermaid & Marlin)	05.03.77
2:18.30	S. Jenner (Mermaid & Marlin)	10.03.78
2:15.32	A. Osgerby (Wigan Wasps)	24.02.79
2:14.78	A. Osgerby (Wigan Wasps)	10.02.80
2:13.35	F. Ross (Bexley)	03.04.83
2:11.91	S. Purvis (Stockton Aquatics)	30.06.84

200 Metres Individual Medley

2:28.30	S. Ratcliffe (Everton)	19.04.69

2:27.48	S. Barnard (Beckenham)	23.03.75
2:27.00	S. Richardson (Beckenham)	13.02.76
2:24.40	A. Kenny (Merton Swordfish)	12.02.77
2:23.53	M. Kelly (Cumbernauld)	06.03.77
2:21.60	S. Davies (Po Plymouth)	03.12.77
2:17.77	S. Davies (Po Plymouth)	11.02.78
2:15.87	S. Davies (Kelly College)	09.02.80

400 Metres Individual Medley

5:14.40	S. Ratcliffe (Everton)	18.04.69
5:11.00	S. Richardson (Beckenham)	16.02.74
5:07.70	S. Barnard (Beckenham)	24.01.76
5:07.10	S. Barnard (Co Cardiff)	02.04.76
5:01.20	S. Davies (Po Plymouth)	16.01.77
5:00.06	S. Davies (Po Plymouth)	12.02.77
4:49.68	S. Davies (Po Plymouth)	04.12.77
4:48.49	S. Davies (Kelly College)	30.03.79
4:43.95	S. Davies (Kelly College)	10.02.80

4×100 Metres Freestyle Club Relay

3:56.54	Stockport Metro	21.11.87
3:56.33	Portsmouth Northsea	19.11.88

Progressive British (Short Course) Records

Men

50 Metres Freestyle

23.33	D. Lowe (England)	12.02.83
23.23	D. Lowe (England)	12.02.83
23.22	D. Lowe (England)	10.02.85
22.88	M. Foster (England)	22.11.86
22.84	M. Foster (England)	24.10.87
22.69	M. Foster (England)	13.02.88
22.57	M. Foster (England)	14.02.88
22.52	M. Fibbens (England)	12.02.89

100 Metres Freestyle

53.90	M. Windeatt (England)	31.03.73
53.80	B. Brinkley (England)	30.03.74
53.60	B. Brinkley (England)	15.03.75
52.94	D. Dunne (England)	05.03.77
52.80	M. Smith (England)	08.05.77
52.00	K. Burns (England)	05.06.78
51.10	M. Smith (England)	05.06.78
50.76	M. Smith (England)	02.01.81
50.59	M. Smith (England)	02.01.81
50.54	M. Smith (England)	10.01.82
50.50	D. Lowe (England)	19.12.82
50.31	D. Lowe (England)	04.04.83
49.86	D. Lowe (England)	04.04.83
49.26	M. Foster (England)	23.11.86
48.97	M. Foster (England)	13.12.87
48.95	M. Fibbens (England)	11.02.89

200 Metres Freestyle

1:59.00	R. Terrell (England)	19.04.69
1:58.10	B. Brinkley (England)	04.09.71
1:56.90	B. Brinkley (England)	31.03.73
1:54.55	B. Brinkley (England)	02.03.74
1:52.71	B. Brinkley (England)	22.03.75
1:52.44	B. Brinkley (England)	15.02.76
1:51.20	A. Astbury (England)	30.03.79
1:50.95	P. Hubble (England)	02.04.82
1:49.59	P. Hubble (England)	16.03.83
1:48.76	K. Boyd (England)	14.12.86
1:48.52	K. Boyd (England)	12.02.89

400 Metres Freestyle

4:14.90	B. Brinkley (England)	23.10.71
4:12.10	B. Brinkley (England)	18.06.72
4:09.70	B. Brinkley (England)	24.02.73
4:09.20	B. Brinkley (England)	29.03.73
4:01.54	B. Brinkley (England)	02.03.74
4:01.40	J. Carter (Scotland)	08.03.75
3:58.85	B. Brinkley (England)	23.03.75
3:58.47	B. Brinkley (England)	14.02.76
3:56.43	B. Brinkley (England)	07.03.76
3:53.31	A. Astbury (England)	29.03.79
3:51.27	P. Easter (Scotland)	03.04.83
3:50.39	A. Astbury (England)	02.12.83
3:46.80	K. Boyd (England)	13.12.86
3:45.33	K. Boyd (England)	12.12.87
3:44.66	K. Boyd (England)	12.12.87

800 Metres Freestyle

8:49.60	B. Brinkley (England)	24.02.73
8:48.50	B. Brinkley (England)	31.03.73
8:42.50	D. Smith (England)	15.04.74
8:27.70	J. Carter (Scotland)	08.03.75
8:23.10	B. Brinkley (England)	13.02.76
8:18.80	D. Parker (England)	23.01.77
8:16.53	S. Lewington (England)	28.03.79
8:14.70	S. Lewington (England)	22.02.80
8:09.03	P. Easter (Scotland)	05.02.82
8:04.12	A. Astbury (England)	07.01.83
7:56.42	D. Stacey (England)	22.11.86
7:54.39	K. Boyd (England)	06.02.87
7:52.61	K. Boyd (England)	13.11.88
7:48.23	K. Boyd (England)	10.02.89

1500 Metres Freestyle

16:47.40	B. Brinkley (England)	24.02.73
16:37.30	B. Brinkley (England)	31.03.73
16:32.70	D. Parker (England)	15.02.75
16:03.90	J. Carter (Scotland)	08.03.75
15:43.78	B. Brinkley (England)	13.02.76
15:39.40	D. Parker (England)	23.01.77
15:30.13	A. Astbury (England)	28.03.79

15:27.30	S. Lewington (England)	22.02.80
15:23.35	D. Stacey (England)	05.02.82
15:22.78	T. Day (England)	18.01.85
15:20.00	T. Day (England)	22.11.85
15:10.12	D. Stacey (England)	22.11.86
15:04.74	T. Day (England)	01.12.86
14:57.36	K. Boyd (England)	10.12.88

50 Metres Backstroke

26.81	M. Peyrebrune (Scotland)	03.04.88

100 Metres Backstroke

1:01.80	A. Davison (England)	10.04.71
1:01.10	M. Richards (Wales)	01.04.72
1:00.70	C. Cunningham (England)	31.03.73
1:00.20	C. Cunningham (England)	30.03.74
1:00.10	S. Harrison (England)	12.02.78
59.88	S. Harrison (England)	10.03.78
58.51	P. Marshall (Scotland)	25.02.79
57.97	P. Marshall (Scotland)	10.02.80
57.68	G. Abraham (England)	04.04.81
57.16	D. Campbell (Scotland)	11.12.82
57.02	G. Robins (England)	16.12.88

200 Metres Backstroke

2:14.20	M. Richards (Wales)	09.04.71
2:13.50	C. Cunningham (England)	30.03.72
2:11.40	C. Cunningham (England)	29.03.73
2:10.60	C. Cunningham (England)	28.03.74
2:10.10	P. Lerpiniere (England)	01.04.76
2:09.40	P. Robinson (England)	30.04.78
2:07.76	P. Marshall (Scotland)	29.03.79
2:07.47	M. Fenner (England)	10.05.81
2:06.95	A. Jameson (England)	07.02.82
2:06.01	D. Campbell (Scotland)	.82
2:05.72	D. Campbell (Scotland)	.82
2:03.60	D. Campbell (Scotland)	12.12.82
2:02.88	D. Campbell (Scotland)	17.12.82
2:02.68	K. Boyd (England)	13.11.88
2:02.04	G. Robins (England)	17.11.88
2:00.07	K. Boyd (England)	04.12.88

50 Metres Breaststroke

28.92	A. Moorhouse (England)	25.01.87
28.24	A. Moorhouse (England)	06.02.87
28.13	A. Moorhouse (England)	13.02.88
27.90	A. Moorhouse (England)	14.02.88

100 Metres Breaststroke

1:09.40	M. O'Connell (England)	30.10.71
1:09.30	M. O'Connell (England)	18.03.72
1:09.10	M. O'Connell (England)	31.03.72
1:08.40	D. Leigh (England)	27.10.72
1:08.30	D. Leigh (England)	27.10.73
1:07.00	D. Leigh (England)	29.03.74
1:06.70	D. Leigh (England)	13.03.75
1:06.36	D. Leigh (England)	23.03.75
1:05.70	L. Atkinson (Wales)	04.03.79
1:01.83	D. Goodhew (England)	09.02.80
1:01.53	A. Moorhouse (England)	05.02.84
1:00.58	A. Moorhouse (England)	06.04.85
59.75	A. Moorhouse (England)	08.02.87

200 Metres Breaststroke

2:33.50	D. Wilkie (Scotland)	10.04.71
2:31.80	D. Wilkie (Scotland)	11.03.72
2:30.50	D. Wilkie (Scotland)	21.03.72
2:25.50	D. Wilkie (Scotland)	18.06.72
2:24.30	D. Leigh (England)	30.03.74
2:23.70	D. Leigh (England)	01.02.75
2:21.64	L. Atkinson (Wales)	11.03.78

2:17.25	D. Goodhew (England)	10.02.80
2:16.88	D. Goodhew (England)	06.04.80
2:16.68	A. Moorhouse (England)	12.11.83
2:15.49	A. Moorhouse (England)	18.12.83
2:15.00	A. Moorhouse (England)	09.03.85
2:14.35	A. Moorhouse (England)	08.04.85
2:13.14	A. Moorhouse (England)	23.01.87
2:12.86	A. Moorhouse (England)	01.03.87
2:12.85	A. Moorhouse (England)	13.02.88
2:10.79	N. Gillingham (England)	11.02.89
2:09.81	N. Gillingham (England)	11.02.89

50 Metres Butterfly

25.48	M. Foster (England)	07.02.86
25.35	M. Fibbens (England)	07.02.87
24.97	M. Foster (England)	07.02.87
24.63	M. Foster (England)	28.02.87
24.48	M. Foster (England)	14.02.88

100 Metres Butterfly

58.90	M. Edwards (England)	29.03.73
57.40	B. Brinkley (England)	17.02.74
57.26	B. Brinkley (England)	16.02.75
57.14	B. Brinkley (England)	22.03.75
56.64	B. Brinkley (England)	06.03.76
56.70	B. Brinkley (England)	25.01.76
55.83	G. Abraham (England)	04.04.81
55.56	P. Hubble (England)	08.01.82
55.45	P. Hubble (England)	08.01.82
54.94	D. Lowe (England)	19.12.82
54.82	P. Hubble (England)	19.03.83
54.77	M. Fibbens (England)	21.11.86
54.00	M. Fibbens (England)	04.02.89

200 Metres Butterfly

2:09.20	J. Mills (England)	31.03.72
2:04.40	B. Brinkley (England)	16.02.74
2:03.86	B. Brinkley (England)	02.03.74
2:03.40	B. Brinkley (England)	16.02.75
2:02.05	B. Brinkley (England)	23.03.75
2:00.36	B. Brinkley (England)	07.03.76
1:59.39	P. Hubble (England)	16.03.83
1:58.81	T. Jones (England)	11.02.89

200 Metres Individual Medley

2:16.40	R. Terrell (England)	19.04.69
2:15.90	D. Wilkie (Scotland)	18.06.72
2:14.60	B. Brinkley (England)	24.02.73
2:13.50	B. Brinkley (England)	17.02.74
2:07.50	B. Brinkley (England)	21.03.75
2:07.31	D. Dunne (England)	28.03.79
2:07.07	J. Randall (England)	05.04.81
2:07.00	S. Poulter (England)	08.01.82
2:06.90	S. Poulter (England)	05.02.82
2:06.83	R. Brew (Scotland)	05.02.82
2:05.97	S. Forrest (England)	04.04.82
2:05.81	P. Easter (Scotland)	04.04.83
2:02.69	R. Brew (Scotland)	08.04.84
2:02.64	P. Brew (Scotland)	12.12.87

400 Metres Individual Medley

4:45.60	B. Brinkley (England)	24.02.73
4:37.77	B. Brinkley (England)	02.03.73
4:36.70	J. Carter (Scotland)	08.03.75
4:35.04	B. Brinkley (England)	22.03.75
4:32.39	D. Cleworth (England)	10.12.78
4:29.24	G. Sykes (England)	25.01.80
4:28.56	G. Sykes (England)	22.02.80
4:26.20	S. Poulter (England)	09.01.82
4:24.96	S. Poulter (England)	06.02.82

4:24.69	S. Poulter (England)	02.04.82
4:24.02	S. Poulter (England)	05.02.83
4:23.92	S. Poulter (England)	07.02.86
4:21.76	T. Day (England)	28.11.86
4:19.83	P. Brew (England)	22.11.87

4×100 Metres Freestyle Relay

3:19.55	GBR	13.12.87

4×100 Metres Medley Relay

3:44.89	GBR	13.12.87

Women

100 Metres Freestyle

1:00.20	D. Hill (England)	30.03.75
59.89	D. Hill (England)	06.03.76
59.37	M. Houston (England)	05.03.77
58.44	S. Davies (England)	11.12.77
57.48	S. Davies (England)	30.03.79
57.27	J. Croft (England)	10.02.80
57.19	J. Croft (England)	08.02.81
56.69	J. Croft (England)	08.02.81
56.59	J. Croft (England)	22.02.81
56.36	J. Croft (England)	15.11.81
55.47	J. Croft (England)	10.01.82
55.27	J. Croft (England)	10.01.82
55.16	J. Croft (England)	03.04.82

200 Metres Freestyle

2:11.70	L. Allardice (England)	29.03.73
2:11.20	S. Edmondson (England)	29.03.74
2:09.90	S. Barnard (England)	29.03.75
2:09.50	S. Barnard (England)	24.01.76
2:08.70	S. Barnard (England)	03.04.76
2:08.20	S. Davies (England)	16.01.77
2:05.76	M. Houston (England)	12.02.77
2:04.13	S. Davies (England)	10.12.77
2:00.81	S. Davies (England)	25.02.79
1:59.90	J. Croft (England)	12.12.81
1:59.40	J. Croft (England)	08.01.82
1:57.95	J. Croft (England)	08.01.82
1:57.15	J. Croft (England)	04.04.82

400 Metres Freestyle

4:42.90	J. Green (England)	26.02.72
4:36.00	J. Green (England)	24.02.73
4:35.20	J. Green (England)	31.03.73
4:34.30	J. Green (England)	22.04.73
4:33.10	J. Green (England)	15.04.74
4:25.10	S. Barnard (England)	24.01.76
4:20.32	S. Davies (England)	09.12.77
4:15.82	S. Davies (England)	28.01.79
4:15.02	J. Willmott (England)	26.01.80
4:12.23	J. Croft (England)	09.01.82
4:10.29	J. Croft (England)	09.01.82
4:08.47	J. Croft (England)	06.02.82
4:04.93	J. Croft (England)	05.04.84

800 Metres Freestyle

9:57.20	S. Jones (Wales)	08.04.71
9:36.80	J. Green (England)	26.02.72
9:24.80	J. Green (England)	24.02.73
9:22.80	J. Green (England)	29.03.73
9:20.80	J. Atkinson (England)	28.03.74
9:18.60	J. Green (England)	30.03.75
9:13.20	A. James (Wales)	22.12.75
9:13.00	S. Barnard (England)	25.01.76
9:09.33	S. Barnard (England)	13.02.76
9:05.10	S. Davies (England)	15.01.77
9:00.68	M. Houston (England)	04.03.77

8:46.06	S. Davies (England)	09.12.77
8:41.50	J. Willmott (England)	25.01.80
8:35.02	J. Willmott (England)	12.12.81
8:27.08	J. Willmott (England)	05.02.82
8:25.00	J. Willmott (England)	02.04.82

1500 Metres Freestyle

19:23.90	C. Bodle (England)	10.06.72
19:00.10	C. Bodle (England)	24.03.74
18:36.00	C. Bodle (England)	31.03.74
17:28.70	A. James (Wales)	22.12.75
16:56.90	J. Willmott (England)	16.12.79
16:37.67	J. Willmott (England)	07.12.80
16:19.23	J. Willmott (England)	20.12.81
16:06.68	S. Hardcastle (England)	10.02.85
16:00.03	S. Hardcastle (England)	23.02.86

100 Metres Backstroke

1:08.40	M. Crook (England)	14.04.73
1:08.00	M. Kelly (England)	28.03.74
1:06.80	J. Beasley (England)	31.03.76
1:06.11	S. Davies (England)	04.12.77
1:05.76	S. Davies (England)	12.02.78
1:05.05	H. Jameson (England)	28.03.79
1:04.83	L. Hall (England)	08.03.80
1:04.71	H. Jameson (England)	07.02.81
1:04.24	B. Rose (Scotland)	09.01.82
1:03.78	C. White (England)	05.02.83
1:03.68	C. White (England)	04.04.83
1:03.58	C. White (England)	08.04.84
1:03.37	C. White (England)	08.04.85

200 Metres Backstroke

2:26.20	M. Kelly (England)	30.03.74
2:25.90	M. Kelly (England)	26.05.74
2:25.10	K. Wilkinson (England)	21.02.76
2:24.34	S. Davies (England)	11.04.76
2:23.50	K. Wilkinson (England)	26.04.76
2:19.63	S. Davies (England)	13.02.77
2:17.79	S. Davies (England)	03.12.77
2:16.30	J. Admans (England)	27.01.80
2:15.16	C. White (England)	02.04.83
2:14.98	C. White (England)	06.04.84
2:14.27	K. Read (England)	10.12.88

50 Metres Breaststroke

33.30	M. Hohmann (England)	12.02.88
32.30	M. Hohmann (England)	23.02.89

100 Metres Breaststroke

1:15.10	D. Harris (England)	19.04.69
1:14.20	M. Kelly (England)	03.04.76
1:12.70	D. Rudd (England)	22.01.77
1:12.56	M. Kelly (England)	11.03.78
1:11.24	M. Kelly (England)	31.03.79
1:10.75	M. Kelly (England)	24.02.80
1:09.85	S. Brownsdon (England)	24.02.81
1:08.96	S. Brownsdon (England)	10.12.88

200 Metres Breaststroke

2:42.30	D. Harris (England)	29.04.69
2:42.20	D. Harrison (England)	18.06.72
2:40.40	M. Kelly (England)	17.01.76
2:39.80	M. Kelly (England)	25.01.76
2:39.50	M. Kelly (England)	31.03.76
2:35.40	D. Rudd (England)	23.01.77
2:35.21	D. Rudd (England)	12.02.77
2:34.49	M. Kelly (England)	28.03.79
2:33.70	M. Kelly (England)	10.02.80
2:32.62	M. Kelly (England)	23.02.80
2:30.82	S. Brownsdon (England)	02.12.84

2:30.72	G. Stanley (England)	28.03.86	2:14.78 A. Osgerby (England)	10.02.80
2:30.69	G. Stanley (England)	22.11.86	2:13.59 A. Osgerby (England)	04.04.81
2:30.34	S. Brownsdon (England)	09.03.87	2:13.35 F. Ross (England)	03.04.83
2:28.53	S. Brownsdon (England)	09.12.88	2:11.91 S. Purvis (England)	30.06.84

100 Metres Butterfly

1:07.00	M. Auton (England)	08.03.69
1:06.70	J. Atkinson (England)	30.03.74
1:06.10	J. Atkinson (England)	06.04.74
1:06.00	E. Taylor (England)	21.02.76
1:05.90	S. Jenner (England)	28.02.76
1:04.30	S. Jenner (England)	13.03.76
1:04.03	S. Jenner (England)	06.03.77
1:03.33	S. Davies (England)	04.12.77
1:02.36	A. Osgerby (England)	25.02.79
1:01.94	A. Osgerby (England)	09.02.80
1:01.43	L. Criddle (England)	01.04.82
1:00.28	C. Cooper (England)	05.04.85

200 Metres Butterfly

2:29.90	J. Machin (England)	31.03.72
2:27.50	J. Jeavons (England)	24.02.73
2:26.30	J. Jeavons (England)	29.03.73
2:24.10	J. Atkinson (England)	14.03.75
2:23.28	J. Atkinson (England)	22.03.75
2:22.80	J. Atkinson (England)	29.03.75
2:21.90	J. Alexander (England)	24.01.76
2:20.70	S. Jenner (England)	02.04.76
2:19.49	D. Simpson (Scotland)	08.02.76
2:18.30	S. Jenner (England)	10.03.78
2:15.32	A. Osgerby (England)	24.02.79

200 Metres Individual Medley

2:28.30	S. Ratcliffe (England)	19.04.69
2:27.48	S. Barnard (England)	23.03.75
2:25.80	A. Adams (Wales)	29.03.75
2:24.40	A. Kenny (England)	12.02.77
2:23.53	M. Kelly (England)	06.03.77
2:21.60	S. Davies (England)	03.12.77
2:17.77	S. Davies (England)	11.02.78
2:15.87	S. Davies (England)	09.02.80

400 Metres Individual Medley

5:14.40	S. Ratcliffe (England)	18.04.69
5:11.00	S. Richardson (England)	16.02.74
5:10.60	A. Adams (Wales)	30.03.75
5:07.70	S. Barnard (England)	24.01.76
5:07.10	S. Barnard (England)	02.04.76
5:01.20	S. Davies (England)	16.01.77
5:00.06	S. Davies (England)	12.02.77
4:49.68	S. Davies (England)	04.12.77
4:48.49	S. Davies (England)	30.03.79
4:43.95	S. Davies (England)	10.02.80

4×100 Metres Freestyle Relay

3:47.61 GBR	13.12.87

4×100 Metres Medley Relay

4:10.82 GBR	13.12.87

Jackie Willmott   Swimming Times

Progressive English (Long Course) Records

NOTE: Records are shown from 1967 after it was decided by the ASA that only metric times would be ratified in future.

Men

50 Metres Freestyle

23.48 D. Lowe	
(Harrow & Wealdstone)	30.01.83
23.41 D. Lowe	
(Harrow & Wealdstone)	16.07.83
23.30 M. Foster (Bo Southend)	01.08.87
23.13 M. Foster (Bo Southend)	22.08.87

100 Metres Freestyle

54.30 A. Jarvis (Otter)	10.08.68
54.30 M. Windeatt (Torquay Leander)	15.07.72
54.20 B. Brinkley (Modernians)	20.07.74
52.30 B. Brinkley (Modernians)	30.08.75
52.23 R. Burrell (Co Southampton)	21.08.79
51.74 R. Burrell (Co Southampton)	22.08.82
51.69 D. Lowe	
(Harrow & Wealdstone)	02.10.82
51.58 D. Lowe	
(Harrow & Wealdstone)	14.07.83
51.32 D. Lowe	
(Harrow & Wealdstone)	24.08.83
51.21 A. Jameson (Co Liverpool)	27.07.86
50.91 A. Jameson (Co Liverpool)	19.08.86
50.78 A. Jameson (Co Liverpool)	20.08.87
50.57 A. Jameson (Co Liverpool)	25.03.88

200 Metres Freestyle

1:58.80 B. Brinkley (Modernians)	06.09.71
1:57.50 B. Brinkley (Modernians)	18.04.72
1:57.00 B. Brinkley (Modernians)	29.08.72
1:56.70 B. Brinkley (Modernians)	29.08.72
1:56.68 B. Brinkley (Modernians)	03.08.73
1:56.42 B. Brinkley (Modernians)	04.09.73
1:56.17 B. Brinkley (Modernians)	19.08.74
1:53.56 B. Brinkley (Modernians)	22.07.75
1:53.07 B. Brinkley (Modernians)	19.07.76
1:51.52 A. Astbury (Leeds Central)	02.10.82
1:51.22 P. Howe (Co Birmingham)	18.09.88

400 Metres Freestyle

4:11.00 B. Brinkley (Modernians)	10.09.71
4:10.00 B. Brinkley (Modernians)	25.06.72
4:06.44 B. Brinkley (Modernians)	01.09.72
4:04.39 B. Brinkley (Modernians)	22.08.74
4:04.03 B. Brinkley (Modernians)	28.08.75
4:01.37 B. Brinkley (Modernians)	19.04.76
3:56.46 A. Astbury (Leeds Central)	16.08.79
3:55.93 A. Astbury (Leeds Central)	10.09.81
3:53.29 A. Astbury (Leeds Central)	04.10.82
3:53.10 K. Boyd (Bo S Tyneside)	21.08.86
3:51.93 K. Boyd (Bo S Tyneside)	21.08.86
3:50.01 K. Boyd (Bo S Tyneside)	23.09.88

800 Metres Freestyle

9:03.70 B. Brinkley (Modernians)	19.12.71
8:42.60 B. Brinkley (Modernians)	28.05.72
8:32.13 D. Parker (Co Coventry)	25.07.75
8:30.26 D. Parker (Co Coventry)	18.04.76
8:20.72 S. Gray (Amateur)	26.05.78
8:16.50 S. Gray (Amateur)	24.08.78
8:13.86 A. Astbury (Leeds Central)	09.04.80
8:13.83 S. Gray	
(Harrow & Wealdstone)	23.05.80
8:12.39 D. Stacey (Co Swansea)	03.08.84
8:01.87 K. Boyd (Bo S Tyneside)	26.03.88

1500 Metres Freestyle

17:09.50 R. Terrell (Co Southampton)	12.07.71
16:39.80 B. Brinkley (Modernians)	28.05.72
16:39.60 B. Brinkley (Modernians)	15.07.72
16:26.94 D. Parker (Co Coventry)	12.04.75
16:16.90 D. Parker (Co Coventry)	24.05.75
15:58.21 D. Parker (Co Coventry)	25.07.75
15:57.45 D. Parker (Co Coventry)	18.04.76
15:46.60 D. Parker (Co Coventry)	20.07.76
15:31.42 S. Gray (Amateur)	24.08.78
15:30.10 D. Stacey (Co Swansea)	03.08.84
15:20.73 K. Boyd (Bo S Tyneside)	03.06.88
15:17.56 K. Boyd (Bo S Tyneside)	24.09.88

50 Metres Backstroke

26.94 N. Harper	
(Harrow & Wealdstone)	10.04.88

100 Metres Backstroke

1:02.20 C. Rushton (Rochdale)	08.08.70
1:01.80 C. Cunningham	
(Co Southampton)	03.03.72
1:01.70 C. Cunningham	
(Co Southampton)	04.03.72
1:01.40 C. Rushton (Madeley College)	16.04.72
1:00.90 C. Cunningham	
(Co Southampton)	18.04.72
1:00.30 C. Cunningham	
(Co Southampton)	15.07.72
59.82 C. Cunningham (Ilford)	25.08.74
59.43 G. Abraham	
(Co Southampton)	28.05.78
58.34 G. Abraham	
(Co Southampton)	11.08.79
58.00 G. Abraham	
(Co Southampton)	12.04.80
57.90 G. Abraham	
(Co Southampton)	20.07.80
57.72 G. Abraham	
(Co Southampton)	24.07.80

200 Metres Backstroke

2:15.50 R. Terrell	
(Co Southampton)	20.07.70
2:13.40 C. Cunningham	
(Co Southampton)	04.03.72
2:13.20 C. Cunningham	
(Co Southampton)	15.04.72
2:11.80 C. Cunningham	
(Co Southampton)	18.04.72
2:09.50 C. Cunningham	
(Co Southampton)	13.07.72
2:09.45 C. Cunningham	
(Co Southampton)	01.08.73
2:08.25 C. Cunningham (Ilford)	23.08.74
2:07.05 J. Davey (Co Milton Keynes)	26.06.82
2:06.61 J. Davey (Co Milton Keynes)	03.08.82
2:05.79 J. Davey (Co Milton Keynes)	03.08.82
2:05.56 G. Binfield (Salford Triple 'S')	27.07.86
2:04.54 G. Binfield (Salford Triple 'S')	27.07.86
2:04.16 J. Davey (Salford Triple 'S')	30.07.87

2:03.79 G. Binfield (Salford Triple 'S') 22.09.88
2:03.56 G. Binfield (Maxwell) 17.08.89

50 Metres Breaststroke
29.44 A. Moorhouse (Co Leeds) 29.01.84
29.01 A. Moorhouse (Co Leeds) 06.05.85
28.96 A. Moorhouse (Co Leeds) 12.04.87
28.91 A. Moorhouse (Co Leeds) 06.06.87
28.75 A. Moorhouse (Co Leeds) 17.04.88

100 Metres Breaststroke
1:09.01 M. O'Connell
         (Co Southampton) 28.08.71
1:08.20 M. O'Connell
         (Co Southampton) 03.03.72
1:07.83 M. O'Connell
         (Co Southampton) 18.04.72
1:06.52 D. Leigh (Oak Street) 01.02.74
1:06.17 D. Leigh (Oak Street) 23.08.74
1:05.32 D. Leigh (Oak Street) 22.07.75
1:05.00 D. Goodhew (Millfield) 02.04.76
1:03.75 D. Goodhew (Beckenham) 21.08.79
1:03.31 D. Goodhew (Beckenham) 24.04.80
1:03.15 A. Moorhouse (Leeds Central) 01.08.82
1:02.93 A. Moorhouse (Leeds Central) 06.10.82
1:02.89 A. Moorhouse (Co Leeds) 30.05.86
1:02.28 A. Moorhouse (Co Leeds) 17.08.86
1:02.13 A. Moorhouse (Co Leeds) 18.08.87
1:01.78 A. Moorhouse (Co Leeds) 26.03.88
1:01.49 A. Moorhouse (Co Leeds) 15.08.89

200 Metres Breaststroke
2:33.40 M. O'Connell
         (Co Southampton) 29.09.71
2:31.30 M. O'Connell
         (Co Southampton) 04.03.72
2:30.30 M. O'Connell
         (Co Southampton) 18.04.72
2:29.96 D. Leigh (Oak Street) 30.08.73
2:24.75 D. Leigh (Oak Street) 30.01.74
2:23.79 D. Leigh (Oak Street) 23.08.74
2:23.38 D. Leigh (Oak Street) 24.07.75
2:20.49 D. Goodhew (Beckenham) 23.08.78
2:19.07 D. Goodhew (Beckenham) 26.05.80
2:18.14 A. Moorhouse (Leeds Central) 07.09.81
2:17.49 A. Moorhouse (Co Leeds) 25.08.83
2:17.03 A. Moorhouse (Co Leeds) 20.04.85
2:16.35 A. Moorhouse (Co Leeds) 28.07.86
2:15.78 A. Moorhouse (Co Leeds) 21.08.87
2:14.58 N. Gillingham
         (Co Birmingham) 23.09.88
2:14.12 N. Gillingham
         (Co Birmingham) 23.09.88
2:12.90 N. Gillingham
         (Co Birmingham) 18.08.89

50 Metres Butterfly
25.58 A. Jameson (Kelly College) 30.07.84
25.20 A. Jameson (Co Liverpool) 07.08.85
25.11 A. Jameson (Co Liverpool) 18.08.86
25.00 A. Jameson (Co Liverpool) 21.09.88

100 Metres Butterfly
58.80 J. Mills (St James) 28.08.71
58.13 J. Mills (St James) 30.08.72
57.95 B. Brinkley (Modernians) 20.08.74
57.50 B. Brinkley (Modernians) 31.03.75
56.68 B. Brinkley (Modernians) 26.07.75
56.53 J. Mills (Sutton & Cheam) 20.07.76
55.52 P. Hubble (Reading) 21.04.79

Andy Jameson

55.15 A. Jameson (Kelly College) 26.05.84
55.04 A. Jameson (Kelly College) 26.05.84
54.59 A. Jameson (Kelly College) 30.07.84
54.28 A. Jameson (Kelly College) 30.07.84
54.24 A. Jameson (Co Liverpool) 07.12.85
54.09 A. Jameson (Co Liverpool) 26.07.86
54.07 A. Jameson (Co Liverpool) 26.07.86
53.67 A. Jameson (Co Liverpool) 18.08.86
53.49 A. Jameson (Co Liverpool) 19.08.87
53.34 A. Jameson (Co Liverpool) 20.09.88
53.30 A. Jameson (Co Liverpool) 21.09.88

200 Metres Butterfly
2:10.10 J. Mills (St James) 07.08.71
2:09.80 B. Brinkley (Modernians) 19.04.72
2:09.60 B. Brinkley (Modernians) 22.04.72
2:09.40 J. Mills (St James) 17.06.72
2:05.60 B. Brinkley (Modernians) 14.07.72
2:05.21 B. Brinkley (Modernians) 03.08.73
2:03.94 B. Brinkley (Modernians) 06.09.73
2:03.84 B. Brinkley (Modernians) 29.03.75
2:02.47 B. Brinkley (Modernians) 24.07.75
2:01.93 B. Brinkley (Modernians) 18.07.76
2:01.49 B. Brinkley (Modernians) 18.07.76
2:01.28 P. Hubble (Reading) 22.04.79
2:00.21 P. Hubble (Slough Dolphins) 11.09.81

200 Metres Individual Medley
2:15.00 R. Terrell (Co Southampton) 11.07.71
2:14.40 R. Terrell (Co Southampton) 03.03.72
2:14.30 R. Terrell (Co Southampton) 19.04.72
2:11.90 R. Terrell (Co Southampton) 13.07.72
2:10.95 B. Brinkley (Modernians) 02.08.73
2:10.89 B. Brinkley (Modernians) 29.08.75
2:10.09 B. Brinkley (Modernians) 03.01.76
2:09.98 D. Cleworth (Co Manchester) 26.05.78
2:09.94 S. Gray
         (Harrow & Wealdstone) 26.05.80
2:08.72 G. Sykes (Co Coventry) 09.08.81
2:07.73 G. Sykes (Co Coventry) 11.09.81
2:07.72 J. Davey (Co Milton Keynes) 27.08.83
2:06.82 S. Willmott (Stockton Aquatics) 28.05.84
2:06.73 J. Davey (Salford Triple 'S') 01.06.86

2:06.51	G. Binfield (Salford Triple 'S')	30.07.86
2:05.67	J. Davey (Salford Triple 'S')	30.07.86
2:05.41	G. Binfield (Salford Triple 'S')	02.08.87
2:05.05	J. Davey (Salford Triple 'S')	28.07.88
2:04.17	J. Davey (Salford Triple 'S')	25.09.88

400 Metres Individual Medley

4:45.70	R. Terrell (Co Southampton)	11.07.71
4:42.70	R. Terrell (Co Southampton)	15.07.72
4:36.29	B. Brinkley (Modernians)	04.08.73
4:27.70	S. Gray (Amateur)	05.08.78
4:27.26	S. Poulter (Wigan Wasps)	01.10.82
4:27.09	S. Poulter (Wigan Wasps)	02.10.82
4:25.38	S. Poulter (Wigan Wasps)	30.07.84
4:24.70	J. Davey (Salford Triple 'S')	30.05.86
4:24.20	J. Davey (Salford Triple 'S')	01.08.87

4×100 Metres Freestyle Club Relay

3:48.50	Co Southampton	04.08.69
3:46.50	Co Southampton	14.07.72
3:45.35	Co Southampton	03.08.73
3:40.90	Modernians	25.08.76
3:38.25	Co Manchester	26.05.78
3:36.51	Beckenham	26.05.78
3:36.50	Co Manchester	01.06.78
3:34.39	Beckenham	25.07.79
3:31.22	Beckenham	25.05.80
3:31.07	Millfield	01.06.86
3:26.38	Co Birmingham	01.08.87

4×100 Medley Club Relay

4:13.50	Nottingham Northern	07.08.71
4:10.08	Co Southampton	14.07.72
4:07.40	Co Southampton	02.08.73
4:07.77	Beckenham	28.05.78
3:58.91	Beckenham	29.05.78
3:57.13	Co Southampton	27.07.79
3:53.00	Beckenham	24.05.80
3:52.80	Beckenham	30.07.88

Women

50 Metres Freestyle

26.48	J. Croft (Wigan Wasps)	27.11.81
26.39	C. Cooper (Potters Bar)	07.12.85
26.19	C. Woodcock (Haywards Heath)	25.03.89
26.01	C. Woodcock (Haywards Heath)	20.08.89

100 Metres Freestyle

1:00.50	A. Jackson (Peel)	18.10.68
1:00.30	D. Hill (Portsmouth Northsea)	07.06.75
1:00.20	S. Edmondson (Co Coventry)	29.05.76
59.58	C. Brazendale (Norbreck Castle)	27.08.76
59.51	C. Brazendale (Norbreck Castle)	10.04.77
59.45	C. Brazendale (Norbreck Castle)	17.04.77
59.34	C. Brazendale (Norbreck Castle)	15.05.77
59.00	C. Brazendale (Norbreck Castle)	10.06.77
57.50	C. Brazendale (Norbreck Castle)	23.08.77
56.60	J. Croft (Wigan Wasps)	31.01.82

200 Metres Freestyle

2:13.50	A. Jackson (Peel)	21.07.70

2:12.20	L. Allardice (Killerwhales)	14.07.72
2:12.00	L. Allardice (Killerwhales)	09.06.73
2:11.19	L. Allardice (Killerwhales)	03.08.73
2:10.98	S. Edmondson (Co Coventry)	28.01.74
2:09.42	S. Edmondson (Co Coventry)	22.08.74
2:09.10	A. Bradshaw (Kingsbury)	30.05.76
2:08.00	S. Barnard (Co Cardiff)	30.05.76
2:06.95	C. Brazendale (Norbreck Castle)	11.04.77
2:06.20	C. Brazendale (Norbreck Castle)	29.04.77
2:04.11	S. Davies (Kelly College)	07.08.78
2:03.23	J. Willmott (Southend on Sea)	26.05.80
2:02.95	J. Croft (Wigan Wasps)	11.07.81
2:00.49	J. Croft (Wigan Wasps)	30.01.82
2:00.08	J. Croft (Wigan Wasps)	17.04.82
1:59.74	J. Croft (Wigan Wasps)	04.10.82

400 Metres Freestyle

4:45.60	S. Williams (Co Exeter)	22.07.67
4:44.50	J. Green (Walsall)	15.04.72
4:43.80	J. Green (Walsall)	18.04.72
4:42.01	S. Edmondson (Hull)	28.05.72
4:36.20	S. Edmondson (Hull)	11.06.72
4:35.40	J. Green (Walsall)	15.07.72
4:35.18	S. Edmondson (Coventry)	01.06.73
4:33.94	J. Green (Walsall)	31.01.74
4:33.77	S. Barnard (Beckenham)	10.08.75
4:30.66	S. Edmondson (Co Coventry)	18.04.76
4:29.00	S. Edmondson (Co Coventry)	30.05.76
4:28.20	M. Houston (Leeds Central)	25.08.76
4:26.60	C. Brazendale (Norbreck Castle)	09.04.77
4:24.83	C. Brazendale (Norbreck Castle)	10.04.77
4:24.09	C. Brazendale (Norbreck Castle)	17.04.77
4:20.56	S. Davies (Po Plymouth)	26.50.78
4:18.59	S. Davies (Kelly College)	25.07.79
4:16.27	J. Willmott (Southend on Sea)	20.04.80
4:15.23	J. Willmott (Southend on Sea)	09.09.81
4:13.94	J. Croft (Wigan Wasps)	31.01.82
4:12.72	J. Willmott (Southend on Sea)	09.05.82
4:11.67	J. Willmott (Southend on Sea)	03.08.82
4:11.55	S. Hardcastle (Southend Synchronettes)	31.07.84
4:10.27	S. Hardcastle (Southend Synchronettes)	31.07.84
4:07.68	S. Hardcastle (Southend Synchronettes)	27.07.86

800 Metres Freestyle

9:49.40	J. Green (Walsall)	12.08.71
9:35.70	J. Green (Walsall)	15.04.72
9:31.40	J. Green (Walsall)	18.04.72
9:31.30	J. Green (Walsall)	13.07.72
9:24.80	J. Green (Walsall)	23.04.73
9:21.48	J. Green (Walsall)	25.01.74
9:12.53	S. Barnard (Beckenham)	28.08.75
9:07.79	C. Brazendale (Norbreck Castle)	11.04.77
9:07.40	L. Heggie (Warrington Warriors)	09.06.77
8:58.87	S. Davies (Po Plymouth)	27.05.78
8:51.40	J. Willmott (Southend & Leigh)	12.08.79
8:38.56	J. Willmott (Southend on Sea)	07.09.81
8:37.22	J. Willmott (Southend on Sea)	11.09.81
8:32.61	J. Willmott (Southend on Sea)	05.08.82

John Davey

8:32.60 S. Hardcastle
(Southend Synchronettes) 03.08.84
8:32.57 S. Hardcastle
(Southend Synchronettes) 10.08.85
8:24.77 S. Hardcastle (Bo Southend) 29.07.86

1500 Metres Freestyle
18:43.20 S. Edmondson (Co Coventry) 16.06.73
18:41.00 N. Muir-Cochrane
(Leeds Central) 02.11.77
17:42.37 M. Charles (Co Coventry) 09.06.78
17:00.03 M. Charles (Co Coventry) 21.12.79
16:46.48 J. Willmott (Southend on Sea) 25.04.80
16:43.95 S. Hardcastle
(Southend Synchronettes) 18.04.85

100 Metres Backstroke
1:08.70 L. Ludgrove (Beckenham) 22.07.67
1:08.61 M. Kelly (Everton) 01.06.73
1:08.57 M. Crook (Co Southampton) 27.04.74
1:08.55 M. Kelly (Everton) 22.08.74
1:08.27 J. Beasley (Halesowen) 24.01.75
1:07.67 B. Roughley (Swinton) 20.08.75
1:06.90 J. Beasley (Junction Ten) 29.05.76
1:06.66 J. Beasley (Junction Ten) 20.07.76
1:06.41 J. Beasley (Junction Ten) 22.01.77
1:05.70 H. Jameson (Kelly College) 15.04.79
1:05.69 K. Read (Stockport Metro) 26.05.85
1:04.52 K. Read (Stockport Metro) 19.08.86
1:04.27 K. Read (Norwich Penguins) 22.09.88

200 Metres Backstroke
2:26.20 W. Burrell (Carlisle Secondary) 09.09.70
2:25.90 J. Beasley (Junction Ten) 25.04.76
2:25.00 S. Davies (Po Plymouth) 01.05.76
2:25.00 K. Wilkinson (Co Coventry) 01.05.76
2:24.20 K. Wilkinson (Co Coventry) 30.05.76
2:21.02 J. Admans (Slough Dolphins) 27.03.78
2:20.64 S. Davies (Po Plymouth) 08.04.78
2:19.30 S. Davies (Po Plymouth) 21.04.78
2:18.94 J. Admans (Slough Dolphins) 28.07.79
2:17.66 J. Admans (Slough Dolphins) 12.09.81
2:16.00 K. Read (Norwich Penguins) 28.05.84
2:14.87 K. Read (Stockport Metro) 30.05.86

50 Metres Breaststroke
33.39 L. Burt (Co Southampton) 30.05.87

100 Metres Breaststroke
1:17.00 D. Harrison (Hartlepool) 07.09.70
1:16.50 D. Harrison (Hartlepool) 01.09.72
1:16.35 C. Jarvis (Modernians) 05.09.73
1:15.48 M. Kelly (Co Cardiff) 15.08.75
1:14.70 C. Jarvis (Modernians) 02.04.76
1:14.47 M. Kelly (Co Cardiff) 18.04.76
1:14.23 M. Kelly (Co Cardiff) 22.07.76
1:13.57 M. Kelly (Co Cardiff) 22.07.76
1:13.20 M. Kelly (Beckenham) 25.03.78
1:13.11 M. Kelly (Beckenham) 25.03.78
1:13.02 M. Kelly (Beckenham) 09.04.78
1:12.75 M. Kelly (Beckenham) 22.04.78
1:11.73 M. Kelly (Beckenham) 22.08.78
1:11.05 S. Brownsdon (RTW Monson) 08.09.81
1:10.39 S. Brownsdon (RTW Monson) 21.08.87

200 Metres Breaststroke
2:45.60 D. Harrison (Hartlepool) 11.09.70
2:45.12 C. Gaskell (Rochdale) 26.01.74
2:44.77 C. Gaskell (Rochdale) 10.04.74
2:42.13 M. Kelly (Co Cardiff) 28.08.75
2:41.96 C. Jarvis (Modernians) 02.04.76
2:41.93 M. Kelly (Co Cardiff) 19.04.76
2:38.60 M. Kelly (Co Cardiff) 29.05.76
2:38.26 D. Rudd (Co Coventry) 21.07.76
2:38.13 M. Kelly (Beckenham) 26.03.78
2:36.98 M. Kelly (Beckenham) 08.04.78
2:35.64 D. Rudd (Co Coventry) 24.04.78
2:34.43 S. Brownsdon (RTW Monson) 03.07.81
2:33.16 S. Brownsdon (Millfield) 04.05.85

50 Metres Butterfly
28.22 C. Cooper (Kelly College) 28.01.84

100 Metres Butterfly
1:07.40 M. Auton (Hartlepool) 14.06.68
1:06.60 J. Jeavons (Melton Mowbray) 15.07.72
1:06.26 J. Atkinson (Darlington) 04.08.73
1:05.48 J. Atkinson (Millfield) 22.08.74
1:05.26 J. Atkinson (Millfield) 25.05.75
1:04.94 S. Jenner (Mermaid & Marlin) 24.04.76
1:04.50 S. Jenner (Mermaid & Marlin) 01.05.76
1:04.44 S. Jenner (Mermaid & Marlin) 15.05.76
1:04.30 J. Atkinson (Millfield) 30.05.76
1:04.20 S. Jenner (Mermaid & Marlin) 03.06.76
1:04.06 S. Jenner (Mermaid & Marlin) 21.07.76
1:03.88 S. Jenner (Mermaid & Marlin) 30.04.77
1:03.76 S. Jenner (Mermaid & Marlin) 25.06.77
1:03.56 S. Jenner (Mermaid & Marlin) 13.05.78
1:03.44 A. Osgerby (Wigan Wasps) 06.08.78
1:03.30 S. Jenner (Mermaid & Marlin) 06.08.78
1:02.90 A. Osgerby (Wigan Wasps) 23.08.78
1:02.74 A. Osgerby (Wigan Wasps) 23.08.78
1:02.58 A. Osgerby (Wigan Wasps) 22.08.79
1:02.32 A. Osgerby (Wigan Wasps) 12.04.80
1:01.87 A. Osgerby (Wigan Wasps) 12.07.83
1:01.56 A. Osgerby (Wigan Wasps) 25.08.83
1:01.48 N. Fibbens
(Harrow & Wealdstone) 02.08.84

200 Metres Butterfly
2:31.60 D. Lansley (Co Southampton) 13.06.70
2:28.00 J. Machin (Gloucester C) 18.04.72
2:26.90 J. Jeavons (Melton Mowbray) 11.06.72
2:26.10 J. Jeavons (Melton Mowbray) 25.06.72
2:23.60 J. Jeavons (Melton Mowbray) 14.07.72

239

2:21.15	J. Atkinson (Millfield)	24.05.75
2:19.50	J. Alexander (Co Cardiff)	29.05.76
2:15.45	S. Jenner (Mermaid & Marlin)	18.08.77
2:15.17	A. Osgerby (Wigan Wasps)	21.07.80
2:14.72	A. Osgerby (Wigan Wasps)	08.09.81
2:14.52	A. Osgerby (Wigan Wasps)	04.10.82
2:13.91	A. Osgerby (Wigan Wasps)	05.10.82
2:13.79	A. Osgerby (Wigan Wasps)	23.07.83
2:13.00	A. Osgerby (Wigan Wasps)	27.08.83
2:11.97	S. Purvis (Stockton Aquatics)	04.08.84

200 Metres Individual Medley

2:29.50	S. Ratcliffe (Everton)	04.04.70
2:26.86	S. Richardson (Beckenham)	25.01.74
2:26.46	S. Davies (Po Plymouth)	26.08.76
2:25.77	M. Kelly (Cumbernauld)	17.04.77
2:24.98	M. Kelly (Cumbernauld)	30.04.77
2:20.99	S. Davies (Po Plymouth)	26.03.78
2:19.75	S. Davies (Po Plymouth)	27.05.78
2:17.55	S. Davies (Kelly College)	02.02.79
2:17.31	S. Davies (Kelly College)	20.04.80

400 Metres Individual Medley

5:15.40	S. Ratcliffe (Everton)	15.08.71
5:13.88	S. Richardson (Beckenham)	06.09.73
5:08.59	S. Richardson (Beckenham)	31.01.74
5:06.71	S. Richardson (Beckenham)	21.08.74
5:04.80	S. Richardson (Beckenham)	01.05.76
5:03.99	S. Richardson (Beckenham)	15.05.76
5:02.10	S. Richardson (Beckenham)	29.05.76
4:54.88	S. Davies (Po Plymouth)	27.03.78
4:47.67	S. Davies (Kelly College)	02.02.79
4:46.83	S. Davies (Kelly College)	26.07.80

4×100 Metres Freestyle Club Relay

4:21.90	Killerwhales	05.08.71
4:17.30	Cheam Ladies	14.07.72
4:13.95	Beckenham	27.08.75
4:13.48	Beckenham	28.08.75
4:11.40	St James	28.08.76
4:05.94	Millfield	29.05.78
4:05.19	Beckenham	29.05.78
4:03.14	Wigan Wasps	28.07.79
4:01.09	Millfield	23.05.80
3:59.35	Wigan Wasps	19.08.82
3:58.44	Millfield	21.07.83
3:57.28	Wigan Wasps	29.05.86
3:56.51	Wigan Wasps	31.05.86

4×100 Metres Medley Club Relay

4:48.90	Beckenham	07.08.67
4:44.40	Co Southampton	14.07.72
4:39.33	Beckenham	27.08.75
4:27.66	Beckenham	28.05.78
4:25.43	Beckenham	26.07.79
4:24.58	Wigan Wasps	25.05.80
4:20.06	Wigan Wasps	20.08.82

Progressive British (Long Course) Records

NOTE: Records are shown from 1967 after it was decided by the ASA that only metric times would be ratified in future.

Men

50 Metres Freestyle

23.41	D. Lowe (England)	16.07.83
23.30	M. Foster (England)	01.08.87
23.13	M. Foster (England)	22.08.87

100 Metres Freestyle

53.40	R. McGregor (Scotland)	29.08.67
52.30	B. Brinkley (England)	30.08.75
52.26	M. Smith (England)	28.08.78
52.23	R. Burrell (England)	21.08.79
51.74	R. Burrell (England)	22.08.82
51.69	D. Lowe (England)	02.10.82
51.58	D. Lowe (England)	14.07.83
51.32	D. Lowe (England)	24.08.83
51.21	A. Jameson (England)	27.07.86
50.91	A. Jameson (England)	19.08.86
50.78	A. Jameson (England)	20.08.87
50.57	A. Jameson (England)	25.03.88

200 Metres Freestyle

2:01.30	A. Jarvis (England)	14.07.68
1:58.80	B. Brinkley (England)	29.09.71
1:57.50	B. Brinkley (England)	18.04.72
1:56.70	B. Brinkley (England)	29.08.72
1:56.68	B. Brinkley (England)	03.08.73
1:56.42	B. Brinkley (England)	04.09.73
1:56.17	B. Brinkley (England)	19.08.74
1:55.21	G. Downie (Scotland)	13.04.75
1:53.56	B. Brinkley (England)	22.07.75
1:53.07	B. Brinkley (England)	19.07.76
1:52.47	G. Downie (Scotland)	19.07.76
1:51.52	A. Astbury (England)	02.10.82
1:51.22	P. Howe (England)	18.09.88

400 Metres Freestyle

4:11.00	B. Brinkley (England)	10.09.71
4:10.00	B. Brinkley (England)	25.06.72
4:06.44	B. Brinkley (England)	01.09.72
4:04.39	B. Brinkley (England)	22.08.74
4:02.88	G. Downie (Scotland)	24.07.75
4:01.37	B. Brinkley (England)	19.04.76
4:01.00	G. Downie (Scotland)	22.07.76
3:58.75	S. Gray (England)	06.08.78
3:56.87	S. Gray (England)	07.08.78
3:56.46	A. Astbury (England)	16.08.79
3:55.93	A. Astbury (England)	10.09.81
3:53.29	A. Astbury (England)	04.10.82
3:53.10	K. Boyd (England)	21.08.86
3:51.93	K. Boyd (England)	21.08.86
3:50.01	K. Boyd (England)	23.09.88

800 Metres Freestyle

9:03.70	B. Brinkley (England)	19.12.71
8:42.60	B. Brinkley (England)	28.05.72
8:41.57	J. Carter (Scotland)	01.02.74
8:33.01	J. Carter (Scotland)	25.08.74
8:32.13	D. Parker (England)	25.07.75
8:30.26	D. Parker (England)	18.04.76
8:23.74	D. Parker (England)	19.07.76
8:20.72	S. Gray (England)	26.05.78
8:17.58	S. Gray (England)	09.08.78
8:16.50	S. Gray (England)	24.08.78
8:13.86	A. Astbury (England)	09.04.80
8:13.83	S. Gray (England)	23.05.80
8:12.39	D. Stacey (England)	03.08.84

8:09.83 T. Day (Wales)	30.07.86
8:01.87 K. Boyd (England)	26.03.88

1500 Metres Freestyle

17:09.50 R. Terrell (England)	12.07.71
16:39.80 B. Brinkley (England)	28.05.72
16:39.60 B. Brinkley (England)	15.07.72
16:34.70 J. Carter (Scotland)	01.02.74
16:17.57 J. Carter (Scotland)	13.04.74
15:54.78 J. Carter (Scotland)	25.08.74
15:46.60 D. Parker (England)	19.07.76
15:39.39 S. Gray (England)	09.08.78
15:31.42 S. Gray (England)	24.08.78
15:30.10 D. Stacey (England)	03.08.84
15:22.76 T. Day (England)	30.07.86
15:20.73 K. Boyd (England)	03.06.88
15:17.56 K. Boyd (England)	24.09.88

50 Metres Backstroke

26.94 N. Harper (England)	10.04.88

100 Metres Backstroke

1:00.70 M. Richards (Wales)	28.08.71
1:00.30 C. Cunningham (England)	15.07.72
59.82 C. Cunningham (England)	25.08.74
59.43 G. Abraham (England)	28.05.78
59.07 G. Abraham (England)	04.08.78
58.48 G. Abraham (England)	09.08.78
58.34 G. Abraham (England)	11.08.79
58.00 G. Abraham (England)	12.04.80
57.90 G. Abraham (England)	20.07.80
57.72 G. Abraham (England)	24.07.80

200 Metres Backstroke

2:17.00 D. Butler (England)	14.07.68
2:13.70 M. Richards (Wales)	31.07.71
2:13.40 C. Cunningham (England)	04.03.72
2:13.20 C. Cunningham (England)	15.04.72
2:11.80 C. Cunningham (England)	18.04.72
2:09.50 C. Cunningham (England)	13.07.72
2:09.45 C. Cunningham (England)	01.08.73
2:08.60 C. Cunningham (England)	19.08.73
2:08.25 C. Cunningham (England)	23.08.74
2:08.13 J. Carter (Scotland)	18.05.75
2:06.87 J. Carter (Scotland)	02.04.76
2:06.79 D. Campbell (Scotland)	21.08.79
2:05.57 D. Campbell (Scotland)	23.05.80
2:05.31 D. Campbell (Scotland)	23.05.80
2:04.78 D. Campbell (Scotland)	26.07.80
2:04.16 J. Davey (England)	30.07.87
2:03.79 G. Binfield (England)	22.09.88
2:03.56 G. Binfield (England)	17.08.89

50 Metres Breaststroke

29.44 A. Moorhouse (England)	29.01.84
29.01 A. Moorhouse (England)	06.05.85
28.96 A. Moorhouse (England)	12.04.87
28.91 A. Moorhouse (England)	06.06.87
28.75 A. Moorhouse (England)	17.04.88

100 Metres Breaststroke

1:09.00 M. O'Connell (England)	28.08.71
1:08.20 M. O'Connell (England)	03.03.72
1:07.80 M. O'Connell (England)	18.04.72
1:06.20 D. Wilkie (Scotland)	29.08.72
1:05.74 D. Wilkie (Scotland)	04.09.73
1:05.60 D. Wilkie (Scotland)	06.04.75
1:04.26 D. Wilkie (Scotland)	22.07.75
1:03.43 D. Wilkie (Scotland)	20.07.76
1:03.31 D. Goodhew (England)	24.04.80
1:03.15 A. Moorhouse (England)	01.08.82

1:02.93 A. Moorhouse (England)	06.10.82
1:02.89 A. Moorhouse (England)	30.05.86
1:02.28 A. Moorhouse (England)	17.08.86
1:02.13 A. Moorhouse (England)	18.08.87
1:01.78 A. Moorhouse (England)	26.03.88
1:01.49 A. Moorhouse (England)	15.08.89

200 Metres Breaststroke

2:32.50 D. Wilkie (Scotland)	17.07.70
2:31.30 M. O'Connell (England)	04.03.72
2:30.30 M. O'Connell (England)	18.04.72
2:28.00 D. Wilkie (Scotland)	15.07.72
2:23.70 D. Wilkie (Scotland)	02.09.72
2:20.94 D. Wilkie (Scotland)	06.09.73
2:19.28 D. Wilkie (Scotland)	06.09.73
2:18.23 D. Wilkie (Scotland)	24.07.75
2:15.11 D. Wilkie (Scotland)	24.07.76
2:14.58 N. Gillingham (England)	23.09.88
2:14.12 N. Gillingham (England)	23.09.88
2:12.90 N. Gillingham (England)	18.08.89

50 Metres Butterfly

25.58 A. Jameson (England)	30.07.84
25.20 A. Jameson (England)	07.08.85
25.11 A. Jameson (England)	18.08.86
25.00 A. Jameson (England)	21.09.88

100 Metres Butterfly

58.80 M. Woodroffe (Wales)	11.07.69
58.13 J. Mills (England)	30.08.72
57.95 B. Brinkley (England)	20.08.74
57.50 B. Brinkley (England)	31.03.75
56.68 B. Brinkley (England)	26.07.75
56.53 J. Mills (England)	20.07.76
55.52 P. Hubble (England)	21.04.79
55.15 A. Jameson (England)	26.05.84
55.04 A. Jameson (England)	26.05.84
54.59 A. Jameson (England)	30.07.84
54.28 A. Jameson (England)	30.07.84
54.24 A. Jameson (England)	07.12.85
54.09 A. Jameson (England)	26.07.86
54.07 A. Jameson (England)	26.07.86
53.67 A. Jameson (England)	18.08.86
53.49 A. Jameson (England)	19.08.87
53.34 A. Jameson (England)	20.09.88
53.30 A. Jameson (England)	21.09.88

Nick Gillingham

241

200 Metres Butterfly

2:07.80	M. Woodroffe (Wales)	13.07.69
2:05.60	B. Brinkley (England)	14.07.72
2:05.21	B. Brinkley (England)	03.08.73
2:03.94	B. Brinkley (England)	06.09.73
2:03.84	B. Brinkley (England)	29.03.75
2:02.47	B. Brinkley (England)	24.07.75
2:01.49	B. Brinkley (England)	18.07.76
2:01.28	P. Hubble (England)	22.04.79
2:00.21	P. Hubble (England)	11.09.81

200 Metres Individual Medley

2:15.00	R. Terrell (England)	11.07.71
2:14.40	R. Terrell (England)	03.03.72
2:14.30	R. Terrell (England)	19.04.72
2:11.90	R. Terrell (England)	13.07.72
2:10.00	D. Wilkie (Scotland)	23.04.73
2:09.61	D. Wilkie (Scotland)	07.09.73
2:08.84	D. Wilkie (Scotland)	07.09.73
2:06.32	D. Wilkie (Scotland)	24.08.74
2:06.25	D. Wilkie (Scotland)	02.04.76
2:06.10	R. Brew (Scotland)	03.10.82
2:05.83	R. Brew (Scotland)	04.10.82
2:04.99	N. Cochran (Scotland)	28.05.84
2:04.13	R. Brew (Scotland)	04.08.84
2:03.76	N. Cochran (Scotland)	06.12.85
2:03.20	N. Cochran (Scotland)	25.03.88

400 Metres Individual Medley

4:45.70	R. Terrell (England)	11.07.71
4:42.70	R. Terrell (England)	15.07.72
4:36.29	B. Brinkley (England)	04.08.73
4:34.23	A. McClatchey (Scotland)	02.04.76
4:33.56	A. McClatchey (Scotland)	15.08.76
4:31.86	S. Gray (England)	04.08.78
4:27.70	S. Gray (England)	05.08.78
4:27.26	S. Poulter (England)	01.10.82
4:27.09	S. Poulter (England)	02.10.82
4:25.38	S. Poulter (England)	30.07.84
4:24.70	J. Davey (England)	30.05.86
4:24.20	J. Davey (England)	01.08.87

4×100 Metres Freestyle Relay

3:37.95	GB – Iredale, Rose, Burns, Smith	10.04.76
3:34.82	GB – Dunne, Smith, Iredale, Brinkley	14.08.76
3:30.10	England – Smith, Burns, Dunne, Burrell	04.08.78
3:28.76	GB – Abraham, Goodhew, Mills, Smith	28.08.78
3:26.98	England – Lowe, Hubble, Osborn, Burrell	01.10.82
3:24.59	GB – Lowe, Lee, Easter, Burrell	02.08.84
3:23.61	GB – Lowe, Lee, Easter, Burrell	02.08.84
3:22.76	GB – Jameson, Foster, Fibbens, Lee	21.08.87
3:21.71	GB – Fibbens, Foster, Lee, Jameson	23.09.88

4×200 Metres Freestyle Relay

8:08.80	GB – Brinkley, Terrell, Bailey, Maher	18.04.72
7:55.60	GB – Brinkley, Mills, Bailey, Cunningham	31.08.72
7:52.90	England – Cunningham, Dexter, Terrell, Brinkley	25.01.74

7:42.55	GB – McClatchey, Brinkley, Jameson, Downie	25.07.75
7:32.11	GB – McClatchey, Dunne, Downie, Brinkley	21.07.76
7:30.00	England – Osborn, Davey, Hubble, Astbury	04.10.82
7:29.22	GB – Cochran, Easter, Davey, Astbury	24.08.83
7:26.83	GB – Cochran, Easter, Howe, Astbury	30.07.84
7:24.78	GB – Cochran, Easter, Howe, Astbury	30.07.84

4×100 Metres Medley Relay

4:04.40	GB – Rushton, O'Connell, Mills, Windeatt	15.04.72
4:01.10	GB – Rushton, O'Connell, Mills, Windeatt	21.04.72
3:58.80	GB – Cunningham, Wilkie, Mills, Windeatt	02.09.72
3:54.13	GB – Cunningham, Wilkie, Nash, Brinkley	25.08.74
3:52.80	GB – Carter, Wilkie, Brinkley, Downie	27.07.75
3:49.56	GB – Carter, Wilkie, Mills, Brinkley	22.07.76
3:49.06	GB – Abraham, Goodhew, Mills, Smith	28.08.78
3:47.71	GB – Abraham, Goodhew, Lowe, Taylor	24.07.80
3:47.39	GB – Harper, Moorhouse, Jameson, Burrell	04.08.84
3:44.85	England – Harper, Moorhouse, Jameson, Lee	30.07.86
3:42.01	GB – Cochran, Moorhouse, Jameson, Lee	23.08.87

Women

50 Metres Freestyle

26.39	C. Cooper (England)	06.12.85
26.19	C. Woodcock (England)	25.03.89
26.01	C. Woodcock (England)	20.08.89

100 Metres Freestyle

1:01.50	A. Jackson (England)	21.04.68
1:00.50	A. Jackson (England)	18.10.68
1:00.30	D. Hill (England)	07.06.75
1:00.20	E. Gray (Scotland)	29.05.76
59.58	C. Brazendale (England)	27.08.76
59.51	C. Brazendale (England)	10.04.77
59.45	C. Brazendale (England)	17.04.77
59.34	C. Brazendale (England)	15.05.77
59.00	C. Brazendale (England)	10.06.77
57.50	C. Brazendale (England)	23.08.77
56.60	J. Croft (England)	31.01.82

200 Metres Freestyle

2:13.50	A. Jackson (England)	21.07.70
2:12.00	L. Allardice (England)	09.06.73
2:11.19	L. Allardice (England)	03.08.73
2:10.02	D. Walker (Scotland)	30.01.74
2:09.42	S. Edmondson (England)	28.08.74
2:09.10	A. Bradshaw (England)	30.05.76
2:08.00	S. Barnard (England)	30.05.76
2:06.95	C. Brazendale (England)	11.04.77
2:06.20	C. Brazendale (England)	29.04.77
2:04.11	S. Davies (England)	07.08.78
2:04.10	J. Willmott (England)	20.04.80

2:03.23 J. Willmott (England) — 26.05.80
2:02.95 J. Croft (England) — 11.07.81
2:00.49 J. Croft (England) — 30.01.82
2:00.08 J. Croft (England) — 17.04.82
1:59.74 J. Croft (England) — 04.10.82

400 Metres Freestyle
4:44.60 L. Allardice (England) — 06.08.71
4:44.50 J. Green (England) — 15.04.72
4:43.80 J. Green (England) — 18.04.72
4:42.10 S. Edmondson (England) — 28.05.72
4:36.20 S. Edmondson (England) — 11.06.72
4:35.40 J. Green (England) — 13.07.72
4:35.18 S. Edmondson (England) — 01.06.73
4:30.14 D. Walker (Scotland) — 31.01.74
4:29.17 D. Walker (Scotland) — 20.08.74
4:29.00 S. Edmondson (England) — 30.05.76
4:28.20 M. Houston (England) — 25.08.76
4:26.60 C. Brazendale (England) — 09.04.77
4:24.83 C. Brazendale (England) — 10.04.77
4:24.09 C. Brazendale (England) — 17.04.77
4:20.56 S. Davies (England) — 26.05.78
4:18.59 S. Davies (England) — 25.07.79
4:16.27 J. Willmott (England) — 20.04.80
4:15.23 J. Willmott (England) — 09.09.81
4:13.94 J. Croft (England) — 31.01.82
4:12.72 J. Willmott (England) — 09.05.82
4:11.67 J. Willmott (England) — 03.08.82
4:11.55 S. Hardcastle (England) — 31.07.84
4:10.27 S. Hardcastle (England) — 31.07.84
4:07.68 S. Hardcastle (England) — 27.07.86

800 Metres Freestyle
9:59.30 S. Davidson (England) — 13.07.68
9:49.40 J. Green (England) — 12.08.71
9:35.70 J. Green (England) — 15.04.72
9:31.40 J. Green (England) — 18.04.72
9:31.30 J. Green (England) — 13.07.72
9:24.80 J. Green (England) — 23.04.73
9:17.41 D. Simpson (Scotland) — 25.01.74
9:12.53 S. Barnard (England) — 28.08.75
9:07.79 C. Brazendale (England) — 11.04.77
9:07.40 L. Heggie (England) — 09.06.77

8:58.87 S. Davies (England) — 27.05.78
8:51.40 J. Willmott (England) — 12.08.79
8:41.88 J. Willmott (England) — 19.04.80
8:38.56 J. Willmott (England) — 07.09.81
8:37.22 J. Willmott (England) — 11.09.81
8:32.61 J. Willmott (England) — 05.08.82
8:32.60 S. Hardcastle (England) — 03.08.84
8:32.57 S. Hardcastle (England) — 10.08.85
8:24.77 S. Hardcastle (England) — 29.07.86

1500 Metres Freestyle
18:43.20 S. Edmondson (England) — 16.06.73
18:19.40 A. James (Wales) — 31.10.76
18:14.40 M. Verth (Scotland) — 24.06.77
17:42.37 M. Charles (England) — 09.06.78
17:00.03 M. Charles (England) — 21.12.79
16:46.48 J. Willmott (England) — 25.04.80
16:43.95 S. Hardcastle (England) — 18.04.85

50 Metres Backstroke
29.90 S. Page (England) — 03.03.89

100 Metres Backstroke
1:08.70 L. Ludgrove (England) — 22.07.67
1:08.61 M. Kelly (England) — 01.06.73
1:08.57 M. Crook (England) — 27.04.74
1:08.55 M. Kelly (England) — 22.08.74
1:08.27 J. Beasley (England) — 24.01.75
1:07.67 B. Roughley (England) — 20.08.75
1:06.90 J. Beasley (England) — 29.05.76
1:06.66 J. Beasley (England) — 20.07.76
1:06.41 J. Beasley (England) — 22.01.77
1:05.98 H. Gallyard (England) — 07.08.78
1:05.83 J. Beasley (England) — 22.08.78
1:05.70 H. Jameson (England) — 15.04.79
1:04.44 B. Rose (Scotland) — 04.10.82
1:03.61 B. Rose (Scotland) — 31.07.84

200 Metres Backstroke
2:26.20 W. Burrell (England) — 09.09.70
2:25.90 J. Beasley (England) — 25.04.76
2:25.00 S. Davies (England) — 01.05.76
2:25.00 K. Wilkinson (England) — 01.05.76
2:24.20 K. Wilkinson (England) — 30.05.76

Sarah Hardcastle Swimming Times

2:21.79 S. Davies (England)	14.08.76
2:21.02 J. Admans (England)	27.03.78
2:20.64 S. Davies (England)	08.04.78
2:19.30 S. Davies (England)	21.04.78
2:18.94 J. Admans (England)	28.07.79
2:18.13 J. Admans (England)	12.04.80
2:17.66 J. Admans (England)	12.09.81
2:16.00 K. Read (England)	28.05.84
2:14.87 K. Read (England)	30.05.86

50 Metres Breaststroke

33.39 L. Burt (England)	30.05.87
33.28 J. Hill (Scotland)	21.08.87
32.94 L. Coombes (England)	18.08.89

100 Metres Breaststroke

1:17.00 D. Harrison (England)	07.09.70
1:16.50 D. Harrison (England)	01.09.72
1:16.35 C. Jarvis (England)	05.09.73
1:15.82 A. Dickie (Scotland)	13.04.74
1:15.48 M. Kelly (England)	15.08.75
1:14.70 C. Jarvis (England)	02.04.76
1:14.47 M. Kelly (England)	18.04.76
1:14.23 M. Kelly (England)	22.07.76
1:13.57 M. Kelly (England)	22.07.76
1:13.20 M. Kelly (England)	25.03.78
1:13.11 M. Kelly (England)	26.03.78
1:13.02 M. Kelly (England)	09.04.78
1:12.75 M. Kelly (England)	22.04.78
1:11.73 M. Kelly (England)	22.08.78
1:11.05 S. Brownsdon (England)	08.09.81
1:10.39 S. Brownsdon (England)	21.08.87

200 Metres Breaststroke

2:45.00 D. Harrison (England)	12.01.72
2:44.25 P. Beavan (Wales)	28.07.72
2:44.20 P. Beavan (Wales)	28.07.72
2:43.11 P. Beaven (Wales)	26.01.74
2:42.13 M. Kelly (England)	28.08.75
2:41.96 C. Jarvis (England)	02.04.76
2:41.93 M. Kelly (England)	19.04.76
2:38.60 M. Kelly (England)	29.05.76
2:38.26 D. Rudd (England)	21.07.76
2:38.13 M. Kelly (England)	26.03.78
2:36.98 M. Kelly (England)	08.04.78
2:35.64 D. Rudd (England)	24.08.78
2:34.43 S. Brownsdon (England)	03.07.81
2:33.16 S. Brownsdon (England)	04.05.85
2:32.43 J. Hill (Scotland)	19.08.87
2:31.51 J. Hill (Scotland)	19.08.87

50 Metres Butterfly

28.22 C. Cooper (England)	28.01.84

100 Metres Butterfly

1:07.40 M. Auton (England)	14.06.68
1:06.60 J. Jeavons (England)	15.07.72
1:06.26 J. Atkinson (England)	04.08.73
1:05.96 K. Wickham (Scotland)	28.01.74
1:05.48 J. Atkinson (England)	22.08.74
1:05.26 J. Atkinson (England)	25.05.75
1:05.09 A. Adams (Wales)	09.08.75
1:04.94 S. Jenner (England)	24.04.76
1:04.50 S. Jenner (England)	01.05.76
1:04.44 S. Jenner (England)	15.05.76
1:04.30 J. Atkinson (England)	30.05.76
1:04.20 S. Jenner (England)	03.06.76
1:04.06 S. Jenner (England)	21.07.76
1:03.88 S. Jenner (England)	30.04.77
1:03.76 S. Jenner (England)	25.06.77
1:03.56 S. Jenner (England)	13.05.78

Jean Hill   Alan Pascoe Ass.

1:03.44 A. Osgerby (England)	06.08.78
1:03.30 S. Jenner (England)	06.08.78
1:02.90 A. Osgerby (England)	23.08.78
1:02.74 A. Osgerby (England)	23.08.78
1:02.58 A. Osgerby (England)	22.08.79
1:02.32 A. Osgerby (England)	12.04.80
1:01.87 A. Osgerby (England)	21.07.83
1:01.56 A. Osgerby (England)	25.08.83
1:01.48 N. Fibbens (England)	02.08.84

200 Metres Butterfly

2:31.60 D. Lansley (England)	13.06.70
2:28.00 J. Machin (England)	18.04.72
2:26.60 M. Brown (Scotland)	08.06.72
2:23.60 J. Jeavons (England)	14.07.72
2:22.79 D. Simpson (Scotland)	25.08.74
2:21.15 J. Atkinson (England)	24.05.75
2:19.50 J. Alexander (England)	29.05.76
2:15.45 S. Jenner (England)	18.08.77
2:15.17 A. Osgerby (England)	21.07.80
2:14.72 A. Osgerby (England)	08.09.81
2:14.52 A. Osgerby (England)	04.10.82
2:13.91 A. Osgerby (England)	05.10.82
2:13.79 A. Osgerby (England)	23.07.83
2:13.00 A. Osgerby (England)	27.08.83
2:11.97 S. Purvis (England)	04.08.84

200 Metres Individual Medley

2:33.00 S. Ratcliffe (England)	14.07.68
2:29.50 S. Ratcliffe (England)	04.04.70
2:26.86 S. Richardson (England)	25.01.74
2:25.01 A. Adams (Wales)	25.05.75
2:24.88 A. Adams (Wales)	08.08.75
2:24.08 A. Adams (Wales)	25.04.76
2:20.99 S. Davies (England)	26.03.78
2:19.75 S. Davies (England)	27.05.78
2:17.82 S. Davies (England)	04.08.78
2:17.55 S. Davies (England)	02.02.79
2:17.31 S. Davies (England)	20.04.80
2:17.21 J. Hill (Scotland)	26.07.86

400 Metres Individual Medley

5:24.50 S. Ratcliffe (England)	13.07.68
5:15.40 S. Ratcliffe (England)	18.08.71
5:13.88 S. Richardson (England)	06.09.73

5:08.59	S. Richardson (England)	31.01.74	
5:06.71	S. Richardson (England)	21.08.74	
5:04.80	S. Richardson (England)	01.05.76	
5:03.99	S. Richardson (England)	15.05.76	
5:02.10	S. Richardson (England)	29.05.76	
4:54.88	S. Davies (England)	27.03.78	
4:52.44	S. Davies (England)	08.08.78	
4:47.67	S. Davies (England)	02.02.79	
4:46.83	S. Davies (England)	26.07.80	

4×100 Metres Freestyle Relay

4:09.50	GB – Allardyce, Pickering, Sutherland, Hill	28.08.71
4:09.00	GB – Allardyce, Pickering, Willington, Brown	21.04.72
4:05.59	England – Jones, Willington, Edmondson, Allardyce	26.01.74
4:03.54	GB Juniors – Hill, Adams, Houston, Vickers	24.04.76
4:00.97	GB – Hill, Bradshaw, Edmondson, Gray	25.07.76
4:00.24	GB – Houston, James, Davies, Brazendale	16.04.77
3:59.55	GB – Motley, Hill, Davies, Brazendale	29.04.77
3:53.27	England – Lovatt, Turk, Brazendale, Davies	05.08.78
3:51.06	GB – Croft, Willmott, Turk, Fibbens	08.09.81

3:50.38	GB – Cooper, Foot, Fibbens, Croft	24.08.83
3:50.12	GB – Croft, Fibbens, Gore, Cripps	31.07.84
3:49.65	England – Cooper, Fibbens, Long, Cripps	27.07.86
3:48.87	England – Pickering, Davies, Woodcock, Coull	17.08.89

4×200 Metres Freestyle Relay

8:15.21	GB – Cripps, Hardcastle, Gilfillan, Croft	26.02.84
8:13.70	England – Cripps, Hardcastle, Mellor, Long	25.07.86

4×100 Metres Medley Relay

4:34.61	GB – Bairstow, Harrison, Jeavons, Allardyce	03.09.72
4:31.68	Scotland – Fordyce, Dickie, Wickham, McGlashan	31.01.74
4:31.41	GB – Kelly, Dickie, Atkinson, Edmondson	24.08.74
4:23.25	England – Beasley, Kelly, Jenner, Hill	18.07.76
4:19.87	England – Gillyard, Kelly, Jenner, Davies	05.08.78
4:19.59	GB – Beasley, Kelly, Cooper, Croft	25.04.80
4:12.24	GB – Jameson, Kelly, Osgerby, Croft	20.07.80

Current Commonwealth Records

Men

100 Metres Freestyle
50.06 M. Stockwell (Australia)   15.08.84

200 Metres Freestyle
1:47.25 D. Armstrong (Australia)   19.09.88

400 metres Freestyle
3:47.15 D. Armstrong (Australia)   23.09.88

800 Metres Freestyle
8:01.49 G. Housman (Australia)   27.03.89

1500 Metres Freestyle
15:04.66 S. Holland (Australia)   20.07.76

100 Metres Backstroke
55.22 S. Murphy (Canada)   01.06.88

200 Metres Backstroke
2:00.48 P. Kingsman (New Zealand)   22.09.88

100 Metres Breaststroke
1:01.49 A. Moorhouse (England)   15.08.89

200 Metres Breaststroke
2:12.90 N. Gillingham (England)   18.08.89

100 Metres Butterfly
53.30 A. Jameson (England)   21.09.88

200 Metres Butterfly
1:57.04 J. Sieben (Australia)   03.08.84

100 Metres Individual Medley
2:01.42 A. Baumann (Canada)   04.08.84

200 Metres Individual Medley
2:01.42 A. Baumann (Canada)   04.03.86

400 Metres Individual Medley
4:17.41 A. Baumann (Canada)   30.07.84

4×100 Metres Freestyle Relay
3:19.68 Australia   02.08.84

4×200 Metres Freestyle Relay
7:15.23 Australia   21.09.88

4×100 Metres Medley Relay
3:39.28 Canada   25.09.88

Tracey Wickham (Australia)

Women

100 Metres Freestyle
56.51 M. Pearson (Australia)   31.07.84

200 Metres Freestyle
1:59.74 J. Croft (England)   04.10.82

400 Metres Freestyle
4:06.28 T. Wickham (Australia)   24.08.78

800 Metres Freestyle
8:22.93 J. McDonald (Australia)   25.09.88

1500 Metres Freestyle
16:06.63 T. Wickham (Australia)   25.02.79

100 Metres Backstroke
1:02.64 N. Livingstone (Australia)   13.08.87

200 Metres Backstroke
2:11.84 N. Livingstone (Australia)   15.08.87

100 Metres Breaststroke
1:08.86 A. Higson (Canada)   23.09.88

200 Metres Breaststroke
2:27.27 A. Higson (Canada)   29.05.88

100 Metres Butterfly
1:01.12 J. Tibbits (Australia)   18.08.85

200 Metres Butterfly
2:10.56 K. Phillips (Australia)   04.08.84

200 Metres Individual Medley
2:15.92 M. Pearson (Australia)   03.08.84

400 Metres Individual Medley
4:44.26 J. Clatworthy (Australia)   18.09.88

4×100 Metres Freestyle Relay
3:46.75 Canada   22.09.88

4×200 Metres Freestyle Relay
8:11.26 Australia   16.08.85

4×100 Metres Medley Relay
4:10.49 Canada   24.09.88

Progressive European (Long Course) Records, 1957–1989

NOTE: On the 1 May, 1957, LEN followed FINA and decided that only long course performances would be accepted for world record purposes.

Men

50 Metres Freestyle
22.52 D. Halsall (Switzerland)   21.07.85
22.47 J. Woithe (GDR)   28.08.87

100 Metres Freestyle
56.10 P. Pucci (Italy)   01.09.58
55.80 G. Dobai (Hungary)   31.07.60
55.70 G. Dobai (Hungary)   18.09.60
55.50 P. Lindberg (Sweden)   09.08.61
55.00 A. Gottvalles (France)   10.08.62
54.40 R. McGregor (GBR)   13.07.63
54.30 P. Lindberg (Sweden)   18.07.63
54.10 R. McGregor (GBR)   31.08.63
54.00 R. McGregor (GBR)   13.09.63
53.90 R. McGregor (GBR)   22.08.64
52.90 A. Gottvalles (France)   13.09.64
52.80 M. Rousseau (France)   05.09.70
52.70 M. Rousseau (France)   31.07.71
52.60 M. Rousseau (France)   15.07.72
52.51 V. Bure (USSR)   14.08.72
52.26 V. Bure (USSR)   28.08.72
51.77 V. Bure (USSR)   03.09.72
51.36 V. Bure (USSR)   25.02.75
51.32 V. Bure (USSR)   28.07.75
51.31 P. Nocke (W Germany)   25.07.76
51.25 M. Guarducci (Italy)   08.09.77
50.79 K. Steinbach (W Germany)   28.08.78
50.55 J. Woithe (GDR)   26.05.80
50.21 J. Woithe (GDR)   26.07.80
50.14 J. Woithe (GDR)   03.02.81
49.95 J. Woithe (GDR)   12.03.82
49.81 J. Woithe (GDR)   28.05.82
49.60 J. Woithe (GDR)   03.08.82
49.58 J. Woithe (GDR)   18.06.83
49.51 S. Caron (France)   21.08.87
49.35 S. Caron (France)   21.08.87
49.24 G. Lamberti (Italy)   17.08.89

200 Metres Freestyle
2:04.80 F. Wiegand (GDR)   03.07.61
2:04.70 G. Hetz (W Germany)   13.08.61
2:04.00 G. Hetz (W Germany)   09.09.61
2:02.60 I. Black (GBR)   29.04.62
2:01.70 G. Hetz (W Germany)   20.05.62
2:00.20 H. Klein (W Germany)   13.10.63
1:58.20 H. Klein (W Germany)   24.05.64
1:57.80 L. Ilicev (USSR)   29.04.67
1:57.60 L. Ilicev (USSR)   01.08.67
1:56.90 L. Ilicev (USSR)   02.04.68
1:56.50 H. Fassnacht (W Germany)   15.08.69
1:56.40 H. Fassnacht (W Germany)   08.09.70
1:55.20 H. Fassnacht (W Germany)   09.09.70
1:53.99 W. Lampe (W Germany)   29.08.72
1:53.97 R. Pyttel (GDR)   04.09.73
1:53.10 P. Nocke (W Germany)   19.08.74
1:52.95 K. Steinbach (W Germany)   11.03.76
1:51.86 P. Nocke (W Germany)   04.06.76
1:51.41 K. Steinbach (W Germany)   19.07.76
1:50.73 A. Krylov (USSR)   19.07.76
1:49.83 S. Kopliakov (USSR)   07.04.79
1:49.81 S. Kopliakov (USSR)   21.07.80
1:49.55 M. Gross (W Germany)   01.08.82
1:49.30 S. Lodziewski (GDR)   15.06.83
1:48.28 M. Gross (W Germany)   21.06.83
1:47.87 M. Gross (W Germany)   22.08.83
1:47.55 M. Gross (W Germany)   08.06.84
1:47.44 M. Gross (W Germany)   29.07.84
1:46.69 G. Lamberti (Italy)   15.08.89

400 Metres Freestyle
4:30.10 B. Nikitin (USSR)   26.08.57
4:28.50 I. Black (GBR)   23.07.58
4:28.40 I. Black (GBR)   20.08.58
4:27.50 I. Black (GBR)   29.04.60
4:21.90 I. Black (GBR)   30.08.60
4:21.80 I. Black (GBR)   31.08.60

8:46.80 A. Mosconi (France)   05.07.67
8:42.00 F. Luyce (France)   21.07.67
8:41.60 W. Lampe (W Germany)   07.08.70
8:41.40 H. Fassnacht (W Germany)   11.09.70
8:38.40 H. Fassnacht (W Germany)   08.08.71
8:38.40 W. Lampe (W Germany)   22.08.71
8:35.50 D. Grozaj (W Germany)   11.08.72
8:35.10 V. Parinov (USSR)   11.08.73
8:32.82 B. Gingsjoe (Sweden)   08.09.73
8:31.30 A. Hargitay (Hungary)   22.12.74
8:30.16 I. Evgrafov (USSR)   02.03.75
8:27.95 R. Strohbach (GDR)   26.07.75
8:24.80 S. Nagy (Hungary)   20.12.75
8:21.50 R. Strohbach (GDR)   13.03.76
8:16.50 I. Kushpeliev (USSR)   04.06.76
8:15.54 Z. Wladar (Hungary)   06.06.76
8:13.35 V. Salnikov (USSR)   20.07.76
8:11.62 V. Parinov (USSR)   06.07.77
8:07.61 V. Salnikov (USSR)   20.08.77
8:06.40 V. Salnikov (USSR)   04.09.77
7:56.49 V. Salnikov (USSR)   23.03.79
7:52.83 V. Salnikov (USSR)   14.02.82
7:52.33 V. Salnikov (USSR)   14.07.83
7:50.64 V. Salnikov (USSR)   04.07.86

Andras Hargitay (Hungary)

4:21.60 F. Wiegand (GDR)   18.05.64
4:18.40 F. Wiegand (GDR)   29.08.64
4:17.20 F. Wiegand (GDR)   14.10.64
4:14.90 F. Wiegand (GDR)   15.10.64
4:14.10 S. Belitz-Geiman (USSR)   16.07.66
4:11.10 F. Wiegand (GDR)   25.08.66
4:10.67 A. Mosconi (France)   02.07.67
4:09.20 A. Mosconi (France)   04.07.67
4:08.20 H. Fassnacht (W Germany)   11.07.69
4:06.90 H. Fassnacht (W Germany)   01.08.69
4:04.00 H. Fassnacht (W Germany)   14.08.69
4:02.60 G. Larsson (Sweden)   07.09.70
4:01.27 B. Gingsjoe (Sweden)   06.09.73
4:01.10 F. Pfutze (GDR)   25.07.75
3:59.60 V. Raskatov (USSR)   12.03.76
3:58.59 F. Pfutze (GDR)   02.06.76
3:58.02 V. Raskatov (USSR)   02.06.76
3:57.56 V. Raskatov (USSR)   22.07.76
3:55.76 V. Raskatov (USSR)   22.07.76
3:54.83 S. Rusin (USSR)   18.08.77
3:54.47 S. Rusin (USSR)   07.07.78
3:53.32 V. Salnikov (USSR)   23.08.78
3:51.94 V. Salnikov (USSR)   23.08.78
3:51.41 V. Salnikov (USSR)   06.04.79
3:51.40 V. Salnikov (USSR)   19.08.79
3:51.20 V. Salnikov (USSR)   24.02.80
3:49.57 V. Salnikov (USSR)   12.03.82
3:49.57 V. Salnikov (USSR)   14.07.82
3:48.32 V. Salnikov (USSR)   19.02.83
3:47.80 M. Gross (W Germany)   27.06.85
3:47.38 A. Wojdat (Poland)   25.03.88
3:46.95 U. Dassler (GDR)   23.09.88

800 Metres Freestyle
9:28.60 G. Montserret (France)   02.09.57
9:25.50 I. Black (GBR)   21.07.58
9:22.70 G. Montserret (France)   29.07.59
9:22.60 J. Katona (Hungary)   02.07.60
9:16.30 G. Hetz (W Germany)   30.04.61
9:08.00 G. Hetz (W Germany)   19.05.62
9:05.40 S. Belitz-Geiman (USSR)   29.10.64
9:03.90 F. Wiegand (GDR)   18.07.65
8:58.70 S. Belitz-Geiman (USSR)   01.08.65
8:47.40 S. Belitz-Geiman (USSR)   03.08.66

1500 Metres Freestyle
18:12.00 G. Montserret (France)   31.07.50
18:06.20 I. Black (GBR)   31.07.58
18:05.80 I. Black (GBR)   06.09.58
17:55.20 J. Katona (Hungary)   18.06.60
17:53.50 J. Katona (Hungary)   02.09.60
17:43.70 J. Katona (Hungary)   03.09.60
17:31.70 G. Hetz (W Germany)   05.08.62
17:30.00 J. Katona (Hungary)   09.08.64
17:27.00 J. Katona (Hungary)   13.09.64
17:01.90 S. Belitz-Geiman (USSR)   01.08.65
16:58.50 S. Belitz-Geiman (USSR)   27.08.66
16:52.70 S. Belitz-Geiman (USSR)   03.08.67
16:46.70 H. Fassnacht (W Germany)   18.08.68
16:36.80 H. Fassnacht (W Germany)   13.07.69
16:32.10 H. Fassnacht (W Germany)   03.08.69
16:23.90 W. Lampe (W Germany)   07.08.70
16:19.90 H. Fassnacht (W Germany)   11.09.70
16:16.01 B. Gingsjoe (Sweden)   04.09.72
16:10.38 A. Bellbring (Sweden)   05.08.73
16:06.01 B. Gingsjoe (Sweden)   08.09.73
15:54.57 F. Pfutze (GDR)   25.08.74
15:42.70 R. Strohbach (GDR)   13.03.76
15:33.49 V. Parinov (USSR)   04.06.76
15:29.45 V. Salnikov (USSR)   20.07.76
15:27.04 V. Salnikov (USSR)   27.03.77
15:16.45 V. Salnikov (USSR)   20.08.77
15:03.99 V. Salnikov (USSR)   26.08.78
14:58.27 V. Salnikov (USSR)   22.07.80
14:56.35 V. Salnikov (USSR)   13.03.82
14:54.76 V. Salnikov (USSR)   22.02.83

50 Metres Backstroke
25.90 I. Polianski (USSR)   24.02.80

100 Metres Backstroke
1:02.90 R. Christophe (France)   14.06.58
1:02.20 R. Christophe (France)   12.07.59
1:02.10 L. Barbier (USSR)   11.09.61
1:01.90 D. Rora (Italy)   30.08.63
1:01.50 V. Mazanov (USSR)   22.09.63
1:01.00 E. Kuppers (W Germany)   16.08.64
1:00.80 E. Kuppers (W Germany)   29.08.64
1:00.00 V. Mazanov (USSR)   23.03.66

247

59.80	R. Matthes (GDR)	23.04.67
58.40	R. Matthes (GDR)	21.09.67
58.00	R. Matthes (GDR)	26.10.68
57.80	R. Matthes (GDR)	23.08.69
57.80	R. Matthes (GDR)	15.04.70
56.90	R. Matthes (GDR)	08.09.70
56.70	R. Matthes (GDR)	04.09.71
56.60	R. Matthes (GDR)	08.04.72
56.30	R. Matthes (GDR)	09.04.72
56.30	R. Matthes (GDR)	04.09.72
56.21	D. Richter (GDR)	21.03.82
56.19	D. Richter (GDR)	06.08.82
55.95	D. Richter (GDR)	06.08.82
55.94	D. Richter (GDR)	18.02.84
55.45	D. Richter (GDR)	26.05.84
55.35	D. Richter (GDR)	27.05.84
55.24	I. Polianski (USSR)	10.08.85
55.17	I. Polianski (USSR)	15.03.88
55.16	I. Polianski (USSR)	16.03.88
55.00	I. Polianski (USSR)	16.07.88

200 Metres Backstroke

2:19.80	W. Wagner (GDR)	06.09.59
2:18.00	W. Wagner (GDR)	15.07.60
2:16.50	L. Barbier (USSR)	04.09.61
2:15.00	E. Kuppers (W Germany)	22.07.62
2:14.80	E. Kuppers (W Germany)	16.08.64
2:12.60	E. Kuppers (W Germany)	22.08.64
2:12.40	V. Mazanov (USSR)	11.05.65
2:11.80	V. Mazanov (USSR)	22.03.66
2:11.20	R. Matthes (GDR)	23.04.67
2:11.10	R. Matthes (GDR)	28.10.67
2:07.90	R. Matthes (GDR)	08.11.67
2:07.50	R. Matthes (GDR)	14.08.68
2:07.40	R. Matthes (GDR)	12.07.69
2:06.40	R. Matthes (GDR)	29.08.69
2:06.10	R. Matthes (GDR)	11.09.70
2:05.60	R. Matthes (GDR)	03.09.71
2:02.80	R. Matthes (GDR)	10.07.72
2:01.87	R. Matthes (GDR)	06.09.73
2:01.78	S. Wladar (Hungary)	15.03.80
2:01.72	S. Wladar (Hungary)	28.06.80
2:00.80	S. Wladar (Hungary)	12.09.81
2:00.65	V. Shemetov (USSR)	18.02.83
2:00.42	S. Zabolotnov (USSR)	04.07.83
2:00.39	S. Zabolotnov (USSR)	15.02.84
1:59.80	D. Richter (GDR)	24.05.84
1:58.41	S. Zabolotnov (USSR)	21.08.84
1:58.14	I. Polianski (USSR)	03.03.85

50 Metres Breaststroke

28.12	D. Volkov (USSR)	19.09.88

100 Metres Breaststroke

1:12.70	V. Svozil (Czechoslovakia)	01.05.57
1:12.20	V. Svozil (Czechoslovakia)	18.08.57
1:11.50	V. Minashkin (USSR)	15.09.57
1:11.40	L. Kolesnikov (USSR)	05.05.61
1:10.80	G. Tittes (GDR)	05.07.61
1:09.80	G. Prokopenko (USSR)	07.07.62
1:09.60	M. Farafanov (USSR)	13.08.63
1:09.20	G. Prokopenko (USSR)	20.10.63
1:09.00	E. Henninger (GDR)	01.03.64
1:07.40	G. Prokopenko (USSR)	26.03.64
1:06.90	G. Prokopenko (USSR)	03.09.64
1:06.70	V. Kosinsky (USSR)	08.11.67
1:06.70	N. Pankin (USSR)	04.04.68
1:06.20	N. Pankin (USSR)	18.04.68
1:05.80	N. Pankin (USSR)	20.04.69

1:05.78	W. Kusch (W Germany)	29.08.72
1:05.50	M. Kriukin (USSR)	28.07.73
1:04.61	M. Kriukin (USSR)	04.09.73
1:04.26	D. Wilkie (GBR)	23.07.75
1:03.43	D. Wilkie (GBR)	20.07.76
1:02.86	G. Moerken (W Germany)	17.08.77
1:02.81	D. Volkov (USSR)	19.02.84
1:02.61	G. Minervini (Italy)	20.08.85
1:02.28	A. Moorhouse (GBR)	17.08.86
1:02.13	A. Moorhouse (GBR)	18.08.87
1:01.78	A. Moorhouse (GBR)	26.03.88
1:01.49	A. Moorhouse (GBR)	15.08.89

200 Metres Breaststroke

2:39.30	L. Kolesnikov (USSR)	19.07.58
2:38.60	K. Enke (GDR)	11.08.59
2:37.40	E. Henninger (GDR)	19.06.60
2:37.30	L. Kolesnikov (USSR)	25.06.61
2:35.60	L. Kolesnikov (USSR)	05.09.61
2:35.40	G. Prokopenko (USSR)	13.04.62
2:34.00	G. Prokopenko (USSR)	13.04.62
2:32.80	I. Karetnikov (USSR)	06.08.62
2:32.40	I. Karetnikov (USSR)	08.08.63
2:31.90	I. Karetnikov (USSR)	11.08.63
2:30.20	G. Prokopenko (USSR)	28.03.64
2:29.60	G. Prokopenko (USSR)	18.05.64
2:28.20	G. Prokopenko (USSR)	15.10.64
2:27.40	V. Kosinsky (USSR)	03.04.68
2:26.50	N. Pankin (USSR)	22.03.69
2:25.40	N. Pankin (USSR)	19.04.69
2:24.55	W. Kusch (W Germany)	20.07.72
2:24.22	N. Pankin (USSR)	14.08.72
2:23.67	D. Wilkie (GBR)	02.09.72
2:20.94	D. Wilkie (GBR)	06.09.73
2:19.28	D. Wilkie (GBR)	06.09.73
2:18.23	D. Wilkie (GBR)	25.07.75
2:15.11	D. Wilkie (GBR)	24.07.76
2:14.27	J. Szabo (Hungary)	21.08.86
2:13.87	J. Szabo (Hungary)	21.08.87
2:13.52	J. Szabo (Hungary)	23.09.88
2:12.90	N. Gillingham (GBR)	18.08.89

50 Metres Butterfly

24.61	F. Henter (W Germany)	22.07.88

100 Metres Butterfly

1:02.30	G. Tumpek (Hungary)	19.08.57
1:02.20	G. Tumpek (Hungary)	08.06.58
1:01.80	F. Dennerlein (Italy)	12.07.59
1:01.20	V. Hopka (Czechoslovakia)	11.03.61
1:01.00	J. Gulrich (Hungary)	01.09.62
1:00.50	N. Kuridja (Yugoslavia)	09.09.62
1:00.20	J. Gulrich (Hungary)	13.09.62
59.50	J. Jiskoot (Holland)	18.09.62
59.30	H. Gregor (GDR)	25.08.64
58.50	A. Depolo (Yugoslavia)	07.08.65
58.40	A. Gordeev (USSR)	08.09.67
58.40	L. Stoklasa (W Germany)	18.08.68
58.00	L. Stoklasa (W Germany)	29.08.68
57.80	V. Nemshilov (USSR)	14.08.69
57.70	H. Lampe (W Germany)	06.09.70
57.50	H. Lampe (W Germany)	08.09.70
56.10	R. Matthes (GDR)	16.04.71
56.00	R. Matthes (GDR)	14.07.71
55.70	R. Matthes (GDR)	03.09.71
55.58	R. Pyttel (GDR)	31.08.74
55.22	R. Pyttel (GDR)	05.06.76
54.75	R. Pyttel (GDR)	20.07.76
54.61	R. Pyttel (GDR)	11.08.79

54.33	P. Arvidsson (Sweden)	03.09.79
54.15	P. Arvidsson (Sweden)	11.04.80
54.00	M. Gross (W Germany)	01.07.82
54.00	M. Gross (W Germany)	23.08.83
53.84	T. Dressler (GDR)	23.05.84
53.78	M. Gross (W Germany)	09.06.84
53.08	M. Gross (W Germany)	30.07.84

200 Metres Butterfly

2:21.40	H. Zierold (GDR)	14.09.57
2:19.50	F. Dennerlein (Italy)	14.07.59
2:18.70	I. Black (GBR)	09.04.60
2:18.00	F. Dennerlein (Italy)	24.04.60
2:16.00	F. Dennerlein (Italy)	02.09.60
2:15.50	G. Hetz (W Germany)	22.07.62
2:14.20	V. Kuzmin (USSR)	23.08.62
2:12.60	F. Dennerlein (Italy)	23.08.62
2:11.20	V. Kuzmin (USSR)	18.05.64
2:10.40	V. Kuzmin (USSR)	22.08.65
2:10.20	V. Kuzmin (USSR)	25.08.66
2:09.40	I. Eriksson (Sweden)	01.08.67
2:08.10	P. Feil (Sweden)	24.07.68
2:08.00	P. Feil (Sweden)	30.07.68
2:07.80	M. Woodroffe (GBR)	13.07.69
2:06.90	H. Fassnacht (W Germany)	22.08.70
2:06.50	H. Fassnacht (W Germany)	10.07.71
2:06.10	H. Fassnacht (W Germany)	10.07.71
2:06.00	H. Fassnacht (W Germany)	07.08.71
2:04.50	H. Fassnacht (W Germany)	29.08.71
2:03.30	H. Fassnacht (W Germany)	31.08.71
2:01.82	R. Pyttel (GDR)	15.03.75
2:01.70	R. Pyttel (GDR)	13.03.76
2:00.21	R. Pyttel (GDR)	03.06.76
1:59.63	R. Pyttel (GDR)	03.06.76
1:59.34	S. Fesenko (USSR)	12.08.79
1:59.19	M. Gross (W Germany)	11.09.81
1:59.00	M. Gross (W Germany)	03.07.82
1:58.85	M. Gross (W Germany)	06.08.82
1:58.37	M. Gross (W Germany)	24.06.83
1:58.22	M. Gross (W Germany)	25.06.83
1:57.05	M. Gross (W Germany)	26.08.83
1:57.01	M. Gross (W Germany)	29.06.85
1:56.65	M. Gross (W Germany)	10.08.85
1:56.24	M. Gross (W Germany)	28.06.86

Michael Gross (W Germany)

Swimming Times

200 Metres Individual Medley

2:16.30	A. Mosconi (France)	20.07.67
2:13.50	F. Wiegand (GDR)	06.11.67
2:13.00	V. Kravchenko (USSR)	15.04.70
2:12.80	R. Matthes (GDR)	11.07.70
2:09.30	G. Larsson (Sweden)	12.09.70
2:07.17	G. Larsson (Sweden)	03.09.72
2:06.32	D. Wilkie (GBR)	24.08.74
2:06.25	D. Wilkie (GBR)	04.04.76
2:05.24	A. Sidorenko (USSR)	09.07.78
2:03.46	A. Sidorenko (USSR)	28.07.79
2:03.46	A. Sidorenko (USSR)	24.02.80
2:03.41	A. Sidorenko (USSR)	11.09.81
2:02.85	A. Sidorenko (USSR)	13.02.82
2:02.48	G. Franceschi (Italy)	27.08.83
2:01.57	T. Darnyi (Hungary)	23.08.86
2:00.56	T. Darnyi (Hungary)	23.08.87
2:00.17	T. Darnyi (Hungary)	25.09.88

400 Metres Individual Medley

5:12.90	V. Stroujanov (USSR)	20.10.57
5:08.80	I. Black (GBR)	06.06.59
5:06.90	B. Nikitin (USSR)	15.04.62
4:53.80	G. Hetz (W Germany)	24.05.62
4:50.20	G. Hetz (W Germany)	12.10.63
4:47.90	F. Wiegand (GDR)	22.08.66
4:47.20	A. Dunaev (USSR)	01.08.67
4:45.30	A. Dunaev (USSR)	03.04.68
4:44.00	M. Holthaus (W Germany)	30.08.68
4:43.00	H. Fassnacht (W Germany)	02.08.69
4:42.50	H. Fassnacht (W Germany)	24.08.69
4:41.80	G. Larsson (Sweden)	07.09.70
4:36.20	G. Larsson (Sweden)	08.09.70
4:34.99	G. Larsson (Sweden)	30.08.72
4:31.98	G. Larsson (Sweden)	30.08.72
4:31.11	A. Hargitay (Hungary)	05.09.73
4:28.89	A. Hargitay (Hungary)	20.08.74
4:26.00	Z. Verraszto (Hungary)	02.04.76
4:25.37	S. Fesenko (USSR)	03.09.77
4:25.25	S. Fesenko (USSR)	09.04.78
4:22.29	S. Fesenko (USSR)	22.08.78
4:21.97	A. Sidorenko (USSR)	22.02.80
4:20.41	G. Franceschi (Italy)	23.08.83
4:19.61	J. Berndt (GDR)	23.05.84
4:18.29	J. Berndt (GDR)	20.08.84
4:15.42	T. Darnyi (Hungary)	19.08.87
4:14.75	T. Darnyi (Hungary)	21.09.88

4×100 Metres Freestyle Relay

3:47.40	USSR	23.07.58
3:47.10	USSR	16.08.59
3:46.90	Hungary	18.09.60
3:45.50	W Germany	24.05.62
3:42.50	France	10.08.62
3:39.20	France	13.09.64
3:38.10	GDR	31.08.65
3:37.00	USSR	22.03.66
3:36.80	GDR	26.08.66
3:35.60	USSR	21.09.67
3:35.60	USSR	03.04.68
3:34.20	USSR	17.10.68
3:32.30	USSR	10.09.70
3:29.72	USSR	28.08.72
3:28.89	USSR	14.03.75
3:26.60	USSR	12.03.76
3:26.57	USSR	16.08.77
3:26.34	Sweden	01.09.79
3:24.39	USSR	02.03.80
3:23.87	W Germany	29.07.81

249

3:21.69 USSR	21.08.81
3:21.48 USSR	08.09.81
3:20.88 USSR	25.08.83
3:20.19 USSR	23.08.84
3:19.17 GDR	21.08.87
3:18.33 USSR	23.09.88

4×200 Metres Freestyle Relay

8:34.70 USSR	03.12.56
8:34.50 USSR	03.08.57
8:27.10 USSR	14.09.57
8:26.90 GBR	28.08.60
8:25.80 France	21.08.62
8:18.40 Sweden	22.08.62
8:16.20 Sweden	17.08.63
8:14.30 Sweden	06.09.64
8:06.80 France	06.09.64
8:00.20 USSR	24.08.66
7:58.60 France	15.07.67
7:58.50 USSR	18.04.69
7:54.50 USSR	24.08.69
7:49.50 W Germany	12.09.70
7:41.69 W Germany	31.08.72
7:39.70 W Germany	21.08.74
7:39.52 USSR	15.03.75
7:39.44 W Germany	26.07.75
7:34.70 USSR	13.03.76
7:33.21 USSR	21.07.76
7:27.97 USSR	21.07.76
7:25.71 USSR	08.03.80
7:23.50 USSR	23.07.80
7:20.40 W Germany	23.08.83
7:15.73 W Germany	30.07.84
7:13.10 W Germany	19.08.87

4×100 Metres Medley Relay

4:16.50 USSR	06.09.58
4:16.10 GDR	18.06.60
4:14.00 USSR	06.08.60
4:11.20 USSR	11.09.61
4:11.10 USSR	24.02.62
4:09.00 GDR	21.08.62
4:07.60 W Germany	28.09.63
4:02.80 USSR	17.05.64
4:00.70 USSR	23.03.66
3:56.50 GDR	07.11.67
3:54.40 GDR	08.09.70
3:53.80 GDR	04.09.71
3:52.12 GDR	04.09.72
3:51.57 W Germany	24.08.74
3:47.29 W Germany	22.07.76
3:46.20 USSR	08.04.79
3:45.99 USSR	20.08.79
3:45.92 USSR	24.07.80
3:44.79 USSR	23.08.81
3:44.23 USSR	12.09.81
3:42.86 USSR	07.08.82
3:42.15 USSR	25.08.84
3:41.51 USSR	22.08.87
3:39.96 USSR	25.09.88

Women

50 Metres Freestyle

25.64 A. Verstappen (Holland)	13.07.83
25.62 K. Otto (GDR)	16.02.86
25.50 T. Costache (Rumania)	14.06.86
25.34 T. Costache (Rumania)	14.06.86
25.31 T. Costache (Rumania)	01.08.86
25.28 T. Costache (Rumania)	23.08.86

100 Metres Freestyle

1:05.00 C. Gastelaars (Holland)	15.01.58
1:03.90 C. Gastelaars (Holland)	17.05.58
1:03.70 C. Gastelaars (Holland)	01.09.58
1:02.90 C. Gastelaars (Holland)	14.07.59
1:02.80 C. Madarasz (Hungary)	02.07.60
1:02.50 C. Madarasz (Hungary)	16.07.60
1:02.40 D. Wilkinson (GBR)	23.06.62
1:02.00 A. Hagberg (Sweden)	18.07.63
1:01.70 A. Hagberg (Sweden)	08.08.63
1:01.50 A. Hagberg (Sweden)	18.08.63
1:01.20 M. Grunert (GDR)	22.08.66
1:00.80 J. Turoczy (Hungary)	19.08.67
1:00.40 J. Turoczy (Hungary)	28.06.68
1:00.20 J. Turoczy (Hungary)	13.07.68
1:00.00 J. Turoczy (Hungary)	08.08.69
59.60 G. Wetzko (GDR)	23.08.69
59.60 G. Wetzko (GDR)	13.04.70
59.60 G. Wetzko (GDR)	07.09.70
59.30 G. Wetzko (GDR)	11.09.70
59.21 G. Wetzko (GDR)	29.08.72
58.60 K. Ender (GDR)	28.05.73
58.25 K. Ender (GDR)	13.07.73
58.12 K. Ender (GDR)	18.08.73
57.61 K. Ender (GDR)	08.09.73
57.54 K. Ender (GDR)	09.09.73
57.51 K. Ender (GDR)	04.07.74
56.96 K. Ender (GDR)	19.08.74
56.38 K. Ender (GDR)	14.03.75
56.22 K. Ender (GDR)	27.07.75
55.73 K. Ender (GDR)	01.06.76
55.65 K. Ender (GDR)	19.07.76
55.41 B. Krause (GDR)	05.07.78
54.98 B. Krause (GDR)	20.07.80
54.79 B. Krause (GDR)	21.07.80
54.73 K. Otto (GDR)	19.08.86

200 Metres Freestyle

2:22.10 C. Schimmel (Holland)	27.06.59
2:21.50 W. Lambour (Holland)	12.06.60
2:21.30 H. Frost (France)	12.07.60
2:20.20 J. Cederqvist (Sweden)	03.05.61
2:18.20 A. Lasterie (Holland)	26.08.61
2:18.00 D. Beneck (Italy)	27.07.65
2:16.20 E. Long (GBR)	11.08.65
2:16.10 E. Long (GBR)	13.08.65
2:15.50 C. Mandonnaud (France)	13.08.66
2:15.00 D. Dorleans (France)	16.08.67
2:14.70 O. Kozikova (USSR)	06.04.68
2:14.40 O. Kozikova (USSR)	06.07.68
2:12.40 C. Mandonnaud (France)	03.08.68
2:10.20 M. Segrt (Yugoslavia)	18.08.68
2:08.90 G. Wetzko (GDR)	24.08.69
2:08.20 G. Wetzko (GDR)	10.09.70
2:07.20 A. Rijnders (Holland)	18.04.72
2:07.05 A. Eife (GDR)	01.09.72
2:06.27 A. Eife (GDR)	01.09.72
2:05.70 A. Eife (GDR)	12.07.73
2:05.64 K. Ender (GDR)	19.08.73
2:05.52 A. Eife (GDR)	05.09.73
2:05.25 A. Franke (GDR)	05.07.74
2:05.14 E. Brigitha (Holland)	25.07.74
2:03.22 K. Ender (GDR)	22.08.74
2:02.27 K. Ender (GDR)	15.03.75
1:59.78 K. Ender (GDR)	02.06.76
1:59.26 K. Ender (GDR)	22.07.76
1:59.04 B. Kause (GDR)	02.07.78
1:58.33 B. Kause (GDR)	24.07.80

1:57.75 K. Otto (GDR)	23.05.84
1:57.55 H. Friedrich (GDR)	18.06.86

400 Metres Freestyle

4:58.50 C. Schimmel (Holland)	27.06.59
4:58.10 C. Schimmel (Holland)	15.07.59
4:57.70 C. Schimmel (Holland)	26.07.59
4:52.40 C. Schimmel (Holland)	08.08.59
4:46.90 J. Cederqvist (Sweden)	03.05.61
4:46.80 C. Mandonnaud (France)	18.02.67
4:45.60 S. Williams (GBR)	22.07.67
4:45.40 E. Ljunggren (Sweden)	20.04.68
4:44.30 M. Kersaudy (France)	20.06.68
4:42.40 E. Ljunggren (Sweden)	01.08.68
4:41.10 C. Mandonnaud (France)	04.08.68
4:40.20 G. Wetzko (GDR)	20.10.68
4:36.10 G. Wetzko (GDR)	15.08.69
4:32.90 E. Sehmisch (GDR)	08.09.70
4:31.90 N. Calligaris (Italy)	20.07.71
4:31.70 H. Bunschoten (Holland)	15.08.71
4:31.30 H. Bunschoten (Holland)	28.08.71
4:31.10 H. Bunschoten (Holland)	19.03.72
4:29.70 A. Rijnders (Holland)	02.07.72
4:29.10 N. Calligaris (Italy)	05.07.72
4:26.70 N. Calligaris (Italy)	25.07.72
4:24.14 N. Calligaris (Italy)	30.08.72
4:22.44 N. Calligaris (Italy)	30.08.72
4:21.79 N. Calligaris (Italy)	07.09.73
4:17.83 A. Franke (GDR)	20.08.74
4:17.00 B. Krause (GDR)	14.03.76
4:11.69 B. Krause (GDR)	03.06.76
4:09.89 P. Thumer (GDR)	20.07.76
4:08.91 P. Thumer (GDR)	17.08.77
4:08.76 I. Diers (GDR)	22.07.80
4:08.58 I. Diers (GDR)	09.09.81
4:08.25 A. Strauss (GDR)	17.06.83
4:08.07 A. Strauss (GDR)	24.08.83
4:07.66 A. Strauss (GDR)	21.08.84
4:06.85 H. Friedrich (GDR)	19.06.86
4:06.39 H. Friedrich (GDR)	20.08.87
4:05.94 H. Friedrich (GDR)	22.09.88
4:05.84 A. Moehring (GDR)	17.08.89

800 Metres Freestyle

10:27.20 M. Kok (Holland)	16.02.57
10:25.30 C. Schimmel (Holland)	15.07.59
10:22.30 C. Schimmel (Holland)	01.08.59
9:55.60 J. Cederqvist (Sweden)	17.08.60
9:53.30 E. Ljunggren (Sweden)	04.08.67
9:45.00 E. Ljunggren (Sweden)	01.08.68
9:43.50 S. Goral (GDR)	16.08.68
9:42.70 M. Hara (Finland)	06.09.68
9:38.00 N. Calligaris (Italy)	10.08.69
9:30.80 K. Neugebauer (GDR)	17.08.69
9:29.10 K. Neugebauer (GDR)	12.09.70
9:23.80 N. Calligaris (Italy)	04.07.71
9:20.90 N. Calligaris (Italy)	21.07.71
9:20.80 N. Calligaris (Italy)	29.08.71
9:17.10 G. Wegner (GDR)	03.09.71
9:16.70 H. Bunschoten (Holland)	18.03.72
9:15.50 H. Bunschoten (Holland)	28.06.72
9:13.40 N. Calligaris (Italy)	29.06.72
9:10.50 G. Wegner (GDR)	12.07.72
9:06.00 N. Calligaris (Italy)	26.07.72
9:02.96 N. Calligaris (Italy)	02.09.72
8:57.46 N. Calligaris (Italy)	03.09.72
8:52.97 N. Calligaris (Italy)	09.09.73
8:52.45 C. Doerr (GDR)	24.08.74
8:47.53 P. Thumer (GDR)	19.04.76

8:40.68 P. Thumer (GDR)	04.06.76
8:37.14 P. Thumer (GDR)	25.07.76
8:35.04 P. Thumer (GDR)	09.07.77
8:32.55 I. Diers (GDR)	27.07.80
8:31.07 A. Sonnenbrodt (GDR)	01.04.83
8:29.61 A. Strauss (GDR)	18.06.83
8:28.36 A. Strauss (GDR)	26.05.84
8:26.52 A. Strauss (GDR)	21.06.86
8:24.77 S. Hardcastle (GBR)	29.07.86
8:19.53 A. Moehring (GDR)	22.08.87

1500 Metres Freestyle

20:03.10 J. Koster (Holland)	27.07.57
19:46.40 C. Schimmel (Holland)	15.07.59
19:23.60 J. Cederqvist (Sweden)	08.09.60
19:02.80 M. Rylander (Sweden)	27.06.61
18:49.90 E. Ljunggren (Sweden)	17.09.67
18:44.60 M. Kersaudy (France)	08.03.69
18:11.60 N. Calligaris (Italy)	10.09.69
18:03.00 L. de Boer (Holland)	24.06.71
17:51.10 N. Calligaris (Italy)	10.07.71
17:46.30 H. Bunschoten (Holland)	17.06.72
17:29.30 N. Calligaris (Italy)	06.07.72
17:18.43 N. Calligaris (Italy)	25.06.73
17:04.20 N. Calligaris (Italy)	01.07.74
16:47.11 A. Maas (Holland)	11.07.77
16:33.56 R. Felotti (Italy)	26.08.79
16:27.89 I. Diers (GDR)	27.08.81
16:13.55 A. Strauss (GDR)	08.01.84

50 Metres Backstroke

29.12 K. Otto (GDR)	22.09.88

100 Metres Backstroke

1:12.40 M. Edwards (GBR)	19.04.58
1:12.30 R. van Velsen (Holland)	20.07.58
1:11.90 J. Grinham (GBR)	23.07.58
1:11.70 R. van Velsen (Holland)	26.07.59
1:11.00 R. van Velsen (Holland)	12.06.60
1:10.90 R. van Velsen (Holland)	10.07.60
1:10.80 N. Steward (GBR)	01.09.60
1:10.60 R. van Velsen (Holland)	19.08.61
1:10.50 R. van Velsen (Holland)	19.08.61
1:10.30 R. van Velsen (Holland)	17.03.62
1:10.20 R. van Velsen (Holland)	05.08.62
1:10.10 R. van Velsen (Holland)	09.09.62

Kornelia Ender (GDR)

1:09.80 C. Caron (France)	23.06.63
1:09.60 C. Caron (France)	14.07.63
1:09.50 C. Caron (France)	05.06.64
1:08.60 C. Caron (France)	14.06.64
1:08.50 C. Caron (France)	13.10.64
1:07.90 C. Caron (France)	14.10.64
1:07.90 A. Gyarmati (Hungary)	03.04.70
1:07.80 T. Lekveishvili (USSR)	06.09.70
1:06.60 A. Gyarmati (Hungary)	11.04.71
1:06.50 A. Gyarmati (Hungary)	11.04.71
1:06.39 A. Gyarmati (Hungary)	02.09.72
1:06.26 A. Gyarmati (Hungary)	02.09.72
1:06.20 E. Brigitha (Holland)	15.04.73
1:06.12 E. Brigitha (Holland)	14.07.73
1:05.93 A. Gyarmati (Hungary)	21.07.73
1:05.39 U. Richter (GDR)	18.08.73
1:04.99 U. Richter (GDR)	04.09.73
1:04.43 U. Richter (GDR)	08.07.74
1:04.09 U. Richter (GDR)	22.08.74
1:03.30 U. Richter (GDR)	23.08.74
1:03.08 U. Richter (GDR)	24.08.74
1:02.60 U. Richter (GDR)	14.03.76
1:01.62 K. Ender (GDR)	03.06.76
1:01.51 U. Richter (GDR)	05.06.76
1:01.51 R. Reinisch (GDR)	20.07.80
1:01.50 R. Reinisch (GDR)	22.07.80
1:00.86 R. Reinisch (GDR)	23.07.80
1:00.59 I. Kleber (GDR)	24.08.84

200 Metres Backstroke

2:38.50 L. de Nijs (Holland)	17.05.57
2:37.50 R. Dobber (Holland)	17.05.59
2:36.20 R. Dobber (Holland)	12.06.60
2:35.60 R. Piacentini (France)	02.08.61
2:35.60 K. Winkel (Holland)	20.08.61
2:34.50 R. Piacentini (France)	04.09.61
2:33.90 R. Piacentini (France)	13.09.61
2:33.80 I. Schmidt (GDR)	15.08.62
2:33.50 C. Caron (France)	13.07.63
2:32.30 K. Winkel (Holland)	01.09.63
2:32.10 C. Caron (France)	08.09.63
2:29.60 C. Caron (France)	18.07.64
2:28.80 C. Caron (France)	19.07.65
2:27.90 C. Caron (France)	16.06.66
2:27.90 B. Duprez (France)	24.08.68
2:27.60 A. Gyarmati (Hungary)	04.04.70
2:27.10 A. Krause (GDR)	06.08.70
2:26.90 A. Gyarmati (Hungary)	22.08.70
2:26.20 W. Burrell (GBR)	09.09.70
2:25.50 A. Gyarmati (Hungary)	10.09.70
2:25.10 A. Gyarmati (Hungary)	29.05.71
2:24.40 A. Gyarmati (Hungary)	29.08.71
2:24.30 A. Gyarmati (Hungary)	19.04.72
2:24.30 A. Groen (Holland)	19.04.72
2:23.70 E. Brigitha (Holland)	04.09.72
2:23.44 C. Herbst (GDR)	04.09.72
2:23.35 A. Kober (W Germany)	04.09.72
2:22.34 A. Eife (GDR)	11.07.73
2:21.66 A. Gyarmati (Hungary)	19.08.73
2:21.13 U. Tauber (GDR)	14.03.74
2:20.27 E. Brigitha (Holland)	26.04.74
2:18.41 U. Richter (GDR)	07.07.74
2:17.35 U. Richter (GDR)	25.08.74
2:16.10 B. Treiber (GDR)	06.06.75
2:15.46 B. Treiber (GDR)	26.07.75
2:14.41 A. Stille (GDR)	29.02.76
2:13.50 A. Stille (GDR)	13.03.76
2:12.47 B. Treiber (GDR)	04.06.76
2:11.77 R. Reinisch (GDR)	27.07.80

2:09.91 C. Sirch (GDR)	07.08.82
2:09.29 E. Egerszegi (Hungary)	25.09.88

50 Metres Breaststroke

31.58 S. Hoerner (GDR)	23.09.88

100 Metres Breaststroke

1:21.10 A. den Haan (Holland)	13.07.57
1:20.30 K. Beyer (GDR)	20.07.58
1:19.60 K. Beyer (GDR)	12.09.58
1:19.10 W. Urselmann (W Germany)	12.03.60
1:19.00 U. Kuper (GDR)	14.07.60
1:18.20 B. Gobel (GDR)	01.07.61
1:18.00 K. Bimolt (Holland)	08.08.64
1:17.20 S. Babanina (USSR)	03.09.64
1:16.50 S. Babanina (USSR)	11.05.65
1:15.70 G. Prozumenshikova (USSR)	17.07.66
1:15.40 G. Prozumenshikova (USSR)	03.04.68
1:14.70 G. Stepanova (USSR)	18.04.71
1:13.79 R. Vogel (GDR)	18.08.73
1:13.74 R. Vogel (GDR)	05.09.73
1:12.91 R. Vogel (GDR)	22.08.74
1:12.55 C. Justen (W Germany)	23.08.74
1:12.28 R. Vogel (GDR)	01.09.74
1:11.93 C. Nitschke (GDR)	02.06.76
1:11.11 H. Anke (GDR)	21.07.76
1:10.86 H. Anke (GDR)	22.07.76
1:10.31 J. Bogdanova (USSR)	22.08.78
1:10.20 U. Geweniger (GDR)	26.05.80
1:10.11 U. Geweniger (GDR)	24.07.80
1:09.52 U. Geweniger (GDR)	20.04.81
1:09.39 U. Geweniger (GDR)	02.07.81
1:08.60 U. Geweniger (GDR)	08.09.81
1:08.51 U. Geweniger (GDR)	25.08.83
1:08.29 S. Gerasch (GDR)	23.08.84
1:08.11 S. Gerasch (GDR)	21.08.86
1:07.91 S. Hoerner (GDR)	21.08.87

200 Metres Breaststroke

2:51.30 A. den Haan (Holland)	04.08.57
2:50.30 A. Lonsbrough (GBR)	25.07.59
2:50.20 W. Urselmann (W Germany)	06.06.60
2:49.50 A. Lonsbrough (GBR)	27.08.60
2:48.00 K. Beyer (GDR)	05.08.61
2:47.70 G. Prozumenshikova (USSR)	11.04.64
2:45.40 G. Prozumenshikova (USSR)	17.05.64

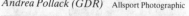

Andrea Pollack (GDR)   Allsport Photographic

2:45.30	G. Prozumenshikova (USSR)	12.09.65
2:44.60	G. Prozumenshikova (USSR)	23.03.66
2:43.00	I. Pozdyakova (USSR)	16.07.66
2:40.80	G. Prozumenshikova (USSR)	23.08.66
2:40.70	G. Stepanova (USSR)	11.09.70
2:40.28	H. Anke (GDR)	18.08.73
2:40.01	R. Vogel (GDR)	07.09.73
2:37.89	A. Schott (GDR)	06.07.74
2:37.44	K. Linke (GDR)	19.08.74
2:34.99	K. Linke (GDR)	19.08.74
2:33.35	M. Koshevaia (USSR)	21.07.76
2:33.32	J. Bogdanova (USSR)	07.04.78
2:33.11	L. Kachusite (USSR)	24.08.78
2:31.42	L. Kachusite (USSR)	24.08.78
2:31.09	S. Varganova (USSR)	30.03.79
2:28.36	L. Kachusite (USSR)	06.04.79
2:28.33	S. Hoerner (GDR)	05.06.85
2:28.20	S. Gerasch (GDR)	28.02.86
2:27.40	S. Hoerner (GDR)	18.08.86
2:26.71	S. Hoerner (GDR)	18.09.88

50 Metres Butterfly

27.54	C. Plewinski France)	23.09.88

100 Metres Butterfly

1:10.50	A. Voorbij (Holland)	04.06.57
1:10.40	M. Heemskerk (Holland)	30.08.60
1:10.00	U. Noack (GDR)	01.04.62
1:09.80	U. Noack (GDR)	14.07.62
1:09.00	A. Kok (Holland)	24.08.62
1:08.70	A. Kok (Holland)	23.03.63
1:06.10	A. Kok (Holland)	01.09.63
1:05.10	A. Kok (Holland)	30.05.64
1:04.50	A. Kok (Holland)	14.08.65
1:04.01	A. Gyarmati (Hungary)	31.08.72
1:03.80	A. Gyarmati (Hungary)	31.08.72
1:03.61	R. Beier (GDR)	01.09.72
1:03.05	K. Ender (GDR)	14.07.73
1:02.31	K. Ender (GDR)	14.07.73
1:02.09	R. Kother (GDR)	21.08.74
1:01.99	R. Kother (GDR)	22.08.74
1:01.88	R. Kother (GDR)	01.09.74
1:01.33	K. Ender (GDR)	09.06.75
1:01.24	K. Ender (GDR)	24.07.75
1:00.13	K. Ender (GDR)	04.06.76
1:00.13	K. Ender (GDR)	22.07.76
59.78	C. Knacke (GDR)	28.08.77
59.46	A. Pollack (GDR)	03.07.78
59.41	T. Kurnikova (USSR)	23.08.84
59.00	K. Otto (GDR)	23.09.88

200 Metres Butterfly

2:38.90	T. Lagerberg (Holland)	13.09.58
2:34.40	M. Heemskerk (Holland)	12.06.60
2:33.50	U. Noack (GDR)	24.09.64
2:25.80	A. Kok (Holland)	21.08.65
2:25.30	A. Kok (Holland)	12.09.65
2:22.50	A. Kok (Holland)	02.08.67
2:21.00	A. Kok (Holland)	25.08.67
2:20.20	H. Lindner (GDR)	12.09.70
2:19.50	R. Kother (GDR)	10.07.72
2:18.32	R. Kother (GDR)	04.09.72
2:17.11	R. Kother (GDR)	04.09.72
2:16.03	R. Kother (GDR)	13.07.73
2:15.47	R. Kother (GDR)	08.09.73
2:13.76	R. Kother (GDR)	08.09.73
2:13.60	R. Kother (GDR)	14.03.76
2:12.84	R. Kother-Gabriel (GDR)	05.06.76
2:11.22	R. Kother-Gabriel (GDR)	05.06.76

2:11.20	A. Pollack (GDR)	09.04.78
2:09.87	A. Pollack (GDR)	05.07.78
2:08.97	I. Geissler (GDR)	01.07.81
2:08.50	I. Geissler (GDR)	08.09.81
2:08.03	I. Geissler (GDR)	19.06.83
2:07.82	C. Polit (GDR)	27.08.83

200 Metres Individual Medley

2:33.90	T. Deviatova (USSR)	13.08.66
2:33.50	S. Steinbach (GDR)	04.03.67
2:32.00	S. Steinbach (GDR)	15.08.67
2:31.10	S. Steinbach (GDR)	08.11.67
2:30.30	S. Steinbach (GDR)	10.03.68
2:30.10	L. Zakharova (USSR)	03.04.68
2:29.60	J. Turoczy (Hungary)	14.07.68
2:27.50	M. Grunert (GDR)	23.08.69
2:27.50	G. Wetzko (GDR)	19.12.71
2:26.90	N. Petrova (USSR)	18.04.72
2:25.45	E. Stoize (GDR)	28.08.72
2:25.39	K. Ender (GDR)	28.08.72
2:23.59	K. Ender (GDR)	28.08.72
2:23.01	K. Ender (GDR)	13.04.73
2:20.51	A. Hubner (GDR)	04.09.73
2:18.97	U. Tauber (GDR)	18.08.74
2:18.30	U. Tauber (GDR)	12.03.76
2:17.14	K. Ender (GDR)	05.06.76
2:16.96	U. Tauber (GDR)	10.07.77
2:15.95	U. Tauber (GDR)	20.08.77
2:15.85	U. Tauber (GDR)	28.08.77
2:15.75	P. Schneider (GDR)	18.03.79
2:14.51	P. Schneider (GDR)	06.08.79
2:13.94	P. Schneider (GDR)	27.02.80
2:13.00	P. Schneider (GDR)	24.05.80
2:11.73	U. Geweniger (GDR)	04.07.81

400 Metres Individual Medley

5:49.00	H. Pechstein (GDR)	16.04.61
5:40.90	M. Heemskerk (Holland)	20.08.61
5:39.40	J. de Nijs (Holland)	26.08.61
5:36.00	M. Heemskerk (Holland)	28.02.62
5:33.10	A. Lasterie (Holland)	29.07.62
5:27.80	A. Lasterie (Holland)	25.08.62
5:26.80	V. Holletz (GDR)	15.10.64
5:25.60	V. Holletz (GDR)	17.10.64
5:25.00	B. Heukels (Holland)	27.08.66
5:22.60	S. Steinbach (GDR)	09.04.67
5:14.90	S. Steinbach (GDR)	02.04.68
5:07.90	E. Stolze (GDR)	06.09.70
5:06.96	E. Stolze (GDR)	31.08.72
5:03.99	N. Calligaris (Italy)	31.08.72
5:01.10	A. Franke (GDR)	19.08.73
4:57.51	G. Wegner (GDR)	06.09.73
4:52.42	U. Tauber (GDR)	21.08.74
4:52.20	U. Tauber (GDR)	07.06.75
4:48.79	B. Treiber (GDR)	01.06.76
4:42.77	U. Tauber (GDR)	24.07.76
4:39.96	P. Schneider (GDR)	08.03.80
4:38.44	P. Schneider (GDR)	27.05.80
4:36.29	P. Schneider (GDR)	26.07.80
4:36.10	P. Schneider (GDR)	01.08.82

4×100 Metres Freestyle Relay

4:22.90	Holland	06.09.58
4:18.20	Holland	11.06.60
4:17.60	GBR	24.08.62
4:15.10	Holland	25.08.62
4:14.00	Sweden	08.08.63
4:12.30	Holland	27.06.64
4:12.00	Holland	15.10.64

4:11.30	USSR	27.08.66	4:47.30 Holland	12.06.60
4:11.30	Italy	17.09.67	4:46.70 GDR	15.07.60
4:09.40	GDR	04.04.68	4:46.40 GDR	06.08.61
4:07.50	Hungary	13.07.68	4:45.00 GDR	24.04.62
4:05.70	GDR	26.10.68	4:44.10 GDR	17.06.62
4:02.60	Hungary	24.08.69	4:43.30 GDR	14.07.62
4:00.80	GDR	11.09.70	4:40.10 GDR	23.08.62
3:58.11	GDR	30.08.72	4:39.10 Holland	28.06.64
3:55.55	GDR	30.08.72	4:39.10 USSR	16.10.64
3:52.45	GDR	08.09.73	4:37.00 Holland	18.10.64
3:52.23	GDR	14.03.75	4:36.40 Holland	25.08.66
3:49.37	GDR	27.07.75	4:35.70 USSR	20.09.67
3:48.80	GDR	02.06.76	4:35.50 Holland	20.04.68
3:45.50	GDR	25.07.76	4:34.80 GDR	23.08.69
3:45.19	GDR	27.07.80	4:30.20 GDR	15.04.70
3:42.41	GDR	21.08.84	4:30.10 GDR	09.09.70
3:40.57	GDR	19.08.86	4:30.00 Holland	18.04.72
			4:27.58 GDR	03.09.72
4×200 Metres Freestyle Relay			4:24.91 GDR	03.09.72
8:02.27	GDR	22.08.83	4:21.70 GDR	18.08.73
7:59.33	GDR	17.08.86	4:16.84 GDR	04.09.73
7:55.47	GDR	18.08.87	4:13.78 GDR	24.08.74
			4:13.41 GDR	05.06.76
4×100 Metres Medley Relay			4:07.95 GDR	18.07.76
4:57.00	Holland	18.05.57	4:06.67 GDR	20.07.80
4:54.00	GBR	25.07.58	4:05.88 GDR	07.08.82
4:52.90	Holland	05.09.58	4:05.79 GDR	26.08.83
4:51.50	Holland	26.07.59	4:03.69 GDR	24.08.84

Progressive World (Long Course) Records, 1956–1989

NOTE: On the 1 May, 1957, FINA decided that only long course performances would be accepted for world record purposes.

Men

50 Metres Freestyle

22.32 T. Jager (USA)	13.08.87
22.23 T. Jager (USA)	25.03.88
22.14 M. Biondi (USA)	24.09.88
22.12 T. Jager (USA)	20.08.89

100 Metres Freestyle

55.40 J. Henricks (Australia)	30.11.56
55.20 J. Devitt (Australia)	19.01.57
54.60 J. Devitt (Australia)	28.01.57
54.40 S. Clark (USA)	18.08.61
53.60 M. dos Santos (Brazil)	20.09.61
52.90 A. Gottvalles (France)	13.09.64
52.60 K. Walsh (USA)	27.07.67
52.60 Z. Zorn (USA)	02.09.68
52.20 M. Wenden (Australia)	19.10.68
51.90 M. Spitz (USA)	23.08.70
51.47 M. Spitz (USA)	05.08.72
51.22 M. Spitz (USA)	03.09.72
51.12 J. Montgomery (USA)	21.06.75
51.11 A. Coan (USA)	03.08.75
50.59 J. Montgomery (USA)	23.08.75
50.39 J. Montgomery (USA)	24.07.76
49.99 J. Montgomery (USA)	25.07.76
49.49 J. Skinner (S Africa)	14.08.76
49.44 J. Skinner (S Africa)	14.08.76
49.36 A. Gaines (USA)	03.04.81
49.24 M. Biondi (USA)	06.08.85
48.95 M. Biondi (USA)	06.08.85
48.74 M. Biondi (USA)	24.06.86
48.42 M. Biondi (USA)	10.08.88

200 Metres Freestyle

2:04.80 J. Konrads (Australia)	18.01.58
2:03.20 J. Konrads (Australia)	05.03.58
2:03.00 T. Yamanaka (Japan)	22.08.58
2:02.20 J. Konrads (Australia)	16.01.59
2:01.50 T. Yamanaka (Japan)	26.07.59
2:01.20 T. Yamanaka (Japan)	24.06.61
2:01.10 T. Yamanaka (Japan)	06.08.61
2:00.40 T. Yamanaka (Japan)	20.08.61
2:00.30 R. Windle (Australia)	21.04.63
1:58.80 D. Schollander (USA)	27.07.63
1:58.50 D. Schollander (USA)	17.08.63
1:58.40 D. Schollander (USA)	24.08.63
1:58.20 H. Klein (W Germany)	24.05.64
1:57.60 D. Schollander (USA)	01.08.64
1:57.20 D. Schollander (USA)	29.07.66
1:56.20 D. Schollander (USA)	19.08.66
1:56.00 D. Schollander (USA)	29.07.67
1:55.70 D. Schollander (USA)	12.08.67
1:54.30 D. Schollander (USA)	30.08.68
1:54.30 M. Spitz (USA)	12.07.69
1:54.20 M. Spitz (USA)	04.09.71
1:53.50 M. Spitz (USA)	10.09.71
1:52.78 M. Spitz (USA)	29.08.72
1:51.66 T. Shaw (USA)	23.08.74
1:51.41 B. Furniss (USA)	18.06.75
1:50.89 B. Furniss (USA)	18.06.75
1:50.32 B. Furniss (USA)	21.08.75
1:50.29 B. Furniss (USA)	19.07.76
1:49.83 S. Kopliakov (USSR)	07.04.79
1:49.16 A. Gaines (USA)	11.04.80
1:48.83 A. Gaines (USA)	19.07.82

Don Schollander (USA)

3:48.32 V. Salnikov (USSR)	19.02.83
3:47.80 M. Gross (W Germany)	29.06.85
3:47.38 A. Wojdat (Poland)	25.03.88
3:46.95 U. Dassler (GDR)	23.09.88

800 Metres Freestyle

9:17.70 J. Konrads (Australia)	11.01.58
9:14.50 J. Konrads (Australia)	22.02.58
8:59.60 J. Konrads (Australia)	10.01.59
8:51.50 M. Rose (Australia)	26.08.62
8:47.40 S. Belitz-Geiman (USSR)	03.08.66
8:47.30 J. Bennett (Australia)	16.01.67
8:46.80 A. Mosconi (France)	05.07.67
8:42.00 F. Luyce (France)	21.07.67
8:34.30 M. Burton (USA)	03.09.68
8:28.80 M. Burton (USA)	17.08.69
8:28.60 G. Windeatt (Australia)	03.04.71
8:23.80 B. Cooper (Australia)	12.01.72
8:17.60 S. Holland (Australia)	05.08.73
8:16.27 S. Holland (Australia)	08.09.73
8:15.88 S. Holland (Australia)	01.02.74
8:15.20 S. Holland (Australia)	17.01.75
8:15.02 S. Holland (Australia)	25.01.75
8:13.68 T. Shaw (USA)	21.06.75
8:09.60 T. Shaw (USA)	13.07.75
8:06.27 S. Holland (Australia)	27.02.76
8:02.91 S. Holland (Australia)	29.02.76
8:01.54 R. Hackett (USA)	21.06.76
7:56.49 V. Salnikov (USSR)	23.03.79
7:52.83 V. Salnikov (USSR)	14.02.82
7:52.33 V. Salnikov (USSR)	14.07.83
7:50.64 V. Salnikov (USSR)	04.07.86

1500 Metres Freestyle

17:28.70 J. Konrads (Australia)	22.02.58
17:11.00 J. Konrads (Australia)	27.02.60
17:05.50 R. Saari (USA)	17.08.63
17:01.80 M. Rose (Australia)	02.08.64
16:58.70 R. Saari (USA)	02.09.64
16:58.60 S. Krause (USA)	15.08.65
16:41.60 M. Burton (USA)	21.08.66
16:34.10 M. Burton (USA)	13.08.67
16:28.10 G. Echevarria (Mexico)	07.07.68
16:08.50 M. Burton (USA)	03.09.68
16:04.50 M. Burton (USA)	17.08.69
15:57.10 J. Kinsella (USA)	23.08.70
15:52.91 R. de Mont (USA)	06.08.72
15:52.58 M. Burton (USA)	04.09.72
15:37.80 S. Holland (Australia)	05.08.73
15:31.85 S. Holland (Australia)	08.09.73
15:31.75 T. Shaw (Australia)	25.08.74
15:27.79 S. Holland (Australia)	25.01.75
15:20.91 T. Shaw (USA)	21.06.75
15:10.89 S. Holland (Australia)	27.02.76
15:06.66 B. Goodell (USA)	21.06.76
15:02.40 B. Goodell (USA)	20.07.76
14:58.27 V. Salnikov (USSR)	22.07.80
14:56.35 V. Salnikov (USSR)	13.03.82
14:54.76 V. Salnikov (USSR)	22.02.83

100 Metres Backstroke

1:02.20 D. Theile (Australia)	06.12.56
1:01.50 J. Monckton (Australia)	15.02.58
1:01.30 R. Bennett (USA)	19.08.61
1:01.00 T. Stock (USA)	11.08.62
1:00.90 T. Stock (USA)	12.08.62
1:00.80 E. Kuppers (W Germany)	28.08.64
1:00.00 T. Mann (USA)	03.09.64
59.60 T. Mann (USA)	16.10.64

1:48.28 M. Gross (W Germany)	21.06.83
1:47.87 M. Gross (W Germany)	22.08.83
1:47.55 M. Gross (W Germany)	08.06.84
1:47.44 M. Gross (W Germany)	29.07.84
1:47.25 D. Armstrong (Australia)	19.09.88
1:46.69 G. Lamberti (Italy)	15.08.89

400 Metres Freestyle

4:27.00 M. Rose (Australia)	27.10.56
4:25.90 J. Konrads (Australia)	15.01.58
4:21.80 J. Konrads (Australia)	18.02.58
4:19.00 J. Konrads (Australia)	07.02.59
4:16.60 T. Yamanaka (Japan)	26.07.59
4:15.90 J. Konrads (Australia)	23.02.60
4:13.40 M. Rose (Australia)	17.08.62
4:12.70 D. Schollander (USA)	31.07.64
4:12.20 D. Schollander (USA)	15.10.64
4:11.80 J. Nelson (USA)	18.08.66
4:11.60 D. Schollander (USA)	18.08.66
4:11.10 F. Weigand (GDR)	25.08.66
4:10.60 M. Spitz (USA)	25.06.67
4:10.60 A. Mosconi (France)	02.07.67
4:09.20 A. Mosconi (France)	04.07.67
4:08.80 M. Spitz (USA)	07.07.67
4:08.20 G. Charlton (USA)	28.08.67
4:07.70 M. Spitz (USA)	23.06.68
4:06.50 R. Hutton (Canada)	01.08.68
4:04.00 H. Fassnacht (W Germany)	14.08.69
4:02.80 J. Kinsella (USA)	20.08.70
4:02.60 G. Larsson (Sweden)	07.09.70
4:02.10 T. McBreen (USA)	25.08.71
4:01.70 B. Cooper (Australia)	12.02.72
4:00.11 K. Krumpholz (USA)	04.08.72
3:58.18 R. de Mont (USA)	06.09.73
3:56.96 T. Shaw (USA)	22.08.74
3:54.69 T. Shaw (USA)	22.08.74
3:53.95 T. Shaw (USA)	19.06.75
3:53.31 T. Shaw (USA)	20.08.75
3:53.08 B. Goodell (USA)	18.06.76
3:51.93 B. Goodell (USA)	22.07.76
3:51.56 B. Goodell (USA)	27.08.77
3:51.41 V. Salnikov (USSR)	06.04.79
3:51.20 V. Salnikov (USSR)	24.02.80
3:50.49 P. Sznidt (Canada)	16.07.80
3:49.57 V. Salnikov (USSR)	12.03.82

59.50	D. Russell (USA)	28.08.67
59.30	C. Hickcox (USA)	28.08.67
59.10	C. Hickcox (USA)	31.08.67
58.40	R. Matthes (GDR)	21.09.67
58.00	R. Matthes (GDR)	26.10.68
57.80	R. Matthes (GDR)	23.08.69
56.90	R. Matthes (GDR)	08.09.70
56.70	R. Matthes (GDR)	04.09.71
56.30	R. Matthes (GDR)	08.04.72
56.30	R. Matthes (GDR)	04.09.72
56.19	J. Naber (USA)	18.07.76
55.49	J. Naber (USA)	19.07.76
55.44	R. Carey (USA)	06.08.83
55.38	R. Carey (USA)	06.08.83
55.19	R. Carey (USA)	21.08.83
55.17	I. Polianski (USSR)	15.03.88
55.16	I. Polianski (USSR)	16.03.88
55.00	I. Polianski (USSR)	16.07.88
54.95	D. Berkoff (USA)	13.08.88
54.91	D. Berkoff (USA)	13.08.88
54.51	D. Berkoff (USA)	24.09.88

200 Metres Backstroke

2:18.80	J. Monckton (Australia)	15.01.58
2:18.40	J. Monckton (Australia)	18.02.58
2:17.90	F. McKinney (USA)	12.07.59
2:17.80	F. McKinney (USA)	25.07.59
2:17.60	C. Bittick (USA)	26.06.60
2:16.00	T. Stock (USA)	24.07.60
2:13.20	T. Stock (USA)	02.07.61
2:11.50	T. Stock (USA)	20.08.61
2:10.90	T. Stock (USA)	10.08.62
2:10.30	J. Graef (USA)	13.10.64
2:09.40	C. Hickcox (USA)	29.08.67
2:07.90	R. Matthes (GDR)	08.11.67
2:07.50	R. Matthes (GDR)	14.08.68
2:07.40	R. Matthes (GDR)	12.07.69
2:06.60	G. Hall (USA)	14.08.69
2:06.40	R. Matthes (GDR)	29.08.69
2:06.30	M. Stamm (USA)	20.08.70
2:06.10	R. Matthes (GDR)	11.09.70
2:05.60	R. Matthes (GDR)	03.09.71
2:02.80	R. Matthes (GDR)	10.07.72
2:01.87	R. Matthes (GDR)	06.09.73
2:00.64	J. Naber (USA)	19.06.76
1:59.19	J. Naber (USA)	24.07.76
1:58.93	R. Carey (USA)	03.08.83
1:58.41	S. Zabolotnov (USSR)	21.08.84
1:58.14	I. Polianski (USSR)	03.04.85

100 Metres Breaststroke

1:12.70	V. Svozil (Czechoslovakia)	01.05.57
1:11.60	C. Lieh-Yung (China)	01.05.57
1:11.50	V. Minashkin (USSR)	15.09.57
1:11.40	L. Kolesnikov (USSR)	05.05.61
1:11.10	C. Jastremski (USA)	02.07.61
1:10.80	G. Tittes (GDR)	05.07.61
1:10.70	C. Jastremski (USA)	28.07.61
1:10.00	C. Jastremski (USA)	30.07.61
1:09.50	C. Jastremski (USA)	03.08.61
1:07.80	C. Jastremski (USA)	20.08.61
1:07.50	C. Jastremski (USA)	20.08.61
1:07.40	G. Prokopenko (USSR)	26.03.64
1:06.90	G. Prokopenko (USSR)	03.09.64
1:06.70	V. Kosinsky (USSR)	08.11.67
1:06.40	J. Fiolo (Brazil)	19.02.68
1:06.20	N. Pankin (USSR)	18.04.68
1:05.80	N. Pankin (USSR)	20.04.69
1:05.68	J. Hencken (USA)	29.08.72

1:05.13	N. Taguchi (Japan)	29.08.72
1:04.94	N. Taguchi (Japan)	30.08.72
1:04.35	J. Hencken (USA)	04.09.73
1:04.02	J. Hencken (USA)	04.09.73
1:03.88	J. Hencken (USA)	31.08.74
1:03.88	J. Hencken (USA)	19.07.76
1:03.62	J. Hencken (USA)	19.07.76
1:03.11	J. Hencken (USA)	20.07.76
1:02.86	G. Moerken (W Germany)	17.08.77
1:02.53	S. Lundquist (USA)	21.08.82
1:02.34	S. Lundquist (USA)	06.08.83
1:02.28	S. Lundquist (USA)	17.08.83
1:02.13	J. Moffett (USA)	25.06.84
1:01.65	S. Lundquist (USA)	29.07.84
1:01.49	A. Moorhouse (GBR)	15.08.89

200 Metres Breaststroke

2:36.50	T. Gathercole (Australia)	28.06.58
2:33.60	C. Jastremski (USA)	28.07.61
2:29.60	C. Jastremski (USA)	19.08.61
2:28.20	C. Jastremski (USA)	30.08.64
2:27.80	I. O'Brien (Australia)	15.10.64
2:27.40	V. Kosinsky (USSR)	03.04.68
2:26.50	N. Pankin (USSR)	22.03.69
2:25.40	N. Pankin (USSR)	19.04.69
2:23.50	B. Job (USA)	22.08.70
2:22.79	J. Hencken (USA)	05.08.72
2:21.55	J. Hencken (USA)	02.09.72
2:20.52	J. Hencken (USA)	24.08.73
2:19.28	D. Wilkie (GBR)	06.09.73
2:18.93	J. Hencken (USA)	24.08.74
2:18.21	J. Hencken (USA)	01.09.74
2:15.11	D. Wilkie (GBR)	24.07.76
2:14.77	V. Davis (Canada)	05.08.82
2:14.58	V. Davis (Canada)	19.06.84
2:13.34	V. Davis (Canada)	02.08.84
2:12.90	M. Barrowman (USA)	03.08.89
2:12.90	N. Gillingham (GBR)	18.08.89
2:12.89	M. Barrowman (USA)	20.08.89

100 Metres Butterfly

1:03.40	G. Tumpek (Hungary)	26.05.57
1:01.50	T. Ishimoto (Japan)	16.06.57
1:01.30	T. Ishimoto (Japan)	07.07.57
1:01.20	T. Ishimoto (Japan)	06.09.57

John Hencken (USA)   Swimming Times

1:01.00 T. Ishimoto (Japan)	14.09.57
1:00.10 T. Ishimoto (Japan)	29.06.58
59.00 L. Larson (USA)	26.06.60
58.70 L. Larson (USA)	24.07.60
58.60 F. Schmidt (USA)	20.08.61
58.40 L. Nicolao (Argentine)	24.04.62
57.00 L. Nicolao (Argentine)	27.04.62
56.30 M. Spitz (USA)	31.07.67
56.30 D. Russell (USA)	29.08.67
55.70 M. Spitz (USA)	07.10.67
55.60 M. Spitz (USA)	30.08.68
55.00 M. Spitz (USA)	25.08.71
54.72 M. Spitz (USA)	04.08.72
54.56 M. Spitz (USA)	04.08.72
54.27 M. Spitz (USA)	31.08.72
54.18 J. Bottom (USA)	27.08.77
54.15 P. Arvidsson (Sweden)	11.04.80
53.81 W. Paulsen (USA)	03.04.81
53.44 M. Gribble (USA)	06.08.83
53.38 P. Morales (USA)	26.06.84
53.08 M. Gross (W Germany)	30.07.84
52.84 P. Morales (USA)	23.06.86

200 Metres Butterfly

2:19.00 M. Troy (USA)	11.07.59
2:16.40 M. Troy (USA)	11.07.59
2:15.00 M. Troy (USA)	11.07.60
2:13.40 M. Troy (USA)	23.07.60
2:13.20 M. Troy (USA)	04.08.60
2:12.80 M. Troy (USA)	02.09.60
2:12.60 C. Robie (USA)	19.08.61
2:12.50 K. Berry (Australia)	20.02.62
2:12.40 C. Robie (USA)	11.08.62
2:10.80 C. Robie (USA)	11.08.62
2:09.70 K. Berry (Australia)	23.10.62
2:08.40 K. Berry (Australia)	12.01.63
2:08.20 C. Robie (USA)	18.03.63
2:06.90 K. Berry (Australia)	29.03.64
2:06.60 K. Berry (Australia)	18.10.64
2:06.40 M. Spitz (USA)	26.07.67
2:06.40 M. Spitz (USA)	12.08.67
2:06.00 J. Ferris (USA)	30.08.67
2:05.70 M. Spitz (USA)	08.10.67
2:05.40 M. Spitz (USA)	22.08.70
2:05.00 G. Hall (USA)	22.08.70
2:03.90 M. Spitz (USA)	27.08.71
2:03.90 M. Spitz (USA)	27.08.71
2:03.30 H. Fassnacht (W Germany)	31.08.71
2:01.87 M. Spitz (USA)	02.08.72
2:01.53 M. Spitz (USA)	02.08.72
2:00.70 M. Spitz (USA)	28.08.72
2:00.21 R. Pyttel (GDR)	03.06.76
1:59.63 R. Pyttel (GDR)	03.06.76
1:59.23 M. Bruner (USA)	18.07.76
1:58.21 C. Beardsley (USA)	30.07.80
1:58.01 C. Beardsley (USA)	22.08.81
1:57.05 M. Gross (GDR)	26.08.83
1:57.04 J. Sieben (Australia)	03.08.84
1:57.01 M. Gross (W Germany)	29.06.85
1:56.65 M. Gross (W Germany)	10.08.85
1:56.24 M. Gross (W Germany)	28.06.86

200 Metres Individual Medley

2:12.40 G. Buckingham (USA)	21.08.66
2:11.30 G. Buckingham (USA)	23.08.67
2:10.60 C. Hickcox (USA)	31.08.68
2:09.60 G. Hall (USA)	17.08.69
2:09.50 G. Hall (USA)	23.08.70
2:09.30 G. Larsson (Sweden)	12.09.70
2:09.30 G. Hall (USA)	06.08.72
2:07.17 G. Larsson (Sweden)	03.09.72
2:06.32 D. Wilkie (GBR)	24.08.74
2:06.32 S. Furniss (USA)	01.09.74
2:06.08 S. Furniss (USA)	23.08.75
2:05.31 G. Smith (Canada)	04.08.77
2:05.24 A. Sidorenko (USSR)	09.07.78
2:03.65 G. Smith (Canada)	24.08.78
2:03.29 J. Vassallo (USA)	06.07.79
2:03.24 W. Barrett (USA)	30.07.80
2:02.78 A. Baumann (Canada)	29.07.80
2:02.25 A. Baumann (Canada)	04.10.82
2:01.42 A. Baumann (Canada)	04.08.84
2:00.56 T. Darnyi (Hungary)	23.08.87
2:00.17 T. Darnyi (Hungary)	25.09.88
2:00.11 D. Wharton (USA)	20.08.89

400 Metres Individual Medley

5:12.90 V. Stroujanov (USSR)	20.10.57
5:08.80 I. Black (GBR)	06.06.59
5:07.80 G. Harrison (USA)	24.06.60
5:05.30 G. Harrison (USA)	24.06.60
5:04.50 D. Rounsavelle (USA)	22.07.60
5:04.30 E. Stickles (USA)	01.07.61
4:55.60 E. Stickles (USA)	18.08.61
4:53.80 G. Hetz (W Germany)	24.05.62
4:51.40 E. Stickles (USA)	30.06.62
4:51.00 E. Stickles (USA)	12.07.62
4:50.20 G. Hetz (W Germany)	12.10.63
4:48.60 R. Roth (USA)	31.07.64
4:45.40 R. Roth (USA)	14.10.64
4:45.30 A. Dunaev (USSR)	03.04.68
4:45.10 G. Buckingham (USA)	06.07.68
4:43.40 G. Hall (USA)	20.07.68
4:39.00 C. Hickcox (USA)	30.08.68
4:38.70 G. Hall (USA)	11.07.69
4:33.90 G. Hall (USA)	15.08.69
4:31.00 G. Hall (USA)	21.08.70
4:30.81 G. Hall (USA)	03.08.72
4:28.89 A. Hargitay (Hungary)	20.08.74
4:26.00 Z. Verraszto (Hungary)	02.04.76
4:23.68 R. Strachan (USA)	25.07.76
4:23.39 J. Vassallo (USA)	04.08.78
4:20.06 J. Vassallo (USA)	22.08.78
4:19.78 R. Prado (Brazil)	02.08.82
4:19.71 J. Berndt (GDR)	25.05.84
4:17.55 A. Baumann (Canada)	17.06.84
4:17.41 A. Baumann (Canada)	30.07.84
4:16.12 D. Wharton (USA)	14.08.87
4:15.42 T. Darnyi (Hungary)	19.08.87
4:14.75 T. Darnyi (Hungary)	21.09.88

4×100 Metres Freestyle Relay

3:46.30 Australia	03.05.58
3:44.40 USA	21.07.59
3:42.50 France	10.08.62
3:39.90 USA	04.07.63
3:36.10 USA	18.08.63
3:33.20 USA	14.10.64
3:32.60 USA	28.08.68
3:32.50 USA	03.09.68
3:31.70 USA	17.10.68
3:28.80 USA	23.08.70
3:26.42 USA	28.08.72
3:25.17 USA	01.09.74
3:24.85 USA	23.07.75
3:21.11 USA	22.08.77
3:19.74 USA	22.08.78
3:19.26 USA	05.08.82

3:19.03 USA	02.08.84
3:17.08 USA	17.08.85
3:16.53 USA	23.09.88

4×200 Metres Freestyle Relay

8:21.60 Japan	22.07.59
8:18.70 Japan	26.07.59
8:17.00 USA	23.07.60
8:16.60 Australia	06.08.60
8:10.20 USA	01.09.60
8:09.80 Japan	21.04.63
8:07.60 USA	10.08.63
8:03.70 USA	19.08.63
8:01.80 USA	28.09.64
7:52.10 USA	18.10.64
7:52.10 USA	12.08.67
7:50.80 Australia	24.07.70
7:48.00 USA	28.08.70
7:45.80 USA	09.08.71
7:43.30 USA	10.09.71
7:35.78 USA	31.08.72
7:33.22 USA	07.09.73
7:30.33 USA	21.07.76
7:23.22 USA	21.07.76
7:20.82 USA	24.08.78
7:20.40 W Germany	23.08.83
7:18.87 USA	30.07.84
7:15.69 USA	30.07.84
7:13.10 W Germany	19.08.87
7:12.51 USA	21.09.88

4×100 Metres Medley Relay

4:17.80 Japan	07.09.57
4:17.20 Japan	28.05.58
4:14.20 Australia	25.07.58
4:10.40 Australia	22.08.58
4:09.20 USA	24.07.60
4:08.20 USA	27.08.60
4:05.40 USA	01.09.60
4:03.00 USA	20.08.61
4:01.60 USA	12.08.62
4:00.10 USA	24.08.63
3:58.40 USA	16.10.64
3:57.20 USA	31.08.67
3:56.50 GDR	07.11.67
3:54.90 USA	26.10.68
3:54.40 GDR	08.09.70
3:50.40 USA	03.09.71
3:48.16 USA	04.09.72
3:47.28 USA	22.07.76
3:42.22 USA	22.07.76
3:40.84 USA	07.08.82
3:40.42 USA	22.08.83
3:39.30 USA	04.08.84
3:38.28 USA	18.08.85
3:36.98 USA	25.09.88

Women

50 Metres Freestyle

25.28 T. Costache (Rumania)	23.08.86
24.98 W. Yang (China)	11.04.88

100 Metres Freestyle

1:01.50 D. Fraser (Australia)	18.02.58
1:01.40 D. Fraser (Australia)	21.07.58
1:01.20 D. Fraser (Australia)	10.08.58
1:00.20 D. Fraser (Australia)	23.02.60
1:00.00 D. Fraser (Australia)	23.10.62
59.90 D. Fraser (Australia)	27.10.62

Dawn Fraser (Australia)

59.50 D. Fraser (Australia)	24.11.62
58.90 D. Fraser (Australia)	29.02.64
58.90 S. Gould (Australia)	30.04.71
58.50 S. Gould (Australia)	08.01.72
58.25 K. Ender (GDR)	13.07.73
58.12 K. Ender (GDR)	18.08.73
57.61 K. Ender (GDR)	08.09.73
57.54 K. Ender (GDR)	09.09.73
57.51 K. Ender (GDR)	04.07.74
56.96 K. Ender (GDR)	19.08.74
56.38 K. Ender (GDR)	14.03.75
56.22 K. Ender (GDR)	26.07.75
55.73 K. Ender (GDR)	01.06.76
55.65 K. Ender (GDR)	19.07.76
55.41 B. Krause (GDR)	05.07.78
54.98 B. Krause (GDR)	20.07.80
54.79 B. Krause (GDR)	21.07.80
54.73 K. Otto (GDR)	23.08.86

200 Metres Freestyle

2:17.70 D. Fraser (Australia)	10.02.58
2:14.70 D. Fraser (Australia)	22.02.58
2:11.60 D. Fraser (Australia)	27.02.60
2:10.50 L. Watson (USA)	19.08.66
2:09.70 P. Kruse (USA)	19.08.66
2:09.50 S. Pedersen (USA)	06.07.68
2:08.80 E. Wetzel (USA)	02.08.68
2:06.70 D. Meyer (USA)	24.08.68
2:06.50 S. Gould (Australia)	01.05.71
2:05.80 S. Gould (Australia)	26.11.71
2:05.21 S. Babashoff (USA)	04.08.72
2:03.56 S. Gould (Australia)	01.09.72
2:03.22 K. Ender (GDR)	22.08.74
2:02.94 S. Babashoff (USA)	23.08.74
2:02.94 S. Babashoff (USA)	31.08.74
2:02.27 K. Ender (GDR)	15.03.75
1:59.78 K. Ender (GDR)	02.06.76
1:59.26 K. Ender (GDR)	22.07.76
1:59.04 B. Krause (GDR)	02.07.78
1:58.53 C. Woodhead (USA)	22.08.78
1:58.43 C. Woodhead (USA)	03.07.79
1:58.23 C. Woodhead (USA)	03.09.79
1:57.75 K. Otto (GDR)	23.05.84
1:57.55 H. Friedrich (GDR)	18.06.86

400 Metres Freestyle

4:45.40	I. Konrads (Australia)	09.01.60
4:44.50	C. von Saltza (USA)	05.08.60
4:42.00	M. Ramenofsky (USA)	11.07.64
4:41.70	M. Ramenofsky (USA)	01.08.64
4:39.50	M. Ramenofsky (USA)	31.08.64
4:39.20	M. Randall (USA)	14.08.65
4:38.00	M. Randall (USA)	26.08.65
4:36.80	P. Kruse (USA)	30.06.67
4:36.40	P. Kruse (USA)	07.07.67
4:32.60	D. Meyer (USA)	27.07.67
4:29.00	D. Meyer (USA)	18.08.67
4:26.70	D. Meyer (USA)	01.08.68
4:24.50	D. Meyer (USA)	25.08.68
4:24.30	D. Meyer (USA)	20.08.70
4:22.60	K. Moras (Australia)	30.04.71
4:21.20	S. Gould (Australia)	09.07.71
4:19.04	S. Gould (Australia)	30.08.72
4:18.07	K. Rothhammer (USA)	22.08.73
4:17.33	H. Greenwood (USA)	28.06.74
4:15.77	S. Babashoff (USA)	22.08.74
4:14.76	S. Babashoff (USA)	20.06.75
4:11.69	B. Krause (GDR)	03.06.76
4:09.89	P. Thumer (GDR)	20.07.76
4:09.39	T. Wickham (Australia)	24.02.78
4:08.91	P. Thumer (GDR)	17.08.78
4:07.66	K. Linehan (USA)	20.08.78
4:06.28	T. Wickham (Australia)	28.08.78
4:05.45	J. Evans (USA)	20.12.87
4:03.85	J. Evans (USA)	22.03.88

800 Metres Freestyle

10:17.70	I. Konrads (Australia)	09.01.58
10:16.20	I. Konrads (Australia)	02.02.58
10:11.80	I. Konrads (Australia)	13.06.58
10:11.40	I. Konrads (Australia)	19.02.59
9:55.60	J. Cederqvist (Sweden)	17.08.60
9:51.60	C. House (USA)	26.08.62
9:47.30	P. Caretto (USA)	30.07.64
9:36.90	S. Finneran (USA)	28.09.64
9:35.80	D. Meyer (USA)	09.07.67
9:22.90	D. Meyer (USA)	29.07.67
9:19.00	D. Meyer (USA)	21.07.68
9:17.80	D. Meyer (USA)	04.08.68
9:10.40	D. Meyer (USA)	28.08.68

Shirley Babashoff (USA)

9:09.10	K. Moras (Australia)	01.03.70
9:02.40	K. Moras (Australia)	18.07.70
8:59.40	A. Simmons (USA)	10.09.71
8:58.10	S. Gould (Australia)	03.12.71
8:53.83	J. Harshbarger (USA)	06.08.72
8:53.68	K. Rothhammer (USA)	03.09.72
8:52.97	N. Calligaris (Italy)	09.09.73
8:50.10	J. Turrall (Australia)	05.01.74
8:47.50	J. Harshbarger (USA)	25.08.74
8:43.48	J. Turrall (Australia)	31.03.75
8:40.68	P. Thumer (GDR)	04.06.76
8:39.63	S. Babashoff (USA)	21.06.76
8:37.14	P. Thumer (GDR)	25.07.76
8:35.04	P. Thumer (GDR)	09.07.77
8:34.86	M. Ford (Australia)	07.01.78
8:31.30	M. Ford (Australia)	21.01.78
8:30.53	T. Wickham (Australia)	23.02.78
8:24.62	T. Wickham (Australia)	05.08.78
8:22.44	J. Evans (USA)	27.07.87
8:19.53	A. Moehring (GDR)	22.08.87
8:17.12	J. Evans (USA)	22.03.88
8:16.22	J. Evans (USA)	20.08.89

1500 Metres Freestyle

20:03.10	J. Koster (Holland)	27.07.57
19:25.70	I. Konrads (Australia)	14.01.59
19:23.60	J. Cederqvist (Sweden)	08.09.60
19:02.80	M. Rylander (Sweden)	27.06.61
18:44.00	C. House (USA)	16.08.62
18:30.50	P. Caretto (USA)	30.07.64
18:23.70	P. Caretto (USA)	12.08.65
18:12.90	P. Caretto (USA)	21.08.66
18:11.10	D. Meyer (USA)	09.07.67
17:50.20	D. Meyer (USA)	20.08.67
17:31.20	D. Meyer (USA)	21.07.68
17:19.90	D. Meyer (USA)	17.08.69
17:19.20	C. Calhoun (USA)	28.08.71
17:00.60	S. Gould (Australia)	12.12.71
16:56.90	S. Gould (Australia)	11.02.73
16:54.14	J. Harshbarger (USA)	25.08.73
16:49.90	J. Turrall (Australia)	09.12.73
16:48.20	J. Turrall (Australia)	09.01.74
16:43.40	J. Turrall (Australia)	13.07.74
16:39.28	J. Turrall (Australia)	03.08.74
16:33.94	J. Turrall (Australia)	25.08.74
16:24.60	A. Browne (USA)	21.08.77
16:14.93	T. Wickham (Australia)	08.02.78
16:06.63	T. Wickham (Australia)	25.02.79
16:04.49	K. Linehan (USA)	19.08.79
16:00.73	J. Evans (USA)	31.07.87
15:52.10	J. Evans (USA)	26.03.88

100 Metres Backstroke

1:12.90	J. Grinham (GBR)	05.12.56
1:12.50	P. Gould (New Zealand)	12.03.58
1:12.40	M. Edwards (GBR)	19.04.58
1:12.30	R. van Velsen (Holland)	20.07.58
1:11.90	J. Grinham (GBR)	23.07.58
1:11.70	R. van Velsen (Holland)	26.07.59
1:11.40	C. Cone (USA)	06.11.59
1:11.00	R. van Velsen (Holland)	12.06.60
1:10.90	R. van Velsen (Holland)	10.07.60
1:10.10	L. Burke (USA)	17.07.60
1:10.00	L. Burke (USA)	04.08.60
1:09.20	L. Burke (USA)	05.08.60
1:09.00	L. Burke (USA)	02.09.60
1:08.90	D. de Varona (USA)	28.07.63
1:08.60	C. Caron (France)	14.06.64
1:08.30	V. Duenkel (USA)	28.09.64

259

1:07.70	C. Ferguson (USA)	14.10.64
1:07.40	A. Fairlie (S Africa)	23.07.66
1:07.30	E. Tanner (Canada)	27.07.67
1:07.10	E. Tanner (Canada)	30.07.67
1:06.70	K. Muir (S Africa)	30.01.68
1:06.40	K. Muir (S Africa)	06.04.68
1:06.20	K. Hall (USA)	23.10.68
1:05.60	K. Hall (USA)	06.07.69
1:05.39	U. Richter (GDR)	18.08.73
1:04.99	U. Richter (GDR)	04.09.73
1:04.78	G. Cook (Canada)	31.01.74
1:04.43	U. Richter (GDR)	08.07.74
1:04.09	U. Richter (GDR)	22.08.74
1:03.30	U. Richter (GDR)	23.08.74
1:03.08	U. Richter (GDR)	24.08.74
1:02.98	U. Richter (GDR)	01.09.74
1:02.60	U. Richter (GDR)	14.03.76
1:01.62	K. Ender (GDR)	03.06.76
1:01.51	U. Richter (GDR)	05.06.76
1:01.51	R. Reinisch (GDR)	21.07.80
1:01.50	R. Reinisch (GDR)	22.07.80
1:00.86	R. Reinisch (GDR)	23.07.80
1:00.59	A. Kleber (GDR)	24.08.84

200 Metres Backstroke

2:39.90	P. Gould (New Zealand)	16.01.57
2:38.50	L. de Nijs (Holland)	17.05.57
2:37.40	C. von Saltza (USA)	01.08.58
2:37.10	S. Tanaka (Japan)	12.07.59
2:34.80	S. Tanaka (Japan)	02.04.60
2:33.50	L. Burke (USA)	15.07.60
2:33.30	S. Tanaka (Japan)	23.07.60
2:33.20	S. Tanaka (Japan)	30.07.61
2:32.10	S. Tanaka (Japan)	03.06.62
2:31.60	S. Tanaka (Japan)	29.07.62
2:29.60	S. Tanaka (Japan)	10.02.63
2:28.90	S. Tanaka (Japan)	18.02.63
2:28.50	S. Tanaka (Japan)	21.02.63
2:28.20	S. Tanaka (Japan)	04.08.63
2:27.40	C. Ferguson (USA)	28.09.64
2:27.10	K. Muir (S Africa)	25.07.66
2:26.40	K. Muir (S Africa)	18.08.66
2:24.40	E. Tanner (Canada)	26.07.67
2:24.10	K. Muir (S Africa)	26.01.68
2:23.80	K. Muir (S Africa)	21.07.68
2:21.50	S. Attwood (USA)	14.08.69
2:20.64	M. Belote (USA)	05.08.72
2:20.58	M. Belote (USA)	04.09.72
2:19.19	M. Belote (USA)	04.09.72
2:18.41	U. Richter (GDR)	07.07.74
2:17.35	U. Richter (GDR)	25.08.74
2:16.33	N. Garapick (Canada)	27.04.75
2:16.10	B. Treiber (GDR)	06.06.75
2:15.46	B. Treiber (GDR)	25.07.75
2:14.41	A. Stille (GDR)	29.02.76
2:13.50	A. Stille (GDR)	13.03.76
2:12.47	B. Treiber (GDR)	04.06.76
2:11.93	L. Jezek (USA)	24.08.78
2:11.77	R. Reinisch (GDR)	27.07.80
2:09.91	K. Sirch (GDR)	07.08.82
2:08.60	B. Mitchell (USA)	23.06.86

100 Metres Breaststroke

1:20.30	K. Beyer (GDR)	20.07.58
1:19.60	K. Beyer (GDR)	12.09.58
1:19.10	W. Urselmann (W Germany)	12.03.60
1:19.00	U. Kuper (GDR)	14.07.60
1:18.20	B. Gobel (GDR)	01.07.61
1:17.90	C. Kolb (USA)	11.07.64

1:17.20	S. Babanina (USSR)	03.09.64
1:16.50	S. Babanina (USSR)	11.05.65
1:15.70	G. Prosumenschikova (USSR)	17.07.66
1:15.60	C. Ball (USA)	28.12.66
1:15.60	C. Ball (USA)	07.07.67
1:14.80	C. Ball (USA)	31.07.67
1:14.60	C. Ball (USA)	19.08.67
1:14.20	C. Ball (USA)	25.08.67
1:13.58	C. Carr (USA)	02.09.72
1:12.91	R. Vogel (GDR)	22.08.74
1:12.55	C. Justen (W Germany)	23.08.74
1:12.28	R. Vogel (GDR)	01.09.74
1:11.93	C. Nitschke (GDR)	02.06.76
1:11.11	H. Anke (GDR)	22.07.76
1:10.86	H. Anke (GDR)	22.07.76
1:10.31	J. Bogdanova (USSR)	22.08.78
1:10.20	U. Geweniger (GDR)	26.05.80
1:10.11	U. Geweniger (GDR)	24.07.80
1:09.52	U. Geweniger (GDR)	10.04.81
1:09.39	U. Geweniger (GDR)	02.07.81
1:08.60	U. Geweniger (GDR)	08.09.81
1:08.51	U. Geweniger (GDR)	25.08.83
1:08.29	S. Gerasch (GDR)	23.08.84
1:08.11	S. Gerasch (GDR)	19.08.86
1:07.91	S. Hoerner (GDR)	21.08.87

200 Metres Breaststroke

2:52.50	A. den Haan (Holland)	18.05.57
2:51.90	A. den Haan (Holland)	03.08.57
2:51.30	A. den Haan (Holland)	04.08.57
2:50.30	A. Lonsbrough (GBR)	25.07.59
2:50.20	W. Urselmann (W Germany)	06.06.60
2:49.50	A. Lonsbrough (GBR)	27.08.60
2:48.00	K. Beyer (GDR)	05.08.61
2:47.70	G. Prosumenschikova (USSR)	11.04.64
2:45.40	G. Prosumenschikova (USSR)	17.05.64
2:45.30	G. Prosumenschikova (USSR)	12.09.65
2:40.80	G. Prosumenschikova (USSR)	22.08.66
2:40.50	C. Ball (USA)	09.07.67
2:39.50	C. Ball (USA)	20.08.67
2:38.50	C. Ball (USA)	26.08.68
2:37.89	A. Schott (GDR)	06.07.74
2:37.44	K. Linke (GDR)	19.08.74
2:34.99	K. Linke (GDR)	19.08.74
2:33.35	M. Koshevaia (USSR)	21.07.76

Linda Jezek (USA)   Allsport Photographic

2:33.32 J. Bogdanova (USSR)	07.04.78
2:33.11 L. Kachusite (USSR)	24.08.78
2:31.42 L. Kachusite (USSR)	24.08.78
2:31.09 S. Varganova (USSR)	30.03.79
2:28.36 L. Kachusite (USSR)	06.04.79
2:28.33 S. Hoerner (GDR)	05.06.85
2:28.20 S. Gerasch (GDR)	28.02.86
2:27.40 S. Hoerner (GDR)	18.08.86
2:27.27 A. Higson (Canada)	28.05.88
2:26.71 S. Hoerner (GDR)	21.09.88

100 Metres Butterfly

1:10.50 A. Voorbij (Holland)	04.08.57
1:09.60 N. Ramey (USA)	28.06.58
1:09.10 N. Ramey (USA)	02.09.59
1:08.90 J. Andrew (Australia)	02.04.61
1:08.80 M. Stewart (Canada)	12.08.61
1:08.20 S. Doerr (USA)	12.08.61
1:07.80 S. Doerr (USA)	02.08.62
1:07.30 M. Stewart (Canada)	28.07.62
1:06.50 K. Ellis (USA)	16.08.63
1:06.10 A. Kok (Holland)	01.09.63
1:05.10 A. Kok (Holland)	30.05.64
1:04.70 S. Stouder (USA)	16.10.64
1:04.50 A. Kok (Holland)	14.08.65
1:04.10 A. Jones (USA)	20.08.70
1:03.90 M. Aoki (Japan)	21.07.72
1:03.80 A. Gyarmati (Hungary)	31.08.72
1:03.34 M. Aoki (Japan)	01.09.72
1:03.05 K. Ender (GDR)	14.04.73
1:02.31 K. Ender (GDR)	14.07.73
1:02.09 R. Kother (GDR)	21.08.74
1:01.99 R. Kother (GDR)	22.08.74
1:01.88 R. Kother (GDR)	01.09.74
1:01.33 K. Ender (GDR)	09.06.75
1:01.24 K. Ender (GDR)	24.07.75
1:00.13 K. Ender (GDR)	04.06.76
1:00.13 K. Ender (GDR)	22.07.76
59.78 C. Knacke (GDR)	28.08.77
59.46 A. Pollack (GDR)	03.07.78
59.26 M. Meagher (USA)	11.04.80
57.93 M. Meagher (USA)	16.08.81

200 Metres Butterfly

2:40.50 N. Ramey (USA)	29.06.58
2:38.90 T. Lagerberg (Holland)	13.09.58
2:37.00 R. Collins (USA)	10.07.59
2:34.40 M. Heemskerk (Holland)	12.06.60
2:32.80 R. Collins (USA)	13.08.61
2:31.20 S. Finneran (USA)	19.08.62
2:30.70 S. Finneran (USA)	25.08.62
2:29.10 S. Pitt (USA)	27.07.63
2:28.10 S. Stouder (USA)	12.07.64
2:26.40 S. Stouder (USA)	02.08.64
2:26.30 K. Moore (USA)	15.08.65
2:25.80 A. Kok (Holland)	21.08.65
2:25.30 A. Kok (Holland)	12.09.65
2:22.50 A. Kok (Holland)	02.08.67
2:21.00 A. Kok (Holland)	25.08.67
2:20.70 K. Moe (USA)	11.07.70
2:19.30 A. Jones (USA)	22.08.70
2:18.60 K. Moe (USA)	07.08.71
2:18.40 E. Daniel (USA)	28.08.71
2:18.40 E. Daniel (USA)	28.08.71
2:18.40 E. Daniel (USA)	10.09.71
2:16.62 K. Moe (USA)	06.08.72
2:15.57 K. Moe (USA)	04.09.72
2:15.45 R. Kother (GDR)	08.09.73
2:13.76 R. Kother (GDR)	08.09.73

Tracy Caulkins (USA) Swimming Times

2:13.60 R. Gabriel (GDR)	14.03.76
2:12.84 R. Gabriel (GDR)	04.06.76
2:11.22 R. Gabriel (GDR)	05.06.76
2:11.20 A. Pollack (GDR)	09.04.78
2:09.87 A. Pollack (GDR)	04.07.78
2:09.87 T. Caulkins (USA)	26.08.78
2:09.77 M. Meagher (USA)	07.07.79
2:07.01 M. Meagher (USA)	16.08.79
2:06.37 M. Meagher (USA)	30.07.80
2:05.96 M. Meagher (USA)	13.01.81

200 Metres Individual Medley

2:27.80 C. Kolb (USA)	21.08.66
2:27.50 C. Kolb (USA)	08.07.67
2:26.10 C. Kolb (USA)	30.07.67
2:25.00 C. Kolb (USA)	18.08.67
2:23.50 C. Kolb (USA)	25.08.68
2:23.07 S. Gould (Australia)	28.08.72
2:23.01 K. Ender (GDR)	13.04.73
2:20.51 A. Huebner (GDR)	04.09.73
2:18.97 U. Tauber (GDR)	18.08.74
2:18.83 U. Tauber (GDR)	10.06.75
2:18.30 U. Tauber (GDR)	12.03.76
2:17.14 K. Ender (GDR)	05.06.76
2:16.96 U. Tauber (GDR)	10.07.77
2:15.95 U. Tauber (GDR)	20.08.77
2:15.85 U. Tauber (GDR)	28.08.77
2:15.09 T. Caulkins (USA)	02.08.78
2:14.07 T. Caulkins (USA)	20.08.78
2:13.69 T. Caulkins (USA)	05.01.80
2:13.00 P. Schneider (GDR)	24.05.80
2:11.73 U. Geweniger (GDR)	04.07.81

400 Metres Individual Medley

5:46.60 S. Ruuska (USA)	27.06.58
5:43.70 S. Ruuska (USA)	01.08.58
5:41.10 S. Ruuska (USA)	24.02.59
5:40.20 S. Ruuska (USA)	17.07.59
5:36.50 D. de Varona (USA)	15.07.60
5:34.50 D. de Varona (USA)	11.08.61
5:29.70 D. de Varona (USA)	02.06.62
5:27.40 S. Finneran (USA)	26.07.62
5:24.70 D. de Varona (USA)	26.07.62
5:21.90 S. Finneran (USA)	28.07.62
5:16.50 D. de Varona (USA)	10.03.64

261

5:14.90	D. de Varona (USA)	30.08.64
5:11.70	C. Kolb (USA)	09.07.67
5:09.70	C. Kolb (USA)	01.08.67
5:08.20	C. Kolb (USA)	19.08.67
5:04.70	C. Kolb (USA)	24.08.68
5:02.97	G. Neall (Australia)	31.08.72
5:01.10	A. Franke (GDR)	18.08.73
4:57.51	G. Wegner (GDR)	06.09.73
4:52.42	U. Tauber (GDR)	21.08.74
4:52.20	U. Tauber (GDR)	07.06.75
4:48.79	B. Treiber (GDR)	01.06.76
4:42.77	U. Tauber (GDR)	24.07.76
4:40.83	T. Caulkins (USA)	23.08.78
4:39.36	P. Schneider (GDR)	08.03.80
4:38.44	P. Schneider (GDR)	27.05.80
4:36.29	P. Schneider (GDR)	26.07.80
4:36.10	P. Schneider (GDR)	01.08.82

4×100 Metres Freestyle Relay

4:16.20	Australia	06.08.60
4:08.90	USA	03.09.60
4:08.50	USA	31.07.64
4:07.60	USA	28.09.64
4:03.80	USA	15.10.64
4:03.50	USA	19.08.67
4:01.10	USA	06.07.68
4:00.80	GDR	11.09.70
4:00.70	USA	09.09.71
3:58.11	USA	18.08.72
3:58.11	GDR	30.08.72
3:55.19	USA	30.08.72
3:52.45	GDR	08.09.73
3:51.99	USA	31.08.74
3:49.37	GDR	26.07.75
3:34.80	GDR	02.06.76

3:44.82	USA	25.07.76
3:43.43	USA	26.08.78
3:42.71	GDR	27.07.80
3:42.41	GDR	21.08.84
3:40.57	GDR	19.08.86

4×200 Metres Freestyle Relay

8:02.27	GDR	22.08.83
7:59.33	GDR	17.08.86
7:55.47	GDR	18.08.87

4×100 Metres Medley Relay

4:57.00	Holland	18.08.57
4:54.00	England	25.07.58
4:52.90	Holland	05.09.58
4:51.50	Holland	26.07.59
4:44.60	USA	06.09.59
4:41.10	USA	02.09.60
4:40.10	GDR	23.08.62
4:39.10	Holland	28.06.64
4:38.10	USA	04.07.64
4:34.60	USA	28.09.64
4:33.90	USA	18.10.64
4:30.00	USA	30.07.67
4:28.10	USA	14.09.68
4:27.40	USA	01.09.70
4:27.30	USA	11.09.71
4:25.34	USA	18.08.72
4:20.75	USA	03.09.72
4:16.84	GDR	04.09.73
4:13.78	GDR	24.08.74
4:13.41	GDR	05.06.76
4:07.95	GDR	18.07.76
4:06.76	GDR	20.07.80
4:05.88	GDR	06.08.82
4:03.69	GDR	24.08.84

Shane Gould (Australia)

Masters Swimming is Here to Stay

by Tony Warn (ASA & GB Masters Committee, Honorary Secretary)

Increasing numbers of people, from all walks of life and of varying abilities and ages now participate in "Masters Swimming". It is a fact that these activities have become the fast-growing section of our sport.

But what is Masters Swimming, and where did it all start?

The first part of this question is probably the easier to answer because those wise men and women of FINA (Federation International de Natation Amateur) — or, in plain English: the world governing body of swimming, have produced a definition!

"The Masters Swimming programme shall promote fitness, friendship, and understanding, through swimming among swimmers, with a minimum age limit of 25, both amateurs and professionals."

In effect, this means that if you are able to swim, and are over the age of 25, you are eligible to compete in Masters events. There is no need for you to be of any set standard. Of course, here in England, you must belong to a swimming club which is affiliated to the ASA (Amateur Swimming Association).

All Masters Swimming events are conducted under the same rules or laws which would normally apply to any other FINA or ASA event. No provision is made for age and, indeed, none would be expected.

Participants in Masters events compete against other swimmers in their own age-group. These groups are usually arranged in five-year bands, commencing with the 25 to 29 age-group and then running through to the 75s to 79s, and then 80 years and over. In the World Championships, and for World Records, the age-groups are still in the five-year age bands, but go through to the 85 to 89 age-group and then 90 and over. Yes, there are World Records for the 90 years and over group!

Although you are competing against swimmers of more or less your own age, you actually swim with competitors who are of a similar standard of ability to your own. The heats (races) are arranged so that the slowest (on submitted entry times), take part in the early heats. These heats then become progressively faster until the final one. Those swimmers who are unable to submit an entry time are either seeded below the slowest entrants in the competition, or below the slowest entrants in their age-group, although some of the events at National level require an entrant to submit a time on his entry form.

Individual events cover a range of distances. Freestyle events (that is, any stroke or style), are usually over 50, 100, 200 and 400 metres. Backstroke, breaststroke, and butterfly events are over 50, 100 and 200 metres. Individual medley events (where the competitor swims four equal length legs of the four strokes — butterfly, backstroke, breaststroke and freestyle), are usually contested over the 100, 200 and 400 metre distances.

Many Masters Swimmers would like to see longer distances catered for in National and District events. But these are precluded at present, on cost of pool and availability considerations.

Relay events are the races which probably give rise to the most interest and excitement. Often, teams will contain swimmers who have never taken part competitively in their lives, but who turn out to make the team up. Sometimes they will win a medal — and then they are *really* hooked. More often than not, these events are comprised of four swimmers, each covering 25 or 50 metres.

The seeding of competitors in time order, irrespective of age, from a competition viewpoint, is probably the greatest single strength and attraction of Masters Swimming, since everyone is able to participate on equal terms, and without embarrassment. It does not matter whether you were a former Olympian, a World Record Holder, or just a recent graduate from a "learn to swim" class — anyone can participate and win.

An interesting oddity about Masters is that everyone wants to get older! Well, they are always looking forward to getting into the next age-group up, where they will once again be the youngest swimmer!

Masters competitions range from races for mums and dads in local club events to World Championships. In between, there are open events promoted by clubs, county, district, National, Great Britain, and European Championships. There is also a thriving programme of inter-county and inter-club competitions.

Records also play an important role in the world of Masters Swimming. What with long course (50 metre pool length), and short course (25 metre pool length), 18 individual events for both ladies and men, and 14 age-groups, there are a total of 1,008 Individual World Records to go for! Add to this the European, Great Britain, English, District, and County Records, and then you have one huge incentive to train and compete.

Having mentioned incentives, why do people become involved in the Masters programme? Firstly, we have the competition swimmers who just love to train and compete — note: not necessarily to win — and have graduated by virtue of becoming older — over 25! Secondly, and probably the largest group are the ex-swimmers, competitive and otherwise, who have re-discovered the sport as their families grow up. The third group are the "learn to swim" and fitness swimming adults, who either want to improve their abilities or fitness. This group are probably the most enthusiastic.

The training régimes of Masters is even more varied than the groups of competitors involved. This training ranges from almost none at all — other than a social swim down at the local pool once or twice a week — right the way through to an incredible ten or a dozen sessions a week, which a budding Olympian would find gruelling. But the average is probably two or three sessions a week with a local club, or in a local authority fitness session.

The training needs of Masters, particularly those with respect to ageing, have recently come under discussion. As a result, a number of Seminars have taken place.

By its very nature, Masters is a social and friendly activity. Most gala sessions last for up to three hours, so there is plenty of time for one to meet old friends, to make new ones, and to gossip — in the kindest meaning of the word — and to recall the past, and make plans for future events.

Masters can be, and very often is, a family event. Not only are the spectators shouting for brothers and sisters, but the same verbal encouragement is heard for mums, dads, grandmas, grand-dads and great grandparents! In what other sport do you find three generations taking part in the same event, with the fourth and youngest looking on?

Let us go back to that earlier question. Where did it all start?

Well, Masters Swimming, as we know it today, had its roots in America in the late 1960s, and Masters Swimming International (MSI), who promoted the first "World Championships" , was constituted in 1983. It is this body to whom claims for World Records are submitted.

It is generally accepted that the first true Masters competitions in this country were staged by the Otter Swimming Club in the late '70s, but of course, in those days it was strictly an event for amateurs.

During the late '70s and early '80s, there was often much heated discussion as to whether professionals should be allowed to compete with amateurs in events. The strange thing was that, at the time, it was the so-called professionals — coaches and the like — who were the most vocal. But when, in 1985, they were finally given the go-ahead to compete, few actually bothered.

But leaving aside all the arguments about amateurs and professionals, it was without doubt the very generous sponsorship and help received from Sun Life that dragged English Masters Swimming into the 1980s. In 1984 we saw the introduction of National and District competitions. This mantle has now been taken over by the TSB, who, like their predecessors, are always looking for innovations and means of encouragement for Masters.

Both the ASA and Great Britain Federation, having seen the rapid growth of interest, formed Masters Committees in 1987. Later the same year, the first Great Britain Masters Championships were staged in Wales.

Currently, events in the UK are limited to swimming. But there is no doubt that, as the need arises and we learn from the experience of other countries, events for Divers, Water Polo players, and Synchronised Swimmers will be introduced.

One last question you might ask: how can I become involved in Masters Swimming?

Visit or call at your local swimming pool and ask if there is a Swimming Club. Contact the club to see if they have either a Masters Section or Masters facilities. But if this approach is not successful, contact the ASA directly for further details of your area.

Starting a Masters Club

by Jane Asher

It was in Norfolk that a small group of swimmers first felt there was a need for a Masters Club. This was decided because there were at least three Masters swimmers in that area who regularly travelled to the English Masters competitions and open meets — and they all belonged to different clubs. So a small committee was formed and its members embarked upon setting up the project.

The Secretary of the proposed club then made enquiries of the County Executive and was told to apply to the Secretary of the ASA, with the result that the District Secretary requested the name of the intended club and a copy of the rules that had been drafted. He put all this information before the District Executive at its next meeting, but of course, all this caused considerable delay.

However, after inspection, the plans were returned, with many suggestions for alterations and additions. The upshot was that the idea was finally accepted and an affiliation was granted.

There were a dozen clubs in the county who were catering for teenage competitors, but very few of them had time or space for adults, although several had among their members one or two Masters swimmers who were enthusiastic enough to train with the youngsters. But these were unable to compete in galas within the existing set-up.

As the English Masters scene widened, local meets proliferated, and other counties and clubs produced relay teams. Bristol and Motherwell Masters were fielding large and happy teams, and at last the Norfolk Masters could take part.

An inaugural meeting was held, to which all interested Masters swimmers were invited. The occasion was embellished by some swimming in a school pool, and over 30 people attended. A Chairman and Committee were elected, and thus the wheels were set in motion.

The primary object of the club was to set up a vehicle enabling people from different clubs to join together under one banner at Masters meets, and to make up relay teams. However, it was not exactly a club in the conventional sense, since it had no home base, no headquarters, and no regular training. Members were recruited on one-day clinics, having circularised all the local clubs, and fun day swims were held. But it was a nebulous body, and very difficult to cater for when transport was hired to distant meets.

Eventually, one training session a week was acquired. This took place at 7 a.m. on Saturdays, at the local pool in Norwich. At first, the cost of hiring this pool was somewhat prohibitive, since there were only about a dozen people who wanted, or were able, to take part on a regular basis. However, the management was approached and proved to be very sympathetic. But the problem of numbers of members was still there. Fortunately, there was a keen and growing body of triathletes in Norwich, and they enjoyed the idea of the early start. This helped solve the problem of numbers and also took care of the financial backing.

There are now various classes of swimmers:

1) Those people for whom the club was originally formed — the highly competitive individuals.

2) The regular trainers who seldom take part in galas, but who are very keen to improve their swimming. They take their training seriously and attend the one-hour clinics run for their benefit in the local pools, in addition to the Saturday morning sessions.

3) There are also other people, who are learning to swim in their later years, and who are equally serious about their new sport. They regularly attend beginners' classes and are being groomed for such competitions as the BLDSA postal swim.

The needs of all these different people are being met, but shortage of cash is still one of the main problems, as it usually is. Perhaps sponsorship is the answer, but there is little to offer in the way of advertisement. Possibly our successful swimmers will gain some publicity through the local media and will thus attract new members to the club.

British Masters Results/Records

Championships, 1988-89
Temple Cowley Pools, Oxford — 14/16 October, 1988

25/29 Years Age Group
Men

50 Metres Freestyle

1	P. Wood (Co Leeds)	25.23
2	A. Exton (Redditch)	25.26
3	M. Brett (Nottingham Leander)	25.36
4	N. Burrows (Portsmouth Northsea)	25.41
5	D. Emerson (Co Leeds)	25.75
6	C. Norrey (Camp Hill Edwardians)	25.77
7	T. Rose (Albyns)	25.89
	R. Collard (Oulton Broad)	
9	S. Thomas (Hull Olympic)	26.24
10	M. Oldershaw (Lutterworth & D)	26.30
11	I. Binns (Co Leeds)	26.55
12	R. Millington (Otter)	26.60
13	N. Tuson (Hoddesdon)	26.64
14	P. Goudie (Otter)	26.67
15	M. Edwards (RAF)	26.72
16	N. Fender (Lutterworth & D)	26.73
17	A. Alexander (Swindon Dolphins)	26.93
18	A. Cooper (Camp Hill Edwardians)	27.20
19	M. Courtney (Otter)	27.39
20	P. Boothman (Lutterworth & D)	27.48
21	M. Ellis (Radford)	27.53
22	J. Cardy (Co Oxford)	27.56
23	M. Barlow (Reading)	27.66
24	C. Milner (Lutterworth & D)	27.80
25	J. Anderson (Gloucester C)	28.57
26	G. Rees (Camden Swiss Cottage)	28.83
27	R. Petitt (Chippenham)	30.14
28	N. Wakelam (Swindon Dolphins)	30.55
29	S. Avanzato (Olympic Salamander)	32.10
30	M. Burnham (Olympic Salamander)	34.14

100 Metres Freestyle

1	N. Goldsworthy (Camden Swiss Cottage)	54.33
2	N. Burrows (Portsmouth Northsea)	54.89
3	C. Norrey (Camp Hill Edwardians)	55.51
4	D. Emerson (Co Leeds)	55.53
5	P. Wood (Co Leeds)	56.00
6	G. Sykes (Redditch)	56.50
7	R. Barker (Otter)	56.73
8	T. Rose (Albyns)	56.85
9	A. Exton (Redditch)	56.95
10	M. Thompson (Redditch)	57.89
11	S. Thomas (Hull Olympic)	58.23
12	R. Collard (Oulton Broad)	58.59
13	M. Oldershaw (Lutterworth & D)	58.83
14	P. Goudie (Otter)	58.95
15	A. Alexander (Swindon Dolphins)	59.60
	M. Courtney (Otter)	
17	B. Seddon (Reading)	59.62
18	R. Armitage (Co Bradford)	59.64
19	G. Acton (Co Bradford)	1:00.06
20	M. Barlow (Reading)	1:00.20
21	M. Maybury (Camp Hill Edwardians)	1:00.22
22	R. Millington (Otter)	1:00.44
23	J. Cardy (Co Oxford)	1:00.79
24	C. Milner (Lutterworth & D)	1:00.84

25	A. Cooper (Camp Hill Edwardians)	1:00.97
26	G. Rees (Camden Swiss Cottage)	1:03.06
27	J. Anderson (Gloucester C)	1:05.57
28	R. Petitt (Chippenham)	1:05.75
29	N. Wakelam (Swindon Dolphins)	1:08.16
30	S. Avanzato (Olympic Salamander)	1:13.29
31	M. Burnham (Olympic Salamander)	1:17.24
32	J. Harber (Swindon Dolphins)	1:19.31

200 Metres Freestyle

1	R. Brew (Maxwell)	1:58.28
2	N. Burrows (Portsmouth Northsea)	1:59.84
3	R. Barker (Otter)	2:03.66
4	A. Exton (Redditch)	2:06.56
5	H. Harcourt (Co Manchester)	2:07.17
6	P. Goudie (Otter)	2:09.90
7	S. Longstaff (Litchfield)	2:11.16
8	M. Barlow (Reading)	2:12.17
9	M. Courtney (Otter)	2:14.50
10	P. Mitchell (Co Newcastle)	2:17.16
11	J. Cardy (Co Oxford)	2:17.39
12	S. Shew (Spencer)	2:24.30
13	S. Avanzato (Olympic Salamander)	2:45.00
14	M. Burnham (Olympic Salamander)	2:51.93
15	J. Harber (Swindon Dolphins)	3:11.00

50 Metres Backstroke

1	M. Brett (Nottingham Leander)	29.77
2	C. Norrey (Camp Hill Edwardians)	29.94
3	M. Oldershaw (Lutterworth & D)	30.53
4	S. Allen (Otter)	30.67
5	M. Edwards (RAF)	31.63
6	J. Prowting (Otter)	32.29
7	P. Bootham (Lutterworth & D)	32.35
8	S. Shew (Spencer)	32.69
9	D. Dickens (Chippenham)	33.02
10	A. Cooper (Camp Hill Edwardians)	33.56
11	A. Alexander (Swindon Dolphins)	36.29
12	J. Anderson (Gloucester C)	36.69
13	M. Burnham (Olympic Salamander)	43.54

100 Metres Backstroke

1	M. Brett (Nottingham Leander)	1:04.07
2	S. Allen (Otter)	1:07.10
3	J. Prowting (Otter)	1:09.27
4	M. Oldershaw (Lutterworth & D)	1:09.62
5	P. Boothman (Lutterworth & D)	1:10.34
6	J. Cardy (Co Oxford)	1:11.70
7	S. Shew (Spencer)	1:12.97
8	A. Cooper (Camp Hill Edwardians)	1:15.84

50 Metres Breaststroke

1	N. Burrows (Portsmouth Northsea)	31.92
2	C. Milner (Lutterworth & D)	32.46
3	P. Morris (Basildon)	32.72
4	R. Collard (Oulton Broad)	32.90
5	N. Fender (Lutterworth & D)	33.42
6	M. Edwards (RAF)	33.90
7	S. Greenstein (Redbridge B)	34.17
8	M. France (Basingstoke)	34.22
9	J. Craib (RAF)	34.44

10	N. Wakelam (Swindon Dolphins)	34.49
11	J. Hutchinson (Camden Swiss Cottage)	34.53
12	N. McLeish (Belgrave)	35.44
13	M. Ellis (Radford)	35.65
14	P. Mitchell (Co Newcastle)	35.77
15	W. Harris (Beckenham)	35.81
16	G. Muller (Camden Swiss Cottage)	36.74
17	A. Richardson (Basingstoke)	36.99
18	S. Avanzato (Olympic Salamander)	42.68
19	J. Harber (Swindon Dolphins)	44.05
20	C. Edwards (Olympic Salamander)	48.66

100 Metres Breaststroke

1	N. Burrows (Portsmouth Northsea)	1:09.15
2	C. Milner (Lutterworth & D)	1:12.61
3	M. France (Basingstoke)	1:14.58
4	P. Wickenden (Hounslow B)	1:15.10
5	J. Craib (RAF)	1:15.50
6	S. Greenstein (Redbridge B)	1:15.72
7	P. Mitchell (Co Newcastle)	1:16.53
8	N. McLeish (Belgrave)	1:17.04
9	M. Watson (Cleveland Police)	1:17.21
10	N. Wakelam (Swindon Dolphins)	1:17.42
11	J. Hutchinson (Camden Swiss Cottage)	1:17.83
12	M. Ellis (Radford)	1:19.70
13	A. Richardson (Basingstoke)	1:23.68
14	G. Muller (Camden Swiss Cottage)	1:23.72
15	R. Petitt (Chippenham)	1:31.76
16	S. Avanzato (Olympic Salamander)	1:34.08
17	J. Harber (Swindon Dolphins)	1:37.90
18	M. Dicker (Reading)	1:39.81
19	C. Edwards (Olympic Salamander)	1:46.95

50 Metres Butterfly

1	P. Morris (Basildon)	26.76
2	M. Brett (Nottingham Leander)	27.80
3	T. Rose (Albyns)	27.93
	A. Morris (Colchester)	27.93
5	A. Exton (Redditch)	27.96
6	N. Burrows (Portsmouth Northsea)	28.14
7	I. Binns (Co Leeds)	28.34
8	N. Burnham (Otter)	28.78
9	J. Cardy (Co Oxford)	28.85
10	J. Craib (RAF)	28.87
11	M. Edwards (RAF)	29.28
12	M. Oldershaw (Lutterworth & D)	29.60
13	N. Fender (Lutterworth & D)	30.08
14	C. Milner (Lutterworth & D)	30.09
15	D. Dickens (Chippenham)	30.39
16	P. Wickenden (Hounslow B)	30.59
17	N. Wakelam (Swindon Dolphins)	32.03
18	R. Pettit (Chippenham)	33.82
19	M. Dicker (Reading)	41.64

100 Metres Butterfly

1	D. Emerson (Co Leeds)	59.71
2	A. Exton (Redditch)	1:00.74
3	N. Burrows (Portsmouth Northsea)	1:01.14
4	G. Sykes (Redditch)	1:01.25
5	S. Thomas (Hull Olympic)	1:01.35
6	P. Wood (Co Leeds)	1:02.32
7	T. Rose (Albyns)	1:02.59
8	H. Harcourt (Co Manchester)	1:04.07
9	M. Maybury (Camp Hill Edwardians)	1:04.31
10	I. Binns (Co Leeds)	1:04.72
11	J. Cardy (Co Oxford)	1:04.97
12	N. Fender (Lutterworth & D)	1:06.44
13	S. Longstaff (Lichfield)	1:07.21
14	P. Goudie (Otter)	1:07.34

15	C. Milner (Lutterworth & D)	1:07.66
16	M. Barlow (Reading)	1:08.70
17	P. Mitchell (Co Newcastle)	1:10:44
18	M. Courtney (Otter)	1:10.81
19	N. Wakelam (Swindon Dolphins)	1:13.03
20	A. Alexander (Swindon Dolphins)	1:13.23
21	G. Rees (Camden Swiss Cottage)	1:22.59
22	R. Petitt (Chippenham)	1:23.94

100 Metres Individual Medley

1	G. Sykes (Redditch)	1:03.00
2	N. Burrows (Portsmouth Northsea)	1:03.64
3	C. Norrey (Camp Hill Edwardians)	1:04.70
4	S. Thomas (Hull Olympic)	1:05.49
5	N. Fender (Lutterworth & D)	1:06.47
6	M. Oldershaw (Lutterworth & D)	1:07.21
7	R. Collard (Oulton Broad)	1:07.48
8	H. Harcourt (Co Manchester)	1:07.60
9	M. Edwards (RAF)	1:07.70
10	S. Allen (Otter)	1:08.35
11	P. Wickenden (Hounslow B)	1:08.54
12	C. Milner (Lutterworth & D)	1:08.99
13	A. Cooper (Camp Hill Edwardians)	1:11.17
14	M. Ellis (Radford)	1:11.24
15	D. Dickens (Chippenham)	1:11.26
16	J. Hutchinson (Camden Swiss Cottage)	1:12.39
17	A. Alexander (Swindon Dolphins)	1:13.35
18	P. Mitchell (Co Newcastle)	1:13.43
19	N. Wakelam (Swindon Dolphins)	1:13.76
20	S. Avanzato (Olympic Salamander)	1:28.67
21	M. Burnham (Olympic Salamander)	1:32.15

Women

50 Metres Freestyle

1	S. Peacock (Co Bradford)	28.70
2	A. Mezen (Albyns)	29.36
3	S. Broadbent (Newquay Cormorants)	29.88
4	J. Allman (Co Chester)	29.99
5	E. Brock (Enfield)	30.47
6	J. Slater (Spencer)	30.84
7	J. Beaumont (Co Bradford)	31.51
8	E. Adams (Bournemouth Dolphins)	31.54
9	V. Smith (Blackpool)	31.62
10	C. Barlow (Reading)	32.06
11	A. Cox (Bramcote Hills)	32.50
12	S. Bulpin (Reading)	33.31
13	E. Edwards (Olympic Salamander)	35.73
14	J. Holliday (Swindon Dolphins)	40.25
15	J. Lane (Kenilworth)	42.67

100 Metres Freestyle

1	L. McLeish (Belgrave)	1:02.29
2	S. Peacock (Co Bradford)	1:04.02
3	S. Broadbent (Newquay Cormorants)	1:04.20
4	E. Brock (Enfield)	1:05.68
5	J. Slater (Spencer)	1:07.53
6	J. Allman (Co Chester)	1:07.62
7	J. Robinson (Bramcote Hills)	1:08.74
8	E. Adams (Bournemouth Dolphins)	1:09.37
9	A. Cox (Bramcote Hills)	1:10.87
10	C. Barlow (Reading)	1:11.82
11	C. Fox (Ashford T)	1:13.26
12	E. Edwards (Olympic Salamander)	1:22.80

200 Metres Freestyle

1	S. Broadbent (Newquay Cormorants)	2:19.21
2	E. Brock (Enfield)	2:19.77
3	S. Peacock (Co Bradford)	2:25.44

4 J. Robinson (Bramcote Hills)   2:26.51
5 J. Slater (Spencer)   2:29.54
6 J. Allman (Co Chester)   2:29.69
7 A. Cox (Bramcote Hills)   2:39.88
8 C. Fox (Ashford T)   2:41.10
9 E. Edwards (Olympic Salamander)   3:08.16

50 Metres Backstroke
1 E. Brock (Enfield)   34.64
2 S. Broadbent (Newquay Cormorants)   34.70
3 K. Wilkinson (Kenilworth)   35.70
4 S. Peacock (Co Bradford)   36.57
5 J. Beaumont (Co Bradford)   38.69
6 L. Davies (Otter)   41.20
7 J. Lane (Kenilworth)   47.73
8 E. Edwards (Olympic Salamander)   49.23

100 Metres Backstroke
1 S. Jenner (Camden Swiss Cottage)   1:13.54
2 S. Broadbent (Newquay Cormorants)   1:14.15
3 J. Allman (Co Chester)   1:15.73
4 E. Brock (Enfield)   1:16.68
5 K. Wilkinson (Kenilworth)   1:18.40
6 A. Cox (Bramcote Hills)   1:22.31
7 S. Peacock (Co Bradford)   1:22.79
8 J. Harber (Swindon Dolphins)   1:28.04
9 L. Davies (Otter)   1:28.13

50 Metres Breaststroke
1 S. Peacock (Co Bradford)   37.82
2 S. Broadbent (Newquay Cormorants)   38.88
3 J. Slater (Spencer)   39.01
4 L. Hogarth (Hull Masters)   39.05
5 E. Adams (Bournemouth Dolphins)   39.84
6 E. Brock (Enfield)   40.13
7 J. Robinson (Bramcote Hills)   40.72
8 J. Sotheby (Co Bradford)   41.34
9 J. Beaumont (Co Bradford)   42.20
10 V. Smith (Blackpool)   42.27
11 C. Barlow (Reading)   42.50
12 L. Davies (Otter)   42.88
13 J. Holliday (Swindon Dolphins)   47.62
14 E. Edwards (Olympic Salamander)   50.83

100 Metres Breaststroke
1 S. Broadbent (Newquay Cormorants)   1:23.15
2 S. Peacock (Co Bradford)   1:24.06
3 J. Slater (Spencer)   1:24.42
4 L. Hogarth (Hull Masters)   1:24.62
5 E. Adams (Bournemouth Dolphins)   1:26.22
6 E. Brock (Enfield)   1:26.36
7 J. Robinson (Bramcote Hills)   1:27.36
8 L. Robinson (Maxwell)   1:29.66
9 L. Davies (Otter)   1:34.32
10 J. Holliday (Swindon Dolphins)   1:44.37

50 Metres Butterfly
1 E. Brock (Enfield)   31.82
2 S. Peacock (Co Bradford)   32.23
3 L. McLeish (Belgrave)   32.35
4 S. Broadbent (Newquay Cormorants)   32.51
5 J. Allman (Co Chester)   33.26
6 E. Adams (Bournemouth Dolphins)   34.20
7 K. Wilkinson (Kenilworth)   34.57
8 J. Slater (Spencer)   34.91
9 R. Binns (Barnet Copthall)   35.89
10 E. Edwards (Olympic Salamander)   45.73

100 Metres Butterfly
1 S. Jenner (Camden Swiss Cottage)   1:07.21
2 E. Brock (Enfield)   1:09.89

3 S. Broadbent (Newquay Cormorants)   1:10.85
4 S. Peacock (Co Bradford)   1:13.63
5 J. Sotheby (Co Bradford)   1:17.00
6 K. Wilkinson (Kenilworth)   1:17.22

100 Metres Individual Medley
1 L. McLeish (Belgrave)   1:11.18
2 S. Broadbent (Newquay Cormorants)   1:12.41
3 E. Brock (Enfield)   1:13.39
4 K. Wilkinson (Kenilworth)   1:16.18
5 S. Peacock (Co Bradford)   1:17.08
6 J. Slater (Spencer)   1:17.34
7 R. Binns (Barnet Copthall)   1:18.00
8 E. Adams (Bournemouth Dolphins)   1:19.01
9 J. Robinson (Bramcote Hills)   1:19.81
10 C. Fox (Ashford T)   1:23.99
11 E. Edwards (Olympic Salamander)   1:35.26

25/34 Years Age Group
Men

4×25 Metres Freestyle Club Relay
1 Co Leeds   1:43.03
2 Otter (white)   1:43.35
3 Lutterworth & D   1:44.42
4 RAF   1:45.29
5 Camp Hill Edwardians   1:45.66
6 Otter (black)   1:45.81
7 Co Bradford   1:46.19
8 Spencer   1:47.29
9 Redditch   1:48.68
10 Redbridge B   1:48.96
11 Swindon Dolphins   1:51.65
12 Nottingham Leander   1:51.89
13 Royal Navy   1:52.75
14 Kenilworth   1:59.40
15 Reading   2:02.67
16 Olympic Salamander   2:17.16

4×25 Metres Medley Club Relay
1 Lutterworth & D   1:56.70
2 Co Leeds   1:57.02
3 Otter (white)   1:57.85
4 RAF   1:59.05
5 Camp Hill Edwardians   1:59.71

Sue Jenner

6	Co Bradford	1:59.96
7	Swindon Dolphins	2:00.00
8	Redbridge B	2:00.21
9	Otter (black)	2:01.46
10	Spencer	2:02.98
11	Co Coventry	2:03.33
12	Nottingham Leander	2:06.47
13	Kenilworth	2:08.01
14	Reading	2:11.15
15	Royal Navy	2:16.12
16	Olympic Salamander	2:47.72
	Redditch	DIS

Women

4×25 Metres Freestyle Club Relay

1	Co Bradford	2:02.89
2	Spencer 'B'	2:04.42
3	Bramcote Hills	2:10.42
4	Reading	2:11.50
5	Poole	2:15.58
6	Olympic Salamander	2:51.79
	Albyns	DIS

4×25 Metres Medley Club Relay

1	Spencer 'A'	2:19.80
2	Co Bradford	2:22.72
3	Albyns	2:23.83
4	Reading	2:27.03
5	Bramcote Hills	2:27.62
6	Poole	2:35.64
7	Spencer 'B'	2:39.92
8	Swindon Dolphins	2:45.52
9	Olympic Salamander	3:38.81

30/34 Years Age Group
Men

50 Metres Freestyle

1	G. Potter (Redbridge B)	25.22
2	B. Ford (Nottingham Leander)	25.69
3	K. Parfoot (Portsmouth Northsea)	25.77
4	W. Hempel (Spencer)	26.22
5	P. Tainty (Camp Hill Edwardians)	26.60
6	S. Nash (Heath Town)	26.64
7	P. Kirk (Otter)	26.80
8	S. Burcham (Kenilworth)	27.03
9	D. Shamp (Spencer)	27.19
10	D. Butler (Spencer)	27.33
11	W. Hayes (Bo Ealing)	27.38
12	K. Sansby (Spencer)	28.21
13	D. Miller (Otter)	28.32
14	A. Burgess (Bournemouth Dolphins)	28.41
15	N. Crowe (Gloucester C)	29.25
16	T. Rowley (Redditch)	32.46
17	G. Robertson (Reading)	32.61

100 Metres Freestyle

1	G. Potter (Redbridge B)	55.30
2	K. Parfoot (Portsmouth Northsea)	56.07
3	W. Hempel (Spencer)	56.76
4	T. Clark (Nottingham Northern)	58.21
5	B. Ford (Nottingham Leander)	58.27
6	P. Tainty (Camp Hill Edwardians)	58.56
7	R. Hughes (Royal Navy)	59.04
8	P. Kirk (Otter)	59.68
9	W. Hayes (Bo Ealing)	59.88
10	T. Allman (Co Chester)	1:00.20
11	A. Burgess (Bournemouth Dolphins)	1:01.08

12	D. Shamp (Spencer)	1:01.31
13	K. Sansby (Spencer)	1:01.32
14	A. Mordue (Bo Sunderland)	1:02.32
15	D. Butler (Spencer)	1:02.72
16	S. Gershon (Harrow & Wealdstone)	1:06.47
17	G. Robertson (Reading)	1:10.94

100 Metres Freestyle

1	K. Parfoot (Portsmouth Northsea)	2:05.08
2	W. Hempel (Spencer)	2:05.60
3	D. Cometson (RAF)	2:10.73
4	T. Allman (Co Chester)	2:11.36
5	A. Burgess (Co Manchester)	2:12.35
6	W. Hayes (Bo Ealing)	2:12.92
7	K. Sansby (Spencer)	2:15.59
8	P. Kirk. (Otter)	2:16.68
9	A. Mordue (Bo Sunderland)	2:20.44
10	D. Butler (Spencer)	2:22.17
11	S. Gershon (Harrow & Wealdstone)	2:25.45
12	G. Robertson (Reading)	2:37.08
13	R. Dennis (Bristol Masters)	2:58.99

50 Metres Backstroke

1	K. Parfoot (Portsmouth Northsea)	29.27
2	T. Clark (Nottingham Northern)	30.00
3	N. McMorrin (Watford)	30.67
4	S. Burcham (Kenilworth)	30.71
5	D. Miller (Otter)	30.89
6	R. Hughes (Royal Navy)	31.24
7	T. Allman (Co Chester)	32.60
8	P. Williams (Kenilworth)	34.70
9	S. Gershon (Harrow & Wealdstone)	34.80
10	D. Butler (Spencer)	34.81

100 Metres Backstroke

1	K. Parfoot (Portsmouth Northsea)	1:03.07
2	S. Burcham (Kenilworth)	1:04.56
3	N. McMorrin (Watford)	1:07.25
4	T. Clark (Nottingham Northern)	1:07.41
5	R. Hughes (Royal Navy)	1:07.65
6	D. Hamm (Brighton)	1:07.80
7	D. Miller (Otter)	1:08.97
8	A. Burgess (Bournemouth Dolphins)	1:09.59
9	N. Smith (Hambleton)	1:09.83
10	P. Kirk (Otter)	1:10.42
11	S. Gershon (Harrow & Wealdstone)	1:13.92
12	D. Shamp (Spencer)	1:13.96
13	F. Bolton (Macclesfield)	1:16.84

50 Metres Breaststroke

1	B. O'Brien (Wellingborough)	32.99
2	M. O'Connell (Co Southampton)	33.14
3	P. Davis (Nottingham Leander)	33.97
4	F. Bolton (Macclesfield)	34.75
5	K. Sansby (Spencer)	35.21
6	D. Cometson (RAF)	35.58
7	G. O'Connell (Gloucester C)	35.71
8	M. How (Bo Waltham Forest)	35.84
9	D. Hamm (Brighton)	36.60
10	M. Gregory (Bristol Masters)	38.81
11	R. Dennis (Bristol Masters)	39.15
12	T. Rowley (Redditch)	42.38

100 Metres Breaststroke

1	B. O'Brien (Wellingborough)	1:10.84
2	M. O'Connell (Co Southampton)	1:12.65
3	P. Davis (Nottingham Leander)	1:14.39
4	K. Sansby (Spencer)	1:16.20
5	F. Bolton (Macclesfield)	1:16.51
6	D. Butler (Spencer)	1:17.90

7	G. O'Connell (Gloucester C)	1:19.61
8	M. How (Bo Waltham Forest)	1:20.19
9	K. McGhie (Bo Ealing)	1:22.13
10	R. Dennis (Bristol Masters)	1:25.63
11	M. Gregory (Bristol Masters)	1:25.97

50 Metres Butterfly

1	K. Parfoot (Portsmouth Northsea)	28.09
2	B. O'Brien (Wellingborough)	28.32
3	T. Clark (Nottingham Northern)	28.36
4	D. Weetman (RAF)	29.46
5	S. Burcham (Kenilworth)	29.83
6	N. Smith (Hambleton)	30.01
7	K. Sansby (Spencer)	30.05
8	D. Shamp (Spencer)	30.29
9	A. Mordue (Bo Sunderland)	30.96
10	F. Bolton (Macclesfield)	32.18
11	M. Gregory (Bristol Masters)	35.71

100 Metres Butterfly

1	T. Clark (Nottingham Northern)	1:02.64
2	P. Tainty (Camp Hill Edwardians)	1:03.68
3	K. Parfoot (Portsmouth Northsea)	1:03.73
4	S. Nash (Heath Town)	1:03.92
5	N. Smith (Hambleton)	1:04.89
6	B. O'Brien (Wellingborough)	1:04.99
7	D. Weetman (RAF)	1:06.60
8	S. Burcham (Kenilworth)	1:07.93
9	D. Shamp (Spencer)	1:08.65
10	A. Burgess (Bournemouth Dolphins)	1:09.23
11	K. Sansby (Spencer)	1:09.73
12	D. Hunt (Poole)	1:11.86
13	N. Crowe (Gloucester C)	1:12.60
14	R. Dennis (Bristol Masters)	1:20.30

100 Metres Individual Medley

1	T. Clark (Nottingham Northern)	1:05.45
2	B. O'Brien (Wellingborough)	1:07.06
3	D. Miller (Otter)	1:07.36
4	A. Burgess (Bournemouth Dolphins)	1:09.06
5	D. Cometson (RAF)	1:09.43
6	W. Hempel (Spencer)	1:10.70
7	K. Sansby (Spencer)	1:10.74
8	S. Burcham (Kenilworth)	1:10.91
9	D. Butler (Spencer)	1:11.01
10	S. Gershon (Harrow & Wealdstone)	1:14.84
11	D. Hunt (Poole)	1:17.00

Women

50 Metres Freestyle

1	A. Jones (Camden Swiss Cottage)	28.40
2	C. Dixon (Hartlepool)	30.20
3	C. Scovell (Worthing)	30.40
4	L. Robinson (Spencer)	31.02
	S. Crissell-Falla (Guernsey)	
6	A. Budynkiewicz (Poole)	31.69
7	L. Weetman (Witney & D)	31.77
8	C. Cox (Bristol Masters)	32.42
9	H. Gore (Poole)	32.69
10	J. Seddon (Co Liverpool)	32.82
11	C. McQuade (Co Bradford)	32.87
12	A. Frost (Bournemouth Dolphins)	33.41
13	A. Doyle (Spencer)	33.88
14	J. Cullin (Falcon)	33.97
15	J. Butler (Harrow & Wealdstone)	34.35
16	M. Price (Burnley)	34.54
17	C. Smith (Weyport Olympians)	35.30
18	H. Sharp (Rugby)	36.13
19	L. Crook (Caldicot)	36.16

20	P. Jones (Gloucester C)	37.09
21	J. Kirk (Bo Burnley CATS)	38.73
22	Z. Rowley (Redditch)	45.32

100 Metres Freestyle

1	A. Jones (Camden Swiss Cottage)	1:01.87
2	C. Scovell (Worthing)	1:07.18
3	L. Robinson (Spencer)	1:07.50
4	S. Crissell-Falla (Guernsey)	1:07.62
5	C. Dixon (Hartlepool)	1:08.04
6	L. Weetman (Witney & D)	1:08.76
7	C. Cox (Bristol Masters)	1:10.90
8	C. Clark (Bramcote Hills)	1:13.00
9	A. Frost (Bournemouth Dolphins)	1:15.19
10	J. Seddon (Co Liverpool)	1:15.29
11	M. Price (Bo Burnley CATS)	1:16.62
12	A. Doyle (Spencer)	1:19.14
13	C. Smith (Weyport Olympians)	1:21.10
14	H. Sharp (Rugby)	1:22.26
15	L. Crook (Caldicot)	1:22.96

200 Metres Freestyle

1	A. Jones (Camden Swiss Cottage)	2:15.72
2	L. Robinson (Spencer)	2:24.62
3	S. Crissell-Falla (Guernsey)	2:25.27
4	C. Cox (Bristol Masters)	2:37.60
5	H. Gore (Poole)	2:40.03
6	C. Clark (Bramcote Hills)	2:40.76
7	A. Frost (Bournemouth Dolphins)	2:45.47
8	M. Price (Bo Burnley CATS)	2:47.70
9	H. Sharp (Rugby)	2:50.93
10	L. Crook (Caldicot)	3:05.46
11	C. Smith (Weyport Olympians)	3:09.85

50 Metres Backstroke

1	C. Dixon (Hartlepool)	34.96
2	A. Budynkiewicz (Poole)	36.23
3	J. Barnes (Radford)	37.07
4	J. Nickerson (Co Coventry)	37.09
5	D. Biddle (Spencer)	37.49
6	J. Britton (Gloucester C)	38.85
7	C. Clark (Bramcote Hills)	40.45
8	C. McQuade (Co Bradford)	42.09
9	M. Price (Bo Burnley CATS)	42.55

100 Metres Backstroke

1	C. Dixon (Hartlepool)	1:16.36
2	D. Biddle (Spencer)	1:21.13
3	J. Seddon (Co Liverpool)	1:22.10
4	A. Budynkiewicz (Poole)	1:22.54
5	L. Robinson (Spencer)	1:24.76
6	J. Nickerson (Co Coventry)	1:25.30
7	J. Butler (Harrow & Wealdstone)	1:25.87
8	A. Doyle (Spencer)	1:28.69
9	H. Sharp (Rugby)	1:37.80

50 Metres Breaststroke

1	J. Barnes (Radford)	37.46
2	H. Gore (Poole)	38.60
3	J. Nickerson (Co Coventry)	40.42
4	A. Frost (Bournemouth Dolphins)	40.89
5	C. Cox (Bristol Masters)	41.03
6	J. Britton (Gloucester C)	42.38
7	C. McQuade (Co Bradford)	44.47
8	J. Cullin (Falcon)	44.55
9	P. Jones (Gloucester C)	45.00
10	M. Price (Bo Burnley CATS)	45.20
11	J. Kirk (Bo Burnley CATS)	48.49

100 Metres Breaststroke

1	J. Barnes (Radford)	1:23.36

2	H. Gore (Poole)	1:23.44
3	C. Cox (Bristol Masters)	1:27.87
4	A. Frost (Bournemouth Dolphins)	1:29.37
5	J. Kirk (Bo Burnley CATS)	1:42.36

50 Metres Butterfly

1	C. Scovell (Worthing)	32.15
2	A. Jones (Camden Swiss Cottage)	32.40
3	S. Crissell-Falla (Guernsey)	33.67
4	L. Robinson (Spencer)	34.41
5	A. Budynkiewicz (Poole)	34.95
6	H. Gore (Poole)	35.10
7	D. Biddle (Spencer)	35.13
8	J. Barnes (Radford)	36.03
9	J. Seddon (Co Liverpool)	36.26
10	A. Bourne (Camp Hill Edwardians)	36.32
11	A. Doyle (Spencer)	36.78
12	C. Clark (Bramcote Hills)	36.84
13	C. McQuade (Co Bradford)	37.91
14	L. Crook (Caldicot)	39.04
15	M. Price (Bo Burnley CATS)	41.45
16	H. Sharp (Rugby)	45.94
17	J. Kirk (Bo Burnley CATS)	45.98

100 Metres Butterfly

1	S. Crissell-Falla (Guernsey)	1:15.29
2	L. Robinson (Spencer)	1:15.75
3	C. Scovell (Worthing)	1:16.89
4	A. Budynkiewicz (Poole)	1:23.05
5	C. Clark (Bramcote Hills)	1:24.81
6	L. Crook (Caldicot)	1:30.99
A.	Doyle (Spencer)	DNF

100 Metres Individual Medley

1	A. Jones (Camden Swiss Cottage)	1:10.52
2	J. Barnes (Radford)	1:16.82
3	C. Cox (Bristol Masters)	1:18.00
4	H. Gore (Poole)	1:19.87
5	C. Scovell (Worthing)	1:22.33
6	C. Clark (Bramcote Hills)	1:23.76
7	C. McQuade (Co Bradford)	1:24.49
8	M. Price (Bo Burnley CATS)	1:26.16
9	L. Crook (Caldicot)	1:34.81
10	H. Sharp (Rugby)	1:37.13
11	J. Kirk (Bo Burnley CATS)	1:38.59

35/39 Years Age Group Men

50 Metres Freestyle

1	J. Mills (Co London Police)	26.65
2	D. McCartney (Ipswich)	27.06
3	S. Johnson (Co Bradford)	27.81
4	A. Chapman (Bristol Masters)	28.09
5	S. Hatfield (Kenilworth)	28.20
6	N. Daymond-John (Deben)	28.34
7	C. Thompson (Co Liverpool)	29.13
8	T. Spray (Shiverers)	29.50
9	I. Mears (Swallowtails)	29.51
	R. Lock (Lutterworth & D)	
11	N. Minns (Hounslow B)	29.65
12	K. Tindall (Hull Masters)	29.68
13	I. Gordon (Bournemouth Dolphins)	29.83
14	B. Bloor (Kingston Royals)	30.28
15	V. Wadley (Spencer)	30.67
16	R. Jones (Royal Navy)	30.74
17	L. Stevens (Stevenage)	31.90
18	T. Carey (Royal Navy)	34.11
19	J. Bayliss (Olympic Salamander)	36.50

100 Metres Freestyle

1	N. Daymond-John (Deben)	1:01.45
2	D. McCartney (Ipswich)	1:01.46
3	S. Bratt (Bristol Masters)	1:02.08
4	A. Chapman (Bristol Masters)	1:02.60
5	S. Hatfield (Kenilworth)	1:03.85
6	S. Johnson (Co Bradford)	1:04.27
7	I. Mears (Swallowtails)	1:04.49
8	T. Spray (Shiverers)	1:05.05
9	N. Minns (Hounslow B)	1:05.57
10	K. Tindall (Hull)	1:06.66
11	V. Wadley (Spencer)	1:07.05
12	M. Appleby (Barnet Copthall)	1:08.33
13	R. Jones (Royal Navy)	1:09.17
14	T. Carey (Royal Navy)	1:17.18
15	J. Watts (Rugby)	1:29.64

200 Metres Freestyle

1	A. Chapman (Bristol Masters)	2:18.75
2	N. Daymond-John (Deben)	2:20.21
3	N. Minns (Hounslow B)	2:24.90
4	D. McCartney (Ipswich)	2:25.44
5	I. Mears (Swallowtails)	2:25.70
6	T. Spray (Shiverers)	2:26.82
7	V. Wadley (Spencer)	2:30.36
8	M. Appleby (Barnet Copthall)	2:31.37
9	R. Jones (Royal Navy)	2:35.78
10	T. Carey (Royal Navy)	2:56.12
11	J. Watts (Rugby)	3:25.88

50 Metres Backstroke

1	S. Hatfield (Kenilworth)	34.06
2	S. Johnson (Co Bradford)	34.28
3	J. Noble (Blackpool)	35.20
4	N. Daymond-John (Deben)	35.35
5	A. Chapman (Bristol Masters)	35.40
6	E. Feakes (Hastings Seagulls)	36.67
7	B. Bloor (Kingston Royals)	37.45
8	I. Mears (Swallowtails)	37.66
9	J. Bayliss (Olympic Salamander)	47.09

100 Metres Backstroke

1	N. Daymond-John (Deben)	1:15.48
2	S. Johnson (Co Bradford)	1:18.03
3	A. Chapman (Bristol Masters)	1:18.91
4	I. Mears (Swallowtails)	1:21.64
5	E. Feakes (Hastings Seagulls)	1:24.62
6	J. Bayliss (Olympic Salamander)	1:43.36

50 Metres Breaststroke

1	S. Bratt (Bristol Masters)	35.02
2	N. Daymond-John (Deben)	35.81
3	I. Gordon (Bournemouth Dolphins)	36.78
4	S. Johnson (Co Bradford)	37.97
5	J. Noble (Blackpool)	38.00
6	S. Hatfield (Kenilworth)	39.23
7	L. Stevens (Stevenage)	40.62
8	I. Mears (Swallowtails)	41.15
9	T. Carey (Royal Navy)	41.33
10	J. Bayliss (Olympic Salamander)	
	R. Gutteridge (Poole)	42.57

100 Metres Breaststroke

1	P. Taylor (Cleveland Police)	1:15.89
2	S. Bratt (Bristol Masters)	1:16.24
3	N. Daymond-John (Deben)	1:20.86
4	J. Noble (Blackpool)	1:21.22
5	I. Gordon (Bournemouth Dolphins)	1:21.43
6	I. Mears (Swallowtails)	1:28.60
7	T. Carey (Royal Navy)	1:30.68

8	L. Stevens (Stevenage)	1:33.22
9	J. Bayliss (Olympic Salamander)	1:33.25
10	R. Gutteridge (Poole)	1:34.39
11	J. Watts (Rugby)	1:58.19

50 Metres Butterfly

1	J. Mills (Co London Police)	27.56
2	A. Chapman (Bristol Masters)	29.81
3	S. Johnson (Co Bradford)	30.21
4	S. Hatfield (Kenilworth)	30.36
5	J. Noble (Blackpool)	31.06
6	I. Mears (Swallowtails)	32.76
7	L. Stevens (Stevenage)	37.54
8	J. Bayliss (Olympic Salamander)	44.69

100 Metres Butterfly

1	J. Mills (Co London Police)	1:02.14
2	A. Chapman (Bristol Masters)	1:07.28
3	S. Bratt (Bristol Masters)	1:10.27
4	N. Minns (Hounslow B)	1:10.82
5	S. Hatfield (Kenilworth)	1:11.46
6	D. McCartney (Ipswich)	1:13.00
7	J. Noble (Blackpool)	1:13.06
8	T. Spray (Shiverers)	1:13.20
9	I. Mears (Swallowtails)	1:14.31

100 Metres Individual Medley

1	N. Daymond-John (Deben)	1:09.65
2	S. Bratt (Bristol Masters)	1:11.80
3	S. Johnson (Co Bradford)	1:12.01
4	S. Hatfield (Kenilworth)	1:12.71
5	J. Noble (Blackpool)	1:13.08
6	C. Thompson (Co Liverpool)	1:15.43
7	I. Mears (Swallowtails)	1:15.96
8	R. Lock (Lutterworth & D)	1:20.25

9	L. Stevens (Stevenage)	1:25.62
10	T. Carey (Royal Navy)	1:29.08
11	R. Jones (Royal Navy)	1:29.90
12	J. Bayliss (Olympic Salamander)	1:37.31

Women

50 Metres Freestyle

1	R. Thomson (Kingston Royal)	30.80
2	L. Powell (Barnet Copthall)	31.80
3	S. Magnall (Bo Burnley CATS)	32.44
4	M. Flook (Reading)	32.48
5	W. Coley (Loughborough)	32.92
6	J. Page (Maxwell)	33.47
7	A. Neale (Camden Swiss Cottage)	33.61
8	B. Bland (Hartlepool)	35.64
9	A. Mellet (Darlington)	36.70
10	R. Knight (Swindon Dolphins)	38.37
11	S. Dawes (Reading)	38.42
12	S. Verball (Olympic Salamander)	47.32

100 Metres Freestyle

1	L. Powell (Barnet Copthall)	1:09.83
2	R. Thomson (Kingston Royals)	1:11.00
3	S. Magnall (Bo Burnley CATS)	1:12.68
4	A. Cork (Slough Dolphins)	1:13.57
5	W. Coley (Loughborough)	1:15.28
6	G. Cackett (Northampton)	1:16.77
7	J. Page (Maxwell)	1:16.83
8	A. Mellett (Darlington)	1:24.45
9	B. Bland (Hartlepool)	1:24.47

200 Metres Freestyle

1	A. Cork (Slough Dolphins)	2:38.10

John Mills

2	L. Powell (Barnet Copthall)	2:40.19
3	M. Purser (Bristol Masters)	2:47.88
4	W. Coley (Loughborough)	2:52.58
5	J. Page (Maxwell)	3:06.66
6	A. Mellett (Darlington)	3:12.32

50 Metres Backstroke

1	A. Cork (Slough Dolphins)	35.40
2	M. Flook (Reading)	35.83
3	S. Cummings (Maxwell)	38.97
4	S. Bloor (Kingston Royals)	40.83
5	B. Bland (Hartlepool)	41.79
6	J. Page (Maxwell)	45.75
7	A. Mellett (Darlington)	45.98
8	S. Verball (Olympic Salamander)	56.91

100 Metres Backstroke

1	A. Cork (Slough Dolphins)	1:15.81
2	M. Flook (Reading)	1:19.57
3	B. Bland (Hartlepool)	1:37.35
4	S. Dawes (Reading)	1:53.98

50 Metres Breaststroke

1	G. Cackett (Northampton)	39.76
2	S. Magnall (Bo Burnley CATS)	41.11
3	R. Knight (Swindon Dolphins)	41.90
4	A. Cork (Slough Dolphins)	42.02
5	Y. Leach (Co Oxford)	43.51
6	J. Page (Maxwell)	43.62
7	C. Hobson (Poole)	46.13
8	S. Cummings (Maxwell)	47.54
9	S. Verball (Olympic Salamander)	49.59
	R. Thomson (Kingston Royals)	DIS
	C. Ryan (Co Chester)	DIS

100 Metres Breaststroke

1	G. Cackett (Northampton)	1:26.48
2	S. Magnall (Bo Burnley CATS)	1:28.84
3	A. Cork (Slough Dolphins)	1:29.46
4	C. Ryan (Co Chester)	1:32.80
5	R. Knight (Swindon Dolphins)	1:33.57
6	Y. Leach (Co Oxford)	1:36.24
7	J. Page (Maxwell)	1:39.08
8	C. Hobson (Poole)	1:44.67
9	S. Verball (Olympic Salamander)	1:50.42

50 Metres Butterfly

1	M. Flook (Reading)	34.68
2	R. Thomson (Kingston Royals)	35.03
3	A. Cork (Slough Dolphins)	36.15
4	S. Magnall (Bo Burnley CATS)	36.28
5	Y. Matthissen (Colchester)	36.38
6	G. Cackett (Northampton)	36.65
7	B. Bland (Hartlepool)	43.17

100 Metres Butterfly

1	A. Cork (Slough Dolphins)	1:18.88

100 Metres Individual Medley

1	A. Cork (Slough Dolphins)	1:17.91
2	R. Thomson (Kingston Royals)	1:20.09
3	S. Magnall (Bo Burnley CATS)	1:22.65
4	G. Cackett (Northampton)	1:22.77
5	W. Coley (Loughborough)	1:24.25
6	Y. Matthissen (Colchester)	1:26.60
7	R. Knight (Swindon Dolphins)	1:31.07
8	J. Page (Maxwell)	1:31.58
9	Y. Leach (Co Oxford)	1:36.12
10	B. Bland (Hartlepool)	1:38.40
11	A. Mellett (Darlington)	1:38.69

35/44 Years Age Group
Men

4×25 Metres Freestyle Club Relay

1	Co Bradford	1:50.65
2	Bristol Masters	1:50.75
3	Otter	1:55.84
4	Spencer	1:57.07
5	Warley Wasps	1:57.08
6	Beckenham	1:59.70
7	Royal Navy	2:07.13
8	Olympic Salamander	2:35.92
	Watford	DIS

4×25 Metres Medley Club Relay

1	Bristol Masters	2:02.02
2	Co Bradford	2:05.92
3	Spencer	2:07.38
4	Otter	2:09.57
5	Watford	2:18.02
6	Beckenham	2:19.79
7	Swindon Dolphins	2:26.58
8	Royal Navy	2:32.80
9	Olympic Salamander	2:59.93

Women

4×25 Metres Freestyle Club Relay

1	Kingston Royals	2:17.33
2	Reading	2:20.37
3	Albyns	2:22.55
4	Bristol	2:28.70
5	Olympic Salamander	2:44.96
	Spencer	DIS

4×25 Metres Medley Club Relay

1	Kingston Royals	2:27.43
2	Reading	2:32.01
3	Bristol Masters	2:33.37
4	Warley Wasps	2:33.41
5	Albyns	2:49.59
6	Olympic Salamander	3:24.75
	Spencer	DIS

40/44 Years Age Group
Men

50 Metres Freestyle

1	B. Lord (Co Coventry)	27.39
2	J. Gordon (Spencer)	27.46
3	D. Hembrow (Kingston Royals)	27.51
4	D. Thompson (Portsmouth Northsea)	28.60
5	D. Hodgetts (Heston)	28.65
6	H. Hanson (Co Bradford)	28.97
7	T. Catterall (Bo Burnley CATS)	28.99
8	M. Thomas (Watford)	30.09
9	P. Stephens (Royal Navy)	30.81
10	J. Webb (Bristol Masters)	31.07
11	R. Barton (Southport)	31.16
12	J. Thorpe (Blackpool)	32.75
13	R. Carroll (Kenilworth)	37.15
14	H. Goforth (Olympic Salamander)	40.65

100 Metres Freestyle

1	D. Hembrow (Kingston Royals)	59.56
2	J. Gordon (Spencer)	59.95
3	D. Thompson (Portsmouth Northsea)	1:00.39
4	B. Lord (Co Coventry)	1:00.55
5	D. Figes (Bristol Masters)	1:03.82

6	P. Stephens (Royal Navy)	1:07.21
7	J. Webb (Bristol Masters)	1:07.56
8	J. Wootton (Co Milton Keynes)	1:08.36
9	P. Williams (Swindon Dolphins)	1:08.50
10	R. Husson (Otter)	1:08.57
11	M. Thomas (Watford)	1:09.01
12	R. Barton (Southport)	1:09.59
13	P. Baker (Beckenham)	1:10.17
14	P. Matthews (Swindon Dolphins)	1:10.26
15	C. Lock (Swindon Dolphins)	1:13.05
16	J. Hillyard (Reading)	1:33.62
17	H. Goforth (Olympic Salamander)	1:36.34

200 Metres Freestyle

1	D. Thompson (Portsmouth Northsea)	2:11.76
2	A. Wilson (Warley Wasps)	2:13.26
3	D. Hembrow (Kingston Royals)	2:13.41
4	J. Gordon (Spencer)	2:13.49
5	T. Catterall (Bo Burnley CATS)	2:21.59
6	D. Figes (Bristol Masters)	2:26.21
7	P. Stephens (Royal Navy)	2:28.31
8	J. Wootton (Co Milton Keynes)	2:34.42
9	J. Webb (Bristol Masters)	2:37.73
10	M. Thomas (Watford)	2:38.07
11	P. Matthews (Swindon Dolphins)	2:42.17
12	P. Williams (Swindon Dolphins)	2:42.39
13	H. Goforth (Olympic Salamander)	3:43.45

50 Metres Backstroke

1	J. Gordon (Spencer)	32.02
2	T. Nesbit (Bo Sunderland)	32.89
3	D. Figes (Bristol Masters)	34.76
4	K. Brown (Co Bradford)	34.77
5	H. Hanson (Co Bradford)	35.30
6	M. Proudfoot (Reading)	37.42
7	J. Webb (Bristol Masters)	37.57
8	R. Husson (Otter)	37.64
9	H. Goforth (Olympic Salamander)	54.39

100 Metres Backstroke

1	J. Gordon (Spencer)	1:09.39
2	T. Nesbit (Bo Sunderland)	1:14.02
3	T. Catterall (Bo Burnley CATS)	1:18.28
4	A. Wilson (Warley Wasps)	1:18.95
5	M. Proudfoot (Reading)	1:24.98
6	H. Goforth (Olympic Salamander)	1:58.81
7	A. Munn (Hull Masters)	2:06.09

John Gordon

50 Metres Breaststroke

1	R. Apel (Spencer)	35.11
2	J. Tomlinson (Colchester)	35.16
3	R. Husson (Otter)	35.83
4	H. Hanson (Co Bradford)	35.98
5	C. Vinter (Colchester)	36.60
6	A. Wilson (Warley Wasps)	36.72
7	M. Crawley (Street & D)	38.62
8	R. Barton (Southport)	39.17
9	T. Catterall (Bo Burnley CATS)	39.60
10	M. Miles (Weyport Olympians)	39.70
11	J. Maddocks (Poole)	42.64
12	H. Goforth (Olympic Salamander)	45.40
13	C. Reynolds (Co Derby)	46.93
14	J. Hillyard (Reading)	47.28
15	A. Munn (Hull Masters)	57.13

100 Metres Breaststroke

1	R. Apel (Spencer)	1:17.53
2	R. Husson (Otter)	1:19.77
3	J. Tomlinson (Colchester)	1:21.60
4	C. Vinter (Colchester)	1:23.35
5	T. Catterall (Bo Burnley CATS)	1:24.76
6	H. Hanson (Co Bradford)	1:25.23
7	R. Barton (Southport)	1:25.66
8	M. Crawley (Street & D)	1:30.04
9	M. Miles (Weyport Olympians)	1:31.56
10	J. Maddocks (Poole)	1:34.04
11	J. Hillyard (Reading)	1:42.71
12	C. Reynolds (Co Derby)	1:43.52
13	H. Goforth (Olympic Salamander)	1:46.58

50 Metres Butterfly

1	D. Hembrow (Kingston Royals)	30.14
2	D. Thompson (Portsmouth Northsea)	30.62
3	M. Crawley (Street & D)	31.86
4	J. Tomlinson (Colchester)	33.45
5	M. Thomas (Watford)	34.10
6	P. Stephens (Royal Navy)	34.21
7	T. Catterall (Bo Burnley CATS)	35.31
8	M. Miles (Weyport Olympians)	37.64

100 Metres Butterfly

1	P. Godfrey (Penarth)	1:04.45
2	D. Thompson (Portsmouth Northsea)	1:07.21
3	B. Lord (Co Coventry)	1:08.73
4	D. Hembrow (Kingston Royals)	1:09.28
5	P. Stephens (Royal Navy)	1:20.05
6	M. Thomas (Watford)	1:21.61
7	J. Thorpe (Blackpool)	1:26.64

100 Metres Individual Medley

1	B. Lord (Co Coventry)	1:08.20
2	D. Thompson (Portsmouth Northsea)	1:09.73
3	T. Catterall (Bo Burnley CATS)	1:13.69
4	H. Hanson (Co Bradford)	1:14.22
5	D. Hodgetts (Heston)	1:15.50
6	P. Stephens (Royal Navy)	1:20.07
7	R. Barton (Southport)	1:20.43

Women

50 Metres Freestyle

1	S. Shrimpton (Exeter)	29.74
2	J. Wilson (Warley Wasps)	31.68
3	C. Fellows (Bristol Masters)	32.65
	P. Cooke (Spencer)	
5	C. Martin-Dye (Watford)	33.60
6	W. Williams (Bournemouth Dolphins)	34.17
7	J. Alden (Barnet Copthall)	34.38

8	V. Neil (Swindon Dolphins)	34.47
9	K. Pavier (Falcon)	35.04
10	J. Boon (Bristol Masters)	35.35
11	S. Reader (Reading)	35.75
12	W. Hooper (Poole)	36.14
13	J. Johnson (Spencer)	36.61
14	J. Hanson (Co Bradford)	37.47
15	S. Husson (Otter)	39.34
16	E. Budden (Reading)	39.58
17	J. Fleming (Kenilworth)	45.39
18	R. Miles (Kenilworth)	48.24

100 Metres Freestyle

1	S. Shrimpton (Exeter)	1:05.72
2	J. Wilson (Warley Wasps)	1:11.70
3	P. Cooke (Spencer)	1:11.74
4	C. Fellows (Bristol Masters)	1:14.22
5	B. Wilkins (Stevenage)	1:15.43
6	J. Alden (Barnet Copthall)	1:17.58
7	W. Williams (Bournemouth Dolphins)	1:21.24
8	H. Hanson (Co Bradford)	1:24.01
9	E. Blower (Hemel Hempstead)	1:24.59
10	J. Fleming (Kenilworth)	1:44.49

200 Metres Freestyle

1	S. Shrimpton (Exeter)	2:30.82
2	G. Adams (W Goldfish)	2:38.10
3	P. Cooke (Spencer)	2:39.04
4	C. Martin-Dye (Watford)	2:48.22
5	W. Williams (Bournemouth Dolphins)	2:48.77
6	J. Alden (Barnet Copthall)	2:53.11
7	W. Hooper (Poole)	3:04.58
8	J. Hanson (Co Bradford)	3:15.76
9	E. Budden (Reading)	3:18.63

50 Metres Backstroke

1	K. Pavier (Falcon)	36.34
2	C. Martin-Dye (Watford)	37.18
3	G. Adams (W Goldfish)	37.95
4	L. Tanner (Slough Dolphins)	40.70
5	B. Wilkins (Stevenage)	41.53
6	J. Johnson (Spencer)	41.77
7	J. Hanson (Co Bradford)	43.38

100 Metres Backstroke

1	K. Pavier (Falcon)	1:20.95
2	C. Martin-Dye (Watford)	1:22.49
3	E. Blower (Hemel Hempstead)	1:28.92
4	L. Tanner (Slough Dolphins)	1:30.44
5	J. Boon (Bristol Masters)	1:34.21
6	J. Hanson (Co Bradford)	1:35.04
7	E. Budden (Reading)	1:51.90

50 Metres Breaststroke

1	F. Jenkins (Southport)	42.05
2	B. Wilkins (Stevenage)	43.31
3	L. Tanner (Slough Dolphins)	48.73
4	J. Fleming (Kenilworth)	50.28
5	R. Miles (Kenilworth)	52.63

100 Metres Breaststroke

1	F. Jenkins (Southport)	1:33.72
2	B. Wilkins (Stevenage)	1:33.96
3	J. Fleming (Kenilworth)	1:49.22

50 Metres Butterfly

1	S. Shrimpton (Exeter)	33.43
2	G. Adams (W Goldfish)	34.46
3	J. Wilson (Warley Wasps)	34.59
4	B. Wilkins (Stevenage)	36.31
5	C. Martin-Dye (Watford)	36.50

6	K. Pavier (Falcon)	36.70
7	L. Tanner (Slough Dolphins)	38.77
8	E. Blower (Hemel Hempstead)	42.94

100 Metres Butterfly

1	S. Shrimpton (Exeter)	1:17.21
2	G. Adams (W Goldfish)	1:17.26
3	B. Wilkins (Stevenage)	1:22.72
4	C. Martin-Dye (Watford)	1:28.23
5	L. Tanner (Slough Dolphins)	1:30.99

100 Metres Individual Medley

1	G. Adams (W Goldfish)	1:17.30
2	B. Wilkins (Stevenage)	1:25.40
3	L. Tanner (Slough Dolphins)	1:28.81
4	J. Alden (Barnet Copthall)	1:29.36
5	P. Cooke (Spencer)	1:29.66
6	E. Blower (Hemel Hempstead)	1:32.00
7	V. Neil (Swindon)	1:33.41
8	J. Hanson (Co Bradford)	1:34.32

45/49 Years Age Group Men

50 Metres Freestyle

1	J. Martin-Dye (Watford)	28.30
2	J. Stewart (Otter)	28.56
3	D. Blakeley (Co Bradford)	28.77
4	R. Lloyd-Mostyn (Otter)	28.80
5	T. Duckworth (Bo Burnley CATS)	29.63
6	S. Godfrey (Leicester)	29.94
7	R. Thomas (Otter)	30.02
8	B. Johnson (Spencer)	30.14
9	J. Lake (Spencer)	30.15
10	K. Ingram (Sparkhill)	30.84
11	P. Sutherland (Beckenham)	31.22
12	H. Adams (Thurrock)	31.50
13	B. Blanden (Royal Navy)	33.04
14	M. Hobdell (Gloucester C)	33.38
15	J. Peto (Wellingborough)	34.50
16	R. Britton (Gloucester C)	35.18
	T. Johnson (Calne Alpha)	35.18
18	E. Boyd-Tuck (Swallowtails)	35.23

100 Metres Freestyle

1	J. Martin-Dye (Watford)	1:01.43
2	J. Stewart (Otter)	1:03.58
3	M. Wake (White Oak)	1:04.74
4	R. Lloyd-Mostyn (Otter)	1:04.96
5	D. Blakeley (Co Bradford)	1:05.00
6	M. Cossins (Scarborough)	1:07.10
7	T. Duckworth (Bo Burnley CATS)	1:07.89
8	K. Ingram (Sparkhill)	1:08.20
9	M. Marshall (Halesowen)	1:09.25
10	B. Blanden (Royal Navy)	1:10.99
11	B. Hey (Marlborough)	1:14.21
12	E. Hack (Gloucester C)	1:14.95
13	V. Hanby (Nottingham Leander)	1:16.86
14	M. Hobdell (Gloucester C)	1:17.55
15	J. Peto (Wellingborough)	1:18.35
16	E. Boyd-Tuck (Swallowtails)	1:20.43
17	T. Johnson (Calne Alpha)	1:22.46
18	R. Morgan (Bottisham)	1:31.44

200 Metres Freestyle

1	A. Galletley (Warrender)	2:16.38
2	M. Wake (White Oak)	2:18.23
3	J. Martin-Dye (Watford)	2:18.57
4	J. Stewart (Otter)	2:22.10
5	C. Doxat (Otter)	2:26.91

6	R. Lloyd-Mostyn (Otter)	2:29.81
7	T. Duckworth (Bo Burnley CATS)	2:29.95
8	K. Ingram (Sparkhill)	2:32.90
9	M. Cossins (Scarborough)	2:33.60
10	M. Marshall (Halesowen)	2:33.88
11	B. Blanden (Royal Navy)	2:38.23
12	E. Hack (Gloucester C)	2:43.64
13	V. Hanby (Nottingham Leander)	2:55.87
14	E. Boyd-Tuck (Swallowtails)	2:57.26
15	J. Peto (Wellingborough)	2:59.87
16	M. Hobdell (Gloucester C)	3:03.64

50 Metres Backstroke

1	J. Lake (Spencer)	33.07
2	R. Thomas (Otter)	33.91
3	J. Stewart (Otter)	34.52
4	R. Reader (Croydon Amphibians)	35.18
5	D. Blakeley (Co Bradford)	35.39
6	R. Lloyd-Mostyn (Otter)	37.14
7	P. Sutherland (Beckenham)	37.77
8	T. Duckworth (Bo Burnley CATS)	38.51
9	H. Adams (Thurrock)	38.88
10	B. Thompson (Barnet Copthall)	40.12
11	R. Morgan (Bottisham)	43.56
12	E. Boyd-Tuck (Swallowtails)	47.18
13	B. Blanden (Royal Navy)	47.71

100 Metres Backstroke

1	J. Lake (Spencer)	1:14.40
2	J. Stewart (Otter)	1:15.70
3	R. Lloyd-Mostyn (Otter)	1:22.02
4	P. Sutherland (Beckenham)	1:27.28
5	B. Thompson (Barnet Copthall)	1:30.99
6	R. Morgan (Bottisham)	1:38.22
7	G. Hales (Hull Masters)	1:45.18
8	E. Boyd-Tuck (Swallowtails)	1:47.93

50 Metres Breaststroke

1	E. Sawyers (Motherwell)	37.36
2	C. Doxat (Otter)	37.45
3	M. Wake (White Oak)	37.75
4	B. Arscott (Colchester)	37.88
5	J. Martin-Dye (Watford)	38.81
6	J. Stewart (Otter)	39.35
7	H. Adams (Thurrock)	40.20
8	G. Hales (Hull)	42.57
9	T. Johnson (Calne Alpha)	42.96
10	E. Boyd-Tuck (Swallowtails)	43.35
11	T. Brooks (Basingstoke)	43.55
12	R. Morgan (Bottisham)	43.98
13	M. Daniel (Bristol Masters)	48.66

100 Metres Breaststroke

1	C. Doxat (Otter)	1:21.06
2	M. Wake (White Oak)	1:21.69
3	E. Sawyers (Motherwell)	1:21.75
4	A. Galletley (Warrender)	1:22.19
5	H. Adams (Thurrock)	1:29.38
6	B. Arscott (Colchester)	1:30.19
7	G. Hales (Hull Masters)	1:32.82
8	T. Johnson (Calne Alpha)	1:36.22
9	T. Brooks (Basingstoke)	1:38.43
10	E. Boyd-Tuck (Swallowtails)	1:39.88
11	R. Morgan (Bottisham)	1:42.07

50 Metres Butterfly

1	R. Lloyd-Mostyn (Otter)	30.58
2	D. Blakeley (Co Bradford)	30.97
3	R. Thomas (Otter)	32.82
4	B. Johnson (Spencer)	33.26

5	M. Wake (White Oak)	33.63
6	S. Godfrey (Leicester)	34.17
7	J. Lake (Spencer)	34.52
8	P. Sutherland (Beckenham)	35.00
9	H. Adams (Thurrock)	36.07
10	T. Duckworth (Bo Burnley CATS)	36.37
11	M. Hobdell (Gloucester)	37.21
12	E. Boyd-Tuck (Swallowtails)	41.42
13	M. Daniel (Bristol Masters)	48.61

100 Metres Butterfly

1	R. Lloyd-Mostyn (Otter)	1:09.33
2	A. Galletley (Warrender)	1:12.89
3	D. Blakeley (Co Bradford)	1:12.90
4	J. Martin-Dye (Watford)	1:13.09
5	M. Wake (White Oak)	1:17.14
6	J. Lake (Spencer)	1:20.11
7	K. Ingram (Sparkhill)	1:21.40
8	H. Adams (Thurrock)	1:25.12
9	P. Sutherland (Beckenham)	1:30.13
10	M. Hobdell (Gloucester C)	1:33.08
11	E. Boyd-Tuck (Swallowtails)	1:41.59
12	R. Morgan (Bottisham)	1:47.53

100 Metres Individual Medley

1	A. Galletley (Warrender)	1:12.36
2	J. Stewart (Otter)	1:13.11
3	C. Doxat (Otter)	1:13.43
4	R. Lloyd-Mostyn (Otter)	1:16.32
5	K. Ingram (Sparkhill)	1:19.18
6	J. Martin-Dye (Watford)	1:19.44
7	T. Duckworth (Burnley)	1:20.77
8	S. Godfrey (Leicester)	1:22.91
9	T. Johnson (Calne Alpha)	1:27.45
10	J. Peto (Wellingborough)	1:30.94
11	E. Boyd-Tuck (Swallowtails)	1:32.54
12	R. Morgan (Bottisham)	1:34.91
	R. Thomas (Otter)	DIS

Women

50 Metres Freestyle

1	N. Kirkendall (Otter)	33.74
2	P. Webster (Kingston Royals)	34.10
3	V. Clark (Albyns)	34.88
4	B. Woodward (Rochford & D)	37.10
5	B. Legg (Chipping Norton)	40.68
6	C. Harridge (Rugby)	47.05
7	M. Gilbert (Olympic Salamander)	56.46

100 Metres Freestyle

1	N. Kirkendall (Otter)	1:14.89
2	P. Webster (Kingston Royals)	1:15.61
3	E. Bromwich (Rugby)	1:18.25

200 Metres Freestyle

1	N. Kirkendall (Otter)	2:48.50
2	P. Webster (Kingston Royals)	2:48.76
3	B. Woodward (Rochford & D)	3:10.17
4	C. Harridge (Rugby)	3:57.58

50 Metres Backstroke

1	C. Winchurch (Southport)	39.02
2	E. Bromwich (Rugby)	43.44
3	S. Cobbold (Olympic Salamander)	45.62
4	B. Legg (Chipping Norton)	48.86

100 Metres Backstroke

1	J. Smith (Watford)	1:27.91
2	B. Woodward (Rochford & D)	1:32.05
3	N. Kirkendall (Otter)	1:33.83

50 Metres Breaststroke

1	E. Bromwich (Rugby)	40.43
2	H. Silcock (Macclesfield)	44.99
3	C. Harridge (Rugby)	47.72
4	S. Cobbold (Olympic Salamander)	47.74
5	B. Legg (Chipping Norton)	51.04
6	M. Gilbert (Olympic Salamander)	58.33

100 Metres Breaststroke

1	E. Bromwich (Rugby)	1:29.29
2	C. Harridge (Rugby)	1:43.47
3	M. Gilbert (Olympic Salamander)	2:21.98

50 Metres Butterfly

1	E. Bromwich (Rugby)	38.47
2	H. Silcock (Macclesfield)	41.55
3	C. Harridge (Rugby)	46.20
4	S. Cobbold (Olympic Salamander)	48.39

100 Metres Butterfly

1	E. Bromwich (Rugby)	1:33.98

100 Metres Individual Medley

1	E. Bromwich (Rugby)	1:26.07
2	H. Silcock (Macclesfield)	1:34.32
3	S. Cobbold (Olympic Salamander)	1:37.78
4	C. Harridge (Rugby)	1:46.70

45+ Years Age Group
Men

4×25 Metres Freestyle Club Relay

1	Otter	1:56.26
2	Watford	1:58.30
3	Motherwell	1:58.33
4	Spencer	2:03.34
5	Bristol Masters	2:05.46

4×25 Metres Medley Club Relay

1	Otter	2:07.68
2	Motherwell	2:14.16
3	Watford	2:16.76
4	Spencer	2:19.53
5	Bristol Masters	2:19.67

Women
4×25 Metres Freestyle Club Relay

1	Olympic Salamander	3:11.72

4 x 25 Metres Medley Club Relay

1	Olympic Salamander	3:36.64

50/54 Years Age Group
Men

50 Metres Freestyle

1	H. Cumberford (Motherwell)	28.66
2	A. Weston (Romsey)	29.30
3	N. Chapman (Watford)	30.36
4	D. Reynolds (Beckenham)	30.40
5	R. Harford (Watford)	30.57
6	A. Gimson (Watford)	30.77
7	R. Burn (Otter)	31.08
8	J. Penswick (Bo Burnley CATS)	33.00
9	M. Kirby (Olympic Salamander)	35.16
10	B. Fleming (Bo Sunderland)	36.29
11	B. Ferriman (Kenilworth)	37.99
12	R. Knight (Shiverers)	39.17

100 Metres Freestyle

1	B. Gyorffy (Bristol Central)	1:04.36
2	H. Cumberford (Motherwell)	1:06.16
3	D. Reynolds (Beckenham)	1:07.88
4	R. Harford (Watford)	1:09.46
5	A. Gimson (Watford)	1:09.60
6	J. MacTaggart (Motherwell)	1:11.80
7	D. Auton (Royal Navy)	1:13.95
8	B. Fleming (Bo Sunderland)	1:24.22
9	R. Knight (Shiverers)	1:28.06

200 Metres Freestyle

1	D. Reynolds (Beckenham)	2:30.11
2	D. Auton (Royal Navy)	2:42.55
3	R. Harford (Watford)	2:43.68
4	J. Penswick (Burnley)	2:46.52
5	N. Chapman (Watford)	2:48.06
6	J. MacTaggart (Motherwell)	2:51.97
7	R. Knight (Shiverers)	3:19.36

50 Metres Backstroke

1	G. Sykes (Co Coventry)	32.17
2	H. Cumberford (Motherwell)	33.09
3	A. Weston (Romsey)	33.60
4	R. Harford (Watford)	34.66
5	R. Burn (Otter)	35.38
6	N. Chapman (Watford)	37.69
7	D. Reynolds (Beckenham)	38.94
8	J. MacTaggart (Motherwell)	39.15
9	B. Fleming (Bo Sunderland)	40.49
10	J. Penswick (Bo Burnley CATS)	43.03
11	B. Ferriman (Kenilworth)	43.91

100 Metres Backstroke

1	G. Sykes (Co Coventry)	1:12.44
2	R. Harford (Watford)	1:16.59
3	H. Cumberford (Motherwell)	1:17.61
4	A. Weston (Romsey)	1:17.83
5	B. Fleming (Bo Sunderland)	1:37.79
6	A. Greenham (Hull Masters)	1:52.31

50 Metres Breaststroke

1	J. MacTaggart (Motherwell)	37.00
2	H. Cumberford (Motherwell)	38.05
3	J. Paterson (Arlington)	39.46
4	T. Hayward (Bristol Masters)	40.05
5	B. Davis (Swindon Dolphins)	40.67
6	J. Penswick (Bo Burnley CATS)	40.90
7	A. Gimson (Watford)	41.14
8	R. Harford (Watford)	42.15
9	M. Kirby (Olympic Salamander)	43.35
10	R. Knight (Shiverers)	43.61
11	R. Robinson (Kenilworth)	44.69
12	A. Greenham (Hull Masters)	45.63
13	M. Gahan (Barnet Copthall)	46.72

100 Metres Breaststroke

1	H. Cumberford (Motherwell)	1:24.83
2	J. MacTaggart (Motherwell)	1:25.18
3	J. Penswick (Bo Burnley CATS)	1:28.95
4	B. Davis (Swindon Dolphins)	1:30.92
5	T. Hayward (Bristol)	1:31.22
6	R. Harford (Watford)	1:31.74
7	M. Kirby (Olympic Salamander)	1:35.28
8	R. Knight (Shiverers)	1:37.42
9	R. Robinson (Kenilworth)	1:40.04
10	A. Greenham (Hull Masters)	1:42.10
11	M. Gahan (Barnet Copthall)	1:45.99

50 Metres Butterfly

1	J. Cardwell (Co London Police)	31.73

2 J. MacTaggart (Motherwell)	34.58
3 J. Paterson (Arlington)	34.97
4 N. Chapman (Watford)	35.05
5 A. Gimson (Watford)	35.66
6 J. Penswick (Bo Burnley CATS)	37.09
7 T. Hayward (Bristol Masters)	37.75
8 R. Knight (Shiverers)	39.64

100 Metres Butterfly

1 R. Knight (Shiverers)	1:33.53
2 T. Collins (Heston)	1:52.11

100 Metres Individual Medley

1 H. Cumberford (Motherwell)	1:16.67
2 R. Harford (Watford)	1:18.32
3 N. Chapman (Watford)	1:20.48
4 J. Penswick (Bo Burnley CATS)	1:22.78
5 A. Gimson (Watford)	1:22.84
6 D. Auton (Royal Navy)	1:23.58
7 M. Kirby (Olympic Salamander)	1:30.30
8 R. Knight (Shiverers)	1:34.69
9 T. Collins (Heston)	1:43.30

Women

50 Metres Freestyle

1 J.Jackson (Potters Bar)	34.98
2 C. Buykx (Swallowtails)	35.53
3 S. Warn (Albyns)	36.74
4 M. Alexander (Sale)	37.74
5 V. Hardman (Heston)	38.26
6 B. Fentiman (Shiverers)	39.29
7 S. Carr (Radcliffe)	39.38
8 M. Wilkinson (Salisbury)	40.63
9 M. Knight (Shiverers)	43.07
10 E. Wain (Oxford C)	46.51
11 J. Orr (Beckenham)	46.73
12 J. Love (Olympic Salamander)	47.58
13 R. Usher (Olympic Salamander)	51.12
14 M. Palumbo (Olympic Salamander)	52.79
15 S. North (Kenilworth)	53.23

100 Metres Freestyle

1 J. Jackson (Potters Bar)	1:20.46
2 S. Warn (Albyns)	1:27.32
3 V. Hardman (Heston)	1:29.75
4 M. Alexander (Sale)	1:30.12
5 S. Carr (Radcliffe)	1:31.81
6 M. Knight (Shiverers)	1:35.06
7 E. Wain (Oxford C)	1:44.82
8 J. Love (Olympic Salamander)	1:44.93
9 J. Orr (Beckenham)	1:44.96
10 R. Usher (Olympic Salamander)	2:02.83
11 S. North (Kenilworth)	2:04.13

200 Metres Freestyle

1 J. Jackson (Potters Bar)	3:05.28
2 B. Fentiman (Shiverers)	3:15.66
3 S. Warn (Albyns)	3:17.86
4 M. Wilkinson (Salisbury)	3:22.48
5 C. Buykx (Swallowtails)	3:28.01
6 S. Carr (Radcliffe)	3:28.31
7 M. Knight (Shiverers)	3:29.95
8 M. Alexander (Sale)	3:32.96
9 E. Wain (Oxford C)	3:52.76
10 J. Orr (Beckenham)	3:54.02
11 R. Usher (Olympic Salamander)	4:18.25

50 Metres Backstroke

1 J. Jackson (Potters Bar)	45.48

2 V. Hardman (Heston)	46.30
3 M. Knight (Shiverers)	48.64
4 J. Orr (Beckenham)	54.42
5 A. Weissand (Barnet Copthall)	56.99
6 M. Palumbo (Olympic Salamander)	1:02.84
7 R. Usher (Olympic Salamander)	1:07.59

100 Metres Backstroke

1 C. Buykx (Swallowtails)	1:29.30
2 M. Knight (Shiverers)	1:44.32

50 Metres Breaststroke

1 M. Wilkinson (Salisbury)	45.69
2 C. Bates (Co Coventry)	47.20
3 A. Weissand (Barnet Copthall)	50.33
4 B. Fentiman (Shiverers)	51.74
5 M. Palumbo (Olympic Salamander)	1:00.55
6 M. Knight (Shiverers)	1:07.19

100 Metres Breaststroke

1 M. Wilkinson (Salisbury)	1:40.82
2 C. Bates (Co Coventry)	1:42.63
3 A. Weissand (Barnet Copthall)	1:52.20
4 M. Alexander (Sale)	2:01.03

50 Metres Butterfly

1 S. Warn (Albyns)	45.88
2 B. Fentiman (Shiverers)	47.74
3 S. Carr (Radcliffe)	48.83
4 M. Knight (Shiverers)	1:03.90

100 Metres Butterfly

1 S. Carr (Radcliffe)	1:58.78

100 Metres Individual Medley

1 V. Hardman (Heston)	1:41.42
2 B. Fentiman (Shiverers)	1:43.18
3 M. Alexander (Sale)	1:49.26
4 S. Carr (Radcliffe)	1:49.66
5 E. Wain (Oxford C)	2:00.28
M. Knight (Shiverers)	DIS

55/59 Years Age Group
Men

50 Metres Freestyle

1 K. Weigh (Blackpool)	30.34
2 T. Holmyard (Bristol Masters)	31.32
3 R. Burns (Motherwell)	31.33
4 S. Banning (Norwich Penguins)	31.81
5 D. Payne (Harrow & Wealdstone)	33.26
6 I. Wilkinson (Salisbury)	34.15
7 D. Mace (Spencer)	34.31
8 E. Mountain (Spencer)	34.51
9 R. Carter (Hornchurch)	36.50
10 J. Jeffery (Reading)	36.93
11 A. Harding (Salisbury)	38.41

100 Metres Freestyle

1 K. Weigh (Blackpool)	1:08.13
2 R. Burrell (Launceston)	1:09.42
3 T. Holmyard (Bristol Masters)	1:10.85
4 S. Banning (Norwich Penguins)	1:11.21
5 R. Burns (Motherwell)	1:11.75
6 E. Mountain (Spencer)	1:18.78
7 D. Mace (Spencer)	1:21.59
8 J. Jeffery (Reading)	1:22.16
9 R. Carter (Hornchurch)	1:30.13

200 Metres Freestyle

1 K. Weigh (Blackpool)	2:36.08

279

2	R. Burrell (Launceston)	2:39.04
3	T. Holmyard (Bristol Masters)	2:40.76
4	S. Banning (Norwich Penguins)	2:41.80
5	E. Mountain (Spencer)	2:58.71
6	D. Mace (Spencer)	3:09.86
7	J. Jeffery (Reading)	3:15.04
8	R. Carter (Hornchurch)	3:30.25

50 Metres Backstroke

1	R. Burrell (Launceston)	36.76
2	R. Burns (Motherwell)	36.80
3	K. Weigh (Blackpool)	37.08
4	N. Trusty (Spencer)	37.51
5	P. Kinsella (W Goldfish)	38.00
6	E. Mountain (Spencer)	41.65
7	S. Banning (Norwich Penguins)	42.32
8	D. Payne (Harrow & Wealdstone)	42.71
9	D. Mace (Spencer)	42.92

100 Metres Backstroke

1	R. Burrell (Launceston)	1:20.30
2	R. Burns (Motherwell)	1:23.16
3	K. Weigh (Blackpool)	1:24.60
4	N. Trusty (Spencer)	1:28.98
5	E. Mountain (Spencer)	1:33.39
6	D. Mace (Spencer)	1:40.69

50 Metres Breaststroke

1	C. Bush (Co Chester)	40.73
2	B. Gell (Bedford)	41.33
3	N. Greenfield (Barnsley)	41.92
4	R. Carter (Hornchurch)	43.01
5	E. Mountain (Spencer)	44.38
6	B. Runham (Co Cambridge)	44.82
7	J. Jeffery (Reading)	46.60

100 Metres Breaststroke

1	C. Bush (Co Chester)	1:30.01
2	N. Greenfield (Barnsley)	1:34.51
3	B. Gell (Bedford)	1:35.77
4	R. Carter (Hornchurch)	1:40.65
5	E. Mountain (Spencer)	1:42.23
6	B. Runham (Co Cambridge)	1:46.50

50 Metres Butterfly

1	S. Banning (Norwich Penguins)	34.36
2	R. Burrell (Launceston)	34.51
3	K. Weigh (Blackpool)	36.49
4	B. Gell (Bedford)	37.79
5	N. Greenfield (Barnsley)	40.38
6	D. Payne (Harrow & Wealdstone)	41.38
7	B. Runham (Co Cambridge)	42.55
8	D. Mace (Spencer)	43.91
9	J. Jeffery (Reading)	47.20

100 Metres Butterfly

1	S. Banning (Norwich Penguins)	1:18.83
2	R. Burrell (Launceston)	1:25.91
3	B. Jackson (Blackpool)	1:30.84
4	C. Bush (Co Chester)	1:35.40
5	N. Greenfield (Barnsley)	1:38.27
6	E. Mountain (Spencer)	1:41.96

100 Metres Individual Medley

1	K. Weigh (Blackpool)	1:19.52
2	R. Burrell (Launceston)	1:21.05
3	T. Holmyard (Bristol Masters)	1:24.28
4	S. Banning (Norwich Penguins)	1:24.77
5	C. Bush (Co Chester)	1:29.71
6	E. Mountain (Spencer)	1:31.70
7	R. Carter (Hornchurch)	1:37.79

8	J. Jeffery (Reading)	1:38.27
9	B. Runham (Co Cambridge)	1:39.75
10	A. Harding (Salisbury)	1:49.99

Women

50 Metres Freestyle

1	J. Asher (Swallowtails)	33.78
2	F. Connolly (Edinburgh)	34.79
3	L. Harding (Salisbury)	41.79
4	P. Baxter (York C)	41.82
5	J. Parkins (Beckenham)	46.62
6	P. Rushworth (Co Bradford)	47.67
7	J. Stobie (Community Education)	48.04
8	M. Simmons (Rochford & D)	48.79
9	J. Morrison (Kenilworth)	54.63
10	A. Dinham (Bristol Masters)	1:01.97

100 Metres Freestyle

1	J. Asher (Swallowtails)	1:13.78
2	F. Connolly (Edinburgh)	1:17.11
3	P. Baxter (York C)	1:32.87
4	M. Simmons (Rochford & D)	1:48.35
5	P. Rushworth (Co Bradford)	1:49.97
6	J. Stobie (Community Education)	1:50.02
7	J. Parkins (Beckenham)	1:52.49
8	A. Dinham (Bristol Masters)	2:17.70

200 Metres Freestyle

1	J. Asher (Swallowtails)	2:45.00
2	F. Connolly (Edinburgh)	2:45.62
3	P. Baxter (York C)	3:18.92
4	L. Harding (Salisbury)	3:25.56
5	P. Rushworth (Co Bradford)	3:51.37
6	M. Simmons (Rochford & D)	3:55.26
7	J. Stobie (Community Education)	4:08.18
8	J. Parkins (Beckenham)	4:08.29
9	A. Dinham (Bristol Masters)	4:48.26

50 Metres Backstroke

1	J. Asher (Swallowtails)	40.38
2	F. Connolly (Edinburgh)	42.72
3	L. Harding (Salisbury)	47.61
4	P. Rushworth (Co Bradford)	54.85
5	J. Stobie (Community Education)	59.18
6	J. Morrison (Kenilworth)	1:04.39
7	A. Dinham (Bristol Masters)	1:20.63

100 Metres Backstroke

1	J. Asher (Swallowtails)	1:30.59
2	F. Connolly (Edinburgh)	1:31.49
3	L. Harding (Salisbury)	1:42.81
4	J. Parkins (Beckenham)	1:58.75
5	P. Rushworth (Co Bradford)	1:59.99
6	J. Stobie (Community Education)	2:23.64

50 Metres Breaststroke

1	F. Connolly (Edinburgh)	42.41
2	J. Asher (Swallowtails)	46.31
3	P. Baxter (York C)	49.81
4	P. Rushworth (Co Bradford)	56.40
5	J. Stobie (Community Education)	59.38
6	J. Morrison (Kenilworth)	59.57
7	A. Dinham (Bristol Masters)	1:17.31

100 Metres Breaststroke

1	F. Connolly (Edinburgh)	1:29.53
2	J. Asher (Swallowtails)	1:38.86
3	P. Rushworth (Co Bradford)	1:58.46
4	J. Stobie (Community Education)	2:08.12
5	J. Morrison (Kenilworth)	2:11.08

6 A. Dinham (Bristol Masters)   2:51.28

50 Metres Butterfly
1 J. Asher (Swallowtails)   37.87
2 F. Connolly (Edinburgh)   40.70
3 P. Rushworth (Co Bradford)   1:00.18
4 J. Stobie (Community Education)   1:13.10

100 Metres Butterfly
1 F. Connolly (Edinburgh)   1:28.32
2 J. Asher (Swallowtails)   1:33.10
3 P. Rushworth (Co Bradford)   2:16.82
4 J. Stobie (Community Education)   DNF

100 Metres Individual Medley
1 F. Connolly (Edinburgh)   1:25.61
2 J. Asher (Swallowtails)   1:27.12
3 P. Baxter (York C)   1:43.18
4 P. Rushworth (Co Bradford)   2:01.01
5 J. Parkins (Beckenham)   2:10.32
6 J. Stobie (Community Education)   2:13.69

60/64 Years Age Group
Men

50 Metres Freestyle
1 A. Miles (Sparkhill)   32.97
2 J. Gibson (Motherwell)   33.45
3 D. Gunnell (Luton)   34.11
4 C. Benfold (Heston)   36.88
5 D. Ward (Kettering)   38.75
6 W. Read-Branker (Bristol Masters)   40.94

100 Metres Freestyle
1 A. Miles (Sparkhill)   1:14.81
2 J. Gibson (Motherwell)   1:19.19
3 R. Gohar (Serpentine)   1:21.49
4 D. Ward (Kettering)   1:23.40
5 W. Read-Branker (Bristol Masters)   1:34.09

200 Metres Freestyle
1 A. Miles (Sparkhill)   2:59.67
2 D. Ward (Kettering)   3:07.50
3 J. Gibson (Motherwell)   3:15.57
4 W. Read-Branker (Bristol Masters)   3:28.88

50 Metres Backstroke
1 J. Gibson (Motherwell)   39.11
2 T. Summers (Newport)   39.37
3 A. Miles (Sparkhill)   42.33
4 D. Ward (Kettering)   46.77

100 Metres Backstroke
1 T. Summers (Newport)   1:26.56
2 D. Ward (Kettering)   1:39.89
3 C. Benfold (Heston)   1:49.81
4 W. Read-Branker (Bristol Masters)   1:57.44

50 Metres Breaststroke
1 R. Golder (Beckenham)   47.58
2 C. Benfold (Heston)   49.71
3 W. Read-Branker (Bristol Masters)   55.83

100 Metres Breaststroke
1 C. Benfold (Heston)   1:52.53

50 Metres Butterfly
1 A. Miles (Sparkhill)   42.38
2 W. Read-Branker (Bristol Masters)   47.96

100 Metres Butterfly
1 D. Gunnell (Luton)   1:51.40
2 W. Read-Branker (Bristol Masters)   2:02.41

100 Metres Individual Medley
1 D. Gunnell (Luton)   1:37.27
2 C. Benfold (Heston)   1:42.00
3 W. Read-Branker (Bristol Masters)   1:50.74
   A. Miles (Sparkhill)   DIS

Women

50 Metres Freestyle
1 O. Hale (Beckenham)   43.30
2 V. Batten (Co Cardiff)   49.65

100 Metres Freestyle
1 O. Hale (Beckenham)   1:38.88
2 V. Batten (Co Cardiff)   1:56.84

200 Metres Freestyle
1 O. Hale (Beckenham)   3:38.16
2 M. Evans (Redbridge B)   3:39.97
3 V. Batten (Co Cardiff)   4:24.89

50 Metres Backstroke
1 O. Hale (Beckenham)   46.05
2 V. Batten (Co Cardiff)   1:12.75

100 Metres Backstroke
1 O. Hale (Beckenham)   1:41.98
2 V. Batten (Co Cardiff)   2:38.08

50 Metres Breaststroke
1 M. Evans (Redbridge B)   49.37
2 V. Batten (Co Cardiff)   59.07

100 Metres Breaststroke
1 M. Evans (Redbridge B)   1:44.12
2 V. Batten (Co Cardiff)   2:13.23

50 Metres Butterfly
1 O. Hale (Beckenham)   59.26

100 Metres Butterfly
1 M. Evans (Redbridge B)   2:03.21

100 Metres Individual Medley
1 M. Evans (Redbridge B)   1:50.81
2 O. Hale (Beckenham)   1:59.95
3 V. Batten (Co Cardiff)   2:27.63

65/69 Years Age Group
Men

50 Metres Freestyle
1 R. Barker (Co Cambridge)   33.93
2 G. Merryweather (Leamington Spa)   36.84
3 P. Foakes (Faversham)   37.74
4 M. McNulty (Middlesbrough)   39.56
5 L. Fabien (Reading)   40.74
6 A. Baxter (York C)   41.75
7 L. Auditt (Chippenham)   42.98
8 M. Berg (Camden Swiss Cottage)   43.15
9 A. Watters (BLDSA)   56.10

100 Metres Freestyle
1 R. Barker (Co Cambridge)   1:16.12
2 G. Merryweather (Leamington Spa)   1:24.11
3 P. Foakes (Faversham)   1:26.27
4 M. Berg (Camden Swiss Cottage)   1:38.36
5 A. Rowley (Highworth)   1:39.99
6 L. Fabien (Reading)   1:45.75

200 Metres Freestyle
1 R. Barker (Co Cambridge)   2:56.34
2 G. Merryweather (Leamington Spa)   3:17.02

281

3	P. Foakes (Faversham)	3:27.79
4	A. Rowley (Highworth)	3:35.74
5	L. Fabien (Reading)	3:51.96

50 Metres Backstroke

1	A. Laylee (Liverpool University)	39.30
2	G. Merryweather (Leamington Spa)	44.78

100 Metres Backstroke

1	A. Laylee (Liverpool University)	1:30.08
2	A. Rowley (Highworth)	2:24.89

50 Metres Breaststroke

1	R. Barker (Co Cambridge)	43.57
2	G. Merryweather (Leamington Spa)	45.63
3	M. Berg (Camden Swiss Cottage)	46.31
4	L. Auditt (Chippenham)	47.10

100 Metres Breaststroke

1	R. Barker (Co Cambridge)	1:39.66
2	G. Merryweather (Leamington Spa)	1:44.74
3	M. Berg (Camden Swiss Cottage)	1:47.20

50 Metres Butterfly

1	G. Merryweather (Leamington Spa)	48.10
2	L. Auditt (Chippenham)	49.74

100 Metres Butterfly

1	M. McNulty (Middlesbrough)	2:14.54
2	A. Watters (BLDSA)	2:42.26

100 Metres Individual Medley

1	R. Barker (Co Cambridge)	1:36.01
2	G. Merryweather (Leamington Spa)	1:36.31
3	L. Auditt (Chippenham)	1:54.12
4	A. Rowley (Highworth)	2:14.84
5	A. Watters (BLDSA)	2:28.68

Women

50 Metres Freestyle

1	D. Cope (Exeter)	38.47
2	B. Condon (Bromley)	43.16
3	B. Sands (Hartlepool)	47.09
4	B. Ivey (Swindon Dolphins)	49.62
5	Y. Hodges (Worcester)	52.68

100 Metres Freestyle

1	D. Cope (Exeter)	1:32.92
2	B. Condon (Bromley)	1:46.17
3	B. Sands (Hartlepool)	1:48.56
4	Y. Hodges (Worcester)	1:58.03

200 Metres Freestyle

1	D. Cope (Exeter)	3:39.81
2	B. Sands (Hartlepool)	3:57.25
3	Y. Hodges (Worcester)	4:15.89
4	B. Condon (Bromley)	4:21.25

50 Metres Backstroke

1	B. Condon (Bromley)	47.12
2	D. Williams (Hounslow B)	56.70
3	B. Ivey (Swindon Dolphins)	56.91
4	B. Sands (Hartlepool)	1:00.62
5	Y. Hodges (Worcester)	1:03.03

100 Metres Backstroke

1	B. Condon (Bromley)	1:52.60

50 Metres Breaststroke

1	D. Williams (Hounslow B)	53.28
2	O. Sutton (Bristol Masters)	54.33
3	B. Ivey (Swindon Dolphins)	1:01.10

4	Y. Hodges (Worcester)	1:01.95
5	N. Chammings (Banstead)	1:02.47
6	B. Sands (Hartlepool)	1:08.13

100 Metres Breaststroke

1	D. Williams (Hounslow B)	1:53.78
2	O. Sutton (Bristol Masters)	2:03.72
3	Y. Hodges (Worcester)	2:17.93
4	N. Chammings (Banstead)	2:27.66

50 Metres Butterfly

1	B. Condon (Bromley)	1:00.81
2	O. Sutton (Bristol Masters)	1:03.70
3	Y. Hodges (Worcester)	1:07.13

100 Metres Individual Medley

1	O. Sutton (Bristol Masters)	2:00.70
2	B. Condon (Bromley)	2:00.98
3	Y. Hodges (Worcester)	2:13.17

70/74 Years Age Group
Men

50 Metres Freestyle

1	G. Huxtable (W Goldfish)	36.52
2	B. Taylor (Southport)	39.57
3	E. Clemett (St Austell)	41.29

100 Metres Freestyle

1	G. Huxtable (W Goldfish)	1:27.36
2	E. Clemett (St Austell)	1:31.70
3	B. Taylor (Southport)	1:33.81

200 Metres Freestyle

1	G. Huxtable (W Goldfish)	3:21.40
2	E. Clemett (St Austell)	3:31.87
3	B. Taylor (Southport)	3:37.22

50 Metres Backstroke

1	G. Huxtable (W Goldfish)	43.79
2	B. Taylor (Southport)	49.22
3	E. Clemett (St Austell)	56.10

100 Metres Backstroke

1	G. Huxtable (W Goldfish)	1:38.87
2	B. Taylor (Southport)	1:50.76
3	E. Clemett (St Austell)	2:06.52

50 Metres Breaststroke

1	E. Clemett (St Austell)	55.34
2	B. Taylor (Southport)	59.36

100 Metres Breaststroke

1	E. Clemett (St Austell)	2:03.44

50 Metres Butterfly

1	E. Clemett (St Austell)	1:04.50

100 Metres Butterfly

1	E. Clemett (St Austell)	2:32.37

100 Metres Individual Medley

1	E. Clemett (St Austell)	1:53.40

Women

50 Metres Freestyle

1	W. van Rysel (Spencer)	45.62
2	S. Margetts (Torquay Leander)	55.22

100 Metres Freestyle

1	W. van Rysel (Spencer)	1:46.36

200 Metres Freestyle
1 W. van Rysel (Spencer) 4:00.22

50 Metres Backstroke
1 W. van Rysel (Spencer) 48.11
2 S. Margetts (Torquay Leander) 1:04.38

100 Metres Backstroke
1 W. van Rysel (Spencer) 1:47.93

50 Metres Breastroke
1 W. van Rysel (Spencer) 1:05.61

50 Metres Butterfly
1 W. van Rysel (Spencer) 1:01.31

100 Metres Individual Medley
1 W. van Rysel (Spencer) 2:09.76

75/79 Years Age Group
Men

50 Metres Freestyle
1 R. Hodges (Worcester) 51.99
2 T. Bidgood (Black Lion) 1:07.06

50 Metres Backstroke
1 R. Hodges (Worcester) 1:03.27
2 T. Bidgood (Black Lion) 1:33.83

50 Metres Breaststroke
1 R. Hodges (Worcester) 58.58
2 W. Wake (Black Lion) 1:01.09
3 T. Bidgood (Black Lion) 1:22.73

100 Metres Breaststroke
1 R. Hodges (Worcester) 2:15.50

50 Metres Butterfly
1 R. Hodges (Worcester) 1:09.64

100 Metres Individual Medley
1 R. Hodges (Worcester) 2:15.76

Women

50 Metres Freestyle
1 N. Yarwood (Urmston) 1:02.55
2 R. Shephard (Otter) 1:04.83

100 Metres Freestyle
1 R. Shephard (Otter) 2:24.24
2 N. Yarwood (Urmston) 2:31.03

200 Metres Freestyle
1 R. Shephard (Otter) 4:58.52
2 N. Yarwood (Urmston) 5:49.07

50 Metres Backstroke
1 D. Weston (Hounslow B) 59.90
2 N. Yarwood (Urmston) 1:05.18

100 Metres Backstroke
1 N. Yarwood (Urmston) 2:27.25
2 R. Shephard (Otter) 2:44.17

50 Metres Breaststroke
1 D. Weston (Hounslow B) 58.41
2 N. Yarwood (Urmston) 1:16.81

100 Metres Breaststroke
1 D. Weston (Hounslow B) 2:14.02
2 N. Yarwood (Urmston) 2:40.42

100 Metres Individual Medley
1 R. Shephard (Otter) 3:10.90

80/99 Years Age Group
Men

50 Metres Freestyle
1 C. Kozlowski (Serpentine) 51.23

50 Metres Breaststroke
1 C. Kozlowski (Serpentine) 59.64

Current (Short Course) Records

Men

50 Metres Freestyle
25–29 B. Archibald (Motherwell) 23.90
30–34 G. Potter (Redbridge B) 24.81
35–39 W. Mills (Beckenham) 25.05
40–44 T. Jarvis (Motherwell) 25.75
45–49 J. Martin-Dye (Watford) 27.34
50–54 S. Clarke (Plaistow U) 27.83
55–59 K. Weigh (Blackpool) 29.68
60–64 J. Hale (Spencer) 30.42
65–69 F. Gentleman (Motherwell) 31.71
70–74 A. Alvarez (Sans Egal) 34.30
75–79 F. Bramhall (Macclesfield) 37.98
80+ C. Kozlowski (Serpentine) 51.23

100 Metres Freestyle
25–29 N. Goldsworthy
  (Camden Swiss Cottage) 53.10
30–34 D. Dunne (Co Southampton) 54.04
35–39 W. Mills (Beckenham) 55.15
40–44 T. Jarvis (Motherwell) 56.28
45–49 J. Martin-Dye (Watford) 1:00.44
50–54 T. Boyes (York C) 1:02.23
55–59 J. Hale (Spencer) 1:06.89

60–64 J. Hale (Spencer) 1:06.98
65–69 F. Gentleman (Motherwell) 1:11.44
70–74 A. Alvarez (Sans Egal) 1:22.22
75–79 J. Cameron (Tayside) 1:49.85
80+ (Not established as yet)

200 Metres Freestyle
25–29 R. Brew (Maxwell) 1:58.28
30–34 D. Dunne (Co Southampton) 2:00.47
35–39 W. Mills (Beckenham) 2:04.37
40–44 A. McGregor (Warrender) 2:10.69
45–49 J. Martin-Dye (Watford) 2:14.38
50–54 T. Boyes (York C) 2:18.56
55–59 K. Weigh (Blackpool) 2:33.08
60–64 J. Hale (Spencer) 2:32.37
65–69 R. Barker (Co Cambridge) 2:56.34
70–74 A. Alvarez (Sans Egal) 3:12.85
75–79 F. Bramhall (Macclesfield) 3:26.53
80+ L. Cherriman (Seaclose) 5:06.72

400 Metres Freestyle
25–29 W. Mills (Beckenham) 4:16.67
30–34 D. Dunne (Co Southampton) 4:15.12
35–39 E. Riach (Motherwell) 4:30.94
40–44 A. Galletly (Warrender) 4:41.22

283

45–49	A. Galletly (Warrender)	4:45.68
50–54	G. Stokes (Spencer)	4:55.99
55–59	K. Weigh (Blackpool)	5:41.60
60–64	F. Gentleman (Motherwell)	5:54.50
65–69	F. Gentleman (Motherwell)	6:05.89
70–74	G. Huxtable (W Goldfish)	6:54.04
75–79	(Not established as yet)	
80+	(Not established as yet)	

50 Metres Backstroke

25–29	K. Parfoot (Portsmouth Northsea)	28.76
30–34	K. Parfoot (Portsmouth Northsea)	29.27
35–39	J. Rogers (Ashton u Lyne)	29.89
40–44	N. Jackson (Southport)	31.03
45–49	G. Sykes (Co Coventry)	31.07
50–54	G. Sykes (Co Coventry)	31.60
55–59	C. Ward (Stockton)	34.65
60–64	J. Hale (Spencer)	36.92
65–69	F. Gentleman (Motherwell)	38.50
70–74	G. Huxtable (W Goldfish)	42.80
75–79	F. Bramhall (Macclesfield)	46.51
80+	L. Cherriman (Seaclose)	1:16.74

100 Metres Backstroke

25–29	K. Parfoot (Portsmouth Northsea)	1:01.26
30–34	K. Parfoot (Portsmouth Northsea)	1:03.07
35–39	E. Riach (Motherwell)	1:04.25
40–44	J. Gordon (Spencer)	1:08.40
45–49	G. Sykes (Co Coventry)	1:08.98
50–54	G. Sykes (Co Coventry)	1:12.44
55–59	R. Burrell (Launceston)	1:20.30
60–64	T. Summers (Newport & Maindee)	1:26.56
65–69	F. Gentleman (Motherwell)	1:26.25
70–74	G. Huxtable (W Goldfish)	1:38.87
75–79	J. McMillan (Tayside)	2:01.87
80+	(Not established as yet)	

50 Metres Breaststroke

25–29	L. Atkinson (Co Cardiff)	30.91
30–34	L. Atkinson (Newport & Maindee)	31.57
35–39	W. Mills (Beckenham) .	32.95
40–44	B. Cracknell (Redbridge B)	33.63
45–49	J. MacTaggart (Motherwell)	35.22
50–54	P. Jervis (Retford)	35.69
55–59	P. Jervis (Retford)	36.70
60–64	P. Jervis (Retford)	37.88
65–69	R. Barker (Co Cambridge)	43.57
70–74	G. Logan (Glasgow)	45.56
75–79	P. Perkins (Scarborough)	55.41
80+	(Not established as yet)	

100 Metres Breaststroke

25–29	D. Wilkie (Warrender)	1:04.91
30–34	D. Wilkie (Warrender)	1:06.83
35–39	R. Apel (Kettering)	1:13.66
40–44	R. Apel (Kettering)	1:15.14
45–49	C. Doxat (Otter)	1:19.20
50–54	T. Walker (Co Chester)	1:21.41
55–59	P. Jervis (Retford)	1:24.84
60–64	P. Jervis (Retford)	1:27.88
65–69	G. Merryweather (Leamington Spa)	1:39.51
70–74	G. Logan (Glasgow)	1:48.10
75–79	J. McMillan (Tayside)	2:06.39
80+	(Not established as yet)	

50 Metres Butterfly

25–29	P. Morris (Basildon)	25.94
30–34	S. Nash (Aston)	27.57
35–39	J. Mills (Co London Police)	27.56
40–44	R. Frame (Scarborough)	29.44
45–49	J. Cardwell (Co London Police)	29.76

Jack Hale

50–54	S. Clarke (Plaistow U)	31.07
55–59	S. Banning (Norwich Penguins)	33.87
60–64	J. Hale (Spencer)	32.48
65–69	F. Gentleman (Motherwell)	42.46
70–74	A. Alvarez (Sans Egal)	41.50
75–79	F. Bramhall (Macclesfield)	57.09
80+	(Not established as yet)	

100 Metres Butterfly

25–29	P. Morris (Basildon)	57.80
30–34	S. Nash (Aston)	1:00.84
35–39	J. Mills (Co London Police)	1:02.14
40–44	P. Godfrey (Co Cardiff)	1:02.74
45–49	R. Lloyd-Mostyn (Otter)	1:09.13
50–54	G. Stokes (Spencer)	1:12.99
55–59	S. Banning (Norwich Penguins)	1:18.76
60–64	J. Hale (Spencer)	1:16.56
65–69	M. McNulty (Middlesbrough)	2:07.40
70–74	A. Alvarez (Sans Egal)	1:59.56
75–79	(Not established as yet)	
80+	(Not established as yet)	

100 Metres Individual Medley

25–29	P. Morris (Basildon)	1:01.08
30–34	D. Wilkie (Warrender)	1:01.60
35–39	W. Mills (Beckenham)	1:04.23
40–44	J. Gordon (Spencer)	1:07.39
45–49	T. Boyes (York C)	1:10.11
50–54	T. Boyes (York C)	1:13.31
55–59	P. Jervis (Retford)	1:18.15
60–64	P. Jervis (Retford)	1:20.02
65–69	F. Gentleman (Motherwell)	1:27.65
70–74	A. Alvarez (Sans Egal)	1:37.61
75–79	F. Bramhall (Macclesfield)	1:51.24
80+	(Not established as yet)	

200 Metres Individual Medley

25–29	N. Burrows (Portsmouth Northsea)	2:16.09
30–34	T. Clarke (Co Newcastle)	2:24.99
35–39	E. Riach (Motherwell)	2:21.51
40–44	D. Thompson (Portsmouth Northsea)	2:29.00
45–49	A. Galletly (Warrender)	2:35.70
50–54	C. Hardy (Loughborough T)	2:54.46
55–59	C. Bush (Co Chester)	3:12.11

60–64	D. Gunnell (Luton)	3:47.39
65–69	G. Merryweather (Leamington Spa)	3:39.91
70–74	A. Alvarez (Sans Egal)	4:03.09
75–79	(Not established as yet)	
80+	(Not established as yet)	

4×50 Metres Freestyle Club Relay

25+	Camp Hill Edwardians	1:41.09
35+	Motherwell	1:48.06
45+	Otter	1:52.73

4×50 Metres Medley Club Relay

25+	Co Leeds	1:54.88
35+	Motherwell	2:00.27
45+	Otter	2:06.76

Women

50 Metres Freestyle

25–29	H. Turk (Gloucester C)	27.50
30–34	A. Jones (Camden Swiss Cottage)	27.60
35–39	S. Shrimpton (Co Exeter)	29.46
40–44	S. O'Neil (Darwen)	29.98
45–49	F. Connolly (Bracknell)	33.96
50–54	B. Walker (Co Chester)	34.20
55–59	J. Asher (Norwich Swan)	33.56
60–64	M. Cunningham (Motherwell)	35.47
65–69	D. Cope (Co Exeter)	38.18
70–74	W. van Rysel (Spencer)	42.40
75–79	V. Cherriman (Seaclose)	45.95
80+	V. Cherriman (Seaclose)	52.43

100 Metres Freestyle

25–29	L. Marshall (Spencer)	1:00.39
30–34	A. Jones (Camden Swiss Cottage)	1:00.02
35–39	S. Shrimpton (Co Exeter)	1:04.72
40–44	S. Shrimpton (Co Exeter)	1:05.72
45–49	F. Connolly (Bracknell)	1:15.91
50–54	F. Connolly (Warrender)	1:17.12
55–59	J. Asher (Norwich Swan)	1:13.78
60–64	M. Cunningham (Motherwell)	1:22.89
65–69	D. Cope (Co Exeter)	1:32.92
70–74	W. van Rysel (BLDSA)	1:43.97
75–79	V. Cherriman (Seaclose)	1:45.53
80+	V. Cherriman (Seaclose)	1:53.70

200 Metres Freestyle

25–29	A. Jones (Camden Swiss Cottage)	2:09.36
30–34	A. Jones (Camden Swiss Cottage)	2:15.72
35–39	S. Shrimpton (Co Exeter)	2:28.33
40–44	S. O'Neil (Darwen)	2:28.35
45–49	P. Webster (Kingston Royals)	2:50.19
50–54	B. Walker (Co Chester)	2:49.21
55–59	F. Connolly (Edinburgh)	2:44.69
60–64	D. Cope (Co Exeter)	3:29.10
65–69	D. Cope (Co Exeter)	3:39.81
70–74	W. van Rysel (Spencer)	3:52.21
75–79	V. Cherriman (Seaclose)	3:52.86
80+	V. Cherriman (Seaclose)	4:19.12

400 Metres Freestyle

25–29	L. Marshall (Spencer)	4:30.49
30–34	A. Jones (Camden Swiss Cottage)	4:41.36
35–39	J. Figes (Bristol Masters)	5:22.24
40–44	S. O'Neil (Darwen)	5:16.58
45–49	M. Clark (RADS)	5:53.94
50–54	F. Connolly (Heart of Midlothian)	5:56.52
55–59	F. Connolly (Edinburgh)	5:44.40
60–64	M. Cunningham (Motherwell)	6:54.11
65–69	W. van Rysel (BLDSA)	7:33.89
70–74	W. van Rysel (Spencer)	7:59.28

| 75–79 | V. Cherriman (Seaclose) | 7:56.05 |
| 80+ | V. Cherriman (Seaclose) | 8:51.10 |

50 Metres Backstroke

25–29	A. Jones (Camden Swiss Cottage)	32.97
30–34	S. Rogers (Stalybridge)	33.72
35–39	S. Rogers (Ashton u Lyne)	33.39
40–44	S. O'Neil (Darwen)	36.34
45–49	M. Arnold (Mansfield)	36.62
50–54	S. Bramham (Co Liverpool)	38.50
55–59	J. Asher (Norwich Swan)	40.38
60–64	W. van Rysel (BLDSA)	44.39
65–69	W. van Rysel (BLDSA)	44.16
70–74	W. van Rysel (Spencer)	45.08
75–79	D. Weston (Hounslow B)	58.63
80+	V. Cherriman (Seaclose)	1:05.08

100 Metres Backstroke

25–29	J. Admans (Slough Dolphins)	1:08.96
30–34	S. Rogers (Stalybridge)	1:13.12
35–39	S. Rogers (Ashton u Lyne)	1:12.85
40–44	J. Whyman (Albyns)	1:19.47
45–49	C. Bye (Eastleigh FP)	1:25.24
50–54	B. Walker (Co Chester)	1:28.10
55–59	F. Connolly (Edinburgh)	1:30.03
60–64	O. Hale (Beckenham)	1:40.23
65–69	W. van Rysel (Spencer)	1:42.92
70–74	W. van Rysel (Spencer)	1:44.02
75–79	V. Cherriman (Seaclose)	2:13.94
80+	V. Cherriman (Seaclose)	2:24.00

50 Metres Breaststroke

25–29	M. Hohmann (Nova Centurion)	34.55
30–34	M. Hohmann (Wigan Wasps)	34.27
35–39	C. Ilman (Co Cambridge)	37.86
40–44	E. Bromwich (Rugby)	39.10
45–49	R. Palmer (Co Oxford)	39.71
50–54	F. Connolly (Warrender)	39.87
55–59	F. Connolly (Edinburgh)	41.45
60–64	M. Cunningham (Motherwell)	48.19
65–69	M. Povey (Gravesend & Northfleet)	48.84
70–74	B. Hooper (Newport & Maindee)	56.93
75–79	E. Hewitt (Heston)	58.00
80+	V. Cherriman (Seaclose)	1:07.65

Willy van Rysel

100 Metres Breaststroke

25–29	M. Hohmann (Nova Centurion)	1:15.62
30–34	M. Hohmann (Wigan Wasps)	1:14.39
35–39	C. Ilman (Co Cambridge)	1:21.50
40–44	E. Bromwich (Rugby)	1:24.96
45–49	D. Ford (Rushmoor Royals)	1:27.77
50–54	F. Connolly (Whitehall)	1:28.94
55–59	F. Connolly (Edinburgh)	1:28.61
60–64	M. Evans (Redbridge B)	1:44.12
65–69	D. Williams (Hounslow B)	1:53.78
70–74	B. Hooper (Newport & Maindee)	2:11.23
75–79	D. Weston (Hounslow B)	2:06.60
80+	V. Cherriman (Seaclose)	2:44.80

50 Metres Butterfly

25–29	H. Turk (Gloucester C)	29.80
30–34	A. Jones (Camden Swiss Cottage)	31.59
35–39	S. Rogers (Ashton u Lyne)	32.09
40–44	G. Adams (W Goldfish)	33.07
45–49	D. Ford (Rushmoor Royals)	38.10
50–54	J. Asher (Norwich Swan)	38.96
55–59	J. Asher (Norwich Swan)	37.87
60–64	M. Cunningham (Motherwell)	46.15
65–69	W. van Rysel (BLDSA)	51.67
70–74	W. van Rysel (BLDSA)	54.80
75–79	V. Cherriman (Seaclose)	1:03.13
80+	V. Cherriman (Seaclose)	1:13.27

100 Metres Butterfly

25–29	S. McDonald (Paisley)	1:05.71
30–34	A. Jones (Camden Swiss Cottage)	1:10.71
35–39	S. Shrimpton (Co Exeter)	1:17.29
40–44	G. Adams (W Goldfish)	1:15.51
45–49	D. Ford (Rushmoor Royals)	1:27.16
50–54	F. Connolly (Heart of Midlothian)	1:31.39
55–59	F. Connolly (Edinburgh)	1:27.88
60–64	(Not established as yet)	
65–69	(Not established as yet)	
70–74	(Not established as yet)	

75–79	(Not established as yet)	
80+	(Not established as yet)	

100 Metres Individual Medley

25–29	A. Jones (Camden Swiss Cottage)	1:08.54
30–34	A. Jones (Camden Swiss Cottage)	1:09.12
35–39	C. Ilman (Co Cambridge)	1:15.23
40–44	S. O'Neil (Darwen)	1:16.08
45–49	R. Palmer (Co Oxford)	1:23.68
50–54	F. Connolly (Warrender)	1:25.37
55–59	F. Connolly (Edinburgh)	1:25.61
60–64	M. Cunningham (Motherwell)	1:37.76
65–69	W. van Rysel (BLDSA)	1:49.22
70–74	W. van Rysel (Spencer)	1:57.95
75–79	V. Cherriman (Seaclose)	2:08.70
80+	V. Cherriman (Seaclose)	2:21.39

200 Metres Individual Medley

25–29	L. McLeish (Belgrave)	2:34.66
30–34	T. Dixon (Hartlepool)	2:46.21
35–39	A. Cork (Slough Dolphins)	2:50.91
40–44	S. O'Neil (Darwen)	2:50.12
45–49	F. Connolly (Whitehall)	3:08.34
50–54	F. Connolly (Whitehall)	3:03.95
55–59	J. Asher (Norwich Swan)	3:23.86
60–64	(Not established as yet)	
65–69	Y. Hodges (Worcester)	4:35.47
70–74	(Not established as yet)	
75–79	(Not established as yet)	
80+	(Not established as yet)	

4×50 Metres Freestyle Club Relay

25+	Camden Swiss Cottage	1:54.32
35+	Bristol Masters	2:16.40
45+	Bristol Masters	2:41.16

4×50 Metres Medley Club Relay

25+	Camden Swiss Cottage	2:08.62
35+	Kingston Royals	2:27.43
45+	Motherwell	3:15.10

Current (Long Course) Records

Men

50 Metres Freestyle

25–29	B. Archibald (Motherwell)	25.16
30–34	G. Potter (Redbridge B)	26.04
35–39	A. Mills (Beckenham)	26.22
40–44	P. Prijdekker (Ealing)	26.35
45–49	I. McLean (Southport)	28.02
50–54	S. Clarke (Plaistow U)	28.26
55–59	K. Weigh (Blackpool)	30.13
60–64	F. Gentleman (Motherwell)	32.51
65–69	J. Hale (Spencer)	33.34
70–74	A. Alvarez (Sans Egal)	35.49
75–79	F. Bramhall (Macclesfield)	40.66
80+	C. Kozlowski (Serpentine)	53.73

100 Metres Freestyle

25–29	N. Burrows (Portsmouth Northsea)	55.70
30–34	P. Rose (Chester le Street)	56.54
35–39	A. Mills (Beckenham)	56.74
40–44	P. Prijdekker (Ealing)	58.00
45–49	J. Martin-Dye (Watford)	1:02.32
50–54	T. Boyes (York C)	1:02.62
55–59	T. Holmyard (Bristol Masters)	1:09.67
60–64	F. Gentleman (Motherwell)	1:15.10
65–69	R. MacAlister (Tynedale)	1:25.03

70–74	A. Alvarez (Sans Egal)	1:20.97
75–79	D. Davey (Faversham)	1:53.95
80+	L. Cherriman (Seaclose)	2:15.99

200 Metres Freestyle

25–29	N. Burrows (Portsmouth Northsea)	2:05.21
30–34	P. Rose (Chester le Street)	2:07.29
35–39	A. Mills (Beckenham)	2:08.89
40–44	P. Prijdekker (Ealing)	2:09.05
45–49	J. Martin-Dye (Watford)	2:18.81
50–54	T. Boyes (York C)	2:20.36
55–59	K. Weigh (Blackpool)	2:36.44
60–64	F. Gentleman (Motherwell)	2:54.41
65–69	J. Hale (Spencer)	2:35.38
70–74	A. Alvarez (Sans Egal)	3:17.64
75–79	F. Bramhall (Macclesfield)	3:49.34
80+	L. Cherriman (Seaclose)	4:55.37

400 Metres Freestyle

25–29	N. Burrows (Portsmouth Northsea)	4:33.85
30–34	A. Chapman (Bristol Masters)	5:02.63
35–39	S. Grossman (Rushmoor Royals)	4:43.92
40–44	P. Prijdekker (Ealing)	4:49.86
45–49	J. Martin-Dye (Watford)	4:59.81
50–54	T. Boyes (York C)	5:03.41
55–59	T. Holmyard (Bristol Masters)	5:42.21

60–64	T. Sweeting (Bury & Elton)	6:25.49
65–69	L. Hoy (Thurrock)	6:52.03
70–74	E. Clemett (St Austell)	7:29.52
75–79	(Not established as yet)	
80+	L. Cherriman (Seaclose)	10:47.44

1000 Metres Freestyle

25–29	M. Jones (Everton)	12:30.70
30–34	D. Cometson (RAF)	12:24.51
35–39	M. Sarsfield (Shepshed)	15:46.82
40–44	A. Pearce (Spencer)	13:04.29
45–49	A. Galletly (Warrender)	12:52.42
50–54	D. Reynolds (Beckenham)	14:08.68
55–59	T. Holmyard (Bristol Masters)	15:18.78
60–64	K. Knapp (Redcar)	17:21.01
65–69	J. Hale (Spencer)	14:27.33
70–74	E. Clemett (St Austell)	19:41.23
75–79	(Not established as yet)	
80+	(Not established as yet)	

50 Metres Backstroke

25–29	C. Norrey (Camp Hill Edwardians)	29.22
30–34	S. Burcham (Kenilworth)	30.13
35–39	D. Hamm (Brighton)	32.17
40–44	J. Gordon (Spencer)	31.69
45–49	J. Lake (Spencer)	32.87
50–54	T. Weston (Romsey)	34.03
55–59	C. Ward (Stockton)	35.21
60–64	T. Summers (Newport & Maindee)	38.53
65–69	J. Hale (Spencer)	32.61
70–74	G. Huxtable (W Goldfish)	43.22
75–79	F. Bramhall (Macclesfield)	49.79
80+	L. Cherriman (Seaclose)	1:17.03

100 Metres Backstroke

25–29	M. Priestley (Co Bradford)	1:04.15
30–34	S. Burcham (Kenilworth)	1:05.91
35–39	J. Rogers (Ashton u Lyne)	1:07.55
40–44	N. Jackson (Southport)	1:09.43
45–49	J. Lake (Spencer)	1:13.68
50–54	C. Hardy (Loughborough T)	1:15.85
55–59	R. Burrell (Launceston)	1:21.16
60–64	T. Summers (Newport & Maindee)	1:27.42
65–69	A. Laylee (Liverpool University)	1:32.59
70–74	G. Huxtable (W Goldfish)	1:45.39
75–79	(Not established as yet)	
80+	(Not established as yet)	

200 Metres Backstroke

25–29	M. McKinney (Comm Education)	2:28.65
30–34	A. Gentleman (Motherwell)	2:28.59
35–39	J. Rogers (Ashton u Lyne)	2:30.17
40–44	J. Gordon (Spencer)	2:36.09
45–49	J. Lake (Spencer)	2:45.65
50–54	N. Trusty (Spencer)	3:13.56
55–59	R. Burrell (Launceston)	2:58.56
60–64	T. Summers (Newport & Maindee)	3:12.06
65–69	J. Hale (Spencer)	2:59.42
70–74	J. McMillan (Tayside)	4:13.37
75–79	(Not established as yet)	
80+	(Not established as yet)	

50 Metres Breaststroke

25–29	D. Millburn (Ealing)	32.77
30–34	S. Papas (Bracknell)	34.22
35–39	K. Browne (Camden Swiss Cottage)	35.15
40–44	R. Apel (Spencer)	34.14
45–49	A. Canham (Broomfield Park)	36.11
50–54	T. Walker (Co Chester)	36.93
55–59	P. Jervis (Retford)	38.88

60–64	P. Jervis (Retford)	39.88
65–69	G. Merryweather (Leamington Spa)	45.28
70–74	R. Romain (Otter)	41.56
75–79	C. Jones (Leith)	52.39
80+	C. Kozlowski (Serpentine)	1:01.04

100 Metres Breaststroke

25–29	B. O'Brien (Wellingborough)	1:11.43
30–34	D. Wilkie (Warrender)	1:08.17
35–39	P. Taylor (Stockton Aquatics)	1:16.80
40–44	R. Apel (Spencer)	1:17.85
45–49	C. Doxat (Otter)	1:22.41
50–54	T. Walker (Co Chester)	1:21.36
55–59	P. Jervis (Retford)	1:30.42
60–64	P. Jervis (Retford)	1:29.74
65–69	G. Merryweather (Leamington Spa)	1:43.68
70–74	R. Romain (Otter)	1:39.19
75–79	D. Davey (Faversham)	2:17.34
80+	(Not established as yet)	

200 Metres Breaststroke

25–29	B. O'Brien (Wellingborough)	2:39.15
30–34	D. Wilkie (Warrender)	2:29.56
35–39	S. Bratt (Bristol Masters)	2:53.87
40–44	R. Apel (Spencer)	2:56.13
45–49	A. Galletley (Warrender)	3:03.60
50–54	T. Walker (Co Chester)	3:01.40
55–59	C. Bush (Chester)	3:29.63
60–64	P. Jervis (Retford)	3:39.35
65–69	J. Frith (Warrender)	3:42.16
70–74	R. Romain (Otter)	3:42.25
75–79	(Not established as yet)	
80+	(Not established as yet)	

50 Metres Butterfly

25–29	T. Rose (Albyns)	27.72
30–34	S. Nash (Heath Town)	28.23
35–39	J. Mills (London Police)	27.78
40–44	P. Prijdekker (Ealing)	28.71
45–49	D. Cherriman (York C)	30.77
50–54	S. Clarke (Plaistow U)	31.82
55–59	R. Burrell (Launceston)	33.63
60–64	F. Gentleman (Motherwell)	41.70
65–69	J. Hale (Spencer)	33.34
70–74	A. Alvarez (Sans Egal)	43.40
75–79	F. Bramhall (Macclesfield)	1:02.50
80+	(Not established as yet)	

100 Metres Butterfly

25–29	T. Rose (Albyns)	1:01.71
30–34	S. Nash (Heath Town)	1:01.98
35–39	J. Mills (London Police)	1:03.16
40–44	T. Jarvis (Motherwell)	1:04.93
45–49	R. Lloyd-Mostyn (Otter)	1:09.21
50–54	G. Stokes (Spencer)	1:13.03
55–59	S. Banning (Norwich Penguins)	1:22.74
60–64	J. Hale (Spencer)	1:19.90
65–69	(Not established as yet)	
70–74	A. Alvarez (Sans Egal)	2:01.46
75–79	(Not established as yet)	
80+	(Not established as yet)	

200 Metres Butterfly

25–29	P. Tainty (Camp Hill Edwardians)	2:28.26
30–34	S. Nash (Heath Town)	2:21.18
35–39	(Not established as yet)	
40–44	T. Pearce (Spencer)	2:45.14
45–49	A. Galletly (Warrender)	2:39.84
50–54	T. Boyes (York C)	2:57.20
55–59	C. Bush (Co Chester)	3:47.05

60–64	J. Hale (Spencer)	3:09.36
65–69	J. Paterson (Bootle & N Liverpool)	4:14.93
70–74	R. Romain (Otter)	3:55.42
75–79	(Not established as yet)	
80+	(Not established as yet)	

200 Metres Individual Medley

25–29	N. Burrows (Portsmouth Northsea)	2:22.62
30–34	D. Wilkie (Warrender)	2:15.89
35–39	D. Hamm (Brighton)	2:36.63
40–44	P. Prijdekker (Ealing)	2:32.23
45–49	A. Galletly (Warrender)	2:34.99
50–54	T. Boyes (York C)	2:40.60
55–59	K. Weigh (Blackpool)	3:04.76
60–64	T. Sweeting (Bury & Elton)	3:29.28
65–69	J. Paterson (Bootle & N Liverpool)	3:45.27
70–74	A. Alvarez (Sans Egal)	4:01.40
75–79	R. Hodges (Worcester)	4:48.68
80+	(Not established as yet)	

4×50 Metres Freestyle Club Relay

25+	Camp Hill Edwardians	1:44.07
35+	Beckenham	1:54.79
45+	Plaistow U	2:02.29

4×50 Metres Medley Club Relay

25+	Otter	1:57.90
35+	Spencer	2:06.17
45+	Spencer	2:21.97

Women

50 Metres Freestyle

25–29	H. Turk (Gloucester Masters)	27.91
30–34	A. Jones (Camden Swiss Cottage)	28.70
35–39	R. Thompson (Kingston)	30.86
40–44	S. O'Neil (Darwen)	30.19
45–49	J. Wilson (Beckenham)	31.13
50–54	S. Bramham (Co Liverpool)	34.90
55–59	J. Asher (Norwich Swan)	34.27
60–64	O. Hale (Beckenham)	42.26
65–69	D. Cope (York C)	38.73
70–74	W. van Rysel (Spencer)	45.07
75–79	O. Banfield (Beckenham)	46.00
80+	V. Cherriman (Seaclose)	53.02

100 Metres Freestyle

25–29	H. Turk (Gloucester Masters)	1:00.97
30–34	A. Jones (Camden Swiss Cottage)	1:01.82
35–39	S. Platt-Rogers (Ashton u Lyne)	1:07.63
40–44	S. O'Neil (Darwen)	1:06.49
45–49	J. Wilson (Beckenham)	1:10.71
50–54	B. Walker (Co Chester)	1:18.82
55–59	J. Asher (Norwich Swan)	1:20.18
60–64	O. Hale (Beckenham)	1:38.95
65–69	B. Condon (Bromley)	1:45.73
70–74	W. van Rysel (Spencer)	1:46.23
75–79	E. Hewitt (Heston)	1:55.72
80+	V. Cheriman (Seaclose)	1:59.22

200 Metres Freestyle

25–29	L. Marshall (Spencer)	2:11.56
30–34	A. Jones (Camden Swiss Cottage)	2:16.21
35–39	L. Powell (Barnet Copthall)	2:35.72
40–44	S. O'Neil (Darwen)	2:28.04
45–49	J. Wilson (Beckenham)	2:49.11
50–54	F. Connolly (Heart of Midlothian)	2:51.24
55–59	J. Asher (Norwich Swan)	2:52.60
60–64	M. Evans (Redbridge B)	3:36.35
65–69	M. Evans (Redbridge B)	3:53.83

70–74	W. van Rysel (Spencer)	4:04.56
75–79	V. Cherriman (Seaclose)	3:52.90
80+	V. Cherriman (Seaclose)	4:16.48

400 Metres Freestyle

25–29	J. Admans (Rushmoor Royals)	4:48.32
30–34	L. Robinson (Spencer)	5:12.27
35–39	S. Magnall (Bo Burnley CATS)	5:48.71
40–44	S. O'Neil (Darwin)	5:19.85
45–49	D. Fairhurst (Wigan Wasps)	6:06.73
50–54	F. Connolly (Heart of Midlothian)	6:04.82
55–59	J. Asher (Norwich Swan)	6:22.55
60–64	O. Hale (Beckenham)	7:34.65
65–69	B. Condon (Bromley)	8:55.21
70–74	W. van Rysel (Spencer)	8:27.16
75–79	V. Cherriman (Seaclose)	8:09.29
80+	V. Cherriman (Seaclose)	9:44.26

1000 Metres Freestyle

25–29	L. Marshall (Spencer)	11:52.66
30–34	A. Jones (Camden Swiss Cottage)	12:48.55
35–39	P. Cooke (Spencer)	15:42.24
40–44	S. O'Neil (Darwen)	14:33.98
45–49	D. Fairhurst (Wigan Wasps)	16:25.20
50–54	M. Wood (Yeovil & D)	19:46.99
55–59	R. Janes (Portsmouth Victoria)	19:29.19
60–64	M. Evans (Redbridge B)	18:42.81
65–69	(Not established as yet)	
70–74	W. van Rysel (Spencer)	22:07.89
75–79	V. Cherriman (Seaclose)	23:39.54
80+	(Not established as yet)	

50 Metres Backstroke

25–29	H. Turk (Gloucester Masters)	33.25
30–34	A. Jones (Camden Swiss Cottage)	34.47
35–39	A. Cork (Slough Dolphins)	35.56
40–44	J. Whyman (Rochford & D)	36.32
45–49	J. Brown (Bristol Masters)	39.31
50–54	S. Bramham (Co Liverpool)	39.75
55–59	J. Asher (Norwich Swan)	40.51
60–64	O. Hale (Beckenham)	45.10
65–69	B. Condon (Bromley)	48.62
70–74	W. van Rysel (Spencer)	46.83
75–79	O. Banfield (Beckenham)	53.26
80+	V. Cherriman (Seaclose)	1:05.74

100 Metres Backstroke

25–29	J. Admans (Rushmoor Royals)	1:10.00
30–34	A. Jones (Camden Swiss Cottage)	1:14.61
35–39	S. Platt-Rogers (Ashton u Lyne)	1:15.46
40–44	J. Whyman (Rochford & D)	1:19.45
45–49	J. Brown (Bristol Masters)	1:26.86
50–54	B. Walker (Co Chester)	1:29.33
55–59	F. Connolly (Edinburgh)	1:34.80
60–64	O. Hale (Beckenham)	1:39.74
65–69	B. Condon (Bromley)	1:53.42
70–74	W. van Rysel (Spencer)	1:47.39
75–79	N. Yarwood (Urmston)	2:36.26
80+	(Not established as yet)	

200 Metres Backstroke

25–29	J. Admans (Rushmoor Royals)	2:25.98
30–34	S. MacDonald (Inverness)	2:52.76
35–39	A. Cork (Slough Dolphins)	2:45.78
40–44	J. Whyman (Albyns)	2:58.53
45–49	J. Brown (Bristol Masters)	3:07.43
50–54	(Not established as yet)	
55–59	J. Asher (Norwich Swan)	3:24.24
60–64	O. Hale (Beckenham)	3:38.22
65–69	B. Condon (Bromley)	4:14.83

70–74	W. van Rysel (Spencer)	4:06.10
75–79	(Not established as yet)	
80+	(Not established as yet)	

50 Metres Breaststroke

25–29	V. Dobbie (Gateshead & Whickham)	36.75
30–34	M. Hohmann (Wigan Wasps)	34.56
35–39	R. Thompson (Kingston)	39.73
40–44	D. Harris (Beckenham)	39.08
45–49	R. Palmer (Co Oxford)	40.57
50–54	F. Connolly (Heart of Midlothian)	42.20
55–59	F. Connolly (Edinburgh)	43.20
60–64	M. Evans (Redbridge B)	50.78
65–69	M. Evans (Redbridge B)	50.26
70–74	B. Swinyard (Beckenham)	59.79
75–79	D. Weston (Heston)	58.32
80+	(Not established as yet)	

100 Metres Breaststroke

25–29	V. Dobbie (Gateshead & Whickham)	1:19.62
30–34	M. Hohmann (Wigan Wasps)	1:14.52
35–39	E. Reid (Co Cambridge)	1:29.15
40–44	D. Ford (Rushmoor Royals)	1:27.50
45–49	D. Ford (Rushmoor Royals)	1:29.17
50–54	F. Connolly (Heart of Midlothian)	1:30.53
55–59	F. Connolly (Edinburgh)	1:34.06
60–64	M. Evans (Redbridge B)	1:51.11
65–69	M. Evans (Redbridge B)	1:50.42
70–74	(Not established as yet)	
75–79	D. Weston (Hounslow B)	2:17.68
80+	(Not established as yet)	

200 Metres Breaststroke

25–29	V. Dobbie (Gateshead & Whickham)	2:52.07
30–34	A. Heath (Spencer)	2:58.96
35–39	E. Reid (Co Cambridge)	3:14.32
40–44	D. Ford (Rushmoor Royals)	3:11.63
45–49	D. Ford (Rushmoor Royals)	3:10.49
50–54	F. Connolly (Heart of Midlothian)	3:14.70
55–59	F. Connolly (Edinburgh)	3:19.65
60–64	M. Evans (Redbridge B)	3:43.72
65–69	M. Ellis (Motherwell)	4:30.71
70–74	(Not established as yet)	
75–79	(Not established as yet)	
80+	(Not established as yet)	

50 Metres Butterfly

25–29	H. Turk (Gloucester Masters)	29.43
30–34	C. Scovell (Shiverers)	32.26
35–39	R. Thompson (Kingston Royals)	34.08
40–44	S. O'Neil (Darwen)	33.31
45–49	J. Wilson (Beckenham)	34.39
50–54	F. Connolly (Heart of Midlothian)	41.67
55–59	J. Asher (Norwich Swan)	39.42
60–64	M. Evans (Redbridge B)	1:02.36
65–69	B. Condon (Bromley)	53.93
70–74	W. van Rysel (Spencer)	57.76
75–79	V. Cherriman (Seaclose)	1:05.26
80+	V. Cherriman (Seaclose)	1:13.71

100 Metres Butterfly

25–29	S. Jenner (Camden Swiss Cottage)	1:07.21
30–34	A. Jones (Camden Swiss Cottage)	1:12.81
35–39	A. Cork (Slough Dolphins)	1:19.56
40–44	G. Adams (W Goldfish)	1:17.36
45–49	J. Wilson (Beckenham)	1:24.49
50–54	F. Connolly (Heart of Midlothian)	1:36.63
55–59	F. Connolly (Edinburgh)	1:30.53

60–64	M. Evans (Redbridge B)	2:24.97
65–69	M. Evans (Redbridge B)	2:08.62
70–74	(Not established as yet)	
75–79	(Not established as yet)	
80+	(Not established as yet)	

200 Metres Butterfly

25–29	S. Jenner (Camden Swiss Cottage)	2:25.58
30–34	A. Heath (Spencer)	2:53.55
35–39	E. Harrison (Nottingham Northern)	3:25.78
40–44	P. Jackson (Howe Bridge)	3:01.44
45–49	V. Buxton (St Helen's)	3:30.28
50–54	F. Connolly (Heart of Midlothian)	3:27.22
55–59	R. Janes (Portsmouth Victoria)	4:37.39
60–64	(Not established as yet)	
65–69	(Not established as yet)	
70–74	(Not established as yet)	
75–79	(Not established as yet)	
80+	(Not established as yet)	

200 Metres Individual Medley

25–29	H. Turk (Gloucester Masters)	2:33.17
30–34	A. Jones (Camden Swiss Cottage)	2:37.66
35–39	A. Cork (Slough Dolphins)	2:50.09
40–44	G. Adams (W Goldfish)	2:52.77
45–49	R. Palmer (Co Oxford)	3:13.93
50–54	F. Connolly (Heart of Midlothian)	3:08.51
55–59	F. Connolly (Edinburgh)	3:11.38
60–64	M. Evans (Redbridge B)	3:58.74
65–69	M. Evans (Redbridge B)	3:57.26
70–74	(Not established as yet)	
75–79	V. Cherriman (Seaclose)	4:38.18
80+	(Not established as yet)	

4×50 Metres Freestyle Club Relay

25+	Gloucester Masters	1:57.43
35+	Barnet Copthall	2:15.55
45+	Rochford & D	2:34.21

4×50 Metres Medley Club Relay

25+	Gloucester Masters	2:13.78
35+	Kingston Royal	2:32.49
45+	Rochford & D	2:53.20

Diana Harris   John Boyd

DIVING
SECTION

The Traditions of Diving

by Ricky Wood (Honorary Secretary, ASA Diving Committee)

"Cor — I'd love to do that!" The speaker has probably just been watching a televised dive, with a slow-motion re-run and an expert commentary. But what would he have seen 100 years ago?

Something very different; things have changed a lot. Broadly, the history of Diving may be sectioned into three periods, which were separated by the World Wars of 1914-18 and 1939-45.

Our 1980s television viewer would hardly suspect that the foundation, laid down around the turn of the century, could be so far removed in concept from what he had just seen. If only we could transport him — first to the Plunge Dive, which swimmers developed from their ordinary swimming dive, and which was the first of its kind to stand as a competitive event. It earned its first Championship in 1893, and it survived for nearly 50 years; even today the Laws of Plunging are contained in Law 401 of the Amateur Swimming Association.

What a significant year 1938 was for the sport! It also heralded and introduced the first diving stage in England. This was a firmboard at the Highgate Pond, in North London.

The old plunge dive paved the way for what is known as the Plain Dive. As its name suggests, it was simply a forward header, with the body straight and the arms extended sideways, and refinements led, in turn, to the names "Swallow" Dive in Europe and "Swan" Dive in the USA. The version in this country, known as the "English Header", did not survive; the required technique made it too difficult to control.

The Plain Dive also had its Championships, which started with a competition for men shortly before the start of the 20th century. It survived the two World Wars until as late as 1961, but its life as such in the Olympic Championships extended only over the 20 years from 1904.

While it is fairly certain that gymnasts introduced "Fancy Diving", in which somersaults and twists were incorporated, it is important to bear in mind that the body was still held straight. Strictly speaking, all early diving was "High Diving", being performed from fixed wooden structures, which varied in height above the water from 4.6 metres to 10 metres. The introduction of "Fancy High Diving" to this country stimulated such excitement generally, that the Amateur Diving Association was inaugurated in 1901, and it existed as a quite separate organisation until its absorption into the then 66-year-old Amateur Swimming Association in 1935. Fancy Dives were first included in competitions in 1903. Men's Plain and Fancy High Diving events pursued their separate courses until they were fused into one event called, simply, High Diving, in the 1928 Olympic Games.

It would appear that the first appearance of a springboard in Britain was delayed until as late as 1923. (F. W. Hobden: *The Art of Springboard Diving*, 1936, p. 213). What, then, prompted the Amateur Diving Association, some two years earlier, to make provisions for certain springboard dimensions? (George Rackham: *Diving Complete*, 1975, p. 21). Springboards were no more than planks fixed at the back and supported — also usually fixed — 4 feet 6 inches from the front end — the fulcrum — so in fact they had very little flexibility.

Women were admitted to Plain Diving competitions just before the First World War, but a further eight years were to elapse before they were admitted to springboard diving, and yet another eight years passed before they had forged their way into Highboard Diving. Even then the range of dives they were allowed to perform was limited for 28 more years!

The period between the two wars was anomalous. In terms of performance, this country was very much in the doldrums, with only very steady and unremarkable progress. Yet this was the period which saw the rise of the USA dominance, which was to last well into the post-1939-45 war period. However, in terms of facilities and technique, there were very significant advances, which did not bear their full fruit until the modern era. The two most outstanding developments were the introduction of tuck and pike positions into diving and the invention of the moveable fulcrum for springboards. The former straight positions of all dives were varied in suitable movements, permitting the body to be bunched up completely (tuck), or to be bent at the hips, but not at the knees

292

(piked). The moveable fulcrum allowed the springboards to be more springy, and this encouraged divers to realise their abilities more adequately, which in turn led to the development of dives of which, hitherto, no-one had even dreamed.

Competitions, too, reflected change by making it compulsory for entrants to perform certain specified dives. Some of them had names which now sound a little odd, like "Isander" (reverse dive) or "Mollberg" (reverse somersault), which were the surnames of the Swedes who introduced them, or "half screw backward" (back dive with a half twist).

They were proud Englishmen who introduced the new Empire Pool, Wembley. It was the first purpose-built indoor pool in England with full diving specifications, designed to host the Empire Games in 1934 and the European Games in 1938, but there were only 98 other pools in the whole country with approved diving facilities. Of these, 67 were outdoor, and thus usable for only a short time each year. Of the indoor baths with springboards, ten had them at heights of 1 metre and 3 metres, five had them at the 1 metre height, only, and two had them at 3 metres. There were 25 baths with "fixed" boards, but only the Empire Pool had boards at both 5 metre and 10 metre heights. There were 18 outdoor venues with fixed boards at 10 metres, almost all of which were at seaside resorts.

At this period, boards were still basically planks. International regulations provided only the required dimensions of springboards, and said they should be "covered along the whole length with coconut matting", and platforms should simply be "covered with coconut matting". The English regulations explained that the springboards used in International and Amateur Swimming Association competitions should be constructed of "Douglas Fir, or of Oregon or British Columbian pine", and the platforms of "Pitch Pine of very straight grain", or of "Teak or other hardwood well seasoned and oiled with linseed oil". Such construction was being recommended in 1951, (Peter Heatly, B.Sc., in a Paper read at the Annual Conference of the National Association of Bath Superintendents), but the author referred with approval to a board built up of three-quarter inch laminations running the full length of the board, which had been introduced from the USA at the 1948 Olympics in London: they rarely warped and were impervious to water.

So, television viewer, this was the diving scene when it became eclipsed by six dark years of World War Two — still a long way from what you have just watched on the "box". But you must move on to the modern era.

One post-war major innovation has revolutionised diving. Springboards were first improved by the application of new materials, particularly fibreglass resin enveloping a wooden core, but by the 1960s wood had been replaced, virtually universally, by an aluminium alloy board from a single manufacturer in the States. This board, now named the Maxiflex, has reached its third generation, and is supported on a sophisticated metal-framed fulcrum made by the same manufacturer. It has done more for the development of springboard diving — and consequently diving generally — than any other single invention connected with the sport. Its phenomenal flexibility can be demonstrated by a good diver, who can depress it a little more than a metre.

The various dives were officially named during the inter-war years in the English, French, and German tongues, but since language was clearly inappropriate for world-wide use, a numbering system was adopted after the 1956 Olympics. This made a description in words of any particular dive unnecessary.

Five judges are normally adequate for most standards of competition, although seven are required for Olympic Games and World Championships. They mark in the range 0 to 10 in half-marks with reference only to the technique and grace of the dive. Each dive has its own difficulty rating — "degree of difficulty" — varying from 1.2 to 3.5, which is calculated under a complex mathematical formula. Any element of bias is avoided by discarding the highest and lowest marks, and in order to arrive at the points scored, the aggregate of the remaining three (or five) marks is multiplied by the degree of difficulty of the dive. If, for instance, the marks awarded for a dive with a degree of difficulty of 1.5 are 5, 5, 6, 6, and 4, one of the sixes and the four are discarded, and the aggregate of the remaining marks — 16 — is multiplied by 1.5 to give 24 points for that dive. A similar calculation is made where there are seven judges, but the result is averaged to three judges for comparison where there are only five officials.

The referee is in charge of the competition, and he ensures that the rules are observed.

Each of the home countries has its own controlling association, but for most international diving — but notably *not* the Commonwealth Games — they combine, as the Amateur Swimming Federation of Great Britain, which organisation is a member of the European and International ruling bodies: LEN (Ligue Europeenne de Natation) and FINA (Federation Internationale de Natation Amateur).

So — back to where we came in, Mr Viewer. What *exactly* is it you'd love to do? If dives with the same number, but different positions (e.g. 103b and 103c), are counted as separate dives — although this may not be done in competitions — you now have a bewildering choice of 544 dives!

	a	b	c	d
1 metre springboard	9	21	28	40
3 metre springboard	11	25	36	37
5 metre platform (and armstand)	10(3)	20(2)	26(5)	36
7½ metre platform (and armstand)	11(4)	24(4)	34(6)	29
10 metre platform (and armstand)	13(4)	27(4)	36(7)	32

The current international programme for divers in Great Britain is geared to the two main events of the year. In 1988, for instance, the premier senior occasions were the European Diving Cup and the Olympic Games. "The Games" are the glamour event of the diving calendar, and for anybody in the sport — whether he or she be competitor, coach, official, or spectator — nothing bears comparison for that person. The meets normally so geared are the Russian "Spring Swallows" in March, and both the Austrian "Volksbank" and the Italian "Bolzano International" in July. A domestic invitational international meet at Crystal Palace in December or January, presently sponsored by the Sun Life Assurance Company, is a showpiece. In May, 1988, a team was also sent to the Can-Am-Mex meet in Florida, USA.

The Olympic Games and the World Championships are regulated by FINA, and are spaced alternately every other year — "Games" in 1988, so "World" in 1990. FINA also has World Age Group competitions. LEN regulates the European Championships (in alternate years between Olympics and World Championships), the European Diving Cup (held annually between 15 March and 15 April), and the European Junior Championships and Youth Diving (held annually in July/August). LEN also introduced Masters Championships in 1987, to be held in alternate years: competitors are grouped in age spans from age 30 upwards.

The dive requirements are the same for all major senior events. Springboard events are performed from the 3 metre board (although 1 metre events will probably be re-introduced in 1990), and all platform events are performed from the 10 metre firmboard. On springboard, women perform ten different dives, and men 11. The first five must cover all five groups — forward, back, reverse, inward, and twist — and their total degree of difficulty must not exceed 9.5. Women then perform five dives, again covering the five groups, but without any restriction of degree of difficulty, and men similarly perform six dives. On platform, women fulfil eight different dives, and men ten. The first four must be from different groups — and it will be recalled that there is the sixth, armstand, group on platform — with a maximum degree of difficulty of 7.6. Women then perform their remaining four dives, which must again be selected from different groups, but without any degree of difficulty, and men similarly execute six dives, taking one from each group. In all events, the first 12 go forward into the final, and they perform eight (or ten or 11) dives again. The diver may change the dives in the final, but there are the same restrictions of degree of difficulty and the requirements of covering all groups and the non-repetition of dives. The winner is the diver who scores most points in the final.

The European Junior Championships are for girls and boys aged 16, 17, or 18, and the European Youth Championships will be introduced in 1989, at the same time as the Junior Championships for girls and boys of 14 or 15. In the Junior Championships, the full Olympic programme of dives is performed, but the 5 metre platform may be used. In the Youth Championships there are eight dives from the 1 metre springboard and six dives from the 5 metre platform. FINA has two Age Group competitions: Group A, ages 16, 17 or 18, in which the full Olympic programme is executed on the 1 metre and 3 metre springboards and on the 5/10 metre platforms, and Group B, ages 14 or 15, in which eight springboard dives are performed at 1 metre and 3 metres and six platform dives are performed at 5/7½ metres.

ASA Championships, 1988–89

The Leisure Centre, Oldham — 3/4 December, 1988 (1 Metre Championships) & Central Park Pool, Plymouth — 19/21 May, 1989

Men

1 Metre Springboard

1 R. Morgan (Highgate)	451.15
2 J. Statham (Barnet Copthall)	447.40
3 A. Byford (Highgate)	422.15
4 R. Grevett (Plymouth C)	377.20
5 A. Bowdery (Southend on Sea)	370.75
6 J. Ramsey (Beaumont)	357.70
7 C. Chester (Oldham)	356.05
8 S. Brown (RTW Monson)	326.60
9 H. Lofti (Iran)	267.25

3 Metre Springboard

1 R. Morgan (Barnet Copthall)	619.70
2 J. Arbon (Essex Cormorants)	599.95
3 G. Morris (Huddersfield)	564.35
4 J. Statham (Southend on Sea)	537.25
5 P. McCord (Southend on Sea)	504.95
6 S. Jackson (Sheffield C)	501.75
7 A. Bowdery (Southend on Sea)	466.00
8 A. Ali (Southend on Sea)	457.60
9 P. Smith (E Kilbride)	451.15

Highboard

1 R. Morgan (Barnet Copthall)	562.30
2 J. Arbon (Essex Cormorants)	474.20
3 J. Statham (Southend on Sea)	427.50
4 P. Smith (E Kilbride)	424.05
5 S. Forrest (Edinburgh)	421.00
6 C. Bratt (Highgate)	365.05

Robert Morgan (left), who won all three titles at this year's championships, is pictured with Britain's leading diver of the '50s and '60, Brian Phelps.

Women

1 Metre Springboard

1	S. Ryan (The Ladies)	333.00
2	L. Ward (The Ladies)	328.15
3	A. Roffey (Leeds Esprit)	325.70
4	T. Miles (The Ladies)	323.05
5	M. Cordey (Oldham)	317.30
6	C. Hughes (Southend on Sea)	300.40
7	K. Wenden (The Ladies)	298.20
8	H. Allen (RTW Monson)	292.95
9	A. Day (Luton Kingfishers)	290.95
10	B. Ackroyd (Southend on Sea)	268.40
11	R. Ainsworth (Mole Valley)	265.00
12	V. Stenning (Southend on Sea)	259.35
13	J. Booth (Huddersfield)	256.10
14	L. Robertson (Bramston)	248.60
15	K. Owen (Mersey)	245.90
16	S. Perry (Luton Kingfishers)	243.95
17	A. Tatch (The Ladies)	239.35
18	T. Wells (Luton Kingfishers)	225.75

3 Metre Springboard

1	N. Bishop (Oldham)	413.95
2	S. Ryan (The Ladies)	411.85
3	K. Shortell (Cheltenham)	408.10
4	L. Ward (The Ladies)	403.25
5	C. Roscoe (The Ladies)	391.00
6	O. Clark (Cheltenham)	389.60
7	T. Miles (The Ladies)	385.60
8	K. Lewis (Po Plymouth)	355.85
9	A. Tatch (Waltham Forest)	346.15
10	N. Cordey (Oldham)	311.30
11	K. Ingram (Dundee)	303.50
12	C. Hughes (Southend on Sea)	303.15
13	A. Bishop (Dundee)	296.45

Highboard

1	S. Ryan (The Ladies)	391.60
2	L. Ward (The Ladies)	337.65
3	T. Miles (The Ladies)	311.85
4	K. Wenden (The Ladies)	299.85
5	C. Haith (Leeds Esprit)	277.15
6	A. Bishop (Dundee)	246.50

Junior Men

1 Metre Springboard

1	A. Bowdery (Southend on Sea)	442.00
2	S. Gladding (Highgate)	417.65
3	A. Byford (Highgate)	390.60
4	M. Buddle (Highgate)	388.20
5	M. Shipman (Bradford Esprit)	380.85
6	S. Callaghan (Luton Kingfishers)	372.90
7	L. Celauro (Southend on Sea)	316.55
8	S. Brown (RTW Monson)	306.70
9	J. Teal (Bradford Esprit)	296.30

3 Metre Springboard

1	A. Byford (Highgate)	477.10
2	A. Ali (Southend on Sea)	475.90
3	S. Gladding (Highgate)	418.35
4	M. Shipman (Bradford Esprit)	417.10
5	S. Brown (RTW Monson)	413.00
6	L. Celauro (Southend on Sea)	392.95
7	J. Teal (Bradford Esprit)	344.50
8	R. Hesling (Southend on Sea)	293.85

Highboard

1	A. Ali (Southend on Sea)	356.85
2	A. Byford (Highgate)	334.95
3	J. Karseras (Cardiff)	316.10
4	M. Shipman (Bradford Esprit)	291.85
5	J. Dundas (Crystal Palace)	286.05
6	L. Celauro (Southend on Sea)	265.95
7	R. Hesling (Southend on Sea)	265.70
8	S. Brown (RTW Monson)	265.30
9	C. Bratt (Highgate)	263.30
10	S. Holloway (Luton Kingfishers)	236.10
11	T. Maguire (Southend on Sea)	229.65
12	D. Bratt (Southend on Sea)	227.25
13	M. Webb (Beaumont)	221.60
14	J. Teal (Bradford Esprit)	200.30
15	D. Neale (Luton Kingfishers)	190.20

Junior Women

1 Metre Springboard

1	A. Roffey (Leeds Esprit)	339.25
2	C. Hughes (Southend on Sea)	324.95
3	Z. Breeze (Leeds Esprit)	317.45
4	A. Tatch (Waltham Forest)	308.80
5	V. Stenning (Southend on Sea)	308.40
6	R. Ainsworth (Mole Valley)	297.65
7	H. Allen (RTW Monson)	297.55
8	K. Wenden (The Ladies)	297.40
9	K. Lewis (Plymouth C)	289.95
10	B. Ackroyd (Southend on Sea)	283.75
11	A. Day (N Bedford)	274.80
12	K. Owen (Mersey)	268.15
13	L. Robertson (Bramston)	267.05
14	J. Ratcliffe (Southend on Sea)	263.60
15	T. Wells (Luton Kingfishers)	262.25

3 Metre Springboard

1	A. Roffey (Leeds Esprit)	413.60
2	C. Hughes (Southend on Sea)	350.50
3	H. Tatch (Waltham Forest)	343.40
4	Z. Breeze (Leeds Esprit)	340.95
5	V. Stenning (Southend on Sea)	336.05
6	A. Tatch (Waltham Forest)	331.70
7	K. Lewis (Po Plymouth)	319.85
8	B. Ackroyd (Southend on Sea)	287.10
9	J. Ratcliffe (Southend on Sea)	271.25
10	S. Freeman (Po Plymouth)	257.30
11	T. Wells (Luton Kingfishers)	255.10

Highboard

1	H. Allen (Southend on Sea)	264.70
2	C. Hughes (Southend on Sea)	247.95
3	K. Wenden (The Ladies)	247.25
4	Z. Breeze (Leeds Esprit)	245.95
5	H. Tatch (Waltham Forest)	243.55
6	A. Tatch (Waltham Forest)	237.65
7	B. Ackroyd (Southend on Sea)	237.00
8	T. Wells (Luton Kingfishers)	235.85
9	J. Ratcliffe (Southend on Sea)	232.10
10	S. Bayliss (RTW Monson)	217.10
11	M. Taylor (Crystal Palace)	183.70
12	S. Freeman (Po Plymouth)	176.95
13	E. Burton (Oldham)	176.70
14	L. Kempster (Luton Kingfishers)	166.50
15	J. Ellis (Southend on Sea)	163.70
16	F. Couttie (Leeds Esprit)	161.30
17	N. Farr (N Bradford)	151.60
18	R. Stutter (Beaumont)	144.00

International Results, 1988–89

Olympic Games, 1988
Seoul, S Korea — 17/20 September, 1988

Men

3 Metre Springboard
Final

1 G. Louganis (USA)	730.80
2 L. Tan (China)	704.88
3 D. Li (China)	665.28

British Competitors

26 G. Morris (GBR)	478.74
29 R. Morgan (GBR)	457.65

Highboard
Final

1 G. Louganis (USA)	638.61
2 N. Xiong (China)	637.47
3 J. Mena (Mexico)	594.39

British Competitors

15 R. Morgan (GBR)	489.27
21 J. Arbon (GBR)	450.18

Women

3 Metre Springboard
Final

1 M. Gao (China)	580.23
2 Q. Li (China)	534.33
3 K. Mc Cormick (USA)	533.19

British Competitors

18 C. Roscoe (GBR)	399.87
26 N. Bishop (GBR)	349.44

Highboard
Final

1 Y. Xu (China)	445.20
2 M. Mitchell (USA)	436.95
3 W. Williams (USA)	400.44

British Competitors

18 C. Roscoe (GBR)	322.35

The Spring Swallows Tournament
Yerevan, USSR — 9/12 March, 1989

Men

3 Metre Springboard
Final

1 P. Jeffries (USA)	644.67
2 A. Ramirez (Cuba)	643.28
3 V. Statsenko (USSR)	642.06

British Competitors

18 R. Morgan (GBR)	551.04
25 J. Statham (GBR)	517.50
30 G. Morris (GBR)	507.45

Highboard
Final

1 A. Dzhavadyan (USSR)	639.03
2 V. Timoshinin (USSR)	627.35
3 M. Scoggins (USA)	588.58

British Competitors

6 R. Morgan (GBR)	552.45
27 S. Forrest (GBR)	392.67

Women

3 Metre Springboard
Final

1 Z. Yuping (China)	515.46
2 I. Lashko (USSR)	513.69
3 G. Quing (China)	507.06

British Competitors

25 S. Ryan (GBR)	382.71

Highboard
Final

1 G. Quing (China)	431.22
2 O. Miroshenko (USSR)	419.40
3 U. Wetzig (GDR)	418.56

British Competitors

16 S. Ryan (GBR)	350.16

European Cup
Zurich, Switzerland — 30 March/2 April, 1989

Men

3 Metre Springboard
Final

1 A. Killat (W Germany)	
2 V. Statsenko (USSR)	
3 S. Lomanowsky (USSR)	

British Competitors

9 R. Morgan (GBR)	519.24

13 G. Morris (GBR)	487.05

Highboard
Final

1 V. Timoshinin (USSR)	
2 J. Hempel (GDR)	
3 R. Morgan (GBR)	

Other British Competitors

17 S. Forrest (GBR)	355.44

Women

3 Metre Springboard
Final
1 D. Krueger (GDR)
2 B. Baldus (GDR)
3 I. Lashko (USSR)
British Competitors
11 S. Ryan (GBR)   376.98

Highboard
Final
1 C. Schmalfuss (GDR)
2 D. Pecher (W Germany)
3 M. Kuehn (W Germany)
British Competitors
9 S. Ryan (GBR)   315.51

The Volksbank International
Vienna, Austria — 7/9 July, 1989

Men

3 Metre Springboard
Final
1 K. Feguson (USA)
2 K. Mena (Mexico)
3 N. Stajkovic (Austria)
British Competitors
15 R. Morgan (GBR)   421.71
27 J. Arbon (GBR)   368.55

Highboard
Final
1 J. Mena (Mexico)
2 P. Jeffries (USA)
3 Q. Wang (China)
British Competitors
5 R. Morgan (GBR)   443.88
18 J. Arbon (GBR)   367.71

Women

3 Metre Springboard
Final
1 G. Xueging (China)
2 B. Bush (Canada)
3 M. Alcala (Mexico)
British Competitors
19 N. Bishop (GBR)   321.24

Highboard
Final
1 X. Xueging (China)
2 A. Dacyshyn (Canada)
3 U. Wetzig (GDR)

20 Nations International
Bozano, Italy — 12/13 July, 1989

Men

3 Metre Springboard
Final
1 K. Ferguson (USA)   624.54
2 V. Goncharov (USSR)   583.23
3 J. Mena (Mexico)   579.69
British Competitors
19 J. Arbon (GBR)   305.64
22 R. Morgan (GBR)   301.23

Highboard
Final
1 J. Tu (China)   580.47
2 O. Wang (China)   531.81
3 S. Haag (GDR)   531.27
British Competitors
6 R. Morgan (GBR)   498.21
20 J. Arbon (GBR)   241.44

Women

3 Metre Springboard
Final
1 A. Gerlach (Hungary)   446.58
2 M. Alcala (Mexico)   442.89
3 J. Ayala (Mexico)   438.18
British Competitors
21 N. Bishop (GBR)   263.67

Highboard
Final
1 C. Nelson (USA)
2 D. Pecher (W Germany)
3 A. Dacyshyn (Canada)

10 Nations Junior International
Athens, Greece — 21/23 July, 1989

Boys

3 Metre Springboard
Final
1 A. Byford (GBR)   344.90
2 L. Celauro (GBR)   279.70
3 B. Thomas (GBR)   247.30

Other British Competitors
5 J. Teal (GBR)   236.00

Highboard
Final
1 A. Byford (GBR)   253.05
2 P. Kaczmarec (Poland)   229.60
3 L. Celauro (GBR)   216.25

Girls

3 Metre Springboard
Final
1 Z. Breeze (GBR)	304.00
2 H. Allen (GBR)	288.75
3 C. Hughes (GBR)	269.25

Highboard
Final
1 K. Despoina (Greece)	232.35
2 H. Allen (GBR)	220.90
3 Z. Breeze (GBR)	210.10

European Junior Championship, 1989
The International Pool, Leeds — 27/30 July, 1989

Junior Men

3 Metre Springboard
Final
1 A. Semeniuk (USSR)	596.70
2 M. Kuhne (GDR)	572.95
3 J. Hempel (GDR)	555.95
British Competitors	
10 A. Ali (GBR)	469.65

Highboard
Final
1 J. Hempel (GDR)	631.75
2 M. Kuhne (GDR)	601.60
3 R. Alvarez (Spain)	601.25
British Competitors	
11 J. Karseras (GBR)	392.90

Boys Age 14-15

3 Metre Springboard
Final
1 S. Zotin (USSR)	381.85
2 A. Wels (GDR)	341.45
3 M. Thrandorf (GDR)	331.05
British Competitors	
5 A. Byford (GBR)	317.40
11 J. Teal (GBR)	230.65

Highboard
Final
1 A. Byford (GBR)	287.05
2 A. Wels (GDR)	275.30
3 S. Zotin (USSR)	266.10
Other British Competitors	
12 L. Celauro (GBR)	203.45

Junior Women

3 Metre Springboard
Final
1 U. Wetzig (GDR)	485.70
2 E. Ivanova (USSR)	453.45
3 C. Bockner (GDR)	431.25
British Competitors	
10 T. Miles (GBR)	351.50
11 O. Clark (GBR)	351.35

Highboard
Final
1 T. Biriukova (USSR)	398.90
2 U. Wetzig (GDR)	389.20
3 I. Voicu (Rumania)	365.70
British Competitors	
9 T. Miles (GBR)	324.45
17 K. Wenden (GBR)	280.50

Girls Age 14-15

3 Metre Springboard
Final
1 C. Schmalfuss (GDR)	335.00
2 D. Lindner (GDR)	328.35
3 C. Hughes (GBR)	296.75
Other British Competitors	
7 Z. Breeze (GBR)	266.40

Highboard
Final
1 D. Lindner (GDR)	266.30
2 C. Schmalfuss (GDR)	251.75
3 H. Allen (GBR)	242.80
Other British Competitors	
5 Z. Breeze (GBR)	231.05

European Championship, 1989
Bonn, W Germany — 12/20 August, 1989

Men

1 Metre Springboard
Final
1 E. Jongejans (Holland)	394.08
2 V. Statsenko (USSR)	378.24
3 A. Gladchenko (USSR)	363.24

3 Metre Springboard
Final
1 A. Killat (W Germany)	672.75
2 A. Gladchenko (USSR)	666.42
3 J. Hempel (GDR)	663.84

British Competitors	
10 R. Morgan (GBR)	532.08
12 J. Arbon (GBR)	504.39

Highboard
Final
1 G. Chogovadze (USSR)	639.69
2 J. Hempel (GDR)	578.43
3 V. Timoshinin (USSR)	572.40
British Competitors	
5 R. Morgan (GBR)	504.81
11 J. Arbon (GBR)	456.33

Women

1 Metre Springboard
Final

1	I. Lashko (USSR)	278.46
2	B. Baldus (GDR)	267.24
3	M. Babkova (USSR)	216.00

3 Metre Springboard
Final

1	M. Babkova (USSR)	514.23
2	B. Baldus (GDR)	510.72

3	S. Alexeeva (USSR)	486.09

British Competitors

13	S. Ryan (GBR)	400.44
14	N. Bishop (GBR)	390.06

Highboard
Final

1	U. Wetzig (GDR)	403.35
2	I. Afonina (USSR)	400.83
3	J. Eichler (GDR)	395.55

Other British Competitors

11	S. Ryan (GBR)	307.59

World Age Group Championships
Madrid, Spain — 24/27 August, 1989

Boys

1 Metre Springboard
Group A
Final

1	D. Panate (USA)	550.35
2	A. Semeniuk (USSR)	539.50
3	M. Murphy (Australia)	524.60

British Competitors

12	A. Ali (GBR)	452.45
24	A. Bowdery (GBR)	399.00

Group B
Final

1	S. Zotin (USSR)	342.00
2	J. Aballi (Cuba)	321.45
3	A. Terrell (USA)	309.40

British Competitors

11	A. Byford (GBR)	277.55

3 Metre Springboard
Group A
Final

1	F. Platas (Mexico)	576.95
2	V. Baranouskiy (USSR)	558.80
3	L. Delgado (Cuba)	538.90

British Competitors

8	A. Ali (GBR)	525.80
22	A. Bowdery (GBR)	400.85

Group B
Final

1	S. Zotin (USSR)	371.95
2	J. Aballi (Cuba)	355.25
3	A. Byford (GBR)	348.25

Highboard
Group A
Final

1	R. Alvarez (Spain)	606.60
2	J. Gil (Spain)	542.90
3	O. Andriuk (USSR)	526.25

British Competitors

18	A. Ali (GBR)	395.10

Group B
Final

1	S. Zotin (USSR)	307.30
2	K. Fix (Canada)	283.05
3	A. Sabbah (Canada)	269.70

British Competitors

4	A. Byford (GBR)	248.60

Girls

1 Metre Springboard
Group A
Final

1	L. Borodulina (USSR)	455.25
2	V. Bergman (USA)	414.15
3	M. Alcala (Mexico)	397.20

British Competitors

14	T. Miles (GBR)	335.90
16	K. Shortell (GBR)	327.65

Group B
Final

1	S. Wigginton (USA)	312.30
2	J. Burkholder (USA)	300.60
3	A. Montminny (Canada)	299.35

British Competitors

14	H. Allen (GBR)	239.55

3 Metre Springboard
Group A
Final

1	E. Richatelli (USA)	450.35
2	V. Bergman (USA)	434.25
3	M. Alcala (Mexico)	433.70

British Competitors

13	T. Miles (GBR)	344.85
20	K. Shortell (GBR)	302.95

Group B
Final

1	I. Vera (USSR)	256.35
2	A. Montminny (Canada)	249.15
3	H. Allen (GBR)	248.00

Highboard
Group A
Final

1	T. Birukova (USSR)	367.10
2	P. Gordon (Canada)	366.05
3	U. Ostbo (Norway)	355.75

British Competitors

13	T. Miles (GBR)	306.15

Group B
Final

1	I. Vera (USSR)	357.45
2	H. Allen (GBR)	335.75
3	Y. Lopez (Puerto Rico)	331.20

Where Are They Now?

Brian Phelps

Brian Phelps was just 13 years old when he made his first international appearance for Great Britain, against Italy in August 1957.

The remarkable international career that followed, ran until 1966, and he was coached throughout by Wally Orner at the Highgate Diving Club.

Gaining a surprise silver medal at the 1958 Commonwealth Games in Cardiff, he finished a mere 3.3 points behind Scotland's Peter Heatly, a veteran of two previous Games. And, within six weeks, he was back in action at the European Championships in Budapest. Despite formidable opposition, and competing before a huge crowd in the famous outdoor Margaret Island Pool, Phelps remained both composed and consistent to take the highboard title. For a boy of 14, he revealed a concentration on the ten metre tower that belied his tender age.

Brian Phelps

His sights were now set on the 1960 Olympic Games. In Rome, Brian briefly led after four rounds of the highboard final, but, in the end, could not quite match the greater tariffs of the two American divers. He did, however, become only the second British male diver to win an Olympic medal when he captured the bronze.

1962 proved remarkably successful for Phelps, as he retained his highboard crown at the European Championships in Liepzig, ahead of local man Rolf Sperling (GDR). Later in the year he took both the springboard and highboard golds at the Commonwealth Games in Perth, Australia; the first diver to complete the double since the Canadian, Alfred Phillips, in 1930.

These tremendous victories made Phelps the most successful British diver of all time, and he was still only 18 years old.

In 1964, Phelps suffered a major disappointment at the Tokyo Olympics, where he finished sixth behind the successful defending platform champion, Robert Webster (USA).

This setback seemd to act as a catalyst to spur him on, and by 1966 he was ready to defend both Commonwealth titles. These Games were held in Kingston, Jamaica, and Phelps became the first diver to retain both titles after a close battle with Australia's Donald Wagstaff, on the three metre springboard. Phelps's tally of gold medals from major championships had risen to six.

The winning European sequence was halted at the 1966 Championships in Utrecht when he lost his highboard crown to Klaus Dibiasi (Italy) by some ten points. After a row over judging, he had to settle for the silver behind the Italian, who later became a legend in the sport himself.

Brian's last major competition was at Crystal Palace in 1967 when David Priestley stopped his run of victories at the National Diving Championships. The defeat marked the end of an era on the domestic and international scene. Phelps had won a total of 14 senior ASA titles, eight junior titles and represented his country on 55 occasions.

In 1965, Brian had married Monica Rutherford, the four-times British Gymnastics Champion and herself an Olympic representative. Their first daughter, Erika, was born in 1967 and Brian quit competitive diving to support his family. He became a professional diver in the Aqua-Show, in Bournemouth, and continued in summer performances for some years. During the winter months he managed to keep working in the entertainment business by touring in a balancing act with Monica. Otherwise, he did some building work on a self-employed basis. In 1972, a second daughter, Mandy, was born.

Three years later the couple took over a disused warehouse and converted it into a gymnasium. They coached children in both gymnastics and trampolining and in 1978, with a by now thriving business, they moved to bigger premises.

Since then, they have coached many trampolinists and gymnasts to international level, including both their daughters. The elder girl, Erika, became World Cup Champion and finished third in the 1980 World Trampolining Championships at the age of 13 (shades of dad!). The younger daughter Mandy won several National Age Group trampolining titles and also represented Great Britain at senior level.

In 1984, they expanded the business still further, opening up a health club, and Brian took up weight-training as a hobby.

Currently, Brian coaches trampolining and weight training, while Monica concentrates on the gymnastics side. Both daughters have helped in the business and have made it a real family enterprise.

Since 1980, Brian has commentated for BBC television on diving and trampolining events, while Monica worked for ITV, covering gymnastics. In 1988 both worked for ITV in Seoul, but have recently moved to Sky Television.

Today, Brian Phelps is a grandfather, a successful businessman, and enjoys snooker and do-it-yourself projects. He has come a long way from the small boy who thrilled crowds all around the world. His broadcasting connections keep him in touch with the sport that brought him international fame, while his coaching involvement is centred around trampolining and gymnastics and he is a National trampolining judge.

Unlike swimming, diving is not a sport where records are set, but Brian made history when he became the youngest ever European Diving Champion in 1958 at the age of 14. He remained undefeated on the highboard in Britain from 1958 to 1966 and, when he retired, the sport lost not only a *big* star, but a character too.

Past Championship Winners, 1883–1989

Junior ASA Championships, 1852–1989

Junior Men

1 Metre Springboard

1984	T. Blott (Beaumont)	407.10
1985	P. McCord (Southend on Sea)	406.95
1986	S. Jackson (Sheffield C)	463.15
1987	A. Ali (Southend on Sea)	454.45
1988	A. Bowdery (Southend on Sea)	442.00

3 Metre Springboard

1952	K. Collin (Isleworth Penguins)	64.56
1953	R. Cann (Blackpool)	71.79
1954	J. Butcher (Highgate)	70.93
1955	C. Giecco (Isleworth Penguins)	71.57
1956	B. Phelps (Highgate)	70.54
1957	B. Phelps (Highgate)	81.40
1958	B. Phelps (Highgate)	85.89
1959	B. Phelps (Highgate)	89.41
1960	B. Phelps (Highgate)	97.32
1961	D. Priestley (Blackpool)	73.94
1962	W. Wood (Highgate)	79.80
1963	K. O'Brien (Highgate)	71.91
1964	K. O'Brien (Highgate)	83.39
1965	C. Walls (Highgate)	75.70
1966	T. Simpson (Highgate)	77.65
1967	G. Hobbs (Highgate)	87.26
1968	G. Hobbs (Highgate)	86.60
1969	B. Wetheridge (Metropolitan)	309.65
1970	C. Naylor (Northern)	283.45
1971	R. Horne (Highgate)	262.30
1972	R. Horne (Highgate)	291.20
1973	C. Snode (Highgate)	282.70
1974	C. Snode (Highgate)	312.90
1975	C. Snode (Highgate)	415.50
1976	D. Pook (Morden Park)	353.80
1977	I. England (Highgate)	378.55
1978	A. Cooper (Highgate)	317.45
1979	P. Powell (Northern)	386.45
1980	D. Mollan (Northern)	346.45
1981	S. White (Highgate)	382.80
1982	S. White (Highgate)	413.90
1983	R. Morgan (Highgate)	488.25
1984	T. Thomas (Metropolitan)	416.15
1985	S. Jackson (Sheffield C)	450.95
1986	S. Jackson (Sheffield C)	465.95
1987	A. Ali (Southend on Sea)	487.00
1988	A. Ali (Southend on Sea)	472.70
1989	A. Byford (Highgate)	477.10

Highboard

1965	C. Walls (Highgate)	61.65
1966	J. Baker (Woolwich)	54.40
1967	C. Walls (Highgate)	78.01
1968	B. Wetheridge (Metropolitan)	74.28
1969	B. Wetheridge (Metropolitan)	210.95
1970	C. Naylor (Northern)	230.50
1971	D. Willison (Hillingdon)	219.35
1972	D. Willison (Hillingdon)	225.30
1973	D. Willison (Hillingdon)	243.05
1974	C. Snode (Highgate)	241.25
1975	C. Snode (Highgate)	319.20
1976	I. England (Highgate)	319.70
1977	I. England (Highgate)	336.40
1978	A. Cooper (Highgate)	286.55
1979	N. Stanton (Beaumont)	309.55
1980	M. Alderman (Co Southampton)	221.75
1981	S. White (Highgate)	319.70
1982	S. White (Highgate)	317.95
1983	R. Morgan (Highgate)	368.55
1984	T. Thomas (Metropolitan)	303.30
1985	S. Forrest (Edinburgh)	324.25
1986	A. Ali (Saxon Crown)	313.30
1987	A. Ali (Southend on Sea)	320.45
1988	A. Byford (Highgate)	358.55
1989	A. Ali (Southend on Sea)	356.85

Junior Women

1 Metre Springboard

1984	R. Spinks (The Ladies)	331.70
1985	L. Ward (Beaumont)	318.90
1986	S. Ryan (The Ladies)	368.15
1987	T. Miles (The Ladies)	349.15
1988	A. Roffey (Leeds Esprit)	339.25

3 Metre Springboard

1952	C. Welsh (Durham C)	71.95
1953	C. Welsh (Durham C)	74.15
1954	A. Woods (Isleworth Penguins)	69.33
1955	J. Gill (Hammersmith)	63.52
1956	E. Nicholson (Fulham)	71.87
1957	V. Borton (Isander)	60.00
1958	M. Watson (Bournemouth Dolphins)	69.73
1959	M. Watson (Bournemouth Dolphins)	82.87
1960	M. Watson (Bournemouth Dolphins)	81.07
1961	M. Austen (Isleworth Penguins)	75.68
1962	M. Austen (Isleworth Penguins)	77.87
1963	K. Rowlatt (Leyton)	79.01
1964	K. Rowlatt (Leyton)	82.02
1965	B. Boys (Canada)	72.26
1966	S. Rowlatt (Leyton)	66.36
1967	S. Rowlatt (Leyton)	70.25
1968	S. Rowlatt (Leyton)	77.91
1969	M. Koppell (Leicester Penguins)	269.15
1970	B. Williams (Hillingdon B)	251.10
1971	H. Koppell (Co Coventry)	266.50
1972	B. Williams (Hillingdon B)	271.95
1973	L. Carwardine (Co Coventry)	274.40
1974	L. Carwardine (Co Coventry)	304.05
1975	C. Bond (Metropolitan)	292.75
1976	S. Hooker (Cheltenham)	308.80
1977	D. Jay (The Ladies)	343.90
1978	A. Childs (Southend on Sea)	290.35
1979	T. Jones (Cheltenham)	320.90
1980	J. Shawcross (Urmston)	310.90
1981	C. Roscoe (The Ladies)	347.10
1982	C. Roscoe (The Ladies)	369.55

1983 L. Brace (North Bedford)	390.10
1984 R. Spinks (The Ladies)	352.55
1985 S. Ryan (The Ladies)	376.05
1986 S. Ryan (The Ladies)	390.95
1987 T. Dart (Southend on Sea)	346.75
1988 A. Montminny (Canada)	382.10
1989 A. Roffey (Leeds Esprit)	413.60

Highboard

1965 B. Boys (Canada)	40.11
1966 J. Parsons (Cardiff)	47.71
1967 J. Abercrombie (Ruislip & Northwood)	48.40
1968 B. Williams (Hillingdon B)	51.81
1969 J. Abercrombie (Ruislip & Northwood)	204.45
1970 B. Williams (Hillingdon B)	212.70
1971 B. Williams (Hillingdon B)	234.40

1972 B. Williams (Hillingdon B)	216.75
1973 J. Adams (Hillingdon B)	216.40
1974 J. Adams (Hillingdon B)	208.75
1975 M. Saunders (Beaumont)	190.20
1976 M. Saunders (Beaumont)	281.80
1977 A. Antill (Metropolitan)	202.50
1978 J. Simpson (Urmston)	163.45
1979 C. Roscoe (The Ladies)	207.50
1980 C. Roscoe (The Ladies)	234.95
1981 C. Roscoe (The Ladies)	260.60
1982 C. Roscoe (The Ladies)	248.70
1983 R. Spinks (The Ladies)	291.00
1984 R. Spinks (The Ladies)	285.10
1985 S. Ryan (The Ladies)	277.70
1986 S. Ryan (The Ladies)	271.00
1987 T. Dart (Southend on Sea)	301.80
1988 H. Allen (RTW Monson)	267.55
1989 H. Allen (Southend on Sea)	264.70

ASA Champions, 1883–1989

Note: The plunging championships held between 1883 and 1946 proved popular as age was no handicap. After a standing plunge from a firm take-off, competitors floated motionless, face downwards, until their breath gave out, or 60 seconds elapsed. A distance achieved was then measured and the winner declared from the best of three attempts.

Men

1 Metre Springboard

1937 C. Tomalin (S Africa)	
1938 C. Tomalin (S Africa)	
1946 F. Hodges (Highgate)	135.85
1947 J. Webb (Highgate)	93.16
1948 P. Elliott (Highgate)	93.35
1949 P. Heatly (Portobello)	128.60
1950 P. Heatly (Portobello)	127.32
1951 P. Heatly (Portobello)	110.09
1952 T. Turner (Highgate)	121.94
1953 T. Turner (Highgate)	113.32
1954 T. Turner (Highgate)	102.31
1955 F. Mercer (Highgate)	110.68
1956 Y. Raanan (Israel)	106.88
1957 K. Collin (Isleworth Penguins)	120.39
1958 P. Squires (Highgate)	124.57
1959 K. Collin (Isleworth Penguins)	132.53
1960 J. Candler (Highgate)	129.21
1961 D. Young (Nelson)	130.40
1962 K. Collin (Isleworth Penguins)	125.68
1963 D. Young (Nelson)	126.88
1964 D. Young (Nelson)	127.39
1965 D. Young (Nelson)	123.58
1966 A. Roberts (Highgate)	126.03
1967 F. Carter (Nelson)	126.35
1968 A. Roberts (Highgate)	130.35
1969 A. Roberts (Highgate)	440.05
1970 A. Gill (Metropolitan)	425.35
1971 T. Simpson (Highgate)	444.80
1972 T. Simpson (Highgate)	474.55
1973 T. Simpson (Highgate)	471.65
1974 T. Simpson (Highgate)	431.00
1975 C. Snode (Highgate)	433.70
1976 C. Snode (Highgate)	477.25
1977 T. Simpson (Highgate)	471.55
1978 B. Wetheridge (Highgate)	454.90
1979 M. Brown (Beaumont)	401.75

1980 A. Jeffs (Highgate)	429.65
1981 N. Stanton (Beaumont)	506.50
1982 R. Dear (Highgate)	460.50
1983 R. Dear (Highgate)	486.65
1984 R. Morgan (Highgate)	496.70
1985 R. Dear (Highgate)	500.10
1986 R. Morgan (Highgate)	541.15
1987 A. Ali (Southend on Sea)	444.90
1988 R. Morgan (Highgate)	451.15

3 Metre Springboard

1935 C. Tomalin (Highgate)	
1936 F. Hodges (Highgate)	
1937 F. Hodges (Highgate)	
1938 F. Hodges (Highgate)	

Peter Heatly

John Boyd

1946	R. Mulinghausen (France)	116.30
1947	L. Kern (Highgate)	105.90
1948	P. Heatly (Portobello)	113.50
1949	P. Heatly (Portobello)	174.91
1950	P. Heatly (Portobello)	176.51
1951	T. Turner (Highgate)	160.67
1952	T. Turner (Highgate)	176.60
1953	T. Turner (Highgate)	135.14
1954	T. Turner (Highgate)	134.29
1955	P. Tarsey (Ealing)	133.43
1956	P. Tarsey (Ealing)	134.02
1957	P. Squires (Highgate)	125.14
1958	K. Collin (Isleworth Penguins)	135.00
1959	P. Squires (Highgate)	150.39
1960	B. Phelps (Highgate)	152.98
1961	B. Phelps (Highgate)	154.80
1962	B. Phelps (Highgate)	152.39
1963	K. Collin (Isleworth Penguins)	128.69
1964	D. Young (Nelson)	139.62
1965	F. Carter (Nelson)	135.96
1966	F. Carter (Nelson)	145.93
1967	F. Carter (Nelson)	140.20
1968	F. Carter (Nelson)	135.31
1969	A. Roberts (Highgate)	468.25
1970	J. Thewlis (Metropolitan)	475.60
1971	C. Walls (Beaumont)	478.30
1972	B. Wetheridge (Metropolitan)	474.95
1973	T. Simpson (Highgate)	512.25
1974	T. Simpson (Highgate)	506.75
1975	C. Snode (Highgate)	536.55
1976	C. Snode (Highgate)	563.60
1977	T. Simpson (Highgate)	507.25
1978	C. Snode (Highgate)	556.65
1979	M. Brown (Beaumont)	466.05
1980	A. Jeffs (Highgate)	437.10
1981	D. Wood (Metropolitan)	507.30
1982	N. Stanton (Beaumont)	570.05
1983	N. Stanton (Beaumont)	618.20
1984	C. Snode (Highgate)	608.10
1985	R. Morgan (Highgate)	605.30
1986	A. Budd (Highgate)	565.85
1987	G. Morris (Huddersfield)	584.95
1988	J. Arbon (Essex Cormorants)	574.30
1989	R. Morgan (Barnet Copthall)	619.70

Highboard

1907	H. Smyrk (Cygnus)
1908	H. Smyrk (Cygnus)
1909	H. Pott (Otter)
1910	H. Pott (Otter)
1911	H. Pott (Otter)
1912	H. Pott (Otter)
1913	G. Gaidzik (USA)
1920	H. Clarke (Wandsworth)
1921	A. Knight (Otter)
1922	A. Knight (Otter)
1923	R. Weil (France)
1924	R. Weil (France)
1925	A. Dickin (Penguin)
1926	A. Dickin (Hammersmith)
1927	H. Aldous (Nine Elms)
1928	W. Burne (Otter)
1929	A. Dickin (Polytechnic)
1930	G. Wild (Highgate)
1931	C. Tomalin (Highgate)
1932	E. Heron (Half Moon, Eire)
1933	C. Tomalin (Highgate)
1934	C. Tomalin (Highgate)

1935	C. Tomalin (Highgate)	
1936	C. Tomalin (S Africa)	
1937	C. Tomalin (S Africa)	
1938	L. Marchant (Highgate)	
1946	L. Marchant (Highgate)	105.43
1947	L. Brunnhage (Sweden)	101.86
1948	G. Ward (Highgate)	87.83
1949	P. Heatly (Portobello)	140.23
1950	P. Heatly (Portobello)	147.64
1951	P. Heatly (Portobello)	142.18
1952	T. Turner (Highgate)	131.25
1953	P. Tarsey (Ealing)	139.59
1954	T. Turner (Highgate)	135.43
1955	P. Squires (Highgate)	135.00
1956	P. Tarsey (Ealing)	138.33
1957	P. Heatl y (Portobello)	139.35
1958	B. Phelps (Highgate)	139.58
1959	B. Phelps (Highgate)	148.61
1960	B. Phelps (Highgate)	157.14
1961	B. Phelps (Highgate)	148.38
1962	B. Phelps (Highgate)	162.23
1963	A. Kitcher (Southampton)	161.08
1964	B. Phelps (Highgate)	165.55
1965	B. Phelps (Highgate)	161.01
1966	B. Phelps (Highgate)	165.52
1967	D. Priestley (Blackpool)	157.30
1968	D. Priestley (Blackpool)	153.45
1969	A. Gill (Highgate)	426.40
1970	P. Drew (Highgate)	446.60
1971	A. Gill (Metropolitan)	421.00
1972	F. Dufficy (Beaumont)	439.95
1973	F. Dufficy (Beaumont)	447.00
1974	M. Brown (Beaumont)	461.85
1975	M. Brown (Beaumont)	471.10
1976	D. Willison (Hillingdon)	429.05
1977	M. Brown (Beaumont)	465.00
1978	M. Brown (Beaumont)	506.40
1979	C. Snode (Highgate)	519.70
1980	P. Drew (Highgate)	401.40
1981	N. Stanton (Beaumont)	448.55
1982	S. White (Highgate)	482.80
1983	C. Snode (Highgate)	585.75
1984	R. Morgan (Highgate)	513.75
1985	J. Arbon (Highgate)	435.00
1986	R. Morgan (Highgate)	571.20
1987	R. Morgan (Highgate)	575.15
1988	J. Arbon (Essex Cormorants)	547.70
1989	R. Morgan (Barnet Copthall)	562.30

Plain

1937	C. Tomalin (S Africa)	
1938	C. Tomalin (S Africa)	
1946	L. Marchant (Highgate)	49.30
1947	L. Marchant (Highgate)	43.70
1948	L. Marchant (Highgate)	49.72
1949	L. Marchant (Highgate)	47.92
1950	L. Marchant (Highgate)	52.81
1951	G. Redfern (Highgate)	38.75
1952	G. Redfern (Highgate)	47.60
1953	P. Elliott (Highgate)	57.28
1954	P. Tarsey (Ealing)	59.11
1955	P. Squires (Highgate)	55.98
1956	P. Squires (Highgate)	57.79
1957	B. Phelps (Highgate)	54.99
1958	K. Collin (Isleworth Penguins)	55.98
1959	P. Squires (Highgate)	67.01
1960	B. Phelps (Highgate)	60.34
1961	B. Phelps (Highgate)	63.77

Plunging

1883	T. Clarke
1884	H. Davenport
1885	H. Davenport
1886	H. Davenport
1887	G. Blake
1888	G. Blake
1889	G. Blake
1890	G. Blake
1891	G. Blake
1892	H. Wilson
1893	S. Dadd
1894	J. McHugh
1895	W. Taylor (Bootle)
1896	W. Allason (Otter)
1897	W. Allason (Otter)
1898	W. Taylor (Bootle)
1899	W. Taylor (Bootle)
1900	W. Taylor (Bootle)
1901	W. Taylor (Bootle)
1902	W. Allason (Otter)
1903	W. Taylor (Bootle)
1904	J. Jarvis (Leicester)
1905	W. Taylor (Bootle)
1906	W. Taylor (Bootle)
1907	H. W. Allason (Otter)
1908	W. Allason (Otter)
1909	W. Allason (Otter)
1910	H. W. Allason (Cambridge University)
1911	H. W. Allason (Cambridge University)
1912	W. Smith (Woodside)
1913	H. Davison (Aston)
1920	H. Davison (Smethwick)
1921	H. W. Allason (Cambridge University)
1922	W. Allason (Otter)
1923	A. Beaumont (Harrogate)
1924	A. Beaumont (Harrogate)
1925	W. Wilson (Liverpool Police)
1926	F. Parrington (Liverpool Police)
1927	F. Parrington (Liverpool Police)"
1928	F. Parrington (Liverpool Police)
1929	F. Parringon (Liverpool Police)
1930	A. Beaumont (Harrogate)
1931	A. Beaumont (Harrogate Amateurs)
1932	A. Beaumont (Harrogate Amateurs)
1933	F. Parrington (Liverpool Police)
1934	F. Parrington (Liverpool Police)
1935	F. Parrington (Liverpool Police)
1936	F. Parrington (Liverpool Police)
1937	F. Parrington (Liverpool Police)
1938	F. Parrington (Liverpool Police)
1946	J. Snow (Croft House)

Women

1 Metre Springboard

1949	E. Child (Plaistow U)	89.12
1950	K. Cuthbert (Willesden)	68.59
1951	A. Long (Ilford)	68.20
1952	C. Welsh (Durham C)	82.89
1953	C. Welsh (Durham C)	84.25
1954	C. Welsh (Durham C)	80.71
1955	C. Welsh (Durham C)	85.38
1956	C. Welsh (Durham C)	80.45
1957	E. Ferris (Mermaid)	102.56
1958	C. Welsh (Durham C)	99.58
1959	N. Thomas (Isleworth Penguins)	106.85
1960	F. Cramp (Isleworth Penguins)	87.68

1961	M. Austen (Isleworth Penguins)	95.97
1962	F. Cramp (Isleworth Penguins)	99.57
1963	N. Leiper (Isleworth Penguins)	100.54
1964	S. Francis (Isander)	93.30
1965	S. Francis (Seven Kings)	97.11
1966	M. Froscher (Mermaid)	103.65
1967	F. Erard (Isleworth Penguins)	107.66
1968	M. Froscher (Mermaid)	94.93
1969	M. Koppell (Leicester Penguins)	295.05
1970	A. Drake (Basildon)	310.85
1971	A. Drake (Basildon)	336.35
1972	H. Koppell (Co Coventry)	353.40
1973	A. Drake (Basildon)	325.65
1974	H. Koppell (Co Coventry)	356.50
1975	H. Koppell (Co Coventry)	334.80
1976	A. Drake (Basildon)	375.15
1977	A. Drake (Beaumont)	389.15
1978	A. Drake (Beaumont)	359.70
1979	D. Jay (The Ladies)	348.25
1980	J. Shawcross (Urmston)	322.35
1981	S. Yeates (Cheltenham)	342.80
1982	S. Yeates (Cheltenham)	389.80
1983	S. Yeates (Cheltenham)	428.85
1984	S. Yeates (Cheltenham)	409.10
1985	S. Yeates (Cheltenham)	413.25
1986	N. Bishop (Northern)	385.25
1987	T. Miles (The Ladies)	382.20
1988	S. Ryan (The Ladies)	333.00

3 Metre Springboard

1935	K. Larsen (Finchley)	
1936	B. Slade (London)	
1937	B. Slade (London)	
1938	B. Slade (London)	
1946	E. Child (Isander)	97.57
1947	P. Winterton (Isander)	89.01
1948	E. Child (Plaistow U)	102.79
1949	E. Child (Plaistow U)	101.15
1950	D. Newman (Mermaid)	106.38
1951	A. Long (Ilford)	107.98
1952	D. Drew (Heston)	120.84
1953	C. Welsh (Durham C)	117.00
1954	C. Welsh (Durham C)	118.39
1955	A. Long (Ilford)	108.31
1956	A. Long (Ilford)	112.61
1957	A. Long (Ilford)	121.20
1958	A. Long (Ilford)	125.40
1959	M. Watson (Bournemouth Dolphins)	128.48
1960	E. Ferris (Mermaid)	137.36
1961	N. Thomas (Isleworth Penguins)	141.71
1962	E. Ferris (Mermaid)	117.88
1963	J. Newman (Isander)	109.08
1964	K. Rowlatt (Leyton)	122.92
1965	J. Stewart (Canada)	131.13
1966	J. Dickens (Co Derby)	118.95
1967	K. Rowlatt (Leyton)	135.10
1968	K. Rowlatt (Leyton)	130.91
1969	B. Boys (Canada)	370.30
1970	A. Drake (Basildon)	354.30
1971	A. Drake (Basildon)	358.60
1972	A. Drake (Basildon)	430.65
1973	H. Koppell (Co Coventry)	416.60
1974	H. Koppell (Co Coventry)	397.50
1975	L. Carwardine (Co Coventry)	375.85
1976	A. Drake (Basildon)	402.15
1977	C. Bond (Metropolitan)	365.40
1978	A. Drake (Beaumont)	368.60
1979	D. Jay (The Ladies)	421.50
1980	A. Drake (Beaumont)	344.80

Joy Newman

1981	A. Childs (Southend on Sea)	407.95
1982	S. Yeates (Cheltenham)	422.55
1983	A. Childs (Southend on Sea)	467.70
1984	A. Childs (Southend on Sea)	420.85
1985	A. Childs (Southend on Sea)	430.30
1986	A. Childs (Southend on Sea)	440.30
1987	A. Childs (Southend on Sea)	436.80
1988	C. Roscoe (The Ladies)	453.90
1989	N. Bishop (Oldham)	413.95

Highboard

1925	B. White (Hammersmith)	
1926	B. White (Hammersmith)	
1927	B. White (Hammersmith)	
1928	B. White (Hammersmith)	
1929	B. White (Hammersmith)	
1930	D. Leach (Jersey)	
1931	D. Leach (Jersey)	
1932	D. Leach (Jersey)	
1933	E. MacReady (Jersey)	
1934	C. Cousens (Coate Amateurs)	
1935	C. Cousens (Coate Amateurs)	
1936	J. Gilbert (Jersey)	
1937	J. Gilbert (Jersey)	
1938	M. Moulton (Isander)	
1946	E. Child (Isander)	34.83
1947	E. Child (Isander)	52.86

1948	A. Hider (Isander)	61.34
1949	E. Child (Plaistow U)	67.55
1950	A. Long (Ilford)	52.04
1951	K. Cuthbert (Willesden)	63.59
1952	A. Long (Ilford)	67.95
1953	A. Long (Ilford)	74.48
1954	A. Long (Ilford)	76.92
1955	C. Welsh (Durham C)	69.80
1956	C. Welsh (Durham C)	76.06
1957	C. Welsh (Durham C)	71.06
1958	C. Welsh (Durham C)	83.70
1959	A. Long (Ilford)	81.17
1960	N. Thomas (Isleworth Penguins)	77.18
1961	N. Thomas (Isleworth Penguins)	91.03
1962	M. Austen (Isleworth Penguins)	89.13
1963	J. Newman (Isander)	103.60
1964	F. Cramp (Isleworth Penguins)	95.96
1965	F. Cramp (Isleworth Penguins)	84.91
1966	F. Cramp (Isleworth Penguins)	83.20
1967	M. Haswell (Co Cardiff)	72.23
1968	M. Haswell (Co Cardiff)	86.17
1969	B. Boys (Canada)	337.65
1970	S. Burrows (Hillingdon B)	302.85
1971	B. Williams (Hillingdon B)	318.30
1972	B. Williams (Hillingdon B)	323.90
1973	H. Koppell (Co Coventry)	331.05
1974	B. Williams (Hillingdon B)	343.45
1975	B. Williams (Hillingdon B)	345.00
1976	F. Hotson (Edinburgh)	300.60
1977	C. Bond (Metropolitan)	329.95
1978	M. Saunders (Beaumont)	351.15
1979	M. Saunders (Beaumont)	336.40
1980	L. Fraser (The Ladies)	341.80
1981	C. Roscoe (The Ladies)	290.80
1982	L. Fraser (The Ladies)	330.60
1983	L. Fraser (The Ladies)	341.15
1984	L. Fraser (The Ladies)	336.05
1985	L. Fraser (The Ladies)	340.85
1986	R. Spinks (The Ladies)	394.15
1987	T. Dart (Southend on Sea)	357.70
1988	J. Tysdale (Canada)	365.20
1989	S. Ryan (The Ladies)	391.60

Plain

1953	C. Welsh (Durham C)	51.35
1954	A. Long (Ilford)	59.85
1955	A. Long (Ilford)	52.00
1956	C. Welsh (Durham C)	54.65
1957	C. Welsh (Durham C)	58.71
1958	A. Long (Ilford)	59.92
1959	E. Ferris (Mermaid)	61.13
1960	E. Ferris (Mermaid)	53.99
1961	M. Austen (Isleworth Penguins)	60.95

Commonwealth Champions, 1930–1986

Men

3 Metre Springboard

1930	A. Phillips (Canada)	147.00
1934	J. B. Ray (England)	117.12
1938	R. Masters (Australia)	126.36
1950	G. Athans (Canada)	169.21
1954	P. Heatly (Scotland)	146.76
1958	K. Collin (England)	126.78
1962	B. Phelps (England)	154.14
1966	B. Phelps (England)	154.55

1970	D. Wagstaff (Australia)	557.73
1974	D. Wagstaff (Australia)	531.54
1978	C. Snode (England)	643.83
1982	C. Snode (England)	631.38
1986	S. Panayi (Australia)	648.33

Highboard

1930	A. Phillips (Canada)	90.60
1934	T. Mather (England)	83.83
1938	D. Tomalin (England)	108.74
1950	P. Heatly (Scotland)	156.07

1954	W. Patrick (Canada)	142.70
1958	P. Heatly (Scotland)	147.79
1962	B. Phelps (England)	168.35
1966	B. Phelps (England)	164.57
1970	D. Wagstaff (Australia)	485.73
1974	D. Wagstaff (Australia)	490.74
1978	C. Snode (England)	538.98
1982	C. Snode (England)	588.54
1986	C. Rogerson (Australia)	600.87

Women

3 Metre Springboard

1930	O. Whitsett (S Africa)	90.10
1934	J. Moss (Canada)	62.27
1938	I. Donnett (Australia)	91.18
1950	E. Child (England)	126.58
1954	A. Long (England)	128.26
1958	C. Welsh (England)	118.81
1962	S. Knight (Australia)	134.72
1966	K. Rowlatt (England)	147.10
1970	B. Boys (Canada)	432.87
1974	C. Shatto (Canada)	430.88
1978	J. Nutter (Canada)	477.33
1982	J. Donnet (Australia)	484.65
1986	D. Fuller (Canada)	513.09

Highboard

1930	P. Stoneham (Canada)	39.30
1934	E. MacReady (England)	30.74
1938	L. Hook (Australia)	36.47
1950	E. Child (England)	70.89
1954	B. McAulay (Australia)	86.55

Chris Snode   Swimming Times

1958	C. Welsh (England)	77.23
1962	S. Knight (Australia)	101.15
1966	J. Newman (England)	98.87
1970	B. Boys (Canada)	352.95
1974	B. Boys (Canada)	361.95
1978	L. Cuthbert (Canada)	397.44
1982	V. Beddoe (Australia)	404.16
1986	D. Fuller (Canada)	431.61

European Champions, 1926–1989

Men

1 Metre Springboard

1989	E. Jongejans (Holland)	794.08

3 Metre Springboard

1926	A. Mund (Germany)	186.42
1927	E. Riebschlager (Germany)	173.86
1931	E. Riebschlager (Germany)	136.22
1934	L. Esser (Germany)	134.74
1938	E. Weiss (Germany)	148.02
1947	R. Heinkele (France)	126.71
1950	H. Aderhold (W Germany)	183.60
1954	R. Brener (USSR)	153.26
1958	L. Ujvari (Hungary)	141.17
1962	K. Mrkwicka (Austria)	147.21
1966	M. Safronov (USSR)	155.27
1970	F. Cagnotto (Italy)	555.21
1974	K. Dibiasi (Italy)	603.51
1977	F. Hoffmann (GDR)	592.20
1981	A. Portnov (USSR)	665.94
1983	P. Georgiev (Bulgaria)	619.80
1985	N. Drozhin (USSR)	635.52
1987	A. Killat (W Germany)	663.18
1989	A. Killat (W Germany)	672.75

Highboard

1926	H. Luber (Germany)	110.80
1927	H. Luber (Germany)	114.86
1931	J. Staudinger (Austria)	111.82
1934	H. Stork (Germany)	98.99
1938	E. Weiss (Germany)	124.67

1947	T. Christiansen (Denmark)	105.55
1950	G. Haase (W Germany)	158.13
1954	R. Brener (USSR)	144.01
1958	B. Phelps (GBR)	143.74
1962	B. Phelps (GBR)	150.81
1966	K. Dibiasi (Italy)	162.92
1970	L. Matthes (GDR)	454.74
1974	K. Dibiasi (Italy)	562.33
1977	V. Aleinik (USSR)	542.31
1981	D. Ambartsumian (USSR)	606.96
1983	D. Ambartsumian (USSR)	605.79
1985	T. Knuths (GDR)	581.46
1987	G. Chogovadze (USSR)	618.48
1989	G. Chogovadze (USSR)	639.69

Women

1 Metre Springboard

1989	I. Lashko (USSR)	278.46

3 Metre Springboard

1927	C. Bornett (Austria)	103.22
1931	O. Jordan (Germany)	77.00
1934	O. Jordan-Densch (Germany)	74.88
1938	B. Slade (GBR)	103.60
1947	M. Moreau (France)	100.43
1950	M. Moreau (France)	155.58
1954	V. Tchumitcheva (USSR)	129.45
1958	N. Krutova (USSR)	124.22
1962	I. Kramer (GDR)	153.57
1966	V. Baklanova (USSR)	135.59

1970	H. Becker (GDR)	420.63	1947 N. Pellissard (France)	60.03
1974	U. Knape (Sweden)	465.57	1950 N. Pellissard (France)	85.67
1977	C. Kohler (GDR)	444.30	1954 T. Karakashyants (USSR)	79.86
1981	Z. Tsrulnikova (USSR)	439.74	1958 A. Karazkaite (USSR)	81.14
1983	B. Baldus (GDR)	494.88	1962 I. Kramer (GDR)	107.96
1985	J. Tsrulnikova (USSR)	514.32	1966 N. Kuznetsova (USSR)	100.93
1987	D. Jongejans (Holland)	466.14	1970 M. Duchkova (Czechoslovakia)	336.33
1989	M. Babkova (USSR)	514.23	1974 U. Knape (Sweden)	408.87
			1977 M. Schopke (GDR)	363.00

Highboard

1927	B. White (GBR)	36.04	1981 K. Zipperling (GDR)	433.05
1931	M. Epply (Austria)	34.28	1983 A. Lobankina (USSR)	455.52
1934	H. Schieche (Germany)	35.43	1985 A. Stusulevich (USSR)	414.27
1938	I. Becken (Denmark)	37.09	1987 E. Miroshina (USSR)	475.50
			1989 U. Wetzig (GDR)	403.35

World Champions, 1973–1986

Men

3 Metre Springboard

1973	P. Boggs (USA)	618.57
1975	P. Boggs (USA)	597.12
1978	P. Boggs (USA)	913.95
1982	G. Louganis (USA)	752.67
1986	G. Louganis (USA)	750.06

Highboard

1973	K. Dibiasi (Italy)	559.53
1975	K. Dibiasi (Italy)	547.98
1978	G. Louganis (USA)	844.11
1982	G. Louganis (USA)	634.26
1986	G. Louganis (USA)	688.58

Women

3 Metre Springboard

1973	K. Kohler (GDR)	442.17
1975	I. Kalinina (USSR)	489.81
1978	I. Kalinina (USSR)	691.43
1982	M. Neyer (USA)	501.03
1986	M. Gao (China)	582.90

Highboard

1973	U. Knape (Sweden)	406.77
1976	J. Ely (USA)	403.89
1978	I. Kalinina (USSR)	412.71
1982	W. Wyland (USA)	438.78
1986	L. Chen (China)	449.67

Olympic Champions, 1904–1988

Men

3 Metre Springboard

1908	A. Zurner (Germany)	85.50
1912	P. Gunther (Germany)	79.23
1920	L. Kuehn (USA)	675.40
1924	A. White (USA)	696.40
1928	P. Desjardins (USA)	185.04
1932	M. Galitzen (USA)	161.38
1936	R. Degener (USA)	163.57
1948	B. Harlan (USA)	163.63
1952	D. Browning (USA)	205.29
1956	R. Clotworthy (USA)	159.56
1960	G. Tobian (USA)	170.00
1964	K. Sitzberger (USA)	159.90
1968	B. Wrightson (USA)	170.15
1972	V. Vasin (USSR)	594.09
1976	P. Boggs (USA)	619.05
1980	A. Portnov (USSR)	905.02
1984	G. Louganis (USA)	754.41
1988	G. Louganis (USA)	730.80

Highboard

1912	E. Adlerz (Sweden)	73.94
1920	C. Pinkston (USA)	100.67
1924	A. White (USA)	97.46
1928	P. Desjardins (USA)	98.74
1932	H. Smith (USA)	124.80
1936	M. Wayne (USA)	113.58
1948	S. Lee (USA)	130.05
1952	S. Lee (USA)	156.28

1956	J. Capilla (Mexico)	152.44
1960	R. Webster (USA)	165.56
1964	R. Webster (USA)	148.58
1968	K. Dibiasi (Italy)	164.18
1972	K. Dibiasi (Italy)	504.12
1976	K. Dibiasi (Italy)	600.51
1980	F. Hoffmann (GDR)	835.65
1984	G. Louganis (USA)	710.91
1988	G. Louganis (USA)	638.61

Plain

1904	G. Sheldon (USA)	12.66
1906	W. Gottlob (Germany)	156.00
1908	H. Johansson (Sweden)	83.75

Women

3 Metre Springboard

1920	A. Riggin (USA)	539.90
1924	E. Becker (USA)	474.50
1928	H. Meany (USA)	78.63
1932	G. Coleman (USA)	87.52
1936	M. Gestring (USA)	89.27
1948	V. Draves (USA)	108.74
1952	P. McCormick (USA)	147.30
1956	P. McCormick (USA)	142.36
1960	I. Kraemer (GDR)	155.81
1964	I. Kraemer (GDR)	145.00
1968	S. Gossick (USA)	150.77
1972	M. King (USA)	450.03
1976	J. Chandler (USA)	506.19

PAST CHAMPIONSHIP WINNERS, 1883–1989

1980 I. Karinina (USSR)	725.91
1984 S. Bernier (Canada)	530.70
1988 M. Gao (China)	580.23

Highboard

1928 E. Pinkston-Becker (USA)	31.60
1932 D. Poynton (USA)	40.26
1936 D. Poynton (USA)	33.93
1948 V. Draves (USA)	68.87
1952 P. McCormick (USA)	79.37
1956 P. McCormick (USA)	84.85
1960 I. Kraemer (GDR)	91.28

1964 L. Bush (USA)	99.80
1968 M. Duchkova (Czechoslovakia)	109.59
1972 U. Knape (Sweden)	390.00
1976 E. Vaytsekhovskaia (USSR)	406.59
1980 M. Jaschke (GDR)	596.25
1984 J. Zhow (China)	435.51
1988 Y. Xu (China)	445.20

Plain

1912 G. Johansson (Sweden)	39.90
1920 S. Fryland-Clausen (Denmark)	34.60
1924 C. Smith (USA)	33.20

Liz Ferris (England), an Olympic Bronze Medallist in the 1960 Games in the springboard event.

WATER POLO SECTION

A Short History of Water Polo

by David Reeves (Secretary/Chief Executive, Amateur Swimming Association)

Since Water Polo requires from its players good swimming ability, plus strength, mobility, and endurance in the water — not to mention ball-handling skills and team tactics — it is not at all surprising that this sport has often been described as the toughest game in the world!

It is a game that attracts devoted loyalty from its participants, and those who pursue it do so for more years than any other team and ball game permits. And since these players stay in the game so long, while their colleagues in other aquatic activities drop out as the years pass, water polo provides the ASA with officials and administrators in numbers which are quite out of proportion to its total participants.

The game was invented in England in the 1860s — allegedly because spectators of the time were becoming bored with continually watching swimming races. Early games were played with three in each team, who scored "goals" by placing a rubber bladder on to floating rafts, which were anchored 60 yards apart!

The first rules of Aquatic Soccer — as it was then known — were drafted in 1876 by a Scotsman, William Watson, and they were used in the first recorded match, promoted by the Bournemouth Premier Rowing Club. By this time there were seven players in each team, and they still had to score by placing a bladder on a raft. This had now become more difficult, as these rafts were defended by "goalkeepers", who stood on the rafts and jumped or dived into the water to prevent the swimming players from scoring — even jumping on to a player with the ball if he came too near to the "goal".

By 1885, the game of water polo was recognised by the Amateur Swimming Association. Teams now consisted of 12 players, caps were introduced to distinguish those taking part, and the goal areas were limited to a maximum width of ten feet. Swimming under water was permitted, and the ball could also be taken under water. There was a significant step in 1888, when a committee was appointed — assumedly by the ASA — to revise the rules, and in 1889, the London Water Polo League was founded. It celebrates its centenary this year.

The first recorded English Club Water Polo Championship Final took place in 1888, when Burton defeated Otter by 3 goals to nil. The first recorded International match was played on 28 July, 1890, in London, when Scotland defeated England by 4 goals to nil. The referee was Mr A. Sinclair, who became President of the London Water Polo League in 1895. The year 1891 saw the first " 'varsity" match played, with Oxford beating Cambridge 4-1.

Curiously, at that time a full blue was awarded to representative players, but somewhere along the way it became a half-blue.

Interest in the sport had begun to spread, and towards the end of the 19th century it had reached as far as America, Germany, France, Belgium and, significantly, Hungary.

Water Polo became an Olympic sport in 1900. Perhaps it was not surprising that, having invented and developed the game over the previous twenty years or so, and with few nations competing internationally, Great Britain should dominate the early Olympic tournaments.

At the 1900 Games in Paris, Great Britain, represented by the Osborne Swimming Club of Manchester, won the Gold Medal, with Belgian and French clubs taking the Silver and Bronze. The 1904 Games were held at St Louis, USA, and American club sides won all three medals. London hosted the Games in 1908, and the Water Polo Tournament became truly international: Great Britain won Gold, Belgium-Silver, and Sweden-Bronze. The pattern was similar at the next Olympics:

1912 Stockholm	— 1 Great Britain	2 Sweden	3 Belgium
1920 Antwerp	— 1 Great Britain	2 Belgium	3 Sweden

The most famous British player during those early Olympic years was Paul Radmilovic, of Weston super Mare. He took part in four Olympic Games: 1908 London, 1912 Stockholm, 1920 Antwerp, and 1924 Paris, winning Gold Medals at the first three.

He was also a member of the Great Britain Gold Medal-winning team in the 4×200 metres Freestyle Relay in 1908. And in 1968, Radmilovic became the first Water Polo player from Great Britain to be honoured at the Swimming Hall of Fame in Florida. Two other players, Charles Smith, of Salford, and George Wilkinson, of Hyde Seal, were the only other British players to win three Olympic Gold Medals.

The game did not develop a great deal until after the Second World War, mainly because matches were played in small and shallow pools, and because the rules dictated that players were not allowed to move after the referee's whistle had blown, and until the ball was put back into play. Any swimming ability a player might have had was therefore nullified, and the big, strong men with good passing and shooting skills became dominant.

The last time Britain competed at the Olympics was in 1956, where they finished last, in Melbourne. Since then there have been Olympic qualification tournaments in the five continents, and Britain has failed to qualify in what is undoubtedly the strongest group: Europe. The Great Britain team in Melbourne was Terry Miller (Plaistow United), Jack Jones (Cheltenham), Gerry Worsell (Sutton & Cheam), Cliff Spooner (Newport), Ron Turner (Penguin), Peter Pass, Bobby Knights, and Neil May (all Polytechnic). Jones captained Britain in three successive Olympics: 1948 in London, 1952 in Helsinki, and 1956 in Melbourne. Some 33 years after their Olympic appearances, Ron Turner and Neil May are still playing for their club teams in the London League — although May has indicated that this will be his final season!

FINA, having been founded as the World Governing Body of Swimming in 1908 (on 19 July, in London), became responsible for the rules of all the Swimming disciplines, including Water Polo. From 1950 onwards, the game has been subject to continual rule changes, which have made it unrecognisable from the earlier activity. Some major changes included the abolition of the "no man moving" rule; control of games by two referees; extension of the playing time to four periods of seven minutes actual playing time; maximum ball possession time of 35 seconds without a shot at goal; and teams having access to six substitute players.

With two referees, a constant changing of players, and tactics mainly based on scoring goals when one team has a player out of the water for fouling, the game has lost a great deal of spectator appeal. But, having said that, Water Polo is still popular throughout the world, particularly in Europe, where the spectators seem to be better educated in the finer tactics and skills of the game. The rule changes have emanated mainly from Europe, where the strength of the International game has shifted very much to Hungary, USSR, Yugoslavia, and Italy, with some intervention from the USA, Holland, and Germany, as the following Olympic Games results indicate:

	1st	2nd	3rd
1948 London	Italy	Hungary	Holland
1952 Helsinki	Hungary	Yugoslavia	Italy
1956 Melbourne	Hungary	Yugoslavia	USSR
1960 Rome	Italy	USSR	Hungary
1964 Tokyo	Hungary	Yugoslavia	USSR
1968 Mexico	Yugoslavia	USSR	Hungary
1972 Munich	USSR	Hungary	USA
1976 Montreal	Hungary	Italy	Holland
1980 Moscow	USSR	Yugoslavia	Hungary
1984 Los Angeles	Yugoslavia	USA	W Germany
1988 Seoul	Yugoslavia	USA	USSR

One of the stars of the immediate post-war Hungarian team, was Dazso Gyarmati, who played his first Olympic Tournament in 1948, and at the age of 37, played his fifth and last Olympic in 1964, with a personal medal tally of three Golds, one Silver, and one Bronze. It is of added interest to note that in the two years prior to his first Olympic appearance, Gyarmati lived in London and played for Kingsbury SC (now disbanded), in the London Water Polo League. His was obviously a talented swimming family, for daughter Andrea won an Olympic Silver Medal for 100 metres Backstroke at the 1972 Olympics in Munich.

At International level, more Water Polo is being played now than ever before. In addition to the Olympic Games Tournament, FINA now promotes World Championships for men and women, World Cups for men and women, and a World Junior Championship for players under 20 years of age was introduced in 1981.

The European Federation (LEN), promotes Senior Championships for both men and women, Junior Championships for players of 19 years and under, and a Youth Championship for players up to 17 years of age. At club level, LEN promotes a National Champions Cup for both sexes, a Cup Winners' Cup, and an Invitation Super Cup, between the winners of the LEN Cup for National Champions and the National Cup Winners. A European Nations Cup, played between countries on a home and away basis is to commence in 1990.

With the almost non-existence of International-sized pitches, and with limited finance available for competition and team training, it is not surprising that the quality of play in Britain lags far behind European and World standards. However, at domestic level, the game is still very much alive, with some 400 clubs running teams in what is now generally accepted as a game for players rather than spectators. The women's game is also gaining in popularity, and in the last five years or so, around 60 clubs have taken up the sport. The National Club Championship, which started back in 1888, is still going strong. It is no longer dominated by Osborne, Hyde Seal, and Plaistow United; the teams to beat in the 1980s are Polytechnic, Sutton & Cheam, and Hammersmith Penguin.

Since World War Two, the ASA have introduced a number of new events into the competitive programme, notably "Inter-District" Championships for juniors (under 18), and boys (under 16). There are now also Club Championships for juniors and boys, and in 1983 an ASA National Women's Club Championship was introduced, which was won by Menzieshill of Dundee. This was not the first time that an English Championship has gone to a Scottish club. This honour also went to Motherwell AS & WPC, who won the ASA Club Water Polo Championship in 1949, defeating Bradford Dolphins by 8 goals to 5 in the final, which was played at Kingsway Baths, Lancaster. They repeated the achievement in 1950, when they defeated Plaistow United. Alas, the County Water Polo Championship, first contested in 1896, is no longer held. This has been replaced by a junior event, which Lancashire, with five Cup Final appearances in the '80s, are proving as difficult to defeat as were their senior predecessors, who won 16 times between 1896 and 1928.

In the 1970s, Oxford caused something of a problem by selecting a woman, Fiona Pixley, an ex-Australian International player, as a member of the team to play Cambridge. The Light Blues refused to play, until it was pointed out to Oxford that they were in contravention of FINA and ASA Law, which stated that competitions "between the sexes shall not take place in public". Fiona reluctantly had to withdraw, but fortunately the incident resulted in the introduction of a match between women's teams into the annual "Oxbridge" sporting calendar.

Eight English clubs: Birkenhead, Birmingham, Cheltenham, Otter, Polytechnic, Sheffield, Sutton & Cheam, and Weston super Mare, formed the first "Premier Invitation Water Polo League" in 1962. The name of the League was changed to the "National Water Polo League" in 1971, and it now encompasses 35 clubs in four divisions. Polytechnic, of London, have been the dominating force in Division One, winning 13 times in the 26 years the League Championship has been held. In 1988, the other Divisions were won by Royton (2), Warley (3), and Tyldesley (4). The National League also organises the British "Deep Water" Championship, the winner of which represents Great Britain in the European National Champions Cup Competition.

Surely it is the final irony that we in Britain, who invented the game, have to organise a tournament with special "deep water" facilities to play European opposition, who would not consider playing the game under any other conditions.

England's International side v. Scotland, 7 October, 1899. Left to right: Back Row: ▷
A.B. Cragg, W.J. Read, P. Ripley, A.G. Robertson, F. Baxter, H.R. Aulton. Front
Row: R. Sharrock, J.A. Jarvis, R. Gray, J.H. Derbyshire, G. Marshall.

ASA Championships, 1988–89

ASA Senior Club

Men

Prelim. Round

Weston s Mare	RAF	W/O
Bristol Central	Warley Wasps	8–5
Co Coventry	Bracknell	7–3
Hamilton	Middlesbrough	18–2
Everton	Warrender	12–9

First Round

Polytechnic	Royton	22-15
Nova Centurion	Bristol Central	7-4
Sutton & Cheam	Purples	21-4
Portobello	Co Coventry	9-7
Hammersmith	Weston s Mare	14-2
Dunfermline	Everton	13-11
Paragon	Hamilton	15-9
Plant Hill	Cheltenham	10-8

Second Round

Plant Hill	Paragon	15-13
Hammersmith	Dunfermline	13-9
Sutton & Cheam	Nova Centurion	W/O
Polytechnic	Portobello	11-10

Semi-finals

Polytechnic	Hammersmith	14-12
Sutton & Cheam	Plant Hill	17-7

Final

Sutton & Cheam	Polytechnic	7-6

Women

Semi-Finals

Co Coventry	Runnymede	17-6
Stretford	Potters Bar	7-6

Final

Co Coventry	Stretford	6-4

ASA Junior Club

First Round

Kings School	Lancaster	7-5

Semi-Finals

Kings School	O.M.W.	9-5
Exeter	Dewsbury	21-8

Final

Kings School	Exeter	8-7

ASA Boys Club

Semi-Finals

Lancaster	Beckenham	17-9
Kings School	Cheltenham	20-5

Final

Lancaster	Kings School	10-8

International Results, 1988–89

Current Internationals

Men (GB): Jerry Birmingham (Polytechnic), Doug Campbell (Dunfermline), Barry Davidson (Polytechnic), Paul Dinsdale (Middlesbrough), Tony Douglas (Middleton), Rob Eastman (Polytechnic), Dave Edwards (Sutton & Cheam), John Gaffney (Hamilton), Andy Knight (Polytechnic), Peter Love (Polytechnic), Ian McCallum (Warrender), Chris Mottley (Nova Centurion), Ian Mountfield (Royton), Stef Radwanski (Sutton & Cheam), Gary Simons (Everton), Charlie Thurley (Sutton & Cheam), Mike Yates (Polytechnic), Mark Shepherd (Sutton & Cheam), Stu Pearson (Sutton & Cheam), Miguel Ortiz (Penguin), Andrew Darlington (Royton).

Women (England): Rosemary Hanton (Stretford), Sarah Webzell (Potters Bar), Claire Sanders (Co Coventry), Helen Nicholson (Potters Bar), Amanda Saville (Potters Bar), Debbie Hipps (Potters Bar), Julie Allsopp (Stretford), Joanne Lunt (Stretford), Susan Langston (Po Plymouth), Susan Webb (Potters Bar), Linzi Mottley (Sheffield Sharks), Nicola Harwood (Beckenham), Lucy Williams (Potters Bar), Rachel Crowder (Co Coventry), Nicola Toone (Stretford), Hillary Sartain (Stretford), Lindsey Green (Potters Bar).

British Results Only

Men

Home Nations Tournament
Walsall — 13/14 January, 1989

England	Ireland	18-7
England	Wales	14-6
England	Scotland	12-5

England won the tournament

TSB International
Crystal Palace — 8 April, 1989

GBR	France	4-8

Six Nations Tournament
Aarhus, Denmark —
28/30 April, 1989

GBR	Czechoslovakia	7-12
GBR	Austria	11-5
GBR	Sweden	8-8
GBR	Poland	4-10
GBR	Denmark	9-10

GBR finished fifth

Euro Qualifying Tournament
Zeist, Holland — 11/15 May, 1989

GBR	Austria	12-7
GBR	Finland	14-3
GBR	Switzerland	17-7
GBR	Holland	7-14

GBR finished second

Seven Nations Tournament
Vienna, Austria — 27/30 July, 1989

GBR	Switzerland	20-5
GBR	Austria	6-7
GBR	Denmark	11-6
GBR	Sweden	10-8
GBR	Israel	9-10
GBR	S Korea	32-0

GBR finished third

European Games
Bonn, W Germany —
12/20 August, 1989

GBR	Hungary	11-12
GBR	Greece	5-7
GBR	Italy	2-14
GBR	Poland	4-10
GBR	Sweden	10-9
GBR	Austria	7-8

GBR finished 15th

Junior Men

Home Nations Tournament
Walsall — 13/14 January, 1989

England	Wales	16-3
England	Ireland	12-10
England	Scotland	8-7

England won the tournament

Five Nations Tournament
Scotland — 14/16 July, 1989

England	Portugal	19-6
England	Scotland	12-4
England	Ireland	15-3
England	Belgium	8-3

England won the tournament

England	France	2-6
England	Greece	14-2
England	Italy	5-8
England	Norway	10-7
England	W Germany	5-6

England finished fifth

Women

Eight Nations Tournament
Antwerp, Belgium — 7/9 July, 1989

England	Canada	3-5
England	Holland	0-14
England	France	10-12
England	Belgium	8-7
England	Sweden	6-5

England finished fifth

Seven Nations Tournament
Rome, Italy — 22/25 March, 1989

| England | Hungary | 4-14 |

Jerry Birmingham

Alan Pascoe Ass.

Past Championship Winners, 1888–1989

ASA Club Finals, 1888–1989

Men

Year	Winner	Runner-up	Score
1888	Burton on Trent	Otter	3–0
1889	Burton on Trent	Amateur	2–0
1890	Hanley	Burton on Trent	6–0
1891	Burton on Trent	Nautilus	3–2
1892	Nautilus	Hanley	3–2
1893	Cygnus	Hanley	3–1
1894	Osborne	Leicester	8–2
1895	Osborne	Leicester	8–1
1896	Osborne	Leicester	3–0
1897	Osborne	People's Palace	9–2
1898	Osborne	People's Palace	3–2
1899	Osborne	St Helens	5–1
1900	Leicester	Hyde Seal	2–1
1901	Osborne	Worthing	6–2
1902	Wigan	Leicester	5–2
1903	Hyde Seal	St Helens	4–2
1904	Hyde Seal	Wigan	4–2
1905	Hyde Seal	Weston s Mare	4–0
1906	Weston s Mare	Polytechnic	6–4
1907	Weston s Mare	Wigan	3–2
1908	Hyde Seal	Polytechnic	5–2
1909	Wigan	Polytechnic	4–3
1910	Wigan	Polytechnic	3–2
1911	Hyde Seal	Wigan	7–6
1912	Hyde Seal	Hornsey	8–2
1913	Hyde Seal	Wigan	4–1
1920	Hyde Seal	Hammersmith	10–1
1921	Weston s Mare	Hyde Seal	11–10
1922	Walsall	Weston s Mare	6–5
1923	Blackburn	Avondale	8–1
1924	Hyde Seal	Weston s Mare	7–5
1925	Weston s Mare	Hyde Seal	6–1
1926	Penguin	Weston s Mare	4–2
1927	Penguin	Harpurhey	4–3
1928	Plaistow U	Walsall	5–3
1929	Plaistow U	Harpurhey	4–3
1930	Plaistow U	Harpurhey	8–2
1931	Plaistow U	Liverpool Police	7–3
1932	Penguin	Coventry	5–4
1933	Coventry	Cheltenham	6–5
1934	Oldham Police	Plaistow U	5–4
1935	Plaistow U	Hyde Seal	5–2
1936	Plaistow U	Oldham Police	4–0
1937	Plaistow U	Polytechnic	7–4
1938	Plaistow U	Otter	5–1
1946	Avondale	Bradford	8–5
1947	Penguin	Otter	2–1
1948	Plaistow U	Bradford	9–6
1949	Motherwell	Bradford	8–3
1950	Motherwell	Plaistow U	7–6
1951	Penguin	Motherwell	5–3
1952	Penguin	Cheltenham	7–5
1953	Plaistow U	Motherwell	6–2
1954	Plaistow U	Cheltenham	6–5
1955	Cheltenham	Plaistow U	6–2
1956	Polytechnic	Cheltenham	9–5
1957	Polytechnic	Cheltenham	5–3
1958	Cheltenham	Polytechnic	7–5
1959	Cheltenham	Polytechnic	6–5
1960	Polytechnic	Otter	10–3
1961	Birkenhead	Penguin	8–7
1962	Cheltenham	Sheffield	9–5
1963	Polytechnic	Sheffield	6–2
1964	Otter	Walsall	6–5
1965	Penguin	Cheltenham	6–5
1966	Birkenhead	Sutton & Cheam	4–3
1967	Walsall	Birkenhead	9–7
1968	Cheltenham	Sutton & Cheam	10–5
1969	Polytechnic	Everton	6–4
1970	Polytechnic	Birkenhead	5–4
1971	Polytechnic	Sutton & Cheam	10–4
1972	Polytechnic	Penguin	4–3
1973	Everton	Polytechnic	7–6
1974	Aston	Polytechnic	6–4
1975	Leamington	Cheltenham	5–4
1976	Polytechnic	Sutton & Cheam	7–6
1977	Polytechnic	Cheltenham	8–6
1978	Polytechnic	Everton	8–2
1979	Polytechnic	Sutton & Cheam	5–4
1980	Sutton & Cheam	Birkenhead	11–6
1981	Polytechnic	Birkenhead	10–8
1982	Polytechnic	Southport	10–7
1983	Birkenhead	Southport	13–7
1984	Maindee Olympic	Polytechnic	10–9
1985	Maindee Olympic	Portobello	11–10
1986	Polytechnic	Portobello	12–9
1987	Polytechnic	Sutton & Cheam	8–4
1988	Polytechnic	Royton	15–5
1989	Sutton & Cheam	Polytechnic	7–6

Women

Year	Winner	Runner-up	Score
1986	Potters Bar	Beckenham	9–8
1987	Co Coventry	Menzieshill	16–7
1988	Co Coventry	Stretford	8–5
1989	Co Coventry	Stretford	6–4

ASA Junior Club Finals, 1947–1989

Competitors must be under the age of 18.

Junior Men

Year	Winner	Runner-up	Score
1947	Plaistow U	Cheltenham	7–4
1948	Plaistow U	Leeds Leander	9–4
1949	Cheltenham	Stafford	8–3
1950	Plaistow U	Cheltenham	6–5
1951	Birkenhead	Middlesbrough	6–4

1952	Plaistow U	Cheltenham	6–4	1971 Cheltenham	Beckenham	4–2
1953	Birkenhead	Cheltenham	7–6	1972 Cheltenham	Everton	10–5
1954	Avondale	Birkenhead	5–4	1973 Sutton & Cheam	Cheltenham	7–2
1955	Sutton & Cheam	Birkenhead	5–1	1974 Sutton & Cheam	Cheltenham	6–5
1956	Shiverers	Wallasey	6–0	1975 Plant Hill	Camp Hill Edw	3–2
1957	Sutton & Cheam	Cheltenham	9–1	1976 Plant Hill	Plymouth	14–3
1958	Sutton & Cheam	Bootle	5–2	1977 Plant Hill	Durham C	8–4
1959	Sutton & Cheam	Cheltenham	6–5	1978 Lancaster	Bedford Modern	7–3
1960	Cheltenham	Sutton & Cheam	8–3	1979 Plant Hill	Warley	9–8
1961	Sutton & Cheam	Birkenhead	6–4	1980 Plant Hill	Durham C	9–4
1962	Lucas	Seven Kings	9–5	1981 Plant Hill	Cheltenham	7–6
1963	Leamington	Wallasey	6–5	1982 Plant Hill	Kings School	7–6
1964	Leamington	Cheltenham	5–1	1983 Havering	Cheltenham	17–11
1965	Sutton & Cheam	York C	3–1	1984 Havering	Royton	13–12
1966	Aston	Thornaby	9–4	1985 Royton	Sutton & Cheam	24–4
1967	Walsall	Thornaby	7–6	1986 Royton	Sutton & Cheam	13–12
1968	Penguin	Birkenhead	5–2	1987 Lancaster	Cheltenham	15–9
1969	Beckenham	Leamington	7–4	1988 Lancaster	Kings School	16–7
1970	Cheltenham	Halifax	5–4	1989 Kings School	Exeter	8–7

ASA Boys Club Finals, 1974–1989

Competitors must be under the age of 16. From 1974–1980 there were no Finals, the winners being produced from League tables.

1974	Plant Hill			1982 Havering	Portobello	14–13
1975	Royton			1983 Royton	Sutton & Cheam	13–8
1976	Walsall			1984 Royton	Co Swansea	5–3
1977	Plant Hill			1985 Lancaster	Exeter	8–5
1978	Plant Hill			1986 Lancaster	Kings School	13–4
1979	Hamilton			1987 Lancaster	Kings School	13–9
1980	Portobello			1988 Kings School	Lancaster	8–4
1981	Portobello	Cheltenham	23–4	1989 Lancaster	Kings School	10–8

European Champions, 1926–1989

Men

1926 Hungary	1954 Hungary
1927 Hungary	1958 Hungary
1931 Hungary	1962 Hungary
1934 Hungary	1966 USSR
1938 Hungary	1970 USSR
1947 Italy	1974 Hungary
1950 Holland	1977 Hungary
	1981 W Germany

1983 USSR
1985 France
1987 France
1989 W Germany

Women
1987 Holland
1989 Holland

World Champions, 1973–1986

Men

1973 Australia	1978 Italy
1975 USSR	1982 USSR
	1986 Yugoslavia

Women
1986 Australia

Olympic Champions, 1900–1988

Men

1900 GBR	1928 Germany	1964 Hungary
1904 USA	1932 Hungary	1968 Yugoslavia
1908 GBR	1936 Hungary	1972 USSR
1912 GBR	1948 Italy	1976 Hungary
1920 GBR	1952 Hungary	1980 USSR
1924 France	1956 Hungary	1984 Yugoslavia
	1960 Italy	1988 Yugoslavia

319

SYNCHRONISED SWIMMING SECTION

Synchronised Swimming Comes of Age

by Irene Williams (Honorary Secretary, ASA Synchronised Swimming Committee)

Surprising as it may seem, forerunners of Synchronised Swimming as we know it today, were staged prior to 1890. It was called "Scientific and Ornamental Swimming" in those days, and it was performed by men, although girls were included in professional displays at Blackpool Tower before the end of the century. Amateur displays were given a few years later, at St George's Baths, London and members of the Otter Swimming Club originated the "Otter Wheel", a prototype of figure formations.

It was in 1906 that Charlie Smith (a famous water polo player), returned from the Olympics with news of the new "trick swimming", to his club in Southport and from then on they have always had some swimmers taking part in this type of swimming, which developed in the '30s to "Ornamental Swimming", and on to Synchronised Swimming as we now know it.

In 1907, an Australian, Annette Kellena, made a tour through the USA, exhibiting in a glass tank of water; and Holland had a Ladies' Team of "Ornamental Swimmers".

After the First World War, "Floatation Teams" were popular in America, Canada, Belgium, Holland, and France, and the American Red Cross used a type of swimming to music.

By the 1920s and '30s, the "Floating Team" era developed in England, including the Polytechnic Ladies and Lewisham Ladies from London. These were pattern formations of ten-12 girls, and the changes in design were signalled by numbers or whistles. Music was played in the background.

In 1925, the first amateur competitions were run in Canada, and these consisted of "stunts", strokes, and sculling. This was followed in US universities by the use of a musical background to water shows, sometimes with a spoken or sung story.

By 1934, Kay Curtis had produced "Modern Mermaids" at the Chicago World Fair, and she introduced Synchronised Swimming more as we know it today. Competitions with floating teams to music were held in France and Germany.

The ASSA of Canada ruled that all routines must be synchronised in 1943. Demonstrations and lectures were held in Europe to promote the sport.

Two years later, in 1945, the AAU of America recognised Synchronised Swimming as a sport, and Annual National Championships have been held ever since. Beulah Gundling and Norma Olsen travelled Europe.

In 1946, Motherwell, Scotland, produced some excellent swimmers, including Cathy Gibson and Nancy Riach, who demonstrated pattern work-strokes and turns to music, with underwater lighting used effectively.

Films were being made by 1947, with such people as Esther Williams, and this stimulated the development of "Aquatic Swimming" all over the world.

Frank Letchford introduced the "Voyagers' Swimming Club" in 1950, and the team swam to live accordion or record-player. Routine times were of any duration, and still mostly pattern swimming: synchronised arm movements with flippers on the feet; solos and duets were introduced, with the team swimming round them. In the same year, Worthing Club produced a maypole item, with 12/14 men and women performing aquatically a near-authentic dance.

KNZB, of Holland, organised its first Synchro Committee in 1952, and the development of the sport was encouraged by Mr Jan Armburst and his wife.

In 1954, Pat Besford helped introduce diving to music at the Metropolitan School of Diving Displays, with Liz Ferris choreographing the Synchronised Swimming section.

1955 saw the introduction of the sport to the Pan American Games; and the first French Championships.

Norma Olsen's Athens Water Follies visited London with AAU Champions on a world tour in 1956. An International Swimming Committee was formed in Holland, with Jan Armburst as President. And FINA recognised the now extremely popular activity.

At the International Festival in Amsterdam in 1958, Metropolitan, London, sent a Solo, Duet, and Team of four. Each competitor had to perform in a stunt competition.

During 1960, Dawn Zajac studied Synchronised Swimming in California, and the following year she founded the Seymour SSC. They held annual competitions, using AAU rules.

In 1964, the first ASA Sub-Committee for Synchronised Swimming was formed in London to promote interest in the sport.

1965 saw the start of various courses being held in different parts of the country, and Pauline McCullough, of Canada, gave demonstrations.

By 1966, the first Award scheme for the sport was introduced, with five grades, and badges for each grade. Examinations for the qualification of Examiners was also introduced.

1967/8 saw the Districts of the ASA forming Synchro Committees. A National Panel of Judges was set up, and a guide for Judges was issued. Competitions started to be held in all the Districts.

In 1969, the first Judges' Conference was held in Newcastle, and we had the first trial for a GB Team. The first National Competition (under FINA Rules), was held in November, 1969 at Marshall Street Baths, London; and we held our first International, against France, in the July.

1970 saw the first ASA Synchro *Handbook* published, and the first Easter Course for swimmers and coaches was held at Crystal Palace.

In 1971, the National Competitions started the present system of circulating round the Districts. The first Four-Nations Competition (GB, Holland, France, West Germany), was held.

The Inter-District competition was started in 1973. Scorers' examinations were also inaugurated. GB came fifth in the first World Championships, in Belgrade.

In 1974, GB won all the Gold medals at the Windmill Trophy in the first European Championships, in Amsterdam. The first International Conference for Judges was staged in Ottowa.

With the inclusion of Switzerland, in 1975, the Four-Nations became the Five-Nations Competition. In this year, also, our Competitions became National Championships, and included awards to juniors. GB took part in the first World Games, in Cali, Colombia. The first Synchro Teachers' Certificate course and examination was held, and a *Teachers' Handbook* was published.

In 1976, an NDO for Synchro was appointed.

In 1977, the Grade "B" and "A" Examinations were revised. Routines are marked in 1/10th points. The first European Symposium was held in Vienna. Trials took place for a Junior Team the following year.

The Advanced Teachers' Certificate was introduced in 1978, and also the Preliminary Teachers' Award. The National Championships were held over two days for the first time.

1979 was the year in which GB took part in the FINA World Cup, in Tokyo.

In 1980, the first Age Group Competitions were held in Nuneaton. GB entered the first Junior European Championships. The Mazda Cars International, between Canada, USA, and GB, was held in Coventry.

In 1981, the first World Coaches' Conference was held in Calgary.

A Festival of Synchronised Swimming was held at Crystal Palace in 1982, and the Coaches' Certificate for Synchro was introduced.

In 1983, GB was represented in the Japan International Age Group Meet.

In the 1984 Olympics, Synchronised Swimming was included for the first time, with Caroline Holmyard and Carolyn Wilson representing GB in Duet, and with Caroline in the Solo. There was a Festival of Synchronised Swimming at Leicester.

The sport was included in the 1986 Commonwealth Games, with Solo and Duet. England being represented by Amanda Dodd and Nicola Shearn, who gained the Silver, while Amanda did likewise in the Solo.

1988 saw Conferences in all the Districts, in preparation for the new two-mark system for Judging routines. A comprehensive training programme was set up and introduced in January, 1989.

As Synchronised Swimming has developed over the last 20 years or so, examination criteria has been revised as necessary, both for swimmers and officials, and the Award scheme updated. Our teams (Senior, Junior, and Age-Group), have competed internationally as England and GB regularly, the programme having gradually increased. A few Home Internationals have been held, but the lack of suitable pools for this purpose has caused problems.

In the Four- and Five-Nations competitions, England won the Dolphin Trophy twice outright, and it is now the property of the ASA.

The Mary Black Award for services to Synchronised Swimming was first awarded in 1977, and the Synchronised Swimmer of the Year Award in 1984.

We now have a number of Awards/Trophies for our Championships, i.e. — The Redwood Team Trophy, The Helen Elkington Trophy for Solo, The Ron Spencer Cup for Duet, The Yvonne Price Cup for Junior Solo, The Holland Trophy for Choreography, all of which are swum for annually.

Georgina Coombs (left) and Nikki Shearn, winners of the 1988–89 ASA National Duet title.
Bristol United Press

ASA Championships, 1988–89

ASA National Senior
Central Baths, Southampton — 5/6 November, 1988

Figures

1	N. Shearn (Bristol Central)	89.38
2	K. Shacklock (Rushmoor Royals)	84.93
3	L. Goodwin (Southport)	81.35
4	S. Northey (Reading Royals)	81.30
5	G. Coombs (Bristol Central)	80.53
6	K. McIntosh (Elgin)	77.80
7	L. Vakil (Rushmoor Royals)	77.76
8	A. Davenport (Walsall)	77.66
9	R. Taylor (Portsmouth Victoria)	77.35
10	C. Geier (Hounslow B)	77.28
11	J. Preston (Barnet Copthall)	76.68
12	L. Skidmore (Bristol Central)	76.38
13	S. Allen (Reading Royals)	76.15
14	K. Wishart (Sale)	75.60
15	S. Richards (Walsall)	75.55
16	J. Luckett (Reading Royals)	75.55
17	V. Maybury (Reading Royals)	75.26
18	E. Clark (Reading Royals)	75.06
19	C. Pember (Barnet Copthall)	75.05
20	L. Webster (Rushmoor Royals)	74.31
21	G. Wigley (Rushmoor Royals)	74.26
22	K. MacAndrew (Barnet Copthall)	74.10
23	A. Alexander (Walsall)	74.06
24	L. Rutter (Reading Royals)	73.10
25	E. Carlsen (Rushmoor Royals)	73.01
26	C. Chambers (Edinburgh)	72.83
27	M. Erraught (Bristol Central)	72.16
28	K. Thompson (Bristol Central)	72.13
29	J. Wells (Rushmoor Royals)	71.96
30	S. Windsor (Exeter)	71.88
31	L. Figes (Bristol Central)	71.60
32	L. Ramatour (Bristol Central)	71.53
33	J. Owen (Nuneaton & Bedworth)	71.08
34	S. Vockins (Reading Royals)	70.73
35	K. Lythgoe (Bristol Central)	70.65
36	P. Shortman (Bristol Central)	70.45
37	R. Scales (Rushmoor Royals)	70.30
38	A. Surch (Sale)	70.05
39	V. Bresnark (Barnet Copthall)	69.93
40	J. Svensen (Reading Royals)	69.88
41	J. Smith (Walsall)	69.83
42	L. Marshall (Seymour)	69.66
43	Z. Vakil (Rushmoor Royals)	69.55
44	L. Parkinson (Co Birmingham)	69.45
45	I. Muxworthy (Edinburgh)	69.40
46	N. Wilson (Reading Royals)	69.35
47	N. Scott-Smith (Dunstable)	69.26
48	L. Smith (Reading Royals)	69.21
49	G. Prewer (Rushmoor Royals)	69.05
50	L. Fishleigh (Reading Royals)	69.03
51	T. Brookes (Walsall)	68.55
52	H. Smith (Reading Royals)	68.33
53	K. Thomas (Abbey Wood)	68.25
54	L. Busby (Abbey Wood)	68.15
55	L. Nickels (Seymour)	68.03
56	J. Whistance (Walsall)	68.03
57	K. Ellis (Walsall)	67.88
58	R. Vakil (Rushmoor Royals)	67.85
59	K. Piercewright (Sale)	67.80
60	C. Hedge (Seymour)	67.76
61	E. Beaumont (Bramston Concordes)	67.46
62	M. Harris (Walsall)	67.43
63	J. Waddilove (Bristol Central)	67.25
64	G. Duncan (Barnet Copthall)	67.21
65	A. Tweedale (Saxon)	67.20
66	H. Whitfield (Walsall)	67.05
67	E. Jones (Co Birmingham)	66.96
68	P. Taylor (Sale)	66.86
69	E. Milne (Sale)	66.81
70	D. Clare (Walsall)	66.71
71	N. Swanscott (Rushmoor Royals)	66.61
72	P. Murphy (Edinburgh)	66.53
73	K. Ryder (Co Birmingham)	66.53
74	R. Hinks (Portsmouth Victoria)	66.53
75	Z. Goldbart (Barnet Copthall)	66.46
76	A. Carlsen (Rushmoor Royals)	66.38
77	M. Shacklock (Rushmoor Royals)	66.33
78	C. Smith (Abbey Wood)	66.23
79	K. Warren (Portsmouth Victoria)	66.21
80	L. le Masurier (Abbey Wood)	66.15
81	F. Haworth (Southport)	66.01
82	M. Beck (Sale)	65.96
83	J. Romer (Barnet Copthall)	65.93
84	L. Zoltonos (Co Birmingham)	65.88
85	R. Ramsay (Rushmoor Royals)	65.88
86	K. Rosser (Jersey Etaile)	65.86
87	S. Bayliss (Co Birmingham)	65.81
88	C. Jones (Rushmoor Royals)	65.73
89	L. Moakes (Troutbeck Bridge)	65.68
90	A. Walls (Co Birmingham)	65.60
91	E. Bennett (Rushmoor Royals)	65.55
92	J. Moreau (Hounslow B)	65.40
93	N. Winwood (Co Birmingham)	65.28
94	J. Lambert (Rushmoor Royals)	65.10
95	E. Coles (Bedford)	64.71
96	V. Cuthbert (Saxon)	64.68
97	C. Allen (Dunstable)	64.55
98	S. Finch (Abbey Wood)	64.30
99	J. Jones (Barnet Copthall)	64.26
100	E. Pollard (Co Newcastle)	64.16
101	D. Heath (Dunstable)	64.03
102	A. Cooper (Barnet Copthall)	63.98
103	J. Allen (Abbey Wood)	63.86
104	J. Baxter (Bramston Concordes)	63.85
105	S. Matthews (Hounslow B)	63.81
106	D. Brooks (Abbey Wood)	63.58
107	J. Matthews (Hounslow B)	63.03
108	M. Parker (Co Newcastle)	62.95
109	C. Perry (Bedford)	62.83
110	L. Watham (Reading Royals)	62.66
111	M. Duncan (Edinburgh)	62.55
112	L. Pettipher (Co Birmingham)	61.93
113	P. Clarke (Bristol Central)	61.61
114	L. Finch (Abbey Wood)	61.61
115	A. Brady (Portsmouth Victoria)	61.41
116	P. Rourke (Reading Royals)	61.30
117	C. Smith (Abbey Wood)	61.25

118	T. Woods (Hounslow B)	60.20
119	S. Dombrick (Hounslow B)	59.98

Solo

1	N. Shearn (Bristol Central)	183.18
2	K. Shacklock (Rushmoor Royals)	175.73
3	G. Coombs (Bristol Central)	169.93
4	S. Northey (Reading Royals)	166.90
5	C. Geier (Hounslow B)	162.28
6	K. McIntosh (Elgin)	162.00
7	L. Skidmore (Bristol Central)	159.78
8	L. Vakil (Rushmoor Royals)	159.36
9	J. Preston (Barnet Copthall)	159.08
10	R. Taylor (Portsmouth Victoria)	158.95
11	A. Davenport (Walsall)	158.86
12	K. Wishart (Sale)	156.80
13	E. Clark (Reading Royals)	155.66
14	J. Luckett (Reading Royals)	155.35
15	S. Allen (Reading Royals)	154.95
16	V. Maybury (Reading Royals)	154.26
17	C. Pember (Barnet Copthall)	153.45
18	S. Richards (Walsall)	153.15
19	K. Thompson (Bristol Central)	151.73
20	E. Carlsen (Rushmoor Royals)	151.41
21	L. Webster (Rushmoor Royals)	150.11
22	K. MacAndrew (Barnet Copthall)	150.10
23	L. Rutter (Reading Royals)	148.70
24	G. Wigley (Rushmoor Royals)	148.66
25	S. Windsor (Exeter)	146.28
26	L. Figes (Bristol Central)	145.40
27	J. Wells (Rushmoor Royals)	145.36
28	R. Scales (Rushmoor Royals)	145.30
29	K. Lythgoe (Bristol Central)	145.05
30	V. Bresnark (Barnet Copthall)	139.13

Junior Placings: (1) C. Geier; (2) L. Skidmore; (3) L. Vakil.

Duet

1	N. Shearn/G. Coombs (Bristol Central)	174.95
2	S. Northey/E. Clark (Reading Royals)	160.98
3	A. Davenport/S. Richards (Walsall)	156.40
4	J. Preston/C. Pember (Barnet Copthall)	155.26
5	F. Hawarth/L. Goodwin (Southport)	152.48
6	K. Wishart/A. Surch (Sale)	151.02
7	M. Erraught/P. Shortman (Bristol Central)	150.90
8	L. Vakil/J. Wells (Rushmoor Royals)	148.66
9	K. Lythgoe/L. Skidmore (Bristol Central)	148.31
10	L. Webster/G. Wigley (Rushmoor Royals)	147.49
11	L. Rutter/J. Svensen (Reading Royals)	147.09
12	L. Figes/K. Thompson (Bristol Central)	145.26
13	C. Geier/J. Moreau (Hounslow B)	144.94
14	J. Whistance/A. Alexander (Walsall)	143.05
15	K. Warren/R. Taylor (Portsmouth Victoria)	142.78

Team

1	Bristol Central	165.92
2	Reading Royals	162.96
3	Rushmoor Royals	161.71
4	Barnet Copthall	155.31
5	Walsall	153.47
6	Abbey Wood	145.66
7	Sale	145.65
8	Co Birmingham	141.40
9	Hounslow B	141.03

ASA National Age-Group (first three)

Halifax Pool — 24/25 September, 1988

12 Years and Under Age Group

Solo

1	L. Finch (Abbey Wood)	103.45
2	M. Shacklock (Rushmoor Royals)	101.78
3	S. Bayliss (Co Birmingham)	101.78

Duet

1	S. Bayliss/N. Calvey (Co Birmingham)	101.44
2	P. Mercer/K. Smith (Abbey Wood)	95.64
3	J. Jones/J. Palmer (Abbey Wood)	95.60

Team

1	Abbey Wood	103.10
2	Hounslow B	98.54
3	Rushmoor Royals	97.96

13/14 Years Age Group

1	L. Vakil (Rushmoor Royals)	121.76
2	J. Wells (Rushmoor Royals)	118.05
3	R. Scales (Rushmoor Royals)	113.50

Duet

1	L. Vakil/J. Wells (Rushmoor Royals)	118.30
2	S. Matthews/J. Moreau (Hounslow B)	109.15

3	R. Ramsey/K. Webber (Rushmoor Royals)	108.74

Team

1	Rushmoor Royals	116.95
2	Reading Royals	111.53
3	Hounslow B	109.71

15/16 Years Age Group

Solo

1	C. Geier (Hounslow B)	125.31
2	L. Rutter (Reading Royals)	121.18
3	L. Skidmore (Bristol Central)	119.98

Duet

1	L. Rutter/J. Svensen (Reading Royals)	120.90
2	K. Lythgoe/L. Skidmore (Bristol Central)	118.45
3	K. MacAndrew/G. Duncan (Barnet Copthall)	118.21

Team

1	Reading Royals	119.49
2	Barnet Copthall	117.98
3	Rushmoor Royals	117.13

International Results, 1988–89

Olympic Games (Finals) 1988
Seoul, S Korea — 26 September/1 October, 1988

Solo

1	C. Waldo (Canada)	200.15
2	T. Ruiz (USA)	197.63
3	M. Kotani (Japan)	191.85
4	M. Hermine (France)	190.10
5	K. Singer (Switzerland)	185.60
6	N. Shearn (GBR)	181.93
7	K. Falassinidi (USSR)	180.65
8	G. Scheller (W Germany)	175.98

Duet

1	M.Cameron/C. Waldo (Canada)	197.71
2	S. Josephson/K. Josephson (USA)	197.28
3	T. Tanaka/M. Kotani (Japan)	190.15
4	K. Schuler/A. Capron (France)	184.79
5	E. Boss/K. Singer (Switzerland)	183.95
6	M. Cherniaeva/T. Titova (USSR)	182.66
7	N. Shearn/L. Goodwin (GBR)	179.07
8	B. Candini/S. Cardenas (Mexico)	176.83

International Meetings (British Placings Only)

Wuppertal, W Germany — 14/15 April, 1989

Junior Solo
2 L. Skidmore
3 C. Geier

Junior Duet
1 L. Skidmore/C. Geier

Age Group Solo
7 J. Wells
10 R. Scales

Age Group Duet
3 J. Wells/R. Scales
6 A. Carlsen/J. Moreau

Team Routines
4 England

Result
2 England

Kerry Shacklock

Paris, France — 10/14 May, 1989

Junior Solo
2 C. Geier

Junior Duet
2 C. Geier/L. Skidmore

Result
2 England

Mallorca, Spain — 23/25 June, 1989

Solo
6 K. Shacklock

Duet
4 K. Shacklock/S. Northey

Result
5 England

Junior World Championships (Finals)
Cali, Colombia — 18/23 July, 1989

Solo

1	B. Dryden (USA)	174.55
2	K. Clark (Canada)	171.60
3	F. Okuno (Japan)	169.65
4	K. Shacklock (GBR)	168.56
5	G. Quelin (France)	166.25
6	O. Pilipchuk (USSR)	163.71
7	M. Tan (China)	161.22
8	M. Both (Holland)	160.99

Duet

1	B. Dryden/J. Sudduth (USA)	172.84
2	K. Clark/K. Closson (Canada)	171.60

3 C. Yamamura/M. Enkaku (Japan)	168.34	6 E. Azarova/N. Gruzdeva (USSR)	164.33
4 K. Shacklock/S. Northey (GBR)	167.60	7 M. Tan/J. Jiang (China)	163.55
5 G. Quelin/C. Leveque (France)	165.64	8 M. Both/S. Braaksma (Holland)	160.07

European Championships (Finals)
Bonn, W Germany — 14/18 August, 1989

Solo

1 K. Falasinidi (USSR)	184.56
2 K. Schuler (France)	182.87
3 K. Singer (Switzerland)	181.83
4 K. Shacklock (GBR)	179.75
5 E. Lopez (Spain)	173.22
6 P. Celli (Italy)	171.09
7 M. Both (Holland)	169.65
8 B. Muellner (Austria)	166.52

Duet

1 K. Schuler/M. Anschbacher (France)	182.50
2 M. Cherniaeva/E. Foschevskaia (USSR)	179.97
3 K. Singer/E. Boss (Switzerland)	179.65
4 K. Shacklock/S. Northey (GBR)	177.32

5 P. Celli/G. Burlando (Italy)	170.79
6 E. Lopez/N. Ayala (Spain)	170.56
7 M. Both/B. Smit (Holland)	169.44
8 D. Eisenhofer/M. Schreib (W Germany)	168.90

Team

1 France	180.36
2 USSR	179.94
3 Switzerland	174.08
4 GBR	173.29
5 Italy	169.89
6 W Germany	168.60
7 Holland	167.93
8 Spain	167.42

Nikki Shearn

Past Championship Winners, 1973–1989

ASA Junior Champions, 1978–1988

Solo

1978	P. Sutton (Reading Royals)	148.08
1979	A. Dodd (Rushmoor Royals)	141.91
1980	T. Cook (Barnet Copthall)	156.56
1981	A. Bowler (Walsall)	175.80
1982	M. Raynsford (Rushmoor Royals)	154.33
1983	N. Batchelor (Rushmoor Royals)	160.23
1984	A. Davenport (Walsall)	149.01
1985	J. Seeburg (Reading Royals)	160.56
1986	S. Northey (Reading Royals)	161.03
1987	K. Shacklock (Rushmoor Royals)	168.13
1988	C. Geier (Hounslow B)	162.28

ASA Champions, 1978–1988

Andrea Holland

Solo

1978	A. Holland (Reading Royals)	156.38
1979	C. Wilson (Rushmoor Royals)	158.38
1980	C. Wilson (Rushmoor Royals)	184.70
1981	C. Wilson (Rushmoor Royals)	175.80
1982	C. Wilson (Rushmoor Royals)	179.15
1983	C. Holmyard (Bristol Central)	181.06
1984	C. Wilson (Rushmoor Royals)	185.28
1985	N. Shearn (Bristol Central)	172.31
1986	N. Shearn (Bristol Central)	178.10
1987	N. Shearn (Bristol Central)	176.83
1988	N. Shearn (Bristol Central)	183.18

Duet

1978	A. Holland/P. Sutton (Reading Royals)	154.13
1979	A. Holland/J. Holland (Reading Royals)	149.21
1980	C. Wilson/S. Kenton (Rushmoor Royals)	178.88
1981	C. Wilson/S. Kenton (Rushmoor Royals)	170.15
1982	C. Holmyard/G. Coombs (Bristol Central)	174.15
1983	A. Dodd/C. Wilson (Rushmoor Royals)	179.20
1984	C. Holmyard/N. Shearn (Bristol Central)	177.10
1985	A. Dodd/J. Dodd (Bristol Central)	171.95
1986	N. Shearn/G. Coombs (Bristol Central)	172.23
1987	G. Coombs/N. Shearn (Bristol Central)	174.11
1988	N. Shearn/G. Coombs (Bristol Central)	174.96

Team

1978	Reading Royals	147.75
1979	Rushmoor Royals	149.55
1980	Rushmoor Royals	171.53
1981	Rushmoor Royals	161.20
1982	Rushmoor Royals	170.05
1983	Rushmoor Royals	170.25
1984	Rushmoor Royals	162.90
1985	Bristol Central	167.58
1986	Bristol Central	161.03
1987	Reading Royals	166.32
1988	Bristol Central	165.92

Commonwealth Champions, 1986

Solo

1986	S. Frechette (Canada)	199.50

Duet

1986	M. Cameron/ C. Waldo (Canada)	199.54

European Champions, 1974–1989

Solo

1974	J. Holland (GBR)	93.82
1977	J. Cox (GBR)	157.63
1981	C. Wilson (GBR)	176.01
1983	C. Wilson (GBR)	180.33
1985	C. Wilson (GBR)	184.63
1987	M. Hermine (France)	188.70
1989	K. Falasinidi (USSR)	184.56

Duet

1974	J. Holland/J. Lane (GBR)	85.50
1977	A. Holland/J. Cox (GBR)	153.91
1981	C. Holmyard/C. Wilson (GBR)	171.41

1983	C. Holmyard/J. Cox (GBR)	174.66
1985	A. Worisch/E. Edinger (Austria)	180.64
1987	M. Hermine/K. Schuler (France)	184.60
1989	K. Schuler/M. Anschbacher (France)	182.50

Team

1974	GBR	88.49
1977	Holland	150.32
1981	GBR	168.65
1983	GBR	168.34
1985	France	171.37
1987	France	178.48
1989	France	180.36

World Champions, 1973–1986

Solo

1973	T. Anderson (USA)	120.46
1975	G. Buzonas (USA)	133.08
1978	H. Vandenburg (Canada)	187.84
1982	T. Ruiz (USA)	192.30
1986	C. Waldo (Canada)	200.03

Duet

1973	T. Anderson/G. Johnson (Canada)	118.39
1975	R. Curren/A. Norrish (USA)	129.43

1978	M. Caulkins/H. Vandenburg (Canada)	183.30
1982	S. Hambrook/K. Kryczka (Canada)	190.54
1986	M. Cameron/C. Waldo (Canada)	196.26

Team

1975	Japan	123.69
1978	USA	182.30
1982	Canada	188.25
1986	Canada	191.20

Olympic Champions, 1984–1988

Solo

1984	T. Ruiz (USA)	198.46
1988	C. Waldo (Canada)	200.15

Duet

1984	T. Ruiz/C. Costie (USA)	195.58
1988	M. Cameron/C. Waldo (Canada)	197.17

Caroline Holmyard (Francis)

LONG DISTANCE SWIMMING SECTION

British Long Distance Swimming

by Trevor Symmons (Honorary General Secretary, B.L.D.S.A.)

The sport of open water Long Distance Swimming stretches back into the distant past, and aquatic achievements are recorded in Roman, Greek, and Assyrian times.

It was in March, 1810, that Lord Byron, while he was becalmed at the mouth of the Hellespont, visited the site of Troy and swam the channel from Sestos to Abydos in imitation of Leander. The next notable date was 1875, when Captain Matthew Webb swam the English Channel from Dover to Calais in a time of 21 hours, 45 minutes.

However, there was no regulatory body for long distance swimming until 1956, when the Association was established. The idea had arisen in the mind of one John Slater, after having successfully swum Windermere in 1955, and having had the experience of distance swimming in Morecambe Bay, Kings Lynn, and the Yorkshire river races.

It soon became apparent that some form of organisation and regulation was necessary for this branch of swimming, which was rapidly growing in popularity. Discussions and meetings took place among four men: Fred Oldman (a Channel swimmer), Trevor Smith and Lewis Craven (both Morecambe Bay swimmers), and John Slater.

In an imaginative and rather ambitious exercise, they formed the British Long Distance Swimming Association in 1956, together with a small band of enthusiastic supporters. They invited another very experienced long distance swimmer, one Philip Rising, to assume the Presidency, a position he held for a period of 14 years. Apart from having taken part in many successful distance swims, Philip had also swum the Channel, and had held the two-way Windermere record over the 21-mile course for several years.

This choice of President was something of a master stroke. With his drive, both financial and practical, together with John Slater's enthusiasm as Secretary, and Trevor Smith's watchful care as Treasurer, the newly-formed Executive Committee made great progress, transforming the fledgling Association into a vibrant branch of the sport of swimming and set it on course for the high level it has reached today.

The first National Long Distance Swimming Championship was held at Windermere over the ten and a half-mile stretch in 1957. This still remains the blue riband of distance swimming in the United Kingdom. The following year, 1958, saw the first National Long Distance Sea Championships being held over an eight-mile course at Torbay — from Torquay to Brixham and back. In 1959, the Association initiated the 23-mile championship course at Loch Lomond. And every year they produced new courses and clubs, as enthusiasm grew. Having innumerable teething problems, which sometimes amounted to actual hostility and obstruction, added to all those ordinary difficulties and hazards of arranging open water events so susceptible to the vagaries of the weather, meant that the Association alternately bludgeoned and sweet-talked its way forward.

As the membership grew, so did the organisation. The trials and tribulations of this fledgling Association were many. The whole story of the numerous anecdotes connected with its difficulties are fascinating to hear, but this short article cannot extend to such detail. It is enough to say that from 1956, when only three local Championships were survivors from a previous era, there are now no less than 11 senior Association Championships and three junior Championships. That total is augmented by senior Championships in excess of 40, and more than 30 for the juniors, which are organised by various clubs and associations affiliated to the BLDSA.

In the mid-term of the Olympic years, the Association has held an International Event at Windermere over 25 kilometres, from Bowness to Lakeside, and thence to Ambleside. Competitors have been attracted from all over the world, and in 1986, FINA promoted the then-proposed event from International status to World Cup status as a prelude to a full-scale World Championship event at some future date. The first-ever World Cup was duly staged very successfully by the Association, and its ebullient members felt that this was in recognition of its long and most satisfactory services to International swimming. It was certainly with great pride that the Association proclaimed that the outright winner was a young Englishman named Marc Newman, who completed the course in a time of six hours, 22 minutes, and six seconds, with another Englishman finishing fourth in the Men's Event. In the Ladies' Event, Bridget Young was third in a time of seven hours, 11 minutes, and 46 seconds, behind the winner from the United States and the second from Hungary.

The very first FINA European Championships are to be held in Yugoslavia in September, 1989 — at which the Association's members will be competing for Great Britain. The next step will be World Championships, and ultimately Olympic Championships.

It is, therefore, perhaps a slight understatement, to refer to the Association's achievements as magnificent; the present position and the growth of the sport must reflect entirely upon the prodigious efforts of those founder-members, as well as the supreme efforts put in so willingly over the years by the Association's Officers and Committee Members.

The aims of the BLDSA are, naturally, to promote Long Distance Swimming, to ensure adequate safety cover, to improve the standards and successes which have already been achieved, and to increase the numbers of persons who enjoy the sport.

The Association possesses its own formal Constitutional Rules. These govern the objects, composition, membership, etc. They also serve as a model and guide for emerging but inexperienced clubs and other Associations.

In addition, the BLDSA recognises and validates members' individual performances

Marc Newman, winner of the first World Cup.

on satisfactory completion of their swims and the necessary form of declaration. It also issues certificates and maintains records.

The Association has a panel of Pilot Lifesavers; this valuable scheme was established in 1960 by Bill Anderson. Such persons qualify by plotting the course, and being in full charge of the boat, crew, and equipment during the swim.

If, after reading the above, you feel impelled to participate in BLDSA's activities, how do you begin? What is the first thing to do? The best idea would be to purchase the Association's *Handbook* from the Honorary Membership Secretary, or you could write to, or ring, the writer of this article. (Names, addresses, and 'phone numbers are appended at the end.) With the *Handbook* you will easily see who carries out which particular duties, how the Championships Rules work, how to qualify as a Pilot Lifesaver, the name and address of your Regional Representative, how to start training and competing, brief descriptions of the various Championship courses — in many cases with accompanying "chartlets" — the current year's programme, and much more. And having digested all this information, you may wish to speak to your Regional Representative, make an approach to your nearest Long Distance club, or just attend some swims to "get the feel of things".

Above all, get swimming! The way in, plus training tips, and almost everything you want to know, is contained in "Advice to New Competitors" in the *Handbook*. Hopefully, by then you will have joined the Association.

The open water swimming season normally commences at the end of May, and it continues to the end of September or early October, purely because of water temperature. Meetings are held every weekend throughout the season, and so wide has the sport grown that several events may well be staged on the same day in different parts of the country. Of course, the Association and Affiliated Clubs strive to avoid this situation, but what with tides and the availability of inland water, it is not always possible to organise the ideal schedule. However, it is a compliment to the sport that the number of events lead to such cases.

The sport of Long Distance Swimming is a happy one, boasting a great number of characters. Obviously, the events bring out the competitive nature in the individual, but, primarily, "you swim the lake" — or the course.

For the majority of keen swimmers, it is an achievement sport, with the placings a secondary consideration — except, perhaps, for the fastest competitors. Naturally, friendly battles are fought out at all levels, with the consequent jokes and comments should you happen to finish ahead of a rival who pipped you last week. Participation as boat crew can have its enjoyable moments as well, and it is very satisfying to "get your swimmer home safely".

Regrettably, there is no up-to-date definitive work on the sport; the Association's *Handbook* is probably the most comprehensive current guide. The only real book of reference was published in 1963 by Routledge and Kegan Paul, and is entitled *Modern Long Distance Swimming*, and was written by Gerald Forsberg. Opportunities to purchase this out-of-print volume are rather rare, but it may still be available from your local library, or could be reserved from another library through the excellent and co-operative exchange system. Gerry Forsberg is one of the most respected men in the sport, and he has swum virtually all of the recognised courses, as well as holding numerous records which were gained throughout his long career. He continues to compete, and contributes articles to various publications. He also writes the regular Long Distance Swimming column in the ASA's *Swimming Times*. I am indebted to him for his assistance with this article.

Well, there you have it. The above is very much just an outline of the sport of Long Distance Swimming. It is a very demanding activity, both physically and mentally; it can be great fun when the sun is shining and the water is warm — it can be uncomfortable when the water temperature is low; but it's very rewarding to stand on the edge of a lake or on a beach and think: "I've swum that!"

So come on in — the water's fine.

Further information is available from the Honorary Membership Secretary, Mrs. P. Morgan, 38 Meadows Drive, East Ayton, Scarborough, North Yorkshire, telephone: 0723-863430, or from the Honorary General Secretary, T.D. Symmons, M Inst.AM, MBIM, 153 The Avenue, Kennington, Oxford OX1 5QZ, telephone: 0865-739310.

ASA Champions, 1877–1989

Note: The men's event was originally known as the "Lords and Commons Race", prior to 1879, as the first cup was presented by a number of Members of Parliament. From 1877 to 1947, apart from the odd occasion, the distance was approximately three miles, but since 1963, when re-established, it has developed into a five mile swim.

Men

Year	Champion	Time
1877	H. Davenport	73:27.00
1878	H. Davenport	76:10.00
1879	H. Davenport	82:27.00
1880	W. Itter	77:00.00
1881	W. Richardson	81:30.00
1882	F. Huntingdon	81:00.00
1883	W. Itter	75:20.00
1884	G. Bell	79:01.00
1885	G. Bell	84:42.00
1886	A. France	80:50.00
1887	A. France	78:10.00
1888	A. France	77:07.00
1889	H. Bowden	85:50.00
1890	W. Henry	75:15.00
1891	A. Ibbott	72:27.00
1892	M. Drake	78:40.00
1893	J. Tyers	77:01.80
1894	J. Tyers	107:06.00
1895	VOID	
1896	W. Green	153:15.00
1897	P. Cavill (Australia)	66:06.35
1898	J. Jarvis (Leicester)	67:58.00
1899	J. Jarvis (Leicester)	69:45.00
1900	J. Jarvis (Leicester)	64:17.00
1901	J. Jarvis (Leicester)	69:04.20
1902	J. Jarvis (Leicester)	73:27.00
1903	J. Jarvis (Leicester)	63:48.20
1904	J. Jarvis (Leicester)	67:32.20
1905	D. Billington (Bacup)	68:55.00
1906	J. Jarvis (Leicester)	63:40.00
1907	R. Radmilovic (Weston super Mare)	69:15.20
1908	F. Springfield (Australia)	70:57.00
1909	H. Taylor (Chadderton)	65:34.00
1910	T. Battersby (Wigan)	63:12.40
1911	M. Champion (New Zealand)	66:11.40
1912	H. Taylor (Hyde Seal)	64:07.40
1913	J. Hatfield (Middlesbrough)	65:27.00
1914	J. Hatfield (Middlesbrough)	65:04.00
1920	H. Taylor (Hyde Seal)	64:55.00
1921	J. Hatfield (Middlesbrough)	68:32.00
1922	E. Peter (Penguin)	67:23.00
1923	J. Hatfield (Middlesbrough)	67:13.00
1924	J. Hatfield (Middlesbrough)	68:25.00
1925	P. Radmilovic (Weston super Mare)	65:06.40
1926	P. Radmilovic (Weston super Mare)	67:35.00
1927	E. Pascoe (Plaistow U)	71:38.40
1928	J. Hatfield (Middlesbrough)	64:44.00
1929	E. Peter (Croydon)	65:02.60
1930	E. Pascoe (Plaistow U)	66:53.80
1931	J. Hatfield (Middlesbrough)	57:22.00
1932	F. Milton (Otter)	53:37.40
1933	F. Milton (Otter)	68:20.00
1934	C. Deane (Penguin)	68:52.60
1935	C. Deane (Penguin)	63:47.40
1936	C. Deane (Penguin)	64:04.80
1937	C. Deane (Penguin)	62:57.60
1938	C. Deane (Penguin)	65:24.20
1947	J. Hale (Hull Kingston)	73:30.20
1963	H. Milton (Otter)	95:22.00
1964	R. Johnson (Sunderland)	105:57.00
1965	H. Milton (Otter)	100:10.00
1966	H. Milton (Otter)	156:10.00
1967	A. Wilson (St James's)	133:20.00
1968	B. Metcalfe (Darlington)	141:09.00
1969	A. Kimber (Clifden)	127:58.00
1970	B. Metcalfe (Darlington)	136:05.00
1971	D. Pratten (Plaistow U)	116:10.00
1972	D. Pratten (Plaistow U)	122:39.00
1973	D. Pratten (Plaistow U)	124:02.00
1974	G. Bell (Teesside)	147:51.00
1975	M. Ashley (Redbridge B)	130:45.00
1976	R. Pavitt (Redbridge B)	126:11.00
1977	R. Sherburn (Westminster Handsworth)	129:12.00
1978	R. Sherburn (Westminster Handsworth)	128:30.00
1979	R. Sherburn (Westminster Handsworth)	117:30.00
1980	R. Sherburn (Westminster Handsworth)	119:00.00
1981	M. Wilby (Darlington Diana)	94:37.00
1982	M. Wilby (Darlington Diana)	109:28.00
1983	M. Wilby (Darlington Diana)	102:09.00
1984	D. Corden (Redditch)	130:54.00
1985	L. Dunsbee (Dover Lifeguard)	106:08.00
1986	L. Dunsbee (Dover Lifeguard)	108:44.00
1987	L. Dunsbee (Dover Lifeguard)	109:55.00
1988	P. Hogg (Co Newcastle)	117:29.00
1989	J. Palfrey (Orpington)	115:18.00

Women

Year	Champion	Time
1920	C. Jeans (Nottingham Ladies)	72:59.40
1921	P. Scott (Roath Park)	66:55.00
1922	C. Jeans (Nottingham Ladies)	67:36.00
1923	H. James (Cunard)	69:46.40
1924	H. James (Cunard)	71:24.40
1925	P. Scott (Roath Park)	71:47.60
1926	M. Hamblen (Hammersmith)	75:17.20
1927	M. Hamblen (Hammersmith)	71:32.00
1928	M. Hamblen (Hammersmith)	69:58.00
1929	G. Vine-Jackman (Hammersmith)	74:07.00
1930	M. Cooper (Mermaid)	72:57.00
1931	M. Cooper (Mermaid)	61:56.00
1932	M. Cooper (Mermaid)	59:04.20
1933	M. Cooper (Mermaid)	66:46.80
1934	S. Browning (Newport)	71:15.80
1935	S. Browning (Newport)	71:27.40
1936	S. Browning (Newport)	70:15.00
1937	M. Allen (Oddicombe)	75:01.00
1938	D. Bassett-Lawke (Northampton)	66:13.80
1947	E. Hill (Croydon Ladies)	84:56.80
1963	M. Gray (Watford)	108:33.00
1964	M. Gray (British Long Distance)	110:03.00

335

ASA CHAMPIONS, 1877–1989

1965	M. Gray (British Long Distance)	112:15.00	
1966	M. Gray (St Albans)	167:16.00	
1967	M. Gray (British Long Distance)	148:58.00	
1968	M. Gray (Loughborough College)	153:30.00	
1969	B. Woodall (Dewsbury)	155:40.00	
1970	B. Woodall (Dewsbury)	160:06.00	
1971	V. Whitworth-Taylor (Walsall)	117:40.00	
1972	V. Whitworth-Taylor (Walsall)	134:26.00	
1973	V. Whitworth-Taylor (Walsall)	129:14.00	
1974	J. Taylor (Walsall)	145:50.00	
1975	W. Brook (Dewsbury)	128:00.00	
1976	W. Brook (Dewsbury)	125:55.00	
1977	G. Clarke (Warrington Dolphins)	141:58.00	

1978	M. Smith (Co Bradford)	141:43.00	
1979	S. Hunt (Rykneld)	126:53.00	
1980	D. Sumner		
	(Harrow & Wealdstone)	117:48.00	
1981	K. Toole (Darlington)	99:16.00	
1982	K. Toole (Darlington)	118:45.00	
1983	K. Toole (Darlington)	110:34.00	
1984	Y. Carter (Wakefield)	131:16.00	
1985	B. Young (Dover Lifeguard)	118:58.00	
1986	L. Brooks (Rotherham Metro)	118:40.00	
1987	L. Brooks (Rotherham Metro)	110:00.00	
1988	B. Young (Dover Lifeguard)	122:09.00	
1989	L. Lee (Rotherham Metro)	118:41.00	

Alan Kimber

Swimming Times

CHANNEL
SWIMMING
SECTION

Channel Swimming at its Best

by Audrey Scott (Honorary Secretary, Channel Swimming Association)

The recorded story of Channel Swimming started in 1875, when Captain Matthew Webb swam from Dover to Calais in 21 hours, 45 minutes, to startle the world and to inspire hardy and courageous people to try and emulate the Captain's feat. After the swim, the Mayor of Dover predicted that "Never will any such feat be performed by anyone else!" Well, he was certainly right for some 36 years, although upwards of 70 attempts were made before Tom Blower's success in 1911, in a time of 22 hours 35 minutes.

The Channel Swimming Association was formed in 1927, following the false claim by Dr Dorothy Logan to have swum the Channel. The first meeting was held on 30 March, 1927, at 6E Beckenhall Mansions, Baker Street, London, with Mr A. Jones in the Chair. Mr A. Bretton became the first Chairman, Mr Jones was elected as Secretary, and Lord Desborough became the first President, while the Mayor of Calais, Mons. A. Vincent, acted as the Association's Delegate in France.

The finances of the Association at that time, give a very good idea of what inflation has done to our currency since those early days. The Financial Statement of 1929 showed a deficit of £7. 5s. 2d — while there was much improvement at the close of the following year. There was 4s. 1d. in hand!

A final meeting in London of the Association was held on 17 September, 1938, at its Headquarters at 54 Chancery Lane, WC2.

But after the war the Association was revived. This was largely under the direction of Inspector Bill Floydd, of the Folkestone Police, following a meeting convened by him on 31 October, 1949. Sadly, most of the early records of the Association were destroyed during the blitz on London, but fortunately the Minute Book survived, and is now in the possession of the Secretary. By 1951, the Association had re-formed at Folkestone, with Ted Maples in the Chair, Bill Floydd as Honorary Secretary, and Ernest Keighley as Treasurer, while Lord Freyburg had accepted the office of President.

It was in 1962 that Commander Gerald Forsburg, OBE, RN (rtd), was elected as President, and twenty-five years later, in 1987, the Association celebrated their Diamond Jubilee, and, at the same time, Commander Forsburg's Silver Anniversary as it's head. In 1973, following the resignation of John Floydd (son of Bill Floydd), as Honorary Secretary, Audrey Scott took on the joint office of both Secretary and Observer Liaison Officer.

The 1989 Committee is: Ray Scott, Chairman; Mike Read, Vice-Chairman; Audrey Scott, Honorary Secretary; Tony Woodroffe, Assistant Secretary; Chris Carter, Honorary Treasurer; Dr Eric Mallett, Honorary Medical Officer; Dr Chris Stockdale, Honorary Committee Doctor; Terry Sutton, Honorary Press Officer. Members: Kevin Murphy, Alison Streeter, Norman Trusty, Mike Oram, David Whyte, Ray Dixon, Molly Gill, and Ian Muir.

The Association's main purpose, today, is to investigate and authenticate the claims of men or women purporting to have swum the English Channel, and very thorough searches are made.

To swim the Channel, is undoubtedly a major achievement. To date, there have been some 4,500 attempts, giving 537 successful solos, 16 two-ways, and two three-ways, by 360 persons: 244 men and 116 women. The King of the Channel, Mike Read, has made no less than 31 crossings, and the Queen of the Channel, Cynthia Nicholas, has been successful 19 times.

Attempts to conquer this formidable stretch, have been made by members of 54 nationalities, 47 of whom have triumphed.

A good time for a crossing is around 13 hours, and a good stroke rate is 65 per minute. So, in order to give you some idea of the physical effort involved, just lie down on a comfortable bench so that your hands cannot reach the floor and whirl your arms in a swimming motion for 13 hours to get in your 51,000 strokes. You may take some salty orange juice to give you realism, and also take the usual nourishment. And when you do it for real you must try to avoid the cold — anything from 50° to 63°F; you will experience sea-sickness, caused by the motion of the waves, you will swallow sea water, breathe diesel fumes from the pilot's boat, experience jelly fish stings, claw your way through thick patches of sea-weed — not to mention nausea from oil slicks, attacks of cramp, sudden fog or high winds, striking pieces of flotsam and jetsam, water in the goggles, swimming across one of the busiest shipping lanes in the world, and negotiating tides of three knots. You feel lonely at night, and you are never free from the anxiety that the pilot and the observer may lose sight of you in the murk of a thick rainy night.

Over the years, the Channel Swimmers Association has gathered a mass of information to assist aspirants today: pilots' expert knowledge of the effect of the wind and tide on a swimmer's course and speed, research in dietetics, and swimming techniques — these have all greatly benefited Channel Swimmers.

Many swims have been made in aid of charities, and as far as this is concerned, pride of place must surely go to Dr Christopher Stockdale, who has raised some £180,000 for various causes.

Relay swims have introduced many people to marathon swimming, and perhaps Kevin Murphy has been the outstanding example in this direction. And 1988 showed a total of 167 relays that succeeded!

Records, of course, are made to be broken, but California's Penny Lee Dean's incredible crossing of seven hours 40 minutes in 1978, has defied all efforts so far. And until 1985, with Philip Rush of New Zealand making a record two-way in 17 hours 56 minutes, no man got within three hours of the two-way of Cindy Nicholas of Canada and Irene van der Laan of Holland.

Philip Rush's epic swim in 1987, of 28 hours 21 minutes for a *three-way* beating, Jon Erikson's by ten hours six minutes, and itself creating five separate records, will stand as a daunting challenge — but for just how long? Philip will surely come back to have a go at Penny's record.

The Rolex Watch Company provide the CSA with a number of their Oyster Perpetuals to ensure the incontestable accuracy of the timing of all swims, and they award one such treasure to the fastest Channel Swimmer of the Year. For this the Association's members are all deeply grateful.

We are proud that the CSA has now established a world-wide camaraderie in what is possibly one of the most demanding of all sports, and perhaps it is the parent to an enduring world-wide friendship.

The ultimate question asked of all marathon swimmers, of course, is still: "Have you done the Channel?" If the answer is "Yes", then metaphorically you immediately stand them upon a pedestal.

Kevin Murphy swimming the Channel in 1980.

Records

Progressive Records

England–France
21:45 M. Webb (GBR)	1875
15:34 E. Temme (GBR)	1934
14:42 F. Chadwick (USA)*	1953
14:06 W. Pickering (GBR)	1955
13:55 F. Chadwick (USA)*	1955
13:33 C. Forsberg (GBR)	1957
12:49 A. Couto (Brazil)	1959
10:23 H. Jensen (Denmark)	1960
9:57 L. Cox (USA)*	1972
9:44 R. D. Hart (USA)	1972
9:36 L. Cox (USA)*	1973
9:03 T. Bischoff (USA)*	1976
8:56 W. Brook (GBR)*	1976
8:45 N. El Shazley (Egypt)	1977
7:40 P. Dean (USA)*	1978

France–England
16:33 E. Tiraboschi (Italy)	1923
14:39 G. Ederle (USA)*	1926
12:40 A. Vierkotter (Germany)	1926
10:50 A. El Rehim (Egypt)	1950
10:35 B. Das (Pakistan)	1961
9:35 B. Watson (GBR)	1964
8:52 R. Charlesworth (GBR)	1982
8:34 L. Dunsbee (GBR)	1984
8:20 E. Johnson (USA)	1985
8:15 P. Rush (New Zealand)	1987
8:05 R. Davey (GBR)	1988

Non-Stop – Two-Way
43:10 A. Abertondo (Argentine)	1961
30:03 T. Erikson (USA)	1965
30:00 J. Erikson (USA)	1975
19:55 C. Nicholas (Canada)*	1977
19:12 C. Nicholas (Canada)*	1979

18:55 C. Nicholas (Canada)*	1982
18:15 I. van der Laan (Holland)*	1983
17:56 P. Rush (New Zealand)	1985
16:10 P. Rush (New Zealand)	1987

Non-Stop – Three-Way
38:27 J. Erikson (USA)	1981
28:21 P. Rush (New Zealand)	1987

Note: *Denotes Female Swimmer

Additional Information

England–France
Fastest Man
7:55 P. Rush (New Zealand)	1987

Fastest Woman
7:40 P. Dean (USA)	1978

France–England
Fastest Man
8:05 R. Davey (GBR)	1988

Fastest Woman
8:48 A. Streeter (GBR)	1987

Greatest Number of Crossings
31 M. Read (GBR) between 1969–1983

Youngest Boy: 11 years, 11 months
11.54 T. Gregory (GBR)	1988

Youngest Girl, 12 years, 118 days
15:28 S. Druce (GBR)	1983

Oldest Man: 67 years, 240 days
18:37 C. Batt (Australia)	1987

Oldest Woman: 45 years, 350 days
18:15 S. Taylor (USA)	1975

The only brother and sister to have swum the Channel — Sally and David Minty.

Jersey Evening Post

SCHOOLS
SECTION

Swimming in Schools

by Marie Bracey (Honorary Press Officer, English Schools Swimming Association

The English Schools' Swimming Association is 40 years old this year. An inaugural meeting was held in London on 14 May, 1949, and the first National Schools Swimming Championships took place at Bethnal Green, London, in 1950. Of course, over the years the format of the Championships has changed, and gradually more disciplines have been introduced. The ESSA now holds five championships a year, including events for water-polo, diving, and synchronised swimming. For purposes of competition and organisation, the country is divided into 12 areas, or divisions, as they are known. Division One covers the very north of England, and Division 12, the very south. The affairs of the ESSA are managed by the Council, headed by a President, who is elected annually. Each Division has a Representative, and there are nine other officers on the Council. In addition, various members can be co-opted for their expertise. Close association is maintained with the ASA through a liaison committee, which meet regularly. The ESSA is also represented on several national bodies, either concerned with swimming, or school sport.

The aim of the ESSA is not only to promote competition for swimmers at school, but also to advance the physical education of school children through the various mediums of the sport, and also to push for the provision of proper facilities. It would be splendid if every school in the country had the use of a nearby pool, or even its very own pool, but this dream is a long way off. There is no consistency in the provision of swimming in schools: some Local Education Authorities actively encourage their schools to go swimming — others seem to discourage it. The ESSA also aims to provide a system of tests and awards to be used in schools and, in conjunction with the ASA, is involved with the promotion of a series of Joint Awards. These are the Rainbow Awards, The Water Skills, the first two grades of the National Challenge Awards, and the Speed Swimming Awards. Full details of these are available from the Awards Organiser (details at the end of article).

The ESSA organises, with Coca Cola Great Britain, the Dolphin Trophy. This Trophy, in passing its silver anniversary milestone, is now one of the longest-running and most successful of schools' sport sponsorships, and is a "learn to swim award" scheme for schools to enter yearly. Its aim is to make every child a safe swimmer before the age of 12. The scheme was re-launched in February, 1988, with the Minister of Sport, Colin Moynihan, MP, present. He commended the English Schools Swimming Association and Coca Cola for their efforts to gain participation from every school in the country housing primary-aged children. The 1988 winners of the Dolphin Trophy received their awards from Adrian Moorhouse at the Windsor Leisure Pool, Berkshire. Children from Brightlands School, Newnham, Gloucestershire, Talbot Combined Junior School, Poole, Dorset, and Morgans Walk Junior School, Hertford, demonstrated their newly-found prowess. It was a day of fun and a celebration of achievement.

It is because the ESSA believes, very firmly, that swimming is an essential part of the child's school curriculum, that it joined with the ASA, the Royal Life Saving Society, and the Central Council of Physical Recreation, in the campaign for the "Teaching of Swimming". This campaign was designed to persuade Parliament to promote swimming actively through new legislation and adequate funding. The Report of the Joint Working Party, titled *Swim For Your Life*, was published in April, 1988. Several thousand copies were circulated to interested bodies and individuals. The campaign now continues with support from inside the House of Commons.

One further way in which the ESSA promotes the teaching of swimming and the provision of facilities, is with the Teaching Bath Scheme. Interest-free loans are available for schools who wish to build learner pools, or refurbish existing pools. Over 430 have received loans to help them build pools.

The English Schools' Swimming Association shares with the ASA a common sponsor in the TSB. All five National Schools Swimming Championships are sponsored by the TSB, and they are held between April and November in different pools around the country.

The main championships of the ESSA are the TSB National Schools' Swimming Championships, held on the last Friday and Saturday in October. These championships are Inter-Divisional, with the Divisions competing for trophies in six age-groups, and also on aggregate. Age limits for ESSA events are taken from midnight 31 August-1 September, in the year of the competition, and at the National Championships, age groups are 12-14 years, 14-16 years, and 16-19 years, for both boys and girls. Rivalry between the divisions is fierce, and the atmosphere in the pool, especially during the final session on Saturday night, is often electric. Each division has a theme tune, which is played for every individual and team winner. Over the last few years, the Floral Dance, for Division Five (Avon, Cornwall, Devon, Glos., Somerset and Wilts.) has been heard many times. Indeed, in 1987 this Division won five of the seven trophies presented. But at the 1988 Championships in Southampton, the tables were turned, and Division Eight (Cambs., Essex, Norfolk, Suffolk, and the London Boroughs of Barking, Havering, Redbridge, and Waltham Forest), took three of the trophies, including the aggregate trophy with 167 points — 16 points clear of Division Five. This was a very fast meet, with Championship Records being broken in 23 events. Many of the team that went to Seoul have been ESSA record-holders in their time. In fact, many of them still hold current ESSA Championship Records, including Nick Gillingham's 1984, 110 yards breaststroke record of 1:06.93. Championships haven't been held in yards pools since, and are not expected to be in the future, so that record is likely to stand for quite some time. Each division is responsible for selecting its own team to compete at the championships, and Trials are held during September. The 1989 championships are in Macclesfield on Friday and Saturday, 27 and 28 October.

The second "swimming" championship organised by the ESSA is the TSB National School Team Championship. Divisional rounds for this event take place in July, and the finals are held on the first Saturday in October. The competition is for relay teams from individual secondary schools. Times from the divisional competitions are forwarded to the National Organiser, and the 12 fastest teams in each age group (same groups for the National Championships), for both freestyle and medley events, are invited to compete at the finals. Over the past few years, Millfield and Kelly have tended to dominate this competition, but at the 1988 Championships, held in Bury, this changed: seven schools divided the 12 trophies between them. The 1989 TSB School Team Competition Championships take place at the new Littledown Pool in Bournemouth on 7 October.

In addition to this, several divisions organise Primary School Team Championships during the summer term. However, these do not lead on to National Championships.

Until 1980, the Diving Championships were held with the School Team Championship, but, in 1981, the two events were split with the first separate Diving Championship held at Crystal Palace. The event always takes place on the third Saturday in November. Each division is represented by a team of six divers, three boys and three girls; one for each group. Again, divisional trials to select the team are usually held in September. The competition consists of eight different voluntary dives, the last three of these forming the final rounds of the competition. The standard of diving can be very high, with some extremely exciting contests. For the past two years, the winning division has been Division 11 (Kent, Surrey, and the London Boroughs of Bexley, Bromley, Croydon, Kingston, Merton, and Sutton). The 1989 TSB Schools Diving Championships are returning to Crystal Palace on Saturday, 18 November.

The first National Water Polo Championships for schools were held at the Sharston Pool, Manchester, in 1977. The competition has gone from strength to strength since then, and interest is maintained throughout the country. Some schools have continued to do well since the very beginning: Bedford Modern School (Division 10), captured the first competition in the 16-19 age group, and also won the 1988 event. The Water Polo Championship starts off with each division holding its own competition between October and February. The divisional champions in two age-groups (12-16 years and 16-19 years), go through to an inter-divisional competition, played during the second weekend in March. The grouping of this section varies from year to year, so that the same teams from one area do not always meet at this stage. Four teams in each age-group go through to the national Finals, played on the 19th Saturday of the year. The 1989 TSB Schools Water Polo Championships were held on 13 May, in Worcester.

The latest event to be organised by the ESSA is the Schools' Synchronised Swimming Championships. The date for this competition varies from year to year, but it is usually around April. The first competition took place in 1981, at Cheadle, where 14 school teams competed. The winners were Dartmouth High, Birmingham. Schools have entered directly to the national finals, although regulations are available to cover regional heats. Teams are made up of between three and eight members, with one half-point added to each team's score for every competitor over three. For the first time, 1989, the new FINA two-tier marking system will be used, and marks will be awarded for technical merit and artistic impression. The TSB Schools Synchronised Swimming Championships for 1989, took place at Canterbury on 22 April. Last year's winners, Wickham Comprehensive, Newcastle upon Tyne, (Division One), who were only 1.4

The winners of the 1989 TSB Schools Synchronised Swimming Championships –
Kendrick School, Reading

Dave Stewart

marks in front of Kendrick School, Reading (Division 12), entered again. But, this year, the tables were turned when Kendrick won the tournament, pushing Wickham into third spot.

Following the National Championships at the end of October, a team is selected to represent the ESSA. Those chosen then compete at the annual Home International, which is sponsored by Speedo. This event, which is commonly known as the WISE match (Wales, Ireland, Scotland and England), is held in March, and is hosted by each of the countries in turn. The teams compete for the Manx Trophy, which has been won by England every year since the start of the competition. But, over the last few years, Scotland has begun to put the pressure on, and at this year's event at Bangor, they came within 16 points of beating the winners. There were some very fine swims from the English entrants, with several championship records broken. Joanne Deakin, of Division Six, was the "English Swimmer of the Meet", following her record-breaking swim in the Intermediate Girls' 100m Backstroke, with a time of 1:06.48. Adrian Moorhouse still holds the Senior Boys' 100m Breaststroke record of 1:06.00 — a time recorded when he represented the English Schools in 1982. The 1990 Speedo Swimming International is due to be held on 24 March, at Cumbernauld and the Scots will be eager for a home victory.

One other major area of International involvement for the ESSA is at the ISF World Schools' Games. The ISF (International School Sport Federation) embraces 48 countries, and gives priority to educational objectives in all its activities. The majority of its events are based on individual school championships at an international level. Every two years, the Gymnasiade (World School Games), is held. This event involves teams from countries within its membership, and incorporates four sports: Athletics, Gymnastics, Rhythmic Gymnastics, and Swimming. Almost 1,000 competitors take part, all under the age of 17, and all in full-time education. ESSA has competed in the last four Gymnasiades, and with some outstanding success. Often, swimmers have returned from the Gymnasiade and have gone on to record personal successes at the ASA National Championships. For some swimmers, it is their first taste of swimming at an international level, and it leads on to further achievements. The last games, in July, 1988, held at Barcelona, took place at the venue which will form the basis of the Olympic facilities in 1992. A team of 11 boys and 11 girls represented the ESSA at the five-day competition, and they were accompanied by three team managers, with Archie Brew, from Kelly College, as coach. The team faced fierce opposition from the Italians, French and Hungarians. One gold, one silver and three bronze were a smaller haul of medals than is usually won by the ESSA, but certainly those swimmers who travelled to Barcelona, rate it as one of the best trips that they had ever made.

The ESSA is also very keen to become involved with swimming for the disabled. A junior International for the Disabled was held in September, 1987, in Glasgow, where a team of 20 youngsters from the north of England represented the Association. It is hoped that a similar event can be arranged in England for September, 1990. This is subject to adequate funding being found.

In order to mark the 40th Anniversary of the English Schools' Swimming Association, a luncheon was held on 14 May, 1989, 40 years to the day since that first meeting. Since 1949, the ESSA has been organising and promoting both competitive swimming in schools and the teaching of swimming throughout England. Competitive swimming is not only at a national or international level, for each of the ESSA Championships have qualifying heats at county and divisional level. Preliminary heats will have been held at schools, sports centres, and swimming pools nationwide. Nearly all these events are organised by teachers in their own time as there are no paid administrators in the ESSA. Many people give quite a lot of their time, in order that school children and young students may have the opportunity to represent their school, division, or country, in so many events.

For further information about school swimming in your area, please contact your Divisional Representative or the organiser for the competition.

Honorary General Secretary: D. Redman, 3 Maybank Grove, Liverpool L17 6DW. Tel: (Home) 051-427 3707; (School) 051-486 1053.

Honorary Treasurer (who deals with the loan scheme): J.B. Beddoe, Holmdale, Far Back Lane, Farnsfield, Newark, Notts. NG22 8JX. Tel: (Home) 0623 882225;

(School) 0623 882494.

Honorary Awards Secretary (who organises the Dolphin Trophy Scheme): N. Bramwell, Brackenridge, Guilsborough Hill, Hollowell, Northants. NN6 8RN. Tel: (Home) 0604 740080; (School) 0604 842185.

Honorary Competitions Secretary (who deals with swimming and diving championships): L. Barber, 48 Ennismore Road, Crosby, Liverpool L23 7UQ. Tel: 051-924 7368.

Honorary Assistant Competitions Secretary (who deals with relay championships and water polo): T.B. Hyde, 20 Pavillion Way, Eastcote, Ruislip HA4 9JN. Tel: (School) 01-207 4323, Ext 228.

Honorary Synchronised Swimming Organiser: Mrs E. Hartley, 49 The Millbank, Ifield, Crawley, West Sussex RH11 0JQ. Tel: (Home) 0293 515519.

Honorary International Organiser: M. Uglow, Southcott Mill, Westleigh, Nr Bideford, Devon EX39 4NH. Tel: 0237 477849; (School) 0237 477611.

Honorary Publicity Secretary (who will send a handbook on receipt of 80p): Mrs M.J. Bracey, Beech Hurst, Forest Road, East Horsley, Surrey KT24 5BL. Tel: 04865 5488.

ASA/ESSA Awards Organiser (who will send you details of all awards on receipt of a large stamped addressed envelope): Miss L.V. Cook, 12 Kings Avenue, Woodford Green, Essex 1G8 0JB.

DIVISIONAL REPRESENTATIVES

Division 1: Cumbria, Northumberland, Tyne and Wear, Cleveland, County Durham:
  Mrs D. Thompson, Highburn House, Jaw Blades, Burnhope, County Durham DH7 0EE. Tel: 0207 521706.

Division 2: Cheshire, Lancashire, Merseyside, Isle of Man:
  N. Spragg, 2 Waltho Avenue, Maghull, Merseyside L31 68E. Tel: (Home) 051-526 2191; (School) 051-526 1378.

Division 3: Humberside North, West and South Yorkshire:
  D. Teale, 8 Ashbrook, Buckingham Street, Hull HU8 8TT. Tel: (School) 0482 51013.

Division 4: Derbyshire, Leicester, Lincs., Northants, Notts., Warwickshire:
  Mrs C.M. Young, 142 Coombe Rise, Oadby, Leicester LE2 5TX. Tel: 0533 716166.

Division 5: Avon, Cornwall, Devon, Glos., Somerset, Wilts.:
  Miss M. Uppington, 35 Ridgeway, Long Ashton, Bristol BS18 9EY. Tel: (Home) 0272 393228.

Division 6: Hereford/Worcs., Shropshire, West Midlands:
  Miss C. Sanders, 45 Minton Road, Harbourne, Birmingham B32 2XE. Tel: (Home) 021-426 4555; (School) 0527 46164.

Division 7: Greater Manchester and Staffs.:
  N. Speake, 28 Peterborough Close, Ashton under Lyne, Tameside OL6 8XW. Tel: (Home) 061-339 5048.

Division 8: Cambs., Essex, Norfolk, Suffolk and Four London Boroughs of Barking, Havering, Redbridge, Waltham Forest:
  G. Redhead, 53 High Street, Wilburton, Ely, Cambs CB6 3RB. Tel: (Home) 0353 740 731.

Division 9: London as comprised by the London Schools' Swimming Association and London Boroughs of Newham, Brent, Ealing, Haringey, and Richmond on Thames.
  E. Godin, 12 Barlby Gardens, Kensington, London W10 5LW. Tel: (Home) 01-969 5377; (School) 01-274 8374.

Division 10: Beds., Bucks., Herts., and an Area Association of Barnet, Enfield, Harrow, Hillingdon, Hounslow:
  Mrs D. Owen, 170 Malvern Avenue, South Harrow HA2 9HD. Tel: (Home) 01-422 3266; (School) 01-204 6564.

Division 11: Kent, Surrey (which includes the six London Boroughs of Bexley, Bromley, Croydon, Kingston upon Thames, Merton and Sutton):
  Mrs M. Cron, Minack, Wises Lane, Borden, Nr Sittingbourne, Kent ME9 8LR. Tel: (Home) 0795 72599; (School) 0795 72895.

Division 12: Berks., Dorset, Hants., Oxon, East/West Sussex and the Channel Isles and Isle of Wight:
  R. Loveman, 37 Westridge Road, Portswood, Southampton SO2 1HP. Tel: (Home) 0703 551000 ; (School) 0703 840025.

National Championships, 1988–89

The Divisions that the competitors are representing, are shown in brackets

Swimming Finals
Central Baths, Southampton — 28/29 October, 1988

Junior Boys

100 Metres Freestyle
Final

1 N. Collins (5)	56.55
2 D. Forster (7)	58.16
3 M. Robilliard (4)	59.11
4 A. Iceton (2)	59.33
5 S. Powell (11)	59.80
6 S. Smalley (3)	1:01.88

Heat Times

1 N. Collins (5)	56.84
2 M. Robilliard (4)	59.40
3 A. Iceton (2)	59.53
4 D. Forster (7)	59.64
5 S. Smalley (3)	1:00.37
6 S. Powell (11)	1:00.38
7 M. Carl (8)	1:00.68
8 N. Watkins (9)	1:00.70
9 C. Barnes (12)	1:01.37
10 D. Mack (1)	1:02.44
11 R. Perry (10)	1:02.61
12 L. Coton (6)	1:03.44

100 Metres Backstroke
Final

1 A. Ruckwood (6)	1:04.64
2 S. Mavin (8)	1:07.23
3 I. Gorst (2)	1:07.56
4 N. Skinner (12)	1:07.91
5 A. Wild (7)	1:08.47
6 D. Paxton (10)	1:08.54

Heat Times

1 A. Ruckwood (6)	1:05.71
2 S. Mavin (8)	1:07.43
3 N. Skinner (12)	1:07.96
4 A. Wild (7)	1:08.28
5 I. Gorst (2)	1:08.30
6 D. Paxton (10)	1:08.67
7 M. Wilson (3)	1:09.34
8 D. Isaac (5)	1:10.42
9 C. Williams (4)	1:10.66
10 A. Shattock (11)	1:12.55
11 M. Yu-Hong (9)	1:12.66
12 M. Gray (1)	1:15.31

100 Metres Breaststroke
Final

1 S. Hamer (2)	1:11.48
2 J. Moreno (12)	1:12.92
3 A. McPeake (1)	1:14.00
4 C. Rippon (4)	1:14.47
5 G. Roberts (8)	1:15.91
6 G. Evans (6)	1:16.02

Heat Times

1 S. Hamer (2)	1:12.74
2 J. Moreno (12)	1:13.76
3 A. McPeake (1)	1:15.43
4 C. Rippon (4)	1:15.86
5 G. Roberts (8)	1:16.18
6 G. Evans (6)	1:16.34
7 I. Croft (11)	1:16.52
8 C. Mee (5)	1:16.66
9 P. Guy (9)	1:16.72
10 M. Colclough (7)	1:17.01
11 A. Peacock (3)	1:21.21
12 M. Belcourt (10)	1:24.50

100 Metres Butterfly
Final

1 P. Palmer (4)	1:02.75
2 D. Brace (10)	1:05.67
3 B. Vickery (11)	1:06.13
4 D. Molloy (12)	1:06.78
5 P. Tyler (6)	1:07.23
6 C. Robinson (7)	1:08.05

Heat Times

1 P. Palmer (4)	1:04.78
2 D. Brace (10)	1:05.79
3 B. Vickery (11)	1:05.88
4 D. Molloy (12)	1:07.50
5 C. Robinson (7)	1:07.54
6 P. Tyler (6)	1:07.71
7 B. White (5)	1:09.04
8 C. Heads (1)	1:09.19
9 D. Gates (2)	1:09.30
10 N. Studd (8)	1:09.74
11 A. Carnegie (3)	1:10.83
12 S. Flin (9)	1:15.70

200 Metres Individual Medley
Final

1 S. Crozier (2)	2:22.63
2 P. Beacham (4)	2:23.17
3 A. Blair (7)	2:25.19
4 I. Winmill (8)	2:27.02
5 R. Murray (5)	2:28.51
6 S. Darling (12)	2:31.49

Heat Times

1 P. Beacham (4)	2:25.37
2 S. Crozier (2)	2:26.00
3 A. Blair (7)	2:27.10
4 I. Winmill (8)	2:27.72
5 R. Murray (5)	2:29.53
6 S. Darling (12)	2:30.12
7 G. Ale (10)	2:31.56
8 S. Watson (11)	2:31.70
9 M. Bowd (6)	2:35.61
10 K. Anderson (1)	2:37.14
11 I. O'Hara (9)	2:48.22
M. Whitton (3)	DIS

4×50 Metres Freestyle Team Relay
Final

1 Division 7	1:47.73
2 Division 8	1:48.08
3 Division 2	1:48.62
4 Division 5	1:49.29

5 Division 12	1:49.51	
6 Division 4	1:50.65	

Heat Times

1 Division 2	1:48.43
2 Division 7	1:48.44
3 Division 8	1:49.02
4 Division 5	1:50.01
5 Division 4	1:50.03
6 Division 12	1:50.19
7 Division 3	1:50.27
8 Division 6	1:50.74
9 Division 11	1:51.88
10 Division 10	1:52.82
11 Division 9	1:54.38
12 Division 1	1:55.88

4×50 Metres Medley Team Relay
Final

1 Division 2	2:00.32
2 Division 12	2:01.26
3 Division 6	2:03.59
4 Division 8	2:04.02
5 Division 4	2:04.59
6 Division 5	2:05.40

Heat Times

1 Division 2	2:01.06
2 Division 12	2:03.44
3 Division 6	2:03.53
4 Division 8	2:04.51
5 Division 4	2:04.62
6 Division 5	2:05.40
7 Division 7	2:05.44
8 Division 11	2:06.03
9 Division 1	2:06.07
10 Division 9	2:09.20
Division 10	DIS
Division 3	DIS

Junior Girls

100 Metres Freestyle
Final

1 D. Salmon (5)	59.29
2 M. Bates (6)	1:00.44
3 D. Palmer (8)	1:00.48
4 J. Mallison (4)	1:00.55
5 A. Gilmore (12)	1:01.82
6 G. Lavin (1)	1:02.47

Heat Times

1 D. Salmon (5)	1:00.08
2 D. Palmer (8)	1:01.00
3 J. Mallison (4)	1:01.17
4 A. Gilmore (12)	1:01.19
5 M. Bates (6)	1:01.70
6 G. Lavin (1)	1:01.75
7 G. Cook (3)	1:02.78
8 J. Hudson (2)	1:02.80
9 T. Hill (11)	1:03.17
10 G. Miller (7)	1:03.38
11 A. Harriott (9)	1:05.65
12 S. Brett (10)	1:07.33

100 Metres Backstroke
Final

1 K. Axford (9)	1:10.26
2 R. Gledhill (3)	1:10.29
3 L. Neale (7)	1:10.53
4 T. Billanie (1)	1:10.74
5 C. Maggs (5)	1:11.74

6 A. Wood (6)	1:12.08

Heat Times

1 R. Gledhill (3)	1:11.08
2 K. Axford (9)	1:11.17
3 L. Neale (7)	1:11.47
4 C. Maggs (5)	1:11.48
5 T. Billanie (1)	1:11.69
6 A. Wood (6)	1:12.06
7 H. Kemball-Cook (8)	1:13.29
8 S. Youd (2)	1:13.89
9 L. Barry (12)	1:14.51
10 S. Dickson (10)	1:14.63
11 S. Clarke (4)	1:15.96
12 A. Pendrich (11)	1:16.12

100 Metres Breaststroke
Final

1 L. Findlay (4)	1:14.60
2 N. Wood (8)	1:17.04
3 J. Marsh (7)	1:18.95
4 J. Lee (10)	1:19.65
5 A. Creasley (9)	1:19.73
6 T. Beattie (2)	1:20.65

Heat Times

1 N. Wood (8)	1:17.71
2 L. Findlay (4)	1:18.48
3 J. Marsh (7)	1:19.61
4 T. Beattie (2)	1:19.76
5 A. Creasey (9)	1:19.91
6 J. Lee (10)	1:20.06
7 M. Hardiman (6)	1:20.14
8 L. Saunders (12)	1:20.65
9 M. Thorn (5)	1:20.70
10 J. Campbell (1)	1:21.55
11 C. Grayson (3)	1:21.62
12 K. Mitchell (11)	1:23.29

100 Metres Butterfly
Final

1 A. MacKay (2)	1:06.21
2 G. Holland (7)	1:06.39
3 P. Trickett (3)	1:08.78
4 M. Williams (11)	1:09.61
5 R. Topley (9)	1:10.15
6 N. Gibbs (5)	1:12.91

Heat Times

1 A. MacKay (2)	1:07.45
2 G. Holland (7)	1:07.55
3 P. Trickett (3)	1:09.48
4 M. Williams (11)	1:09.57
5 R. Topley (9)	1:10.86
6 N. Gibbs (5)	1:11.78
7 T. Pickwell (6)	1:11.90
8 E. Strange (12)	1:12.35
9 E. Cooke (1)	1:12.45
10 S. Read (10)	1:13.19
11 C. Cleaver (4)	1:14.29
12 J. Corn (8)	1:14.74

200 Metres Individual Medley
Final

1 Z. Harrison (8)	2:26.09
2 J. Birkett (4)	2:27.92
3 V. Horner (1)	2:30.40
4 G. Palmer (2)	2:34.16
5 D. Lane (6)	2:34.58
6 L. Wyatt (11)	2:35.11

Heat Times

1 Z. Harrison (8)	2:28.19

2	J. Birkett (4)	2:29.60
3	V. Horner (1)	2:30.63
4	D. Lane (6)	2:33.52
5	L. Wyatt (11)	2:34.23
6	G. Palmer (2)	2:34.35
7	G. Slater (7)	2:36.78
8	C. Willmott (10)	2:39.50
9	T. Cooper (5)	2:40.23
10	L. Earl (9)	2:40.29
11	D. Perrian (12)	2:41.54
12	J. Sugden (3)	2:44.61

4×50 Metres Freestyle Team Relay
Final

1	Division 4	1:52.96
2	Division 1	1:55.45
3	Division 7	1:56.46
4	Division 11	1:57.43
5	Division 8	1:57.65
6	Division 5	1:57.68

Heat Times

1	Division 4	1:54.56
2	Division 1	1:55.38
3	Division 8	1:55.61
4	Division 7	1:55.74
5	Division 11	1:57.21
6	Division 5	1:57.24
7	Division 6	1:58.08
8	Division 2	1:59.27
9	Division 3	1:59.34
10	Division 12	1:59.46
11	Division 9	1:59.66
12	Division 10	2:02.55

4×50 Metres Medley Team Relay
Final

1	Division 4	2:06.78
2	Division 8	2:08.18
3	Division 7	2:09.40
4	Division 1	2:10.84
5	Division 6	2:11.54
6	Division 2	2:11.98

Heat Times

1	Division 4	2:07.96
2	Division 8	2:08.35
3	Division 7	2:10.43
4	Division 1	2:11.14
5	Division 6	2:11.19
6	Division 2	2:11.73
7	Division 5	2:12.06
8	Division 12	2:12.79
9	Division 3	2:13.51
10	Division 9	2:13.56
11	Division 10	2:15.93
12	Division 11	2:16.53

Intermediate Boys

100 Metres Freestyle
Final

1	A. Shortman (5)	51.81
2	P. Frith (7)	54.37
3	J. Leveridge (3)	54.94
4	G. Warwick (1)	55.17
5	P. Chick (9)	55.26
6	D. Hill (10)	56.16

Heat Times

1	A. Shortman (5)	52.13
2	P. Frith (7)	55.05

3	J. Leveridge (3)	55.30
	G. Warwick (1)	
5	P. Chick (9)	55.43
6	D. Hill (10)	55.65
7	L. Grenyer (11)	55.78
8	P. Edwards (8)	56.03
9	L. Radwell (4)	56.76
10	A. Nannini (12)	56.88
11	M. Wolfenden (2)	57.57
	S. Wort (6)	DIS

100 Metres Backstroke
Final

1	S. Mellor (2)	1:02.22
2	I. Jeffery (5)	1:02.95
3	P. Hinxman (11)	1:04.27
4	M. Hampton (8)	1:04.36
5	H. Lewisman (12)	1:04.76
6	J. Wallis (4)	1:04.92

Heat Times

1	S. Mellor (2)	1:02.63
2	I. Jeffery (5)	1:03.92
3	P. Hinxman (11)	1:04.34
4	M. Hampton (8)	1:04.49
5	H. Lewisman (12)	1:04.61
6	J. Wallis (4)	1:04.69
7	A. Fry (7)	1:04.73
8	A. Jones (3)	1:05.44
9	N. English (10)	1:05.53
10	J. Fitzgerald (9)	1:06.14
11	P. Simpson (1)	1:07.02
12	A. Wooldridge (6)	1:07.08

100 Metres Breaststroke
Final

1	R. Maden (7)	1:04.18
2	I. Swift (3)	1:08.14
3	N. Poole (12)	1:08.17
4	T. Maddocks (8)	1:08.25
5	W. O'Gorman (5)	1:09.70
6	J. Moorfoot (1)	1:10.92

Heat Times

1	R. Maden (7)	1:06.20
2	N. Poole (12)	1:08.27
3	T. Maddocks (8)	1:08.85
4	I. Swift (3)	1:08.93
5	W. O'Gorman (5)	1:10.43
6	J. Moorfoot (1)	1:10.65
7	S. Hutchinson (4)	1:10.79
8	M. Baker (10)	1:12.54
9	K. Lancaster (2)	1:12.93
10	S. Lacon (6)	1:13.84
11	D. Potter (11)	1:17.01
12	H. Logue (9)	1:18.05

100 Metres Butterfly
Final

1	C. Robinson (8)	58.91
2	D. Hedley (1)	59.77
3	K. Crosby (2)	1:00.56
4	C. Yeo (4)	1:00.83
5	D. Claridge (6)	1:01.28
6	C. Baker (7)	1:02.17

Heat Times

1	D. Hedley (1)	1:00.31
2	C. Robinson (8)	1:00.67
3	K. Crosby (2)	1:01.08
4	C. Yeo (4)	1:02.27
5	D. Claridge (6)	1:02.32

6 C. Baker (7)	1:02.45
7 S. Houlton (10)	1:02.58
8 A. Chamberlain (5)	1:03.11
9 D. Case (9)	1:03.87
10 M. Simpkins (12)	1:04.14
11 S. Giles (11)	1:06.06
12 K. Swainson (3)	1:08.63

200 Metres Individual Medley
Final

1 S. Patch (4)	2:13.83
2 S. Lee (8)	2:15.32
3 D. Entwistle (7)	2:16.03
4 D. Smith (6)	2:17.00
5 M. Billam (3)	2:17.57
6 S. Morris (5)	2:18.17

Heat Times

1 S. Patch (4)	2:16.03
2 D. Entwistle (7)	2:16.47
3 S. Lee (8)	2:16.50
4 D. Smith (6)	2:17.89
5 M. Billam (3)	2:18.08
6 S. Morris (5)	2:18.10
7 R. Laidlow (1)	2:18.96
8 D. Belcourt (10)	2:19.47
9 S. Adamson (12)	2:22.83
10 D. Pye (2)	2:23.94
11 A. Webster (11)	2:26.61
12 J. Stennett (9)	2:27.16

4×50 Metres Freestyle Team Relay
Final

1 Division 5	1:39.67
2 Division 12	1:41.71
3 Division 1	1:41.76
4 Division 8	1:41.78
5 Division 4	1:42.14
6 Division 7	1:43.87

Heat Times

1 Division 5	1:41.57
2 Division 8	1:41.89
3 Division 12	1:42.60
4 Division 1	1:43.21
5 Division 4	1:43.44
6 Division 7	1:43.85
7 Division 2	1:44.29
8 Division 10	1:45.62
9 Division 9	1:45.86
10 Division 6	1:46.38
11 Division 11	1:46.39
12 Division 3	1:46.50

4×50 Metres Medley Team Relay
Final

1 Division 5	1:52.55
2 Division 8	1:53.92
3 Division 7	1:53.97
4 Division 12	1:55.55
5 Division 3	1:55.81
6 Division 1	1:57.00

Heat Times

1 Division 8	1:55.03
2 Division 7	1:55.09
3 Division 5	1:55.80
4 Division 12	1:56.04
5 Division 3	1:56.13
6 Division 1	1:56.38
7 Division 4	1:57.62
8 Division 2	1:58.07

9 Division 9	1:58.14
10 Division 10	1:58.53
11 Division 11	2:00.43
12 Division 6	2:00.47

Intermediate Girls

100 Metres Freestyle
Final

1 A. Clarke (5)	59.37
2 G. Brooke (9)	59.40
3 D. Morgan (1)	59.54
4 J. Andrews (10)	59.60
5 E. Brooks (8)	1:00.72
6 S. Littlewood (7)	1:01.19

Heat Times

1 A. Clarke (5)	59.25
2 G. Brooke (9)	59.71
3 D. Morgan (1)	1:00.59
4 J. Andrews (10)	1:00.61
5 S. Littlewood (7)	1:00.73
6 S. Kench (2)	
E. Brooks (8)	1:00.91
8 C. Saunders (12)	1:01.55
9 H. Lawrence (11)	1:01.62
10 C. Piggott (6)	1:01.76
11 A. Sobolewski (4)	1:03.44
12 S. Knights (3)	1:03.85

100 Metres Backstroke
Final

1 J. Deakin (6)	1:06.08
2 E. Firbank (1)	1:07.77
3 L. Gahan (5)	1:08.50
4 T. Sullivan (2)	1:09.28
5 K. Johnson (8)	1:09.81
6 L. Racster (12)	1:09.84

Heat Times

1 J. Deakin (6)	1:05.91
2 E. Firbank (1)	1:07.89
3 L. Gahan (5)	1:08.64
4 T. Sullivan (2)	1:09.60
5 K. Johnson (8)	1:09.83
6 S. Green (11)	1:10.16
7 L. Racster (12)	1:10.30
8 F. Cover (3)	1:10.78
9 C. Gould (10)	1:11.06

Emma Brooks   Artwood Photography

10	B. Turner (7)	1:11.21
11	J. Burnage (4)	1:12.59
12	K. Bond-Vaughn (9)	1:14.68

100 Metres Breaststroke
Final

1	R. Gillat (3)	1:14.96
2	H. Alder (10)	1:15.17
3	M. Young (8)	1:15.45
4	H. Goddard (5)	1:15.86
5	A. Whittle (7)	1:15.91
6	L. Janes (12)	1:16.46

Heat Times

1	H. Alder (10)	1:15.51
2	A. Whittle (7)	1:15.87
3	H. Goddard (5)	1:16.25
4	R. Gillatt (3)	1:16.34
5	L. Janes (12)	1:16.38
6	M. Young (8)	1:16.90
7	K. Seaborn (2)	1:17.37
8	R. Swain (4)	1:17.46
9	K. Marley (11)	1:19.62
10	C. Whitfield (1)	1:19.95
11	C. Brooks (6)	1:20.01
12	K. Jackson (9)	1:20.37

100 Metres Butterfly
Final

1	S. McGill (12)	1:04.67
2	J. Dowling (2)	1:05.06
3	H. Jepson (3)	1:05.21
4	M. George (8)	1:05.68
5	J. Crewdson (7)	1:08.65
6	L. Richards (1)	1:09.10

Heat Times

1	S. McGill (12)	1:06.06
2	H. Jepson (3)	1:06.08
3	J. Dowling (2)	1:06.83
4	M. George (8)	1:07.21
5	J. Crewdson (7)	1:08.00
6	L. Richards (1)	1:08.42
7	J. Corbett (6)	1:08.53
8	J. Carter (10)	1:08.93
9	M. Trudgeon (5)	1:10.30
10	S. Preaman (9)	1:10.47
11	C. Dancer (11)	1:11.12
12	K. Mellors (4)	1:12.15

200 Metres Individual Medley
Final

1	H. Osborne (6)	2:23.48
2	S. Vick (3)	2:24.26
3	J. Drewitt (10)	2:25.66
4	E. Burns (11)	2:25.72
5	P. Richardson (12)	2:28.69
6	E. Rumbold (8)	2:31.60

Heat Times

1	H. Osborne (6)	2:25.47
2	S. Vick (3)	2:27.48
3	P. Richardson (12)	2:28.18
4	J. Drewitt (10)	2:28.56
5	E. Burns (11)	2:28.63
6	E. Rumbold (8)	2:29.80
7	E. O'Sullivan (5)	2:30.45
8	R. Rowan (2)	2:31.92
9	V. Crane (9)	2:32.43
10	H. Gorman (4)	2:34.03
11	C. Caulfield (7)	2:35.57
12	S. Bevan (1)	2:36.77

4×50 Metres Freestyle Team Relay
Final

1	Division 8	1:51.30
2	Division 10	1:52.11
3	Division 11	1:52.35
4	Division 2	1:53.03
5	Division 5	1:53.29
6	Division 6	1:54.47

Heat Times

1	Division 8	1:51.88
2	Division 10	1:52.79
3	Division 11	1:53.22
4	Division 5	1:53.30
5	Division 2	1:53.79
6	Division 6	1:54.40
7	Division 12	1:54.67
8	Division 7	1:54.83
9	Division 1	1:56.18
10	Division 3	1:56.55
11	Division 4	1:57.16
12	Division 9	1:59.01

4×50 Metres Medley Team Relay
Final

1	Division 8	2:03.24
2	Division 12	2:04.20
3	Division 3	2:04.73
4	Division 10	2:05.31
5	Division 2	2:06.77
6	Division 6	2:07.65

Heat Times

1	Division 8	2:05.38
2	Division 3	2:05.56
3	Division 12	2:05.82
4	Division 10	2:06.31
5	Division 6	2:06.82
6	Division 2	2:07.27
7	Division 7	2:07.32
8	Division 1	2:08.17
9	Division 5	2:08.42
10	Division 11	2:10.27
11	Division 4	2:13.84
12	Division 9	2:15.15

Senior Boys

100 Metres Freestyle
Final

1	R. Tozer (5)	52.59
2	D. Gatland (11)	53.06
3	M. Levine (3)	53.24
4	W. Howarth (12)	53.45
5	A. Steel (10)	55.87
6	T. Morgan (7)	56.44

Heat Times

1	D. Gatland (11)	54.24
2	R. Tozer (5)	54.31
3	M. Levine (3)	54.43
4	W. Howarth (12)	54.46
5	A. Steel (10)	55.44
6	T. Morgan (7)	55.62
7	M. Osteritter (8)	56.24
8	D. Sharrock (2)	56.64
9	J. Swain (4)	56.65
10	P. Williams (1)	57.00
11	D. Coley (6)	57.71
12	J. Cornwall (9)	58.54

100 Metres Backstroke
Final

1	M. O'Connor (7)	58.72
2	N. Sherringham (3)	1:01.35
3	N. Bridge (5)	1:01.40
4	M. Hooper (12)	1:02.13
5	C. Dunmore (4)	1:02.60
6	J. Hunter (1)	1:03.99

Heat Times

1	M. O'Connor (7)	1:01.47
2	N. Bridge (5)	1:02.05
3	M. Hooper (12)	1:02.08
4	N. Sherringham (3)	1:02.74
5	C. Dunmore (4)	1:03.10
6	J. Hunter (1)	1:03.90
7	P. Taylor (11)	1:05.43
8	J. Chatten (8)	1:06.13
9	R. Smale (10)	1:06.87
10	M. Waring (2)	1:10.74
11	D. Hall (6)	1:11.18

100 Metres Breaststroke
Final

1	T. Ashwell (8)	1:06.12
2	T. Evans (4)	1:06.41
	J. Hender (2)	
4	J. Lant (3)	1:06.94
5	M. Driscoll (11)	1:07.59
6	G. McPeake (1)	1:08.57

Heat Times

1	T. Evans (4)	1:06.76
2	T. Ashwell (8)	1:07.03
3	J. Hender (2)	1:07.41
4	M. Driscoll (11)	1:08.19
5	J. Lant (3)	1:08.49
6	G. McPeake (1)	1:08.53
7	M. Wynn (5)	1:09.09
8	P. McQuaid (7)	1:09.63
9	A. Green (12)	1:11.21
10	J. Thacker (6)	1:11.25
11	J. Cheshire (10)	1:15.96

Tim Ashwell   Artwood Photography

100 Metres Butterfly
Final

1	R. Leishman (5)	56.80
2	M. Weighton (7)	58.31
3	B. Rees (10)	58.52
4	J. Gray (11)	58.80
5	R. Beacham (4)	59.21
6	M. Jones (12)	59.68

Heat Times

1	R. Leishman (5)	58.20
2	M. Weighton (7)	58.32
3	J. Gray (11)	59.17
4	R. Beacham (4)	59.20
5	B. Rees (10)	59.31
6	M. Jones (12)	59.53
7	A. Myers (2)	59.55
8	G. Mavin (8)	59.97
	S. Wyer (3)	
10	M. Fellows (6)	1:01.69
11	P. Buswell (9)	1:02.41
12	S. Noddings (1)	1:03.56

200 Metres Individual Medley
Final

1	I. Stewart (3)	2:08.39
2	D. Warren (1)	2:10.97
3	S. Wainwright (5)	2:12.52
4	A. Clarke (7)	2:12.73
5	T. Lewis (10)	2:14.00
6	A. Murdock (4)	2:18.31

Heat Times

1	D. Warren (1)	2:11.39
2	I. Stewart (3)	2:11.88
3	S. Wainwright (5)	2:13.15
4	A. Clarke (7)	2:13.43
5	T. Lewis (10)	2:14.41
6	A. Murdock (4)	2:15.08
7	R. Stapleton (9)	2:17.09
8	P. King (12)	2:19.19
9	J. Drummond (2)	2:22.77
10	S. Curran (8)	2:31.24
	J. Brownhill (11)	DIS

4×50 Metres Freestyle Team Relay
Final

1	Division 5	1:38.49
2	Division 12	1:39.12
3	Division 7	1:39.37
4	Division 3	1:39.48
5	Division 11	1:40.54
6	Division 4	1:41.90

Heat Times

1	Division 12	1:40.15
2	Division 7	1:40.46
3	Division 5	1:40.67
4	Division 3	1:41.07
5	Division 4	1:41.09
6	Division 11	1:41.73
7	Division 1	1:42.30
8	Division 10	1:42.69
9	Division 8	1:42.83
10	Division 9	1:45.68
11	Division 2	1:46.06
	Division 6	DIS

4×50 Metres Medley Team Relay
Final

1	Division 5	1:49.50
2	Division 3	1:50.02

3 Division 7	1:50.36
4 Division 12	1:51.53
5 Division 2	1:52.96
6 Division 11	1:54.21
Heat Times	
1 Division 5	1:51.79
2 Division 12	1:52.45
3 Division 7	1:52.47
4 Division 3	1:52.57
5 Division 2	1:53.03
6 Division 11	1:53.31
7 Division 4	1:53.73
8 Division 1	1:54.07
9 Division 8	1:54.87
10 Division 10	1:57.21
11 Division 6	1:58.89
12 Division 9	1:59.20

Senior Girls

100 Metres Freestyle
Final

1 J. Wilkinson (2)	58.69
2 C. Woodcock (12)	58.79
3 A. Kindon (6)	59.66
4 P. Herron (1)	59.88
5 N. Cumbers (5)	1:00.24
6 H. Tooke (8)	1:01.42
Heat Times	
1 C. Woodcock (12)	59.43
2 J. Wilkinson (2)	59.75
3 P. Herron (1)	1:00.18
4 A. Kindon (6)	1:00.32
5 N. Cumbers (5)	1:00.89
6 H. Tooke (8)	1:00.91
7 D. Churchman (3)	1:01.04
8 L. Hawking (4)	1:01.72
9 A. Derby (10)	1:01.74
10 G. Bryant (11)	1:04.01
11 W. Curtis (7)	1:11.16

100 Metres Backstroke
Final

1 H. Slatter (5)	1:06.52
2 C. Huddart (7)	1:06.87
3 L. Jackson (2)	1:07.92
4 J. Kelly (12)	1:08.40
5 P. Rickard (1)	1:10.27
6 L. Lennon (4)	1:11.44
Heat Times	
1 H. Slatter (5)	1:07.41
2 C. Huddart (7)	1:08.37
3 L. Jackson (2)	1:08.60
4 J. Kelly (12)	1:08.74
5 P. Rickard (1)	1:09.28
6 L. Lennon (4)	1:09.62
7 J. Austin (10)	1:09.74
8 A. Sedgebeer (8)	1:10.18
9 K. Haugh (11)	1:11.88
10 L. Morris (6)	1:11.94
11 N. Shirley (3)	1:13.18

100 Metres Breaststroke
Final

1 A. Baker (8)	1:13.02
2 J. Travis (7)	1:15.87
3 R. Newey (6)	1:16.47
4 S. Tinsley (2)	1:16.63

Jane Wilkinson

5 A. Bird (5)	1:17.34
6 T. Watkinson (4)	1:18.34
Heat Times	
1 A. Baker (8)	1:13.81
2 J. Travis (7)	1:15.76
3 S. Tinsley (2)	1:16.54
4 R. Newey (6)	1:16.68
5 A. Bird (5)	1:17.34
6 T. Watkinson (4)	1:17.55
7 A. Day (10)	1:17.81
8 E. Turner (12)	1:18.52
9 S. Embleton (1)	1:21.45
10 J. Kellington (3)	1:21.80
11 S. Marsh (11)	1:21.92
12 J. Ferrett (9)	1:26.92

100 Metres Butterfly
Final

1 N. Bates (8)	1:04.94
2 D. Evans (7)	1:05.36
3 N. Sommers (9)	1:06.19
4 A. Jones (2)	1:06.21
5 S. Buxton (4)	1:06.47
6 A. Duffy (1)	1:07.77
Heat Times	
1 N. Bates (8)	1:05.95
2 N. Sommers (9)	1:06.17
3 D. Evans (7)	1:06.47
4 A. Jones (2)	1:06.65
5 S. Buxton (4)	1:06.90
6 A. Duffy (1)	1:07.35
7 R. Thomas (10)	1:07.54
8 S. Jamison (3)	1:07.65
9 A. Cashmore (6)	1:07.86
10 A. Sanderson (12)	1:08.53
11 E. Nathan (5)	1:09.54
12 S. Warriner (11)	1:11.92

200 Metres Individual Medley
Final

1 R. Bowden (12)	2:21.16
2 J. Riegal (10)	2:24.55
3 M. Hollingsworth (7)	2:25.27
4 J. Harrison (3)	2:25.45
5 Z. Blake (5)	2:26.62

6 S. Solly (4)	2:27.76	

Heat Times

1 J. Harrison (3)	2:25.55
2 J. Riegal (10)	2:25.60
3 R. Bowden (12)	2:26.02
4 Z. Blake (5)	2:26.47
5 M. Hollingsworth (7)	2:27.60
6 S. Solly (4)	2:28.48
7 E. Archer (8)	2:28.74
8 C. Upton (11)	2:28.95
9 N. Ballard (9)	2:30.77
10 J. Robinson (2)	2:31.73
11 H. Morgan (6)	2:33.66
12 S. Bowman (1)	2:33.89

4×50 Metres Freestyle Team Relay

Final

1 Division 8	1:49.61
2 Division 12	1:50.15
3 Division 1	1:53.29
4 Division 5	1:53.33
5 Division 4	1:53.51
6 Division 7	1:55.63

Heat Times

1 Division 8	1:50.54
2 Division 12	1:51.11
3 Division 5	1:53.49
4 Division 1	1:53.57
5 Division 4	1:54.39
6 Division 7	1:54.42
7 Division 2	1:54.54
8 Division 10	1:54.97
9 Division 6	1:54.98
10 Division 11	1:56.14
11 Division 3	1:58.89

4×50 Metres Medley Team Relay

Final

1 Division 8	2:03.43
2 Division 12	2:05.18
3 Division 5	
Division 2	2:06.17
5 Division 6	2:06.45
6 Division 7	2:06.91

Heat Times

1 Division 8	2:04.70
2 Division 12	2:05.50
3 Division 2	2:06.39
4 Division 6	2:06.97
5 Division 5	2:07.28
6 Division 7	2:07.91
7 Division 10	2:08.25
8 Division 4	2:09.15
9 Division 11	2:11.89
10 Division 3	2:11.94
Division 1	DIS

Diving Finals

Copthall Stadium, Hendon — 19 November, 1988

Junior
Boys

1 J. Teal (3)	260.75
2 L. Celauro (8)	256.80
3 S. Holloway (10)	233.65
4 N. Dickinson (11)	219.70
5 T. Maguire (9)	188.85
6 M. T. Smith (4)	152.00

Girls

1 H. Allen (11)	281.30
2 A. Tatch (8)	229.05
3 B. Hawkes (5)	214.45
4 N. Fan (10)	190.25
5 H. Jeyes (4)	158.90
6 S. French (12)	152.95

Intermediate
Boys

1 A. Ali (9)	361.70
2 A. Byford (11)	344.90
3 S. Gladding (12)	328.80
4 M. Shipman (3)	295.20
5 S. Callaghan (10)	288.30
6 C. Bratt (8)	233.80

Girls

1 R. Ainsworth (11)	258.35
2 C. Hughes (8)	241.65
3 A. Day (10)	237.35

Adam Bowdery

Alan Pascoe Ass.

4 K. Owen (2)	224.95
5 B. Tomlinson (7)	189.00
6 S. Freeman (5)	175.10

Senior
Boys

1 A. Bowdery (11)	353.35
2 J. Ramsey (10)	317.50
3 A. Smith (3)	290.80
4 C. Chester (2)	257.80

5	J. Bellan (5)	248.95	2	T. Miles (9)	328.15
6	S. Moore (4)	218.75	3	O. Clark (5)	324.10
			4	N. Cordey (2)	254.55
Girls			5	J. Booth (3)	238.00
1	S. Ryan (12)	329.40	6	E. Seddon (4)	189.95

Antonio Ali (right) pictured with coach Kim White, following his stunning Intermediate Boys title win.   Alan Pascoe Ass.

Water Polo Finals
The Pool, Worcester — 13 May, 1989

12–16 Years
Boys   **16–19 years**
Trinity, Croydon (12) v Kings School (6)   Kings School (10) v Trinity, Croydon (4)

Synchronised Swimming Final
Kingsmead Pool, Canterbury — 22 April, 1989

Girls

Team			
1 Kendrick, Reading	72.42	3 Whickham, Newcastle on Tyne	68.32
2 Mayfield, Portsmouth	69.36	4 Henry Box, Witney	67.34
		5 Greenbank High, Southport	66.86
		6 Alleynes High, Stone	65.50

ASA Club Directory

All clubs affiliated to the ASA are listed in alphabetical order within their respective District, by: Year of formation; Club Secretary — name and address; Coaching staff; Membership figures; and a selection of thdir leading swimmers by age group. Clubs that did not respond to the questionnaires, even though they were requested to do so by the ASA, are shown by name only.

For the general government of the sport, the ASA is divided into five Districts, comprising the following:

Midland District — The West Midlands Metropolitan County of the Counties of Bedford, Cambridge, Derby, Hereford/Worcester, Leicester, Lincoln, Norfolk, Northampton, Nottingham, Shropshire, Suffolk, Warwick, Buckinghamshire and Oxfordshire as lie north of latitude 51deg. 37'. Such portions of Staffordshire as lie south of latitude 53deg., except the City of Stoke on Trent, and that portion of the County of Humberside which is south of the Humber and River Ouse.

Northern District — Cheshire, Cumbria, Lancashire, and Isle of Man, together with such portions of Staffordshire as lie north of latitude 53deg. Also the City of Stoke on Trent.

North-Eastern District — The Counties of Durham, Northumberland and York.

Southern District — Berkshire, such portions of Buckinghamshire and Oxfordshire as lie south of latitute 51deg. 37', the Channel Islands, Essex, Hampshire, Hertfordshire, Kent, Middlesex, Surrey and Sussex.

Western District — Cornwall, Devon, Dorset, Gloucestershire, Somerset and Wiltshire.

Midland District

Honorary Secretary: M. Rutter, 50 Gavden Road, Pedmore, Stourbridge, West Midlands DY9 9HN

ABINGDON (Oxford & North Bucks)

ALFRETON & DISTRICT (Derbys)

APPLEBY FRODINGHAM (Lincs)

ARNOLD (Notts)

ARROW (Worcs)

ASHBOURNE & DISTRICT (Derbys)

ASTON (Warwicks)

ATHERSTONE & DISTRICT (Warwicks)

AVON NEPTUNES (Warwicks)
Formed 1978
Club Sec: D. Collis, Brookside House, Fosse Way, Moreton Morrell. *Chief Coach:* W. Stowe
Members: 238.

AYLESBURY & DISTRICT (Oxford & North Bucks)
Formed 1930
Club Sec: Mrs T. Maxwell, 18 Penrith Way, Aylesbury, Bucks, HP21 7JZ. *Chief Coach:* M. Willis
Leading Members: S. Bishop, C. Blake, J. Bradbury, N. Burnham, P. Byrnes, W. Carner, S. Chilton, A. Colbeck, P. Ettrick, G. Evans, S. Evans, T. Griffin, R. Henley, M. Jordon, J. Kinane, E. Mallard, W. Munge, I. Murgatroyd, T. Ridgeway, D. Soley, M. Spicers, J. Tilly, I. Trimm, E. Williams, C. Windebank.

AYLSHAM VIKINGS (Norfolk)
Formed 1976
Club Sec: Mrs G. Cripwell, 67 Holman Road, Aylsham, Norwich, NR11 6DN. *Chief Coach:* D. Poynton
Members: 106.*Leading Members:* Elizabeth Aldous (9), Katherine Aldous (10), Sandra Burdett (16), James Campbell (9), Mark Clayton (9), Stuart Cripwell (9), Alistair Cubbitt (12), James Cubbitt (12), Bella Durrant (9), Angela Durrent (15), Kate Edlington (10), Sarah Edlington (14), Clare Fox (13), Richard Gilding (17), Sarah Hamspon (12), Thomas Hampson (9), Bruce Hannah (10), James Nesbitt (15), Hannah Nisbett (9), Isla Nisbett (14), Jeffrey Parkhurst (16), Kim Phillips (18), Ian Poynton (13), Richard Surridge (10), Debra Worboys (9).

BANBURY (Oxford & North Bucks)
Club Sec: Mrs G. Hughes, 3 Hereford Way, Banbury, Oxon, OX16 7FT. *Chief Coach:* A. Hale
Members: 140. *Leading Members:* Ian Burn (18), Hannah Church (13), Richard Gillingham (17), Katie Greenland (14), Nicholas Greenland (12), Richard Hale (16), Lisa Harvey (12), Ben Hughes (12), Matthew Hughes (15), Alex Lane (18), Charles Lane (16), Amy Musgrove (18), Thomas Musgrove (15), Marcus Noon (17), Sarah Perks (19), Paul Sabin (13), Hazel Starsmore (13), Robert Starsmore (15), Paul Swift (15), Edward Thornhill (15).

BANBURY WPC (Oxford & North Bucks)

BARTON UPON HUMBER & DISTRICT NEPTUNE (Lincs)
Formed 1964
Club Sec: Mrs J. Bee, 2 Prince Philip Drive, Barton upon Humber, DN18 6AZ.
Members: 155.

BECCLES TOWN (Suffolk)
Formed 1902
Club Sec: D. Alexander, Hill Farm, Mundham, Norwich, NR14 6EN. *Chief Coach:* Mrs J. Horton
Members: 115. *Leading Members:* Dawn Alexander (26), Keith Alexander (16), Claire Byles (14), Helen Byles (12), Cheryl Campling (12), Debbie Fisher (15), James Godbold (23), Jonathan Godbold (16), Diane Henderson (16), Kelly Holmes (10), Carrie Horton (18), Andrew Knights (12), Richard Lear (36), Christopher Machin (17), Donna Machin (14), Joanna Machin (11), Morgan Murray (12), Stuart Quinn (14), James Riseborough (11), Michael Talbot (14), Christopher Thrower (12), Mark Thrower (14), Sandra Wheatley (10), James Wilson (13), Louise Wyles (14).

BEDFORD (Beds)
Formed 1904
Club Sec: R. Draycott, 25 Albion Place, Rushden, Northants, NN10 0RF. *Chief Coach:* A. Jackson
Members: 300.

BEDFORD EAGLES (Beds)
Formed 1977
Club Sec: Mrs C. Seber, 6 Partridge Place, Cranfield, MK43 0BP. *Chief Coach:* Mrs P. de Quincey
Leading Members: Paul Boddey (12), David Bush (14), Sherre Corp (14), Darren Goff (11), Steven Goff (13), Mark Ruffles (13), Paul Ruffles (12), Robert Seber (14), Mercedes Uder (14), Tina Williams (15), Thomas Woods (13).

BEDFORD HIGH SCHOOL (Beds)

BEDFORD MASTERS (Beds)
Formed 1986
Club Sec: Miss H.S. Wilson, Flat C, 6 Clapham Road, Bedford, MK41 7PP.
Members: 170.

BEDFORD MODERN SCHOOL (Beds)

BEDFORD WPC (Beds) *Formed* 1980
Club Sec: S. Monico, 13 Weaver Close, Bedford, MK41 7YR.
Members: 40. *Leading Members:* Austin Atkins, Paul Barclay, Tony Booth, Paul Bradbury, Tim Bradbury, Simon Browning, Mark Bulleridge, Pete Carpenter, Adrian Cattley, Torben Cattley, Mike Claridge, Andy Cuss, Mark Dickinson, Keith Everley, Jon Harmer, Dave Hurley, Adrian Irbe, Andy Irvine, Justin Irvine, Steve Monico, Giles Perry, Tom Perry, Ian Stupple, Tim Whiteham, Frank Wright.

BEDWORTH OTTERS ALLIANCE (Warwicks) *Formed* 1976
Club Sec: J.H. Bacon, 65 Cleveland Road, Bulkington, Warwicks, CV12 9PA.
Members: 350. *Leading Members:* Claire Allen (10), Karen Arnold (12), Claire Barnes (14), Michelle Beale (16), Karen Blackham (17), Daniel Bottrill (12), Yvonne Brown (17), Paul Cutler (13), David Ellis (21), David Ganley (16), Kaye Ganley (14), Jonathan Gidlow (15), Nicola Griffin (14), Ian Hemmingway (14), Andrew Jackson (16), Kay Lucas (15), Marc Lucas (17), Rachel Lucas (12), Malcolm McSheffrey (13), Ian Smith (14), Ian Stew (11), Paulette Stew (15), Claire Thompson (13), Sheena Thompson (39), Melanie Wiltshire (14).

BELGRAVE (Leics) *Formed* 1914
Club Sec: Mrs U. Beck, 47 Ploughmans Lea, East Goscote, Leics, LE7 8ZR. *Chief Coach:* A. King
Members: 175. *Leading Members:* Nicholas Adkins (14), Aarti Amin (13), Ian Brown (25), Graham Budge (11), Craig Campbell (20), Ian Elliott (22), Max Gibbon (14), Christopher Goode (13), J. Greenhill (27), Ann-Marie Harriman (15), Jackie Harriman (13), Kieran Harrison (20), Faye Kettell (12), Ross Kettell (11), Lee Kilby (19), Angela Liquorish (17), Lou McLeish (27), Angela Mee (14), Clare Salmon (14), Emma Skinner (16), Jonathan Sleath (15), Paul Sleath (19), Robert Taylor (18), Daniel Ward (14), Taryn Ward (12).

BELPER MARLIN (Derbys) *Formed* 1970
Club Sec: Miss J. Pickering, 4 Belle Villas, Brickyard Lane, Kilburn, Derbys. *Chief Coach:* R. Maskrey
Members: 120. *Leading Members:* Edward Baker (14), Donna Briddon (13), Jeremy Brough (17), David Chamberlain (14), Steven Chamberlain (14), Martin Devenport (15), Ashley Fox (13), Elaine Fox (10), Dinah Hodson (13), Mark Lawson (13), Sally Lawson (11), James Maskrey (15), Carly Mathews (10), Jemma Mathews (13), Andrew Mosley (16), Carl Perry-Taylor (18), Claire Perry-Taylor (11), Kelly Rafferty (12), Haley Rossington (15), Sarah Rossington (12), Mark Sheard (13), Jayne Slack (14), Craig Tarling (13), Galvin Tarling (18), Haley Thorne (14).

BICESTER (Oxford & North Bucks) *Formed* 1950
Club Sec: Mrs C. Richardson, 5 The Spinney, Launton, Oxon, OX6 0EP. *Chief Coach:* I. Cox
Members: 100. *Leading Members:* Niki Bland (18), Fiona Boyer (13), Karen Coolin (15), Neil Cox (18), Joanne Croxton (15), Dominic Deacon (15), Claire Evans (15), Laura Fernandes (13), Chris Goodgame (15), Jonathan Grant (10), Chris Griffith (11), Charlotte Hammond (13), Claire Hannent (14), Hannah Jobling (11), Rachel Jobling (9), Andrew Myton (19), Peter Phillips (9), Richard Proctor (14), Ben Richardson (9), Clarissa Shepherd (13), Jonathon Smith (14), Neil van den Broek (10), Ben Vine (14), Ian Whiting (23), Andrew Wiggins (16).

BIGGLESWADE (Beds) *Formed* 1966
Club Sec: Mrs K. Griffiths, 56 Beech Avenue, Biggleswade, Beds. *Chief Coach:* Y. Hanks
Leading Members: Sharon Adams (14), Diane Brinkler (21+), Kelly Brinkler (8), James Buckingham (10), David Chessum (15), Rebecca Constant (12), Steve Constant (21+), Derek Cruft (13), Lee Cruft (9), Kim Curtis (12), Helen Gurney (9), Karen Harries (12), Eleanor Kingdon (9), Gregory Lawrence (9), Jamie Lawrence (11), Adrian Lear (21+), Lynne McCreath (10), Carl Maplecroft (16), Colin Marshall (11), Karl Marshall (13), Christopher Mason (9), Stephen Mason (13), Sonia Spearing (15), Elaine Taylor (21+), Michelle York (13).

BILSTON (Staffs)

BINGHAM LEISURE CENTRE (Notts)

BIRCOTES PENGUINS (Notts) *Formed* 1978
Club Sec: Mrs L. Ridgway, 8 Arundell Walk, Bircotes, Doncaster, DN11 8QZ. *Chief Coach:* Mrs W. Short
Members: 136. *Leading Members:* Neil Annable (12), Tracey Belfitt (16), Scott Bower (14), Lee Burgess (11), Sarah Cartwright (16), Damien Edwards (14), Lee Fairclough (14), Jonathan Fisher (18), Rebecca Goodwin (13), Mark Harrington (15), Lucy Hilton (15), Simon Kane (18), Kerry Lee (13), Suzanne Powell (15), Kelly Qualter (11), Lee Qualter (12), Michael Riddell (13), James Roberts (12), Toni Rousell (14), Maria Spate (17), Adrian Taylor (12), Lyndsey Taylor (12), Stephen Taylor (12), Steven Watkins (14), Jon Paul Watson (11).

BIRMINGHAM CENTRAL (Warwicks) *Formed* 1926
Club Sec: Mrs V. Neal, 47 Overgreen Drive, Kingshurst, Birmingham, B37 6EZ.
Members: 94.

BIRMINGHAM & DISTRICT SWIMMING & WPC (Worcs)

BIRMINGHAM DC (Warwicks)

BIRMINGHAM LADIES (Warwicks)

BIRMINGHAM POST OFFICE & CIVIL SERVICE (Warwicks)
Formed 1906

Club Sec: D. Ryan, 126 Solihull Lane, Hall Green, Birmingham, B28 9LY.   *Chief Coach:* D. Ryan
Members: 30. *Leading Members:* Jonathon Baker (10), Helen Bates (16), Paul Beech (22), Helen Davis (16), Ian Griffiths (18), Jenny Helme (10), Michael Neal (16), Sharon Pristleton (10), John Shields (10), Linda Spooner (22).

BIRMINGHAM UNIVERSITY (Warwicks)

BIRSTALL (Leics)

BLETCHLEY & DISTRICT (Oxford & North Bucks)

BLOXWICH (Staffs)

BLUEBIRD (Worcs)
Formed 1980

Club Sec: Mrs H.V. Brown, 2 Tythebarn Drive, Kingswinford, DY6 0DS.   *Chief Coach:* Miss J. Wilding
Members: 350.

BOLDMERE (Warwicks)
Formed 1895

Club Sec: P. Mellors, 8 Halton Road, Sutton Coldfield, B73 6NP.   *Chief Coach:* Mrs E.M. Perkins
Members: 351. *Leading Members:* Miriam Cohen (12), Benjamin Desanges (9), Deena Elsharief (9), Joseph Gledhill (13), Robert Greenwood (12), Susan Harden (14), Scott Horton (11), Andrew Howells (16), Ruth Kitchen (14), Michael Leeming (14), Esther Liggins (11), Frederick Matthews (15), Andrew Mellington (15), Faye Mellington (13), Lee Owen (15), Miles Parker (17), Colin Reoch (16), Estella Roberts (14), Julia Robinson (12), Peter Robinson (14), Hazel Sayer (12), Sarah Smart (14), Kate Stickney (15), Jacqueline Widdowson (16), Victoria Widdowson (15).

BOSTON (Lincs)
Formed 1890

Club Sec: Dr B.P. Hunt, "Saddlers Mead", Northlands, Sibsey, Lincs, PE22 0UA. *Chief Coach:* D. Wilmott
Members: 400.

BOTTISHAM (Cambs)
Formed 1982

Club Sec: Mrs J. Osbourn, 11 Poplars Close, Burwell, Cambridge, CB5 0ET.   *Chief Coach:* D. Hunt
Members: 135. *Leading Members:* Anna Beadle (12), Yvonne Beadle (13), Leon Beer (10), Emma Bendon (13), Daniel Bethell (11), Christopher Brown (13), Daniel Clarke (18), Suzy Crisp (16), Simon Flack (13), Adrian Fox (18), Julian Fox (18), Richard Fuller (10), Tim Griffin (15), Jemma Hardiment (14), Alice Howard (12), Kate Jackson (10), Jo McAllister (10), Laura McAllister (13), Tim Mills (13), David Osbourn (15), Lizzy Osbourn (13), Susan Round (14), Christine Saunders (11), Paul Swan (13), Helen Woodward (13).

BOURNE END JUNIOR SPORTS CLUB (Oxford & North Bucks)
Formed 1972

Club Sec: R.M.A. Strudwicke, 21 Furlong Road, Bourne End, Bucks, SL8 5AE.   *Chief Coach:* E. Vine
Members: 81. *Leading Members:* Mark Barnett (9), Michelle Bobbett (15), Emma Cordingley (13), Jason Evans (15), Craig Fines-Allin (15), Birgit Hauffe (12), Trevor Hoggan (20), Catherine Holcroft (11), Sara Jacklin (17), Paul Lasenby (16), Peter Lasenby (12), Samantha Little (17), Laura McClintock (13), Michelle Martin (12), Samantha Martin (13), Daniel Mee (13), Alexandra Paine (14), Kathryn Paterson (11), Zoe Reynolds (11), Natalie Smith (16), Torkjell Stromme (16), Jeremy Wood (8), Katie Wood (10), Karen Wright (13).

BRAMCOTE HILLS (Notts)

Club Sec: Mrs J. Casemore, 28 Ilkeston Road, Stapleford, Notts.   *Chief Coach:* I. Guilor
Members: 300. *Leading Members:* Paul Anderson (13), Peter Bishop (17), Jason Carter (10), Suzanne Clarke (13), Andrew Corbett (14), Richard Corrall (13), Gemma Coulter (11), Richard Ford (15), Dave Hamilton (18), Fiona Harrison (17), Chris Hart (11), Caroline Haywood (12), Kathryn Haywood (18), Robert Hextor (14), Charlotte Higton (14), Samantha Koban (13), Alex Milne (14), Stephen Morley (10), Rebecca Owen (15), Suzanne Rigby (11), Matthew Robinson (20), Simon Robinson (19), Andrew Shaw (12), Claire Watterson (14), David Wright (13).

BRAUNSTONE (Leics)

BRECKLAND SYNCHRO (Norfolk)
Formed 1987

Club Sec: Mrs L. Williams, 36 Nunsgate, Thetford.   *Chief Coach:* Mrs P. Barton
Members: 28.

BRECKLAND WPC (Norfolk)
Formed 1983

Club Sec: N.A. Brooks, "Wyndon", Church Road, East Harling, Norwich.   *Chief Coach:* M. Hansell
Members: 20.

BRETTON DOLPHINS (Cambs)
Formed 1983

Club Sec: Mrs A. Perry, 42 Eyrescroft, Bretton, PE3 8ES.   *Chief Coaches:* D. Sanders, R. Spraggon
Members: 53. *Leading Members:* Chris Baverstock (13), Karen Burrows (16), Keith Burrows (17), Karen Chisnell (12), Kristy Clark (10), John Colbert (12), Debbie Copeland (11), Helen Copeland (10), Kathryn Francis (10), Michelle Francis (13), Tina Gallogby (13), Brenda Green (15), Jennifer Hill (10), Cheryl Martinez (12), Maralyn Martinez (10), Carl Regan (10), Eleanor Rice (12), Kirsty Sampson (12), Martin

Sanders (13), Richard Sanders (11), Robert Sanders (15), Jane Spraggon (16), Richard Taylor (11), Chris Walton (12), Amy Whittaker (10).

BRIERLEY HILL (Staffs) *Formed* 1961
Club Sec: Mrs J. Hill, 16A Oakfield Road, Wordsley, West Midlands, DY8 5XS.
Members: 270. *Leading Members:* Michelle Bates (14), Natasha Boots (13), Sharon Churchman (15), Emma Green (13), Martin Griffiths (12), Stephen Hackett (14), Timothy Hadley (12), David Hall (17), Natalie Hawkes (13), Duncan Haywood (16), Louise Hill (16), Gareth Homer (13), Catriona Jephcott (16), Matthew Jephcott (13), Christopher Jones (11), Helen Jones (15), Paul Langford (14), Daniel Philpotts (14), Jessica Philpotts (13), Leslie Plant (17), Neil Ramage (17), Adam Smith (13), Neil Tandy (15), Joanne Wall (19), James Webster (17).

BRITISH RAIL SPORTS (Derbys)

BRITISH TELECOM RESEARCH LABS (Suffolk)

BROADWAY (Staffs) *Formed* 1982
Club Sec: Mrs L. Payne, 39 Ganton Road, Bloxwich, West Midlands, WS3 3XQ. *Chief Coach:* L. Robinson
Members: 250. *Leading Members:* James Aspinall (12), Emma Bagnall (13), Stephen Ball (15), Richard Barr (12), Rebecca Bradbury (15), James Brain (11), Piers Brown (17), Soames Brown (14), Craig Emery (15), Simon Gentry (15), Marie Hardiman (14), Jeremy Jones (20), Laura Mitchell (11), Brett Moss (11), Iain Payne (13), Sarah Payne (15), Samantha Phillips (11), Julie Price (18), Hannah Pymm (11), Adrian Strange (18), Dave Swift (24), Teresa Taylor (13), Hayden Wakeling (17), Paul Westley (13), David White (13).

BROMSGROVE (Worcs)

BUCKINGHAM CYGNETS (Oxford & North Bucks)

BUCKINGHAM & DISTRICT (Oxford & North Bucks)

BURNTWOOD (Staffs)

BURTON (Derbys) *Formed* 1878
Club Sec: Mrs K. Sessions, 69 Valley Rise, Swadlincote, Staffs, DE11 0QE. *Chief Coach:* S. Barrett
Members: 108. *Leading Members:* Samantha Adshead (11), Charlotte Beswick (14), Ian Brister (14), John Clarke (29), Jennifer Cooke (12), Colette Freeman (18), Lynne Goodhead (18), Jonathan Gosling (9), James Greenlee (12), Matthew Haywood (12), David Hughes (10), Lee Hyde (11), James Leeman (12), Fay McCallion (16), Jon Mann (14), Jon Milton (11), Martin Murphy (9), Robert Page (19), Helen Pratt (10), Helen Proctor (12), Richard Stanbridge (18), Debbie Wakelin (12), Guy Whittaker (11), Matthew Wiseman (10), Sophie Wiseman (13).

BURY ST EDMUNDS (Suffolk) *Formed* 1923
Club Sec: Mrs P. Neate, 15 Bury Park Drive, Bury St Edmunds, Suffolk. *Chief Coach:* D.P. Hopson
Members: 200. *Leading Members:* Meg Boothby (15), Harriet Brooke (13), Ziggi Jane Clark (12), Laurence Crichton (14), Oliver Crichton (14), James Desira (11), Kerry Francksen (15), Angela Graystone (26), Anna Jackson (12), Brian Kenworthy (29), Michael Kerry (13), Michelle McCullum (13), Diane Mackay (15), Susan Mendham (14), Francis Neal (16), Helen Neal (13), Joseph Onslow (13), Sarah Pack (14), Alistair Peagram (11), Gordon Pratley (15), Mark Pratley (13), Michael Ransom (25), Stephen Rogers (14), Susie Ruddock (16).

BUXTON & DISTRICT (Derbys) *Formed* 1973
Club Sec: Mrs M. Dyson, "Braeside", Whitehough, Chinley, Cheshire. *Chief Coach:* R. Davies
Members: 160. *Leading Members:* Daniel Ashton (12), Kirsty Birkinshaw (16), Michael Birkinshaw (14), Crispin Brightmore (16), Daniel Chelton (13), Iain Dyson (17), Alistair Fitzgerald (14), Lindsey Hambleton (11), Graham Hardman (16), Christopher Hoare (14), Neeta Hoare (10), Paul Houghton (16), Ruth Hoyle (13), Kirsty Mellor (16), Cathy Mone (14), Richard Mycock (13), Mark Nadin (21), Alan Rapley (19), Nicola Rapley (16), Mark Robinson (14), Paula Rogers (17), Stuart Taylor (12), Stuart Thornhill (10), Abigail Trivett (13), Charles Trivett (16).

CALVERTON (Notts) *Formed* 1978
Club Sec: T. Brentnall, 5 Church Street, Cropwell Bishop, Nottingham. *Chief Coach:* L. Capewell
Members: 108. *Leading Members:* Matthew Atkinson (13), Daniel Bamford (13), Nigel Bartholomew (19), Andrew Bevins (13), Julie Camm (17), Michelle Camm (14), Nicola Camm (17), Christopher Capewell (22), Helen Croome (17), Nathan Gerry (14), Rochele Greenway (13), Jason Knight (19), Gareth Lewis (17), Kerry Lewis (14), Louise Mancer (16), Rachel Neale (13), James Patterson (11), Stuart Peace (14), Colin Pierpoint (14), Tracy Pierpoint (17), Marie Sparrow (21), Carol Suffolk (14), Marie Sulley (15), Martin Sulley (14), Paul Tindall (13).

CAMBRIDGE UNIVERSITY (Cambs)

CAMP HILL EDWARDIANS (Warwicks)

C.A.R.I.T.A.S. (Oxford & North Bucks)

CARR VALE (Derbys)

Calverton S.C.

CARLTON FORUM (Notts)
Formed 1968
Club Sec: M. Gilliver, 289 Oakdale Road, Carlton, Nottingham, NG4 1BP.   *Chief Coach:* J. Bragg
Members: 148. *Leading Members:* Craig Bradshaw (15), Jonathon Daniels (9), Tanya Daniels (10), Jon Paul de Balsi (11), Lucia de Balsi (16), Helen Fryer (9), David Fryman (12), Helen Gorman (16), James Greensmith (12), Suzanne Haines (14), Kate Hardy (12), Rebekah Hardy (17), Christopher Ireland (9), Nicola Jephson (14), Matthew Jones (12), Shelly Jones (9), Wendy Lang (18), Alison MacIntosh (16), Steven Melboure (10), Alexander Piziura (11), Dale Powis (19), Phillippa Powis (15), Richard Seals (16), Danielle Sheppard (15), Simon Steele (11).

CHASE (Staffs)
Formed 1974
Club Sec: Mrs C. Davies, 33 Lloyd Street, Cannock, Staffs, WS11 1HG.   *Chief Coach:* K.L. Selvey
Members: 220. *Leading Members:* Helen Barklam (13), Steven Davies (13), David Evans (17), Matthew Evans (19), Sean Hickman (19), Adrian Hill (15), Katherine Hill (14), Maria Hollingsworth (17), Alison Jacques (12), Heidi Leek (13), Joanne Leek (11), Sonia Leek (11), Adam McLean (10), Richard McLean (11), Natalie Marsh (13), Carl Mellor (13), Jason Mellor (11), Lucy Neale (14), Karen Perry (15), Julie Shield (13), Lorraine Shield (13), Caroline Smith (14), Mark Stevens (13), Dean Swinnerton (13), Clare Tolley (17).

CHATTERIS KINGFISHER (Cambs)

ESLYN HAY WPC (Staffs)

CHESTERFIELD (Derbys)

CHESTERFIELD GLASSWORKS R.C. (Derbys)

CHESTERFIELD TUBE CO. LTD. (Derbys)

CHIPPING NORTON & DISTRICT (Oxford & North Bucks)

CHURCH STRETTON (Shropshire)

CITY OF BIRMINGHAM (Warwicks)
Formed 1985
Club Sec: Mrs L. Harbison, "Yew Tree Cottage", Truemans, Heath Lane, Shirley.   *Chief Coach:* B. Prime
Leading Members: Catherine Bailey (17), James Bainbridge, Claire Brookes (17), Guy Bullpitt (21), Daniel Claridge (16), Joanna Corbett (15), Joanna Coull (16), Matt Fellows (19), Nick Gillingham (22), Martin Harris (19), Louise Heath (17), Tim Jones (22), Lindsey Kilgour (15), Alison Kindon (17), Graham Minns (23), Gerald Morgan (15), Heather Osborne (16), Sharon Page (18), Caroline Piggott (16), Jamie Randell (15), Arran Stevens (19), Debby Tubby (19), Lee Tyson, Alison Warner (17), Alex Wooldridge.

CITY OF CAMBRIDGE (Cambs)

CITY OF COVENTRY (Warwicks) *Formed* 1975
Club Sec: Mrs J.M. Nickerson, "The Squirrels", 324 Lower Eastern Green Lane, Eastern Green, Coventry, CV5 7DT. *Chief Coach:* N. Sellwood
Members: 800. *Leading Members:* Jane Adkins (14), Cheryl Armstrong (17), Paul Beacham (15), Robert Beacham (20), Claire Brookes (17), Stewart Clamp (16), Darran Dyke (23), Lisa Eyles (17), Dale Grassby (12), Blayne Hughes (14), Amanda Lucas (17), Phillip McGillion (19), Michelle Mahiques (16), Jenny Mallison (14), Robert Millay (16), David Moreton (16), Fiona O'Reilly (15), David Parker (18), Stuart Parker (16), Simon Penny (23), Michael Poole (17), Kay Pountney (16), Neil Randle (15), Elizabeth Spokes (16), Claire Wallis (16).

CITY OF DERBY (Derbys) *Formed* 1983
Club Sec: Mrs B.I. Randle, 83 St Albans Road, Derby, DE3 3JN. *Chief Coach:* J. Randall
Members: 200.

CITY OF ELY (Cambs)

CITY OF LEICESTER (Leics) *Formed* 1978
Club Sec: Mrs J. Hammond, 5 Lutterworth Road, Leicester, LE2 6GT. *Chief Coach:* M. Parker
Members: 61. *Leading Members:* Paul Aucott (13), Simon Aucott (16), Joanne Baker (18), Lisa Baxter (19), Julie Beadnall (15), Craig Campbell (20), James Cole (23), Susan Davis (15), Tara Evatt (16), Louise Footitt (15), Stephen Fryett (20), Alistair Gilbert (15), Luke Hammond (17), Stuart Henson (23), Joanne Hutchinson (15), Luke Jacobs (16), Melanie Lister (16), Paul McCloud (15), Louise McLeish (27), Ross Martin (23), Spencer Martin (18), Claire Salmon (15), Claire Stubley (14), Katie Vines (13), David Wright (16).

City of Leicester S.C.

CITY OF LINCOLN PENTAQUA (Lincs) *Formed* 1972
Club Sec: Mrs D. Fearn, 21 Park Avenue, Lincoln. *Chief Coach:* I. Turner
Members: 200. *Leading Members:* T. Atkin (18), P. Balfour (14), H. Barton (25), R. Birch (14), J. Birkett (15), H. Bretton (15), A. Chadderton (18), N. Clover (15), E. Davison (13), E. Driffill (14), T. Driffill (10), D. Goodwin (18), D.G. Hayes (10), J.P. Hayes (11), A. McLeish (16), K. Palmer (12), P. Palmer (15), A. Plummer (14), R. Rook (12), H. Shipley (11), M. Spackman (10), S. Strahan (14), T. Wainwright (15), J. Young (18).

CITY OF MILTON KEYNES (Oxford & North Bucks)   *Formed* 1980
Club Sec: Mrs S. Pearson, 35 Osborne Street, Wolverton, MK12 5HH.   *Chief Coach:* A. Patterson
Members: 140. *Leading Members:* Ben Antell (13), Lindsey Balch (18), Alison Brimson (12), Amanda
Brimson (14), Jackie Broome (16), Sheryl Cahill (15), Alison Casey (11), David Casey (13), Greg Cavill
(14), Alison Chipperfield (10), John Craib (26), Kerrie Day (16), David Furness (15), Kay Jones (16), Brian
Kingston (14), David Kingston (15), Erin Lee (12), Darren Lynham (19), Jo-Anne Pearson (12), Stuart
Pearson (14), Julian Reed (19), George Smith (15), Emma Spadaccini (13), Martin West (18), Paul Wrenn
(12).

CITY OF OXFORD (Oxford & North Bucks)   *Formed* 1984
Club Sec: Mrs P. Sutton, 8 Dents Close, Marston, Oxford, OX3 0NP.   *Chief Coach:* J. Glenn
Members: 180. *Leading Members:* Stuart Baker (15), Briony Ballard (12), Rebecca Brown (18), Netta
Cohen (14), Helen Cowan (15), Philip Cox (16), Nicholas Cross (15), Sarah Gardiner (13), Matthew
Gomez (23), Julian Green (18), Emma Leighfield (16), Hagan Lewisman (17), Claire Nash (15), Donald
Reid (12), Marie Royal (24), Marcus Simpkins (15), Deborah Simpson (16), Abby Smith (12), Ian Stott
(11), Ellen Strange (14), Debbie Sutton (14), Keith Sutton (12), Diana Tothill (17), Lindsey Walker (14),
Zoe Walters (12).

CITY OF PETERBOROUGH (Cambs)   *Formed* 1936
Club Sec: Mrs J. Sloan, c/o Regional Pool, The Embankment, Peterborough.   *Chief Coach:* B. Brinkley
Members: 120. *Leading Members:* Ann Aure (15), Gina Chapman (14), Clive Dunnett (13), Anna Garratt
(16), Nicola Gockel (16), Liza Gripton (13), Joan Groom (17), Neil Henson (11), Nicola Herron (13),
Stephen Hill (16), Gina Hovell (16), Mark Johnson (13), Mike King (19), Tom Kirk (13), Gary Mavin (18),
Steve Mavin (14), Jamie Piercewright (21), Joan Runnacles (13), Francis Schultz (11), Lesley Shedd (13),
Neil Sloan (14), Madeline Sowerby (11), Simon Taylor (18), Jeremy Wallis (17), Mark Williams (16).

CLEETHORPES & DISTRICT (Lincs)   *Formed* 1977
Club Sec: Mrs L. Beck, 2 West Street, Cleethorpes.   *Chief Coaches:* Mrs Killeal, Mr Perkins
Members: 120. *Leading Members:* Amber Bensley (16), Liam Clarley (13), Vonni Clifton (24), Steven
Clipsham (14), Lindsay Crawford (12), Anna Grundy (15), Nick Grundy (13), Robert Holden (16), Andrew
Johnson (18), Richard Johnson (15), Paul Leggett (22), Liz McCluskie (14), Alison McDonnell (13),
Mathew Melia (17), Sam Mellors (16), Andrew Neal (16), Robert Ornsby (21), Caroline Robinson (11),
Jenny Robinson (13), Alex Rowe (19), Richard Sheard (11), H. Taylor (12), Paul Whitfield (15), Mark
Woods (20), Caroline Wright (13).

COALVILLE (Leics)   *Formed* 1947
Club Sec: Mrs M. Crane, "The Bungalow", Main Street, Nailstone, Warkwicks, CV13 0QB.
Leading Members: Victoria Allen (11), Kathryn Austen (15), Andrew Betts (12), Kelly Butler (14), N.
Chantrill, Dean Clarke (15), Zoe Clarke (11), Kathryn Crane, Robert Crane (13), Stephen Crane, Helen
Darby (16), Jennifer Darby (13), Neil Darby (13), Ryan Dennis (13), Christopher Fox (11), James Garner
(11), Kevin Joyce (16), Ester Lincoln (13), Lorraine Lincoln, Garry Morris, Paula Rice (11), Carl Shilliam
(15), Beverley Smith (12), Paula Stretton (12).

CODSHALL (Staffs)

COLTON HILLS (Staffs)

CORBY (Northants)   *Formed* 1963
Club Sec: G.D. Isaac, 3 Howe Crescent, Corby,Northants, NN17 2RY.   *Chief Coach:* S.J. Earthy
Members: 120. *Leading Members:* Lisa Abbott (16), Heidi Bothel (17), Martin Cochrane (15), Richard
Cochrane (11), Jacqueline Cole (13), Hayley Collis (12), Neil Collis (14), Scott Ewing (19), Paul Hammond
(13), Hayley Kennedy (14), Kelly Little (13), Caroline McKinnon (14), Mark McNulty (13), Paul McNulty
(14), Emma Martin (11), John Matthews (14), George Mitchell (18), Greg Newton (16), Richard Smith (12),
Ella Wagstaff (15), Tracey Webster (18), Gary Wilkinson (15), Paul Wilkinson (13).

COSELEY (Staffs)   *Formed* 1964
Club Sec: R. Taylor, 4 Fountain Lane, Coseley, West Midlands.   *Chief Coaches:* T.M. Poole, J. Taylor
Members: 208. *Leading Members:* Matthew Adamson (11), Emma Beasley (12), Rebecca Brownsword
(11), Andrew Cashmore (14), Paul Cashmore (16), Emma Cook (12), Andrew Cox (14), Steven Denham
(13), Neil Elwell (13), Kerrie Hancox (13), Mark Harris (16), Tim Harris (11), Christopher Hodgkiss (10),
Kristian Martin (13), Charlotte Penn (11), Faye Penn (14), Allison Poole (14), Jonathan Poole (10), Anna
Reed (15), Ian Sherwood (15), Joanne Taylor (13), Scott Taylor (18), Sarah Theaker (15), Michael Vance
(14), Adrian Watkins (11).

COURT (Shropshire)

COVENTRY MORRIS (Warwicks)

COVENTRY WORKS SPORTS ASSOCIATION (Warwicks)

CRIPPS (Northants)   *Formed* 1977
Club Sec: Mrs M.L. Borrill, 11 Croughton Close, Kingsthorpe, NN2 8NZ.   *Chief Coach:* D. Billingham
Leading Members: Jonathan Baker (11), Philippa Best (14), Vanessa Burn (15), Ian Buswell (13), Stephen
Buswell (15), Clare Butterfield (21), Samantha Hillyard (14), Christopher Keal (19), Peter Knott, Gary Luck

(28), Alistair McPherson (15), Martin Mansell (28), Rachel Robins (14), Andrew Robinson (14), Kirsten Sear (12), Giles Shaxted (11), Robert Snedker (20), Julie Street (16), Sharon Street (18), Susan Sturgess (16), Katie Whitmill (14), Peter Withrington (12), Stephen Withrington (9), Sarah Jayne Woodhall (13), Louise Woolliscroft (12).

DARLASTON (Staffs)

DAVENTRY & DISTRICT (Northants)
Formed 1962
Club Sec: A. Colsey, "Toad Hall", 4 The Willows, Daventry, NN11 5PY. *Chief Coach:* K. Magee
Members: 300. *Leading Members:* Caroline Barker (16), Nigel Barker (15), Craig Billingham (18), Pipa Bowler (11), Louise Colsey (14), Sarah Colsey (16), Gareth Deacon (15), Rachel Dicks (14), Damien Green (13), Simon Green (13), Julie Hemmings (13), Simon Hemmings (16), Matthew Henderson (16), Carolyn Hicks (15), Alison Luck (12), Mark Lupton (21), Grant Mitchell (11), Rachel Parkin (11), Tara Setterfield (10), Paula Taylor (14), Joanne Tite (18), Adrian Turner (20), Joanna Warltier (12), Jonathan Wood (11), Ashley Woodcock (11).

DEBEN (Suffolk)
Formed 1972
Club Sec: Mrs S.J. Bacon, 6 Burkitt Road, Woodbridge, Suffolk, IP12 4JL.
Members: 270. *Leading Members:* Sarah Bealton, Jill Chatten, Susan Clarke (14), Laura Cotton (12), Hannah Davies, Neal Daymond-John, Katy Ellis (14), Neil Flowers (14), Mark Girling (13), Christopher Hawood (14), Clare Holmes (14), Alastair Howard (15), Michael Howard (12), Craig Lawes (12), Paul Lawes (16), Adrian Mills (15), Rachel Mills (13), David Murrell (16), Damon Solis (14), Susan Stockton, Matthew Thompson, Christopher Warner (13), Steven Warner (11), Debbie Watson (11), Neal Watson (14).

DEEPINGS (Lincs)
Formed 1977
Club Sec: Mrs E. Kelly, Horseshoe Cottage, Park Road, Peterborough. *Chief Coach:* D. Mann
Members: 200. *Leading Members:* C. Baldwin (16), K. Baldwin (12), M. Bremner (14), W. Casterton (11), A. Chapman (11), K. Chapman (13), D. Cooper (11), C. Devonport (13), H. Dobbs (14), J. Goode (11), M. Goode (13), M. Griffin (13), S. Griffin (14), P. Holley (12), H. Lesage (12), S. Rea (12), A. Roberts (15), A. Robertson (17), K. Rome (11), J. Smith (16), S. Smith (10), M. Swain (18), G. Townson (10), L. Wales (13), T. Wallis (20).

DERBY BRITISH RAIL (Derbys)

DERBY CITY TRANSPORT (Derbys)

DERBY PHOENIX (Derbys)
Formed 1964
Club Sec: D.G. Copperthwaite, 34 Linacres Drive, Chellaston, Derby, DE7 1XH. *Chief Coach:* D.G. Collins
Members: 185. *Leading Members:* Andrew Bell (16), Louise Bell (13), Ian Beswick (12), Jamie Cresswell (15), Emma Day (13), Samantha Hamlett (16), Catherine Hemsworth (14), Mark Hollingsworth (16), Wendy Hollingsworth (18), Thomas Johnston (16), Hannah Kelly (16), Mark Malia (15), Karan Martin (15), Andrew Meacham (11), Helen Moore (12), Richard Moore (14), Karl Morley (18), Angela Moss (11), Stuart Moss (14), Marie Rose (16), Vicky Rowlands (12), Gary Smith (17), Kyle Whitlam (16), Debbie Wing (14), Michelle Wing (17).

DERBY SCHOOL OF DIVING (Derbys)
Formed 1974
Club Sec: Mrs V.M. Seddon, 3 North Avenue, Darley Abbey, Derby, DE3 1EZ. *Chief Coach:* Mrs N. Pipes
Members: 24. *Leading Members:* Thomas Atkinson (12), Laura Collier (11), Kerry Harvey (17), Philip Horton (20), Helen Jeyes (13), Simon Moore (19), Erica Seddon (17), Martin Smith (15).

DEREHAM & DISTRICT (Norfolk)
Formed 1975
Club Sec: Mrs R. Adcock, "Shrublands", Westfield Road, East Dereham, Norfolk. *Chief Coach:* W. Blyth
Members: 130. *Leading Members:* Christopher Angell (10), Kieran Barnard (13), Carolyn Blyth (16), Carly Buck (11), Ben Clarke (15), David Clarke (13), Amanda Doherty (14), Rachel Gunton (11), Ian Hargreaves (17), Ruth Keele (12), Ross McDermott (12), Neil Morris (17), Carl Nelson (15), Christopher Ponton (10), Juliet Ponton (16), Nicola Rumble (17), Oliver Skinner (11), Kieron Smith (15), Stacey Smith (12), Virginia Smith (12), Chanel Studd (11), Christina Wake (10), James Wake (11), Lisa White (16), Joanne Wright (12).

DESFORD DOLPHINS SYNCHRO (Leics)

DOLPHIN (Notts)

DOVE VALLEY (Staffs)
Formed 1985
Club Sec: S. Hughes, High Park Farm, Stone Heath, Leigh, Staffs, ST10 4PG. *Chief Coach:* B. Murray
Members: 140. *Leading Members:* Marc Alcock (15), Rachael Armett (11), Elaine Ball (12), Adam Brown (10), Andrew Brown (13), Stephen Chadfield (12), Catherine Dodd (12), Adele Gibson (13), Rebecca Gibson (13), Rupert Hough (16), Josephine Hughes (15), Nigel Hughes (14), Sarah Joynes (12), Abigail Lear (12), Matthew Lear (11), Kelly Lewis (14), Paul Marrow (10), Thea Mathias (14), Janet Murray (14), Chris Murtagh (14), Laura Sims (9), Liz Tench (15), Chloe Timmis (9), Joanna Tweddle (13), Caroline Waite (17).

DOWNHAM MARKET (Norfolk)
Formed 1975
Club Sec: Mrs B. Law, 226 Broom Hill, Downham Market.
Members: 170.

DROITWICH DOLPHINS (Worcs) *Formed* 1955
Club Sec: Mrs A.H. Gerwitz, 4 Singer Hill, Droitwich, Worcs, WR9 8SN.
Members: 130. *Leading Members:* Jocelyn Collins (11), James Davies (12), Mathew Fellows (19), Sally Garbett (12), Helen Gerwitz (15), Graeme Harkins (21), Julie Harvey (13), Simon Hillson (19), Peter Jarvis (11), Sarah Jarvis (12), Neil Jenkins (17), Emma Jones (10), Ian Leadbetter (13), Michelle Leadbetter (10), Nicola Osborne (18), Susan Osborne (16), Jayne Rhodes (14), Philip Rhodes (12), Carol Savage (15), John Sherring (42), Lindsey Sherring (13), Tracey Sherring (13), Mark Turner (21), Alison Warner (17), Michelle Woodbury (14).

DRONFIELD DOLPHINS (Derbys) *Formed* 1980
Club Sec: S. Pryke, 16 Sheards Close, Dronfield Woodhouse, SI8 5NJ. *Chief Coach:* R. Carr
Members: 106. *Leading Members:* M. Bartrim (14), D. Carr (13), A. Cooke (11), G. Cooke (15), R. Cooke (13), J. Fisher (15), S. Hopkins (11), A. Jewitt (12), R. Johnson (12), M. Jones (12), S. Ledbetter (10), A. Lunn (12), N. Marsden (14), S. Marsden (15), R. Mason (12), S. Ollerenshaw (12), C. O'Neill (16), L. O'Neill (15), J. Pryke (12), E. Southall (12), M. Taylor (15), W. Taylor (13), K. Thomson (12), H. Tomlinson (14), K. Wilkinson (13).

DUDLEY CENTRAL (Worcs)

DUDLEY METRO (Worcs) *Formed* 1977
Club Sec: Mrs C. Evans, 30 Metfield Croft, Kingswinford. *Chief Coaches:* E. Gorton, T. Green
Members: 110. *Leading Members:* Nicholas Amphlett (12), Michelle Bates (14), Kate Beardsmore (14), Sharon Churchman (15), Jenny Glynn (15), Martin Griffiths (12), Sarah Guest (12), Stephen Hacker (14), Timothy Hadley (12), David Hall (17), Kerry Hancox (13), Stephen Handley (13), Chris Harvey (12), Natalie Hawkes (13), Carl Holloway (16), Laura James (13), Eve Millard (12), Mark Morris (16), Stephen Pratt (13), Scott Raybould (11), Adelle Rowley (12), Samantha Smart (14), David Smith (16), Andrew Sparry (17), Jo-Anne Taylor (13).

DUNSTABLE (Beds) *Formed* 1975
Club Sec: Mrs V. Holt, 14 The Heath, Leighton Buzzard, Beds. *Chief Coach:* M. Henderson
Members: 159. *Leading Members:* Shaun Anniss (10), Linda Bavister (11), Paul Bavister (13), Caroline Bender (15), Patrick Butterworth (20), Emma Crawford (18), Jennie Gomersal (14), Sarah Gomersal (17), Clare Haddacks (16), Mark Haddacks (14), Gayle Hetterley (16), Craig Holt (16), Glyn Jackson (18), Tony McLellan (14), Lynsey Moore (12), Iain Morris (16), Karen Morris (13), Kelly Reay (13), Emma Roch (16), Vicky Roch (14), Paul Rollason (12), Neil Sherriff (14), Steve Sherriff (18), Alan Smith (16), James Toyer (18).

EAST ANGLIAN SWALLOW TAILS (Norfolk) *Formed* 1987
Club Sec: Mrs J. Asher, 38 Keswick Road, Cringleford, Norwich, NR4 6UG. *Chief Coach:* Mrs J. Asher
Members: 90. *Leading Members:* Linda Ashby (41), Jane Asher (58), Seymour Banning (56), Edward Boyd-Tuck (49), Martin Bull (29), Carol Buykx (51), Tony Byford (42), Philip Coghlan (38), Richard Collinson (43), Christine Comer (31), Philip Cotton (33), Joy Dalkin (31), Geoff Eagles (33), Angela Graystone (26), Linda Hewett (28), Edna Hitchborn (62), Julie Jago (27), Jim Masterson (69), Idris Mears (38), Anne Moore (54), Rex Morgan (48), Liz Read (39), Barry Ryan (42), Tony Sword (52), Karen Wooliscroft (33).

ECKINGTON (Derbys) *Formed* 1976
Club Sec: L. Ayling, 29 Main Road, Renishaw, Sheffield, S31 9UX. *Chief Coach:* D.G. Bellamy
Members: 199. *Leading Members:* Joanne Armitage (13), Zoe Baker (13), Ian Barker (11), John Bennett (17), Caroline Bissell (15), Nick Burdett (18), Jane Burnage (16), Jamie Charlesworth (12), Sally Clarke (15), Leigh Daveran (19), Matthew Freeston (14), Sarah Hodson (15), Paul Jones (17), Gareth Lloyd (17), Gemma McCall (14), Sian McCall (11), Spence Nichols (15), Dawn Radford (15), Lisa Shepherd (14), Dale Spencer (16), Carl Storey (14), Helen Wallace (14), Mark Wallace (14), Jamie Whiteley (15), Elizabeth Wright (16).

ENDERBY (Leics) *Formed* 1984
Club Sec: Mrs S. Ince, 7 Kingsfield Road, Cosby, Leicester, LE9 5SW. *Chief Coach:* A. Marston
Members: 150. *Leading Members:* Colin Bartlette (17), Louise Bent (13), Nicola Blake (16), Ashley Glew (17), Rachel Gorman (14), Natalie Harby (15), Marcus Hayes (15), Kirsten Hewitson (15), Annabel Hudson (18), Michelle Hurst (15), Joanne Ince (14), Daniel Johnson (11), Sally Johnson (14), Graham Marshall (18), Carl Marston (12), Gareth Metcalf (12), Simon Mottram (13), David Parker (10), Neil Parker (11), David Patterson (13), Deniece Sargeant (11), Glenn Sargeant (13), Justin Weir (15), Lee Wilford (11), Robert Williams (15).

EREWASH VALLEY (Derbys)

ETWALL EAGLES (Derbys) *Formed* 1980
Club Sec: Mrs D.R. Woollands, 4 Downham Close, Mickleover, Derbys. *Chief Coach:* A. Hawkins
Members: 100. *Leading Members:* Mark Arjoo (17), Neil Arjoo (14), James Bland (11), Joanna Carmichael (12), Kate Carmichael (10), Andrew Curry (13), Paul Dakin (11), Andrew Elliott (16), Rhys Hancock (9), Amanda Harris (11), Neil Harrison (16), Paul Hawkins (16), Emma Hodgkinson (14), Richard Jarvis (17), Andrew McGallan (12), Katherine Parker (17), Phillip Peake (19), Mark Sharratt (20), Katherine Spain

(15), Ben Speed (13), Lucy Speed (12), Iain Stevenson (11), Joseph Tuckwell (13), Sarah Wedgebury (17), Sarah Woollands (14).

EVESHAM SWIMMING & WPC (Worcs)
Formed 1890

Club Sec: Mrs B. Holder, 26 Princess Road, Evesham, WR11 4QG.   *Chief Coach:* N. Crowe
Members: 200. *Leading Members:* Rachel Amor (16), Andy Anderson (19), Amanda Barnes (16), Hannah Bean (14), James Bean (16), Christine Clarke (32), Trevor Clarke (34), Joanne Deakins (16), David Eales (12), Helen Eales (10), Suz Hampson (14), Suz Henderson (26), David James (18), James Kimberley (12), Michelle Kimberley (16), Roland Lee (24), Katie Moore (14), Jon Ostler (17), Louise Palfrey (18), Debbie Richardson (19), Anna Salcedo (14), Daniel Salcedo (18), Keith Shindler (16), David Storer (14), Scott Walford (13).

FAKENHAM INVADERS (Norfolk)

Club Sec: Mrs J. Barrett, 33 Rudham Stile Lane, Fakenham, Norfolk, NR21 8JN.   *Chief Coach:* E. Mason
Members: 120. *Leading Members:* Mark Barrett (16), Rebecca Brunton (14), Naomi Cane (12), Nathan Defew (12), Andrew Edge (13), Matthew Ellis (11), Clare Francis (14), Duncan Gilhooly (12), Victoria Howard (12), Dionne Lawrence (11), Debbie Myhill (14), Donna Myhill (12), Andrew Norman (14), Sarah Palmer (13), Catherine Pegg (16), Steven Pegg (18), Sam Sharp (16), Barry Smith (13), David Smith (14), Colin Stark (15), Jane Stark (16), Sonya Swift (12), Andrew Teage (13), Simon Thompson (21), Sarah Wright (16).

FALCON (Derbys)
Formed 1957

Club Sec: C. Rolle, 36 Polperro Way, Hucknall, Nottingham, NG15 6JS.   *Chief Coach:* K. Oldham
Members: 80. *Leading Members:* Louise Curtis (17), Richard Curtis (14), Jenifer Davey (12), Marcus Drabble (15), Simon Drabble (12), David Edwards (27), Victoria Hodgeman (11), Mathew Lancaster (12), Rachel Lancaster (15), Greg Oldham (14), Karen Oldham (12), Kath Pavier (42), Linda Pavier (18), Sean Pike (19), Ben Pollitt (12), Michael Pollitt (14), Richard Pugsley (16), Martin Richardson (12), Andrew Rolle (13), Chris Rolle (15), Robert Shelton (20), Andrew Sheppard (17), Claire Williams (13), Claire Yates (17), Susan Yates (15).

FELIXSTOWE (Suffolk)
Formed 1985

Club Sec: M. Williams, 154 Grange Road, Felixstowe, Suffolk.   *Chief Coaches:* J. Hughes, R. Loosemore
Members: 240. *Leading Members:* Kirsty Aberclein (10), Tamsin Aberclein (12), Nicholas Attwell (15), Stacy Burt (11), Vaughan Clarke (10), David Coulson (16), Michelle Davis (15), Nicola Fulcher (11), Martin Gallagher (10), James Gosling (11), Kate Hollis (12), Noel Hughes (13), Gordon Humphries (13), Allison Kelly (14), Emma Loosemore (10), Nicola Loosemore (14), Jackie Nightingale (12), Adam Pearse (10), Keith Songhurst (14), Till Songhurst (16), Paul Stefan (10), Dean Symonds (10), David Thorpe (14), Gavin Tonks (13), Andrew Williamson (16).

FREDERICK GOUGH (Lincs)
Formed 1972

Club Sec: Mrs V.P. Harrison, 8 De Aston Square, Scunthorpe, South Humberside, DN15 8JL.
Members: 250.

GAINSBOROUGH (Lincs)
Formed 1898

Club Sec: Mrs L. Higgins, 9 North Marsh Road, Gainsborough, DN21 2RN.   *Chief Coach:* P. Donnelly
Members: 350. *Leading Members:* Paul Airs (16), Kate Bartle (13), Rebecca Bashforth (13), Paul Brownless (20), Andrew Charlesworth (17), Neil Chester (10), Damian Cox (12), Leon Cox (14), Louise Donnelly (18), Philip Donnelly (16), Jari Goddard (26), Faith Grocock (12), Andrew Higgins (13), Lisa Hunt (12), Daniel King (13), Sarah King (12), Liza McRoberts (13), Rosina Marks (13), Jeanette Morris (14), Steve Morris (17), Jane Parry (11), Sarah Parsonage (13), Paula Spence (15), Daniel Taylor (14), Alan Walker (25).

GAINSBOROUGH LADIES (Lincs)
Formed 1905

Club Sec: Mrs J. Wooffitt, 99 Lea Road, Gainsborough, Lincs, DN21 1AB.
Members: 304. *Leading Members:* Nicola Allbones (9), Karen Amoss (12), Lindsay Amoss (14), Amy Atkin (10), Kate Bartle (13), Rebecca Bashforth (13), Abigail Chorlton (12), Claire Daly (9), Faith Grocock (12), Joanne Houghton (9), Nikki Howitt (10), Lisa Hunt (12), Liza McRoberts (13), Rosina Marks (13), Sarah Parsonage (13), Vicky Turner (9).

G.E.C. (Staffs)

GIPPING (Suffolk)

GLANFORD (Lincs)

GORWAY SYNCHRO (Staffs)

GRANTHAM (Lincs)

Club Sec: Mrs J. Hobson, 13 The Haverlands, Gonerby Hill Foot, Grantham.   *Chief Coach:* D. Cressey
Members: 220. *Leading Members:* Adam Arnott (9), Laura Caley (12), Suzanne Carter (14), Gordon Cooley (17), Natasha Finlow (15), Hayley Fountain (14), Jacqueline Fulcher (11), Nicholas Gibson (14), Matthew Haw (14), Simon Howitt (11), Stephen Lambley (17), Benjamin Lester (16), Tracey Norton (11), Zoe Norton (14), Claire Robinson (12), Ian Robinson (17), Michael Robinson (16), Paul Robinson (13),

Pollyanna Sims (13), Ross Skinner (11), Natalie Toon (10), James Waling (13), Karen White (13), Beverley Wilson (17), Spencer Wright (17).

GREAT BARR (Warwicks)

GREAT YARMOUTH (Norfolk) *Formed* 1919
Club Sec: Mrs P.M. Hollis, 10 Osborne Avenue, Great Yarmouth, Norfolk.   *Chief Coach:* R. Caton
Members: 404. *Leading Members:* Nadine Barford (15), Andrew Bloomfield (13), Rachel Calver (16), James Carter (14), Debra Carvell (17), Jamie Durrant (18), Adam Funnell (14), Michael George (16), Rachel Hollis (16), Donna Kitchener (15), James Knowles (15), Samantha Ladbrook (12), Carl Millican (14), Clare Read (13), Ben Roper (15), Jane Russell (11), Gavin Symonds (18), Iain Taylor (17), Richard Taylor (16), Suzanne Taylor (12), Carl Thompson (13), Oliver Thompson (11), Tracy Vardy (14), Louise Williams (15), Alexis Williamson (12).

Great Yarmouth S.C. — The opening day of the pool, 22 July, 1922.

GREEN ARROW SYNCHRO (Notts) *Formed* 1971
Club Sec: R. Hardy, 62 Bracadale Road, Rise Park, Nottingham, NG5 5EG.   *Chief Coach:* E. Walters
Members: 20. *Leading Members:* Helen Basford (10), Julie Basford (14), Amanda Boam (13), Caroline Cartledge (13), Karen Dales (14), Carolyn Davis (16), Anne Marie Fitzwater (12), Nichola Hardy (12), Lesley Leavesley (18), Samantha Lees (14), Sarah Lockwood (17), Kirsty Marchant (13), Sarah Precious (14), Rebecca Priest (11), Jaime Rippon (12), Hannah Scott (14), Molly Sears-Piccavey (13), Nichola Shephard (13), Victoria Tippett (11), Rachel Whitemore (14).

GRIMSBY ALEXANDRA (Lincs) *Formed* 1902
Club Sec: Mrs M. Taylor, 3 Harlech Way, Great Grimsby, South Humberside.   *Chief Coach:* Mrs V. Rowell
Members: 555. *Leading Members:* Ann Blanchard (22), Clair Devine (12), Claer Dierking (14), Gail Elkington (16), Sara Fursman (16), Joanne Gill (13), Nichola Goodchild (15), Julie Harrison (15), Jacqui Kirk (24), Alison Muir (15), Alison Rowell (15), Helen Rowell (23), Karen Sirl (16), Christine Taylor (25), Louisa Teanby (12), Lisa Thompson (15), Rachel Thompson (18), Joanne Waddingham (15).

GRIMSBY DOLPHINS (Lincs) *Formed* 1896
Club Sec: R. Creese, 100 Springbank, Grimsby, South Humberside, DN34 4DB.   *Chief Coach:* C. Playle

GRIMSBY MERMAIDS (Lincs) *Formed* 1927
Club Sec: Mrs S. Shotton, 36 Warwick Road, Cleethorpes, South Humberside.*Chief Coach:* Miss S. Bartle
Members: 450. *Leading Members:* Susan Bartle (19), Nicola Bird (15), Lucy Blakey (13), Eve Burley (10), Charlotte Dale (7), Danielle Elford (11), Roxanne Elford (9), Kristan Harness (9), Elisabeth Henrickson (10), Stephanie Henrickson (7), Laura Hickson (11), Abbe Jackson (11), Jody Jackson (10), Aislim Jerem (13), Corinne Lingard (14), Ann Owen (17), Julie Rea (14), Lucy Rolf (11), Claire Schofield (14), Kate Shotton (11), Kerry Skudder (13), Caroline Turner (13), Claire Wiliams (13), Donna Williams (15), Emma Wilson (11).

GRIMSBY SANTA MARINA (Lincs) *Formed* 1969
Club Sec: D.A. Shephard, 5 Grasby Crescent, Grimsby, DN37 9HE. *Chief Coach:* F. Roberts
Members: 300. *Leading Members:* Richard Barber (15), Mark Berry (12), Claire Cheetham (13), Sarah Connis (13), Caroline Corken (11), Jane Corlett (14), Paula Fleming (17), Richard Foster (15), Katherine Hardy (16), Sarah Hardy (19), Jason Ives (19), Gillian Lockhart (24), Stuart Morgan (15), Neil Parker (12), Andrew Porter (12), Nicola Ranyard (15), Steven Ranyard (13), Karen Richardson (26), Jane Ringrose (16), Richard Scott (15), Celia Shephard (14), Martin Stark (14), Michael Waller (17), Dean Wilkinson (17), Lee Wilkinson (19).

HADEN HILL (Worcs) *Formed* 1977
Club Sec: R.L. Edwards, 9 Hall Lane, Hagley, West Midlands, DY9 9LL. *Chief Coach:* B. Charles
Members: 70. *Leading Members:* Liann Andrews (13), Karl Barton (15), Elizabeth Beighton (14), Emma Beighton (10), Andrea Bennett (13), Andy Davies (17), Helen Davies (13), Gareth Evans (14), Joanne Green (14), Caroline Grove (17), Steven Hackett (11), Kerry Harris (14), Nicholas Healey (13), Steven Hickman (15), Paul Hughes (12), Stuart Hunt (10), Kate Moore (12), Adam Ruckwood (15), Bryan Sherwood (12), Ceri Sidaway (17), David Sigerson (12), Martin Stockin (14), David Willets (13), Jane Willets (11), Angela Wood (15).

HADLEIGH (Suffolk) *Formed* 1971
Club Sec: Mrs C. Webber, 11 The Causeway, Boxford, Essex, CO6 5JR. *Chief Coach:* D. Bartholomew
Members: 170. *Leading Members:* Martin Bartholomew (19), Marcus Bennett (14), Marie Benstead (16), Keith Brown (10), Andrew Greenacre (16), Nicola Harvey (15), Wendy Harvey (17), Rebecca Hines (18), Stephen Mitchell (26), Sacha Mullett (18), Gavin Peters (15), Scott Peters (12), Emma Pople (10), Shane Richardson (12), Vickie Richardson (16), Simon Sheldrick (9), Ellen Stock (12), Laura Tibble (9), Jonathan Watsham (10), Mike Watsham (42), Robert Watsham (12), Helen Watson (12), Naomi Webber (11), Philip Williams (15), Chris Wise (19).

HALESOWEN (Worcs) *Formed* 1963
Club Sec: Mrs P. Baynham, 27 Mount Street, Halesowen, B63 4NN. *Chief Coach:* T. Walker
Members: 400. *Leading Members:* Claire Baynham (13), Esme Bedford (11), Sarah Bowcott (12), Lisa Burras (15), Andrew Butler (14), Nikki Davis (18), David Doran (18), Mathew Doran (15), Stewart Downing (14), Steven Handley (13), Julie Hitchmough (15), Tracy Hitchmough (13), Carl Holloway (16), Ian James (24), Laura James (13), Guy Jameson (18), Neil Jones (19), Stuart Jones (16), Alison Kindon (17), Andrew Papworth (11), Peter Ramage (15), Judith Smart (15), Rachael Smith (13), Rebecca Smith (14), April Wicketts (11).

HALESWORTH & DISTRICT (Suffolk) *Formed* 1972
Club Sec: J. Weaver, 10 The Street, Wissett, Halesworth, Suffolk, H19 0JE. *Chief Coach:* T. Hales
Members: 200. *Leading Members:* Cathy Block (10), Claire Bushell (11), Lucy Cantwell (19), Marie Cantwell (14), Mark Denny (15), Vicky Fletcher (11), Zoe Foster (12), Adam Friday (13), Stacey Friday (10), Stephen Gardam (13), Paul George (12), Sally Hales (16), Darren Harris (15), Kate Monk (16), Angeline Page (13), Steven Page (17), James Read (14), Lawrence Sherwood (15), Kelly Stammers (13), Niqui Stammers (17), Wendy Stammers (11), Jane Weaver (14), Richard Weaver (12), Michael Welby (10), Rose Williams (16).

HANDSWORTH (Warwicks)

HANDSWORTH GRAMMAR SCHOOL OLD BOYS (Warwicks)

HARBORNE (Warwicks)

HAVERHILL (Suffolk) *Formed* 1931
Club Sec: Mrs B. Hartshorn, 8 Coltsfoot Close, Wickhambrook, Newmarket. *Chief Coach:* A. Lee
Members: 300. *Leading Members:* Darryl Alexander (19), Elaine Archer (17), Dawn Baldry (13), Melanie Berry (19), Steven Butler (13), Lisa Clark (19), Denise Farrant (16), Mark Harding (14), Sarah Hartshorn (14), Julian Lee (19), Spenser Lee (16), John McKenny (14), Thomas McKenny (16), Clare Martin (14), Mark Osterritter (17), David Pipe (15), Sarah Saward (16), Dawn Sewell (15), Joanna Smith (13), Charlotte Squire (17), Paul Squire (17), Mark Tuhill (15), Helen Whitcombe (13), Alison Woodley (21).

HEANOR (Derbys)

HEATH TOWN (Staffs) *Formed* 1933
Club Sec: Mrs S. Green, 20 Raymond Gardens, Wednesfield, WV11 3JH. *Chief Coach:* J. Barber
Members: 250. *Leading Members:* Jacqueline Emery (10), Sean Grundy (16), Nicholas Icke (11), Stephen Jarvis (15), Jane Lester (16), Sandra Lester (21), Andrea Morris (13), Jason Morris (18), Elizabeth Myers (11), Stephen Newell (16), Lisa Parton (11), Claire Perry (12), Nicola Pitt (14), Sharon Pugh (13), Alison Sutcliffe (17), Sally Sutcliffe (15), Claire Turner (15), Andrew Welsh (15), Richard Welsh (10), Jonathan Williams (16).

HEATH TOWN WPC (Staffs)
Club Sec: P. Ferguson, Beckbury Stores, Beckbury, Shifnal, Shropshire.

HELLESDON SEAGULL SYNCHRO (Norfolk)

HENLOW PENGUINS (Beds)
Formed 1975

Club Sec: Mrs J. Spencer, 33 Vicarage Close, Langford, Beds.   *Chief Coach:* P. Cramer
Members: 36. *Leading Members:* Nicholas Cage (11), Sharron Cage (14), Brodie Clement (13), Marcus Clement (11), Emily Collis (12), Nicola Collis (9), Abigale Davies (12), Paul Gravell (12), Alison Gudgin (10), Claire Gudgin (14), Mark Jaggard (15), Nicola Jaggard (10), Richard James (15), Kathy Jones (12), Claire Knightley (14), Christopher Lawrence (15), Richard Lawrence (13), Alison Morse (12), Christopher Peacock (12), Jason Scoot (12), Julia Sellers (14), Claire Spencer (15), Steven Spencer (13), Anne-Marie Wills (15), Paul Wrench (9).

HEREFORD DOLPHINS WPC (Derbys)

HIBERNIA (Staffs)

HIGHLEY & DISTRICT (Shropshire)

HINCKLEY (Leics)

HOPE VALLEY (Derbys)

HORNCASTLE OTTERS (Lincs)

HOUGHTON REGIS (Beds)
Formed 1977

Club Sec: H. Wenman, 96 Manor Road, Barton le Clay, MK45 4NS.   *Chief Coach:* J. Honey
Members: 95. *Leading Members:* Scott Addy (11), Helen Arthur (10), Graham Behtley (14), Michael Bishop (13), Neil Blain (8), Nina Blain (10), Jenny Briggs (9), Sally Briggs (9), Rachel Buxton (17), Gareth Clancy (11), Jacky Clarke (17), Vanessa Clarke (15), Joanne Currant (15), Andrew Delaney (12), Kevin Delaney (9), Nick Durrans (11), Sean Exall (11), Jane Fisher (17), Mandy Ford (16), Joanne Hearn (13), Lisa Hearn (10), David Hicks (10), Elaine Honey (17), Amy Kever (8), Michelle Kever (9).

HUCKNALL & LINBY WELFARE (Notts)

HUNSTANTON SEAGULLS (Norfolk)
Formed 1920

Club Sec: Mrs A.J. Dawson, 1 Lincoln Street, Hunstanton, Norfolk, PE36 6AS.   *Chief Coach:* S. Peacock
Members: 250.

HUNTINGDON (Cambs)

ILKESTON (Derbys)
Formed 1972

Club Sec: Mrs S. Reeve, 52 Lower Stanton Road, Ilkeston, DE7 4LN.   *Chief Coach:* Mrs E. Dent-Smith
Members: 300. *Leading Members:* Angela Beagley (11), Allison Bednall (14), Clair Boam (15), Allison Carter (15), Racheal Chambers (15), Richard Clarke (15), Adam Coleman (12), Neil Cox (15), Racheal Edwards (16), Charlotte Ellis (16), Damon Ellis (13), Scott Finney (11), Adrian Gilcott (16), Nathan Gilcott (13), Kelly Grainger (13), Mark Grainger (17), Mark Hardy (14), Louisa King (16), Steven Riley (16), Dean Sherwin (18), Julie Sisson (11), Mark Smith (18), Peter Stephenson (12), Brian Turnbull (24), Emma Walker (15), Darren Young (15).

IMMINGHAM PILGRIMS (Lincs)

IPSWICH (Suffolk)
Formed 1884

Club Sec: Mrs R. Noller, 428 Norwich Road, Ipswich, Suffolk, IP1 5DU.   *Chief Coach:* D. Champion
Members: 463. *Leading Members:* Tim Ashwell (17), Hayley Barbour (13), Adam Beany (10), Ian Carr (10), Rachel Cooke (13), Julien Crewe (14), Verity Cutting (13), Sally Eade (15), Adam Fairbrother (10), Jane Gooch (15), Marie Gosling (15), Gemma Green (12), Rachel Hamilton (18), Isabelle Kenning (11), Paul Laws (15), Brett Lumis (10), Ann Minter (12), Claire Parker (17), Karen Pickering (17), Simon Robinson (11), Neil Studd (13), Shan Wassermeyer (13), Barry Watchman (12), Catherine White (11), Adam Whitely (11).

IPSWICH & DISTRICT HANDICAPPED PERSONS (Suffolk)
Formed 1964

Club Sec: Miss I. Pratt, 50 York Crescent, Claydon, Ipswich, IP6 0DR.   *Chief Coach:* Mrs P. Smith
Members: 190.

JUNCTION TEN (Staffs)
Formed 1983

Club Sec: Mrs G.M. Banks, 10 Arley Grove, Penn, Wolverhampton, WV4 4QX.   *Chief Coach:* A. Robinson
Members: 46. *Leading Members:* Corrina Banks (9), Victoria Banks (12), Joanne Brown (10), Shaun Brown (9), Craig Coley (10), Ross Coley (8), Richard Edge (9), Sally Evans (13), Richard Fletcher (12), Louise Handley (13), Claire Harris (11), Debbie Harris (9), Joanne Harris (7), Emma Jukes (8), Christopher Lane (11), Gavin Lewis (11), Craig Lockley (10), Sarah Lyons (11), Danielle Perkins (9), Robert Risker (10), Stuart Slater (9), Richard Smith (9), Carl Stephenson (12), Gareth Williams (9).

KENILWORTH (Warwicks)

KETTERING (Northants)
Formed 1916

Club Sec: Mrs M. Chaucer, 3 St Mary's Road, Kettering, Northants.   *Chief Coach:* J. Freeman
Members: 193. *Leading Members:* K. Boddington (26), W. Chalker (14), J. Crick (12), E. de Schoolmeester (14), M. de Schoolmeester (16), C. Dunmore (18), T. Evans (17), A. Freeman (14), S. Freeman (12), A. Gaggini (14), J. Gaggini (16), N. Gaggini (19), K. Grove (13), C. Hamilton (17), S. Harris (20), A. Hyde (13), C. Labrum (14), S. Moniget (22), E. Morley (13), J. Oldfield (12), G. Pateman (18), T. Pateman (16), J. Prior (13), L. Radwell (15), N. Stockham (14).

KIDDERMINSTER (Worcs)   *Formed* 1900
Club Sec: Mrs G. Bullingham, 12 Hardy Avenue, Kidderminster, DY10 3QY.   *Chief Coach:* R. Chapman
Members: 160. *Leading Members:* Jason Atkin (19), Helen Babb (19), Mathew Bishop (11), Louise
Bourne (11), Claire Bullingham (12), Mark Bullingham (14), Andrew Chapman (26), James Chapman (23),
Oliver Cox (13), Richard Cutler (10), Rachel Gore (21), Amanda Harrington (19), Christopher Holmes
(18), David Markham (13), Belinda Pengelly (12), Laura Phillips (11), David Price (13), Richard Vaux (14),
Robert Waite (14), Paul Wear (18), Claire Weston (17), Sarah Weston (14), Anabel Wilson (10), Claire
Winmill (13).

KIDLINGTON & GOSFORD (Oxford & North Bucks)   *Formed* 1974
Club Sec: Mrs R.M. Burch, 34 Temple Street, Oxford, OX4 1JS.   *Chief Coach:* M. Edwards
Members: 200.

KIMBERLEY (Notts)

KINETON & DISTRICT (Warwicks)

KINGSBURY AQUARIUS (Warwicks)   *Formed* 1974
Club Sec: Mrs J.E. Gatland, 24 Kingsbury Road, Curdworth, B76 9EP.   *Chief Coach:* Mrs J.E. Gatland
Leading Members: Charlotte Baldry (11), Kevin Barton (12), Paul Chadwick (14), Andrew Claridge (13),
Edwin Claridge (10), Dylan Collins (15), Luke Collins (11), Marc Davis (17), Christopher Ellis, Katie Foist
(14), Jayne Forgham (15), Ann Freeman (18), Deb Gatland (21), Amanda Gill (14), Alison Hill (16),
Matthew Hill (12), Siôn Hill (15), Clare Hubbard (15), Kathryn Hubbard (11), Emma Husselbee (15),
Duncan Niblett (11), Emma Rose (16), Gemma Smith (13), Colin Ward (17), Darrel Young (18).

KINGS HEATH (Warwicks)

KING'S LYNN (Norfolk)   *Formed* 1901
Club Sec: Mrs P. Cesar, 40 Woodland Gardens, North Wootton, Norfolk, PE30 3PX.
Members: 160. *Leading Members:* Jonathan Booty (13), Sally Boswell (16), William Cesar (11), Neil
Clarke (15), Paula Clarke (17), James Crussell (13), Mark Crussell (11), Jody Cundy (11), Robert Dyke
(12), Paul Ellen (17), Karen Emmerson (15), Joanna Ford (13), Jonathan Gray (17), Justin Gray (13),
Emma Hogson (14), Mark Hornigold (15), Helen Leman (13), Carl Peach (11), Jason Shaw (17), Helga
Simons (11), Kristina Simons (16), Donna Simpson (16), Debbie Skitt (15), Karen Smith (13), Karen
Sparks (11), Alexandra Taylor (9).

KING'S LYNN GLADIATORS (Norfolk)

KINGS SCHOOL WPC (Lincs)

KINGTON DOLPHINS (Derbys)

KNIGHTON FIELDS (Leics)   *Formed* 1910
Club Sec: Mrs B.C. Bush, 109 Pendlebury Drive, Leicester, LE2 6GT.   *Chief Coach:* G. Benford
Members: 200. *Leading Members:* Julian Allen (10), Paul Aucott (12), Simon Aucott (16), Joanne Baker
(18), Julie Beadnall (15), Claire Bradshaw (13), David Clarke (14), Stephen Fryett (20), Alastair Gilbert
(15), Liz Green (19), Luke Hammond (17), Nicola Heather (10), Stephen Heather (12), Samantha Keating
(9), Nicola Mason (18), Ian Robinson (22), Ian Seaton(12), Stuart Sharp (11), Helen Smith (13), Tara
Whitehead (9), Paul Willoughby (10).

LEAMINGTON SPA (Warwicks)   *Formed* 1885
Club Sec: Mrs H. Jelfs, 29 Nightingale Lane, Beechwood Gardens, Coventry.   *Chief Coach:* J. Cotterill
Members: 556. *Leading Members:* Sophie Anderson (15), Tim Anderson (13), Paul England, Clare Evison
(15), Christopher Good (10), Samantha Good (13), Louise Gould (16), Faye Hickman (14), Aran Jackson
(11), Simon Malka (10), Stewart Nunn, Matthew Parker (10), Clare Raynor (13), Kelly Sanders (13), Lucy
Sanders (11), Tamsin Slack (12), Matthew Smith (11), Victoria Smith (13), Penny Storrie (15), Louise
Thing (12), Louise Thomas (16), Philip Valley (13), Lena Walsgrove (15), Keith Woodhead (16), Lynn
Woodhead (11).

LEDBURY & DISTRICT (Derbys)   *Formed* 1976
Club Sec: M. Forshaw, 25 Shepherds Close, Ledbury, Herefordshire.   *Chief Coach:* A.Loveitt
Members: 170. *Leading Members:* Craig Ahern (18), Mark Davies (12), Kerrie Douglas (13), Maxine
Edwards (11), Ian Forshaw (12), Jenny Forshaw (15), James Gardner (15), Ceri Griffiths (15), Simon
Hewitt (11), Kate Jones (12), Luke Jones (14), Philippa Jones (18), Douglas Kirkpatrick (14), Andrew
Meredith (14), Lee Meredith (11), Emma Moore (13), Katherine Moore (12), Charlotte Newey (14),
Rachael Newey (17), James O'Donnell (16), Mark Robinson (15), Catherine Slater (13), Jonathan Slater
(14), Jason Snape (19), Sian Thomas (14).

LEICESTER (Leics)   *Formed* 1881
Club Sec: Mrs P.A. Everett, 14 Haybrooke Road, Silbey, Leics, LE12 7QR.
Members: 200. *Leading Members:* Richard Bailey (13), Ruth Edwards (19), Clare Evans (12), Tara Evatt
(16), Sharon Everett (22), Steven Everett (13), Lynne Fenton (12), Mark Fletcher (20), Louise Footitt (15),
Kathryn Jarvis (18), Alison Jones (18), Debbie Lee (14), Malcolm McArthur (12), Amanda Mansfield (15),
Troy Muddimer (16), Jean Preston (17), Christopher Shepherd (11), Paul Shepherd (15), Paul Smith (11),

Claire Stubley (14), Christopher Talbot (21), Alistair Taylor (15), Daniel Walley (14), Jonathan Walthoe (14), Philip Young (18).

LEICESTER DC (Leics)

LEICESTER NEPTUNE (Leics)

LEICESTER PENGUINS (Leics) Formed 1960
Club Sec: Mrs R. Kellett, 132 Victoria Park Road, Leicester, LE2 1XD.
Members: 380. Leading Members: Joanna Baines (18), Lisa Baxter (19), Robert Bishop (22), Karen Brewin (14), Richard Brewin (12), Stuart Carr (12), Caroline Cleaver (14), Jo Ann Collins (14), John Crowcroft (14), Susan Davis (15), Holly Evans (14), David Goadby (20), Philip Godfrey (20), Joanne Hutchinson (15), Luke Jacobs (16), Martin Knifton (16), Julie Lehane (13), Melanie Lister (16), Christopher Pears (15), Allison Peasgood (16), Michael Robilliard (14), Andrew Stockton (19), Katie Vines (13), Gareth Wilson (16), David Wright (16).

LEICESTER SYNCHRO (Leics) Formed 1970
Club Sec: Mrs A.W. Clark, 4 Grange Drive, Grange Park, Burbage, Leics. Chief Coach: Mrs A.W. Clark
Members: 14. Leading Members: Rachel Brant (14), Tracey Flynn (14), Karyn Henson (18), Marissa Henson (16), Andrea Hunt (18), Melanie Shilton (15), Dawn Shipway (16), Cassandra Soulsby (13), Helen Tyler (18).

LEIGHTON BUZZARD (Beds) Formed 1923
Club Sec: Mrs C. Simmonds, 8 Hydrus Drive, Leighton Buzzard, Beds. Chief Coach: J. Bellis
Leading Members: Richard Anniss (13), Nicola Ayers (18), Matthew Blades (14), Jonathan Brown (23), Simon Calvert (24), Lesley Campbell (22), Michael Cheval (14), Paul Cheval (17), William Day (14), Jenny Dilley (16), Christine Edwards (13), Debbie Francis (12), Julie Graham (18), Kirsty Gudgeon (15), Anna Hewitt (16), Christopher Howell (13), Hannah Kimble (12), Annette Miles (11), Matthew Minor (14), Paul Munford (15), Lee Trabucchi (12), Zoe Trabucchi (15), Justin Vroone (19), Melanie Wells (14), Ruth Werner (14).

LEOMINSTER KINGFISHER (Derbys)

LEWSEY CENTRE (Beds) Formed 1977
Club Sec: Mrs P. Harrington, 79 Macaulay Road, Luton, Beds, LU4 0LP. Chief Coach: Mrs P. Harrington
Members: 42. Leading Members: Tracey Edwards (18), Jane Foster (16), Paul Foster (19), Kelvin Freemantle (14), Derrick Gunnel (61), Pauline Harrington (42), Teresa Harrington (13), Simon Lewis (13), Victoria Lewis (10), Paul McNamara (11), Ian Murray (31), Marion Peters (42), Alan Powell (42), Paul Stanley (11), Bill Ward (43).

LICHFIELD (Staffs) Formed 1968
Club Sec: Mrs C. Hickinbotham, 5 Wyrley Close, Lichfield, Staffs, WS14 9DA. Chief Coach: R. Johnson
Members: 150. Leading Members: Katie Eaves (12), Francine Hamilton (16), Jane Hickinbotham (15), Sarah Holgate (13), James Hunt (13), Esther Jennings (12), Alastair Johnson (14), Simon Longstaff (28), Steven McCausland (13), Ailsa McDonald (16), Emma McLeod (15), Matthew Minton (12), Carla Morgan (10), Ian Morgan (18), Matthew Morgan (16), Simon Morgan (13), Martin Plant (14), Mala Rajput (13), Renu Rajput (12), Gavin Stockton (11), Andrew Stonehouse (15), Joanna Tipper (15), David Turner (16), Abby Wakeling (14), Stephanie Wilkins (11).

LINCOLN (Lincs) Formed 1901
Club Sec: A. Butler, 84 Abbey Road, Baroney, Lincoln, LN3 5XD.
Members: 220.

LINCOLN IMPS DC (Lincs)

LINCOLN LADIES (Lincs) Formed 1940
Club Sec: Mrs M.E. Ellis, "Mayfair", Lincoln Road, Nettleham, Lincoln. Club Coaches: Mrs A. Carveth, Mrs M. Ellis, Mrs E. Moon
Members: 111.

LINCOLN VULCANS (Lincs) Formed 1973
Club Sec: J.D. Marsh, "Oakapple", Church Lane, Owmby by Spital, Lincoln, LN2 3HN.
Chief Coaches: G. Jeffries, M. Vickers
Members: 200. Leading Members: Katie Allen (11), Chris Beck (17), Anna Bell (11), Nigel Burley (11), Helen Chaplin (10), Paul Chaplin (13), Heather Cousins (16), Rachel Critchley (12), Karen Derry (13), Nick Gant (13), Janet Hairsine (12), Ashley Harrison (21), Kerry Hogarth (16), Stuart Horsley (17), Nicola Jeffries (17), Lizzie Jenns (12), James King (15), Stuart Patch (16), Kerrie Pells (17), Vicki Rogers (12), Caroline Sewell (16), Ian Smith (17), James Toyne (11), Clare Turton (15), Joanne Ward (16).

LINGS WPC (Northants) Formed 1983
Club Sec: D.P. Billingham, 5 Wantage Close, Hackleton, Northants, NN7 2AG. Chief Coach: F. Steele
Members: 13. Leading Members: Duncan Billingham, Keith Bishop, Alan Curtis, Geoff Davies, Kevin Dewhay, Tony Greene, Chris Hale, Phil Harris-Ward, Paul Johnson, Dan Kightley, Martin Mansell, Fred Steele.

LINSLADE CRUSADERS (Beds) *Formed* 1982
Club Sec: Mrs P. Swaithes, 27 Linwood Grove, Leighton Buzzard, Beds, LU7 8RP.
Chief Coaches: M. Sedgwick, P. Swaithes
Members: 240. *Leading Members:* Robert Bird (14), Mark Chambers (13), Cara Chastney (13), Claire Compton (10), Timothy Ewart (11), Darren Goodyear (13), Paul Griffin-Jorgensen (15), Julie Harris (14), Miles Hill (10), Anthony Jessup (11), David Jessup (9), Kerry Jones (9), Martin Jones (11), Nichola Jones (13), Sarah Jones (9), James Knights (13), Simon Patterson (9), Andrew Phillips (12), Edward Robinson (16), Michaela Solesbury (10), Darryl Swaithes (17), Gayle Swaithes (12), Simon Teste (8), Natasha Watson (11), Helen Whatmore (9).

LODDON WHITE DOLPHIN (Norfolk)

LONG EATON (Derbys)

LONG STRATTON (Norfolk)

LOUGHBOROUGH COLLEGES (Leics)

LOUGHBOROUGH TOWN (Leics)

LOUTH (Lincs)

LOWESTOFT (Suffolk) *Formed* 1903
Club Sec: D. Kemp, 52 Gunton Drive, Lowestoft. *Chief Coach:* B. Rivett
Members: 200. *Leading Members:* Barry Brooks (17), Julie Brooks (20), Lisa Cone (14), Ian Edwards (13), Michelle Elliston (11), Paul Freear (15), Rachel Freear (13), Neil Godbold (17), Sarah Godbold (10), Matthew Haltell (12), Hannah Kemball-Cook (13), Stephen Kemball-Cook (15), Simon Muirhead (10), Sarah Newell (16), Mark Newnham (20), Kris Osborne (10), Jodie Pike (11), Catherine Poulter (17), Katrina Rayner (13), Samantha Rayner (15), Mark Schroder (14), Paul Walpole (12), Stephen Waters (13), Julie West (16).

LUCAS (Warwicks) *Formed* 1927
Club Sec: Mrs A. Turner, 109 Neville Road, Shirley, Solihull, B90 2QX. *Chief Coach:* V. Tonks
Members: 65. *Leading Members:* Naomi Baker (12), Rachall Baker (14), Paul Beech (24), Mark Bollard (12), Samantha Bollard (9), Steven Cheshire (22), Sophia Cubello (8), Philip Day (36), Clare Gasby (10), Ian Griffiths (19), Louise Hughes (12), John Ison (20), Ben King (11), Dan King (9), Kirsty Morrison (9), Rachael Parr (9), Simon Peckover (15), Kay Reid (12), Victoria Reid (11), Mark Robinson (13), Joanne Skellum (12), Mark Skellum (13), Glen Turner (15), Faye Williams (9).

LUDLOW DOLPHINS (Shropshire)
Club Sec: N. Morse, Burf House, Abdon, Shropshire, SY7 9HU. *Chief Coach:* P. Morris
Members: 50.

LUTON (Beds)
Club Sec: Mrs S.A. Carter, 232 Stockingstone Road, Luton, Beds, LU2 7DG. *Chief Coach:* D.R. Williams
Members: 357. *Leading Members:* Gary Ale (13), Joanna Carter (16), Sarah Chew (12), Paula Dean (12), Joanne Drewitt (16), Mathew Harnham (14), David Hill (16), Stuart Houlten (16), Christian Lapihuska (15), Joanne Lee (13), Simon Lewis (14), Ryan Perry (15), Spencer Prichard (12), Michael Pullen (18), Andrew Slough (12), Sonia Spearing (16), Andrew Steel (19).

LUTON KINGFISHER SYNCHRO & DC (Beds) *Formed* 1963
Club Sec: J.F. Pollard, 4 Saxtead Close, Luton, Beds, LU2 9SQ.
Members: 250.

LUTTERWORTH & DISTRICT (Leics)

MALVERN (Worcs)

MANSFIELD (Notts) *Formed* 1905
Club Sec: G.C. Flint, 49 Greendale Avenue, Edwinstowe, Notts.
Members: 200. *Leading Members:* Lee Adams (17), Zoe Anderson (16), Lisa Atkins (19), Mark Atkins (16), Melanie Boot (14), Clive Brookes (15), Alex Flint (16), Tristan Formon (17), Angela Holmes (19), Paul Holmes (17), Paul Hopkinson (15), Sally Kemp (14), Alison Lewis (14), Jonathan Mitchell (16), Robert Mitchell (18), Rebecca Ram (16), Andrew Roe (21), Stephen Roe (14), Peter Sabin (15), Sarah Sabin (18), Nicola Steudel (18), Sue Train (16), Claire Wiffen (16), Marie Wigley (16), Wayne Wigley (18).

MANSFIELD & DISTRICT DISABLED (Notts)
Club Sec: Mrs E.N. Peat, 35 Yew Tree Avenue, Forest Town, Mansfield, NG19 0JF.

MARCH MARLINS (Cambs) *Formed* 1965
Club Sec: Mrs J. Hill, 8 The Greys, March, Cambs. *Chief Coach:* B. Butler
Members: 150. *Leading Members:* Karlinda Andrew (17), Anna Baker (12), Christopher Butler (10), Jonathan Butler (13), Ian Darrington (12), Katie Darrington (11), Caroline Hill (11), Katie Hill (13), Keith Jarman (13), Matthew Jarman (15), Isla McCraig (11), Darren Mott (10), Paul Newton (11), Richard Nightingale (13), Wayne Palmer (13), James Parr (10), Susan Peat (18), Katy Richards (14), Simon Rooke (17), Stephen Rooke (16), Stuart Sawyer (10), Lara Stockbridge, Melanie Trayford (13), Sadie Wales (11), Shaun Wright (21).

MARINA DISABLED GREAT YARMOUTH (Norfolk)
Club Sec: Mrs P. Powley, 48 Crosstead, Great Yarmouth, Norfolk, NR30 4AP.

MARKET DRAYTON & DISTRICT (Shropshire) *Formed* 1972
Club Sec: Mrs V. Taylor, 13 Caernarvon Close, Market Drayton. *Chief Coach:* D. Taylor
Members: 200.

MARKET HARBOROUGH (Leics) *Formed* 1988
Club Sec: Mrs V. Dunton, 121 Western Avenue, Market Harborough, Leics. *Chief Coach:* I. Johnson
Members: 300. *Leading Members:* Nicola Avins (17), Ian Bowles (12), Lydia Broome (11), Jessica Bulley (11), Edward Burbridge (11), Zoe Coles (13), Carl Cook (19), Alison Dodd (11), Katherine Dodd (17), James Dunton (14), Rebecca Foxon (12), Steven Foxon (12), Natalie Gerard (17), Michelle Grainger (11), Alison Haynes (13), Simon Lewis (13), Nicholas Lowe (18), Steven Perry (13), Michelle Peterson (12), Steven Peterson (14), Jaime Reed (12), David Robinson (21), Peter Swaine (11), Maria Szakatics (15), Lloyd Woodhouse (15), Peta Woodhouse (17).

MATLOCK & DISTRICT (Derbys) *Formed* 1938
Club Sec: I. Bowler, "Inglenook", Four Lane Ends, Wingfield Road, Oakerthorpe, Derbys.
Chief Coaches: D. Bannister, A. Hitchcock
Members: 200. *Leading Members:* Matthew Allison (11), Robert Allison (17), Esther Boadle (15), Elaine Bowler (19), Martin Cantrill (17), Anna Dewey (12), Claire Ellis (13), Matthew Ellis (15), Alexander Finch (11), Madelaine Greaves (9), Rachel Harvey (14), Caroline Heald (12), Colin Hitchcock (17), Julie Hitchcock (14), Jackie Jarvis (14), James Knowles (15), Lisa Knowles (16), David Manning (13), David Richardson (13), Caroline Salmons (13), Ian Shepherd (15), Samantha Starbuck (11), Kirsty Starkey (14), Richard Taylor (17), Mark Warman (13).

MATLOCK WPC (Derbys)

MAXWELL, AYLESBURY (Oxford & North Bucks) *Formed* 1979
Club Sec: W. Ashton, Aylesbury Vale District Council, The Mall, Friars Square, Aylesbury.
Chief Coach: M. Wakely
Members: 300. *Leading Members:* Georgina Benham (16), Gary Binfield (22), Lucy Brailey (12), Sarah Brailey (14), Robin Brew (27), John Brown (22), Alexandra Buddle (13), Joanne Buddle (15), Julian Chappell (22), Stephen Chappell (19), David Collins (16), Craig Corbett (19), Jessica Cotton (12), Richard Every (19), Chris Hendren (17), Rhona Jack (14), Simon Kennady (14), Gavin Morgan (12), Natalie Ping (13), Deborah Powell (15), Loren Snelson (16), Richard Stevens (12), Stuart White (14), Andy Williams (13), Mark Williams (15).

MELTON MOWBRAY (Leics) *Formed* 1964
Club Sec: R. Lee, 31 Willcox Drive, Melton Mowbray. *Chief Coach:* T. Wilde
Members: 210.

MILDENHALL & DISTRICT SHARKS (Suffolk) *Formed* 1973
Club Sec: Mrs J. Brackenbury, 40 Raven Close, Mildenhall, IP28 7LF. *Chief Coach:* Mrs L. Franklin
Members: 160. *Leading Members:* Tiernan Boland (11), Simon Brackenbury (12), Conrad Burgess (16), Nathan Burgess (14), Naomi Cocksedge (13), Stephen Dick (10), David Edwards (15), Louisa Edwards (13), Stuart Gee (14), Marcus Hamill (19), Lynne Jones (12), Paul Leonard (15), Alex Logan (14), Rebecca Logan (16), Alan Martin (16), Katie Minns (14), Katie Pearson (17), Daniel Reynolds (10), Karen Robinson (15), John Rowell (12), Elizabeth Sangster (13), Julie Sharp (16), Ethan White (13), Joshua White (14), Michelle Workman (17).

MODERNIANS (Beds) *Formed* 1965
Club Sec: Mrs C.M. Wilson, 124 Goldington Road, Bedford. *Chief Coach:* C. Wilson
Members: 700. *Leading Members:* Sharon Bloss (14), Dave Cartledge (28), Karen Cox (15), Alison Day (18), Amanda Day (15), Neil French (16), Angela Graystone (24), Ian Graystone (26), Jo Irons (15), Anita King (17), Nicky King (15), Sarah King (14), Ian Millard (16), Lucy Miller (14), Claire Mortlock (16), Darren O'Rourke (18), Kyran Parker (19), Stephen Perugi (18), Philip Pope (15), Mark Richardson (16), Lorna Sainsbury (15), Marcel Scholten (22), Neil Whitehorn (15), Anne Wilson (27), Helen Wilson (28).

MUSKHAM (Notts)

NECHELLS (Warwicks)

NENE WOMEN'S WPC (Northants)

NETTLEHAM (Lincs) *Formed* 1970
Club Sec: K.R. Bennett, 9 Washdyke Lane, Nettleham, Lincs, LN2 2PT. *Chief Coach:* Mrs M. Herrick
Members: 150.

NEWARK (Notts) *Formed* 1935
Club Sec: R.S. Bolus, 38 Orchard Way, Balderton, Newark, Notts, NG24 3LU. *Chief Coach:* T. Mallender
Members: 340. *Leading Members:* Anthony Bates (16), Cathrine Bates (11), Richard Birch, Vicky Birch (11), Carl Faisey (16), Adrian Gibson (18), Simeon Hansard (12), Steven Hansard (18), Nichola Hearn (11), Jemma Hendley (16), Vannessa Hunt (11), Jamie Kettleborough (22), Edward Lawrence (10), Jane Lawrence (12), James Mayle (14), Nichola Poulton (14), Emberson Roe (12), Stephanie Roe (13),

Amanda Scott (13), Ross Skinner (11), Ben Thompson (12), Damien van Alderwesen (16), Mathew van Alderwesen (15), Dawn Whitehead (20), Julie Wing (15).

NEWMARKET (Suffolk)
Formed 1918
Club Sec: Mrs I. Cockerton, 95 St Philips Road, Newmarket, Suffolk, CB8 0ES. *Chief Coach:* T. Camplin
Members: 127. *Leading Members:* David Beddington (14), Michelle Broadhead (12), Sarah Broadhead (9), Laura Camplin (15), Alison Chapman (13), Carrie Cockerton (9), Jason Collins, John Collins, Clare Cowling (14), Sarah Cowling (12), Joanne Dyson (10), Anthony Hall (13), Alex King (10), Luke King (13), Keir Levell (15), Zena Levell, Nicola Lockwood (13), Stuart McClean (10), Garry Marshall (10), Alex Martin (14), James Martin (11), Jenny Parr (12), Paul Shaw (12), Elizabeth Spurling (8), Ben Topp (10).

NEWMARKET SYNCHRONETTES (Suffolk)

NEWPORT & DISTRICT (Shropshire)
Formed 1969
Club Sec: Mrs M. Rudd, 8 Vineyard Road, Newport, Shropshire, TF10 7DA. *Chief Coach:* Mrs S. Churm
Members: 143.

NEWPORT & WREKIN DISTRICT SYNCHRO (Shropshire)
Formed 1983
Club Sec: Mrs J. Jones, 3 Oaklands Drive, Trench, Telford, Shropshire. *Chief Coach:* P. Hurdley
Members: 60. *Leading Members:* Emma Chiva (10), Amanda Dalby (12), Victoria Doran (10), Colette Dutton (12), Louise Dutton (10), Nicola Dyson (12), Tracey Fielding (10), Janine Fletcher (15), Helen Greenwood (12), Louise Greenwood (8), Karen Handley (11), Abigail Hurdley (11), Suzanna Hurdley (8), Catherine Kiernan (10), Heather Lane (11), Laura Morgan (10), Johanna Phelps (10), Karen Pocock (8), Maria Stamp (12), Suzanne Stamp (10), Claire Turner (10), Katy Vickers (11), Davinnia Wickstead (11), Karen Wright (15), Vicky Yates (14).

NEWPORT PAGNELL (Oxford & North Bucks)
Formed 1890
Club Sec: Mrs P. Mount, 68 Annesley Road, Newport Pagnell, Bucks. *Chief Coach:* D. Jones
Members: 220. *Leading Members:* Nicholas Blake (17), Anthony Forster (16), Michael Hackett (14), Robin Hackett (12), Andrew Hall (12), Gareth Jones (16), Christopher Larr (16), Lewis Maulding (12), Naomi May (14), Nyree May (16), Justin Mount (16), Rebecca Mount (13), Carol Ann Neale (14), Nigel Oxtoby (15), Ross Oxtoby (12), Clare Paybody (14), Victoria Pike (15), Domonic Pullman (15), Alison Reece (13), Helen Reece (16), Jennifer Robertson (16), Stuart Robertson (13), Clare Slessor (13), Jane Smith (17), Mathew Wooton (13).

NEXUS (Northants)
Formed 1982
Club Sec: Mrs E.M. Grahame-Wright, 68 Thrapston Road, Finedon. *Chief Coach:* K. Boddington
Members: 45. *Leading Members:* Andrew Avery (11), Kevin Boddington (25), Martin Cochrane (14), Lucy Crane (15), Marie Dunkley (12), Stuart Gannon (20), Gemma Grahame-Wright (13), Claire Harris (16), Hayley Kennedy (13), Daniel Luke (13), Jason Luke (12), Andrew McDougall (14), Mark McInulty (12), Craig Mills (16), Gary Mlls (14), Caroline Moore (14), Sarah Noble (15), Mark Northen (11), Lisa Pickersgill (16), Richard Smith (12), Robert Starkey (14), Jackie Thompson (20), David Webster (13), Gary Wilkinson (14), Paul Wilkinson (12).

NORTHAMPTON (Northants)
Formed 1971
Club Sec: M.J. Nicholson, 18 Woodland Avenue, Overstone, Northants, NN6 0AJ. *Chief Coach:* D. Day
Members: 719. *Leading Members:* Anne Marie Adkinson (15), Darren Coates (17), Mark Elvy (17), Martin Flowers (23), Claire Harris (16), Shellie Harrison (22), Richard Jewitt (13), Maria Kelly (17), Nina McCrossan (13), Tim McCrossan (13), John Maher (18), Grant Mayhook (15), Hannah Middleton (11), Rachel Newall (14), Sally Ann Nicholson (17), Sarah Noble (15), Julie Prince (13), Alex Pygott (15), Joanna Reed (13), Matthew Small (15), Daniel Stanbury (11), Sarah Thompson (14), Duncan Timbs (11), Alex Wray (12).

NORTH BEDFORD DC (Beds)
Formed 1978
Club Sec: Mrs L. Carter, 4 Tithe Barn Road, Wootton, Bedford. *Chief Coach:* Mrs D. Whitworth
Members: 28. *Leading Members:* Gary Canzano (6), Andrew Carter (11), Dawn Carter (13), Natalie Devereux (13), Elizabeth Evans (12), Natalie Farr (13), Nique Gipson (12), Louise Haddon (12), Philip Haddon (8), Bethan Hopewell (12), Ceri Hopewell (14), Jamie Hughes (10), Hannah Josty (11), Vicki Kent (12), Sarah King (14), Claire Mascello (11), Kirstin O'Connor (13), Lewis O'Connor (9), Paula Osborne (15), Katie Parkin (11), Rebecca Parkin (10), Bethan Phillips (14), Henry Ransby (14), Vicky Roberts (12), Catherine Talbot (10).

NORTHFIELD (Warwics)

NORTHGATE BRIDGNORTH (Shropshire)
Formed 1977
Club Sec: Mrs S.E. Hopkins, 17 Paulbrook Road, Bridgnorth, Shropshire. *Chief Coach:* W. Davidson
Members: 182. *Leading Members:* Simon Ashworth, Laura Choppin, Antony Cleobury, Karen Darby, Rebecca Davidson, Mark Gibbons, Lucy Gould, Sharon Heighway, Jonathan Hives, David Holding, Simon Hooper, Nicola Jarman, Victoria Kite, Shaun Lyle, Darren McCloskey, Ian Marshall, Tom Newbrook, Ian Onions, Michael Owen, Rebecca Skan, Kevin Thomas, Victoria Thomas, Harriet Thompson, Edward Vernon, Jillian Waterworth.

NORTON (Warwicks)

NORWICH CENTRAL (Norfolk)
Formed 1966
Club Sec: S. Parker, 8 Latimer Road, Norwich, NR1 2RW.
Chief Coach: S. Parker
Members: 12.

NORWICH PENGUINS (Norfolk)
Formed 1930
Club Sec: P.R. Keen, 4 Horseshoe Close, New Costossoy, Norwich, NR5 0SF. *Chief Coach:* F. Kirby
Members: 1500. *Leading Members:* Anna Baker (18), Kate Berry (15), James Boags (15), Kerry Boucher (16), Rachel Carey (16), Paul Easter (26), Paul Edwards (16), Stewart Feek (14), Helen Gill (13), Zoe Harrison (14), Lucy Keen (12), David Luff (12), Beverley Marshall (13), Joseph Moor (13), Richard Moulson (20), Annie Rigby (12), Melissa Riseborough (12), Nick Rounce (14), Pamela Tate (15), Stewart Wells (15), Brian Woods (19), Aron Woamer (13).

NORWICH SWAN (Norfolk)
Formed 1880
Club Sec: Mrs C. Joy, "Sol Y Sombra", 66 Shakespeare Way, Taverham, Norwich. *Chief Coach:* J. Swift
Members: 1100. *Leading Members:* Heidi Banks (15), Sandra Banks (19), Kerry Bradfield (13), Neil Bradfield (15), Ben Bridgeman (14), Nicola Brown (14), James Chapman (12), Alison Clark (13), Graham Edmunds (21), Claire Hansen (16), Douglas Hudson (16), James Hudson (12), Russell Human (13), Richard Ireson (15), Clare Jarvis (18), Robert Joy (12), Wendy King (18), Leanne Knights (12), Simon Knox (15), Craig Lovatt (19), Sarah Miller (11), Kevin Postle (16), Paul Russell (17), William Thompson (14), Andrew Weston (21).

NOTTINGHAM (Notts)
Formed 1880
Club Sec: Mrs S. Birchmore, 11 Broadhurst Avenue, Nottingham, NG6 0HX. *Chief Coach:* R. Roberts
Members: 330. *Leading Members:* Simon Binnie (20), Claire Bowler (15), Tracey Cawthan (17), Susan Evans (11), Rachel Fox (12), Simon Hall (9), Paul Jackson (17), Alan Jones-Barlow (13), Lee Jukes (16), Jason Knight (19), Charlotte Littlewood (11), Samantha Littlewood (15), Michael Lockwood (11), Richard Lockwood (13), Hannah McLeod (16), Dawn Miller (15), Helen Readman (11), Keith Richardson (27), Chris Roberts (27), Gail Sansom (14), Daniel Sheldon-Smith (14), Kay Sheldon-Smith (12), Adrian Wakelin (15), Andrew Wyles (13), Melanie Young (20).

NOTTINGHAM & DISTRICT POST OFFICE (Notts)

NOTTINGHAM LEANDER (Notts)
Formed 1947
Club Sec: M. Waters-Marsh, 45 Walcote Drive, West Bridgford, Nottingham. *Chief Coach:* T. Holmes
Members: 350. *Leading Members:* P. Abell (25), R. Bennett (10), J. Buckley (13), Tim Evans (13), B. Ford (30), S. Fowler (16), K. Grange (14), M. Hanby (17), D. Harper (17), L. Hett (18), N. James (16), D. King (19), M. Kirk (16), H. Koban (16), G. Langham (13), T. Langham (13), A. Musson (15), J. Musson (13), R. Nicklins (16), M. Roe (16), H. Sanderson (20), J. Sheppard (15), K. Watson (14), C. Williams (14), C. Yeo (17).

NOTTINGHAM NORTHERN
Formed 1908
Club Sec: Mrs E. Mandeville, 7 Revesby Road, Woodthorpe, Nottingham, NG5 4LJ. *Chief Coach:* J. Tyler
Members: 280. *Leading Members:* Elizabeth Arnold (16), Jennifer Botterill (12), Rachel Bridger (15), Lindsay Godber (12), Philip Hardy (12), Suzanne Henderson (12), Maggie Hohman (33), Tim Reddish (32), Carl Rippon (14), Joanne Terry (16).

NOVA CENTURION (Notts)
Formed 1977
Club Sec: K. Heathcote, 9 Farm View, Ordsall, Retford, Notts, DN22 7UJ. *Chief Coach:* W. Furniss
Members: 100. *Leading Members:* Craig Alderson (15), Dean Anscombe (17), Rachel Bennet (19), Susan Buxton (17), Sarah Carley (17), Maria Donaghy (15), Helen Gorman (17), Glen Hall (16), Michael Hanby (17), Louise Hawkin (17), Carl Heathcote (17), Steven Hutchinson (15), Nicola James (16), James Kearney (17), Nicola Kennedy (20), Heidi Koban (16), Lisa Marchant (15), Alasdair Murdoch (18), Duncan Murdoch (15), Alec Musson (15), Simon Robinson (19), Heather Sanderson (20), Alasdair Skellern (20), Joanne Terry (16), Carl Yeo (17).

NUNEATON (Warwicks)
Formed 1890
Club Sec: J. Keeley, 4 Chelsea Close, Nuneaton, CV11 6ND. *Chief Coach:* T. Freeman
Members: 550. *Leading Members:* Cheryl Armstrong (16), Ian Armstrong (13), Dean Beasley (11), Stuart Coppock (13), Alex Dawson (12), Ian Dawson (10), Caroline Dyall (12), Dale Freeman (12), Greg Freeman (10), Claire Halls (13), Claire Handley (13), Emma James (11), Victoria McCormack (10), Edward Mowe (12), Kelly Paggett (10), Michael Pagget (12), Adam Reynold (15), Gregory Rowley (13), James Smith (16), Donna Taylor (11), James Taylor (13), Geoffy Terrell (11), Joanne Walton (13), Gregory Warren (12), Laura Wheeler (13).

NUNEATON & BEDWORTH SYNCHRO (Warwicks)

OADBY & WIGSTON (Leics)
Formed 1966
Club Sec: Mrs L. Kazakevics, 1 Hampton Close, The Meadows, Wigston. *Chief Coach:* M. Hodges
Members: 160. *Leading Members:* Rowan Arnot (12), Samantha Bott (16), Leon Bree (11), Simon Chamberlain (17), Louise Colebourne (11), Samantha Colebourne (12), Dale Copley (12), Sam Dearlove (12), Melanie Earnaker (16), Richard Earnaker (13), Carley Ferguson (11), Zoe Ferguson (13), Zoe Francis (13), Daniel Frost (13), Ian Hodges (17), Mark Hodges (14), Diane Morris (16), Estelle Philips (12), Mathew Rudback (15), Paul Sawbridge (13), Katie Scott (12), Scot Towers (11), Chris Upex (10), Claire White (13), Sarah White (15).

OAKENGATES & DISTRICT (Shropshire)

OAKHAM SCHOOL (Leics)

OLDBURY (Worcs) *Formed* 1934
Club Sec: R. Jones, 99 Apsley Road, Oldbury, West Midlands. *Chief Coach:* M. Parsons
Members: 150. *Leading Members:* Lindsay Andrews (13), Nicola Atkin (11), Justin Bland (16), Marie Bould (12), Mark Browne (10), Andrew Chapman (18), Gareth Comerford (11), Wayne Cowley (16), Emma-Jane Day (10), Andrew Dennies (16), Anthony Hall (21), Abigail Jones (12), Chris Knight (17), Alan Merris (23), Alison Peakman (10), Julie Rickers (17), Rebbeca Simms (11), Stuart Simpson (22), Joanne Siviter (17), Marcus Smith (15), Marc Soulsby (15), Rachel Soulsby (12), Matthew Stayen (16), Richard Stokes (17), Katie Williams (13).

OLLERTON OTTERS (Notts)

ORION (Warwicks) *Formed* 1967
Club Sec: Mrs S. Taylor, 14 Gunner Lane, Rubery, Birmingham, B45 9EP. *Chief Coach:* B. Spiers
Members: 600. *Leading Members:* Miriam Allott (18), Andrew Caves (12), Matthew Cockbill (14), Andrew Compton (14), Paul Farrell (12), Lloyd Griffiths (16), Sarah Harris (13), Louise Heath (13), Matthew Hinton (13), Joanna Hunt (13), John Longvill (16), Mark McGarry (16), Melanie McQuade (15), Gemma Mitchell (12), Glen Mitchell (15), Michele Need (16), Christian Phelps (16), Caroline Piggott (16), Julia Piggott (13), Charlotte Robertson (16), Stephen Spiers (15), Rebecca Spratt (12), Shelley Taylor (13), Nick Tromans (17), Chris Warburton (15).

OSWESTRY OTTERS (Shropshire) *Formed* 1977
Club Sec: Mrs C. Hibbert, Ty Draw, Glyn Ceiriog, Llangollem, Clywd, LL20 7AA. *Chief Coach:* D. Hobbs
Members: 100.

OULTON BROAD SWIMMING & DC (Suffolk) *Formed* 1929
Club Sec: Mrs J. Butters, 7 The Street, Blundeston, Lowestoft, NR32 5AA. *Chief Coach:* Mrs J. Green
Members: 175.

OUNDLE & DISTRICT (Northants) *Formed* 1986
Club Sec: Mrs J.E. Lamb, Toll Farm, Ramsey Hollow, Ramsey, PE17 1YE. *Chief Coach:* C. Dedynski
Members: 55. *Leading Members:* Philip Baxter (14), Melanie Bradley (18), Kerry Chapman (13), Belinda Cobb (14), Juliet Corn (16), Kyle Duggan (15), Natalie Duggan (15), Charlie Dunmore (19), Jim Evans (18), Anita Freeman (14), Nick Gaggini (19), Kerry Griggs (15), Lee Holgate (19), Stewart Miller (18), Spencer Moore (18), Greg Newton (16), Nigel Parish (19), Giles Pateman (19), Lee Radwell (16), Matthew Rolfe (16), Fiona Skipworth (13), Joanne Smith (16), Mark Smith (16), Ian Wallace (15), Kerry Walton (12).

Oundle & District S.C.

OXFORD UNIVERSITY (Oxford & North Bucks)
Formed 1900

Club Sec: N. Skipper, Wolfson College, Linton Road, Oxford.   *Chief Coach:* S. Green

Members: 30. *Leading Members:* Kevin Barrett (18), Nick Bullock (14), Janet Cartmeil (22), Annette Chandler (26), Joanne Edwards (18), Stefan Green (20), Gavin Hill (21), Susan Hill (18), Mike Hodgson (21), Lisa Jones (22), Sadie King (23), Steven Lord (20), Meredith Miller (19), Jane Mountjoy (18), Sheila Nolan (18), Ken Oliphant (18), Sian Pilling (21), Jon Price (20), Rob Pullan (20), Ronald Roberts (21), Neal Skipper (27), Karen Sutton (20), Penny Tattershaw (20), Gary Woods (18), Phil Young (22).

OXFORD UNIVERSITY PRESS (Oxford & North Bucks)

PEAK SYNCHRO (Derbys)

PERRY BEECHES (Warwicks)
Formed 1984

Club Sec: J. Phelps, 149 Birmingham Road, Wylde Green, Sutton Coldfield.   *Chief Coach:* B. Phelps

Members: 200. *Leading Members:* Penny Arnold (11), Catherine Bailey (17), Gavin Brettal (12), Marion Buckley (21), Guy Bulpitt (20), Danny Claridge (16), Joanna Corbett (14), Joanna Coull (15), Martin Cramp (15), Julie Gordon (10), Richard Herbert (13), Vicky Jones (12), Graham Minns (20), Heather Osborne (15), Wendy Phelps (14), Tracy Pickwell (14), Jamie Randall (14), Stuart Sanders (11), Nathan Shaw (14), Rhian Taylor (11), Richard Wardle (12), Alison Warner (17), Helen Washborne (17), Justin Whittles (16), David Williams (14).

PERSHORE (Worcs)

PERSHORE & DISTRICT DISABLED (Worcs)
Club Sec: Mrs S. Blowers, The Bungalow, Drakensbridge Road, Eckington, Worcs.

PERTON (Staffs)

PETERBOROUGH SYNCHRO (Cambs)

PHOENIX (Staffs)

PLECK DIPPER (Staffs)

PORTLAND (Notts)
Formed 1931

Club Sec: S. Poole, "Greylands", 31 Lenton Avenue, The Park, Nottingham.   *Chief Coach:* Mrs M. Gill

Members: 80. *Leading Members:* Bryony Butcher (10), John Butt (28), Anthony Clark (11), Natalie Clark (14), Paul Cresswell (11), Richard Grainger (10), Clare Gretton (12), Tim Harrison (24), Paul Hodgkinson (11), Sarah Humphrey (11), Sharon Humphrey (13), Lee Jackson (11), Mark Johnson (15), Martin Johnson (31), Vanessa Kerlow (14), Nicola McFarlane (13), Duncan McNulty (11), Stephen Moore (24), Fiona Pickford (11), Thomas Pickford (12), Lorraine Robertson (16), Philip Robertson (13), Laura Whitworth (14), Kay Williamson (11).

PUTTERIDGE CENTRE (Beds)
Formed 1980

Club Sec: Mrs C. Smith, 361 Ashcroft Road, Stopsley, Luton, Beds.   *Chief Coach:* Mrs J. Smith

Members: 150. *Leading Members:* Lynsey-Ann Abbitt (10), Marc Barnes (13), Stephen Breen (11), James Carter (13), Joanne Carter (10), David Clarke (30+), Gary Cooke (10), Nancy Ewers (15), Debbie Maynard (15), Lisa Misson (16), Tim Misson (15), Cherie Pattman (13), Nicola Porter (12), Andrew Roberts (15), Lynne Roberts (16), Elizabeth Smith (12), Lee Smith (16), Nigel Smith (14), Matthew Spendley (16), Joanne Spicer (14), Kelly Sturgeon (13), Sarah Vincent (14), Steven Walters (15), Philip Warren (14), Claire Watkins (10).

RADFORD (Notts)

REDDITCH (Worcs)
Formed 1901

Club Sec: Mrs V. McAuliffe, 22 Brotherton Avenue, Webheath, Redditch, Worcs.   *Chief Coach:* G. Sykes

Members: 290. *Leading Members:* Billy Bott (9), Nina Bott (13), Steve Craner (14), Rebecca Craner (16), Sara Crompton (13), Andrew Exton (26), Paul Fitzpatrick (16), Neil Goodman (11), Neil Graham (13), Adele Hughes (13), Ann Laight (12), Jon Laight (13), Daniel McAuliffe (14), Chris Mitchell (14), Katie Picone (26), Zoe Plant (13), Justine Reading (17), Christian Robinson (11), Jamie Salter (13), Peter Saville (42), Sharon Southern (20), Gareth Sykes (27), Clive Taylor (13), Angela Watson (11), Robert Williams (11).

REMORA (Lincs)

RETFORD (Notts)
Formed 1900

Club Sec: C. Broad, 32 Orchard Crescent, Tuxford, Notts, NG22 0LU.   *Chief Coach:* M. Holton

Members: 375.

RIPLEY (Derbys)
Formed 1973

Club Sec: P.M. Eaton, 21 Waingroves Road, Ripley, Derbys, DE5 9TB.   *Chief Coach:* D. Wickland

Leading Members: Alison Butlin (17), Jason Carlin (19), Rachel Cox (12), Alan Eaton (18), Garth Ethelston (13), Kevin Gear (13), Charlotte Gibbs (11), Julian Gibbs (12), Jeremy Johnson (17), Sally Johnson (13), Lynne Knowles (17), Jennifer Morton (14), Julie Nuton (11), Mark Nuton (15), Kirsty Oldroyd (15), Edward Parker (11), Erica Power (10), Rebecca Power (12), Lee Richmond (15), Paul Richmond (12), Ilya Romaine (17), Richard Taylor (11), Nicola Wickland (17), Christopher Wright (15), Emma Wright (15).

ROLLS ROYCE, DERBY (Derbys)

ROLLS ROYCE, HUCKNALL (Notts)

ROSS & DISTRICT (Derbys) *Formed* 1975
Club Sec: D. Brown, 4 Silver Birches, Ross on Wye, Herefordshire. *Chief Coach:* Mrs T. Pulsford
Members: 200. *Leading Members:* Steven Amand (13), Tracey Barlow (13), Alex Brown (10), Paul Bundy (10), Sarah Clark (15), Neil Devereux (13), Caroline Eaton (14), Cathy Goodwin (13), Lindsay Griffiths (13), Ann Hargreaves (13), Susan Hargeaves (15), Alan Hughes (10), Dafydd Hughes (12), Mark Leett (14), Genny MacCallum (13), Scott MacCallum (10), Emma Marjrett (14), Alex Masters (11), Jamie Masters (11), Rachel Mayer (14), Stuart Pratlett (14), Pete Shelton (10), Helen Thompson (13), Michael Wasfold (12), Stephen Williams (13).

ROTHWELL (Northants) *Formed* 1972
Club Sec: Mrs P. Thompson, 59 Desborough Road, Rothwell, NN14 2JG.
Members: 90.

ROVER (Warwicks)

ROYAL HOSPITAL SCHOOL (Suffolk)

RUGBY (Warwicks) *Formed* 1970
Club Sec: Mrs S. Harrison, 23 Ennerdale Close, Daventry, Northants, NN11 5EF.
Chief Coaches: G. Croad, N. Lines, E. Thompson
Members: 350. *Leading Members:* Zoe Adnitt (11), Amy Boyes (10), Elaine Bromwich (47), Lorna Cave (22), Emma Cramphorn (14), Elspeth Fair (17), James Faulkner (12), Damion Flavell (14), Nicholas Flavell (16), Caroline Grannell (9), Marie Griffiths (14), Carole Harridge (46), Nigel Harridge (22), Sarah Joughin (12), Norman Lines (47), Simon Rigg (22), Susan Smith (16), Karen Taylor (17), James Thompson (18), Linzi Walden (12).

RUGELEY (Staffs)

RUSHCLIFFE (Notts)

RUSHDEN (Northants)
Club Sec: Mrs A. Denton, 2C Fern Road, Rushden, Northants, NN10 9AU.

RYKNELD SHARLEY PARK (Derbys)

ST IVES (Cambs) *Formed* 1973
Club Sec: R.H. Goscomb, 18 Sheepfold, St Ives, Cambs, PE17 4FY. *Chief Coach:* P. Coleman
Members: 250. *Leading Members:* Steve Ankin (17), Sarah Ashley (10), Judy Attwood (12), Nicky Banks (16), Sarah Chamberlain (18), Mandy Christy (21), Amanda Coleman (14), Robert Coleman (16), Simon Coleman (21), Paul Coombs (13), Shona Eldridge, Paul Gregory (10), Christian Humphreys (13), Tim Jenner (12), Hazel Johnson (14), John Kirkpatrick (10), Peter Kirkpatrick (14), Shaun Levitt (21), Alistair Lowe (11), Matthew O'Connell (10), Ian Quest (15), Charlotte Reynolds (12), Debbie Selsby (15), Donna Selsby (13), Alison Tanton (12).

ST JAMES, KING'S LYNN (Norfolk) *Formed* 1977
Club Sec: J.C. Toll, 63 Milton Avenue, Kings Lynn, Norfolk, PE30 2QQ.
Members: 90.

ST JOHNS (Derbys)

SALOPIA (Shropshire) *Formed* 1986
Club Sec: D.H. Ashworth, 43 Ludlow Road, Bridgnorth, Shropshire. *Chief Coach:* W.D. Davidson
Members: 250.

SAXON SYNCHRO (Beds)

SCUNTHORPE ANCHOR (Lincs) *Formed* 1972
Club Sec: Mrs P.A. Guntrip, 54 Chiltern Crescent, Scunthorpe, DN17 1TJ. *Chief Coach:* G. Dale
Members: 144.

SCUNTHORPE & DISTRICT (Lincs)

SCUNTHORPE WPC (Lincs)
Club Sec: W. Sowerby, Kirmington House, Kirmington, South Humberside. *Chief Coach:* M. Wright
Members: 16. *Leading Members:* Sonya Holmes (20), Gerard Leitch (20), Roger Leitch (34), Keith Mundell (30), Mark Snowden (33), Rick Snowden, William Sowerby (23), Mark Welch (34), Martin Welch (30), Sean Welch (32), Simon Welch (33), Dean Wilkinson (16), Lee Wilkinson (19), Mick Wright (43), Simon Wright (13).

SEVERN STREET (Warwicks) *Formed* 1892
Club Sec: S. Reader, 45 Gibbins Road, Selly Oak, Birmingham, B29 6PQ. *Chief Coach:* A. Deeley
Members: 56. *Leading Members:* G. Delaney (20), B. Dosanjh (11), S. Dosanjh (12), A. Downes (20), R. Downes (18), L. Hallal (11), P. Hibberd (37), D. Holland (45), S. Kelly (14), B. Lees (38), V. Lees (12), B. Maguire (11), N. McCaffery (11), L. McGill (11), D. McMohome (40), J. Millson (11), K. Morrissey (11), P.

Rainbow (13), J. Richards (20), S. Richards (17), C. Scott (10), N. Shepherd (18), J. Thomas (15), M. White (11), D. Yates (10).

SHEPSHED (Leics)
Formed 1972
Club Sec: Mrs L. Jackson, 19 Lansdowne Road, Shepshed. *Chief Coach:* C. Butler
Members: 95. *Leading Members:* Amanda Adams (11), Vaughan Adams (15), Jemma Atkins (13), Robert Blanchard (11), Julia Butler (13), Madeline Butler (15), Sara Dunn (16), Steven Dunn (14), John Fox (13), Hilary Griffin (14), Melony Gubb (10), Emma Hollingworth (12), Scott Jacques (17), Van Johnson (9), Emma Jones (15), Laura Jones (10), John Murphy (9), Gareth Seymour (17), Laura Slater (12), Phillipa Slater (9), Anthia Tainton (10), Naomi Taylor (15), Deborah Tooley (16), Richard Weedon (12), Kenton Wye (16).

SHERWOOD COLLIERY (Notts)
Formed 1934
Club Sec: Mrs C. Gibson, 20 Prestwold Avenue, Forest Town, NG19 0DB. *Chief Coach:* A. Harwood
Members: 250. *Leading Members:* David Barksby (11), Gavin Barlow (18), Guy Barlow (16), Sally Barlow (10), Nickie Bennett (9), Elizabeth Bonner (13), Claire Dillon (15), Claire Flowers (13), Andrew Gibson (14), Joanne Gibson (16), Kieron Hall (16), Steven Hall (15), Richard Hardwick (9), Mark Holloway (11), Victoria Johnson (14), Christopher Navin (13), Joanne Potter (15), David Riley (12), Andrew Shead (13), Gavin Walker (13), Susan Walker (16), Dean Whitcombe (15), Richard Williams (13), David Winfield (10), Lisa Wood (12).

SHREWSBURY (Shropshire)
Formed 1888
Club Sec: Mrs A. Cox, 21 Burnham Avenue, Shrewsbury, Shropshire, SY2 5LL. *Chief Coach:* D. Williams
Members: 86. *Leading Members:* Nicola Breach (15), Claire Carter (15), Rebecca Cox (14), Robert Cox (13), Alison Cumming (15), Anna Davies (14), Tomas Dodds (15), Juliet Eden (11), Joanne Evans (15), Stephanie Farmer (19), Andrew Gibson (22), Steven Harris (14), Adam Houlston (10), Emma Hughes (14), Guy Johnson (22), Simon Morgans (15), Lorraine Morris (17), Suzanna Pope (15), Lucy Purcell (14), Philip Rodenhurst (16), Steven Rogers (14), Simon Smith (14), Hannah Wilby (12), Karen Wilderspin (13), Emma Wright (16).

SHREWSBURY LADIES (Shropshire)
Formed 1912
Club Sec: Mrs P. Simpson, 173 Ellesmere Road, Shrewsbury. *Chief Coach:* Mrs W. Wilkinson
Members: 270.

SIRENS LADIES WPC (Derbys)
Formed 1986
Club Sec: Mrs J. Clayton, 33 Mill Street, Ilkeston, DE7 8GG. *Chief Coach:* P. Clayton
Members: 20.

SKEGNESS (Lincs)
Formed 1988
Club Sec: H. Moore, 9 Burdett Close, Skegness, Lincs. *Chief Coach:* D. Parker
Members: 50. *Leading Members:* Kay Anson (11), David Blanchard (9), Steven Blanchard (12), Rachel Brooks (11), Ricky Broome (17), Andrew Daybell (14), Victoria Dixon (9), Samantha Epton (9), Neil Fisher (11), Nicola Fowlston (13), Joanne Foxon (11), Jenny Halliday (11), Mark Hargreaves (10), David Hopkins (15), David Horry (22), Gareth Hunt (11), Thomas Jenkins (11), Gary Moore (15), Donna Scholz (13), Kay Scholz (11), Julie Tanner (16), Tracey Tanner (13), Cassie Taylor (12), Katrina Taylor (10), Paul Wilkinson (13).

SLEAFORD (Lincs)
Formed 1937
Club Sec: P. Onyon, 10 Grantham Road, Sleaford, Lincs, NG54 7NB.
Members: 154.

SOLIHULL (Warwicks)
Formed 1963
Club Sec: Mrs I.P. Badger, 51 Seven Star Road, Solihull, B91 2BZ. *Chief Coach:* R.M. Floyd
Members: 550. *Leading Members:* Nicolas Beard (17), Diane Brades (29), Simon Brades (29), Louise Brocklesby (18), Peter Feilden (15), Alastair Forbes (15), Fiona Freeborough (11), Michael Gill (25), Jamie Hamer (12), Max Harberson (12), Cary Holloway (13), Christian Holloway (15), Nina Jones (16), Simon Moseley (12), Rachel Nock (13), Simon Pemberton (18), Ella Pountney (14), Kay Pountney (16), Duncan Richardson (11), James Smith (13), Joanne Smith (16), Justin Smith (14), Matthew Statham (18), Leanne Turgoose (16), Mark Walsh (18).

SOLIHULL TRIATHLON CLUB (Warwicks)
Formed 1988
Club Sec: A. Wilson, 98 Solihull Road, Shirley, West Midlands, B90 3HS.
Members: 20.

SOUTHAM (Warwicks)

SOUTH LINCS (Lincs)
Formed 1977
Club Sec: L. Beasley, "Westview", Northgate, Pinchbeck, Lincs, PE11 3TB. *Chief Coach:* R. Pates
Members: 95. *Leading Members:* Michelle Beck (19), Jane Belding (13), Mark Coley (13), Steph Fulcher (11), Cheryl Futter (14), Jacqueline Gray (14), Mathew Gregory (13), Lee Holgate (19), Mandy Houghton (14), Tamsin Hurley (14), Jenny Kyriakou (14), Joby Luckett (14), Sean McConnell (16), Stew Miller (18), Clair O'Dell (12), Sarah Pates (19), Mathew Rolfe (15), Helen Roulston (16), Karen Sanderson (22), Brett Shepherd (12), Mark Smith (15), Sally Tuffs (11), Andrew Wallace (13), Ian Wallace (15), Richard Wallace (12).

SOUTHWELL (Notts)

SPALDING (Lincs)   *Formed* 1935
Club Sec: T. Ainley, 13 Greenfields, Holbeach, Spalding, Lincs, PE12 7BJ.   *Chief Coach:* K. Sanderson
Leading Members: Abigail Ainley (13), Gwyneth Ainley (11), Catherine Briers (9), Martin Croft (11), Cheryl Futter (14), Lyndsey Futter (12), Nicola Gibson (13), John Henson (12), Philip Henson (10), Ben Hoare (9), Peter Hopkin (9), Emily Horner (10), Ben Howling (9), Darren Jessop (11), Iain Randall (10), Susan Robson (9), Catherine Rolfe (11), Jonathan Smith (12), Charlotte Steel (10), Siobhan Steel (12), Victoria Steel (12), Zannah Stibbins (11), Chris Taylor (13), Maryse Tennant (9), Chris Wardell (13).

SPARKHILL (Warwicks)

SPONDON (Derbys)   *Formed* 1968
Club Sec: Mrs J. Beswick, 179 Duffield Road, Darley Abbey, Derby.   *Chief Coach:* M. Merritt
Members: 42. *Leading Members:* Charlotte Beswick (14), Christopher Cheney (17), Karen Cheney (14), Emma Clements (16), Colin Dahill (18), Karenina Jarram (18), Adam Marshall (18), Simon Mason (23), Rachael Seymour (17).

STAFFORD (Staffs)   *Formed* 1892
Club Sec: Mrs B. Blood, "Shenstone", Newport Road, Great Bridgeford.   *Chief Coach:* R.F. Barker
Members: 149.

STAFFORD APEX (Staffs)   *Formed* 1982
Club Sec: B. Chandler, 12 Meadow Ridge, Radford Bank, Stafford.   *Chief Coaches:* J. Shenton, J. Walker
Members: 70.

STAFFORD LADIES (Staffs)   *Formed* 1900
Club Sec: Mrs M. Buckingham, 9 Howard Road, Rising Brook, Stafford, ST17 9EW.
Members: 180.

STANTONBURY (Oxford & North Bucks)   *Formed* 1977
Club Sec: D. Steadman, 73 Stokenchurch Place, Bradwell Commord.   *Chief Coach:* E. Mallory
Members: 250.

STETCHFORD (Warwicks)

STONE & DISTRICT (Staffs)

STOURBRIDGE (Worcs)   *Formed* 1967
Club Sec: P. Boden, 4 Rathmore Close, Norton, Stourbridge, West Midlands.   *Chief Coach:* J. Vaughn
Members: 265. *Leading Members:* Nicholas Amphlett (11), James Bainbridge (15), Kathryn Beardsmore (14), Lisa Carter (19), Ruth Clements (11), Jenny Glynn (15), Kerry Glynn (12), Trudy Goodwin (13), Jonathan Green (14), Julie Green (11), David Gregg (14), Sarah Guest (12), Gemma Hadley (11), Chris Harvey (12), Karen Harvey (17), Stephen Hathaway (11), Lyndsey Kilgour (16), Debbie Lane (15), Eve Millard (12), Richard O'Brien (12), Steven Pratt (13), Scott Raybould (11), Adelle Rowley (12), Samantha Smart (14), David Smith (16), Gary Smith (19), Andrew Sparry (17), Arran Stevens (19), Lee Tyson (16), Alex Wooldridge (15).

STOURPORT (Worcs)   *Formed* 1975
Club Sec: Mrs P. Male, 29 Catterbutts, Abberley, Worcester, WR6 6BX.   *Chief Coach:* D. Burgess
Members: 188. *Leading Members:* Tony Adams (20), Elizabeth Allen (14), Leigh Bolton (14), Richard Bolton (16), Lynsey Burford (11), Paul Camden (21), Shelley Davies (12), Kristian Durden (10), Caroline Francis (13), Andrew Gilbert (10), Sally Green (16), Alexander Hopkins (14), Mark Kinsella (13), Rebecca McDonald (13), Helen McKittrick (13), Mathew Male (12), Andrea Mowbray (16), Christian Parkes (18), Jacob Pearson (14), Sara Pedersen (13), Steven Roe (21), Hayley Rowan (11), Andrew Steward (18), Elizabeth Swift (13), Joan Wagstaff (18).

STOWMARKET (Suffolk)   *Formed* 1888
Club Sec: Mrs W.E. Flinter, 73 Hillside, Stowmarket, Suffolk, IP14 2BA.   *Chief Coach:* Mrs K. Lynch
Members: 60. *Leading Members:* Mark Ames (11), Tom Ames (8), Ruth Barber (10), Gareth Bishop (10), Richard Boxall-Hunt (15), Robin Boxall-Hunt (14), Michelle Cockayne (16), Matthew Connick (12), Debbie Fairbourne (14), Kirstie Flinter (15), Sally Friston (10), Nicola Griffiths (13), Debbie Hart (14), Mandy Hart (12), Sarah Holdich (10), Alice Jenkins (11), Peter Lynch (10), Susan Marshall (15), Karl Meadows (15), Clive Mitson (10), Norman Morrison (16), Catherine Paton (10), Kelly Peachment (12), Andrew Thorndyke (12), Leesa Wilson (10).

STRATFORD-UPON-AVON (Warwicks)   *Formed* 1932
Club Sec: Mrs S. Jones, 19 Roebuck Park, Alcester, Warwicks, B49 5EF.   *Chief Coach:* J. Russell
Members: 406. *Leading Members:* Georgina Aplin (13), Melissa Barr (12), Mark Baxter (26), Gareth Challoner (12), Melissa Elliot (13), Paul Gallagher (22), Lois Hazzledine (12), Matthew Holmes (14), Claire Humberstone (18), Fraser Jones (13), Jonathan Leybourne (11), Victoria Mealings (14), Alex Morris (18), Sally Ann Nealings (19), Julian Poyner (18), Jamie Salisbury (12), Kate Salisbury (15), Steven Sims (13), Andrew Smith (17), Amy Wardle (13), Sarah Weatherhead (19), Christopher White (15), Elizabeth White (20), Richard White (17), Helen Williamson (12).

SUDBURY & DISTRICT (Suffolk) *Formed* 1950
Club Sec: Mrs C. Wells, 29 Suffolk Road, Sudbury, Suffolk, CO10 6UN. *Chief Coach:* N. Stemp
Members: 120. *Leading Members:* Heidi Bennett (15), Roger Duncombe, Cherry Fisher (12), Kate Graham, Karl Grimwade, Jon Hearnden (15), Lisa Hearnden (12), Tanya Hunt (14), Emily Johnson (16), Richard Johnson, Pauline Kennedy, Stuart McLellan, James Marshall, Laurence Milton, Daniel Minnis (10), Matthew Minnis (12), Margaret Nolan, Craig Paley (15), John Paley, Lindsey Peacock (14), Hayley Spooner (15), Mike Vickers, Roger Wells (16), Kevin Whybrow, Timothy Whybrow (11).

SUTTON COLDFIELD TRIPLE 'S' (Warwicks) *Formed* 1974
Club Sec: Mrs G. Brown, 3 Boswell Road, Sutton Coldfield, B74 2NB. *Chief Coach:* S. Bridges
Leading Members: Kate Boswell (14), Rebecca Boswell (17), Piers Burford (14), Graham Campbell (12), Mark Cooper (15), Lee Coton (13), Mark Deakin (18), Steven Ford (13), Natalie Friel (11), Andrew Hamilton (10), Clare Henderson (16), Joseph Hess (15), Kevin Kain (24), Lucy Ketteridge (13), Adam Kowalski (18), Sally Latham (10), Sarah Latham (10), Vicky Luckhurst (12), Daniel McDermott (10), Claire Moffett (15), Gerald Morgan (15), Lucy Rollason (20), Craig Trevis (12), Jo Wilkinson (15), Emma Yates (10).

SUTTON COLDFIELD TUDOR (Warwicks)

SUTTON IN ASHFIELD (Notts) *Formed* 1929
Club Sec: Mrs K. Hutchings, 49 Charnwood Street, Sutton in Ashfield, Notts. *Chief Coach:* A. Urch
Members: 112. *Leading Members:* Jennifer Ball (13), Adrian Bradbury, Martin Bradbury (13), Georgina Clamp (12), Grant Cooper (14), Steven Cooper (15), Ian Crampton (15), Michelle Cupit (16), Paul Goodwin (12), Sally Greaves (15), Wendy Greaves (12), Neal Hopkinson (12), Paul Hopkinson (15), Tracey Keeling (13), Simon Langton (16), Amanda Layton (14), Lisa Mills (15), Andrew Paxton (15), M. Perry (12), Lisa Radford (12), Catherine Selby (14), Ian Vernon (13), Jane Vernon (14), Lisa Watson, David Wilson.

SWADLINCOTE (Derbys) *Formed* 1983
Club Sec: R. Whiteland, 66 Winchester Drive, Midway, Derbys, DE11 7LT. *Chief Coach:* D. West
Members: 200. *Leading Members:* Robert Allcote (12), Stewart Batchelor (11), Richard Booth (16), Paul Brown (12), Richard Cornell (14), Katherine Cripwell (12), Mark Dissington (11), Martyn Dissington, Richard Fletcher (11), Jonathan Hart (17), Elizabeth Hogg (17), Edward Kemp (10), Nicola Meakin (13), David Page (15), Lee Poulton (11), Mitchell Poulton (10), Claire Poxon (21), Victoria Sherratt (10), Jenny Steele (16), Martyn Stretton (15), Helen Toone (14), Olivia Topliss (10), Carl Winfield (15), Jeanne Woollett (18), Benjamin Young (14).

SWALLOWS DC (Warwicks)

SWANS, ST NEOTS (Cambs)

SYSTON TOWN (Leics)

TAMWORTH (Staffs)

TENBURY (Worcs) *Formed* 1965
Club Sec: Miss J. Snowden, 45 Dunnington Avenue, Kidderminster, DY10 2YT. *Chief Coach:* J. Greatham

THETFORD DOLPHINS (Norfolk) *Formed* 1974
Club Sec: Mrs M. Rex, 10 Hardy Close, Thetford, Norfolk, IP24 1LF. *Chief Coach:* G. Charlesworth
Members: 80. *Leading Members:* Elizabeth Atkins (10), James Barrett (11), Sarah Boyden (11), Julie Brand (13), Simon Britcher (12), Jamie Courtman (15), Steven Currie (14), Dominic Donald (15), Peter Edmunds (14), Simon Elliston (14), Martin Gale (19), Jackie Hunt (13), Alan Jones (15), Ross Jones (13), Heidi Lakin (15), Cy Martin (13), Linda Miller (16), Nadine Morgan (15), Edward Mundy (12), Joanne Neath (17), Ashley Rex (14), Chris Wellington (12), Emma Williams (12), Julie Williams (12), Colin Young (16).

TIPTON (Staffs)

TRENTON DOLPHINS (Lincs) *Formed* 1979
Club Sec: C.A. Haw, 3 Northolme, Gainsborough, Lincs, DN21 2QN. *Chief Coach:* C. Pitchforth
Members: 350. *Leading Members:* Lucy Ball (9), Sarah Ball (13), Charlotte Batty (12), Sara Dugmore (14), Michael Duke (15), Stephen Duke (12), Deborah Graham (15), Sonya Holmes (19), Claire Jackson (13), Neil Jackson (10), Claire Laughton (13), Paul Marcroft (15), Nichola Marriott (12), Vicky Neal (10), Richard Nelsey (9), Steven Paine (13), James Priestley (12), Claire Ridley (14), Stuart Ridley (12), Mark Smith (25), Karen Stanham (10), David Taylor (13), Steven Taylor (17), Lee Wills (11), Helen Woodward (13).

TRENT VALLEY SYNCHRO (Staffs)

TREONTE DOLPHINS (Derbys) *Formed* 1980
Club Sec: T. Graham, 2 Langley Drive, Kegworth, Derby, DE7 2DN. *Chief Coach:* Mrs L. Seymour
Members: 170. *Leading Members:* Anthony Allcock (11), Antony Ball (11), Helen Bexton (13), Sarah Bexton (15), Simon Brown (13), Holly Cooke (18), Edward Crisp (18), Lisa Dennis (16), Mark Flinders (15), Sarah Flinders (12), Greg Freer (11), Alex Graham (11), Tom Graham (13), Emma Griffin (16), James Griffin (18), Sarah Griffin (11), Kevin Harrison (16), Nicola Harrison (13), Emma Higgs (12), Shelley

Higgs (13), Kevin Lever (14), James Parry (15), Joanne Riddell (17), Rachael Seymour (17), Andrew Simmons (20).

TRIDENT (Derbys)   Formed 1977
Club Sec: C. Snaith, Arcadian House, Rempstone, Loughborough, Leics.   Chief Coach: D. Brown
Members: 200. Leading Members: Chris Andrews (13), Robert Andrews (11), Elliot Austin (14), Nancy Beardsall (11), Sarah Beresford (11), William Beresford (19), Ian Bexon (14), Lee Bostock (12), Jessica Byrne (10), Paul Cockayne (12), Richard Cockayne (10), Nina Cockcroft (18), Rachel Culling (12), Tom Gutteridge (12), Celia Hall (13), Jon Hollingsworth (13), Sarah Hulse (13), Neil Meadows (17), Neil Paling (19), Anne Richardson (23), Clare Robinson (11), Clare Scothern (13), Andrew Thornton (13), Sarah Wills (13), Alison Wood (17).

TUPTON HALL SCHOOL (Derbys)   Formed 1971
Club Sec: R.A. Bannister, 32 Lindale Road, Dunston, Chesterfield.   Chief Coach: R.A. Bannister
Members: 20. Leading Members: Bee Bennett (11), Martin Cantrill (16), Matthew Douch (15), Andrew Gore (15), Peter Gore (13), Rachel Hage (11), Jennie Horbury (14), Clare Lee (15), Stephanie Lilley (13), Faye Mallender (13), Alan Marsh (27), Clare Revel (15), Chris Sellars (22), Alison Sims (14), Sarah Smith (14), Richard Taylor (16), Nicki Valentine (16), Jane Walker (14), Nicky Walton (14), Sarah Weir (16).

UPPINGHAM SCHOOL (Leics)

VICTORIA PARK DC (Derbys)

VIKINGS (Suffolk)

WALSALL DC (Staffs)

WALSALL SWIMMING & WPC (Staffs)   Formed 1884
Club Sec: Mrs V. Davies, 30 Chapel Street, Pelsall, West Midlands, WS3 4LW. Chief Coach: M. Hepwood
Leading Members: Marcus Alsop (15), Claire Asson (13), Emma Avery (15), Michael Bowd (13), Karen Bowen, Peter Bunday (19), Lee Chipchase (11), Donna Clift (14), Andrew Dawson (15), Kate Dugmore (14), Stuart Dugmore (15), Darran Dyke (23), Kieron Etheridge (14), Nick Gillingham (22), Richard Gudgin (12), Julie Harris (17), Karen Harris (15), Rachel Harvey (12), Tim Jones (22), Kate Leibe (12), Linsay Ruddell (15), Chris Taylor (10), Mark Tift (15), Jenny Turner (12), Peter Vaughan (11).

WALSALL SYNCHRO (Staffs)   Formed 1972
Club Sec: Mrs M.L. Bates, 25 Leveson Avenue, Cheslyn Hay, Walsall.   Chief Coach: Miss M. Salt
Members: 52. Leading Members: Sarah Adams (16), Anne Alexander (18), Jenny Atthey (13), Lesley Bates (12), Teresa Brookes (18), Dawn Clare (16), Faye Crawford (13), Angela Davenport (19), Faye Dutton (10), Catherine Ellis (16), Jacqui Ford (11), Esther Gregory (10), Melanie Harris (14), Shelley Howles (16), Alyson Hunt (16), Lisa Perham (16), Emma Price (13), Susan Richards (18), Jenny Smith (16), Andrea Sparkes (10), Victoria Thane (13), Kerry Tolley (14), Rachel Varden (13), Helen Vincent (13), Jeanna Whistance (16).

WANTAGE WHITE HORSES (Oxford & North Bucks)   Formed 1981
Club Sec: A. Temple, Windshiels, Belmont, Wantage, Oxon, OX12 9AS.   Chief Coach: D. Moorwood
Members: 110. Leading Members: Melissa Bence (14), Lisa Carson (14), Claire Cavanagh (14), Alison Cox (15), Alistair Cox (18), Steve Croall (17), Chris Eddings (15), Alun Edwards (13), Ceri Edwards (11), Jenny Freeth (14), Claire Greenfield (18), Jessica Harrison (12), Andrew Jones (21), Jackie King (15), Richard King (13), John Marsh (11), Emma Morris (13), Ruth O'Donnell (14), Edward O'Neill (14), Mark O'Neill (14), Jamie O'Sullivan (12), Nick Smith (17), Gordon Syme (13), Lisa Vokins (18), Dean Wall (14).

WARLEY WASPS (Worcs)

WARWICKS CONSTABULARY (Warwicks)

WARWICK UNIVERSITY (Warwicks)

WAVENEY (Suffolk)

WAVENEY OTTERS (Norfolk)

WEDNESBURY (Staffs)

WEDNESBURY WPC (Staffs)

WELLINGBOROUGH (Northants)
Club Sec: Mrs J. Avery, 13 Woodlands Road, Irchester, Northants, NN9 7BW.   Chief Coach: R. Driver
Members: 244. Leading Members: Darren Bason (19), Aaron Beasley (16), Jamie Bishop (16), Craig Brown (20), Jason Donner (15), Lesley-Anne Driver (15), Stuart Gannon (21), Gemma Grahame-Wright (13), Mark Hollyman (23), Barry King (16), Danny Lloyd (16), Daniel Luke (14), Andrew McDougall (14), Craig Mills (17), Gary Mills (15), Caroline Moore (15), Barry O'Brien (32), Theresa Parry (17), Michael Penney (19), Lisa Pickersgill (17), Matthew Rawson (15), Robert Starkey (15), Jackie Thompson (21), David Webster (13), Matthew Whittaker (16).

WELLINGTON (Shropshire)   Formed 1950
Club Sec: M.S. Nicholls, 52 Broomfield Road, Admaston, Telford, TF5 0AS.   Chief Coach: E. Glazebrook
Members: 260. Leading Members: Andrew Aldridge (13), Olivia Baker (10), Jonathon Coit (10), Robert

383

Corbett (20), Jennifer Davies (21), Janine Fletcher (15), Andrew Galloway (18), Simon Harris (16), Mark Nicholls (26), Helen Picken (18), Stuart Spence (20), Mathew Toogood (10).

WELLS & DISTRICT SCHOOLS (Norfolk) — Formed 1967
Club Sec: Mrs A. Doyle, 9 Marsh Lane, Wells next Sea, Norfolk. *Chief Coach:* Mrs G.T. Ashworth
Members: 85. *Leading Members:* Jonathan Ashworth (19), Sally Ashworth (18), Jethro Borthwick (10), Stuart Court (10), Michael Cox (13), Ashley Dack (11), Timothy Doyle (12), Stephanie Glover (16), Alice Griffith-Jones (12), Sam Griffith-Jones (13), Caroline Jarvis (15), Stephanie Jarvis (16), Iain McCallum (11), Robert McCallum (15), Carl Neale (12), Charlotte O'Neill (13), Karen Smith (17), Sonya Smith (12), Anne-Marie Smithers (17), Kenton Terrington (16), Alex Whitaker (15), Amy Whitaker (12), Matthew Whitaker (16), Elaine Wickers (17), Sarah Wickers (13).

WEST BROMWICH (Staffs) — Formed 1898
Club Sec: R. Yates, 30 Johnston Street, West Bromwich, West Midlands, B70 7LW. *Chief Coach:* J. Juiles
Members: 165. *Leading Members:* Kay Baker (13), Lee Bates (11), Katie Burkitt (13), Jayne Cadman (13), Michael Chalton (18), Scott Coombes (12), Dean Crumpton (13), Glenn Crumpton (13), Caroline Davies (28), Lucy Doggett (10), Emma Fell (17), Tristan Graham (10), Chris Grice (13), Matthew Jones (14), Marcus Law (15), Chris Malborn (13), Stephen Malborn (14), Rachel Martin (15), Sarah Martin (15), Leigh Morris (13), David Owen (14), Carla Pitt (10), Matthew Sunderland (11), Kirsty Trentham (13), Sharon Trentham (11).

WEST MIDLANDS GAS (Warwicks)

WEST MIDLANDS POLICE (Warwicks)

WEST MIDLANDS TRAVEL (Warwicks)

WESTMINSTER HANDSWORTH (Warwicks) — Formed 1885
Club Sec: E.J. Blight, 72 Jerrard Drive, Sutton Coldfield, West Midlands, B75 7TJ.
Members: 100. *Leading Members:* Jonathon Allsopp (24), Claire Bird (24), Helen Caffrey (14), Barbara Checkley (18), Michelle Colley (30), Claire Collins (26), Gabriel Fisher (15), Caroline Harnett (26), Janice Hazeldine (21), Richard Martin (28).

WHITCHURCH (Shropshire) — Formed 1984
Club Sec: Mrs S. McKeon, 20 Highfields Avenue, Whitchurch, Shropshire. *Chief Coach:* J. Thomas
Members: 80.

WILLENHALL (Staffs)

WISBECH (Cambs)

WITNEY & DISTRICT (Oxford & North Bucks) — Formed 1975
Club Sec: Mrs D. Forster, 13 Woodstock Road, Witney,Oxon, OX8 6EA. *Chief Coach:* J. Sadler
Members: 135. *Leading Members:* Laura Barry (13), Robin Beckwith (13), Antony Beer (16), Stephen Bowen (16), Alex Chapman (16), Sarah Cooper (14), Jonathan Dennis (15), Chloe Dobson (14), Helen Dobson (16), Stephen Ebbs (22), Wendy Fifield (12), Stuart Forster (13), William Howarth (18), Lindsay James (16), Ben Martin (14), John Pengilly (14), Jane Perrin (16), Colin Pettifer (18), Rachel Rathbone (14), Jonathan Sadler (17), Tim Sadler (14), Catherine Saunders (16), Ross Sharp-Dent (12), Neal Skipper (27), Jonathon Weeden (17).

WOLVERHAMPTON (Staffs)

WOMBOURNE (Staffs) — Formed 1985
Club Sec: Mrs D. Jenks, 108 Wombourne Park Estate, Wombourne, WV5 0LR. *Chief Coach:* D. Porter
Members: 185. *Leading Members:* Steve Carter (10), Claire Collins (25), Paul Delaney (11), Neil Ellwell (13), Dean Flavell (12), Lyndsey Flavell (13), Ben Greaves (9), Christopher Gwynn (9), Sara Hemming (15), Simeon Hemming (17), Christopher Howie (16), David Hughes (13), Helen Hunter (15), Louise Hunter (17), Adrian James (17), Nichole Molyneux (10), Suzanne Molyneux (10), Helen Pithouse (13), Rachel Pronauskas (10), Nadine Rawcliffe (13), Neil Smallman (17), Victoria Smallman (12), Mary Spiers (10), Louise Tomlinson (12), Nicola Wearing (14).

WOODHALL SHARKS (Lincs) — Formed 1983
Club Sec: Mrs K. Lamberton, "Belvedere", Woodhall Spa, Lincoln. *Chief Coach:* Mrs M. Morley
Members: 120. *Leading Members:* Laura Ball (15), Joanne Barnes (14), Tara Barnes (16), Georgiana Bidgood (15), Adrian Burnett (17), Steven Charlton (14), Alex Cochran (16), Rebecca Curt (16), Stuart Curt (17), James Goodhand (13), Terry Hastings (18), Karen Hollingsworth (16), Nicola Knowles (12), Ian Laing (18), Andrew Lamberton (13), Clare Lamberton (15), Sean Lovett (16), Tracey Mills (14), James Morton (13), Amanda Morton-Jones (24), Iwan Peverett (14), Anka Robins (15), Emma Scarborough (12), Samantha Tyte (14), Mark Vater (16).

WORCESTER (Worcs) — Formed 1924
Club Sec: Mrs P.M. Lunn, 27 Beverley Way, Malvern Link, Worcs, WR14 1LA. *Chief Coach:* N. Martin
Members: 250. *Leading Members:* Jenny Arnold (13), Samantha Arnold (16), Christopher Bell (12), Suzanne Burchell (15), Daniel Bussey (10), Matthew Caffrey (14), Charles Cox (15), Matthew Evans (12), Simon Evans (16), Amanda Ferebee (14), David Godber (16), Karen Haines (14), James Hubbard (15),

Thomas Kirby (11), Kirsty Lunn (13), Mike Maddicks (23), Gregg Murfin (11), Phenice Newman, Phillipa Rawlings (11), Julian Ruane (19), Kara Ruane (16), Ian Sharpe (18), Nora Taylor (17), David Tulacz (16), Victoria Wheeler (13).

WORKSOP DOLPHINS (Notts)
Formed 1976

Club Sec: Mrs C. Hall, The Pinfold, Sheffield Road, South Anston, Sheffield.   *Chief Coach:* R. Coupe
Members: 130. *Leading Members:* Sarah Bint (14), James Clarke (20), Mark Conroy (17), Phillip Covill (19), Theron Denyer (16), James Downie (14), Sally-Anne Downie (14), Sally Gray (15), Damian Harris (17), Georgina Hobson (15), Angela Hopwood (17), Daniel Jackson (15), Rachael Jackson (13), Andrew Jefferson (18), Richard Jennings (19), Joanne Morris (5), Zoe Morris (14), David Payne (15), Richard Payne (13), Mark Perkins (16), Cathy Snowden (16), Helen Claire Stone (18), Helen Tansey (15), Amanda Wilson (19), Nicola Wilson (15).

WORLDS END (Warwicks)

WULFRUNIANS (Staffs)
Formed 1970

Club Sec: S. Lacon, "Emandale", Langley Road, Lower Penn, Wolverhampton.   *Chief Coach:* M. Ayre
Members: 50. *Leading Members:* Neil Bourne (14), Dominic Forsythe (14), Natalie Forsythe (12), Bethan Golland (14), Kathryn Harenett (11), Emma Harrison (15), Lyndon Hollinshead (22), Guy Jameson (18), Christopher Lacon (13), Simon Lacon (16), Julian Littleton (18), Heidi Morgan (18), Jayne Nicklin (21), Lucy O'Gorman (15), Stephen Penham (13), Anna Reid (15), Jonathan Robinson (14), Katie Richardson (14), William Russell (22), Kerry Stamp (17), Nick Thacker (23), Claire Tolley (17), Mark Tolley (14), Michael Vance (13), Magnus Weighton (17).

North Eastern District

Honorary Secretary: F. Latimer, 62 Teviotdale Gardens, Newcastle on Tyne, NE7 7PX

AIREBOROUGH (Yorkshire) *Formed* 1967
Club Sec: Mrs G. Smith, 18 Westway Park, Guiseley, LS20 8JX. *Chief Coach:* S. MacAlister
Members: 500.

AIRDALE & WHARFDALE (Yorkshire)
Club Sec: Mrs F.M. Hill, 14 Birklands Road, Shipley, West Yorkshire BD18 3BY. *Formed* 1968

ALDWICK (Yorkshire)

ALNWICK & DISTRICT (Northumberland & Durham) *Formed* 1980
Club Sec: Mrs D. A. Mills, 19 Glovers Green, Alnwick, Northumberland. *Chief Coach:* M. Barrow
Leading Members: Aiden Barron (10), Charlotte Bickmore (12), Joanne Carter (13), Alistair Gaines (12), Joanne Gaines (11), Jon Gaines (11), Marie Gaines (10), Catherine Green (11), Nicholas Green (14), Thomas Green (10), Michael Hamilton (14), Sophie Heslop (10), Sarah Howey (10), Victoria Howey (10), Caroline Kerr (14), Patrick Matheson (10), Anne Mills (11), Robert Mills (15), Caroline Munden (10), Christopher Munden (12), Craig Straughan (10), Emma Straughan (11), Jamie Temple (15),

ALNWICK DOLPHINS (Northumberland & District)

AMBLEFORTH COLLIERY (Yorkshire)

ARMLEY LADIES (Yorkshire)

ARMTHORPE & DISTRICT (Northumberland & District) *Formed* 1973
Club Sec: Mrs G. Christian, 379A Goodison Boulevard, Doncaster. *Chief Coach:* T. Firbank
Members: 450. *Leading Members:* Ian Andrews (15), Melanie Barnett (13), Tim Bevington (15), Jamie Christian (17), Jenny Christian (15), Louise Clayton (14), Vicky Credland (11), Richard Dawson (17), Julie Eland (16), Trevor Eland (13), Richard Ellis (16), Sarah Felters (16), Adam Firbank (16), Simon Firbank (14), Tina Gale (14), Alison Hardy (13), Matthew Hardy (15), Carys Hughes (14), Alison Lynch (17), Vanessa Murray (15), Andrew Norburn (16), Michael Parkinson (14), Helen Smith (16), Brooke Stevenson (12), Ian White (17).

ASHINGTON (Northumberland & Durham) *Formed* 1979
Club Sec: Mrs K. Dickinson, 23 Haldane Street, Ashington, Northumberland. *Chief Coach:* G. Dickinson
Members: 115. *Leading Members:* Eleanor Crate (13), Sharon Crate (17), Kathleen Dickinson (26), Gordon Dickinson (29), Nicola Dodds (14), Graeme Finn (13), Gary Garncjarjyk (22), Brett Johnston (11), William Jones (36),Mark Mather (15), Lesley Muller (14), Alison Pakroham (12), Jane Pakroham (13), Ricky Potter (18), Philip Robertson (15), Alan Robinson (35), Ian Robinspn (12), Susan Smith (21), Lucy Stephenson (13), Joanna Swarbrick (15), Leila Swarbrick (13), Kelly Todd (12), Stephen Williamson (17), Dave Young (43), Paula Young (14).

ATTERCLIFFE 1879 (Yorkshire)

BARNSLEY (Yorkshire) *Formed* 1879
Club Sec: Mrs K. Singleton, 14 Harewood Avenue, Barnsley, S70 6QR. *Chief Coach:* R. Ellis
Members: 350. *Leading Members:* David Austin (16), Lee Austin (12), Gavin Batty (11), Malcolm Beaumont, Richard Blackshaw (10), Alison Bradbury (13), Jannine Elliker (14), Alison Foy (16), Catherine Foy (13), Norman Greenfield, Sara Holt (14), David Oliver (10), Shaun Parker (19), Helen Parkin (11), Sarah Roscoe (13), Emma Skews (14), Mark Wade (16).

BARNSLEY METRO (Yorkshire) *Formed* 1974
Club Sec: I. Walker, 54 Wharfedale Road, Pogmoor, Barnsley, S75 2LJ. *Chief Coach:* M. Chafer
Members: 50. *Leading Members:* Shona Alison (12), Gavin Batty (11), Melanie Bright (15), Michelle Chafer (14), Laura Count (11), David Driver (10), Jannine Elliker (14), Nina Frost (15), Rachel Gallagher (11),Claire Hamby (12), Darren Main (13), David Main (13), Belinda Middlemore (13), Louise Middlemore (11), Steven Mouncey (15), Claire Orman (16), Helen Parkin (11), Emma Priest (12), Sarah Roscoe (14), Jamie Rowlett (12), Helen Shirt (17), Thomas Swales (17), Gary Walker (14), Julie Walker (12).

BARNSLEY OLYMPIC (Yorkshire)

BEACON BARRACUDA (Yorkshire)

BERWICK (Northumberland & Durham)

BEVERLEY LADIES (Yorkshire)

BEVERLEY MEN (Yorkshire)

BILLINGHAM FORUM (Northumberland & Durham) *Formed* 1968
Club Sec: I. J. Archibald, 6 Emsworth Drive, Eaglescliffe, Cleveland, TS16 0NS. *Chief Coach:* A. Janes
Members: 150. *Leading Members:* Lindsey Barthram (11), Stuart Begg (28), Clare Bulman (16), Ian Davison (10), Ian Gill (14), Alison Hall (12), Richard Hall (10), Lisa Harbron (14), Carrie Harrison (11), Kylie Jackson (11),Brian Kenny (15), Julia McGuren (10), Neil McGuren (12), Karen Mack (12), Vanessa

Mack (16), Elizabeth Morgan (14), Helen Peterson (16), David Robson (10), Neil Routledge (11), Karen Shields (13), Nicholas Smith (15), Emma Taylor (10), Sarah Taylor (11), Stephen Walton (19), Paul Wright (15).

BINGLEY (Yorkshire)
Formed 1900

Club Sec: Mrs M. Gibson, 15 Branksome Drive, Nabwood, Shipley, West Yorkshire.   *Chief Coach:* T. Hill
Members: 130. *Leading Members:* Craig Bealey (14), Andrew Beech (13), Richard Bennett (13), Holly Blues (12), Mark Edon (11), Michelle Edon (15), Susan Frost (11), Elizabeth Ibbotson (11), Sam Ibbotson (15), Philip Jessop (16), Andrew Morley (11), Sarah Normington (11), Louise Oates (12), Rebecca Owen (15), Joel Pitchforth (16), Catherine Portas (11), Andrew Poynter (11), Kirsten Poynter (15), Sarah Poynter (12), Julie Reynolds (14), David Scrivener (10), Leoni Stead (14), Lisa Stead (12), Georgina Taylor (10), Ian Wright (16).

BIRTLEY (Northumberland & Durham)

BISHOP AUCKLAND (Northumberland & Durham)
Formed 1968

Club Sec: Mrs G. Best, 2 Balmer Hill, Gainford, Co. Durham.   *Chief Coach:* R. White
Members: 225. *Leading Members:* Richard Attley (18), Trevor Barnes (23), Samantha Bean (15), Stephen Best (23), Gemma Body (12), Leanne Body (16), Louise Brown (12), Lee Carey (14), Mark Cooper (14), Rachel Craddock (13), Richard Craddock (15), Alan Dale (14), Paul Foulds (13), Ralph Foulds (16), Elizabeth Kipling (16), Duncan Lorraine (18), Sarah Niven (12), Karen Penman (16), Justine Redfern (13), Linzi Redfern (16), Carla Rispin (12), Angela Spark (17), David Warton (14), Paul Weir (15), Sarah Wilkinson (12).

BLAYDON & DISTRICT (Northumberland & Durham)
Club Sec: I. Craig, The Old Rectory, Rectory Lane, Winlaton, Tyne & Wear.   *Chief Coach:* A. Prendergast
Members: 40.

BLYTH (Northumberland & Durham)
Formed 1935

Club Sec: Mrs M. Harrison, 10 Jubilee Road, Blyth, Northumberland.   *Chief Coach:* P. Maddison
Leading Members: Emma Blakely (12), Matthew Blakely (10), Graeme Calder (11), Lisa J. Davison (11), Terence France (18), Alan Guest (12), Marie Hawkes (12), Stephen Hawkes (15), Mark Hopkins (13), Anthony Keenan (24), Graeme Kenny (14), Gary Maddison (19), Lynne Maddison (16), Jill Parkin (14), Neil Parkin (14), Damian Railston (17), Marc Rigden (11), David Smith (13), Michelle Smith (10), Rachel Smith (12), Hannah M. Stafford (15), Heidi E. Stafford (14), Phillip Thompson (14), Joanne Waugh (12), Laura Wilson (12).

BOLDON COMMUNITY (Northumberland & Durham)
Formed 1978

Club Sec: H. Stenton, 27 Holland Park Drive, Jarrow, Tyne & Wear, NE32 4U.   *Chief Coach:* D. Simpson
Members: 240. *Leading Members:* Louise Archer (13), Steven Archer (11), David Bell (21), Janet Bell (2), David Borsberry (15), Christine Cowie (24), Andrew Fairweather (19), Paul Fairweather (21), Philip Gibbs (12), Rosalind Gibbs (10), Michelle Harrison (15), Joanne Hart (17), Sara Lawson (12), Jayne O'Neil (22), Ian Reay (15), Martyn Robson (12), Nicola Robson (15), Rebecca Rodgers (14), Geoff Simpson (22), Judith Smith (16), Amanda Stenton (21), Gary Stenton (15), Raymond Stenton (17), Simon Tripcony (17), Paul Udale (12).

BOROUGH OF KIRKLEES (Yorkshire)
Formed 1982

Club Sec: B. G. Hall, Prudential House, 69 New Street, Huddersfield.   *Chief Coach:* M. H. Mosey
Members: 220. *Leading Members:* Craig Barraclough (16), Caroline Battye (14), Mark Botterill (19), Robert Carruthers (13), James Collins (14), Gillian Cook (15), Matthew Coulson (13), Sally Dickens (14), Mark Ennis (15), Eliz Firth (13), Jill Fleetwood (12), Ruth Haigh (11), Jill Harrison (17), Leigh Jamieson (12), Helen Jeason (17), Joe Leveridge (16), Stefan Lodge (15), Alex Mallinson (13), Darren Matel (18), Justy Phillips (14), Robert Pilling (18), Daniel Scedding (11), Susan Smith (13), Simon Summers (15), Kevin Wilkin (14), Neal Wilkin (16).

BOROUGH OF SOUTH TYNESIDE (Northumberland & Durham)
Formed 1979

Club Sec: A. Kay, 7 Southfield Road, South Shields, Tyne & Wear.   *Chief Coach:* J. F. Hayes
Members: 300. *Leading Members:* Martin Adair (15), Shelley Bentham (13), Kevin Boyd (22), John Bradley (20), Helen Brand (11), Angie Braund (12), Alan Brown (11), Julie Charlton (13), Lynne Charlton (12), Ian Cook (15), Jill Drysdale (20), Elizabeth Durham (10), John Durham (11), Steven Durham (14), Martin Fenner (27), Philip Hardy (12), Mandy Ivison (18), Jackie Kay (13), Kenny Nesworthy (14), Samantha Nicholson (11), Robert Oughton (12), Colin Ovington (20), Nicholas Stock (10), John Thompson (12), Victoria Wright (13).

BOROUGH OF SUNDERLAND (Northumberland & Durham)
Formed 1986

Club Sec: J.D. Hidle, 12 Rock Lodge Gardens, Roker, Sunderland, SR6 9NU.   *Chief Coach:* B. Pollard
Members: 230. *Leading Members:* David Bartell (11), Parl Bartell (15), Sharon Bell (12), Neil Cooke (11), Emma Cutter (14), Paul Dinsdale (29), Stephen Forster (14), Veryan Hickman (12), David Hidle (16), Helen Hidle (18), Anthony Hodgson (15), Robert Howe (16), Steven Howe (19), Amanda Lowery (12), Victoria Marshall (10), Andrea Newby (15), Geoff Peart, Gail Quinn (14), Peter Reed (14), Clare Swanston (11), Allan Westray (14), Ian Wilson (19), Lynne Wilson (20), Paul Worthington (12), Lousie Wright (11).

BRADFORD DC (Yorkshire)

BRADFORD DOLPHIN (Yorkshire)   *Formed* 1888
Club Sec: Mrs P. A. Llewellyn, 8 Radfield Road, Bradford, BD6 1BZ.   *Chief Coach:* M. Horner
Members: 190. *Leading Members:* Sarah Bass (14), Jason Bebb (17), Gayle Benson (14), Barry Booth (12),Sharon Brown (15), Catherine Eddison (11), Amanda Griffin (15), James Griffin (11), Jenifer Hall (15), Martin Hall (17), Leanne Haworth (13), Darren Heald (16), Nicola Hilliam (13), Mathew Holroyd (14), Alex Kay (17), John Kay (14), Daren Martell (17), Emma Midgeley (15), Kate Milnes (12), Rob Pilling (17), Richard Sheriff (12), Claire Swatman (12), Sally Townend (13), Lindsey Wall (16), Sara Ward (14).

BRADFORD GIRLS GRAMMAR SCHOOL (Yorkshire)

BRADFORD GRAMMAR (Yorkshire)

BRADFORD LONG DISTANCE (Yorkshire)

BRADFORD SCHOOLS (Yorkshire)

BRIDLINGTON (Yorkshire)   *Formed* 1977
Club Sec: Mrs K. Lloyd, 11 Marton Road, Bridlington, Y016 5AQ.   *Chief Coach:* Mrs M. Greenall
Members: 108. *Leading Members:* Simon Bedlow (11), Peter Bowtell (10), Sharon Bowtell (16), Sam Brewitt (10), James A. Brown (15), Nigel Burton (13), Christopher Cammiss (14), Neil Cammiss (12), Billie-Jean Clark (15), Sarah-Jane Clark (9), Cara Craven (10), Marie Edmond (11), Stuart Edmond (14), James Gardner (13), Matthew Kerslake (16), Mark Marshall (17), Caroline Neely (10), Paul Newsome (11), Martin Petch (10), Richard Petch (12), Richard Royal (9), Ashley Simpson (12), Rachael Simpson (10), Dean Whittington (19), Kirstie York (12).

BRIGHOUSE (Yorkshire)

BRITISH FOLIO FELLOWSHIP (Yorkshire)

BROOMPARK CROFT HOUSE (Yorkshire)

BRUNNER SCHOOL (Northumberland & Durham)

CALDERDALE (Yorkshire)   *Formed* 1975
Club Sec: Mrs B. Naylor, 4 Lees Moor Road, Cullingworth, Bradford, BD13 5HG.
Members: 40. *Leading Members:* Scott Ayscough (14), Sara Byrne (13), Zoe Cooper (15), Karen Crabtree (26), Jo Dixon (12), Claire Fox (13), Jill Gatehouse (12), Karen Green (14), Mark Halstead (15), Gemma Holmes (15), Shelley Holmes (13), Sarah Jessop (17), Linda Morris (30), Angela Ralph (11), Faye Wall (15).

CALDER VALLEY (Yorkshire)

CAMBRIDGE LADIES (Yorkshire)   *Formed* 1918
Club Sec: Miss S. Beever, 72 Rawthorpe Lane, Dalton, Huddersfield, HD5 9NU.
Members: 144.

CASTLEFORD (Yorkshire)

CHAPLETOWN (Yorkshire)

CHESTER LE STREET (Northumberland & Durham)   *Formed* 1975
Club Sec: Mrs M. Foster, 68 Kingsmere North Lodge, Chester le Street.   *Chief Coach:* J. Renshaw
Members: 175. *Leading Members:* Richard Bewley (12), Lisa Blewitt (16), Andrew Burke (10),Andrew Collett (12), Kevin Dick (23), Ruth Emerson (17), Nicholas Foster (14), Sarah Frostwick (13), Christopher Harrison (12), Emma James (12), Helen James (10), Paula McArtney (11), David McNulty (20), Gareth Owen (12), Jaqui Owen (15), Adam Palmer (17), Naomi Palmer (15), Kevin Renshaw (23), Nicola Robinson (13), Tracy Sim (16), Sarah Stonehouse (10), Robert Thomas (15), John Thubron (15), Michelle Turnbull (14), Lisa Ward (10).

CITY OF BRADFORD (Yorkshire)
Club Sec: Mrs B. Thompson, 18 Coley View, Northowram, Halifax.   *Chief Coach:* I. Armiger
Members: 194. *Leading Members:* Sarah Bass (14), Sharon Brown (14), Helen Dick (11), Catherine Eddison (11), Josephine Fannon (20), Amanda Griffin (15), James Griffin (11), Martin Hall (17), Matthew Holroyd (14), Richard Illingworth (16), Alex Kay (17), John Kay (14), Emma Midgley (15), Kate Milnes (12), Lois Partington (12), Claire Swatman (12), Craig Thompson (17), Sally Townend (13), Lindsey Wall (16).

CITY OF BRADFORD ESPRIT SCHOOL OF DIVING (Yorkshire)

CITY OF BRADFORD WPC (Yorkshire)

CITY OF HULL (Yorkshire)

CITY OF LEEDS (Yorkshire)   *Formed* 1963
Club Sec: D. Plowman, 4 Ringwood Gardens, Leeds, LS14 1AW.   *Chief Coach:* T. Denison
Members: 250. *Leading Members:* Paula Adams (15), David Akers (17), Susan Brooksbank (21), Jonathan Broughton (21), Dawn Churchman (18), Andrew Clayton (16), Carl Cockcroft (19), Ian Cotton (19), John Davey (25), Tony Day (24), Steven Dronsfield (18), Jayne Farnsworth (17), Helen Frank (18), Jane Gorst (20), Richard Greenwood (21), Jason Gregory (17), Sheldon Hanton (19), Alison McKellican

Chester le Street S.C. winning the "Top Club" Award at the Gateshead Open Meet, February, 1989

City of Bradford W.P.C. — Yorkshire Champions, 1980.

(21), Neil Metcalfe (20), Adrian Moorhouse (24), James Parrack (21), Andrew Pearce (22), Evan Stewart (19), Adeline Thorpe (15),Philip Wilkinson (16).

CITY OF NEWCASTLE-ON-TYNE (Northumberland & Durham)
Formed 1978
Club Sec: Mrs C. Foggo, 42 Hallington Mews, Killingworth, Newcastle. *Chief Coach:* I. Oliver
Members: 350. *Leading Members:* Lee Bennett (18), Alastair Boyd (22), Jill Campbell (14), David Carr (20), Lucy Clarke (15), Joanne Davey (17), Martin Douglas (15), Mark Duffy (20), Samantha Embleton (17), Emily Firth (15), Samantha Foggo (15), Steven Foggo (18), Pippa Herron (17), Tim Hobbs (18), Paul Hogg (27), Alastair Johnson (22), Simon Kelly (14), Daryl Mason (18), Paul Mitchell (27),Steven Proud (16), Janice Russell (19), Tony Stephenson (16), Helen Storey (15), Chris Sultman (16), Ian Trinder (16).

CITY OF SHEFFIELD (Yorkshire)

CLEVELAND POLICE (Northumberland & Durham)

CLUB (Yorkshire)
Formed 1899
Club Sec: S. Moss, 24 North Avenue, Otley, West Yorkshire. *Chief Coach:* M. Armstrong
Members: 200. *Leading Members:* Elina Arter (13), Alison Bown, Simon Calvert (17), Graham Dunn, James Finlay (9), Jason Healeas (12), Matthew Healey (20), Noel Horner (9), Damian Johnstone (13), Alison Kirby (9), Claire Kirby (12), Amy Littlewood (10), Peter Lodge, Sally Macgill, Sally Macgill (10), Ben Riley (11), Julie Saunders (17), David Spence (18), Rebecca Spence (15), James Stamp (17), Karen Stamp (13), Paula Todd (12), Janet Wilson.

COLNE VALLEY (Yorkshire)

CONSETT (Northumberland & Durham)

CROOK & WILLINGTON (Northumberland & Durham)
Formed 1976
Club Sec: E. P. Fayle, 2 Butwell Terrace, Hamsterley, Bishop Auckland. *Chief Coach:* A. Hills
Members: 135.

DARLINGTON (Northumberland & Durham)
Formed 1882
Club Sec: Mrs V. J. McNichol, 19 Albatross Way, Darlington, Co. Durham. *Chief Coach:* J. Moore
Members: 350. *Leading Members:* Paul Angelidi (11), Mandy Baker (9),Stephanie Bevan (16), Kwan Burachati (13), Simone Carbett (12), Andrew Carnegie (13), Grant Cockerill (14), Stephen Coulthard (11), Dawn Craven (13), Andrew Henderson (10), Craig Hollifield (11), Kevin Kelso (15), Glenda McNichol (11), Mark Monument (10), Craig Nicholson (9), Simon Noddings (17), Nicola Pardoe (10), Samantha Peacock (11), Nicola Scott (10), Brian Sharkey (16), Gavin Smith (11), Stephen Turner (14), Lyndsey Vincent (14), Helen Worth (15).

DARLINGTON DOLPHIN MASTERS (Northumberland & Durham)

DAWOON COLLIERY (Northumberland & Durham)

DEARNE DOLPHINS (Yorkshire)

DEARNE WPC (Yorkshire)

DENABY & CONISBOROUGH (Yorkshire)

DERWENTSIDE (Northumberland & Durham)
Formed 1987
Club Sec: Mrs J. Collins, 8 West Acre, Blackhill, Consett, Co. Durham. *Chief Coach:* P. Remmonds
Members: 251. *Leading Members:* Ellen Castling (11), Susan Colling (14), Stuart Craig (11), Lee Dalzell (12), David Dick (11), Paul Dixon (14), Alexander Dobson (11),Helen Downes (14), Alyson Duffy (18), Philip Greves (15), Jonathon Hunter (17), Sarah Hunter (14), Laura Jackson (13), Lesley-Anne Johnston (12), Gillian Lavin (14), Jonathon Leech (13), Ian Little (14), Mark McCamley (17), Deborah Morgan (15), Grant Pearson (15), Scott Reed (14), John Robertson (12), Scott Watson (14), Caroline Whitfield (16), Alastair Wight (12).

DERWENT VALLEY (Yorkshire)

DEWSBURY (Yorkshire)
Formed 1875
Club Sec: R. Stead, 161 Hollin Lane, Cringlestone, Wakefield, WF4 3EG. *Chief Coach:* T. L. Wilkinson
Members: 200.

DEWSBURY DOLPHINS (Yorkshire)
Formed 1979
Club Sec: Dr J. C. France, 13 Chapel Close, Thornhill, Dewsbury. *Chief Coach:* P. Rushworth
Members: 68. *Leading Members:* Craig Barraclough (15), Nicola Bogue (15), Robert Carruthers (13), Noel Craven (10), Jill Fleetwood (11), Richard France (15), Alister Gaunt (13), Kay Godbold (11), Alan Greenwood (62), Abigail Henry (12), David Hill (20), Ian Jackson (12), Joe Leveridge (15), Isla McCleery (15), Alexander Mallison (12), Christopher Murrey (13), Emma Murrey (10), Leigh Oates (14), Helen Smith (18), Rebecca Smith (10), Richard Smith (14), Daniel Spedding (11), Paul Spedding (14), Karl Squire (17), Simon Wilson (15).

DONCASTER (Yorkshire)

DONCASTER DARTES (Yorkshire)
Formed 1979
Club Sec: K. Smith, 6 Grange Road, Bessacarr, Doncaster, DN4 6SA. *Chief Coach:* P. Bright

Members: 180. *Leading Members:* Ian Andrews (15), Tim Bevington (15), Spencer Binks (14), Robin Butler (11), Jamie Christian (17), Jenny Christian (15), Victoria Credland (11), Hywel Davies (11), Trevor Eland (13), Richard Ellis (16), Adam Firbank (16), Simon Firbank (14), Stephen Hall (16), Neil Hambleton (14), Matthew Hardy (15), Carys Hughes (14), Vanessa Murray (15), Andrew Norburn (16), Michael Parkinson (14), Christopher Rix (13), Mathew Rix (11), Helen Smith (16), Brooke Stephenson (12), Pamela Trickett (14), Greg Vercant (10).

DONCASTER & DISTRICT LIFEGUARD (Yorkshire)

DONCASTER METRO (Yorkshire)

DRIFFIELD (Yorkshire)　　　　　　　　　　　　　　　　　　　　　　　　*Formed* 1984
Club Sec: Mrs C. Hughes, 26 Laburnum Avenue, Cranswick. *Chief Coaches:* W. Crawford, Mrs S. Kemp
Members: 67. *Leading Members:* Michael Billinton (12), Elizabeth Donohue (9), Jayne Goodlass (15), Alex Harrison (10), Coby Kemp (14), Damian Kemp (15), Andrew Keryakoplis (8), Alexandra King (10), Emma King (15), Sarah Owen (13), Martin Petch (10), Richard Petch (12),Louise Savage (17), Helen Sawdon (13), Kate Wylie (15), Steven Young (10).

DRONFIELD DOLPHINS (Yorkshire)

DURHAM CITY SWIMMING & WPC (Northumberland & Durham)　　　　　*Formed* 1861
Club Sec: W. B. Johnson, 10 Cookes Wood, Broompark, Durham, DH7 7RL. *Chief Coach:* K. Walton
Members: 320. *Leading Members:* Alistair Banks (11), Lucy Chivers (11), Victoria Christian (13), Steven Clark (11), Paul Fairless (10), Barry Foster (18), Neil Foster (15), Helen Hampton (14), Judith Hampton (11), Andrew Holloway (12), Sarah Holloway (18), Christopher Johnson (14), Malcolm Johnson (12), Joanne Liddle (15), David Lister (15), Rebecca Parker (10), Adam Pearson (10), Nicola Robinson (10), Mark Rochester (14), Natalie Scott (10), Nicholas Scott (14), Jeffrey Waugh (12), Steven Waugh, Phillipa West (12), Victoria Wood (12).

DURHAM COUNTY POLICE (Northumberland & Durham)　　　　　　　*Formed* 1977
Club Sec: K. W. Blakey, c/o Durham Police, Personnel and Training Department, Aykloy Heads, Durham.
Members: 25. *Leading Members:* Philip Atess (27), Graham Bell (32), Kevin Blakey (27), Ian Butler (28), Kevin Clayton (27), Paul Etherington (26), Alex Frances (29), Alison Hart (24), Angela Irving (24), Beverley Lerner (28), Timothy Lerner (28), Nicola MacDonald (28), Stuart Maughan (33), David Middleness (25), Nigel Miller (32), Anthony Mole (26), Steve Mulvey (24), Ian Proud (28), David Scott (27), Leigh Smith (26), Paul Taylor (32), Robin Trounson (32).

DURHAM SCHOOL (Northumberland & Durham)

DURHAM UNIVERSITY (Northumberland & Durham)

EAST LEEDS (Yorkshire)　　　　　　　　　　　　　　　　　　　　　　*Formed* 1986
Club Sec: Mrs D. Crossley, 28 Broomhill Drive, Leeds LS17 6JJ. *Chief Coach:* J. Thompson
Members: 150. *Leading Members:* Jane Alexander (12), Liane Dwyer (11), Sarah Fisher (15), John Henderson (13), Katharine Horgan (12), Nicholas Horner (9), Paul Kelly (15), Gavin Meadows (12), Louise Monkhouse (11), Jane Powell (18), Andrew Roberts (17), Laura Stafford (13), Lindsey Stafford (11), Victoria Staveley (12), Louise Summerfield (10),Chris Tutin (12), Paul Wardell (10).

EBOR JUNIORS (Yorkshire)

EDLINGON (Yorkshire)　　　　　　　　　　　　　　　　　　　　　　　*Formed* 1971
Club Sec: Mrs A. Jutrzenka, 31 Cecil Avenue, Warmsworth, Doncaster, DN4 9QP. *Chief Coach:* P. Shott
Members: 281.

ELLAND (Yorkshire)

ESTON (Northumberland & Durham)

FELLING (Northumberland & Durham)

FILEY & DISTRICT (Yorkshire)

FORGEMASTERS (Yorkshire)

GATESHEAD & WHICKHAM (Northumberland & Durham)　　　　　　　*Formed* 1989
Club Sec: Mrs C. Holmes, 28 Thornley Close, Whickham, Newcastle Upon Tyne. *Chief Coach:* P. Donnelly
Members: 300*Leading Members:* Scott Amos (17), Craig Ballard (21), Felicity Bennett (13), David Chaney (21), Ian Davison (11), Verity Dobbie (29), Sonia Harrison (11), Scott Holmes (16), Vicki Horner (13), Nicola Kinsey (11), Darren Little (15), Steven Little (16), David Molloy (14), Emma-Lou Morrison (15), Helen O'Halleron (11), Lynne Poulton (20), Simon Rochester (15), Steven Scott (14), Jonathan Shaw (11), Gillian Thompson (15), Kerry Thompson (13), Catherine Todd (14), Kathleen Turner (13), Louise Wigham (14), David Williams (11).

GOOLE (Yorkshire)　　　　　　　　　　　　　　　　　　　　　　　　　*Formed* 1908
Club Sec: N. Penistone, 43 Langrick Avenue, Howden, Humberside. *Chief Coach:* Mrs P. Nichols
Members: 300. *Leading Members:* R. Addinal (30+), S. Anderson (20), C. Clegg (13), S. England (18), K. Gibbons (13), L. Gunther (28), P. Gunther (17), L. Habron (12), M. Hannan (30+), N. Holmes (16), J.

Hutton (13), W. Hutton (30+), H. Langton (18), P. Nichols (30+), N. Penistone (26), P. Penistone (20), A. Raddings (13), K. Thompson (28), E. Youle (13).

GOSFORTH (Northumberland & Durham)
Formed 1970

Club Sec: Mrs A. Hastings, 10 Bromley Court, Kingston Park, Gosforth, NE3 2YH. *Chief Coach:* J. McCorie
Members: 120. *Leading Members:* Amy Austin (15), Claire Batey, Neil Benett (10), Andrew Betts (14), Richard Betts (16), Daniel Chambers (12), Louise Cook (13), Gideon Court (16), Christopher Dayson (17), Julia Dayson (14), Christopher Haddow (12), Ben Hale (12), Jenny Hall (13),Sandra Hastings (13), Alison Hope (14), Laura Johnson (12), Angus Knox (17), Caroline Lovelock (14), Lorraine McEwan (17), Michele Peasten (14), Helen Shields (13), Neil Taylor (13), Daniel Toms (14), Katy Toms (12), Joanne Young (16).

GUISBOROUGH (Northumberland & Durham)

HALIFAX (Yorkshire)
Formed 1864

Club Sec: Mrs A. Armitage, 4 Trimmingham Lane, Halifax, HX2 7PT. *Chief Coach:* L. Holroyd
Members: 300. *Leading Members:* Liam Ackroyd (12), Clare Addis (13), Christopher Armitage (11), Deborah Armitage (15), Kirstie Ashworth (17), Martin Ashworth (16), Jasen Burke (26), Kirsty Devine (15), Tony Fawthrop (27), Polly Henry (13), Sean Hepworth (18), Lisa Knowles (14), Alexandra Marshall (14), Marcus Moody (11), Richard Ridealgh (13), Ben Shaw (13), Michael Shaw (15), Nicola Shaw (14), Neal Sherwood (14), Russell Sherwood (17), Christopher Short (33), Craig Sutcliffe (16), Joanne Teal (17), Keely Thornton (12), James Wilson (13).

HALTEMPRICE (Yorkshire)

HALTWHISTLE (Northumberland & Durham)

HAMBLETON SWIM SQUAD (Yorkshire)
Formed 1979

Club Sec: A. E. Pook, 8 Hambleton Cottages, Carlton Husthwaite, Thirsk. *Chief Coach:* D. Smith
Members: 250. *Leading Members:* Steven Abbott (24), Caroline Banks (14), Claire Bennett (15), Chris Blackburn (12), Charlotte Boynton (12), Emily Boynton (12), Jonathan Burnett (14), Jonathan Charge (16), Chris Charlton (17), Helen Charlton (14), Chris Dale (18), Mark Gibbon (17), Janine Grange (17), Cheryl Hutchinson (11), Marcia Jackson (14), Claire Lazenby (14), Richard Lazenby (17), Lee Murray (13), Michael Ormerod (17), Karen Pickersgill (12), Nigel Smith (32), Paul Smith (13), Andrew Thomas (14), Georgina Toll (11), Sarah Whitcher (13).

HARROGATE DISTRICT (Yorkshire)
Formed 1898

Club Sec: Mrs J. Wilgos, 48 Studley Road, Harrogate, North Yorkshire, HG1 5JU. *Chief Coach:* B. Wilgos
Members: 60. *Leading Members:* Jenny Buffin (11), Jane Button (16), Chris Charlton (18), David Cherriman (40+), Ruth Childs (15), Mark Dalloway (13), Kate Dingwall (14), Jane Goymer (13), James Holyland (10), Ross McVey (14), Steve McVey (10), Christian Marsden (12), Joanne Marwood (14), Betty Jo Miller (11), Andrew Mullins (13), Helen Mullins (15), Jenny Mullins (11), Claudio Peral (10), Fabio Peral (12), Ben Shaw (13), Naomi Shaw (10), Alan Smith (18), Madeleine Smith (14), Kate Tipping (10), Rebecca Wilkinson (14).

HARTLEPOOL (Northumberland & Durham)
Formed 1920

Club Sec: Mrs S. M. Black, 38 Lancelot Street, Hartlepool, Cleveland, TS26 8QL. *Chief Coach:* B. Ridley
Members: 350. *Leading Members:* Aiden Bew (13), Duncan Bew (16), Christopher Bird (12), Alison Bland (12), Brenda Bland (40), Jonathon Bratt (10), Elizabeth Carter (14), David Cox (11), Steven Cox (16), Mark Davies (11), Tina Dixon (34), Allan Gray (12), Martin Gray (17), Michael Gray (15), Paul Gray (16), Julie Harrison (10), Stephen Herbert (14), Claire Jenkison (13), Danny King (15), Kim McGill (13), Katy Picken (14), Martin Sancaster (13), Betty Sands (70), Darren Turnbull (11), Michael Weed (18).

HATHERSAGE & DISTRICT (Yorkshire)
Formed 1936

Club Sec: Mrs J. Moseley, Lawnside, Bamford, Near Sheffield.
Members: 150. *Leading Members:* Caroline Carlisle (14), Robert Carlisle (12), Philip Dixon (12), Fiona Jackson (12), Louise Jackson (14), Jennifer Parkin (11), Mark Simpson (15), Peter Simpson (14), Fiona Tweedie (12).

HETTON (Northumberland & Durham)
Formed 1972

Club Sec: Mrs J. Middlemiss, Burdon Pass, Seaton, Seaham, Co. Durham. *Chief Coach:* J. Evans
Members: 350. *Leading Members:* Joanne Ayre (14), Marie Bleanch (15), Paula Burns (13), Julie Cottee (14), Craig Cummings (14), Ian Gouge (17), Frances Guy (14), Victoria Guy (13), Jill Kent (18), Andrea Lloyd (16), Alex McCall (18), Richard McElroy (12), Stephen McElroy (19), Kerry Marshall (12), Clare Middlemiss (16), Marc Middlemiss (13), Melanie Reed (17), Neil Richardson (17), Michael Robinson (15), Alan Smith (17), Stephen Smith (15), Michael Stevenson (10), Lynne Storey (12), Anya Thompson (16), David Wilkinson (13).

HOLBECK (Yorkshire)
Formed 1898

Club Sec: D. Robinson, 104 Castle Ings Gardens, Leeds, LS12 5EF.
Members: 98.

HOLME VALLEY (Yorkshire)

HUDDERSFIELD (Yorkshire)
Formed 1862

Club Sec: Mrs A. Hesselden, 58 Hill Grove, Salendine Nook, Huddersfield. *Chief Coach:* P. Cartwright
Members: 325.

HUDDERSFIELD BATHS (Yorkshire)

HUDDERSFIELD BOROUGH (Yorkshire)
Club Sec: Mrs E. Lockwood, 47 South Parade, Elland, West Yorkshire.   *Chief Coach:* F. Sykes
Members: 120. *Leading Members:* James Battye (13), Jonathan Battye (15), Amanda Bradshaw (16), Matthew Coulson (13), Robert Fox (16), Christopher Haigh (12), Damian Haigh (12), Jonathan Haigh (14), Nathan Haigh (10), Richard Haigh (15), Stuart Haldenby (11), Janine Knight (12), Sonia Lockwood (11) Stefan Lodge (15), Lynette Manning (11), Neil Moore (18), Nikki O'Flaherty (14), Victoria Podgorski (15), Anna Smith (15), Jessica Sullivan (12), Daniel Tao (12), James Tattersall (14), Robert Walker (12), Adrian Walters (10), Katie Whittaker (11).

HUDDERSFIELD OTTERS (Yorkshire)   *Formed* 1919
Club Sec: Mrs L. Firth, 130 Cowcliffe Hill Road, Cowcliffe, Huddersfield.   *Chief Coach:* J. S. Bonds
Members: 152.

HUDDERSFIELD SCHOOL (Yorkshire)

HULL CITY (Yorkshire)   *Formed* 1894
Club Sec: P. Brown, 77 Corona Drive, Hull, HU8 OHA.
Members: 40 families.

HULL KINGSTON (Yorkshire)

HULL MASTERS (Yorkshire)

HULL NEPTUNE (Yorkshire)

HULL OLYMPIC (Yorkshire)   *Formed* 1952
Club Sec: P. Boyd, 18 Cayton Road, Gillshill Road, Hull, HU8 OHD.   *Chief Coach:* R. Darley
Leading Members: Mark Billiam (15), Stephen Billiam (13), Rosaland Brett (10), James Brown (15), Christopher Cannell (18), Laura Clarke (12), Belinda Darley (17), James Draper (12), Anthony Dunn (13), Andrew Edwards (14), James Elbourne (13), Philip Elbourne (10), Julie Ellis, Richard Garbutt (16), Rebecca Garton (11), Sarah Garton (14), Carl Hale (17), Heidi Holmes (12), Sara Knights (17), Jill Newton (14), Stuart Smalley (14), Jane Sugden (14), Lee Toomey (17), Naomi Wood (13), Philip Wray (11).

HULL WPC (Yorkshire)

HULL WORKS (Yorkshire)

ILKLEY (Yorkshire)   *Formed* 1885
Club Sec: Mrs. J. Smith, Wyndham Close, 14 Clifton Road, Ilkley, LS29 8TT.
Chief Coaches: J. Cheetham, Mrs. M. Hunter, Mrs. A. Purser
Members: 150. *Leading Members:* Andrew Bailey (14), Kirstie Bennett (12), Emma Colman (16), Paula Colman (13), Bobby Diggles (13), Elizabeth Diggles (10), Sarah Fell (17), Catherine Fisher (18), Robert Griffin (18), Thomas Griffin (11), Richard Hey (12), Matthew Hodgson (13), Karl Howes (10), Timothy Lee-Gallon (12), Thomas Moore (10), Christopher Owen (15), Clare Pennock (14), Kate Pennock (11), Julie Phillips (12), Catherine Smith (21), Christopher Stanley (15), Caroline Storer (17), Heather Stubbs (18), Luke Wray (12).

KEIGHLEY (Yorkshire)

KILLINGWORTH SHARKS (Northumberland & Durham)

KINGFISHER, SCARBOROUGH (Yorkshire)   *Formed* 1979
Club Sec: Mrs C. M. Hampshire, 21 Newlands Park Grove, Scarborough.   ˙ *Chief Coach:* B. Eade
Members: 400. *Leading Members:* Simon Beevers (21), Craig Birkinshaw (13), Mark Bond (10), Hannah Brooks (15), Kate Connell (15), Lee Craven (14), Alison Davies (14), Christopher Davies (15), Karen Davison (17), David Farragher (14), Joanne Hampshire (17), Peter Hobden (11), Carole Jordan (12), Rowan Leebetter (13), James Mann (11), Garry Moment (15), Carl Morley (15), Gillian Palmer (13), Andrew Short (15), Rachael Smith (11), Amanda Thornton (13), Katie Thornton (11), Joanne Titley (12), Karen Titley (10), James Torkington (15).

KINGSTON-UPON-HULL (Yorkshire)

KIPPAX (Yorkshire)   *Formed* 1975
Club Sec: Mrs L. D. Harland, 47 Haighside Drive, Rothwell, Leeds, LS26 OUR.   *Chief Coach:* C. Bulmer
Members: 195. *Leading Members:* C. Bellwood (12), M. Bimrose (13), P. Bimrose (16), D. Blakeley (16), J. Burton (12), C. Cockroft (18), A. Cox (11), S. Cryer (11), F. Dickinson (14), S. J. Dixon (12), R. Farrell (14), L. Goodall (12), R. Goodall (12), R. Green (11), P. Hall (18), L. Hatty (12), P. Howard (14), S. Johnston (11), C. Knee (10), F. Manson (13), A. Nicholson (13), S. Starbuck (10), R. Walker (12), A. Wanbon (10), S. White (10).

KIPPAX KIPPERS SYNCHRO (Yorkshire)   *Formed* 1987
Club Sec: Mrs A. Telfer, 18 Kempton Road, Kippax, Leeds.   *Chief Coaches:* M. Telfer, I. Watson
Members: 48. *Leading Members:* Verity Baumanis (12), Kathrine Black (9), Julie Bond (11), Fiona Broadbent (11), Fiona Broomfield (12), Nicola Broomfield (10), Maria Chaplin (12), Michelle Cowell (8), Claire Cox (12), Jennifer Drever (6), Claire Dunwell (11), Laura Herbert (13), Sonyar Herbert (12), Victoria

Kingfisher, Scarborough S.C.

Kippax S.C.

Mills (11), Madeline Peacock (12), Lucy Pearson (11), Lindsey Pemberton (10), Sally Pemberton (8), Shelley Pickersgill (13), Elizabeth Roberts (12), Kirstie Ruston (11), Amy Stephenson (8), Emma Stephenson (11), Lisa Telfer (10), Vicki Telfer (11).

KNOTTINGLEY (Yorkshire)
Formed 1968
Club Sec: P. Wray, 54 Wakefield Road, Ackworth, Pontefract.   *Chief Coach:* Mrs C. A. Robbins
Members: 287. *Leading Members:* Robert Barlow (15), Richard Berry (15), Susan Brown (14), Matthew Carr (15), Julie Davies (15), Jaclyn Hayes (10), Adele Holtom (13), Lisa Langton (11), Kevin Leigh (18), Stephen Malpass (13), Louise Peart (14), Richard Penty (14), Stuart Purves (16), Craig Richards (14), Andrew Stones (18), Tracy Trinder (14), Lesley Tucker (23), David Whitelaw (14), Tracy Whittam (15), Paul Wilson (10), Andrew Wray (11), Emma Wray (13), Mark Wyard (14).

LEEDS & DISTRICT (Yorkshire)

LEEDS ESPRIT SCHOOL OF DIVING (Yorkshire)

LOFTUS DOLPHINS (Northumberland & Durham)
Formed 1988
Club Sec: Mrs B. Wilkinson, 53 Chestnut Close, Saltburn, Cleveland, TS12 1PE. *Chief Coach:* J. Wilkinson
Members: 52 *Leading Members:* Charlotte Armstrong (12), Ian Bulman (13), Neil Bulman (12), Sheila Carey (13), Stuart Danby (12), Rachel Flattley (13), Stephen Fox (11), Terry Fox (14), Stephen Gittins (11), Ruth Harland (11), Claire Harris (14), Harry Heathcock (41), Simon Jackson (12), Alan Moore (12), Claire Palmer (14), James Sanderson (10), Katie Smith (11), Ben Tyreman (10), Ian Verrill (11), Angela Webster (13), John Whitwell (11), Diane Wilkinson (13), Ian Wilkinson (12), Karen Wilkinson (13), Lee Wilson (13).

MACCABI (Yorkshire)

MIDDLESBROUGH (Northumberland & Durham)
Formed 1886
Club Sec: Mrs M. Harvey, 3 Newby Close, Acklam Hall Estate, Middlesbrough.   *Chief Coach:* S. Balmer
Members: 360. *Leading Members:* Chris Baines (13), Mark Butler (16), Ester Casson (14), Anna Clinkard (15), Rachel Clinkard (18), Jonathan Dale (12), Lisa Darks (12), Stephen Davidson (15), Mark Easby (12), Paul Floyd (16), Jonathan Harbron (13), Gillian Hodgson (15), Stephen Lancaster (13), Jillian Marsh (14), Joanne Morris (26), Richard Parry (12), Adam Petson (12), Helen Pluck (16), Jenny Robinson (13), Philip Rodgers (10), Caroline Salvin (14), Simon Ward (15), Richard Waterson (18), Tracey Waterson (15), Richard Williams (15).

MIDDLESBROUGH LADIES (Northumberland & Durham)

MINSTHORPE MARLINS (Yorkshire)
Formed 1985
Club Sec: Mrs M. Stevenson, 10 Shaw Close, South Elmsall, Pontefract.   *Chief Coach:* B. Mosey
Members: 85. *Leading Members:* Louise Allen (10), Joanne Birkin (18), Leanne Birkin (15), Sam Burton (11), Emma Coyle (14), Joanne Coyle (16), Julie Coyle (12), Nigel Hawkins (14), John Hewitt (22), Yvonne Horne (10), Jon Jamieson (15), Leigh Jamieson (12), Lyndsay Jones (10), Karen Lomas (14), Craig McDougall (10), Lee McDougall (12), Clare Picton (13), Craig Robinson (13), Andrew Somerfield (13), Andrea Stevenson (19), Lisa Tindall (9), Paula Tindall (8), Jonathan Tuffrey (13), Ruth Turner (10), Clare Yates (11), Paul Yates (12).

MORLEY (Yorkshire)

MORPETH (Northumberland & Durham)

NEWBURN (Northumberland & Durham)
Formed 1970
Club Sec: J. Knight, 10 Hawthorn Way, Ponteland, Newcastle Upon Tyne.   *Chief Coach:* T. Briggs
Members: 200. *Leading Members:* Paul Armstrong (15), Craig Beswick (19), Tracey Anne Billanie (14), Russell Bowman (23), Ian Brooks (13), Debbie Bulman (16), Kevin Davison (17), Colin Dermand (12), Scott Dickinson (11), Rachael Dryden (11), Claire Ewles (14), David Ewles (17), Rachael Hope (14), Kirsten Knight (17), Andrea McLoughlin (15), Claire Marshall (12), Julie Richardson (15), Stuart Rolph (10), Susan Rolph (11), Paula Stoves (13), Richard Stoves (15), Steven Tomkinson (14), Peter Wilkinson (16), Gary Wilson (22), Steven Woodward (17).

NEWCASTLE UNIVERSITY (Northumberland & Durham)

NEW EARSWICK (Yorkshire)

NORTH ALLERTON (Northumberland & Durham)

NORTH RIDING COLLEGE (Yorkshire)

NORTHUMBERLAND (Northumberland & Durham)
Formed 1861
Club Sec: Miss C. Laws, 23 Eastfield Road, Benton, Newcastle Upon Tyne.   *Chief Coach:* Miss C. Laws
Members: 50.

NORTHUMBRIA POLICE (Northumberland & Durham)

OTLEY (Yorkshire)

OTTERS, AIREBOROUGH (Yorkshire)
Formed 1984
Club Sec: Mrs L. Jenkinson, 25 Park Road, Guiseley, LS20 8AR.
Members: 180.

PETERLEE (Northumberland & Durham)

PILKINGTON RECREATION (Yorkshire)

POCKLINGTON DOLPHINS (Yorkshire) *Formed* 1963
Club Sec: Mrs C. Huzzard, "Cedar Lodge", York Road, Shiptonthorpe, York. *Chief Coach:* P. Hopwood
Members: 120. *Leading Members:* Andrew Barber (27), Lance Barr (13), John Brooks (25), Michael Brunt (11), Daniel Cartwright (16), Julie Clark (15), Gillian Curley (13), Jane Curley (15), Caroline Dearing (13), Paul Dearing (11), Jaqui Hindwell (16), John Hindwell (13), Claire Holmes (11), Daniel Huzzard (15), Kristian Huzzard (12), Sally Huzzard (11), Darren Jackson (11), Alan Kendra (24), Daniel Owen (11), Ian Pickering (12), Nicholas Pimm (12), Victoria Price (12), David Salmon (22), Richard Salmon (16), Richard Theakston (12).

PONTEFRACT (Yorkshire) *Formed* 1986
Club Sec: Mrs A. Ellway, 58 Knottingley Road, Pontefract, WZ8 2LD. *Chief Coach:* B. Jubb
Members: 300. *Leading Members:* I. Blackman (14), R. Carol (12), J. Charlton (9), M. Charlton (14), Fiona Darly (11), Georgina Ellis (12), Kate Ellway (10), Ruth Ellway (12), Sarah Gommerson (12), Stephanie Gordon (14), K. Gordon (10), D. Huckell (13), C. Hughes (12), Ben Hunter (10), Ruth Hunter (13), Debbie Jackson (10), Emma Jarvis (14), R. Jarvis (12), Helen Latham (13), M. Lee (13), Cassey Mullinger (11), Jessica Mullinger (10), R. Murray (13), R. Page (12), P. White (17).

PUDSEY (Yorkshire)

REDCAR (Northumberland & Durham) *Formed* 1949
Club Sec: Mrs J. Appleby, 56 West Dyke Road, Redcar, Cleveland, TS10 1HQ. *Chief Coach:* K. Morrison
Members: 150. *Leading Members:* Lorraine Brettle (11), Neil Brettle (10), Andrew Carling (13), Alexandra Clitheroe (9), Chris Clitheroe (11), Rachel Curwen (13), Mark Dale (21), Mark Dawson (17), Emma Dowse (11), Kerry Dowse (16), Mark Easton (15), Ron Fletcher (42), Jamie Ives (10), Chris Jones (15), Karl Knapp (63), Daniel McGurk (11), Richard Morrison (15), Michelle Nicholls (17), Stuart Nicholls (10), Matthew Petite (10), Dorothy Scott (34), David Stewart (12), John Stewart (10), Rebecca Surrell (11), Louise Wiggins (17).

RICHMOND DALES (Northumberland & Durham) *Formed* 1976
Club Sec: Mrs E. R. Pearson, 7 Beechfield Road, Richmond, North Yorkshire, DL10 4PJ.
Members: 200.

RIPON (Yorkshire)

ROSSINGTON (Yorkshire) *Formed* 1966
Club Sec: Mrs G. P. Norton, 6 Sharlston Gardens, Littleworth Park, Rossington. *Chief Coach:* G. Murden
Members: 250. *Leading Members:* Mark Binnington (11), Christy Branningan (18), Rebecca Brown (14), Christopher Bush (13), Alan Edmondson (12), Timothy Gleeson (15), Stephen Greene (13), Amy Grogan (13), Duane Grogan (15), Neil Hambleton (14), Jackie Hofton (14), Daniel McNamee (14), Kathryn Milne (12), Alison Moore (13), Stephen Moore (13), Lee Murden (18), Jacqui Norton (15), John Pearson (13), Shireen Pearson (16), Michael Portor (10), Deborah Powell (14), Lynn Powell (11), Michele Simm (14), Spencer Wilkinson (11), Sian Wilson (10).

ROTHERHAM (Yorkshire)

ROTHERHAM METRO (Yorkshire) *Formed* 1977
Club Sec: Mrs D. Billington, 10 Boyd Road, Wath Upon Dearne, Yorks. *Chief Coach:* C. Cunningham
Members: 200. *Leading Members:* Richard Beaumont (13), Darren Brailsford (14), Robin Clements (13), Anthony Cooper (9), Fiona Cover (17), Andrew Dales (10), Glyn Davies (21), Nicola Elliott (9), Eleanor Gambles (15), Kirstie Harrison (14), Louise Hitchings (9),Richard House (14), Paul Keens, Julia Marshall (17), Ross Martin (10), Lee North (15), Warren Osborne (9), Justine Peace (14), Claire Pursehouse (12), Andrew Simpson (9), Ian Swift (16), Craig Thompson (15), Ian White (17), Joanne Wordsworth (10), Paul Wordsworth (12).

ROTHERHAM NEPTUNES (Yorkshire)

ROUNDHAY LEISURE (Yorkshire)

ROWNTREE (Yorkshire)

ROYAL GRAMMAR SCHOOL (Northumberland & Durham)

ROSTON (Yorkshire)

RUTHERFORD (Northumberland & District)

RYDALE (Yorkshire)

SALTBURN & MARSKE (Northumberland & Durham) *Formed* 1972
Club Sec: Mrs H. Cook, 5 Frobisher Close,Marske by the Sea, Cleveland. *Chief Coach:* W. Cook
Members: 100. *Leading Members:* Darren Barker (16), Mark Burdon (16), Graham Cook (13), Rebecca Cook (15), Sarah Cook (16), Simon Cook (14), Antony Corrie (18), Liam Daniels (17), Alyson Faughey (16), Neil France (17), Fleur Harding (14), Daniel Hill (14), Lucy Hill (17), Fay Howard (13),Karl

Jakubowiak (15), David Jolly (16), Timothy Luckhurst (15), David Maddison (17), Christopher Monan (11), Stephen Monan (13), Andrew Spight (17), Lee Thompson (14), Richard Unthank (15), Lee Willard (15), Alison Wilson (16).

SALTBURN WPC (Northumberland & Durham)

SCARBROUGH (Yorkshire)
Formed 1893

Club Sec: Mrs J. Brooksbank, "Que Sera", North Street, Flixton, Yorks.   *Chief Coach:* S. Greetham

Members: 243. *Leading Members:* Joanne Allison (14), Carly Atkinson (10), Simon Bedlow (11), Sarah Bell (15), Jonathan Best (13), Lee Best (14), Gene Brooksbank (12), Hayley Chadwick (16), Jon Cheshire (17), Billie Jean Clarke (15), Nicola Crowe (14), Mary Davies (13), Karen Davison (17), Daniel Emmerson (14), Robert Fisher (15), Amanda Jessop (15), Jonathan Lucas (13), Andrew Mitchell (18), Darren Mitchell (16), James Pearce (18), Lee Simpson (16), Dyan Squires (12), Richard Thraves (21), Lorraine Wilkie (16), Kirstie York (12).

SCARBOROUGH CASTLE LONG DISTANCE (Yorkshire)
Formed 1979

Club Sec: Mrs P. Morgan, 38 Meadow Drive, East Ayton, Scarborough.   *Chief Coach:* D. Morgan

Members: 40. *Leading Members:* Selina Clayton (11), Alexia Dunn (17), Lindsay Dunn (9), Tony Hartley (40), Amanda Jessop (15), Eve Jessop (40), David Morgan (25), Pam Morgan (52), Ann Robinson (16), Jane Robinson (22), Adele Seamarks (12), Jeff Seamarks (40), Margaret Smith (41), Brian Tyson (31), Katie Tyson (26), Andrew Wharton (14), Pete Winchester (45).

SCISSETT YOUTH (Yorkshire)

SEDGEFIELD & DISTRICT 75 (Northumberland & Durham)
Formed 1975

Club Sec: G. Robson, 23 Butterwick Court, Newton Aycliffe, Co. Durham.   *Chief Coach:* R. Stobbart

Members: 187.

SELBY (Yorkshire)

Club Sec: Mrs L. Wadsworth, 30 Barlby Crescent, Selby.   *Chief Coaches:* B. Lawrence, L. Wadsworth

Members: 300.

SHEFFIELD CITY (Yorkshire)
Formed 1962

Club Sec: Mrs R. F. Bacon, 23 Newfield Lane, Dore, Sheffield, S17 3DB.   *Chief Coach:* G. Mettam

Members: 130.

SHEFFIELD & DISTRICT (Yorkshire)

SHEFFIELD DC (Yorkshire)

SHEFFIELD DOLPHINS (Yorkshire)
Formed 1973

Club Sec: J. Martin, 40 Norris Road, Hillsborough, Sheffield, S6 4QS.   *Chief Coach:* E. Motley

Members: 21. *Leading Members:* N. Aldgate, L. Bates, A. Browning, R. Burgess, R. Cankwell, A. Cornes, M. Kelly, S. Kelly, D. Leighton, N. Leighton, J. McKenna, J. Martin, C. Motley, E. Motley, P. Parsons, M. Pegg, P. Reader, K. Simpson, D. Walker, S. Welch, J. White.

SHEFFIELD NALGO (Yorkshire)
Formed 1911

Club Sec: J. W. Weston, 51 Oldfield Road, Sheffield, South Yorkshire, S6 6DS.   *Chief Coach:* A. Lindley

Members: 123. *Leading Members:* Jason Austin (23), Judith Axelby (13), Frazer Birch (14), Stuart Brayne (16), Victoria Brighton (11), Stratton Brock (17), Lynne Brooks (24), Melanie Clark (15), Caroline Couldwell (28), Debbie Daly (20), Karen Dearns (27), Sally Gough (10), Scott Hargreaves (15), Sarah Hodgson (18), Simon Hodgson (15), Matthew Johnson (15), Helen Khan (16), Ben Lafferty (18), Andrew Littlewood (22), Claire Malcolmson (12), Sally Malcolmson (15), Karen Mellor (20), Christine Shaw (36), Neil Sherringham (18), Heather Wilkins (11).

SHEFFIELD TELEPHONES (Yorkshire)

SHEFFIELD TRANSPORT (Yorkshire)

SHEFFIELD UNIVERSITY (Yorkshire)

SHEFFIELD WORKS (Yorkshire)

SKIPTON (Yorkshire)
Formed 1906

Club Sec: F. W. Hardcastle, 48 Greenacres, Skipton, North Yorkshire, BD23 1BU.   *Chief Coach:* E. Nutton

Members: 211. *Leading Members:* Diane Binns (15), M. Broadley, Angela Coates, O. Davies, Joanna Davy (15), Rachel Davy, Leo Doyle, Tao Doyle (12), Jane Green, S. Howarth, Andrew Maude (18), Daniel Maude (16), Karen Moorhouse, Alison Pickles (15), John Pickles (16), David Preston (18), S. Rogers, Christopher Smith (14), Paul Spensley (16), L. Taylor, Neil Townson, Daniel Whitaker, P. Whitaker, G. Wilkins, C. Yull.

SKIPTON DOLPHINS (Yorkshire)

SOUTH HOLDERNESS (Yorkshire)

SOUTH HUNSLEY (Yorkshire)
Formed 1976

Club Sec: J. Walker, 10 Ganton Way, Willerby, Hull, HU10 6NJ.

Members: 77.

Skipton S.C.

SOUTH SHIELDS (Northumberland & Durham)

SOUTH TYNESIDE METRO (Northumberland & Durham)

SOUTH YORKSHIRE POLICE (Yorkshire)

SOWERBY BRIDGE (Yorkshire) *Formed* 1880
Club Sec: R. Wood, 134 Pye Nest Road, Halifax, West Yorkshire, HX2 7HS. *Chief Coach:* J. Ingham
Members: 84. *Leading Members:* Virginia Carroll (17), Alison Cooper (12), Julie Eccles (10), Debbie Hodgson (10), Peter Ingham (36), Joanne Lake (15), James Pitchforth (11), Mark Rushby (16), Michael Rushby (36), Peter Rushby (38), Ian Shaw (9), Michael Shaw (14), Neal Sherwood (14), Russell Sherwood (16), Rachel Webster (10).

SOWERBY BRIDGE LADIES (Yorkshire) *Formed* 1917
Club Sec: Miss C. Thomas, 126 Pye Nest Road, Halifax, Yorks. HX2 7HX. *Chief Coach:* Mrs A. Ackroyd
Members: 109. *Leading Members:* V. Carroll, J. Eccles, D. Hodgson.

SPA (Yorkshire)

SPENBOROUGH (Yorkshire) *Formed* 1890
Club Sec: Mrs L. Dewhurst, "Fair View", Kester Road, White Lee, Batley. *Chief Coach:* B. Morse
Leading Members: Janine Armitage (14), Angela Banks (17), Sharon Barraclough (12), Richard Booth (12), Frazer Bowman (12), Mark Bowman (12), Neil Bowman (13), Mark Briggs (20), Mandy Brummitt (15), Jenny Carter (12), Debbie Church (14), Jackie Church (17), Emma Dewhurst (10), Christopher Dickens (11), Sally Dickens (14), Andrew England (12), Stephen Ferriday (20), Robert Gosling (13), Tony Gosling (10), Helen Louise Jackson (12), Gayle Pannett (12), Leanne Pannett (10), Jethro Pickard (15), Matthew Pickard (19), Michael Thornborrow (14).

STARBRECK CENTENARY (Yorkshire)

STOCKSBRIDGE PENTAQUA (Yorkshire)

STOCKTON (Northumberland & Durham) *Formed* 1876
Club Sec: P. McGann, 174 Ragpath Lane, Stockton on Tees, Cleveland. *Chief Coach:* B. Candler
Members: 220. *Leading Members:* A. Bell (14), K. Bell (16), M. Best (11), H. Farr (13), A. Ferguson (15), M. Ferguson (17), P. Harding (10), C. Iley (10), M. Johnson (14), M. Laidler (10), K. McDougall (11), K. McGann (13), N. McGann (15), C. Pearson (36), M. Stockdale (17), I. Taylor (13), L. Taylor (17), S. Thomas (11), A. Walton (14), D. Walton (17), C. Ward (57), P. Wilson (14), R. Wilson (11), J. Yarrow (14), K. Yarrow (16).

STOCKTON AQUATICS (Northumberland & Durham)   *Formed* 1978
Club Sec: Mrs C. Dawson, 146 Newton Road, Great Ayton, North Yorkshire.   *Chief Coach:* D. Carthy
Members: 107. *Leading Members:* Andrew Aitken (16), Jane Armstrong (13), David Beddard (13), Elaine Cook (14), David Dawson (14), Peter Doherty (26), Catherine Doyle (13), Emma Firbank (16), Stuart Lane (16), Jamie Moorfoot (15), Louise Mutch (15), Duane Newton (15), Kristen Oakley (15), Samantha Purvis (22), Ian Richards (11), Laura Richards (16), Antony Robinson (17), Paul Simpson (16), Kelly Smith (13), Philip Taylor (13), Louise Taylor (15), Adam Wallace (11), Lee Wardell (13), Brian West (13), Cheryl Wilson (12).

STOKESLEY (Northumberland & Durham)   *Formed* 1976
Club Sec: J. A. Hill, 46A Hilton Road, Seamer, Middlesbrough, Cleveland.   *Chief Coach:* T. Smith
Members: 398. *Leading Members:* J. Blackburn (14), S. Blackburn (12), J. Bonnington (12), T. Brown (11), F. Chapman (12), M. Chapman (15), R. Corry (19), T. Dawson (17), J. Dixon (14), H. Gerrard (11), K. Harding (14), I. Heseltine (18), L. Hill (15), V. Hill (12), K. Holley (14), M. Holley (12), A. Hutchinson (11), J. Levick (10), S. Newcombe (10), H. Purnell (13), T. Shipley (9), F. Taylor (10), S. Walker (10), J. Walton (14), S. Walton (17).

SUNDERLAND SWIM CENTRE SYNCHRO (Northumberland & Durham)   *Formed* 1986
Club Sec: Mrs A. Willis, 54 Broadmeadows, East Herrington, Sunderland.   *Chief Coach:* J. Pollard
Members: 30 *Leading Members:* Samantha Bean (15), Stephanie Bean (13), Faye Clark (9), Nicola Hope (11), Sarah Hughes (10), Helen Lindsey (13), Helen Mason (13), Anna Miller (15), Ruth Miller (11), Abigail Naugher (9), Sharon Patrick (10), Vikki Proud (9), Melisa Smith (10), Emma Todd (13), Lindsay Whiteoak (12), Joanne Willis (15), Dawn Winlow (10), Gayle Winlow (10), Pamela Wood (13), Naomi Wright (12).

SUNDERLAND TEACHERS (Northumberland & Durham)   *Formed* 1950
Club Sec: C. W. Pullen, 9 Ashton Way, East Herrington, Sunderland, SR3 3RX.

SWIMMING FOR HEALTH (Yorkshire)

THIRSK & DISTRICT (Northumberland & Durham)   *Formed* 1971
Club Sec: P. Whitaker, "Hollycroft", Croft Heads, Sowerby, North Yorkshire.   *Chief Coach:* M. Dixon
Members: 200. *Leading Members:* Darren Binks (15), Simon Bird (15), Rebecca Blackwell (12), Kate Bottomley (17), Marie Clayton (16), Anne Codling (18), Andrew Gospel (13), Nicola Jenkins (12), Scott Keningley (13), Iain Milner (11), Suzie Mitchell (16), Stephen Pickford (11), Colin Purvis (16), Helen Purvis (14), Graham Smurthwaite (14), Helen Smurthwaite (12), Helen Stead (14), Andrew Thomas (15), Michael Thomas (11), Robert Triffitt (10), Paul Watson (10), John Wharton (10), Deborah Williamson (14), Stephanie Worley (11).

THORNABY (Northumberland & Durham)

THORN PARK (Yorkshire)   *Formed* 1971
Club Sec: W.N. Darby, 26 Lindley Drive, Bradford, BD7 4JU.   *Chief Coach:* W. N. Darby
Members: 38.

TODMORDEN (Yorkshire)   *Formed* 1958
Club Sec: J. Stansfield, 8 Dale Avenue, Todmorden, Lancs, OL14 6BA.   *Chief Coach:* D. Sutcliffe
Members: 140. *Leading Members:* Gary Costello (16), Michelle Dawson (20), Kelly Deakin (11), Claire Fowler (11), Sarah Godsman (15), Shaun Godsman (13), Amy Hallgarth (11), Catherine Helliwell (14), Michael Herbert (11), Daniel Howarth (15), Heather Hudson (9), Helen Hudson (12), Martin Kipping (11), Janine Knight (12), Louise Lancashire (11), Kirsty Lapish (12), Ian Marshall (17), Emma Noble (11), Jayne Smith (20), Garry Sutcliffe (14), Karen Sutcliffe (16), Marc Thornton (12), Stuart Thornton (10), Carolyn Veevers (12), Christian Worsley (13).

TRINITY & ALL SAINTS COLLEGE (Yorkshire)

TYNEDALE (Northumberland & Durham)

TYNEMOUTH (Northumberland & Durham)

WAKEFIELD (Yorkshire)

WAKEFIELD & DISTRICT (Yorkshire)

WAKEFIELD KINGFISHER (Yorkshire)

WALLSEND (Northumberland & Durham)   *Formed* 1912
Club Sec: G. Brown, 11 Forrest Road, Wallsend, Tyne & Wear, NE28 8QF.
Members: 80.

WASHINGTON (Northumberland & Durham)

WATH WPC (Yorkshire)   *Formed* 1978
Club Sec: B. W. Taylor, 62 Newby Crescent, Balby, Doncaster, DN4 9BG.   *Chief Coach:* J. Hemmingway
Members: 15.

WESTOE LADIES (Northumberland & Durham)

WETHERBY & DISTRICT (Yorkshire)   *Formed* 1976
Club Sec: K. Beaumont, 6 Kings Meadow Grove, Wetherby, LS27 4FR.   *Chief Coach:* B. C. White

Members: 170. *Leading Members:* Andrew Atkinson (17), Helen Atkinson (15), Simon Atkinson (12), David Beaumont (10), Peter Beaumont (12), Michael Brown (10), Victoria Carter (10), Harriet Chapman (10), Nicolas Clark (18), Sarah Crinson (10), Anna Eason (12), Sian Hall (11), Louise Hardcastle (17), Sally Hardcastle (10), David Lee (12), Steven Lockwood (12), Jane McNulty (16), Claire Marley (12), Anna Nissbet (12), Claire Parker (11), Gemma Richards (10), Paul Ruddy (10),Kirsty Ward (12), Marcus Ware (18), Andrew White (17).

WHITBY SEALS (Northumberland & District)
Club Sec: Mrs G. Marshall, 40 Mayfield Road, Whitby, North Yorkshire.

Formed 1960
Chief Coach: H. Russell

Members: 237. *Leading Members:* Dawn Beeforth (14), Karen Beeforth (12), Mary Davies (13), Sarah Drummond (10), Alistair Duke (13), Andrea Duke (16), Karen Duke (11), Karl Fenwick (19), Mark Fenwick (20), Jamie Fuller (16), Adrian Fusco (11), Lindsay Harper (11), Nicola Howarth (12), Paul Keyworth (12), Darren Marshall (16), Graham Marshall (13), Kate Mercer (11), Nicola Mercer (14), Ewan Patterson (12), Ross Patterson (10), Danielle Russell (13), Matthew Russell (16), Lee Simpson (16), Rachel Stuart (11), Lee Wilson (20).

WILKINSON FURN. SOCIETY (Yorkshire)

YEARSLEY (Yorkshire)

YORK CITY BATHS (Yorkshire)
Sec: A. Baxter, 24 The Garlands, York, YO3 6YZ.

Formed 1882
Chief Coach: N. Juba

Members: 850. *Leading Members:* Caroline Banks (15), Richard Batterby (15), Kerry Chaloner (15), Helen Douthwaite (16), Martyn Falkous (17), Charlotte Grayson (14), David Gregory (12), Gary Hague (19), Jason Hague (17), Faye Heppell (14), Vicki Himsworth (13), Robert Jamison (15), Sarah Jamison (17), Adam Jones (16), David Legge (21), Rebecca Morton (13), Phil Potter (12), Lee Quickmire (12), Kelly Reed (14), Neil Savage (20), Paul Shackley (25), Chris Sharpe (17), Bronwen Simmonds (16), Ian Stewart (19), Sarah Turner (16).

Northern District

Honorary Secretary: T. Cooper, 23 Nazeby Avenue, Liverpool, L23 0SN.

ACCRINGTON (North Lancs) *Formed* 1911
Club Sec: Mrs L. Whittle, 46 Limefield Street, Accrington, Lancashire, BB5 2AF. *Chief Coach:* D. Hogan
Members: 200. *Leading Members:* David Adams (16), Stevie Baron (12), Carol Bell (12), Sarah Bramhill (12), Jason Brierley (18), Alex Bullock (17), Helen Bullock (17), Nicholas Bullock (19), Philip Bullock (13), Jane Burton (13), Damian Davenport (10), Peter Foulds (11), Kirsty George (11), Liam George (12), Linzi George (16), Paul Harrison (12), Adam Hogan (12), Melissa Hogan (12), Andrew Holden (16), Simon Holden (16), Anna Newell (10), Natasha Newell (17), Laura Simpson (13), Adam Whitehead (18), Gillian Yates (10).

ALSAGER BRIDGESTONE (North Midlands) *Formed* 1979
Club Sec: Mrs B. Cooper, 10 Clowes Avenue, Alsager, Stoke On Trent. *Chief Coach:* E. Hawkins
Members: 150. *Leading Members:* Emma Bailey (14), Suzanne Brunt (14), Alison Cooper (14), Denise Davis (16), Robert Edgell (11), Andrew Frost (17), Lisa Goode (12), Craig Hambrook (17), Elizabeth Harrison (12), Susan Harrison (17), Gail Hendry (17), Scott Hendry (15), Philip Hulme (18), Neil Jackson (43), Emma James (11), Thomas Marshall, Stephen Molyneux (13), Janine Morgan (20), Derek Pedley (15), Robert Sarson (17), Marc Sherwood (15), Simon Sherwood (12), Claire Skorupinska (16), Helen Smallwood (14), Patrick Woodhead (14).

APPLEBY (Cumbria)

AQUA 90 (Liverpool & District)

AQUADIS (Cheshire)

ASHTON CENTRAL (Central Lancs) *Formed* 1977
Club Sec: Mrs E. Holmes, 181 Princess Road, Ashton in Makerfield. *Chief Coach:* A. Grundy
Members: 197. *Leading Members:* Joanne Banks (17), Spencer Glover (20), Andrew Gow (15), Andrew Hughes (10), Michael Nolan (18), Emma Pilling (13), Mark Ray (17), Matthew Ritchie (11), Ian Whitehead (14), Barry Woodall (12).

ASHTON UNDER LYNE (Central Lancs)

ATHERTON (Central Lancs)
Club Sec: Mrs D. Rowland, 29 Hillside Avenue, Atherton, M29 9LX. *Chief Coach:* A. Cowburn
Members: 169. *Leading Members:* Carol Baddley (12), Lesley Charlesworth (16), Paul Cowburn (10), Karen Derbyshire (15), Jackie Ellis (17), Daniel Forster (14), Keith Gabbitas (12), Neil Gabbitas (14), Barry Goodwin (13), Deborah Greensmith (15), Andrew Hickson (17), Christian Hunt (15), Joanne Hurst (11), Alison Peat (14), Helen Reed (11), Beverley Rowland (12), Donna Rowland (14), Michael Sharples (14), Jonathan Sutton (15), Katherine Sutton (15), Lisa Thompson (11), Phillip Thompson (15), Haydn Vaughan (15), Joanne Wilcock (16), Katherine Winstanley (11).

AUTOMOTIVE (Liverpool & District)

BACUP (Central Lancs)

BARROW BEAVER (Cumbria) *Formed* 1882
Club Sec: Mrs S. Wilson, "Wilmoran", North Scale, Walney Island, Cumbria. *Chief Coach:* D. NcNamee
Members: 450. *Leading Members:* S. Brewer (14), C. Calvert (13), C. Corkill (13), M. Corkill (9), I. Devlin (16), M. Dewey (9), E. Docker (11), A. Dower (13), S. Harrison (12), J. Hockwell (15), K. Hopkins (11), J. Johnson (18), G. Kilburn (16), M. Knagg (23), A. McNamee (19), L. Mounsey (14), I. Plumb (11), G. Queen (10), A. Robson (11), B. Sutcliffe (10), D. Thomas (14), A. Waite (10), G. Walker (14), J. Wilson (13), R. Wood (9).

BARROW LONG DISTANCE (Cumbria)

BEAVER (Liverpool & District)

BEBINGTON (Liverpool & District) *Formed* 1974
Club Sec: R.K. Robinson, 8 Nelson Croft, Bebington, Wirral, Merseyside. *Chief Coach:* W.E. Swaby
Members: 100. *Leading Members:* Mary-Louise Adamson (15), Alex Baker (11), Pippa Cook (18), Christopher Edge (11), Alex Fryer (17), Natalie Hardy (13), Sonja Hardy (16), Andrew Haselgrove (14), Elizabeth Henderson (16), Paul Herbert (14), Adrian Ingram (11), Philip Ingram (16), Kate Jackson (12), Stephanie Jackson (11), David Jones (10), Catherine Lightfoot (14), Liam Morgan (12), Andrew Olds (13), David Phillips (12), Stuart Phillips (17), Andrew Pimbley (12), Carole Schofield (13), Michelle Thompson (11), Jaqueline West (16), Siobhan Winter (11).

BICC INSTRUCTION (Liverpool & District) *Formed* 1951
Club Sec: L.S. Pryde, 37 Poplar Grove, Prescot, Merseyside, L35 5AY.
Members: 247. *Leading Members:* J. Barron, G.T. Brown, A.M. Burns, J.T. Comerford, J. Doward, C.G. Fairclough, V.L. Frodsham, A. Grisedale, F. Hankin, E.J. Head, G. Humphreys, J.T. Jeffs, B. Kulshaw, V. Kirk, C.D. Kitto, S. Kitto, I. Lucas, R. Lucas, F. Lynam, B. Lyon. T. Powell, L.S. Pryde, C. Riley, J. Riley, R. Wiltshire.

BICC Instruction S.C. — Committee, Officials and Teachers in the deep end.

BIDDULPH *Formed* 1973
Club Sec: Mrs C. Wheawall, 23 Lyndhurst Drive, Brown Lees, Biddulph. *Chief Coach:* G.J. Kirkham
Leading Members: Steven Allen (18), David Ball (15), Christopher Bean (16), Andrew Beard (27), Hilary Bradbury (26), Craig Edwards (22), Jason Eggerton (16), Julie Eggerton (20), Alison Fisher (18), Paula Fisher (16), John Fleming (15), Lesley Gallimore (36), Matthew Griffiths (17), Mark Johnson (24), Steven Jones (21), Geoffrey Kirkham (32), David Lacey (37), Andrew Lawton (16), Mark Ludlow (15), Cheryl Mann (14), Julie Millins (13), Victoria Oxford (14), Lisa Sharman (15), Mark Stevens (14), Ruth Williams (15).

BIRKENHEAD (Liverpool & District)

BIRKENHEAD CEC (Liverpool & District)

BIRKENHEAD CWS (Liverpool & District)

BLACKBURN CENTURIONS (Central Lancs)

BLACKPOOL (North Lancs)

BOLTON (North Lancs)

BOLTON BRIDGEMAN (Bolton & District) *Formed* 1901
Club Sec: Mrs I.B. Williams, 17 Clayton Street, Bolton, BL2 1NJ. *Chief Coach:* Mrs C.A. Waldram
Members: 245.

BOLTON DOLPHINS (Bolton & District)

BOLTON SCHOOL (Bolton & District)

BONUS (Cumbria)

BOOTLE & NORTH LIVERPOOL (Liverpool & District) *Formed* 1889
Club Sec: Mrs D. Winrow, 28 Fouracres, Maghull, Merseyside, L31 7BP. *Chief Coach:* W. Stevens
Members: 100. *Leading Members:* Edward Clements (13), Mathew Davidson (13), Glynn Davies (17), Kimberley Edwards (13), Melanie Edwards (16), Neil Grundy (15), Caroline Hayes (12), Greg Hedger (16), Stuart Ingram (14), A. Knight (17), Julie Knight (18), Tony Lawless (13), Katrina McCormack (15), Helen McEvoy (15), Sara McEvoy (18), Stephen McKenzie (12), Kathryn Mawdsley (17), Joanne Moore (16), Tina Porter (13), David Roddy (14), Joanne Rogers (12), Brian Stevens (15), Helen Wilson (17), K. Winrow (20), Debbie Woods (18).

BORDER CITY (Cumbria) *Formed* 1921
Club Sec: A.A. Dane, 1 Naworth Drive, Carlisle, Cumbria, CA3 0DD. *Chief Coach:* G. Allan
Members: 150.

BOROUGH OF BURNLEY C.A.T.S. (Central Lancs) *Formed* 1976
Club Sec: A.D. Moorhouse, 8 Singleton Avenue, Read, Burnley, BB12 7PJ. *Chief Coach:* A.D. Moorhouse.
Members: 100. *Leading Members:* Sara Atkinson (14), Tracy Beattie (14), Vanessa Blackburn (17), Rachel Brown (16), Daniel Crossley (16), Simon Crozier (14), Jayne Dowling (15), Lee Downham (17), John Drummond (18), Andrew Fletcher (16), Tracy Gee (15), Stuart Hamer (14), Joane Hudson (14), Karon Jackson (16), Peter Jones (19), Emma Lang (12), Timothy Lee (14), Nicola Magnall (13), Joane Robinson (18), Rachel Rowan (17), Steven Smith (22), Steven Walker (15), Simon Walmsley (16), Joanna Waterworth (18), Mark Whittam (13).

BRIDGEFIELD (Liverpool & District)

BROADWAY (Central Lancs) *Formed* 1968
Club Sec: Mrs G. Marr, 25 Nina Drive, Moston, Manchester, M10 9SA. *Chief Coach:* W. Andrew
Members: 120.

BROOKVALE (Liverpool & District)

B.S.A.D., NORTH WEST (Manchester & District)

BURNLEY (Central Lancs) *Formed* 1887
Club Sec: J. Yates, 76 Whalley Road, Read, Burnley, Lancashire. *Chief Coach:* M. Roper
Members: 125. *Leading Members:* Stephen Airey (11), Anthony Brown (14), Martin Brown (11), Rachel Brown (16), Andrew Comstive (5), Kelsey Duckworth (5), Mark Gill (12), Brian Hargreaves (10), Nicola Magnall (13), Susan Magnall (5), Alexandra Milburn (10), David Milburn (11), Victoria Parkinson (11), Caroline Porter (11), Marian Price (5), Charlotte Rigby (11), Margaret Roper (5), Sarah Stevenson (13), David Sturrock (10), Jane Taylor (14), Janet Taylor (12), Ian Terry (14), Barnaby Thompson (11), Gregory Thompson (13), Paul Wood (12).

BURY & ELTON (Central Lancs)

CARLISLE CITY (Cumbria) *Formed* 1944
Club Sec: Mrs M.L. Hollick, 10 Longthwaite Road, Wigton, Cumbria, CA7 9JR. *Chief Coach:* C. Kidd
Members: 254. *Leading Members:* P. Anderson (12), K. Brown (13), K. Daniels (15), R. Edwards (12), A. Fearon (16), D. Fearon (13), D. Frame (18), H. Gradwell (17), J. Judge (15), N. Karge (15), A. Kidd (14), C. Lancaster (18), M.Y. Little (20), C. Ludwig (15), J. Miller (18), S. Morgan (14), D. Patterson (14), C. Reardon (16), N. Reid (19), C. Rodgers (13), D. Rodgers (16), L. Scougall (15), S. Smith (17), M. Telford (17), L. Tickell (17).

Carlisle City S.C. — Craig Lancaster, Jacqui Miller, Helen Gradwell and Myles Little.

CARNFORTH & DISTRICT OTTERS (North Lancs)
Formed 1978
Club Sec: R.G. White, 5 Browfoot Close, Carnforth, Lancashire, LA5 9XT. *Chief Coach:* P. Goymer
Members: 185. *Leading Members:* Faye Beattie (15), Martin Cooke (15), Stella Dixon (14), Danny Fitzgerald (15), Ian Gorst (14), Jane Gorst (21), Kerry Goymer (15), Emma Gudgeon (12), Paul Hartley (13), Simon Hartley (15), Emma King (14), Deborah Longley (12), Mark Longley (14), Helen Morris (17), John Morris (20), Sarah Nisbet (17), Matthew Nolan (13), Paul Rickerby (24), Anna Stevenson (12), Matthew Thoms (12), Philip White (12), Sally White (16), Sarah Williams (13), Matthew Wilson (13), Nicholas Wilson (14).

CASTLETON (Central Lancs)

CELLARMEN (Manchester & District)

CHADDERTON (Central Lancs)
Formed 1894
Club Sec: B. Edge, 76 Holly Grove, Chadderton, Lancashire, OL9 0DQ. *Chief Coach:* J. Entwistle
Members: 250. *Leading Members:* Annette Ahern (15), Ryan Ahern (12), Matthew Aspden (10), Richard Bailey (13), Lynn Beswick (22), Graham Bucknell (15), Kristina Clay (16), Naomi Coulston (14), Emma Exon (12), Vickie Griffin (13), Alison Haigh (12), Dawn Hepburn (11), Michelle Huskinson (11), Lesley Ibbotson (13), Liza Jackson (14), Paul Jackson (10), Richard Jackson (14), Clare Joyce (13), Debbie Joyce (10), Kristian Lee (15), Kirsty Lees (13), Mandy Lees (16), Lisa Saxon (14), Martin Tighe (13), Nicola Young (15).

CHALLENGE LIVERPOOL (Liverpool & District)

CHALLENGE MANCHESTER (Manchester & District)

CHALLENGE ST HELENS (Liverpool & District)

CHEADLE & DISTRICT (North Midlands)
Formed 1968
Club Sec: Mrs B. Turner, 16 Dilhorne Road, Forsbrook, Stoke on Trent, ST11 9DJ. *Chief Coach:* A. Stone
Members: 248. *Leading Members:* Carl Baker (16), Joanne Bate (12), Andy Berrisford (14), Dan Berrisford (18), John Blood (12), Philip Brown (15), Lee Carnwell (12), Louise Carnwell (10), Joanna Clarke (17), Amy Cope (10), Laura Cope (12), Melissa Cosson (12), Tim Edwards (18), Duncan Ellis (12), Richard Ellis (9), Jane Heralny (14), Ben Jary (13), Rob Keates (13), Andy Powell (16), Paula Sherratt (13), Jamie Tait (15), Ian Thompson (17), Joanna Underwood (15), Iain Wood (11), Glenys Wood (14).

CHESHIRE CONSTABULARY (Cheshire)

CHESTER BREAKAWAY (Cheshire)

CHESTNUT LODGE (Liverpool & District)

CITY OF CHESTER (Liverpool & District)
Formed 1896
Club Sec: F. Morris, 6 Rosewood Avenue, Upton, Chester, CH2 2JG. *Chief Coach:* N. Longridge
Members: 750. *Leading Members:* Steven Ashton (18), Greg Barnham (15), Sarah Cunruff (13), Andrew Davies (16), Niall Evans (15), Mark Hulse (15), Beverley Jones (17), Debbie Jones (15), Elizabeth Jones (16), Keri Jones (15), Rachel Kench (15), Sarah Kench (16), Helen Mansfield (18), Lynsay Potter (15), Jill Roberts (17), Lynsay Smart (16), Shona Smart (18), Alyn Smith (16), Colin Smith (18), Jason Wender (18), Andrew Whitby (15), Greg Williams (15), Mark Wolfenden (15), Julie Wright (17), Sarah Youd (15).

CITY OF LIVERPOOL (Liverpool & District)
Formed 1974
Club Sec: T. Tanstall, 23 Cherry Lane, Aughton, Ormskirk, L39 5EH. *Chief Coach:* D. Jameson
Members: 300. *Leading Members:* N. Beeley (11), S. Brainham (51), J. Burgess (14), S. Burgess (11), L. Caddick (15), S. Formby (11), S. Gale (15), C. Halsall (13), C. Hayes (12), J. Howell (12), A. Jameson (24), P. Knight (16), V. Long, H. McEvoy (15), D. Parry (13), S. Parry (12), D. Potter (11), R. Rayworth (12), A. Riley (14), B. Riley (15), D. Rimmer (14), J. Sim (13), B. Swaine (11), J. Tinsley (37), S. Tulley (13), K. Williamson (12).

CITY OF MANCHESTER (Manchester & District)

CLARENDON (Bolton & District)

CLITHEROE & DISTRICT (North Lancs)

COCKERMOUTH (Cumbria)
Formed 1978
Club Sec: D. Salmon, 13 Dale View, Cockermouth, Cumbria, CA13 9EN. *Chief Coach:* C. Laidlow
Members: 150. *Leading Members:* Kathryn Burke (12), Antony Bush (13), John Dougall (13), Susan Dougall (11), Jacqueline Emmerson (13), Tina Fletcher (14), Ian Gould (14), Peter Haley (18), Craig Harrison (15), Louise Harrison (17), Paul Hodgson (20), Richard Laidlow (16), Amanda Lee (15), Elizabeth Lorton (17), Emily Lorton (11), Olivia Lorton (15), Paul Messenger (17), Ciaran Owens (12), Louise Salmon (12), Judith Smith (12), Paul Wainwright (17), Helen Walsh (21), Kevin Walsh (18), Louise Watson (13), Matthew Woodcock (12).

COLNE (Central Lancs)
Formed 1912
Club Sec: J. Croxall, 2 Holme Close, Earby, North Colne, Lancashire. *Chief Coach:* J. McCartan
Members: 150. *Leading Members:* Tony Catterall (44), Joe Chambers (12), Rachel Crowther (13), Andrew Croxall (19), Lesley Croxall (17), Philip Croxall (20), Jayne Dowling (15), Jolene Dowling (10), Philip Downing (11), Karen Driver (17), Andrew Higginbottom (11), Claire Higginbottom (13), Laura

Hornby (9), Craig McDonald (12), James McDonald (9), Kate Reynolds (15), Jessica Shuttleworth (11), Steve Smith (21), Andrew Stobbs (10), Geoff Stobbs (30), Sheryl Sweeney (12), Rebecca Tomkins (14), Steven Walker (15), Emma Wilkinson (11), Jimmy Wilson (15).

CONGLETON (Cheshire)   Formed 1936
Club Sec: Mrs C. Banner, "Y-B-Sad", 122 Holmes Chapel Road, Congleton.   Chief Coach: P. Axson
Members: 250. Leading Members: David Bailey (9), Ivan Barber (17), Ben Brampton (11), Jenny Capon (11), Sarah Cheetham (9), Liam Conroy (9), Rachael Cope (15), Stephen Cousins (13), Charles Cropper (15), Andrew Dean (11), Philip Dean (13), Mathew Field (11), Helen Godley (11), Claire Greenwood (11), Claire Harper (11), Nicholas Howe (15), Pamela Maddock (15), Josephine Mayburey (15), Debbie Mellor (13), Joanne Morris (11), Caroline Moss (13), Beverly Plant (11), Christopher Plant (13), Rebecca Salt (11), Michael Whitehurst (13).

COPELAND (Cumbria)   Formed 1986
Club Sec: Mrs J. Mossop, Picketthow Farm, Egremont, Cumbria, CA22 2UD.   Chief Coach: C.W. Griffin
Members: 142. Leading Members: Michael Asbridge (15), Esther Barry (15), Leanne Cottier (11), Kerry Dawson (15), Gillian Gainford (12), Daniel Hawkrigg (15), Philip Hawkrigg (14), Josephine Marshall (15), Kathryn Marshall (13), Jonathan Mean (12), Richard Musgrave (11), Angela Osman (13), Vanessa Osman (15), Graeme Parkin (16), Steven Parkin (14), Christina Pattinson (11), Tracy Penrice (17), Trudy Penrice (15), Martin Pickup (18), Heidi Ritson (12), Paula Scott (14), Ryan Taylor (12), Rhona Watson (14), Andrew Westhead (13), Naomi Wilson (12).

CREWE BOROUGH (Cheshire)

CITY OF STOKE-ON-TRENT (North Midlands)   Formed 1968
Club Sec: D. Taylor, 109 Ulverston Road, Newstead, Burton.   Chief Coaches: G. Clarke, S. Whittaker
Members: 140. Leading Members: Carl Baker (15), Joanne Bate (12), Andrew Berrisford (13), Donna Bruce (13), Adrian Clarke (17), Joanne Clowes (14), Beth Cooper (14), Tim Edwards (18), Duncan Ellis (12), Nicola Gallimore (15), Jane Heraghty (14), Michelle Jones (14), Cheryl Mann (14), Kirstee Moorcroft (17), Vicky Oxford (14), Diane Poole (16), Andrew Roberts (14), Patrick Roberts (14), Tim Roberts (16), Andrew Sharp (20), P. Sharp (17), Robert Shaw (15), Mark Stevens (14), Ian Thompson (17), Joanne Underwood (14).

CROMPTON CLASSICS (Central Lancs)   Formed 1918
Club Sec: Mrs P. Sutcliffe, 52 Edward Road, Shaw, Oldham, OL2 7EY.   Chief Coach: N. Hilton
Members: 200.

CROSBY (Liverpool & District)   Formed 1963
Club Sec: Mrs D. Thomas, 34 York Avenue, Crosby, Liverpool 23.   Chief Coach: J. Roberts
Members: 200. Leading Members: Dominic Batty (12), Emily Chadwick (12), Andrew Chestnut (11), Gareth Couldray (17), Richard Couldray (15), Christine Cunningham (18), Helen Cunningham (13), Michael Cunningham (17), Alexandra Davies (10), John Delamere (14), Helen Hale (13), Colin Harrison (15), Alan Hill (19), Dawn Leatherbarrow (17), Julia McGuire (15), David Maddock (15), Sarah Maddock (9), Nicola Martin (16), Joanne Mugrond (16), Neville Roberts (21), Christopher Sanders (11), Gareth Shepherd (12), Rachael Shepherd (10), Stephen Simpson (10), John Tanner (12).

DALTON DOLPHINS (Cumbria)

DANE VALLEY (Cheshire)

DARWEN (Central Lancs)   Formed 1932
Club Sec: Mrs I. Ingham, 102 Livingstone Road, Blackburn, BB2 6NE.   Chief Coach: A. Wilkinson
Members: 200. Leading Members: Douglas Aspden (13), Andrew Bolton (15), Emma Bury (15), Andrew Farnworth (15), Natalie Farnworth (12), Rebecca Haworth (15), Clair Higginbottom (13), Graeme Hunter (11), David Ingham (10), Joanne Martin (13), Jonathan Metcalfe (11), Sarah Metcalfe (15), Vicky Miller (14), Sarah Myers (15), Julie O'Neil (19), Sandra O'Neil (43), Mark Pearson (11), Craig Ridgeway (15), John Robinson (19), Barbara Rodgerson (14), Helen Rushton (13), Matthew Rushton (11), Elizabeth Taylor (17), Mark Warren (15), Kristine Wilkinson (17).

DAVENPORT & DISTRICT (Central Lancs)

DAVEY HUME MASTERS (Manchester & District)

DIDSBURY COLLEGE OF EDUCATION (Manchester & District)

DOLPHIN, CARLISLE (Cumbria)   Formed 1947
Club Sec: E.A. Ayress, "Samarkand", Orton Road, Carlisle, Cumbria, CA2 7TP.   Chief Coach: A. Ayress
Members: 50.

DOLPHIN, CHEADLE (North Midlands)

DOLPHIN DIVING (Manchester & Distrct)

DOLPHIN, LIVERPOOL GENTS (Liverpool & District)

DOUGLAS (Isle of Man)   Formed 1882
Club Sec: Mrs V.A. Ward, Silver Creek, Litergy Cripperty, Union Mills.   Chief Coach: Mrs C. Cooil

Members: 256. *Leading Members:* Suzanne Brown (15), David Bushe (17), Shirley Carine (30), Joanne Clague (13), Leonie Cooil (10), Marcus Cooil (15), Jonathan Cretney (12), Martine Fleming (15), Voirrey Howland (13), Christine Johnson (15), Alan Jones (11), Miranda Kinrade (19), Philippa Kinrade (13), Russell McCann (12), Jason Macaulay (13), Jennifer Morris (11), Lynsey Morris (14), Mark Osborn (19), Caroline Ruscoe (14), John Ruscoe (16), Nicola Sims (13), Graham Stigant (28), Shane Stigant (26), Alan Stockdale (25), Kelly Unsworth (11).

DROYLESDEN & DISTRICT (Central Lancs)

DUKINFIELD MARLINS (Central Lancs)

ECCLES (Central Lancs)

ELLESMERE PORT (Liverpool & District)
Formed 1968
Club Sec: Mrs S.C. Cooke, 40 Greenfield Road, Little Sutton, Cheshire.　　*Chief Coach:* Mrs H. Smith
Members: 360.

EVERTON (Liverpool & District)
Formed 1865
Club Sec: F. Lunney, 59 The Beeches, Liverpool, L18 3LT.　　*Chief Coach:* N. Blythin
Members: 280. *Leading Members:* B. Bradley (13), A. Carbery (12), M. Chidlow (13), D. Cottrell (12), N. Cowell (14), J. Culshaw (11), J. Dacre (14), S. Frederick (14), A. Hamlyn (14), L. Jackson (18), M. Jones (29), H. Lancaster (14), J. Lee (14), A. Lunney (12), S. Maddock (9), C. Maddocks (15), P. Maxwell (13), D. Park (13), T. Parr (13), N. Robb (15), C. Roland (13), K. Rowe (15), L. Smith (14), S. Turley (13), A. Wylie (22).

FAILSWORTH (Central Lancs)
Formed 1984
Club Sec: C. Hobbs, 15 Paddock Lane, Failsworth, Manchester, M35 0NY.　　*Chief Coach:* L. Howman
Members: 75. *Leading Members:* Edward Bright (10), Marie Chadderton (12), Laura Coyle (9), Robert Coyle (15), Matthew Davies (9), Nicola Jackson (12), Darren Jones (11), Stella Kenyon (13), Laura Madden (10), Donna Marlborough (10), Rachael Stimpson (11), Joanne Swallow (14), Michele Tarpey (13), Mark Tippman (12).

FARNWORTH (Bolton & District)

FENCIBLES (Isle of Man)

FLEETWOOD & DISTRICT (North Lancs)
Formed 1975
Club Sec: A. Stout, 1 Ridgeway Drive, Cleveleys, Blackpool.　　*Chief Coach:* J. Medd
Members: 440. *Leading Members:* Anne Beaumont (15), Darren Bradford (16), Ian Chappell (22), Marcus Cook (17), Catherine Cowburn (14), Gregory Cowburn (17), Debbie Gore (22), Anna Gray (14), Nick Grundy (15), Cherie Knight (13), Leslie Masters (20), Alex Myers (19), Elliot Myers (19), Colette Newsham (18), Helen Oates (13), Paul Ramsbottom (24), Robert Schofield (24), Kathryn Scott (23), Maria Scott (24), Sarah Swettenham (15), Michelle Wheeler (22), Jared Whiteside (13), David Williams (24), Richard Williams (25), David Williamson (16).

FORMBY (Liverpool & District)

FORMBY PRIMARY SCHOOLS (Liverpool & District)

FOURWAYS (Manchester & District)

FRIENDS OF STOCKPORT SCHOOL (Manchester & District)

GARSTANG (North Lancs)
Formed 1980
Club Sec: S. Mortimer, 15 Garstang Road, Garstang, Preston.　　*Chief Coach:* Mrs J. Barnes
Members: 180. *Leading Members:* Melissa Barnes (11), Lynsey Bracegirdle (11), Daniel Burrow (16), Nicola Burrow (18), Jenifer Clarke (13), Daniel Collinson (10), Daniel Crook (10), Jayne Cuff (11), Jonathon Cuff (14), Deborah Garstang (18), Mark Haslem (15), Dean Hesketh (14), Neil Hesketh (16), Martha Ingleby (11), Kathleen Jemson (12), Ian McKean (12), Kirsten Mackin (14), Christopher Miller (11), Claire Miller (12), Susan Miller (14), Matthew Mortimer (14), Judith Newsholme (23), Caroline Porter (10), James Riley (11), Amy Swarbrick (12).

GARSTON (Liverpool & District)
Formed 1908
Club Sec: S. Rothwell, 48 Manor Road, Wallasey, Merseyside, L44 1BY.　　*Chief Coach:* A. Christie
Members: 400. *Leading Members:* Nicola Allister (16), Rebecca Allister (11), Timothy Allister (15), Michael Ball (13), Elizabeth Bromilow (16), Anthony Christie (12), Eleanor Cooke (12), Heddy Cringle (14), James Cummins (13), Kevin Danily (13), John Jackson (13), Paula Jackson (11), Stephen James (13), Claire Knox (12), Fiona Lawlor (13), Joanne MacAskill (12), Karen Pickering (12), Lisa Roberts (18), Anita Wakefield (12).

G.E.C./B.A.C. (Liverpool & District)

G.H. LEE (Liverpool & District)

GLOSSOP (Manchester & District)

GOODLASS (Liverpool & District)

GRANGE OVER SANDS (Cumbria)

Garston S.C. — Team photo taken in 1919. Austin Rawlinson, the former backstroke champion of England and only title-holder ever to become the ASA President, is shown, back row, in centre of swimmers.

GREATER MANCHESTER EAST SCOUTS (Manchester & District)

GREATER MANCHESTER POLICE (Manchester & District)

GREAT HARWOOD OTTERS (Central Lancs)   *Formed* 1962
Club Sec: Mrs M. Hilton, 20 Westcliffe, Great Harwood, Lancashire.   *Chief Coach:* R. Ward
Members: 99. *Leading Members:* Jennifer Allen, Paul Allen, Ben Baron (13), Rachel Bellas (17), Mark Boardman (13), David Burrows (11), Martin Counsell (10), Carla Dewell (9), Helen Duckworth (12), Stephen Ellis (15), Vicky Gill (9), Emma Hayes (10), Catherine Hilton (13), Rachel Hudson (13), Leanne Kelly (10), Gregor Methven, Carol Miller, Steven Miller (16), Shellie Pirrie (12), Mark Potter (12), Janette Procter, Paul Rutter (11), Ian Tunstall (9), Bianca Verity (13), Rachel Ward (11).

GREEN PARK (Liverpool & District)   *Formed* 1986
Club Sec: P. Edwards, 14 Stangate, Green Park, Maghull.   *Chief Coaches:* D.R. Bayliff, B. Williams
Members: 60. *Leading Members:* Stephen Bayliff (13), Andrew Bird (14), Fiona Broadfoot (12), David Charnley (11), Jane Charnley (8), Chris Edwards (14), Sarah Edwards (10), Andrew Evans (10), Colin Filby (10), Stewart Filby (12), Ian Gibson (10), Simon Gibson (12), Lisa Hamblett (14), Ian Harrison (16), Stephen Harrison (13), Paul Lange (13), Stephen Lange (14), Katie Orr (13), Andrew Parker (8), Graham Parker (11), Mark Rimmer (10), Nichola Roe (11), Jennifer Thomas (10), Steven Thomas (12), Nicholas Williams (16).

HAMBLETT SPECIAL SCHOOL (Liverpool & District)
Club Sec: J.E. Mawdsley, Hamblett School, Rainford Road, St Helens, WA10 6DX.

HARPURNEY (Central Lancs)   *Formed* 1910
Club Sec: Mrs D. Matthews, 12 Boardman Fold Road, Alkrington, M24 1GD.   *Chief Coach:* D. Evert
*Members:*150. *Leading Members:* Lyndsay Allen (11), Helen Anderson (15), Lee Armstrong (10), David Bailey (16), Sally Dickinson (14), Rachel Dyce (11), Andrew Evans (15), David Evans (12), Nicola Finnerty (15), Chantel Green (11), Damien Green (13), Natalie Horn (12), Andrea Jackson (13), Claire Jepson (11), David Pontifract (16), Andrew Poole (11), Yvonne Porter (12), Steven Powell (15), Peter Roberts (10), Claire Scott (15), Antony Shatliff (15), Hassan Soitani (16), Michael Stanton (12), Sara Walker (12), Kerry Walsh (12).

HASLINGDEN (Central Lancs)   *Formed* 1936
Club Sec: Mrs E. Haworth, 252 Grane Road, Haslingden.   *Chief Coach:* B. Till
Members: 180. *Leading Members:* Ian Baxter (12), John Buckley (12), Paul Buckmaster (13), Andrew Fletcher (16), Katie Foster (11), Sarah Grundy (10), Samantha Hargreaves (13), Jill Haworth (17), Mark

Haworth (16), Joanne Hood (10), Karen Hood (13), Ian McAllister (13), Alister Millington (13), Samantha Muldowney (12), Andrew Parrott (13), Heather Parrott (10), Andrew Scanlon (14), Paul Scanlon (16), Amanda Sedgwick (12), Nadine Till (12), Rachael Whittaker (10), Simon Whittaker (12), Kirsty Wilkinson (16), Paul Wright (10), Shelly Wright (14).

HAZEL GROVE & BRAMHALL SARACENS (Central Lancs) — Formed 1972
Club Sec: E.J. Bentley, 8 Kintore Avenue, Hazel Grove, Stockport, SK7 4QJ.   *Chief Coach:* L. Jones
Members: 250.

HESWALL (Cheshire)

HEVERSHAM (Cumbria)

HINDLEY (Central Lancs) — Formed 1970
Club Sec: P. Ainge, 12 Rushmoor Avenue, Ashton in Makerfield, Lancashire.   *Chief Coach:* K.J. O'Leary
Members: 260. *Leading Members:* Stuart Ainge (12), Roger Ashcroft (16), Stuart Bell (13), Mark Colclough (14), Andrew Crossland (12), Sarah Crossland (15), Nicholas Cunliffe (15), Kelly Donohue (13), Roy Draper (13), Lisa Edward (12), Donna Forshaw (15), Douglas Heaton (17), Andrew McCulloch (12), Joanne Marsh (14), Kathy O'Hare (12), Lyndsey O'Hare (14), Brendan O'Leary (15), Kay Ryding (12), Paul Smith (14), Carrie Stirrup (16), Nicole Thornley (12), Anita Whittle (17), James Wilde (13), Kathryn Wilson (16), Philip Yeldon (15).

HORWICH (Liverpool & District)

HORWICH LEISURE CENTRE (Central Lancs)
Club Sec: Mrs V. Uttley, 5 Kiln Brow, Bromley Cross, Bolton, BL7 9NR.   *Chief Coach:* B. Hodgkinson
Members: 300. *Leading Members:* Paul Frith (15), Philip Hackett (15), Catherine Jones (13), Carl Mann (20), Philip Stewart (13), Paul Sumner (19), Zoe Whittle (16), Alexandra Wilkinson (12).

HOWE BRIDGE ACES (Central Lancs) — Formed 1979
Club Sec: S. Holmes, 29 Hesketh Street, Leigh, Lancashire, WN7 4SN.   *Chief Coach:* T. Boardman
Members: 130. *Leading Members:* Andrew Arnold (18), Justin Arnold (17), Sarah Barnes (12), Samantha Berry (10), David Boardman (19), Michelle Cook (12), Howard Davies (15), Matthew Hamlett (13), Michael Hardy (11), Craig Holmes (12), Richard Holmes (14), Patricia Jackson (42), Christian Jones (17), Kay Lythgoe (12), Alison Mather (17), Karen Mather (11), Bobby Morse (13), Donna Morris (11), Craig Rogers (15), Robin Sinclair (13), Victoria Skipworth (12), Marcus Sloan (12), Leanne Stafford (10), Gregg Stott (11), Rachael Wylie (13).

HOWE BRIDGE MARLINS (Central Lancs) — Formed 1979
Club Sec: D. Reason, 11 Longcroft, Astley, Manchester, M29 7EN.
Members: 50. *Leading Members:* Kay Barton (21), Suzanne Bretnall (22), Joanne Colley (14), Andrew Hurst (14), M. Hurst (17), Yendle Jeruis (14), Cliff Kelleher (40), Derek Pritchard (24), Dave Reason (44), Jennifer Warburton (21), A. Worden (18).

Hoylake S.C. — shown winning the Vosene Trophy, 1985.

HOYLAKE (Liverpool & District)   *Formed* 1931
Club Sec: D. Booth, "Heathmoor", Highfields, Heswall, Wirral, L60 7TF.   *Chief Coach:* J. Tinsley
Members: 253. *Leading Members:* Kerry Booth (14), Stuart Brown (13), Sally Burgess (10), Kathy Burrows (22), Hayley Chapman (13), Jon Hart (11), Paul Hitchman (11), Sian Hughes (14), Colin Jackson (17), Graham Jackson (14), Greg James (13), Neil Kemp (20), Nicola Logan (12), Andy Nolan (26), Rachel Peters (14), Ray Pote (19), Rebecca Rayworth (12), Simon Reed (16), Kirsty Roberts (18), Wanda Roberts (17), Mark Sanchez (15), Jenny Simm (13), Ben Swaine (10), Daniel Wallwork (13), Matthew Wallwork (15).

HUNT (Liverpool & District)

HUYTON (Liverpool & District)   *Formed* 1973
Club Sec: E. Grimes, 69 Court Hey Drive, Liverpool, L16 2NB.   *Chief Coach:* P. Philips
Members: 400.

HYDE SEAL (Central Lancs)   *Formed* 1895
Club Sec: Mrs L. Allman, 64 Stockport Road, Gee Cross, Hyde, Cheshire.   *Chief Coach:* Mrs J. Harris
Members: 100. *Leading Members:* Brent Allman (13), Kevin Bennett (31), Terrell Bolton (13), Lisa Brown (11), Louise Clegg (11), Emma Collingwood (18), Louise Collingwood (17), Robert Collins (13), Christopher Driver (14), Clair Driver (11), Darren Driver (16), Stephen Gregory (10), Ursula Grimsham (14), Paul Harris (30), Bradley Hart (10), Lewis Hart (14), Kieran Hartley (18), Claire Henshall (12), Jenny Hill (12), Adrian Johnson (13), Hayley Johnson (11), Gareth Lawson (10), Paul Murphy (9), Jill Sidebottom (18), Gary Spencer (19).

ISLE OF MAN SCHOOLS (Isle of Man)

IVRI (Manchester & District)

KENDAL (Cumbria)   *Formed* 1945
Club Sec: Mrs L. Williams, 145 Lingmoor Rise, Kendal, Cumbria, LA9 7PL.   *Chief Coach:* C. Hayton
Members: 400. *Leading Members:* Andrew Cotton (13), Rachel Elleray (14), Grant Fawcett (19), Daniel Fitzgerald (15), Niall Gallagher (18), Darren Gibson (15), Simon Hartley (15), Beverley Hayton (17), Dawn Hayton (19), Jennifer Hetherington (13), Shauna Hodges (18), Jeremy Hoggarth (19), Gareth Hudson (15), Scott Hudson (19), Catherine Lee (18), Katy Lilley (16), Kim Lowther (14), Samantha Siddall (16), Sonya Studholme (14), Steve Varcoe (21), Rebecca Ward (14), Sarah Williams (13), Julian Wilson (17), Marcus Wilson (15), Philip Winstanley (16).

KIRBY STEPHEN & DISTRICT (Cumbria)   *Formed* 1967
Club Sec: Mrs J. Keogh, 15 High Street, Kirkby Stephen, Cumbria.
Members: 150.

KIRKBY (Liverpool & District)

KIRKHAM AND WESHAM (North Lancs)   *Formed* 1956
Club Sec: Mrs J. Kirkham, Pendle View, Fleetwood Road, Esprick.   *Chief Coach:* Mrs R. Butterworth
Members: 200. *Leading Members:* Tamsin Ainscough (13), Mark Allison (11), Claire Barton (14), Michelle Bleasdale (9), Caroline Bradley (12), Andrew Butterworth (14), Christopher Butterworth (15), Matthew Gibb (15), Mark Gilbertson (13), Louise Green (14), Elizabeth Griffin (9), Richard Gunderson (12), Melanie Harling (11), Luke Harris (15), Lee Harrison (13), David Hassall (13), Louise Hassall (15), Lyndsey Hilton (12), Tony Holgate (16), Stephen Jones (13), Christopher Kenwood (17), Katie Phillips (17), Alexandra Severns (14), Jonathan Severns (12), Christopher Smith (9), James Smith (11).

KNOWSEY (Liverpool & District)   *Formed* 1978
Club Sec: Mrs L. Ellis, 12 Owen Road, Rainhill, Merseyside.
Members: 90.

KNUTSFORD & DISTRICT (Cheshire)

LANCASHIRE CONSTABULARY (Lancs)

LANCASTER CITY (North Lancs)   *Formed* 1889
Club Sec: R.G. Holt, 118 Westminster Road, Morecambe, LA3 1SH.   *Chief Coach:* P. Johnson
Members: 175. *Leading Members:* Vicky Bailey (17), Catherine Beesley (13), Niel Bowers (19), Colin Burgess (17), Steven Burgess (19), Kerrie Davies (16), Ryzard Detko (29), Rachel Dewhurst (13), Jayne Dillon (14), Ceri Hall (14), Christopher Hartley (16), Danny Johnson (22), Simon Jones (11), Mark Leamy (18), Shaun Love (15), Robert Lucas (18), Lee McNiell (16), Paula Mather (15), Lindsay Queally (16), Danny Rothschild (13), Claire Sandham (16), Caroline Stansfield (12), Sharon Stansfield (16), Kirsteen Wilson (14), Graeme Woodhouse (16).

LANCASTER UNIVERSITY (North Lancs)   *Formed* 1983
Club Sec: J. Brown, c/o Athletics Union, University of Lancaster.   *Chief Coach:* W. Holmes
Members: 40. *Leading Members:* J. Ainscow (21), D. Bissett (19), J. Brown (20), L. Chalk (21), M. Cumber (19), C. Escott (20), C. Fearn (22), C. Harper (22), R. Harper (29), S. Howard (20), M. Jeffery (20), M. Lamb (18), A. Lee (19), S. Lewis (21), K. McCool (21), D. McKenna (22), K. Marshall (19), L. Moss (20), L. Philpott (22), M. Powell (18), M. Smith (21), K. Stride (20), L. Tatersfield (21), G. Vickers (21), N. Wilson (20).

LEASOWE (Cheshire)

LEEK (North Midlands)

LEYLAND BARRACUDAS (North Lancs)   *Formed* 1974
Club Sec: I. Dickinson, 48 St James Gardens, Ulnes Walton, Leyland, PR5 3XB.   *Chief Coach:* S. Mills
Leading Members: A. Armstrong (12), C. Banks (17), H. Blakley (16), K. Cann (13), D. Castle (10), J.
Castle (11), P. Collier (16), I. Dickinson (24), R. Doyle (11), D. Farragher (11), M. Gale (20), D. Hey (15),
R. Horrocks (13), A. Jolly (14), S. Mills (25), I. Mouille (14), C. Pickles (12), G. Robinson (12), K. Robinson
(13), P. Sanderson (17), L. Stringer (12), C. Sutherland (15), J. Thompson (21), N. Valverde (11), N.
Wilkinson (13).

LITHERLAND (Liverpool & District)

LIVERPOOL (Liverpool & District)

LIVERPOOL PENGUINS (Liverpool & District)   *Formed* 1964
Club Sec: Mrs S. Williams, 6 Wyndale Close, Liverpool, L18 7JX.   *Chief Coach:* Mrs B. Fagan
Members: 600. *Leading Members:* Nicola Beeley (11), Jonathan Brodigan (15), Paul Burke (11), David
Carr (11), Paul Cox (22), Andrew Dawson (12), Derek Dawson (13), Michelle Dutton (11), Jill Fagan (20),
Michael Green (16), David Holt (12), Ian Ingman (21), Sarah Kirwan (14), Philip Knight (15), Alison Mollard
(16), Stephen Parry (11), Colin Peters (15), David Potter (11), Adam Riley (14), Bryan Riley (15), Daniel
Snowdon (11), Jonathan Tunstall (13), Chris Walker (12), Karen Wrigley (13), Paul Wrigley (11).

LIVERPOOL SCHOOLS (Liverpool & District)

LIVERPOOL SCHOOLS SYNCHRO (Liverpool & District)

LIVERPOOL UNIVERSITY (Liverpool & District)

LYDIATE CITY JUNIOR SCHOOL P.T.A. (Liverpool & District)

LYTHAM ST ANNES (North Lancs)

MACCLESFIELD (Cheshire)   *Formed* 1893
Club Sec: Mrs C.E. Moore, 66 Thirlmere, Ivy Bank Farm Estate, Macclesfield.   *Chief Coach:* D.J.A. Higgins
Members: 486.

MAGHULL & LYDIATE FAMILY CLUB (Liverpool & District)

MAGHULL RATEPAYERS (Liverpool & District)

MAGHULL SCHOOLS (Liverpool & District)

MANCHESTER COUNTY SCHOOL (Manchester & District)

MANCHESTER DISABLED ATHLETIC CLUB (Manchester & District)
Club Sec: Mrs J.S. Bruce, 18 Slateacre Road, Gee Cross, Hyde, SK14 5LB.

MANCHESTER SCHOOL SPORTS ASSOCIATION (Manchester & District)

MANCHESTER UNITED SALFORD TRIPLE 'S' (Manchester & District)   *Formed* 1979
Club Sec: Mrs M. Robinson, 16 Briarfield Road, Worsley, Manchester.   *Chief Coach:* C. Rushton
Members: 200. *Leading Members:* Jamie Dargie (15), Lee Delaney (18), Andrew Fry (16), Spencer Glover
(19), Ian Hardern (20), Claire Huddart (18), Sue Littlewood (16), Paul Locke (15), Andrea Murphy (16),
Anthony Quinn (17), Martin Wells (17), Anthony Wild (15).

MARLINS (North Lancs)   *Formed* 1974
Club Sec: Mrs J. Grimes, 42 The Hawthorns, Eccleston, Chorley, Lancashire.   *Chief Coach:* F. Turner
Members: 70. *Leading Members:* Lucy Abercrombie (15), Nicola Adam (16), Catherine Ash (14), James
Ash (16), Sarah Bond (15), Amy Borland (11), Vicky Callan (13), Stuart Christie (20), Stuart Foster (16),
Mark Greenhalgh (12), Chris Hamer (17), Emma Holmes (11), Jamie Holmes (15), Caroline Jackson (14),
Karen Jones (11), Ian Reid (14), Rebecca Rodman (14), Robert Scott (18), Stephen Taylor (14), David
Tennant (13), Debbie Turner (19), Anna Wade (10), Zoe Wade (15), Jill Walmsley (12), Ceri Sian Williams
(12).

MARPLE (Central Lancs)   *Formed* 1936
Club Sec: Mrs A. Newton, 14 Elmley Close, Offerton, Stockport, SK2 5XE.   *Chief Coach:* S. Hishmurgh
Members: 250. *Leading Members:* John Bagshaw (18), Nick Bagshaw (16), Charlotte Bennett (12), Chris
Campion (13), Debbie Campion (16), Kate Carpenter (14), Andrew Cheshire (13), Christine Dixon (10),
Michelle Dixon (10), Sara Dixon (13), Alison Fawkes (15), Chris Fawkes (12), Andrew Goodall (18), Bryan
Goodall (16), Nick Goodall (11), Katherine Greaves (14), Matthew O'Connor (18), Lynda Patrick (15),
Mark Richards (11), Victoria Scholes (10), Laura Singleton (11), Jennifer Spence (9), Matthew Webster
(16), Jane Williams (14), Nicki Williams (10), Claire Wilson (13).

MERE OAKS SCHOOL (Manchester & District)

MERMAIDS (Liverpool & District)

MERSEY DC (Liverpool & District)   *Formed* 1964
Club Sec: M. Rae, 1 Grassendale Court, Liverpool, L19 0NJ.   *Chief Coaches:* Miss J. Barlow, M. Davies

Members: 19. *Leading Members:* Andrew Bacon (12), Mark Barlow (16), Ian Calland (12), Jayne Currin (18), Carl Highton (10), Gary Highton (14), Neil Jackson (15), Christian Jacobsen (11), Nicola Jacobsen (11), Stephen Jacobsen (13), Peter Krol (12), Alan Laine (30), Jennifer McLoughlin (10), Graham Morris (25), Karen Owen (15), Dean Stanton (12), Christopher Swift (12), Daniel Turner (12), Clair White (15).

MERSEYSIDE ADVENTURE (Liverpool & District)

MERSEYSIDE FIRE SERVICE (Liverpool & District)

MERSEYSIDE POLICE (Liverpool & District)

MERSEYSIDE SCHOOLS (Liverpool & District)

MORECAMBE AND HEYSHAM (North Lancs)   *Formed* 1930
Club Sec: G.D. Sunderland, 8 Russell Drive, Torrisholme, Lancashire, LA4 6NR. *Chief Coach:* R. Allinson
Members: 35.

NANTWICH (Cheshire)

NANTWICH SYNCHRO (Cheshire)

NAPIER & ENGLISH ELECTRIC (Cheshire)

NELSON (North Lancs)   *Formed* 1913
Club Sec: E. Howley, 36 Mansfield Avenue, Brierfield, Nelson, Lancashire. *Chief Coach:* D.L. Short
Members: 120. *Leading Members:* Sara Atkinson (14), Craig Bateman (11), Tracey Beattie (14), Fiona Corrigan (15), Clare Crowther (10), Daniel Dawson (13), Sophie Driver (12), John Drummond (18), Stuart Hamer (14), Jane Hancock (12), Heather Holden (15), Paul Jackson (11), Joanne Parkinson (11), Linda Parkinson (13), Paul Rowan (12), Rachel Rowan (16), Matthew Short (18), Daniel Smith (13), Michael Turner (10), David Wesson (14), Simon Wesson (12), Daniel Whitham (10), Donna Whitham (13), Mark Whitham (13), Victoria Whittam (12).

NEPTUNE (Liverpool & District)   *Formed* 1907
Club Sec: N.T. Haslehurst, 3 Hillam Road, Wallasey, Merseyside, L45 8LD. *Chief Coach:* N.T. Haslehurst
Members: 55.

NESTON (Liverpool & District)

NEWCASTLE, STAFFS (North Midlands)   *Formed* 1908
Club Sec: I.B. Faulkner, "Betarn", Hill Crescent, Alsagers Bank, Stoke-on-Trent. *Chief Coach:* A. Faulkner
Members: 200. *Leading Members:* John Bradbury (17), Stuart Breeze (14), David Corbett (10), Andrea Dudd (15), Matthew Earp (10), Nicola Edwards (14), Claire Ellis (13), Karen Emery (10), Joy Faulkner (11), Helen James (12), Sarah James (16), Karin Jones (10), Robert Lofthouse (13), Alison Mayer (16), James Mayer (11), Joanne Mayer (13), Susan Nicholls (13), Alison Potts (15), Alan Rapley (18), Philip Smith (16), Kelly Sylvester (12), Jamie Tait (15), Julie Underwood (11), Mark Wareham (17), James Whitehead (13).

NEW KINGFISHER (Cheshire)

NEWTON HALL (North Lancs)

NEWTON LE WILLOWS (Liverpool & District)   *Formed* 1979
Club Sec: B. Scatterson, 6-8 Aldridge Drive, Burtonwood, Cheshire, WA5 4NP. *Chief Coach:* G. Moore
Members: 65. *Leading Members:* Lynsey Adams (9), Alexandra Blackburn (11), Alexandra Blackburn (10), Susanne Boardman (14), Dawn Fairhurst (12), Ian Fairhurst (14), Vicki Fairhurst (10), John Flannery (11), Jane Gilchrist (14), Andrew Hilton (9), James Howe (14), Matthew Howe (12), Mark Hughes (9), Jeanett Kelly (13), Naomi Kelly (12), Dean Price (15), Simone Price (11), Andrew Roughley (14), Nicholas Roughley (11), Christopher Scatterson (11), Stephen Scatterson (14), Lynsey Shalcross (12), Jonathan Skeech (9), David Wilson (11), Fiona Wilson (14).

NORBRECK CASTLE (North Lancs)   *Formed* 1960
Club Sec: P. Guite, 79 Lytham Road, Preston. *Chief Coach:* F. Naylor
Members: 41. *Leading Members:* Richard Andrews (10), Diane Beezley (9), Stephen Beezley (8), Julie Bradshaw (25), Victoria Clifford (9), Mark Godfrey (9), Lee Hampson (13), Clive Hughes (18), Andrew Marsh (11), Steven Maskett (11), Sarah Normyle (7), Francis Parish (11), Robert Parish (9), Steven Pedley (14), Kerry Rigby (11), Mark Shaw (10), Oliver Sinclair (11), Martyn Smith (13), Michelle Smith (10), Lisa Snaith (11), Christine Swarbrick (11), Charlotte Thomas (9), Samantha Weber (13), Zoe White (9).

NORRIS BANK (Manchester & District)

NORTH EAST LIVERPOOL (Liverpool & District)

NORTHERN DIVING (Manchester & District)

NORTHWICH (Cheshire)   *Formed* 1915
Club Sec: J. Denton, 24 Prospect Drive, Davenham, Northwich, Cheshire. *Chief Coach:* F. Yarwood
Members: 650. *Leading Members:* Andrew Bancroft (15), Simon Bancroft (13), Simon Barlow (15), Kate Bayly (14), Jerry Birtles (17), Leah Bowden (14), Matthew Burgess (15), Richard Burgess (13), Matthew

Butler (19), Stephen Carter (19), Adam Christie (19), Diane Clegg (22), Duncan Cooper (14), Jonathan Dean (18), Catherine Dewsbury (12), Steven Forster (15), Sarah Gregory (13), Bethan Haeney (10), Jane Hamilton (14), Scott Lester (12), Ben Palin (13), Ruth Radcliffe (11), Haley Warren (18), Nicola Wright (17), Julie Yarwood (19).

NORTON (Cheshire)

NORWESTERN FINCLUB (Cheshire)

OLDHAM (Central Lancs)
Club Sec: Mrs C. Holland, 14 Balmoral Avenue, Royton, Lancashire, OL2 6NY.   *Chief Coach:* G. Delaney
Members: 300. *Leading Members:* Christopher Angrave (15), Matthew Angrave (12), John Askew (10), Matthew Batters (13), Alison Briggs (16), Julia Briggs (18), Graham Cooper (22), Darren Driver (15), Stacy Durkin (13), Nicky Fletcher (12), Mark Harrison (27), David Heap (14), Angela Holland (13), Gayle Holland (14), Colin Hudson (23), Darren Hudson (16), Lee Kent-Brown (16), Joanne Kent-Brown (12), Janina Makowski (13), Lee Middleton (16), Mark Nanyn (13), Vicky Quigley (14), Rachel Shaw (13), Richard Slater (23), Tim Summers (23).

OLDHAM BOYS BRIGADE (Central Lancs)

OLDHAM DC (Central Lancs)   *Formed* 1986
Club Sec: C.J. Slough, Valley View Cottage, 33 Grafton Street, Stalybridge.   *Chief Coach:* F.E. Jessop
Members: 55. *Leading Members:* Phillip Barrow (16), Naomi Bishop (21), Vicki Broadbent (11), Emily Burton (13), Craig Chester (18), David Cocker (10), Nicole Cordey (17), Helen Dukes (21), Chris Haigh (10), Gavin Hopwood (14), Madelaine Hopwood (13), Ben McKeer (11), Michael Pawsey (10), Stuart Perks (17), Chris Slough (17), Liane Tennant (22), Beki Tomlinson (14), Paul Waite (11), Jenny Wheeldon (13).

OLD TRAFFORD (Manchester & District)   *Formed* 1904
Club Sec: Mrs J. Hoyle, 51 Manor Road, Stretford, Manchester, M32 9HT.
Members: 640.

ONWARD DOLPHIN (Central Lancs)   *Formed* 1969
Club Sec: B.G. Youngman, 4 Withy Tree Grove, Denton, M34 1BP.   *Chief Coach:* A. Davenport
Members: 260.

ORMSKIRK & DISTRICT (Liverpool & District)   *Formed* 1975
Club Sec: Mrs V. Howlin, 81 South Meade, Green Park, Maghull, L31 8EQ.   *Chief Coach:* J. Howlin
Members: 250. *Leading Members:* Dianne Brack (16), Paul Carroll (11), Christopher Chalk (12), Edward Clayton (13), Mary Clayton (15), Christina Cowan (15), Andrew Davidson (18), Mark Davidson (17), Christopher Gerrard (17), Joanne Gray (14), Lisa Hamblett (15), Andrew Harkness (14), John Howlin (15), Lisa Howlin (12), Emma Jordan (11), Christopher Nash (15), Michael Nash (11), Amanda Owens (15), Matthew Robinson-Powell (12), Lynne Sims (18), David Summers (11), Lyndsey Sumner (14), Bryan Tunstall (12), Graeme Tunstall (10), Mark Waring (17).

ORMSKIRK FAMILY CLUB (Liverpool & District)

OTIS ELEVATOR (Liverpool & District)

PARBOLD (Manchester & District)

PAROGON (North Midlands)

PARTINGTON (Manchester & District)

PATHFINDERS (Liverpool & District)

PEEL (Isle of Man)

PENDLE DISTRICT (North Lancs)

PENKETH (Liverpool & District)

PENRITH (Cumbria)

PENRITH AQUATIC (Cumbria)

PICTON (Liverpool & District)

PILKINGTONS (Liverpool & District)

PIONEER 79 (North Lancs)   *Formed* 1979
Club Sec: M.J. Holden, 94 Openshaw Drive, Blackburn, Lancashire.   *Chief Coach:* D. Brown
Members: 180. *Leading Members:* Philippa Baron (14), Helen Beardmore (12), Sarah Bibby (14), Simon Bibby (11), Samantha Blair (11), Gordon Cassie (15), Yvonne Greenwood (17), Jeffrey Helm (12), Dominic Holden (12), Simon Holroyd (15), Caroline Horrocks (14), Owen Hurcombe (15), Simone Kenyon (14), Suzanne Kenyon (17), Tammy Lightowler (11), Mark Lundy (19), John McKeown (12), Hannah McLean (11), Joanne Martin (13), Lisa Parker (10), Jonathan Penson (11), Julian Ricards (14), Richard Thompson (15), Andrew Wilkinson (13), Alisa Willan (14).

PIPELINE (Liverpool & District)

PIRANHA (North Lancs)   *Formed* 1978
Club Sec: P.S. Rigby, "Merecroft", 176 Liverpool Road, Penwortham, Lancashire.   *Chief Coach:* B. Evitts
Members: 500. *Leading Members:* Belinda Bamber (22), Janet Cragg (13), Darren Critchley (23), Lesley Duckett (13), Andrew Goodier (16), Samantha Green (13), Paul Haworth (16), Victoria Heald (14), Niall le Coustre (15), Sarah Muncaster (14), Susan Pask (19), David Peart (14), Melanie Shaw (13), Tracy Sullivan (16), Hayley Thistlethwaite (16).

PLANT HILL HIGH SCHOOL (Manchester & District)

PORPOISE (Liverpool & District)

POYNTON DIPPERS (Manchester & District)

PRESCOTT (Liverpool & District)   *Formed* 1967
Club Sec: Mrs C. Rowlands, 2 Whitmoore Close, Rainhill, Merseyside, L35 6PQ.
Leading Members: Joanne Bainbridge (14), Peter Bainbridge (10), David Boyle (15), Nicola Boyne (13), Andrea Brislen (12), Barbara Coole (17), David Cowan (19), Nicola Doddridge (15), Samantha Doddridge (11), Leslie Fisher (12), Nicole Harris (15), Stuart Hitchmough (14), Shan Liptrot (11), Michael MacAuley (22), Alison Middleton (14), Elizabeth Naylor (13), Nicholas Nugent (18), Catherine Riley (14), Rachael Rowlands (16), Karyn Sharkey (15), Peter Sharkey (11), Stephen Twiss (18), Rebecca Wallace (10), Nicola Watson (12), Neil Williams (13).

PRESTON (North Lancs)

PROGRESS (Central Lancs)

RADCLIFFE (Central Lancs)   *Formed* 1890
Club Sec: Miss J. Owens, 35 Cunningham Drive, Bury, BL9 8PP.   *Chief Coach:* I. Gray
Members: 250. *Leading Members:* Helen Bailey (13), Lisa Chadwick (13), Stephanie Chadwick (15), David Gray (14), Stephen Harding (11), Andrew Hurst (15), David Killoran (16), Robert Lewis (14), David Lomas (15), Anna McDaid (15), Mark Maffia (13), Brent Newey (14), Craig Newey (16), Michael Oakes (14), Mathew Percival (17), Caroline Plummer (23), Greg Plummer (24), David Preston (15), Paul Preston (13), Martin Raggett (17), Jennie Reeves (16), Karen Simmister (23), Roy Sinclair (18), Marie Sue (13), Andrew Wilson (14).

RAINHILL & DISTRICT (Liverpool & District)

RAMSBOTTOM (Central Lancs)   *Formed* 1972
Club Sec: Mrs S. Kenyon, 4 Beech Acre, Ramsbottom, Bury, Lancashire.   *Chief Coach:* R. Wesolowski
Members: 200. *Leading Members:* Bree Carruthers (13), Dru Carruthers (11), Ross Carruthers (10), Andrew Cox (16), Chris Cox (18), Julie Goulding (15), Lyndsay Greenhough (12), Jonathan Grundy (12), Mark Howe (16), Mandy Hynes (15), Alex Jackson (14), Andrew Jackson (12), Paul Kalogirou (10), Rebecca Littlewood (11), Sue Littlewood (16), Andrea Newton (13), Gemma Peters (13), Chris Smith (16), Graham Smith (11), Mark Smith (14), Lee Stringfellow (13), Emma Wesolowski (11), Ann Willis (16), Ellen Willis (15), Margaret Willis (12).

RAMSEIAN (Isle of Man)

RAVEN MOSS (Manchester & District)

RAWTENSTALL (North Lancs)

REDDISH (Central Lancs)

RIBBLESDALE MASTERS (North Lancs)

ROCHDALE (Central Lancs)

ROCHDALE AQUABEARS (Central Lancs)   *Formed* 1979
Club Sec: J. Whittaker, 3 Arnold Avenue, Hopwood, Heywood, Lancashire.   *Chief Coach:* D. Crouch
Members: 600. *Leading Members:* Allan Blair (15), Rachael Blair (13), Steven Dawson (16), Timmy Earl (15), Steven Fielding (15), Anna Fogo (13), John George (18), Ralph Hall (14), Paul Harwood (14), Julia Hayter (14), Nicola Heed (15), Mark Howson (16), Andrew Jackson (16), Tina Jameson (13), Lisa Johnson (15), Richard Lyon-Hayes (13), Richard Maden (17), Christel Meredith (14), Donna Meredith (16), Chris Mills (13), Andrew Morgan (18), Trevor Morgan (17), William Reece (14), Jayne Travis (17), Jessica Turnbull (14).

ROLLS ROYCE (North Lancs)

ROMILEY MARINA (Manchester & District)   *Formed* 1973
Club Sec: G. Kelly, 19 Bowland Road, Woodley, Stockport, Cheshire.   *Chief Coach:* G. Smith
Members: 350. *Leading Members:* Laura Cook (10), Alison Smith (16).

ROSEGROVE (North Lancs)

ROYTON (Central Lancs)

ROYTON BLUE FINS LONG DISTANCE (Central Lancs)

413

RUNCORN (Liverpool & District)

ST ANNE'S (North Lancs)

ST HELENS (Liverpool & District)

ST HELENS SCHOOL (Liverpool & District)

ST MARYS (Central Lancs)

SADDLEWORTH (Central Lancs)

SALE (Central Lancs)

SALFORD CITY (Manchester & District)

SANDBACH DOLPHINS SYNCHRO (Cheshire)

SANDBACH SHARKS (Cheshire) *Formed* 1978
Club Sec: Mrs G. Gibson, 58B Marsh Green Road, Elworth, CW11 9JX. *Chief Coach:* S. Wrigley
Members: 107. *Leading Members:* Jenny Astles (17), Mark Austin (14), Simon Boulton (20), Vanessa Cliffe (13), Rachel Davies (14), Mark Ellis (18), Niel Findley (16), Jane Garratt (16), Mathew Gibson (14), Craig Guildford (16), Lisa Jeff (18), Lorraine Jones (14), Emma Knox (13), Adam Parkinson (13), Stephanie Parkinson (11), Wayne Ravenscroft (18), Sarah Richardson (13), Debbie Roberson (14), Nigel Roberson (16), Andy Rowlands (14), David Rowlands (11), Marcus Royle (13), Steve Sutton (16), John Tothill (14), Joanna Waddilove (17).

Sandbach Sharks S.C. — Team group from 1985–86.

SATELLITE (Manchester & District) *Formed* 1973
Club Sec: Mrs J. Pengelly, 83 South West Avenue, Macclesfield, Cheshire. *Chief Coach:* V. Mellor
Members: 200. *Leading Members:* Alex Bennett (12), Fiona Black (18), Philippe Calais (30), David Cooper (18), Simon Cooper (17), Helen Corlett (16), Chris Davies (16), Carol Duff (14), Daniel Gates (14), Ruth Hoyle (13), Andrew Iceton (15), Tony Martin (19), Simon Mellor (19), Steven Mellor (16), Cathy Mone (14), Georgina Palmer (14), Matthew Patrick (12), Emma Pengelly (14), Rachel Pengelly (17), Georgina Price (15), Alison Seaborn (18), Kathryn Seaborn (15), Daniel Sharrock (18), Christopher Taylor (13), Abigail Trivett (13).

SCOTCHBARN POOL LADIES (Liverpool & District)

SEFTON (Liverpool & District)

SKELMERSDALE (Liverpool & District)

SOUTHERN (Liverpool & District)) Formed 1979
Club Sec: Mrs S. Brown, 112 Ballarcriy Park, Colby, Isle of Man.
Members: 176. *Leading Members:* Ben Alcock (12), David Batty (14), David Brown (13), Marcus Cooil (14), Ruth Crellin (12), Jackie Cullden (15), David Glover (24), Mark Gorry (16), Stephen Gorry (14), Paul Maltby (15), Cerian Mellor (12), Nicholas Pledger (14), Alexandra Skillicorn (12), Andrew Skillicorn (14), Jennifer Ware (13).

SOUTH MANCHESTER (Manchester & District)

SOUTHPORT (North Lancs) Formed 1878
Club Sec: W.G. Lea, 20 Marshside Road, Southport, PR9 9TH. *Chief Coach:* J. Basterra
Members: 650. *Leading Members:* Philip Basterra (16), Nicholas Bennet (16), Zac Brigg (15), John Burgess (14), Stephen Burgess (15), Victoria Burgess (17), Thomas Cropper (9), Sally Formby (11), Lucy Gibson (14), Nicholas Gibson (17), Charlotte Halsall (14), Neil Jackson (43), Colin Knell (18), Victoria Lang (15), Ian McClean (48), David Melling (30), Daniel Morgan (14), Robert Newman (20), Diane Rimmer (14), Derek Rodgers (10), Damian Stanley (16), Sarah Waring (25), Mark Webster (18), Matthew Whittaker (15), Kate Williamson (12).

SOUTHPORT SCHOOLS (North Lancs)

STALYBRIDGE (Manchester & District) Formed 1887
Club Sec: G. Davies, 53 Hutton Avenue, Ashton Under Lyne, Lancashire. *Chief Coach:* B. Ward
Members: 160. *Leading Members:* Peter Andrew (9), Michael Bradbury (13), David Clayton (14), Christian Cooper (18), Sharon Etchells (16), Alastair Goddard (9), Andrew Goddard (16), Andrew Green (10), Philip Haworth (24), Andrew Kay (21), Michael Kays (9), Richard Lawrence (11), Andrew Moore (15), Andrew Morris (13), Anna Moss (9), Katie Normington (9), Hannah Smee (9), Rebecca Smee (14), Katie Tawse (11), Karen Taylor (13), Suzan Taylor (15), Helen Tonge (12), Sarah Turner (12), Natalie Walker (13), Craig Ward (17).

STOCKPORT (Manchester & District) Formed 1886
Club Sec: Mrs W. Bowlas, 177 Petersburg Road, Stockport, SK3 9RA. *Chief Coach:* Mrs J. Hallworth
Members: 330. *Leading Members:* Claire Bates (12), Lee Beveridge (15), Nicole Beveridge (11), Richard Bristol (11), Alex Buller (17), Laura Cooke (10), Alex Crangle (12), Jane Garner (14), Sarah Hallworth (12), Kate Hardman (11), Lesley Henderson (14), James Hutchinson (12), Lisa Kettle (15), Daniel Mather (11), Ryan Newbould (14), Simon Potts (12), Joanne Rogers (13), Cathryn Silke (10), Elizabeth Silke (12), Philip Stackhouse (16), Dacre Staines (12), Andrew Sturmey (10), Daniel Sutton (10), Kerry Sutton (12), Emma Weedon (12).

STOCKPORT METRO (Central Lancs)

STRETFORD (Manchester & District) Formed 1888
Club Sec: G. McNeil, 13 Whalley Avenue, Davyhulme, Manchester, M31 1QL. *Chief Coach:* B. Coley
Members: 600. *Leading Members:* B. Alderson (12), J. Alderson (11), S. Butler (15), G. Calderbank (15), H. Cassidy (12), N. Caverly (13), J. Crewdson (16), P. Crewdson (19), T. Dillon (13), P. Foster (13), R. Garner (11), B. Gosling (15), K. Hawcroft (11), G. Murray (13), S. Purcell (15), M. Redman (20), J. Rodgers (13), C. Singleton (16), L. Singleton (12), A. Smith (14), C. Teasdale (11), R. Thorley (20), C. Venables (18), W. Wardle (15), K. Williams (13).

SWINTON (Central Lancs)

TADPOLES (Manchester & District)

TAMESIDE SYNCHRO (Manchester & District)

TANHOUSE TENANTS (Liverpool & District)

TARLETON & DISTRICT (North Lancs)

THINGWALL SCHOOL (Cheshire)

TRAFFORD PARK (Manchester & District) Formed 1946
Club Sec: R.H. Way, 10 Ilkley Drive, Davyhulme, Manchester, M31 2DB.

TRINITY SYNCHRO (Cumbria)

TRINITY TRAINERS (Cumbria)

TROUTBECK BRIDGE (Cumbria)

TUNSTALL (North Midlands)

28TH WALLASEY SCOUT GROUP (Cheshire)

TYLDESLEY (Central Lancs) Formed 1876
Club Sec: Mrs K. Giles, 2 Greenland Close, Astley, Tyldesley, Manchester 29. *Chief Coach:* P. Fairhurst
Members: 200. *Leading Members:* Paul Bailey (18), Hayley Bowker (17), Christopher Charlson (16), Damien Clarke (14), Suzanne Coleman (16), Joanne Colley (15), Jack Davidson (20), Stephen Davidson (22), Jennifer Fairhurst (10), Melanie Fairhurst (13), Lesley Foulds (14), Maria Giles (16), Rachel Giles (16), Rachel Hall (15), Paul Howarth (13), Samantha McCormick (13), Christopher Mills (20), David

O'Donnell (13), Stephen Pritchard (16), Leanne Stafford (10), Troy Stevens (17), Nicola Taylor (13), Daniel Toone (16), Michael Toone (16), Edward Wallbank (17).

ULVERSTON (Cumbria)

URMSTON (Central Lancs) Formed 1933
Club Sec: D.A. Collins, 63 Chassen Road, Flixton, Manchester, M31 1DU.   Chief Coach: P. Deighton
Members: 196. Leading Members: K. Ashton (12), Joanne Bentley (14), Suzanne Bentley (12), C. Brook (17), A. Cassels (9), H. Cassels (12), F. Chen (11), M. Chen (12), R. Harris (12), P. Jackson (30), Lisa Jones (13), David Lavelle (14), E. Milne (16), C. Ogden (17), M. Pearson (12), P. Pickwell (14), S. Pickwell (10), S. Richardson (11), Nigel Sanders, I. Shaw (33), K. Shaw (30), A. Thomas (11), C. Wibberley (30), M. Woodcock (17), N. Yarwood (77).

WALLASEY (Liverpool & District) Formed 1890
Club Sec: Mrs J. Farrell, 43 Green Lane, Wallasey, Merseyside, L45 8JG.   Chief Coach: R. Steen
Members: 240. Leading Members: Stephen Bellis (13), Lucy Blesenzka (10), Clare Brough (14), Adam Carter (10), Clare Davies (15), Shona Fallows (14), Katie Finney (13), Sarah Gale (15), Stephen Gale (11), John Hamilton (21), Elizabeth Hansen (10), Ursula Hartley (20), Ian Herbert (9), Angela Jennings (12), Sean Kehoe (27), Darren Kostanczuk (12), Trevor Morgan (14), Vanessa Morris (15), Craig Murray (9), Andrew Pearce (24), Anthony Rosso (13), Stephanie Schultz (12), Victoria Smerdon (11), Mark Sopp (14), Peter Scott (19).

WALTON DOLPHINS (Liverpool & District)

WARRINGTON (Liverpool & District)

WARRINGTON & DISTRICT LIFEGUARDS (Liverpool & District)

WARRINGTON DOLPHINS (Liverpool & District)

WARRINGTON S&R CLUB (Liverpool & District)

WARRINGTON WARRIORS (Liverpool & District) Formed 1972
Club Sec: R. Warburton, 95 Cliftonville Road, Woolston, Warrington, WA1 4BJ.   Chief Coach: D. Moore
Members: 250. Leading Members: Patricia Alcock (14), Louise Appleton (16), Neil Cooper (18), Rachel Cooper (15), David Cowan (19), Kevin Crosby (16), Paul Daintith (15), Angela Dean (15), Paul Dean (14), Ruth Garry (16), Philip Grainger (14), Matthew Hickey (16), James Kirkin (16), Diane Lancaster (15), Judy Lancaster (17), Kevin Lancaster (15), Alison Mackay (15), Gillian McMichael (13), Karen Nuttall (17), Richard Padgett (14), Philip Parry (15), Sadie Preece (16), Gary Stephens (22), Clare Wanbon (15), Karen Wrigley (14).

WEST CRAVEN (North Lancs)

WEST DERBY (Liverpool & District)

WESTHOUGHTON SPORTS CENTRE (Central Lancs)

WEST KIRBY (Liverpool & District) Formed 1900
Club Sec: N. Murthwaite, 29 Ambleside Close, Thingwall, Wirral, L61 3XG.   Chief Coach: C. Tranter
Members: 120.

WEST KIRBY CHALLENGE (Liverpool & District)

WEST LANCASHIRE (Liverpool & District)

WEST LANCASHIRE COUNTY SCOUTS (Liverpool & District)

WHITWORTH (Central Lancs) Formed 1972
Club Sec: Mrs A. Hoyle, 1 Tonacliffe Terrace, Whitworth, Rochdale, Lancashire, OL12 8SU.
Members: 150.

WIDNES (Central Lancs)

WIGAN WASPS (Central Lancs) Formed 1976
Club Sec: J. Hodges, International Pool, Library Street, Wigan.   Chief Coach: K. Bewley
Members: 150. Leading Members: Patrick Blake (23), Suki Brownsdon (22), Catherine Caulfield (16), Ian Clayton (17), Mary Clayton (15), Beverley Collier (17), June Croft (26), Donna Evans (17), Nicola Gwynne (19), Stephen Hodkinson (15), Margaret Hohmann (32), Samantha Purvis (22).

WILMSLOW & DISTRICT (Manchester & District)

WINSFORD (Cheshire)

WIRRAL AQUARIUS (Liverpool & District)

WIRRAL MASTERS (Liverpool & District)

WITHNELL (North Lancs) Formed 1950
Club Sec: M. Cawood, 23 Cartmel Drive, Hoghton, Lancashire, PR5 0LN.   Chief Coach: M. Barrow
Members: 130. Leading Members: G. Barrow (22), M. Barrow (27), C. Brakewell (16), J. Brakewell (14), K. Brakewell (11), T. Bullen (12), G. Cawood (17), I. Chew (14), C. Clegg (13), C. Critchley (13), J. Hassen

(18), B. Heskin (11), L. Jones (9), M. Jones (12), S. Kenyon (20), A. Kirby (13), S. Kirby (11), K. Marsden (12), P. Marsden (14), E. Smith (14), E. Stanton (15), M. Trumper (19), D. Turner (17), K. Turner (15), A. Wilkinson (14).

WOODCHURCH (Cheshire)

WOODEND (Liverpool & District)

WOOLTON (Liverpool & District)

WORKINGTON (Cumbria)   *Formed* 1935
Club Sec: M. Kirkbride, 4 Loweswater Avenue, Workington, Cumbria, CA14 3LA.   *Chief Coach:* J.J. Hill
Members: 134. *Leading Members:* Lynne Ashcroft (11), Malana Burgess (13), Louise Cain (11), David Chapman (19), Peter Chapman (15), Cathy Fawcett (11), Alison Greenbank (12), David Gregg (11), Andrew Gregory (10), Trevor Gregory (17), Richard Hurley (12), Simon Ingram (17), Samantha Jennings (15), Steven Light (15), Sarah Little (16), David Lowes (10), Craig Matthews (13), Emma Reay (10), Laura Sharpe (10), Alison Smith (13), Anthony Stalker (13), Ben Tatters (12), Lucy Tatters (14), Jodie Walker (10), Diane Wilson (15).

WORSLEY (Manchester & District)

WYTHENSHAWE (Central Lancs)

YORK HOUSE NURSERY (Liverpool & District)

Southern District

Honorary Secretary: J. Lewis, 28 Hillview Avenue, Hornchurch, Essex, RM11 2QW

ABBEY COURT SCHOOL (Kent)

ABBEY SCHOOL (Berks & Bucks)

ABBEYWOOD SYNCHRO (Kent)   *Formed* 1980
Club Sec: Miss L. Holdsworth, 32 Brewery Road, Plumstead, London, SE18.   *Chief Coach:* A. Bell
Members: 26. *Leading Members:* Natalie Ash (12), Debbie Brooks (14), Sian Brown (14), Lisa Busby (15), Michelle Daniels (11), Nia Davis (10), Michelle Delieu (14), Lisa Finch (13), Samantha Finch (15), Janice Jones (13), Louise le Masurier (15), Katie McNicholas (10), Lucy McNicholas (13), Pippa Mercer (13), Samantha Norris (13), Joanna Ogbourne (13), Caroline Smith (16), Kerry Smith (12), Katie Thomas (15), Jody Veryard (13), Kelly Veryard (11), Janine West (11), Samantha Whale (13), Bethany Whorlow (10), Melanie Whorlow (16).

ACTON (Middlesex)

ADDINGTON (Surrey)   *Formed* 1959
Club Sec: Mrs T. Moore, 17 Cator Crescent, New Addington, Surrey, CR0 0BL.   *Chief Coach:* S.J. Hopper
Members: 166.

ALBATROSS DC (Berks & Bucks)

ALBYNS (Essex)

ALDERSHOT (Hants)   *Formed* 1982
Club Sec: Mrs G. Judge, "Casju", Northfield Close, Aldershot, Hants, GU12 4QL.   *Chief Coach:* J. Judge
Members: 60.

ALPHA (Middlesex)   *Formed* 1911
Club Sec: Mrs M.H. Newman, 6 Oaklands Road, London, N20 8BA.   *Chief Coach:* Mrs H. Rawlinson
Members: 100.

ALTON & DISTRICT (Hants)   *Formed* 1969
Club Sec: J. Knight, 1 Goodwyns Green, Alton, Hants, GU34 2NS.   *Chief Coach:* C.Meckiffe
Leading Members: Ryan Annetts (17), Chris Armstong (16), Nick Barrett (11), Mark Bruce (15), John Campbell (34), Simon Compton (20), James Cunningham (11), Alison Dickenson, Janina Dowding (15), Lisa Dowding (11), Helen Fairclough (12), Stuart Freeman (15), Luke Gamble (13), Karren Gerry (12), Barnaby Joy (13), Gareth Kenny (12), Alison McHarg (14), Sarah Mackett (16), Andrew Milne (14), Jonathan Tricker (15), Beverley Warner (12), Diane Warner (14), Steven Welton (17), Christopher Worsley, Jonathan Worsley (13).

AMERSHAM (Berks & Bucks)   *Formed* 1966
Club Sec: A. Wright, 3 Woodlands Drive, Beaconsfield, Bucks.   *Chief Coach:* M. Holt
Members: 270. *Leading Members:* Zoe Ambler (16), Graham Andrews (15), Jacqui Andrews (17), Charles Bagot (16), Vanessa Bagot (20), Conrad Hill (11), Russell Hill (16), Keturah Hughes (13), Christy Johnson (16), Victoria Leigh (15), Annabel Liversedge (14), Andrew Marshall-Taylor (18), Stephen Marshall-Taylor (15), Catherine Moloney (19), Andrew Moore (23), Vanessa Moore (15), Christian Palmer (16), Richard Peever (18), Debbie Rawson (14), Victoria Rawson (17), Abbie Spindler (14), Alexander Todd (15), Emily Worthington (15), Anthony Wright (13), Iain Wright (15).

ANACONDA (Middlesex)

ANDOVER (Hants)   *Formed* 1938
Club Sec: Mrs P.A. Kemp, 10 Beresford Close, Andover, Hants, SP10 2HN.   *Chief Coach:* G. Wardell
Members: 335. *Leading Members:* Andrew Bushell (16), Stuart Bushell (15), Sally Dearden (21), David Gregory (18), Michael Gregory (13), Robert Gregory (16), Christopher Hooper (11), Sarah Law (16), Emma Maskell (12), Justin Moss (13), Mark Parkins (18), Andrew Price (16), Victoria Roberts (11), Mark Stepney (17), Emma Tatlock (13), Naomi Thomas (10), Jennifer Waite (15), Mark Waite (11), Mark White (12), Emma Wickens (17), Lisa Williams (15), Claire Wiltshire (14), Christopher Woodgate (12), Nicola Woodgate (11), Glenn Woodthorpe (18).

ANDOVER MARLINS DC (Hants)

ANGLIA PENTATHLON CLUB (Herts)

APPLEMORE & WATERSIDE (Hants)

AQUALINA SYNCHRO (Herts)   *Formed* 1968
Club Sec: Mrs M. Romer, 14 Pear Tree Dell, Letchworth, Herts, SG6 2SW.   *Chief Coach:* Mrs D. King
Members: 37. *Leading Members:* Faye Ashworth (12), Natasha Beech (13), Natalie Cocks (11), Samantha Cocks (14), Cheryl Didd (12), Margaret Dixon (13), Natasha Dudley (13), Leah Grundy (13), Rebecca Hughes (11), Deborah King (10), Catherine Lane (10), Coriander McVeigh (12), Eleanor McVeigh (10), Stephanie Marshall (12), Joanne Palmer (10), Hannah Rees (11), Julie Romer (16), Cori Saunderson (10), Emma Sproat (11), Clare Thurgood (10), Louise Winch (12).

AQUARIUS NATURISTS (Surrey)   *Formed* 1979
Club Sec: D.E. Wells, 33 Edward Road, Croydon, Surrey, CR0 6DZ.
Members: 160.

ARMY CASUALS (Hants)

ASHFORD TOWN (Kent)   *Formed* 1900
Club Sec. Mrs G. Lawrence, 37 Jemmett Road, Ashford, Kent, TN23 2QD.   *Chief Coach:* C. Wood
Members: 225. *Leading Members:* Mark Amos (17), Darryl Bartholomew (10), Jonathon Colledge (10), Vicky Earl (16), Alison Found (18), Carolyn Fox (27), Matthew Fraser (11), Jackie Hallworth (9), Victoria Hayes (10), Andrew Hayward (21), Stacey Haywood (11), Richard Hodgetts (16), Kevin Ludlow (23), Hannah Macey (13), Rachael Macey (14), Sarah Norris (12), Craig Sadler (16), Rebecca Sadler (13), Mark Stanton (20), Jacqueline Tottey (11), Karen Vermeulan (12), Lisa Vermeulan (12), John West (14), Grahame White (13), Stephen White (11).

ASTRA (Middlesex)

ATLANTIS (Sussex)   *Formed* 1985
Club Sec: Mrs A.D. Geale, 27 Kingfisher Way, Horsham, Sussex.   *Chief Coaches:* Mrs. J. Phillips, A. Purchase, Mrs A. Geale
Members: 75. *Leading Members:* Sarah Cargill (13), Martin Geale (16), Simon Geale (13), Georgina Hackney (13), Tom Hackney (10), Caroline Hall (13), Julia Hall (10), James Holt (10), Lindy Hotze (11), Jason Ingold (13), Sarah Jones (14), Wendy King (12), Edward Kite (13), Georgina Kite (11), Roddy Lanning (12), Esther Levin (15), Ruth Levin (14), Sally Phillips (18), Daniel Purchase (12), Ian Robbs (13), Peter Sissons (10), John Stebbings (17), Martin Stebbings (15), Elizabeth Tyler (12), Kevin Walls (15).

AVONDALE (Surrey)
Club Sec: J.H. Hurworth, 18 Springfield Avenue, London, SW20 9JX.   *Chief Coaches:* D. Falcini, R. Leach
Members: 20.

BANSTEAD TITANS (Surrey)

BARKING (Essex)   *Formed* 1926
Club Sec: Mrs C. Case, 165 Gorse Way, Rush Green, Romford, Essex, RM7 0SA.   *Chief Coach:* C. Stripe
Members: 300. *Leading Members:* David Auger (14), Scott Bradley (15), Natasha Brooks (15), Nigel Carr (15), Darren Case (15), Alex Clapper (15), Elizabeth Clapper (13), Andrew Clark (14), Trevor Cook (16), Nicola Couch (16), Martin Dentry (19), Gary Donovan (21), Michelle Ford (15), Catherine Fordham (13), William Gray (14), Andrew Harrington (25), Vicki Hawkes (15), Mathew Heil (14), Vicki Heil (17), Claire Penrose (17), Donna Pugh (15), Samantha Reading (17), Paul Speller (17), Daniel Spinks (15), Zoe White (14).

BARNET (Middlesex)   *Formed* 1908
Club Sec: P.B. Shaw, 1 Bramber Road, N12 9ND.   *Chief Coach:* W.J. Kelly
Leading Members: Timothy Abson (12), Warren Chew (13), Gregory Clifford (11), Nicholas Clifford (9), John Cole (13), Daniel Dunbar (12), Ian Gillard (12), Domonic Grime (11), Nicholas Grime (11), Chantele Hart (8), Shelena Hart (10), John Hinds (10), Stuart Hinds (11), Andrew Inniarov (12), Ceri Jones (11), Rhodri Jones (13), Warren Kerwin (13), James Martin (11), Penny Martin (10), Annabel Price (12), Edward Price (10), Alex Smith (11), Nicky Symonds (13), Ben Williams (11), Jessica Willis (10).

BARNET COPTHALL (Middlesex)   *Formed* 1978
Club Sec: D.E. Telford, 60 Brookfield Crescent, Mill Hill, London NW7 2DG.   *Chief Coach:* D. Campbell
Members: 230. *Leading Members:* Mikel Arzoz (16), Calvin Biss (17), Daniel Brace (13), André Fabik (16), Mike Fibbens (20), Sarah Garrett (22), Lisa Graham (20), Allan Greig (20), Mikaela Harley (13), Sam Holland (14), Aleks Hughes (14), Stuart Jamieson-Pate (15), Victoria Jamieson-Pate (12), Steve Lack (15), Victor Leon (23), Damian lo Cascio (19), Francis Lumby (15), Piers Martin (13), Mark Matthews (22), Colin Moxham (15), Dalia Nissim (19), Mike Oscher (21), Jeremy Roberts (13), Liza Sutton (12), Zoe Sutton (12), David Tapnack (13).

BARNET COPTHALL DC (Middlesex)

BARRACUDA (Surrey)   *Formed* 1973
Club Sec: K. Canham, 25 Rosehillpark West, Sutton, Surrey, SM1 3LA.   *Chief Coach:* D. Griffiths
Members: 100. *Leading Members:* Patrick Allen (20), Carolyn Allenden (12), James Barrett (16), Tom Barrett (14), Mark Buller (12), Claudia Gin (14), James Gray (13), Lee Greatorex (14), Julie Griffiths (20), Lesley Harris (20), Warren Harris (20+), Susan Howard (12), Clare Huntor (13), Kevin Kersey (20+), Duncan Kester (14), Gethin Lanford (20+), Glen Lawson (13), Debbie Leyser (12), Kelly Nicoll (15), Elizabeth Perkins (14), Carolyn Pewtress (15), Nigel Scrivener (14), Dave Shamp (20+), Karen Tedder (14), Samantha Weedon (14).

BASILDON (Essex)

BASINGSTOKE & DISTRICT (Hants)   *Formed* 1970
Club Sec: Mrs U.M. Payne, 96 Puikerton Road, Basingstoke, Hants, RG22 6RN.   *Chief Coach:* M. France
Members: 150. *Leading Members:* Gavin Bridger (12), Jason Bridger (16), Eric Butcher (19), James Essen (17), Martin France (26), Bjorn Gastou (11), Anne Marie Jackson (17), Catherine Lambert (14),

Gavin Littleford (11), Daniel Loxton (15), Kevin Lucas (14), Robert Lucas (11), Tanya Nawacott (18), Samantha Naylor (12), Thomas Northam (15), Stephen Paton (20), Ursula Payne (14), Andrew Richardson (30), Jonathan Rottier (18), Richard Satchwell (14), Rebecca Sharman (11), Samantha Stratton (11), Sarah Stratton (14), Kevin Taylor (12), Rachel Ward (16).

BASINGSTOKE WPC (Hants)   Formed 1974
Club Sec: N. Paton, 61 Beech Way, Basingstoke, Hants, RG23 8LS.
Members: 30. Leading Members: M. Bastable (25), A. Hankin (23), G. Holdcroft (34), P. Kerry (35), G. Lay (29), A. McLauglin (39), S. Moss (22), J. Naylor (16), N. Paton (22), S. Paton (19), I. Remfry (17), A. Richardson (30), J. Rottier (17), J. Savage (22), I. Simmons (25), L. Tocher (14), D. Trewmella (22), A. Tullet (22), S. Turner (19), T. Wilson (28).

BATTERSEA JACULATOR LIFE SAVING (Surrey)

BATTERSEA PARK SCHOOL (Surrey)

BATTERSEA PEGASUS (Surrey)

BEACHFIELD (Kent)   Formed 1986
Club Sec: Mrs P. Swain, "The Cottage", The Broadway, Sheerness, Kent.   Chief Coach: L. Ludgrove
Members: 60. Leading Members: Caroline Alcock (14), Stacey Barney (12), Louise Butcher (12), Mark Currie (12), Darren Fuller (13), Helen Kidd (14), Terry Kidd (12), Damien le Grys (10), Samantha le Grys (15), Cathryn Maguire (13), Kerri Maguire (15), Darren Middleton (15), Natasha O'Brien (12), Bradley Parker (11), Brett Parker (15), Darren Potter (16), Stuart Potter (12), Jody Roberts (11), Lucie Rogers (14), Marie Saunders (15), Paul Saunders (16), Tony Saunders (13), Bobbie Taylor (14), Brent Ward (10), Imogen Ward (12).

BEACON (Sussex)   Formed 1976
Club Sec: Mrs J. Neech, Towners Hill, Tollwood Road, Crowborough.   Chief Coach: Mrs H. Brown
Members: 200. Leading Members: A. Brackpool (17), J. Brackpool (14), C. Brand (11), M. Chivers (10), J. Cornford (12), R. Cornford (10), A. Coveney (12), R. Cox (13), A. Featherstone (13), K. Fenner (19), A.M. Keily (12), R. Lacey (19), J. Latreille (14), A. Marriott (12), A. Miller (13), M. Miller (16), A. Parker (20), B. Rose (56), C. Sampson (35), J. Sampson (9), C. Stanbridge (13), K. Thorpe (15), L. Willatts (18), R. Woods (12), D. York (11).

BEAUMONT DIVING ACADEMY (Herts)   Formed 1968
Club Sec: B. Roberts, 32 Firs Walk, Tewin Wood, Old Welwyn, Herts.   Chief Coach: D. Beaumont
Members: 48. Leading Members: David Bonsall (17), Hannah Chapman (12), Michelle Cox (11), Caron Gidley (13), Emma Jackson (17), Katherine Lees (11), Philip Meekins (15), Christine Morgan (11), Graham Owen (26), James Ramsey (18), Beverly Sawyer (18), Ruth Stutter (14), Adrian Timbers (11), Gregory Timbers (9), Stuart Timbers (12), Mark Webb (15), Alexander Williamson (11), Domonic Williamson, Gary Woodfine (12), Ryan Woodfine (9).

BEAU SEJOUR (Channel Islands)   Formed 1978
Club Sec: Mrs A. Frankland, Beau Sejour Swimming Club, c/o Beau Sejour Centre, Amherst, St Peter Port, Guernsey.   Chief Coaches: Mrs A. Frankland, Mrs D. le Noury
Leading Members: Chris Adkins (14), Sarah Chambers (12), James Chester (15), Trudi Clarkson (14), John Elder (15), Nicole Falla (12), Kieran Fawcett (13), Lucy Fawcett (15), Marina Finetti (13), Stefano Finetti (15), Peter Frankland (14), Adrian Gidney (15), Matthew Hutchinson (14), Simon Jackson (12), Hayley Lavenne (14), Ian le Pelley (12), Louise McGowan (15), Claire Matthews (12), Harriet Morgan (13), Barnaby Paul (13), Sean Rowe-Hagans (15), Adrian Sarchet (15), Neil Stewart (16), Shelley Torode (13), Helen Watts (13).

BEAVER (Kent)

BECKENHAM (Kent)   Formed 1893
Club Sec: Mrs P. Cameron, 55 Coniston Road, Bromley, Kent, BR1 4JG.   Chief Coach: T. Ross
Members: 800. Leading Members: Karen Axford (14), Ngaiu Ballard (17), Justin Brownhill (18), Elizabeth Burns (16), Murray Buswell (27), Peter Buswell (17), Maureen Cameron (26), Iain Campbell (24), Peter Chick (16), Jackie Elliott (23), Douglas Gatland (18), Alasdair Green (16), Sheelagh Green (16), Leon Grenyer (16), Neil Grenyer (19), Michelle Hadden (20), Nicola Harwood (22), Mimi Kowalski (20), Zara Long (19), Jacqui Pitt (16), Nicola Sommers (18), Russell Stapleton (17), Catherine Upton (17), Lucy Williams (27), Lynda Wyatt (14).

BECONTREE (Berks & Bucks)   Formed 1971
Club Sec: S. Hahn, 19 Shafter Road, Dagenham, Essex, RM10 8AJ.   Chief Coaches: T. Baisden, J. Oram
Members: 252. Leading Members: Graham Bailes (17), Wanda Bailes (16), Paul Bainbridge (18), Jane Comper (15), Susan Cottrell (12), Laraine Evans (28), Laura Humphries (13), Michelle Humphries (16), Hanna Keep (11), Darren Keevil (14), Katie Kennell (11), Lynsey Kennell (15), James Lardner (11), Shayne McFadden (16), Eleanor Neeves (11), John Oram (14), Nikki Oram (13), Westley Price (10), Dawn Read (14), Jeff Richardson (11), Leanne Ridgeon (10), Greg Rowe (15), Amanda Soles (19), Deanne Soles (16), Anita Trail (18).

BERKHAMSTEAD (Herts)

Becontree S.C. — Jubilee Trophy Winners, 1988.

BETHNAL GREEN (Middlesex)

BEXHILL (Sussex)   *Formed* 1896
Club Sec: Mrs K. Elliott, 83 Grange Court Drive, Bexhill on Sea, East Sussex.
Members: 116. *Leading Members:* Karen Ball (12), Chris Blunt (12), Emma Buontempo (14), Matthew
Dadd (14), Hanna Day (11), Katy Day (15), Nicola Drake (12), Jeremy Fielder (14), Jenny Humpage (16),
Kirsty Mathews (15), Catherine Morgan (12), Andrew Sayers (11), David Sayers (12), Mark Sayers (14),
Robert Shaw (11), Robert Stevens (12), Robin Thompson (12), Andrew Umpleby (15), Natalie Wells (11),
Andrew Wilson (16), Kelly Wilson (14), Jonathan Wise (14), Alison Wright (13), Kirsty Young (12), Toby
Young (13).

BEXLEY (Kent)   *Formed* 1968
Club Sec: Mrs J.M. Scott, 48 Norman Hurst Avenue, Bexley Heath, Kent.   *Chief Coach:* A. Pearce
Members: 150.

BEXLEY DC (Kent)

BEXLEY WPC (Kent)   *Formed* 1960
Club Sec: F.G. Holehouse, 15 Turnberry Way, Orpington, Kent, BR6 8DR.   *Chief Coach:* R.Cufley
Members: 60. *Leading Members:* B. Anstead (22), D. Archer (26), P. Ashenden (18), G. Beckley (25), M.
Binns (30), D. Clifford (21), I. Cross (15), M. Cross (18), R. Cufley (15), R. Cufley (42), L. Dunsbee (21), D.
Foulger (16), S. Foulger (14), S. Hill (32), S. Langman (26), S. Lippert (22), G. Murrell (47), M. Nelson (30),
P. Tollefson (36), S. Wardell (25), D. Watson (24), D. Westofel (26), A. Wheatley (25), R. Wickham (22),
M. Winters (26).

BIRCHINGTON (Kent)   *Formed* 1973
Club Sec: Mrs H. Epps, Rose Bay House, 17 Minnis Road, Birchington, Kent, CT7 9SE.
Leading Members: Graham Bay (15), Peter Bay (13), Andrew Buckley (10), Steven Cunningham (12),
Brendon Dean (16), Nicola Dean (14), Kevin Fearn (13), Emma French, James French (10), Joanna
Fulton (13), Steven Green (11), Louise Jones (15), Marc Lawrance (12), Ian McCabe (13), Christopher
McDermott (12), Bryn Powis (11), Melanie Powis (14), Steven Ridge (13), Samantha Seager (12), Carra
Taft (9), Anna Watkins (10), Sarah Watkiss (11), Maxine Whitling (10), Trudie Whitling (12), Louise
Williams (13).

BISHOP'S STORTFORD (Herts)   *Formed* 1884
Club Sec: Mrs K.A. Valentine, 15 Norman Avenue, Bishop's Stortford, Herts.   *Chief Coach:* D. Newby
Members: 400. *Leading Members:* Rachel Ainsworth (13), Nicholas Baker (12), Paul Batteburg (27),

Matthew Bonham (17), Clare Burrows (12), Donna Cook (14), Anthony Forsyth (17), Steven Fullbrook (13), Matthew Jackson (14), Neil Jackson (15), Christopher Livermore (15), Christine Miller (16), Paul Milton (9), Wendy Milton (12), Matthew Page (12), David Paxton (14), Graeme Paxton (11), Jane Somer (15), Tim Somer (11), Jennifer Stock (16), Kay Stoddart (12), Paul Stoddart (14), Richard Symons (14), Jo Valentine (13), Jo Wymer (18).

BISHOP'S STORTFORD COLLEGE (Herts)

BLACK LION SPORTS CENTRE (Kent)
Club Sec: Mrs L.A. Jordan, 20 Grasmere Grove, Frindsbury, Rochester, Kent.   *Formed* 1897
Chief Coach: C. Whiting
Members: 120. *Leading Members:* Jamie Barclay (11), Dean Baura (21), Lucy Chidley (15), Emma Colyer (13), Sam Colyer (12), John Connolly (20), Martin Connolly (16), Sheelagh Dunn (14), Nicola Goode (16), Kate Harman (11), Kirsty Haugh (17), Lorna Haugh (15), Nolan Heatler (14), Andrew Kilgannon (11), Tracey Kilganon (14), Anthea Ludlow (16), Sadie McGowan (12), Christian Phillips (16), Lee Relcert (16), Peter Richardson (16), Donna Stanley (15), John Walsh (16), Maria Wickham (13), Michelle Williams (15), Paul Woodland (12).

BLUE MARLINS OF ELMBRIDGE (Surrey)

BOGNOR REGIS (Sussex)
Club Sec: E. Whitehand, 8 Trundle View Road, Barnham, Sussex, PD22 0JZ.   *Formed* 1965
Chief Coach: C. Adams
Members: 250. *Leading Members:* Nick Brown (14), John Burnham (15), Catherine Carmen (12), Jon Etherington (16), Wayne Gill (15), Julia Gingell (15), Stephen Green (15), Lisa Harmer (15), Ian Herechuk (13), Rachel Jeffery (11), Ben Keayes (16), Sam Keayes (14), Jamie Kincaid (16), Emma Nevitt (14), Lucy Newman (16), Jacob Pope (14), Reuben Pope (15), Nicola Simmons (11), Sharon Waggott (11), Michelle Warner (13), Becky Wheeler (14), Hannah Whitehand (12), Matthew Whitehand (16), Paul Whitehand (19), Debbi Wright (21).

BOREHAMWOOD (Herts)

BOROUGH OF BRENT (Middlesex)

BOROUGH OF SOUTHEND (Essex)
Club Sec: P. Slatford, 32 Parkanaur Avenue, Thorpe Bay, Essex, SS1 3HY.   *Formed* 1985
Chief Coach: M. Higgs
Members: 65. *Leading Members:* Paul Adams (13), Kevin Allwork (11), Lorraine Banks (16), Mandy Banks (14), Kelly Blackshaw (14), Julie Brignall (12), Giles Brown (14), Keeley Brown (14), Nigel Brown (23), Sarah Chandler (10), Paul Clark (21), Adam Fitzgerald (20), Mark Foster (19), Sarah Hardcastle (20), Paul Howell (18), Karen Leggott (15), Darren Lidlow (14), Jamie Lidlow (11), Ann Matheron (11), Jayne Matheron (15), Michelle Ryan (19), Alison Sedgebeer (18), Hiroshi Sheraton (16), Tei Sheraton (20), Tanya Vannini (20).

BOROUGH OF WALTHAM FOREST (Essex)
Club Sec: S. Mundy, 29 Forest View Road, London, E17 4EJ.   *Formed* 1985
Chief Coach: K. Ayres
Members: 300. *Leading Members:* Matthew Bracey (13), Mark Briggs (16), Elizabeth Brock (27), Danny Bullock (19), Leigh Carr (13), Richard Clement (13), Paul Cooper (14), Julie Cornell (13), Daniel Edwards (17), Michael Fielding (13), Jamie Fleet (18), Kevin Fleet (16), Maxine George (15), Michaela Harley (14), Niel Harper (24), Anna Heales (13), Cheryl Hurst (17), Elizabeth Impey (26), Stephen Lack (16), Louise Lawrence (13), Ian Manning (14), Mark Rothenberg (16), Daniel Smith (13), Heather Vassallo (32), Caroline Wright (15).

BOURNEMOUTH DOLPHINS (Hants)
Club Sec: Mrs M. Howe, 23 Osborne Road, Winston, Bournemouth, BH9 2JJ.   *Formed* 1952
Chief Coach: L. Dormer
Members: 280. *Leading Members:* Douglas Adams (24), Elaine Adams (26), Colin Andrews (16), Barry Atfield (13), Daniel Christ (23), Robert Cornish (15), Laura Dormer (14), Luke Dormer (15), Simon Frend (17), Peter Goody (20), Caroline Green (18), Katie Groom (12), Howard Hawkes (11), Ian Jones (17), Alan Manns (17), Derek Manns (15), David Molloy (19), Clare Rimmer (14), Amanda Small (16), Kirsty Stevens (17), Mathew Swarbrick (12), Tarah Tomei (16), Elaine Turner (17), Rachel Williams (21), Kaleena Wilson (12).

BOYS BRIGADE, REDBRIDGE (Essex)
Club Sec: H.G. Pearson, 28 Woodstock Gardens, Seven Kings, Ilford, Essex, IG3 9SZ.   *Formed* 1967
Members: 282.

BOYS BRIGADE, WALTHAM FOREST (Essex)

BRACKNELL (Berks & Bucks)
Club Sec: R. Elliott, 5 Beckett Close, Wokingham, RG11 1YZ.   *Formed* 1961
Chief Coach: Mrs R. Gallop
Members: 180. *Leading Members:* Amie Bagshaw (11), Peter Barlow (18), Gary Bennett (21), Jonathan Berry (12), Sarah Colby (13), Adrian Collett (18), Stuart Collett (16), Gavin Collier (17), Lee Cooper (16), Sharron Davies (26), Katy Dawson (15), Susan Dullard (12), Jackie Elliott (14), Jason Ellis (14), Jeanette Gunstone (22), Lee Johnson (16), Sarah Power (13), Anita Rentall (14), Andrew Rose (26), Simon Rose (14), Karen Senior (17), Paula Senior (16), Paul Smith (15), Emma Tattum (16), Alex Watson (13).

BRACKNELL SPORTS CENTRE (Berks & Bucks)

BRACKNELL WPC (Berks & Bucks)   *Formed* 1975
Club Sec: N. Paton, 61 Beech Way, Basingstoke, Hants, RG23 8LS.
Leadings Members: M. Bastable (25), D. Butler (27), A. Hankin (23), G. Holdcroft (34), P. Kerry (35), K. Khanfir (25), G. Lay (29), A. McLaughlin (39), S. Moss (22), J. Naylor (16), S. O'Donnell (30), N. Paton (22), S. Paton (19), I. Remfry (17), A. Richardson (30), J.Rottier (17), J. Savage (22), I. Simmons (25), L. Tocher (14), D. Trewmella (22), A. Tullet (22), S. Turner (19), T. Wilson (28).

BRAINTREE & BOCKING (Essex)   *Formed* 1977
Club Sec: Mrs L.A. Digby, 8 Convent Lane, Braintree, Essex, CM7 6RN.   *Chief Coach:* M. Gosling
Members: 150. *Leading Members:* Keith Abbott (15), Andrew Aley (16), Nicholas Bartlett (10), Paul Clark (21), Steven Digby (18), Helen Goodwin (13), Lynn Halliday (17), Susan Halliday (15), Stefan Haylock (11), Andrew Kyle (16), Michelle Leech (16), Yvette Lester (16), Magnus Long (10), Natasha Long (14), Paul Loring (18), Ian McKenzie (17), Andrew Macleod (10), Stuart Notman (14), Nicole Outhwaite (13), Craig Peterson (13), Lee Peterson (15), Joanne Roberts (10), Barnaby Scothern (11), James Taylor (10), Sian Williams (10).

BRAMBLETYE SCHOOL (Sussex)   *Formed* 1976
Club Sec: A.C. Callender, Brambletye, East Grinstead, Sussex, RH19 3PD.
Members: 220.

BRAMSTON CONCORDES SYNCHRO (Essex)   *Formed* 1977
Club Sec: Mrs S. Stewart, "Rydings", Norman Hill, Terling, Chelmsford, Essex.   *Chief Coach:* D. Deer
Members: 19. *Leading Members:* Caroline Baker (14), Joanne Baxter (16), Elise Beaumont (19), Lisa George (14), Emma Harvey (10), Zena Reeve (13), Shona Scorah (14), Tracey Scorah (17), Gunilla Thyeten (16), Kerry Tilson (17), Sarah Turbutt (15), Wendy Turbutt (12).

BRAMSTON DC (Essex)

BRENT CENTRE (Middlesex)   *Formed* 1967
Club Sec: Mrs J. Nield, 73 Eton Grove, Kingsbury, London, NW9 9LE.   *Chief Coach:* R. Game
Members: 65.

BRENTFORD & CHISWICK (Middlesex)

BRENTWOOD (Essex)

BRIGHTON (Sussex)   *Formed* 1860
Club Sec: Mrs M. Tuppen, 17 Wanderdown Road, Ovingdean, Brighton, Sussex.   *Chief Coach:* B. Dray
Members: 550. *Leading Members:* Michele Baldwin (15), Calvin Barnes (14), Steven Barrett (19), Michael Benny (15), Fiona Burton (15), Nigel Carrucan (22), Tracy Castle (17), Paula Cook (19), Teresa Dray (16), Richard Forrester (12), David Hamm (34), Christopher Hook (11), Steven Killick (20), Dean Orchard (18), Scott Orchard (15), Cassie Palmer (12), Luke Palmer (10), Nikki Pierce (14), Tanya Pierce (11), Andrew Robinson (15), Matthew Voyce (19), Scott Walder (10), Kathy Watson (15), James Wheeler (11), Joan Wheeler (34).

BRIGHTON DOLPHIN (Sussex)   *Formed* 1891
Club Sec: Mrs M.E. Ottaway, 8 Starford Court, Starford Avenue, Brighton. *Chief Coach:* Mrs M.E. Ottaway
Members: 731. *Leading Members:* Jose Adam (48), Jean Caplin (59), Lisa Custance (19), Linda Doidge (34), Marie Edwards (40), Melanie Eldridge (43), Helen Gold (15), Paul Grimwood (32), Guy Harris (20), Ray Herridge (40), Linda Isaac (32), Stuart Longrigg (19), Lynn MacKenzie (45), Kelly Medhurst (12), Suzy Medhurst (14), David Milford (14), Antony Neve (19), Karen Smith (20), Susan Smog (19), Bridget Snowden (25), Avon Spry (41), Neil Tasker (51), Christopher Thorneley (16), James Touhig (13), Joan Tyler (69).

BRIGHTON POLYTECHNIC AQUATICS (Sussex)

BRITANNIA (Essex)   *Formed* 1986
Club Sec: G. Childs, 122 Pinkerton Road, Basingstoke, Hants, RG22 6RN.
Members: 140. *Leading Members:* Dominic Bhargaua (11), Marcus Bhargaua (13), Stephanie Clark (13), Daniel Edwards (9), Emma Edwards (11), Sarah Edwards (13), Bryce Gibson (12), Donna Gibson (11), Mark Gibson (10), Tramayne Gibson (11), Vicky Harrington (12), Gillian Hills (9), Jeremy Jones (11), Mathew Jones (9), Roger Jones (9), Stewart le Madechal (14), Emma Lock (12), Ceri May (10), Claire May (14), Gemma Pearce (14), Andrew Pettican (14), Luke Pettican (13), Jonathon Shepherd (12), Wendy Smith (9), Clare Urwin (10).

BRITISH PETROLEUM (Middlesex)

BRITISH TELECOM, SOUTH LONDON (Kent)   *Formed* 1965
Club Sec: J.E. Sheeprash, 130 Dunleery Road, Mottingham, London, SE9 4HS.
Members: 45.

BROADSTAIRS (Kent)   *Formed* 1920
Club Sec: Mrs S.A. Watson, 29 Albert Road, St Peters, Broadstairs, Kent.   *Chief Coach:* Mrs P. Shepherd
Members: 140. *Leading Members:* Benjamin Aslett (12), Jonathan Aslett (16), Nicola Batchelor (12), Lee Cousins (9), Virginia Ellis (16), Tracey Farrant (16), Adrian Grant (10), Sarah Griffiths (13), Collette

Houghton (17), Kathryn Lovelock (10), Andy McElvey (25), Shaun Miles (16), Steven Moffit (14), Charlotte Pollack (9), Rachel Pollack (9), Derek Read (17), Ann Shepherd (22).

BROMLEY (Kent)
Formed 1898
Club Sec: Mrs J. Michael, Park Road, Bromley, Kent. *Chief Coach:* J. Carrington
Members: 130. *Leading Members:* Beverley Adams (15), Charles Armstrong (13), Sharon Armstrong (16), Alan Bevan (11), Susan Bruce (13), Zoe Bruce (12), Sarah Carrington (13), Simon Carrington (12), Karen Crowdy (15), Joanne Dawson (12), Paul Dotter (12), Laura Flaherty (14), Alex Freelove (15), Cathy Legge (11), Frances Legge (13), Andrew Mason (16), Robert Orange (15), Suzanne Orange (17), Samantha Ore (13), Jeremy Parks (15), Matthew Parks (13), Tim Radley (15), Claire Steel (14), Tiffany Steel (12), Matthew Wright (11).

BROOMFIELD PARK (Middlesex)
Formed 1903
Club Sec: Mrs M. Molloy, 79 Caversham Avenue, Palmers Green, London. *Chief Coach:* W.A. Oakes
Members: 398. *Leading Members:* Sarah Adams (15), Joanne Barnett (13), Simon Barnett (16), Natalie Beeson (20), Darryl Birch (17), Jeremy Birch (20), Victoria Bowler (14), Oliver Clifford (12), Andrew Crowfoot (20), Catherine Fair (12), Nicholas Fair (15), Jennifer Fletcher (11), Nicholas Fusedale (13), Ruth Green (12), Daniel King (17), David Mabey (20), Daniel Molloy (13), Matthew Molloy (20), Rebecca Molloy (16), Rosalyn Oakes (16), Diane Penwill (22), Darren Peters (14), Nigel Richardson (15), Alexie Riedl (15), Lucy Wells (13).

BROXBOURNE (Herts)
Formed 1957
Club Sec: Mrs G.E. Haylock, "Woodbury", Yewlands, Hoddesdon, Herts. *Chief Coach:* Mrs C. Pelley
Members: 335. *Leading Members:* Paul Beattie (14), John Bladon (23), James Conway (10), Justin Evans (14), Karen Evitt (14), Russell Gayler (22), Richard Glen (14), Ian Hardcastle (10), Adele Harrow (16), Claire Howell (14), Tamlyn Hughes (12), Vanessa Mattin (19), Natasha Millett (16), Laura Moffett (11), Russell Moffett (14), Craig Morgan (14), Andrew Quy (13), Jonathan Palmer (13), Martin Palmer (15), Stephanie Pearmain (13), Lisa Roberts (16), Richard Webb (15), David Wheatley (11), Diane Williams (23).

B.S.A.D. SURREY (Surrey)

BUNTINGFORD (Herts)

BURGESS HILL & DISTRICT (Sussex)

BURRSWOOD (Kent)

BUSHEY (Herts)
Formed 1929
Club Sec: Mrs F. Todd, 29 Newberries Avenue, Radlett, Herts, WD7 7EJ. *Chief Coach:* Mrs C. Litherland
Leading Members: Stuart Adams (16), Jason Baker (11), Wendy Cook (23), Zoe Cook (24), Karen Earley (14), John Ford (12), Lesley Hine (17), Robert Hines (8), Lesley Kershaw (21), Tony Lissaman (16), Andrea Litherland (14), Julia Litherland (17), Ryan McCarthy (15), Alison McCulloch (16), Anna Mindel (10), Paul Mindel (8), Charlotte Montague (10), Heather O'Connell (15), Julie O'Connell (11), Edward Smith (8), Philip Smith (10), Colin Smyth (13), Jackie Southam (13), Edward Stormont (17), Clare Todd (13).

CALDICOTT SCHOOL (Berks & Bucks)

CAMDEN SWISS COTTAGE (Middlesex)
Formed 1950
Club Sec: Mrs B. Pickett, 13 Clovelly Gardens, Bush Hill Park, Enfield, Middlesex. *Chief Coach:* D. Hobbs
Members: 250. *Leading Members:* Claire Baggett (22), Ayshea Dullforce (17), Nigel Goldsworthy (28), Edwin Goodson-Piper (18), Sue Jenner (29), Alyson Jones (33), Chris Mason (22), Ian Meakin (23), Stuart Owen (17), Dave Picken (20), Matthew Pickett (17), Steve Russell (22).

CANTERBURY (Kent)
Formed 1880
Club Sec: Mrs J. Rownes, 15 Hawe Close, Canterbury, CT2 7DL. *Chief Coach:* T. Smith
Members: 600.

CANVEY ISLAND (Essex)
Formed 1974
Club Sec: Mrs C. Carlson, 12 Briarswood, Canvey Island, Essex, SS8 9UD. *Chief Coach:* P. Eveleigh
Members: 152. *Leading Members:* Lynsey Armitage (13), Danny Carlson (14), Louise Carlson (12), Nolan Collins (14), Claire Green (15), Anna Guthrie (15), Brian Heller (12), Kelly Hoyles (13), Sarah Keegan (15), Emma Ling (15), Hayley Middleton (14), Marc Miller (16), Peter Miller (16), Julia Mullett (15), Catherine Old (12), Louise Skurr (18), Steven Skurr (11), James Thomas (13), Karl Topel (18), Philip Whitehead (30), Marc Wilkinson (14), Carrie Wood (23), Maria Wood (16), Samantha Wood (14), Trevor Wood (22).

CAWPRA (Surrey)

CETACEA AQUATIC ART SCHOOL (Sussex)
Formed 1972
Club Sec: Mrs A. Rayment, 12 Wellington Way, Horley, Surrey, RH6 8JH. *Chief Coach:* Mrs A. Oldaker
Members: 33. *Leading Members:* Julliette Adshead (16), Katherine Adshead (11), Samantha Adshead (13), Sandra Baker (52), Karen Bates (14), Tracey Childs (14), Melanie Davey (14), Sarah Davy (10), Diane Eggitt (14), Esther Figueiredo (16), Alison Followell (14), Rosie Griffiths (12), Angela Matthews (20), Natalie Menzies (16), Joanna Pierce (14), Esta Powell (13), Abigail Rayment (12), Catrina Scott (11),

Natalie Scully (11), Tamara Scully (10), Paula Sherriff (13), Ashley Terry (15), Julie Thorn (23), Anna Thorpe (15), Katie Tong (13).

CHALFONT OTTERS (Berks & Bucks) *Formed* 1987
Club Sec: Mrs S.M. Nickolds, 3 High Close, Rickmansworth, Herts, WD3 4DZ. *Chief Coach:* P. Dover
Members: 210. *Leading Members:* Matthew Abercrombie (16), James Baker (13), Michael Burgess (12), Sophie Dawkins (16), Rebekah George (15), James Hearn (16), Jacky Lawrence (14), Mark Lock (15), Kirstie McEwen (14), Jo Manton (14), Kate Merritt (13), Mark Merritt (12), Charlotte Moss (12), Katie Nicholson (13), Claire Nickolds (15), Paula Nickolds (16), Martin Parnington (13), Daniel Power (15), Charlotte Roberts (12), Lauren Stent (14), Iain Tait (15), Jo Todd (17), Clare Walter (12), Emma Walter (14), John Way (16).

CHASE FARM ASTHMATIC (Middlesex)

CHEAM LADIES (Surrey) *Formed* 1930
Club Sec: Mrs L. Wiggins, 55 Chiltern Road, Sutton, Surrey, SM2 5QU.
Members: 120. *Leading Members:* Sue Bishop (20), Claire Bowden (15), Joanne Bowering (14), Nicola Bowering (12), Faye Chown (12), Amanda Clarke (11), Avril Collins (29), Heather Cross (12), Laura Dick (12), Jane Dickinson (11), Belinda Eade (18), Helena Evison (13), Charlotte Fenn (10), Lindsay Foster (13), Samantha Fountain (12), Karen Griffith (17), Sarah Griffith (14), Ruth Izard (15), Tracey Krapper (15), Rachel Purton (13), Alison Rooke (14), Karen Sargent (18), Tamsyn Tremeer (10), Terri Veal (17), Emma Wiggins (13).

CHELMSFORD (Essex) *Formed* 1908
Club Sec: A.F. Jordan, 1 Torquay Road, Springfield, Chelmsford, Essex. *Chief Coach:* R. Springett
Members: 540. *Leading Members:* Nicola Cannon (12), Chris Cardozo (16), Joanna Crockford (11), Sean Eveleigh (20), Lesley Fair (12), Natasha Fox (13), Simon Fox (11), Andrew Goodman (11), Jane Gregory (14), Daniel Hill (13), Karen Milton (20), Andrew Moss (15), Samantha Moss (13), Lisa Noakes (15), Richard Olley (15), Robert Olley (19), James Poll (12), Neil Raven (22), Chris Richards (15), Andrew Robinson (28), Katy Salmon (15), Julian Snow (15), Ryan Springett (12), Joanne Thrussell (15), Dean Walker (13).

CHELMSFORD HALL SCHOOL (Sussex)

CHELSEA & KENSINGTON (Middlesex)

CHESHUNT (Herts) *Formed* 1967
Club Sec: Mrs C. McGolpin, 19 Bencroft, Cheshunt, Herts, EN7 6BE. *Chief Coach:* Mrs M.C. George
Members: 150. *Leading Members:* Giselle Biasin (15), Aimeé Blease (16), Robert Brown, Iain Bulloch (15), Sarah Doe (10), Paula Dredge (12), Faye Ewen (14), Nigel Fletcher (13), Teresa Gill (10), Christopher Hayden (11), Stephen Hill (13), Paul Jenkins (14), Simon Jenkins (11), Michelle McGolpin (14), Natalie McGolpin (13), Stacey Pellicci (14), Matthew Rust (17), Ben Thurnell (15), Kirsty Travers (12), James Waite (11), Kirsty Willis (13), Ian Wimpenny (12), Joanna Wimpenny (15), Danielle Wood (10), Stuart Wood (11).

CHICHESTER AREA YOUTH (Sussex) *Formed* 1970
Club Sec: Mrs H.M. Billington, Chaddesley Cott, Chestnut Avenue, Chichester. *Chief Coach:* D. Rosen
Members: 268.

CHICHESTER CORMORANTS (Sussex) *Formed* 1956
Club Sec: Miss V.A. Caton, 20 Market Close, Barnham, West Sussex, PO22 0LH. *Chief Coach:* C. Rees
Members: 180. *Leading Members:* Kerrin Arens (11), Emma Barber (15), Michael Barber (13), Samantha Barnes (15), Helen Batchelar (13), Nic Batchelar (14), Alison Bilham (11), Andrew Brook (11), Irene Caton (13), Elaine Cruttenden (14), Kerrin Cruttenden (12), Georgina Doughty (13), Michael Hanhan (16), Natasha Honywood (15), Thomas Isted (10), Carl Johnson (16), Martin Johnson (18), Alex K-Barnard (14), Lucy K-Barnard (11), Charlotte Martin (11), George Osborne (12), John Railton (20), Karen Rees (20), Nicola Rees (18).

CHILTERN SYNCHROS (Berks & Bucks)

CHINGFORD (Essex) *Formed* 1964
Club Sec: P.R. Wright, 12 Kings Head Hill, Chingford, London, E4 7LU. *Chief Coach:* A. Peatling
Members: 150. *Leading Members:* Karen Allard (15), Michelle Bartle (18), Neil Bartle (15), Lindsey Boraster (13), Richard Branchflower (18), Catherine Davis (15), Claire Gilder (14), Jenny Haylett (14), John Herbert (14), Martin Horne (16), Martin How (31), Adele Kellerman (14), Louise Lawrence (13), Michael Lawrence (18), David Mundy (17), Sara Parsall (15), Joanne Regnier (17), Julie Sheridan (18), Mark Sheridan (22), Daniel Smith (13), Karl Swain (15), Heather Vassallo (29), Russell Vinn (15), Grant Willmott (16), Caroline Wright (15).

CHIPSTEAD VALLEY (Surrey)

CHRISTCHURCH (Hants)

CHRISTS HOSPITAL SCHOOL (Sussex)

CITIZENS SWIMMING & WPC (Middlesex) *Formed* 1919
Club Sec: J.D. Allan, City of London School, Queen Victoria Street, London, EC4U 3AL.

Members: 20. *Leading Members:* J. Allan (41), D. Bryan (25), P. Bryan (23), J. Coghill (20), B. Coppins (23), P. Edwards (20), J.P. Gaume (21), M. Goldbart (23), V.G. William (26), A. Kerr (18), K. Lanstein (22), J. Levine (20), M. Ortiz (23), J. Read (21), N. Rissbrook (22), C. Smith (33), C. Taylor (26), H. Turner (27), V.G. William (26).

CITY OF LONDON GIRLS SCHOOL (Middlesex)

CITY OF LONDON POLICE (Middlesex)

CITY OF LONDON SCHOOL (Middlesex)

CITY OF ROCHESTER (Kent)
Formed 1896
Club Sec: Mrs J.C. Smith, 278 Thong Lane, River View Park, Gravesend, Kent. *Chief Coach:* R. Brown
Members: 164. *Leading Members:* Kathy Batts (29), Stuart Beacher (24), Jonathan Brown (22), Alexandra Burgess (9), Mark Burgess (14), Natasha Cooper (11), Tara Cooper (13), Matthew Cosgrove (11), Joanna Cox (18), Aaron Davis (9), Rebecca Davoodbhoy (15), Mikaela Holland (15), Paul Holland (17), Vanessa Kelly (11), Susan Lawrence (17), Natalie Leppard (9), Malcolm Long (22), Donna Loveridge (14), Simon Martin (15), Ian Smith (19), Cheryl Speller (15), Clare Stone (11), Mark Warner (12), Sarah Wichall (13), Stuart Woodward (16).

CITY OF ST ALBANS (Herts)
Formed 1963
Club Sec: Mrs H. Gorman, 43 Walton Street, St Albans, Herts, AL1 4DQ. *Chief Coach:* Mrs P.J. Martin
Members: 430. *Leading Members:* Beth Baxter (11), Giles Baxter (17), Suzanna Bradburn (13), Lee Clark (13), Samantha Crawley (17), Megan Crowther (16), Jefferson Doyle (10), Lise Evans (12), Neil Evans (13), Nick Grubb (17), Denice Hawkins (11), Christopher Hayhurst (11), Simon Hayhurst (20), Tom Hickman (12), Stuart Jellows (12), Graham Martin (24), Andrew Mortimer, Judith Oliver (16), Anthony Powell (13), Louise Robson (16), Martin Robson (14), Elizabeth Scales (15), Maria Schwartzenberger (11), Matthew Segall (17), Edward Whalley (15).

CITY OF SOUTHAMPTON (Hants)
Formed 1963
Club Sec: Mrs M. Loveman, 37 Westridge Road, Portswood, Southampton. *Chief Coach:* D. Heathcock
Members: 646. *Leading Members:* Stewart Adamson (15), Becky Bowden (19), Lorraine Coombes (28), Sarah Crook (17), James Flint (14), Martin Flint (16), Matthew James (14), Mark Jones (16), Jo Kelly (18), John Langdown (23), Steve Lock (16), Sophie Lockyer (13), Rowena Loveman (16), Tricia Loveman (22), David Major (15), James Moreno (13), Julian Plumley (25), Glen Prentice (14), Adrian Sadler (15), Lisa Sonn (14), Lynsay Stroud (12), Jenny Waite (14), Mark Whittaker (15), Justine Williamson (16), Charles Wilson (21).

CITY OF WESTMINSTER (Middlesex)
Formed 1893
Club Sec: G.R. Plumb, Flat 5, 15 Portman Square, London, W1H 9HD. *Chief Coach:* G.R. Plumb
Members: 27. *Leading Members:* R. Hardy (57), C. Kozlowski (81), G. Plumb (17), G. Plumb (71), K. Wyatt (40).

CLACTON ON SEA (Essex)
Formed 1931
Club Sec: G. Tapper, 17 Eastcliff Avenue, Clacton, Essex. *Chief Coach:* G. Morris
Members: 400. *Leading Members:* Bruce Barnard (11), Alison Beales (16), Zoe Cray (15), Esther Davidson (13), Ivan Drinkwater (17), Neil Drinkwater (17), James Fairchild (11), Julie Goodman (13), Neil Green (14), Lesa Grindrod (16), Paul Howie (14), Laura Hunt (10), Katy Karsten (8), Jonathon Martin (18), Danielle Morley (10), Adrian Morris (25+), Robert Newman (14), Michael Oates (10), Steven Roberts (11), Glynn Roberts (13), Deborah Smith (13), Juliet Smith (24), Lynette Ward (11), Nick Westlake (25+), Dale Windle (9).

COBHAM HALL SCHOOL (Kent)

COELACANTH MASTERS (Essex)

COLCHESTER (Essex)
Formed 1884
Club Sec: Miss E.A. Baines, 48 Gainsborough Road, Colchester, Essex. *Chief Coaches:* R. Howkins, I. Johnson, R. Nicholson
Members: 200. *Leading Members:* Helen Bell (17), Stephen Casey (15), Margaret Chester (14), Martin Collins (18), Sarah Collins (15), Debbie Cooper (17), Stephen Cooper (16), Anthony Dennis (15), Ruth Eddy (14), David Francis (23), Dominic Howkins (15), Julian Howkins (13), Graham Hymus (19), Keri Johnson (15), Ross Johnson (12), Clare Kelly (14), Donna Keys (16), Ross Khevett (12), Sally Levett (14), Julie Longman (15), Faye Miller (15), Sacha Munro (14), Lee Troman (15), Richard Vinter (10), Michell Young (16).

COOPERS CO & COBURN SCHOOL (Essex)

COULSDON SPORTS & SOCIAL (Surrey)
Formed 1974
Club Sec: Mrs B. Tomlinson, 83 Onslow Gardens, Wallington, Surrey. *Chief Coach:* G. Tomlinson
Members: 32.

CRANBROOK & DISTRICT (Kent)

CRANLEIGH (Surrey)

CRANLEIGH WPC (Surrey)

CRAWLEY (Sussex) *Formed* 1964
Club Sec: G.J.N. Oxlade, 108 Grattons Drive, Pound Hill, Crawley, Sussex. *Chief Coach:* J. Hartley
Members: 292. *Leading Members:* Lucy Benson (13), Tim Briggs (18), Joanne Clothier (12), Sarah Clothier (11), Sharon Crowhurst (12), Claire Drackford (12), Alistaire Green (18), Nicky Green (16), Matthew Gunston (14), Michelle Hall (10), Warren Hall (14), Zoe Ladd (14), Joanna Langston (15), David Molloy (14), Lorraine Moore (19), Lisa Morgan (17), Chris Oxlade (17), Vicky Paice (13), Gary Paskell (13), Colin Payne (16), Dawn Shadwell (16), Dionne Smith (12), Anne Wareing (15), Alexa White (10), Matthew Wood (18).

CRESCENT (Kent)

CROYDON (Surrey)

CROYDON AMPHIBIANS (Surrey) *Formed* 1979
Club Sec: Mrs L. Packman, South Shaw, High Road, Chipstead, Surrey, CR3 3QN.
Members: 300. *Leading Members:* Adam Bates (12), Iain Bates (14), Steven Butler (16), Andrew Collins (18), Jennifer Evans (11), Ryan Ferguson (11), Caroline Hide (13), Graham Hughes (11), Damian Kiernander (12), Simon Letts (16), Lauren McFie (14), Julia Macartney (13), Tristanne Maquire (14), Justin Packman (14), Sarah Payne (14), Ben Pitts (14), Ray Reader (5), Sally Rhodes (14), Christopher Smith (11), Jonathon Smith (13), Lorraine Smith (14), Neil Sterling (14), Kate Wanstall (15), Jenny Whiting (15), Kim Williams (17).

Croydon Amphibians

CROYDON Y.M.C.A. (Surrey)
Club Sec: K. Hynes, 1 Lansdowne Road, Croydon, Surrey. *Chief Coach:* K. Hynes
Members: 450.

CRYSTAL PALACE DC (Kent)

DACORUM METRO DIVING SCHOOL (Herts)

DAGENHAM (Essex)

DARTFORD DISTRICT (Kent) *Formed* 1912
Club Sec: Mrs C. Wade, 80 Glenhurst Avenue, Bexley, Kent, DA5 3QN. *Chief Coach:* H. Kwong
Members: 360.

DEAL & DISTRICT (Kent) *Formed* 1970
Club Sec: Mrs K. James, 58 Gladstone Road, Deal, Kent, CT14 7ET.

DIDCOT (Berks & Bucks) *Formed* 1969
Club Sec: R. Hayes, 61 Meadow Way, Didcot, Oxon, OX11 0AX. *Chief Coach:* R.W. Hayes
Members: 150.

DOLPHIN (Surrey)

DORKING (Surrey) *Formed* 1976
Club Sec: Mrs S. Hulbert, 9 Chalkpit Terrace, Dorking, Surrey, RH4 1HX.
Members: 140. *Leading Members:* Sharon Adams (15), Jessica Barkley (16), Joanne Buss (12), Nicola Cann (15), Philip Cann (13), Marnie Ebdon (18), Richard Ellis-Smith (18), Marie Fidler (15), Philip Gatland (16), Katharine Hawkins (13), Alan Kearton (12), Adrian Lloyd (15), Neil McMahon (15), Daniel Morris (17), Claire Moyce (16), Alison Osmond (14), David Post (17), Richard Price (19), Mary-Anne Remington (14), Graeme Smith (14), Jackie Smith (16), Andrew Taylor (17), Peter Taylor (18), Doric Wells (13), Elizabeth West (14).

DOUAI SCHOOL (Berks & Bucks)

DOVER LIFEGUARD (Kent)

DUKE OF YORK SCHOOL (Kent)

DUNMOW (Essex) *Formed* 1979
Club Sec: Mrs S. Ayre, 14 Venmore Drive, Dunmow, Essex. *Chief Coach:* R. Banham
Members: 77. *Leading Members:* Matthew Ayre (14), Clare Banham (13), Paul Barron (13), Sam Barron (11), James Bennett (14), Graham Bullock (13), Jane Catchpole (14), Andrew Cox (17), Timothy Davison (13), Oliver Flexman (10), Peter Gray (12), Gary Harwood (16), Jenny Harwood (12), Paul Lamb (14), Elizabeth Page (15), Christopher Pannell (14), Paul Pannell (11), Lucy Roberts (13), Toby Shoolbred (12), Paul Stevenson (15), Kate Vaughan (15), Polly Vaughan (16), Francis Wallington (15), Stewart Wallington (17), Paul Whiffen (17).

EASTBOURNE (Sussex)

EASTBOURNE COLLEGE (Sussex) *Formed* 1968
Club Sec: Dr R.C. Edmondson, Powell House, 22 Grange Road, Eastbourne. *Chief Coach:* F. Bagshaw
Members: 30. *Leading Members:* A. Abdulai (15), M. Abdulai (15), J. Bishop (14), P. Bodharante (16), R. Bromley (14), J. Croft (16), J. Donaldson (17), A. Evans (14), T. Foulds (16), P. Gardiner (17), M. Hafemile (14), E. Heale (16), R. Heale (17), O. Hunt (15), R. Kaiser (17), M. Kirby (18), O. Landerer (18), M. Ling (14), S. Mason (18), E. Norman (16), S. Nowell (14), M. Piper (18), N. Smith (17), M. Trott (14), S. Trott (17).

EASTERN OTTERS (Middlesex)

EAST GRINSTEAD (Sussex) *Formed* 1912
Club Sec: Mrs E. Savage, 19 Hurst Farm Road, East Grinstead. *Chief Coaches:* F. Ludman, R. Ludman
Members: 500. *Leading Members:* Guy Barham (16), Scott Barham (13), Dominic Broad (11), Naomi Broad (13), Chrissie Dean (11), Matthew Disney (18), Neil Garrido (10), Robert Harvey (15), Julie Hayward (11), Alex Herbert (12), Russell Herbert (15), Suzanne Hill (15), Emma Kirby (15), Tom Ludman (17), Edward Lunniss (13), John Mulvey (14), Natalie Napier (15), Kay Parker (25), Andrew Pearce (15), Julie Rees (21), Sarah Slattery (13), Abigail Sweet (12), Jamie Sweet (11), Sarah Windle (15), Helen Withecombe (13).

EAST HAM (Essex)

EASTLEIGH, FLEMING PARK (Hants) *Formed* 1905
Club Sec: F. Blakeway, 53 Rownhams Road, Waybush, Southampton, Hants. *Chief Coach:* D. Dunne
Members: 800.

EASTNEY (Hants)

EDMONTON PHOENIX (Middlesex) *Formed* 1968
Club Sec: M.D. Steward, 72 Trinity Avenue, Bush Hill Park, Enfield, EN1 1HS. *Chief Coach:* C. Wilton
Members: 285. *Leading Members:* Daniel Bond (12), Dean Boyce (12), Philip Brown (13), Richard Brown (14), Stephen Brown (11), Mandy Claydon (14), Niel Claydon (12), Penny Drew (15), Nichola Elves, Mark Furmston (13), Andrew McParland (12), Clare Magee (15), Natalie Magee (15), Gary Mitchell (13), Sally Muir (15), Clare O'Dea (16), Adam Renvoize (15), David Schilder (15), Hazel Smith (16), James Smith (13), Michelle Spikesley (14), Faye Swain (13), Clare Travis, Christina Whellams (16), David Young (16).

ELMBRIDGE PHOENIX (Surrey) *Formed* 1908
Club Sec: B. Lamberton, 98 Kings Road, Walton on Thames, Surrey, KT12 2RD. *Chief Coach:* C. Everitt
Members: 120. *Leading Members:* Caroline Alden (15), Mike Bullen (24), Dan Comfort (13), Helen Coxon (13), Kirsty Craze (10), Neil Craze (11), Mike Dyde (24), Peter Falcini (24), Tara Harrop (9), Gary Hicks (17), Jane Holmes (13), Bethan Howells (11), Dylan Howells (14), Frankie Lamberton (11), Douglas Law (9), Michelle McDermot (16), Tammy McDermott (8), Simon Muir (14), James Nicholson (12), Angela Rudolph (14), Paulo Samothrakis (9), Andrew Taft (13), David White (14), Katie White (9), Taigh Wilson (13).

ELSTREE NEPTUNE (Herts)

ELTHAM (Kent) *Formed* 1967
Club Sec: C. Wetherly, 143 Howarth Road, Abbey Wood, London. *Chief Coaches:* J. Callaway, D. Minde
Members: 80.

ENFIELD (Middlesex) *Formed* 1903
Club Sec: Mrs S.K. Steggles, 207 Galliard Road, Edmonton, London, N9 7NP. *Chief Coach:* J. Lowe
Members: 140. *Leading Members:* Liz Brock (26), Hazel Smith (16).

EPPING FOREST DISTRICT (Essex) *Formed* 1977
Club Sec: M.J. Sedgebeer, 5 Roding Drive, Kelvedon Hatch, Brentwood, Essex. *Chief Coach:* T. Nicholls
Members: 121. *Leading Members:* Richard Cole (11), Steven Cornwall (11), Joanne Eaton (12), Andrew
Elliott (15), Gillian Ennever (20), Georgina Felby (11), Jonathan Frootko (12), Michael Frootko (14),
Natasha Frootko (10), Philip Kennedy (18), Richard Kent-Woolsey (20), Amy Lovell (14), Jonathan
Millership (12), Penny Mitchell (17), Zoe Morley (13), Matthew Nicholls (18), Tony Pearman (9), Alison
Sedgebeer (17), Robert Sedgebeer (13), Vanessa Smith (14), Susie Stuitbke (10), Annabel Taylor (14),
Georgina Taylor (11), Grant Twine (16), Nicole Twynham (12), Emma White (11).

EPSOM DISTRICT (Surrey) *Formed* 1947
Club Sec: Mrs J. Bridgman, 104 Reigate Road, Ewell, Surrey, KT17 3DZ. *Chief Coach:* B. Smethhurst
Members: 130. *Leading Members:* Louise Alexander (22), Gregg Allan (12), Melanie Bridgman (15),
Michael Brugnoli (19), James Corbett (18), Claire Craven (19), David Craven (16), Ian Daws (11), Simon
Daws (14), Paul Dobson (19), Sarah Dobson (17), Robert Gallie (15), Mandy Gee (16), Gavin Ingram (17),
Paul James (12), Damon Jevons (18), Lorraine Jevons (15), Joanne McHafee (19), Carrie O'Leary (14),
Dale Simpson (23), Blair Smethurst (17), Michelle Stenhouse (15), Gary Vlaeminck (15), Laura Wilson
(11), Linda Wyatt (14).

EPSOM & EWELL (Surrey) *Formed* 1938
Club Sec: Mrs C.M. Opher, "Treffen", 18 Green Lanes, West Ewell, Surrey. *Chief Coach:* C. Opher
Members: 230. *Leading Members:* Julie Andrews (17), Stephen Beadle (19), Claire Evans (15), Simon
Fletcher (16), Sara Glanville-Taylor (20), Andrew Hall (15), Andrew Howe (11), Emma Johnson (13), Ben
Kitchener (18), Paul Kitchener (20), Colin McCoy (17), Caroline Mitchell (15), Sarah Mitchell (19), Paul
Moore (15), Paul Murrell (23), Ian Newcastle (26), Rachel Park (15), Ian Rothwell (20), Darren Russell
(15), Gavin Russell (13), Nancy Skelton (14), Neil Skelton (16), Diana Steven (20), Tony Stone (20), Alex
Waite (13).

ERITH & DISTRICT (Kent) *Formed* 1912
Club Sec: A.B. Bedford, 120 Brook Street, Erith, Kent, DA8 1JF.
Members: 170. *Leading Members:* Mark Bragg (20), John Burdett (16), Roy Burdett (12), Claire Conner
(15), Paul Dodson (19), Tracey Dodson (14), Martin Eastaugh (15), Lee Gilbert (11), Heidi Green (10),
Zak Green (13), Suzie Groce (16), Sammy Hayes (18), Miriam Hogan (13), John Murray (25), Lorraine
Newitt (18), Jenny Newton (25), Luciana Romagndo (23), Philip Rush (17), Mark Russell (16), Rebecca
Russell (13), Marnie Thackray (17), Alison Walker (11), Keith Walker (13), Liz Watkins (17), Jamie Wilcox
(11).

ESSEX CORMORANTS DIVING SCHOOL (Essex)

ESSEX POLICE (Essex)

ETON COLLEGE (Berks & Bucks) *Formed* 1888
Club Sec: P.K. Manley, Hornby House, Willowbrook, Eton, Windsor, Berks. *Chief Coach:* P.K. Mansley
Members: 1260. *Leading Members:* S. Carver (15), E. Charles (14), J. Ferguson (17), A. Leslie, J.
Livingstone-Wallace (17), S. Livingstone-Wallace (15), A. Nannini (15), J. Price (17), T. Price (17), M.
Rawlence (15), R. Russell (16), S. Taseer (16), J. Tenouf-La (15).

ETON HOUSE SCHOOL FOR BOYS (Essex)

FAIRFIELD (Surrey) *Formed 1945*
Club Sec: Mrs I. Evans, 83 The Ridgeway, Sutton, Surrey. *Chief Coach:* I. Reeves
Members: 100.

FAREHAM NOMADS (Hants) *Formed 1978*
Club Sec: C. Wilson, 53 Kiln Road, Fareham, Hants, PO16 7UH. *Chief Coach:* M. Rogers
Members: 350. *Leading Members:* Katie Allen (15), Charlotte Arm (13), Kathryn Barnes (13), Simon
Barnes (16), Louise Berridge (16), Steve Berry (21), Katie, Broomfield (13), Sarah Cox (25), Janette
Crowe (18), Sarah Davies (16), Caroline Fisher (15), Colin Green (15), Adrian Hillman (13), Bethan
Jenkins (12), Richard Lee (21), Simon Lee (25), Jon Longman (17), Alan Mitchinson (11), Claire New (20),
Matthew Norman (16), Jo Stunt (16), Robert Sunderland (14), Claire Tromans (12), Mike Wakefield (21),
David White (14).

FARNBOROUGH (Hants) *Formed 1983*
Club Sec: Miss C. Dalton, c/o 36 Evergreen Road, Frimley, Surrey.
Members: 250.

FARNHAM (Surrey)

FARNHAM TRIATHLON (Surrey)

FAVERSHAM (Kent)

FELTHAM (Middlesex)
Formed 1966
Club Sec: R.A. Bridge, 35 Benedict Drive, Bedfont, Middlesex, TW14 8JH.   *Chief Coach:* K. Bridge
Members: 250. *Leading Members:* Danny Ashley (18), Joan Baker (10), Caroline Bligh (17), Sara Clements (15), Jason Collins (15), Clare Deacon (11), Timothy Don (11), Richard Evans (21), Roderick Fontain (13), John Gorman (11), Niel Greathead (18), Stuart Hayes (10), Wayne Humphrey (16), J. Lynch (18), C. McKay (23), Joanne Pearce (11), Sarah Pooley (11), Clare Punter (12), Julie Punter (14), Stephanie Reed (13), Sarah Reghelini (16), James Richardson (13), Yolande Roberts (12), Scott Searle (20), Edward Thorne (11).

FELTON FLEET SCHOOL (Surrey)

FINCHLEY SCHOOL OF SWIMMING & LIFE SAVING (Middlesex)

FINSBURY (Middlesex)

FOLKESTONE & HYTHE SCOUTS COUNCIL (Kent)

FOLKESTONE SPORTS CENTRE (Kent)

FORWARD HILLINGDON SQUAD (Middlesex)
Formed 1977
Club Sec: T. Watson, 63 Heath Road, Hillingdon, Middlesex.   *Chief coach:* S. Lewington
Members: 142. *Leading Members:* Karen Adams, Mark Beveridge, Clare Bishop, Arlette Boyd, Colin Burksfield, Stewart Clegg, Mark Creasy, Chris Farren, Duncan Farrowsmith, Wanda Field, Emma Hansford, Chris Jennings, Dominique McPherson, Marc McPherson, Michelle Maunders, Scott Meachum, Chris Moulson, Sally Prier, Graham Rough, James Rumsey, Elian Sabba, Mark Skyrme, Robert Skyrme, Jonathan Wong, Paula Wood.

FULHAM (Middlesex)
Formed 1946
Club Sec: R.A. Luckett, 25 Clifford House, Edith Villas, London, W14 8UG.   *Chief Coach:* Miss C. Gomm
Members: 250.

FURZEFIELD DC (Herts)

GALAGOS (Middlesex)

GAV/BP KENT COMETS (Kent)

GODALMING (Surrey)
Formed 1975
Club Sec: Mrs R. Napper, 6 Windsor Close, Onslow Village, Guildford.   *Chief Coach:* Mrs E. Sprake
Members: 190. *Leading Members:* James Albery, Julia Antonini, Laura Antonini, David Archer, Benjamin Bailey, Ross Bailey, Naomi Browne, Annaliese Burton, Harry Charles, David Cox, Robin Dew, Neil Edwards, Benjamin Highfield, Felicity Lee, Rebecca Lloyd, Lucy Mullan, James Mustill, Richard Shapley, Alexie Sommer, Jonathan Stevens, Andrew St John-Seymour, Linda Stollery, John Tomkins, Alex von Haselberg, Tamsin Wilson.

GOSPORT DOLPHINS (Hants)
Formed 1975
Club Sec: D.G. Taylor, 66 Rowner Road, Gosport, Hants, PO13 9RG.   *Chief Coach:* Mrs M. Taylor
Members: 200. *Leading Members:* Gillian Bennett (15), Lesley Bennett (18), Robert Bennett (19), David Chandler (14), Nigel Davis (11), Emma Dowdle (12), Peter Fairhurst (16), Roger Fairhurst (16), Femke Hawksworth (13), Rory Macleod (13), Lara McNeil (14), Neil McRoberts (10), Sarah Marsh (11), Nicola Power (21), Michael Spoor (16), Stephen Taylor (16), Paul Tolputt (16), Iain Wallace (11), Chris White (14), Kevin White (13), Mark White (15), Emma Widdop (14), Sarah Widdop (17), Charlotte Wilson (12), Rebecca Wilson (15).

GOSPORT ST VINCENT (Hants)
Formed 1987
Club Sec: Mrs E. Nash, 124 Chantry Road, Gosport, Hants.   *Chief Coach:* Mrs V. Pointon
Members: 30. *Leading Members:* Chris Barrett (10), Michelle Beckwith (11), Wayne Cross (13), Mark Davis (9), Aaron Giles (11), Trevor Giles (13), David Godfrey (10), William Godfrey (14), Andrew Groth (10), Gareth Jenkins (10), Ella Kilgour (9), Sally Kilgour (12), Louise Marlow (10), Sarah Martin (11), Katie May (11), Louise Nash (11), Janine O'Gorman (11), Zoe O'Gorman (9), Lyndsey Sharpe (12), Darren Sheard (15), Donna Sumpner (15), David Thomson (13), Scott Thomson (10), Anthony Wellington (15), Jamie Wellington (13).

GRAVESEND & NORTHFLEET (Kent)
Formed 1912
Club Sec: Mrs A. Hatherly, 68 Northdown Road, Longfield, Kent.   *Chief Coach:* S. Winn
Members: 325. *Leading Members:* Colin Arundell (14), Kevin Arundell (11), Zillah Beaumont (14), Paul Blair (16), Frances Burgin (12), Lee Caller (15), Elizabeth Dadson (14), Samantha Davidson (21), Richard Davis (14), David Godwin (12), Wendy Godwin (14), Juliette Hatfield (14), Ann Hatherly (51), Lisa Hatherly (21), Frances Hillier (36), Sean Holden (11), Simon King (15), Alan Leeming (31), Hayley Lucas (14), Zena Money (12), Maud Povey (65), Kate Start (14), Caroline Warren (23), Rebecca Winn (14), Claire Yendell (14), Neil Young (13).

GRAVESHAM LIFE SAVING (Kent)

GREENFORD & DISTRICT SCOUTS (Middlesex)

GREENWICH (Kent)

GREENWICH BOROUGH MARINERS (Kent) *Formed* 1910
Club Sec: Mrs T.R. McKelvey, 175 Axminster Crescent, Welling, Kent, DA16 1EX. *Chief Coach:* G. Ross
Members: 220. *Leading Members:* Georgina Brooks (15), Liam Duff (12), Samantha Fensome (12), Louise Goodfellow (18), Vikky Grane (15), David Graves (15), Tara Hill (14), Alison Howells (18), Kelly Jackson (15), William Jolin (12), John Lee (21), Ian Miller (16), Suzanne Orman (16), James Pauling (12), Ansela Pendrich (13), Suzanne Pendrich (11), Elizabeth Reid (14), Emma Rickard (13), Simon Shering (13), Sarah Smith (12), Paul Vickers (14), Gary Waddilove (14), Ian Walker (15), Terry Ward (25), Daniel Warren (13).

GUERNSEY (Channel Islands) *Formed* 1866
Club Sec: Mrs M. Hubert, La Villette, St Martins, Guernsey. *Chief Coach:* Mrs J. Guille
Members: 350. *Leading Members:* Sue Crissel-Falla (10), Emma Davies (13), Simon Dowdney (22), Mark Freear (15), Tony Fulgoni (18), Lisa Guille (25), Samantha Herridge (12), Claire Hudson (15), Susie Hudson (14), Simon Kneebone (22), Damian Lee (12), Darragh Lee (13), Siobhan Lee (16), Daniel Lintell (15), Tim Lowe (22), Sally McGhee (14), Wendy Machon (22), Stephen Mann (16), Susan Mann (13), Paul Nettleship (15), Emma Ryan (15), Gary Smith (18), John Tomlin (16), Michelle Tomlin (17), Simon Watson (17).

GUILDFORD CITY (Surrey) *Formed* 1889
Club Sec: R.G. Moys, 26 Irwin Road, Guildford, GU2 5PP. *Chief Coach:* F. Rhode
Members: 240. *Leading Members:* Joanne Alden (12), Gemma Dunlop (15), Kitty Edbrooke (19), Kate McCarthy (13), Michelle Read (12), Simon Read (12), Karen Stewardson (19), Fleur Stredwick (13), Dawn Suckling (13), Kieron Taylor (17), Samantha Witts (15).

HABERDASHERS ASKE'S SCHOOL (Herts)

HAGGERSTON (Middlesex)

HALCYON NATURISTS (Hants)

HALLIWICK PENGUINS (Middlesex)

HALSTEAD (Essex) *Formed* 1965
Club Sec: L. Gorse, 14 Bois Hall Gardens, Halstead, Essex. *Chief Coach:* M. Finch
Members: 60. *Leading Members:* J. Balaam (16), S. Balaam (13), E. Beaumont (18), A. Chaplin (14), H. Chaplin (12), G. Chapman (20), C. Cowell (12), N. Cox (14), C. Fawkes (12), M. Finch, P. Gladwin (15), E. Hughes (13), P. Hughes (14), T. Rayner (12), J. Scott-Robinson (18), C. Sizer (13), P. Slee (12), T. Swallow (20), S. Traube (14), S. Wickes (12), A. Wood (12), C. Wright (16), G. Wright (13).

HAMMERSMITH PENGUINS (Middlesex)

HAMPSHIRE CONSTABULARY SPORTS & SOCIAL (Hants)

HAMPSTEAD SCHOOL OF DIVING & LIFE SAVING (Middlesex)

HARINGEY BOROUGH (Middlesex)

HARLOW (Essex)

HARPENDEN (Herts) *Formed* 1962
Club Sec: D.H.D. Russell, 29 Barnfield Road, Harpenden, Herts, AL5 5TH.
Members: 220.

HARROW SCOUTS & GUIDES (Middlesex)

HARROW & WEALDSTONE (Middlesex)

HART (Hants) *Formed* 1968
Club Sec: Mrs P. Stow, 23 Adams Drive, Fleet, Hants, GU13 9DZ. *Chief Coach:* Mrs S. Horn
Members: 400. *Leading Members:* Bruce Andrews (25), David Brinck (21), Richard Brinck (23), Charlotte Byrne (15), Helen Chambers (15), Anita Dye (17), Louise Dye (20), Mark Dye (16), Kylie Gyertson (14), Roynan Hastings (18), Joanne Holton (18), Kevin Hough (12), Sharon Hough (15), Warren Jesse (14), Kevin Long (19), Nicholas Mellor (14), Elizabeth Murray (14), Joanne Northwood (14), Grant Perks (13), Helen Ramsay (18), Margaret Ramsay (16), Helen Sanderson (17), Melissa Stow (12), Christopher Townsley (12), Karen Wooldridge (19).

HARTLEY & DISTRICT (Kent)

HARWICH, DOVERCOURT & PARKSTONE (Essex)

HASLEMERE (Surrey) *Formed* 1971
Club Sec: Mrs J. Ashford, 3 Rozeldene, Hindhead, Surrey, GU26 6TW. *Chief Coach:* Mrs I. Sanderson
Members: 250. *Leading Members:* Simon Ash (13), Catherine Ashford (15), Elizabeth Ashford (18), Robert Blackaby (13), Debora Clarke (14), Simon Day (13), Catherine Denard (12), Naomi Gould (12), Beth Grant (11), Claire Morris (14), Thomas Nicholson (17), William Nicholson (16), David O'Brien (11), Cato Pedder (16), Geoffrey Pedder (12), Margaretha Pedder (9), Kim Sanderson (17), Craig Saunders (11), Rachel Sherrington (10), Robert Stemp (17), Kirsten Webster (16), Jessica Wright (13).

HASTINGS SEAGULL (Sussex)
Formed 1969

Club Sec: Mrs K.G. Honeysett, 3 Shirley Drive, St Leonards on Sea, East Sussex.   *Chief Coach:* D. Guy
Members: 450. *Leading Members:* Clive Benson (25), Steven Brown (16), Natalie Campion-Smith (13), James Cocker (18), Joanna Cocker (20), Margaret Croft, Katherine Curl (14), Kevin Day (13), Michael Day (16), Rebecca Driscoll (12), Ivan Durham (14), Ted Feakes, Lisa Guy (12), Andrew Harley (18), Louise Henham (13), Andrew Hudson (16), Emma Hurst (18), Sarah McGlone (14), Andrea Nash (16), Todd Pappaiouannou (15), Tim Pearce, Tony Powell, Leigh Sherrington (16), Hayley Southwood (14), Steven Torrance (13).

HATFIELD (Herts)
Formed 1966

Club Sec: W. Jolley, 3 Hyburn Close, Bricket Wood, St Albans, Herts.   *Chief Coach:* T. MacGuinness
Members: 400. *Leading Members:* Louis Bull (18), Alexis Cooper (9), Mark Dare (11), James Day (18), Chris Dunn (43), Heather Fouracres (18), Nicola Gale (19), Richard Gale (17), Sheena Gale (15), Gavin Green (12), Adrian Hill (15), Rebecca Hill (17), Gaynor Hodnett (12), Jonathan Holmes (14), Imogen Jolley (17), Jessica Lane (10), Alison Lawrence (17), Ruth MacKenzie (11), Nicola More (14), Duncan Ogilvie (10), Susan Reed (13), Gary Sharpe (13), Réamonn Smale (17), Kathryn Smith (17), Christian Williamson (14).

HAYES & HARLINGTON (Middlesex)

HAYWARDS HEATH (Sussex)
Formed 1976

Club Sec: Mrs B. Davies, 24 Summerhill Lane, Haywards Heath, Sussex.   *Chief Coach:* K. Banfield
Members: 350. *Leading Members:* Clare Amer (14), Mark Bermingham (10), Steven Cale (17), Gillian Davies (10), Suzanne Davies (12), Anthony Gimson (51), Elizabeth Griffin (16), Keith Hotton (13), Paul Hotton (8), Paul Kember (11), Charlotte Leahy (13), Kieron Leahy (9), Paul Maclean (16), Louisa Mant (11), Alice Mills (12), Matti Nurklik (16), Vicky Paice (13), Nicola Rankin (13), Andrew Rees (21), Paul Richardson (13), Tara Smith (11), Helen Sommerton (9), Liam Tucknott (12), Ben Weeks (13), Caroline Woodcock (16).

HEMEL HEMPSTEAD (Herts)

Club Sec: Mrs A. Syddal, Pembroke, Cerimaes Meadow, Hemel Hempstead.   *Chief Coach:* B. Robson
Members: 180. *Leading Members:* Nicholas Ablett (13), Alex Beller (12), Graham Booth (20), Matthew Brooks (12), Ian Colmer (20), Emma Cooksey (12), Nicola Dainton (12), Ian Evans (14), Sarah Foster (11), Alex Gibbon (14), Charlotte Gibson (15), Sarah Herbert (14), Mark Kelly (12), Michelle Kent (18), Simon Knight (12), Joanna Mutton (14), Sean Newman (19), Faye Norris (13), Sarah Randall (17), Langley Sharp (13), Kevin Sinclair (13), Richard Stratum (13), Louise Syddall (13), Emma Vogel (15), Karen White (14).

HEMEL HEMPSTEAD WPC (Herts)

HENDON (Middlesex)
Formed 1958

Club Sec: Miss B.A. Atkin, 15 Hillfield Avenue, The Hyde, Hendon, NW9 6NY.
Members: 120.

HENLEY ON THAMES (Berks & Bucks)
Formed 1976

Club Sec: Mrs V.J. Clark, 16 King James Way, Henley on Thames, Oxon.   *Chief Coach:* D. Davies
Members: 101. *Leading Members:* Nick Csemiczky (14), Chris Darke (10), Nick Darke (14), Jenna Davies (10), Andrew Fletcher (12), Lucy Goodall (14), Nicola Johnstone (15), Nicola Leaver (10), Stuart Neild (14), Joanna Parkerson (15), Isla Pearce (14), Sophia Pierce (15), Rhiannon Preston (11), William Quinton (17), Emma Rowlett (14), Rebekah Rowlett (17), Elizabeth Scott (13), Laura Scott (12), Mark Scourse (13), Andrew Sibon (13), John Andrew Smith (12), Louise Stanbrook (15), Richard Stanbrook (12), Joanna Summerland (12), Daniel Wood (16).

HERNE BAY (Kent)

HERTFORD (Herts)

HESTON (Middlesex)

HIGHGATE DC (Middlesex)
Formed 1928

Club Sec: R.J. Leighton, 160 Marks Road, Romford, Essex.   *Chief Coach:* M. Edge
Members: 35.

HIGHGATE LIFE BUOYS (Middlesex)

HILLINGDON DIVING SCHOOL (Middlesex)

HILLINGDON SOUTH (Middlesex)

HITCHIN (Herts)
Formed 1886

Club Sec: W.E. Harmer, 37 Ninesprings Way, Hitchin, Herts, SG4 9NR.   *Chief Coach:* D.W. Cook
Members: 250. *Leading Members:* Colin Bayles (30), Lindsay Cook (19), Rachel Cook (16), Stephen Cook (21), Joanna Corby (18), Rachel Corby (17), Russell Harmer (24), Matthew Harrington (15), Paul Harrington (18), Sarah Hunt (17), Adrian Hutton (17), Catherine Jenkins (17), Darren Kolek (16), Beverley Larman (13), Lucie Lohrey (14), Julie Marlow (18), Sarah Marlow (16), Stephen Monk (16), Graham

Munro (18), Jonathan Nixon (15), Anthony Rhodes (17), Stephen Symmons (30+), Andrew Watson (20), Stuart Watson (17), Karen Young (18).

HODDESDON (Herts)　　　　　　　　　　　　　　　　　　　　　　　　*Formed* 1895
Club Sec: Mrs M. Moore, 30 Benford Road, Hoddesdon, Herts, EW11 8LL.　　　　　*Chief Coach:* J. Lowe
Members: 185. *Leading Members:* Robert Ager (11), John Brett (23), Danny Brinkley (11), Leyla Butterfield (11), Julie Downes (9), Lee Downes (15), Jo-Anne Elbourn (11), Amanda Greig (15), Neal Guilliotte (13), Ryan Ingrey (11), Kathrine Leadbeater (11), Julie Lowe (34), Allen Martin (24), Tracey Martin (17), Keith Mason (11), Laura Mason (13), Ian Monksfield (22), Annalee Moore (14), Colin Moore (17), Natalie Morgan (9), Laurence Osborn (15), Nicholas Rogers (14), Lorrainne Scheuber (15), Neal Tuson (28), Mark Warner (29).

HORLEY (Surrey)

HORNCHURCH (Essex)

HORSHAM (Sussex)

HOUNSLOW BOROUGH (Middlesex)　　　　　　　　　　　　　　　　　　*Formed* 1980
Club Sec: M. Straight, 12 Mowbray Crescent, Egham, Surrey.　　　　　*Chief Coach:* M.J. Staight
Leading Members: Sharon Aldridge (17), Sarah Aylott (16), Tania Cleveland (15), James Collins (16), Sharon Duggan (15), Nicki Eldridge (14), Sarah Higgins (16), Trevor Hodes (21), David Knight (18), Danny McClaughlin (13), Shawn McClaughlin (15), Julie Martin (18), Jannie Minnock (18), Peter O'Sullivan (21), Paul Pederzolli (16), Julie Punter (15), Yolande Roberts (13), Dilan Senatillene (14), Rachael Shurey (15), Andrew Singh (16), Sarah Thomson (15), Sean Tierney (15), Natalie Vafardis (13), Neal Williams (17), Graeme Woolgar (18).

HOUNSLOW BOROUGH SYNCHRO SQUAD (Middlesex)

HUNGERFORD (Berks & Bucks)

HURRICANES (Berks & Bucks)

HURSTPIERPOINT COLLEGE (Sussex)

HURST SCHOOL (Hants)

HYTHE (Kent)　　　　　　　　　　　　　　　　　　　　　　　　　*Formed* 1975
Club Sec: Mrs V. Nash, 3 Mill Fields Road, Hythe, Kent, CT21 4DH.　　　　*Chief Coach:* J. Hammond
Members: 300. *Leading Members:* Nan Banfield (10), Gavin Brown (10), Doreen Burgess (16), Emma Chambers (11), Clare Clayton (16), Tom Collins (12), Natasha Derrick (19), Tania Derrick (18), Ben Gray (12), Wendy Hughes (21), Conrad Krawczyk (10), Heather Morden (13), Louise Mothersele (9), Antony Nannini (16), Claudia Nannini (12), John Nash (17), Robert Oates (13), Ben Painter (15), Nathan Painter (19), Helen Smith (12), Joseph Strinatti (11), Angela Sturdy (18), Matthew Thurley (13), John Whenday (15), Jeremy Yeo (10).

IBIS, READING (Berks & Bucks)

IBIS (Middlesex)

I.B.M. SOUTH HAMPSHIRE (Hants)

ILFORD (Essex)　　　　　　　　　　　　　　　　　　　　　　　　*Formed* 1920
Club Sec: H. Greenstein, 11 Somersby Gardens, Redbridge, Ilford, Essex, 1G4 5DY.
Members: 327. *Leading Members:* Donna Aitken (14), Ross Andrews (13), Emma Bethell (14), Nicola Bowdidge (14), Leon Brand (15), Keelie Brooks (13), Martin Brooks (17), Lee Bushell (17), Peter Corke (13), Duncan Ferreira (15), Emma Gains (16), Steven Greenstein (27), Susan Greenstein (23), Charles Harris (17), Clare Harris (19), Mark Harris (20), Mark Harrisson (15), Andrew Hill (12), Mark Howlett (14), Bradley Jones (11), Mark Jowers (15), Clare Sadler (13), Mark Sadler (15), Andrea Smith (13), Danny Young (13).

ILFORD DC (Essex)

IMPERIAL COLLEGE SWIMMING & WPC (Middlesex)

INTERNATIONAL SCHOOL OF LONDON (Middlesex)

ISLE OF THANET (Kent)

ISLE OF WIGHT (Hants)

ISLEWORTH PENGUIN (Middlesex)

ISLINGTON BOROUGH (Middlesex)

JERSEY (Channel Islands)　　　　　　　　　　　　　　　　　　　*Formed* 1865
Club Sec: Mrs M. Mesch, Rue de Dammes, St Clements, Jersey. *Chief Coaches:* R.N. Hasfall, T. Sordson
Members: 120. *Leading Members:* Natasha Abels (16), Simon Abels (15), Rachel Blythe (11), Rebecca Brewer (12), Nicklas Collins (11), Zoe de Carteret (12), Jane Dryden (15), Susan Goodson (12), Brett Grover (17), Kim Grover (16), Russel Hocquard (17), Steve Hopkins (17), Robert Huish (11), Tracy Huish

433

(16), Melanie le Saint (16), Christian Love (14), Greg McDonald (16), Rachel Morris (17), Joanne Morton (16), Christian Mourant (12), Richard Nicolle (17), Solenn Pastourel (10), Dean Rabaste (12), Kirsteen Taylor (10), Joanne Wills (14).

JERSEY D.I.P.S. (Channel Islands)

JERSEY ETAILE SYNCHRO (Channel Islands)   Formed 1976
Club Sec: A. Johnson, Fort View House, Pico Road, St Saviour, Jersey.
Members: 50. *Leading Members:* E. Cann (10), N. Donnelly (16), A. Jones (13), C. McLaughlin (14), V. Osborne (14), S. Pastourel (10), N. Risebrow (15), K. Rosser (18), J. Stayte (9), M. Taylor (14), J. Wills (13).

JERSEY LONG DISTANCE (Channel Islands)   Formed 1974
Club Sec: P.N. Gravett, "Wissant View", 1 Mark Close, Rue de la Croix, St Clement, Jersey.
Chief Coach: Mrs S. Minty-Gravett
Members: 45. *Leading Members:* Raulin Amy (14), Den Arnold (41), Trevor Billingsley (40), Denise Billingsley (35), Sarah Bland (13), Aimee Crook (11), Hazel Firbank (35), Richard Flambard (20), George Gaudin (44), Peter Gravett (46), Tracy Harris (24), Marion Harvey (26), Maurice Lakeman (63), Karryna McLaughlin (13), Jean Paul Madelenat (48), David Minty (25), Leslie Minty (70), Sally Minty-Gravett (31), Andrew Munns (26), Suzanne Munns (32), Marcus Nobes (18), James Rhodes (17), Kathryn Rosser (18), Ian Rumens (17), Alison Streeter (25), Gary Tobin (20).

JOHN LEWIS PARTNERSHIP (Middlesex)

KENT COUNTY CONSTABULARY (Kent)

KENT FIRE BRIGADE (Kent)

KILLERWHALES, HAVERING (Essex)

KINGFISHER (Kent)

KINGFISHER WPC (Surrey)

KINGSFERRY (Kent)

KINGS LANGLEY (Herts)   Formed 1973
Club Sec: Mrs M. Stavrou, 44 Rymill Close, Bovingdon, Herts, HP3 0JA.   *Chief Coach:* D. Moore
Members: 135. *Leading Members:* Vanessa Barnes (18), Kate Barnett (9), Claire Biggs (14), Christine Evans (14), Katherine Everitt (11), Helen Fee (12), Mark Gilmore (13), Simon Gilmore (17), Amanda Green (16), Leon Halford (15), Ian Hayter (12), Robert Ingleby (9), Lisa Keys (11), Rachael McCann (16), Mark McGinty (9), Owen McGinty (11), Jason Mancey-Jones, Gary Mayger (22), Graham Riddick (18), Lucy Rosenthal (12), Claire Sheldrake (14), Lynsey Thomas (10), Martin Wiggs (12), Keiron Williamson (12).

KING'S SCHOOL, CANTERBURY (Kent)   Formed 1945
Club Sec: Dr N.J. Bridge, c/o 25 The Precincts, Canterbury, CT1 2ES.   *Chief Coach:* R.E. Barham
Members: 65. *Leading Members:* M.R.J. Craddock (14), R.J.T. Craig (14), J.G.S. Doust (14), C.P. Dwyer (15), M.T. Edlmann (13), J.A.N. Faulkner (13), R.J. Francis (14), D.P.P. Godfrey (17), J.M. Grimes (15), P.A. Higgins (15), N.J.H. King (14), J. Kingsland (13), N.D. Lawrence (16), W.A. Manning (15), M. Montgomery (17), J.J. Morse (17), R.J. Norris (14), C.J. Pearce (14), J.H.J. Phipson (13), S. Santry (16), J.J.F. Stobbs (16), J.R.P. Thomson (17), N.H. Turner (15), M.D.A. Willis-Jones (15), K.W. Yeoh (16).

KINGSTON GRAMMAR SCHOOL (Surrey)

KINGSTON LADIES (Surrey)

KINGSTON ROYALS (Surrey)   Formed 1981
Club Sec: Mrs A. Sadler, 14 Pony Chase, Knipp Hill, Cobham, Surrey.   *Chief Coach:* J. Dobinson
Members: 500.

LADIES DC (Essex)

LADIES DC, BARNET (Middlesex)

LAING SPORTS (Herts)

LAMBETH (Surrey)   Formed 1959
Club Sec: J.H. Whyton, Flat 6B, Christchurch Road, London, SW2 3EX.   *Chief Coach:* W.Hagman
Members: 50. *Leading Members:* Stewart Billings (23), Steve Bromwich (15), Steve Burchmore (29), Christopher Burden, Barnaby Day, Keiran Day, Sebastian Day, Kevin Harman (28), Neil Harman (25), Elizabeth Harvey, Paul Innis, Pearl Manifold, Jasper Myles, Siobhan Myles, Julia Purcell, William Purcell, Claire Reeves, Kelly Robinson, Terry Robinson (25), Sam Smith, Sarah Smith, Maria Thompson, Julie Watson, Kyla West, Edward White.

LAMBETH WPC (Surrey)

LEANDER (Surrey)

434

LEATHERHEAD (Surrey)　　　　　　　　　　　　　　　　*Formed* 1975
Club Sec: Mrs W.A. Prevost, "Riverslea", Hamm Court, Weybridge, Surrey.　　*Chief Coach:* S. Davis
Members: 260. *Leading Members:* Tim Arnell (12), Paul Belk (12), Kari Bell (14), Lesley Bray (20), Christopher Cardwell (14), Rosie Chitty (16), Gillian Emery (16), Fiona Greswell (15), Laura Greswell (13), Claire Jeffs (15), Graeme Keith (16), Natasha Kelley (14), Martin Kowalski (11), Paul Lewis (15), Julie Mercer (12), Richard Osborne (11), Richard Pepper (13), Michael Rayner (15), Alistair Shattock (14), Lucy Shaw (14), Lee Slater (15), Richard Stannard (15), Phillipa Stanyard (12), Paul Taylor (14), Lucy Webster (16).

LEA VALLEY CYGNETS SYNCHRO (Herts)　　　　　　　　　　*Formed* 1974
Club Sec: Mrs Y. Price, "Roseneath", 39 Carnaby Road, Broxbourne.　　*Chief Coach:* Miss J.M. Price
Members: 18.

LENSBURY (Surrey)

LETCHWORTH (Herts)
Club Sec: Mrs S. Merry, 88 Willian Way, Letchworth, Herts, SG6 2HY.　　*Chief Coach:* Mrs S. Goldsmith
Leading Members: Vicky Cadwallader (10), Daniel Cochran (9), Susan Croft (15), Zoe Dallimore (12), Daniel Debtuck (14), Helen Eele (9), Jonathan Eele (11), Helen Goldsmith (13), Sarah Goldsmith (11), Carey Haigh (16), Jill Hardy (30), Matthew Lockyer (13), Adrian Mariados (9), Stephen Mariados (14), Terry May, Jennifer Newbould (12), Richard Osborne (13), Kathryn Reeves (13), Lorraine Roby (12), Mark Slavoy (16), Greg Steel (10), Gareth Stutely (10), Sam Wickramasinghe (8), Graham Wright (16), Peter Young (10).

LEWES (Sussex)　　　　　　　　　　　　　　　　　　*Formed* 1975
Club Sec: D. Jones, 47 Spences Lane, Lewes, East Sussex, BN7 2HF.　　*Chief Coach:* Mrs C. Parfect
Members: 300.

LEWISHAM (Kent)

LEWISHAM LADIES & LADYWELL (Kent)

LEYTON (Essex)

LICENSED VITUALLERS SCHOOL (Berks & Bucks)

LITTLEHAMPTON (Sussex)　　　　　　　　　　　　　　*Formed* 1983
Club Sec: Mrs L. Jones, 4 Dinsdale Gardens, Rustington, Littlehampton.　　*Chief Coach:* Mrs J. Foster
Members: 170. *Leading Members:* Philip Brooke (14), Alison Brown (13), Emma Brunning (11), Thomas Chalmers (12), Gillian Clarke (10), Caroline Corfield (13), Michael Corfield (12), Simon Feldwick (10), Ken Flint (12), Callum Foster (18), Edward Hiscock (14), Leigh Hunt (14), Barry James (20), David Lawallee (14), Jenny Lee (12), Louise McCartney (14), Leigh Martin (13), Sally Mills (34), Tamsin Oliver (13), Bruce Pearce (24), Mark Saxton (14), Susan Scott (10), Daniel Shelverton (15), Wendy Umney (16), Tony Watson (10).

LLOYDS (Middlesex)

LONDON BOROUGH OF EALING (Middlesex)

LONDON BOROUGH OF ENFIELD WPC (Middlesex)　　　　　*Formed* 1967
Club Sec: K. Hall, 19 Elmscott Gardens, London, N21.
Members: 30.

LONDON BOROUGH OF GREENWICH (Kent)

LONDON CENTRAL YMCA (Middlesex)

LONDON HOSPITAL (Middlesex)

LORD WANDSWORTH COLLEGE (Hants)

LYMINGTON (Hants)　　　　　　　　　　　　　　　　*Formed* 1892
Club Sec: J.C. Sims, 18 Park Road, Lymington, Hants.　　*Chief Coach:* Miss J. Davis
Members: 180. *Leading Members:* Wilf Adams (50), Joss Crouch (50), Jenny Davis (24), Joanna Dean (11), Natasha Dean (15), James Dunsden (11), Adrian Glasspool (15), Ian Glasspool (13), Sandra Harris (18), Len Jackson (40), Mark Jackson (16), Theresa Jackson (13), James Letchford (15), Rob Letchford (13), Nick Martin (13), Pam Poulton (21), Nick Radcliff (15), Zoe Reossin (11), Hayley Saunders (9), Karen Saunders (17), Karen Sims (15), Andy Tibbert (13), Steven Tompkin (13), Sandra Tools (11), C. Webb (15).

MACCABI UNION (Middlesex)

MAIDENHEAD (Berks & Bucks)

MAIDENHEAD COLLEGE (Berks & Bucks)

MAIDSTONE (Kent)　　　　　　　　　　　　　　　　*Formed* 1844
Club Sec: A. Baker, 28 Briar Fields, Weavering, Maidstone, Kent, ME14 5UZ.　　*Chief Coach:* B. Ludgrove
Members: 146. *Leading Members:* Stuart Baker (16), Victoria Baker (13), Susan Byrne (14), Caroline

Fielder (15), Christa Gammon (14), Heidie Gammon (13), Simon Giles (16), Michelle Holman (10), Richard Howe (14), Elizabeth Mepstead (14), Sarah Mepstead (10), Adam Page (10), Niel Peeper (10), Stuart Peeper (13), Douglass Reid (10), Elizabeth Saul (16), Michael Smith (17), Jodie Stafford (10), Kelly Stafford (12), Grant Strachen (15), Jo Tew (16), Darren Wetheridge (14), Daniel Wigg (10), Sarah Wooldridge (21), Simon Wooldridge (21).

MARGATE (Kent)
Formed 1974
Club Sec: Mrs S. Southworth, 12 Eastchurch Road, Cliftonville, Kent, CT9 3EN.   Chief Coach: J. White
Members: 82. Leading Members: Gemma Bailey (11), David Brackenborough (17), Nolan Cocks (12), Brenda Crosswell (17), Samantha Dallman (10), Rebecca Hammond (15), Louise Hickson (13), Jamie Knight (12), Mark Lawless (14), Justin Legge (17), Florrie Miles (12), Gregg Miles (10), Lee Miles (15), Scott Miles (11), Sarah Moore (11), Dale Owens (10), Kelly Potter (11), Jake Rostron (14), Daniel Rowe (13), Paul Rowland (15), Lorraine Sansom (13), Louise Stapley (10), Marissa Summers (16), Lynn Titmus (11), James Ward (11).

MARLOW (Berks & Bucks)
Formed 1980
Club Sec: Mrs L. Wilson, "Highbank", Springfield Lane, Marlow, Bucks, SL7 2LB.   Chief Coach: D. Evans
Members: 140.

MATURE ADULTS (Middlesex)

MERTON PISCES WEST PARK (Surrey)
Formed 1979
Club Sec: Mrs R. Kavanagh, 141 West Way, London, SW20 9LT.   Chief Coach: H.G. Green
Members: 35. Leading Members: N. Bellord (12), G. Caro (15), J. Caro (15), D. Cowan (16), L. Cowan (13), R. Giffiths (16), L. Gray (12), M. Green (18), J. Hatton (10), D. Jamel (14), S. Jamel (14), P. Jones (12), L. Kavanagh (10), D. Lawson (16), J. Letkey (15), G. Marshall (9), K. Prothero (9), D. Siggery (20), C. Torlan (13), M. Torlan (12), J. Voss (16), K. Voss (14), S. Voss (14), N. Webb (14), J. Wood (10).

MERTON SCHOOL OF DIVING (Surrey)

MERTON SWORDFISH (Surrey)

METROPOLITAN DIVING SCHOOL (Middlesex)

METROPOLITAN POLICE (Middlesex)

METROPOLITAN POLICE TRAINING SCHOOL (Middlesex)

MIDDLESEX HOSPITAL (Middlesex)

MIDHURST & DISTRICT (Sussex)

MID-SUSSEX SYNCHRO CLUB (Sussex)
Formed 1983
Club Sec: Mrs S. Cooper, 5 Wye Close, Broadfield, Crawley, RH11 9QZ.   Chief Coach: Mrs G. Hillman
Members: 45. Leading Members: Clare Amer, Leanne Amey, Lucy Bush, Amy Clark, Jane Clark, Nicola Cooper, Petra Cooper, Catherine Croney, Alex Dann, Phillippa Dann, Kirsty Eke, Liz Fitzsimmons, Suzy Halson, Julie Hillman, Mandy Hillman, Toni Hillman, Nicola Hunter, Emma Jones, Alex Kindell, Emma Norledge, Anna Ramsden, Kim Rogers, Masiel Villaverde, Sharon West, Charlotte Woodard.

MINNOWS (Kent)

MITCHAM CLARION (Surrey)

MOIRA HOUSE SCHOOL (Sussex)

MOLE VALLEY DC (Surrey)
Formed 1987
Club Sec: S. McKee, 12 Bourne Drive, off Batsworth Road, Mitcham, Surrey.   Chief Coach: J. Bull
Members: 20. Leading Members: Roz Ainsworth (16), Andrew Byford (14).

MORDEN PARK (Surrey)

MOTE PARK (Kent)
Formed 1970
Club Sec: Mrs V. Coddington, 1 Barrel Arch Close, Marden, Maidstone.   Chief Coach: Mrs C. Shipp
Members: 80. Leading Members: Craig Anderson (20), Rachel Camp (12), Sarah Camp (13), Mark Chittenden (12), Christopher Coddington (14), Julia Coddington (12), Harry Cole (14), Jimmy Cole (11), Clare Coleman (15), Lydia Goulding (15), Daniel Hatcher (14), Lisa Holmes (11), Lloyd Kent (9), Nichola King (15), Paul Roper (17), Simon Roper (13), Leanne Ross (14), Hannah Smith (15), David Stolton (10), Matthew Stolton (13), Charlotte Tobin (10), Darren Tobin (14), Caroline Upton (14), Catherine Upton (17), Claire Upton (14).

NATIONAL WESTMINSTER BANK (Middlesex)

NATURIST FOUNDATION (Kent)

NAUTILUS (Surrey)
Formed 1959
Club Sec: Mrs J. Hickley, 40 Taunton Lane, Old Coulsdon, Surrey, CR3 1SE.
Members: 264.

NEWBURY (Berks & Bucks)
Formed 1948
Club Sec: Mrs J. Hopkins, "Midway", The Ridge, Cold Ash, Newbury, Berks.   Chief Coach: Mrs B. Hart

Members: 198. *Leading Members:* Keith Arlott (14), Stuart Bryant (16), Christian Carley (10), Andrew Edwards (13), Anna Edwards (13), Linda Freeman (17), Lee Gollop (12), Ian Harber (19), Duncan Hart (18), Mathew Hart (17), Alison Hathrill (16), Kevin Hathrill (18), Joanna Hayward (14), Penny McGeorge (15), Neil Phillips (16), Marc Pinder (17), Andrew Scott (12), Hannah Shepherd (16), Kate Shepherd (12), Emma Stacey (10), Paul White (15).

NEWHAM SYNCHRONETTES (Essex)   *Formed* 1981
Club Sec: A.P.H. Dunning, 23 Morley Road, Stratford, London, E15 3HF.   *Chief Coach:* Mrs L. Springett
Members: 20. *Leading Members:* Sandra Dunning (21), Jacqueline Pease-Cox (12), Victoria Pease-Cox (15).

NEW MILTON (Hants)   *Formed* 1977
Club Sec: Mrs M.J. Annetts, 47 South Street, Pennington, Lymington, Hants.   *Chief Coach:* R. Jarvis
Members: 150. *Leading Members:* Michael Bycroft (15), Darren Chamberlain (9), Rebbecca Chamberlain (9), Zoe Chamberlain (12), Michael Dawson (12), James Doran (9), Sarah Gannaway (16), Andrew Glasspool (14), Zoe Hatchett (12), Claire Holiday (9), Abigail Hughes (9), Andrew Hughes (10), Gina Martin (13), Nicola Martin (18), Gail Richardson (15), Nicola Rowe (11), Warren Rowe (9), Martin Scott (20), Rachael Southey (11), Philip Tennant (12), Samantha Tennant (14), James Waller (9), Sam Walton (10), Jamie Wearn (10), Sara Wearn (12).

NONSUCH (Surrey)

NORTHUMBERLAND PARK (Middlesex)

OASIS (Middlesex)

OJAYS (Kent)   *Formed* 1984
Club Sec: Mrs H. Cross, 17 Cloonmore Avenue, Orpington, Kent.   *Chief Coaches:* M. Besford,
C. Castle, J. Cooper, E. Powis
Members: 130. *Leading Members:* Mark Allan (10), Louise Bell (9), Gemma Besford (12), Steven Besford (13), Natalie Betts (12), Laura Beveridge (9), Helen Brown (11), Timothy Buick (12), Nicola Castle (8), Dawn Collette (12), Andrew Gammon (11), Stuart Hawes (9), Niomi Hawney (11), Julienne Hunter (10), Nicola Hunter (12), Ian Jarvis (12), Alexander Kuness (9), Christopher Lofts (11), Andrew Miller (11), Saul Penhallow (13), Mark Pettyfer (9), Nigel Pointer, Timothy Powis (11), Victoria Powis (13), Richard Scorer (10), Helen Wyatt (11).

OLD CHOLMELIANS SWIMMING & WPC (Middlesex)

OLD MID WHITGIFTIANS (Surrey)

OLD STORTFORDIANS WPC (Herts)   *Formed* 1927
Club Sec: M.R. Claridge, 16 The Pyghtle, Turvey, Bedford, MK43 8ED.
Members: 28.

OLD VICTORIANS WPC (Channel Islands)   *Formed* 1976
Club Sec: R.J. Parker, Le Clos du Puits, Route D'Ebenezer, Trinity.   *Chief Coach:* P. Pitcher
Members: 15.

OLD WHITGIFTIANS (Surrey)

OLYMPIC SALAMANDER (Middlesex)

ORPINGTON (Kent)   *Formed* 1965
Club Sec: D. Comrie, 20 Warren Gardens, Chelsfield, Orpington, Kent, BR6 6JD.   *Chief Coach:* C. Perry
Members: 201. *Leading Members:* Dominic Bill (18), Julian Bunclark (12), Kristin Castle (14), Robert Czaplinski (15), Sarah Dennis (14), Jo Edwards (18), Polly Epton (13), Simon Henley (14), Nicola Hine (13), Emma Hulls (14), Elizabeth Kilbey (13), David Kingsland (11), Helen Lydall (12), Helen Morris (15), Stephen Morris (17), Simon Mullinger (17), Justin Palfrey (17), Steven Parker (18), Tim Powis (11), Mark Thorne (17), Jonathan Tickner (14), Lara Whitfield (13), Steven Wilson (15).

OTTER (Middlesex)   *Formed* 1869
Club Sec: C.J. Stewart, "Clyvers", Toys Hill, Westerham, Kent, TN16 1QE.   *Chief Coach:* A. Batt
Members: 230. *Leading Members:* Robert Alderton (30), Stephen Allen (28), Robert Barker (26), Joanne Breare (29), Nigel Burnham (28), Mary Chamberlain (28), Mark Courtney (30), Lesley Davies (28), Guy Davis (20), Tim Frazer (30), Iain Gerrard (31), Paul Goudie (30), Stephen Hirst (28), Jim Mackenzie (35), David Miller (31), Robert Millington (26), Julian Plumley (25), Marcus Plumley (27), Felicity Porritt (23), John Prowting (27), Ed Reynolds (30), Paulo Rosetti (19), Loretta Sollars (23), Lucinda Spicer (31), Graham Stark (23).

OXHEY HORNETS (Herts)

PANGBOURNE COLLEGE (Berks & Bucks)

PEARL ASSURANCE (Middlesex)

PETWORTH & DISTRICT (Sussex)

PINNER & HEADSTONE SCOUTS (Middlesex)

PIRANHA (Kent)

Club Sec: Mrs L. Chamberlain, 7 Leverholme Gardens, Eltham, London. *Chief Coach:* Miss L. Ellis
Members: 54. *Leading Members:* Lee Barnard (8), Bridget Barnes (12), Simon Barnes (9), Richard Beaumont (14), Emma Brozdowski (10), Jeffrey Bull (14), Colin Chamberlain (16), Graeme Chamberlain (8), Kate Clarke (10), Allen Davis (11), Fay Delahoy (13), Laura Evans (13), Paul Finnegan (12), Claire Freeman (10), Anthony Fox (10), Richard Jones (12), Shelley Keable (9), Steven Keable (11), Christopher Kelly (10), Joanne Kelly (12), Keziban Osman (14), Serkan Osman (11), Lucy Rogers (11), Jodie Street (11), Nicholas Watts (12).

PLAISTOW UNITED (Essex)

Formed 1908
Club Sec: F. Willmott, 53 Melbourne Road, East Ham, London, E6 2RU. *Chief Coach:* P. McNeil
Members: 150.

POLLARDS (Surrey)

POLYTECHNIC SWIMMING & WPC (Middlesex)

PORTSMOUTH (Hants)

Formed 1875
Club Sec: S.C. Tilbury, 22 Windsor Road, Waterlooville, Hants, PO7 6BA.
Members: 100.

PORTSMOUTH NORTHSEA (Hants)

Formed 1928
Club Sec: Mrs J. Cole, 4 Brightside, Waterlooville, Hants, PO7 7BA. *Chief Coach:* C. Nesbit
Members: 350. *Leading Members:* Gillian Atkins (18), Marc Clements (14), Ryan Copping (16), Annabel Gilmore (13), Adrian Godwin (12), Eileen Hall (19), Mike Hooper (17), Ken Joy (23), Joanne McHerg (15), Emma Platt (18), Zoe Platt (15), Lynda Racster (15), James Ralph (15), Grant Robins (19), Nick Robinson (18), Madeleine Scarborough (24), Nick Skinner (13), Janine Taylor (17), Dave Thompson (42), Mike Watt (15), Steve Wellington (22), Alan Weltch (14), Justin Whitbread (15), Robert Wilkes (22), Gareth Williams (17).

PORTSMOUTH VICTORIA (Hants)

POSEIDON WPC (Channel Islands)

POTTERS BAR (Herts)

POTTERS BAR SYNCHRO (Herts)

PURPLES WPC (Middlesex)

QUEEN ELIZABETH GIRLS SCHOOL (Middlesex)

RAINHAM SCOUTS & GUIDES (Kent)

RAMSGATE (Kent)

Formed 1912
Club Sec: Mrs A.C. Martin, 6 Northumberland Avenue, Margate, Kent, CT9 3PB.
Members: 69. *Leading Members:* Robert Addley (10), Philip Brounsell (15), Lorna Cribbens (15), Sandra Fasham (13), Aaron Gilerington (11), Rebecca Hammond (15), Andrew Herman (12), Mark Herman (15), Darren Hudson (11), Katie Jarrett (9), Simon Knight (12), Carrie Martin (12), Mary Martin (13), Rebecca Miller (13), James Pashley (13), Rebecca Pashley (15), Julia Rouse (14), Antony Russell (7), Andrew Scarr (11), Kerry Smith (12), Rouan Smith (12), Jamie Summers (7), Tracy Summers (10).

READING (Berks & Bucks)

READING LIFE SAVING (Berks & Bucks)

READING ROYALS SYNCHRO (Berks & Bucks)

Club Sec: Mrs S. Wathen, 57 Redwood Avenue, Woodley, Reading, Berks. *Chief Coach:* J. Hawthorne
Members: 60. *Leading Members:* Sam Allen (19), Julie Audoire (14), Tamsin Buckley (14), Karen Childs (15), Emma Clark (18), Louise Fishleigh (15), Belinda Harrison (15), Kate Jones (16), Joanne Luckett (18), Sam Luckett (12), Jolie McQuillan (15), Linda Macrae (14), Vicky Maybury (17), Sarah Northey (17), Penny Rourke (15), Kirsty Runnals (15), Louise Rutter (17), Joanne Seeburg (20), Diana Singh (14), Helen Smith (15), Lindsay Smith (17), Naomi Taylor (14), Susie Vockins (18), Lisa Wathen (15), Nicola Wilson (19).

READING SCHOOL (Berks & Bucks)

READING SYNCHRO ACADEMY (Berks & Bucks)

Formed 1980
Club Sec: Mrs J. Hulbert, "Fourways", Micklands Road, Caversham. *Chief Coach:* Mrs A. Dudding
Members: 25. *Leading Members:* M. Allen (14), K. Butler (11), R. Cherry (17), C. Dalton (15), E. Flawn (13), A. Frasinski (13), K. Hayes (9), S. Healy (13), A. Hulbert (12), C. Kelham (12), S. Kennedy (12), S. Kilvert-Jones (11), K. Lowman (14), J. Murray (11), N. Murray (8), E. Palles-Clark (9), M. Palles-Clark (10), S. Parry (11), J. Paske (11), J. Pitman (13), S. Rivers (20), K. Speirs (10), J. Tinker (18), A. White (13), R. Yates (12).

READING UNIVERSITY (Berks & Bucks)

READING UNIVERSITY DC (Berks & Bucks)

Reading Royals Synchro S.C.   Reading Chronicle

READING YOUTH (Berks & Bucks)

REDBRIDGE (Essex)   *Formed* 1958
Club Sec: H.A. Fox, 22 Langham Drive, Romford, Essex, RM6 4TD.   *Chief Coach:* H.A. Fox
Members: 300. *Leading Members:* Frances Alvarez (48), Paul Alvarez (53), Johanna Augustine (14), Roy
Barnes (50), Lyn Batterhum (32), James Beach (15), Gemma Brook (13), Emma Carl (11), Martin Carl
(14), Toni Edward (10), Margaret Evans (65), Christopher Harrison (13), Ian Jones (19), Roland Kanner
(25), James Kemp (15), John Leigh (55), Laura Matthews (19), Maxine Merrion (10), Carol Mooney (38),
Laurence Nunn (15), William Price (38), Andrew Tomsett (25), Nicola Wallman (13), Keith Ward (29).

REDBRIDGE ASCLS (Essex)

REDBRIDGE BOROUGH (Essex)   *Formed* 1976
Club Sec: G. Matthews, Fullwell Cross Swimming Pool, High St, Barkingside.   *Chief Coach:* G. Matthews
Members: 126. *Leading Members:* Johanna Augustine (15), James Beach (16), Emma Brooks (15), Laura
Brooks (10), Emma Carl (11), Martin Carl (14), Lyndsey Dilley (13), Paul Fishbaum (17), Andrew Hamill
(17), Charles Harris (18), Mark Harris (20), Christopher Harrison (13), Paul Hayward (20), Kirstie Herbert
(12), Simon Jayham (22), Ian Jones (18), James Kemp (16), Emma Marham (21), Laura Matthews (19),
Daryl Newell (22), Karen Poole (18), JonPaul Sherriff-Geary (11), Nicholas Sinclair (13), Nicola Wallman
(13), Lynda Watkins (14).

REDHILL & REIGATE (Surrey)   *Formed* 1887
Club Sec: Mrs M. West, The Clockhouse, Partridge Lane, Newdigate, Surrey.   *Chief Coach:* Mrs Y. Millar
Members: 200. *Leading Members:* Simon Aplin (17), Adrian Burr (14), Caroline Burrage (13), Barry
Cannon (14), Nicola Cannon (12), Elizabeth Collins (23), Amy Cullen (14), Sacha Cunningham (15),
Marcus Doller (24), Sarah Foot (16), Philip Gatland (16), Emma Gudge (14), Philip Gudge (15), Michelle
Harker (17), Stephen Hodgson (13), David King (12), Katie Marr (15), Dale Millar (22), Joanne Money
(15), Angela Stacey (13), Joanna Stone (16), Alison Streeter (25), Karl Streeter (23), Nicholas Walker
(13), Scott Wright (12).

REDHILL & REIGATE MARLINS (Surrey)   *Formed* 1920
Club Sec: L. Stratton, 22 Colesmead Road, Redhill.   *Chief Coaches:* Mrs Knight, Mrs Stratton, Mr Palmer
Leading Members: Rosalind Allen, Andrew Boxall, Martin Brown, Stephanie Brown, David Campion,
Rebecca Cash (16), Simon Dawes, Helen Grainger, Robert Hazell, Ben Jones, Hannah Jones, Matthew
Jones, Vicky Kemp, Ruth Main (15), Zoe Main, Amy Marpole, Scott Marpole, Philip Martyn, Kim Nicholls,
Kirsty Nicholls, Lucy Prentice (17), Alison Puttick, Patrick Roche, Iain Russell, Steven Walter.

REGENT TIGERS (Channel Islands)   Formed 1983
Club Sec: Mrs R. Furzer, La Maison de la Palloterie, St Martin, Jersey.   *Chief Coach:* P. du Feu
Members: 505. *Leading Members:* Raulin Amy, Jane Beadle, Matthew Brehant, Stephanie Christie, Martin Colley, Abigail Corbet, Heidi Corbet, Philippe Falle, Catherine Furzer, Heidi Georgelin, Lee Henry, Andrea Hussey, Neil Hussey, Glen Militis, Simon Militis, Julie Millow, Matthew Munns, Joanne O'Boyle, Richard Phillips, Paul Pitcher, Claire Powell, Julian Simpson, Richard Stead, Sarah Jane Stirling, Rebecca Wise.

RICHMOND LADIES (Surrey)

RICHMOND UPON THAMES (Surrey)   Formed 1883
Club Sec: Mrs B. Adams, 1 Beechrow, Church Road, Ham, Richmond.   *Chief Coach:* K. Parry
Members: 60. *Leading Members:* Nicola Adams (13), Natasha Beal (10), Colin Chilcott (10), Paul Chilcott (16), Nicole Docker (14), Robert Francis (11), Daniel Hartley (13), Rachel Hathaway (14), Ian Hepburn (16), Damien Marks (13), Rosalind Marks (16), Vicki Morris (10), Sian Packer (10), Ben Parton (12), Toby Ramsay (10), Ailsa Rothwell (10), Suzanne Rye (13), Donna Thompson (12), Lena Thompson (14), Paul Young (13).

RICHMOND WPC (Surrey)

RICKMANSWORTH MASONIC SCHOOL (Herts)

RICKMANSWORTH SCHOOL (Herts)

RINGMER (Sussex)   Formed 1982
Club Sec: Mrs R. Chandler, "Brambles", Ham Lane, Ringmer, BN8 5SB.
Members: 160.

RINGWOOD (Hants)   Formed 1926
Club Sec: D. Caile, 17 New Road, Ringwood, Hants, BH24 3AU.   *Chief Coach:* K. Caile
Members: 200. *Leading Members:* Russell Berry (14), Ali Caile (14), Simon Cloke (16), Peter Coysh (9), Karl Creasey (13), Peter Croucher (13), Haley Davies (12), Michelle Foresbury (13), Caroline Fraser (13), David Fraser (14), Caroline Gledhill (15), Sarah Gledhill (13), Jonathan Hiett (13), Richard Hiett (10), Michelle Jones (10), Tony Larkin (13), Lorraine Manson (10), Neil Manson (11), Richard Morton (10), Sally Anne Pierson (9), Amanda Redwood (11), Sarah Redwood (12), Joanna Smith (10), Richard Trim (11), Mathew Winchester (12).

RIVERMEAD (Middlesex)

RIVERSIDE (Kent)   Formed 1960
Club Sec: N. Brooks, 189 Malling Road, Snodland, Kent, ME6 5EE.
Members: 35.

R.L.S.S. JERSEY (Channel Islands)

R.L.S.S. KENT (Kent)   Formed 1960
Club Sec: P. O'Connell, 42 Amherst Road, Rochester, Kent, ME1 2AR.

ROEDEAN SCHOOL (Sussex)

ROCHFORD & DISTRICT (Essex)   Formed 1979
Club Sec: R. Frith, 43 Woodside Chase, Hawkwell, Essex, SS5 4NB.   *Chief Coach:* S. Ham
Members: 414. *Leading Members:* Susan Adams (14), Natalie Clark (16), Richard Clarke-Irons (18), Matthew Dixon (15), Hazel Drew (15), Guy Gray (19), Charlie Green (16), Shelley Hatton (18), Sarah Heaton (14), Faye Jennings (14), Simon Livesey (14), Victoria Longhurst (13), Emma Mackley (13), Sarah Mackley (15), Craig Maddocks (13), Tony Maddocks (16), Sarah O'Flanagan (14), Ian Parrott (12), Steven Purdy (16), Trevor Purdy (14), Thomas Reddick (14), Scott Reed (15), Suzie Ridler (16), Graham Thomas (16), Justine Worman (14).

ROMFORD TOWN (Essex)   Formed 1900
Club Sec: K. Debney, 15 Broadway, Gidea Park, Romford, Essex, RM2 5NS.   *Chief Coach:* G. Straight
Members: 250. *Leading Members:* Chris Barry (11), Stephen Barry (13), Nicolas Beth (14), Darren Bigmore (19), Lara Clarke (14), Nicky Clifford (14), Alison Cornell (14), Debbie Cornell (12), Mark Edmonds (19), Julie Farabee (15), Gavin Francis (11), Anna Gadsdon (14), Charles Gadsdon (12), Mark Hatfull (11), Russell Hulett (12), Vicky Lescombe (22), Michelle Lomax (11), Catherine Neville (11), Lauren Pittard (13), Charmain Smith (13), Shane Smith (15), Paul Springfield (12), Paul Thoroughgood (14), Adrian Vickers (20), Guy Wakefield (14).

ROMSEY (Hants)   Formed 1948
Club Sec: D. Coombs, 4 The Bungalow, Winchester Road, Crampmoor.   *Chief Coach:* S. Harrison
Members: 50. *Leading Members:* Annie Bainbridge (11), Robert Baker (8), Michael Batchelor (22), Susan Batchelor (15), Judy Brooks (13), Nicola Capell (11), Helen Carter (11), Bret Coombs (15), Simon Coughlin (11), Charmain Ewald (10), Vanessa Gibbs (18), Anthony Girdlestone (16), Murray Hodges (13), Sarah Lockyer (16), Andrew Norgate (11), Jonathon Pawlik (10), Roy Potter (20), Paul Rose (12), Timothy Sadler (11), Tamsin Saxton (12), Becky Scovell (13), Helen Smith (16), Julia Smith (15), Stephen Watkins (13), Tony Weston (52).

ROXETH DISTRICT SCOUTS (Kent)

ROYAL NAVY, PORTSMOUTH (Hants) *Formed* 1974
Club Sec: A.P. Bell, 21 Barlow Close, Hill Head, Fareham, Hants, PO14 3SL. *Chief Coach:* A.P. Bell
Members: 22. *Leading Members:* A. Atkinson (29), T. Barker (27), A. Bell (33), B. Blauden (44), J. Daniel (19), G. Duncan (19), P. Hasker (32), R. Heatly (26), P. Hingson (21), A. Knowles (23), C. Logan (24), R. Loram (22), R. Marshall (41), S. Mead (21), S. Murphy (20), S. Price (14), S. Price (47), C. Rowsell (20), P. Stephens (41), G. Tobin (23), P. Walter (36), D. Wood (18).

ROYAL NAVY SCHOOL (Surrey)

ROYAL TUNBRIDGE WELLS MONSON (Kent) *Formed* 1901
Club Sec: J.M. Burton, 49 Wilman Road, Tunbridge Wells, Kent, TN4 9AL. *Chief Coach:* M.D. Geer
Leading Members: Edward Benn (13), Richard Benn (16), Andrew Berwick (15), Suki Brownsdon (23), Joanne Butler (19), Louisa Cousins (12), Mark Edwards (12), Emma Fry (16), Wilton Fry (17), Julian Gray (18), Simon Handley (15), Claire Harvey (19), Rebecca Harvey (11), Bjorn Hoffman (14), Kieron Jones (12), Kirsty Kirkness (15), Samantha Kirkness (13), Elizabeth Lesemore (11), Jackie Luckings (29), Garry Picton (21), Simon Reeve (15), Nicola Sargent (11), Alex Silvestone (11), Simon Whibberley (15), Ian Wynn (15).

Royal Tunbridge Wells Monson — The youngest team to swim the Channel.

ROYSTON (Herts)

RUISLIP JUNIOR SWIMMING SCHOOL (Middlesex)

RUISLIP & NORTHWOOD (Middlesex) *Formed* 1964
Club Sec: Mrs E.M. Brum, 124 Bury Street, Ruislip, Middlesex, HA4 7TH. *Chief Coach:* D. Dix
Members: 300. *Leading Members:* Joanna Austin (15), Mariam Bamford (14), Andrew Beech (16), Gregory Buck (13), Philip Buck (12), Helen Bucknill (13), Jason Clarke (16), Russell Clarke (13), Gemma Gardner (13), Abigail Green (15), Stephen Greenwood (12), Carolyn Hawkins (16), Steven Hawkins (14), Amanda Heath (31), Reggie Housego (12), Charles Nash (31), Karen O'Dea (19), Tricia O'Donoghue (13), Graeme Perry (18), Kate Ryan (14), Philip Searle (15), Victoria Short (16), Colleen Wilson (17), Danny Wilson (15), Gary Woffington (15).

RUNNYMEDE (Essex)

RUSHMOOR ROYALS (Hants) *Formed* 1974
Club Sec: Mrs P. Harding, 40 Gilbert Road, Camberley, Surrey. *Chief Coach:* G. Gorvin
Members: 250. *Leading Members:* Tony Attfield (13), Graham Chamberlain (16), Sarah Coatsworth (16),

Stephen Cockarill (17), Russel Crampin (15), Gary Dressell (18), Chris Fawn (15), Claire Fawn (15), Sue Fawn (18), Duncan Gorvin (15), Nicola Gorvin (13), Donna Harding (16), Line Mieling (16), Ken Mitsumizo (16), Shizuka Mitsumizo (15), Barbara Nunn (14), Mia Pozzo (14), Alison Sanderson (18), Stewart Tyson (16), Lilian van Teffelen (16).

RUSHMOOR ROYALS SYNCHRO (Hants) Formed 1966
Club Sec: Mrs E.V. Russell, Crowsley, Hutton Road, Ash Vale, Aldershot, Hants, GU12 5HA.
Chief Coaches: Mrs D. Burdett, M.C.P. Firmin
Members: 142. *Leading Members:* Claire Allen (13), Emma Bennett (15), Karen Broadbent (16), Adele Carlsen (14), Emma Carlsen (17), Penelope Cooper (16), Sophie Curwen (14), Paula Davies (14), Kate Hodgson (15), Caroline Jones (16), Joanne Lambert (16), Georgina Prewer (16), Rachel Ramsay (15), Rebecca Scales (15), Megan Shacklock (13), Kerry Shacklock (18), Michelle Swansborough (13), Helen Swanscott (13), Laila Vakil (15), Zarina Vakil (21), Gemma Warner (13), Katie Webber (14), Lynette Webster (17), Josephine Wells (15), Grace Wigley (17).

Rushmoor Royals Synchro S.C.

ST ALBANS DC (Herts) Formed 1970
Club Sec: Mrs A. Allam, 10 St Stephens Close, St Albans, Herts.   *Chief Coach:* T. Salvidge
Members: 22. *Leading Members:* Mark Allam (10), Sally Chapman (14), Bronwen Curtis (10), Nicholas Denny (16), Robert Hardy (16), Elizabeth Hook (14), Clive Jackson (15), Lois Kane (10), Adrian Manistre (16), Carl Miles (14), Neil Miles (12), Sarah Osborne (14), Rebecca Pearce (16), Yvonne Pearce (14), Jonathan Reed (14), Susan Talbot (14), Simon Wadsworth (12), Cheryl Woodhouse.

ST DUNSTANS COLLEGE (Kent) Formed 1888
Club Sec: S. Holt, St Dunstans College, Stanstead Road, Catford, London.   *Chief Coach:* S. Holt
Leading Members: Vincent Acors (15), Nicholas Alford (16), Matthew Allen (15), Martin Beedham (16), Robin Beedham (17), Robert Billings (17), Stephen Billings (18), Matthew Boyle (15), Peter Chick (16), Hugo Davis (15), Simon Elliott (16), Paul Ginger (18), Christopher Glynne (18), Alasdair Green (16), Romolo Hella (17), Christopher Jones (17), Stephen Langsdown (18), Matthew Locke (16), Ian Morgan (15), Sheldon Perrin (15), Christopher Sells (17), Simon Tilling (16), Christopher White (18), Christopher Winter (17), Mark Winter (15).

ST GEORGES (Middlesex)

ST JAMES (Surrey) Formed 1878
Club Sec: P.M. Topley, 5 Ryedale, Dulwich, London, SE22.   *Chief Coaches:* P.M. Topley, J. Williams
Members: 100. *Leading Members:* Stephen Allen (29), Brian Anstead (20), Gurkan Arabaji (28), Gary Beckley (27), Dave Blackmore (38), Stephen Bromwich (16), Simon Canham (13), Alan Clark (33), Robert

Cotton (23), Barry Coupar (24), Robert Coupar (27), Terry Coupar (27), Mark Courtney (30), Douglas Golder (29), Paul Goudie (30), Kevin Harman (27), Keith Langan (31), Trevor Langan (25), Anthony Lavery (31), Richard Norman (23), Terry Robinson (26), Robert Stamp (23), Abigail Tobley (25), Portia Wiggins (13), John Williams (36).

ST JOHNS (Sussex)

ST LAWRENCES COLLEGE (Kent

ST MARKS SCHOOL (Berks & Bucks)

ST MARYS COLLEGE (Middlesex)

ST PANCRAS LADIES (Middlesex)

ST PAULS GIRLS SCHOOL (Middlesex)

ST. PAULS SCHOOL (Surrey)

SAFFRON WALDON (Essex) *Formed* 1911
Club Sec: Mrs R.J. Weston, 42 Old Mill Road, Saffron Walden, Essex, CB11 3ER.
Members: 178. *Leading Members:* Michael Bell (16), David Buckingham (16), Karen Buckingham (13), Robert Cootes (10), Jill Crawford (14), Lisa Curtis (16), Clive Ellen (14), Fiona Ellen (11), Karen Everitt (15), Louise Everitt (13), Clare Fisher (9), Stuart Harvey (12), Christopher Hayes (12), Ben Head (10), Samantha Head (12), Sarah Jacobs (16), Marko Jevtic (15), Richard Loveday (14), Graham Mummery (10), Jason Perry (13), Richard Sawkins (14), Joanna Start (10), Melanie Suckling (12), Ellie Weir (9), Emma Weston (11).

Saffron Waldon S.C.

SANS EGAL (Essex) *Formed* 1953
Club Sec: J. Brockett, 379 Manford Way, Chigwell, Essex. *Chief Coach:* N. Clark
Members: 800. *Leading Members:* A. Baroni (22), A. Burton (24), J. Burton (21), K. Chesney (12), S. Chesney (12), S. Count (11), D. Cracknell (14), L. Dilley (14), P. Fishbaum (16), D. Forman (10), A. Hastings (10), K. Herbert (12), J. Hooker (11), P. McDonald (14), B. Rees (12), L. Rogers (10), A Russ (15), E. Ryan (15), D. Watkins (12), J. Watkins (10), L. Watkins (14), D. Willis (12), K. Willis (9), G. Worth (12), R. Worth (9).

SAXON CROWN, LEWISHAM (Kent) *Formed* 1975
Club Sec: Mrs K. Grimshaw, 89 Upwood Road, Lee, London, SE12 8AL. *Chief Coach:* F. Grimshaw
Members: 486. *Leading Members:* Mandy Andrews (18), Dean Baker (13), Kerry Baker (10), Michael Belton (14), David Bridson (12), Claire Callan (13), Andrew Clarke (13), Tony Crane (11), Peter Dickson

(15), Sharon Dillon (18), Gabor Doby (11), Rich Grimshaw (23), Donna Harding (11), Lisa Harding (14), Helen Johnson (13), Rebecca Killick (12), Iain O'Hara (13), Nicola O'Hara (11), Mitchell Lee (10), Owen Levett (14), Claud Manga (23), Tina Noble (14), Debbie Walker (14), Tammy Walker (13), Anita West (10).

SCHWEPPES, SIDCUP (Kent)   *Formed* 1963
Club Sec: E. Fendt, 148 Amherst, Drive, St Mary Cray, Orpington, Kent, BR5 2HL.
Members: 42. *Leading Members:* Gaynor Bright (30), Ed Alexander Fendt (32), Edward Andrew Fendt (11), Sarah Louise Fendt (13), Ted Fendt (50), V. Alison Fendt (21), Stephanie Fern-King, Jaqueline Gray (21), William Gray (32), Margaret Harris (30), Alison King (21+), David King (7), Beryl Loxley (21+), Jane Loxley (21+), Harvey Ponder (48).

Schweppes, Sidcup

SCOTT LIDGETT (Surrey)

SEA BYRD (Middlesex)

SEACLOSE (Hants)   *Formed* 1980
Club Sec: C.C. Gaches, "Brooklyn", The Shute, Newchurch, Isle of Wight.   *Chief Coach:* J. Hollidge
Members: 445. *Leading Members:* Greg Adams (17), Sam Bernard (12), Gemma Blackman (11), Claire Boll (14), Adam Evans (18), Yvette Evans (16), Richard Gaches (11), Simon Gaskell (14), Gemma James (12), Michelle Jeffery (15), Duncan Lockhart (14), Rebecca Logan (16), Paul Moreton (16), Mark Painter (11), Alec Patterson (12), Nicole Patterson (18), David Pay (16), Samantha Scott (13), Andrew Smith (14), Jeremy Smith (15), Russell Stant (13), Charlotte Stone (13), Philippa Ventress (13), Chris Whitbread (18), Steven Williams (13).

SEAGULLS (Hants)

SELLINDGE (Kent)   *Formed* 1975
Club Sec: Mrs P. Huckstepp, "Hawthorn", Barrow Hill, Sellindge, Ashford, Kent.
Members: 80.

SERPENTINE (Middlesex)

SEVENOAKS (Kent)   *Formed* 1915
Club Sec: Mrs P.D. Carrie, 62 Pilgrims Way East, Otford, Sevenoaks, Kent.   *Chief Coach:* P. Edwards
Members: 287. *Leading Members:* Stuart Andrews (14), David Armitage (11), Philip Armitage (17), Kimi Beloso (15), Mark Boyden (20), Fiona Brown (17), Lydia Cevik (12), Claire Dawes (11), Alison Dewyner (17), Michael Dominguez (13), Claire Edwards (14), Neil Gordon (19), Nigel Gunn (21), Heather Guy (16), Christopher Hinsley (13), Genevieve Mead (13), Josephine Metcalf (13), Julian Metcalf (14), Caroline Mills (12), Edward Mills (15), Rachel Owens (13), Kate Parkinson (15), Emma Sharpe (12), David Simpson (14), Nick Varley (19).

SEYMOUR SYNCHRO SWIMMING SCHOOL (Middlesex) *Formed* 1961
Club Sec: Mrs D. Zajac, 18 Garden City, Edgware, Middlesex. *Chief Coach:* Mrs D. Zajac
Members: 40. *Leading Members:* Charlotte Hedge (17), Lisa Marshall (16), Una Mulligan (19), Georgina Plumb (17).

SHANKLIN TOWN REGATTA (Hants)

SHEERNESS SWIMMING & LIFE GUARD (Kent)

SHIVERERS (Sussex) *Formed* 1920
Club Sec: T.A. Spray, Flat 1, 21 Montefiore Road, Hove, East Sussex, BN3 1RD. *Chief Coach:* I. Newell
Members: 730. *Leading Members:* Stephen Akers (18), Dennis Allen (15), Chris Bailey (16), Andy Bell (13), Samantha Bourton (18), Graham Buss (17), Danny Carter (13), Helen Clifford (15), Gary Cohen (11), James Collins (12), Karen Dieffenthaller (22), Helen Drewitt (14), Martin Geale (16), Chris Goldsmith (12), Emma Goldsmith (12), Debbie Harman (16), Adam Harper (18), Tracey Hemblade (14), James Huxtable (16), Paul McDavitt (17), Nicola Matthews (15), Marianne Proe (17), David Swayne (15), Lucie Turner (18), Linette Wheeler (13).

SILVER STAR LADIES (Essex) *Formed* 1946
Club Sec: Mrs E.M. Nicholls, 155 Mitcham Road, East Ham, E6 3NG.
Members: 60.

SITTINGBOURNE & MILTON (Kent) *Formed* 1896
Club Sec: Mrs S.M. Langford, Cryalls Farm Cottage, Cryalls Lane, Sittingbourne. *Chief Coach:* R. Lewis
Members: 180. *Leading Members:* Danny Batchelor (11), Mark Bunting (12), Paul Carey (14), Gavin Cripps (10), Justin Cripps (9), Michelle Cross (10), Sarah Davies (11), Neil Elmer (12), John Emmerson (10), Ian Jerram (13), Cecily Jilks (14), Claire Kelly (10), Gareth Langford, Paul Lederer, Laurence Parker (9), Jane Patching (12), Sally Patching, Anna Rhodes (12), Matthew Thompson (10), Christine Whyman (8), Sarah Whyman (10), Claire Wicks (10), Lynn Wicks (9), Timothy Williams (13), Nathan Wiseman (13).

SIX HILLS (Herts) *Formed* 1985
Club Sec: Mrs M.F. Cooke, 3 Swangley's Lane, Knebworth, Herts, SG3 6AA.
Members: 621. *Leading Members:* Karen Burlison (13), Natalie Cocks (11), Samantha Cocks (14), Paul Comley (28), Peter Cooke (22), Carl de Courcy (10), Michelle de Courcy (11), Matthew Dunn (14), Stuart Ellis (22), Alison Fenner (18), Michelle Fouracres (15), Mark Franklin, Craig Hunter (28), James Jeffery (9), Ian Johnstone (31), Martin Lindsey (12), Paul Lindsey (14), Neil McLellan (11), Hannah Rees (11), Adrian Smale (13), Andrea Smale (12), Helen Soloman (15), Jean Southren (19), Jenny Williams (12), Richard Williams (10).

SLOUGH DOLPHINS (Berks & Bucks) *Formed* 1937
Club Sec: P.T. Hughes, 21 Crispin Way, Farnham Common, Bucks, SL2 3UD. *Chief Coach:* J. Tibballs
Members: 120. *Leading Members:* J. Admans, S. Anderson, K. Coates, A. Cork, S. Foster, D. Hawthorne, M. Hemmings, K. Hope, H. Hughes, S. Humphreys, D. Johnson, V. Jones, J. Moffatt, C. Mogridge, D. Mogridge, N. Morris, N. Morton, H. Nalletamby, R. Pratt, K. Rogers, P. Smith, H. Thompson, A. Webb, G. Webb, B. Wojas.

SMITH SWIM SQUAD (Sussex)

SOLENT (Hants) *Formed* 1962
Club Sec: Mrs M. Collett, 108 Lackford Avenue, Totton, Southampton, Hants, S04 4DH.
Members: 30. *Leading Members:* Bob Allen (40+), Denis Arnold (40+), John Ayling (60+), Dave Clothier (40), Mary Collett (41), Michael Collett (15), Peter Collett (50), Oihna Davies (40+), Catherine Dowman (18), Gerald Forsberg (70+), Simon Lee (20+), Barry Love (50+), Denis Medlycott (40+), Tony Moorey (40+), Roy Neene (50+), Jean Ramshaw (40+), Maurice Ralph (40+), Brian Rann (50+), James Rann (20+), Keith Richards (50+), Alison Streeter (20+), Willy van Rysel (70+), Anne White (40+).

SOUTHAMPTON DC (Hants) *Formed* 1979
Club Sec: Mrs S.H. Alderman, 38 Chadwell Avenue, Sholing, Southampton. *Chief Coach:* M. Alderman
Members: 20. *Leading Members:* Sarah French (14), Sheila Morrison (20), Jenny Nightingale (16), Natasha Willard (15).

SOUTHAMPTON PENGUINS (Hants) *Formed* 1963
Club Sec: Mrs E. Basford, 7 Rampart Road, Bitterue Manor, Southampton.
Members: 130.

SOUTHAMPTON UNIVERSITY WPC (Hants)

SOUTHEND ON SEA (Essex) *Formed* 1894
Club Sec: Mrs J. Swift, 191A High Street, Great Wakering, Essex. *Chief Coaches:* E. Clarke, G. Stopford
Members: 500. *Leading Members:* Nicola Blake (13), Denise Bridge (15), Keith Bridge (17), Gary Clarke (18), Karen Clarke (16), Emma Day (12), Christian Hall (12), Mathew Halsey (16), Tristan Hardley (13), Andrew Jamison (13), Gareth Jenkins (14), Sian Jenkins (17), Chris Jones (14), Lindsay Jones (16), Kane Lucas (12), Amanda Morrant (18), John Newton (15), Joanna Sansome (13), Sarah Schofield (15), Mark Sedgwick (11), Keith Swift (15), Michelle Swift (12), Angela Walpole (11), David Walpole (13), Martyn Wiley (18).

SOUTHEND SYNCHRONETTES (Essex)

SOUTHGATE (Middlesex) *Formed* 1940
Club Sec: A. Wilkie, 64 Meadway, London, N14 6NH. *Chief Coach:* S. Woolhead
Members: 350.

SOUTH LÔNDON (Surrey) *Formed* 1908
Club Sec: Mrs V. Studholme. *Chief Coach:* J. Snelling
Members: 160. *Leading Members:* Sarah Burman (15), Esme Clarke (10), Jena Collins (16), Toby Collins (18), Richard Gledhill (42), Katherine Heffernan (15), Ben Jones (15), Paul McWheeny (18), Clare Martin (12), Marian Martin (11), Michael Martin (16), Sinaed Martin (15), John Sextone (50), Bob Spicer (60+), Daniel Studholme (12), Jamie Studholme (10), John Whyton (23), Megan Willis (25+), Cyril Wood (60+), Dean Yeoman (10), Keith Yeoman (12), Sebastian Yeoman (10).

SOUTHWARK (Sussex)
Club Sec: Mrs M. Cooper, 11 Borrett Close, Pasley Estate, Walworth, London. *Chief Coach:* G. Light
Members: 100. *Leading Members:* Dean Annun (13), Shane Annun (11), Lee Bedford (11), Alan Bratton (18), Sarah Bratton (14), Paul Colledge (8), Neil Cooper (10), Paul Cooper (15), Barry Corrigan (14), Danny Corrigan (13), Laurie Griffith-Jones (15), David Harrison (12), William Holden (13), Arnet Knight (12), Tessa Knight (14), Bernard O'Brien (12), Sarah Wash (13), Matthew Wheeler (12).

SOUTH WIGHT (Hants) *Formed* 1981
Club Sec: Mrs S. Godwin, "Hideaway", Talbot Road, Sandown, Isle of Wight. *Chief Coach:* A. Ayres
Members: 293. *Leading Members:* Sarah Ayres (15), Kevin Batchelor (17), Duncan Brown (14), Fiona Brown (10), Sharon Brown (15), Allison Dalrymple (13), Gavin Dalrymple (14), April Dixley (10), Tom Edmunds (16), Charlene Frankling (11), Susan Graves (11), Chris Hagger (14), Julia Hagger (16), Steven Hall (11), Michelle Lakin (13), Joanne Lane (13), Carol Lidington (14), Tracie Lidington (17), Martin Lovett (31), Kate Newnham (10), Martin Newnham (12), Susan Newton (12), Stephen Parsonage (15), Natasha Porter (10), Ray Stevens (14).

SPENCER SWIM TEAM (Surrey) *Formed* 1977
Club Sec: J.S. Gordon, 24 Emerson Court, Wimbledon Hill Road, London. *Chief Coach:* J.S. Gordon
Members: 80. *Leading Members:* Godfrey Admans (35), Robert Apel (45), Pauline Cooke (42), Peter Dorrell (45), Carol Everitt (34), John Gordon (44), Clair Griffiths (30), Jack Hale (67), Otto Hamelink (28), Amanda Heath (32), Carole Hunt (27), Sarah Hunt (27), John Lake (49), Dave Mace (56), Lynn Marshall (28), Barney Miller (60), Eric Mountain (60), Justin Palfrey (18), Tony Pearce (43), Steve Shew (30), Peter Stephens (42), Allison Streeter (25), Jeff Tanner (53), Norman Trusty (56), Willy van Rysel (72).

Spencer Swim Team — 1984 group, including Linda Ludgrove (left).

SPLASH CLUB (Surrey)

SPRINGFORD (Middlesex) *Formed* 1978
Club Sec: Mrs C. Folkard, 93 Stratton Road, Sunbury on Thames. *Chief Coach:* Mrs C. Bennett
Members: 90.

STAINES (Middlesex) *Formed* 1967
Club Sec: T. Wright, 17 Lincoln Way, Sunbury on Thames, Middlesex. *Chief Coach:* G. Gravett
Members: 400. *Leading Members:* Michael Eade (14), Joanne Exall (9), Jenny Gannon (10), Lynne Goodhead (15), Neil Goodhead (16), David Hills (30), Neil Hinton (12), Laura Hodgson (10), Michael Howe (15), Clare McCormick (15), Alistair McGee (11), Antony Mammous (15), Nicholas Mammous (16), Jason Nixon (13), Joanna Norman (20), Alison Penn (13), Steven Penn (16), Julian Robinson (18), Gareth Robinson (15), Vanessa Stamp (16), Richard Steel (9), John Verrinder (19), Stephen Wale (19), Joseph Wells (15), Terry Wright (28).

STAR DC (Surrey)

STARFISH (Essex)

STEVENAGE (Herts) *Formed* 1962
Club Sec: P. Maris, 3 Dewpond Close, Stevenage, Herts. *Chief Coach:* D. Parker
Members: 120. *Leading Members:* Sarah Ades (14), Nick Bradley (18), Jacky Cameron (13), Mark Collins (12), Hayley Fennick (13), Nicola Fennick (13), Davina Garrod (15), Catherine George (13), Vanessa Hall (15), Timothy Highsted (14), David Hills (13), Sarah Hills (15), Mark Hoffman (11), Andrew Hoiles (16), Jeffrey Hunter (13), Jamie Hunting (12), Gary King (13), Emma Lindridge (14), Paul Morgan (13), Julie Oakley (17), Paul Rayner (15), Peter Robinson (13), Paul Sheard (11), Vicky Tremaine (12), Nicola Voyce (11).

STOCK EXCHANGE (Middlesex) *Formed* 1924
Club Sec: A.H. Kilgour, BNP Securities, 8-13 King William Street, London, EC4N 7EX.
Members: 20.

STOKE NEWINGTON (Middlesex)

STORT VALLEY (Herts)
Club Sec: N.A.H. Coulson, 6 The Chase, Bishops Stortford, Herts, CM23 3HT.

STREATHAM (Surrey)

SURVIVE & SAVE CLUB (Middlesex)

SUSSEX UNIVERSITY (Sussex) *Formed* 1984
Club Sec: S.P. Henderson, c/o Sports Fed., University of Sussex, Lewes Road, Falmer, Brighton.
Members: 50. *Leading Members:* Mark Barnes (19), Tamsin Bowra (20), Nir Danai (24), Deanne Debeer (21), Karen Dieffenthaller (21), David Groiser (22), Simon Henderson (25), Ulrika Hotopp (23), Paul Mason (22), Donna Murray (21), Rob Pearce (21), Mike Rau (19), Anna Rimini (22), Paul Thomas (19), Phil Vigor (22).

SUTTON & CHEAM (Surrey)
Club Sec: R. Pearson, 84 Grange Road, Cheam, Surrey, SM2 6SW. *Chief Coach:* Mrs Thurley
Members: 200. *Leading Members:* Garry Alsted (19), Paul Anjos (28), Adrian Brown (17), David Craven (16), Tony Croft (23), Dave Edwards (30), Matt Gregory (19), Mark Hamilton (11), Paul Humphries (19), David Kimber (16), Stephen McGregor (15), Greg Moore (19), Stephen Moorhouse (23), Barry Morgan (16), Peter Padella (33), James Pearson (25), Stuart Pearson (21), Stefan Radwanski (33), Stuart Russell (16), Mark Shepherd (26), Ian Spooner (23), Graham Stark (23), Charles Thurley (21), Ian Uren (22), Neil Uren (20).

SWAN (Essex)

TATE & LYLE (Essex)

TEDDINGTON (Middlesex) *Formed* 1978
Club Sec: Mrs P. Hoare, 20 Cranmer Road, Hampton Hill, Middlesex. *Chief Coach:* G. Pines
Members: 260. *Leading Members:* Simon Acton-Bond (14), Philip Attwood, Samantha Beasley-Suffolk (14), Claire Bebbington (11), Josephine Booth (14), Sam Brown (14), Keith Darby (12), Adam Grice (11), Stephen Hoare (12), William Hughes (12), Rutsuko Ito (13), Hiroyuki Kado (14), Joel Kelly (16), Julia Kershaw (16), Emma Komlosy (12), Alexander Lucas (13), Jody Moore (11), Alistair Paul (19), Matthew Rees (12), Greg Meagher, Russell Ryan, Gary Sloan (19), Susan Walker (14), Deborah Watson (12), Lucy Whittaker (15).

THAMES VALLEY TRIATHLETES (Berks & Bucks)

THANET VIKINGS (Kent) *Formed* 1977
Club Sec: S. Lee, 5 Devonshire Gardens, Margate, Kent. *Chief Coach:* R. Hitchcock
Members: 115. *Leading Members:* Caroline Barsley (14), Thomas Boeckx (13), Lisa Butler (10), Sheryl Butler (11), Natalie Forrest (13), Charlotte Goldsmith (10), Adam Highsted (14), Rebecca Highsted (13), Emma Jarrett (11), Matthew Jury (15), Robert Lee (12), Nichola Linington (15), Chris McAvoy (15), Alex

Mott (10), Deborah Murray (16), Richard Murray (14), Julian Oldfield (17), Emma Peeling (10), James Peeling (11),, Sandra Sacre (15), Anna Shearer (9), Sarah Skuse (12), Shelly Smart (16), Emma Taylor (10), Ben Vickery (14).

THANET WPC (Kent)
Formed 1935
Club Sec: C. Boreham, 107 Church Path, Deal, Kent, CT14 9UD. *Chief Coach:* T. Fitzgerald
Members: 21. *Leading Members:* G. Banning (30), S. Barnacle (17), A. Barrs (15), C. Boreham (39), R.A. Charlesworth (25), G. Cooper (33), T. Fitzgerald (38), R. Gibson (17), G. Hadlow (24), S. Hards (17), A. Mac (26), P. Martin (16), K. Peake (45), M. Phillpot (18), W. Reeves (20), P. Rice (24), N. Rickett (25), M. Rye (17), A. Small (15), M. West (15), B. Wilson (26).

36 ENGINEERS (Kent)

THOMAS GUY (Surrey)

THREE RIVERS (Herts)
Formed 1973
Club Sec: Mrs A. Worth, 149 Highfield Way, Rickmansworth, Herts, WD3 2PL.
Members: 200.

THURROCK (Essex)
Formed 1963
Club Sec: C. Goodrum, 2 Jefferies Way, Corringham, Essex. *Chief Coach:* I. Tripp
Members: 110. *Leading Members:* Andrew Bell (16), Andrea Bird (15), Kristian Brook (15), Emma Brown (14), Paul Coster (15), Rachel Dennett (14), Kevin Depree (16), Anthony Diprose (16), Lisa Evans (15), Caroline Hall (14), Andrew Harris (15), Tim Hart (17), Adrian Hughes (11), Claire Jones (13), Kara Langston (13), Paul Leahy (13), Stephen Miles (13), Ryan Milington-Jones (13), Esther Morris (13), Steven Murphy (20), Nicola Ryder (13), Sharon Say (14), Dominic Tidey (13), Colin Waterman (15), Andrew Westwood (15).

TIGERSHARKS (Surrey)

TONBRIDGE (Kent)
Formed 1890
Club Sec: R.W. Bannister, 11 Foalhurst Close, Tonbridge, TN10 4HA. *Chief Coach:* R. Ashdown
Members: 240. *Leading Members:* Mary Ashdown (34), Richard Ashdown (34), Sarah Carter (14), Neil Declemy (15), Nick Foard (16), Joanna Hogg (12), Beverley Homewood (12), Ian Jackson (14), Neil King (19), Toni Manuel (16), Sarah Marks (16), Jenny Marshall (14), Ashley Mills (16), Douglas Mills (12), Stephanie Mills (18), Caroline Mogben (14), Ashley Moon (14), Christina Read (14), Joel Rennie (15), Kristean Rennie (12), John Ridley (21), Wendy Singleton-Green (18), Helen Wenbourne (16), Matt White (13), Jenny Wright (14).

Tonbridge S.C.

TOWER HAMLETS (Middlesex) *Formed* 1964
Club Sec: J. Watts, 20 Windsor House, Roman Road, London. *Chief Coaches:* B. Fitzpatrick, B. Humphreys
Members: 80. *Leading Members:* Lucy Adcock (12), Kelly Bouvier (19), Gemma Carpel (11), Melissa Carpel (14), James Collett (11), Georgina Cross (13), Michael Fanning (17), Joe Farrugia (13), Daniel Fellows (11), David Fellows (14), Roy Ferebee (13), Danny Frayne (10), Carey Grant (10), Karen Hardy (13), Nicola Henry (12), Nancy Jeffrey (11), Mike O'Donaghue (14), Leann Powell (10), Brett Treend (11), Darren Treend (13), Jade Vickers (10), Nicole Warren (12), Stephen Warren (15), Dawn Watts (19).

TRING (Herts)

TRINITY SCHOOL (Surrey)

TURTLES (Kent)

UNIVERSITY OF ESSEX (Essex)

UNIVERSITY OF LONDON (Middlesex)
Club Sec: D. Grant, 47 Twisden Road, Kentish Town, London, NW5 1DL. *Chief Coach:* J. Hartley
Members: 80. *Leading Members:* Ruth Anson (20), Claire Baggett (22), Robert Bennett (20), Xenia Boergen (22), Claire Butler (21), Betty Coombs (23), Claire Craven (20), Jackie Elliott (22), Steve Forrest (25), Louise Furlonger (19), Mark Gillett (20), David Grant (22), Malory Greene (24), Julian Halcox (23), Mary Jackets (22), Adam Korn (22), Ian Meakin (22), Erica Parry (23), James Pearson (25), Peter Penniffer (20), Steven Russell (22), Karen Sargent (20), Neale Spence (20), Andrew Thomas (19), David Townsend (20).

UPS CLUB (Surrey)

UXBRIDGE (Middlesex) *Formed* 1940
Club Sec: Mrs C.E. Ratcliffe, 33 Ladygate Lane, Ruislip, Middlesex, HA4 7QT.
Members: 120.

VERULAM (Herts) *Formed* 1979
Club Sec: Mrs M. Keys, 18 Wych Elms, St Albans, Herts. *Chief Coaches:* A. Rawson, Mrs A. Robinson
Members: 240. *Leading Members:* Ryan Beszant (10), Emma Bradstock (13), Kevin Brammer (10), Nicola Brammer (14), Marcelle Buck (14), Luciano Casazza (13), Jill Chapman (14), Paul Chapman (16), Andrew Cummins (14), Lisa Jones (10), Simon Keys (14), Laura McCullough (12), Mark Neville (13), Ryan Rawson (16), Louise Robb (10), Neill Robb (13), Elizabeth Robey (12), Brett Robinson (16), Michaela Robinson (14),David Stacey (11), Jonathan Stacey (15), Christa Upjohn (13), David Upjohn (10), Adrian Vyse (17), Nicholas Vyse (14).

WALTHAM ABBEY (Essex)

WALTHAM FOREST (Essex)

WALTHAM FOREST DC (Essex) *Formed* 1983
Club Sec: Mrs M. Banks, 72 Heathcote Grove, Chingford, London, E4 6SF. *Chief Coach:* Miss L. Fraser
Members: 100. *Leading Members:* Adel Ahmet, Denice Baker (9), Julie Banks (13), Claire Crutchfield (11), Sarah Crutchfield (9), Abigail Fitch (12), Stephen Hill (11), Michelle Hopkins (11), Abigail Johnston (16), Kevin Livock (13), Daniel Medlock (9), Sarah Medlock (12), David Morgan (10), Gary Newman (17), Lindsey Pearson (10), Stuart Pearson (14), Faye Richards (9), Claire Smith (10), Kate Stonell (9), Alison Tatch (14), George Tatch (12), Helen Tatch (14).

Waltham Forest D.C. — Alison Tatch, Julie Banks, Helen Tatch.

WALTHAM FOREST DOLPHINS (Essex)

WALTHAMSTOW (Essex)

WANDSWORTH (Surrey)

WARE (Herts)

WATFORD (Herts)   Formed 1902
Club Sec: O. Roberts, 5 Stanbury Avenue, Watford, Herts, WD1 3HW.
Members: 170. *Leading Members:* Andrew Allum (15), Stefan Battle (17), Eleanor Brooks (17), Sarah Broughton (13), Allan Bulman (15), Megan Bush (13), Robert Dempsey (13), Ian Gregory, Angela Grimley (12), Kerry Johnson (14), Suzannah McGrath (10), Stuart McIntosh (14), Anoushka Martin (14), Cordelia Martin-Dye, Graham Martin-Dye (11), John Martin-Dye, Sarah Martin-Dye (20), Steven Martin-Dye (18), Anthony Meyler (13), Paul Meyler (11), Russell Munro (11), Jayne Skerm (11), Darren Smith (11), Joanne Tearle (14), Zoe Tearle (10), Mark Whitehead (14).

WELLCOME CLUB (Kent)

WELWYN GARDEN (Herts)   Formed 1960
Club Sec: B. Milton, 62 Hardings, Welwyn Garden City, Herts.   *Chief Coach:* T. Cheng
Members: 250.

WESSEX WYVERN MODERN PENTATHLON (Berks & Bucks)

WEST HAM (Essex)

WEST HILL PARK SCHOOL (Hants)

WESTMINSTER (Middlesex)

WESTRIDGE (Hants)

WEST WIGHT (Hants)   Formed 1969
Club Sec: C. Johnson, "Littlemead", Copselane, Freshwater, Isle of Wight.   *Chief Coach:* A. Collins
Members: 45. *Leading Members:* Danny Attree (14), Helen Attree (12), Victoria Belgrove (11), Keira Blunn, Emma Carter (13), Philip Collinson (14), Tracey Creagh (12), Steven Ellis (9), James Frampton (14), Clare Griffin (25), Tina Hunt (12), Leigh Johnson (14), Lewis Johnson (10), Neil Lewis (9), David McDine (20), Wayne Nicholls (10), Lee Nichols (12), Jamie Reurtherine (10), Gareth Roughly (10), David Russell (17), Martine Sampson (16), Paula Sampson (11), Gary Watson (25), Stuart Whalley (14), Emma Wray (20).

WEST WYCHHAM DIVING & SYNCHRO (Kent)

WEY VALLEY (Surrey)   Formed 1978
Club Sec: Mrs J. Sunderland, "Penshurst", Pursers Lane, Peaslake.   *Chief Coach:* Mrs T. Denardo
Members: 75. *Leading Members:* Daniel Bennett, Jonathan Brane, Emily Cawthorne, Lindsey Clapp, Mark Clapp, Lydia Cuss, Catherine de Nardo (18), Erika Feszt (17), Yolika Feszt (18), Stuart Fowler, Jenny Harkman, Lizzie Harkman, Andrew Hayward, Jessica Medding, Jane Mitchinson, Edward Pepper, Gerald Pepper, Laura Sampson, Emily Sunderland, Matthew Sunderland, Vicky Taylor (16), Ben Welton, Douglas Whitfield, Emma Yarrow.

WHITE OAK (Kent)   Formed 1967
Club Sec: Mrs A. Salliss, "Wildernesse", Stonehouse Road, Halstead, Sevenoaks. *Chief Coach:* M. Bush
Members: 262. *Leading Members:* Russell Barlow (15), Amanda Bearfoot (12), Mark Boyle (22), Stephen Cox (13), Paul Farrer (13), Lynda Ford (13), Ryan Godfrey (15), Katie Howard (13), Matthew Howard (10), James Ireland (11), Alan Kelly (13), Laura Kennedy (10), Harvey Langman (19), Richard Law (15), Adam McFarlane (17), Claire McInnes (12), Steve Salliss (22), Julie Scott (18), Rachael Scott (11), Graham Smith (22), Richard Spice (15), David Straker (23), Daniel Stubbington (9), Dennis Whyment (10), Chris Wood (19).

WIGHT AQUATICS (Hants)

WILSONS (Surrey)

WIMBLEDON & MERTON (Surrey)   Formed 1922
Club Sec: M.J. Bennett, 46 Kenley Road, Merton Park, London, SW19 3JQ. *Chief Coach:* Mrs J. Andrews
Members: 215. *Leading Members:* Robert Antrobus (u15), Duncan Benedett (u16), Ben Christie (u14), Alison Crook (u17), Jason Davies (u16), Kathryn Edwards (u10), Chris Egan, Becky Grant (u13), Isha Hawkins (u11), Sian Lea (u15), Theodor Mills (u12), Becky O'Carroll (u13), Sarah O'Carroll (u16), Mark Perrett (u16), Nicholas Pickover (u16), Jarl Redington (u16), Mark Sams (u13), Thomas Savage (u10), Anna Stoddart (u14), Jessica Stoddart (u16), Barry Taylor (u17), Diane Taylor, Jeremy Tombs (u14), Mark Williams, Sonia Woolsey (u18).

WINCHESTER CITY PENGUINS (Hants)

WINCHESTER SYNCHRO (Hants)   Formed 1976
Club Sec: Miss S.C. Bulbrooke, 6 Brooklyn Close, Otterbourne, Hants.   *Chief Coach:* Mrs D.W. Bulbrooke
Members: 35. *Leading Members:* Karen Bailey (17), Sandra Bohle (17), Alison Bougard (16), Claire

Bougard (18), Vanessa Bulbrooke (18), Amanda Cairns (12), Alana Challis (11), Lisa Dugdale (11), Rachel Head (16), Lisa Herridge (14), Sarah Hockey (20), Emily Hodgkinson (12), Nancy Hodgkinson (14), Gillian Howse (16), Sam Jenner (19), Heidi Jones (9), Quita Jones (14), Joanna Ling (11), Elizabeth Miller (21), Nicole Miller (20), Shona Payne (14), Carolyn Showell (16), Clare Smart (17), Lexi Welsh (15), Emma Wilcock (12).

WINDLESHAM HOUSE SCHOOL (Sussex)

WINDSOR (Berks & Bucks)
Formed 1909
Club Sec: Mrs A. Gates, 7 Stewart Close, Fifield, Maidenhead, Berks, SL6 2PD. *Chief Coach:* D. Holding
Members: 420. *Leading Members:* Angus Baldwin (14), Caroline Bell (12), Simon Brett (17), Tara Capp (13), Stewart Carroll (19), Helen Chambers (15), Dawn Clark (13), Vanessa Clark (14), Ian Cox (12), Julie Holden (16), Julian Hughes (15), David Humber (16), Michael Kirby (11), Choi Man (17), Alex Marshall (12), Luke Muir (11), Neil Piddington (12), David Rippon (18), David Rolph (16), Kerin Rolph (18), Ian Russell (18), Annelies Simmons (15), Darren Snellgrove (15), Philip Starr (12), Paul Trice (11).

WITHAM DOLPHINS (Kent)
Club Sec: Mrs R.N. Port, 28 Harvey Road, Great Totham, Essex, CM9 8QA. *Chief Coach:* Mrs C. Miller
Members: 77.

WOKING (Surrey)
Formed 1935
Club Sec: Mrs V. Twilley, 2 Greenway Close, West Byfleet, Surrey, KT14 6QZ. *Chief Coach:* Mrs C. Kelly
Members: 190. *Leading Members:* James Ankers (12), Michael Byerts (12), Lyndsay Cameron (11), Samantha Deakin (13), Nicholas Dearden (14), Susan Finney (12), Ruth Gahagan (12), Julie Gallacher (16), Jackie Kellie (12), Neil Kellie (10), Paula Kelly (20), John Mould (20), Lara Murphy (17), James Naylor (17), Chris O'Brien (10), Joanna Pearce (13), Simon Pepper (16), Georgina Phelps (10), Susanna Ross (11), Charles Watford (12), Duncan Webb (11), Matthew West (16), Mark Wingate (13), Kate Woods (11), Andrew Wrigley (14).

WOKINGHAM (Berks & Bucks)

WOOD GREEN (Middlesex)

WOODSIDE & THORNTON HEATH (Surrey)
Formed 1980
Club Sec: Mrs J.H. Ure, 2 Coombe Wood Hill, Purley, Surrey, CR2 1JN. *Chief Coach:* M. Moylan
Members: 250. *Leading Members:* Andrew Barker (17), Claire Bashford (15), John Blackburn (18), Natasha Blake (14), Sharon Blake (12), Karen Brandrick (12), Lisa Goddard (16), Kelly Gray (14), Douglas Hathaway (12), Kirsty Hathaway (15), Adam Higgins (12), Robert Higgins (13), Seamus Higgins (15), Lisa Hutchinson (16), Katie Love (15), Paul Lowe (12), Andrew Macrae (17), Jonathan Pirks (13), Sara Pirks (16), Nicola Plumb (12), Matthew Porter (16), Simon Porter (14), Marie Trafford (11), Sarah Trafford (15), John Whyton (23).

WORTHING (Sussex)
Formed 1890
Club Sec: Mrs E. Roberts, 2 Kilmore Close, Findon, West Sussex, BN14 0RU. *Chief Coach:* A.G. Barnett
Members: 687.

WYCOMBE DISTRICT (Berks & Bucks)
Formed 1957
Club Sec: Mrs K. King, 41 Wrights Lane, Prestwood, Bucks, HP16 0LQ. *Chief Coach:* B. Johnston
Members: 320. *Leading Members:* John Aperchis (16), Mark Baker (15), Simon Beveridge (12), Tammy Brandon (12), Marina Brynen (13), Lisa Calladine (16), Mark Cary (16), Caroline Gould (15), Peter Gould (17), Neil Hartstone (13), Rob Hutchinson (36), Daniel Jenner-Bull (13), Tom Kean (23), Kerry King (12), Jason Lancaster (14), Tony Lewis (18), Ben Rees (17), Hannah Ridgway (12), Dominick Shaw (14), Claire Shevels (12), Louise Sweeney (17), Rachel Thomas (17), Andrea Varney (12), David White (19), Kevin Wills (13).

YOUNG BRITONS (Essex)

Western District

Honorary Secretary: I. Martin, 32 Birch Grove, Chippenham, Wilts.

ABBEY (Dorset)

APOLLO (Somerset)

AQUARIANS (Avon)

AVON COUNTY SCOUTS (Avon)

AVON & SOMERSET CONSTABULARY (Avon)   *Formed* 1974
Chairman: G. Cutting, Police Station, Staple Hill, Bristol, BS16 5LX.

AVON SWIFTS (Avon)

BACKWELL (Somerset)   *Formed* 1974
Club Sec: T. Jeal, 7 St Austell Close, Nailsea, Avon, BS19 2US.   *Chief Coach:* G. Moore
Members: 50. *Leading Members:* Ross Addicott (13), Mike Ashman (22), Wayne Clarke (15), Nicola Elliott (13), Ivan Moore (19), Andrew Peckham (17), Laura Peckham (15), Joanne Pickup (14), Steven Pickup (12), Jonathan Ratcliffe (16), Tim Redfearn (22), Lisa Reynolds (17), David Trounce (16).

BARNSTAPLE (Devon)   *Formed* 1932
Club Sec: Mrs J. Squire, 45 Fort Street, Barnstaple, North Devon, EX32 8BJ.   *Chief Coach:* D. Davies
Members: 400. *Leading Members:* Catherine Beer (13), Amanda Coates (13), Claire Coates (17), Matthew Collins (13), Andrew Cotton (10), Jon Davies (19), Matthew Davies (16), Katie Emmons (12), Mark Fewings (11), Lynsey Fisher (15), Donald Gatfield (10), Duncan Gillard (12), Ben Haslett (14), Kimberley Haslett (12), Tim Haslett (17), Bobby Hinton (12), Melissa Hinton (13), Neil McDonald (13), Chris Mee (14), Louise Powe (11), Tracy Purchase (22), Ross Smith (11), Fiona Thomas (11), Claire Weyman (12), Patricia Williams (22).

BATH DOLPHIN (Somerset)   *Formed* 1899
Club Sec: M. Deacon, "The Retreat", Forester Road, Bath.   *Chief Coaches:* S. Charlton, P. Sartain
Members: 400. *Leading Members:* Anthony Bond (17), Nicki Brake (13), Paul Brake (14), Ainsley Charlton (17), Rachel Charlton (13), Stephen Faulkner (15), Gavin Frankcom (14), Jay Furze (14), Edward Gooding (11), Annabel Holmes (13), Bryony Hunt (13), James Justice (14), Shaun Justice (11), Jackie Liddiard (18), Jonathon Liddiard (16), Tooni Mahto (13), Jonathon Marshall (12), Lucy Marshall (11), David Maynard (14), Rachel Morrison (13), Andrew Shore (13), Rachael Toogood (15), Ian Wilkins (20), Vicki Williams (15), Rachel Yates (22).

BATH UNIVERSITY (Somerset)

BEAUFORT (Gloucester)   *Formed* 1984
Club Sec: Mrs V. Fuller, 17 Elderwood Way, Tuffley, Gloucester.   *Chief Coach:* P. Ruiz
Members: 212. *Leading Members:* Scott Booth (14), Teresa Bradley (13), Ian Cheape (19), Jamie Cheape (16), Stuart Cheape (20), Rachel Chequer (17), Phillip Clegg (19), David Elkins (16), Lee Griffin (13), Lisa Griffin (12), Paul Griffin (16), David Guy (13), Steve Guy (10), Helen Knight (11), Julianne Marriott (15), Karl Marriott (12), Lee Merritt (12), Mark Merrett (15), Christopher Moss (11), Andrew Ruiz (19), Becky Ruiz (14), Zoe Ruiz (16), Karen Taylor (18), Louisa Wallis (14).

BENDIX PENGUIN OLYMPIC (Avon)

BERE REGIS (Dorset)

BISHOPSWORTH (Gloucester)

BISHOP WORDSWORTH SCHOOL (Wiltshire)

BLANDFORD FORUM (Dorset)   *Formed* 1953
Club Sec: Mrs D. Alner, 44 Barnes Close, Blandford Forum, Dorset.   *Chief Coaches:* D. Alner, K. Alner
Members: 150. *Leading Members:* Clive Asplen (13), Sarah Brooks (15), Tammy Bryant (14), Mark Fielding (15), Jane Fishlock (18), Michael Harper (11), Thomas Harper (11), Katherine Hopper (14), Nicholas Hopper (13), Ian Ingram (16), Keith Ingram (19), Odette Neilson (13), Claire Norris (11), Charlotte Payne (14), Matthew Pike (12), Emma Pindel (13), Robert Sealey (15), Chris Sheppard (13), David Smith (12), Nicholas Spong (13), Laura Stickly (13), Luke Tetley (14), Sharon Usher (11), Melanie Westwood (13), Claire Wiley (13).

BODMIN & DISTRICT (Cornwall)   *Formed* 1973
Club Sec: D. Comer, Trewiston Lodge, Higher Trewint, St Minver, Cornwall.   *Chief Coach:* P. Goldman
Members: 217. *Leading Members:* Belinda Alecock (12), Sarah Bickers (17), Mark Bicknell (13), Verity Blake (12), Chris Comer (14), Jemima Cripps (14), Rebecca Dickinson (17), Matthew East (10), Heidi Hicks (13), Sharron Hill (14), Patrick Hornsey (17), Lindsey Hughes (14), Victoria Keat (15), Phillip Lane (14), Shari-Louise Lovidge (11), Clare McCombie (14), Joanna McCombie (12), Charlotte Mayor (15), Kathryn Peslod (19), Mirriam Simmons (14), Katy Skea (11), Jeremy Spencer (18), Gale Thomas (13), Andrew Tozer (15), Kerry Webb (15).

Bodmin & District S.C. — First Division finalists, Speedo Western League, 1988

BOVINGTON (Dorset)

BOYS BRIGADE, BRISTOL (Avon)

BRADFORD ON AVON (Wiltshire) *Formed* 1975
Club Sec: Mrs B.M. Smith, 86 Downs View, Bradford on Avon, Wilts, BA15 1PW. *Chief Coach:* J. Sloan
Members: 320. *Leading Members:* Andrew Ballinger (11), Liz Ballinger (12), James Bancroft (21), Sara Catt (14), Caroline Cole (15), Julia Dotchin (13), Mark Dotchin (15), Jessica Fagg (10), Sally Fagg (15), Tim Harris (17), Daryk Hives (13), Rona Lunt (16), Shaun McCann (14), Ian McDougall (13), Nicky McDougall (15), Steve McDougall (16), Matt McMinn (15), Hanna Maslin (13), Laura Owen (17), Amanda Painter (18), Harry Sargant (11), Kate Sargant (15), Joel Scott (13), Kirsty Sloan (18), Paul Woodward (19).

BRIDGWATER (Somerset) *Formed* 1894
Club Sec: Mrs Y.M. Lock, 7 Penarth Road, Bridgwater, Somerset, TA6 7ED. *Chief Coach:* G. Lock
Members: 240. *Leading Members:* Alistair Back (18), David Lock (17), Joanne O'Mahoney (19), Louise Spooner (17).

BRIDPORT (Dorset) *Formed* 1898
Club Sec: R.M. Everley, 5 Claremont Gardens, Bridport, Dorset, DT6 3AX. *Chief Coach:* W. Alexander
Members: 91. *Leading Members:* W. Alexander (25), A. Halson (25).

BRIDPORT LADIES (Dorset) *Formed* 1921
Club Sec: Mrs J. Tiltman, 90 St Andrews Road, Bridport, Dorset. *Chief Coach:* Mrs S. Tattershall
Members: 98.

BRISTOL CENTRAL (Avon) *Formed* 1937
Club Sec: R.K. Thompson, 17 Benville Avenue, Coombe Dingle, Bristol. *Chief Coaches:* P. Holmyard, P. Sherman, M. Shortman
Members: 200. *Leading Members:* Nikki Ball (15), Annette Bird (17), Katharine Britton (17), Rebecca Britton (15), Dave Bush (22), Joyce Cave (67), Georgie Coombs (22), Maria Erraught (19), Derek Figes (40), Lynne Figes (16) Ian Gibbons (17), Tony Holmyard (57), Mark Jones (28), Katrina Lythgoe (17), Nichola Shearn (22), Austyn Shortman (16), Mick Shortman (21), Penny Shortman (18), Louise Skidmore (16), Richard Sleight (15), Karen Thompson (15).

BRISTOL GRAMMAR SCHOOL (Avon)

BRISTOL MASTERS (Avon) *Formed* 1985
Club Sec: A.B. Hayward, "Westway", School Lane, Barrow Guerney, Bristol, BS19 3RZ.
Members: 45.

453

Bristol Central Synchro S.C. — ASA National Team Champions, 1988–89.

BRISTOL NORTH (Avon) *Formed* 1922
Club Sec: B. Dunning, 70 Dongola Road, Bristol, BS7 9HP. *Chief Coach:* J. Wilkins
Members: 200. *Leading Members:* L. Bryan (14), P. Bye (13), S. Bye (16), C. Chivers (13), S. Dunning (16), S. Ford (17), M. Foster (16), P. Hammond (15), S. Harris (12), D. Lewis (13), K. Lucas (16), P. Maber (20), S. Mallor (14), N. Pearce (14), N. Powell (18), G. Puttergill (16), K. Puttergill (14), L. Rogers (12), J. Silcox (15), N. Silcox (13), C. Staddon (17), C. Staddon (20), N. Sweet (14), S. Wilkins (22), J. Wring (13).

BRIXHAM (Devon) *Formed* 1928
Club Sec: G. Head-Rapson, 1 Southdown Avenue, Brixham. *Chief Coach:* F. Bradfield
Members: 415. *Leading Members:* Neil Artz (13), Janine Bond (15), Alice Bull (14), Lynne Crocker (16), Kevin Dart (22), Ian Davies (15), Darren Edwards (13), Kelly Ems (13), Christopher Hannaford (12), Ian Hicks (13), Natasha Lomas (20), Simon Longthorpe (13), Andrea Lugg (18), Melanie Lugg (11), Ashley McInally (12), Claire Morris (13), Jon-Paul Passmore (14), Julia Pedrick (12), Ryan Pedrick (14), Mark Plumridge (20), Sarah van den Brouck (13), Danielle Waller (12), Sacha Waller (14), Darry Wiggington (15), Robert Wiggington (14).

BROCKWORTH (Gloucester)

BURNHAM-ON-SEA (Somerset) *Formed* 1978
Club Sec: Mrs L. Chilton, "Sheridan Cottage", Wellsway, Blackford, Wedmore. *Chief Coach:* M. Gardner
Members: 250. *Leading Members:* Richard Blood (12), Lesley Dear (14), Michelle Drew (12), Rachel Evans (12), Stephen Evans (14), Daisy Ford (16), Andrew Gardner (13), Zoe Helbrow (15), Charlotte

Hutchings (13), Louise Jones (15), Andrew Lacaster (12), Martin Lee (12), John Murphy (13), Jay Parsons (11), Kerri Paul (12), Keith Pratt (14), Nicola Puddy (15), Andrew Pusill (15), Alison Rands (15), Jethro Skinner (12), Catherine Stewart (14), Rosemary Stewart (12), Iona White (16), Tim Whittle (18), Christopher Young (12).

BUTLER & TANNER (Somerset)

CALNE ALPHA FOUR (Wiltshire)　　　　　　　　　　　　　　　　　　　　*Formed* 1976
Club Sec: Mrs G.M. Moore, 32 Churchill Avenue, Melksham, Wilts, SN12 7JN.　　　*Chief Coach:* B. Nicol
Members: 100. *Leading Members:* Tom Ashpole (14), Neil Bartram (10), Donna Comley (21), Anna Dyke (14), Richard Ferris (14), Sophia Forsey (13), Julie Gerken (13), Kevin Hatchman (11), Tracey Hatter (18), David Hayward (30), Peter Hayward (29), Benjamin Hutchings (15), Damon Ingram (12), David Jacomb (23), Timothy Jacomb (14), Trevor Johnson (47), Johanna Lund (14), Helen Mead (10), Patrick Miley (27), Joanne Moore (18), Stuart Moore (20), Karan Parker (12), Lynne Pitfield (22), Richard Rowlands (30), Martin Vowden (14).

Calne Alpha Four W.P.C.

CARADON (Cornwall)　　　　　　　　　　　　　　　　　　　　　　　　　*Formed* 1973
Club Sec: Mrs M. Ball, 16 Morview Road, Widegates, Looe, Cornwall.　　　*Chief Coach:* M. Green
Members: 170. *Leading Members:* Caroline Andrew (17), Samantha Astin (13), Daren Ball (17), Nicola Ball (14), Chris Barrell (13), Amand Bendle (14), Leanne Burnett (15), Hannah Coe (12), Martyn Cole (13), Paul Day (14), Rebecca Elliott (12), Sarah Ford (10), Kyan Frith (12), Sam Heaton (12), Jonathon Hess (12), Andrew Jackson (11), Gary Johns (14), Robert Johns (17), Brendon Lee (13), Amanda Low (13), Charlie Low (15), Zoe Pote (13), Mark Preston (18), Benji Sharp (10), Lindsey Walke (13).

CARN BRAE (Cornwall)

CHAFYN GROVE SCHOOL (Wiltshire)

CHARD & DISTRICT (Somerset)

CHEDDAR DOLPHINS (Somerset)

CHELTENHAM (Gloucester)　　　　　　　　　　　　　　　　　　　　　*Formed* 1887
Club Sec: Mrs A. Davies, 6 The Rise, Shipton Oliffe, Cheltenham, Gloucester.　　　*Chief Coach:* J. Coe
Members: Jason Baldrey (15), Graham Brookhouse (26), Dave Cummings (21), Kate Davis (14), Simon Emm (23), Matthew Fletcher (18), Ian Gibson (18), Tina Griffiths (30), Debbie Ireland (14), Cheryl Johnson (22), Linda Kilminster (14), Wendy Kilminster (15), Dave Morris (16), Kevin Morris (25), Dave Shill (18), Paul Shilling (14), Emma Simpson (15), Guilia Staiano (12), Lorna Stanley (15), Edward Steel (16), Ian Sweet (18), Carol Taylor (18), Alison Viveash (16), Louise Waite (14), Mark Weaver (14).

CHIPPENHAM (Wiltshire)   *Formed* 1877
Club Sec: Mrs M. Lewis, "Gate House", Stanley Lane, Chippenham, Wilts.   *Chief Coach:* Mrs M. Evans
Members: 300. *Leading Members:* Susan Callaway (22), Katie Chambers (12), Andy Chapman (34), Emma Cowley (17), Emma Davison (20), Alan Drinkwater (23), Katherine Goodall (12), James Humphries (18), Michael Humphries (16), Owen Liversidge (14), Emer McCarron (15), Darren McMillan (13), Tim Mason (14), David Mays (18), Angela Moorhouse (14), Darren Moorhouse (16), Sally Normington (13), Emma Phillimore (12), Mark Rees (12), Tina Wales (11), Alan Ward (13), Steven Ward (18), Amanda White (14), Emma Wyatt (19), Alan Zenklusen (13), Steven Zenklusen (16).

CHRISTCHURCH PARRS (Dorset)

CINDERFORD & DISTRICT (Gloucester)

CINDERFORD & DISTRICT SYNCHRO (Gloucester)

CIRENCESTER (Gloucester)

CITY OF BRISTOL (Avon)   *Formed* 1984
Club Sec: R.T. Dykes, 10 Stonewell Park Road, Congresbury, Avon.   *Chief Coach:* E. Henderson
Members: 72. *Leading Members:* Wayne Clarke (15), Paula Clements (14), Jeremy Curry (18), Mark Dunston (16), Felicity Dutfield (15), Sara Dykes (17), Naomi Dymock (14), Nicola Elliot (13), Simon Jones (13), Ralph McQuillan (12), Caroline Maggs (15), Terri Parsons (15), Steven Pickup (12), Penny Porter (11), Lee Portingale (14), Jonathon Ratcliffe (16), Lynsey Rogers (12), Michael Shackcloth (18), Richard Shackcloth (16), Alex Smailes (16), Ian Sparks (22), Caroline Staddon (17), Julie Stannet (14), Alan Stokes (16), Tim Westlake (28).

CITY OF EXETER (Devon)

CITY OF PLYMOUTH (Devon)

CLEVEDON (Somerset)   *Formed* 1928
Club Sec: Mrs J.A. Ellis, 5 Tennyson Avenue, Clevedon, Avon, BS21 7UQ.   *Chief Coach:* M. Addicott
Members: 209.

CLIFTON COLLEGE (Avon)

CLIFTON HIGH SCHOOL (Avon)

CORMORANTS (Cornwall)

CORMORANTS SYNCHRO (Cornwall)

CORSHAM (Wiltshire)

DARTMOUTH (Devon)   *Formed* 1893
Club Sec: Mrs J. Wallis, 32 Venn Way, Stoke Fleming.   *Chief Coaches:* Mrs F. Bailey, Mrs S. Strudwick
Members: 75.

DAWLISH (Devon)   *Formed* 1863
Club Sec: Mrs R. Martin, 25 Higher Drive, Dawlish, South Devon.   *Chief Coach:* N. Storey
Members: 175. *Leading Members:* Nick Acton (10), Sarah Beer (15), James Blackmore (12), Simon Bloomfield (15), Rebecca Cockram (12), Sally Fletcher (15), Lia Giovanovits (14), Steven Glenister (13), Darren Goldby (11), Mark Grimwood (15), Neil Grimwood (13), Matthew Halse (11), Katherine Keeley (12), Clair Llewellen (12), Darren Maddick (12), Gary Martin (9), Warren Masters (14), Neil Osborne (10), Alex Ramsden (12), Justine Steer (16), Peter Storey (16), Michael Symons (12), Tanya Symons (15), Cameal Townsend (9), Damon Townsend (9).

DEAN CLOSE SCHOOL (Gloucester)

DEANE DOLPHIN (Gloucester)

DEVIZES (Wiltshire)

DEVON & CORNWALL POLICE (Devon)

DEVONPORT (Devon)   *Formed* 1863
Club Sec: D. Gregory, 21 Cherry Tree Drive, Brixton, Plymouth, PL8 2DD.   *Chief Coach:* Mrs B. Dixon
Members: 400. *Leading Members:* Joanne Anderson (15), Donna Bowden (14), Helen Coleman (21), Jonathon Dare-Williams (17), Neil Dare-Williams (14), Deborah Dixon (18), Paul Dixon (15), Helen Easterbrook (15), Michael Edgecombe (14), Kathryn Foster (11), Paul Foster (14), Andrew Holmes (21), Natalie Jewell (14), Suzanne Lannie (27), Carl McGowan (10), Dawn Milton (18), Glenn Milton (16), Kathryn Nugent (12), Philip Nugent (16), Raymond Parsons (15), Claire Perry (14), Michael Potham (17), Michelle Potham (13), Leslie Pritchard (17), Kerrie Thirlby (10).

DINNATON (Devon)   *Formed* 1986
Club Sec: Mrs I.J. Welton, 223 Ridgeway, Plympton, Plymouth, Devon.   *Chief Coach:* N. Lowden
Members: 50. *Leading Members:* Becky Austin (13), Tanya Austin (11), Jackie Bance (13), Joanne Bance (10), Vicky Bartlett (12), Amy Brightwell (12), Louise Brightwell (15), Jeff Butler (16), Andrew Colquhoun (13), Andrew Denham (11), Tammy Docking (10), Carla Drage (12), Simon Dry (11), Fiona Fisher (10),

Mark Hedges (13), Marcus Lemin (14), Ralph Lowden (16), Niall Milner (10), Andrew Moore (11), Alex Rowse (12), Sally Sinclair (13), Edward Thorpe (10), Martin Townsend (11), Geoff Walters (13), Rachel Welton (12).

DIPPERS (Avon)

DORCHESTER (Dorset)

DORCHESTER YOUTH SERVICE (Dorset)   *Formed* 1977
Club Sec: Mrs E. Cummins, 37 Grosvenor Road, Dorchester, Dorset, DT1 2BD.   *Chief Coach:* D. Hewitt
Members: 120.

DORSET SCHOOLS (Dorset)

DOWTY (Gloucester)

DURRINGTON & DISTRICT (Wiltshire)

EXETER CITY (Devon)   *Formed* 1988
Club Sec: D.H. Gillard, 30 Hamilton Avenue, Exeter, EX2 6BQ.   *Chief Coach:* P.J. Gilpin
Members: 500.

EXETER SYNCHRO (Devon)   *Formed* 1985
Club Sec: Mrs C. Bates, 122 Wardrew Road, Exeter, Devon.   *Chief Coaches:* M. Hooper, J. Northrop, J. Waters
Members: 60. *Leading Members:* Rosie Bates (11), Emma Copus (13), Lucy Cordery (13), Catherine Forth (16), Claire Gatcum (11), Helen Gatcum (11), Anna Gouch (14), Eloise Hall (13), Ruth Hall (12), Jo Hargreaves (13), Sarah Hooper (13), Karina Jones (11), Sarah Jones (13), Lyn Kenyon (19), Charlotte King (12), Nicola Mills (13), Clare Mulvihill (16), Lyndsey Seward (10), Tamsin Seward (13), Clare Thorne (13), Kellie Thorne (11), Sarah Vincent (16), Claire Waters (10), Debbie Weatherhead (12), Sarah Windsor (16).

EXMOUTH (Devon)   *Formed* 1893
Club Sec: Miss D. Snowshall, 17 Wessex Close, Topsham, Exeter.
Leading Members: Matthew Bater (10), Nigel Chase (12), Rachael Clements (11), Jonathan Daniels (15), Chloe Flint (15), Kim Franks (15), Oliver Jardine (11), Mark Keilty (14), Anthony Laye (12), Sophie Laye (15), Ian Leyland (13), Kevan Murphy (18), James Pike (12), Rebecca Pike (10), Steve Pond (18), Jane Quilter (11), Cheryl Sinclaire (15), Mark Stevens (15), Karen Thomas (17), Lisa Thomas (13), Karen Tomsett (10), Lucy Tyrrell (13), Zoe Walpole (10), Joann Wolstenholme (13), Wesley Woltman (14).

EXMOUTH (Devon)

EXTON JUNIORS (Devon)   *Formed* 1977
Club Sec: Mrs J. Milton, "East The Water", Exton, Exeter.
Members: 60.

FERNDOWN FLAMINGOES (Dorset)   *Formed* 1983
Club Sec: L. Fransen, 31 Barnes Crescent, Wimborne, Dorset.   *Chief Coach:* D. Bolton
Members: 25. *Leading Members:* Julia Bolton (21), Lisa Bolton (18), Tanya Bolton (15), Marion Challis (14), Zoe Davey (14), Christine Fairfax, Julia Fransen (14), Chloe Fullen (12), Louise Goodman (12), Hannah Grayson (12), Céline Hacchè, Danielle Hacchè, Michelle Howlett (16), Sandra Howlett (15), Rachel Johnson (11), Amanda King (18), Sandra Lawrence (13), Gemma McColl (14), Emma McLouphlin, Samatha Moir (15), Sara Pertlin, Kate Rogers (16), Caroline Saunders (14), Kelly Watson, Stephanie Wood.

FERNDOWN SYNCHRO (Dorset)

1ST KEYNSHAM SCOUTS (Somerset)

FRAMPTON COTTERELL COM.A.S. (Avon)

FROME

GLOUCESTER CITY (Gloucester)   *Formed* 1900
Club Sec: E.S. Murray, 64 Pacrets Road, Bishops Cleeve, Gloucester.   *Chief Coach:* H. Meinike
Members: 300. *Leading Members:* J. Barnacle (16), S. Buckley (15), R. Bulpin (15), J. Deakins (17), O. Gallienne (16), H. Goddard (16), P. Griffiths (18), M. Haynes (14), J. Hipwell (12), L. Joseph (13), P. Martin (14), S. Morris (16), R. Murray (14), E. O'Sullivan (16), K. Parker (13), E. Peatman (13), P. Pederzolli (17), A. Rolley (20), D. Rolley (21), R. Smart (19), H. Turk (28).

GLOUCESTER CONSTABULARY (Gloucester)

HAYLE (Cornwall)

HELSTON (Cornwall)   *Formed* 1969
Club Sec: Mrs S. Hoy, 43 Osborne Park, Helston, Cornwall.   *Chief Coach:* Mrs C. Raines
Members: 300. *Leading Members:* Craig Billing (11), Jake Boey (11), Sam Boey (12), William Boey (12), Elly Burnard (10), Louis Burnard (10), Peter Carr (12), Tracy Carroll (14), Clare Dale (12), Emma Downham (12), Ceri Drew (12), Catriona Grant (9), Fionn Howieson (9), Max Hoy (10), Jack Opie (11),

Rebecca Raines (10), Clare Rodwell (11), Helen Rodwell (13), Demelza Rogers (12), Jenny Search (13), Lizzy Search (10), Hannah Steer (12), Ben Swanson (11), Daniel Waite (10), Sarah Warry (14).

HENLEAZE (Avon) *Formed* 1919
Club Sec: Mrs M. Harris, 18 Mayfield Park, Fishponds, Bristol, BS16 3NN. *Chief Coach:* H. Rose
Members: 450. *Leading Members:* Bridget Canney, Alan Chilcott (14), Chris Dunning (26), Anne Marie Fowler (16), Charlotte Fowler (13), Luke Harding (11), Jayne Harris (21), Michael Hayes (14), Carol Holloway (40), Kate McLaren (11), Laura Marshall (13), Rachel Mitchell (13), James Passmore (12), Victoria Pike (16), Kate Reed (12), Matthew Rice (14), Sonia Robertson (14), Huw Rose (30), Alison Rowles (18), Simon Rowles (23), Kerry Skrine (12), Dave Strong (25), Rob Wilkins (25).

HEREFORD (Gloucester)

HIGHWORTH (Gloucester) *Formed* 1968
Club Sec: Mrs E.A. Hunt, 83 Henley Drive, Highworth, Swindon, Wilts. *Chief Coach:* F. Ranson
Members: 130. *Leading Members:* Samantha Allen (14), Pauline Archibald (17), Russel Bond (16), Steven Bond (18), William Bowman (18), Nicola Brown (18), Robert Cooke (14), Neil Craggs (11), Carol Fry (13), Nicola Hidden (14), Zoe Hidden (11), Kathryn Hunt (19), Heide Jelleyman (16), Joanne Jelleyman (19), Rachel Jones (13), Paul Mercer (15), Andrea Mulford (12), Samantha Mulford (16), Paul Newall (13), Richard Newall (10), Robert Ranson (15), Claire Simpkins (12), Mark Simpkins (10), Christopher Trewhella (12), Andrea Worsnip (17).

HMS SEA HAWKE (Cornwall)

HONITON (Devon)

ILFRACOMBE (Devon) *Formed* 1880
Club Sec: Mrs A. McEwan, 10 Chambercombe Park Terrace, Ilfracombe. *Chief Coach:* S. Capron
Members: 240. *Leading Members:* Kersty Brind (15), Robert Brind (14), James Capron (12), Thomas Capron (10), Michael Catlin (15), Craig Churchill (12), Ian Churchill (14), Russell Clement (11), Joanna Crookes-West (14), Ian Cudmore (15), Nicholas Cudmore (11), Matthew de Havilland (13), Carolyn Edwards (13), Nicola Edwards (11), Lucy Gaisford (14), Heather Ground (12), Matthew Ground (14), Miles Hamer (11), Sonja Hamer (14), Lyndsey Hutchings (14), Linda McGuirk (15), Phillip Manning (18), James Mitchell (10), Helen Morgan (14), Andrew Neale (15).

ILMINSTER (Somerset)

JUNIOR LEADERS REGIMENT (Dorset)

Kelly College John Lyne

KELLY COLLEGE (Devon) *Formed* 1977
Club Sec: R. Govier, c/o Kelly College, Tavistock, Devon, PL14 0HZ. *Chief Coach:* A.F. Brew
Members: 44. *Leading Members:* Elaine Archer (17), Joanne Austin (18), Chris Bird (21), Paul Brew (24), Rachael Brinn (18), Alison Cashmore (17), Bridget Chalmers (17), Neil Collins (15), Nicola Cumbers (19), James Eldridge (17), Lucy Findlay (15), Laura Gahan (15), Alistair Irwin (19), Jonathan Kerr (18), Richard Laidlaw (16), Rik Leishman (20), Jonathan Lynas (17), Jeffrey Ong (17), Ian Panting (20), Hannah Paull (16), Joanne Pearson (17), Debbie Salmon (15), Helen Slatter (19), Hayley Tooke (17), Michael Wynn (19).

KEYNSHAM (Somerset)
Club Sec: Mrs P.C. Dove, 121 Hurn Lane, Keynsham, Avon. *Chief Coaches:* Mrs L. Bullard, M. Ellaby
Members: 130. *Leading Members:* Martin Balcombe (16), James Burston (14), Joanne Coventry (16), Paul Denner (17), Claire Dove (14), Nicholas Ellaby (17), Mark Francis (12), Heide French (11), Nicholas Goodland (18), Nigel Harris (21), Lucy Hunt (13), Tracey Jennings (11), David Lloyd (15), Karen McGaul (17), Kirsteen McGaul (15), Rebecca Manley (12), Gary Parsons (16), Chris Pears (13), Emily Pears (11), Richard Smart (11), Katherine Stoate (11), Sharon Thomas (13), Jenny Wheatley (12), Amy White (12), Rebecca White (14).

KEYNSHAM RED CROSS (Somerset)

KINGSDOWN (Avon) *Formed* 1983
Club Sec: B.W.H. Maurice, 187 Cranbrook Road, Redland, Bristol, Avon. *Chief Coach:* B. Maurice
Members: 55. *Leading Members:* Dominic Barry (10), Debbie Collins (13), Luke Duncan (10), Poppy Edwards (12), Anna Gibbs (10), Katy Gibbs (12), Richard Jenkins (9), Imogen Lang (12), Thomasin Lang (11), Matthew Lillie (17), Helen Masters (13), James Masters (18), Daniel Maurice (14), Nathan Maurice (12), Penny Porter (11), Lois Roger-Jones (12), Abby Scott-Wilson (11), Paul Shields (12), Amy Tigg (8), Katy Tigg (10), Matty Tigg (11), Claire Vaughan (13), Peter Wright (11), Sally Young (11).

KINGSDOWN SCHOOL (Wiltshire)

KINGS COLLEGE, TAUNTON (Somerset)

KINGS SCHOOL, BRUTON (Somerset)

KINGSTEIGNTON (Devon) *Formed* 1979
Club Sec: L. Wilkinson, 12 Oak Greenhill Park, Kingsteignton. *Chief Coach:* P. Terrill
Members: 260. *Leading Members:* Michelle Bromley (15), Adam Cornish (18), Elizabeth Cousins (12), Helen Coxall (17), Darrin Crocombe (11), Karon Crocombe (11), Neil Edwards (13), Louise Franklin (11), Amy Geary (13), David Hambly (16), Zoe Hambly (16), Amanda Holmes (11), James Jenner (18), Jeffrey Jenner (11), Sarah Pack (14), Claire Pike (13), Susan Rundle (16), Amanda Russell (14), Charlotte Sawyer (12), Alia Serhan (11), Andrew Slaney (18), Adrian Stokes (14), Amanda Thomas (13), Wendy Thomas (15), Fredrick Wood (12).

LAMORNA (Devon)

LAUNCESTON (Cornwall) *Formed* 1982
Club Sec: Mrs J.E. McGhee, Western House, Lane End, Lamerton, Devon. *Chief Coach:* Mrs V.H. Astley
Members: 140. *Leading Members:* Anthony Astley (12), Helen Caudwell (16), Naomi Clements (14), Alan Duff (12), Jane Evely (13), Robert Evely (15), Amanda Grey (12), Matthew Jeffries (13), Drystan Jones (15), Veryan Jones (14), Stephen Leach (14), Bethany Lewitt (10), Katharine McGhee (16), Elizabeth Mason (11), Sally Nash (14), Ian Newbury (10), Hannah Rattray (11), Mark Storey (13), Matthew Storey (18), Michael Storey (17), Kellie Towl (12), Richard Trace (14), Katie Walke (17), Peta Waymouth (11), Benjamin Wiggins (15).

MALMESBURY MARLINS (Wiltshire)

MARLBOROUGH (Wiltshire) *Formed* 1958
Club Sec: H.C. Yeoman, Bexton Lodge, Rawlingswell Lane, Marlborough. *Chief Coach:* Mrs V. Clark
Members: 505. *Leading Members:* Andy Allen (21+), Stewart Allen (21+), Holly Berry (13), Ian Bevan (16), Emilie Came (12), Samantha Cheverall (11), Helen Duckham (21+), Joel Duckham (10), Dean Evans (12), Emma Fishlock (14), Jane Fishlock (19), Andy Kerr (20), Heather McNamee (10), Andrew Manley (11), Cheryl Morris (10), Alistair Southern (11), Chris Stuart (14), Alison Walters (15), Sarah White (17), Chris Williams (14), Louise Williams (12), Andrew Wilson (17), Carolyn Wootton (15), Mike Wootton (18), Nick Wootton (16).

MARLBOROUGH COLLEGE (Wiltshire)
Club Sec: Master In Charge of Swimming, Marlborough College, Wilts. *Chief Coach:* M. Evans
Members: 40. *Leading Members:* Will Alston (14), Barnaby Boss (16), Mathew Critchen-Brown (15), Max Dahele (18), Michael Davis (14), Dominic Ebel (14), Tom Fisher (15), Vincent Goh (15), Giles Haycock (14), Sebastian Henagulph (17), Joe Hill (15), Piers Jennings (14), Justin King (15), Dominic Liversidge (15), Patrick Lusty (17), James McGrigor (17), Jasper Morgan (16), David Mott (16), Tom Newton-Dunn (16), Nicholas Oxborrow (15), Greg Page (16), Simon Petrovitch (15), Adam Taylor (14), Peter Vaughan (14), Charles Wale (17).

MELKSHAM (Wiltshire)
Formed 1959

Club Sec: Mrs E.J. Millard, Hill View, 91 Sandridge Road, Melksham, Wilts.   *Chief Coach:* R. Fogden
Members: 250. *Leading Members:* Paul Ashman (14), Martin Bailey (22), Paul Bailey (20), Yvonne Bodkin (14), Alexander Brennan (17), Christopher Brennan (18), Kate Brookes (25), Kevin Broom (12), Avril Burbidge (13), Colin Burbidge (15), Russell Crumpler (11), Carolyn Dolman (21), Joy Dolman (14), Robert Hodgson (10), Steven Hodgson (12), Clair Jordan (11), Paul Millard (23), Lee Mortimar (14), Anna Scholfield (11), Sophie Schofield (14), Hayley Sibley (9), Kevin Sibley (14), Morven Sinclair (13), Clare Tapliss (12), Rebecca Whittick (15).

MENDIP (Somerset)
Formed 1968

Club Sec: Mrs V. Atkins, 44 Devonshire Road, Weston super Mare, BS23 4EL.   *Chief Coach:* P. Moore
Members: 170. *Leading Members:* Katherine Airey (16), Debbie Atkins (17), Elizabeth Barnetson (11), Katie Barnetson (11), Arthur Bassingham (11), Sarah Bassingham (14), Andrew Dawson (12), Luke Dawson (11), Jaki Dors (16), Sarah Dransfield (11), Mark Gonsalves (20), Karen Hart (14), Chris Hawkins (13), Charlotte Hill (16), Simon Jones (13), Andrew Lee (10), Mathew Lee (18), Rebecca Lee (10), Elizabeth Mitchell (14), Kathryn Mitchell (13), Jonathan Moore (10), Melanie Moore (17), Dale Moran (14), Jamie Sutton (17), Tim Westlake (29).

MENDIP DISABLED (Somerset)

MERRYWOOD & QUEENSDALE SCHOOL (Avon)

MILLFIELD SCHOOL (Somerset)
Formed 1968

Club Sec: L.P. Garratt, Millfield School, Street, Somerset, BA16 0YD.   *Chief Coach:* L.P. Garratt
Members: 125. *Leading Members:* Jamie Beale (17), Richard Birch (16), Nick Bridge (18), Scott Darling (14), Mark Eastment (13), Caroline Foot (24), Vicki Goodwin (14), Gail Harvey (15), Ruth Holland (12), James Ley (17), Owen Llewellyn (17), Emily Nathan (17), William O'Gormon (15), Jonathan Rayner (14), Julie Ricketts (14), Caroline Roberts (18), Rupert Ronca (13), Hiroshi Sheraton (15), Marcus Smallbone (16), Scott Squire (15), Julian Thomlinson (17), Richard Tozer (18), Kirstie Unsworth (16), Simon Wainwright (17), Emma Wilkinson (19).

Millfield School — Swimming squad, Summer Term, 1988   Eric Purchase

MINEHEAD (Avon)

NEWENT (Gloucester)

NEWQUAY CORMORANTS (Cornwall)
Formed 1968

Club Sec: Mrs C. Jepson, 27 Mayfield Crescent, Newquay, Cornwall, TR7 2DH.   *Chief Coach:* J. Cridland
Members: 180. *Leading Members:* David Annear (16), Toby Beard (12), Sheryl Broadbent (28), Neil Davison (15), Fiona Gaslonde (15), Lee Harding (13), Beverley Hogg (16), Amanda Jepson (25), Peter Landstrom (11), Russell Mullins (10), Philip Nelson (17), Kristina Newell (12), Lesley Ogden (16), Jo Ann Oliver (13), Gareth Owen (16), Jamie Owen (14), Jennifer Phillips (19), Rachael Pyett (13), Timothy Ramsden (11), Gavin Randell (18), Lindsey Randell (16), Daniel Smith (11), Matthew Wickham (10), Stephanie Wickham (13), Andrew Willmott (10).

NEWTON ABBOT (Devon)   *Formed* 1972
Club Sec: Mrs J.A. Vanstone, 2 Margaret Road, East Ogwell, Devon, TQ12 6AE. *Chief Coach:* B. Jarman
Leading Members: Claire Barron (14), James Davis (20), Richard Davis (24), Darren England (15), Wayne England (16), Cathryn Evison (13), Patricia Franklin (12), Emma Gilpin (15), Keri Green (15), Anna Martin (18), John Martin (23), Nigel Murch (23), Emma Peck (13), Ian Price (19), Nick Prouse (26), Paul Rhodes (20), Elizabeth Richards (11), Mandy Ridgway (22), Lydia Roscoe (13), Tim Seabrook (20), Graham Simpson (24), Karl Spreckley (23), Elizabeth Thomas (14), Simon Truscott (26), Suzanne Vine (13).

NIPPERS (Somerset)

NORTH DEVON (Devon)   *Formed* 1977
Club Sec: Mrs T.M. Pote, 32 Willoway Lane, Braunton, Devon, EX33 1BS. *Chief Coach:* D. Spratt
Members: 265. *Leading Members:* Melissa Arrowsmith (14), Rhodri Arrowsmith (13), Louise Benjafield (12), Kieran Brown (11), Paul Campbell (13), Paul Cawsey (27), Amber Clarke (10), Leon Clarke (11), Lee Ellis (12), Keith Gammon (15), Pauline Henry (12), Stuart Henry (16), Claire Hillson (13), Sarah Hillson (17), Debbie Howse (13), Rebecca Jordan (10), Chris Maud (14), Diane Maud (16), Kirsty Parkhouse (16), Chris Pote (14), Philip Pote (9), Paul Simpson (12), Nick Squire (13), Michelle Thorn (14), Nicholas Thorn (13).

NORTH DEVON DOLPHINS (Devon)

NORTON RADSTOCK (Somerset)

OAKHAMPTON OTTERS (Devon)

ODDICOMBE (Devon)   *Formed* 1922
Club Sec: Mrs E. Lake, Milton House, Higher Warberry Road, Torquay, Devon. *Chief Coach:* D.J. Roberts
Members: 250. *Leading Members:* Gail Adams (16), Andrew Bosley (10), Jonathan Bosley (17), Claire Boxall (14), Linda Clark (14), Matthew Clark (17), Peter Coish (17), Cara Cox (17), Jonathan Crocker (19), Ben Dommett (10), Matthew Dusgate (15), Paul Hogg (13), Damian Hunt (15), Paula Kerslake (15), Ben Lake (15), Andrew Lawton (10), Charlotte Litchfield (12), Sara Netherway (13), Philip O'Connell (14), Kirsty Paddon (17), Glen Port (16), Toby Smith (17), Jennifer Stephenson (14), Tracey Strainge (15), Christianne Williamson (15).

PAIGNTON (Devon)   *Formed* 1900
Club Sec: Mrs C. Humphreys, 2 Porlock Way, Paignton. *Chief Coach:* I. Throgmorton
Members: 650. *Leading Members:* Andrew Babbage (10), Lewis Babbage (10), Andrew Beesley (10), Sarah Bowser (12), Andrew Cole (19), Marcia Coleman (14), Andrew Cooke (10), Emma Davies (10), Paul Edwards (16), Sam Glasser (12), Carmen Goodchild (11), Michelle Greening (13), Robert Greening (16), Lydia Harris (11), Dawn Helps (15), Michael Hewitt (17), Clare Hunter (15), Matthew Lowe (14), Joanne Newton (10), Gaynor Oakden (18), Donna Plumridge (22), Mark Proctor (20), Lisa Swift (11), Chantelle Throgmorton (19), Derek Wyatt (23).

PAULTON (Somerset)

PENZANCE (Cornwall)   *Formed* 1863
Club Sec: Mrs A. Hughes, 12 Barton Close, Heamoor, Penzance, Cornwall. *Chief Coach:* J. Saulter
Members: 300. *Leading Members:* Ben Childs (13), Tom Childs (16), Mark Evered (16), Lara Hanken (17), Fenella Hilditch (17), Greg Hine (14), Matthew Hoyle (16), Tim Hoyle (14), Nick McKenzie (19), Ross McKenzie (14), Rebecca May (11), Katrina Moore (12), Natasha Moore (14), Abigail Nicholas (12), Michele Rescorca (21+), Jessica Ryan (13), Sam Ryan (12), Andrew Saulter (19), Tim Saulter (14), Jackie Stevenson (21+), Tamsyn Scott (13), Sasha Thomas (21+), Tamsin Thomas (21+), Emma Trevonon (13), Hara Trevonon (15).

PEWSEY (Wiltshire)

PLYMOUTH LEANDER (Devon)   *Formed* 1965
Club Sec: Mrs C. Tremellen, 7 Earls Wood Close, Earlswood, Plymouth. *Chief Coach:* Mrs S. Butler
Members: 450. *Leading Members:* Marcus Barton (19), Peter Barton (16), Matthew Beal (11), Jennie Burchell (15), Matthew Butler (13), James Carter (16), Jackie Chiles (21), James Davies (23), Scott Fairey (14), Neil Goldfinch (16), Amanda Higgins (12), Neal Ivey (11), Stuart Larkins (22), Andrew Lyon (15), Sarah McQuarry (13), June Porter (26), Tim Porter (22), Nicola Rutter (12), Simon Rutter (14), Simon Senior (20), Lyn Sirey (16), Christopher Tapscott (12), Alexandra Tremellen (14), Claire Trippier (21), Sophie Wright (25).

POOLE (Dorset)   *Formed* 1931
Club Sec: Mrs C. Honor, 53 St Osmund Road, Parkstone, Poole, Dorset. *Chief Coach:* I. Pritchard
Members: 450. *Leading Members:* Alison Bud, Julie Cooke (16), Paula Cooke (14), Karen Fletcher (13), Julia Hansford (17), James Harris (12), Paula Hartwell, Mark Hawkins (15), Ryan James (14), Hilary Johnson, Juan Londono (12), Paul Maddocks (16), Simon Maddocks (13), Paul Mason, Marc Newman, Rebecca Nicholas (15), Louise O'Brien (13), Lynda Racster (16), Susan Racster (14), Catherine Stevenson (12), Richard Storah (12), Keith Tyler (11), Nicholas Valentine (14), Claire Weldon (12), Lisa Willcocks (15).

PORTISHEAD (Somerset)   *Formed* 1932
Club Sec: V. Adamson, 6 Drakes Way, Portishead, Bristol, BS20 9LB.
Members: 105.

PORTLAND DOLPHINS (Dorset)

PORT OF PLYMOUTH (Devon)   *Formed* 1862
Club Sec: W.J. Baker, 183 Bridwell Road, Weston Mill, Plymouth, PL5 1AG.
Members: 575. *Leading Members:* Richard Baker (26), Lisa Bartlett (14), Stephen Blake (21), Della Booth (15), Nicola Bowden (14), Nicholas Broad (14), Charlotte Campbell (14), Fleur Campbell (12), Michael Dowding (14), Katy Holleran (16), Kevin Jones (17), Stephane Kolinsky (11), Andrew Mann (14), Richard Moore (25), James Oliver (12), Sharon Price (19), Ian Pring (26), Kevin Richards (17), Helen Rickett (15), Susan Rickett (17), Jon Rudd (18), Simon Smith (14), Lee Walker (16), Kathy Weir (22), Rachel Welton (12).

PORTWAY (Gloucester)   *Formed* 1949
Club Sec: Mrs C. Vincent, Poole Street, Avonmouth, Bristol.   *Chief Coach:* L. Smith
Members: 200. *Leading Members:* Tom Alger (15), Scott Anstey (19), Nick Brace (11), Sarah Bruton-Gibney (15), Niki Carmichael (12), Zoe Carmichael (15), Matthew Chaplin (10), Mark Davies (16), Rachel Gallop (11), Julian Gard (13), Emma Hanks (13), Jamie Lavis (10), Zoe Lavis (12), Lucy O'Brien (12), Fiona Paddon (14), Gary Paviour (11), Louise Paviour (14), Michael Petch (11), Louise Reeves (11), Lisa Scadding (13), Nicola Scadding (11), Tyrone Tippins (13), Sharon Vincent (11), Lisa Wills (14), Paul Wood (16).

QUEENS COLLEGE, TAUNTON (Somerset)

RAF LYNEHAM (Wiltshire)

RNAS COLDROSE (Cornwall)
Club Sec: Swimming Pool Manager, Sports Centre, RNAS Coldrose, Heaton, Cornwall.

ST ANDREWS, FILTON (Avon)

ST AUSTELL & DISTRICT (Cornwall)
Club Sec: Mrs S. Smith, School House, Carthew, St Austell, Cornwall.   *Chief Coach:* H. Richards
Members: 300. *Leading Members:* Tracey Chard (11), Tristan Clark (12), E.V. Clemett (72), Mark Cocks (11), Claire Dunstan (13), Jackie Evans (10), Peter Hoar (18), Richard Horne, Sharon Lagor (18), Tony Lambert (41), Karen Legg (13), Helen Leigh (13), Matthew Leigh (14), Brett Marsh (13), Hannah Morden (13), Andrea Patterson (13), Scott Patterson, Lucy Penhalligan (10), Lynne Phillips (12), Helen Richards (21), Peter Rogers (12), Tarryn Rowe (11), Julie Smith (10), Carl Sturt, Peter Thornton.

ST PAUL'S COLLEGE (Gloucester)

SALCOMBE (Devon)

SALISBURY (Wiltshire)   *Formed* 1908
Club Sec: Mrs R. Lancaster, 14 Beatrice Road, Salisbury, Wilts.   *Chief Coach:* M. Muddiman
Members: 400. *Leading Members:* Allan Adlam (12), Nick Beauchamp (24), Rachel Benson (12), Gemma Brewer (11), Phillip Burdes (15), Darryl Cherrett (11), Alexander Cox (13), Matthew Cox (13), Rachel Fanner (19), Melissa Gale (14), Heather Gilbert (13), Stewart James (14), Tim Kent-Robinson (13), Mark Learnihan (11), Paul Mernagh (16), Kevin Muddiman (24), Gareth Noble (12), Joanne Orchard (15), Michelle Parkes (22), Joanne Roberts (11), Andrew Smith (19), Brendan Smith (20), Linsey Spaven (13), Richard Thompson (23), Castelle Webb (12).

SEVON GROUP OF SWIMMERS (Gloucester)

SHELBURNE SHARKS (Gloucester)   *Formed* 1981
Club Sec: Mrs W.P. Ilsley, 68 Kingscote Road West, Upper Hatherley.   *Chief Coach:* A. Williams
Members: 25.

SHEPTON MALLET (Somerset)

SMITHS INDUSTRIES LIMITED (Gloucester)

SOMERSET SCOUTS (Somerset)

SOUNDWELL (Gloucester)   *Formed* 1962
Club Sec: T. Blackwell, 42A Oakleigh Gardens, Oldland Common, Bristol.   *Chief Coach:* C. Pritchard
Members: 460. *Leading Members:* Paul Bond (16), Katie Britton (11), Jemma Colette (11), Matthew Cox (13), Karen Fellows (16), Richard Ford (11), Tom Hawkins (11), Paul Hennys (20), Laura Hocks (11), John Lewis (13), Matthew Maulding (11), Charles Morgan (11), Tabitha Philpott (15), Mark Robinson (15), Robert Scott (15), Andrew Sessions (11), Rebecca Thunhurst (13), Susannah Thunhurst (11), Clare Watts-Jones (14), Mark Watts-Jones (16), Susan White (11), Andrew Wilmott (14).

SOUTH MOLTON (Devon)   *Formed* 1945
Club Sec: Mrs P.A. Miller, 10 Broad Close, North Molton, Devon, EX36 3JD.   *Chief Coach:* N. Miller
Members: 195.

SOUTH WILTSHIRE GRAMMAR SCHOOL (Wiltshire)

SOUTHWOLD (Gloucester) *Formed* 1973
Club Sec: H. Adams, 7 Cherry Road, Chipping Sudbury, Bristol, BS17 6JH. *Chief Coach:* J. Scanlan
Members: 324. *Leading Members:* Charlotte Bidwell (10), David Boulton (10), Matthew Bragg (15), Mark Cahill (15), Jeremy Curry (18), Chris Dawes (13), Tracey Dawes (10), David Haskins (10), Emma Haskins (14), Neil Holloway (18), Toby Holloway (17), Phillip Howe (17), Stephen Isles (17), Hayley Johnson (12), Nick Judd (16), Helen Marshall (10), Mike Norman (23), Sam Rushent (10), Kirstie Seymour (16), Ian Shackcloth (10), Michael Shackcloth (18), Richard Shackcloth (16), Claire Smith (16), Martin Stephens (11), Emma Vincent (14).

SPINNER ASTHMATIC (Cornwall)

STREET (Somerset)

STROUD DOLPHINS (Gloucester)

SUPPORTERS (Gloucester)

SWINDON (Wiltshire)
Club Sec: V. Mills, 1 Westmorland Road, Swindon, SN1 2ND. *Chief Coach:* T. Bowditch
Members: 200. *Leading Members:* James Bishop (17), Julie Bishop (32), David Blackmor (17), Stuart Bowditch (13), Karen Brealey (19), Martin Brealey (14), Lisa Cleary (18), Paul Daultrey (11), Simon Davey (13), Rhian Evans (13), Joanne Fisher (13), Nicola Fisher (14), Jennifer Gleeson (13), Richard Gleeson (15), Kelly Kitchener (13), Steven Leech (12), Andrew Minton (15), Kevin Minton (13), Pamela Ovendon (15), Clive Page (13), Ian Page (14), Donna Scarr (12), Karen Scarr (15), Matthew Webb (16), Michael Webb (14).

SWINDON DOLPHINS (Wiltshire)

SWINDON LIFESAVING CLUB (Wiltshire)

TAUNTON (Somerset) *Formed* 1883
Club Sec: Mrs G.P. Berryman, 17 Queensdown, Creech St Michael, Somerset. *Chief Coach:* R. Howse
Members: 500. *Leading Members:* S. Badley (15), G. Berryman (12), R. Berryman (13), L. Chidgey (13), E. Freudenberg (13), N. Heys (12), S. Heys (14), E. Hooper (11), E. Hooper (13), T. Hooper (16), A. Howse (18), I. Howse (15), K. Johnson (12), C. Lake (15), D. Lake (11), R. Lauer (12), D. Palmer (22), G. Perks (24), C. Rawlings (20), J. Rawlings (22), E. Searle (16), M. Shephard (13), M. Shephard (14), J. Soloman (14), I. Usher (17).

TAUNTON SCHOOL (Somerset)

TEIGNMOUTH (Devon) *Formed* 1974
Club Sec: Mrs J. Hammond, "Madeley", Upper Hermosa Road, Teignmouth, Devon, TQ14 9JW.
Members: 190.

TEWKESBURY (Gloucester)

THAMESDOWN DIVING CLUB (Wiltshire) *Formed* 1984
Club Sec: Mrs E. Head, 54 Kellsborough Avenue, Wroughton. *Chief Coach:* M. Sutton
Members: 40. *Leading Members:* Kate Aldridge (9), Louise Guy (11), Simon Guy (13), Jonathan Baker (4), Victoria Baker (8), James Black (11), Amanda Brain (10), Helen Burnett (7), Matthew Deer (9), James Henly (14), Martin Henly (11), Tristan Morten-Spencer (12), Lucy Nicholls (12), Nathan Pryor (7), Victoria Pryor (9), Danny Roberts (9), James Stevens (11), Clive Vandervelde (14), Phillip Vandervelde (16), Sharon Vandervelde (10), Gareth Woolley (10).

THAMESDOWN TIGERSHARKS (Wiltshire) *Formed* 1975
Club Sec: J. Hudson, 4 Bydemill Gardens, Highworth, Swindon, Wilts, SN6 7BS. *Chief Coach:* D. Lyles
Members: 300. *Leading Members:* Samantha Blyth (12), Nicola Boon (13), Geoff Dyball (18), Paul French (14), Joanne Fuller (12), Glen Hanley (13), Paul Hillier (16), Nick Hudson (23), Sally Hudson (19), Declan Kevener (18), Paul Milburn (14), Alison Millard (16), Joanne Millard (14), Lee Morgan (15), Zoe Morgan (12), Karl Mutton (14), Dawn Newman (12), Craig Nicholas (14), Chris Strong (25), Gary Tanner (23), Daniel Thurley (14), Anne Watkins (14), David Wilson (14), Sarah Wilson (16), Jane Woodward (13).

THORNBURY (Gloucester) *Formed* 1968
Club Sec: Mrs J.G. Shepherd, 53 St Kingsmark Avenue, The Danes, Chepstow. *Chief Coach:* B. Pollard
Members: 300. *Leading Members:* Matthew Bird (16), Jane Constable (16), Matthew Craddy (13), Nichola Cuff (11), Chris Davies (13), Melonie Forrest (15), Michael Gribb (15), Michael Grove (12), Steve Hodges (16), Kevin Jay (14), David Kershaw (13), Mike Kershaw (15), Charlotte Leslie (11), Bethan Lewis (15), David Lewis (13), Kate McLevey (15), Andrew McMorinne (11), Simon Mundy (13), Peter Shepherd (11), Andrew Vittle (10), Lora White (11).

THORNLOW TORNADOES (Dorset) *Formed* 1982
Club Sec: D. Hamilton, 4 Cunningham Close, Wyke Regis, Weymouth, Dorset. *Chief Coach:* P. Daniels
Members: 460. *Leading Members:* Sam Alderton (18), Gary Barter (17), Vicky Brook (11), Natasha Coupe (12), Ben Daniels (12), Simon Davies (15), Beverley Dunford (13), George Fridd (13), Hayley Hamilton

(15), Philip Hanger (15), Rhys Hanger (12), Philip Hogan (14), Mark Jarvis (16), Michele Jarvis (10), Paul Jarvis (12), Janet Kirby (11), Gavin Lamb (11), Gail Lloyd (12), Rachel Masters (11), Mathew Newman (19), Lisa Palmer (12), Dawn Perriam (14), Tim Rose (19), Lee Samways (11), Ricky Wood (15).

TISBURY (Wiltshire)   *Formed* 1964
Club Sec: R. Allsopp, 7 Churchill Estate, Tisbury, Wilts.   *Chief Coach:* P. Betts
Members: 100. *Leading Members:* Joanna Betts (11), Louise Betts (13), Peter Betts (41), Lisa Cope (15), Kay Croucher (15), Gary Davis (14), Adele Dearden (22), Jacquie Dearden (19), Paul Dix (19), Jonathon Gray (16), Steve Hudson (33), Tony Hughes (19), Tony Jenn (39), Catherine Morris (16), Ian Morris (14), Emma Penson (13), Nicky Porter (14), Gary Price (11), Shanna Ricketts (12), Vincent Stone (10), Julie Walton (28), Melodie Walton (30), Dee Wareham (12), Julian Webb (30), Stephanie Wells (14).

TIVERTON (Devon)   *Formed* 1925
Club Sec: S. Redwood, 13 Bampfylde Close, Tiverton, Devon.   *Chief Coach:* J. Cridland
Members: 356. *Leading Members:* Michelle Bisiker (10). Andrew Blake (13), Alison Clarke (16), Janet Franklin (5), Rebecca Hagley (10), Stephanie Hawkins (15), Suzanne Hawkins (13), Andrew Hill (18), Bryony Hogg (11), Karen Howard (5), David Isaac (14), Emma Kingston (5), Alison Loosemore (16), Kathryn Loosemore (13), Becky Mardon (15), Ben Mardon (12), Sophie Maunder (15), Andrew Oswald (11), Emma Redwood (11), Marie Stark (13), Natasha Stone (14), Vicky Treeby (11), Ben White (14), Simon White (18), Samantha Yarnton (11).

TOPSHAM (Devon)

TORQUAY LEANDER (Devon)   *Formed* 1897
Club Sec: M.P. Garros, "Ellemar", New Road, Teignmouth, Devon.   *Chief Coach:* C. Trudgeon
Members: 385. *Leading Members:* Joanne Baker (13), Paul Baker (10), Paul Blake (16), Andrew Boulton (13), Stephen Boxall (16), Lee Boyle (15), Helen Cottey (13), Katie Fortune (14), Tony Furneaux (19), Mark Hindom (14), Paul Hindom (17), Ian Jeffrey (17), Stephen Margetts (14), Kirsty Northcott (15), Sarah Northcott (17), Ashley Noyce (17), Russell Page-Dove (10), Martin Saunders (18), Gary Spencer (12), Gina Westlake (15), Mark Westlake (13), Kevin Wheeler (17), Dawn Winston (13), Simon Wood (11), Mark Wray (15).

TORRIDGESIDE (Devon)

TOTNES (Devon)
Club Sec: Mrs J. Veale, Broomborough House Farm, Totnes, Devon.   *Chief Coach:* J. Harris
Leading Members: Nicholas Baillie, Cherr Bissell, Charlotte Dalzell, Rachel Doble, Jessica Evered, Jonathan Evered, Kirsty Evered, Simon Gale, Chris Hubble, Tracy King, Helen Payne, Greg Pearson, Clair Pedrick, Ian Pedrick, Sheree Putt, Trudy Rowe, Helen Sloman, Zoe Tapper, Simon Veale, Ian Watson, Karen Watson, Kathrine Wier, May Wintle.

TRICORN (Dorset)

TROWBRIDGE (Wiltshire)

Thornbury S.C. — Members of the junior team, 1988.

TRURO CITY (Cornwall)   *Formed* 1973
Club Sec: Mrs M. Carter, Lanner Farm, Cusgarne, Truro, Cornwall, TR4 8RW.   *Chief Coach:* R. Sutton
Members: 220. *Leading Members:* Simon Ashenden (15), Stephanie Bell (11), Andrew Bicknell (10), Lorraine Bishop (13), Andrew Carter (17), Cathy Dash (12), Paul Davies (16), Rachel Goss (17), Tamsin Greener (13), David Hocking (14), Jo Hocking (17), David King (22), Peter King (15), Nick Polkinghorne (17), Robbie Polkinghorne (15), Dominic Pullen (12), Julia Raines (17), Lindsey Randall (16), Claire Raven (13), James Stiff (14), David Stone (12), Graham White (17), Vicky Wilson (15), Chantal Worden (12), Sarita Worden (12).

UNIVERSITY OF BRISTOL (Avon)

WANSDYKE DISABLED (Somerset)

WAREHAM & DISTRICT (Dorset)   *Formed* 1956
Club Sec: F.J. Stokes, 45 Stowell Crescent, Wareham, Dorset, BH20 4PU.
Members: 300.

WARMINSTER & DISTRICT (Wiltshire)   *Formed* 1973
Club Sec: Mrs P.A. Selby, 1 Cowleaze Lane, Edington, Westbury, Wilts, BA13 4PB.
Members: 167. *Leading Members:* Simon Ager (15), Paula Antliffe (16), Louise Armes (17), Matthew Armes (14), Richard Baker (12), Nicola Brewer (14), Kirstie Button (10), Joanne Cox (16), Tim Curtis (15), Ross Dewey (11), Simon Farrell (9), Michelle Genevieve (14), Terry Goodsman (12), Suzanne Griffin (14), Sheryl Grist (14), Alison Hinton (10), Julia Hutton (12), Marion Kinman (27), Shane Lulham (12), Paul Macfarlane (12), Nicola Otterwell (14), Steven Payne (15), Mark Plumridge (19), David Price (14), Amanda Rhodes (16).

WELLS (Somerset)

WELLS CATHEDRAL SCHOOL (Somerset)

WESSEX DIVING CLUB (Dorset)   *Formed* 1976
Club Sec: Mrs J. Latham, 117 Pinehurst Road, West Moors, Wimborne, Dorset.   *Chief Coach:* P. Morris
Members: 51. *Leading Members:* Tina Ayles (12), Alison Bartlett (11), Gemma Brooks (12), Ryan Brooks (9), Katie Cremins (14), Rachel Cronk (19), Lorraine Exley (12), Martin Frewier (13), Katrina Goodwin (13), Valerie Green (18), Col Holland (17), Derek Holland (18), Tracey Jorden (14), Paul Luthier (14), Mathew McGuire (10), Sarah Mainstone (14), Ella Morris (13), Claire Rafferty (12), Richard Sheridan (12).

WESSEX WPC (Dorset)

WESTBURY (Wiltshire)

WEST DORSET LEISURE CENTRE (Dorset)

WESTON SUPER MARE (Somerset)   *Formed* 1880
Club Sec: Mrs M. Reed, 8 St Peters Avenue, Uphill, Weston super Mare.   *Chief Coach:* B. Bewley
Members: 325. *Leading Members:* Chris Baker (13), Darren Baker (15), Sarah Baker (18), Karen Balmond (14), Yvonne Chandler (16), James Clark (11), Claire Connis (9), Mark Dunstone (16), Andrew Fowler (14), Frances Gansden (10), James Hadley (9), Stephanie Hadley (11), Leila Hasham (10), Mark Horsley (10), Patricia Horsley (14), Dawn Jones (12), David McKenzie (10), Mathew Parkes (12), Chris Rickard (11), Anthony Rowlands (11), Cherilyn Rowlands (14), Su Staines (16), Andrew Wallace (16), Ruth Wallace (10), Amanda Willett (12).

WEYMOUTH (Dorset)
Club Sec: Mrs S. Short, 5 Creech Way, Weymouth, Dorset, DT3 5RE.   *Chief Coach:* Mrs J. Hewitt
Members: 450. *Leading Members:* Peter Birchill (14), Ian Bulns (18), Kelly Burnage (12), Jon Desmond (17), Paul Desmond (21), Owen Finnie (17), Kelly Foster (14), Clive Gilbert (17), Laura Grant (14), Faye Hickman (15), Russell Hickman (16), Rowena Howell (17), Rebecca Kelly (15), Fraser Knight (19), Lynn Mesney (18), Chris Middle (19), Marianne Middle (17), Louise Miles (13), Alex Nichols (14), Andrew Redhead (14), Jane Salmon (14), Mark Saunders (17), Michael Short (18), Kate Thomas (15), Seth Why (17).

WEYPORT OLYMPIANS (Dorset)   *Formed* 1985
Club Sec: D. Hamilton, 4 Cunningham Close, Wyke Regis, Dorset, DT4 9HL.   *Chief Coach:* Mrs J. Hewitt
Members: 60. *Leading Members:* Samantha Alderton (17), Gary Barter (17), Kelly Burnage (12), Ian Burns (20), Jon Desmond (18), Paul Desmond (22), Sian Edwards (21), Owen Finnie (17), Kelly Foster (14), Lee Freeman (15), Clive Gilbert (17), Laura Grant (14), Hayley Hamilton (15), Faye Hickman (15), Vicky Horton (13), Rowena Howell (17), Mark Jarvis (16), Alistair Knight (16), Phil Mesney (17), Marianne Middle (18), Alex Nichols (14), Dawn Perriam (14), Jane Salmon (14), Mark Saunders (18), Seth Why (17).

WILTSHIRE WOMENS INSTITUTE (Wiltshire)

WIMBORNE (Dorset)   *Formed* 1969
Club Sec: Mrs S. Burke, 28 The Vineries, Wimborne, Dorset, BH21 2PX.   *Chief Coach:* R. Burke
Members: 100.

WINCANTON (Somerset)   *Formed* 1978
Club Sec: Mrs C. Chilcott, Barrow Lane Farm, Charlton Musgrove, Wincanton, Somerset.
Members: 290.

WOOTTON BASSETT (Wiltshire)   *Formed* 1973
Club Sec: Mrs S. Brooks, 1 Elm Grove, Nine Elms, Shaw, Swindon, SN5 9PG.   *Chief Coach:* R. Jones
Members: 200. *Leading Members:* Jessica Angell (12), Nigel Bell (16), Julie Brooks (15), Peter Brooks (12), Adrian Burden (18), Matthew Chandler (11), Susanne Davies (15), Paul Davis (13), Steve Davis (10), David Dunn (16), Zoë Franklin (13), Mark Hopkins (20), Dean Jones (13), Kara Jones (17), Carol Lees (15), Kirsty Lees (12), Katie Mitchell (10), Abigail Reeve (12), Caroline Roe (17), Katherine Roe (19), Ian Saunders (15), Abby Williams (14), David Williams (15), Peter Williams (13), Stuart Wright (13).

WROUGHTON (Wiltshire)

WYCLIFFE COLLEGE (Gloucester)

YEOVIL & DISTRICT (Somerset)
Club Sec: Mrs D. White, "Towans", 52 Constable Close, Yeovil, Somerset.   *Chief Coach:* Mrs R. Johnson
Leading Members: Greg Battarbee (13), Neil Battarbee (16), Anna Bower (16), Fiona Campbell (15), Andrew Chamberlain (16), Rachel Creed (13), Natalie Davis (12), Helen Dycer (17), David Gubbins (14), Lee Ann Hedges (11), Paul Hilditch (16), David Johnson (19), Sally Johnson (13), Sian Jones (15), Christopher Mapp (11), James Mak (16), Creole Palmer (17), Paul Perry (12), Andrew Pinder (15), Richard Pinder (13), Claire Rowe (15), Claire Small (15), Karen Small (15), Kevin Tribe (13), Alan Woodward (15).

British Swimming Coaches Association: Directory

The British Swimming Coaches Association was originally formed in 1964, at which time the majority of swimming coaches were either part time professionals or enthusiastic amateurs. In the '70s, swimming coaching took on a totally professional aspect as clubs and local authorities realised that producing the very best for swimmers at all levels, was indeed, a full time role, which called for considerable skill both in coaching and management.

Membership of the BSCA has grown correspondingly, and the recent changes to the constitution reflect the desire for an efficient and professional organisation.

The last decade has seen the ASA and the BSCA forge favourable links towards the progression of the Sport. Indeed, the two bodies, through a Joint Liaison Committee, actively discuss and develop new ideas for the betterment of Swimming at all levels.

With many Founder Members and Contributors to the Associations development over the last quarter of a century, expected to make the trip from far and wide to Yorkshire, the 1990 BSCA Conference, in Bradford, will be a nostalgic affair. It is indeed fitting that the 25th AGM will be held in White Rose Country, the home of one of the Founder Members, and most prolific supporters over the years, George Bole, from Huddersfield. George coaches to this day, and although now across the Atlantic in St Petersburg, Florida, is still an active member of the coaching fraternity.

So what can the BSCA offer coaches within the country? The answer to this question is numerous and can by fully obtained from our administrative Secretary Joanne Pearse. But it is the voice of British Coaches, and is working hard to move the sport successfully into the 21st Century as swimming competes in the sporting market place.

British Swimming Coaches Association — Officers 1989

President: **Dormer, Laurie** "Yule Cottage", Milky Down, Hightown, Ringwood, Hampshire. Tel: 0425 471147.
Vice President: **Fox, Harold** 22 Langham Drive, Chadwell Heath, Romford, Essex. Tel: 01 590 4607.
Treasurer: **Presbury, Peter** 16 Clare Lodge Close, Bransgore, Christchurch, Dorset. BH23 8NG. Tel: 0425 72285.
Memberships: **Presbury, Moya** 16 Clare Lodge Close, Bransgore, Christchurch, Dorset. BH23 8NG. Tel: 0425 72285.
Secretary: **Bush, Paul** Leeds International Pool, Westgate, Leeds, West Yorkshire. LS1 4PH. Tel: 0532 421959/443713/438696. Fax: 0532 426761 or Fax: 0532 421321. 51 Woodside Drive, Churwell, Leeds, West Yorkshire LS27 9NL. Tel: 0532 528315.
Administration: **Pearce, Joanne** 32 Slade Close, Sully, South Glamorgan. Tel: 0222 531114.

Executive Committee 1989

Pay, Bob "Pays", 31 Deerings Drive, Joel Street, Old Eastcote, Pinner, Middlesex. HA5 2HZ. Tel: Home: 01 429 0620. S: 01 863 3198.
Sellwood, Nick 53 Pinewood Avenue, Meadow Rise, Edgehill, Woodend, Near Atherstone, Warwickshire. Tel: 0827 873563.
McGill, John 244 Willingale Road, Loughton, Essex IG10 2BX. Tel: 01 508 0183.
Brew, Archie Kelly College, Tavistock, Devon. Tel: Office: 0822 612010. Home: 0752 793252.
Drew, Mike 35 Priory Road, Stanford le Hope, Essex. Tel: 03756 71852.
Stripe, Colin 29 Cornell Way, Collier Way, Romford, Essex. Tel: Home: 0708 48750. Office: 01 595 1229.
Kirby, Fred 3 Primula Drive, Eaton, Norwich, NR4 7LZ. Tel: 0603 507465.
Lord, Wally 5 Broomie Knowe Gardens, Bonnyrigg, Midlothian, Scotland. Tel: 031 667 7211 Ext 202.

Firman, Viv 74 Whitwell Road, Southsea, Hampshire. Tel: 0705 733635.

Williams, Bryn 80 Penlan Road, Llandough, Nr Penarth, Wales CF6 1LU. Tel: 0222 701170.

Longridge, Neil 6 Elizabeth Crescent, Queens Park, Chester. Tel: 0244 679026.

BSCA Accountant:

James, Robert 11 Imperial Court, St Leonards Road, Windsor, Berkshire SL4 3RE. Tel: 0344 412121 Ext 229.

ISTC Representative:

Wilson, Charlie 124 Goldington Road, Bedford MK40 3EH. Tel: 0234 67555 or 0582 415214.

Coaches

Adams, Chris (Bognor Regis) 14 Norbren Avenue, North Bersted, Bognor Regis. Tel: 860857.

Adams, Douglas (Bournemouth Dolphins) 14 Morevale Road, Mordown, Bournemouth.

Analox Instruments, Unit 8, Goldhawk Industrial Estate, Brackenbury, London W6 0BQ. Tel: 01 749 7635.

Ansell, David (Bethnal Green Sharks) 31 Morpeth Street, Bethnal Green, London E2 0PS. Tel: 01 980 7369.

Ansell, Tony (Bethnal Green Sharks) 71 Graham Road, Hackney, London E8 1PB. Tel: 01 923 0419.

Armiger, Ian (Bradford Schools) Bingley Baths, Bingley BD16 2LF.

Asher, Jane (Jets) 38 Keswick Road, Cringleford, Norwich NR4 6UG. Tel: 0603 52268.

Atkinson, Leigh (Newport & Maindee) 9 Thornwood Close, Llanishen, Cardiff. Tel: 763296.

Austin, David 5 Kempton Close, Lawrence Drive, Ickenham, Middlesex.

Ayers, Kevin

Bagshaw, F.J. (Eastbourne Colleges) 291 Sraside, Eastbourne, East Sussex BN22 7NU. Tel: 0323 638853.

Bailey, Rick 73 Shakespeare Drive, Shirley, Solihull, West Midlands.

Bance, Dave (Goldfins) 127 Frobisher Drive, Saskatoon, Saskatchewan, Canada. Tel: 306 2427311.

Banks, Denise Flat 4, 18A Valkyrie Road, Westcliff on Sea, Essex. Tel: 0702 334506.

Barker, Gwyneth 40 Oak Street, Abertillery, Gwent NP3 1TF.

Barnes, Joan "Ashbourne", Cartford Lane, Little Eccleston, Preston PR3 0YP. Tel: 0995 70262.

Bates, Carol 26 Golf Drive, Nuneaton, Warwickshire.

Batten, Bryan "Red Cottage", Broadway, Laleham, Middlesex TW18 1SB. Tel: 0784 52390.

Batterbury, Paul 11 Maze Green Road, Bishop's Stortford, Hertfordshire CM23 2QZ.

Berryman, Ronald (Hatfield) 10 Smallwood Close, Wheathampstead, Hertfordshire AL4 8TW. Tel: 0582 832776.

Bewley, Brian R. (Weston super Mare) 15 Chalfont Road, Weston super Mare BS22 8AN. Tel: 0934 624129.

Bewley, Keith (Wigan Wasps)

Black, John (Co Hull) 48 Strathmore Avenue, Hull. Tel: 804528.

Blythin, Neil (Everton) 207 Bridge Lane, Bootle, Merseyside L30 3SN. Tel: 051 525 2587.

Bole, George (Fellow member).

Booth, Amanda 6 Deyne Street, Salford M5 5WT.

Brew, Archie (Kelly College) Kelly College, Tavistock, Devon.

Bridges, Stephen J. (Manchester U Salford) 35 Bedford Drive, Sutton Coldfield, West Midlands.

Briggs, Tom 15 Ingram Drive, Chapel Park, Newcastle upon Tyne.

Brinkley, Brian 247 Peterborough Road, Fadcet, Peterborough, Cambridgeshire.

Brookehouse, Ray (Sparkhill) 47 Bilbury Road, Hall Green, Birmingham B28 0HG. Tel: 021 777 3318.

Brystow, Terry 29 Thornhill Close, Houghton Regis, Dunstable.

Buchanan, Keith 30 North Circular Road, Lisburn, Co Antrim.

Burgess, Neil Flat 7, Thanet House, 101 Nags Head Road, Ponders End, Enfield. Tel: 01 340 8055 x 2339.

Burrows, Roy (Hoylake) 8 The Goose Green, Meols, Wirral L47 6BQ. Tel: 051 632 2160.

Burt, Peter (Reading) 5 Geoffreyson Road, Caversham, Reading RE4 7HS.

Bush, Michael A. 1 Chapel Hill, Crayford, Kent DA1 4BY.

Bush, Paul 51 Woodside Drive, Churwell, Leeds 1. Tel: 0532 443713.

Calleja, David (Stockport Metro) Flat 1, 48 Tatton Road, South Heaton, Chapel, Stockport. Tel: 061 474 4481.

Campion, Eddie (Dolphin) "Sarto", Ashleigh Drive, Blackrock, Cork, Ireland. Tel: 021 293037.

Champion, David (Ipswich) 35 Sproughton Court, Sproughton, Ipswich IP8 3AJ. Tel: 0473 462507.

Chapman, Michael 24 Seven Acres Road, Preston, Weymouth, Dorset DT3 6DQ. Tel: 0305 832448.

Clark, Anne (Leicester Synchro) 4 Grange Drive, Grange Park, Leicestershire LE10 2JR.

Clark, Ian D. (Beckenham) 84 Glebe Way, West Wickham, Kent BR4 0SA.

Clark, Nigel (Sans Egal) 12 Rise Cottages, Widford, Ware, Hertfordshire. Tel: 0279 842610.

Clarke, Joyce (Hounslow B) 16 Roxborough Avenue, Isleworth, Middlesex TW7 5HG.

Clay, Arthur F. (Edmonton) "Pin-Hi", Lippitts Hill, High Beech, Loughton, Essex. Tel: 01 807 8760.

Coley, Brian (Stretford) 11 Penrith Avenue, Sale, Cheshire. Tel: 061 969 8766.

Collinson, Ernest (Leeds) 50 Greenhill Lane, Leeds, West Yorkshire. Tel: 0532 637040.

Corry, Ian (Lisburn) 29 Thornhill Park, Belfast.

Cousins, Capt Jack (Southend on Sea) 20B Carlton Avenue, Westcliff on Sea, Essex, SS0 0QD. Tel: 0702 343779.

Cracknell, Robert (Ilford) 104 Riverdene Road, Ilford, Essex.

Cross, Neville 7 Inverleigh Gardens, Edinburgh EH3 5PU.

Cryer, Steve Anthony (Orpington) "The Grange", c/o Eltham College, Mottingham, London. Tel: 01 857 4456.

Dale, Gerald 334 Abergele Road, Old Colwyn, Colwyn Bay, Clwyd. Tel: 0492 533233.

Darby, W.N. (Bradford Schools) 26 Lindley Drive, Bradford BD7 4JQ.

Davis, Steve (Leatherhead) 29 May Close, Chessington, Surrey KT9 2AP. Tel: 01 397 9556.

Delaney, Thomas G. (Oldham) 536 Broadway, Chadderton, Oldham OL9 9NJ. Tel: 0616 820638.

Denison, Terry (Co Leeds) 39 Green Hill Drive, Leeds. Tel: 0532 639678.

Derrick, John (Hythe) 8 Hillside Street, Hythe, Kent.

Dickinson, Gordon (Ashington) 23 Haldane Street, Ashington, Northumberland NE63 8SF. Tel: 855413.

Dix, Dennis 67 Seaford Close, Ruislip, Middlesex HA4 7HH.

Dixon, Ann (Hereford) 13 Wyelands Close, Hereford HR2 6DH. Tel: 0432 51657.

Dobinson, James (Kingston Royals) 11 Collingwood Avenue, Tolworth, Surrey KT5 9PT. Tel: 01 337 3671.

Docker, David 7 Woodland Rise, Sutton Coldfield, West Midlands.

Donnelly, Patrick (Gateshead & Whickham) 8 Derwent Terrace, Annfield Plain, Stanley, Co Durham.

Dormer, Laurie "Yule Cottage", Milky Down, Hightown, Ringwood, Hampshire. Tel: 0425 45440.

Dover, Peter (Chalfont Otters) 55 Glebe Road, Chalfont St Peter, Buckinghamshire. Tel: 0753 888283.

Downie, William 170 Swinston Hill Road, Dinnington, South Yorkshire S31 7SB. Tel: 0909 562786.

Drew, Michael (Killerwhales) 35 Priory Road, Stanford le Hope, Essex SS17 7EW.

Duane, Win (Colchester/Brentwood) 28 Barfield Road, Weston, Mersea, Colchester CO5 8QT. Tel: 0206 382970.

Dudley, George (Potters Bar) 83 Sunnybank Road, Potters Bar EN6 2NZ.

Du Feu, Paul (Regent Tigers) 28 Midnale Road, St Helier, Jersey, CI.

Dummer, Terence 22 Slade Road, Barry, South Glamorgan. Tel: 0446 738644.

Dummer, William 22 Slade Road, Barry, South Glamorgan. Tel: 0446 738644.

Dyer, John (Leeds) 31 Planetrees Street, Allerton, Bradford BD15 7DL.

Earle, Eddie (Camden Swiss Cottage) Flat 4, 223 North Gower Street, London NW1 2NR. Tel: 01 380 1149.

Eddy, John (Walthamstow) 26 Gwynne Park Avenue, Woodford Bridge, Essex IG8 8AB. Tel: 01 989 8950.

Ellis, Sidney 9 St Alphege Road, Edmonton, London N9 8BU. Tel: 01 804 8991.

Entwistle, John 2 Albert Street, Bury, Greater Manchester BL9 7BH.

Esmond, Chris "Kitelands", 110 Wyke Road, Weymouth, Dorset.

Evitts, Brian (Piranha) 75 Ellenbrook Road, Boothstown, Worsley, Manchester.

Firman, Viv (Portsmouth Northsea) 74 Whitwell Road, Southsea, Hampshire PO4 0QS. Tel: 733636.

Fodden, David (Co Leeds) 190 Crossgates Ring Road, Leeds LS15 8RF.

Fox, Harold (Redbridge B) 22 Langham Drive, Romford, Essex. Tel: 01 590 4607.

Franklin, L. 2 Cathedral View Park, Witchford, Ely, Cambridgeshire. Tel: 0353 661492.

Gallop, Rosa (Bracknell) 33 Holland Gardens, Fleet. Hampshire.

Garratt, Lawrence P. (Millfield) "The White Cottage", 15 Bere Lane, Glastonbury, Somerset. Tel: 0458 32377.

Geer, Michael D. (RT W Monson) 24 John Street, Tunbridge Wells TV4 9RR. Tel: 0892 26784.

Geeves, Barry (Olympic Salamander) 44 Connaught Road, High Barnet, Barnet EN5 2PY. Tel: 01 441 3982.

Gilchrist, Thomas (Longridge Towers) c/o Berwick Fire Station, Ord Road, Tweedmouth.

Gillies, Pamela J. (King's Lynn Gladiators) 11 Charlock Whisson Close, King's Lynn, Norfolk.

Gilpin, Peter 85 Bamburgh Close, Washington, Tyne & Wear. Tel: 091 415 1032.

Gold, Jamie A 18 Avenue Road, London W6 5DW.

Goldman, Philip (Bodmin) "Hauteville", 96 Fore Street, Newquay, Cornwall TR7 1EY. Tel: 0637 876065.

Gosling, M. (Stirling) 34 Goldstream Avenue, Dumblane, Stirling. Tel: 0786 70544.

Graham, Malcolm 13 Harrington Close, Windsor, Berkshire SL4 4AD. Tel: 0753 867176.

Gray, Maurice (St Pauls School) The Flat, Putney Swimming Pool, Dryburgh Road, Putney. Tel: 01 758 2405.

Green, Michael (Caradon) 34 Crodon Gardens, Ernesettley, Plymouth, Devon PL5 2RQ. Tel: 364022.

Greyson, Ian (Stockport Metro) Petersgate Centre, St Petersgate, Stockport.

Grimshaw, Fred 89 Upwood Road, Lee, London SE12 8AL. Tel: 01 852 1634.

Hannelly, Pauline The Orchard, Stekley, Buckinghamshire.

Hargrave, Diane 46 Molesey Road, Hersham, Walton on Thames, Surrey. Tel: 0932 227141.

Harley, Andrew (Army) UKLF School of P&RT, Bulford Camp, Bulford, Wiltshire. Tel: 0980 3371.

Hart, Colin Richard 21 Ashgrove Road, Redland, Bristol BS6 6NA.

Hart, Sybille (Newbury) "Byways", 34 Andover Road, Newbury, Berkshire.

Hartley, James A. (Crawley) 49 The Millbank, Ifield, Crawley, West Sussex RH11 0JQ. Tel: 0293 515519.

Hawkins, Eric 13 Audley Road, Alsager, Stoke on Trent, Staffordshire ST7 2L0. Tel: 936 378473.

Hayes, Paddy 132 Beach Road, South Shields, Tyne & Wear NE33 2NE. Tel: 091 456 1647.

Hepwood, Mick (Walsall) 120 Stuarts Green, Redlake Drive, Pedmore, Stourbridge. Tel: 0902 714029.

Herbert, Joan 30 Kenwood Road, Leicester.

Hewitson, Keith (Co Leicester) 20 Maurice Drive, Countesthorpe, Leicester LE8 3PH Tel: 774427.

Higgs, Mike (Bo Southend) 283 High Street, Great Wakering, Essex.

Hobbs, David (Camden Swiss Cottage) 5 Stanley Road, Edmonton, London N9 9AD. Tel: 01 807 1581.

Hogarth, Lynne (Hull Masters) 71 Ransfield Avenue, Brough, Hull HU15 1BE.

Holden, Susan 162 Waterloo Walk, Sulgrave, Washington, Tyne & Wear.

Hood, Peter 1A Blenheim Road, Reading, Berkshire RG1 5NG. Tel: 0734 669563.

Hopson, David (Bury St Edmunds) 137 York Road, Bury St Edmunds, Suffolk IP33 3EE.Tel: 0284 60767.

Horsfall, Roy Noel "Neuville", Victoria Road, St Clements, Jersey, CI. Tel: 24134.

Hughes, John (Felixstowe). 27 Henley Court, Henley Road, Ipswich, Suffolk IP1 3SD Tel: 0473 57017.

Hunt, Douglas (Bottisham) "The Whitehouse", Main Road, Morton, Derbyshire.

Hunter, Stuart (Newark) 14 Wellington Road, Newark, Nottinghamshire NG24 1NJ.

Ivison, Muriel (Bo S Tyneside) 50 Morpeth Avenue. South Shields, Tyne & Wear. Tel: 0914 566901.

Jameson, Diane (Co Liverpool) 114 Chesterfield Road, Great Crosby, Liverpool L23 9TT. Tel: 051 924 2698.

James, Robert 11 Imperial Court, St Leonards Road, Windsor, Berkshire. Tel: 0344 412121.

Johnson, James 10 Buckstone Mount, Alwoodley Park, Leeds LS17 5HS. Tel: 0532 692740.

Johnson, Michael 6 Thirlmere Drive, Lymm, Cheshire.

Jones, Kenneth 19 Meadow View, Sealand Manor, Deeside, Clwyd. Tel: 0244 812922.

Jones, Lesley (Hazel Grove/Bramhall) 8 Hillcroft Road, High Lane, Stockport SK6 8HN. Tel: 0663 65714.

Jones, Oliver 18 Station Road, Mochder, Clwyd.

Kenney, Paraic 73 Lakeshore Drive, Castlebar, Co Mayo, Ireland.

Kirby, Fred 3 Primula Drive, Eaton, Norwich NR4 7LZ. Tel: 0603 507465.

Kovacs, Leonart (Bradford Schools) 208 Hainworth Wood Road, Keighley BD21 5BS.

Kwong, Hector (Dartford) 43 Tudor Avenue, Stanford le Hope, Essex SS17 8BX. Tel: 0375 640477.

Lack, Robert (Barnet Copthall) 92 Larkswood Road, Chingford, London E4 9DU. Tel: 01 529 7685.

Lander, Geoffrey, D. "Woodcroft", Broad Road, Hambrook, Sussex PO18 8RF.

Loftus, Peter (West Kent) 18 St Margarets Street, Rochester, Kent. Tel: 0634 44400

Longridge, Neil 6 Elizabeth Crescent, Queens Park, Chester. Tel: 0244 679026.

Lyles, David 23 Timothy Lane, Batley, West Yorkshire WF17 0BA. Tel: 444934.

McCortick, Graeme W. (Hounslow B) "Baths Cottage", Clifden Road, Brentford, Middlesex. Tel: 01 847 3329.

McCullagh, David 244 Lundsire Road, Dublin 12, Ireland.

McGill, John 244 Willingdale Road, Loughton, Essex IG10 2BX. Tel: 01 508 0183.

McGregor, Ian (Warrender) 54 Albion Road, Leith, Edinburgh EH7 5QZ. Tel: 031 661 8097.

McGuinness, Brian J. 11 Ashdown Way, High Crompton, Oldham, Lancashire OL2 7UL. Tel: 061 627 0648

McNeil, Alex 74 North Grange Road, Bearsden, Dumbartonshire.

MacGuinness, Tony (Hatfield) 122 Travellers Lane, Hatfield, Herts. Tel: 0707 264487.

MacKinney, Ian (Brentwood) c/o The Brentwood Centre, Doddington Road, Brentwood. Tel: 0277 261448.

Maddison, Peter 8 Kingsdale Avenue, Blyth, Northumberland NE24 4EN.

Marjoram, James (Hammersmith) 258 Russell Court, Woburn Place, London WC1H 0NF. Tel: 01 278 9979.

Martin, Pamela (Co St Albans) 19 Ridgmont Road, St Albans, Hertfordshire AL1 3AG.

Masters, John (Rhymney Valley) 8B St Cenydd Road, Trecenydd, Caerphilly, Mid Glamorgan. Tel: 0222 864427.

Matthews, Gordon (Redbridge B) "Baths Cottage", 470 High Road, Ilford, Essex IG1 1DE. Tel: 01 478 1606.

Maurice, Brian (Kingsdown) 187 Cranbrook Road, Redland, Bristol BS6 7DF. Tel: 240573.

Meadows, Ron 38 Commercial Road, Staines, Middlesex.

Medd, Jim (Fleetwood) 36 Hathaway Road, Fleetwood FY7 7JH. Tel: 70818.

Melia, Norman (Cleethorpes & District) 11 Weelsby Road, Grimsby, South Humberside DN32 0QA. Tel: 0472 78085.

Minns, Richard Alex (Leeds Polytechnic) 6 Westfield Gardens, Christchurch, Dorset BH23 4SF. Tel: 0425 272535.

Moore, John (Darlington) 1 Kenilworth Court, Woodham Village, Newton Aycliffe. Tel: 0325 311726.

Moore, Terry (Oundle & D) 14 Turnpike Close, Wisbech, Cambridgeshire PE13 3UR.

Moorhouse, Alan D. (Bo Burnley CATS) 8 Singleton Avenue, Read, Burnley, Lancashire. BB12 7PJ. Tel: 0254 393621.

Morewood, D. (Wantage White Horses) 31 Belmont, Wantage, Oxfordshire.

Morris, Anthony (Abingdon) 38 Besseleigh Road, Abingdon, Oxfordshire OX13 6DX. Tel: 730254.

Mosey, M. (Kirklees) 12 Ashford Court, Hightowton, Huddersfield, West Yorkshire. Tel: 604427.

Moulsen, Leslie (Norwich Penguins) 103 Tuckwood Lane, Norwich NR4 6BG. Tel: 0603 57752.

Muff, Brian (Bradford Schools) 11 Straygate Green, Bradford, West Yorkshire.

Muir, Celia Anne Arena UK, Manor Lane, Holmes Chapel, Cheshire. Tel: 0477 34024.

Muir, Cochrane N. 75 Stoneybank Gardens, Musselburgh EH21 6TG.

Mullins, John 23 Swanland Hill, North Ferriby, North Humberside.

Nesbitt, Chris (Portsmouth Northsea) 43 Burgoyne Road, Southsea, Hampshire.

Newby, Duncan 27 Mayfield Park, Bishop's Stortford, Hertfordshire CM23 4JL.

Newton, Colin 12 Halifax Way, Brabazon Drive, Christchurch BH23 4TX.

Nicholls, Joan (Worcester) Virginia House, Powick, Worcester. Tel: 0905 830223.

Oakes, William 47 Hillside Gardens, Barnet, Hertfordshire EN5 2NO. Tel: 01 449 5058.

Oliver, Ian (Co Newcastle) 3 Limetrees Gardens, Gateshead NE9 5BE. Tel: 091 477 2259.

Parker, Michael (Co Leicester) 12 Laundon Close, Groby, Leicester. Tel: 0533 29011.

Pay, Bob "Pays", 31 Deerings Drive, Joel Street, Old Eastcote, Pinner. Tel: 01 429 0620.

Pearce, Donald (Co Leeds) 62 Half Mile Lane, Leeds LS13 1NJ.

Pears, Barry (Leicester Penguins) 5 Alexandra Street, Narborough, Leicestershire LE9 5DD. Tel: 0760 848737.

Peters, Ralph (Wycombe) "New House", Wilton Lane, Jordons, Buckinghamshire HP9 2RF.

Pettengell, David J. 5 Robin Close, Billericay, Essex CM12 05J.

Peyrebrune, Mike 18 Henderland Road, Edinburgh.

Phelps, Michael J. 6 Cooks Orchard, Gloucester GL1 3JY. Tel: 422070.

Porter, Martin (Jeddah) 30 Bader Avenue, Thornaby, Cleveland TS17 0HQ. Tel: 0642 761928.

Powell, Lindsay (Barnet Copthall) 97 Abbots Gardens, East Finchley, London N2 0JJ.

Presbury, Peter (Bournemouth Dolphins) 16 Clare Lodge Close, Bransgore, Christchurch, Dorset. Tel: 0425 72285.

Prime, Barry (Co Birmingham) 21 Adswood Lane East, Cale Green, Stockport.

Pritchard, Catherine (Soundwell) Flat 3, 15 Clouds Hill Road, St George, Bristol B55 4LD. Tel: 0272 541441.

Pritchard, Ian (Poole) 16 Pen Deri Close, Maes Y Garn, Oakdale, Gwent NP2 0J0. Tel: 495 225852.

Pulsford, Trixie (Ross & D) "Aldanti", Ledbury Road, Ross on Wye, Herefordshire. Tel: 0989 64088.

Purchase, Steve (Co Leeds) Leeds International Pool, Westgate, Leeds LS1 4PH.

Rescorla, Julia "Tolverne", 11 Kings Road, Penzance, Cornwall TR18 4LH.

Rhodes, Paul (Bradford Schools) 1 Killinghall Avenue, Bradford BD2 4SA.

Robbins, Paul A. (Deben) 71 High Road, Layer de la Haye, Colchester, Essex.

Rolfe, Ron 100 Oakleigh Road North, Whetstone, London N20 0TH.

Ross, Anthony D. 55 Erith Road, Bexley Heath, Kent DA7 6BS. Tel: 0322 529483.

Ross, George A. 121 Rydal Drive, Bexley Heath, Kent DA7 5DX. Tel: 01 304 4550.

Rowe, Elizabeth (Cleethorpes & D) 25 Cumberland Avenue, Grimsby, Humberside. Tel: 0472 77434.

Runnalls, Lesley (Reading) 4 Spring Cottages, Sonning on Thames, Berkshire RG4 0TL. Tel: 0734 693389.

Seery, Martin (Tynemouth) 35A Percy Park, North Shields NE30 4JX. Tel: 091 258 5840.

Sellwood, Nick 53 Pinewood Avenue, Wood End, Atherstone, Warwickshire. Tel: 0827 873563.

Skelly, Edward L.R. 5 Rathmore Crescent, Bangor, N. Ireland BT19 1DG.

Smith, Jeff (Bradford Schools) 92 Ashbourne Way, Bradford BD2 4DV.

Smith, John 10 Larklands, Longthorpe, Peterborough, Cambridgeshire PE3 6LL. Tel: 0733 263592.

Smith, Rodney (Co Coventry) 15 Roland Mount, Holbrooks, Coventry CV6 4HP.

Sollars, Loretta "April Cottage", Horsham Road, Cranleigh, Surrey GU6 8DT. Tel: 0483 273753.

Sparkes, Audrey E.A. (Potters Bar) 23 Peplins Way, Brookmans Park, Hatfield AL9 7UR. Tel: 0707 55603.

Staight, Gary (Romford T) 48 Shepherds Close, Chadwell Heath, Romford RM6 5AH. Tel: 01 598 8652.

Stark, William 34 Porchester Road, Bingham, Nottingham NG13 8ES. Tel: 0949 38257.

Stewart, Maxwell (Co Bradford) 17 Banksfield Close, Yeardon, Yorkshire LS19 7LW. Tel: 0532 506818.

Stripe, Colin Dagenham Pool, Althorphe Way, Dagenham, Essex. Tel: 01 595 1229.

Summers, Derek 233 Norbury Crescent, Norbury, London SW16 4LF. Tel: 01 764 7994.

Sykes, Gareth (Co Coventry) 116C Earisdon Avenue, South Coventry CVJ 6DN. Tel: 0203 691088.

Tait, Eric John 21 Pearnville View, Leeds LS8 3DJ.

Taylor, James (Hounslow B) 57 Larkhill Lane, Formby, Liverpool L37 1LU. Tel: 0704 871751.

Tripp, Iain 33 Springfield Road, Grays, Essex RM16 2QM. Tel: 0375 376559.

Watford, Susan (Bingham) 2 Stathern Road, Eastwell, Melton Mowbray, Leicestershire. Tel: 0949 61256.

Weetman, Larry (Bournemouth Dolphins) 6 Evershot Road, Bournemouth BH8 9PB. Tel: 0202 510637.

Wells, Ian 19 Ingrestre Street, Hereford. Tel: 0432 272512.

Wilkinson, John (Bradford Schools) 40 Hawes Road, Bradford BD5 9AW.

Willey, Stephen (Bournemouth Dolphins) 50 Parkwood Road, Bournemouth, Dorset BH5 2BL. Tel: 420896.

Williams, Bryn 8 Oakwood Close, Llandough, Nr Penarth, Wales. Tel: 0222 701170.

Williams, G.M. (Co Southampton) 11 Sykend Lane, Hordle, Lymington, Hampshire. Tel: 0703 220138.

Willianson, Brian "Hazeldene", Ballinaneeshagh, Waterford, Ireland. Tel: 051 73901.

Wilson, Charlie 124 Goldington Road, Bedford MK40 3EH. Tel: 0234 67555.

Wooley, Ian (Crewe Neptune) 174 Willoughby Road, Bottesford, Scunthorpe, South Humberside. Tel: 0724 861469.

Worthington, George (Bo Kirklees) 42 Bankfield Park Avenue, Taylor Hill, Huddersfield.

Wybrow, George (Fin Club) 27 Sherwood Road, Macclesfield, Cheshire SK11 7RR. Tel: 611224.

The Institute of Swimming Teachers and Coaches: Aims and Objectives

by Brian Relf (Secretary)

The ISTC was inaugurated in 1975 to provide a service to qualified ASA swimming teachers and coaches. It now has a membership of 9,000, which is increasing each year. Membership is open to holders of the Teaching or Coaching Certificates, Amateur Swimming Association and/or Royal Life Saving Society in all disciplines of the sport, and also to holders of equivalent qualifications of other bodies, approved by the Board of Directors.

The Institute publishes a Directory of Membership, which is made available to local authorities and other appropriate bodies concerned with the employment of swimming teachers and coaches. A comprehensive public liability and personal accident insurance cover, including contractual and products liability cover, is provided for members. This is essential for practising teachers and coaches. The Institute also negotiates discount facilities with companies who supply equipment and services, which may be of assistance to members in their swimming activities.

Initially, the Institute was administered by the Management Committee, made up of three members appointed by the ASA Committee and two elected by the membership. But in 1983, the ASA changed the status of the Institute by forming a Limited Company, to be administered by a Board of Directors: five of its members appointed by the ASA Committee and four elected from the Institute's Regional Committees.

The officers of the Institute are the Chairman, the Financial Director, and the Secretary. These are responsible for the day-to-day running of the affairs in accordance with the policy and within the budget approved by the Board.

In 1976, seminars were held in each of the Sports Council Regions, plus Scotland, Ireland and Wales, resulting in the establishment of Regional Committees. These are now responsible for the organisation of two or three seminars each year; which provide opportunities for in-service training and also allow members to comment on proposed changes to the ASA Educational System. In addition, the Institute appoints representatives to the ASA National Technical Committee, thus setting up a useful channel of communication, and enabling the opinions of the "grass roots" to be considered by those responsible for the initiation of the future policy of the Amateur Swimming Asssociation. The ASA Districts have welcomed ISTC representatives on to their committees, which has provided a very helpful liaison, and a number of worthwhile joint projects have been arranged. Two of these are the Southern Counties Tutors' Conference and the Midland District Centenary Education Conference.

The ISTC provides every individual teacher and coach with a collective identity, which is made evident by the use of designated letters after the member's name: AIST/AISC (Associate), or FIST/FISC (Fellow). Focal centres are organised in the regions, where teachers and coaches can meet to join in those activities which interest them. They are also able to discuss matters of mutual concern, and can exchange ideas and technical information. Lectures, seminars, conferences, and discussions enable members to keep in touch with each other, as well as hearing about any new developments in the swimming world.

The official journal of the ASA and ISTC, *The Swimming Times*, is sent to each member every month. It contains details of regional activities, articles of particular interest to teachers and coaches, and technical papers to assist with the development of the sport.

Membership is for a 12-month period from the date of receipt of application. Forms can be obtained from the Secretary, ISTC Ltd., Lantern House, 38 Leicester Road, Loughborough, Leics. LE11 2AG. Tel: 0509 264357.

Lifesaving

by Sandra Caldwell and Peter Owen

Although there is no doubt that swimming is a sport which can be undertaken by almost anyone, and, indeed, can be of great benefit to many people, there is another important aspect which cannot be overlooked — that of *safety*. With current trends towards fitness and the expansion of the leisure industry, more and more people are becoming involved in water-based activities.

It is not surprising that statistics show that more accidents and fatalities occur among non-swimmers than swimmers — although, on occasions, the latter group is just as susceptible as any other. In many instances, particularly in open areas such as rivers, canals, and lakes, it is a fact that a proportion of drownings occur *close* to the bank. With the correct training, a land-based rescue can be performed, using a reaching or throwing aid such as a stick or article of clothing, thus avoiding the unnecessary risk of other persons endangering themselves by entering the water. The natural progression from learning to swim would therefore seem to be learning to save lives.

In Victorian times, the annual toll of 2,000 needless deaths by drowning, convinced William Henry for the need of a Life Saving Society, and in 1891 "The Swimmers' Life Saving" was founded. This later became "The Life Saving Society", with Mr Henry as its first Chief Secretary. In 1901, the Society was honoured when His Majesty King Edward VII consented to become Patron, and in 1904 he granted permission for the use of the title "Royal". This organisation has since grown to become a recognised leader in lifesaving education, with programmes being conducted in over 50 Commonwealth and other countries.

The Society was incorporated by Royal Charter in 1924, and was recognised in 1960 by the granting of a Supplemental Charter, which defined a Commonwealth Council and autonomous Member Branches in Australia, Canada, New Zealand, and the United Kingdom.

Here in the United Kingdom, work is divided into three areas: water safety education, teaching water rescue and resuscitation skills, and the training of lifeguards, who work both in swimming pools and on beaches and inland waterways. Over half a million people participate annually in the RLSS UK programmes; there are close links with both national and international educational and recreational organisations, and full co-operation is maintained with the emergency services — the Police and HM Coastguard — in the provision of RLSS UK Lifeguard services.

The Society is closely allied with other organisations. This is in order to perpetuate the aims founded nearly a century ago, and it is one of several bodies, including the Amateur Swimming Association, which form a Joint Consultative Committee. One of this Committee's first achievements was the launching of what is now known as the ASA/RLSS Lifesaving Certificate. This was developed by the Society to meet the lifesaving needs of those undertaking ASA Preliminary Teachers', Teachers', and Advanced Teachers', Certificate courses. In addition, the Committee publishes specific advice on swimming pool hire and insurance for swimming clubs and other pool hirers. The ASA/RLSS Lifesaving Certificate was expressly designed by the Society as a lifesaving test for swimming teachers and others responsible for the conduct of programmed swimming sessions. The Society was also instrumental in the setting up of a joint liaison body with the leisure industry's foremost professional management bodies, in order that standards of supervision in swimming pools could be improved. Steps were first taken in 1973, when the Sports Council published a Technical Unit for Sport Bulletin entitled *Public Indoor Swimming Pools*. It was not until 1988, however, that comprehensive guidance was issued jointly by the Health and Safety Commission and the Sports Council in the safety guidance booklet, *Safety in Swimming Pools*.

The Society was represented on the working party responsible for producing this document, which, during consultations, most frequently, suggested the RLSS Pool Bronze Medallion as a suitable qualification for those providing a comprehensive service at a pool. 1989 sees the launching of the Pool Lifeguard Bronze Medallion, which takes into account the objectives of this latest guidance.

To the world of swimming, in general, the Society also has much to offer. Its Award Schemes offer a diversity of activity which can often be taken up by those swimmers who grow dissatisfied with just perfecting strokes or swimming distances, or who lose interest in the competitive side of the sport.

The Award Schemes are broken into the following broad areas:

Aquapack   First steps in lifesaving for children.

Resuscitation   Land-based Resuscitation Awards from basic to advanced levels.

Open Water   Bridges the gap between indoor lifesaving and active lifeguard service.

Specialist   ASA/RLSS Lifesaving Certificate and Police Service Awards.

Lifesaving   A progression of awards, all requiring land and water-based skills, and knowledge.

Teaching and Coaching   An organised scheme to ensure standard education throughout the Society's spheres of activity.

Lifeguarding   A co-ordinated active lifeguard service, comprising affiliated groups, which supervise other water users and provide safety patrols in both inland and coastal, indoor and open water. This group has its own award structure, which reflects the special skills necessary.

The Society holds two National Championships each year. The Lifesaving Champions feature club and school, junior and senior categories, and are held in indoor conditions. The National Lifeguard Championships are held in open water, and feature tests specific to the specialised equipment and techniques that the lifeguards use. The Society also has an international UK team which, in 1988, was highly successful at the Asia Pacific World Lifesaving Championships.

There is always the risk that an accident can occur when swimming, and the Society teaches people how to look after themselves and help others in the aquatic environment. Whereas, to be able to lifesave in the water, a person must first know how to swim. One aspect of rescue which everyone can learn — whether swimmers or non-swimmers, young or old — is that of resuscitation. Near-drowning, or indeed, any other serious accident, can cause the casualty to cease breathing, and shortly afterwards the heart may stop. The most important technique in this situation is that of Cardio Pulmonary Resuscitation (CPR), and this is taught and examined in the Society's Resuscitation Certificates.

If you are interested in becoming involved in any area of the Society's work, please contact:

The Royal Life Saving Society UK, Mountbatten House, Studley, Warwickshire B80 7NN. Tel: (052785) 3943.

Extracts from Laws of the Sport

Constitutional Laws

2. Objects
The objects of the ASA shall be to: Promote the teaching and practice of swimming, diving, synchronised swimming and water polo, and stimulate public opinion in favour of providing proper accommodation and facilities for them: Draw up, publish and enforce uniform laws for the control and regulation of amateur swimming, diving, synchronised swimming and water polo championships and competitions in England, and deal with any infringement thereof.

3. Membership
The ASA shall comprise the following members: Honorary members, members of clubs which are affiliated to Districts, members of bodies directly affiliated to the ASA and members of associate bodies.

5. Affiliation
Each District shall comprise:

Clubs – The affiliated clubs whose headquarters are situated within the District's boundaries. A club which is a member of a body directly affiliated to the ASA shall not be regarded as an affiliated club for competition purposes unless it is also directly affiliated to a District.

Except with the agreement of both Districts concerned and the approval of the ASA Committee, a club may affiliate only to the District in which its headquarters are situated.

Local Associations – A Local Association is an association of clubs all of which are affiliated to a District and whose headquarters are within an area defined by the District.

Each club and each individual member comprising a Local Association shall count as a unit for affiliation purposes.

Private Associations – A Private Association is an affiliated association, the individual member clubs of which may or may not be affiliated to a District. Clubs which are not directly affiliated to a District are not regarded as affiliated clubs for competition purposes.

A Private Association may affiliate to the District in which the majority of its clubs operate or that in which its headquarters are situated.

When the scope of its activities make affiliation to a District inappropriate a Private Association may apply to affiliate direct to the ASA at a fee to be fixed by the ASA Committee at its first meeting in each year. The fee, which shall be due on March 31st, shall be shared equally among the five Districts.

Schools Swimming Association – An Association which consists solely of schools shall be eligible to affiliate without fee to the District in which the majority of its units are situated. An association so affiliated shall not be entitled to a delegate to the Council of the District but shall become entitled if the fee prescribed by the District is paid. In all other respects a Schools Swimming Association shall be regarded as a Private Association.

6. Special Affiliations
The following Associations shall be eligible to affiliate direct to the ASA at a fee to be fixed by the ASA Committee at its first meeting in each year. The fee which shall be due on March 31st shall be shared equally among the five Districts.

Royal Navy ASA, Army Swimming Union, Royal Air Force SA, English Schools SA, British Students Sports Federation, British Swimming Coaches Association, Royal Life Saving Society.

Upon affiliation the above organisations shall be entitled to one representative on the ASA Council.

A Club whose headquarters are overseas and whose members have British citizenship shall be eligible to affiliate direct to the ASA Committee at its first meeting in each year.

Such affiliation shall not confer the normal rights and privileges of an affiliated club.

7. Honorary Membership
On a proposal of the ASA Committee, the ASA Council may grant honorary membership of the ASA to persons who have given distinguished service to the Association.

8. ASA Certificate
The certificate of the Association shall be presented to: The retiring President of the ASA, a retiring member of the ASA Committee, provided that no person may receive more than one such certificate, an individual on the recommendation of the ASA Committee in recognition of a special performance or service rendered to the Association, an individual as provided for in the championship conditions. The Certificate shall not be issued for any other purpose unless authorised by the ASA Council or Committee.

11. Government
The following shall be members of the Council of the ASA: The President, Life Presidents and Past Presidents of the ASA (A Past President of the ASA may be removed from membership of the Council on a resolution passed by four fifths of the members of the Council); the Hon. Treasurer, the Hon. Legal Adviser and the Hon. Medical Adviser; the President, the Hon. Secretary and the Hon. Treasurer of each District; the nominee for the office of President of the ASA; District representatives elected in the ratio of one for every sixty paid affiliated clubs or fraction thereof greater than one half. Every representative shall be either a Past President of a District or a delegate entitled to represent a club at meetings of the District, and shall be

elected at the Annual General Meeting of the District, which shall be held in the month of January in each year; a representative of each of such of the following organisations as may be affiliated: The Royal Navy Amateur Swimming Association, the Army Swimming Union, the Royal Air Force Swimming Association, the English Schools' Swimming Association, The British Students Sports Federation, the British Swimming Coaches Association and the Royal Life Saving Society; a representative of the following Associate body: The Institute of Swimming Teachers and Coaches Ltd.

13. Special Meetings

A Special meeting of the Council shall be summoned: If a resolution to that effect is passed by the Council at the Annual Council Meeting, or on the receipt by the Secretary of a written request from at least three Districts stating the reason for such meeting, or at the request of two-thirds of the ASA Committee.

A special or adjourned meeting of the Council shall be held in the same District as that in which the preceding Annual Council Meeting was held. Unless otherwise directed by the Council a special meeting shall be held within twenty-eight days of the passing of the resolution or receipt of the request.

14. Notice of Meetings

The Secretary shall notify all those entitled to attend a Council Meeting, stating where and when it will be held. The District Hon. Secretary shall send a copy of the agenda paper to the District representatives at least ten days before the meeting.

A summons for an adjourned meeting of the Council shall be sent out so that those entitled to attend shall receive seven clear days' notice. It shall not be necessary to circulate an agenda.

15. Officers

The Council shall, at its Annual Council Meeting, elect the following Officers: President (who shall be nominated by the Districts in the following rotation: South, North, Midlands, South, West and North East); Hon. Treasurer, Hon. Legal Adviser and Hon. Medical Adviser. These, together with the Secretary of the Association, shall be the Officers and shall be indemnified against risk and expense out of the property of the ASA for acts and things done by them in the normal performance of their duties as Officers or servants of the ASA but not further or otherwise.

The Council shall at its Annual Meeting appoint Auditors, alternatively Council may delegate the appointment to the ASA Committee.

16. Life Presidents

The Council may elect, on nominations received from the ASA Committee, one or more Life Presidents in order to recognise meritorious service in the Association, provided that the total number of Life Presidents does not exceed five.

17. District Representatives

The number of representatives to which a District shall be entitled shall be determined by the number of club affiliation fees shown as received in its financial statement, made up to the 30th September prior to the Annual Council Meeting of the ASA. Arrears of affiliation fees paid for previous years and shown in the District financial statement shall be included for this purpose.

In the event of a representative or officer of any District being unable to attend, a substitute, who shall also be a member of the Council of the District, may be appointed.

No substitute may be appointed for a Past President of the ASA but when the President and/or nominee for the President are officers of their Districts they may be substituted.

18. Annual Report and Agenda

The ASA year shall end on 30th September.

The agenda of the Annual Council Meeting and audited financial statement for the year last past, together with the report of the ASA Committee, which shall include a list of its rulings and recommendations, shall be forwarded to the Hon. Secretary of each District and directly affiliated body not later than the 4th January.

The report shall be forwarded by each District, together with its own annual report and financial statement, to the Hon. Secretaries of all affiliated clubs and all other members of the District Council at least ten days before its Annual General Meeting.

37. Technical Committees

Committee Hon. Secretaries shall notify all those entitled to attend meetings giving at least seven days notice, stating where and when they will be held and sending the relevant papers and agenda.

Except for committees created under laws 31 and 35.18, the President, Hon. Treasurer and Secretary shall be ex-officio members of all committees, but the secretary shall have no power to vote.

38. Diving Committee

May consist of eight members, four to form a quorum. Each District shall have its nominated representative. Specialist members to a maximum of three may be appointed by the ASA Committee at its first meeting. Nominations may be submitted by the Districts. If any District representative is unable to attend a meeting the District concerned may appoint a substitute.

In addition, a National Development Officer shall serve on this Committee, and the Institute of Swimming Teachers and Coaches Ltd also may nominate one representative to serve in an advisory capacity, both without power to vote.

The duties of the Committee shall be to: Appoint from among themselves at their first meeting, a Chairman and Hon. Secretary; advise the ASA Committee on all matters relating to diving and submit recommendations concerning facilities and equipment; appoint all officials for ASA Diving Championships and submit to the ASA Committee nominations for international appointments; conduct training courses; compile the ASA list of diving officials; deal with all matters relating to the ASA Teachers Certificate for Diving, including the compilation of a panel of Examiners therefore; advise the ASA Committee on the selection of divers to represent England in international events, and if authorised, make such selections; produce a manual on diving. The Committee may co-opt for this purpose.

39. Education Committee
May consist of twelve members, seven to form a quorum. Each District shall have its nominated representative. Specialist members to a maximum of seven may be appointed by the ASA Committee at their first meeting. Nominations may be submitted by the Districts.

In addition, the Education Officer shall serve on this Committee, and the Institute of Swimming Teachers and Coaches Ltd also may nominate one representative, both without power to vote.

The duties of the Committee shall be to: Appoint from among themselves at their first meeting, a Chairman and Hon. Secretary; produce swimming publications, books, films, film strips and loops and other educational matter published in the name of the Association; deal with all matters relating to the following ASA teaching awards for swimming: Club Instructors Certificate, Preliminary Teaching Certificate, Teachers Certificate, Advanced Teachers Certificate, Preliminary Teachers, Teachers and Advanced Teachers Certificates for the Disabled; compile the ASA list of Moderators, Tutors and Senior Tutors for swimming; conduct training courses for teachers; deal with any other educational swimming matter referred to it by the ASA Committee.

41. Masters Committee
May consist of eight members, four to form a quorum. Each District shall have its nominated representative. Specialist members to a maximum of three may be appointed by the ASA Committee at its first meeting. Nominations may be submitted by the Districts. If any District representative is unable to attend a meeting the District concerned may appoint a substitute.

In addition, a National Development Officer may serve on this Committee, and the Institute of Swimming Teachers and Coaches Ltd also may nominate one representative to serve in an advisory capacity, both without power to vote.

The duties of the Committee shall be to: Appoint from among themselves at the first meeting a Chairman and Hon. Secretary; advise the ASA Committee on all matters relating to Masters swimming and submit recommendations for methods for improving the standard of Masters swimming; appoint a committee of management for the ASA National Masters Swimming Championships; give advice on all Masters Swimming Championships; deal with such matters as may be decided from time to time by the ASA Committee.

42. Medical Advisory Committee
May be appointed by the ASA Committee each year. It shall comprise not less than 10 medical practitioners, four to form a quoram, including the ASA Medical Adviser and the Medical Advisors of each of the Districts. Its functions shall be to: Appoint from among themselves at the first meeting a Chairman and Hon. Secretary; to consider any case in which a prohibited substance has been found in a body fluid of a competitor and to advise the Chairman of the NJT whether or not there are any extenuating circumstances. Also to advise the ASA Committee on any matter relating to the use and misuse of drugs which may be referred to it.

43. Public Relations Committee
May consist of not more than six members, three to form a quorum. Each District shall have its nominated representative, and one specialist member may be appointed by the ASA Committee. Nominations may be submitted by the Districts. If a District representative is unable to attend a meeting the District concerned may appoint a substitute.

The Committee shall: Appoint from among themselves at the first meeting, a Chairman and Hon. Secretary who shall be styled Public Relations Officer; advise the ASA Committee on all matters with regard to public relations; publish an annual diary of events; organise and conduct such exhibitions, displays and campaigns on a national basis as may be required by the ASA Committee.

44. Scientific Advisory Committee
May consist of such persons as may be appointed by the ASA Committee at its first meeting in each year.

The duties of the Committee shall be to: Appoint from among themselves at the first meeting, a Chairman and Hon. Secretary; collect, sort and distribute scientific information relating to swimming training, initiate and control scientific experiments; act in an advisory capacity to the ASA Committee in scientific matters.

45. Selection Committee
May consist of five persons, one from each District, whose sole function shall be to select swimmers to represent England in international matches.

46. Swimming Committee
May consist of eight members, four to form a quorum. Each District shall have its nominated representative. Specialist members to a maximum of three may be appointed by the ASA Committee at its first meeting. Nominations may be submitted by the Districts. If any District representative is unable to attend a meeting, the District concerned may appoint a substitute.

In addition, a National Development Officer may serve on this Committee, and the Institute of Swimming

Teachers and Coaches Ltd also may nominate one representative to serve in an advisory capacity, both without power to vote.

The duties of the Committee shall be to: Appoint from among themselves at the first meeting, a Chairman and Hon. Secretary; advise the ASA Committee on all matters relating to swimming and submit recommendations for methods for improving the standard of swimming; conduct courses for swimmers and coaches; compile the ASA list of swimming officials; appoint a Committee of Management for the ASA National Swimming Championships and Age Group Competitions; give advice on all Age Group Competitions; recommend the appointment of team officials for interational and other representative fixtures; appoint a sub-committee of six, of whom one shall be a representative nominated by the Institute of Swimming Teachers and Coaches Ltd, to be responsible for all coaching affairs, and to: draw up syllabuses for the ASA Swimming Coaches Certificate and the ASA Club Coaches Certificate examinations; appoint examiners, and conduct the examinations of coaches for these certificates; deal with any other matters concerning swimming coaching which may be referred to them by the ASA Committee; appoint a committee to be responsible for swimming officials on a national basis. The committee shall comprise a secretary who shall be appointed from nominations submitted by the Districts and one nominated representative of each of the Districts and the Combined Services. The Committee shall: Draw up syllabuses for the Swimming Officials theory and practical examinations; arrange for the preparation and marking of the written examination papers and for overall superintendence of the practical examinations; deal with any other matters concerning the appointment of swimming officials which may be referred to it by the ASA Committee.

47. Swimming Facilities Committee

May consist of eight persons, four to form a quorum. Each District shall have its nominated representative. Specialist members to a maximum of three may be appointed by the ASA Committee at its first meeting. Nominations may be submitted by the Districts. If any District representative is unable to attend, the District concerned may appoint a substitute.

The duties of the Committee shall be to: Appoint from among themselves at the first meeting, a Chairman and Hon. Secretary; implement the Objects of ASA Law 2.2. Stimulate public opinion in favour of providing proper accommodation and facilities; obtain wherever possible suitable facilities for the training of our competitive swimmers; maintain active liaison with The Sports Council and the Regional Sports Councils; disseminate technical information and propaganda.

48. Synchronised Swimming Committee

May consist of eight members, four to form a quorum. Each District shall have its nominated representative. Specialist members to a maximum of three may be appointed by the ASA Committee at its first meeting. Nominations may be submitted by the Districts. If any District representative is unable to attend a meeting the District concerned may appoint a substitute.

In addition, a National Development Officer may serve on this Committee, and the institute of Swimming Teachers and Coaches Ltd, also may nominate one representative to serve in an advisory capacity, both without power to vote.

The duties of the Committee shall be to: Appoint from among themselves at the first meeting, a Chairman and Hon. Secretary; advise the ASA Committee on how best to encourage synchronised swimming as a recreational pursuit, and on the technique to be adopted for this type of swimming, particularly for beginners; conduct training courses; produce a manual of Synchronised Swimming.

49. Water Polo Committee

May consist of eight members, four to form a quorum. Each District shall have its nominated representative. Specialist members to a maximum of three may be appointed by the ASA Committee at its first meeting. Nominations may be submitted by the Districts. If any District representative is unable to attend a meeting, the District concerned may appoint a substitute.

In addition, a National Development Officer shall serve on the Committee, without power to vote.

The duties of the Committee shall be to: Appoint from among themselves at the first meeting a Chairman and Hon. Secretary; supervise the work of the Referees and Rules Committee, the Women's Water Polo Committee and the National Water Polo Coaches Association, all as described hereafter, advise the ASA Committee on all matters relating to water polo and submit recommendations for improving the standard of water polo; conduct training courses; compile the ASA list of water polo referees; appoint officials, as required, for ASA championship matches, and submit similar nominations to the ASA Committee for international appointments; select water polo teams to represent England in international matches; appoint a Referees and Rules Committee of six members of whom one shall be nominated by the Water Polo Committee and one by each District. In the event of a District representative being unable to attend a meeting, a substitute may be appointed. Each member must be or have been a Referee recognised by a County or District Association. This Committee shall elect its own Chairman and Secretary.

The duties of this Committee shall be to: Establish and improve the standards of refereeing throughout the ASA by: Conducting an examination for referees; maintaining a standard system of grading of referees; issuing and disseminating interpretations and rulings in cases which the meaning or application of the Rules of Water Polo causes difficulty; issuing a code of practice for use by Referees; establish and maintain a register of qualified Referees; recommend Referees for the FINA and LEN Lists; recommend proposals for amending the Rules of Water Polo; arrange an Annual Conference of Water Polo Referees; prepare an Annual Report; appoint a Women's Water Polo Committee of six members one of whom shall be nominated by the Water Polo Committee and the remaining five members shall be from nominations received from affiliated clubs. The Committee shall elect its own Chairman and Secretary.

The duties of this Committee shall be to: Conduct the Women's Water Polo Championships; advise the Water Polo Committee on all matters relating to Women's Water Polo and submit recommendations for improving the standard of play; deal with any matters relating to Women's Water Polo delegated by the Water Polo Committee; prepare an Annual Report; supervise the work of the National Water Polo Coaches Association, whose objects are to establish and improve standards of Water Polo coaching nationally by: Developing a grading system for coaches; producing an examination syllabus incorporating the latest coaching techniques available, in conjunction with ASA; producing a coaching manual to include coaching techniques required for examination candidates and advice on improving the general standard of coaching; establishing a list of qualified coaches, the staffing and promotion of coaching courses for coaches and would be coaches at all levels; managing the Water Polo Coaches Certificate Examinations; liaising with other bodies to provide up-to-date information on rule changes, tactical innovations and new coaching techniques; organising an Annual Conference for Water Polo coaches; preparing an Annual Report.

Advertising
53. Advertising at Events Promoted by the ASA

Technical Equipment, Costumes – it is not permitted to wear any visible item in the form of advertising other than the trademark of the manufacturer not exceeding 16 sq cm in area.

Hats – may carry two advertisements, including that of manufacturer. These may up to 16 sq cm in area each and may be two of manufacturer, or one of manufacturer and one of commercial sponsor.

Poolside Equipment Towels and bags – may carry two advertisements as for hats above, up to 600 sq cm each in size, but letters may not exceed 10 cm in height, and the actual name of manufacturer or commercial sponsor may not exceed 50 sq cm: Towels and bags supplied before 1st January, 1989 are exempt from this ruling.

Tracksuits and Officials' Uniforms – may carry two advertisements on the top and two on the trousers or skirt as for hats, and may not exceed 16 sq cm, each in area. The logo of the manufacturer or commercial sponsor may be repeated as well but the same name may be used only once on each article of clothing.

Body Advertisement is not allowed in any way whatsoever.

General. No slogans may be used in advertising, nor names of products involving tobacco or alcohol. In all cases of doubt, advertisements should be submitted to the Secretary of the ASA for approval.

Referees at events organised under ASA Laws shall control advertising.

General Competition Laws
101. Eligibility

A competitor is eligible to compete in competitions unless he has competitive swimming as his sole occupation or business on which he is financially dependent for living.

Any competitor eligible to compete shall be registered with the ASA in accordance with Law 110.

An eligible competitor shall not compete against a person ineligible to compete except in Masters competitions, lifesaving competitions approved by the ASA, or when in the Services, and then only in Inter-Service competitions. Breach of this Law should be dealt with under the Judicial Laws.

102. Swimming and Trust Funds

Any financial advantage accruing to a swimmer from his athletic fame or competitive results shall be paid into a swimming fund, or legally established trust fund, administered by the Hon. Treasurer of the ASA who will also pay all legitimate claims from the fund.

103. Club Members

The competing members of any club wishing to affiliate to a District must be eligible to compete as defined in Law 101.1 except for those members competing in Masters competitions, and every affiliated club shall have a published rule to that effect.

104. Reinstatement

A person who is ineligible to compete may apply at any time to the District to which his club is affiliated, to be reinstated as an eligible competitor. The District may grant the application if it is satisfied that he complies with Law 101.1 and has not claimed the balance of his swimming or trust fund.

105. Competitions under ASA Laws

All galas, contests and exhibitions held or sponsored by an affiliated body shall be held under ASA Laws.

All advertisements, entry forms, programmes, tickets and official notices shall include the following words: 'Affiliated to the . . . (District) . . . Counties ASA, Under ASA Laws.'

106. Permits

An unaffiliated body or a person wishing to sponsor a gala, contest or exhibition under ASA Laws must obtain a permit from the District Hon. Secretary.

Application for the permit must be made on the official form and must be received by the District Hon. Secretary at least twenty-eight days before the event, accompanied by a fee of £10 or such similar sum as the District may decide.

The application must state: The date, time and place of the meeting or event; full details of all events on the programme; the guaranteed value of each prize; the amount of entry fee for each event, the entry fee must include admission, the date for the closing of entries; an undertaking to comply with ASA Laws; if the meeting includes an open handicap event the name of the official handicapper. A permit may be refused without a reason being stated. Any gala, contest or exhibition for which a permit has been issued shall be held under ASA Laws and all advertisements, entry forms, programmes, tickets and official notices shall include the following words: 'By permit of the . . . (District) . . . Counties ASA, Under ASA Laws.'

The permit shall be signed by the District Hon. Secretary and be available for inspection at the gala, contest or exhibition for which it was granted. A report of all permits issued or refused shall be made to the next meeting of the District Executive.

A permit shall not be granted: To a suspended person; to an individual, except where the meeting is in aid of a stated charity approved by the District, in which case a copy of the financial statement, duly audited, must be sent to the District Hon. Secretary within one month of the date of the meeting; to a club eligible for affiliation which has previously been granted a permit; for a competition, contest or exhibition to be held in a place of public entertainment such as a theatre, music hall, circus, variety exhibition or any other form of mixed entertainment.

107. Galas held in another District

An affiliated body wishing to hold a gala, contest or exhibition outside the District to which it is affiliated shall obtain permission of its District and of the District in which the event is to be held.

108. Gala Advertisements

A District Hon. Secretary may require the withdrawal of an advertisement which, in his opinion, is misleading or incorrect. He shall report such action to the next meeting of the District Executive.

A participant in a gala, contest or exhibition shall not be advertised under a misleading or incorrect title. The word 'champion' may only be used provided the championship title is also quoted, and the championship is one recognised by the ASA.

109. Right to Participate

Any competitor may join as many clubs as he wishes, but he is allowed to represent only one at a time.

No club shall prevent a member from belonging to another club or competing for another club. No person or club may promote or take part in an open competition which has a condition preventing a swimmer from competing because he is a member of more than one club.

Any competitor who temporarily or permanently changes his residence to another country may join a club affiliated to the respective Member in the new country.

Any competitor who wishes to represent a club in another country must make a written declaration of his intention to his former club and to the new club. The right to represent the new club may be allowed after a minimum of one month following the request.

111. Open Competitions

An open competition is a competition to which entry is not limited to members of any one club. A promoter may, however, impose other restrictions on entry. An inter-club contest is not regarded as an open competition if: It involves not more than eight clubs, each of which has been individually invited by the promoter who has supplied the conditions, and the whole event takes place in one pool on one occasion, and the contest does not form part of a series of such events, the results of which are aggregated or considered together to decide the eventual winner, e.g. as in a league competition.

The promoter of an open competition may, at his discretion, refuse to accept any entry. If he does so he must, if requested by the entrant, give the reasons for his refusal in writing. An entry, having been accepted, may be returned at any time if it is found that the information given on the entry form is incorrect in a material particular.

Entrants to an open competition shall complete an **entry form** which must contain at least the following information:

For **individual events** the entrants must register name and registration number. A declaration that he is an eligible competitor, unless the event is a Masters event open also to ineligible competitors. A declaration that he accepts the promoter's conditions. The name of an affiliated club of which he is a member in the name of which he wishes to compete and which has been included on his registration form.

For **team events** the name of the team. A declaration by the team manager that: (a) All the members from whom his team is to be selected are registered, and eligible to be members of the team, (b) he accepts on behalf of the team the promoter's conditions, (c) all members of his team comply with any age conditions. A declaration signed by the team manager that the information given is correct.

If the entry form does not state the **promoter's conditions**, they shall be made available by the promoter on request.

Incomplete or Inaccurate Information. If the information required is not given fully or is found to be materially incorrect, the entry shall be void and the entry fee forfeited unless the information is completed or fully corrected by the closing date for entries.

Competitors. An entrant is regarded as a competitor in an event as soon as his entry has been accepted. He ceases to be a competitor if his entry is returned or he withdraws before the event is started.

Unregistered Swimmers in Open Team Competitions. If, between the submission of an entry for an open team competition and the start of the competition, a team manager finds that, because of withdrawals of swimmers originally selected, he has insufficient registered members to complete his team, he may include unregistered members provided that: They are otherwise eligible to compete, the promoter and the referee are informed before the contest starts and given the names of the unregistered swimmers, the team manager ensures that they are registered within 14 days. Such swimmers shall be permitted to swim in only one gala before being registered, but may be allowed to swim in up to 3 rounds of one competition without the production of his registration card. The promoter shall notify the Registrar of the names and clubs of the swimmers.

Exemptions from Registration. Open competitions under ASA Laws which are promoted by any one of the following affiliated private associations and restricted to its own members shall be exempt from the requirement for the swimmers to be registered: The three Service Associations separately or in combination, The English Schools SA, its Divisions and area Associations, British Students Sports Federation, Air Training Corps, Army Cadet Force Association, The Boys' Brigade, British Blind Sport, The British Deaf Sports Council, British Long Distance Swimming Association, The British Polytechnics Sports Association, British Rail, British Sports Association for the Disabled, The Church Lads' and Church Girls' Brigade, The Civil Service SA, The Fire Service Sports and Athletic Association, The Girl Guides Association, The Independent Schools Association, Modern Pentathlon Association of Great Britain, Police Athletic Association, Scout Association, Sea Cadet Corps.

District Associations may grant exemptions from registration to affiliated private associations connected with bodies not mainly concerned with swimming.

116. Championships

The word 'Championship' shall be used only in connection with the championships of the ASA, a District Association, a County Association, or one of the bodies directly affiliated to the ASA. It may also be used in connection with the name of a locality, to which area entries to the championship shall be confined.

A club may promote a championship confined to its own members, and it may promote an open championship, in which case the title shall be qualified by the addition of a local name. The District shall decide the title and rules governing a local championship.

117. Mixed Competitions

With the following exceptions, a contest between the sexes shall not take place in public: A team race or team diving contest in which each team consists of the same number of each sex as each other team, a school contest confined to school children under the age of sixteen years.

118. Masters Competitions

Competitions held under ASA Laws where competitors are required to be 25 years and over on the day of the competition shall be designated as Masters Competitions. Persons who are not eligible to compete under Law 101 who are members of affiliated clubs may compete if the promoter's rules so provide. They shall be subject to the same rules and conditions as the eligible competitors.

Where Masters competitions are held concurrently with other championships and competitions, swimmers under the age of 25 years must not compete with or be seeded with Masters competitors.

119. Underwater Competitions/Exhibitions

No underwater competition or exhibition shall take place at any event promoted under ASA Laws unless such is undertaken by an approved Sub-Aqua organisation which will be responsible for carrying out the necessary safeguards.

Where there are underwater movements in a swimming, diving, water polo or synchronised swimming event these do not constitute an underwater competition but the competitors shall at all times be within the view of the officials.

120. Competitions by Children

A child under the age of nine as on 31st December in the year of competition shall not take part in any open event held under ASA Laws (see also Law 313).

121. Costumes

The costumes of all competitors shall be in good moral taste and suitable for the individual sports discipline. All costumes shall be non-transparent.

The referee of a competition has the authority to exclude any competitor whose costume does not comply with this rule.

122. Smoking Ban

At all events promoted by the ASA smoking shall not be permitted in any area designated for competitors, either prior to or during competitions.

123. Banned Drugs

A competitor in an event under ASA Laws shall not use any drug or other substance which is on the FINA List of Banned Subtances in force at the time of the competition.

It shall be an offence for any person other than a medical practitioner treating him to aid, abet, or incite a competitor to use a banned substance. Offenders shall be reported to the Chairman of the NJT.

A copy of the current FINA List of Banned Substances shall be available to each competitor in any competition where drug testing is to be carried out.

127. Prizes

All prizes for an open competition shall be purchased before the competition is held, and shall be of full advertised value. A competitor, being of opinion that his prize is not of the full advertised value, may protest to the referee of the competition, as provided in Law 208.

International Events and Qualification
131. International Competitions

Are those in which the teams taking part have been selected by the governing bodies of the sport in the countries which they represent.

They shall be held under the Laws of the Federation Internationale de Natation Amateur (FINA).

132. English Qualification

A team may only be designated as an English team and represent England if it has been selected by and managed by the ASA.

Anyone wishing to swim for England shall be an individual of British nationality and born in England, or born of English parents, or a naturalised British citizen who shall have lived continuously in England for at least one year.

If a competitor has represented England it is to be considered that he has chosen an English qualification and he will be under the control of the ASA and cannot represent another country until he officially changes his national qualification.

A competitor wishing to change his national qualification from one national governing body to the ASA shall have lived continuously in England and been under the jurisdiction of the ASA for at least one year and may thereafter apply to the Secretary of the ASA for a change of his national qualification.

A member of an affiliated club may join a club affiliated to another FINA member. When competing in the competitions of the foreign club he shall be under the jurisdiction of that club and its national association.

A competitor who has two nationalities according to the laws of the respective nations shall, for the purpose of international competition, choose one national qualification and be under the control of the governing body of the chosen country.

A body affiliated to the ASA under Law 5 shall not also be affiliated to any other members of FINA.

133. Foreign Tours

Only members of the ASA, as defined in Law 3, who are registered with the ASA may compete in any competitions in a country outside Great Britain which is a member of FINA. The laws of the FINA member under which the competition is held shall apply.

Notice of all tours abroad shall be given to the Secretary of the ASA at least 1 month before the tour starts giving full details of the itinerary and the names and registration numbers of those likely to take part.

Additional swimmers may also be included in the tour providing their names and registration numbers are given to the Secretary of the ASA prior to departure.

All such teams or individual swimmers or officials shall remain within the jurisdiction of the ASA during the period of time from their departure from until their return to England. Any team, individual swimmer, or official alleged to have been guilty of misbehaviour or unfair practice during such period, shall, within 30 days of such return, be reported to the Secretary of the ASA, who shall bring the report to the notice of the ASA Committee. In such cases that Committee shall have all the powers vested in a District Judicial Tribunal.

The Secretary of the ASA, having established that the arrangements are in order shall issue a permit.

134. Visits and Tours of Swimmers from outside Great Britain

Clubs or individuals arranging for the visits of swimmers from outside Great Britain shall submit particulars of the proposed arrangements to the Secretary of the ASA before such arrangements are definitely concluded, and he in turn shall furnish such information to the District Association of the Club or clubs concerned. The information required is: The name of the club promoting and responsible for the visit, an assurance that the visit has been approved by the National Association to which the visiting club is affiliated, the financial arrangements, a certificate from the National Association that all competing members of a visiting team are eligible, any other information requested by the Secretary of the ASA.

In the case of a water-polo match, the ASA Water Polo Committee shall appoint the referee at the expense of the promoter unless a referee from a country not concerned is agreed upon by the competing clubs.

135. Home International Representation

No swimmer shall ever represent more than one of the Home Countries except:

In the case of the Commonwealth Games where if a swimmer has dual qualification for the Commonwealth Games, or the qualification for his first international country has lapsed, he may be chosen for another country in these Games with the permission of the first international country.

If a swimmer has been resident in another Home Country for a minimum period of twelve months he may represent that country provided his first international country agrees.

Laws of Racing
301. Officials

A decision of the Referee on a question of fact shall be final, except in regard to placings where an agreed decision on placings by the placing judges shall be final.

Where the placing judges disagree, the decision of the Referee on the placings where they differ shall be final.

Where approved automatic judging and timing equipment, including any secondary system associated with it, is in use, the decision of the Referee on the correctness of its operation shall be final.

The Referee's application of ASA Laws and the promoter's conditions must be accepted at the time, but may be the subject of a protest.

Judges shall not act as timekeepers in the same event.

A professional may act as an official in any swimming contest under the ASA Laws, subject to those conditions governing the appointment of amateur officials.

For all open competitions there shall be: A Referee, a Starter, a Check Starter for handicap races.

Not less than two Placing Judges and such additional judges as may be necessary to bring to the notice of the referee any instance in which a swimmer fails to comply with ASA Laws or the promoter's conditions during a race.

Not less than two Turning Judges for each turning or take-over line other than the finishing line.

A Chief Timekeeper and at least one Timekeeper for each lane, except in a competition where times are not required for determining race results. Competitors Stewards, a Recorder.

302. Duties and Powers of Officials

The Referee shall: Give a decision in accordance with Law 303.2.5 when the placings of the judges are inconsistent with the timings recorded by the timekeepers. Give a decision where the appropriate officials fail to agree. In cases where the placing judges disagree, he shall give a decision on the placings that differ. Before each event, satisfy himself that all competitors and officials are in their places and aware that the event is about to start and signal to the starter when he so satisfied. Disqualify any competitor for any violation of the rules that he personally observes or which is reported to him by other authorised officials and inform the placing judges, after consultation with the officials concerned.

The Starter shall: In a minor competition, where authorised by the Referee, satisfy himself that the competitors are on their correct stations and are aware of what they have to do, have control of the competitors from the time they are handed over to him by the Referee until a valid start has been made. With the concurrence of the referee, disqualify competitors for delaying the start, for disobeying an order or for any other misconduct taking place at the start. Have power to decide whether the start is valid, subject only to the decision of the Referee. Have power to recall the competitors at any time after the signal to start has been given in accordance with Law 304.2.1.

The Check Starter shall: In a handicap event, disqualify any competitor who starts before his number is called unless he returns to his starting place on the side of the bath or in the water under his original station and starts afresh. He shall report such disqualification to the Referee.

The Chief Timekeeper shall: Before the commencement of the competition, arrange for a check on the accuracy of the watches to be used. Assign each timekeeper to the lane for which he will be responsible. If necessary, direct a reserve timekeeper to time the lane of a timekeeper whose watch fails to start, stops prematurely or who for any other reason is unable to record the time. Should there be no reserve timekeeper available, he should time the lane himself. Collect from each timekeeper the time recorded, record the official time for each lane and report it to the referee. Inspect the watches, if necessary, and after each event give a signal when the watches are to be reset.

A Timekeeper shall: Take the time of the competitor assigned to him by starting his watch when the starting signal is given and stopping it when his competitor has completed the course. After each race, and before consulting with any other timekeepers on his lane, record the time on his report card. Present his watch for inspection if requested. He shall not reset his watch until he receives the signal from the Chief Timekeeper. Wherever possible, for events of 400m or longer except for relays and medley events, record the number of laps completed by his competitor and keep him informed of the remaining laps to be completed by displaying for observation of the competitor at the finishing end of the pool, lap cards bearing numbers. Give a warning signal when his competitor has two lengths plus 5m to swim to the finish in events of 400m or longer except for relays or medley events. The warning signal may be pistol shot, whistle or bell.

The Placing Judges shall: Take up positions where, in all events and at all times, they have a clear view of the whole of the course and be in line with the finish when it is taking place. With the concurrence of the Referee, disqualify for fouling. Act as turning judges at the finishing line. After each event individually record and then decide the order of finishing and report it to the Referee.

The Turning Judges shall: Report to the Referee any competitor who, between the commencement of the last armstroke before touching for the turn or take over and the end of the first armstroke after the turn, fails to comply with the relevant ASA Laws. In Breaststroke events the Turning Judges shall be responsible for observing the competitor until his head has broken the surface of the water after the turn.

The Stroke Judges shall: Report to the Referee any competitor who fails to comply with ASA Law regarding the stroke conditions of the competition.

The Competitors Stewards shall: Wear a distinguishing badge. Be responsible for behaviour in the dressing rooms and report misbehaviour to the Referee. Be responsible, where necessary, for arranging the competitors into heats. Be responsible for ensuring that the competitors are on the correct stations prior to each event, (but see 302.2.1). Carry out any duties delegated by the Referee in respect of any entry card system in operation for that competition.

The Recorder shall: Record the places and times on a results sheet when the race results are handed to him. Extract the names of the swimmers for any swim-off or the final and arrange them in accordance with ASA Law. Arrange for the early announcement of the names of swimmers for any swim-off or the final so that they may be warned and, when this has been done, pass the list of names so announced to the other officials concerned.

303. Decision of the Times and Placings

When using **automatic judging and timing equipment** which is started by the starting signal and is stopped by the competitor at the end of the course.

Where approved automatic judging and timing equipment has been provided, it shall be used to determine the winner and placings and the times for each lane. The results and times so determined shall have precedence over the decisions of human judges and timekeepers provided the Referee is satisfied that it operated correctly. When the approved system incorporates a secondary recording system, which supports the primary system, and is started by the same starting equipment as the primary system but terminated by appointed timekeepers, the times recorded by the secondary system shall be deemed official times in the event of failure of the approved equipment.

Where there is any failure in whole, or in part of the approved equipment the following procedure shall be adopted: Record all available automatic times and places, record all human times and places.

The official time for all competitors having automatically recorded times shall be those times. The official times for all competitors not having automatically recorded times shall be the manually recorded times.

To determine the official place and time of a competitor in a race, the following procedure shall apply:

A competitor having an automatically recorded place must retain that place in relation to other competitors having automatically recorded places.

A competitor not having an automatically recorded place but having an automatically recorded time shall be given a place in the order of finishing by comparing that time with the automatically recorded times of the other competitors.

No automatically recorded order of finishing may be altered, except that all competitors having the same automatically recorded time shall be tied in the order of finishing.

A competitor having neither an automatically recorded place nor an automatically recorded time shall be given a place in the order of finishing in accordance with the human placings. He shall be given the manually recorded time, adjusted as necessary in accordance with Law 303.2.5, with a zero added in the second decimal place if necessary.

A competitor having an automatically recorded place but not having an automatically recorded time shall retain that place in the order of finishing. His time shall be determined by reference to his manually recorded time.

When approved automatic timing to 1/1000th of a second is used, the third decimal place shall not be recorded or used, all competitors making the same time by the operation of this law shall be considered tied.

When approved automatic timing to 1/100th of a second is used, the timings shall be as recorded.

When using **human Judges and Timekeepers**, crystal controlled handheld electronic timers are recognised for record purposes, provided that the crystal has an accuracy of thirty parts in a million or better. Timers with LED displays must be fitted with a means of checking the battery. Timers with the LCD type must have the battery renewed in a period of not exceeding twelve months irrespective of the type of battery used. Such electronic timers are not to be regarded as approved electronic timing apparatus, as referred to previously. They shall be read to 1/100th of a second when all the watches concerned are designated electronic timers. When they are used in conjunction with watches they shall be read to 1/10th of a second, and where there is a second decimal point other than a '0' ring the time shall be raised to the next highest 10th.

Where three timekeepers are used for a lane, if the times recorded by two timekeepers agree, that shall be the accepted time, but in cases where the times recorded by all three timekeepers disagree, that recorded by the middle watch shall be accepted.

Where two timekeepers are used for a lane, if the times recorded do not agree, then the slower of the times recorded shall be the accepted time.

Where one timekeeper only is used for a lane, then his recorded time shall be the accepted time.

If the times registered by the timekeepers do not agree with the decision of the placing judges, the times for the competitors concerned shall be added together and divided by the number of such competitors who shall be credited with that time, raised, if necessary to the nearest tenth or hundredth (as appropriate under paragraph 303.2.1) of a second slower. It is not permissable to announce times which do not support the classifications made to the placing judges.

Should a competitor be disqualified during or following an event, such disqualification shall be recorded in the official results but no time or place shall be recorded.

A disabled swimmer shall not be disqualified in a competition in a case where the disability prevents him from complying with the rules of a particular stroke.

304. Starting

Starts. Where the promoters decide and so publish in the rules of the competition and publicly announce at the event, the procedure detailed in Law 304.2.2 and 304.2.3, may be suspended in that a swimmer shall be disqualified for any false start as defined in Law 304.2.1.

The starter shall, when starting an event, take up a position on the side of the pool where the competitors can hear the starting signal and the timekeepers can see or hear it.

The Referee shall signal that the event is about to start by a series of short sharp blasts on his whistle. When he is satisfied that the competitors and the appropriate officials are ready, he shall give a single, long blast whereupon the competitors starting from the side of the pool shall take up their positions on the back of the starting block or a short pace back from the starting line and competitors starting in the water shall immediately enter the water and take up their positions for the start. The Referee shall then signal to the starter, by means of a raised hand, that he may proceed to start the race. In a minor competition where the Referee deems it expedient he may delegate his functions in relation to the start to the Starter.

On the preparatory command from the starter 'Take Your Marks', the competitors shall immediately take up a starting position either on the front of the starting blocks or line, or as required to conform to the relevant parts of ASA laws 307, 308, 309 and 310 and shall remain stationary until the starter gives the starting signal.

In a scratch race, the starting signal may be by shot, whistle, the word 'Go' or klaxon. In handicap races the starting signal shall be given by the word 'Go' followed by the counting of the seconds until all competitors in the race have started.

For deaf swimmers, the starter should make adequate provision after consultation with the competitors or their representatives.

False Starts in Scratch Races: If after the command 'take your marks', a swimmer leaves his starting place before or is moving when, the starting signal is given it shall be a false start.

In the event of a first or second false start: the starter shall call back the swimmers by repeating the starting signal, whereupon the false start rope shall be dropped. If the Referee decides that a start is false, although the Starter has decided that it was valid, he shall blow his whistle, whereupon the Starter shall repeat the starting signal.

After two false starts in a race the Starter shall warn the swimmers that at the third attempt the race will proceed, irrespective of further infringement, and any swimmer who is not stationary in his starting position when the starting signal is given will be disqualified by the Starter, whether or not he was a previous offender.

Wherever Practical A rope shall be provided to stop the swimmers in the event of a false start.

It shall be suspended across the pool from fixed stands 15m in front of the starting end, attached to the stands by a quick release mechanism.

If the rope is not operated automatically by the repetition of the starting signal it shall be released by a designated official in response to that signal.

305. Heats and Finals

When the number of competitors exceeds the number of lanes available, heats, any necessary swim off to resolve ties, and a final, shall be swum or alternatively results may be decided on heat time classification, without finals, if the conditions of the competition are so agreed and published. To be eligible for the final of an event, a competitor must have competed in the heats, if any.

Except with the consent of all the competitors affected, a heat or final shall not be started before the advertised time, if any, of starting, or the stipulated interval, if any, between rounds has elapsed.

When all events at a gala start at the same end of the pool, stations shall count from the right facing the course from the starting end. When the events at a gala do not all start from the same end of the pool but all events finish at the same end of the pool, stations shall count from the right facing the course from the finishing end.

Heats: *Scratch Races.* The promoter, at his option, shall arrange the programme order of the competitors by draw or by seeding on times given on the entry forms.

Handicap Races. The promoter shall arrange the competitors in handicap order, or in heats in handicap order, with the limit competitor (being the one who has the longest start) on the right facing the course.

Where heats are necessary the finalists shall be the competitors accomplishing the fastest times in the heats, subject where necessary to the concurrence of the judges as to placing in the heats. Where the number of finalists exceeds the number of available lanes by reason of a dead heat or equal time, unless the promoters conditions allow for a lesser number of finalists than there are lanes in the pool, all the competitors concerned in a dead heat or equal time shall swim off for the remaining lane(s).

In handicap races the qualifying time shall be the gross time of the competitor concerned.

Finals: *Scratch Races.* The stations of the competitors shall be decided on the spearhead system which provides that the competitor who qualified with the fastest time in the heats is stationed in the centre lane and the other competitors in the remaining lanes on the left and right alternately according to their respective times. If there is no centre lane the fastest qualifying competitor shall be placed in the lane immediately to the right of the centre of the course and the remaining competitors to the left and right according to their respective times.

Handicap Races. The competitors shall be placed in handicap order.

In the event of a dead heat in the final, the competitors may, with the consent of the Referee, divide the prize or prizes, or compete again at such time and place as he may direct.

Team Races: The rules relating to heats and finals shall apply to team events, except that swimmers may be freely interchanged for each round.

The team of a competitor whose feet, or hands in the case of a swimmer starting in the water, have lost touch with his starting place before his preceeding partner touches the end shall be disqualified, unless the competitor in default returns to his starting place at the wall. It shall not be necessary to remount the starting platform. Running takeovers are not permitted.

A swimmer in a team race shall not be permitted to swim more than one leg.

306. The Race

Swimming Over. When only one competitor reports for an event he shall, to qualify as the winner, complete the whole distance and comply with the laws governing style, turning and finishing.

Standing or Walking. A competitor may not walk during a race.

He may – in a Freestyle race only – stand for the purpose of resting.

Fouling. A foul is any action by a swimmer as a result of which another swimmer in the same event suffers an unfair disadvantage. Should a foul endanger the chance of success of a competitor, the Referee shall have power to allow him to compete in the final. Should a foul occur in a final,the Referee may order it to be re-swum. Should the foul be intentional the Referee shall report the matter to the Chairman of the DJT (Law 204). In all events when turning, a swimmer is not permitted to take a stride or step from the bottom of the pool nor may he leave the water. Where there are lane ropes, a swimmer must finish in the lane in which he started. A breaststroke swimmer shall not be disqualified if he submerges for not more than one stroke for the purpose of returning to his lane. Goggles may be worn. After completing the race a swimmer must remain in the water in his own lane until released by the Referee or other official authorised by him.

Illegal Pool Entry A non-competitor who, in the opinion of the Referee or a judge, deliberately enters the water while a race is in progress, except to go to the assistance of a swimmer in distress, shall be reported by the Referee to the Chairman of the DJT. Anyone whose deliberate action causes someone to enter the water involuntarily during a race shall be similarly reported.

A relay team shall be disqualified from a race if a member of the team enters the water while the race is in progress unless he does so for the purpose of starting his leg.

307. Freestyle

A competitor may start with a plunge or jump, or in the water holding the rail or side of the pool or other starting place. A competitor may swim any style or styles and rules relating specifically to Breaststroke, Butterfly, and Backstroke swimming shall not apply. In Freestyle turning and finishing the swimmer may touch the wall with any part of his body.

308. Breaststroke

A competitor may start with a plunge or jump, or in the water, facing the course, and holding the rail or side of the pool or other starting place, with both hands.

From the beginning of the first arm stroke after the start and after each turn the body shall be kept on the breast and the shoulders shall be in line with (parallel to) the water surface.

All movements of the hands and feet shall be simultaneous and in the same horizontal plane without alternating movement except at each turn and upon the finish of the race when the touch may be made with the hands at different levels.

Hands shall be pushed forward together from the breast, and shall be brought back on or under the surface of the water. Except at the start and at the turns, the hands shall not be brought back beyond the hip line.

In the leg kick the feet shall be turned outward in the backward movement. Up or down movements of the legs or feet in the vertical plane in the form or a 'dolphin' kick are not permitted.

At each turn and upon the finish of the race, the touch shall be made with both hands simultaneously, not necessarily at the same level, either at, above or below the water level. The shoulders shall remain in the horizontal plane.

During each complete cycle of one arm stroke and one leg kick, some part of the head of the swimmer shall break the surface of the water, except that after the start and after each turn the swimmer may take one arm stroke completely back to the legs and one leg kick while wholly submerged before returning to the surface.

FINA Interpretation of the Breaststroke Law After the start and after each turn, the swimmer is permitted as previously, to take one arm stroke completely back to the legs and return the arms to the original forward position, followed by one leg kick, while wholly submerged. The head must break the surface of the water during the first part of the second arm stroke, that is, before the hands begin to turn inward at the widest part of the second arm stroke.

During each cycle after the first, part of the swimmer's head must actually come out of the water, it is no longer sufficient for the head to remain above the level of the calm water surface, with the possibility of a wave covering the top of the head. It is important that part of the head actually be exposed directly to the air.

FINA Rule SW 7.3 now explicitly states that the hands may not come down beyond the hipline after the first armstroke at the completion of the start and each turn. This does not represent a drastic departure from the previous rule, but is merely intended to ensure that throughout the race the swimmer does not glide underwater with the arms flat or nearly flat against the side of the body, as is normal after the start and turns. The swimmer should get the benefit of any doubt relating to the position of the hipline.

Although the rule has not been changed, there has been inconsistent interpretation of SW 7.3 regarding the recovery portion of the armstroke. The hands must be pushed forward together from the breast on, under, or over the water. A butterfly-style recovery is not permissible.

At each turn and at the finish, the swimmer no longer must touch with his hands at the same level. However, the rule that the shoulders must remain in the horizontal plane has not changed. The head may now be submerged immediately prior to the turn or finish, so long as the head broke the surface of the water at some point during the last cycle preceding the turn or finish.

309. Butterfly

A competitor may start with a plunge or jump, or in the water, facing the course, and holding the rail, or side of the pool or other starting place, with both hands.

All movements of the hand shall be simultaneous. The arms shall be brought forward over the water and brought back on or under the surface.

The body shall be kept on the breast with the shoulders horizontal from the beginning of the first arm stroke after the start and after the turn.

All movements of the feet shall be executed in a simultaneous manner. Simultaneous up and down movements of the legs and feet in the vertical plane are permitted. The legs or feet need not be at the same level but no alternating movement is permitted.

At each turn and upon the finish of the race, the touch shall be made with both hands simultaneously, either at, above or below the water level. The shoulders shall remain in the horizontal plane.

At the start and at turns, a swimmer is permitted one or more leg kicks and one arm pull under the water, which shall bring him to the surface.

310. Backstroke

Competitors shall line up in the water facing the starting end with hands on the end, rail or starting grips. The feet, including the toes, shall be under the surface of the water. Standing in or on the gutter or bending the toes over the lip of the gutter is prohibited.

At the starting signal they shall push off and swim on their backs throughout the race, except during turns. The hands shall not be released before the starting signal has been given. While required to be on the back, the shoulders of the competitors shall not roll more than 90° from the horizontal.

When touching at the turn and at the finish, the touch shall be made by the head, shoulder, foremost hand or arm. The turn shall begin when the competitor correctly touches the end of the course and shall end when his feet lose contact with the end of the course at the push off.

Wherever possible backstroke turn indicators shall be provided by means of flagged ropes suspended across the pool 1.8m above the water surface from fixed supports or stands set 5m from each end wall of the pool.

Clarification of Turn: it is permissible to turn over beyond the vertical after the foremost part of the body has touched, for the purpose of executing the turn, but the swimmer shall have returned past the vertical to a position on his back before the feet have left the wall.

311. Medley Events

Shall consist of equal legs on four strokes in the following order: *Individual Medley* – Butterfly, Backstroke, Breaststroke, Freestyle. *Medley Relay* – Backstroke, Breaststroke, Butterfly, Free-style.

In Medley Events, Freestyle shall be any stroke other than Butterfly, Backstroke or Breaststroke.

ASA Calendar, 1989–90

Swimming

Major International Events
1990

Jan 25-30	Commonwealth Games	Auckland, New Zealand
Jul 26-29	European Junior Championships	Dunkirk, France
Jul 29-Aug 5	Goodwill Games	Seattle, USA
Aug 9-12	European Open Cup	Rome, Italy

FINA Swimming World Cup
1989

Nov 29-Dec 1	Montreal, Canada
Dec 3-5	Orlando, USA

1990

Jan 5-7	Perth, Australia
Feb 2-4	Paris, France
Feb 5-7	Berlin, GDR
Feb 9-11	Bonn, W Germany
Feb 13-14	Gothenburg, Sweden
Feb 16-18	Venice, Italy

International Open Meets — Overseas
1990

Jan 26-28	International Championships	Geneva, Switzerland
Mar 24-25	Grand Prix du Printemps	Brussels, Belgium
Apr 14-15	8 Nations Junior International	Vittel, France
Apr 14-15	7 Nations Youth International	W Germany
Apr 20-22	CIJ Meet Lux 90	Luxemburg
Apr 28-29	3 Nations Junior Meet	Gera, GDR
May 5-6	European Community Club Championships	Italy
May 7-8	Ulster Games	Belfast, N Ireland
May 19-20	Belgian Swim Cup	Brussels, Belgium
May 20	International Arena Sprint Cup	Heidelberg, W Germany
Jun 1-3	International Meet of Monte Carlo	Monte Carlo, Monaco
Jun 2-3	Turnier de Nations	Vienna, Austria
Jun 15-17	International de Canet	Canet en Roussillon, France
Jun 15-17	Swedish Swim Games	Falun, Sweden
Jun 22-24	Chiasso Meet	Chiasso, Switzerland
Nov 9-11	Elektroimpex Meet	Budapest, Hungary
Nov 16-18	Seven Hills Meet	Rome, Italy

International Open Meets — Home
1989

Nov 4	International Invitation Meet	Leighton Buzzard

1990

Apr 7-8	Spring Trophy (GB, Holland, Sweden, W Germany)	Coventry
Apr 14-16	Multi Nations Meet	Southend on Sea
Apr 14-16	Multi Nations Open	Portsmouth Northsea
Nov 3	International Invitation Meet	Leighton Buzzard

National Championships/Competitions
1990

Mar 10-11	GB Club Championships — Preliminary Rounds	Regional
Apr 13-14	GB Club Championships	Regional
Jun 15-17	Scottish ASA Open Championships	Edinburgh
Jul 20-22	Welsh National Championships	Cardiff
Jul 26-29	ASA National Championships	Crystal Palace
Jul 30-Aug 4	ASA National Age Group Competition	Leeds
Sep 9	Speedo League Final	Leeds
Oct 26-27	ESSA National Championships	Luton
Nov 3	Inter County Knockout — 1st Rounds	Regional
Nov 15-18	ASA Winter Championships	Coventry
Nov 24	Inter County Knockout — Final	Coventry

British Grand Prix
1989

Sep 29-Oct 1	Gloucester

Oct 20-22		Dundee
Nov 3-5		Cumbernauld
Dec 1-3		Barnet
1990		
Feb 23-25		Leicester
Mar 16-18		Southampton
May 26-28	Final	Leeds

District Events
1990

Mar 3	Inter Counties Championships	Coventry
Mar 12-13	Individual & Team Competitions	Midland District
Mar 19-20	Individual & Team Competitions	Midland District
Apr 7-8	Age Group Competitions	Scarborough
Apr 21	Inter County Age Group Competition	Crystal Palace
Apr 21-22	Age Group Competitions	Felling
May 5-6	Age Group Competitions	Gloucester
May 5-7	General Championships	Crystal Palace
May 12	Inter County Championships	Crystal Palace
May 12-13	Age Group Competitions	Newcastle
May 13	General Championships	Crystal Palace
May 19	Age Group Competitions	Bristol
May 19-20	General Championships	Crystal Palace
May 26-27	Inter Association Age Group Competition	Everton Park
May 26-28	General Championships	Crystal Palace
Jun 2-3	Inter Association Age Group Competition	Everton Park
Jun 9-10	Long Course Championships	Leeds
Jun 9-10	Championships & Age Group Championships	Wigan
Jun 16-17	Long Course Championships	Leeds
Jun 16-17	Championships & Age Group Championships	Wigan
Jun 23	Age Group Team Competitions	Keynsham
Jun 23-24	Long Course Championships & Junior Competitions	Coventry
Jun 30-Jul 1	Long Course Championships & Junior Competitions	Coventry
Sep 8	Teams Competition	Felling
Sep 15	Schools Competition	Midland District
Oct 6-7	Winter Championships	Wigan
Oct 20-21	Championships	Plymouth
Oct 20-21	Short Course Championships	Hull
Oct 20-21	Short Course Championships	Midland District

Other Open Meets
1989

Nov 11	Open Gala	E Grinstead
Nov 11	Graded Meet	Co Newcastle
Nov 11-12	Potential Champions	Manchester U Salford
Nov 12	"B" Grade Gala	Dudley Metro
Nov 12	Big "M" Meet	Rochdale Aquabears
Nov 18	Open Meet	Letchworth
Nov 18	Mini Open Sprint Meet	Thurrock
Nov 19	Open Meet	White Oak
Nov 19	Big "M" Meet	Rochdale Aquabears
Nov 25	Open Meet	Lewes
Nov 26	Sprints Gala	Barking
Nov	Aggregate Sprint Individual Medley	Romford T
Nov	400m Open Meet	N Devon
Nov	Junior Open	Stockton Aquatics
Nov	"B" Grade Gala	Piranha
Nov	Open Meet	Co Lincoln Pentaqua
Nov	Junior Open Meet	Ipswich
Dec 3	Fox's Inter Cities Gala	Co Leicester
Dec 9	Newburn Sprint Meet	Newburn
Dec 9	"B" Grade Open Meet	Sheffield C
Dec 9	Open "200" Meet	Stevenage
Dec 16	Open "200" Meet	Stevenage
Dec 16	Open Meet	Co Oxford
Dec 17	Shrimps Meet	Co Newcastle
Dec	Christmas Meet	Co Bradford
Dec - Feb 90	4×Distance Development Meets	Co Leeds

1990

Jan	5	York Graded Meet	York City Baths
Jan	6	Long Distance Gala	Nottingham
Jan	6-7	3rd Designated Open Age Group Competition	Luton
Jan	20-21	Annual Open Meet	Derby
Jan	20-22	Maxwell Open	Maxwell
Jan	21	Novices Sprint Meet	Billingham
Jan	21	Open Meet	Dudley Metro
Jan	27	Graded Age Groups — Part 1	Melton Mowbray
Jan	27-28	Northolt Swimerama	Forward Hillingdon
Jan	27-28	Gateshead Short Course Meet	Gateshead & Whickham
Jan	28	Open Sprint Meet	Nottingham Leander
Jan		Young Age Group Sprint Gala	Redbridge B
Jan		Age Group Open Meet	Brighton
Jan		New Year Open Meet	N Devon
Jan		200/400 Meet	Bo Kirklees
Jan		Graded Gala	Rotherham Metro
Feb	10-11	Age Group Open Meet	Piranha
Feb	11	Open Meet	Haden Hill
Feb	24	Graded Age Groups — Part 2	Melton Mowbray
Feb	24	"C" Grade Open Meet	Hart
Feb		Junior Open Meet	Bishop Auckland
Feb		"B" Grade Meet	Co Leeds
Feb		Open Meet	Co Newcastle
Feb		Age Group Distance Meet	Derwentside
Feb		Distance Meet	Harrogate D
Feb		"B" Grade Competition	Co Chester
Feb		Shrimps Gala	Colne
Feb		Open Meet	Wycombe
Feb	- Mar	Age Group Open Meet	Stockton Aquatics
Mar	3	"C" Grade Open Meet	Hart
Mar	4-11	Age Group "200" Meet	Broadway
Mar		Evesham Biathlon	Evesham Swimming & WPC
Apr	14-16	Open Meet	Co Milton Keynes
Apr	14-16	Open Meet	Rotherham Metro
Apr	14-16	Open Meet	Chase
Apr	14-16	Swim Festival	Yeovil
Apr	29	Open Meet	Nuneaton
Apr		Spring Meet	Rochdale Aquabears
Apr		Age Group Meet	Co Leeds
Apr		Graded Meet	Derwentside
Apr		DARTES Open	Doncaster DARTES
Apr		Jarvik Meet	York City Baths
Apr		Senior Open Meet	Walsall Swimming & WPC
Apr		Sprints Meet	Thornlow Tornadoes
May	5-6	Gateshead Junior Meet	Gateshead & Whickham
May	18	Spring Open Meet	Co Milton Keynes
May		Island Championships	Guernsey
May		Open Meet	Chase
May		Tuliptime Open Meet	S Lincs
May		Open Meet	Orion
Jun	2	Corne Motors Age Group Open Meet	Bo Southend
Jun	8-10	Annual Open Meet	Thurrock
Jun	mid	Age Group Open Meet	Orpington
Jun	17	100 Gala	Nottingham
Jun	23-24	Open Meet	Rushmoor Royals
Jun		Royal Mail Open Meet	Bristol Central
Jun		Sprint Meet	Thamesdown Tigersharks
Jun		"Last Chance" Age Group Open Meet	Barnet Copthall
Jun	30-Jul 1	Open Meet	Satellite
Jul	15	Open Biathlon	Dorking
Jul	21	M.A. Skinner Sprint Meet	Bo Southend
Jul		Open Meet	Derwentside
Jul		Open Meet	Pioneer '79
Jul		Midsummer Open Meet	Eckington
Aug	4	110th Birthday Fast Water Meet	Nottingham
Sep	1	Perpetual Trophy	Nottingham
Sep	16	Newburn Biathlon	Newburn

Sep 17	Biathlon	Dartford D
Sep 22	Autumn Open Age Sprint Meet	Bo Southend
Sep 30	Annual Open Meet	Co Oxford
Sep	Open Meet	Leamington Spa
Sep	Hay Trophy Gala	Leicester
Sep	Open Meet	Lincoln Vulcans
Sep	Open Meet	Rugby
Oct 6	Open Meet	Grimsby Santa Marina
Oct 12 or 19	Graded Open Meet	Hull Olympic
Oct 13-14	Open Meet	Darlington
Oct 14	Open Meet	Leicester Penguins
Oct 20	Open Meet	Grimsby Santa Marina
Oct 22	Staffs Moorlands Sprint Meet	Cheadle & D
Oct	"C" Grade Open Meet	South Wight
Nov 7	Mini Open Sprint Meet	Thurrock
Nov 10	PIP Open Sprint Meet	Bo Southend
Nov 18	Open Meet	White Oak
Nov	Open Meet	Co Lincoln Pentaqua
Dec 8	Newburn Sprint Meet	Newburn
Dec	Open Meet	Torquay Leander

Masters Swimming

Major International Events
1990

Aug 6-13	World Championships	Rio de Janeiro, Brazil

International Open Meets — Overseas
1990

Mar 31-Apr 1	Finnish Open Masters Championships	Pori, Finland
May 26-27	International Masters	Baja, Hungary
Jun 7-8	Scandinavian Open Masters	Espoo, Finland
Aug 31-Sep 2	International Masters	Vichy, France

International Open Meets — Home
1990

Apr 6-8	Welsh Masters	Cardiff

National Championships/Competitions
1990

Oct 19-21	ASA Masters	Barnet
Nov 2-4	GB Masters	Cardiff

District Events
1990

Feb 24-25	Masters Long Course	Crystal Palace
Oct 7		Tiverton

Other Open Meets
1989

Nov 19	Masters Open Meet	Brixham
Nov	Masters Competition	Co Chester
Nov	London Masters Open Meet	Spencers
1990		
Jan	Distance Open Meet	Co Liverpool
Mar 10	Masters Relay Gala	Sudbury & D
Mar 11	Masters Open Meet	Basingstoke D
Mar 17	Spring Masters	Stockport
Mar 29	Annual Masters Meet	Co Oxford
Nov 11	London Masters Open Meet	Spencers

Diving

Major International Events
1990

Jan 25-30	Commonwealth Games	Auckland, New Zealand
Jul 20-Aug 5	Goodwill Games	Seattle, USA

National Championships/Competitions
1990

	National Junior & Senior Championships	TBA

	National Age Group Competition, 3m	TBA
	National Junior & Senior Championships 1m/3m/10m	TBA
	National Age Group Competition 1m/5m	TBA

District Events
1990

Mar 10	3m Springboard "F"	Crystal Palace
Mar 17	Inter Counties Championships	Midland District
Mar 17	Highboard Championships	Midland District
Apr 7	Highboard "F" & Junior Championships	Crystal Palace
Apr 7	3m Springboard Championships & Age Group Comp	Midland District
Apr 8	Junior & Senior Highboard Championships	Wigan
Apr 14	Open 3m Springboard Competitions	Oldham
Jun 2	3m Springboard Age Group	Crystal Palace
Jun 2	Junior Springboard Championships	Oldham
Jun 9-10		Cheltenham
Sep 8	1m Age Group Competitions	Midland District
Sep 15	1m Springboard Junior Competitions	Crystal Palace
Sep 15	Senior Springboard Championships	Oldham
Sep 15-16		Poole
Sep 22	1m Springboard Age Groups	Crystal Palace
Sep 22	1m Springboard Championships	Sharston
Sep 29	1m Springboard Senior Competitions	Crystal Palace
Sep 29	1m Championships	Midland District
Oct 20	Highboard Age Groups	Crystal Palace
Nov 3	Age Group Competitions	Burnley

Synchronised Swimming

Major International Events
1990

Jan 25-30	Commonwealth Games	Auckland, New Zealand
Jul 20-Aug 5	Goodwill Games	Seattle, USA

International Meets — Home
1990

Aug 16-19	European Junior Championships	Leicester

National Championships/Competitions
1990

Mar 25	Inter District Competitions	Crystal Palace
Aug 4	National Senior Solo Championships	Leicester
Sep 29-30	National Age Group Competition	Leicester
Nov 3-4	National Championships	Halifax

District Meets
1990

Mar 17	Age Group Competitions	Southern District
Mar 28	Age Group Competitions	Southern District
May 19	Age Group Competitions	Midland District
Jun 16	Championships	Midland District
Jul 15	Inter County Competition	Crystal Palace
Oct 6	Championships	Horwich
Oct 13	Championships	Southern District

Other Open Meets
1990

Mar	Essex Championships	Newham Synchronettes
Jul 1	Steel City Open Synchro Competition	Sheffield NALGO
Aug	Kippax Kippers Synchro Gala	Kippax Kippers

Water Polo

Major International Events
1990

Jan 25-30	Commonwealth Games	Auckland, New Zealand

Other Championships/Competitions
1990

Mar 16-17	4 Home Nations Tournament — Senior	Cardiff
Mar 16-17	4 Home Nations Tournament — Junior	Cardiff

Mar 23-25	Boys Inter District Championships	Walsall
Mar 23-25	Under-20 Inter District Championships	Walsall
Apr 21	Boys Club Championship Final	TBA
Apr 21	Womens Club Championship Final	Potters Bar
Jul 21	Mens Club Championship Final	TBA
Jul 21	Junior Mens Club Championship Final	TBA
Nov 10	County Junior Championship Final	TBA

District Championships
1990

| Jul 12 | Club Final | Crystal Palace |

Long Distance Swimming

International Open Meets — Home
1990

| Aug 11 | International | Windermere |

District Events
1990

Jul 7	8 Miles	Torbay
Jul 14	Two Way — Senior, 6 Miles	Bala
Jul 15	One Way — Junior, 3 Miles	Bala
Sep 1	10½ Miles	Windermere